PSYCHOLOGY

AP* EDITION

PSYCHOLOGY

SECOND EDITION

SAUNDRA K. CICCARELLI

Gulf Coast Community College

J. NOLAND WHITE

Georgia College & State University

Prentice Hall

Boston   Columbus   Indianapolis   New York   San Francisco   Upper Saddle River

Amsterdam   Cape Town   Dubai   London   Madrid   Milan   Munich   Paris   Montreal   Toronto

Delhi   Mexico City   Sao Paulo   Sydney   Hong Kong   Seoul   Singapore   Taipei   Tokyo

Editorial Director: Craig Campanella
Editor in Chief: Jessica Mosher
Sponsoring Editor: Amber Mackey
Editorial Assistant: Paige Clunie
Director of Marketing: Brandy Dawson
Executive Marketing Manager: Jeanette Koskinas
Marketing Assistant: Shauna Fishweicher
Managing Editor: Maureen Richardson
Senior Production Project Manager: Harriet Tellem
AV Production Project Manager: Maria Piper
Line Art: Precision Graphics
Anatomical Line Art: Peter Bull Art Studio
Senior Operations Specialist: Sherry Lewis
Senior Art Director: Nancy Wells
Text and Cover Designer: Anne Demarinis/DeMarinis Design LLC

Photographer, Student Images: Shayle Keating Photography
Manager, Visual Research: Beth Brenzel
Photo Researchers: Susanna Lesan, Kathy Ringrose, Sheila Norman
Manager, Rights and Permissions: Zina Arabia
Image Permission Coordinator: Debbie Latronica
Manager, Cover Visual Research & Permissions: Karen Sanatar
Cover Art: Getty Images
Text Research and Permissions: Lisa Black
Copy Editor: Donna Mulder
Media Project Manager: Paul DeLuca
Supplements Editor: Virginia Livsey
Full-Service Project Management: Preparé Inc./ Cécile Billioti de Gage
Composition: Preparé Inc.
Printer/Binder: Courier Kendallville
Cover Printer: Lehigh-Phoenix Color/Hagerstown

*AP and Advanced Placement Program are trademarks registered and/or owned by the College Board, which was not involved in the production of, and does not endorse, this product.

We would like to thank all of the students who allowed us to use their photos in our book.
Credits and acknowledgments from other sources and reproduced, with permission, in this text book appear on pages C-1–C-4.

Library of Congress Cataloging-in-Publication Data
Ciccarelli, Saundra K.
  Psychology / Saundra K. Ciccarelli; J. Noland White. —2nd AP ed.
    p. cm.
  Includes bibliographical references and index.
  ISBN-13: 978-0-205-78617-6
  ISBN-10: 0-205-78617-0
  1. Psychology—Textbooks. I. White, J. Noland. II. Title.
BF121.C52 2011
150—dc22
                        2009052043

10 9 8 7 6

Prentice Hall
is an imprint of

www.pearsonhighered.com

AP* Edition High School Binding
ISBN-13: 978-0-205-78617-6
ISBN-10: 0-205-78617-0

Brief Contents

Contents

1

The Science of Psychology 2

2

The Biological Perspective 46

3
Sensation and Perception 88

4
Consciousness: Sleep, Dreams, Hypnosis, and Drugs 132

5 Learning 174

6 Memory 218

7

Cognition: Thinking, Intelligence, and Language 260

8

Motivation and Emotion 306

13
Psychological Therapies 514

14
Social Psychology 554

Preface

Dear Reader,

Teachers and students alike experience frustration when students are unprepared for class. One of our goals in writing this text was to focus on motivating students to learn. We wrote in a style that draws students into an ongoing dialogue and introduces them to psychology—its history, its breadth, its mysteries, and its applications. In this AP* Edition, we provide some exciting new tools to help students prepare for and succeed on the AP Psychology Exam, including a correlation to the College Board's AP Psychology topics and learning objectives, along with quizzes and chapter tests with questions formatted like those students will experience on the AP Exam. We organized chapters so they closely follow the order of topics in the AP Psychology Course Description booklet.

We also want to see students inspired to use the study materials that accompany their text. Students want to do well; they are motivated when goals are clearly laid out, and when they know that content will "be on the test." By creating an integrated learning and assessment package, we encourage students to focus on the learning objectives presented, and assist teachers in continually assessing students' progress in mastering these objectives. This integrated format enables students to understand the content, and teachers to track progress and address the specific needs of their classes.

We are deeply indebted to the hundreds of reviewers who have taken the time to give insightful feedback and suggestions for this project, especially the numerous AP Psychology teachers who have helped us shape this AP* Edition.

Sincerely,

Sandy Ciccarelli

Noland White

FOR ADVANCED PLACEMENT PSYCHOLOGY

Our goals with this new AP* Edition were to create the most useful tool possible to introduce AP students to the study of psychology and to prepare them for success on the Advanced Placement (AP) Psychology Exam. Response from students and teachers using the second edition has been very gratifying—particularly the feedback from students who are reading our text and are excited by this introduction to the fascinating field of psychology. For this AP* Edition, we have retained the approach of the second edition, and we have made specific changes and additions to tailor the text to AP Psychology classes. We have paid special attention to the presentation, adjusting it throughout to be more relevant, appropriate, and clear and understandable for high school AP students. In addition, we have created specific tools to help AP students prepare for the AP Psychology Exam.

Correlation to the College Board's AP Topics and Learning Objectives

In the AP Psychology Course Description booklet (Acorn Book), the College Board provides a list of 14 topics, or major content areas, that are covered on the AP Psychology Exam. Each topic is accompanied by several learning objectives that AP students should be able to meet in order to succeed on the AP Exam. This new AP* Edition addresses each of the topics and learning objectives described in the AP Psychology Course Description booklet. With AP students in mind, this text utilizes several organizational features that readily identify the specific content areas that correlate with the key AP Psychology topics and learning objectives. These features include:

Comprehensive AP* Correlation Guide
On pages xix-xxiii you will find a comprehensive correlation guide that provides the page reference indicating where this text addresses each of the 14 AP Psychology topics and the associated learning objectives.

AP* PSYCHOLOGY TOPICS AND LEARNING OBJECTIVES	Ciccarelli/White's *Psychology,* AP* Edition, 2e
1. History and Approaches	Chapter 1 & Appendix B
Recognize how philosophical perspectives shaped the development of psychological thought.	p. 6
Describe and compare different theoretical approaches in explaining behavior: • structuralism, functionalism, and behaviorism in the early years; • Gestalt, psychoanalytic/psychodynamic, and humanism emerging later; • evolutionary, biological, and cognitive as more contemporary approaches.	pp. 6–17
Recognize the strengths and limitations of applying theories to explain behavior.	pp. 5–6
Distinguish the different domains of psychology: • biological, clinical, cognitive, counseling, developmental, educational, experimental, human factors, industrial-organizational, personality, psychometric, and social.	pp. 17–18, B-5–B-10

AP* Discuss psychology's abiding interest in how heredity, environment, and evolution work together to shape behavior.

▶

AP Icons
Integrated into each chapter, these icons call out where we address each AP Psychology learning objective.

1

The Science of Psychology 2

Table of Contents
We have organized the chapters to closely follow the order of topics, or major content areas, as they are organized in the College Board's AP Psychology Course Description.

PRACTICE **QUIZ:** PREPARING FOR THE AP* EXAM

Directions: Read each of the questions or incomplete sentences below. Then choose the or completes the sentence.

1. Although Chien's parents have told him that he attended his grandmother's funeral when he was 9 years old, he has no memory of the funeral. Freud would most likely argue that Chien's memory of the funeral is in the _____.
   a. ego
   b. superego
   c. conscious mind
   d. unconscious mind
   e. preconscious mind

2. Which of Freud's parts of the personality is most like a director?
   a. Id
   b. Ego
   c. Superego
   d. Conscience
   e. Unconscious

Built-In Preparation and Practice for the AP Psychology Exam
AP students will benefit from plenty of practice with questions formatted and style like those on the AP Exam: multiple-choice questions with five-answer choices and free-response questions. This text provides numerous opportunities for AP students to test their understanding and to practice and develop good test-taking skills.

Practice Quiz: Preparing for the AP Exam
Multiple-choice quizzes are included in each chapter at the end of every major section to help students think critically and apply their understanding of crucial content. These multiple-choice quizzes are presented in the same five-answer format used on the AP Exam.

TEST YOURSELF: PREPARING FOR THE AP* EXAM

✓•⌐ **Practice** on **MyPsychLab**   **Ready for your test?** More quizzes

PART I: MULTIPLE-CHOICE QUESTIONS ·

Directions for Part I: Read each of the questions or incomplete sentences belov or completes the sentence.

1. In which sequence does a neural impulse travel through a neuron?
   a. Dendrite, soma, axon
   b. Dendrite, axon, soma
   c. Soma, dendrite, axon
   d. Soma, axon, dendrite
   e. Axon, soma, dendrite

2. What happens when a cell's action potential has ended?
   a. Negative sodium ions enter the cell
   b. Positive potassium ions enter the cell
   c. Activated dendrites stimulate the cell
   d. The cell returns to its resting potential
   e. The cell is ready to receive another neural impulse

3. Beta blockers serve as a(n) _____ by blocking the effects of neurotransmitters that stimulate the heart.
   a. agonist
   b. inhibitory synapse
   c. antagonist
   d. synaptic vesicle
   e. reuptake

PART II: FREE-RESPONSE QUESTION

Directions for Part II: Read the essay question that follows. Then, respond to the question in a clear, concise essay. Do not simply list facts. Instead, present a thorough argument based on your critical consideration of the topic. Use proper psychological terminology as necessary.

Briefly describe how someone might use each of the lobes of the cortex listed below while riding a bicycle. For each lobe, include a general description of the function it performs and an example of how that function relates to riding a bicycle:
   a. Occipital lobe
   b. Temporal lobe
   c. Frontal lobe
   d. Parietal lobe

Test Yourself: Preparing for the AP Exam
A sample test is found at the end of every chapter. The chapter test contains multiple-choice questions and a free-response question, both styled after AP Exam format. Answers to all practice quizzes and end-of-chapter tests are in the Answer Key found in the back of the book. The Answer Key also includes criteria for a successful free-response essay.

ENSURE STUDENT SUCCESS ON THE AP EXAM:

AP* Test Prep Guide by Brenda Fonseca (Mesa Community College) includes a chapter summary and AP Exam style practice exams structured around the chapter learning objectives. An innovative Study Hints section helps students with the most difficult to understand concepts from every chapter. Each chapter's visual summary is included. The AP* Test Prep Guide is perforated and three-hole-punched so students can pull out and use the pages they need. Available for purchase.

CORRELATION GUIDE TO
AP* PSYCHOLOGY **TOPICS**

AP* PSYCHOLOGY TOPICS AND LEARNING OBJECTIVES	Ciccarelli/White's *Psychology*, AP* Edition, 2e

1. History and Approaches
Chapter 1 & Appendix B

Recognize how philosophical perspectives shaped the development of psychological thought.	p. 6
Describe and compare different theoretical approaches in explaining behavior: • structuralism, functionalism, and behaviorism in the early years; • Gestalt, psychoanalytic/psychodynamic, and humanism emerging later; • evolutionary, biological, and cognitive as more contemporary approaches.	pp. 6–17
Recognize the strengths and limitations of applying theories to explain behavior.	pp. 5–6
Distinguish the different domains of psychology: • biological, clinical, cognitive, counseling, developmental, educational, experimental, human factors, industrial-organizational, personality, psychometric, and social.	pp. 17–18, B-5–B-10
Identify the major historical figures in psychology (e.g., Mary Whiton Calkins, Charles Darwin, Dorothea Dix, Sigmund Freud, G. Stanley Hall, William James, Ivan Pavlov, Jean Piaget, Carl Rogers, B. F. Skinner, Margaret Floy Washburn, John B. Watson, Wilhelm Wundt).	pp. 6–11

2. Research Methods
Chapter 1 & Appendix A

Differentiate types of research (e.g., experiments, correlational studies, survey research, naturalistic observations, and case studies) with regard to purpose, strengths, and weaknesses.	pp. 22–28
Describe how research design drives the reasonable conclusions that can be drawn (e.g., experiments are useful for determining cause and effect; the use of experimental controls reduces alternative explanations).	pp. 22–32
Identify independent, dependent, confounding, and control variables in experimental designs.	pp. 28–31
Distinguish between random assignment of participants to conditions in experiments and random selection of participants, primarily in correlational studies and surveys.	pp. 30–32
Predict the validity of behavioral explanations based on the quality of research design (e.g., confounding variables limit confidence in research conclusions).	pp. 30–32
Distinguish the purposes of descriptive statistics and inferential statistics.	pp. 26–28, A-1–A-11
Apply basic descriptive statistical concepts, including interpreting and constructing graphs and calculating simple descriptive statistics (e.g., measures of central tendency, standard deviation).	pp. 26–28, A-2–A-8
Discuss the value of reliance on operational definitions and measurement in behavioral research.	pp. 28–30
Identify how ethical issues inform and constrain research practices.	pp. 35–36
Describe how ethical and legal guidelines (e.g., those provided by the American Psychological Association, federal regulations, local institutional review boards) protect research participants and promote sound ethical practice.	pp. 35–36

3. Biological Bases of Behavior
Chapters 1 & 2

Identify basic processes and systems in the biological bases of behavior, including parts of the neuron and the process of transmission of a signal between neurons.	pp. 49–57
Discuss the influence of drugs on neurotransmitters (e.g., reuptake mechanisms).	pp. 55–57
Discuss the effect of the endocrine system on behavior.	pp. 79–80
Describe the nervous system and its subdivisions and functions: • central and peripheral nervous systems; • major brain regions, lobes, and cortical areas; • brain lateralization and hemispheric specialization.	pp. 48, 59–64, 68–79
Recount historic and contemporary research strategies and technologies that support research (e.g., case studies, split-brain research, imaging techniques).	pp. 65–68, 71–72, 76–79
Discuss psychology's abiding interest in how heredity, environment, and evolution work together to shape behavior.	p. 16
Predict how traits and behavior can be selected for their adaptive value.	pp. 16–17
Identify key contributors (e.g., Paul Broca, Charles Darwin, Michael Gazzaniga, Roger Sperry, Carl Wernicke).	pp. 16, 76–79

4. Sensation and Perception	Chapter 3
Discuss basic principles of sensory transduction, including absolute threshold, difference threshold, signal detection, and sensory adaptation.	pp. 90–92
Describe sensory processes (e.g., hearing, vision, touch, taste, smell, vestibular, kinesthesis, pain), including the specific nature of energy transduction, relevant anatomical structures, and specialized pathways in the brain for each of the senses.	pp. 93–113
Explain common sensory disorders (e.g., visual and hearing impairments).	pp. 99–100, 104–106
Describe general principles of organizing and integrating sensation to promote stable awareness of the external world (e.g., Gestalt principles, depth perception).	pp. 115–121
Discuss how experience and culture can influence perceptual processes (e.g., perceptual set, context effects).	pp. 123–124
Explain the role of top-down processing in producing vulnerability to illusion.	pp. 122–124
Discuss the role of attention in behavior.	pp. 114–115
Challenge common beliefs in parapsychological phenomena.	pp. 125–126
Identify the major historical figures in sensation and perception (e.g., Gustav Fechner, David Hubel, Ernst Weber, Torsten Wiesel).	pp. 91–92, 97–98

5. States of Consciousness	Chapter 4
Describe various states of consciousness and their impact on behavior.	pp. 135–169
Discuss aspects of sleep and dreaming: • stages and characteristics of the sleep cycle; • theories of sleep and dreaming; • symptoms and treatments of sleep disorders.	pp. 135–150, 167–169
Describe historic and contemporary uses of hypnosis (e.g., pain control, psychotherapy).	pp. 151–153
Explain hypnotic phenomena (e.g., suggestibility, dissociation).	pp. 151–153
Identify the major psychoactive drug categories (e.g., depressants, stimulants) and classify specific drugs, including their psychological and physiological effects.	pp. 156–165
Discuss drug dependence, addiction, tolerance, and withdrawal.	pp. 154–155 (various aspects also addressed with different substances, pp. 156–165)
Identify the major figures in consciousness research (e.g., William James, Sigmund Freud, Ernest Hilgard).	pp. 134, 147–150, 152–153

6. Learning	Chapter 5
Distinguish general differences between principles of classical conditioning, operant conditioning, and observational learning (e.g., contingencies).	pp. 177–209
Describe basic classical conditioning phenomena, such as acquisition, extinction, spontaneous recovery, generalization, discrimination, and higher-order learning.	pp. 177–185
Predict the effects of operant conditioning (e.g., positive reinforcement, negative reinforcement, punishment, schedules of reinforcement).	pp. 186–194
Predict how practice, schedules of reinforcement, and motivation will influence quality of learning.	pp. 196–199
Interpret graphs that exhibit the results of learning experiments.	pp. 181, 187, 196–199, 205
Provide examples of how biological constraints create learning predispositions.	p. 200
Describe the essential characteristics of insight learning, latent learning, and social learning.	pp. 204–209
Apply learning principles to explain emotional learning, taste aversion, superstitious behavior, and learned helplessness.	pp. 183–184, 194, 206–207
Suggest how behavior modification, biofeedback, coping strategies, and self-control can be used to address behavioral problems.	pp. 201–202
Identify key contributors in the psychology of learning (e.g., Albert Bandura, John Garcia, Ivan Pavlov, Robert Rescorla, B. F. Skinner, Edward Thorndike, Edward Tolman, John B. Watson).	pp. 177, 183–187, 204–209

AP* Psychology Topics and Learning Objectives	Ciccarelli/White's *Psychology*, AP* Edition, 2e

7. Cognition	Chapters 6 & 7
Compare and contrast various cognitive processes: • effortful versus automatic processing; • deep versus shallow processing; • focused versus divided attention.	pp. 221–234, 262–265, 272–274
Describe and differentiate psychological and physiological systems of memory (e.g., short-term memory, procedural memory).	pp. 224–234
Outline the principles that underlie effective encoding, storage, and construction of memories.	pp. 220–222, 226–230, 239–241
Describe strategies for memory improvement.	pp. 229, 235–239
Synthesize how biological, cognitive, and cultural factors converge to facilitate acquisition, development, and use of language.	pp. 294–298
Identify problem-solving strategies as well as factors that influence their effectiveness.	pp. 266–269, 271–274
List the characteristics of creative thought and creative thinkers.	pp. 272–274
Identify key contributors in cognitive psychology (e.g., Noam Chomsky, Hermann Ebbinghaus, Wolfgang Köhler, Elizabeth Loftus, George A. Miller).	pp. 224, 228, 240, 246, 287–289, 294–295

8. Motivation and Emotion	Chapters 8 & 9
Identify and apply basic motivational concepts to understand the behavior of humans and other animals (e.g., instincts, incentives, intrinsic versus extrinsic motivation).	pp. 308–309, 315–316
Discuss the biological underpinnings of motivation, including needs, drives, and homeostasis.	pp. 310–312
Compare and contrast motivational theories (e.g., drive reduction theory, arousal theory, general adaptation theory), including the strengths and weaknesses of each.	pp. 310–312, 313–319
Describe classic research findings in specific motivation systems (e.g., eating, sex, social)	pp. 320–327
Discuss theories of stress and the effects of stress on psychological and physical well-being.	pp. 348–381
Compare and contrast major theories of emotion (e.g., James-Lange, Cannon-Bard, Schachter two-factor theory).	pp. 332–336
Describe how cultural influences shape emotional expression, including variations in body language.	pp. 329–331
Identify key contributors in the psychology of motivation and emotion (e.g., William James, Alfred Kinsey, Abraham Maslow, Stanley Schachter, Hans Selye).	pp. 310, 316, 320, 328, 329, 330, 332-335, 347, 358, 367

9. Developmental Psychology	Chapters 10 & 11
Discuss the interaction of nature and nurture (including cultural variations) in the determination of behavior.	pp. 387–388
Explain the process of conception and gestation, including factors that influence successful fetal development (e.g., nutrition, illness, substance abuse).	pp. 391–396
Discuss maturation of motor skills.	p. 399
Describe the influence of temperament and other social factors on attachment and appropriate socialization.	pp. 408–412
Explain the maturation of cognitive abilities (e.g., Piaget's stages, information processing).	pp. 401–406
Compare and contrast models of moral development (e.g., Kohlberg, Gilligan).	p. 418
Discuss maturational challenges in adolescence, including related family conflicts.	pp. 416–419
Characterize the development of decisions related to intimacy as people mature.	pp. 422–423
Predict the physical and cognitive changes that emerge as people age, including steps that can be taken to maximize function.	pp. 420–422
Describe how sex and gender influence socialization and other aspects of development.	pp. 413–415
Identify key contributors in developmental psychology (e.g., Mary Ainsworth, Albert Bandura, Diana Baumrind, Erik Erikson, Sigmund Freud, Carol Gilligan, Harry Harlow, Lawrence Kohlberg, Konrad Lorenz, Jean Piaget, Lev Vygotsky).	pp. 401, 405, 408, 409, 410, 411, 418, 423, 437, 444, 447

10. Personality — Chapter 11

Compare and contrast the major theories and approaches to explaining personality: psychoanalytic, humanist, cognitive, trait, social learning, and behavioral.	pp. 436–455
Describe and compare research methods (e.g., case studies and surveys) that psychologists use to investigate personality.	pp. 456–464
Identify frequently used assessment strategies (e.g., the Minnesota Multiphasic Personality Inventory [MMPI], the Thematic Apperception Test [TAT]), and evaluate relative test quality based on reliability and validity of the instruments.	pp. 459–464
Speculate how cultural context can facilitate or constrain personality development, especially as it relates to self-concept (e.g., collectivistic versus individualistic cultures).	pp. 455, 457–458
Identify key contributors to personality theory (e.g., Alfred Adler, Albert Bandura, Paul Costa and Robert McCrae, Sigmund Freud, Carl Jung, Abraham Maslow, Carl Rogers).	pp. 437, 443–445, 447, 448, 449, 452, 454

11. Testing and Individual Differences — Chapter 7 & Appendix A

Define intelligence and list characteristics of how psychologists measure intelligence: • abstract versus verbal measures; • speed of processing.	pp. 275–279
Discuss how culture influences the definition of intelligence.	pp. 281–283
Compare and contrast historic and contemporary theories of intelligence (e.g., Charles Spearman, Howard Gardner, Robert Sternberg).	pp. 275–277
Explain how psychologists design tests, including standardization strategies and other techniques to establish reliability and validity.	pp. 277–283
Interpret the meaning of scores in terms of the normal curve.	pp. 280–281, A-2–A-8
Describe relevant labels related to intelligence testing (e.g., gifted, cognitively disabled).	pp. 284–288
Debate the appropriate testing practices, particularly in relation to culture-fair test uses.	pp. 281–283
Identify key contributors in intelligence research and testing (e.g., Alfred Binet, Francis Galton, Howard Gardner, Charles Spearman, Robert Sternberg, Louis Terman, David Wechsler).	pp. 275–278, 287

12. Abnormal Behavior — Chapter 12

Describe contemporary and historical conceptions of what constitutes psychological disorders.	pp. 474–476
Recognize the use of the *Diagnostic and Statistical Manual of Mental Disorders* (DSM) published by the American Psychiatric Association as the primary reference for making diagnostic judgments.	pp. 481–482
Discuss the major diagnostic categories, including anxiety and somatoform disorders, mood disorders, schizophrenia, organic disturbance, personality disorders, and dissociative disorders, and their corresponding symptoms.	pp. 484–508
Evaluate the strengths and limitations of various approaches to explaining psychological disorders: medical model, psychoanalytic, humanistic, cognitive, biological, and sociocultural.	pp. 477–480
Identify the positive and negative consequences of diagnostic labels (e.g., the Rosenhan study).	pp. 483–484
Discuss the intersection between psychology and the legal system (e.g., confidentiality, insanity defense).	p. 477

13. Treatment of Abnormal Behavior — Chapter 13

Describe the central characteristics of psychotherapeutic intervention.	pp. 516–517
Describe major treatment orientations used in therapy (e.g., behavioral, cognitive, humanistic) and how those orientations influence therapeutic planning.	pp. 518–534, 541–545
Compare and contrast different treatment formats (e.g., individual, group).	pp. 516–517, 531–534, 539, 540
Summarize effectiveness of specific treatments used to address specific problems.	pp. 519, 523, 528, 531, 536–539, 540–545
Discuss how cultural and ethnic context influence choice and success of treatment (e.g., factors that lead to premature termination of treatment).	pp. 538–539
Describe prevention strategies that build resilience and promote competence.	p. 540
Identify major figures in psychological treatment (e.g., Aaron Beck, Albert Ellis, Sigmund Freud, Mary Cover Jones, Carl Rogers, B. F. Skinner, Joseph Wolpe).	pp. 517, 518, 521, 526, 528, 530, 536, 545

AP* Psychology Topics and Learning Objectives	Ciccarelli/White's *Psychology*, AP* Edition, 2e
14. Social Psychology	Chapters 1, 9, & 14
Apply attribution theory to explain motives (e.g., fundamental attribution error, self-serving bias).	pp. 574–575
Describe the structure and function of different kinds of group behavior (e.g., deindividuation, group polarization).	p. 560
Explain how individuals respond to expectations of others, including groupthink, conformity, and obedience to authority.	pp. 557–564
Discuss attitudes and how they change (e.g., central route to persuasion).	pp. 566–571
Predict the impact of the presence of others on individual behavior (e.g., bystander effect, social facilitation).	pp. 564, 588–591
Describe processes that contribute to differential treatment of group members (e.g., in-group/out-group dynamics, ethnocentrism, prejudice).	pp. 576–581
Articulate the impact of social and cultural categories (e.g., gender, race, ethnicity) on self-concept and relations with others.	pp. 40, 371, 579–580
Anticipate the impact of behavior on a self-fulfilling prophecy.	pp. 579–580
Describe the variables that contribute to altruism, aggression, and attraction.	pp. 582–591
Discuss attitude formation and change, including persuasion strategies and cognitive dissonance.	pp. 566–571
Identify important figures in social psychology (e.g., Solomon Asch, Leon Festinger, Stanley Milgram, Philip Zimbardo).	pp. 557, 562, 570–571, 574, 583, 586-587, 590

Upon publication, this text was correlated to The College Board's Psychology Course Description dated May 2010, May 2011. We continually monitor The College Board's AP Course Description for updates to exam topics. For the most current AP Exam Topic correlation for this textbook, visit PearsonSchool.com/AdvancedCorrelations

LEARNER-CENTERED APPROACH
Curiosity and Dialogue

In recent years there has been an increased focus on a more learner-centered approach in education. A learner-centered approach encourages dialogue and recognizes the importance of actively engaging students inside and outside the classroom. The first edition of this textbook came about because we recognized the importance of motivating students to read. When we say "read," we mean that we want students to be *absorbed* in reading the text, and not to just skim the pages looking for answers to some study-guide questions—or even worse—to attempt to cram in a huge amount of reading on the night before an exam. We have written in a style that draws the students into an ongoing dialogue about psychology. We also want to inspire students to use the study materials integrated with the text and have designed this edition using art, photos, and other features that will engage students and draw them to these additional resources. Our goal is to awaken students' curiosity and to energize their desire to learn more; we are delighted with the feedback from students and teachers who have used our text and who tell us this approach is working.

Chapter Opening Prologues are designed to capture student interest immediately. Taken from a case study or recent event in the news, these openers engage students in the material from the very start of the chapter. The design truly captures the imagination of students and adds to the appeal of the chapter content.

What Were We Talking About? Forgetting

Why do we ▶ forget things? And why do we forget some things but not others?

Why do we forget things? And why do we forget some things but not others?

6.10 Why do we forget?

Think for a minute: What would it be like if people didn't forget anything? At first, the answer seems to be that such a phenomenal memory would be great, right? Anything people learned would always be there. But what if people *couldn't* forget? That is exactly the problem experienced in the case of A. R. Luria's (1968) famous *mnemonist*, Mr. S. (A mnemonist is a memory expert or someone with exceptional memory ability.) Mr. S. was a performing mnemonist, astonishing his audiences with lists of numbers that he memorized in minutes. But Mr. S. found that he *was unable to forget* the lists. He also could not easily separate important memories from trivial ones, and each time he looked at an object or read a word, images stimulated by that object or word

Student Voice Questions encourage students to stop, to clarify, and to think critically. Written by students for students, these questions create a dialogue between the text and the reader and encourage students to ask similar questions in the classroom or online. Cited by students and teachers alike as a truly unique and key feature of the first edition, for the second edition we highlight photographs of students who used the Ciccarelli text in their introductory class and who provided questions, comments, and invaluable feedback on the book.

more likely to show physical changes such as obesity, resistance to insulin, high blood pressure, and elevated levels of triglycerides three years after the initial measurements of hostility had been made (Raikkonen et al., 2003).

  What about people who don't blow their top but try to keep everything in instead? Wouldn't that be bad for a person's health?

Type C A third personality type was identified by researchers Temoshok and Dreher (1992) as being associated with a higher incidence of cancer. **Type C** people tend to be very pleasant and try to keep the peace but find it difficult to express emotions, especially negative ones. They tend to internalize their anger and often experience a sense of despair over the loss of a loved one or a loss of hope. They are often lonely. These personality characteristics are strongly associated with cancer, and people who have cancer and this personality type often have thicker cancerous tumors as well (Eysenck, 1994; Temoshok & Dreher, 1992). Just as the stress of hostility puts the cardiovascular systems of Type A people at greater risk, the internalized negative

◀ What about people who don't blow their top but try to keep everything in instead? Wouldn't that be bad for a person's health?

It is often difficult for students to make connections from topics in one chapter to topics in other chapters. To help students identify interrelated concepts, throughout each chapter, whenever one topic has a relationship to another within the text, a (L)(I)(N)(K) symbol is shown that includes specific chapter and page number cross references. These links refer to content covered within the same chapter, in earlier chapters, or in subsequent chapters—giving students a real sense of the connections throughout the text material.

136   CHAPTER 4

The Rhythms of Life: Circadian Rhythms The sleep–wake cycle is a **circadian rhythm**. The term actually comes from two Latin words, *circa* ("about") and *diem* ("day"). So a circadian rhythm is a cycle that takes "about a day" to complete.

  For most people, this means that they will experience several hours of sleep at least once during every 24-hour period. The sleep–wake cycle is ultimately controlled by the brain, specifically by an area within the *hypothalamus*, the tiny section of the brain that influences the glandular system. (L)(I)(N)(K) *to Chapter Two: The Biological Perspective, pp. 70–71.*

it as basically a rectangular door. We do the same thing with a triangle and a circle—although when we look at them from different angles they cast differently shaped images on our retina, we experience them as a triangle and a circle because of shape constancy.

perception the method by which the sensations experienced at any given moment are interpreted and organized in some meaningful fashion.

size constancy the tendency to interpret an object as always being the same actual size, regardless of its distance.

shape constancy the tendency to interpret the shape of an object as being constant, even when its shape changes on the retina.

THE CONSTANCIES: SIZE, SHAPE, AND BRIGHTNESS

There's an old cartoon that shows a very large man speaking to a very small man. He's saying, "Excuse me for shouting—I thought you were much farther away." This cartoon makes use of the concept of a perceptual constancy* for size. **Size constancy** is the tendency to interpret an object as always being the same size, regardless of its distance from the viewer (or the size of the image it casts on the retina). So if an object that is normally perceived to be about 6 feet tall appears very small on the retina, it will be interpreted as being very far away.

  Another perceptual constancy is the tendency to interpret the shape of an object as constant, even when it changes on the retina. This **shape constancy** is why a person still perceives a coin as a circle even if it is held at an angle that makes it appear to be an oval on the retina. Dinner plates on a table are also seen as round, even though from the angle of viewing they are oval. (See Figure 3.14.)

*Constancy: something that remains the same, the property of remaining stable and unchanging.

With the diversity of today's classroom, many ESL students' lack of vocabulary can be a big stumbling block. We have found that if a word is defined at the end of the page on which it occurs, students stand a far better chance of understanding the content of what they are reading. In this text, **Vocabulary Terms** are defined at the bottom of the page on which they first appear. Feedback on the placement of these terms from ESL students has been very positive; they say it helps them to better understand the chapter content as a whole.

Psychological terms included in the **Running Glossary** are set in bold type in the text and defined in the page margins.

New **Explore/Watch/Listen/Practice Icons** integrated in the text lead to Web-based expansions on topics, allowing teachers and students access to extra information, videos, podcasts, and simulations. The icons are not exhaustive; many more resources are available than those highlighted in the book, but the icons draw attention to some of the most high-interest materials available at **www.mypsychlab.com**. See page (xxxvi) for more information on **MyPsychLab**™ and for access information.

NEW ✳–Explore

Expands on chapter content, providing students with greater details on compelling topics, such as the case of Phineas Gage, right- and left-handedness, phantom limb pain, hypnosis, the case of David Reimer, and much more.

> ✳ **Explore** with a timeline of important dates in psychology. **www.mypsychlab.com**

both description and explanation, as is the case with experimental psychologists who design research to find explanations for observed (described) behavior. Therapists, of course, would be more interested in controlling or influencing behavior and mental processes, although the other three goals would be important in getting to this goal.

Although these goals have not really changed over the years, since psychology's beginnings, the methods of achieving them certainly have changed. In the next section, we'll take a look at the early pioneers in psychology. ✳–**Explore** on **MyPsychLab**

NEW 👁–Watch

Highlights classic content from Penn State Media, such as video clips on John Watson, Harry Harlow, and Jean Piaget, as well as contemporary clips on alcoholism, anatomy of a human brain, bullying, and more.

> 👁 **Watch** classic video footage of John Watson, Rosalie Rayner, and Little Albert. **www.mypsychlab.com**

associated with early and late maturation in puberty. She and her husband, Harold Jones, published the first educational television course in child development in 1952. After a long and distinguished career, Mary Cover Jones died on July 22, 1987, at the age of 90 (Rutherford, 2000). 👁–**Watch** on **MyPsychLab**

Questions for Further Thought

1. What difficulties might early women psychologists like Mary Cover Jones have faced in a field and a culture dominated by men?

NEW ((•–Listen

Each chapter has a link to a *Psychology in the News* podcast, providing high-interest topics and support for a variety of learning styles.

> ((•● **Listen** to the Psychology in the News podcast. **www.mypsychlab.com**

difficulty in communicating with others, often refusing to look at another person). **LINK** *to Chapter Ten: Development Across the Life Span, p. 403.* People who are autistic may also fail to learn to speak at all, and they normally do not like to be touched. ((•–**Listen** on **MyPsychLab**

In ABA, skills are broken down to their simplest steps and then taught to the child through a system of reinforcement. Prompts (such as moving a child's face back to look at the teacher or the task) are given as needed when the child is learning a skill

NEW ✓•–Practice

Provides information on practice quizzes, tests, downloadable flashcards, and other online study resources for AP students.

> **TEST** YOURSELF: PREPARING FOR THE AP* EXAM   ANSWERS ON PAGE AK-1.
>
> ✓•–**Practice** on **MyPsychLab**   **Ready for your test?** More quizzes and a customized study plan. **www.mypsychlab.com**
>
> PART I: MULTIPLE-CHOICE QUESTIONS
>
> *Directions for Part I: Read each of the questions or incomplete sentences below. Then choose the response that best answers the question or completes the sentence.*
>
> 1. Algorithms are a type of _____.
>   a. heuristic
>   b. mental set
>   c. rule of thumb
>   d. mechanical solution
>   e. means-end analysis
>
> 4. Which of the following questions would be most likely to produce divergent thinking?
>   a. What is a stapler?
>   b. How do you spell *stapler*?
>   c. What is a stapler's main use?
>   d. What does a stapler look like?
>   e. How many uses can you think of for a stapler?

Concept Maps and Practice Quizzes are included in each chapter at the end of every major section. Concept mapping is a key study tool for AP students, and its use is encouraged in the American Psychological Association assessment guidelines. The NEW section-level maps help make connections and encourage AP students to stop, review, and reinforce their learning before moving on. The NEW AP Exam style multiple-choice questions now offer five-answer choices, giving AP students the opportunity to apply their understanding and practice for the AP Exam.

Test Yourself Sample exams are found at the end of every chapter. These end-of-chapter tests contain multiple-choice questions with five answer choices and a free response question to replicate the experience AP students will have on the AP Exam. Answers to all multiple-choice questions in the practice quizzes and end-of-chapter tests are in the Answer Key found in the back of the book. For each free response question, the Answer Key contains a list of criteria for a successful essay.

1 CHAPTER SUMMARY

What Is Psychology?

1.1 What defines psychology as a field of study and what are psychology's four primary goals?

* Psychology is the scientific study of behavior and mental processes.
* The four goals of psychology are description, explanation, prediction, and control.

* Humanism, which focuses on free will and the human potential for growth, was developed by Maslow and Rogers, among others, as a reaction to the deterministic nature of behaviorism and psychoanalysis.
* Cognitive psychology is the study of learning, memory, language, and problem solving.
* Biopsychology emerged as the study of the biological bases of behavior.

Visual Summaries at the end of each chapter provide students with a graphic summary of content covered in the more detailed section-level concept maps and in the end-of-chapter bulleted summaries. By pulling the content together in this highly visual manner, students can better understand the connections and grasp how the chapter material fits together.

Other features of each chapter are special sections covering interesting topics related to the material, especially topics of diversity and cultural interest. These are not set off from the text in boxes, and the authors refer to these features in the chapter content, making it more likely that students will read the enriching material. The test bank, practice quizzes, and the tests at the end of each chapter include questions on this material, further encouraging students to read the chapter. Each section ends with Questions for Further Study that allows students to think critically about the content they have just read.

Classic Studies in Psychology

Harlow and Contact Comfort

As psychologists began to study the development of attachment, they at first assumed that attachment to the mother occurred because the mother was associated with satisfaction of primary drives such as hunger and thirst. The mother is always present when the food (a primary reinforcer) is presented, so the mother becomes a secondary reinforcer capable of producing pleasurable feelings. **LINK** *to Chapter Five: Learning, p. 190.* Psychologist Harry Harlow felt that attachment had to be influenced by more than just the

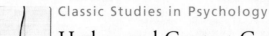

Psychology in the News

Stem Cells: New Hope for Damaged Brains?

Scientists have been researching the possibility of transplanting **stem cells** to repair damaged or diseased brain tissue. (See Figure 2.7.) Stem cells can become other cells, such as blood cells, nerve cells, and brain cells (National Institutes of Health, 2007). An ongoing controversy concerns the source of such stem cells, which can be obtained from human embryos, either from terminated pregnancies or fertilization clinics. Many people are opposed to the idea of putting embryos to this use, even if stem cell research promises cures for diseases,

Current Issues in Psychology

A Look at Abnormality in Various Cultures

As mentioned earlier, what's normal in one culture may be abnormal in another culture. In the **sociocultural perspective** of abnormality, abnormal behavior (like normal behavior) is seen as the product of behavioral shaping within the context of family influences, the social group to which one belongs, and the culture within which the family and social group exist. In particular, cultural differences in abnormal behavior must be addressed when psychological professionals are attempting to treat members of a culture different from that of the professional. **Cultural relativity** is a term that refers to the need to consider the unique characteristics of the culture in which a person with a disorder

Applying Psychology to Everyday Life:
Reflections on Mirror Neurons

You have probably heard the old phrase, "monkey see, monkey do." Neuroscientists have now discovered that the phrase "monkey see, monkey *cortex* do" is more appropriate. Psychologist Giacomo Rizzolatti and his colleagues at the University of Parma, Italy, while using implanted electrodes to examine neural activity in macaque monkeys, made an interesting discovery (Rizzolatti et al., 1996). The researchers wanted to determine which neurons were specifically involved in controlling the movement of the hands.

LEARNING OUTCOMES AND ASSESSMENT
Goals and Standards

In recent years many college and university psychology departments have been focusing on core competencies and how methods of assessment can better enhance students' learning. In response, the American Psychological Association (APA) established 10 recommended goals for the undergraduate psychology major. Specific learning outcomes were established for each of the 10 goals, and suggestions were made on how best to tie assessment practices to these goals. In writing this text, we have used the APA goals and assessment recommendations as guidelines for structuring content and integrating the teaching and homework materials. For details on the APA learning goals and assessment guidelines, please see **http://www.apa.org/**.

8 Learning Objectives

- **8.1** How do psychologists define motivation, and what are the key elements of the early instinct and drive-reduction approaches to motivation?

- **8.2** What are the characteristics of the three types of needs?

- **8.3** What are the key elements of the arousal and incentive approaches to motivation?

- **8.4** How do Maslow's humanistic approach and self-determination theory explain motivation?

- **8.5** What happens in the body to cause hunger, and how do social factors influence a person's experience of hunger?

- **8.6** What are some problems in eating behavior, and how are they affected by biology and culture?

- **8.7** What are the three elements of emotion?

- **8.8** How do the James-Lange and Cannon-Bard theories of emotion differ?

- **8.9** What are the key elements in cognitive arousal theory, the facial feedback hypothesis, and the cognitive-mediational theory of emotion?

- **8.10** What is the positive psychology movement?

Based on APA recommendations, each chapter is structured around detailed **Learning Objectives**. For the second edition the learning objectives have been streamlined and the wording has been revised to encourage more critical thinking of key concepts. All of the supplementary materials are also organized around these objectives, making the text a fully integrated system of study. Teachers can choose which objectives are important in the scope of their course and have the flexibility when using the supplementary material to pick the content they want their students to focus on.

APA UNDERGRADUATE LEARNING GOALS AND OUTCOMES   CICCARELLI CONTENT

1. Knowledge Base of Psychology

Demonstrate familiarity with the major concepts, theoretical perspectives, empirical findings, and historical trends in psychology.

1.1 Characterize the nature of psychology as a discipline.

1.2 Demonstrate knowledge and understanding representing appropriate breadth and depth in selected content areas of psychology: theory and research representing general domains, the history of psychology, relevant levels of analysis, overarching themes, and relevant ethical issues.

1.3 Use the concepts, language, and major theories of the discipline to account for psychological phenomena.

1.4 Explain major perspectives of psychology (e.g., behavioral, biological, cognitive, evolutionary, humanistic, psychodynamic, and sociocultural).

Ch 1: 1.1–1.5 and Applying Psychology: A Reflection on Mirror Neurons
Ch 2: 2.1–2.5, 2.6–2.11
Ch 3: 3.1–3.11
Ch 4: 4.1–4.8
Ch 5: 5.1–5.5, 5.7–5.11
Ch 6: 6.1–6.12
Ch 7: 7.1, 7.3, 7.6–7.9
Ch 8: 8.1–8.9
Ch 9: 9.1–9.3, 9.7–9.10, 9.13
Ch 10: 10.2–10.5, 10.7–10.12
Ch 11: 11.1–11.8
Ch 12: 12.1–12.10
Ch 13: 13.1–13.10
Ch 14: 14.1–14.12
Major concepts all reinforced with online homework tools, and teacher's resource and assessment package

2. Research Methods in Psychology

Understand and apply basic research methods in psychology, including research design, data analysis, and interpretation.

2.1 Describe the basic characteristics of the science of psychology.

2.2 Explain different research methods used by psychologists.
   a. Describe how various research designs address different types of questions and hypotheses.
   b. Articulate strengths and limitations of various research designs.
   c. Distinguish the nature of designs that permit causal inferences from those that do not.

2.3 Evaluate the appropriateness of conclusions derived from psychological research.
   a. Interpret basic statistical results.
   b. Distinguish between statistical significance and practical significance.
   c. Describe effect size and confidence intervals.
   d. Evaluate the validity of conclusions presented in research reports.

2.4 Design and conduct basic studies to address psychological questions using appropriate research methods.
   a. Locate and use relevant databases, research, and theory to plan, conduct, and interpret results of research studies.
   b. Formulate testable research hypotheses, based on operational definitions of variables.
   c. Select and apply appropriate methods to maximize internal and external validity and reduce the plausibility of alternative explanations.
   d. Collect, analyze, interpret, and report data using appropriate statistical strategies to address different types of research questions and hypotheses.
   e. Recognize that theoretical and sociocultural contexts as well as personal biases may shape research questions, design, data collection, analysis, and interpretation.

2.5 Follow the APA Code of Ethics in the treatment of human and nonhuman participants in the design, data collection, interpretation, and reporting of psychological research.

2.6 Generalize research conclusions appropriately based on the parameters of particular research methods.
   a. Exercise caution in predicting behavior based on limitations of single studies.
   b. Recognize the limitations of applying normative conclusions to individuals.
   c. Acknowledge that research results may have unanticipated societal consequences.
   d. Recognize that individual differences and sociocultural contexts may influence the applicability of research findings.

Ch 1: 1.6–1.12 and Classic Studies in Psychology: Mary Cover Jones and Little Peter and Teresa Amabile and the Effect of Extrinsic Reward on Creativity
Ch 2: 2.5 and Classic Studies in Psychology: Through the Looking Glass: Spatial Neglect
Ch 3: Classic Studies: The Visual Cliff
Ch 4: Psychology in the News: Murder While Sleepwalking
Ch 5: 5.11 and Classic Studies: Biological Constraints of Operant Conditioning
Ch 6: Classic Studies: Elizabeth Loftus and Eyewitnesses and Current Research on Alzheimer's Disease
Ch 7: 7.2, 7.4–7.5 and Classic Studies: Terman's Termites
Ch 8: Classic Studies: The Angry/Happy Man
Ch 10: 10.1, 10.6, 10.10 and Classic Studies: Harlow and Contact Comfort
Ch 11: 11.9 and Classic Studies: Geert Hofstede's Four Dimensions of Cultural Personality
Ch 13: Current Issues: What Is EMDR?
Ch 14: Classic Studies: Brown Eyes, Blue Eyes and Latané and Darley
Appendix A: Statistics A.1–A.6
Appendix B: Applied Psychology B.7
Methodology reinforced with online homework tools, and teacher's resource and assessment package

APA UNDERGRADUATE LEARNING GOALS AND OUTCOMES   **CICCARELLI CONTENT**

3. Critical Thinking Skills in Psychology

Respect and use critical and creative thinking, skeptical inquiry, and, when possible, the scientific approach to solving problems related to behavior and mental processes.

3.1 Use critical thinking effectively.

3.2 Engage in creative thinking.

3.3 Use reasoning to recognize, develop, defend, and criticize arguments and other persuasive appeals.

3.4 Approach problems effectively.

Ch 1: 1.13–1.14 and Using Critical Thinking: Does Astrology Work?
Ch 2: Applying Psychology to Everyday Life: Reflections on Mirror Neurons
Ch 3: Thinking Critically about ESP
Ch 4: 4.8–4.10
Ch 5: 5.6, 5.11
Ch 7: 7.10–7.11 and Psychology in the News: Artificial Intelligence (AI)
Ch 8: 8.5–8.6
Ch 9: 9.2 and 9.8 and Current Issues: Suicide in America
Ch 10: 10.2, 10.10 and Current Issues: The Facts and Myths about Immunizations
Ch 11: 11.8–11.9 Applying Psychology: Personality Testing on the Internet
Ch 12: 12.1 and Current Issues: Was "Sybil" a True Multiple Personality?
Ch 13: 13.5, 13.7–13.8, 13.11 and Applying Psychology to Everyday Life: Should Antidepressants Be Prescribed for Children and Adolescents?
Ch 14: 14.8, 14.12–14.13 Applying Psychology: Anatomy of a Cult
Critical-thinking skills reinforced with online homework tools, and teacher's resource and assessment package

4. Application of Psychology

Understand and apply psychological principles to personal, social, and organizational issues.

4.1 Describe major applied areas of psychology (e.g., clinical, counseling, industrial/organizational, school, health).

4.2 Identify appropriate applications of psychology in solving problems.

4.3 Articulate how psychological principles can be used to explain social issues and inform public policy.

4.4 Apply psychological concepts, theories, and research findings as these relate to everyday life.

4.5 Recognize that ethically complex situations can develop in the application of psychological principles.

Introduction: How to Study
Ch 1: 1.5, 1.14, study skills and Applying Psychology to Everyday Life: Stereotypes, Athletes, and College Test Performance
Ch 2: Psychology in the News: Stem Cells: New Hope for Damaged Brains? and Applying Psychology to Everyday Life: Reflections on Mirror Neurons
Ch 4: 4.17 and Psychology in the News: Murder While Sleepwalking and Applying Psychology to Everyday Life: Are you Sleep Deprived?
Ch 5: 5.11 and Applying Psychology to Everyday Life: Can You Really Toilet Train Your Cat?
Ch 6: 6.12
Ch 7: 7.11 and Applying Psychology to Everyday Life: Mental Exercises for Better Cognitive Health
Ch 8: 8.10 and Psychology in the News: The Biology of Obesity and Applying Psychology to Everyday Life: A How-To of Happiness?
Ch 9: 9.2, 9.6–9.9 and Applying Psychology to Everyday Life: Focus on Wellness
Ch 10: 10.11 and 10.12 and Applying Psychology to Everyday Life: ADHD—Not Just for Children
Ch 11: 11.8–11.9 and Applying Psychology to Everyday Life: Personality Testing on the Internet
Ch 12: 12.10 and Applying Psychology to Everyday Life: Seasonal Affective Disorder
Ch 13: 13.1, 13.5, 13.7, 13.9, 13.11
Ch 14: 14.13 and Applying Psychology to Everyday Life: Anatomy of a Cult
Appendix B: Applied Psychology
Applications reinforced with online homework tools, and teacher's resource and assessment package

5. Values in Psychology

Value empirical evidence, tolerate ambiguity, act ethically, and reflect other values that are the underpinnings of psychology as a science.

5.1 Recognize the necessity for ethical behavior in all aspects of the science and practice of psychology.

5.2 Demonstrate reasonable skepticism and intellectual curiosity by asking questions about causes of behavior.

5.3 Seek and evaluate scientific evidence for psychological claims.

5.4 Tolerate ambiguity and realize that psychological explanations are often complex and tentative.

5.5 Recognize and respect human diversity and understand that psychological explanations may vary across populations and contexts.

5.6 Assess and justify their engagement with respect to civic, social, and global responsibilities.

5.7 Understand the limitations of their psychological knowledge and skills.

Ch 1: 1.12–1.14 and Applying Psychology to Everyday Life: Stereotypes, Athletes, and College Test Performance
Ch 4: 4.8–4.9
Ch 8: 8.5–8.6 and Psychology in the News: The Biology of Obesity
Ch 9: 9.8–9.9
Ch 10: 10.2, 10.4, 10.8
Ch 11: 11.8
Ch 12: 12.1
Ch 13: 13.11
Ch 14: 14.4, 14.7–14.9, 14.11–14.12 and Classic Studies: Brown Eyes, Blue Eyes and Latané and Darley
Values reinforced with content in teacher's resource and assessment package

APA UNDERGRADUATE LEARNING GOALS AND OUTCOMES   **CICCARELLI CONTENT**

6. Information and Technological Literacy

Demonstrate information competence and the ability to use computers and other technology for many purposes.

6.1   Demonstrate information competence at each stage in the following process: formulating a researchable topic, choosing relevant and evaluating relevant resources, and reading and accurately summarizing scientific literature that can be supported by database search strategies.

6.2   Use appropriate software to produce understandable reports of the psychological literature, methods, and statistical and qualitative analyses in APA or other appropriate style, including graphic representations of data.

6.3   Use information and technology ethically and responsibly.

6.4   Demonstrate basic computer skills, proper etiquette, and security safeguards.

Ch 1: 1.6–1.12, and Classic Studies in Psychology: Mary Cover Jones and Little Peter and Teresa Amabile and the Effect of Extrinsic Reward on Creativity
Ch 2: 2.5, and Psychology in the News: Stem Cells: New Hope for Damaged Brains? Classic Studies in Psychology: Through the Looking Glass: Spatial Neglect
Ch 3: Classic Studies: The Visual Cliff
Ch 4: Classic Studies: REM Madness
Ch 5: Classic Studies: Biological Constraints of Operant Conditioning
Ch 6: Classic Studies: Elizabeth Loftus and Eyewitnesses and Current Research on Alzheimer's Disease
Ch 7: Classic Studies: Terman's Termites
Ch 8: Classic Studies: The Angry/Happy Man
Ch 10: Classic Studies: Harlow and Contact Comfort
Ch 11: Classic Studies: Geert Hofstede's Four Dimensions of Cultural Personality
Ch 13: Current Issues: What Is EMDR?
Ch 14: 14.2–14.5, 14.8–14.13 and Classic Studies: Brown Eyes, Blue Eyes and Latané and Darley
Appendix A: Statistics
Information and technological literacy reinforced with online homework tools, and teacher's resource and assessment package

7. Communication Skills

Communicate effectively in a variety of formats.

7.1   Demonstrate effective writing skills in various formats (e.g., essays, correspondence, technical papers, note taking) and for various purposes (e.g., informing, defending, explaining, persuading, arguing, teaching).

7.2   Demonstrate effective oral communication skills in various formats (e.g., group discussion, debate, lecture) and for various purposes (e.g., informing. defending, explaining, persuading, arguing, teaching).

7.3   Exhibit quantitative literacy. Demonstrate effective interpersonal communication skills.

7.4   Exhibit the ability to collaborate effectively.

Ciccarelli Student Voice questions
Narrative of the text—like a dialogue between author and reader
Test bank essay questions
Instructor's Resource Manual—see student assignments, lecture launchers, and classroom activities sections
Ciccarelli online homework and assessment tools

8. Sociocultural and International Awareness

Recognize, understand, and respect the complexity of sociocultural and international diversity.

8.1   Interact effectively and sensitively with people from diverse backgrounds and cultural perspectives.

8.2   Examine the sociocultural and international contexts that influence individual differences.

8.3   Explain how individual differences influence beliefs, values, and interactions with others and vice versa.

8.4   Understand how privilege, power, and oppression may affect prejudice, discrimination, and inequity. Recognize prejudicial attitudes and discriminatory behaviors that might exist in themselves and others.

Ch 1: 1.13, 1.14
Ch 7: 7.10–7.11
Ch 8: 8.5, 8.6, 8.10
Ch 9: 9.5–9.6, 9.15–9.16
Ch 10: 10.8
Ch 11: 11.8
Ch 12: 12.1 and Current Issues in Psychology: A Look at Abnormality in Various Cultures
Ch 13: 13.8, 13.11
Ch 14: 14.1, 14.3–14.5, 14.7–14.9, 14.12–14.13 and Classic Studies: Brown Eyes, Blue Eyes and Latané and Darley
Diversity issues also covered in online homework tools, and teacher's resource and assessment package

APA UNDERGRADUATE LEARNING GOALS AND OUTCOMES   **CICCARELLI CONTENT**

9. Personal Development

Develop insight into their own and others' behavior and mental processes and apply effective strategies for self-management and self-improvement.

9.1 Reflect on their experiences and find meaning in them.

9.2 Apply psychological principles to promote personal development.

9.3 Enact self-management strategies that maximize healthy outcomes.

9.4 Display high standards of personal integrity with others.

Ch 1: 1.16, study skills section

Ch 7: Applying Psychology to Everyday Life: Mental Exercises for Better Cognitive Health

Ch 8: 8.10 and Applying Psychology to Everyday Life: A How-To of Happiness?

Ch 11: 11.4, 11.12, 11.14, 11.17 and Applying Psychology to Everyday Life: Focus on Wellness

Ch 12: 12.4–12.5, 12.7, 12.9, 12.12–12.13

Ch 11: Applying Psychology to Everyday Life: Personality Testing on the Internet

Ch 12: Applying Psychology to Everyday Life: Seasonal Affective Disorder

Appendix B: Applied Psychology

10. Career Planning and Development

Pursue realistic ideas about how to implement their psychological knowledge, skills, and values in occupational pursuits in a variety of settings.

10.1 Apply knowledge of psychology (e.g., decision strategies, life span processes, psychological assessment, types of psychological careers) to formulating career choices.

10.2 Identify the types of academic experience and performance in psychology and the liberal arts that will facilitate entry into the workforce, post-baccalaureate education, or both.

10.3 Describe preferred career paths based on accurate self-assessment of abilities, achievement, motivation, and work habits.

10.4 Identify and develop skills and experiences relevant to achieving selected career goals.

10.5 Demonstrate an understanding of the importance of lifelong learning and personal flexibility to sustain personal and professional development as the nature of work evolves.

Ch 1: 1.5

Appendix A: Statistic A.7

Appendix B: Applied Psychology B.1–B.6

Career planning content also found in online homework tools, and teacher's resource and assessment package

TEACHING AND LEARNING PACKAGE
Integration and Feedback

The AP* Test Bank was revised extensively by Cathy Alsman and Katey Baruch (Ivy Tech Community College), and Jason Speigelman (Community College of Baltimore County), as well as Noland White (GCSU) and Fred Whitford (Montana State University). The AP* Test Bank contains multiple-choice questions with five answer choices and free response questions to prepare students for the AP Exam. The AP* Test Bank includes a two-page Total Assessment Guide that lists all of the test items in an easy-to-reference grid. The Total Assessment Guide organizes all test items by learning objective and question type.

An additional test bank feature currently not found in any other introductory psychology texts is the inclusion of rationales for the correct answer and the key distracter in the multiple-choice questions. The rationales help teachers reviewing the content to further evaluate the questions they are choosing for their tests, giving them the option to use the rationales as an answer key for their students. Feedback from current customers indicates this unique feature is very useful for ensuring test quality and quick response to student queries.

It is increasingly true today that as valuable as a good textbook is, it is still only one element of a comprehensive learning package. The teaching and component package that accompanies *Psychology*, AP* Edition, 2e, is the most comprehensive and integrated on the market. We have made every effort to provide high-quality teacher supplements that will save preparation time and will enhance the time spent in the classroom. My coauthor, Noland White from Georgia College & State University, has overseen the development of each of the components of the teaching and assessment package by working directly with the authors and reviewers to ensure consistency in quality and content. We are grateful to the participants of numerous focus groups who helped guide the revisions for different elements of the integrated package, as well as those teachers and students who reviewed the first and second edition supplements and provided wonderful feedback.

FOR THE TEACHER

Some of the teacher supplements and resources for this book text are available electronically for download on the Instructor Resource Center (IRC) to qualified adopters. Upon adoption or to preview the online resources, please go to PearsonSchool.com/Advanced and select "Online Teacher Supplements." You will be required to complete a one-time registration subject to verification. Upon verification of educator status, access information and instructions will be sent via email.

Learning Objective	Factual (Multiple Choice)	Conceptual (Multiple Choice)	Applied (Multiple Choice)	True/False Questions	Short Answer Questions	Essay Questions
5.1- What is learning?	1, 2	3, 4, 5		152		180
5.2- What is classical conditioning and who first studied it?	6, 7, 8, 9, 10, 11			153		
5.3- What are the important concepts in classical conditioning?	13, 14, 18, 19, 20		12, 15, 16, 17, 21, 22	154	167	181
5.4- What was Pavlov's classic experiment in conditioning?	23, 27, 28, 30, 31, 32, 33	24, 34	25, 26, 29	155, 156, 157	169, 173	179
5.5- What is a conditioned emotional response?	35, 42, 43, 44, 49, 50, 51, 53, 54	45, 47	36, 37, 38, 39, 40, 41, 46, 48, 52	158, 159	168, 172	177, 183
5.6- Why does classical conditioning work?		55, 56, 57, 58, 59	60	160	175	
5.7- What is operant conditioning and	63, 64, 65	61, 62, 66		161		178

Chapter 5 Learning — TOTAL ASSESSMENT GUIDE

Answer Key

1. **a** Explanation: Alterations due to a genetic blueprint w examples omaturation. (Page 166-167, Conceptual, LO 5.1)

2. **b** Explanation: The food acted as an unconditioned sti automatically evoked the conditioned response. Foo causes one to salivate. (Page 167, Applied, LO 5.3)

3. **b** Explanation: The UCS was a loud noise because it a evoked a fear response. (Page 167, Applied, LO 5.5)

4. **b** Explanation: Thorndike was known for his work wit (Page 176, Factual, LO 5.7

The AP* Test Bank has been thoroughly revised in response to reviewer feedback. It has also been analyzed line by line by an editor and a copy editor in order to ensure clarity, accuracy, and delivery of the highest quality assessment tool.

> *Unbelievable and cutting edge. I truly enjoy these resources and see them as a leading the pack—other textbooks are going to be far behind. They offer a new fresh way to teach. These resources allow both a rookie and an experience teacher to stay on their toes and get excited to use these tools.*
> —Joe Geiger, Carl Sandburg High School

The AP* Test Bank comes with **TestGen**, a powerful assessment generation program that helps teachers easily create and print quizzes and exams. Teachers can readily access existing questions and edit, create, and store using a simple interface. Data on each question provides information regarding difficulty level and page number. In addition, each question maps to the text's major section and learning objective.

Completely NEW Interactive PowerPoint Slides by Derek Borman (Mesa Community College) bring the powerful Ciccarelli/White design right into the classroom, drawing students into the lecture and providing wonderful interactive activities, visuals, and videos. A video walk-through is available and provides clear guidelines for using and customizing the slides.

The slides are built around the text learning objectives and offer multiple pathways or links between content areas.

Icons utilized throughout the slides indicate interactive exercises, simulations, and activities that can be accessed directly from the slides if teachers want to use these resources in the classroom.

- **AP* Teacher's Resource DVD**
  This DVD offers all the major teacher's resources in one place. The DVD contains the Teacher's Resource Manual, Test Bank, TestGen, highly visual Interactive PowerPoint slides, and more traditional secondary PowerPoint Slides.

  I commend the fact that the complete package is so well thought out and targeted to true AP level instruction. It sets a new benchmark in textbook package design, it is student-centric and instructor friendly. It is superior to other "AP" focused texts, most notably because all of its resources are designed to not only to engage students, but also to give them greater ownership over their learning.
  —John Billingslea, Franklin High School

- **AP* Teacher's Resource Manual,** authored by Diane Ashe and Debra Hollister (Valencia Community College), offers an exhaustive collection of resources. For each chapter, there are activities, exercises, assignments, handouts, and demos for in-class use, as well as guidelines on integrating the many Pearson media resources into your classroom. With specific resources for teaching AP Psychology, this resource saves prep work and helps instructors maximize their classroom time.

- **Introductory Psychology Teaching Films Boxed Set**
  An easy-to-use multi-DVD set of videos contains 100 short video clips (5 to 15 minutes in length) from many of the most popular video sources for psychology content, such as *ABC News, Films for the Humanities* series, PBS, Pennsylvania State Media Sales Video Classics, and more! Available for purchase.

ONLINE OPTIONS
for *Psychology, AP* Edition, 2e* for *Students and Teachers*

Clearly established goals • Focused instruction • Effective learning

Across the country, a trend is emerging: high school class sizes are increasing and available resources can't keep pace; in some instances, they are even decreasing. The result—a teacher's time stretched to its limit as never before. At the same time, continual feedback is an important component of successful student progress. The APA strongly recommends student self-assessment tools and the use of embedded questions and assignments (see http://www.apa.org/ed/eval_strategies.html for more information). In response to these demands, Pearson's **MyPsychLab** offers students useful and engaging self-assessment tools and offers teachers flexibility in assessing and tracking student progress.

WHAT IS MyPsychLab?

MyPsychLab is an online learning and assessment tool that enables teachers to assess student performance and adapt course content—without investing additional time or resources. Students benefit from an easy-to-use site where they can test themselves on key content, track their progress, and utilize individually tailored study plans. **NEW** to **MyPsychLab**:

- *NEW* time line feature
- *NEW* survey tool
- *NEW* flash cards
- *NEW* podcasting tool
- *NEW* video clips, animations, and podcasts
- Continued improvements to design, course content, and grading system based on direct customer feedback

ASSESSMENT AND ABILITY TO ADAPT

MyPsychLab is designed with teacher flexibility in mind—you decide the extent of integration into your class—from independent self-assessment for students to total course management. By transferring teachers' most time-consuming tasks—content delivery, student assessment, and grading—to automated tools, **MyPsychLab** enables teachers to spend more quality time with students. For ideas on incorporating **MyPsychLab**, see the AP* Teacher's Resource Manual and **www.mypsychlab.com**.

Some time-saving features for teachers integrating **MyPsychLab** into their class and curriculum: Teachers are provided with the results of the diagnostic tests—delineated by individual student results as well as an aggregate report of their entire class.

In addition to those activities that students can access in their customized study plans, teachers are provided with extra lecture notes, video clips, and activities that reflect the content areas with which their class is still struggling. Teachers can bring these resources to class or easily post them online for students to access.

Now available in MyPsychLab *NEW* **MyClassPrep for teachers:** Finding, sorting, organizing, and presenting your teacher resources is faster and easier than ever before with **MyClassPrep.** This fully searchable database contains hundreds and hundreds of our best teacher resources, such as lecture launchers and discussion topics, in-class and out-of-class activities and assignments, handouts, as well as video clips, photos, illustrations, charts, graphs, and animations. Teachers can search or browse by topic, and it is easy to sort your results by type, such as photo, Word document, or animation. You can create personalized folders to organize and store what you like, or you can download resources. Teachers can even present material in class directly from **MyClassPrep!**

Upon textbook purchase, students and teachers are granted access to **MyPsychLab.** High school teachers can obtain preview or adoption access for **MyPsychLab.**

- Ask your sales representative for a Preview Access Code Card (ISBN 0-13-111589-8). Adoption Acess
- Register online at www.PearsonSchool.com/Access_Request, using Option 3

or

- Ask you sales representative for an Adoption Access Code Card (ISBN 0-13-214300-3)

For more information on MyPsychLab go to **www.mypsychlab.com**

DEVELOPMENT STORY
Insight and Collaboration

The creation of the Ciccarelli/White *Psychology* and the components for both the first and second editions is the result of the most extensive development investment in a textbook that this discipline has ever experienced. Over 1,000 educators and students have contributed. Over 250 manuscript reviewers provided invaluable feedback. Expert reviewers in critical topic areas provided feedback on the currency and accuracy of the research. A full-time development editor analyzed feedback from our customers and reviewers and worked with the authors, editing the prose line by line for clarity. More than 100 focus-group participants contributed to decisions regarding text organization and content coverage as well as pedagogical innovation. Student reviewers have been involved in evaluating the clarity of the writing style and the value of the in-text learning tools and assessment features—you will see many of these student reviewers in the photos included with the student voice questions in the margins of the text. We are grateful to all who provided feedback on changes for the second edition text as well as suggested updates to the design—which we hope you find as inviting as we do!

AP* EDITION REVIEWERS

Cindy Dvorak, Schaumburg High School
Bernard Beins, Ithaca College
Susan Spencer, Northern Highlands Regional High School
Bradley Cravens, Dr. Phillips High School
Terri Lindenberg, Lake Park High School
Wiliam Elmhorst, Marshfield High School
Jann Longman, Liberty High School
Beth Cooper, University of Tennessee
John Billingslea, Franklin High School
Mary Jean Voigt, Boylan High School
Laura Brandt, Adlai E. Stevenson High School
Beth Burkhead, Career Center High School
Margaret Davidson, Rockwall Heath High School

James Denson, Kempsville High School
Audrey Erickson, Moorhead High School
Joseph Geiger, Carl Sandburg High School
Jay Heilman, Prospect High School
Eileen Hermansen, Rancho Bueno Vista High School
Karen Lozzi, Whitman-Hanson Regional High School
Kathleen Manz, Voorhees High School
Robert Nelson, J.J. Pearce High School
Mary Spilis, Lapeer East High School
Larry Stombaugh, Career Center High School
Desi Vuillaume, Carl Sandburg High School
Debra Adams, Osceolo High School
Jennifer O'Meara, Floyd B Buchanan High School
Cara Terry, Lakewood High School
Stacy Wrenn, Chamberlain High School

AP* EDITION FOCUS GROUP PARTICIPANTS

Chris Weiss, Divine Savior Holy Angels High School
Angela Darrenkamp, Owen J. Roberts High School
Ryan Wallace, Owen J. Roberts High School
Joe Geiger, Carl Sandburg High School

Hilary Rosenthal, John Hersey High School
Daria Schaffeld, Prospect High School
Peter Masciopinto, Glenbrook South High School
Sejal Vaughn, Glenbrook South High School
Patsy Brooks, Dobyns-Bennett High School

INSTRUCTORS

Alabama
Lisa D. Hager, Spring Hill College
Royce Simpson, Spring Hill College

Arizona
Olga Carranza, Pima Community College–Desert Vista
Mike Todd, Paradise Valley Community College
Deborah Van Marche, Glendale Community College

California
Patricia Alexander, Long Beach City College
Ronald Barrett, Loyola Marymount University
John Billimek, California State University–Long Beach
Jessica Cail, Long Beach City College
David Campbell, Humboldt State University
Linda Chaparro, Oxnard College
Kimberley Duff, Cerritos College
Vera Dunwoody, Chaffey College
Mark Eastman, Diablo Valley College
Michael Feiler, Merritt College
Maria Fitzpatrick, Chaffey College
Lenore Frigo, Shasta College
Gregg Gold, Humboldt State University
Mark Harmon, Reedley College–Clovis Center
Ann Hennessey, Los Angeles Pierce College
Melissa Holmes, San Joaquin Delta College
Karin Hu, City College of San Francisco
Senqi Hu, Humboldt State University
Lori Hubbard-Welsh, California State University–Chico
Steve Isonio, Golden West Community College
Inna Kanevsky, San Diego Mesa College
Randy Martinez, Cypress College
Terry Maul, San Bernardino Valley College
Lee Merchant, Modesto Junior College
Arthur Olguin, Santa Barbara City College
Fernando Ortiz, Santa Ana Community College
Jeff Pedroza, Santa Ana College
Michelle Pilati, Rio Hondo College
Scott Reed, California State University–Chico
Angela Sadowski, Chaffey College
Harry Saterfield, Foothill College
Cindy Selby, California State University–Chico
Alan Spivey, Shasta College
Mark Stewart, American River College
Joan Thomas-Spiegel, Los Angeles Harbor College
Inger Thompson, Glendale Community College
Herkie Williams, El Camino College–Compton Center
Dean Yoshizumi, Sierra College

Colorado
Layton Curl, Metropolitan State College
Karla Gingerich, Colorado State University
Jan Hickman, Westwood College
Misty Hull, Pikes Peak Community College
Diane Martichuski, University of Colorado at Boulder
Lisa Routh, Pikes Peak Community College
Frank Vattano, Colorado State University

Connecticut
Marlene Adelman, Norwalk Community College
Moises Salinas, Central Connecticut State University
Lawrence Venuk, Naugatuck Valley Community College

Florida
Melissa Acevedo, Valencia Community College–West
Kathleen Bey, Palm Beach Community College–Central
Gary Bothe, Pensacola Junior College
Kelvin Faison, Pasco Hernando Community College
Jodi Grace, St. Thomas University
Peter Gram, Pensacola Junior College
Joe Grisham, Indian River Community College
Marlene Grooms, Miami Dade College–Homestead Campus
Gregory Harris, Polk Community College
Sheryl Hartman, Miami Dade Community College
Debra Hollister, Valencia Community College
James Jakubow, Florida Atlantic University
Manuel Mares, Florida National College
Glenn J. Musgrove, Broward Community College–Central Campus
Jeanne O'Kon, Tallahassee Community College
Jennifer P. Peluso, Florida Atlantic University
Jeanine Plowman, Florida State University
Lawrence Siegel, Palm Beach Community College–South
Wayne Stein, Brevard Community College–Melbourne
Patricia Stephenson, Miami Dade Community College
Richard Townsend, Miami Dade Community College
Barbara Van Horn, Indian River Community College
Steven Zombory, Palm Beach Atlantic University

Georgia
Sheree Barron, Georgia College & State University
Deb Briihl, Valdosta State University
Kristen Diliberto-Macaluso, Berry College
Dan Fawaz, Georgia Perimeter College
Deborah Garfin, Georgia State University
Adam Goodie, University of Georgia
Amy Hackney, Georgia Southern University
John Lindsay, Georgia College & State University
Antoinette Miller, Clayton State University

Hawaii
Robert Dotson, Honolulu Community College

Idaho
Randy Simonson, College of Southern Idaho

Illinois
Elizabeth Arnott-Hill, Chicago State University
Rachel Berry, Southeastern Illinois College
Paula J. Biedenharm, Aurora University
Martha Bonne, Joliet Junior College
Lorelei Carvajal, Triton College
David Das, Elgin Community College
Joseph Ferrari, DePaul University
Renae Franiuk, Aurora University
Pablo Gomez, DePaul University
Christine Grela, McHenry County College
Susan Harris-Mitchell, College of DuPage
Suzanne Hester, Oakton Community College
Charmaine Jake-Matthews, Prairie State College
Lynnel Kiely, Harold Washington College
Shari Larson, College of Lake County
Karen Owens, College of Lake County
Deborah Podwika, Kankakee Community College
Eric Rogers, College of Lake County

Ada Wainwright, College of DuPage
Joan Warmbold-Boggs, Oakton Community College

Indiana
Cathy Alsman, Ivy Tech Community College–Terre Haute
Dan Dickman, Ivy Tech Community College of Indiana
Patricia Kemerer, Ivy Tech Community College–Fort Wayne
Darrell Rudmann, Indiana East University
Don Shull, Ivy Tech–Evansville
Deb Stipp-Evans, Ivy Tech Community College–Gary
Colin William, Ivy Tech Community College–Lafayette
Martin Wolfger, Ivy Tech Community College of Indiana

Iowa
Tim Boffeli, Clarke College
Lee Skeens, Southeastern Community College
Susan Troy, Northeast Iowa Community College

Kansas
Deborah Allen, Fort Scott Community College
Diane Kappen, Johnson County Community College
Rupert Klein, Kansas State University
John Sanders, Garden City Community College
Joe Slobko, Garden City Community College

Kentucky
Sabra Jacobs, Big Sandy Community and Technical College–
    Prestonburg

Louisiana
Brett Heintz, Delgado Community College
Mike Majors, Delgado Community College–City Park
Jack Palmer, University of Louisiana–Monroe
Mary Boone Treuting, Louisiana State University–Alexandria

Maryland
Patrick Allen, College of Southern Maryland
Katherine Helfrich, Frederick Community College
Cynthia Koenig, St. Mary's College of Maryland
Misty Kolchakian, Anne Arundel Community College

Massachusetts
Marcelle Bartolo-Abela, Holyoke Community and Baypath Colleges
Shirley Cassarra, Bunker Hill Community College
Pamela Ludemann, Framingham State College
Chitra Ranganathan, Framingham State College

Michigan
Gregory Cutler, Bay de Noc Community College
Michael Drissman, Macomb Community College–South
Mary Eberly, Oakland University
Cassandra George-Sturges, Washtenaw Community College
Terri Heck, Macomb Community College–South
Patricia Lanzon, Henry Ford Community College
Shawn Talbot, Kellogg Community College
Michael Vargo, Grand Rapids Community College

Minnesota
Dawn Albertson, Minnesota State University–Mankato
Ivonne Tjoe Fat, Rochester Community and Technical College

Mississippi
Collin Billingsley, Northeast Mississippi Community College
Shaila Khan, Tougaloo Community College
Randy Vinzant, Jones County Junior College

Missouri
John Gambon, Ozarks Technical College
Matthew Westra, Metropolitan Community College–Longview

Nebraska
Patrick Dolan, Drew University
Jean Mandernach, University of Nebraska, Kearney
Keith Matthews, Northeast Community College
James Thomas, University of Nebraska–Omaha

New Hampshire
Mark Henn, University of New Hampshire

New Jersey
Fred Bonato, Saint Peter's College
Deborah Fish Ragin, Montclair State University
Joan Rafter, Hudson County Community College
John Ramirez, Middlesex County College
Darla Silverman, Sussex County Community College
Jonathon Springer, Kean University
Jordan Vosmik, Drew University
Anthony Zoccolillo, DeVry University

New Mexico
Katherine Demitrakis, Albuquerque Tech–Vocational Institute
Andrea Ericksen, San Juan College
Sarah Erickson, University of New Mexico
Jim Johnson, Central New Mexico Community College
Marisa McLeod, Santa Fe Community College
Brian Parry, Mesa State College
Ron Salazar, San Juan College

New York
Miles Groth, Wagner College
Melvyn King, SUNY–Cortland
Joe Lao, Teachers College, Columbia University
Michael Magee, Brooklyn College
George Meyer, Suffolk County Community College–Ammerman

North Carolina
Beth Barton, Coastal Carolina Community College and University of
    North Carolina–Wilmington
Shirley Kuhn, Pitt Community College
Julie Lee, Cape Fear Community College
Michele Mathis, Cape Fear Community College
Micha Pitzen, Coastal Carolina Community College
John Schulte, Cape Fear Community College
Stephanie Williford, Coastal Carolina Community College

Ohio
Leslie Angel, Sinclair Community College
Ronald Craig, Cincinnati State College
Lorry Cology, Owens Community College
Chris Cunningham, Bowling Green State University
Diane Feibel, University of Cincinnati–Raymond Walters College
Carolyn Kaufman, Columbus State Community College
Elaine McLeskey, Belmont Technical College
Keith Syrja, Owens Community College

Oklahoma
James Hunsicker, Southwestern Oklahoma State University
Mike Knight, University of Central Oklahoma
Jerrie Scott, Rose State College

Oregon

Barbara DeFilippo, Lane Community College

Pennsylvania

Joseph Hardy, Harrisburg Area Community College
Daniel Klaus, Community College of Beaver County
Sonya Lott-Harrison, Community College of Philadelphia
Barbara Radigan, Community College of Allegheny County
Cathy Sigmund, Geneva College
Peter Zubritzky, Community College of Beaver County

Rhode Island

Thomas Malloy, Rhode Island College

South Carolina

Dan Bellack, Trident Technical College
Devin Byrd, University of South Carolina–Aiken
William House, University of South Carolina–Aiken
Laura May, University of South Carolina Aiken
Nancy Simpson, Trident Technical College

South Dakota

Gabe Mydland, Dakota State University

Tennessee

Erskine Ausbrooks, Dyersburg State Community College
Vivian Grooms, Jackson State Community College
Michelle Merwin, University of Tennessee–Martin
Aubrey Shoemaker, Walters State Community College

Texas

Dr. Joyce Bateman-Jones, Central Texas College
Robert Benefield, East Texas Baptist University
Diane Boudreaux-Kraft, Houston Community College–Southwest
Patrick Carroll, University of Texas–Austin
Monica Castator, Navarro College
Dr. Ili Castillo, Houston Community College–Northwest
Jane Cirillo, Houston Community College–Southeast
Wanda Clark, South Plains College
Perry Collins, Wayland Baptist University
Mary Cordell, Hill College–Hillsboro
Michael Devoley, Lonestar College–Montgomery
Wendy Domjan, University of Texas–Austin
Daniel Fox, Sam Houston State University
James Francis, San Jacinto College–South
Perry Fuchs, University of Texas–Arlington
Michael Garza, Brookhaven Community College
Robert C. Gates, Cisco Junior College
Jerry Green, Tarrant County College–Northwest
Brooke Hall, Lamar State College
Richard Harland, West Texas A&M University
Rose Hattoh, Austin Community College–South Austin
Helen Just, St. Edward's University
Judith Keith, Tarrant County Community College–Northeast
Shirin Khosropour, Austin Community College
Richard Kirk, Texas State Technical College
Irv Lichtman, Houston Community College–Northeast
Nancey Lobb, Alvin Community College
Don Lucas, Northwest Vista College
Lynn New, East Texas Baptist University
Annette Nolte, Tarrant County College–Northwest
Jane Ogden, East Texas Baptist University
Julie Penley, El Paso Community College
Jean Raniseski, Alvin Community College

Cynthia Reed, Tarrant County College–Northeast
Eric Reittinger, Texas A&M University
Karen Saenz, Houston Community College–Southeast
David Shepard, South Texas Community College
Sangeeta Singg, Angelo State University
Lynn Skaggs, Central Texas College
Peggy Skinner, South Plains College
Christopher L. Smith, Tyler Junior College
Jeanne Spaulding, Houston Community College–Northwest
Genevieve Stevens, Houston Community College–Central
Donna Thompson, Midland College
Cheryl Willard, Lee College
Tom Wood, Sam Houston State University
Melissa Wright, Victoria College
Andrea Zabel, Midland College
Clare Zaborowski, San Jacinto College–Central

Utah

Leigh Shaw, Weber State University
David Yells, Utah Valley State College

Virginia

Jeffrey Clark, Virginia Union University
Rosalyn King, Northern Virginia Community College–Loudoun
Molly Lynch, NOVA–Manassas
Bethany Marcus, ECPI College of Technology
James O'Brien, Tidewater Community College
Theresa Tuttle, ECPI College of Technology

Washington

Pamela Costa, Tacoma Community College
Craig Cowden, Tacoma Community College
Brian Smith, Seattle Central Community College
Connie Veldink, Everett Community College

West Virginia

Chris LeGrow, Marshall University

Wisconsin

Andrew Berns, Milwaukee Area Technical College
Regan Gurung, University of Wisconsin–Green Bay
Kathleen Kavanaugh, Milwaukee Area Technical College
Bart Van Voorhis, University of Wisconsin–La Crosse
Carmen Wilson-Van Voorhis, University of Wisconsin–La Crosse

Supplements Review Conference Participants

Cathy Alsman, Ivy Tech Community College–Terre Haute
Derek Borman, Mesa Community College
Brenda Fonseca, Mesa Community College
John Gambon, Ozarks Technical Community College
Debra Hollister, Valencia Community College
Jason Spiegelman, Community College of Baltimore County
Fred Whitford, Montana State University

Text Focus Group

John Creech, Collin County Community College
Vera Dunwoody, Chaffey College
Dan Fawaz, Georgia Perimeter College
Dan Grangaard, Austin Community College
Wayne Hall, San Jacinto College–Central
Susan Hornstein, Southern Methodist University
Shirin Khosropor, Austin Community College
Irv Lichtman, Houston Community College
Michael McCoy, Cape Fear Community College
Wendy Mills, San Jacinto College–North

Annette Nolte, Tarrant County College
Laura Overstreet, Tarrant County College
Gloria Scheff, Broward Community College
Nancy Simpson, Trident Technical College
Joe Tinnin, Richland College
Andrea Zabel, Midland College

Reviewer Conference Participants
Dan Bellack, Trident Technical College
Jane Cirillo, Houston Community College Southeast
Vera Dunwoody, Chaffey College
Perry Fuchs, University of Texas, Arlington
Amy Hackney, Georgia Southern University
Jennifer Peluso, Florida Atlantic University
Cynthia Reed, Tarrant County College–Northeast
Stephanie Williford, Coastal Carolina Community College

Supplements Focus Groups
Kristin Anderson, Houston Community College–Southwest
Susan Anderson, University of South Alabama.
Melissa Avecedo, Valencia Community College
Mike Barber, Lake City Community College
Kathy Bey, Palm Beach Community College
Jack Chuang, San Jacinto College–Central
Jane Cirillo, Houston Community College–Southeast

Wanda Clark, South Plains College
Perry Collins, Wayland Baptist
Jacqueline Cuevas, Midwestern State
Barbara DeFilippo, Lane Community College
Ann Ewing, Mesa Community College
Brenda Fonesca, Mesa Community College
Dan Grangaard, Austin Community College
Sheryl Hartman, Miami Dade College
Karen Hoblit, Victoria College
Debra Hollister, Valencia Community College
Shirin Khospour, Austin Community College
Irv Lichtman, Houston Community College–Northeast
Jerry Marshall, Green River Community College
Marisa McLeod, Santa Fe Community College
Fred Miller, Portland Community College
Jennifer Peluso, Florida Atlantic University
Skip Pollock, Mesa Community College
Genevieve Stevens, Houston Community College–Central
Larry Symon, Western Washington University
Richard Townsend, Miami Dade College
Madeline Wright, Houston Community College–Central
Charles Verschoor, Miami Dade Community College
Andrea Zabel, Midland College
Clare Zaborowski, San Jacinto College–South

STUDENT REVIEWERS

Maribel Acevedo
Everton Allen
Nancy Alvarez
Carolina Amaye
Tiffany Anglin
Vincent Appellaniz
Vanessa Armendariz
Julie Asher
Jennifer Astor
Tracy Marie Augustine
Thomas Baker
Darren Bardot
Chris Beard
Michelle Birreland
Lisa Bosecker
Sean Boyle
Glenn Brown
Tiffany Brown
Robert Bundy
Mike Burns
Amanda Bussell
Kelly Butler
Chris Chappell
Yvronis Charles
Gina Chedid
Alexander Cobin
Alina Cole
Valentine Collade
Lindsey Cook
Jennifer Crisp
Stephen Cromwell
Zuzanna Dabek
Tara Danny

Melissa Linn Davis
Jessica Decker
Joanna DePierro
Kelly Dickinson
Laura Duffy
Margaret Easches
Adel Ebraheey
Christina Falcon
Jennifer Feld
Ericka Ferrias
Ashley Fleming
Tara Fossetta
Kalofa Fregini
James Frier
Norelis K. Garcia
Ryan Gaynor
Matthew Gensler
Amanda Giancaspro
Veronica Gonzales
Maria G. Gonzalez
David Green
Maria Guzman
Cassandra Hanley
Rochelle Harris
Meredith Hawkins
Britney Hayes
Brent Heiligenthal
Laura Herrera
Elisa Holden
Cameron Humericlehouse
Megan Hutchinson
Danielle Marie Ikonomides
Akeem James

Leslie Joiner
Barri-Lyn Jones
Marianne Joseph
Francine Kelly
Victoria A. King
Tracy Klopfer
Mark Kurtovic
Tim Lancaster
Danna Lowe
Noemi Maldonado
John Martin
Nelida Martinez
Chris Meda
Rebecca Miller
Esther Monzon
Gricelda Moreno
Melissa Muldowney
Candace Murphy
Catherine Murphy
Charline Nacius
Shalay Nash
Christopher Ortiz
Zenaida Oyola
Arturo Perez
Sarah Marie Perez
Christina Petruzzelli
Nina Pomeroy
Shana Prado
Evan Prout
Kyle Prunyi
Amanda Ramirez
Natalia M. Ramos
Andria Randazzo

Elizabeth Restrepo
Lisa Rieck
Alexandra Rivera
Jessica Rodriguez
Pierre A. Saintable
Joni Saladino
Alondra Santos
Bethany Schimborski
Bryan Scott
Patricia Shacler
Brenda Smith
Valerie Smith
Paul Sobczau
Morgan Solles
Jennine Stewart
Matthew Stone
Brittany Stork
Matthew Taylor
Luke Thema
Alexis Trematerra
Danielle Vanardsdale
Samantha Vitello
Sara Watson
Meredith Werbler
Jack Wilkinson
Daniel Wilson
Amanda Wright
Sharee Wright
Anthony Yetto
Kacie Young
Shaira Yrel

Acknowledgments

It seems like only yesterday that my longtime friend and Prentice Hall superstar, Cindy Sullivan, talked me into writing a textbook. We were in a wonderful little restaurant in Panama City, Florida, along with two other Prentice Hall people. Maybe it was the smell of the salt air wafting onto the veranda where we were having lunch. Maybe it was the crab cakes or possibly the key lime pie. Maybe it was the wine, but something made me say yes. Cindy, thank you for believing in me and gently prodding me into this whole endeavor. (Okay, maybe it was more like a giant shove.) My husband, Joe Ciccarelli, and my young adult offspring Al and Liz deserve thanks for putting up with my working at odd hours of the day and night.

Yolanda de Rooy and Leah Jewell supported and advised me, and both of these lovely people put a tremendous amount of support behind the first edition of the text and this second edition—thank you both so much. I have to thank Jessica Mosher, the editor who never quits and apparently sleeps very little and somehow manages to have a life squeezed into the spare moments between trips to visit schools. Special thanks to Jeanette Koskinas for a fantastic marketing campaign. Thank you again to Rochelle Diogenes for moral support and great guidance behind the scenes.

Anne DeMarinis is the designer extraordinaire who pulled all of this together to create what I modestly think is one of the most visually appealing textbooks to ever grace a student's desk. I also owe special thanks to Maria Piper, who coordinated the art program and kept her cool through many rounds of corrections, and John Christiana, creative design director, who fielded all of our many design ideas and changes. Harriet Tellem, a bastion of production know-how and good sense, kept us all on track (not an easy job!).

Thank you to all of my supplement authors who waited patiently for the final, final versions of this edition so that they could finish revising all of their work.

And, of course, I can't forget Noland White, my co-author, buddy, and Grand High Expert who helped in many ways to make this edition soar to new heights. Last, but most certainly not least, to my friend and developmental editor, Susanna Lesan, who poured over every word of this text, kept me relatively sane (I'm a psychologist, there's only so much one can do in that regard)—once again, I could not have done it without you. Thank you from the bottom of my heart!

Sandy Ciccarelli
Gulf Coast Community College
Panama City, Florida
sciccarelli@gulfcoast.edu

would like to personally thank:

My wife and best friend Leah and our wonderful children, Sierra, Alexis, and Landon, for their patience and loving support throughout this project despite the many nights and weekends that I was working;

My colleagues in the Department of Psychology at Georgia College & State University, for their encouragement, frequent discussions, and feedback;

Jessica Corley, for her hard work and assistance in the chapter-by-chapter research for this edition;

Both my current and past students for the inspiration and encouragement they have offered;

Everyone who has worked so hard on updating and revising the supplements, including Cathy Alsman, Katey Baruth, Derek Borman, Brenda Fonseca, John Gambon, Debra Hollister, Jason Spiegelman, Fred Whitford, Ginny Livsey, and LeeAnn Doherty;

Sandy Ciccarelli, for her support, advice, and for being such a great lead author and collaborator for me to work with as a co-author;

Jessica Mosher, for her enthusiasm and guidance in this new endeavor and for never failing to be there when I needed additional support or direction;

Leah Jewell, Susanna Lesan, Harriet Tellem, John Christiana, Anne DeMarinis, Amanda Bacher, Jessica Kupetz, Jeanette Koskinas, Karen Scott, Ashley Fallon, Rosaria Cassinese, Craig Campanella, Amber Mackey, Jackie Moya, Paige Clunie, Paul Deluca, Cécile Billioti de Gage, and all of the other Pearson and associated staff, for making this such a great experience.

Noland White
Georgia College & State University
Milledgeville, Georgia
noland.white@gcsu.edu

About the Authors

SAUNDRA K. CICCARELLI is a Professor of Psychology at Gulf Coast Community College in Panama City, Florida. She received her Ph.D. in Developmental Psychology from George Peabody College of Vanderbilt University, Nashville, Tennessee. She is a member of the American Psychological Association and the Association for Psychological Science. Originally interested in a career as a researcher in the development of language and intelligence in developmentally delayed children and adolescents, Dr. Ciccarelli had publications in the *American Journal of Mental Deficiency* while still at Peabody. However, she discovered a love of teaching early on in her career. This led her to the position at Gulf Coast Community College, where she has been teaching Introductory Psychology and Human Development for over 27 years. Her students love her enthusiasm for the field of psychology and the many anecdotes and examples she uses to bring psychology to life for them. Before writing this text, Dr. Ciccarelli authored numerous ancillary materials for several introductory psychology and human development texts.

J. NOLAND WHITE is an Associate Professor of Psychology at Georgia College & State University (GCSU) in Milledgeville, Georgia. He received both his B.S. and M.S. in Psychology from GCSU and joined the faculty there in 2001 after receiving his Ph.D. in Counseling Psychology from the University of Tennessee. As a licensed psychologist, Dr. White has worked as a consultant in a variety of settings, including adult mental health, developmental disabilities, and juvenile justice. Back on campus, he has an active lab and with his students is currently investigating the psychophysiological characteristics and neuropsychological performance of adults with and without ADHD. Outside of the lab, Dr. White is engaged in collaborative research examining the effectiveness of incorporating iPods and podcasting in and out of the college classroom to facilitate student learning. In April 2008, he was a recipient of the GCSU Excellence in Teaching Award.

Important Dates in Psychology

Use this timeline to get a better understanding of key dates in the history of psychology.

1929 Hans Berger introduces EEG method for studying the human brain.

1906 Ivan Pavlov publishes his findings on classical conditioning.

1906 Ramon y Cajal discovers that the nervous system is composed of individual cells.

1920 Francis Sumner becomes the first African American to receive a Ph.D. in psychology at Clark University.

1920 Watson and Rayner publish the "Little Albert" experiment.

1921 The first neurotransmitter, acetylcholine, is discovered.

1921 The Rorschach Inkblot Test is developed.

1921 Allport proposes a trait theory of personality.

360 Plato writes the *Theaetetus* examining theories of perception, knowledge, and truth.

350 Aristotle writes *De Anima* about the relationship of the soul to the body.

1848 Phineas Gage suffers brain damage and provides a famous case study of the effects of brain damage.

1859 Charles Darwin publishes the theory of natural selection, which influences the field of evolutionary psychology.

1884 James-Lange theory of emotion proposed.

1900 Freud publishes *The Interpretation of Dreams*.

1908 Yerkes-Dodson law proposed to explain relationship between performance and arousal.

B.C.E. 400   **C.E. 1650**   **1860**   **1900**   **1920**

430 Hippocrates proposes that mental illnesses are caused by an imbalance of four major fluids in the human body.

1649 Descartes publishes *The Passion of the Soul,* outlining the pineal gland as the seat of the soul.

1860 Gustav Fechner is often credited with performing the first scientific experiments that would form the basis for experimentation in psychology.

1861 Broca's Area and its role in speech production is discovered.

1874 Wernicke's Area and its role in language comprehension is discovered.

1890 William James publishes his book, *Principles of Psychology.*

1892 Structuralism first discovered by Wundt and Titchener.

1894 Margaret Floy Washburn is the first woman to receive a Ph.D. in psychology at Cornell University.

1904 Spearman proposes a general factor of intelligence.

1905 Mary Whiton Calkins becomes the first president of the American Psychological Association.

1905 Freud proposes his psychosexual theory of personality development.

1905 The first IQ test, the Simon-Binet, was created.

1911 Thorndike discovers the Law of Effect.

1912 Gestalt psychology first developed by Max Wertheimer.

1912 The intelligence quotient is developed by William Stern.

1913 Carl Jung develops his theory of the collective conscious.

1930 Tolman and Honzik demonstrate latent learning in rats.

1930 Jean Piaget proposes four stages of cognitive development.

1933 Sigmund Freud proposes the concepts of id, ego, and superego.

1934 Lev Vygotsky proposes concept of zone of proximal development.

1935 Henry Murray creates the Thematic Apperception Test.

1935 Prefrontal lobotomy developed by Dr. Antonio Egas Moniz.

1915 Freud first proposes the concept of defense mechanisms.

1879 Wilhelm Wundt establishes the first psychological laboratory in Leipzig, Germany.

1950 Eric Erikson proposes his psychosocial stages of personality development.

1951 Soloman Asch's classic study on conformity conducted.

1952 The first edition of the *Diagnostic and Statistical Manual of Mental Disorders (DSM)* is published.

1952 Chlorpromazine first drug treatment introduced for the treatment of schizophrenia.

1943 Hull proposes drive reduction theory of motivation.

1942 Carl Rogers develops client-centered therapy.

1942 The Minnesota Multiphasic Personality Inventory is created.

1938 B.F. Skinner introduces the concept of operant conditioning.

1938 Electroconvulsive shock first used on a human patient.

1939 Clark and Clark classic study on prejudice conducted.

1961 Carl Rogers creates the concepts of ideal self, real self, conditional positive regard, and unconditional positive regard.

1961 Muzafer Sherif conducts the "Robber's Cave" study.

1967 Seligman demonstrates learned helplessness in dogs.

1967 Holmes and Rahe create the Social Readjustment Rating Scale.

1967 Beck proposes a cognitive theory for explaining depression.

1968 Roger Sperry demonstrates hemispheric specialization with split-brain patients.

1977 The stress-vulnerability model of schizophrenia proposed by Zubin and Spring.

1977 Thomas and Chess conduct studies of different types of infant temperament.

1978 Elizabeth Loftus puts into question the validity of eyewitness testimony with discovery of misinformation effect.

1979 Mary Ainsworth uses the Strange Situation experiment to study infant attachment styles.

1979 Thomas Bouchard begins the Minnesota study of twins reared apart to identify the influence of genetics and the environment on personality traits.

1994 Herrnstein and Murray publish *The Bell Curve*.

1995 Goleman proposes idea of emotional intelligence.

2000 The DSM-IV-TR is published.

2002 New Mexico is the first state to allow licensed psychologists to prescribe drug treatments for psychological disorders.

1940   1960   1970   1990   2000

1948 Alfred Kinsey begins survey research on sexual behavior.

1953 The American Psychological Association publishes the first edition of *Ethical Standards in Psychology*.

1954 Abraham Maslow proposes a hierarchy of needs to describe human motivation.

1955 Albert Ellis proposes rational emotive behavioral therapy.

1956 Hans Selye proposes the General Adaptation Syndrome to describe responses to stress.

1959 Festinger and Carlsmith publish their study on cognitive dissonance.

1959 Harlow and Zimmerman demonstrate the importance of contact comfort with their study on infant monkeys.

1962 The serial position effect discovered by memory researcher Bennett Murdock.

1962 Cognitive arousal theory of emotion proposed by Schachter and Singer.

1963 Albert Bandura's "Bobo doll" study is conducted.

1963 Stanley Milgram conducts his classic study on obedience.

1963 Lawrence Kohlberg creates his theory of moral development.

1966 Masters and Johnson introduce four stages of sexual response cycle.

1973 Flora Rita Schreiber publishes the book *Sybil*, detailing the life of a woman with dissociative identity disorder.

1974 Friedman and Rosenman discover link between heart disease and Type-A personality.

1974 The PET scan is first introduced as a brain imaging technique.

1981 David Wechsler begins to devise IQ tests for specific age groups.

1983 Gardner first proposes his theory of multiple intelligences.

1985 Robert Sternberg proposes the triarchic theory of intelligence.

1989 Albert Bandura proposes the concept of reciprocal determinism.

1996 McCrae and Costa propose the Big Five Personality dimensions.

1997 Elisabeth Kübler-Ross publishes *On Grief and Grieving*, exploring the process of grieving through expansion of her theory of the five stages of death from *On Death and Dying* (1969).

2004 Alexander Storch presents possibility of obtaining stem cells from adults to repair damaged neural tissue.

2009 U.S. President Barack Obama lifts federal funding limits on scientific research involving human stem cells.

Introduction

Secrets for Surviving AP Psychology: How to Improve Your Grades

WARNING: READING THE FOLLOWING MATERIAL MAY LEAD TO HIGHER GRADES AND LOWER ANXIETY!

I want to make better grades, but sometimes it seems that no matter how hard I study, the test questions turn out to be hard and confusing and I end up not doing very well. Is there some trick to getting good grades?

Many students would probably say that their grades are not what they want them to be. They may make the effort, but they still don't seem to be able to achieve the higher grades that they wish they could earn. A big part of the problem is that despite many different educational experiences, students are rarely taught how to study. Many students in high school and college have developed a system of taking notes, reading the textbook, and reviewing for exams that has worked pretty well in the past, but what worked in previous years may not work in now, when the expectations from teachers are higher and the workload is far greater. There are five things students need to know in order to do their absolute best in any advanced course:

- Their particular learning style.

- How to read a textbook and take notes so that they're understandable and memorable the first time.

- How to take useful notes during lectures.

- How to study efficiently for exams.

- How to write good term papers.

This Introduction presents various techniques and information for maximizing knowledge and skills in each of these five areas.

Learning Styles: Different Strokes for Different Folks

Life would be so much easier, if everyone learned new information in exactly the same way. Teachers would know exactly how to present material so that all students would have an equal opportunity to learn. Unfortunately, that just is not the way it works—people are different in many ways, and one of the ways they differ is in the style of learning that works best for each person.

What exactly is a **learning style**? In general, a learning style is the particular way in which a person takes in information (Dunn et al., 1989, 2001; Felder, 1993, 1996; Felder & Spurlin, 2005). People take in information in several ways: through the eyes, by reading text or looking at charts, diagrams, and maps; through the ears, by listening, talking things out, and discussing things with others; and through the sense of touch and the movement of the body, by touching things, writing things down, drawing pictures and diagrams, and learning by doing (Barsch, 1996).

TYPES OF LEARNING STYLES

Learning styles are often classified based on personality theories or theories of intelligence. The number of different learning styles varies with the theory, but most theories of learning styles include **visual learners**, who learn best by seeing, reading, and looking at images; **auditory learners**, who learn best by hearing and saying things out loud; **tactile learners**, who need to touch things; **kinesthetic learners**, who prefer to learn by doing and being active; and **social learners**, who prefer to learn with other people or in groups (Dunn et al., 1989). Most people will find that they have one dominant, or most powerful, learning style along with one or two secondary styles. Notice that several of the learning styles described would work well together: Auditory learners and social learners, for example, work well together, as do tactile and kinesthetic learners, because they are both hands-on kinds of learners. Many theories simply divide people into four basic styles of learning (Barsch, 1996; Dunn et al., 1989; Jester, 2000):

- **Visual/Verbal.** These people learn best when looking at material, particularly things that are written down. Reading the textbook, using classroom notes, and having a teacher who uses overhead projections, writes on the board, or uses visual multimedia presentations are very helpful. Visual/verbal learners, because they focus on reading and taking notes, tend to learn best when studying alone rather than in a group.
- **Visual/Nonverbal.** These visual learners learn best through the use of diagrams, pictures, charts, videos, and other image-oriented material rather than printed text. This type of learner, like the visual/verbal learner, also prefers to study alone.
- **Auditory/Verbal.** Auditory/verbal learners take in information best by listening. Group discussions and a lecture format in which the teacher talks about the subject are of the most benefit to this style of learning.
- **Tactile/Kinesthetic.** This style of learner needs a "hands-on" opportunity to learn. Lab classes are very good ways for this type of learner to absorb material. Teachers who do lots of demonstrations and use field experiences outside of the classroom are good for this style of learner. Some kinesthetic learners benefit from writing notes during a lecture or from writing a summary of their lecture notes afterward.

Notice that the social aspect of learning (studying alone or with others) is included as a part of the description of these four styles. Students who know their learning style can adapt their study habits and note-taking to methods that work best for that style. Finding out one's style is accomplished by taking a simple test. There are a number of online assessments for learning styles, or your school's counseling center may have tests available. Here are a few online assessment sites:

Auditory learners need to listen in addition to other forms of learning. This student is listening to an audio recording of the textbook she is reading while she looks at the figures and pictures.

learning style   the particular way in which a person takes in information.

visual learners   people who learn best by seeing, reading, and looking at images.

auditory learners   people who learn best by hearing and saying things out loud.

tactile learners   people who need to touch objects in order to learn about them.

kinesthetic learners   people who prefer to learn by doing and being active.

social learners   people who prefer to learn with other people or in groups.

The Barsch Learning Styles Inventory (Barsch, 1996):
   http://www.wou.edu/provost/aalc/learning/barsch_ls_inventory.php
   (from Western Oregon University)

The VARK Questionnaire (Fleming & Mills, 1992):
   www.vark-learn.com/English/page.asp?p=questionnaire

Memletics Learning Styles Questionnaire (Advanogy.com, 2007)
   www.learning-styles-online.com/inventory

LEARNING STYLES AND LEARNING

Does knowing one's learning style really help improve learning? The research findings have produced mixed results thus far, with some finding support for the idea that matching learning styles to teaching styles produces improvement (Braio et al., 1997; Drysdale et al., 2001; Dunn et al., 1986, 1995; Ford & Chen, 2001), but a large survey of the research in this field found little consistent support (Coffield et al., 2004).

From the teacher's point of view, the possibility of different student learning styles present a very practical problem. Teachers must teach to the most common level of understanding and may not be able to easily teach for multiple learning styles. The typical teacher may not have a lot of classroom time to do demonstrations, write things on the board, or spend time in discussions, for example. For a student, however, knowing one's learning style can have an impact on note-taking, studying, and reading the textbook. Table 1 presents some study tips for visual,

Some people need to learn in the presence of others, making study groups such as this one an ideal format for the social learner. What are some other study methods that a social learner might use?

Table 1   Study Tips for Different Learning Styles

VISUAL/VERBAL	VISUAL/NONVERBAL	AUDITORY	TACTILE/KINESTHETIC
Use different colors of high-lighter for different sections of information in text or notes.	Make flash cards with pictures or diagrams to aid recall of key concepts.	Join or form a study group or find a study partner so that you can discuss concepts and ideas.	Sit near the front of the class-room and take notes by jotting down key terms and making pictures or charts to help you remember what you are hearing.
Use flash cards of main points or key terms.	Make charts and diagrams and sum up information in tables.	Talk out loud while studying or into a tape or digital audio recorder that you can listen to later.	When you study, read informa-tion out loud while walking back and forth.
Write out key information in whole sentences or phrases in your own words.	Use different highlighter colors for different information but do symbols and diagrams as well as key terms and ideas.	Make speeches.	Study with a friend.
When looking at diagrams, write out a description.	Visualize charts, diagrams, and figures.	Record the lectures (with permission). Take notes on the lecture sparingly, using the recording to fill in parts that you might have missed.	While exercising, listen to audio recordings that you have made containing important information.
Use "sticky" notes to remind yourself of key terms and information, and put them in the notebook or text or on a mirror that you use frequently.	Redraw things from memory.	Read notes or text material into a tape or digital audio recorder or get study materials on tape, on disc, or as audio files (e.g., MP3's, .wav, etc.) and listen while exercising or doing other chores.	Write out key concepts on a large board or poster.
Visualize spellings of words or facts to be remembered.	Study alone in a quiet place.	When learning something new, state the information in your own words out loud or to a study partner.	Make flash cards, using different colors and diagrams, and lay them out on a large surface. Practice putting them in order.
Rewrite things from memory.			Make a three-dimensional model.
Study alone in a quiet place.			Spend extra time in the lab.
			Go to outside areas such as a museum or historical site to gain information.
			Trace letters and words to remember key facts.
			Use musical rhythms as memory aids, putting information to a rhyme or a tune.

auditory, and tactile/kinesthetic learners. All of the techniques listed in this table are good for students who wish to improve both their understanding of a subject and their grades on tests.

Notice that all four of the learning styles make use of some similar methods but in different ways. For example, drawing graphs, charts, and diagrams is a good technique for the visual/nonverbal and the tactile/kinesthetic learners, and both types of visual learners tend to do better when studying alone to improve concentration, whereas both the auditory and the tactile/kinesthetic learners benefit from studying with others and "talking it out."

No matter what the learning style, students must read the textbook to be successful in the course. The next section deals with how to read textbooks for understanding rather than just to "get through" the material.

Reading Textbooks: Textbooks Are Not Meatloaf

There are two common mistakes that people make in regard to reading a textbook. The first mistake is simple: Many people don't bother to read the textbook before going to the class that will cover that material. Trying to get anything out of a class without reading the material first is like trying to find a new, unfamiliar place without using a map or any kind of directions. It's easy to get lost. This is especially true because of the assumption that most teachers make when planning their classes: They assume that the students have already completed the assignment. The teachers then use the class to go into detail on the information the students supposedly got from the reading. If the students haven't done the reading, the teacher's lesson isn't going to make a whole lot of sense.

Before reading any chapter in a text, you should survey the chapter by reading the outline and the section headings.

The second mistake that most people make when reading textbook material is to try to read it the same way they would read a novel: They start at the first page and read continuously. With a novel, it's easy to do this because the plot is usually interesting and people want to know what happens next, so they keep reading. It isn't necessary to remember every little detail—all they need to remember are the main plot points. One could say that a novel is like meatloaf—some meaty parts with lots of filler. Meatloaf can be eaten quickly, without even chewing for very long.

With a textbook, the material may be interesting but not in the same way that a novel is interesting. A textbook is a big, thick steak—all meat, no filler. Just as a steak has to be chewed to be enjoyed and to be useful to the body, textbook material has to be "chewed" with the mind. You have to read slowly, paying attention to every morsel of meaning.

So how do you do that? Probably one of the best-known reading methods is called SQ3R, first introduced by F. P. Robinson in a book called *Effective Study* (1946). The letters S-Q-R-R-R stand for:

Survey   Look at the chapter you've been assigned to read.

- Take a look at the outline at the beginning of the chapter or whatever opening questions, learning objectives, or other material the author has chosen to let you, the reader, know what the chapter is about.

- Flip through the chapter and read the headings of each section, and look at the tables, figures, graphs, and cartoons to get an idea about the kinds of things that you will be learning.

- Finally, quickly read through the chapter summary if there is one.

It might sound like it takes too much time to do this, but you should just be skimming at this point—a couple of minutes is all it should take. Why do this at all? Surveying the chapter, or "previewing" it, as some experts call it, helps you form a framework in your head around which you can organize the information in the chapter when you read it in detail. In Chapter Six, organization is listed as one of the main ways to improve your memory for information. Think of it this way: As mentioned earlier, if you are going to drive to a new place, it's helpful to have a road map to give you an idea of what's up ahead. Surveying the chapter is giving yourself a "road map" for the material in the chapter.

Question After previewing the chapter, read the heading for the first section. *Just the first section!* Try to think of a question based on this heading that the section should answer as you read. For example, in Chapter One there's a section titled "Pavlov, Watson, and The Dawn of Behaviorism." You could ask yourself, "What did Watson do for psychology?" or "What is behaviorism?" Some textbooks even include questions at the start of many sections. In this text, there is a list of learning objectives for the key concepts in the chapter in the form of questions that can be used with the SQ3R method. There are also student questions that can serve the same purpose. These questions, which are based on the author's years of hearing and answering similar questions from students in the classroom, will be in blue type in the margin, often with the picture of a typical student who is asking the question. Now when you read the section, you aren't *just* reading—you're reading to *find an answer*. That makes the material much easier to remember later on.

Read Now read the section, looking for the answer to your questions. As you read, take notes by making an outline of the main points and terms in the section. This is another area where people make a big mistake. They assume that using a highlighter to mark words and phrases is as good as writing notes. One of the author's former students is conducting research on the difference between highlighting and note-taking, and her preliminary findings are clear: Students who write their own notes during the reading of a text or while listening to a lecture scored significantly higher on their exam grades than students who merely used a highlighter on the text (Boyd & Peeler, 2004). Highlighting requires no real mental effort (no "chewing," in other words), but writing the words down yourself requires you to read the words in depth and understand them. In Chapter Seven, Cognition: Thinking, Intelligence, and Language, you'll learn more about the value of processing information in depth.

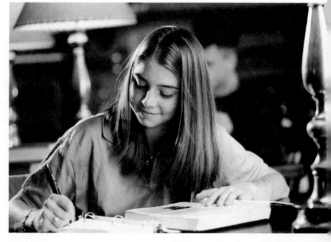

As you read, take notes. Write down key terms and try to summarize the key points of each paragraph and section in the chapter. These notes will be useful when you later review the chapter material.

Recite It may sound silly, but reciting *out loud* what you can remember from the section you've just read is another good way to process the information more deeply and completely. How many times have you thought you understood something, only to find that when you tried to tell it to someone, you didn't understand it at all? Recitation forces you to put the information in your own words, just as writing it down in the form of notes does. Writing it down accesses your visual memory; saying it out loud gives you an auditory memory for the same information. If you have ever learned something well by teaching it to someone else, you already know the value of recitation. If you feel self-conscious about talking to yourself, talk into a tape or digital audio recorder—it makes a great way to review while exercising.

Now repeat the Question, Read, and Recite instructions for each section, taking a few minutes' break after every two or three sections. Why take a break? There's a process that has to take place in your brain when you are trying to form a permanent memory for information, and that process takes a little bit of time. When you take a break every 10 to 20 minutes, you are giving your brain time to do this process. Doing this avoids a common problem in reading texts in which when you find yourself reading the same sentence over and over again because your brain is too overloaded with trying to remember what you just read to continue reading.

Recall/Review   Finally, you've finished reading the entire chapter. If you've used the guidelines listed previously, you'll only have to read the chapter in this depth once instead of having to read it over and over throughout the year and just before exams. Once you've read the chapter, take a few minutes to try to remember as much of what you learned while reading it as you can. A good way to do this is to take any practice quizzes that might be available, either in your text or in a student workbook that goes with the text. Many publishers have Web sites for their textbooks that have practice quizzes available online. If there are no quizzes, read the chapter summary in detail, making sure that you understand everything in it. If there's anything that's confusing, go back to that section in the chapter and read again until you understand it.

Reading textbooks in this way means that you only have to read them once. When it comes time for the AP exam, all you will have to do is carefully review your notes to be ready for the exam—you won't have to read the entire textbook all over again. What a time-saver!

How to Take Notes: Printing Out PowerPoint Slides Is Not Taking Notes

Remember the study showing that highlighting is not as effective as note-taking (Boyd & Peeler, 2004)? One of this researcher's earliest studies was a comparison of students who took notes by hand while listening to a lecture with PowerPoint slides and students who printed out the PowerPoint slides and merely used a highlighter to stress certain ideas on the printout. Students taking notes by hand scored an average of one letter grade higher on exams than did the students who used a highlighter on the printouts. PowerPoint slides are not meant to be notes at all; they are merely talking points that help the teacher follow a particular sequence in lecturing. Typically, the teacher will have more to say about each point on the slide, and that is the information students should be listening to and writing down. In Table 1, the suggestions to use highlighters of different colors are not meant to replace taking notes but instead to supplement the notes you do take.

TAKING NOTES WHILE READING THE TEXT

How should you take notes? As stated earlier, you should try to take notes while reading the chapter by writing down the main points and the vocabulary terms *in your own words* as much as possible. It's important to put the information in your own words because that forces you to think about what you are reading. The more you think about it, the more likely it is that the concepts will become a part of your permanent memory. Remembering to use the techniques for your particular learning style is important, too. For example, auditory learners should try to state ideas out loud in their own words as well as writing them down.

TAKING NOTES IN CLASS

Taking notes in class is a slightly different procedure. First, you should have your notes from the reading in front of you, and it helps to leave plenty of space between lines to add notes from the class. As mentioned in the section on how to read a textbook, a major mistake made by many students is to come to the class without having read the material first. This is an EXTREMELY BAD IDEA. In case that didn't sink in the first time, let me repeat it: **Extremely Bad Idea**. If you come to the class totally unprepared, you will have no idea what is important enough to write down and what is just the teacher's asides and commentary. Reading the material first gives you a good idea of exactly what is important in the lecture and reduces the amount of notes you take.

If you are an auditory learner, ask the teacher if you can bring a tape or digital audio recorder to class and record the lesson. That allows you to both listen in class and then listen to the recording to write down notes later on. Visual learners (especially those who are nonverbal) and tactile learners should try to jot down diagrams, charts, and other visual aids along with written notes.

When you have good notes taken while reading the text and from the lectures, you will also have ready-made study aids for preparing to take exams. The next section deals with the best ways to study for exams.

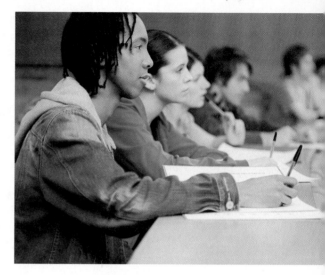

Here are two things that teachers love to see: attentive looks and note-taking during the class. How should these students have prepared before coming to this class?

Studying for Exams: Cramming Is Not an Option

There is a right way to study for a test, believe it or not. Here are some good things to remember when preparing for an exam, whether it's a quiz, a unit test, a midterm, or the AP exam (Carter et al., 2002; Reynolds, 2002):

- *Timing is everything:* One of the worst things that students do is waiting until the last minute to study for the exam. Remember the analogy about "chewing" the steak? (Just as a steak has to be chewed to be enjoyed and to be useful to the body, textbook material has to be "chewed" with the mind.) The same concept applies to preparing for an exam: You have to give yourself enough time. If you've read your text material and taken good notes as discussed in the previous sections, you'll be able to save a lot of time in studying for the exam, but you still need to give yourself ample time to go over all of those notes. One helpful thing to do is to make a study schedule in which you plan out (at least a week before the exam) the hours of the day during which you intend to study and the topics you will cover in those hours. Always give yourself more time than you think you will need, just in case something comes up at the last minute to throw off your schedule: unexpected company, car trouble, or other unforeseen events that might require you to forgo studying for one night.

- *Find out as much as you can about the type of test and the material it will cover.* The type of test can affect the way in which you want to study the material. An objective test, for example, such as multiple choice or true/false, is usually fairly close to the text material, so you'll want to be very familiar with the wording of concepts and definitions in the text, although this is not a suggestion to memorize a lot of material. These kinds of tests can include one of three types of questions:

    - **Factual:** Questions that ask you to remember a specific fact from the text material. For example, "Who built the first psychological laboratory?" requires that you recognize a person's name. (The answer is Wilhelm Wundt.)

Could this be you? The scattered materials, the frantic phone call to a friend; the tense and worried facial expression are all hallmarks of that hallowed yet useless student tradition, cramming. Don't let this happen to you.

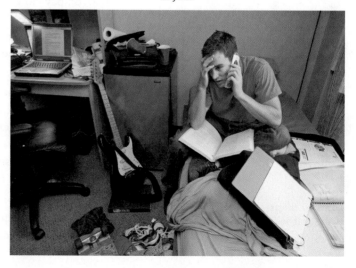

- **Applied:** Questions that ask you to use, or apply, information presented in the text. For example, consider the following question from Chapter Five, Learning:

  Stephanie, a young child, developed a fear of white coats as a result of painful shots given to her by doctors and nurses dressed in white coats. The fact that she was not only afraid of white coats worn by doctors and nurses but also those worn by photographers is an example of _____.

    a. extinction
    b. reinforcement
    c. stimulus discrimination
    d. spontaneous recovery
    e. stimulus generalization

  This question requires you to take a concept (in this case, the concept of stimulus generalization) and apply it to a real-world example.

- **Conceptual:** Questions that demand that you think about the ideas or concepts presented in the text and demonstrate that you understand them by answering questions like the following: "Freud is to _____ as Watson is to _____." (The answers could vary, but a good set would be "the unconscious" and "observable behavior.")

Notice that although memorizing facts might help on the first type of question, it isn't going to help at all on the last two. Memorization doesn't always help on factual questions either, because the questions are sometimes worded quite differently from the text. It is far better to understand the information rather than be able to "spit it back" without understanding it. "Spitting it back" is memorization; understanding it is true learning.

Subjective tests, such as essay tests and short answer exams, require that you not only be able to recall and understand the information from the course but also that you are able to organize it in your own words. To study for a subjective test means that you not only need to be familiar with the material, you also need to be able to write it down. Make outlines of your notes. Rewrite both reading and lecture notes and make flash cards, charts, and drawings. Tactile learners can practice putting the flash cards in order. If you are an auditory or kinesthetic learner, you should talk out loud or study with someone else and discuss the possible questions that could be on an essay test.

Other helpful advice is to look at old tests (if the teacher has made them available) to see what kinds of questions are usually asked. If this is not possible, make sure that you pay close attention to the kinds of questions asked on the first exam so that you will know how to prepare for future tests. Write out your own test questions as if you were the teacher. Not only does this force you to think about the material the way it will appear on the test, it also provides a great review tool.

- *Use SQ3R.* You can use the same method that you used to read the text material to go over your notes. Skim through your notes to get an overview of the material that will be on the test. Try to think of possible test questions that the teacher might include on an exam. Reread your notes, referring back to the text if necessary. Recite the main ideas and definitions of terms, either out loud, into an audio recorder, or to a friend or study group. Review by summarizing sections of material or by making an outline or flash cards that you can use in studying important concepts.

- *Use the concept maps provided.* When surveying the chapter, make sure you look over the concept maps provided at the end of each major section of the chapter (just before the practice quizzes in most cases). **Concept maps** are a visual organization

concept maps a visual representation of the relationships between key concepts, terms, and ideas.

of the key concepts, terms, and definitions that are found in each section and are an excellent way to "see" how various concepts are linked together (Carnot et al., 2001; Novak, 1995; Wu et al., 2004). They are also a great way to review the chapter once you have finished reading it, just to check for understanding—if the concept maps don't make sense, then you've missed something and need to go back over that section. You can also make your own concept maps as you take notes on the chapter. A guide to making concept maps, developed at the University of Illinois at Urbana-Champaign, can be found at **http://classes.aces.uiuc.edu/ ACES100/Mind/Cmap.html.**

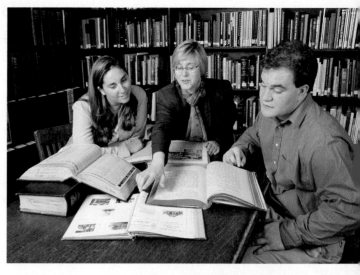

- *Take advantage of all the publisher's test materials.* Practice does help, and most textbooks come with a study guide or a Web site (such as MyPsychLab, see page xxxvi). Those materials should have practice quizzes available—take them. The more types of quiz questions you try to answer, the more successful you will be at interpreting the questions on the actual exam. You'll also get a very good idea of the areas that you need to go back and review again.

- *Make use of the resources.* If you find that you are having difficulty with certain concepts, go to the teacher well in advance of the exam for help. (This is another good reason to manage your study time so that you aren't trying to do everything in a few hours the night before the exam.) Your school or community may have an academic help center with people who can help you learn to study, organize your notes, or tutor you in the subject area.

Many students studying for exams ignore one of the most valuable resources to which they have access: the teacher. Most teachers are happy to answer questions or schedule time for students who are having difficulty understanding the material.

- *Don't forget your physical needs.* Studies have shown that not getting enough sleep is very bad for memory and learning processes (Stickgold et al., 2001). Try to stop studying an hour or so before going to bed at a reasonable time to give your body time to relax and unwind. Get a full night's sleep if possible. Do eat breakfast; hunger is harmful to memory and mental performance. A breakfast heavy on protein and light on carbohydrates is the best for concentration and recall (Benton & Parker, 1998; Pollitt & Matthews, 1998; Stubbs et al., 1996).

Holding your eyes open is not going to help you study when you are this tired. Sleep has been shown to improve memory and performance on tests, so get a good night's sleep before every exam.

- *Use your test time wisely.* When taking the test, don't allow yourself to get stuck on one question that you can't seem to answer. If an answer isn't clear, skip that question and go on to others. After finishing all of the questions that you can answer easily, go back to the ones you have skipped and try to answer them again. This accomplishes several things: You get to experience success in answering the questions that you can answer, which makes you feel more confident and relaxed; other questions on the test might act as memory cues for just the information you need for one of those questions you skipped; and once you are more relaxed, you may find that the answers to those seemingly impossible questions are now clear because anxiety is no longer blocking them.

The next section gives some helpful information about another form of assessment: the term paper.

Writing Papers: Planning Makes Perfect

There are several steps involved in writing a paper, whether it be a short paper or a long one. You should begin all of these steps well in advance of the due date for the paper (not the night before):

1. *Choose a topic.* The first step is to choose a topic for your paper. In some cases, the teacher may have a list of acceptable topics, which makes your job easier. If that is not the case, don't be afraid to go to your teacher and talk about some possible topics. Try to choose a topic that interests you, one that you would like to learn more about. The most common mistake students make is to pick a topic that is far too broad. For example, the topic "mental retardation" could fill a book. A narrower topic might be one type of mental retardation discussed in detail. Again, your teacher can help you narrow down your topic choices.

2. *Do the research.* Find as many sources as you can that have information about your topic. Don't limit yourself to encyclopedias or textbooks. Go to your school library and ask the librarian to point you in the direction of some good scientific journals that would have information about the topic.

3. *Take notes.* While reading about your topic, make note cards. On the back of the note card (a 3 × 5 card), write the reference that will go along with the reading. (You might also start a document on the computer and type your references into the document as you read, but that only works if you have your computer with you while reading.) References for psychology papers are usually going to be in APA (American Psychological Association) style, which can be found at **www.apastyle.org**. Write your notes about the reading on the front of the note card. Some people prefer two note cards, one for the notes and one for the reference, so that they can sort them separately.

4. *Decide on the thesis.* The thesis is the central message of your paper—the message you want to communicate to your audience—which may be your teacher, your classmates, or both, depending on the nature of the assignment. Some papers are persuasive, which means they are trying to convince the reader of a particular point of view, such as "Mental retardation is not caused by immunizations." Some papers are informative, providing information about a topic to an audience that may have no prior knowledge, such as "There are several ways to prevent mental retardation."

5. *Write an outline.* Using your notes from all your readings, create an outline of your paper—a kind of "road map" of how the paper will go. Start with an introduction (e.g., a brief definition and discussion of what autism is). Then decide what the body of the paper should be. If your paper is about a type of mental retardation, for example, your outline would include sections about the different causes of that type of retardation. The last section of your outline should be some kind of conclusion. For example, you might have recommendations about how parents of a mentally retarded child can best help that child to develop as fully as possible.

6. *Write a first draft.* Write your paper using the outline and your notes as guides. If using APA style, place citations with all of your statements and assertions. Failure to use citations (which point to the particular reference work from which your information came) is also a common mistake that many students make. Remember not to plagiarize. Plagiarizing is copying information from a source without stating that it is a quotation but instead letting it seem as if it is something you wrote yourself. When you use a source, you are supposed to explain the information that you are using in your own words and cite the source, as in the following example:

Teachers are a good source of suggestions for paper topics—they know the kind of information they want to be reading and grading in the wee hours of the night.

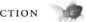

In one study comparing both identical and fraternal twins, researchers found that stressful life events of the kind listed in the SRRS were excellent predictors of the onset of episodes of major depression (Kendler & Prescott, 1999).

The reference section would have the following citation: Kendler, K. S., & Prescott, C. A. (1999). A population-based twin study of lifetime major depression in men and women. *Archives of General Psychiatry, 56*(1), 39–44.

7. *Let it sit.* Take a few days (if you have been good about starting the paper on time) to let the paper sit without reading it. Then go back over the paper and mark places that don't sound right and need more explanation, a citation, or any other changes. This is much easier to do after a few days away from the paper; your errors will be more obvious.

8. *Write the revised draft.* Some people do more than one draft whereas others do only a first draft and a final. In either case, revise the draft carefully, making sure to check your citations.

Strategies for Improving Your Memory

Everyone needs a little memory help now and then. Even memory experts use strategies to help them perform their unusual feats of remembering. These strategies may be unique to that individual, but there are many memory "tricks" that are quite simple and available for anyone to learn and use. A memory trick or strategy to help people remember is called a **mnemonic** from the Greek word for memory. Here are a few of the more popular mnemonics, some of which may sound familiar:

- *Linking.* Make a list in which items to be remembered are linked in some way. If trying to remember a list of the planets in the solar system, for example, a person could string the names of the planets together like this: *Mercury* was the messenger god, who carried lots of love notes to *Venus*, the beautiful goddess who sprang from the *Earth's* sea. She was married to *Mars*, her brother, which didn't please her father *Jupiter* or his father *Saturn*, and his uncle *Uranus* complained to the sea god, *Neptune*. That sounds like a lot, but once linked in this way, the names of the planets are easy to recall in proper order.

- *The peg word method.* In this method, it is necessary to first memorize a series of "peg" words, numbered words that can be used as keys for remembering items associated with them. A typical series of peg words is:
  - One is a bun
  - Two is a shoe
  - Three is a tree
  - Four is a door
  - Five is a hive
  - Six is bricks
  - Seven is heaven
  - Eight is a gate
  - Nine is a line
  - Ten is a hen

  To use this method, each item to be remembered (e.g., on a grocery list) is associated with a peg word and made into an image. If the items to be remembered are cheese, milk, eggs, bread, and sugar, the series of images might be a bun with a big wedge of cheese in it, a shoe with milk pouring out of it, a tree with eggs hanging from it, a door made of a slice of bread, and a hive with little bags of sugar flying

In ancient times, people actually had to write or type their first, second, and sometimes third drafts on real paper. The advent of computers with word-processing programs that allow simple editing and revision have no doubt saved a lot of trees from the paper mill. This also means there is no good excuse for failing to write a first draft and for proofreading one's work.

mnemonic a strategy or trick for aiding memory.

As this student studies, he may be turning the concepts he is learning into images. Using imagery is an excellent mnemonic.

around it instead of bees. The images are bizarre, and that actually helps cement the memory. When retrieving the list, all the person has to do is recite, "One is a bun, cheese. Two is a shoe, milk . . ." and so on, and the images will pop up readily.

- *The method of loci (LOW-kee)*. This method, often credited to the ancient Romans and sometimes called the Roman Room Method, was actually invented by the Greeks. In both cultures, orators and speech makers used this method to keep track of the points they wanted to make in their speeches, which were often quite long and involved. There were no cue cards or teleprompters, so they had to rely on memory alone. In this method, the person pictures a very familiar room or series of rooms in a house or other building. Each point of the speech is then made into an image and "placed" mentally in the room at certain locations. For example, if the first point was about military spending, the image might be a soldier standing in the doorway of the house throwing money out into the street. Each point would have its place, and all the person would need to do to retrieve the memories would be to take a "mental walk" around the house.

- *Verbal/rhythmic organization*. How do you spell relief? If when spelling a word with an *ie* or an *ei* in it, you resort to the old rhyme "I before E except after C, or when sounded as A as in neighbor or weigh," you have made use of a verbal/ rhythmic organization mnemonic. "Thirty days hath September, April, June, and November . . ." is another example of this technique. Setting information into a rhyme aids memory because it uses verbal cues, rhyming words, and the rhythm of the poem itself to aid retrieval. Sometimes this method is accomplished through making a sentence by using the first letters of each word to be remembered and making them into new words that form a sentence. The colors of the rainbow are ROY G. BIV (red, orange, yellow, green, blue, indigo, and violet). The notes on the musical staff are "Every Good Boy Does Fine." There are countless examples of this technique.

- *Put it to music (a version of the rhythmic method)*. Some people have had success with making up little songs, using familiar tunes, to remember specific information. The best example of this? The alphabet song.

This Introduction has covered several different ways to help you get more out of not only your psychology class but also your other courses. If you follow the advice given in this section for reading, taking notes, studying, writing papers, and improving your memory, you will find that making good grades will be easier than ever before and that you will actually remember a great deal of what you've studied long after the last final exam is over.

Other Resources

There are some excellent books and Web resources available for help in maximizing your studying. Three excellent books are the following:

Carter, C., Bishop, J., Kravits, S. L., & D'Agostino, J. V. (ed. consultant). (2002). *Keys to college studying: Becoming a lifelong learner.* Upper Saddle River, NJ: Prentice Hall.

Carter, C., Bishop, J., & Kravits, S. L. (2006). *Keys to success: Building successful intelligence for college, career, and life* (5th ed.). Englewood Cliffs, NJ: Prentice Hall. **http://www.ucc.vt.edu/stdyhlp.html**

Reynolds, J. (2002). *Succeeding in college: Study skills and strategies.* Upper Saddle River, NJ: Prentice Hall.

Web sites

The Virginia Polytechnic Institute and State University has a good online site at **http://www.ucc.vt.edu/stdyhlp.html**

Another good source created by Joe Landsberger is the Web site Study Guides and Strategies, available at **http://www.studygs.net**

A good resource for the background behind concept maps and how to use them is at **http://cmap.ihmc.us/Publications/ResearchPapers/TheoryCmaps/Theory UnderlyingConceptMaps.htm**

PSYCHOLOGY

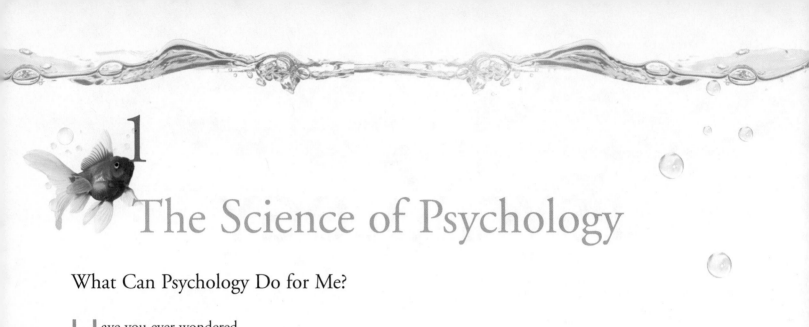

1

The Science of Psychology

What Can Psychology Do for Me?

Have you ever wondered . . .

. . . why using common sense doesn't always work?

. . . how you could develop a better memory?

. . . if psychics really communicate with the dead?

. . . why it's so easy for little children to learn another language when it's so hard for adults?

. . . what happens when you faint?

. . . if ESP really exists?

. . . why you find some people attractive but not others?

. . . why some people become serial killers?

. . . why you get nervous?

. . . what scores on an IQ test really mean?

. . . how the salesperson managed to talk you into buying more than you wanted to buy?

. . . how different men and women really are?

. . . why you sleep and why you dream?

. . . if hypnosis is real?

. . . why buying lottery tickets can be so addictive?

. . . why people tend to get sick right before final exam week?

. . . why identical twins aren't so identical when it comes to their personalities?

If you've ever been curious about any of these questions, this book is for you. Psychologists study all of these things and more. If you've puzzled about it, thought about doing it, or actually done it, chances are psychology has an explanation for it.

Why study psychology? Psychology not only helps you understand why other people do the things they do, but it also helps you better understand yourself and your reactions to other people. Psychology can help you understand how your brain and body are connected, how to improve your learning abilities and memory, and how to deal with the stresses of life, both ordinary and extraordinary. In studying psychology, an understanding of the methods psychologists use is important because research can be flawed, and knowing how research should be done can bring those flaws to light. Finally, the critical thinking that psychology and its methods of research promote can be used to evaluate not just research but also claims of all kinds, including those of advertisers and politicians.

1 Learning objectives

Study Help Note: For each section of every chapter in this text there are numbered learning objectives. These learning objectives represent the key concepts that students should be able to recognize, discuss, analyze, and use after reading the chapter. They appear at the beginning of each chapter, at the beginning of each relevant section in the chapter, and in the chapter summary.

These are your learning objectives for this chapter:

- **1.1** What defines psychology as a field of study and what are psychology's four primary goals?

- **1.2** How did structuralism and functionalism differ, and who were the important people in those early fields?

- **1.3** What were the basic ideas and who were the important people behind the early approaches known as Gestalt, psychoanalysis, and behaviorism?

- **1.4** What are the basic ideas behind the seven modern perspectives, as well as the important contributions of Skinner, Maslow, and Rogers?

- **1.5** How does a psychiatrist differ from a psychologist, and what are the other types of professionals who work in the various areas of psychology?

- **1.6** Why is psychology considered a science, and what are the steps in using the scientific method?

- **1.7** How are naturalistic and laboratory settings used to describe behavior, and what are some of the advantages and disadvantages associated with these settings?

- **1.8** How are case studies and surveys used to describe behavior, and what are some drawbacks to each of these methods?

- **1.9** What is the correlational technique, and what does it tell researchers about relationships?

- **1.10** How are operational definitions, independent and dependent variables, experimental and control groups, and random assignment used in designing an experiment?

- **1.11** How do the placebo and experimenter effects cause problems in an experiment, and how can single-blind and double-blind studies control for these effects?

- **1.12** What are the basic elements of Amabile's creativity experiment?

- **1.13** What are some ethical concerns that can occur when conducting research with people and animals?

- **1.14** What are the basic principles of critical thinking, and how can critical thinking be useful in everyday life?

What Is Psychology?

THE FIELD OF PSYCHOLOGY

Some people believe psychology is just the study of people and what makes them tick. Psychologists do study people, but they study animals, too. What makes people and animals "tick" is what goes on inside their bodies and brains as well as what they do.

1.1 What defines psychology as a field of study and what are psychology's four primary goals?

Psychology is the scientific study of behavior and mental processes. *Behavior* includes all of our outward or overt actions and reactions, such as talking, facial expressions, and movement. The term *mental processes* refers to all the internal, covert activity of our minds, such as thinking, feeling, and remembering. Why "scientific"? To study behavior and mental processes in both animals and humans, researchers have to observe them. Whenever a human being is observing anyone or anything, there's always a possibility the observer will see only what he or she expects to see. Psychologists don't want to let these possible biases* cause them to make faulty observations. They want to be as precise and measure as carefully as they can, so they use the scientific method to study psychology.

psychology the scientific study of behavior and mental processes.

_____

*Biases: personal judgments based on beliefs rather than facts.

PSYCHOLOGY'S GOALS

Every science has goals. In physics, the goals concern learning how the physical world works. In astronomy, the goals are to chart the universe and understand both how it came to be and what it is becoming. In psychology, there are four goals that aim at uncovering the mysteries of human and animal behavior: description, explanation, prediction, and control.

Description: What Is Happening?   The first step in understanding anything is to give it a name. *Description* involves observing a behavior and noting everything about it: what is happening, where it happens, to whom it happens, and under what circumstances it seems to happen.

For example, a teacher might notice a young girl in his second-grade classroom who is behaving oddly. She's not turning in her homework, her grades are slipping badly, and she seems to have a very negative attitude toward school.

That's *what* she is doing, observed in her outward behavior and her possible feelings. The description of what she is doing gives a starting place for the next goal: *Why* is she doing it?

Explanation: Why Is It Happening?   To find out why the girl is doing all these things, the teacher would most likely ask the school counselor to administer some tests. Her parents might be asked to take her to a pediatrician to make sure there is no physical illness, such as an allergy. They might also take her to a psychologist to be assessed. In other words, they are trying to understand or find an *explanation* for her behavior. Finding explanations for behavior is a very important step in the process of forming theories of behavior. A *theory* is a general explanation of a set of observations or facts. The goal of description provides the observations, and the goal of explanation helps to build the theory.

Theories, especially when strengthened by scientific evidence, help us to explain the world around us. However, when a theory has not been tested, it shouldn't be taken as fact. Researchers may have many different theories about a person's unusual behavior, and all of their theories may be based on careful observation and facts, but until scientific tests are performed, there's no way to tell if any of the theories are correct. A good theory will structure future research by allowing researchers to test whether or not the theory holds true in a variety of situations.

If all the tests seem to indicate the young girl has a learning problem, such as dyslexia (an inability to read at expected levels for a particular age and degree of intelligence), the next step would be trying to predict what is likely to happen if the situation stays the same.

Prediction: When Will It Happen Again?   Determining what will happen in the future is a *prediction*. In the example, the psychologist or counselor would predict (based on previous research into similar situations) that this little girl will probably continue to do poorly in her schoolwork and may never be able to reach her full learning potential. Clearly, something needs to be done to change this prediction, which is the point of the last of the four goals of psychology: changing or modifying behavior.

Control: How Can It Be Changed?   The focus of *control*, or the modification of some behavior, is to change a behavior from an undesirable one (such as failing in school) to a desirable one (such as academic success).

In the example of the young girl, certain learning strategies can be used to help children (or adults) who have dyslexia improve their reading skills (Aylward et al., 2003; Shaywitz, 1996). The psychologist and educators would work together to find a training strategy that works best for this particular girl.

The researcher in the foreground is watching the children through a one-way mirror to get a description of their behavior. Observations such as these are just one of many ways that psychologists have of investigating behavior. Why is it important for the researcher to be behind a one-way mirror?

◄ **AP*** Recognize the strengths and limitations of applying theories to explain behavior.

Not all psychological investigations will try to meet all four of these goals. In some cases, the main focus might be on description and prediction, as it would be for a personality theorist who wants to know what people are like (description) and what they might do in certain situations (prediction). Some psychologists are interested in both description and explanation, as is the case with experimental psychologists who design research to find explanations for observed (described) behavior. Therapists, of course, would be more interested in controlling or influencing behavior and mental processes, although the other three goals would be important in getting to this goal.

Although these goals have not really changed over the years, since psychology's beginnings, the methods of achieving them certainly have changed. In the next section, we'll take a look at the early pioneers in psychology. ✱⌐Explore on MyPsychLab

Psychology Then: The History of Psychology

IN THE BEGINNING: WUNDT, INTROSPECTION, AND THE LABORATORY

How long has psychology been around?

Psychology is a relatively new field in the realm of the sciences, only about 130 years old. It's not that no one thought about what makes people tick before then; on the contrary, there were philosophers,* medical doctors, and physiologists** who thought about little else. Aristotle, who lived from 384–322 B.C., wrote about the relationship of the soul to the body (with the two being aspects of the same underlying structure) in *De Anima* as well as other works (Durrant, 1993; Everson, 1995). Plato (427–347 B.C.), Aristotle's teacher, felt the soul could exist separately from the body, a view that has become known as *dualism* (Jackson, 2001). René Descartes, a seventeenth-century French philosopher and mathematician, agreed with Plato and believed that the pineal gland (a small organ at the base of the brain) was the seat of the soul (Kenny, 1968, 1994). Philosophers tried to understand or explain the human mind and its connection to the physical body, while medical doctors and physiologists wondered about the physical connection between the body and the brain. For example, physician and physicist Gustav Fechner is often credited with performing some of the first scientific experiments that would form a basis for experimentation in psychology with his studies of perception (Fechner, 1860), and physician Hermann von Helmholtz (von Helmholtz, 1852, 1863) performed groundbreaking experiments in visual and auditory perception. ⓁⒾⓃⓀ *to Chapter Three: Sensation and Perception, pp. 97, 104.*

▶ 1.2 How did structuralism and functionalism differ, and who were the important people in those early fields?

It really all started to come together in a laboratory in Leipzig, Germany, in 1879. It was here that Wilhelm Wundt (VILL-helm Voont, 1832–1920), a physiologist, attempted to apply scientific principles to the study of the human mind. In his laboratory, students from around the world were taught to study the structure of the human mind. Wundt believed that the mind was made up of thoughts, experiences, emotions, and other basic elements. In order to inspect these nonphysical elements, students had to learn to think objectively about their own thoughts—after all, they could hardly read someone else's mind. Wundt called this process **objective introspection,** the process of objectively examining and measuring one's own thoughts and mental activities (Rieber & Robinson,

✱ **Explore** with a timeline of important dates in psychology.
www.mypsychlab.com

AP* Recognize how philosophical perspectives shaped the development of psychological thought.

How long has ▶
psychology
been
around?

AP* Describe and compare different theoretical approaches in explaining behavior.

AP* Identify the major historical figures in psychology.

objective introspection the process of examining and measuring one's own thoughts and mental activities.

---

*Philosophers: people who seek wisdom and knowledge through thinking and discussion.
**Physiologists: scientists who study the physical workings of the body and its systems.

2001). For example, Wundt might place an object, such as a rock, into a student's hand and have the student tell him everything that he was feeling as a result of having the rock in his hand—all the sensations stimulated by the rock.

This was really the first attempt by anyone to bring objectivity* and measurement to the concept of psychology. This attention to objectivity, together with the establishment of the first true experimental laboratory in psychology, is why Wundt is known as the "father of psychology."

TITCHENER AND STRUCTURALISM IN AMERICA

One of Wundt's students was Edward Titchener (1867–1927), an Englishman who eventually took Wundt's ideas to Cornell University in Ithaca, New York. Titchener expanded on Wundt's original ideas, calling his new viewpoint **structuralism** because the focus of study was the structure of the mind. He believed that every experience could be broken down into its individual emotions and sensations (Brennan, 2002). Although Titchener agreed with Wundt that consciousness, the state of being aware of external events, could be broken down into its basic elements, Titchener also believed that objective introspection could be used on thoughts as well as on physical sensations. For example, Titchener might have asked his students to introspect about things that are blue rather than actually giving them a blue object and asking for reactions to it. Such an exercise might have led to something like the following: "What is blue? There are blue things, like the sky or a bird's feathers. Blue is cool and restful, blue is calm . . ." and so on.

In 1894, one of Titchener's students at Cornell University became famous for becoming the first woman to receive a Ph.D. in psychology (Goodman, 1980; Guthrie, 2004). Her name was Margaret F. Washburn, and she was Titchener's only graduate student for that year. In 1908 she published a book on animal behavior that was considered an important work in that era of psychology, *The Animal Mind* (Washburn, 1908).

Structuralism was a dominant force in the early days of psychology, but it eventually died out in the early 1900s, as the structuralists were busily fighting among themselves over just which key elements of experience were the most important. A competing view arose not long after Wundt's laboratory was established, shortly before structuralism came to America.

WILLIAM JAMES AND FUNCTIONALISM

Harvard University was the first school in America to offer classes in psychology in the late 1870s. These classes were taught by one of Harvard's most illustrious instructors, William James (1842–1910). James began teaching anatomy and physiology, but as his interest in psychology developed, he began teaching psychology almost exclusively (Brennan, 2002). His comprehensive textbook on the subject, *Principles of Psychology*, is so brilliantly written that copies are still in print (James, 1890, 2002).

Unlike Wundt and Titchener, James was more interested in studying the importance of consciousness to everyday life than he was in actually analyzing consciousness. He believed that the scientific study of consciousness itself was not yet possible. Conscious ideas are constantly flowing in an ever-changing stream, and once you start thinking about what you were just thinking about, what you were thinking about is no longer what you *were* thinking about, it's what you *are* thinking about, and . . . excuse me, I'm a little dizzy. I think you get the picture, anyway.

Instead, James focused on how the mind allows people to *function* in the real world—how people work, play, and adapt to their surroundings, a viewpoint he called **functionalism.** (He was heavily influenced by naturalist Charles Darwin's ideas about

German physiologist Wilhelm Wundt participates in an experiment in his laboratory as students look on.

Structuralists would be interested in all of the memories and sensations this woman is experiencing as she smells the rose.

structuralism early perspective in psychology associated with Wilhelm Wundt and Edward Titchener, in which the focus of study is the structure or basic elements of the mind.

functionalism early perspective in psychology associated with William James, in which the focus of study is how the mind allows people to adapt, live, work, and play.

---

*Objectivity: expressing or dealing with facts or conditions as they really are without allowing the influence of personal feelings, prejudices, or interpretations.

Mary Whiton Calkins, despite being denied a Ph.D. degree by Harvard because she was a woman, became the first female president of the American Psychological Association and had a successful career as a professor and researcher. Archives of the History of American Psychology–The University of Akron

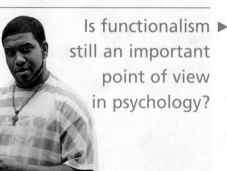

Is functionalism still an important point of view in psychology? ▶

natural selection, in which physical traits that help an animal adapt to its environment and survive are passed on to its offspring, becoming part of the animal's traits. We'll discuss Darwin and natural selection in more detail later in this chapter.) If physical traits could aid in survival, James thought, why couldn't behavioral traits do the same? Animals and people whose behavior helped them to survive would pass those traits on to their offspring, perhaps by teaching or even by some mechanism of heredity.* (Remember that this was early in the days of trying to understand how heredity worked.) For example, a behavior such as avoiding the eyes of others in an elevator can be seen as a way of protecting one's personal space—a kind of territorial protection that may have its roots in the primitive need to protect one's home and source of food and water from intruders (Manusov & Patterson, 2006) or as a way of avoiding what might seem like a challenge to another person.

One of James's early students was Mary Whiton Calkins, who completed every course and requirement for earning a Ph.D. but was denied that degree by Harvard University because she was a woman. She was allowed to take those classes as a guest only. Calkins eventually established a psychological laboratory at Wellesley College. Her work was some of the earliest research in the area of human memory and the psychology of the self. In 1905, she became the first female president of the American Psychological Association (Furumoto, 1979). Unlike Washburn, Calkins never earned the elusive Ph.D. degree despite a successful career as a professor and researcher (Guthrie, 2004).

This might be a good place to point out that women were not the only minority to make contributions in the early days of psychology. In 1920, for example, Francis Cecil Sumner became the first African American to earn a Ph.D. in psychology at Clark University. He eventually became the chair of the psychology department at Howard University and is assumed by many to be the father of African American psychology (Guthrie, 2004). Kenneth and Mamie Clark worked to show the negative effects of school segregation on African American children (Lal, 2002). Hispanic psychologist Jorge Sanchez conducted research in the area of intelligence testing, focusing on the cultural biases in such tests. Since those early days, psychology has seen an increase in all minorities, although the percentages are still far too small when compared to the population at large.

Is functionalism still an important point of view in psychology?

In the new field of psychology, functionalism offered an alternative viewpoint to that of the structuralists. But like so many of psychology's early ideas, it is no longer a major perspective. Instead, we can find elements of functionalism in the modern fields of *educational psychology* (studying the application of psychological concepts to education) and *industrial/organizational psychology* (studying the application of psychological concepts to businesses, organizations, and industry), as well as other areas in psychology. Ⓛ Ⓘ Ⓝ Ⓚ *to Appendix B: Applied Psychology.* Functionalism also played a part in the development of one of the more modern perspectives, evolutionary psychology, discussed later in this chapter.

GESTALT PSYCHOLOGY: THE WHOLE IS GREATER THAN THE SUM OF ITS PARTS

Meanwhile, back in Germany, other psychologists were attacking the concepts of psychology in yet another way. Max Wertheimer (VERT-hi-mer), like James, objected to the structuralist point of view, but for different reasons. Wertheimer felt that psychological events such as perceiving** and sensing† could not be broken down into any smaller elements and still be properly understood. You can take a compact disc player

---

*Heredity: the transmission of traits and characteristics from parent to offspring through the actions of genes.

**Perceiving: becoming aware of something through the senses.

†Sensing: seeing, hearing, feeling, tasting, or smelling something.

apart, for example, but then you no longer have a CD player—you have a pile of unconnected bits and pieces. As a melody is made up of individual notes that can only be understood if the notes are in the correct relationship to one another, so perception can only be understood as a whole, entire event. Hence, the familiar slogan, "The whole is greater than the sum of its parts." The Gestalt psychologists believed that people naturally seek out patterns ("wholes") in the sensory information available to them. See Figure 1.1 for an example of Gestalt perceptual patterns.

Figure 1.1 A Gestalt Perception
The eye tends to "fill in" the blanks here and see both of these figures as circles rather than as a series of dots or a broken line.

1.3 What were the basic ideas and who were the important people behind the early approaches known as Gestalt, psychoanalysis, and behaviorism?

Wertheimer and others devoted their efforts to studying sensation and perception in this new perspective, **Gestalt psychology.** *Gestalt* (Gesh-TALT) is a German word meaning "an organized whole" or "configuration," which fit well with the focus on studying whole patterns rather than small pieces of them. Today, Gestalt ideas are part of the study of *cognitive psychology*, a field focusing not only on perception but also on learning, memory, thought processes, and problem solving; the basic Gestalt principles of perception are still taught within this newer field (Ash, 1998; Kohler, 1992; Wertheimer, 1982). ⓁⒾⓃⓀ *to Chapter Three: Sensation and Perception, pp. 115–117.* The Gestalt approach has also been influential in psychological therapy, becoming the basis for a major therapeutic technique called *Gestalt therapy.* ⓁⒾⓃⓀ *to Chapter Thirteen: Psychological Therapies, pp. 522–523.*

Gestalt psychology early perspective in psychology focusing on perception and sensation, particularly the perception of patterns and whole figures.

SIGMUND FREUD'S THEORY OF PSYCHOANALYSIS

It should be clear by now that psychology didn't start in one place and at one particular time. People of several different viewpoints were trying to promote their own perspective on the study of the human mind and behavior in different places all over the world. Up to now, this chapter has focused on the physiologists and philosophers who became interested in psychology, with a focus on understanding consciousness but little else. The medical profession took a whole different approach to psychology.

What about Freud? Everybody talks about him when they talk about psychology. Are his ideas still in use?

Sigmund Freud had become a noted physician in Austria while the structuralists were arguing, the functionalists were specializing, and the Gestaltists were looking at the big picture. He was a medical doctor—a neurologist, someone who specializes in disorders of the nervous system—and he and his colleagues had long sought a way to understand the patients who were coming to them for help.

Freud's patients suffered from nervous disorders for which he and other doctors could find no physical cause. Therefore, it was thought, the cause must be in the mind, and that is where Freud began to explore. He proposed that there is an *unconscious* (unaware) mind into which we push, or *repress*, all of our threatening urges and desires. He believed that these repressed urges, in trying to surface, created the nervous disorders in his patients (Freud et al., 1990). ⓁⒾⓃⓀ *to Chapter Eleven: Theories of Personality, pp. 437–438.*

Freud stressed the importance of early childhood experiences, believing that personality was formed in the first six years of life; if there were significant problems, those problems must have begun in the early years.

Some of his well-known followers were Alfred Adler, Carl Jung, and his own daughter, Anna Freud. Anna Freud began what became known as the ego movement in psychology that produced one of the most famous psychologists in the study of personality development, Erik Erikson. ⓁⒾⓃⓀ *to Chapter Ten: Development Across the Life Span, pp. 411–412.*

What about Freud? Everybody talks about him when they talk about psychology. ◄ Are his ideas still in use?

Psychoanalyst Sigmund Freud walks with his daughter Anna, also a psychoanalyst.

psychoanalysis the theory and therapy based on the work of Sigmund Freud.

behaviorism the science of behavior that focuses on observable behavior only.

Freud's ideas are still influential today, although in a somewhat modified form. He had a number of followers in addition to those already named, many of whom became famous by altering his theory to fit their own viewpoint, but his basic ideas are still discussed and debated. (L)(I)(N)(K) *to Chapter Eleven: Theories of Personality, pp. 437–443.*

Freudian **psychoanalysis,** the theory and therapy based on Freud's ideas, has been the basis of much modern *psychotherapy* (a process in which a trained psychological professional helps a person gain insights into and change his or her behavior), but another major and competing viewpoint has actually been more influential in the field of psychology as a whole.

PAVLOV, WATSON, AND THE DAWN OF BEHAVIORISM

Ivan Pavlov, like Freud, was not a psychologist. He was a Russian physiologist who, working with dogs, had shown that a reflex (an involuntary reaction) such as salivation, which is normally produced by actually having food in one's mouth, could be caused to occur in response to a totally new and formerly unrelated stimulus,* such as the sound of a bell. He would ring the bell, give the dogs food, and they would salivate. After several repetitions, the dogs would salivate to the sound of the bell *before* the food was presented—a learned (or "conditioned") reflexive response (Klein & Mowrer, 1989). This process was called *conditioning.* (L)(I)(N)(K) *to Chapter Five: Learning, p. 177.*

Physiologist Ivan Pavlov uses a dog to demonstrate the conditioned reflex to students at the Russian Military Medical Academy.

In the early 1900s, psychologist John B. Watson had tired of the arguing among the structuralists; he challenged the functionalist viewpoint, as well as psychoanalysis, with his own "science of behavior," or **behaviorism** (Watson, 1924). Watson wanted to bring psychology back to a focus on scientific inquiry, and he felt that the only way to do that was to ignore the whole "consciousness" issue and focus only on *observable behavior*—something that could be directly seen and measured. He had read of Pavlov's work and thought that conditioning could form the basis of his new perspective of behaviorism.

Of Babies and Rats Watson was certainly aware of Freud's work and his views on unconscious repression. Freud believed that all behavior stems from unconscious motivation, whereas Watson believed that all behavior is learned. Freud had stated that a *phobia,* an irrational fear, is really a symptom of an underlying, repressed conflict and cannot be "cured" without years of psychoanalysis to uncover and understand the repressed material.

Watson believed that phobias are learned through the process of conditioning and set out to prove it. He took a baby, known as "Little Albert," and taught him to fear a white rat by making a loud, scary noise every time the infant saw the rat, until finally seeing the rat caused the infant to cry and become fearful (Watson & Rayner, 1920). Even though "Little Albert" was not afraid of the rat at the start, the experiment worked very well—in fact, "Little Albert" became afraid of other white and fuzzy things, including a white rabbit and a sealskin coat.

This sounds really bizarre—what does scaring a baby have to do with the science of psychology?

This sounds really bizarre—what does scaring a baby have to do with the science of psychology? ▶

---

*Stimulus: anything that causes an organism to have a reaction or response.

Watson wanted to prove that all behavior was a result of a stimulus–response relationship such as that described by Pavlov. Because Freud and his ideas about unconscious motivation were becoming a dominant force, Watson felt the need to show the world that a much simpler explanation could be found. Although scaring a baby sounds a little cruel, he felt that the advancement of the science of behavior was worth the baby's relatively brief discomfort. One of Watson's graduate students later decided to repeat Watson and Rayner's study but added training that would "cancel out" the phobic reaction of the baby to the white rat. For more on this research, see the section on Classic Studies in Psychology that follows.

Behaviorism, like psychoanalysis, is still a major perspective in psychology today. It has also influenced the development of other perspectives, such as *cognitive psychology*.

American psychologist John Watson is known as the Father of Behaviorism. Behaviorism focuses only on observable behavior.

Classic Studies in Psychology
Psychologist Mary Cover Jones and "Little Peter"

Mary Cover was born on September 1, 1897. She graduated from Vassar in 1919 with her bachelor's degree. Rosalie Rayner, John B. Watson's graduate assistant and future wife, was a fellow Vassar graduate and a friend. Mary Cover attended one of Watson's weekend lectures and came away determined to pursue a graduate degree in psychology. Her master's degree was completed in 1920 under the supervision of Watson. In that same year she married another graduate student, Harold Jones (Rutherford, 2000).

Mary Cover Jones was fascinated with the "Little Albert" study and wanted to explore the concept of learned phobias. Beginning with a child known as "Little Peter," Jones began by duplicating Watson and Rayner's 1920 study. She was able to create the same kind of phobic reaction in Peter that had developed in Albert, but she used a white rabbit instead of a rat (Jones, 1924).

Once the child was conditioned to fear the rabbit, Jones began a process called *counterconditioning*, in which the old conditioning (fear of the rabbit) would be replaced, or countered, by new conditioning. Peter was brought into one corner of a room, while the rabbit was placed in the opposite corner. Peter was then given some food (something he liked quite a bit). Although Peter may have been nervous to have the rabbit in the far corner, the food was right in front of him. He began to eat and experienced the pleasurable sensations associated with eating. This pattern was repeated over several sessions, with the rabbit being brought a little closer each time. Eventually, Peter was no longer showing any fear of the rabbit at all.

How did this work? In Watson and Rayner's original experiment, the white rat was paired with a scary noise. The scary noise caused a fear response, and eventually the rat caused the same fear response because of association with the noise. In Jones's study, this is exactly how Peter came to fear the rabbit. But then the rabbit was paired with yet another stimulus, food, which causes pleasure, not fear. After enough pairings of the food with the rabbit, the newer association of rabbit/food/pleasure replaced the old association of rabbit/noise/fear. The old fear response had been "countered."

Mary Cover Jones went on to become one of the early pioneers of behavior therapy. She was also a key figure in the Oakland Growth Study, a study of 200 fifth- and sixth-grade children that followed their development from the beginning of puberty to the end of adolescence. It is her work that is often cited when textbooks talk about the benefits and problems

Mary Cover Jones, one of the early pioneers of behavior therapy, earned her master's degree under the supervision of John Watson. She had a long and distinguished career, including in 1952 the publication of the first educational television course in child development.

Watch classic video footage of John Watson, Rosalie Rayner, and Little Albert.
www.mypsychlab.com

associated with early and late maturation in puberty. She and her husband, Harold Jones, published the first educational television course in child development in 1952. After a long and distinguished career, Mary Cover Jones died on July 22, 1987, at the age of 90 (Rutherford, 2000). **Watch** on **MyPsychLab**

Questions for Further Thought

1. What difficulties might early women psychologists like Mary Cover Jones have faced in a field and a culture dominated by men?

2. What kinds of behavior or issues might have been thought inappropriate for women to study in the early days of psychology?

1.2–3

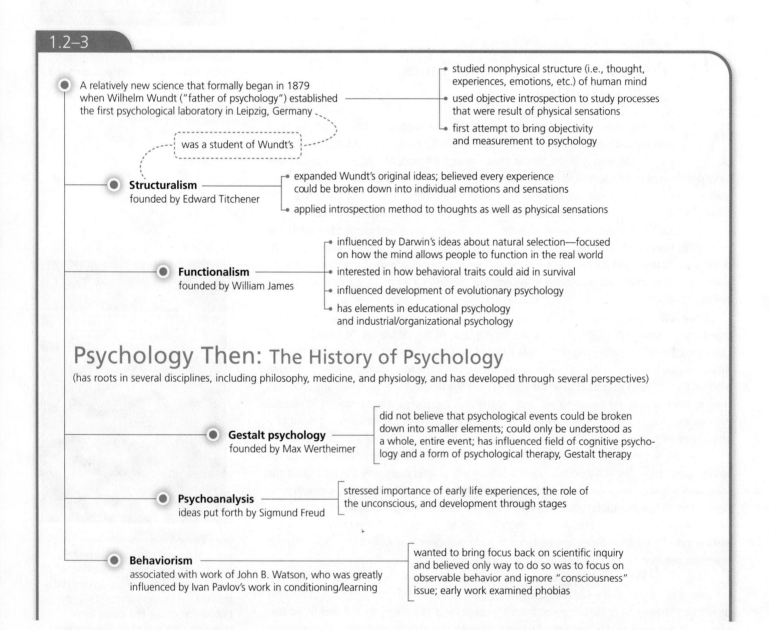

A relatively new science that formally began in 1879 when Wilhelm Wundt ("father of psychology") established the first psychological laboratory in Leipzig, Germany

- studied nonphysical structure (i.e., thought, experiences, emotions, etc.) of human mind
- used objective introspection to study processes that were result of physical sensations
- first attempt to bring objectivity and measurement to psychology

was a student of Wundt's

Structuralism
founded by Edward Titchener

- expanded Wundt's original ideas; believed every experience could be broken down into individual emotions and sensations
- applied introspection method to thoughts as well as physical sensations

Functionalism
founded by William James

- influenced by Darwin's ideas about natural selection—focused on how the mind allows people to function in the real world
- interested in how behavioral traits could aid in survival
- influenced development of evolutionary psychology
- has elements in educational psychology and industrial/organizational psychology

Psychology Then: The History of Psychology
(has roots in several disciplines, including philosophy, medicine, and physiology, and has developed through several perspectives)

Gestalt psychology
founded by Max Wertheimer

did not believe that psychological events could be broken down into smaller elements; could only be understood as a whole, entire event; has influenced field of cognitive psychology and a form of psychological therapy, Gestalt therapy

Psychoanalysis
ideas put forth by Sigmund Freud

stressed importance of early life experiences, the role of the unconscious, and development through stages

Behaviorism
associated with work of John B. Watson, who was greatly influenced by Ivan Pavlov's work in conditioning/learning

wanted to bring focus back on scientific inquiry and believed only way to do so was to focus on observable behavior and ignore "consciousness" issue; early work examined phobias

Directions: Read each of the questions or incomplete sentences below. Then choose the response that best answers the question or completes the sentence.

1. Which of the following early psychologists would have been most likely to agree with the statement, "The study of the mind should focus on how it allows us to adapt to our surroundings"?
   a. Wilhelm Wundt
   b. William James
   c. John Watson
   d. Sigmund Freud
   e. Ivan Pavlov

2. Which early perspective would have been least likely to agree with the structuralist perspective?
   a. Introspectionism
   b. Functionalism
   c. Psychoanalysis
   d. Gestalt
   e. Behaviorism

3. With which psychological relationship were ancient philosophers like Aristotle and Plato most concerned?
   a. The relationship between mind and body
   b. The relationship between sensation and perception
   c. The relationship between a stimulus and a response
   d. The relationship between environment and behavior
   e. The relationship between conscious and unconscious urges

4. Why was psychologist Mary Whiton Calkins denied a Ph.D. from Harvard University?
   a. She was a woman.
   b. She was a functionalist.
   c. She was a poor researcher.
   d. She was an African American.
   e. She was a student of William James.

5. A general explanation of a set of observations or facts is known as a _____.
   a. description
   b. control
   c. prediction
   d. perception
   e. theory

Psychology Now: Modern Perspectives

1.4 What are the basic ideas behind the seven modern perspectives, as well as the important contributions of Skinner, Maslow, and Rogers?

Even today, there isn't one single perspective that is used to explain all human behavior and mental processes. There are actually seven modern perspectives, with two of those being holdovers from the early days of the field.

PSYCHODYNAMIC PERSPECTIVE

Freud's theory is still with us today in use by many professionals in therapy situations. It is far less common today than it was a few decades ago, however, and even those who use his techniques modify them for modern use. In the more modern **psychodynamic perspective,** the focus is still on the unconscious mind and its influence over conscious behavior and on early childhood experiences, but with less of an emphasis on sex and sexual motivations and more emphasis on the development of a sense of self and the discovery of other motivations behind a person's behavior.

Freud had a number of followers who took his original ideas and modified them to their own perspectives. Their students continued to modify those theories until today we have a kind of neo-Freudianism (Freud et al., 1990; Meadow & Clevans, 1978). Therapists often speak of Freudian complexes and use much of his terminology in their work with clients. Part of the reason that Freudian concepts are so enduring is the lack of any scientific way to test them and, therefore, show them to be either useful or useless. (L⃝I⃝N⃝K⃝) *to Chapter Eleven: Theories of Personality, pp. 437–443.* Nevertheless, despite the lack of testability, Freud's theory continues to appeal to many modern theorists.

psychodynamic perspective modern version of psychoanalysis that is more focused on the development of a sense of self and the discovery of other motivations behind a person's behavior than sexual motivations.

Behaviorist B. F. Skinner puts a rat through its paces. What challenges might arise from applying information gained from studies with animals to human behavior?

BEHAVIORAL PERSPECTIVE

Like psychoanalysis, behaviorism is still also very influential. When its primary supporter, John B. Watson, moved on to greener pastures in the world of advertising, B. F. Skinner became the new leader of the field.

Skinner not only continued research in classical conditioning, but he also developed a theory of how voluntary behavior is learned called *operant conditioning* (Skinner, 1938). In this theory, behavioral responses that are followed by pleasurable consequences are strengthened, or *reinforced*. For example, a child who cries and is rewarded by getting his mother's attention will cry again in the future. Skinner's work is discussed in much greater depth in Chapter Five. Ⓛ Ⓘ Ⓝ Ⓚ *to Chapter Five: Learning, pp. 187–199.* In addition to the psychodynamic and behavioral perspectives, there are five newer perspectives that have developed within the last 50 years.

HUMANISTIC PERSPECTIVE

One of the newer perspectives, often called the "third force" in psychology, was really a reaction to both psychodynamic theory and behaviorism. In the early to mid-1900s, if you were a psychologist you were either a psychoanalyst or a behaviorist—there weren't any other major viewpoints to rival those two. Behaviorism was seen as a very "mechanical" theory—stimulus goes in, response comes out, and what happens in the middle is of no interest. The environment determines behavior, and the individual has little input into his or her development. Psychoanalysis wasn't mechanistic, but in that theory the workings of the physical body (in the form of sexual and aggressive instincts) determine behavior, and the individual, once again, has little to do with his or her own destiny.

Some professionals began to develop a perspective that would allow them to focus on people's ability to direct their own lives. These theorists wanted to shift the focus to the aspects of human nature that make us uniquely human—our appreciation for beauty, for example. In a very real sense, then, this approach owes far more to the early roots of psychology in the field of philosophy rather than the more scientific fields of medicine and physiology. Humanists held the view that people have *free will*, the freedom to choose their own destiny. Two of the earliest and most famous founders of this view were Abraham Maslow (1908–1970) and Carl Rogers (1902–1987).

Both Maslow and Rogers emphasized the human potential, the ability of each person to become the best person he or she could be (Maslow, 1968; Rogers, 1961). They believed that studying animals in laboratories (as the behaviorists did) or people with nervous disorders (as the psychoanalysts did) could not lead to a better understanding of this human potential for *self-actualization*, as Maslow termed it—achieving one's full potential or ideal self. Today, humanism is still very influential in psychotherapy. Ⓛ Ⓘ Ⓝ Ⓚ *to Chapter Thirteen: Psychological Therapies, pp. 520–523.*

COGNITIVE PERSPECTIVE

Cognitive psychology, which focuses on how people think, remember, store, and use information, became a major force in the field in the 1960s. It wasn't a new idea, as the Gestalt psychologists had themselves supported the study of mental processes of learning. The development of computers (which just happened to make great models of human thinking), the work of Piaget with children, Chomsky's analysis of Skinner's views of language, and discoveries in biological psychology all stimulated an interest in studying the processes of thought. The **cognitive perspective** with its focus on memory, intelligence, perception, thought processes, problem solving, language, and learning has become a major force in psychology. **LINK** *to Chapter Seven: Cognition: Thinking, Intelligence, and Language, pp. 260–305.*

Within the cognitive perspective, the relatively new field of **cognitive neuroscience** includes the study of the physical workings of the brain and nervous system when engaged in memory, thinking, and other cognitive processes. Cognitive neuroscientists use tools for imaging the structure and activity of the living brain, such as magnetic resonance imaging (MRI), positron emission tomography (PET), and functional MRI (fMRI). **LINK** *to Chapter Two: The Biological Perspective, pp. 66–68.* The emerging field of brain imaging is an important one in the study of cognitive processes.

SOCIOCULTURAL PERSPECTIVE

Another modern perspective in psychology is the **sociocultural perspective,** which actually combines two areas of study: *social psychology*, which is the study of groups, social roles, and rules of social actions and relationships; and *cultural psychology*, which is the study of cultural norms,* values, and expectations. These two areas are related in that they are both about the effect that people have on one another, either individually or in a larger group, such as a culture (Peplau & Taylor, 1997). **LINK** *to Chapter Fourteen: Social Psychology, pp. 554–600.* Russian psychologist Lev Vygotsky (1978) also used sociocultural concepts in forming his sociocultural theory of children's cognitive development. **LINK** *to Chapter Ten: Development Across the Life Span, p. 405.*

The sociocultural perspective is important because it reminds people that how they and others behave (or even think) is influenced not only by whether they are alone, with friends, in a crowd, or part of a group, but also by the social norms, fads, class differences, and ethnic identity concerns of the particular culture in which they live. *Cross-cultural research* also fits within this perspective. In cross-cultural research, the contrasts and comparisons of a behavior or issue are studied in at least two or more cultures. This type of research can help illustrate the different influences of environment (culture and training) when compared to the influence of heredity (genetics, or the influence of genes on behavior).

For example, in a classic study covered in Chapter Fourteen (pp. 470, 472–474), researchers Darley and Latané (1968) found that the presence of other people actually *lessened* the chances that a person in trouble would receive help. The phenomenon is called the bystander effect and it is believed to be the result of *diffusion of responsibility*, which is the tendency to feel that someone else is responsible for taking action when others are present. But would this effect appear in other cultures? Shorey (2001), in his discussion of the brutal beating death of a Somali prisoner in a Canadian military facility while bystanders looked on without acting, suggests that it just might. But is Canadian culture too similar to our own to lead us to this conclusion? Would another culture very different from Western culture show the same effect? This is exactly the kind of question that the sociocultural perspective, using cross-cultural research, asks and attempts to answer.

---

*Norms: standards or expected behavior.

cognitive perspective modern perspective that focuses on memory, intelligence, perception, problem solving, and learning.

cognitive neuroscience study of the physical changes in the brain and nervous system during thinking.

sociocultural perspective perspective that focuses on the relationship between social behavior and culture.

EARLIEST DEFICIT

5 YEARS LATER (SAME SUBJECTS)

STG   DLPFC

These brain scans highlight gray matter loss in the brains of very early-onset, adolescents with schizophrenia over a five-year period, highlighting one focus of the biological perspective.

AP* Discuss psychology's abiding interest in how heredity, environment, and evolution work together to shape behavior.

AP* Predict how traits and behavior can be selected for their adaptive value.

That explains why people don't like bitter stuff, like the white part of an orange peel, but that's really a physical thing. How would the evolutionary perspective help us understand something psychological like relationships?

biopsychological perspective perspective that attributes human and animal behavior to biological events occurring in the body, such as genetic influences, hormones, and the activity of the nervous system.

evolutionary perspective perspective that focuses on the biological bases of universal mental characteristics that all humans share.

BIOPSYCHOLOGICAL PERSPECTIVE

Biopsychology, or the study of the biological bases of behavior and mental processes, isn't really as new a perspective as one might think.

In the **biopsychological perspective,** human and animal behavior is seen as a direct result of events in the body. Hormones, heredity, brain chemicals, tumors, and diseases are some of the biological causes of behavior and mental events. ⓁⒾⓃⓀ *to Chapter Two: The Biological Perspective, pp. 53–64.*

For example, evidence is mounting for a biological cause (perhaps even genetic) for *schizophrenia,* a mental disorder involving delusions (false beliefs), hallucinations (false sensory impressions), and extremely distorted thinking (Brzustowicz et al., 2004; Maziade et al., 1997). ⓁⒾⓃⓀ *to Chapter Twelve: Psychological Disorders, pp. 501–504.*

EVOLUTIONARY PERSPECTIVE

As you've seen by now, biology isn't the only force that determines and drives human behavior. Just as some researchers examine the effects of biological factors (like genetics) on behavior and others examine the effects of environmental factors (like parenting) on behavior, still other researchers examine potential links between human behavior and Charles Darwin's theory of evolution. The **evolutionary perspective** focuses on the biological bases for universal mental characteristics that all humans share. It seeks to explain general mental strategies and traits, such as why we lie, how attractiveness influences mate selection, why fear of snakes is so universal, and why people like music and dancing, among many others.

In this perspective, the mind is seen as a set of information-processing machines, designed by the same process of natural selection that Darwin (1859) first theorized, allowing human beings to solve the problems faced in the early days of human evolution— the problems of the early hunters and gatherers. For example, *evolutionary psychologists* (psychologists who study the evolutionary origins of human behavior) would view the human behavior of not eating substances that have a bitter taste (such as poisonous plants) as an adaptive* behavior that evolved as early humans came into contact with such bitter plants. Those who ate the bitter plants would die, while those who spit them out survived to pass their "I don't like this taste" genes on to their offspring, who would pass the genes on to their offspring, and so on, until after a long period of time there is an entire population of humans that naturally avoid bitter-tasting substances.

That explains why people don't like bitter stuff, like the white part of an orange peel, but that's really a physical thing. How would the evolutionary perspective help us understand something psychological like relationships?

Relationships between men and women are one of the many areas in which evolutionary psychologists conduct research. For example, in one study researchers surveyed individuals about their relationships with the opposite sex, asking the participants how likely they would be to forgive either a sexual infidelity or an emotional one (Shackelford et al., 2002). Evolutionary theory would predict that men would find it more difficult to forgive a woman who was physically intimate with someone else than a woman who was only emotionally involved with someone because the man wants to be sure that the children the woman bears are his (Geary, 2000). Why put all that effort into providing for children who could be another man's offspring? Women, on the other hand, should find it harder to forgive an emotional infidelity, as they are always sure that their children are their own, but (in evolutionary terms, mind you) they need the emotional loyalty of the men to provide for those children (Buss et al., 1992; Daly

*Adaptive: having the quality of adjusting to the circumstances or need; in the sense used here, a behavior that aids in survival.

et al., 1982). The results of the study bore out the prediction: Men found it harder to forgive a partner's sexual straying and were more likely to break up with the woman than if the infidelity were purely emotional; for women, the opposite results were found. Another study concerning mating found that women seem to use a man's kissing ability to determine his worthiness as a potential mate (Hughes et al., 2007).

Psychological Professionals and Areas of Specialization

There are a number of professionals who work in the field of psychology. These professionals have different training, different focuses, and may have different goals from the typical psychologist.

1.5 How does a psychiatrist differ from a psychologist, and what are the other types of professionals who work in the various areas of psychology?

A **psychiatrist** has a medical (M.D. or D.O.) degree and is a medical doctor who has specialized in the diagnosis and treatment of psychological disorders. Psychiatrists can prescribe medicine in addition to providing therapy and counseling, and they typically work in private practice or hospital settings.

A **psychoanalyst** is usually either a psychiatrist (M.D.) or a psychologist (Ph.D., Psy.D., or Ed.D.) who has special training in the theories of Sigmund Freud and his method of psychoanalysis. Psychoanalysts, like psychiatrists, usually work in private practice or hospital settings. **LINK** *to Appendix B: Applied Psychology.* (Like the term *therapist*, the label of *psychoanalyst* is not protected by federal or state law and anyone—trained or not—may use this label. If you are looking for a therapist of any type, always ask to see the person's credentials.)

A **psychiatric social worker** is trained in the area of social work and usually possesses a Master of Social Work (M.S.W.) degree, and often has obtained a professional license, such as a Licensed Clinical Social Worker (L.C.S.W.). These professionals focus more on the environmental conditions that can have an impact on mental disorders, such as poverty, overcrowding, stress, and drug abuse. They work out of clinics, hospitals, and social service organizations.

Psychologists with an evolutionary perspective would be interested in how this couple selected each other as partners.

How might using hand puppets help these young children talk about the problems in their lives?

psychiatrist a medical doctor who has specialized in the diagnosis and treatment of psychological disorders.

psychoanalyst either a psychiatrist or a psychologist who has special training in the theories of Sigmund Freud and his method of psychoanalysis.

psychiatric social worker a social worker with some training in therapy methods who focuses on the environmental conditions that can have an impact on mental disorders, such as poverty, overcrowding, stress, and drug abuse.

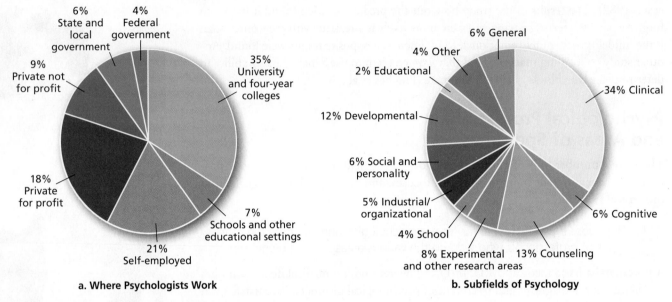

a. Where Psychologists Work

b. Subfields of Psychology

Figure 1.2 Work Settings and Subfields of Psychology

(a) There are many different work settings for psychologists. Although not obvious from the chart, many psychologists work in more than one setting. For example, a clinical psychologist may work in a hospital setting as well as teach at a university or college. (Tsapogas et al., 2006) (b) This pie chart shows the specialty areas of psychologists who recently received their doctorates. (Hoffer et al., 2007)

Note: Due to rounding, percentages may not total to 100 percent.

A **psychologist** has no medical training but has a doctorate degree. (A person with a master's degree might be a counselor, therapist, or researcher but is typically not referred to as a psychologist.) Psychologists undergo intense academic training, learning about many different areas of psychology before choosing an area in which to specialize. Because the focus of their careers can vary so widely, psychologists work in many different vocational* settings. Figure 1.2a shows the types of settings in which psychologists work. Although typically psychologists cannot prescribe medications, in some states psychologists can go through special training in the prescription of drugs for certain psychological disorders. Psychologists in the counseling profession must be licensed to practice in their states.

AREAS OF SPECIALIZATION

You said not all psychologists do counseling. But I thought that was all that psychologists do—what else is there?

Although many psychologists do participate in delivering therapy to people who need help, there is a nearly equal number of psychologists who do other tasks: researching, teaching, designing equipment and workplaces, and developing educational methods, for example. Also, not every psychologist is interested in the same area of human—or animal—behavior and most psychologists work in several different areas of interest, as shown in Figure 1.2b, Subfields of Psychology.

There are many other areas as well, as psychology can be used in fields such as health, sports performance, legal issues, business concerns, and even in the design of equipment, tools, and furniture. To learn more about psychology's different domains, get a more detailed look at some of the areas in which psychological principles can be applied, and view a listing of careers that can benefit from a degree in psychology, see ⓁⒾⓃⓀ to *Appendix B: Applied Psychology*.

> You said not all psychologists do counseling. But I thought that was all that psychologists do—what else is there?

AP* Distinguish the different domains of psychology.

psychologist a professional with an academic degree and specialized training in one or more areas of psychology.

———————————

*Vocational: having to do with a job or career.

1.4   1.5

- **Psychodynamic** —— focuses on the role of the unconscious mind and its influence on conscious behavior, based on Freud's theory   early childhood experiences, development of sense of self, and other motivations

- **Behavioral** —— focuses on how behavioral responses are learned through classical or operant conditioning
  based on early work
  of Watson and later B.F. Skinner

- **Humanistic** —— focuses on human potential, free will, and possibility of self-actualization
  two pioneers are Carl Rogers
  and Abraham Maslow

- **Cognitive** —— focuses on memory, intelligence, perception, thought processes,
  has roots in   problem solving, language, and learning
  Gestalt psychology

Psychology Now: Modern Perspectives

(No one single perspective is used to explain all human behavior and processes)

- **Sociocultural** —— focuses on the behavior of individuals as the result of the presence (real or imagined) of other individuals, as part of groups, or as part of a larger culture

- **Biopsychological** —— focuses on influences of hormones, brain structures and chemicals, disease, etc.; human and animal behavior is seen as a direct result of events in the body

- **Evolutionary** —— focuses on the biological bases for universal mental characteristics, such as why we lie, how attractiveness influences mate selection, the universality of fear, and why we enjoy things like music and dance

Types of Psychological Professionals

(people working in the field of psychology have a variety of training experiences and different focuses)

- **psychiatrist**

  - medical doctor (M.D. or D.O.) who specializes in diagnosis and treatment of psychological disorders; can prescribe medication

- **psychoanalyst**

  - usually a psychiatrist or psychologist who has special training in theories of Freud

- **psychiatric social worker**

  - has training in area of social work (M.S.W.) and often has a professional license to practice (L.C.S.W.)

- **psychologist**

  - has a doctorate degree (Ph.D., Psy.D., or Ed.D.) and works with either humans or animals in a variety of settings based on the area of specialization

  - must be licensed to practice independently; typically does not prescribe medications but can go through specialized training to do so in some states

PRACTICE QUIZ: PREPARING FOR THE AP* EXAM

ANSWERS ON PAGE AK-1.

Directions: Read each of the questions or incomplete sentences below. Then choose the response that best answers the question or completes the sentence.

1. Which of the following pairs represents the two psychology perspectives that were also part of the historical beginnings of psychology?
   a. Humanism and behaviorism
   b. Behaviorism and psychodynamics
   c. Psychodynamics and humanism
   d. Humanism and cognitive psychology
   e. Cognitive psychology and psychodynamics

2. Elsie suffered a stroke and had to be hospitalized. While in the hospital, she talked in funny, garbled words and seemed to think that she was being held against her will. Which of the following perspectives best explains Elsie's odd behavior?
   a. Behaviorism
   b. Sociocultural psychology
   c. Psychodynamics
   d. Biopsychology
   e. Evolutionary psychology

3. Which perspective would a researcher be taking if she were studying the way children store and retrieve information?

(continued)

a. A psychoanalytic perspective
b. A behaviorist perspective
c. A humanist perspective
d. An evolutionary perspective
e. A cognitive perspective

4. Which of the following professionals in psychology focuses most on the environmental conditions that affect mental disorders?
   a. Psychiatrist
   b. Psychologist
   c. Psychoanalyst
   d. Professor of psychology
   e. Psychiatric social worker

5. Dr. Roaden works in a hospital assessing, evaluating, and treating patients who present with symptoms of various mental illnesses. The treatments often involve the prescribing of medications, though she also performs counseling as part of her job. Dr. Roaden is most likely _____.
   a. a personality psychologist
   b. a developmental psychologist
   c. a psychiatrist
   d. a psychiatric social worker
   e. an experimental psychologist

Psychology: The Science

WHY PSYCHOLOGISTS USE THE SCIENTIFIC METHOD

Have you ever played the "airport game"? You sit at the airport (bus terminal, doctor's office, or any other place where people come and go and you have a long wait) and try to guess what people do for a living based only on their appearance. Although it's a fun game, the guesses are rarely correct. People's guesses also sometimes reveal the biases that they may have about certain physical appearances: men with long hair are musicians, people wearing suits are executives, and so on. Like the airport game, psychology is concerned with the study of people and their behavior. Unlike the airport game, though, psychology is about trying to determine facts and reduce uncertainty and bias.

The scientific method can be used to determine if children who watch violence on television are more likely to be aggressive than those who do not.

1.6 Why is psychology considered a science, and what are the steps in using the scientific method?

In psychology, researchers want to see only what is really there, not what their biases might want them to see. The way to do that is by using the **scientific method,** a system for reducing bias and error in the measurement of data.

The first step in any investigation is to have a question to investigate, right? So the first step in the scientific method is this:

1. **Perceiving the Question:** You notice something interesting happening in your surroundings for which you would like to have an explanation. An example might be that you've noticed that your younger siblings seem to get a little more aggressive with each other after watching a particularly violent children's cartoon program on Saturday morning. You wonder if the violence in the cartoon could be creating the aggressive behavior in your siblings. This step is derived from the goal of description: What is happening here?

   Once you have a question, you want an answer. The next logical step is to form a tentative* answer or explanation for the behavior you have seen. This tentative explanation is known as a **hypothesis.**

2. **Forming a Hypothesis:** Based on your initial observations about what's going on in your surroundings, you form an educated guess about the explanation for your observations, putting it into the form of a statement that can be tested in some way. Going back to the previous example, you might say, "Children who watch violent cartoons will become more aggressive."

   The next step is testing the hypothesis. People have a tendency to notice only things that agree with their view of the world, a kind of selective percep-

scientific method system of gathering data so that bias and error in measurement are reduced.

hypothesis tentative explanation of a phenomenon based on observations.

---

*Tentative: something that is not fully worked out or completed as yet.

tion called *confirmation bias.* Ⓛ Ⓘ Ⓝ Ⓚ *to Chapter Seven: Cognition: Thinking, Intelligence, and Language, p. 272.* For example, if a person is convinced that all men with long hair are musicians, that person will tend to notice only those long-haired men who are musicians and ignore all the long-haired men who are plumbers, lawyers, or computer scientists. The scientific method is designed to overcome the tendency to look at only the information that confirms people's biases by forcing them to actively seek out information that might *contradict* their biases (or hypotheses). So when you test your hypothesis, you are trying to determine if the factor you suspect has an effect and that the results weren't due to luck or chance. That's why psychologists keep doing research over and over—to get more evidence that hypotheses are "supported."

3. **Testing the Hypothesis:** The method you use to test your hypothesis will depend on exactly what kind of answer you think you might get. You might make more detailed observations or do a survey in which you ask questions of a large number of people, or you might design an experiment in which you deliberately change one thing to see if that adjustment causes changes in the behavior you are observing. In the example, the best method would probably be an experiment in which you select a group of children, show half of them a cartoon with violence and half of them a cartoon with no violence, and then find some way of measuring aggressive behavior in the two groups.

   What do you do with the results of your testing? Of course, testing the hypothesis is all about the goal of getting an explanation for behavior, which leads to the next step.

4. **Drawing Conclusions:** Once you know the results of your hypothesis testing, you will find that either your hypothesis was supported—which means that your little experiment worked, or your measurements supported your initial observations—or it wasn't supported, which means that you need to go back to square one and think of another possible explanation for what you have observed. (Could it be that Saturday mornings make children a little more aggressive? Or Saturday breakfasts?)

   The results of any method of hypothesis testing won't be just the raw numbers or measurements. Any data that come from your testing procedure will be analyzed with some kind of statistical method that helps to organize and refine the data. Ⓛ Ⓘ Ⓝ Ⓚ *to Appendix A: Statistics.* You have come to some conclusion about your investigation's success or failure, and you want to let other researchers know what you have found.

   Why tell anyone what happened if it failed?

   Just because one experiment or other study did not find support for the hypothesis does not necessarily mean that the hypothesis is incorrect. Your study might have been poorly designed, or there might have been factors not under your control that interfered with the study. But other researchers are asking the same kinds of questions that you might have asked. They need to know what has already been found out about the answers to those questions so that they can continue investigating and adding more knowledge about the answers to those questions. Even if your own investigation didn't go as planned, that tells other researchers what *not* to do in the future. So the final step in any scientific investigation is reporting the results.

5. **Report Your Results:** At this point, you would want to write up exactly what you did, why you did it, how you did it, and what you found, so that others can learn from what you have already accomplished—or failed to accomplish.

◀ Why tell anyone what happened if it failed?

replicate   in research, repeating a study or experiment to see if the same results will be obtained in an effort to demonstrate reliability of results.

observer effect   tendency of people or animals to behave differently from normal when they know they are being observed.

Another reason for reporting your results is that even if your research gave you the answer you expected, your investigation might have been done incorrectly, or the results might have been a fluke or due to chance alone. So if others can **replicate** your research (do exactly the same study over again and get the same results), it gives much more support to your findings. This allows others to predict behavior based on your findings as well as use the results of those findings to modify or control behavior, the last two goals in psychology.

This might be a good place to make a distinction between questions that can be scientifically or empirically studied and those that cannot. For example, "What is the meaning of life?" is not a question that can be studied using the scientific or empirical method. Empirical questions are those that can be tested through direct observation or experience. For example, "Has life ever existed on Mars?" is a question that scientists are trying to answer through measurements, experimentation, soil samples, and other methods. Eventually they will be able to say with some degree of confidence that life could have existed or could not have existed. That is an empirical question, because it can be supported or disproved by gathering real evidence. The meaning of life, however, is a question of belief for each person. One does not need proof to *believe*, but scientists need proof (in the form of objectively gathered evidence) to *know*.

In psychology, researchers try to find the answers to empirical questions. Questions that involve beliefs and values are best left to philosophy and religion.

AP*   Differentiate types of research with regard to purpose, strengths, and weaknesses.

AP*   Describe how research design drives the reasonable conclusions that can be drawn.

Researcher Jane Goodall watches chimpanzees behave in their natural environment. How might her presence have affected the behavior of the chimpanzees?

DESCRIPTIVE METHODS

1.7   How are naturalistic and laboratory settings used to describe behavior, and what are some of the advantages and disadvantages associated with these settings?

There are a number of different ways to investigate the answers to research questions, and which one researchers use depends on the kind of question they want to answer. If they want to simply gather information about what has happened or what is happening, they would want a method that gives them a detailed description.

Naturalistic Observation   Sometimes all researchers need to know is what is happening to a group of animals or people. The best way to look at the behavior of animals or people is to watch them behave in their normal environment. That's why animal researchers like Jane Goodall went to the areas where chimpanzees lived and watched them eat, play, mate, and sleep in their own natural surroundings. In order to study people, researchers might want to observe them in their workplaces, homes, or on playgrounds. For example, if a researcher wanted to know how adolescents behave with members of the opposite sex in a social setting, she might go to the mall on a weekend night.

What is the advantage of naturalistic observation? It allows researchers to get a realistic picture of how behavior occurs because they are actually watching that behavior. In a more artificial setting, like a laboratory, they might get behavior that is contrived or artificial rather than genuine. Of course, there are precautions that must be taken. In many cases, animals or people who know they are being watched will not behave normally anyway, in a process called the **observer effect,** so often the observer needs to remain hidden from view. When researching humans, this is often a difficult thing for researchers to do. In the mall setting with the teenagers, a researcher might find that pretending to read a book was a good disguise, especially if she wore glasses to hide her eye movements. Then she would be able to observe teenagers' natural behavior at the mall, and the teens wouldn't know they were being watched. In other cases, researchers might use one-way mirrors, or they might actually become participants in a group, a technique called **participant observation.**

Are there disadvantages? Unfortunately, yes. One of the disadvantages of naturalistic observation is the possibility of **observer bias.** That happens when the person doing the observing has a particular opinion about what he or she is going to see or expects to see. If that is the case, sometimes that person sees only those actions that support that expectation and ignores actions that don't fit. A way around that is to have *blind observers*: people who do not know what the research question is and, therefore, have no preconceived notions about what they "should" see. It's also a good idea to have more than one observer, so that the various observations can be compared.

Another disadvantage is that each naturalistic setting is unique and unlike any other. Observations that are made at one time in one setting may not hold true for another time, even if the setting is similar, because the conditions are not going to be exactly the same time after time—researchers don't have that kind of control over the natural world. For example, famed gorilla researcher Diane Fossey had to battle poachers who set traps for the animals in the area of her observations (Mowat, 1988). The presence and activities of the poachers affected the normal behavior of the gorillas she was trying to observe.

Laboratory Observation   Sometimes observing behavior in animals or people is just not practical in a natural setting. For example, a researcher might want to observe the reactions of infants to a mirror image of themselves and record the reactions with a camera mounted behind the one-way mirror. That kind of equipment might be difficult to set up in a natural setting. In a laboratory observation, the researcher would bring the infant to the equipment, controlling the number of infants and their ages as well as everything else that goes on in the laboratory.

As mentioned previously, laboratory settings have the disadvantage of being an artificial situation that might result in artificial behavior—both animals and people often react differently in the laboratory than they would in the real world. The main advantage of this method is the degree of control that it gives to the observer.

Both naturalistic and laboratory observations can lead to the formation of hypotheses that can later be tested.

1.8   How are case studies and surveys used to describe behavior, and what are some drawbacks to each of these methods?

Case Studies   Another descriptive technique is called the **case study,** in which one individual is studied in great detail. In a case study, researchers try to learn everything they can about that individual. For example, Sigmund Freud based his entire theory of psychoanalysis on his numerous case studies of his patients in which he gathered information about their childhoods and relationships with others from the very beginning of their lives to the present. ⓛⓘⓝⓚ *to Chapter Eleven: Theories of Personality, p. 437.*

The advantage of the case study is the tremendous amount of detail it provides. It may also be the only way to get certain kinds of information. For example, one famous case study was the story of Phineas Gage, who had a large metal rod driven through his head and suffered a major personality change as a result (Damasio et al., 1994). Researchers couldn't study that with naturalistic observation, and an experiment is out of the question. Imagine anyone responding to an ad in the newspaper that read:

Wanted: 50 people willing to suffer nonfatal brain damage for scientific study of the brain. Will pay all medical expenses.

At the top is a computer-generated reconstruction of the damaged skull of Phineas Gage. The red area shows the path taken by the steel rod driven through his skull by an explosion in 1848. At the bottom is a model of his head and next to it the actual skull.

participant observation   a naturalistic observation in which the observer becomes a participant in the group being observed.

observer bias   tendency of observers to see what they expect to see.

case study   study of one individual in great detail.

It's pretty certain that anyone who actually answered that ad might already be suffering from some rather extensive brain damage. Case studies are also good ways to study things that are rare, such as multiple personality (now called *dissociative identity disorder*).

The disadvantage of the case study is that researchers can't really apply the results to other similar people. In other words, they can't assume that if another person had the same kind of experiences growing up that he or she would turn out just like the person in their case study. People are unique and have too many complicating factors in their lives to be that predictable. So what researchers find in one case won't necessarily apply or generalize to others. Another weakness of this method is that case studies are a form of detailed observation and are vulnerable to bias on the part of the person conducting the case study, just as observer bias can occur in naturalistic or laboratory observation. ✺⬚Explore on MyPsychLab

Surveys   Sometimes what psychologists want to know about is pretty personal and potentially embarrassing to research subjects. The only way to find out about very private (covert) behavior is to ask questions.

In the survey method, researchers will ask a series of questions about the topic they are studying. Surveys can be conducted in person in the form of interviews or on the telephone, the Internet, or with a questionnaire. The questions in interviews or on the telephone can vary, but usually the questions in a survey are all the same for everyone answering the survey. In this way, researchers can ask lots of questions and survey literally hundreds of people.

That is the big advantage of surveys, aside from their ability to get at private information. Researchers can get a tremendous amount of data on a very large group of people. Of course, there are disadvantages. One disadvantage is researchers have to be very careful about the group of people they survey. If they want to find out what high school students think about politics, for example, they can't really ask every single high school student in the entire United States. But they can select a **representative sample** from that group. They could randomly* select a certain number of students from several different high schools across the United States, for example. Why randomly? Because the sample has to be *representative* of the **population,** which is the entire group in which the researcher is interested. If researchers selected only students from schools in Massachusetts, for example, they would most likely get different opinions on politics than they might get from students attending schools in Oklahoma. But if they survey a lot of high schools and select their *participants* (people who are part of the study) randomly, they will be more certain of getting answers that a broad selection of students would typically give.

That brings up the other major disadvantage of the survey technique: People aren't always going to give researchers accurate answers. The fact is, people tend to misremember things, distort the truth, and may lie outright—even if the survey is an anonymous** questionnaire. Remembering is not a very accurate process sometimes, especially when people think that they might not come off sounding very desirable or socially appropriate. Some people deliberately give the answer they think is more socially correct rather than their true opinion, so that no one gets offended, in a process

✺**Explore** the fascinating Phineas Gage case study. **www.mypsychlab.com**

"Next question: I believe that life is a constant striving for balance, requiring frequent tradeoffs between morality and necessity, within a cyclic pattern of joy and sadness, forging a trail of bittersweet memories until one slips, inevitably, into the jaws of death. Agree or disagree?"

representative sample   randomly selected sample of subjects from a larger population of subjects.

population   the entire group of people or animals in which the researcher is interested.

---

*Randomly: in this sense, selected so that each member of the group has an equal chance of being chosen.

**Anonymous: not named or identified.

called *courtesy bias*. Researchers must take their survey results with a big grain of salt*—they may not be as accurate as they would like them to be.

Both the wording of survey questions and the order in which they appear on the survey can affect the outcome. It is difficult to find a wording that will be understood in exactly the same way by all those who read the question. For example, questions can be worded in a way that the desired answer becomes obvious (often resulting in courtesy bias–type answers), or a question that appears at the end of a survey might be answered quite differently than if it had appeared at the beginning. ✱⌐Explore on MyPsychLab

✱Explore with a simulation on observational studies, the scientific method. **www.mypsychlab.com**

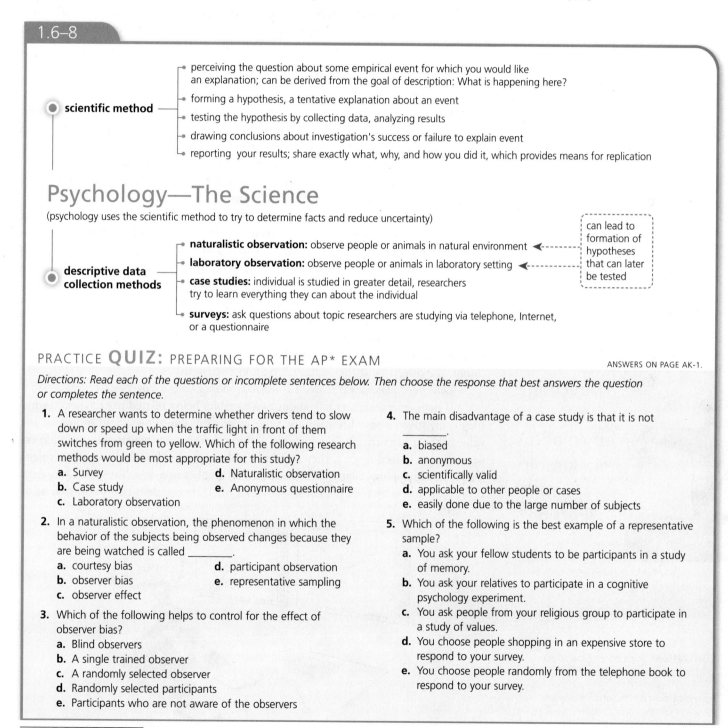

1.6–8

scientific method
- perceiving the question about some empirical event for which you would like an explanation; can be derived from the goal of description: What is happening here?
- forming a hypothesis, a tentative explanation about an event
- testing the hypothesis by collecting data, analyzing results
- drawing conclusions about investigation's success or failure to explain event
- reporting your results; share exactly what, why, and how you did it, which provides means for replication

Psychology—The Science
(psychology uses the scientific method to try to determine facts and reduce uncertainty)

descriptive data collection methods
- **naturalistic observation:** observe people or animals in natural environment
- **laboratory observation:** observe people or animals in laboratory setting
- **case studies:** individual is studied in greater detail, researchers try to learn everything they can about the individual
- **surveys:** ask questions about topic researchers are studying via telephone, Internet, or a questionnaire

can lead to formation of hypotheses that can later be tested

PRACTICE QUIZ: PREPARING FOR THE AP* EXAM

ANSWERS ON PAGE AK-1.

Directions: Read each of the questions or incomplete sentences below. Then choose the response that best answers the question or completes the sentence.

1. A researcher wants to determine whether drivers tend to slow down or speed up when the traffic light in front of them switches from green to yellow. Which of the following research methods would be most appropriate for this study?
- **a.** Survey
- **b.** Case study
- **c.** Laboratory observation
- **d.** Naturalistic observation
- **e.** Anonymous questionnaire

2. In a naturalistic observation, the phenomenon in which the behavior of the subjects being observed changes because they are being watched is called _____.
- **a.** courtesy bias
- **b.** observer bias
- **c.** observer effect
- **d.** participant observation
- **e.** representative sampling

3. Which of the following helps to control for the effect of observer bias?
- **a.** Blind observers
- **b.** A single trained observer
- **c.** A randomly selected observer
- **d.** Randomly selected participants
- **e.** Participants who are not aware of the observers

4. The main disadvantage of a case study is that it is not _____.
- **a.** biased
- **b.** anonymous
- **c.** scientifically valid
- **d.** applicable to other people or cases
- **e.** easily done due to the large number of subjects

5. Which of the following is the best example of a representative sample?
- **a.** You ask your fellow students to be participants in a study of memory.
- **b.** You ask your relatives to participate in a cognitive psychology experiment.
- **c.** You ask people from your religious group to participate in a study of values.
- **d.** You choose people shopping in an expensive store to respond to your survey.
- **e.** You choose people randomly from the telephone book to respond to your survey.

---

*Big grain of salt: a phrase meaning to be skeptical; to doubt the truth or accuracy of something.

FINDING RELATIONSHIPS

The methods discussed so far only provide descriptions of behavior. There are really only two methods that allow researchers to know more than just a description of what has happened: correlations and experiments. Correlation is actually a statistical technique, a particular way of organizing numerical information so that it is easier to look for patterns in the information. This method will be discussed here rather than in the statistics appendix found at the back of this text because correlation, like the experiment, is about finding relationships. In fact, the data from the descriptive methods just discussed are often analyzed using the correlational technique. To read more about descriptive and inferential statistics, and to learn how to use statistical concepts in psychological research, be sure to see (LINK) to *Appendix A: Statistics.*

AP* Distinguish the purposes of descriptive statistics and inferential statistics.

AP* Apply basic descriptive statistical concepts, including interpreting and constructing graphs and calculating simple descriptive statistics.

1.9 What is the correlational technique, and what does it tell researchers about relationships?

Correlations A **correlation** is a measure of the relationship between two or more variables. A *variable* is anything that can change or vary—scores on a test, temperature in a room, gender, and so on. For example, researchers might be curious to know whether or not cigarette smoking is connected to life expectancy—the number of years a person can be expected to live. Obviously, the scientists can't hang around people who smoke and wait to see when those people die. The only way (short of performing a really unethical and lengthy experiment) to find out if smoking behavior and life expectancy are related to each other is to use the medical records of people who have already died. (For privacy's sake, the personal information such as names and social security numbers would be removed, with only the facts such as age, gender, weight, and so on available to researchers.) Researchers would look for two facts from each record: the number of cigarettes the person smoked per day and the age of the person at death.

Now the researcher has two sets of numbers for each person in the study that go into a mathematical formula (LINK) to *Appendix A: Statistics,* to produce a number called the **correlation coefficient**. The correlation coefficient represents two things: the direction of the relationship and its strength.

Direction? How can a mathematical relationship have a direction?

Whenever researchers talk about two variables being related to each other, what they really mean is that knowing the value of one variable allows them to predict the value of the other variable. For example, if researchers found that smoking and life expectancy are indeed related, they should be able to predict how long someone might live if they know how many cigarettes a person smokes in a day. But which way does that prediction work? If a person smokes a lot of cigarettes, does that mean that he or

Direction? ▶
How can a
mathematical
relationship
have a
direction?

correlation a measure of the relationship between two variables.

correlation coefficient a number derived from the formula for measuring a correlation and indicating the strength and direction of a correlation.

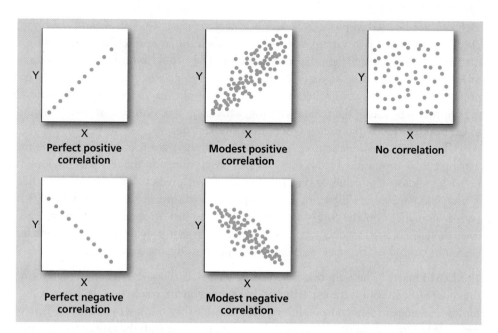

Figure 1.3

Five scatterplots showing direction and strength of correlation. It should be noted that perfect correlations, whether positive or negative, rarely occur in the real world.

she will live a longer life or a shorter one? Does life expectancy go up or down as smoking increases? That's what is meant by the *direction* of the relationship.

In terms of the correlation coefficient (represented by the small letter *r*), the number researchers get from the formula will either be a positive number or a negative number. If positive, the two variables increase in the same direction—as one goes up, the other goes up; as one decreases, the other also decreases. If negative, the two variables have an inverse* relationship. As one increases, the other decreases. If researchers find that the more cigarettes a person smoked, the younger that person was when he or she died, that would mean that the correlation between the two variables is negative. (As smoking goes up, life expectancy goes down—an inverse relationship.)

The strength of the relationship between the variables will be determined by the actual number itself. That number will always range between +1.00 and −1.00 The reason that it cannot be greater than +1.00 or less than −1.00 has to do with the formula and an imaginary line on a graph around which the data points gather, a graph called a scatterplot (see Figure 1.3). If the relationship is a strong one, the number will be closer to +1.00 or to −1.00. A correlation of +.89 for example, would be a very strong positive correlation. That might represent the relationship between scores on the SAT and an IQ test, for example. A correlation of −.89 would be equally strong but negative. That would be more like the correlation researchers would probably find between smoking cigarettes and the age at which a person dies.

Notice that the closer the number is to zero, the weaker the relationship becomes. Researchers would probably find that the correlation coefficient for the relationship between people's weight and the number of freckles they have is pretty close to zero, for example.

Go back to the cigarette thing—if we found that the correlation between cigarette smoking and life expectancy was high, does that mean that smoking causes your life expectancy to be shortened?

Not exactly. The biggest error that people make concerning correlation is to assume that it means one variable is the cause of the other. Remember that *correlation does not prove causation*. Although adverse health effects from cigarette smoking account for approximately 438,000 deaths each year in the United States alone, correlation by

---

*Inverse: opposite in order.

Go back to the cigarette thing—if we found that the correlation between cigarette smoking and life expectancy was high, does that mean that ◄ smoking causes your life expectancy to be shortened?

experiment a deliberate manipulation of a variable to see if corresponding changes in behavior result, allowing the determination of cause-and-effect relationships.

operational definition definition of a variable of interest that allows it to be directly measured.

✱ **Explore** with a simulation on distinguishing independent and dependent variables. **www.mypsychlab.com**

AP* Identify independent, dependent, confounding, and control variables in experimental designs.

AP* Distinguish between random assignment of participants to conditions in experiments and random selection of participants, primarily in correlational studies and surveys.

AP* Discuss the value of reliance on operational definitions and measurement in behavioral research.

---

itself can not be used to prove causation (Centers for Disease Control and Prevention, 2009). Just because two variables are related to each other, researchers cannot assume that one of them causes the other one to occur. They could both be related to some other variable that is the cause of both. For example, cigarette smoking and life expectancy could be linked only because people who smoke may be less likely to take care of their health by eating right and exercising, whereas people who don't smoke may tend to eat healthier foods and exercise more than smokers do.

To sum up, a correlation will tell researchers if there is a relationship between the variables, how strong the relationship is, and in what direction the relationship goes. If researchers know the value of one variable, they can predict the value of the other. If they know someone's IQ score, for example, they can predict about what score that person should get on the SAT—not the exact score, just a reasonable estimate. Also, even though correlation does not prove causation, it can provide a starting point for examining causal relationships with another type of study, the experiment.

The Experiment   The only research method that will allow researchers to determine the cause of a behavior is the **experiment.** In an experiment, researchers deliberately manipulate (change in some purposeful way) the variable they think is causing some behavior while holding all the other variables that might interfere with the experiment's results constant and unchanging. That way, if they get changes in behavior (an effect, in other words), they know that those changes must be due to the manipulated variable. For example, remember the discussion of the steps in the scientific method. It talked about how to study the effects of watching violent cartoons on children's aggressive behavior. The most logical way to study that particular relationship is by an experiment.

First, researchers might start by selecting the children they want to use in the experiment. The best method to do that is through random selection of a sample of children from a "population" determined by the researchers—just as a sample would be selected for a survey. Ideally, researchers would decide on the age of child they wanted to study—say, children who are 3 to 4 years old. Then researchers would go to various day care centers and randomly select a certain number of children of that age. Of course, that wouldn't include the children who don't go to a day care center. Another way to get a sample in the age range might be to ask several pediatricians to send out letters to parents of children of that age and then randomly select the sample from those children whose parents responded positively.

▶ **1.10** How are operational definitions, independent and dependent variables, experimental and control groups, and random assignment used in designing an experiment?

The Variables   Another important step is to decide on the variable the researchers want to manipulate (which would be the one they think causes changes in behavior) and the variable they want to measure to see if there are any changes (this would be the effect on behavior of the manipulation). Often deciding on the variables in the experiment comes before selection of the participants or subjects. ✱ **Explore** on **MyPsychLab**

In the example of aggression and children's cartoons, the variable that researchers think causes changes in aggressive behavior is the violence in the cartoons. Researchers would want to manipulate that in some way, and in order to do that they have to define the term *violent cartoon*. They would have to find a cartoon that contains violence or make one. Then they would show that cartoon to the participants and try to measure their aggressive behavior afterwards. In measuring the aggressive behavior, they would have to define exactly what they mean by "aggressive behavior" so that it can be measured. This definition is called an **operational definition** because it specifically names the operations (steps or procedures) that the experimenter must use to control or measure the variables in the experiment. An operational definition of aggressive behavior might be a checklist of very specific actions such as hitting, pushing, and so on that an observer can mark off as the children do the items on the list. If the observers were just told to look for "aggressive behavior," the researchers would probably get half a dozen or more different interpretations of what aggressive behavior is.

The name for the variable that is manipulated in any experiment is the **independent variable** because it is *independent* of anything the participants do. The participants in the study do not get to choose or vary the independent variable, and their behavior does not affect this variable at all. In the preceding example, the independent variable would be the presence or absence of violence in the cartoons.

The response of the participants to the manipulation of the independent variable *is* a dependent relationship, so the response of the participants that is measured is known as the **dependent variable.** Their behavior, if the hypothesis is correct, should *depend* on whether or not they were exposed to the independent variable, and in the example, the dependent variable would be the measure of aggressive behavior in the children. The dependent variable is always the thing (response of subjects or result of some action) that is measured to see just how the independent variable may have affected it.

The Groups   *If researchers do all of this and find that the children's behavior is aggressive, can they say that the aggressive behavior was caused by the violence in the cartoon?* No, what has been described so far is not enough. The researchers may find that the children who watch the violent cartoon are aggressive, but how would they know if their aggressive behavior was caused by the cartoon or was just the natural aggressive level of those particular children or the result of the particular time of day they were observed? Those sorts of *confounding variables* (variables that interfere with each other and their possible effects on some other variable of interest) are the kind researchers have to control for in some way. For example, if most children in this experiment just happened to be from a pretty aggressive family background, any effects the violent cartoon in the experiment might have had on the children's behavior could be confused (confounded) with the possible effects of the family background. The researchers wouldn't know if the children were being aggressive because they watched the cartoon or because they liked to play aggressively anyway.

The best way to control for confounding variables is to have two groups of participants: those who watch the violent cartoon, and those who watch a nonviolent cartoon for the same length of time. Then the researchers would measure the aggressive behavior in both groups. If the aggressive behavior is significantly greater in the group that watched the violent cartoon (statistically speaking), then researchers can say that in this experiment, violent cartoon watching caused greater aggressive behavior.

The group that is exposed to the independent variable (the violent cartoon in the example) is called the **experimental group,** because it is the group that receives the experimental manipulation. The other group that gets either no treatment or some kind of treatment that should have no effect (like the group that watches the nonviolent cartoon in the example) is called the **control group** because it is used to *control* for the possibility that other factors might be causing the effect that is being examined. If researchers were to find that both the group that watched the violent cartoon and the

The act of hitting each other with toy swords could be part of an operational definition of aggressive behavior.

If researchers do all of this and find that the children's behavior is aggressive, can they say that the aggressive behavior was caused by the violence in the cartoon?

independent variable   variable in an experiment that is manipulated by the experimenter.

dependent variable   variable in an experiment that represents the measurable response or behavior of the subjects in the experiment.

experimental group   subjects in an experiment who are subjected to the independent variable.

control group   subjects in an experiment who are not subjected to the independent variable and who may receive a placebo treatment.

group that watched the nonviolent cartoon were equally aggressive, they would have to assume that the violent content did not influence their behavior at all.

The Importance of Randomization   As mentioned previously, random selection is the best way to choose the participants for any study. Participants must then be assigned to either the experimental group or the control group. Not surprisingly, **random assignment** of participants to one or the other condition is the best way to ensure control over other interfering, or *extraneous*, variables. Random assignment means that each participant has an equal chance of being assigned to each condition. If researchers simply looked at the children and put all of the children from one day care center or one pediatrician's recommendations into the experimental group and the same for the control group, they would run the risk of biasing their research. Some day care centers may have more naturally aggressive children, for example, or some pediatricians may have a particular client base in which the children are very passive. So researchers want to take the entire participant group and assign each person randomly to one or the other of the groups in the study. Sometimes this is as simple as picking names out of a hat. ◉┤**Watch** on **MyPsychLab**

1.11   How do the placebo and experimenter effects cause problems in an experiment, and how can single-blind and double-blind studies control for these effects?

Experimental Hazards: The Placebo Effect and the Experimenter Effect   There are a few other problems that might arise in any experiment, even with the use of control groups and random assignment. These problems are especially likely when studying people instead of animals, because people are often influenced by their own thoughts or biases about what's going on in an experiment. For example, say there is a new drug that is supposed to improve memory in people who are in the very early stages of *Alzheimer's disease* (a form of mental deterioration that occurs in some people as they grow old). ⓛⓘⓝⓚ *to Chapter Six: Memory, pp. 253–254.* Researchers would want to test the drug to see if it really is effective in helping to improve memory, so they would get a sample of people who are in the early stages of the disease, divide them into two groups, give one group the drug, and then test for improvement. They would probably have to do a test of memory both before and after the administration of the drug to be able to measure improvement.

Let me see if I've got this straight. The group that gets the drug would be the experimental group, and the one that doesn't is the control group, right?

Right, and getting or not getting the drug is the independent variable, whereas the measure of memory improvement is the dependent variable. But there's still a problem with doing it this way. What if the researchers do find that the drug group had greater memory improvement than the group that received nothing? Can they really say that the drug itself caused the improvement? Or is it possible that the participants who received the drug *knew* that they were supposed to improve in memory and, therefore, made a major effort to do so? The improvement may have had more to do with participants' *belief* in the drug than the drug itself, a phenomenon* known as the **placebo effect**: The expectations and biases of the participants in a study can influence their behavior. In medical research, the control group is often given a harmless substitute for the real drug, such as a sugar pill or an injection of salt water, and this substitute (which has no medical effect) is called the *placebo*. If there is a placebo effect, the control group will show changes in the dependent variable even though the participants in that group received only a placebo.

---

*Phenomenon: an observable fact or event.

◉ **Watch** classic video footage of Konrad Lorenz on controlling an experiment. **www.mypsychlab.com**

AP* Predict the validity of behavioral explanations based on the quality of research design. ▶

Let me see if I've got this straight. The group that gets the drug would be the experimental group, and the one that ▶ doesn't is the control group, right?

random assignment process of assigning subjects to the experimental or control groups randomly, so that each subject has an equal chance of being in either group.

placebo effect the phenomenon in which the expectations of the participants in a study can influence their behavior.

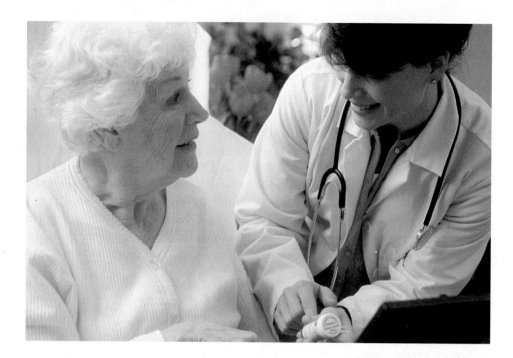

This elderly woman has Alzheimer's disease, which causes a severe loss of recent memory. If she were given a drug to improve her memory, the researcher could not be certain that any improvement shown was caused by the drug rather than by the elderly woman's belief that the drug would work. The expectations of any person in an experimental study can affect the outcome of the study, a phenomenon known as the placebo effect.

Another way that expectations about the outcome of the experiment can influence the results, even when the participants are animals rather than people, is called the **experimenter effect**. It has to do with the expectations of the experimenter, not the participants. As discussed earlier in the section about naturalistic observations, sometimes observers are biased—they see what they expect to see. Observer bias can also happen in an experiment. When the researcher is measuring the dependent variable, it's possible that he or she could give the participants clues about how they are supposed to respond—with body language, tone of voice, or even eye contact. Although not deliberate, it does happen. It could go something like this in the example: You, the Alzheimer's patient, are in the experimenter's office to take your second memory test after trying the drug. The experimenter seems to pay a lot of attention to you and to every answer that you give in the test, so you get the feeling that you are supposed to have improved a lot. So you try harder, and any improvement you show may be caused only by your own increased effort, not by the drug. That's the experimenter effect: The behavior of the experimenter caused the participant to change his or her response pattern.

Single-Blind and Double-Blind Studies   Fortunately, there are ways to control for these effects. The classic way to control for the placebo effect is to give the control group an actual placebo—some kind of treatment that doesn't affect behavior at all. In the drug experiment, the placebo would have to be some kind of sugar pill or saline (salt) solution that looks like and is administered just like the actual drug. The participants in both the experimental and the control groups would not know whether or not they got the real drug or the placebo. That way, if their expectations have any effect at all on the outcome of the experiment, the experimenter will be able to tell by looking at the results for the control group and comparing them to the experimental group. Even if the control group improves a little, the drug group should improve significantly more if the drug is working. This is called a **single-blind study** because while the experimenter knows which participant is taking which treatment, the participants are "blind" to the treatment they receive.

experimenter effect   tendency of the experimenter's expectations for a study to unintentionally influence the results of the study.

single-blind study   study in which the subjects do not know if they are in the experimental or the control group.

For a long time, that was the only type of experiment researchers did in psychology. But researchers Robert Rosenthal and Lenore Jacobson reported in their 1968 book, *Pygmalion in the Classroom*, that when teachers were told that some students had a high potential for success and others a low potential, the students showed significant gains or decreases in their performance on standardized tests depending on which "potential" they were supposed to have (Rosenthal & Jacobson, 1968). Actually, the students had been selected randomly and randomly assigned to one of the two groups, "high" or "low." Their performances on the tests were affected by the attitudes of the teachers concerning their potential. This study and similar studies after it highlighted the need to have both the experimenter and the research participants be "blind." So in a **double-blind study** neither the participants nor the person or persons measuring the dependent variable know who got what. That's why everything in a double-blind experiment gets coded in some way, so that only after all the measurements have been taken can anyone determine who was in the experimental group and who was in the control group.

Other Experimental Designs   In the field of developmental psychology, researchers are always looking for the ways in which a person's age influences his or her behavior. The problem is that age is a variable that cannot be randomly controlled. In a regular experiment, for example, participants can be randomly assigned to the various conditions: drug or placebo, special instructions or no special instructions, and so on. But participants cannot be randomly assigned to different age groups. It would be like saying, "Okay, these people are now going to be 20, and these others will be 30."

To get around this problem, researchers use alternative designs (called *quasi-experimental designs*) that are not considered true experiments because of the inability to randomly assign participants to the experimental and control groups (Gribbons & Herman, 1997). These designs are discussed more fully in Chapter Ten, Ⓛ Ⓘ Ⓝ Ⓚ *to Chapter Ten: Development Across the Life Span, pp. 386–387.*

For a good example of a typical experiment, read the following section about Dr. Teresa Amabile's experiment in creativity and rewards.

Classic Studies in Psychology

Teresa Amabile and the Effect of Extrinsic Reward on Creativity

1.12 What are the basic elements of Amabile's creativity experiment?

A very good example of an experiment is a classic study by famed Harvard Business College professor, Dr. Teresa Amabile. Amabile (1982) has made great strides in the study of creativity in both children and adults. In her 1982 study, she randomly selected a group of girls from a local public school. The girls ranged in age from 7 to 11. Dr. Amabile randomly divided them into two groups, an experimental group and a control group. She arranged to have an "art party" at the school after regular class hours and set up an empty classroom as her "laboratory." In this classroom she placed all the materials the children would need to make collages—poster board, paste, and numerous shapes and colors of construction paper. (A collage is just bits of paper or pictures glued onto a poster or paper—no drawing skills are necessary.)

Her hypothesis was that the girls who created art for an *extrinsic* (external) reward, such as toys, would be significantly less creative than the girls who created art for its own sake, or who have *intrinsic* (internal) motivation. On the day of the art party for the experimental group, she showed the children all the materials they would be using and *told them that the best three collages would win prizes*. This instruction was actually one part of her independent variable because she wanted to manipulate the children into believing that they were creating art for an extrinsic reward.

On a different day, she brought the girls in her control group into the same classroom with the same materials, but she told these children that the prizes she showed them at the beginning would be raffled off by drawing names out of a hat at the end of the party. So these children had the same materials, the same amount of time, and the same prizes—but they were making their collages purely for the fun of it, or because of intrinsic motivation.

At the end of the party for *both* groups, she actually raffled off the prizes. It wasn't important that the children in the experimental group actually *win* the prizes with their art, only that they *believed that they would*.

Now all the basic elements of an experiment were in place: the hypothesis (the prediction), the independent variable (the two different sets of instructions), the experimental group (the ones who were told they could win prizes), and the control group (the ones just having fun). From her hypothesis, Amabile's dependent variable has to be how creative the artwork of the children in both groups actually was, but how could she measure something as subjective as creativity?

This is where cleverness comes in. Amabile got several local artists, art critics, and art teachers to come in after the children were gone. She had taped all of the collages (with all the identifying information on the back and, therefore, invisible) to the walls of the school corridors. Each "judge" rated each piece of artwork for its creativity, and then Amabile collected the ratings for each collage, averaged them, and came up with a "creativity score" that she could analyze with statistics. (L)(I)(N)(K) *to Appendix A: Statistics.*

Amabile's hypothesis was indeed supported by the results of her study. The judges' scores for the experimental group (who all believed they were competing for prizes) were consistently and significantly lower than the scores for the control group (Amabile, 1982). She concluded that creativity is decreased when reward is in the picture in the form of prizes or money (as her studies with adults have shown).

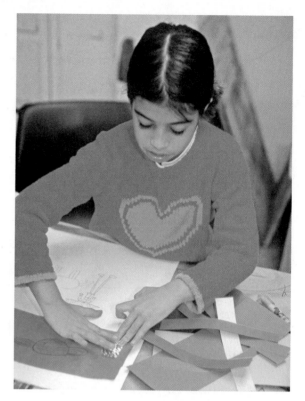

This girl is putting together a collage, using materials very similar to those used in Amabile's classic experiment.

Questions for Further Discussion

1. In thinking about how researchers control for biases in experiments, why did Dr. Amabile ask several local artists and art critics to judge the collages after the children had gone? (Hint: There are two important effects being controlled by Dr. Amabile's decision.)

2. How might the particular school from which Dr. Amabile selected her participants have been an interfering factor in the experiment?

3. How can parents and educators encourage creativity without the use of external rewards?

1.9–12

correlation
- is a measure of relationship between two or more variables (anything that can change or vary)
- produces a value called the *correlation coefficient* that represents both direction and strength of relationship
- does not prove causation—variables can be related but you cannot assume that one of them causes the other to occur

Finding Relationships

(different ways to find out more than just descriptions of behavior)

operational definition: specifically names the steps or procedures used to control or measure the variable in the experiment
- independent variable is the variable that is manipulated, it is independent of anything participants do
- dependent variable is the measure used to evaluate the manipulation of the independent variable

groups
- **experimental:** gets the independent variable or experimental manipulation
- **control:** receives no treatment or treatment that should not have an effect

random assignment to conditions is the best way to assure control over extraneous variables or confounding variables, variables that interfere with each other, and/or on the variable of interest

experiments
the only research method that will allow researchers to determine the cause of a behavior by deliberately manipulating some variable and measuring changes in the variable of interest

hazards
- **placebo effect:** participants' beliefs or expectations about a study can influence their behavior
- **experimenter effect:** experimenter's biases can affect or influence participants' behavior

can be controlled through single-blind (participants "blind" to treatment/condition) and double-blind studies where the experimenter measuring the dependent variable does not know the treatment/condition associated with the data

---

PRACTICE **QUIZ:** PREPARING FOR THE AP* EXAM

ANSWERS ON PAGE AK-1.

Directions: Read each of the questions or incomplete sentences below. Then choose the response that best answers the question or completes the sentence.

1. Which of the following correlation coefficients would indicate the strongest relationship between two variables?
   a. +0.75
   b. +0.50
   c. 0
   d. −0.25
   e. −0.90

2. In an experiment to test the effects of a new drug designed to enhance memory, the experimenter gives orange juice mixed with the drug to one group of subjects and orange juice mixed with a placebo to the other group. She then measures the memory skills of both groups by means of a memory test. In this study, the independent variable would be _____.
   a. the placebo
   b. the presence or absence of the drug in the orange juice
   c. the experimenter
   d. the participants' scores on the memory test
   e. the participants

3. Dr. MacInerney is conducting a research study that explores the relationship between the temperature of a room in which an exam is taken and the students' performance on that exam. 50 students take the exam in a 50-degree room, 50 students take the exam in a 70-degree room, and 50 students take the exam in a 90-degree room. When the test is over, he compares the results of each group of students. Which of the following is the dependent variable in this study?
   a. The students' exam scores
   b. The amount of studying each student did in preparation for the exam
   c. The temperature of the rooms
   d. The distribution of men and women in each of the exam rooms
   e. The amount of natural light found in each exam room

4. In which type of study do neither the experimenter nor the participants know who is in the control group and who is in the experimental group?
   a. A correlational study
   b. A single-blind study
   c. A double-blind study
   d. An observational study
   e. A triple-blind study

5. Randomly assigning participants to different experimental conditions allows experimenters to _____.
   a. eliminate the effect of observer bias
   b. reduce the impact of the experimenter effect
   c. generalize an experimental result across all populations
   d. control the effects of extraneous variables
   e. recruit participants from a variety of different locations and backgrounds

Ethics of Psychological Research

The study that Dr. Watson did with "Little Albert" and the white rat seems pretty cruel, when you think about it. Do researchers still do that kind of study today?

Actually, as psychology began to grow and more research with people was being done, psychologists began to realize that some protections had to be put in place. No one wanted to be thought of as a "mad scientist," and if studies were permitted that could actually harm people, the field of psychology might die out pretty quickly. **L I N K** *to Chapter Five: Learning, p. 183; Chapter Fourteen: Social Psychology, pp. 561–564.* Scientists in other areas of research were also realizing that ethical treatment of the participants in studies had to be ensured in some way. Ethical treatment means that people who volunteer for a study will be able to expect that no physical or psychological harm should come to them.

1.13 What are some ethical concerns that can occur when conducting research with people and animals?

Universities and colleges (where most psychological research is carried out) usually have *institutional review boards*, groups of psychologists or other professionals who look over each proposed research study and judge it according to its safety and consideration for the participants in the study. These review boards look at all aspects of the proposed research, from the written materials that explain the research to the potential subjects to the equipment that may be used in the study itself.

THE GUIDELINES FOR DOING RESEARCH WITH PEOPLE

There are quite a few ethical concerns when dealing with human subjects in an experiment or other type of study. Here is a list of the most common ethical guidelines:

1. **Rights and well-being of participants must be weighed against the study's value to science.** In other words, people come first, research second.

2. **Participants must be allowed to make an informed decision about participation.** This means that researchers have to explain the study to the people they want to include before they do anything to them or with them—even children—and it has to be in terms that the participants can understand. If researchers are using infants or children, their parents have to be informed and give their consent. This is known as *informed consent.* Even in single- or double-blind studies, it is necessary to tell the participants that they may be members of either the experimental or the control group— they just won't find out which group they were actually in until after the experiment is concluded.

3. **Deception must be justified.** In some cases, it is necessary to deceive the participants because the study wouldn't work any other way. The participants have to be told after the study exactly why the deception was important. This is called *debriefing.*

4. **Participants may withdraw from the study at any time.** The participants must be allowed to drop out for any reason. Sometimes people get bored with the study, decide they don't have the time, or don't like what they have to do, for example. Young children are particularly likely to decide not to play. Researchers have to let them go, even if it means having to get more participants.

◀ The study that Dr. Watson did with "Little Albert" and the white rat seems pretty cruel, when you think about it. Do researchers still do that kind of study today?

AP* Identify how ethical issues ◀ inform and constrain research practices.

AP* Describe how ethical and ◀ legal guidelines protect research participants and promote sound ethical practices.

"He says he wants a lawyer."

5. **Participants must be protected from risks or told explicitly of risks.** For example, if researchers are using any kind of electrical equipment, care must be taken to ensure that no participant will experience a physical shock from faulty electrical equipment.

6. **Investigators must debrief participants, telling the true nature of the study and expectations of results.** This is important in all types of studies but particularly in those involving a deception.

7. **Data must remain confidential.** Freud recognized the importance of confidentiality, referring to his patients in his books and articles with false names. Likewise, psychologists and other researchers today tend to report only group results rather than results for a single individual, so that no one could possibly be recognized (American Psychological Association, 2002).

Psychologists also study animals to find out about behavior, often drawing comparisons between what the animals do and what people might do under similar conditions.

But why not just study people in the first place?

Some research questions are extremely important but difficult or impossible to answer by using human participants. Animals live shorter lives, so looking at long-term effects becomes much easier. Animals are also easier to control—the scientist can control diet, living arrangements, and even genetic relatedness. The white laboratory rat has become a recognized species different from ordinary rats, bred with its own kind for many decades until each white rat is essentially a little genetic "twin" of all the others. Animals also engage in much simpler behavior than humans do, making it easier to see the effects of manipulations. But the biggest reason that researchers use animals in some research is that animals can be used in ways that researchers could never use people. For example, it took a long time for scientists to prove that the tars and other harmful substances in tobacco cause cancer because they had to do correlational studies with people and experiments only with animals. There's the catch—researchers can do many things to animals that they can't do to people. That might seem cruel at first, but when you think that without animal research there would be no vaccines for deadly diseases, no insulin treatments for diabetics, no transplants, and so on, then the value of the research and its benefits to humankind far outweigh the hazards to which the research animals are exposed.

There are also ethical considerations when dealing with animals in research, just as there are with humans. With animals, though, the focus is on avoiding exposing them to any *unnecessary* pain or suffering. So if surgery is part of the study, it is done under anesthesia. If the research animal must die in order for the effects of some drug or other treatment to be examined in an autopsy, the death must be accomplished humanely. Animals are used in only about 7 percent of all psychological studies (Committee on Animal Research and Ethics, 2004).

Critical Thinking

What good is all this focus on science and research going to do for me? I live in the real world, not a laboratory.

The real world is full of opportunities for scientific thinking. Think about all the commercials on television for miracle weight loss, hair restoration, or herbal remedies for arthritis, depression, and a whole host of physical and mental problems. Wouldn't it be nice to know how many of these claims people should believe?

But why not ▶ just study people in the first place?

What good is all this focus on science and research going ▶ to do for me? I live in the real world, not a laboratory.

Wouldn't you like to know how to evaluate claims like these and possibly save yourself some time, effort, and money? That's exactly the kind of "real-world" problem that critical thinking can help sort out. ((•—[Listen on **MyPsychLab**

((•● **Listen** to the Psychology in the News podcast. **www.mypsychlab.com**

THE CRITERIA FOR CRITICAL THINKING

1.14 What are the basic principles of critical thinking, and how can critical thinking be useful in everyday life?

According to Beyer (1995), **critical thinking** means making reasoned judgments. The word *reasoned* means that people's judgments should be logical and well thought out. There are four basic criteria* for critical thinking that people should remember when faced with statements about the world around them (Gill, 1991; Shore, 1990):

1. **There are very few "truths" that do not need to be subjected to testing.** Although people may accept religious beliefs and personal values on "faith," everything else in life needs to have supporting evidence. Questions that can be investigated empirically should be examined using established scientific methods. One shouldn't accept anything at face value but should always ask, "How do you know that? What is the evidence?"

2. **All evidence is not equal in quality.** One of the most important steps in critical thinking and one that is often overlooked is evaluating how evidence is gathered before deciding that it provides good support for some idea. For example, there are poorly done experiments, incorrect assumptions based on correlations rather than experiments, and studies in which there was either no control group or no attempt made to control for placebo effects or experimenter effects.

3. **Just because someone is considered to be an authority or to have a lot of expertise does not make everything that person claims automatically true.** One should always ask to see the evidence rather than just take some expert's word for anything. How good is the evidence? Are there other alternative explanations? For example, Linus Pauling, a famous and respected scientist, made claims about the benefits of vitamin C for curing the common cold. Although research is beginning to support the idea that vitamin C may help fight cancer, research has also found that even larger doses of this vitamin don't cure the common cold (Padayatty & Levine, 2001).

4. **Critical thinking requires an open mind.** Although it is good to be a little skeptical, people should not close their minds to things that are truly possible. At the same time, it's good for people to have open minds but not so open that they are gullible** and apt to "swallow anything." Critical thinking requires a delicate balance between skepticism and willingness to consider possibilities—even possibilities that disagree with previous judgments or beliefs. For example, scientists have yet to find any convincing evidence that there was once life on Mars. That doesn't mean that scientists totally dismiss the idea of life on Mars, just that there is no convincing evidence *yet*. I don't believe that there are Martians on Mars, but if I were shown convincing evidence, I would have to be willing to change my thinking—as difficult as that might be.

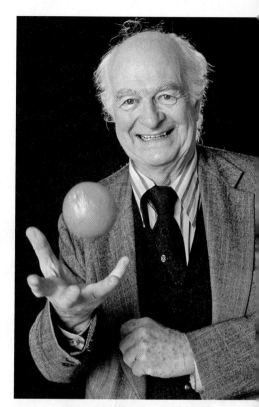

Linus Pauling is a two-time winner of the Nobel Prize. He proposed the use of vitamin C supplements to prevent the common cold, but scientific evidence has repeatedly failed to find support for his belief.

---

*Criteria: standards on which a judgment or decision may be based.
**Gullible: easily fooled or cheated.

critical thinking making reasoned judgments about claims.

PSEUDOPSYCHOLOGIES: WHY DO PEOPLE FALL FOR FAKERY?

I guess I understand about the importance of critical thinking—there seems to be a lot of people out there who will fall for anything.

Actually, you might be surprised by the people who fall for the dumbest-sounding scams. Intelligent, well-educated people often fall prey to faulty reasoning, just like everyone else does. Con artists and scammers know the flaws in human nature pretty well, and that's how they survive.

Some of the easiest things to fall for are the **pseudopsychologies,** systems of explaining human behavior that are not based on scientific evidence and that have no real value other than being entertaining (Bunge, 1984). Because people like to try to understand themselves, they often participate in these activities.

One false system is *palmistry*, or the reading of palms. There is overwhelming evidence that the lines of the palm have absolutely no relationship to personality and cannot predict the future (Ben-Shakhar et al., 1986; Dean et al., 1992), yet many people still believe that palm readers are for real. What about handwriting? Surely one's personality would be revealed in handwriting? The pseudopsychology called *graphology*, or the analysis of personality through handwriting, even has respectable companies using handwriting analysis to select prospective employees, yet graphologists score close to zero on tests of accuracy in personality measurement (Ben-Shakhar et al., 1986).

Astrology is another popular pseudopsychology that attempts to predict the future and explain personality by using the positions of the stars and planets at the moment of birth. But does it work? Here's an example of critical thinking applied to astrology:

1. **Are astrologers' charts up-to-date?** The basic astrological charts were designed over 3,000 years ago. The stars, planets, and constellations are no longer in the same positions in the sky, due to changes in the rotation of the Earth's axis over long periods of time—over 24 degrees in just the last 2,000 years (Dean & Kelly, 2000; Kelly, 1980). So a Gemini is really a Cancer and will be a Leo in another 2,000 years.

2. **What exactly is so important about the moment of birth?** Why not the moment of conception? What happens if a baby is born by cesarean section and not at the time it would have been born naturally? Is that person's whole life screwed up?

3. **Why would the stars and planets have any effect on a person? Is it gravity?** The body mass of the doctor who delivers the baby has a far greater gravitational pull on the infant's body than the moon does. (Maybe people should use skinny obstetricians?)

Research also shows no connection between astrological signs and personality, careers, skills, marriage rates, divorce rates, or even physical characteristics (Dean & Kelly, 2000; Kelly, 1980). Studies of thousands of predictions by astrologers showed that only a very small percentage of those predictions actually came true (Dean & Kelly, 2000), and the ones that did come true were very vague or easily guessed from current events ("I predict that a famous star will have plastic surgery this year.") ✳ Explore on **MyPsychLab**

I guess I understand ▶ about the importance of critical thinking—there seems to be a lot of people out there who will fall for anything.

pseudopsychologies systems of explaining human behavior that are not based on or consistent with scientific evidence.

This is a map of sixteenth-century astrologer Tycho Brahe's earth-centered universe. He rejected Copernicus's notion that the planets, including the earth, revolved around the sun, preferring his own theory that the earth was the center of the universe.

✳ **Explore** phrenology. Can your skull explain certain personality traits? **www.mypsychlab.com**

1.13   1.14

guidelines for research with humans
- rights and well-being of participants must be weighed against the study's value to science
- participants must be allowed to make an informed decision about participating (informed consent)
- deception must be justified
- participants may withdraw from the study at any time
- participants must be protected from risks or told explicitly of risks
- investigator must debrief participants, telling the true nature of the study and expectations of results
- data must remain confidential

Ethics of Psychological Research

(psychological scientists have a primary goal of protecting the health and welfare of their animal or human participants)

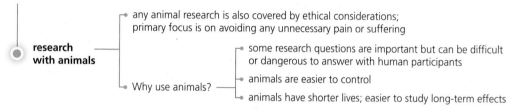

research with animals
- any animal research is also covered by ethical considerations; primary focus is on avoiding any unnecessary pain or suffering
- Why use animals?
  - some research questions are important but can be difficult or dangerous to answer with human participants
  - animals are easier to control
  - animals have shorter lives; easier to study long-term effects

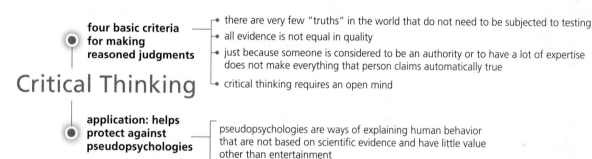

four basic criteria for making reasoned judgments
- there are very few "truths" in the world that do not need to be subjected to testing
- all evidence is not equal in quality
- just because someone is considered to be an authority or to have a lot of expertise does not make everything that person claims automatically true
- critical thinking requires an open mind

Critical Thinking

application: helps protect against pseudopsychologies
- pseudopsychologies are ways of explaining human behavior that are not based on scientific evidence and have little value other than entertainment

PRACTICE QUIZ: PREPARING FOR THE AP* EXAM

ANSWERS ON PAGE AK-1.

Directions: Read each of the questions or incomplete sentences below. Then choose the response that best answers the question or completes the sentence.

1. Which of the following is not a common ethical rule of psychological research?
   a. Data must remain confidential.
   b. Participants must give informed consent.
   c. Participants may withdraw from the study at any time.
   d. Deception cannot be used in any studies on human beings.
   e. The rights and well-being of the participants must come first.

2. According to the American Psychological Association's research guidelines, participants in an experiment must _____.
   a. remain blind to their experimental condition
   b. be debriefed about the purpose of the study
   c. receive monetary payment in exchange for participation
   d. complete the entire experiment once they have begun it
   e. give a written endorsement of the study before the results are published

3. Which of the following is not a reason why scientists use animals in research?
   a. Animals' lives are easier to control than humans' lives are.
   b. It is easier to see the effect of manipulations in animals than in humans.

   c. Long-term effects are more immediately visible in animals than in humans.
   d. Researchers are allowed to treat animals in ways that they cannot treat people.
   e. Results of experiments on animals are consistently stronger than results of experiments on humans.

4. Dr. Hirose is a member of an institutional review board. In her capacity as a board member, Dr. Hirose is responsible for _____.
   a. judging completed research studies to approve or reject their conclusions
   b. judging research studies in progress to determine the level of bias present
   c. judging whether candidates should receive doctoral degrees in psychology
   d. judging proposed research studies according to safety and ethics guidelines
   e. judging completed research papers for inclusion in national professional journals

(continued)

5. Which of the following is an example of informed consent?

a. A person agrees to participate in a study after waiving his right to privacy.

b. A person agrees to participate in a study after taking a psychology course.

c. A person agrees to participate in a study after receiving an explanation of the study.

d. A person agrees to participate in a study after being told what the results are expected to be.

e. A person agrees to participate in a study after being paid in advance for his participation.

AP* Articulate the impact of social and cultural categories on self-concept and relations with others.

Applying Psychology to Everyday Life: Stereotypes, Athletes, and Test Performance

It seems that many people have a negative stereotype of student athletes—that they are graded and promoted on the basis of their ability on the athletic field and not on the basis of classroom performance. Evidence does exist for poorer performance on academic tests of athletes when compared to nonathletes in college (National Collegiate Athletic Association, 2002; Purdy et al., 1982; Upthegrove et al., 1999). If you are an athlete, can that negative stereotype actually have a negative impact on your test performance? Wesleyan University researchers Matthew Jameson, Robert Diehl, and Henry Danso have some evidence that such stereotypes can have just that kind of negative impact (Jameson et al., 2007).

Could knowing that other people might think your success in school is due to your athletic ability and not to your intelligence make you perform poorly on an academic test?

In their experiment, 72 male college athletes were given an intellectual test. Half of the athletes answered a brief questionnaire before taking the test, whereas the other half received the same questionnaire after taking the test. The questionnaire asked three questions, with the third question being, "Rate your likelihood of being accepted to the university without the aid of athletic recruiting." This item was designed to bring the negative stereotype of athletes ("dumb jocks") to the forefront of students' minds, creating a "high threat" for that stereotype.

The results? Those students who answered the "high threat" question *before* the intellectual test scored significantly lower on that test than those who answered the question *after* the test. The researchers also found a correlation between the students' exposure to the "high threat" stereotype condition and accuracy on the intellectual test: The more students believed that they got into college primarily because of their ability in sports (based on their rating of that third question), the worse they performed on the subsequent test. Jameson and colleagues concluded that obvious negative stereotypes in higher education may be an important cause of the tendency of college athletes to underperform in academics.

Questions for Further Discussion

1. In this experiment, which group was the experimental group and which was the control? What was the independent variable? The dependent variable?

2. What might educators do to try to prevent the effect of the "dumb jock" negative stereotype on student athletes?

1 CHAPTER SUMMARY

What Is Psychology?

1.1 What defines psychology as a field of study and what are psychology's four primary goals?

* Psychology is the scientific study of behavior and mental processes.
* The four goals of psychology are description, explanation, prediction, and control.

Psychology Then: The History of Psychology

1.2 How did structuralism and functionalism differ, and who were the important people in those early fields?

* In 1879 psychology began as a science of its own in Germany with the establishment of Wundt's psychology laboratory. He developed the technique of objective introspection.
* Titchener, a student of Wundt, brought psychology in the form of structuralism to America. Structuralism died out in the early twentieth century. Margaret F. Washburn, Titchener's student, was the first woman to receive a Ph.D. in psychology in 1894 and published *The Animal Mind*.
* William James proposed a countering point of view called functionalism, that stressed the way the mind allows us to adapt.
* Functionalism influenced the modern fields of educational psychology, evolutionary psychology, and industrial/organizational psychology.
* Some noted early psychologists were women and other minorities, such as Margaret Washburn, Mary Whiton Calkins, Francis Cecil Sumner, Kenneth and Mamie Clark, and Jorge Sanchez.

1.3 What were the basic ideas and who were the important people behind the early approaches known as Gestalt, psychoanalysis, and behaviorism?

* Wertheimer and others studied sensation and perception, calling the new perspective Gestalt (an organized whole) psychology.
* Freud proposed that the unconscious mind controls much of our conscious behavior in his theory of psychoanalysis.
* Watson proposed a science of behavior called behaviorism, which focused only on the study of observable stimuli and responses.
* Watson and Rayner demonstrated that a phobia could be learned by conditioning a baby to be afraid of a white rat.

Classic Studies in Psychology: Psychologist Mary Cover Jones and "Little Peter"

* Mary Cover Jones later demonstrated that a learned phobia could be counterconditioned.

Psychology Now: Modern Perspectives

1.4 What are the basic ideas behind the seven modern perspectives, as well as the important contributions of Skinner, Maslow, and Rogers?

* Modern Freudians such as Anna Freud, Jung, and Adler changed the emphasis in Freud's original theory into a kind of neo-Freudianism.
* Skinner's operant conditioning of voluntary behavior became a major force in the twentieth century. He introduced the concept of reinforcement to behaviorism.

* Humanism, which focuses on free will and the human potential for growth, was developed by Maslow and Rogers, among others, as a reaction to the deterministic nature of behaviorism and psychoanalysis.
* Cognitive psychology is the study of learning, memory, language, and problem solving.
* Biopsychology emerged as the study of the biological bases of behavior.
* The principles of evolution and the knowledge we currently have about evolution are used in this perspective to look at the way the mind works and why it works as it does. Behavior is seen as having an adaptive or survival value.

Psychological Professionals and Areas of Specialization

1.5 How does a psychiatrist differ from a psychologist, and what are the other types of professionals who work in the various areas of psychology?

* Psychiatrists are medical doctors who provide diagnosis and therapy for persons with mental disorders, whereas psychoanalysts are psychiatrists or psychologists with special training in the theory of psychoanalysis.
* Psychiatric social workers are social workers with special training in the influences of the environment on mental illness.
* Psychologists have academic degrees and can do counseling, teaching, and research and may specialize in any one of a large number of areas within psychology.
* There are many different areas of specialization in psychology, including clinical, counseling, developmental, social, and personality as areas of work or study.

Psychology: The Science

1.6 Why is psychology considered a science, and what are the steps in using the scientific method?

* The scientific method is a way to determine facts and control the possibilities of error and bias when observing behavior. The five steps are perceiving the question, forming a hypothesis, testing the hypothesis, drawing conclusions, and reporting the results.

1.7 How are naturalistic and laboratory settings used to describe behavior, and what are some of the advantages and disadvantages associated with these settings?

* Naturalistic observations involve watching animals or people in their natural environments but have the disadvantage of lack of control.
* Laboratory observations involve watching animals or people in an artificial but controlled situation, such as a laboratory.

1.8 How are case studies and surveys used to describe behavior, and what are some drawbacks to each of these methods?

* Case studies are detailed investigations of one subject, whereas surveys involve asking standardized questions of large groups of people that represent a sample of the population of interest.
* Information gained from case studies cannot be applied to other cases. People responding to surveys may not always tell the truth or remember information correctly.

1.9 What is the correlational technique, and what does it tell researchers about relationships?

- Correlation is a statistical technique that allows researchers to discover and predict relationships between variables of interest.

- Positive correlations exist when increases in one variable are matched by increases in the other variable, whereas negative correlations exist when increases in one variable are matched by decreases in the other variable.

- Correlations cannot be used to prove cause-and-effect relationships.

1.10 How are operational definitions, independent and dependent variables, experimental and control groups, and random assignment used in designing an experiment?

- Experiments are tightly controlled manipulations of variables that allow researchers to determine cause-and-effect relationships.

- The independent variable in an experiment is the variable that is deliberately manipulated by the experimenter to see if related changes occur in the behavior or responses of the participants and is given to the experimental group.

- The dependent variable in an experiment is the measured behavior or responses of the participants.

- The control group receives either a placebo treatment or nothing.

- Random assignment of participants to experimental groups helps to control for individual differences both within and between the groups that might otherwise interfere with the experiment's outcome.

1.11 How do the placebo and experimenter effects cause problems in an experiment, and how can single-blind and double-blind studies control for these effects?

- Experiments in which the subjects do not know if they are in the experimental or control groups are single-blind studies, whereas experiments in which neither the experimenters nor the subjects know this information are called double-blind studies.

Classic Studies in Psychology: Teresa Amabile and the Effect of Extrinsic Reward on Creativity

1.12 What are some basic elements of Amabile's creativity experiment?

- Dr. Teresa Amabile's experiment explored the relationship of rewards and creativity by promising a reward to one group of children for being creative (the experimental group) and not to a second group of children, who were being creative for fun (the control group).

- Her conclusion was that external rewards have a negative effect on creativity.

Ethics of Psychological Research

1.13 What are some ethical concerns that can occur when conducting research with people and animals?

- Ethical guidelines for doing research with human beings include the protection of rights and well-being of participants, informed consent, justification when deception is used, the right of participants to withdraw at any time, protection of participants from physical or psychological harm, confidentiality, and debriefing of participants at the end of the study.

- Animals in psychological research make useful models because they are easier to control than humans, they have simpler behavior, and they can be used in ways that are not permissible with humans.

Critical Thinking

1.14 What are the basic principles of critical thinking, and how can critical thinking be useful in everyday life?

- Critical thinking is the ability to make reasoned judgments. The four basic criteria of critical thinking are that there are few concepts that do not need to be tested, evidence can vary in quality, claims by experts and authorities do not automatically make something true, and keeping an open mind is important.

- Faulty reasoning and a failure to use critical thinking can lead to belief in false systems such as palmistry and graphology.

Applying Psychology to Everyday Life: Stereotypes, Athletes, and Test Performance

- Athletes were given an intellectual test either before or after being exposed to a stereotyping question designed to increase their awareness of negative stereotypes toward student athletes. Those exposed to the stereotyping question before taking the intellectual test scored much lower than those who were exposed to the question after taking the test, implying that obvious negative stereotypes in higher education may be an important cause of the tendency of student athletes to underperform in academics.

TEST YOURSELF: PREPARING FOR THE AP* EXAM   ANSWERS ON PAGE AK-1.

✔●—[**Practice** on **MyPsychLab**   **Ready for your test?** More quizzes and a customized study plan. **www.mypsychlab.com**

PART I: MULTIPLE-CHOICE QUESTIONS

Directions for Part I: Read each of the questions or incomplete sentences below. Then choose the response that best answers the question or completes the sentence.

1. Which early theorist developed his perspective on psychology by basing it on Darwin's "survival of the fittest" doctrine?
   a. Wilhelm Wundt
   b. William James
   c. John Watson
   d. Sigmund Freud
   e. Max Wertheimer

2. "The whole is greater than the sum of the parts" is a statement associated with the perspective of _____.
   a. introspectionism
   b. functionalism
   c. psychoanalysis
   d. Gestalt psychology
   e. evolutionary psychology

3. Jenna suffers from the nervous tic of washing her hands repeatedly and being unable to resist washing them again and again. Which perspective would explain Jenna's hand-washing behavior as a result of repressed conflicts?
   a. Humanism
   b. Behaviorism
   c. Biopsychology
   d. Cognitive perspective
   e. Psychodynamic perspective

4. In which setting do the majority of psychologists work?
   a. Hospitals
   b. Private (for profit) practices
   c. Universities and four-year colleges
   d. Private (not for profit) practices
   e. Schools and other educational settings

5. The main advantage of laboratory observation is _____.
   a. the degree of control it allows the observer
   b. the degree of participation it allows the observer
   c. the elimination of the observer effect
   d. the opportunity to use participant observation
   e. the reduction in the effect of observer bias

6. A researcher designs an experiment to test the effects of playing video games on memory. What would be the dependent variable?
   a. The participants' scores on a memory test
   b. The hours spent playing video games
   c. The version of the memory test completed
   d. The type of video game participants played
   e. The participants' memories before the experiment

7. Double-blind studies control for _____.
   a. the observer effect and observer bias
   b. random selection and random assignment
   c. the placebo effect and the experimenter effect
   d. confounding variables and participant bias
   e. independent variables and dependent variables

8. Sarah wants to study levels of self-confidence in teens. Which of the following research methods is best suited to Sarah's study?
   a. Survey
   b. Case study
   c. Experiment
   d. Laboratory observation
   e. Naturalistic observation

9. Jamal is studying the psychological effects of eating disorders, and he has sent surveys about eating habits to a representative sample of hundreds of people across the country. Which of the following problems is most likely to inhibit Jamal's research?
   a. The survey is not a double-blind research technique.
   b. The research does not make use of random assignment.
   c. The results of the research will not be easily replicable.
   d. Not all respondents are likely to suffer from an eating disorder.
   e. Some respondents will answer the survey untruthfully or inaccurately.

10. Which of the following could be an operational definition of "excitement"?
    a. Enthusiasm
    b. An emotion
    c. Increased heart rate
    d. A feeling of anticipation
    e. An emotion experienced by someone who is looking forward to something.

PART II: FREE-RESPONSE QUESTION

Directions for Part II: Read the essay question that follows. Then, respond to the question in a clear, concise essay. Do not simply list facts. Instead, present a thorough argument based on your critical consideration of the topic. Use proper psychological terminology as necessary.

Qing is a 12-year-old girl who has just moved to the United States from China. She is struggling academically and socially, and she has trouble learning the traditions and expectations of her new home. She has become withdrawn and moody. However, she has always enjoyed painting, and art class is the one thing that still brings a smile to her face. In an essay, discuss how each of the following psychological perspectives would explain Qing's behavior:
   a. Psychodynamic perspective
   b. Behavioral perspective
   c. Sociocultural perspective
   d. Cognitive perspective
   e. Biopsychological perspective

1.1
Psychology
(is the scientific study of behavior and mental processes)

- has methods for studying phenomena
- has four primary goals
  - describe
  - explain
  - predict
  - control

1.2–3   p. 12

Psychology Then: The History of Psychology
(has roots in several disciplines, including philosophy, medicine, and physiology, and has developed through several perspectives)

- A relatively new science that formally began in 1879 when Wilhelm Wundt ("father of psychology") established the first psychological laboratory in Leipzig, Germany

  was a student of Wundt's

  - **Structuralism**
    founded by Edward Titchener
  - **Functionalism**
    founded by William James
  - **Gestalt psychology**
    founded by Max Wertheimer
  - **Psychoanalysis**
    ideas put forth
    by Sigmund Freud
  - **Behaviorism**
    associated with work
    of John B. Watson,
    who was greatly influenced by
    Ivan Pavlov's work
    in conditioning/learning

1.4   p. 19

- **Psychodynamic**
  based on Freud's theory
- **Behavioral**
  based on early work
  of Watson
  and later B.F. Skinner
- **Humanistic**
  two pioneers are
  Carl Rogers
  and Abraham Maslow
- **Cognitive**
  has roots in
  Gestalt psychology

Psychology Now:
Modern Perspectives
(No one single perspective is used to explain all human behavior and processes)

- **Sociocultural**
- **Biospsychological**
- **Evolutionary**

5 YEARS LATER (SAME SUBJECTS)

STG   DLPFC

1.5   p. 19

Types of
Psychological Professionals
(people working in the field of psychology have a variety
of training experiences and different focuses)

- **psychiatrist**
- **psychoanalyst**
- **psychiatric social worker**
- **psychologist**

1.6–8   p. 25

Psychology—The Science

(psychology uses the scientific method to try to determine facts and reduce uncertainty)

scientific method
- perceiving the question
- forming a hypothesis
- testing the hypothesis
- drawing conclusions
- reporting your results

descriptive data collection methods
- naturalistic observation
- laboratory observation
- case studies
- surveys

1.9–12   p. 34

correlation
- is a measure of relationship between two or more variables
- produces a value called the *correlation coefficient*
- does not prove causation

Finding relationships

(different ways to find out more than just descriptions of behavior)

experiments
the only research method that will allow researchers to determine the cause of a behavior by deliberately manipulating some variable and measuring changes in the variable of interest

- **operational definition** specifically names the steps or procedures used to control or measure the variable in the experiment
- **groups**
- **hazards**

1.13   p. 39

guidelines for research with humans
- rights and well-being of participants must be weighed against the study's value to science
- participants must be allowed to make an informed decision about participating (informed consent)
- deception must be justified
- participants may withdraw from the study at any time
- participants must be protected from risks or told explicitly of risks
- investigator must debrief participants, telling the true nature of the study and expectations of results
- data must remain confidential

Ethics of Psychological Research

(psychological scientists have a primary goal of protecting the health and welfare of their animal or human participants)

research with animals

"He says he wants a lawyer."

1.14   p. 39

four basic criteria for making reasoned judgments
- there are very few "truths" in the world that do not need to be subjected to testing
- all evidence is not equal in quality
- just because someone is considered to be an authority or to have a lot of expertise does not make everything that person claims automatically true
- critical thinking requires an open mind

Critical Thinking

application: helps protect against pseudopsychologies
pseudopsychologies are ways of explaining human behavior that are not based on scientific evidence and have little value other than entertainment

2

The Biological Perspective

Half a Mind?

Michelle M. is a 29-year-old woman who holds a part-time job and loves to read, watch movies, and spend time with her family. She has the amazing ability to tell you exactly what day of the week on which any particular calendar date fell, and she's a whiz at playing solitaire. If you were to look at her, you would see that in addition to wearing glasses (like so many other people), Michelle's right wrist is a bit bent and slightly twisted. She can use this hand just fine, although she is actually left-handed. She wears a brace to support her right leg.

You might think that Michelle is very lucky to be so normal, since the weakness on her right side might indicate that she had suffered a moderate stroke at some time in her past, but you'd be wrong. Michelle is more than lucky—she's astonishing. The weakness in her right side comes from the fact that Michelle was born with only half a brain—the right half—and nothing but a fluid-filled cavity in the left side of her skull.

Michelle's case has fascinated doctors who study the brain. Her condition has existed since the womb, when some unknown accident caused the left side of her brain to fail to develop, while the right side grew normally. The left side of the brain, as you will see later in this chapter, normally controls skills such as speech, reading, analytical thinking, and understanding abstract concepts. Michelle, with no left brain, can do all of those things well with the exception of abstraction—she's a pretty detail-oriented, concrete person (Doidge, 2007).

How can Michelle function so normally when she's missing half of her brain? That's just one mystery that we will explore in the pages to come.

Why study the nervous system and the glands? How could we possibly understand any of our behavior, thoughts, or actions without knowing something about the incredible organs that allow us to act, think, and react? If we can understand how the brain, the nerves, and the glands interact to control feelings, thoughts, and behavior, we can begin to truly understand the complex organism called a human being.

2 Learning Objectives

- **2.1** What are the nervous system, neurons, and nerves, and how do they relate to one another?

- **2.2** How do neurons use neurotransmitters to communicate with each other and with the body?

- **2.3** How do the brain and spinal cord interact?

- **2.4** How do the somatic and autonomic nervous systems allow people and animals to interact with their surroundings and control the body's automatic functions?

- **2.5** How do psychologists study the brain and how it works?

- **2.6** What are the different structures of the bottom part of the brain and what do they do?

- **2.7** What are the structures of the brain that control emotion, learning, memory, and motivation?

- **2.8** What parts of the cortex control the different senses and the movement of the body?

- **2.9** What parts of the cortex are responsible for higher forms of thought, such as language?

- **2.10** How does the left side of the brain differ from the right side?

- **2.11** How do the hormones released by glands interact with the nervous system and affect behavior?

An Overview of the Nervous System

AP* Describe the nervous system and its subdivisions and functions. ▶

2.1 What are the nervous system, neurons, and nerves, and how do they relate to one another?

This chapter will discuss a very complex system of cells, organs, and chemicals that work together to produce behavior, thoughts, and actions. The first part of this complex arrangement is the **nervous system**, a network of cells that carries information to and from all parts of the body. Before beginning the discussion on the cells that make up the nervous system, take a look at Figure 2.1. This figure shows the organization of the various parts of the nervous system and will help in understanding how all the different parts work together in controlling the way people and animals think, act, and feel.

nervous system an extensive network of specialized cells that carries information to and from all parts of the body.

Figure 2.1 An Overview of the Nervous System

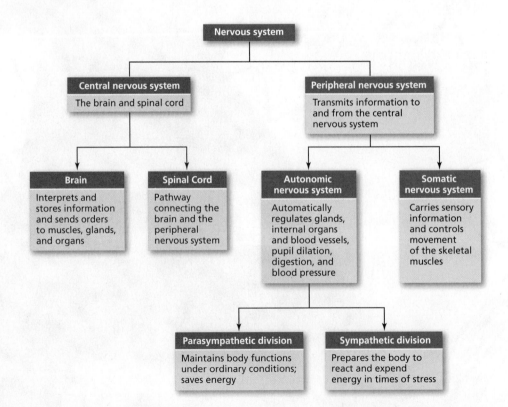

Neurons and Nerves: Building the Network

The field of **neuroscience** is a branch of the life sciences that deals with the structure and functioning of the brain and the neurons, nerves, and nervous tissue that form the nervous system. It was Santiago Ramón y Cajal, a doctor studying slides of brain tissue, who in 1887 first theorized that the nervous system was made up of individual cells (Ramón y Cajal, translation, 1995). Biological Psychology or Behavioral Neuroscience is the branch of neuroscience that focuses on the biological bases of psychological processes, behavior, and learning. ✱⌐Explore on MyPsychLab

STRUCTURE OF THE NEURON—THE NERVOUS SYSTEM'S BUILDING BLOCK

Although the entire body is composed of cells, each type of cell has a special purpose and function and, therefore, a special structure. Skin cells are flat, but muscle cells are long and stretchy. Most cells do have three things in common: a nucleus, a cell body, and a cell membrane holding it all together. The **neuron** is the specialized cell in the nervous system that receives and sends messages within that system. Neurons are one of the messengers of the body, and that means that they have a very special structure.

The parts of the neuron that receive messages from other cells are called the **dendrites**. The name *dendrite* means "branch," and this structure does indeed look like the branches of a tree. The dendrites are attached to the cell body, or **soma**, which is the part of the cell that contains the nucleus and keeps the entire cell alive and

✱ **AP*** Identify basic processes and systems in the biological bases of behavior.

✱ **Explore** Cajal's influence and discoveries at **www.mypsychlab.com**

neuroscience a branch of the life sciences that deals with the structure and function of neurons, nerves, and nervous tissue.

Biological Psychology/Behavioral Neuroscience branch of neuroscience that focuses on the biological bases of psychological processes, behavior, and learning.

neuron the basic cell that makes up the nervous system and that receives and sends messages within that system.

dendrites branchlike structures that receive messages from other neurons.

soma the cell body of the neuron responsible for maintaining the life of the cell.

Figure 2.2 The Structure of the Neuron

The electron micrograph on the left shows neurons with axons and dendrites extending from them.

functioning. The **axon** (from the Greek for "axis") is a fiber attached to the soma, and its job is to carry messages out to other cells. (See Figure 2.2.)

Most people think that the brain is made up entirely of neurons. They may also have heard the old saying that people use only 10 percent of their brains. Neither statement is true, however. People use every cell in the brain for *something*. The fact is that neurons make up only 10 percent of the cells in the brain. The other 90 percent of the brain is composed of **glial cells** that serve as a sort of structure on which the neurons develop and work and that hold the neurons in place. There are several different types of glial cells that perform various functions, such as getting nutrients to the neurons, cleaning up the remains of neurons that have died, communicating with neurons and other glial cells, and providing insulation for neurons. Recent research has found that some types of glial cells affect both the functioning of neurons and their structure and also "give birth" to new neurons during prenatal development (Breedlove et al., 2007; Bullock et al., 2005).

Neurons aren't found only in the brain. If they are spread all throughout the human body, how are they kept separated? The answer is simple. Two special types of glial cells, called *oligodendrocytes* and *Schwann cells*, generate a layer of fatty substances called **myelin**. (Oligodendrocytes produce myelin in the brain and spinal cord; Schwann cells produce myelin in the neurons of the body.) Myelin wraps around the shaft of the axons, forming a protective sheath. It's really the axons that do the bulk of the traveling through the body, with the somas clumped together near the spinal cord. So the axons of those various neurons can travel together throughout the body and never really touch each other directly. It's very similar to the concept of a laptop power cable. Within the cable are lots of copper wires coated in plastic. The plastic serves the same insulating purpose for the wires as the myelin sheath does for the axons. Bundled all together, they form a cable that is much stronger and less vulnerable to breakage than any wire alone would be. It works the same way in the nervous system. Bundles of myelin-coated axons travel together in "cables" called **nerves**.

A few other facts about myelin: It not only insulates the neuron, but it also offers a little protection from damage and speeds up the neural message traveling down the axon. As shown in Figure 2.2, sections of myelin bump up next to each other on the axon, similar to the way sausages are linked together. The places where the myelin seems to bump are actually small spaces on the axon called nodes, which are not covered in myelin. When the electrical impulse that is the neural message travels down an axon coated with myelin, it "jumps" between the myelin sheath sections to the places where the axon is accessible at the nodes. That makes the message go much faster down the coated axon than it would down an uncoated axon of a neuron in the brain. This myelin sheath is a very important part of the neuron. The disease called *multiple sclerosis* damages the myelin sheath, which leads to a loss of function in those damaged cells (Allen, 1991).

In addition to the myelin sheath produced by the Schwann cells, axons of neurons found in the body are also coated with a thin membrane called the *neurilemma*, or Schwann's membrane. This membrane, which surrounds the axon and the myelin sheath, serves as a tunnel through which damaged nerve fibers can repair themselves. That's why a severed toe might actually regain some function and feeling if sewn back on in time. Unfortunately, axons of the neurons in the brain and spinal cord do not have this coating and are, therefore, more likely to be permanently damaged.

Exactly how does this "electrical message" work inside the cell?

axon tubelike structure that carries the neural message to other cells.

glial cells cells that provide support for the neurons to grow on and around, deliver nutrients to neurons, produce myelin to coat axons, clean up waste products and dead neurons, influence information processing, and, during prenatal development, influence the generation of new neurons.

myelin fatty substances produced by certain glial cells that coat the axons of neurons to insulate, protect, and speed up the neural impulse.

nerves bundles of axons coated in myelin that travel together through the body.

Exactly how does this "electrical message" work inside the cell? ▶

GENERATING THE MESSAGE WITHIN THE NEURON—THE NEURAL IMPULSE

A neuron that's at rest—not currently firing a neural impulse or message—is actually electrically charged. The inside of the cell is really a semiliquid (jelly-like) solution in which there are charged particles, or *ions*. There is a semiliquid solution surrounding the outside of the cell as well that also contains ions. While there are both positive and negative ions inside and outside of the cell, the catch is that the ions inside the cell are mostly negatively charged, and the ions outside the cell are mostly positively charged. The cell membrane itself is *semipermeable*. This means some substances that are outside the cell can enter through tiny openings, or *gates*, in the membrane, while other substances in the cell can go outside. The negatively charged ions inside the cell, however, are so big that they can't get out, which leaves the inside of the cell primarily negative when at rest. Outside the cell are lots of positively charged sodium ions, but they are unable to enter the cell membrane when the cell is at rest—the ion gates that would allow them in are closed. But because the outside sodium ions are positive and the inside ions are negative, and because opposite electrical charges attract each other, the sodium ions will cluster around the membrane. This difference in charges is an electrical potential. ❋ Explore on MyPsychLab

When a cell is resting (a state called the **resting potential**, because the cell is at rest), the sodium ions are outside the cell. The sodium ions cannot enter when the cell is at rest, because even though the cell membrane has all these gates, the *particular* gates for the big sodium ions aren't open yet. But when the cell receives a strong enough stimulation from another cell (meaning that the dendrites are activated), the cell membrane opens up those *particular* gates, one after the other, all down its surface, allowing the sodium ions to rush into the cell. That causes the inside of the cell to become mostly positive and the outside of the cell to become mostly negative, because many of the positive sodium ions are now inside the cell—at the point where the first gate opened. This electrical charge reversal will start at the part of the axon closest to the soma (the first gate) and then proceed down the axon in a kind of chain reaction. (Picture a long hallway with many doors in which the first door opens, then the second, and so on all the way down the hall.) This electrical charge reversal is known as the **action potential** because the electrical potential is now in action rather than at rest. Each action potential sequence takes about one-thousandth of a second, so the neural message travels very fast—from 2 miles per hour in the slowest, shortest neurons to 270 miles per hour in other neurons. (See Figure 2.3.)

Now the action potential is traveling down the axon. When it gets to the end of the axon, something else happens—the message will get transmitted to another cell—that will be discussed momentarily. Meanwhile, what is happening to the parts of the cell that the action potential has already left behind? How does the cell get the sodium ions back outside? Remember, the action potential means that the cell is now positive inside and negative outside at the point where the gate opened. Several things happen to return the cell to its resting state. First, the sodium ion gates close immediately after the action potential has passed, allowing no more sodium ions to enter. The cell membrane also literally pumps the positive sodium ions back outside the cell, kicking them out until the next action potential opens the gates again. This pumping process is a little slow, so another type of ion gets into the act. Small, positively charged potassium ions inside the neuron move rapidly out of the cell after the action potential passes, helping to more quickly restore the inside of the cell to a negative charge. Now the cell becomes negative inside and positive outside, and the neuron is capable of "firing off" another message. Once the sodium pumps finish

❋ **Explore** with a simulation of neurons and neurotransmitters.
www.mypsychlab.com

resting potential   the state of the neuron when not firing a neural impulse.

action potential   the release of the neural impulse consisting of a reversal of the electrical charge within the axon.

Figure 2.3 **The Neural Impulse Action Potential**

In the graph, voltage readings are shown at a given place on the neuron over a period of 20 or 30 milliseconds (thousandths of a second). At first the cell is resting; it then reaches threshold and an action potential is triggered. After a brief hyperpolarization period, the cell returns to its resting potential.

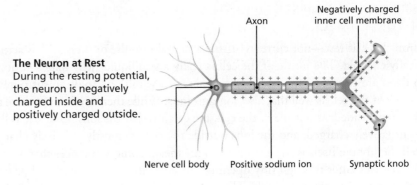

The Neuron at Rest
During the resting potential, the neuron is negatively charged inside and positively charged outside.

Axon

Negatively charged inner cell membrane

Nerve cell body   Positive sodium ion   Synaptic knob

Nerve impulse →

Movement of sodium ions

Sodium ions, along with potassium ions, move outside membrane

Sodium ions enter next segment of axon

The Neural Impulse
The action potential occurs when positive sodium ions enter into the cell, causing a reversal of the electrical charge from negative to positive.

The Neural Impulse Continues
As the action potential moves down the axon toward the axon terminals, the cell areas behind the action potential return to their resting state of a negative charge as the positive sodium ions are pumped to the outside of the cell, and the positive potassium ions rapidly leave.

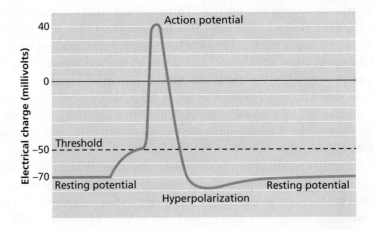

pumping out the sodium ions, the neuron can be said to have returned to its full resting potential.

To sum all that up, when the cell is stimulated, the first gate opens and the electrical charge *at that gate* is reversed. Then the next gate opens and *that* charge is reversed, but in the meantime the *first* gate has been closed and the charge is returning to what it was when it was at rest. The action potential is the *sequence* of gates opening all down the length of the cell.

So if the stimulus that originally causes the neuron to fire is very strong, will the neuron fire more strongly than it would if the stimulus were weak?

Neurons actually have a threshold for firing, and all it takes is a stimulus that is just strong enough to get past that threshold to make the neuron fire. Here's a simple version of how this works: Each neuron is receiving many signals from other neurons. Some of these signals are meant to cause the neuron to fire, whereas others are meant to prevent the neuron from firing. The neuron constantly adds together the effects of the "fire" messages and subtracts the "don't fire" messages, and if the "fire" messages are great enough, the threshold is crossed and the neuron fires. When a neuron does fire, it fires in an **all-or-none** fashion. Neurons are either firing at full strength or not firing at all—there's no such thing as "partial" firing of a neuron. It would be like turning on a light switch—it's either on or it's off. Once the switch is turned to the on position, the light will come on. When it's turned to the off position, the light is off.

So what's the difference between strong stimulation and weak stimulation? A strong message will cause the neuron to fire repeatedly (as if someone flicked the light switch on and off as quickly as possible), and it will also cause more neurons to fire (as if there were a lot of lights going on and off instead of just one). The latter point can be demonstrated quite easily. Just touch lightly on the palm of your hand. You feel a very light pressure sensation. Now push hard in the same spot. You will feel a much stronger pressure sensation, and you can see with your own eyes that more of the skin on the palm of your hand is pushed in by your touch—more skin involved means more neurons firing.

Now that we know how the message travels within the axon of the cell, what is that "something else" that happens when the action potential reaches the end of the axon?

SENDING THE MESSAGE TO OTHER CELLS: THE SYNAPSE

2.2   How do neurons use neurotransmitters to communicate with each other and with the body?

Look once again at Figure 2.2 on page 49. The end of the axon actually fans out into several shorter fibers called **axon terminals**. The tip of each axon terminal has a little knob on it. Figure 2.4 shows this knob blown up to giant size. Notice that the knob (called the **synaptic knob** or sometimes the *terminal button*) is not empty. It has a number of little saclike structures in it called **synaptic vesicles**. The word *vesicle* is Latin and means a "little blister" or "fluid-filled sac."

Inside the synaptic vesicles are chemicals suspended in fluid, which are molecules of substances called **neurotransmitters**. The name is simple enough—they are inside a neuron and they are going to transmit a message. Next to the synaptic knob is the dendrite of another neuron (see Figure 2.4). Between them is a fluid-filled space called the **synapse** or the **synaptic gap**. Instead of an electrical charge, the vesicles at the end of the axon contain the molecules of neurotransmitters, whereas the surface of the dendrite right next to the axon contains special little locks called **receptor sites**. These locks have a special shape that allows only a particular molecule of neurotransmitter to fit into it, just as only a particular key will fit into a keyhole. (The end of the axon containing the neurotransmitters is also called the presynaptic membrane, and the surface of the receiving neuron is called the postsynaptic membrane.)

How do the neurotransmitters get across the gap? Recall the action potential making its way down the axon after the neuron has been stimulated. When that action potential, or electrical charge, reaches the synaptic vesicles, the synaptic vesicles release their neurotransmitters into the synaptic gap. The molecules then float across

◀ So if the stimulus that originally causes the neuron to fire is very strong, will the neuron fire more strongly than it would if the stimulus were weak?

Now that we know how the message travels within the axon of the cell, what is that "something else" that ◀ happens when the action potential reaches the end of the axon?

all-or-none   referring to the fact that a neuron either fires completely or does not fire at all.

axon terminals   branches at the end of the axon.

synaptic knob   rounded areas on the end of the axon terminals.

synaptic vesicles   saclike structures found inside the synaptic knob containing chemicals.

neurotransmitter   chemical found in the synaptic vesicles that, when released, has an effect on the next cell.

synapse (synaptic gap)   microscopic fluid-filled space between the synaptic knob of one cell and the dendrites or surface of the next cell.

receptor sites   holes in the surface of the dendrites or certain cells of the muscles and glands, which are shaped to fit only certain neurotransmitters.

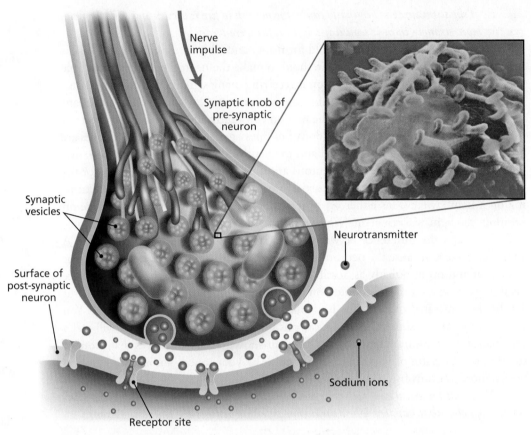

Nerve
impulse

Synaptic knob of
pre-synaptic
neuron

Synaptic
vesicles

Neurotransmitter

Surface of
post-synaptic
neuron

Sodium ions

Receptor site

Figure 2.4 The Synapse
The nerve impulse reaches the synaptic knobs, triggering the release of neurotransmitters from the synaptic vesicles. The molecules of neurotransmitter cross the synaptic gap to fit into the receptor sites that fit the shape of the molecule.

the synapse and many of them fit themselves into the receptor sites, activating the next cell. It is this very activation that stimulates, or releases, the action potential in that cell. It is important to understand that the "next cell" may be a neuron, but it may also be a cell on a muscle or a gland. Muscles and glands have special cells with receptor sites on them, just like on the dendrite of a neuron.

So far, we've been talking about the synapse as if neurotransmitters always cause the next cell to fire its action potential (or, in the case of a muscle or gland, to contract or start secreting its chemicals). But the neurons must have a way to be turned *off* as well as on. Otherwise, when a person burns a finger, the pain signals from those neurons would not stop until the burn was completely healed. Muscles are told to contract or relax, and glands are told to secrete or stop secreting their chemicals. The neurotransmitters found at various synapses around the nervous system (and there are at least 50 to 100 identified neurotransmitters and theoretically several times that number exist) can either turn cells on (called an *excitatory* effect) or turn cells off (called an *inhibitory* effect), depending on exactly what synapse is being affected. Although some people refer to neurotransmitters that turn cells on as *excitatory* neurotransmitters and the ones that turn cells off as *inhibitory* neurotransmitters, it's really more correct to refer to **excitatory synapses** and **inhibitory synapses**. In other words, it's not the neurotransmitter itself that is excitatory or inhibitory, but rather it is the effect of that neurotransmitter that is either excitatory or inhibitory at the receptor sites of a particular synapse.

excitatory synapse   synapse at which a neurotransmitter causes the receiving cell to fire.

inhibitory synapse   synapse at which a neurotransmitter causes the receiving cell to stop firing.

I think I understand the synapse now, but will knowing about neurotransmitters and synapses help me in the real world?

Most people have used drugs of some sort at some point in their lives. Knowing how and why drugs affect us can help us understand why a doctor might prescribe a particular drug or why certain drugs are dangerous and should be avoided. Because molecules of various drugs, if similar enough in shape to the neurotransmitters, can fit into the receptor sites on the receiving neurons just like the neurotransmitters do, drugs can affect what happens in the synapse in two ways. **Agonists** are chemical substances that can mimic or enhance the effects of neurotransmitters on the receptor sites of the next cell, which can result in an increase or decrease in the activity of the receiving cell, depending on what the effect of the original neurotransmitter (excitatory or inhibitory) was going to be. So if the original neurotransmitter was excitatory, the effect of the agonist will be to increase that excitation. If it was inhibitory, the effect of the agonist will be to increase that inhibition. For example, there are drugs that bind to receptors in the heart muscle (called *beta* receptors) that act as agonists by increasing the action of the neurotransmitter that stimulates the contractions of certain heart valves. Digoxin, which comes from the foxglove plant, is one example of this kind of agonist drug.

Other drugs act as **antagonists**, chemical substances that block or reduce a cell's response to the action of other chemicals or neurotransmitters. Although an antagonist might sound like it has only an inhibitory effect, it is important to remember that if the neurotransmitter that the antagonist affects is inhibitory itself, the result will actually be an *increase* in the activity of the cell that would normally have been inhibited; the antagonist *blocks* the inhibitory effect.

Beta blockers are drugs that are used to control high blood pressure and (as the name suggests) serve as antagonists by blocking the effects of the neurotransmitters that stimulate the heart's contractions. This results in slower heart contractions and lowered blood pressure. Two examples of commonly prescribed beta blockers are propranolol (Inderal®) and metaprolol (Lopressor®). In the following discussion of specific types of neurotransmitters, there are more examples of agonists and antagonists and how they affect the nervous system.

NEUROTRANSMITTERS, MESSENGERS OF THE NETWORK

The first neurotransmitter to be identified was named *acetylcholine.* It is found at the synapses between neurons and muscle cells. Acetylcholine serves to stimulate the skeletal muscles to contract but actually slows contractions in the heart muscle. If acetylcholine receptor sites on the muscle cells are blocked in some way, then the acetylcholine can't get to the site and the muscle will be incapable of contracting—paralyzed, in other words. This is exactly what happens when *curare,* a drug used by South American Indians on their blow darts, gets into the nervous system. Curare's molecules are just similar enough to fit into the receptor site without actually stimulating the cell, making curare an antagonist for acetylcholine.

What would happen if the neurons released too much acetylcholine? The bite of a black widow spider does just that. Its venom stimulates the release of excessive amounts of acetylcholine and causes convulsions and possible death. Black widow spider venom is an agonist for acetylcholine. Acetylcholine is also found in the hippocampus, an area of the brain that is responsible for forming new memories, and low levels of acetylcholine have been associated with Alzheimer's disease, the most common type of dementia. (LINK) *to Chapter Six: Memory, pp. 253–254.*

◄ I think I understand the synapse now, but will knowing about neurotransmitters and synapses help me in the real world?

◄ **AP*** Discuss the influence of drugs on neurotransmitters.

The venom of the black widow spider causes a flood of acetylcholine to be released into the body's muscle system, causing convulsions.

agonists chemical substances that mimic or enhance the effects of a neurotransmitter on the receptor sites of the next cell, increasing or decreasing the activity of that cell.

antagonists chemical substances that block or reduce a cell's response to the action of other chemicals or neurotransmitters.

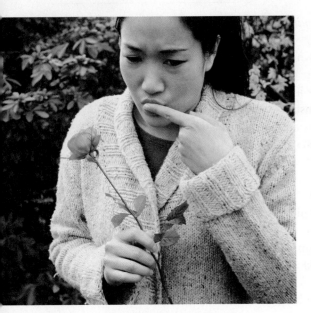

The look on this young woman's face clearly indicates that she has experienced pain in her finger. Pain is a warning signal that something is wrong, in this case that touching the thorns on the stem of the rose was a bad idea. What might be some of the problems encountered by a person who could feel no pain at all?

Although acetylcholine was the first neurotransmitter found to have an excitatory effect at the synapse, the nervous system's major excitatory neurotransmitter is *glutamate*. Like acetylcholine, glutamate plays an important role in learning and memory, and may also be involved in the development of the nervous system.

Another neurotransmitter is *GABA*, or γ-*aminobatyric acid* (or *gamma-aminobutyric acid*). Whereas glutamate is the major neurotransmitter with an excitatory effect, GABA is the most common neurotransmitter producing inhibition in the brain. GABA can help to calm anxiety, for example, by binding to the same receptor sites that are affected by tranquilizing drugs and alcohol. In fact, the effect of alcohol is to enhance the effect of GABA, which causes the general inhibition of the nervous system associated with getting drunk. This makes alcohol an agonist for GABA. (L I N K) *to Chapter Four: Consciousness: Sleep, Dreams, Hypnosis, and Drugs, p. 159.*

Serotonin is a neurotransmitter found in the lower part of the brain that can have either an excitatory or inhibitory effect, depending on the particular synapses being affected. It is associated with sleep, mood, and appetite. For example, low levels of serotonin activity have been linked to depression. (L I N K) *to Chapter Twelve: Psychological Disorders, p. 499.*

Dopamine is found in the brain and, like serotonin, can have different effects depending on the exact location of its activity. If too little dopamine is released in a certain area of the brain, the result is Parkinson's disease—the disease currently being battled by former boxing champ Muhammad Ali and actor Michael J. Fox (Ahlskog, 2003). If too much dopamine is released in another area, the result is a set of symptoms that may be part of a serious mental disorder called schizophrenia (Akil et al., 2003). Please note, this example oversimplifies the role of neurotransmitters in mental disorders. Many disorders are due to multiple causes and/or variations in multiple neurotransmitters. (L I N K) *to Chapter Twelve: Psychological Disorders, pp. 501–504.* (See Table 2.1 for a list of some neurotransmitters and their functions.)

Some neurotransmitters directly control the release of other neurotransmitters. These special neurotransmitters are called *neural regulators* or *neural peptides* (Agnati et al., 1992), and one that researchers know a little about is endorphin. *Endorphins* are pain-controlling chemicals in the body. When a person is hurt, a

Table 2.1   Neurotransmitters and Their Functions

NEUROTRANSMITTERS	FUNCTIONS
Acetylcholine	Excitatory or inhibitory; involved in arousal, attention, memory and controls muscle contractions.
Serotonin	Excitatory or inhibitory; involved in mood, sleep, and appetite.
GABA (gamma-aminobutyric acid)	Major inhibitory neurotransmitter; involved in sleep and inhibits movement.
Glutamate	Major excitatory neurotransmitter; involved in learning, memory formation, and nervous system development.
Norepinephrine	Mainly excitatory; involved in arousal and mood.
Dopamine	Excitatory or inhibitory; involved in control of movement and sensations of pleasure.
Endorphins	Inhibitory neural regulators; involved in pain relief.

neurotransmitter that signals pain is released. When the brain gets this message, it triggers the release of endorphins. The endorphins bind to receptors that open the gates on the axon. This causes the cell to be unable to fire its pain signal, and the pain sensations eventually lessen. For example, you might bump your elbow and experience a lot of pain right at first, but the pain will quickly subside to a much lower level. Sports players may injure themselves during an event and yet not feel the pain until after the event when the endorphin levels go down.

The name *endorphin* comes from the term *endogenous morphine*. (*Endogenous* means "native to the area"—in this case, native to the body.) Scientists studying the nervous system found receptor sites that fit morphine molecules perfectly and decided that there must be a natural substance in the body that has the same effect as morphine. Endorphins are the reason that heroin and the other drugs derived from opium are so addictive—when people take morphine or heroin, their bodies neglect to produce endorphins. When the drug wears off, they are left with no protection against pain at all, and *everything* hurts. Known as withdrawal, this pain is why most people want more heroin, creating an addictive cycle of abuse. ⓁⒾⓃⓀ *to Chapter Four: Consciousness: Sleep, Dreams, Hypnosis, and Drugs, p. 162.*

If the neurotransmitters are out there in the synaptic gap and in the receptor sites, what happens to them when they aren't needed anymore?

CLEANING UP THE SYNAPSE: REUPTAKE AND ENZYMES

The neurotransmitters have to get out of the receptor sites before the next stimulation can occur. Some just diffuse away but most will end up back in the synaptic vesicles in a process called **reuptake**. (Think of a little suction tube, sucking the chemicals back into the vesicles.) That way, the synapse is cleared for the next release of neurotransmitters. Some drugs, like cocaine, affect the nervous system by blocking the reuptake process. See Figure 2.5 for a visual representation of how dopamine is affected by cocaine.

There is one neurotransmitter that is not taken back into the vesicles, however. Because acetylcholine is responsible for muscle activity, and muscle activity needs to happen rapidly and continue happening, it's not possible to wait around for the "sucking up" process to occur. Instead, an enzyme* specifically designed to break apart acetylcholine clears the synaptic gap very quickly (a process called enzymatic degradation). There are enzymes that break down the other neurotransmitters as well.

The neurotransmitter serotonin helps regulate and adjust people's moods, but in some people the normal process of adjustment is not working properly. In some people, serotonin is either not produced or not released in great enough amounts, so it can't fully activate the receptors on the next neuron, leaving the person in a state of depression. Most of the drugs used to treat this condition are called SSRIs (selective serotonin reuptake inhibitors). SSRIs block the reuptake of serotonin, leaving more serotonin available in the synapse to bond with the receptor sites. Eventually, this elevates mood and lifts the depression. Although doctors used to "taper off" the use of antidepressants after the person's depression had lifted, new research has found that keeping a person on a maintenance dose of the drug helps prevent future episodes of depression (Geddes et al., 2003; Taylor et al., 2004).

This section covered the neuron and how neurons communicate. The next section looks at the bigger picture—the nervous system itself. Before reading on, try answering the following questions to test your memory.

---

*Enzyme: a complex protein that is manufactured by cells.

◄ **If the neurotransmitters are out there in the synaptic gap and in the receptor sites, what happens to them when they aren't needed anymore?**

Figure 2.5 Reuptake of Dopamine
Dopamine is removed from the synapse by reuptake sites. Cocaine acts by blocking dopamine reuptake sites, allowing dopamine to remain active in the synapse longer.

AP✱ Discuss the influence of drugs ◄ on neurotransmitters (e.g., reuptake mechanisms).

---

reuptake   process by which neurotransmitters are taken back into the synaptic vesicles.

2.1–2

The nervous system is a network of cells that carries information to and from all parts of the body; **neuroscience** is the field of study that deals with the structure of the brain and components of the nervous system

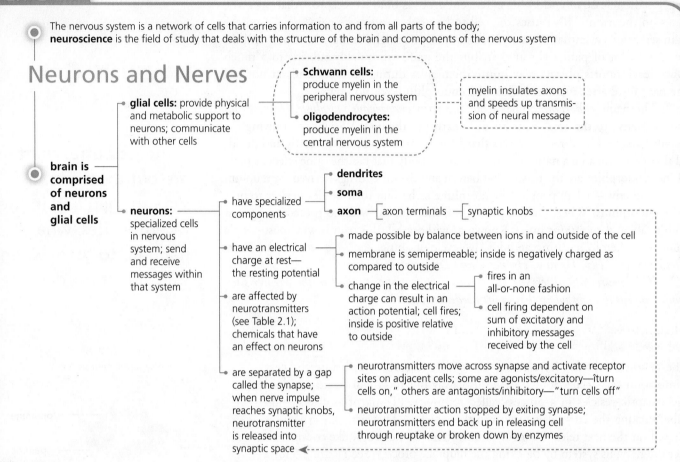

Neurons and Nerves

- **brain is comprised of neurons and glial cells**
  - **glial cells:** provide physical and metabolic support to neurons; communicate with other cells
    - **Schwann cells:** produce myelin in the peripheral nervous system
    - **oligodendrocytes:** produce myelin in the central nervous system
      - myelin insulates axons and speeds up transmission of neural message
  - **neurons:** specialized cells in nervous system; send and receive messages within that system
    - have specialized components
      - **dendrites**
      - **soma**
      - **axon** — axon terminals — synaptic knobs
    - have an electrical charge at rest—the resting potential
      - made possible by balance between ions in and outside of the cell
      - membrane is semipermeable; inside is negatively charged as compared to outside
      - change in the electrical charge can result in an action potential; cell fires; inside is positive relative to outside
        - fires in an all-or-none fashion
        - cell firing dependent on sum of excitatory and inhibitory messages received by the cell
    - are affected by neurotransmitters (see Table 2.1); chemicals that have an effect on neurons
    - are separated by a gap called the synapse; when nerve impulse reaches synaptic knobs, neurotransmitter is released into synaptic space
      - neurotransmitters move across synapse and activate receptor sites on adjacent cells; some are agonists/excitatory—îturn cells on," others are antagonists/inhibitory—"turn cells off"
      - neurotransmitter action stopped by exiting synapse; neurotransmitters end back up in releasing cell through reuptake or broken down by enzymes

---

PRACTICE QUIZ: PREPARING FOR THE AP* EXAM

ANSWERS ON PAGE AK-1.

Directions: Read each of the questions or incomplete sentences below. Then choose the response that best answers the question or completes the sentence.

1. Which part of the neuron receives messages from other cells?
- **a.** Axon
- **b.** Dendrite
- **c.** Soma
- **d.** Myelin
- **e.** Nucleus

2. Which of the following statements about the activity of neurons is true?
- **a.** A weak message can be used to stimulate a myelinated neuron, but a strong message is needed to stimulate a demyelinated neuron.
- **b.** A weak message can be used to stimulate a sensory neuron, but a strong message is needed to stimulate a motor neuron.
- **c.** A strong message received by a neuron will cause the neuron to generate a stronger action potential.
- **d.** A strong message will cause the release of neurotransmitters from the neuron, while a weak message will cause the release of hormones form the neuron.
- **e.** A strong message received by a neuron will cause the neuron to fire repeatedly, in a faster fashion.

3. When the neuron's action potential occurs, ____ ions are rushing into the axon through openings on the membrane.
- **a.** sodium
- **b.** potassium
- **c.** chloride
- **d.** oxygen
- **e.** ammonium

4. When the action potential reaches the end of the axon terminals, it causes the release of ____.
- **a.** an electrical spark that sets off the next neuron
- **b.** positively charged ions that excite the next cell
- **c.** positively charged ions that inhibit the next cell
- **d.** negatively charged ions that inhibit the next cell
- **e.** neurotransmitters that excite or inhibit the next cell

5. When an antagonist drug affects an inhibitory neurotransmitter, it ____.
- **a.** increases the inhibitory effect
- **b.** increases the activity of the cell
- **c.** paralyzes the system
- **d.** neutralizes the cell
- **e.** does not affect the cell

6. Which of the following neurotransmitters is associated with sleep, mood, and appetite?
- **a.** Acetylcholine
- **b.** GABA
- **c.** Serotonin
- **d.** Endorphin
- **e.** Glutamate

The Central Nervous System—The "Central Processing Unit"

The **central nervous system (CNS)** is composed of the brain and the spinal cord. Both the brain and the spinal cord are composed of neurons and glial cells that control the life-sustaining functions of the body as well as all thought, emotion, and behavior.

2.3   How do the brain and spinal cord interact?

THE BRAIN

The brain is the true core of the nervous system, the part that makes sense of the information received from the senses, makes decisions, and sends commands out to the muscles and the rest of the body. Later parts of this chapter will cover the brain in more detail. Without the spinal cord, however, the brain would be useless.

THE SPINAL CORD

The **spinal cord** is a long bundle of neurons that serves two vital functions for the nervous system. Look at the cross-sectional view of the spinal cord in Figure 2.6. Notice that it seems to be divided into two areas, one around the outside and one inside the cord. If it were a real spinal cord, the outer section would appear to be white and the inner section would seem gray. That's because the outer section is composed mainly of myelinated axons and nerves, which appear white, whereas the inner section is mainly composed of cell bodies of neurons, which appear gray. The purpose of the outer section is to carry messages from the body up to the brain and from the brain down to the body. It is simply a message "pipeline."

The Reflex ARC: Three Types of Neurons   The inside section, which is made up of cell bodies separated by glial cells, is actually a primitive sort of "brain." This part of the spinal cord is responsible for certain reflexes—very fast, lifesaving reflexes. To understand how the spinal cord reflexes work, it is important to know there are three basic types of neurons: **afferent (sensory) neurons** that carry messages from the senses to the spinal cord, **efferent (motor) neurons** that carry messages from the spinal cord to the muscles and glands, and **interneurons** that connect the afferent neurons to the motor neurons (and make up the inside of the spinal cord and much of the brain itself). (See Figure 2.6.) Touch a flame or a hot stove with your finger, for example, and an afferent neuron will send the pain message up to the spinal column where it enters into the central area of the spinal cord. The interneuron in that central area will then receive the message and send out a response along an efferent neuron, causing your finger to pull back. This all happens very quickly. If the pain message had to go all the way up to the brain before a response could be

2 Sensory neurons excite interneurons in the dorsal gray portion of the spinal cord.

Sensory neuron

To the brain

3 Interneurons excite motor neurons in the ventral gray portion of the spinal cord.

4 Motor nerves exit the spinal cord, excite the muscle, and initiate a movement.

1 Flame stimulates pain receptors (sensory neurons).

Figure 2.6 The Spinal Cord Reflex
The pain from the burning heat of the candle flame stimulates the afferent nerve fibers, which carry the message up to the interneurons in the middle of the spinal cord. The interneurons then send a message out by means of the efferent nerve fibers, causing the hand to jerk away from the flame.

◄ **AP***   Describe the nervous system and its subdivisions and functions.

central nervous system (CNS)   part of the nervous system consisting of the brain and spinal cord.

spinal cord   a long bundle of neurons that carries messages between the body and the brain and is responsible for very fast, lifesaving reflexes.

afferent (sensory) neuron   a neuron that carries information from the senses to the central nervous system.

efferent (motor) neuron   a neuron that carries messages from the central nervous system to the muscles of the body.

interneuron   a neuron found in the center of the spinal cord that receives information from the afferent neurons and sends commands to the muscles through the efferent neurons. Interneurons also make up the bulk of the neurons in the brain.

This electronmicrograph shows a motor neuron making contact with muscle fibers.

((•● **Listen** to the Psychology in the News podcast. **www.mypsychlab.com**

reflex arc the connection of the afferent neurons to the interneurons to the efferent neurons, resulting in a reflex action.

neuroplasticity the ability within the brain to constantly change both the structure and function of many cells in response to experience or trauma.

stem cells special cells found in all the tissues of the body that are capable of becoming other cell types when those cells need to be replaced due to damage or wear and tear.

> If the spinal cord is such an important link between the body and the brain, what happens if it is damaged? ▶

made, the response time would be greatly increased and more damage would be done to your finger. So having this kind of **reflex arc** controlled by the spinal cord alone allows for very fast response times. (A good way to avoid mixing up the terms *afferent* and *efferent* is to remember "<u>a</u>fferent neurons <u>a</u>ccess the spinal cord, <u>e</u>fferent neurons <u>e</u>xit.") The pain message does eventually get to the brain, where other motor responses may be triggered, like saying "Ouch!" and putting the finger in your mouth.

If the spinal cord is such an important link between the body and the brain, what happens if it is damaged?

Damage to the central nervous system was once thought to be permanent. Neurons in the brain and spinal cord were not seen as capable of repairing themselves. When people recovered from a stroke, for example, it was assumed that healthy brain cells took over the function of the damaged ones. Scientists have known for a while now that some forms of central nervous system damage can be repaired by the body's systems, and in recent years great strides have been made in repairing spinal cord damage. The brain actually exhibits a great deal of **neuroplasticity**, the ability to constantly change both the structure and function of many cells in the brain in response to experience and even trauma (Neville & Bavelier, 2000; Rossini et al., 2007; Sanders, Weber-Fox, & Neville, 2008)). Scientists have been able to *implant* nerve fibers from outside the spinal cord onto a damaged area and then "coax" the damaged spinal nerves to grow through these "tunnels" of implanted fibers (Cheng et al., 1996). The first human trials have already begun (Blits & Bunge, 2006; Bunge & Pearse, 2003). It is also now known that the brain can change itself quite a bit by adapting neurons to serve new functions when old neurons die or are damaged. Dendrites grow and new synapses are formed in at least some areas of the brain, as people learn new things throughout life (Abraham & Williams, 2003). And as in the case of Michelle M. from the opening story, it is actually possible to live a relatively normal life with a substantial amount of brain tissue missing.

Researchers are constantly looking for new ways to repair the brain. For a look at a new and promising treatment for people with diseases such as Parkinson's, Alzheimer's, and damage from strokes, read the following Psychology in the News section. ((•—|**Listen** on **MyPsychLab**

Psychology in the News

Stem Cells: New Hope for Damaged Brains?

Scientists have been researching the possibility of transplanting **stem cells** to repair damaged or diseased brain tissue. (See Figure 2.7.) Stem cells can become other cells, such as blood cells, nerve cells, and brain cells (National Institutes of Health, 2007). An ongoing controversy concerns the source of such stem cells, which can be obtained from human embryos, either from terminated pregnancies or fertilization clinics. Many people are opposed to the idea of putting embryos to this use, even if stem cell research promises cures for diseases, such as Parkinson's and Alzheimer's, or the repair of damaged spinal cords or brain tissue.

On August 9, 2001, President George W. Bush announced his decision to allow federal funding of stem cell research using human embryonic stem cells but only on cell lines already in existence. In 2004, House representatives proposed a bill called the Stem Cell Research Enhancement Act, which would have allowed researchers to use stem cells taken from donated embryos that came from fertilization clinics and would be discarded if not used. In the summer of 2006, President Bush vetoed this bill. On June 20, 2007, President Bush once again vetoed the bill (American Association for the Advancement of Science, 2007). On March 9, 2009, President Barack Obama reversed the 2001 limitations on stem cell lines, creating new hope for researchers (CBS/AP, 2009).

Stem cells are found in many of the organs of the body and also in the bone marrow. A study conducted by neurologist Alexander Storch of the University of Ulm in Germany and his colleagues may hold hope for the future of stem cell treatments without the controversial need to use human embryonic tissue (Hermann et al., 2006). In this study, the researchers were able to convert bone marrow stem cells from mice into cells resembling neural stem cells. The authors go on to describe the possibility of such conversion taking place in adult bone marrow stem cells.

Stem cells that are not embryonic tend not to be as "plastic"—they want to form into cells of the tissues in which they are found. Scientists are working to find ways to increase the plasticity of nonembryonic stem cells, such as those obtained from bone marrow, so that future generations may have hope that "permanent" brain damage may become a thing of the past (Croft & Przyborski, 2006; Maisel et al., 2007).

Questions for Further Discussion

1. If stem cells can be used to create tissues other than nerves and neurons, what other kinds of diseases might become treatable?

2. What ethical considerations might arise from doing bone marrow stem cell research with human volunteers?

3. How might the recent changes in stem cell research affect cancer research?

The Stem Cell
These cells develop into all other blood cells, including red, white, and platelets

Red Blood Cells
These cells supply oxygen to the organs and body tissues

White Blood Cells
These cells help the body fight off infections

Platelets
The platelets aid in blood clotting

Figure 2.7 The Stem Cell
Stem cells are basic cells that differentiate into specific types of cells, such as these blood cells. Stem cells can also become other types of cells, such as brain cells and nerve cells.

Microphotograph of a bone marrow stem cell.

The Peripheral Nervous System—Nerves on the Edge

Okay, that takes care of the central nervous system, except for the detail on the brain. How does the central nervous system communicate with the rest of the body?

The term *peripheral* refers to things that are not in the center or that are on the edges of the center. The **peripheral nervous system** or **PNS** (see Figure 2.8) is made up of all the nerves and neurons that are not contained in the brain and spinal cord. It is this system that allows the brain and spinal cord to communicate with the sensory systems of the eyes, ears, skin, and mouth and allows the brain and spinal cord to control the muscles and glands of the body. The PNS can be divided into two major systems, the **somatic nervous system** and the **autonomic nervous system (ANS)**.

2.4   How do the somatic and autonomic nervous systems allow people and animals to interact with their surroundings and control the body's automatic functions?

THE SOMATIC NERVOUS SYSTEM

One of the parts of a neuron is the soma, or cell body (the word *soma* means "body"). The somatic nervous system is made up of the **sensory pathway**, which is all the nerves carrying messages from the senses to the central nervous system (those nerves containing

Okay, that takes care of the central nervous system, except for the detail on the brain. How ◀ does the central nervous system communicate with the rest of the body?

peripheral nervous system (PNS)   all nerves and neurons that are not contained in the brain and spinal cord but that run through the body itself.

somatic nervous system   division of the PNS consisting of nerves that carry information from the senses to the CNS and from the CNS to the voluntary muscles of the body.

autonomic nervous system (ANS)   division of the PNS consisting of nerves that control all of the involuntary muscles, organs, and glands.

sensory pathway   nerves coming from the sensory organs to the CNS consisting of afferent neurons.

Figure 2.8 The Peripheral Nervous System

Brain
(CNS)

Spinal
cord
(CNS)

Nerves
(PNS)

motor pathway   nerves coming
from the CNS to the voluntary muscles,
consisting of efferent neurons.

**sympathetic division (fight-or-flight
system)**   part of the ANS that is responsible for reacting to stressful events and
bodily arousal.

parasympathetic division   part of the
ANS that restores the body to normal functioning after arousal and is responsible for
the day-to-day functioning of the organs
and glands.

afferent neurons), and the **motor pathway**, which is all of the nerves carrying messages from the central nervous system to the voluntary, or skeletal,* muscles of the body—muscles that allow people to move their bodies (those nerves composed of efferent neurons). When people are walking, raising their hands in class, picking a flower to smell, or directing their gaze toward a pretty picture, they are using the somatic nervous system. (As seen in the discussion of spinal cord reflexes, although these muscles are called the voluntary muscles, they can move involuntarily when a reflex response occurs. They are called "voluntary" because they *can* be moved at will but are not limited to only that kind of movement.)

Involuntary** muscles, such as the heart, stomach, and intestines, together with glands such as the adrenal glands and the pancreas are all controlled by clumps of neurons located on or near the spinal column. (The words *on* or *near* are used quite deliberately here. The neurons *inside* the spinal column are part of the central nervous system, not the peripheral nervous system.) These large groups of neurons near the spinal column make up the *autonomic nervous system*.

THE AUTONOMIC NERVOUS SYSTEM

The word *autonomic* suggests that the functions of this system are more or less automatic, which is basically correct. Whereas the somatic division of the peripheral nervous system controls the senses and voluntary muscles, the autonomic division controls everything else in the body—organs, glands, and involuntary muscles. The autonomic nervous system is divided into two systems, the **sympathetic division** and the **parasympathetic division**. (See Figure 2.9.) (For a visual representation of how all the various sections of the nervous system are organized, look back at Figure 2.1 on page 48.)

The Sympathetic Division   The sympathetic division of the autonomic nervous system is primarily located on the middle of the spinal column—running from near the top of the ribcage to the waist area. It may help to think of the name in these terms: The *sympathetic* division is in *sympathy* with one's emotions. In fact, the sympathetic division is usually called the *fight-or-flight system* because it allows people and animals to deal with all kinds of stressful events. **LINK** *to Chapter Nine: Stress and Health, p. 349.* Emotions during these events might be anger (hence, the term *fight*) or fear (that's the *flight* part, obviously) or even extreme joy or excitement. Yes, even joy can be stressful. The sympathetic division's job is to get the body ready to deal with the stress.

What are the specific ways in which this division readies the body to react? (See Figure 2.9.) The pupils seem to get bigger, perhaps to let in more light and, therefore, more information. The heart starts pumping faster and harder, drawing blood away from nonessential organs such as the skin (so at first the person may turn pale) and sometimes even the brain itself (so the person might actually faint). Blood needs lots of oxygen before it goes to the muscles, so the lungs work overtime, too (the person may

---

*Skeletal: having to do with the bones of the body, or skeleton.
**Involuntary: not under deliberate control.

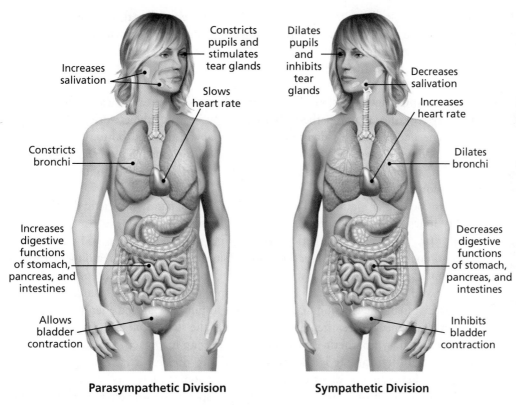

Increases salivation

Constricts pupils and stimulates tear glands

Slows heart rate

Constricts bronchi

Increases digestive functions of stomach, pancreas, and intestines

Allows bladder contraction

Parasympathetic Division

Dilates pupils and inhibits tear glands

Decreases salivation

Increases heart rate

Dilates bronchi

Decreases digestive functions of stomach, pancreas, and intestines

Inhibits bladder contraction

Sympathetic Division

Figure 2.9 **Functions of the Parasympathetic and Sympathetic Divisions of the Nervous System**

begin to breathe faster). One set of glands in particular receives special instructions. The adrenal glands will be stimulated to release certain stress-related chemicals (members of a class of chemicals released by glands called *hormones*) into the bloodstream. These stress hormones will travel to all parts of the body, but they will only affect certain target organs. Just as a neurotransmitter fits into a receptor site on a cell, the molecules of the stress hormones fit into receptor sites at the various target organs—notably, the heart, muscles, and lungs. This further stimulates these organs to work harder. (There are other hormones for other functions that have nothing to do with stress. For more about hormones and glands, see the last section in this chapter, The Chemical Connection: The Endocrine Glands.)

But not every organ or system will be stimulated by the activation of the sympathetic division. Digestion of food and excretion* of waste are not necessary functions when dealing with stressful situations, so these systems tend to be "shut down" or inhibited. Saliva, which is part of digestion, dries right up (ever try whistling when you're scared?). Food that was in the stomach sits there like a lump. Usually, the urge to go to the bathroom will be suppressed, but if the person is really scared the bladder or bowels may actually empty. The sympathetic division is also going to demand that the body burn a tremendous amount of fuel, or blood sugar.

Now, all this bodily arousal is going on during a stressful situation. If the stress ends, the activity of the sympathetic division will be replaced by the activation of the parasympathetic division. If the stress goes on too long or is too intense, the person

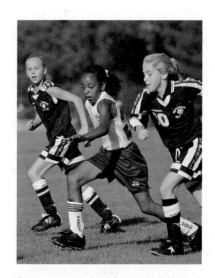

These young soccer players are using their senses and voluntary muscles controlled by the somatic division of the peripheral nervous system. What part of the autonomic nervous system are these girls also using at this time?

---

*Excretion: in this sense, the act of eliminating waste products from the body.

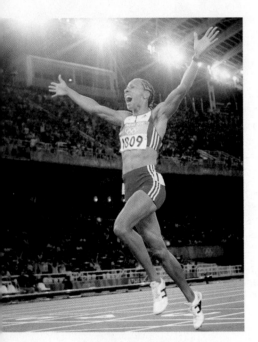

British runner Kelly Holmes at the 2004 Summer Olympics in Athens, Greece. Her sympathetic nervous system is still in high gear in response to her emotional state.

might actually collapse (as a deer might do when being chased by another animal). This collapse occurs because the parasympathetic division overresponds in its inhibition of the sympathetic activity. The heart slows, blood vessels open up, blood pressure in the brain drops, and fainting can be the result.

The Parasympathetic Division If the sympathetic division can be called the fight-or-flight system, the parasympathetic division might be called the eat-drink-and-rest system. The neurons of this division are located at the top and bottom of the spinal column, on either side of the sympathetic division neurons (*para* means "beyond" or "next to" and in this sense refers to the neurons located on either side of the sympathetic division neurons).

In looking at Figure 2.9, it might seem as if the parasympathetic division does pretty much the opposite of the sympathetic division, but it's a little more complex than that. The parasympathetic division's job is to restore the body to normal functioning after a stressful situation ends. It slows the heart and breathing, constricts the pupils, and reactivates digestion and excretion. Signals to the adrenal glands stop because the parasympathetic division isn't connected to the adrenal glands. In a sense, the parasympathetic division allows the body to put back all the energy it burned—which is why people are often very hungry *after* the stress is all over.

The parasympathetic division does more than just react to the activity of the sympathetic division. It is the parasympathetic division that is responsible for most of the ordinary, day-to-day bodily functioning, such as regular heartbeat and normal breathing and digestion. People spend the greater part of their 24-hour day eating, sleeping, digesting, and excreting. So it is the parasympathetic division that is normally active. At any given moment, then, one or the other of these divisions, sympathetic or parasympathetic, will determine whether people are aroused or relaxed.

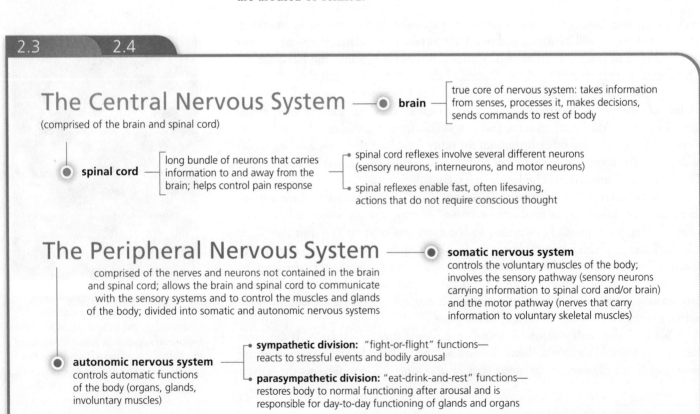

2.3   2.4

The Central Nervous System
(comprised of the brain and spinal cord)

brain — true core of nervous system: takes information from senses, processes it, makes decisions, sends commands to rest of body

spinal cord — long bundle of neurons that carries information to and away from the brain; helps control pain response

- spinal cord reflexes involve several different neurons (sensory neurons, interneurons, and motor neurons)
- spinal reflexes enable fast, often lifesaving, actions that do not require conscious thought

The Peripheral Nervous System
comprised of the nerves and neurons not contained in the brain and spinal cord; allows the brain and spinal cord to communicate with the sensory systems and to control the muscles and glands of the body; divided into somatic and autonomic nervous systems

somatic nervous system
controls the voluntary muscles of the body; involves the sensory pathway (sensory neurons carrying information to spinal cord and/or brain) and the motor pathway (nerves that carry information to voluntary skeletal muscles)

autonomic nervous system
controls automatic functions of the body (organs, glands, involuntary muscles)

sympathetic division: "fight-or-flight" functions—reacts to stressful events and bodily arousal

parasympathetic division: "eat-drink-and-rest" functions—restores body to normal functioning after arousal and is responsible for day-to-day functioning of glands and organs

Directions: Read each of the questions or incomplete sentences below. Then choose the response that best answers the question or completes the sentence..

1. If you burn your finger, which of the following central nervous system components will receive the message last?
   a. The brain
   b. The spinal cord
   c. Afferent neurons
   d. Efferent neurons
   e. Interneurons

2. If you are typing on the computer keyboard, the motions of your fingers on the keys are probably being controlled by _____.
   a. the autonomic nervous system
   b. sensory pathway neurons
   c. motor pathway neurons
   d. autonomic neurons
   e. peripheral neurons

3. The neurons of the motor pathway control _____.
   a. stress reactions
   b. organs and glands
   c. involuntary muscles
   d. voluntary muscles
   e. emotion and behavior

4. Which of the following is NOT a function of the sympathetic division?
   a. Increasing digestive activity to supply fuel for the body
   b. Dilating the pupils of the eyes
   c. Increasing the heart rate
   d. Increasing the activity of the lungs
   e. Preparing the body to handle stress

5. Which of the following would be active if you are sleeping?
   a. Sympathetic division
   b. Parasympathetic division
   c. Somatic division
   d. Motor division
   e. Autonomic division

Peeking Inside the Brain

2.5   How do psychologists study the brain and how it works?

AP* Recount historic and contemporary research strategies and technologies that support research.

In ancient times, many early "scientists" would dissect the brains of those who had died—both animals and people—to try to see how the brain worked. The problem, of course, is that it is impossible tell what a structure in the brain is supposed to do if it's dead. This method did, however, meet some success. In 1861, French surgeon Paul Broca performed autopsies and located the speech center of the brain. How can scientists find out what the various parts of the brain do? ◉⊣**Watch** on **MyPsychLab**

◉ **Watch** classic video on Wilder Penfield and electric brain stimulation. **www.mypsychlab.com**

CLINICAL STUDIES

Without having access to a functioning brain, several researchers studied the image of the brain. Leonardo da Vinci drew sketches of the brain. Santiago Ramon y Cajal used sketches and advanced staining methods to study the brain and how neurons communicate. So how do researchers study human brain function? It should be obvious that researchers can't destroy areas of the brains of human beings. But they can test people who already have brain damage and assess what they can or cannot do. It isn't an ideal way to study the brain, however, as no two case studies of human brain damage are likely to be in exactly the same area of the brain and involve exactly the same amount of damage.

One way to get some idea of what the various areas of the brain control is to study animals or people with damage to those areas. In animals, that may mean damaging a part of the brain deliberately. Then researchers test the animal to see what has happened to its abilities. Or they may electrically stimulate some particular area of the animal's brain and watch the result. Both the destruction and stimulation of brain tissue are accomplished by the same basic process. After the animal is anesthetized, a thin wire insulated everywhere but the very tip is surgically inserted into the brain of the test animal. If brain tissue is to be destroyed, an electrical current strong enough to kill off the neurons at the tip of the wire is sent through it. This is called **deep lesioning**. (When cells are destroyed on the surface of the brain or just below, this process is sometimes called *shallow lesioning*.)

If researchers only want to stimulate that area of the brain, the electrical current will be much milder, causing the neurons to react as if they had received a message.

deep lesioning   insertion of a thin, insulated wire into the brain through which an electrical current is sent that destroys the brain cells at the tip of the wire.

This is called *electrical stimulation of the brain*, or *ESB*. Of course, animals aren't people even though some people treat them that way, and researchers can't be sure that a human brain is going to function exactly like the brain of a lower animal.

THE EEG

A fairly harmless way to study the activity of the living brain is to record the electrical activity of the cortex just below the skull. This has been done for years, using a device called an **electroencephalograph (EEG)**. Small metal disks electrodes are placed directly on the scalp, using a jelly-like substance to help conduct the electrical messages from the cortex just below. These electrodes are connected to an amplifier and then to a computer to view the information. (Older devices had amplifiers connected to pens that traced activity on graph paper.) The resulting electrical output forms waves that indicate many things, such as stages of sleep, seizures, and even the presence of tumors. The EEG can also be used to determine which areas of the brain are active during various mental tasks that involve memory and attention.

As can be seen in Figure 2.10a, very fast, irregular waves called *beta waves* indicate waking activity (third and sixth lines in Figure 2.10a). Slightly more regular and slower waves called *alpha waves* are a sign of relaxation, *theta waves* are associated with drowsiness and sleep, whereas much slower, larger waves called *delta waves* indicate a deep stage

electroencephalograph (EEG)
equipment designed to record the brain-wave patterns produced by electrical activity of the surface of the brain.

a.   b.   c.   d.   e.

Figure 2.10 **Studying the Brain**

These are four methods researchers use to study the brain: EEGs, CT scans, MRIs, and PET scans. (a) An example of an EEG readout. (b) A CT scan (colored by a computer) showing the detail of a center cross section of the brain. (c) An MRI (colored by a computer) showing enhanced detail of the same view of the brain as in the CT scan. (d) A PET scan showing activity of the brain, using colors to indicate different levels of activity; areas that are very active are white, whereas areas that are inactive are dark blue. (e) An fMRI tracking oxygen levels in the brain shows which areas of the brain are active.

of sleep (the "delta" waves in the graphic are likely an artifact due to an eyeblink, not sleep. The waveforms are also covered in more detail in Chapter 4). (L)(I)(N)(K) *to Chapter Four: Consciousness: Sleep, Dreams, Hypnosis, and Drugs, pp. 139–141.*

Scientists have recently developed a new technique involving the way EEG recordings are interpreted (Makeig et al., 2004). The process allows identification of individual signals coming from the different areas of the brain and is called *Independent Component Analysis (ICA)*. ICA allows a more detailed and precise interpretation of the signals coming from different areas of the brain's surface. Another technique based on the EEG uses *event-related potentials*, or *ERPs*. In ERP research, the results of multiple presentations of a stimulus are recorded and then averaged to remove the variations in random brain activity that occur in the background of any single EEG recording. The result is a measurement of the electrical potential of the brain related to the stimulus event itself or an event-related potential. ERPs are being investigated for several different uses. For example, one study has looked at the possibility of using ERPs to follow the progression of Alzheimer's disease (Katada et al., 2003), whereas another area of research involves using ERPs as a method of lie detection (Mertens & Allen, 2007; Rosenfeld et al., 2004).

CT SCANS

The EEG only allows researchers to look at the activity of the surface of the brain. Scientists now have several ways to look inside the human brain without harm to the person. One way is to take a series of X-rays of the brain, aided by a computer. This is called a **CT scan** (CT stands for computed tomography, or mapping "slices" of the brain by computer). CT scans can show stroke damage, tumors, injuries, and abnormal brain structure. (See Figure 2.10b.)

MRI SCANS

As good as a CT scan can be, it still doesn't show very small details within the brain. A newer technique called **magnetic resonance imaging**, or **MRI**, provides much more detail, even allowing doctors to see the effects of very small strokes. (See Figure 2.10c.) The person getting an MRI scan will be placed inside a machine that generates a powerful magnetic field. The magnetic field allows the computer to create a three-dimensional image of the brain and display "slices" of that image on a screen.

PET SCANS

While CT and MRI scans can show the structure of the brain, researchers who want to see the brain in action may use a **PET scan** (positron emission tomography). (See Figure 2.10d.) In this method, the person is injected with a radioactive glucose (a kind of sugar). The computer detects the activity of the brain cells by looking at which cells are using up the radioactive glucose and projecting the image of that activity onto a monitor. The computer uses colors to indicate different levels of activity. Areas that are very active usually show up as white or very light, whereas areas that are inactive are dark blue. With this method, researchers can actually have the person perform different tasks while the computer shows what his or her brain is doing during the task.

FUNCTIONAL MRI (fMRI)

Although traditional MRI scans only show structure, there is a technique called *functional MRI (fMRI)* in which the computer tracks changes in the oxygen levels of the blood (see Figure 2.10e). By placing this picture of where the oxygen goes in the brain on top of the picture of the brain's structure, researchers can tell what areas of

computed tomography (CT) brain-imaging method using computer-controlled X-rays of the brain.

magnetic resonance imaging (MRI) brain-imaging method using radio waves and magnetic fields of the body to produce detailed images of the brain.

positron emission tomography (PET) brain-imaging method in which a radioactive sugar is injected into the subject and a computer compiles a color-coded image of the activity of the brain, with lighter colors indicating more activity.

AP* Describe the nervous system and its subdivisions and functions. ▶

medulla the first large swelling at the top of the spinal cord, forming the lowest part of the brain, which is responsible for life-sustaining functions such as breathing, swallowing, and heart rate.

the brain are active. By combining such images taken over a period of time, a sort of "movie" of the brain's functioning can be made (Lin et al., 2007). Functional MRIs can give more detail, tend to be clearer than PET scans, and are fast becoming an incredibly useful tool for research into the workings of the brain.

Okay, now I understand a little more about how we look inside the brain. What exactly IS inside the brain?

From the Bottom Up: The Structures of the Brain

Now it's time to look at the various structures of the brain, starting from the bottom and working up to the top. (A word of caution: This text won't be discussing every single part of the brain, only the parts interesting to psychologists as explorers of human behavior. Many parts of the brain also overlap in their functions, but a full understanding of the brain is not truly possible within one chapter of an introductory psychology text.)

2.6   What are the different structures of the bottom part of the brain and what do they do?

THE HINDBRAIN

Medulla   The **medulla** (which, oddly enough, means "marrow" or "inner substance") is located at the top of the spinal column. In Figure 2.11, it is the first "swelling" at the top of the spinal cord, just at the very bottom of the brain. This is the part of the brain that a person would least want to have damaged, as it controls life-sustaining functions such as heartbeat, breathing, and swallowing. (Remember the actor Christopher Reeve, who played the lead in the original *Superman* movies and Dr. Virgil Swann in the *Smallville* television series? After a fall from horse, his spinal

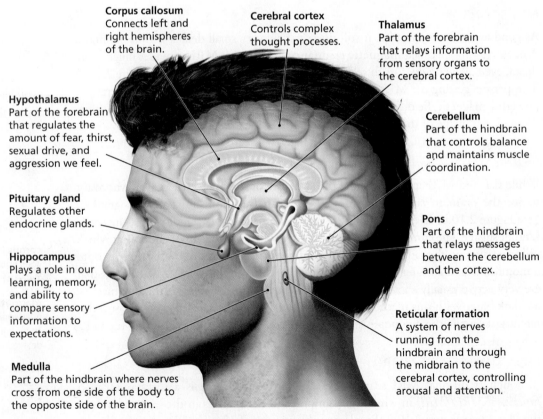

Corpus callosum
Connects left and right hemispheres of the brain.

Cerebral cortex
Controls complex thought processes.

Thalamus
Part of the forebrain that relays information from sensory organs to the cerebral cortex.

Hypothalamus
Part of the forebrain that regulates the amount of fear, thirst, sexual drive, and aggression we feel.

Cerebellum
Part of the hindbrain that controls balance and maintains muscle coordination.

Pituitary gland
Regulates other endocrine glands.

Pons
Part of the hindbrain that relays messages between the cerebellum and the cortex.

Hippocampus
Plays a role in our learning, memory, and ability to compare sensory information to expectations.

Reticular formation
A system of nerves running from the hindbrain and through the midbrain to the cerebral cortex, controlling arousal and attention.

Medulla
Part of the hindbrain where nerves cross from one side of the body to the opposite side of the brain.

Figure 2.11 **The Major Structures of the Human Brain**

cord was damaged. The damage was very serious because it was high enough to involve part of the medulla, leaving him paralyzed and unable to breathe on his own [McDonald et al., 2002]. The upper part of the spinal cord and the lower part of the brain are highly interconnected.) It is in the medulla that the sensory nerves coming from the left and right sides of the body cross over, so that sensory information from the left side of the body goes to the right side of the brain and vice versa.

Pons   The **pons** is the larger "swelling" just above the medulla. This term means "bridge," and the pons is indeed the bridge between the lower parts of the brain and the upper sections. As in the medulla, there is a crossover of nerves, but in this case it is the motor nerves carrying messages from the brain to the body. This allows the pons to coordinate the movements of the left and right sides of the body. (It will be useful to remember these nerve crossovers when reading about the functions of the left and right sides of the brain in a later part of this chapter.) The pons also influences sleep, dreaming, and arousal. The role that the pons plays in sleep and dreams will be discussed in more detail in Chapter Four. ⓁⓘⓃⓚ *to Chapter Four: Consciousness: Sleep, Dreams, Hypnosis, and Drugs, p. 148.*

The Reticular Formation   The **reticular formation (RF)** is an area of neurons running through the middle of the medulla and the pons and slightly beyond. These neurons are responsible for people's ability to attend to certain kinds of information in their surroundings. Basically, the RF allows people to ignore constant, unchanging information (such as the noise of an air conditioner) and become alert to changes in information (for example, if the air conditioner stopped, most people would notice immediately).

The reticular formation is also the part of the brain that helps keep people alert and aroused. One part of the RF is called the *reticular activating system (RAS)*, and it stimulates the upper part of the brain, keeping people awake and alert. When a person is driving along and someone suddenly pulls out in front of the vehicle, it is the RAS that brings that driver to full attention. It is also the system that lets a mother hear her baby cry in the night, even though she might sleep through other noises. The RAS has also been suggested by brain-scanning studies as a possible area involved in attention-deficit hyperactivity disorder, in which children or adults have difficulty maintaining attention to a single task (Durston, 2003).

Studies have shown that when the RF of rats is electrically stimulated while they are sleeping, they immediately awaken. If the RF is destroyed (by deep lesioning, for example), they fall into a sleeplike coma from which they never awaken (Moruzzi & Magoun, 1949; Steriade & McCarley, 1990). The RF is also implicated in comas in humans (Plum & Posner, 1985).

Cerebellum   At the base of the skull, behind the pons and below the main part of the brain, is a structure that looks like a small brain. (See Figure 2.11 on page 68.) This is the **cerebellum** (meaning "little brain"). The cerebellum is the part of the lower brain that controls all involuntary, rapid, fine motor movement. People can sit upright because the cerebellum controls all the little muscles needed to keep them from falling out of their chair. It also coordinates voluntary movements that have to happen in rapid succession, such as walking, diving, skating, gymnastics, dancing, typing (once it has been learned well), playing a musical instrument, and even the movements of speech. Learned reflexes, skills, and habits are also stored here, which allows them to become more or less automatic. Because of the cerebellum, people don't have to consciously think about their posture, muscle tone, and balance.

So if your cerebellum is damaged, you might be very uncoordinated? Yes. In fact, in a disease called *spinocerebellar degeneration* the first symptoms are tremors, an unsteady

This pitcher must count on his cerebellum to help him balance and coordinate the many fine muscle commands that allow him to pitch the baseball accurately and swiftly. What other kinds of professions depend heavily on the activity of the cerebellum?

pons   the larger swelling above the medulla that connects the top of the brain to the bottom and that plays a part in sleep, dreaming, left–right body coordination, and arousal.

reticular formation (RF)   an area of neurons running through the middle of the medulla and the pons and slightly beyond that play a role in general arousal, alertness, and sleep.

cerebellum   part of the lower brain located behind the pons that controls and coordinates involuntary, rapid, fine motor movement.

So if your cerebellum is damaged, you might be ◀ very uncoordinated?

Explore with a simulation on the lower brain structures.
www.mypsychlab.com

walk, slurred speech, dizziness, and muscle weakness. The person suffering from this disease will eventually be unable to walk, stand, or even get a spoon to his or her own mouth (Schöls et al., 1998). These symptoms are similar to what one might see in a person who is suffering from alcohol intoxication. **Explore on MyPsychLab**

2.7 What are the structures of the brain that control emotion, learning, memory, and motivation?

STRUCTURES UNDER THE CORTEX

The cortex, which is discussed in detail later in this chapter, is the outer wrinkled covering of the brain. But there are a number of important structures located just under the cortex and above the brain stem. Each of these structures plays a part in our behavior. (See Figure 2.12.)

Limbic System The **limbic system** (the word *limbic* means "marginal," and these structures are found in the inner margin of the upper brain) includes the thalamus, hypothalamus, hippocampus, and amygdala. In general, the limbic system is involved in emotions, motivation, and learning.

Thalamus Have you ever had to go to the emergency room of a hospital? You may find yourself getting past the receptionist, but most of the time you will have to wait to see a triage nurse before you ever get to see the doctor—if you ever get to see the doctor. (The word *triage* refers to a process for sorting injured people into groups based on their need for or likely benefit from immediate medical treatment.) Triage nurses will ask people questions about their complaints. They may be able to partially treat minor complaints before the person sees a doctor. Then they will send the person to a treatment room with the equipment that might be needed for the ailment, and eventually the person will see a doctor.

limbic system a group of several brain structures located under the cortex and involved in learning, emotion, memory, and motivation.

Thalamus
Part of the forebrain that relays information from sensory organs to the cerebral cortex.

Mamillary body
Neurons that act as a relay station, transmitting information between fornix and thalamus.

Fornix
Pathway of nerve fibers that transmits information from hippocampus to the mamillary bodies.

Hypothalamus
Part of the forebrain that regulates the amount of fear, thirst, sexual drive, and aggression we feel.

Amygdala
Influences our motivation, emotional control, fear response, and interpretations of nonverbal emotional expressions.

Hippocampus
Plays a role in our learning, memory, and ability to compare sensory information to expectations.

Figure 2.12 **The Limbic System**

The **thalamus** ("inner chamber") is in some ways similar to a triage nurse. This somewhat round structure in the center of the brain acts as a kind of relay station for incoming sensory information. Like a nurse, the thalamus might perform some processing of that sensory information before sending it on to the part of the cortex that deals with that kind of sensation—hearing, sight, touch, or taste. Damage to the thalamus might result in the loss or partial loss of any or all of those sensations. (L)(I)(N)(K) *to Chapter Three: Sensation and Perception, p. 109.*

The sense of smell is unique in that signals from the neurons in the sinus cavity go directly into special parts of the brain called **olfactory bulbs**, just under the front part of the brain. Smell is the only sense that does not have to pass through the thalamus.

Hypothalamus　A very small but extremely powerful part of the brain is located just below and in front of the thalamus (see Figure 2.12). The **hypothalamus** ("below the inner chamber") regulates body temperature, thirst, hunger, sleeping and waking, sexual activity, and emotions. It sits right above the *pituitary gland*, which is called the "master gland" because it controls the functions of all the other endocrine glands that will be discussed later in this chapter. The hypothalamus controls the pituitary, so the ultimate regulation of hormones lies with the hypothalamus.

Hippocampus　The **hippocampus** is the Greek word for "seahorse," and it was given to this structure of the brain because the first scientists who dissected the brain thought it looked like a seahorse. Research has shown that the hippocampus is instrumental in forming long-term (permanent) memories that are then stored elsewhere in the brain (Bigler et al., 1996). As mentioned earlier, acetylcholine, the neurotransmitter involved in muscle control, is also involved in the memory function of the hippocampus. People who have Alzheimer's, for example, have much lower levels of acetylcholine in that structure than is normal, and the drugs given to these people boost the levels of acetylcholine. The hippocampus is located within the temporal lobes on each side of the brain, and electrical stimulation of the temporal lobe may produce memory-like or dream-like experiences.

The hippocampus may be very close to the area of the brain where the memories for locations of objects are stored as well. Researchers have found that the right parahippocampal gyrus, located alongside the right hippocampus, is more active when a person is planning a travel route (Maguire et al., 1998), which might explain why elderly people who develop memory problems associated with deterioration of the hippocampus also tend to forget where they live, where they parked the car, and similar location problems. Deterioration in the hippocampal area may spread to or affect other nearby areas.

Amygdala　The **amygdala** ("almond") is an area of the brain located near the hippocampus. These two structures seem to be responsible for fear responses and memory of fear. Information from the senses goes to the amygdala before the upper part of the brain is even involved, so that people can respond to danger very quickly, sometimes before they are consciously aware of what is happening. In 1939 researchers found that monkeys with large amounts of their temporal lobes removed—including the amygdala—were completely unafraid of snakes and humans, both normally fear-provoking stimuli (Klüver & Bucy, 1939). This effect came to be known as the *Klüver-Bucy syndrome*. Rats that have damaged amygdala structures will also show no fear when placed next to a cat (Maren & Fanselow, 1996). Case studies of humans with damage to the amygdala also show a link to decreased fear response (Adophs et al., 2005).

What about Michelle M. from the story at the beginning? Was she missing any of these structures?

This young man's thirst is regulated by his hypothalamus.

thalamus　part of the limbic system located in the center of the brain, this structure relays sensory information from the lower part of the brain to the proper areas of the cortex and processes some sensory information before sending it to its proper area.

olfactory bulbs　two projections just under the front of the brain that receive information from the receptors in the nose located just below.

hypothalamus　small structure in the brain located below the thalamus and directly above the pituitary gland, responsible for motivational behavior such as sleep, hunger, thirst, and sex.

hippocampus　curved structure located within each temporal lobe, responsible for the formation of long-term memories and the storage of memory for location of objects.

amygdala　brain structure located near the hippocampus, responsible for fear responses and memory of fear.

AP*　Recount historic and contemporary research strategies and technologies that support research.

What about Michelle M. from the story at the beginning? Was she missing any of these structures?

Michelle M. did have some abnormalities in a few of these structures, but her greatest "missing piece" was one-half of a very important brain structure, the cortex. The next section explores the cortex and its functions.

THE CORTEX

As stated earlier, the **cortex** ("rind" or outer covering) is the outermost part of the brain, which is the part of the brain most people picture when they think of what the brain looks like. It is made up of tightly packed neurons and actually is only about one-tenth of an inch thick on average (Fischl et al., 2001; MacDonald et al., 2000; Zilles, 1990). The tissue appears grayish pink because the tightly packed neural bodies are gray and the small blood vessels appear pink. The cortex is very recognizable surface anatomy because it is full of wrinkles. ◉─Watch on **MyPsychLab**

Why is the cortex so wrinkled?

The wrinkling of the cortex allows a much larger area of cortical cells to exist in the small space inside the skull. If the cortex were to be taken out, ironed flat, and measured, it would be about 2 to 3 square feet. (The owner of the cortex would also be dead, but that's fairly obvious, right?) As the brain develops before birth, it forms a smooth outer covering on all the other brain structures. This will be the cortex, which will get more and more wrinkled as the brain increases in size and complexity. This increase in wrinkling is called *corticalization* and is the real measure of human intelligence.

◉ **Watch** a video podcast of a real human brain's surface anatomy.
www.mypsychlab.com

▶ Why is the cortex so wrinkled?

cortex outermost covering of the brain consisting of densely packed neurons, responsible for higher thought processes and interpretation of sensory input.

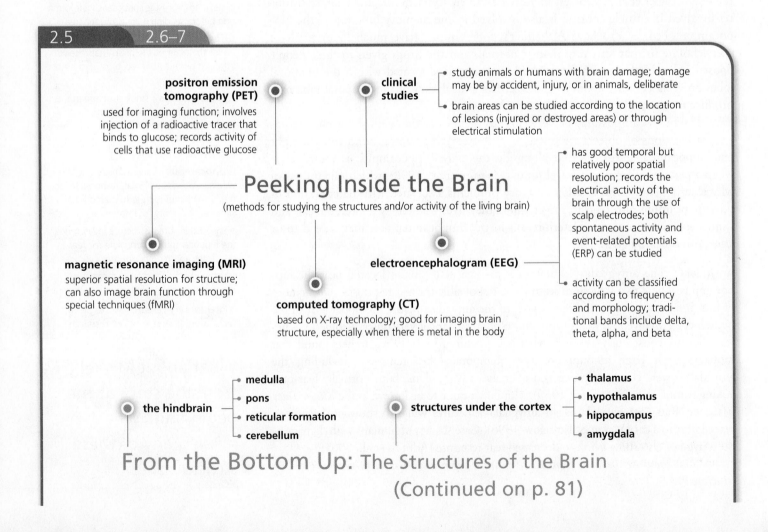

2.5   2.6–7

Peeking Inside the Brain
(methods for studying the structures and/or activity of the living brain)

positron emission tomography (PET)
used for imaging function; involves injection of a radioactive tracer that binds to glucose; records activity of cells that use radioactive glucose

clinical studies
- study animals or humans with brain damage; damage may be by accident, injury, or in animals, deliberate
- brain areas can be studied according to the location of lesions (injured or destroyed areas) or through electrical stimulation

magnetic resonance imaging (MRI)
superior spatial resolution for structure; can also image brain function through special techniques (fMRI)

computed tomography (CT)
based on X-ray technology; good for imaging brain structure, especially when there is metal in the body

electroencephalogram (EEG)
- has good temporal but relatively poor spatial resolution; records the electrical activity of the brain through the use of scalp electrodes; both spontaneous activity and event-related potentials (ERP) can be studied
- activity can be classified according to frequency and morphology; traditional bands include delta, theta, alpha, and beta

the hindbrain
- medulla
- pons
- reticular formation
- cerebellum

structures under the cortex
- thalamus
- hypothalamus
- hippocampus
- amygdala

From the Bottom Up: The Structures of the Brain

(Continued on p. 81)

Directions: Read each of the questions or incomplete sentences below. Then choose the response that best answers the question or completes the sentence.

1. Which of the following techniques uses a radioactive sugar to look at the functioning of the brain?
   a. EEG
   b. CT
   c. MRI
   d. PET
   e. ESB

2. Which brain structure is most responsible for our balance, posture, and muscle tone?
   a. Medulla
   b. Hippocampus
   c. Reticular formation
   d. Pons
   e. Cerebellum

3. Which brain structure would most likely result in death if damaged?
   a. Medulla
   b. Cerebellum
   c. Reticular formation
   d. Pons
   e. Hypothalamus

4. If you were to develop a rare condition in which signals from your eyes were sent to the area of the brain that processes sound, and signals from the ears were sent to the area of the brain that processes vision, which part of the brain would most likely be damaged?
   a. Hippocampus
   b. Hypothalamus
   c. Thalamus
   d. Amygdala
   e. Pons

5. If you have problems storing long-term memories, the damage is most likely in the ____ area of the brain.
   a. hippocampus
   b. hypothalamus
   c. cerebellum
   d. amygdala
   e. thalamus

2.8 What parts of the cortex control the different senses and the movement of the body?

The Lobes and Their Specialties The cortex is divided into two sections called the **cerebral hemispheres**, which are connected by a thick, tough band of neural fibers (axons) called the **corpus callosum** (literally meaning "hard bodies," as calluses on the feet are hard). (See Figure 2.11 on page 68.) The corpus callosum allows the left and right hemispheres to communicate with each other. Each hemisphere can be roughly divided into four sections by looking at the deeper wrinkles, or fissures, in its surface (see Figure 2.13). (Remember, Michelle M.'s left hemisphere never developed—she had only the right hemisphere, and so only the right-side lobes.)

Occipital Lobes At the base of the cortex, toward the back of the brain is an area called the **occipital lobe** (the term *occipital* refers to the rear of the head). This area processes visual information from the eyes in the *primary visual cortex.* The *visual association cortex*, also in this lobe, is the part of the brain that helps identify and make sense of the visual information from the eyes. The famed neurologist Oliver Sacks once had a patient who had a tumor in his right occipital lobe area. He could still see objects perfectly well and even describe them in physical terms, but he could not identify them by sight alone. For example, Sacks once gave him a rose to look at. The man turned it around and around and began to describe it as a "red inflorescence" of some type with a green tubular projection. Only when he held it under his nose (stimulating the sense of smell) did he recognize it as a rose (Sacks, 1990). Each area of the cortex has these association areas that help people make sense of sensory information.

Have you ever wondered why people "see stars" sometimes after being hit in the back of the head? Because the area of the brain at the back of the head processes vision, any stimulation to that area will be interpreted as vision—hence, the "stars."

Parietal Lobes The **parietal lobes** (*parietal* means "wall") are at the top and back of the brain, just under the parietal bone in the skull. This area contains the **somatosensory cortex**, an area of neurons (see Figure 2.14) running down the front of the parietal lobes on either side of the brain. This area processes information from the skin and internal body receptors for touch, temperature, and body position. The somatosensory cortex is laid out in a rather interesting way—the cells at the top of the

◄ **AP*** Describe the nervous system and its subdivisions and functions.

cerebral hemispheres the two sections of the cortex on the left and right sides of the brain.

corpus callosum thick band of neurons that connects the right and left cerebral hemispheres.

occipital lobe section of the brain located at the rear and bottom of each cerebral hemisphere containing the visual centers of the brain.

parietal lobes sections of the brain located at the top and back of each cerebral hemisphere containing the centers for touch, taste, and temperature sensations.

somatosensory cortex area of neurons running down the front of the parietal lobes responsible for processing information from the skin and internal body receptors for touch, temperature, body position, and possibly taste.

Figure 2.13 **The Lobes of the Brain: Occipital, Parietal, Temporal, and Frontal**

This boxer must rely on his parietal lobes to sense where his body is in relation to the floor of the ring and the other boxer, his occipital lobes to see his target, and his frontal lobes to guide his hand and arm into the punch.

temporal lobes areas of the cortex located just behind the temples containing the neurons responsible for the sense of hearing and meaningful speech.

frontal lobes areas of the cortex located in the front and top of the brain, responsible for higher mental processes and decision making as well as the production of fluent speech.

brain receive information from the bottom of the body, and as one moves down the area, the signals come from higher and higher in the body. It's almost as if a little upside-down person were laid out along this area of cells. (See Figure 2.14.)

Temporal Lobes The beginning of the **temporal lobes** (*temporal* means "of or near the temples") are found just behind the temples of the head. These lobes contain the *primary auditory cortex* and the *auditory association area*. If a person receives a blow to the side of the head, that person will probably "hear" a ringing sound. Also found in the left temporal lobe is an area that in most people is particularly involved with language. Oddly enough, the sense of taste also seems to be processed in the temporal lobe, deep inside a fold of the cortex, rather than anywhere in the parietal lobe (Fresquet et al., 2004).

Frontal Lobes These lobes are at the front of the brain, hence, the name **frontal lobes**. (It doesn't often get this easy in psychology; feel free to take a moment to appreciate it.) Here are found all the higher mental functions of the brain—planning, personality, memory storage, complex decision making, and (again in the left hemisphere in most people) areas devoted to language. The frontal lobe also helps in controlling emotions by means of its connection to the limbic system. Phineas Gage, who was mentioned in Chapter One (p. 23), suffered damage to his frontal lobe. He lacked emotional control because of the damage to this lobe's connection with the limbic system structures, particularly the amygdala. People with damage to the frontal lobe may also experience problems with performing mental tasks, getting stuck on one step or one wrong answer and repeating it over and over again (Goel & Grafman, 1995).

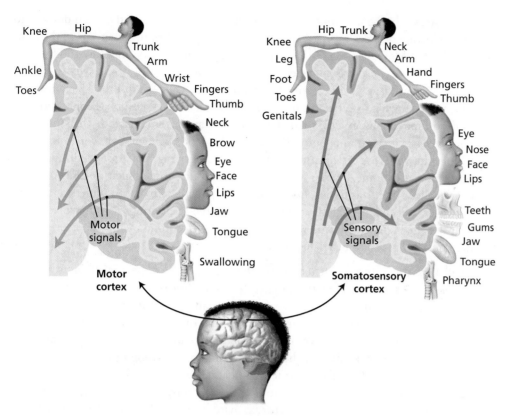

Figure 2.14 The Motor and Somatosensory Cortex

The motor cortex in the frontal lobe controls the voluntary muscles of the body. Cells at the top of the motor cortex control muscles at the bottom of the body, whereas cells at the bottom of the motor cortex control muscles at the top of the body. Body parts are drawn larger or smaller according to the number of cortical cells devoted to that body part. For example, the hand has many small muscles and requires a larger area of cortical cells to control it. The somatosensory cortex, located in the parietal lobe just behind the motor cortex, is organized in much the same manner and receives information about the sense of touch and body position.

The frontal lobes also contain the **motor cortex**, a band of neurons located at the back of each lobe. (See Figure 2.14.) These cells control the movements of the body's voluntary muscles by sending commands out to the somatic division of the peripheral nervous system. The motor cortex is laid out just like the somatosensory cortex, which is right next door in the parietal lobes.

You've mentioned association cortex a few times. Do the other lobes of the brain contain association cortex as well?

THE ASSOCIATION AREAS OF THE CORTEX

2.9 What parts of the cortex are responsible for higher forms of thought, such as language?

Association areas are made up of neurons in the cortex that are devoted to making connections between the sensory information coming into the brain and stored memories, images, and knowledge. In other words, association areas help people make sense of the incoming sensory input. Although the association areas in the occipital and temporal lobes have already been mentioned, much of the brain's association cortex is in the frontal lobes. Some special association areas are worth talking about in more detail.

You've mentioned association cortex a few times. Do the other lobes of the brain contain association cortex as well?

motor cortex section of the frontal lobe located at the back, responsible for sending motor commands to the muscles of the somatic nervous system.

association areas areas within each lobe of the cortex responsible for the coordination and interpretation of information, as well as higher mental processing.

Broca's Area   In the left frontal lobe of most people is an area of the brain devoted to the production of speech. (In a small portion of the population, this area is in the right frontal lobe.) More specifically, this area allows a person to speak smoothly and fluently. It is called *Broca's area* after nineteenth-century neurologist Paul Broca, who first studied people with damage to this area (Leonard, 1997). Damage to Broca's area causes a person to be unable to get words out in a smooth, connected fashion. People with this condition may know exactly what they want to say and understand what they hear others say, but they cannot control the actual production of their own words. Speech is halting and words are often mispronounced, such as saying "cot" instead of "clock" or "non" instead of "nine." Some words may be left out entirely, such as "the" or "for." This is called **Broca's aphasia**. *Aphasia* refers to an inability to use or understand either written or spoken language (Goodglass et al., 2001). (Stuttering is a somewhat different problem in getting words *started*, rather than mispronouncing them or leaving them out, but may also be related to Broca's area.)

Wernicke's Area   In the left temporal lobe (again, in most people) is an area called *Wernicke's area*, named after the physiologist and Broca's contemporary, Carl Wernicke, who first studied problems arising from damage in this location. This area of the brain appears to be involved in understanding the meaning of words (Goodglass et al., 2001). A person with **Wernicke's aphasia** would be able to speak fluently and pronounce words correctly, but the words would be the wrong ones entirely. For example, Elsie suffered a stroke to the temporal lobe, damaging this area of the brain. In the emergency room the nurse tried to take her blood pressure, and when the cuff inflated, Elsie said, "Oh, that's so Saturday hard." Now, what does "Saturday hard" mean? Neither the nurse nor Elsie's daughter could figure that one out, but Elsie *thought* she was making sense. She also had trouble understanding what the people around her were saying to her. In another instance, Ernest suffered a stroke at the age of 80 and developed complete aphasia. As he recovered, he showed some telltale signs of Wernicke's aphasia. In one instance, he asked his wife to get him some milk out of the air conditioner. When she told him that he surely meant to say "refrigerator" he got angry and told her he knew what he was saying, "Now get me some milk out of the air conditioner, woman!"

Classic Studies in Psychology

Through the Looking Glass: Spatial Neglect

Dr. V. S. Ramachandran reported in his fascinating book, *Phantoms in the Brain* (Ramachandran & Blakeslee, 1998), the case of a woman with an odd set of symptoms. When Ellen's son came to visit her, he was shocked and puzzled by his formerly neat and fastidious* mother's appearance. The woman who had always taken pride in her looks, who always had her hair perfectly done and her nails perfectly manicured, looked messy and totally odd. Her hair was uncombed on the left side. Her green shawl was hanging neatly over her right shoulder but hanging onto the floor on the left. Her lipstick was neatly applied to the right side of her lips, and *only to the right side—the left side of her face was completely bare of makeup!* Yet her eyeliner, mascara, and rouge were all neatly applied to the right side of her face.

What was wrong? The son called the doctor and was told that his mother's stroke had left her with a condition called **spatial neglect**, in which a person with damage to the right

---

*Fastidious: having demanding standards, difficult to please.

AP* Identify key contributors to the study of the brain. ▶

AP* Recount historic and contemporary research strategies and technologies that support research. ▶

Broca's aphasia   condition resulting from damage to Broca's area, causing the affected person to be unable to speak fluently, to mispronounce words, and to speak haltingly.

Wernicke's aphasia   condition resulting from damage to Wernicke's area, causing the affected person to be unable to understand or produce meaningful language.

spatial neglect   condition produced by damage to the association areas of the right hemisphere resulting in an inability to recognize objects or body parts in the left visual field.

parietal and occipital lobes of the cortex will ignore everything in the left visual field. Damage to areas of the frontal and temporal lobes may also play a part along with the parietal damage. Spatial neglect can affect the left hemisphere, but this condition occurs less frequently and in a much milder form than right-hemisphere neglect (Heilman et al., 1993; Corbetta et al., 2005; Springer & Deutsch, 1998).

This woman was not blind on the left side—she just would not notice anything there unless her attention was specifically called to it. Her son found that when he pointed out the condition of her makeup to her, she was able to recognize it. He found that she also ignored all of the food on the left side of her plate unless her attention was specifically called to it.

When the doctor examined this woman, he tried to get her to notice her left side by holding up a mirror. She responded correctly when asked what the mirror was and she was able to describe her appearance correctly, but when an assistant held a pen just within the woman's reach, reflected in the mirror on her left side, she tried to reach *through the mirror* to get the pen with her good right hand. When the doctor told her that he wanted her to grab the real object and not the image of it in the mirror, she told him that the pen was *behind* the mirror and even tried to reach around to get it.

Clearly, persons suffering from spatial neglect are not blind at all. They simply can no longer perceive the world in the same way as other people do. For these people, the left sides of objects, bodies, and spaces are somewhere "through the looking glass."

Questions for Further Discussion

1. If a person with spatial neglect only eats the food on the right side of the plate, what could caregivers do to help that person get enough to eat?

2. What other odd things might a person with spatial neglect do that a person with normal functioning would not? What other things might a person with spatial neglect fail to do?

cerebrum the upper part of the brain consisting of the two hemispheres and the structures that connect them.

THE CEREBRAL HEMISPHERES: ARE YOU IN YOUR RIGHT MIND?

I've heard that some people are right-brained and some are left-brained. Are the two sides of the brain really that different?

Most people tend to think of the two cerebral hemispheres as identical twins. Both sides have the same four lobes and are arranged in much the same way. But language seems to be confined to only the left hemisphere in about 90 percent of the population (Toga & Thompson, 2003). What other special tasks do the two halves of the **cerebrum** (the upper part of the brain consisting of the two hemispheres and the structures connecting them) engage in, and how do researchers know about such functions?

2.10 How does the left side of the brain differ from the right side?

Split-Brain Research Roger Sperry was a pioneer in the field of hemisphere specialization. He won a Nobel Prize for his work in demonstrating that the left and right hemispheres of the brain specialize in different activities and functions (Sperry, 1968). In looking for a way to cure epilepsy (severe muscle spasms or seizures resulting from brain damage), Sperry cut through the corpus callosum, the thick band of neural fibers that joins the two hemispheres. In early research with animals, this technique worked and seemed to have no side effects. The first people to have this procedure done also experienced relief from their severe epileptic symptoms, but testing found that (in a sense) they now had two brains in one body.

The special testing involves sending messages to only one side of the brain, which is now possible because the connecting tissue, the corpus callosum, has been cut. Figure 2.15 shows what happens with a typical split-brain patient.

I've heard that some people are right-brained and some are left-brained. Are the two sides of the brain really that different?

◄ **AP*** Describe the nervous system and its subdivisions and functions.

◄ **AP*** Recount historic and contemporary research strategies and technologies that support research.

◄ **AP*** Identify key contributors to the study of the brain.

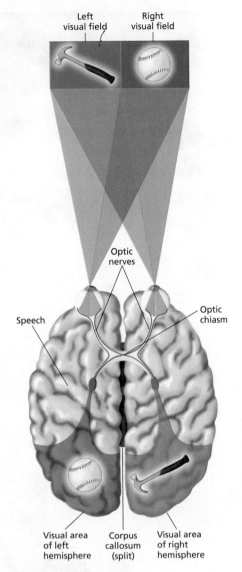

Left visual field

Right visual field

Optic nerves

Speech

Optic chiasm

Visual area of left hemisphere

Corpus callosum (split)

Visual area of right hemisphere

Figure 2.15 The Split-Brain Experiment

Roger Sperry created this experiment to demonstrate the specialization of the left and right hemispheres of the brain.

So there really are left-brained and right-brained people? And how could Michelle M. talk and read without a left hemisphere? ▶

Table 2.2 Specialization of the Two Hemispheres

LEFT HEMISPHERE	RIGHT HEMISPHERE
Controls the right hand	Controls the left hand
Spoken language	Nonverbal
Written language	Visual-spatial perception
Mathematical calculations	Music and artistic processing
Logical thought processes	Emotional thought and recognition
Analysis of detail	Processes the whole
Reading	Pattern recognition
	Facial recognition

In a split-brain patient, if a picture of a ball is flashed to the right side of the screen, the image of the ball will be sent to the left occipital lobe. The person will be able to say that he or she sees a ball. If a picture of a hammer is flashed to the left side of the screen, the person will not be able to <u>verbally</u> identify the object or be able to state with any certainty that something was seen. But if the left <u>hand</u> (controlled by the right hemisphere) is used, the person can point to the hammer he or she "didn't see." The right occipital lobe clearly saw the hammer, but the person could not <u>verbalize</u> that fact (Sperry, 1968). By doing studies such as these, researchers have found that the left hemisphere specializes in language, speech, handwriting, calculation (math), sense of time and rhythm (which is mathematical in nature), and basically any kind of thought requiring analysis. The right hemisphere appears to specialize in more global (widespread) processing involving perception, visualization, spatial perception, recognition of patterns, faces, emotions, melodies, and expression of emotions. It also comprehends simple language but does not produce speech.

Springer and Deutsch (1998) found that, in general, the left hemisphere processes information in a sequence and is good at breaking things down into smaller parts, or performing analysis. The right hemisphere, by contrast, processes information all at once and simultaneously, a more global or holistic* style of processing. Remember the discussion in Chapter One of the early days of psychology, the structuralists, and the Gestalt psychologists? One could almost say that the left hemisphere of the brain is a structuralist who wants to break everything down into its smallest parts, and the right side of the brain is a Gestaltist, who wants to study only the whole. (See Table 2.2.)

So there really are left-brained and right-brained people? And how could Michelle M. talk and read without a left hemisphere?

Actually, unless one is a split-brain patient, the two sides of the brain are always working together as an integrated whole. For example, the right side might recognize someone's face, while the left side struggles to recall the person's name. People aren't

―――――――

*Holistic: relating to or concerned with complete systems or wholes.

really left- or right-brained, they are whole-brained. And in the case of Michelle M., neuroscientists think that her right hemisphere was able to "learn" what would normally be left hemisphere tasks through Michelle's own actions and her parents' constant encouragement—neuroplasticity in action!

The separate functions of the left and right sides of the brain are often confused with handedness, or the tendency to use one hand for most fine motor skills. While most right-handed people also have their left hemisphere in control of their other fine motor skills, such as speech, a few right-handers actually have their language functions in the right hemisphere, in spite of the dominance of the left hemisphere for controlling the right hand. Among left-handed people, there are also many who, although right-brain dominant for motor control, still have their language functions on the left side of the brain. Why? How much time do you have? There are far too many theories of why we use one hand over the other to cover in this text. ✸ Explore on MyPsychLab

✸ **Explore** curious facts about right and left handedness.
www.mypsychlab.com

The Chemical Connection: The Endocrine Glands

How do the glands fit into all of this? Aren't there more glands than just the adrenal glands? How do they affect our behavior?

Glands are organs in the body that secrete chemicals. Some glands, such as salivary glands and sweat glands, secrete their chemicals directly onto the body's tissues through tiny tubes, or ducts. This kind of gland affects the functioning of the body but doesn't really affect behavior. Other glands, called **endocrine glands**, have no ducts and secrete their chemicals directly into the bloodstream. The chemicals secreted by this type of gland are called **hormones**. As mentioned earlier in the chapter when talking about the sympathetic division of the autonomic nervous system, these hormones flow into the bloodstream, which carries them to their target organs. The molecules of these hormones then fit into receptor sites on those organs to fulfill their function, affecting behavior as they do so.

◄ How do the glands fit into all of this? Aren't there more glands than just the adrenal glands? How do they affect our behavior?

2.11 How do the hormones released by glands interact with the nervous system and affect behavior?

The hormones affect behavior and emotions by controlling muscles and organs such as the heart, pancreas, and sex organs. Some theories of emotion state that the surge in certain hormones actually triggers the emotional reaction (Izard, 1988; Zajonc, 1980, 1984). ⓛⓘⓝⓚ *to Chapter Eight: Motivation and Emotion, p. 329.* Some of the hormones produced by endocrine glands also influence the activity of the brain, producing excitatory or inhibitory effects (Mai et al., 1987).

◄ **AP*** Discuss the effect of the endocrine system on behavior.

THE PITUITARY, MASTER OF THE HORMONAL UNIVERSE

The **pituitary gland** is located in the brain itself, just below the hypothalamus. The hypothalamus (see p. 379) controls the glandular system by influencing the pituitary. That is because the pituitary gland is the *master gland*, the one that controls or influences all of the other endocrine glands. One part of the pituitary controls things associated with pregnancy, such as production of milk for nursing infants and the onset of labor, as well as the levels of salt and water in the body. Another part of the pituitary secretes several hormones that influence the activity of the other glands.

endocrine glands glands that secrete chemicals called hormones directly into the bloodstream.

hormones chemicals released into the bloodstream by endocrine glands.

pituitary gland gland located in the brain that secretes human growth hormone and influences all other hormone-secreting glands (also known as the master gland).

Most notable of these hormones is a *growth hormone* that controls and regulates the increase in size as children grow from infancy to adulthood.

As the master gland, the pituitary forms a very important part of a feedback system, one that includes the hypothalamus and the organs targeted by the various hormones. The balance of hormones in the entire endocrine system is maintained by feedback from each of these "players" to the others.

THE PINEAL GLAND

The **pineal gland** is also located in the brain, near the back. It secretes a hormone called *melatonin* primarily at night, which tracks day length and influences the sleep-wake cycle in humans and some animals. (LINK) *to Chapter Four: Consciousness: Sleep, Dreams, Hypnosis, and Drugs, p. 136.*

THE THYROID GLAND

The **thyroid gland** is located inside the neck and secretes a hormone called *thyroxin* that regulates metabolism (how fast the body burns its available energy).

PANCREAS

The **pancreas** controls the level of blood sugar in the body by secreting *insulin* and *glucagons*. If the pancreas secretes too little insulin, it results in *diabetes*. If it secretes too much insulin, it results in *hypoglycemia*, or low blood sugar, which causes a person to feel hungry all the time and often become overweight as a result.

THE GONADS

The **gonads** are the sex glands, including the **ovaries** in the female and the **testes** in the male. They secrete hormones that regulate sexual behavior and reproduction. They do not control all sexual behavior, though. In a very real sense, the brain itself is the master of the sexual system—human sexual behavior is not controlled totally by instincts and the actions of the glands as in some parts of the animal world but also by psychological factors such as attractiveness.

THE ADRENAL GLANDS

Everyone has two **adrenal glands**, one on top of each kidney. The origin of the name is simple enough; *renal* comes from a Latin word meaning "kidney" and *ad* is Latin for "to," so *adrenal* means "to or on the kidney." Each adrenal gland is actually divided into two sections, the *adrenal medulla* and the *adrenal cortex*. It is the adrenal medulla that releases ephinephrine and norepinephrine when people are under stress and that aids in sympathetic arousal.

The adrenal cortex produces over 30 different hormones called *corticoids* (also called steroids) that regulate salt intake, help initiate* and control stress reactions, and also provides a source of sex hormones in addition to those provided by the gonads. One of the most important of these adrenal hormones is *cortisol*, released when the body experiences stress, both physical stress (such as illness, surgery, or extreme heat or cold) and psychological stress (such as an emotional upset). (LINK) *to Chapter Nine: Stress and Health, p. 349.* Cortisol is important in the release of glucose into the bloodstream during stress, providing energy for the brain itself, and the release of fatty acids from the fat cells that provide the muscles with energy.

---

*Initiate: begin or start.

pineal gland endocrine gland located near the base of the cerebrum; secretes melatonin.

thyroid gland endocrine gland found in the neck; regulates metabolism.

pancreas endocrine gland; controls the levels of sugar in the blood.

gonads sex glands; secrete hormones that regulate sexual development and behavior as well as reproduction.

ovaries the female gonads.

testes the male gonads.

adrenal glands endocrine glands located on top of each kidney that secrete over 30 different hormones to deal with stress, regulate salt intake, and provide a secondary source of sex hormones affecting the sexual changes that occur during adolescence.

- **the cortex**
  the outermost, wrinkled layer of the brain; comprised of left and right hemispheres, connected by corpus callosum; each hemisphere can be further divided into four lobes
  - frontal lobes
  - temporal lobes
  - parietal lobes
  - occipital lobes

- **the association areas of the cortex**
  devoted to making connections between incoming sensory information and stored memories, images, and knowledge; damage to right association areas can result in spatial neglect where person fails to recognize the left side of the visual field
  - **Brocaís area:** found in left frontal lobe; devoted to speech production; damage to this area can result in Broca's aphasia
  - **Wernicke's area:** found in the left temporal lobe; plays a role in understanding the meaning of words

The Structures of the Brain (continued)

- **the cerebral hemispheres**
  some brain functions governed by one hemisphere more than the other; differences found due to work of various researchers (e.g., Sperry's split-brain studies; work of Springer & Deutsch)
  - **left hemisphere** specializes in tasks that involve sequence and analysis (language, speech, handwriting, math)
  - **right hemisphere** processes information in a more global sense (perception; visualization; spatial perception; recognition of patterns, faces, and emotional expression)

- **glands** are organs in the body that secrete chemicals; some affect functioning of the body but not behavior; others have widespread influence on the body and behavior

The Chemical Connection:
The Endocrine Glands

- **endocrine glands** secrete chemicals called *hormones* into bloodstream; affect behavior and emotions by influencing the activity of the brain and by controlling muscles and organs such as the heart, pancreas, and sex organs
  - **pituitary gland**
  - **pineal gland**
  - **thyroid gland**
  - **pancreas**
  - **gonads**
  - **adrenal glands**

PRACTICE QUIZ: PREPARING FOR THE AP* EXAM

ANSWERS ON PAGE AK-1.

Directions: Read each of the questions or incomplete sentences below. Then choose the response that best answers the question or completes the sentence.

1. In which of the following lobes of the brain would you find the primary auditory cortex?
   - **a.** Left frontal
   - **b.** Right frontal
   - **c.** Temporal
   - **d.** Occipital
   - **e.** Parietal

2. The higher mental functions, such as planning, personality, and complex decision making, are found in the _____ lobe.
   - **a.** frontal
   - **b.** parietal
   - **c.** temporal
   - **d.** corpus
   - **e.** occipital

3. In an old *Twilight Zone* episode, a man wakes up one morning to find that people around him are using words that make no sense to him, and they also don't seem to understand him. His wife tells him that their son forgot his dinosaur today, and when he looks puzzled, she holds up the son's lunchbox and repeats, "You know, his dinosaur." This man's predicament is most like which of the following disorders?
   - **a.** Wernicke's aphasia
   - **b.** Broca's aphasia
   - **c.** Apraxia
   - **d.** Spatial neglect
   - **e.** Auditory disinhibition syndrome

4. When Dr. Ramachandran's spatial neglect patient was asked to reach for the pen on her left side, she _____.
   - **a.** reached to the wrong side of the mirror
   - **b.** said she couldn't see the pen
   - **c.** successfully grabbed the pen
   - **d.** said that she couldn't reach behind the mirror to get it
   - **e.** tried to reach through the mirror

5. If you are a split-brain patient, which of the following would be TRUE according to Roger Sperry's research?
   - **a.** Objects in your left visual field would be easily named
   - **b.** Objects in your left visual field are invisible
   - **c.** Objects in your right visual field would be easily named
   - **d.** Objects in your right visual field are invisible
   - **e.** Images from the left visual field will not make it past the optic chiasm, and will be 'reflected' to the left cerebral cortex

6. Andrew was always hungry. The doctor told his parents that Andrew's _____ was/were producing too much insulin, causing low blood sugar.
   - **a.** pituitary gland
   - **b.** adrenal glands
   - **c.** thyroid gland
   - **d.** pancreas
   - **e.** gonads

As this boy imitates the motions his father goes through while shaving, certain areas of his brain are more active than others, areas that control the motions of shaving. But even if the boy were only <u>watching</u> his father, those same neural areas would be active—the neurons in the boy's brain would <u>mirror</u> the actions of the father he is observing.

Applying Psychology to Everyday Life: Reflections on Mirror Neurons

You have probably heard the old phrase, "monkey see, monkey do." Neuroscientists have now discovered that the phrase "monkey see, monkey *cortex* do" is more appropriate. Psychologist Giacomo Rizzolatti and his colleagues at the University of Parma, Italy, while using implanted electrodes to examine neural activity in macaque monkeys, made an interesting discovery (Rizzolatti et al., 1996). The researchers wanted to determine which neurons were specifically involved in controlling the movement of the hands. They discovered that the same neurons that fired when the monkeys clutched a piece of food would also fire when the monkeys merely *watched the researchers* handle food. These premotor cortex neurons, which fire when an animal performs an action but also when an animal observes that same action being performed by another, are called **mirror neurons**. Brain-imaging techniques in human studies indicate that we, too, have mirror neurons (Buccino, et al., 2001; Buccino et al., 2004; Iacoboni et al., 1999) and in other parts of the frontal and parietal cortex (Breedlove et al., 2007).

Psychologists are very excited about what the existence of mirror neurons means for social interaction and its influence on the brain and perception. Have you ever winced and ducked when watching someone in a soccer game get hit? Blame those mirror neurons. Do you see someone looking happy and feel you just have to smile also? Mirror neurons again—monkey see, monkey *feel*. Researchers have known for decades that in the first few weeks of life human infants will imitate (although quite unconsciously) the facial expressions of adults (Meltzoff, 1990, 2007; Meltzoff & Moore, 1989). Now mirror neurons seem to provide the neurological explanation for why infants can do this. We are apparently social creatures from the very beginning, reacting to the mere sight of what we see others doing.

Does the knowledge researchers are gathering about mirror neurons have any practical applications? Some studies find that when a stroke patient needs to relearn a motor skill, watching another person perform that skill can be effective in regaining it (Binkofski & Buccino, 2006; Ertelt et al., 2007).

Experts in the field of *autism*, a disorder that is primarily social, are now becoming convinced that autism may be due at least in part to a faulty mirror system in the brain (Dapretto et al., 2006; Oberman et al., 2005; Oberman & Ramachandran, 2007). Autistic people may not like to touch or be touched, do not communicate well if at all, and tend not to make eye contact. In one study (Dapretto et al., 2006), autistic children and nonautistic children were asked to imitate the facial expressions they saw in a series of pictures, and researchers measured neural activity in the mirror neuron system. Although both groups of children were able to imitate the expressions in the pictures, the autistic children showed no neural activity in the mirror system while doing so. The control group of nonautistic children *did* show such mirror system activity. The researchers believe that this lack of a normally functioning mirror system in the autistic children may help explain why autistic people have difficulty with empathy (the ability to understand the emotions of others) as well as with language skills. Their mirror neuron systems respond only to what they themselves do and not to what they see other people doing—autistic people are "locked out" of that system of social reflection.

The implications for therapy with psychological disorders have not yet been fully explored. Could having depressed patients watch others enjoying themselves and laughing lift the depression? If a child with an intense fear of dogs watched someone calmly pet and play with a dog, would that help the child become less afraid? Is it possible that effective exercises could be developed to train or correct the defective mirror neuron systems of autistic children and adults, thereby enabling them to communicate and interact with others more socially? The future is ours to see—through the looking glass of social interactions.

mirror neurons neurons that fire when an animal or person performs an action and also when an animal or person observes that same action being performed by another.

Questions for Further Discussion

1. What are some other psychological disorders that might be treated by having the affected person observe someone else's behavior or facial expression?

2. In what ways might mirror neurons be involved in how children learn to speak and form words?

2 CHAPTER SUMMARY

An Overview of the Nervous System

2.1 What are the nervous system, neurons, and nerves, and how do they relate to one another?

- The nervous system is a complex network of cells that carries information to and from all parts of the body.

Neurons and Nerves: Building the Network

2.2 How do neurons use neurotransmitters to communicate with each other and with the body?

- The brain is made up of two types of cells, neurons and glial cells.

- Neurons have dendrites, which receive input, a soma or cell body, and axons that carry the neural message to other cells.

- Glial cells separate, support, and insulate the neurons from each other and make up 90 percent of the brain.

- Myelin insulates and protects the axons of neurons that travel in the body. These axons bundle together in "cables" called nerves. Myelin also speeds up the neural message.

- Neurons in the peripheral nervous system are also coated with neurilemma, which allows the nerves to repair themselves.

- A neuron contains charged particles called ions. When at rest, the neuron is negatively charged on the inside and positively charged on the outside. When stimulated, this reverses the charge by allowing positive sodium ions to enter the cell. This is the action potential.

- Neurons fire in an all-or-nothing manner. It is the speed and number of neurons firing that tell researchers the strength of the stimulus.

- Synaptic vesicles in the end of the axon terminal release neurotransmitter chemicals into the synapse, or gap, between one cell and the next. The neurotransmitter molecules fit into receptor sites on the next cell, stimulating or inhibiting that cell's firing. Neurotransmitters may be either excitatory or inhibitory.

- The first known neurotransmitter was acetylcholine. It stimulates muscles, is involved in arousal and attention, and helps in memory formation. Curare is a poison that blocks its effect.

- GABA is the major inhibitory neurotransmitter; high amounts of GABA are released when drinking alcohol.

- Serotonin is associated with sleep, mood, and appetite.

- Dopamine is associated with Parkinson's disease and schizophrenia.

- Endorphins are neural regulators that control our pain response.

- Most neurotransmitters are taken back into the synaptic vesicles in a process called reuptake.

- Acetylcholine is cleared out of the synapse by enzymes that break up the molecules.

The Central Nervous System— The "Central Processing Unit"

2.3 How do the brain and spinal cord interact?

- The central nervous system consists of the brain and the spinal cord.

- The spinal cord serves two functions. The outer part of the cord transmits messages to and from the brain, whereas the inner part controls lifesaving reflexes such as the pain response.

- Spinal cord reflexes involve afferent neurons, interneurons, and efferent neurons, forming a simple reflex arc.

- Great strides are being made in spinal cord repair and the growth of new neurons in the central nervous system.

Psychology in the News: Stem Cells: New Hope for Damaged Brains?

- Research suggests that stem cells can be obtained from adult bone marrow, making the repair and replacement of damaged neurons more feasible.

The Peripheral Nervous System— Nerves on the Edge

- The peripheral nervous system is all the neurons and nerves that are not part of the brain and spinal cord and that extend throughout the body.

- There are two systems within the peripheral nervous system, the somatic nervous system and the autonomic nervous system.

2.4 How do the somatic and autonomic nervous systems allow people and animals to interact with their surroundings and control the body's automatic functions?

- The somatic nervous system contains the sensory pathway, or neurons carrying messages to the central nervous system, and the motor pathway, or neurons carrying messages from the central nervous system to the voluntary muscles.

- The autonomic nervous system consists of the parasympathetic division and the sympathetic division. The sympathetic division is our fight-or-flight system, reacting to stress, whereas the parasympathetic division restores and maintains normal day-to-day functioning of the organs.

Peeking Inside the Brain

2.5 How do psychologists study the brain and how it works?

- We can study the brain by using deep lesioning to destroy certain areas of the brain in laboratory animals or by electrically stimulating those areas (ESB).

- We can use case studies of human brain damage to learn about the brain's functions but cannot easily generalize from one case to another.

- The EEG allows researchers to measure the electrical activity of the surface of the brain through the use of electrodes placed on the scalp.
- CT scans are computer-aided X-rays of the brain and show a great deal of brain structure.
- MRI scans use a magnetic field and a computer to give researchers an even more detailed look at the structure of the brain. A related technique, fMRI, allows researchers to look at the activity of the brain.
- PET scans use a radioactive sugar injected into the bloodstream to track the activity of brain cells, which is enhanced and color-coded by a computer.

From the Bottom Up: The Structures of the Brain

2.6 What are the different structures of the bottom part of the brain and what do they do?

- The medulla is at the very bottom of the brain and top of the spinal column. It controls life-sustaining functions such as breathing and swallowing. The nerves from each side of the body also cross over in this structure to opposite sides.
- The pons is above the medulla and acts as a bridge between the lower part of the brain and the upper part. It influences sleep, dreaming, arousal, and coordination of movement on the left and right sides of the body.
- The reticular formation runs through the medulla and the pons and controls our wakefulness and arousal.
- The cerebellum is found at the base and back of the brain and coordinates fine, rapid motor movement, learned reflexes, posture, and muscle tone.

2.7 What are the structures of the brain that control emotion, learning, memory, and motivation?

- The thalamus is the relay station that sends sensory information to the proper areas of the cortex.
- The hypothalamus controls hunger, thirst, sleep, sexual behavior, sleeping and waking, and emotions. It also controls the pituitary gland.
- The limbic system consists of the thalamus, hypothalamus, hippocampus, amygdala, and the fornix.
- The hippocampus is the part of the brain responsible for storing memories and remembering locations of objects.
- The amygdala controls our fear responses and memory of fearful stimuli.

2.8 What parts of the cortex control the different senses and the movement of the body?

- The cortex is the outer covering of the cerebrum and consists of a tightly packed layer of neurons about one-tenth of an inch in thickness. Its wrinkles, or corticalization, allow for greater cortical area and are associated with greater intelligence.
- The cortex is divided into two cerebral hemispheres connected by a thick band of neural fibers called the corpus callosum.
- The occipital lobes at the back and base of each hemisphere process vision and contain the primary visual cortex.
- The parietal lobes at the top and back of the cortex contain the somatosensory area, which processes our sense of touch, temperature, and body position. Taste is also processed in this lobe.
- The temporal lobes contain the primary auditory area and are also involved in understanding language.

- The frontal lobes contain the motor cortex, which controls the voluntary muscles, and are also where all the higher mental functions occur, such as planning, language, and complex decision making.

2.9 What parts of the cortex are responsible for higher forms of thought, such as language?

- Association areas of the cortex are found in all the lobes but particularly in the frontal lobes. These areas help people make sense of the information they receive from the lower areas of the brain.
- An area called Broca's area in the left frontal lobe is responsible for producing fluent, understandable speech. If damaged, the person has Broca's aphasia in which words will be halting and pronounced incorrectly.
- An area called Wernicke's area in the left temporal lobe is responsible for the understanding of language. If damaged, the person has Wernicke's aphasia in which speech is fluent but nonsensical. The wrong words are used.

Classic Studies in Psychology: Through the Looking Glass: Spatial Neglect

- Spatial neglect comes from damage to the association areas on one side of the cortex, usually the right side. A person with this condition will ignore information from the opposite side of the body or the opposite visual field.

2.10 How does the left side of the brain differ from the right side?

- Studies with split-brain patients, in which the corpus callosum has been severed to correct epilepsy, reveal that the left side of the brain seems to control language, writing, logical thought, analysis, and mathematical abilities. The left side also processes information sequentially.
- The right side of the brain processes information globally and controls emotional expression, spatial perception, recognition of faces, patterns, melodies, and emotions.

The Chemical Connection: The Endocrine Glands

2.11 How do the hormones released by glands interact with the nervous system and affect behavior?

- Endocrine glands secrete chemicals called hormones directly into the bloodstream, influencing the activity of the muscles and organs.
- The pituitary gland is found in the brain just below the hypothalamus. It has two parts, the anterior and the posterior. It controls the levels of salt and water in the system and, in women, the onset of labor and lactation, as well as secreting growth hormone and influencing the activity of the other glands.
- The pineal gland is also located in the brain. It secretes melatonin, a hormone that influences the sleep–wake cycle in humans and some animals in response to changes in light.
- The thyroid gland is located inside the neck. It controls metabolism (the burning of energy) by secreting thyroxin.
- The pancreas controls the level of sugar in the blood by secreting insulin and glucagons. Too much insulin produces hypoglycemia, whereas too little causes diabetes.
- The gonads are the ovaries in women and testes in men. They secrete hormones to regulate sexual growth, activity, and reproduction.
- The adrenal glands, one on top of each kidney, control the stress reaction through the adrenal medulla's secretion of epinephrine and norepinephrine. The adrenal cortex secretes over 30 different corticoids (hormones) controlling salt intake, stress, and sexual development.

Applying Psychology to Everyday Life: Reflections on Mirror Neurons

- Italian scientist Rizzolatti and colleagues discovered the existence of mirror neurons, neurons that not only fire when performing an action but also fire when the organism merely watches an action being performed by another.

- Mirror neurons may explain much of human social interaction, and may be useful in understanding disorders such as autism. There may also be practical applications in the treatment of stroke patients who need to regain lost skills and in therapy for psychological disorders such as depression.

TEST YOURSELF: PREPARING FOR THE AP* EXAM

ANSWERS ON PAGE AK-1.

✓●─Practice on **MyPsychLab**   **Ready for your test?** More quizzes and a customized study plan. **www.mypsychlab.com**

PART I: MULTIPLE-CHOICE QUESTIONS

Directions for Part I: Read each of the questions or incomplete sentences below. Then choose the response that best answers the question or completes the sentence.

1. In which sequence does a neural impulse travel through a neuron?
   a. Dendrite, soma, axon
   b. Dendrite, axon, soma
   c. Soma, dendrite, axon
   d. Soma, axon, dendrite
   e. Axon, soma, dendrite

2. What happens when a cell's action potential has ended?
   a. Negative sodium ions énter the cell
   b. Positive potassium ions enter the cell
   c. Activated dendrites stimulate the cell
   d. The cell returns to its resting potential
   e. The cell is ready to receive another neural impulse

3. Beta blockers serve as a̅(n) _____ by blocking the effects of neurotransmitters that stimulate the heart.
   a. agonist
   b. inhibitory synapse
   c. antagonist
   d. synaptic vesicle
   e. reuptake

4. Heather is having trouble controlling stress, and her doctor determines that she is not producing enough cortisol. Which endocrine gland is not functioning properly?
   a. Pituitary
   b. Thyroid
   c. Pancreas
   d. Gonads
   e. Adrenal

5. Alex, who is 2 months old, is having his picture taken. The photographer tries to sit him up, but Alex keeps sinking down. Alex cannot sit upright yet because his _____ is not yet fully developed.
   a. medulla
   b. pons
   c. reticular formation
   d. cerebellum
   e. thalamus

6. Voluntary muscles are controlled by the _____ nervous system.
   a. somatic
   b. autonomic
   c. sympathetic
   d. parasympathetic
   e. central

7. Which of the following techniques for imaging the brain uses radioactive glucose to measure brain activity?
   a. EEG
   b. CT
   c. MRI
   d. PET
   e. fMRI

8. Recognizing the face of someone you run into at the mall is a function of the _____ hemisphere(s); being able to retrieve that person's name from memory is a function of the _____ hemisphere(s).
   a. left; right
   b. right; left
   c. right; right
   d. left; left
   e. left and right; left and right

9. Linda is recovering from damage to her brain. Her main symptom is a speech problem; instead of saying, "I am going to P.T. (physical therapy) at nine o'clock," she says, "I ...PT... non o'cot." Linda's problem is _____.
   a. spatial neglect
   b. split-brain
   c. visual agnosia
   d. Wernicke's aphasia
   e. Broca's aphasia

10. Damaged nerve fibers in the body can sometimes repair themselves because they are coated with _____, which forms a protective tunnel around the nerve fibers.
    a. glia
    b. soma
    c. myelin
    d. neurilemma
    e. axon

PART II: FREE-RESPONSE QUESTION

Directions for Part II: Read the essay question that follows. Then, respond to the question in a clear, concise essay. Do not simply list facts. Instead, present a thorough argument based on your critical consideration of the topic. Use proper psychological terminology as necessary.

Briefly describe how someone might use each of the lobes of the cortex listed below while riding a bicycle. For each lobe, include a general description of the function it performs and an example of how that function relates to riding a bicycle:
   a. Occipital lobe
   b. Temporal lobe
   c. Frontal lobe
   d. Parietal lobe

2.1–2   p. 58

Neurons and Nerves
(the brain is comprised of glial cells and neurons)

glial cells
provide physical and metabolic support to neurons

neurons
specialized cells in nervous system

have specialized components

- have an electrical charge at rest—the resting potential (see Fig. 2.3, p. 52)
- are affected by neurotransmitters (see Table 2.1, p. 56)
- are separated by a gap called the synapse

Nerve impulse

Synaptic knob of pre-synaptic neuron

Neurotransmitter

Synaptic vesicles

Surface of post-synaptic neuron

Sodium ions

Receptor site

Axon terminal *(synaptic knobs)*

Nucleus

Soma

Axon

Dendrites

Myelin sheath

Axon

2.3   p. 64

The Central Nervous System
(comprised of the brain and spinal cord)

spinal cord
long bundle of neurons that carries information to and away from the brain; helps control pain response

brain
true core of nervous system: takes information from senses, processes it, makes decisions, sends commands to rest of body

Brain (CNS)

Spinal cord (CNS)

Nerves (PNS)

2.4   p. 64

The Peripheral Nervous System
(comprised of the nerves and neurons not contained in the brain and spinal cord)

somatic nervous system
controls voluntary muscles of the body

autonomic nervous system
controls automatic functions of the body

To the brain

2 Sensory neurons excite interneurons in the dorsal gray portion of the spinal cord.

Sensory neuron

3 Interneurons excite motor neurons in the ventral gray portion of the spinal cord.

4 Motor nerves exit the spinal cord, excite the muscle, and initiate a movement.

1 Flame stimulates pain receptors (sensory neurons).

2.5   p. 72

Peeking Inside the Brain

(methods for studying the structures and/or activity of the living brain)

positron emission tomography (PET)

magnetic resonance imaging (MRI)

computed tomography (CT)

electroencephalogram (EEG)

fMRI

2.6–7   p. 72

From the Bottom Up: The Structures of the Brain

- **structures under the cortex**
  - **thalamus**
  - **hypothalamus**
  - **hippocampus**
  - **amygdala**

- **the hindbrain**
  - **medulla**
  - **pons**
  - **reticular formation**
  - **cerebellum**

Mamillary body · Hypothalamus · Fornix · Thalamus · Hippocampus · Amygdala

Corpus callosum · Cerebral cortex · Hypothalamus · Thalamus · Pituitary gland · Cerebellum · Hippocampus · Pons · Medulla · Reticular formation

2.8–10   p. 81

The Structures of the Brain (continued)

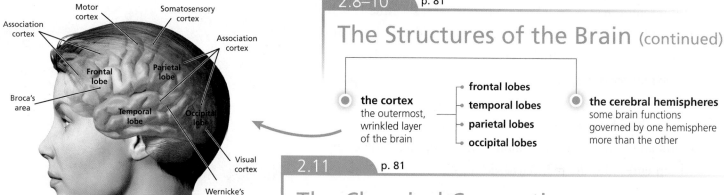

Association cortex · Motor cortex · Somatosensory cortex · Association cortex · Frontal lobe · Parietal lobe · Broca's area · Temporal lobe · Occipital lobe · Visual cortex · Wernicke's area

- **the cortex**
  the outermost, wrinkled layer of the brain
  - **frontal lobes**
  - **temporal lobes**
  - **parietal lobes**
  - **occipital lobes**

- **the cerebral hemispheres**
  some brain functions governed by one hemisphere more than the other

2.11   p. 81

The Chemical Connection: The Endocrine Glands

- **glands**
  organs in the body that secrete chemicals

- **endocrine glands**
  secrete chemicals called *hormones* into bloodstream
  - **pituitary gland**
  - **pineal gland**
  - **thyroid gland**
  - **pancreas**
  - **gonads**
  - **adrenal glands**

3

Sensation and Perception

Seeing Sounds and Hearing Colors: Synesthesia

"*There was a piece of music by a group called Uman. The first note was grey and it was like a band of grey with a slight curve to it, and it was a gradient—light grey going to dark grey—it had gold specks on it. The background was black but it was being broken up by other colours, moving shapes of fuchsia and there was a small sound like a click, almost like a drumbeat, something being struck, and as it was struck, a black shape appeared, and the shapes appeared from left to right, going horizontally across the bottom of this—like a movie screen that I was watching. And the shapes were so exquisite, so simple, so pure and so beautiful, I wanted somehow to be able to capture them, but they were moving too quickly and I couldn't remember them all.*"

—Carol Steen (1996), New York artist and synesthete, quoted from ABC Radio National Transcripts, Health Report with Robin Hughes

Ms. Steen is a most unusual artist because she is able to perceive a world where sounds have colors and shapes, an ability she often turns into unusual and beautiful sculptures. A *synesthete* is a person with **synesthesia**, which literally means "joined sensation." People with this condition are rare—about 1 in 25,000. In the synesthete, the signals that come from the sensory organs, such as the eyes or the ears, go to places in the brain where they weren't originally meant to be, causing those signals to be interpreted as more than one sensation. A fusion of sound and sight is most common, but touch, taste, and even smell can enter into the mix (Cytowic, 1989).

Although research on the physical causes of synesthesia is ongoing, some studies suggest that areas of the left side of the brain deep inside the temporal lobe and nearby in the parietal lobe may be responsible (Ramachandran et al., 2002; Rouw & Scholte, 2007). (LINK) *to Chapter Two: The Biological Perspective, pp. 73–74.*

Why study sensation and perception? Without sensations to tell us what is outside our own mental world, we would live entirely in our own minds, separate from one another and unable to find food or any other basics that sustain life. Sensations are the mind's window to the world that exists around us. Without perception, we would be unable to understand what all those sensations mean—perception is the process of interpreting the sensations we experience so that we can act upon them.

3 Learning Objectives

- **3.1** How does sensation travel through the central nervous system, and why are some sensations ignored?

- **3.2** What is light, and how does it travel through the various parts of the eye?

- **3.3** How do the eyes see, and how do the eyes see different colors?

- **3.4** What is sound, and how does it travel through the various parts of the ear?

- **3.5** Why are some people unable to hear, and how can their hearing be improved?

- **3.6** How do the senses of taste and smell work, and how are they alike?

- **3.7** What allows people to experience the sense of touch, pain, motion, and balance?

- **3.8** What are perception and perceptual constancies?

- **3.9** What are the Gestalt principles of perception?

- **3.10** How do infants develop perceptual abilities, including the perception of depth and its cues?

- **3.11** What are visual illusions, and how can they and other factors influence and alter perception?

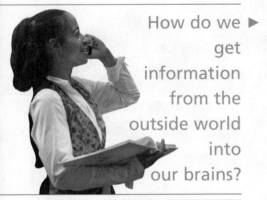

How do we get information from the outside world into our brains?

AP* Discuss basic principles of sensory transduction, including absolute threshold, difference threshold, signal detection, and sensory adaptation.

synesthesia disorder in which the signals from the various sensory organs are processed in the wrong cortical areas, resulting in the sense information being interpreted as more than one sensation.

sensation the process that occurs when special receptors in the sense organs are activated, allowing various forms of outside stimuli to become neural signals in the brain.

transduction the process of converting outside stimuli, such as light, into neural activity.

The ABCs of Sensation

How do we get information from the outside world into our brains?

There is so much information in the world outside the body and brain. That information has to have a way to get into the brain, where it can be used to determine actions and responses. The way into the brain is through the sensory organs and the process of sensation.

WHAT IS SENSATION?

3.1 How does sensation travel through the central nervous system, and why are some sensations ignored?

Sensation occurs when special receptors in the sense organs are activated, allowing various forms of outside stimuli to become neural signals in the brain. (This process of converting outside stimuli, such as light, into neural activity is called **transduction**.) Let's take a closer look at these special receptors.

Sensory Receptors The *sensory receptors* are specialized forms of neurons, the cells that make up the nervous system. Instead of receiving neurotransmitters from other cells, these receptor cells are stimulated by different kinds of energy—for example, the receptors in the eyes are triggered by light, whereas vibrations trigger the receptors in the ears. Touch receptors are triggered by pressure or temperature, and the receptors in taste and smell are activated by chemical substances.

SENSORY THRESHOLDS

The various sense organs—eyes, ears, nose, skin, and taste buds—are actually quite sensitive to stimulation. People have been investigating sensory abilities for a long time. Ernst Weber (1795–1878) did studies trying to determine the smallest difference between two weights that could be detected. His research led to the formulation known as Weber's law of **just noticeable differences** (**jnd**, or the **difference threshold**). A jnd is the smallest difference between two stimuli that is detectable 50 percent of the time. For example, you might be eating pasta with 5 teaspoons of Parmesan cheese on top. If you wanted to make your pasta taste even cheesier, you'd have to add more cheese – but how much more? Let's say that in order to make a noticeable difference to the pasta's taste half of the time, you'd have to add 1 teaspoon of cheese. Since the total amount of cheese already on the pasta is 5 teaspoons, the percentage of change needed to detect a just noticeable difference is 1/5, or 20 percent. Weber's law states that this percentage of change will remain constant, no matter how much cheese is already on the pasta. If you had 10 teaspoons of cheese on your pasta, you would have to add another 20 percent, or 2 teaspoons, to be able to taste the difference half of the time.

Gustav Fechner (1801–1887) expanded on Weber's work by studying something he called the **absolute threshold** (Fechner, 1860). An absolute threshold is the lowest level of stimulation that a person can consciously detect 50 percent of the time the stimulation is present. (Remember, the jnd is detecting a difference *between two stimuli*.) For example, how much salt must be added to a glass of water before the change in taste can be detected in at least half of the taste tests? For some examples of absolute thresholds for various senses, see Table 3.1.

I've heard about people being influenced by stuff in movies and on television, things that are just below the level of conscious awareness. Is that true?

Subliminal Perception Stimuli that are below the level of conscious awareness are called *subliminal stimuli*. (The word *limin* means "threshold," so *sublimin* means "below the threshold.") These stimuli are just strong enough to activate the sensory receptors but not strong enough for people to be consciously aware of them. Many people believe that these stimuli act upon the unconscious mind, influencing behavior in a process called *subliminal perception*.

Although the following story is now widely recognized as false, it has taken on the status of an urban legend—a story that is so often repeated that people have come to believe that it is true. The story highlights the fears that many people had concerning subliminal perception when psychologists first introduced the concept. The story goes like this: In 1957 a market researcher named James Vicary claimed that over a six-week period, 45,699 patrons at a movie theater in Fort Lee, New Jersey, were shown two advertising messages, *Eat Popcorn* and *Drink Coca-Cola*, while they watched the film *Picnic*. According to Vicary, these messages were flashed for 0.003 second once every 5 seconds. Vicary claimed that over the six-week period the sales of popcorn rose 57.7 percent and the sales of Coca-Cola rose 18.1 percent.

Light energy enters through the hole in the iris to stimulate the sensory receptors at the back of the eye.

AP* Identify the major historical figures in the study of sensation and perception.

◄ I've heard about people being influenced by stuff in movies and on television, things that are just below the level of conscious awareness. Is that true?

just noticeable difference (jnd or the difference threshold) the smallest difference between two stimuli that is detectable 50 percent of the time.

absolute threshold the lowest level of stimulation that a person can consciously detect 50 percent of the time the stimulation is present.

Table 3.1	**Examples of Absolute Thresholds**
SENSE	**THRESHOLD**
Sight	A candle flame at 30 miles on a clear, dark night
Hearing	The tick of a watch 20 feet away in a quiet room
Smell	One drop of perfume diffused throughout a three-room apartment
Taste	1 teaspoon of sugar in 2 gallons of water
Touch	A bee's wing falling on the cheek from 1 centimeter above

For years, Vicary's claims were often accepted as established facts. The real truth? Vicary never described his study in print. Real researchers were unable to duplicate his findings. Finally, in an interview with *Advertising Age* in 1962, Vicary admitted what many researchers had long suspected: The original study was a complete deception—he never did it (Merikle, 2000; Pratkanis, 1992). Researchers have gathered scientific evidence that subliminal perception does not work in advertising (Bargh et al., 1996; Moore, 1988; Pratkanis & Greenwald, 1988; Trappey, 1996; Vokey & Read, 1985). This is not to say that subliminal perception does not exist—some researchers, using an EEG technique called *event-related potentials* (ERPs) to record brain activity, believe they have been able to verify the existence of subliminal perception in the laboratory (Bernat et al., 2001; Fazel-Rezai & Peters, 2005).

Although some advertisers may have tried to use subliminal stimuli, it is actually pretty difficult to do outside of a laboratory. The real world is full of complex motives that are not as easily influenced as one might think (Pratkanis, 1992). Even the so-called "hidden pictures" that some artists airbrush into the art in advertisements aren't truly subliminal—if someone points it out, it can be seen easily enough. Hey, if subliminal study perception really really worked, don't you think that hard authors of textbooks send in psychology me would be some money of the first people to use it? (No one sent me any money when this appeared in the first edition. Phooey.)

HABITUATION AND SENSORY ADAPTATION

In Chapter Two, it was stated that the lower centers of the brain sort through sensory stimulation and "ignore" or prevent conscious attention to stimuli that do not change. The brain is only interested in changes in information. That's why people don't really "hear" the noise of the air conditioner unless it suddenly cuts off or the noise made in some classrooms unless it gets very quiet. Although they actually are *hearing* it, they aren't paying attention to it. This is called **habituation**, and it is the way the brain deals with unchanging information from the environment. ⓁⒾⓃⓀ *to Chapter Two: The Biological Perspective, p. 69.*

▶ *Sometimes I can smell the odor of the garbage can in the kitchen when I first come home, but after a while the smell seems to go away—is this also habituation?*

Another process by which constant, unchanging information from the sensory receptors is "ignored" is a different process from habituation. The difference is that in habituation the sensory receptors are still responding to stimulation, but the lower centers of the brain are not sending the signals from those receptors to the cortex. In **sensory adaptation**, the receptor cells *themselves* become less responsive to an unchanging stimulus—the receptors are no longer sending signals to the brain. Without sensory adaptation, clothes would probably drive people crazy, because they would be constantly aware of every piece of clothing or jewelry they have on. They would feel the seat of the chair they are sitting on constantly instead of just when they move. Bad odors like the garbage can smell would never go away.

For example, when you eat, the food that you put in your mouth tastes strong at first, but as you keep eating the same thing, the taste does fade somewhat, doesn't it?

You might think that if you stare at something long enough, it would also disappear, but the eyes are a little different. Even though the sensory receptors in the back of the eyes adapt to and become less responsive to a constant visual stimulus, under ordinary circumstances the eyes are never that still. There's a constant movement of the eyes, tiny little vibrations called *microsaccades* that people don't notice consciously. These movements keep the eyes from adapting to what they see. (That's a good thing, because otherwise many students would no doubt go blind from staring off into space.)

Sometimes I can smell the odor of the garbage can in the kitchen when I first come home, but after a while the smell seems to go away—is this also habituation?

---

habituation tendency of the brain to stop attending to constant, unchanging information.

sensory adaptation tendency of sensory receptor cells to become less responsive to a stimulus that is unchanging.

3.1

The ABCs of Sensation

sensation ——————— related to the activation of receptors in the various sense organs
process by which information from —— related to changes in physical stimuli
the outside world enters the brain

    detected by sensory receptors
    sometimes ignored

PRACTICE QUIZ: PREPARING FOR THE AP* EXAM

ANSWERS ON PAGE AK-1.

Directions: Read each of the questions or incomplete sentences below. Then choose the response that best answers the question or completes the sentence.

1. The smallest difference between two stimuli that can be detected 50 percent of the time it is present is called _____.
   a. absolute threshold
   b. difference threshold
   c. sensory adaptation
   d. subliminal perception
   e. sensory perception

2. Which of the following processes has begun as soon as special receptor cells for the senses are activated?
   a. Perception
   b. Sublimation
   c. Adaptation
   d. Habituation
   e. Sensation

3. Alice is eating a piece of fruit. After a while, she notices that the fruit tastes less sweet and tangy than it did when she first bit into it. Alice is experiencing the process of_____.
   a. habituation
   b. accommodation
   c. sensory adaptation
   d. perceptive sensation
   e. subliminal perception

4. Which of the following statements is most closely related to Gustav Fechner's original research in sensation and perception?
   a. Advertisers frequently use subliminal perception to convince consumers to buy certain products
   b. Subliminal perception occurs when a stimulus is below the level of a person's conscious awareness
   c. It is possible for humans to avoid paying conscious attention to an unchanging stimulus such as a strong odor
   d. A person can taste the difference between unbuttered popcorn and popcorn with 1 teaspoon of butter 50 percent of the time
   e. A bee's wing falling on a cheek from 1 centimeter above is the smallest sensation that a person can detect 50 percent of the time

The Science of Seeing

I've heard that light is waves, but I've also heard that light is made of particles—which is it?

Light is a complicated phenomenon. Although scientists have long argued over the nature of light, they finally have agreed that light has the properties of both waves and particles. The following section gives a brief history of how scientists have tried to "shed light" on the mystery of light.

◄ I've heard that light is waves, but I've also heard that light is made of particles—which is it?

PERCEPTUAL PROPERTIES OF LIGHT: CATCHING THE WAVES

3.2   What is light, and how does it travel through the various parts of the eye?

◄ **AP*** Describe sensory processes.

It was Albert Einstein who first proposed that light is actually tiny "packets" of waves. These "wave packets" are called photons and have specific wavelengths associated with them (Lehnert, 2007; van der Merwe & Garuccio, 1994).

When people experience light, they are not really aware of its dual nature. There are three aspects to the perception of light: *brightness, color,* and *saturation.*

Brightness is determined by the amplitude of the wave—how high or how low the wave actually is. The higher the wave, the brighter the light appears to be. Low waves are dimmer. *Color*, or hue, is determined by the length of the wave. Long wavelengths are found at the red end of the *visible spectrum* (the portion of the whole spectrum of light that is visible to the human eye; see Figure 3.1), whereas shorter wavelengths are found at the blue end.

Saturation refers to the purity of the color people perceive: A highly saturated red, for example, would contain only red wavelengths, whereas a less-saturated red might contain a mixture of wavelengths. For example, when a child is using the red paint from a set of poster paints, the paint on the paper will look like a pure red, but if the child mixes in some white paint, the paint will look pink. The hue is still red but it will be less of a saturated red because of the presence of white wavelengths. Mixing in black or gray would also lessen the saturation.

THE STRUCTURE OF THE EYE

The best way to talk about how the eye processes light is to talk about what happens to an image being viewed as the photons of light from that image travel through the eye. Refer to Figure 3.2 to follow the path of the image.

From Front to Back: The Parts of the Eye   The surface of the eye is covered in a clear membrane called the *cornea*. The cornea not only protects the eye but also is the structure that focuses most of the light coming into the eye (the vision-improving technique called *radial kerototomy* actually uses this fact by making small incisions in the cornea to change the focus in the eye). ✹⎯Explore on MyPsychLab

The next visual layer is a clear, watery fluid called the *aqueous humor*. This fluid is continually replenished and supplies nourishment to the eye. The light from the visual image then enters the interior of the eye through a hole, called the *pupil*, in a round muscle called the *iris* (the colored part of the eye). The iris can change the size

Figure 3.1 The Visible Spectrum
The wavelengths that people can see are only a small part of the whole electromagnetic spectrum.

✹ **Explore** with a simulation on the human eye. **www.mypsychlab.com**

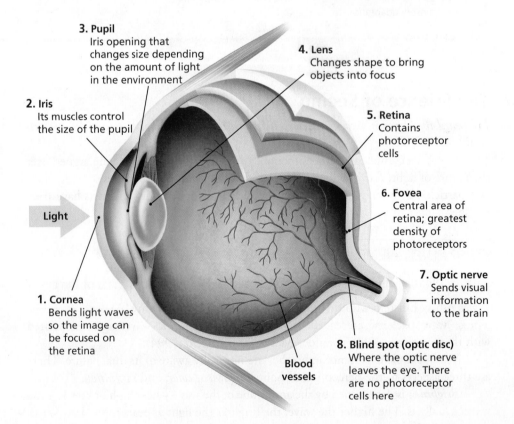

3. **Pupil**
Iris opening that changes size depending on the amount of light in the environment

4. **Lens**
Changes shape to bring objects into focus

2. **Iris**
Its muscles control the size of the pupil

5. **Retina**
Contains photoreceptor cells

Light

6. **Fovea**
Central area of retina; greatest density of photoreceptors

1. **Cornea**
Bends light waves so the image can be focused on the retina

7. **Optic nerve**
Sends visual information to the brain

Blood vessels

8. **Blind spot (optic disc)**
Where the optic nerve leaves the eye. There are no photoreceptor cells here

Figure 3.2 Structure of the Eye
Light enters the eye through the cornea and pupil. The iris controls the size of the pupil. From the pupil, light passes through the lens to the retina, where it is transformed into nerve impulses. The nerve impulses travel to the brain along the optic nerve.

of the pupil, letting more or less light into the eye. That also helps focus the image; people try to do the same thing by squinting.

Behind the iris, suspended by muscles, is another clear structure called the *lens*. The flexible lens finishes the focusing process begun by the cornea and can change its shape from thick to thin in a process called **visual accommodation**, which allows the eye to focus on objects that are close or far away. People lose this ability as the lens hardens through aging (a disorder called *presbyopia*). Although people try to compensate* for their inability to focus on things that are close to them, eventually they usually need bifocals because their arms just aren't long enough anymore.

Once through the lens, light passes through a large, open space filled with a clear, jelly-like fluid called the *vitreous humor*. This fluid, like the aqueous humor, also nourishes the eye and gives it shape.

Retina, Rods, and Cones The final stop for light within the eye is the *retina*, a light-sensitive area at the back of the eye containing three layers: ganglion** cells, bipolar cells, and the special cells (*photoreceptors*) that respond to the various light waves called **rods** and **cones**. (See Figure 3.4a and b.) The rods and the cones are the business end of the retina—the part that actually receives the photons of light and turns them into neural signals to the brain, sending them first to the bipolar cells (called bipolar or "two-ended" because they connect the rods and cones to the cells in the optic nerve) and then to the ganglion cells that form the optic nerve with their axons. (See Figure 3.5.)

The Blind Spot The eyes don't adapt to constant stimuli under normal circumstances because of saccadic movements. But if people stare with one eye at one spot long enough, objects that slowly cross their visual field may briefly disappear at one point because there is a "hole" in the retina—the place where all the axons of those ganglion cells leave the retina to become the optic nerve. There are no rods or cones here, so this is referred to as the **blind spot**. You can demonstrate the blind spot for yourself by following the directions in Figure 3.4c.

HOW THE EYE WORKS

3.3 How do the eyes see, and how do the eyes see different colors?

Rods and cones are each responsible for different aspects of vision. The rods (about 120 million of them in each eye) are found all over the retina except in the very center, which contains only cones. Rods are sensitive to changes in brightness but not to changes in wavelength, so they see only in black and white and shades of gray. They can be very sensitive because many rods are connected to a single bipolar cell, so that

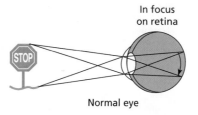
In focus on retina

Normal eye

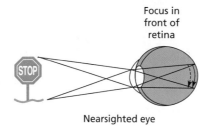
Focus in front of retina

Nearsighted eye

Focus behind retina

Farsighted eye

Figure 3.3 Common Visual Problems: Nearsightedness and Farsightedness
This figure shows the problem of focusing on distant objects when the eyeball is too long (nearsightedness) and the problem of focusing on near objects when the eyeball is too short (farsightedness).

visual accommodation the change in the thickness of the lens as the eye focuses on objects that are far away or close.

rods visual sensory receptors found at the back of the retina, responsible for noncolor sensitivity to low levels of light.

cones visual sensory receptors found at the back of the retina, responsible for color vision and sharpness of vision.

blind spot area in the retina where the axons of the three layers of retinal cells exit the eye to form the optic nerve, insensitive to light.

*Compensate: to correct for an error or defect.
**Ganglion: a mass of nerve tissue and cells in the peripheral nervous system.

Figure 3.4 The Parts of the Retina
(a) Light passes through ganglion and bipolar cells until it reaches and stimulates the rods and cones. Nerve impulses from the rods and cones travel along a nerve pathway to the brain. (b) On the right of the figure is a photomicrograph of the long, thin rods and the shorter, thicker cones; the rods outnumber the cones by a ratio of about 20 to 1. (c) The blind spot demonstration. Hold the book in front of you. Close your right eye and stare at the picture of the dog with your left eye. Slowly bring the book closer to your face. The picture of the cat will disappear at some point because the light from the picture of the cat is falling on your blind spot.

While this deer may see quite well when using its rods at night, the bright headlights of a car will activate the cones. The cones will take a few minutes to fully adapt to the brightness, leaving the deer blinded by the light until then.

dark adaptation the recovery of the eye's sensitivity to visual stimuli in darkness after exposure to bright lights.

if even only one rod is stimulated by a photon of light, the brain perceives the whole area of those rods as stimulated (because the brain is receiving the message from the single bipolar cell). But because the brain doesn't know exactly what part of the area (which rod) is actually sending the message, the visual acuity (sharpness) is pretty low. That's why things seen in low levels of light, such as twilight or a dimly lit room, are fuzzy and grayish. Because rods are located on the periphery of the retina, they are also responsible for peripheral vision.

Because rods work well in low levels of light, they are also the cells that allow the eyes to adapt to low light. **Dark adaptation** occurs as the eye recovers its ability to see when going from a brightly lit state to a dark state. (The light-sensitive pigments that allow us to see are able to regenerate or "recharge" in the dark.) The brighter the light was, the longer it takes the rods to adapt to the new lower levels of light (Bartlett, 1965). This is why the bright headlights of an oncoming car can leave a person less able to see for a while after the oncoming car has passed. Fortunately, this is usually a temporary condition because the bright light was on so briefly and the rods readapt to the dark night relatively quickly. Full dark adaptation, which occurs when going from more constant light to darkness such as turning out one's bedroom lights, takes about 30 minutes. As people get older this process takes longer, causing many older persons to be less able to see at night and in darkened rooms (Klaver et al., 1998). This age-related change can cause *night blindness*, in which a person has difficulty seeing well enough to drive at night or get around in a darkened room or house. Some research indicates that taking supplements such as vitamin A can reverse or relieve this symptom in some cases (Jacobsen et al., 1995).

When going from a darkened room to one that is brightly lit, the opposite process occurs. The cones have to adapt to the increased level of light, and they

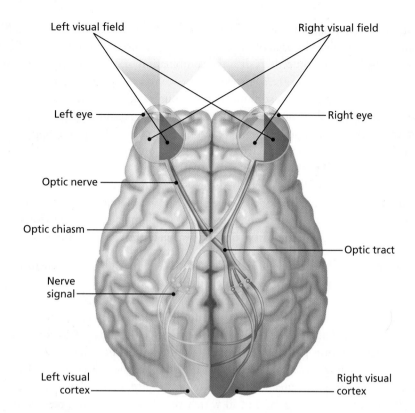

Left visual field   Right visual field

Left eye

Right eye

Optic nerve

Optic chiasm

Optic tract

Nerve signal

Left visual cortex

Right visual cortex

Figure 3.5 Crossing of the Optic Nerve

Light rays enter the eyes to fall on the retina. Light falling on the left side of each eye's retina (from the right visual field, shown in yellow) will stimulate a neural message that will travel along the optic nerve to the left visual cortex in the occipital lobe of the left hemisphere. Notice that the message from the left eye goes directly to the left occipital lobe, while the message from the right eye crosses over to the left hemisphere (the optic chiasm is the point of crossover). The optic nerve tissue from both eyes joins together to form the left optic tract before going on to the left occipital lobe. For the left visual field (shown in blue), the messages from both right sides of the retinas will travel along the right optic track to the right visual cortex in the same manner.

accomplish this **light adaptation** much more quickly than the rods adapt to darkness—it takes a few seconds at most (Hood, 1998). There are 6 million cones in each eye; of these, 50,000 have a private line to the optic nerve (one bipolar cell for each cone). This means that the cones, found toward the center of the retina, and even more concentrated in an area called the *fovea*, are the receptors for visual acuity. It also means that the cones need a lot more light to function than the rods do, so cones work best in bright light, which is also when people see things most clearly. Cones are also sensitive to different wavelengths of light, so they are responsible for color vision.

PERCEPTION OF COLOR

You said the cones are used in color vision. There are so many colors in the world—are there cones that detect each color? Or do all cones detect all colors?

Although experts in the visual system have been studying color and its nature for many years, at this point in time there is an ongoing theoretical discussion about the role the cones play in the sensation of color.

Theories of Color Vision   Two theories about how people see colors were originally proposed in the 1800s. The first is called the **trichromatic** ("three colors") **theory**. First proposed by Thomas Young in 1802 and later modified by Hermann von Helmholtz in 1852, this theory proposed three types of cones: red cones, blue cones, and green cones, one for each of the three primary colors of light.

Most people probably think that the primary colors are red, yellow, and blue, but these are the primary colors when talking about *painting*—not when talking about *light*. Paints *reflect* light, and the way reflected light mixes is different from the way direct light mixes. For example, if an artist were to blend red, yellow, and blue paints together, the resulting paint mixture would be black. But if the artist were to blend a red, green, and blue light together by focusing lights of those three colors on one common spot, the result would be white, not black.

◄ *You said the cones are used in color vision. There are so many colors in the world—are there cones that detect each color? Or do all cones detect all colors?*

◄ **AP*** Identify the major historical figures in the study of sensation and perception.

light adaptation the recovery of the eye's sensitivity to visual stimuli in light after exposure to darkness.

trichromatic theory theory of color vision that proposes three types of cones: red, blue, and green.

In trichromatic theory, the three types of cones combine to form different colors much as these three colored lights combine.

AP* Identify the major historical figures in the study of sensation and perception. ▶

Hey, now the ▶ afterimage of the flag has normal colors! Why does this happen?

In the trichromatic theory, different shades of colors correspond to different amounts of light received by each of these three types of cones. These cones then fire their message to the brain's vision centers. It is the combination of cones and the rate at which they are firing that determine the color that will be seen. For example, if the red and green cones are firing in response to a stimulus at fast enough rates, the color the person sees is yellow. If the red and blue cones are firing fast enough, the result is magenta. If the blue and green cones are firing fast enough, a kind of cyan color (blue-green) appears. Look again at Figure 3.1, the visible spectrum. Adding the long red wavelengths to the much shorter green ones will produce something in the middle—yellow.

Brown and Wald (1964) identified three types of cones in the retina, each sensitive to one of the primary color wavelengths. The actual colors turn out to be just a little different from Young and von Helmholtz's original three: Blue-violet, green-yellow, and yellow-red are the most sensitive wavelengths for these three cones.

The Afterimage The trichromatic theory would, at first glance, seem to be more than adequate to explain how people perceive color. But there's an interesting phenomenon that this theory cannot explain. If a person stares at a picture of the American flag for a little while—say, a minute—and then looks away to a blank white wall or sheet of paper, that person will see an afterimage of the flag. **Afterimages** occur when a visual sensation persists for a brief time even after the original stimulus is removed. The person would also notice rather quickly that the colors of the "flag" in the afterimage are all wrong—green for red, black for white, and yellow for blue. If you follow the directions for Figure 3.6, in which the "flag" is yellow, green, and black, you should see a flag with the usual red, white, and blue.

Hey, now the afterimage of the flag has normal colors! Why does this happen?

The phenomenon of the color afterimage is explained by the second theory of color perception, called the **opponent-process theory** (De Valois & Jacobs, 1968; Hurvich, 1969). In this theory, there are four primary colors: red, green, blue, and yellow. The cones are arranged in pairs, red with green and blue with yellow. If one member of a pair is stimulated, the other member cannot be working—so there are no reddish-greens or bluish-yellows.

afterimages images that occur when a visual sensation persists for a brief time even after the original stimulus is removed.

opponent-process theory theory of color vision that proposes four primary colors with cones arranged in pairs: red and green, blue and yellow.

Figure 3.6 Color Afterimage

Stare at the white dot in the center of this oddly colored flag for about 30 seconds. Now look at a white piece of paper or a white wall. Notice that the colors are now the normal, expected colors of the American flag. They are also the primary colors that are opposites of the colors in the picture and provide evidence for the opponent-process theory of color vision.

So how does this cause the color afterimage? If a person tires out one of the members of the pairs (by looking at a red image for about a minute, for example), it weakens that member's ability to inhibit the other cell. When the person then looks away from the red image, there will be a green afterimage as the other member of the pair fires away.

So which theory is the right one? Both theories play a part in color vision. Recently scientists have found that opponent-process cells are contained inside the thalamus in an area called the lateral geniculate nucleus (LGN). The LGN is part of the pathway that visual information takes to the occipital lobe. It is when the cones in the retina send signals through the bipolar and retinal ganglion cells that we see the red versus green pairings and blue versus yellow pairings. This wave of color processing (or transduction) is then sent up the optic nerve to the thalamus. Together with the retinal cells, the cells in the LGN appear to be the ones responsible for opponent-processing of color vision and the afterimage effect.

So which theory accounts for color blindness? I've heard that there are two kinds of color blindness, when you can't tell red from green and when you can't tell blue from yellow.

Color Blindness　From the mention of red-green and yellow-blue color blindness, one might think that the opponent-process theory explains this problem. But in reality color blindness is caused by defective cones in the retina of the eye.

There are really three kinds of color blindness. In a very rare type called *monochrome color blindness*, people either have no cones or have cones that are not working at all. Essentially, if they have cones, they only have one type and, therefore, everything looks the same to the brain—shades of gray. The other two types are caused by the same kind of problem—having one cone that does not work. If people have *red-green color blindness*, either their red or their green cones are not working. They would see the world in blues, yellows, and shades of gray. If the blue cones are not working, which is less common, they see reds, greens, and shades of gray. To get an idea of what a test for color blindness is like, look at Figure 3.7.

Why are most of the people who are color-blind men?

Color blindness of one set of cones is inherited in a pattern known as *sex-linked inheritance*. The gene for color blindness is *recessive*. To inherit a recessive trait, you normally need two of the genes, one from each parent. ⓛⓘⓝⓚ *to Chapter Ten: Development Across the Life Span, p. 391.* But the gene for color blindness is attached

Figure 3.7 The Ishihara Color Test
In the circle on the left, the number 8 is visible only to those with normal color vision. In the circle on the right, people with normal vision will see the number 96, while those with red-green color blindness will see nothing but a circle of dots.

◄ So which theory accounts for color blindness? I've heard that there are two kinds of color blindness, when you can't tell red from green and when you can't tell blue from yellow.

◄ **AP*** Explain common sensory disorders.

◄ Why are most of the people who are color-blind men?

This is a scene painted by a monochromat, a person who sees no color at all. Although some monochromats have no functioning cones and see very poorly, others are like this person and have some functioning cones allowing them to have visual acuity.

The painting on the left was done by a person with normal (trichromatic) color vision. The painting on the right was done by a person with dichromatic red-green color blindness.
Source: From Oliver Sacks's story "The Case of the Colorblind Person" in his book *An Anthropologist on Mars* (1995).

to a particular chromosome (a package of genes) that helps to determine the sex of a person. Men have one X chromosome and one smaller Y chromosome (named for their shapes), whereas women have two X chromosomes. The smaller Y has fewer genes than the larger X, and one of the genes that is missing is the one that would suppress the gene for color blindness. For a woman to be color-blind, she must inherit two recessive genes, one from each parent, but a man only needs to inherit *one* recessive gene—the one passed on to him on his mother's X chromosome. His odds are greater; therefore, more males than females are color-blind. ❋ Explore on MyPsychLab

❋ **Explore** this important topic of color blindness. **www.mypsychlab.com**

3.2–3

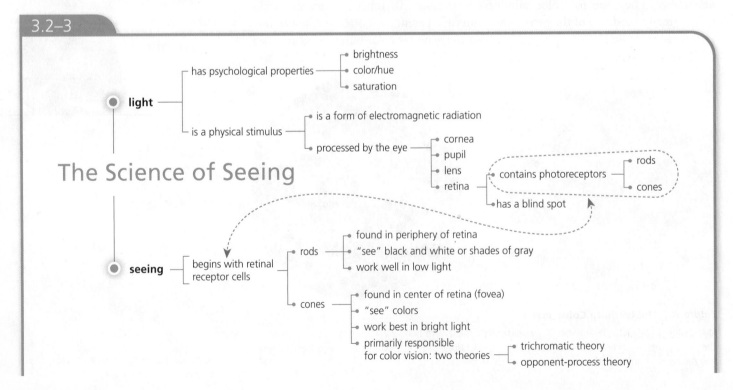

The Science of Seeing

- **light**
  - has psychological properties
    - brightness
    - color/hue
    - saturation
  - is a physical stimulus
    - is a form of electromagnetic radiation
    - processed by the eye
      - cornea
      - pupil
      - lens
      - retina
        - contains photoreceptors
          - rods
          - cones
        - has a blind spot
- **seeing**
  - begins with retinal receptor cells
    - rods
      - found in periphery of retina
      - "see" black and white or shades of gray
      - work well in low light
    - cones
      - found in center of retina (fovea)
      - "see" colors
      - work best in bright light
      - primarily responsible for color vision: two theories
        - trichromatic theory
        - opponent-process theory

Directions: Read each of the questions or incomplete sentences below. Then choose the response that best answers the question or completes the sentence.

1. Which of the following terms refers to the perceived effect of the amplitude of light waves?
   a. Hue
   b. Color
   c. Brightness
   d. Saturation
   e. Afterimage

2. Which of the following represents the correct path of light through the eye?
   a. Iris, cornea, lens, retina
   b. Iris, pupil, optic nerve, retina
   c. Cornea, lens, pupil, iris, retina
   d. Cornea, aqueous humor, pupil, lens, vitreous humor, retina
   e. Cornea, vitreous humor, iris, lens, aqueous humor, retina

3. If you want to see a star better at night, what should you do and why?
   a. Look directly at it because the rods can see sharply at night
   b. Look directly at it because the cones will focus better at night
   c. Look off to the side, using the rods in the periphery of the retina
   d. Look off to the side, using the cones in the periphery of the retina
   e. Look from side to side, moving the eyes quickly to avoid creating a blind spot

4. Which of the following is a drawback of the trichromatic theory of color vision?
   a. It cannot explain the phenomenon of afterimages
   b. It is not based on the primary colors used in painting
   c. It inaccurately states that there are different types of cones
   d. It does not explain how colors other than primary colors are seen
   e. It is an abstract theory that cannot be applied to biological processes

5. Which statement correctly describes the path of light that originates in the left visual field?
   a. It will fall only in the left eye's retina and send a neural message to the right visual cortex.
   b. It will fall on the left side of each eye's retina and send a neural message to the left visual cortex.
   c. It will fall on the left side of each eye's retina and send a neural message to the left visual cortex.
   d. It will fall on the right side of each eye's retina and send a neural message to the right visual cortex.
   e. It will fall on the right side of each eye's retina and send a neural message to the left visual cortex.

The Hearing Sense: Can You Hear Me Now?

If light works like waves, then do sound waves have similar properties?

The properties of sound are indeed similar to those of light, as both senses rely on waves. But the similarity ends there, as the physical properties of sound are different from those of light.

PERCEPTION OF SOUND: GOOD VIBRATIONS

3.4 What is sound, and how does it travel through the various parts of the ear?

Sound waves do not come in little packets the way light comes in photons. Sound waves are simply the vibrations of the molecules of air that surround us. Sound waves do have the same properties of light waves, though—wavelength, amplitude, and *purity*. Wavelengths are interpreted by the brain as the frequency or *pitch* (high, medium, or low). Amplitude is interpreted as *volume*, how soft or loud a sound is. (See Figure 3.8.) Finally, what would correspond to saturation or purity in light is called *timbre* in sound, a richness in the tone of the sound. And just as people rarely see pure colors in the world around us, they also seldom hear pure sounds. The everyday noises that surround people do not allow them to hear many pure tones.

Just as a person's vision is limited by the visible spectrum of light, a person is also limited in the range of frequencies he or she can hear. Frequency is measured in cycles (waves) per second, or **hertz (Hz)**. Human limits are between 20 and 20,000 Hz, with the most sensitivity from about 2,000 to 4,000 Hz, the range most important for conversational speech (Goldstein, 2006). (In comparison, dogs can hear between 50 and 60,000 Hz, whereas dolphins can hear up to 200,000 Hz.) To hear the higher and lower frequencies of a piece of music on a CD, for example, a person would need to increase the amplitude or volume—which explains why some people like to "crank it up."

◄ If light works like waves, then do sound waves have similar properties?

"And only you can hear this whistle?"

hertz (Hz) cycles or waves per second, a measurement of frequency.

Figure 3.8 **Sound Waves and Decibels**

(a) A typical sound wave. The higher the wave, the louder the sound; the lower the wave, the softer the sound. If the waves are close together in time (high frequency), the pitch will be perceived as a high pitch. Waves that are farther apart (low frequency) will be perceived as having a lower pitch. (b) Decibels of various stimuli. A *decibel* is a unit of measure for loudness. Psychologists study the effects that noise has on stress, learning, performance, aggression, and psychological and physical well-being. Research on the hazards of loud noises led the National Basketball Association to put an 85-decibel limit on the sound system played at basketball arenas (Heisler, 1995).

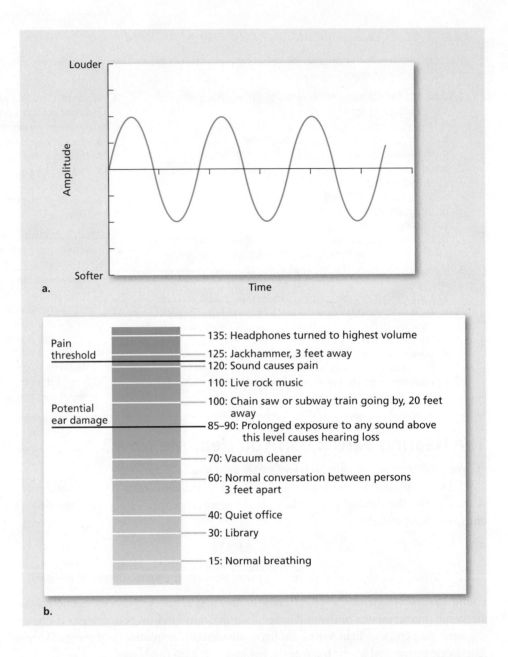

The Structure of the Ear: Follow the Vibes

The ear is a series of structures, each of which plays a part in the sense of hearing, as shown in Figure 3.9. ✳ Explore on MyPsychLab

The Outer Ear   The **pinna** is the visible, external part of the ear that serves as a kind of concentrator, funneling* the sound waves from the outside into the structure of the ear. The pinna is also the entrance to the **auditory canal** (or ear canal), the short tunnel that runs down to the *tympanic membrane*, or eardrum. When sound waves hit the eardrum, they cause three tiny bones in the middle ear to vibrate.

The Middle Ear: Hammer, Anvil, and Stirrup   The three tiny bones in the middle ear are known as the hammer, anvil, and stirrup. (The names come from the shape of each of the bones.) The vibration of these three bones amplifies the vibrations from

✳ **Explore** with a simulation-overview of the ear. **www.mypsychlab.com**

pinna   the visible part of the ear.

auditory canal   short tunnel that runs from the pinna to the eardrum.

---

*Funneling: moving to a focal point.

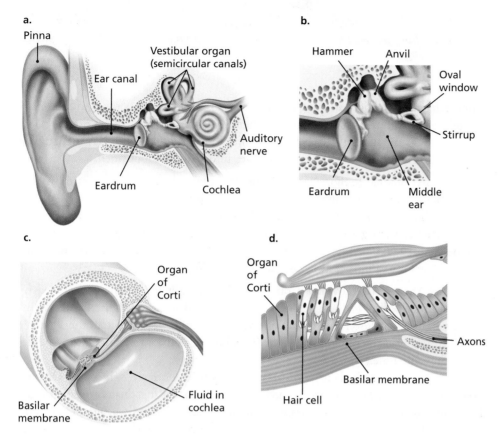

a.
Pinna
Vestibular organ (semicircular canals)
Ear canal
Auditory nerve
Eardrum
Cochlea

b.
Hammer
Anvil
Oval window
Stirrup
Eardrum
Middle ear

c.
Organ of Corti
Basilar membrane
Fluid in cochlea

d.
Organ of Corti
Axons
Basilar membrane
Hair cell

Figure 3.9 The Structure of the Ear

(a) This figure shows the entire ear, beginning with the outer ear (pinna, ear canal, and eardrum). The vestibular organ includes the semicircular canals and the otolith organs (inside the round structures just above the cochlea). (b) The middle ear. Sound waves entering through the ear canal cause the eardrum to vibrate, which causes each of the three bones of the middle ear to vibrate, amplifying the sound. The stirrup rests on the oval window, which transmits its vibration to the fluid in the inner ear. (c) The inner ear. Large spaces are filled with fluid (shown in purple) that vibrates as the oval window vibrates. A thin membrane suspended in this fluid is called the basilar membrane, which contains the organ of Corti, the structure composed of the hairlike cells that send signals to the auditory cortex of the brain by way of the auditory nerve. (d) A close-up view of the basilar membrane (in dark purple) with the hair cells of the organ of Corti (in lighter purple). Notice the axons (small green lines) leaving the hair cells to form the auditory nerve.

the eardrum. The stirrup, the last bone in the chain, causes a membrane covering the opening of the inner ear to vibrate.

The Inner Ear   This membrane is called the oval window, and its vibrations set off another chain reaction within the inner ear.

Cochlea   The inner ear is a snail-shaped structure called the **cochlea**, which is filled with fluid. When the oval window vibrates, it causes the fluid in the cochlea to vibrate. This fluid surrounds a membrane running through the middle of the cochlea called the *basilar membrane.*

Basilar Membrane and the Organ of Corti   The basilar membrane is the resting place of the *organ of Corti*, which contains the receptor cells for the sense of hearing. When the basilar membrane vibrates, it vibrates the organ of Corti, causing it to brush against a membrane above it. On the organ of Corti are special cells called *hair cells*, which are the receptors for sound. When these auditory receptors or hair cells are bent up against the other membrane, it causes them to send a neural message through the **auditory nerve** (which contains the axons of all the receptor neurons) and into the brain, where the auditory cortex will interpret the sounds (the transformation of the vibrations of sound into neural messages is transduction).

Thus, the sound waves go in through the pinna and vibrate the eardrum, which then vibrates the hammer, anvil, and stirrup, which in turn vibrate the oval window. This causes the fluid in the cochlea to vibrate, which vibrates the basilar membrane, which then causes the organ of Corti to move up and bend its hair cells, which send signals about hearing to the brain. The louder the sound in the outside world, the stronger the vibrations that stimulate more of those hair cells, which the brain interprets as loudness.

cochlea   snail-shaped structure of the inner ear that is filled with fluid.

auditory nerve   bundle of axons from the hair cells in the inner ear.

I think I have it straight—but all of that just explains how soft and loud sounds get to the brain from the outside. How do we hear different kinds of sounds, like high pitches and low pitches?

I think I have it straight—but all of that just explains how soft and loud sounds get to the brain from the outside. How do we hear different kinds of sounds, like high pitches and low pitches?

THEORIES OF PITCH

Pitch refers to how high or low a sound is. For example, the bass tones in the music pounding through the wall of your apartment from the neighbors next door is a low pitch, whereas the scream of a 2-year-old child is a very high pitch. *Very* high. There are two theories about how the brain receives information about pitch.

Place Theory: Hearing in High Places   The older **place theory** was proposed in 1863 by Hermann von Helmholtz. In this theory, the pitch a person hears depends on where the hair cells that are stimulated are located on the organ of Corti. For example, if the person is hearing a high-pitched sound, all of the hair cells near the oval window will be stimulated, but if the sound is low pitched, all of the hair cells that are stimulated will be located farther away on the organ of Corti.

Frequency Theory: The Lowdown on Pitch   The **frequency theory**, developed by Ernest Rutherford in 1886, states that pitch is related to how fast the basilar membrane vibrates. The faster this membrane vibrates, the higher the pitch; the slower it vibrates, the lower the pitch. (In this theory, all of the auditory neurons would be firing at the same time.)

So which theory is right? It turns out that both theories are right up to a certain point. In the case of place theory, research has found that for this theory to be right, the basilar membrane has to vibrate unevenly—which it does when the frequency of the sound is *above* 1,000 Hz. For the frequency theory to be correct, the neurons associated with the hair cells would have to fire as fast as the basilar membrane vibrates. This only works up to 1,000 Hz, because neurons simply can't fire any faster than 1,000 times per second.

The frequency theory works for low pitches, and place theory works for moderate to high pitches. Is there another explanation? Yes, and it is the **volley principle**, which accounts for pitches from about 400 Hz up to about 4000 Hz (Breedlove et al., 2007; Klein & Thorne, 2007). In this explanation, groups of auditory neurons take turns firing in a process called volleying. If a person hears a tone of about 3000 Hz, it means that three groups of neurons have taken turns sending the message to the brain—the first group for the first 1000 Hz, the second group for the next 1000 Hz, and so on.

TYPES OF HEARING IMPAIRMENTS

Hearing impairment is the term used to refer to difficulties in hearing. A person can be partially hearing impaired or totally hearing impaired, and the treatment for hearing loss will vary according to the reason for the impairment.

3.5   Why are some people unable to hear, and how can their hearing be improved?

Conduction Hearing Impairment   *Conduction hearing impairment* means that sound vibrations cannot be passed from the eardrum to the cochlea. The cause might be a damaged eardrum or damage to the bones of the middle ear (usually from an infection). In this kind of impairment, hearing aids may be of some use in restoring hearing.

Nerve Hearing Impairment   In *nerve hearing impairment*, the problem lies either in the inner ear or in the auditory pathways and cortical areas of the brain. Normal aging causes loss of hair cells in the cochlea, and exposure to loud noises can damage hair cells. *Tinnitus* is a fancy word for an extremely annoying ringing in one's ears, and it can also be caused by infections or loud noises—including loud music in headphones, so you might want to turn down that music player!

AP*   Explain common sensory disorders.

pitch   psychological experience of sound that corresponds to the frequency of the sound waves; higher frequencies are perceived as higher pitches.

place theory   theory of pitch that states that different pitches are experienced by the stimulation of hair cells in different locations on the organ of Corti.

frequency theory   theory of pitch that states that pitch is related to the speed of vibrations in the basilar membrane.

volley principle   theory of pitch that states that frequencies from about 400 Hz to 4000 Hz cause the hair cells (auditory neurons) to fire in a volley pattern, or take turns in firing.

Because the damage is to the nerves or the brain, nerve hearing impairment cannot be helped with ordinary hearing aids, which are basically sound amplifiers. A new technique for restoring hearing to those with nerve hearing impairment makes use of an electronic device called a *cochlear implant*. This device bypasses the outer and middle ears by sending signals from a microphone worn behind the ear to a sound processor worn on the belt or in a pocket, which then translates those signals into electrical stimuli that are sent to a series of electrodes implanted directly into the cochlea, allowing transduction to take place and stimulating the auditory nerve. (See Figure 3.10.)

a.

b.

Figure 3.10 Cochlear Implant

(a) In a cochlear implant, a microphone implanted just behind the ear picks up sound from the surrounding environment. A speech processor, attached to the implant and worn outside the body, selects and arranges the sound picked up by the microphone. The implant itself is a transmitter and receiver, converting the signals from the speech processor into electrical impulses that are collected by the electrode array in the cochlea and then sent to the brain. (b) This child is able to hear with the help of a cochlear implant. Hearing spoken language during the early years of a child's life helps in the development of the child's own speech.

((•● **Listen** to the Psychology in the News podcast. **www.mypsychlab.com**

The brain then processes the electrode information as sound. With an implant, people can hear others' speech and their own speech to a degree that allows more communication with others. ((•●⎡**Listen** on **MyPsychLab**

3.4–5

The Hearing Sense

- **sound**
  - has psychological properties
    - **volume** —⎡larger wave amplitudes associated with louder volume
    - **frequency or pitch** —⎡shorter wavelengths = more waves per second = higher frequencies
    - **timbre** —⎡increase in number of sounds results in greater richness
  - is a physical stimulus
    - comprised of sound waves
      - have wavelengths and wavelike properties that can be measured
      - result in vibrations of air molecules
    - processed by the ear
      - **outer ear**
      - **middle ear**
      - **inner ear**
    - processing can be impaired

PRACTICE **QUIZ:** PREPARING FOR THE AP* EXAM

ANSWERS ON PAGE AK-1.

Directions: Read each of the questions or incomplete sentences below. Then choose the response that best answers the question or completes the sentence.

1. Which of the following properties of sound is most similar to the color or hue of light?
   a. Pitch
   b. Volume
   c. Purity
   d. Timbre
   e. Clarity

2. Which of the following represents the correct path of sound through the ear?
   a. Basilar membrane, auditory canal, hammer, anvil, stirrup, cochlea, auditory nerve
   b. Basilar membrane, hammer, anvil, stirrup, tympanic membrane, organ of Corti
   c. Tympanic membrane, basilar membrane, hammer, anvil, stirrup, organ of Corti
   d. Tympanic membrane, organ of Corti, hammer, anvil, stirrup, cochlea, eardrum
   e. Tympanic membrane, hammer, anvil, stirrup, cochlea, basilar membrane, auditory nerve

3. Which theory explains how we hear sounds above 4,000 Hz?
   a. Place theory
   b. Volley theory
   c. Adaptive theory
   d. Frequency theory
   e. Conduction theory

4. If the bones of Shawndra's middle ear begin to deteriorate, Shawndra will most likely develop a _____.
   a. nerve hearing impairment
   b. tinnitus hearing impairment
   c. conduction hearing impairment
   d. stimulation hearing impairment
   e. brain pathway hearing impairment

5. Which of the following would be the most effective treatment for someone suffering from nerve hearing impairment?
   a. A tinnitus amplification device (TAD)
   b. A cochlear implant
   c. A standard hearing aid
   d. An ossicular boosting implant (OBI)
   e. There is no effective way to help restore the hearing of someone with nerve hearing impairment.

Chemical Senses: It Tastes Good, but It Smells Terrible

3.6 How do the senses of taste and smell work, and how are they alike?

The sense of taste (taste in food, not taste in clothing or friends) and the sense of smell are very closely related. Have you ever noticed that when your nose is all stopped up, your sense of taste is affected, too? That's because the sense of taste is really a combination of taste and smell. Without the input from the nose, there are actually only four, and possibly five, kinds of taste sensors in the mouth.

GUSTATION: HOW WE TASTE THE WORLD

Taste Buds   *Taste buds* are the common name for the taste receptor cells, special kinds of neurons found in the mouth that are responsible for the sense of taste, or **gustation**. Most taste buds are located on the tongue, but there are a few on the roof of the mouth, the cheeks, and under the tongue as well. How sensitive people are to various tastes depends on how many taste buds they have; some people have only around 500, whereas others have 20 times that number. The latter are called "supertasters" and need far less seasoning in their food than those with fewer taste buds (Bartoshuk, 1993).

So taste buds are those little bumps I can see when I look closely at my tongue?

No, those "bumps" are called *papillae*, and the taste buds line the walls of these papillae. (See Figure 3.11.)

Each taste bud has about 20 receptors that are very similar to the receptor sites on receiving neurons at the synapse. ⓛⓘⓝⓚ *to Chapter Two: The Biological Perspective pp. 53–54.* In fact, the receptors on taste buds work exactly like receptor sites on neurons—they receive molecules of various substances that fit into the receptor like a key into a lock. Taste is often called a chemical sense because it works with the molecules of foods people eat in the same way the neural receptors work with neurotransmitters. When the molecules (dissolved in saliva) fit into the receptors, a signal is fired to the brain, which then interprets the taste sensation.

gustation   the sensation of a taste.

◄ So taste buds are those little bumps I can see when I look closely at my tongue?

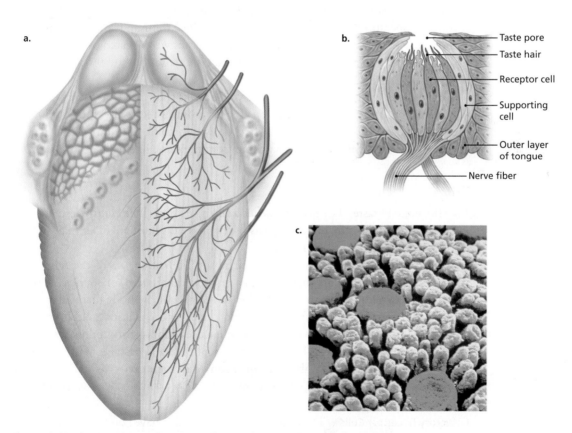

Figure 3.11 The Tongue and Taste Buds—A Crosscut View of the Tongue

(a) The right side of this drawing shows the nerves in the tongue's deep tissue. (b) The taste bud is located inside the papillae and is composed of small cells that send signals to the brain when stimulated by molecules of food. (c) Microphotograph of the surface of the tongue, showing two different sizes of papillae. The taste buds are located under the surface of the larger red papillae, whereas the smaller and more numerous papillae form a touch-sensitive rough surface that helps in chewing and moving food around the mouth.

> **What happens to the taste buds when I burn my tongue? Do they repair themselves? I know when I have burned my tongue, I can't taste much for a while, but the taste comes back.**

What happens to the taste buds when I burn my tongue? Do they repair themselves? I know when I have burned my tongue, I can't taste much for a while, but the taste comes back.

Actually, in general, the taste receptors get such a workout that they have to be replaced every 10 to 14 days (McLaughlin & Margolskee, 1994). And when the tongue is burned, the damaged cells no longer work. As time goes on, those cells get replaced and the taste sense comes back. Ever wonder why some people make a point of cleaning their tongue? The coating that people get on their tongue is no doubt partly composed of dead taste cells.

The Five Basic Tastes   In 1916 a German psychologist named Hans Henning proposed that there are four primary tastes: sweet, sour, salty, and bitter. In 1996, Lindemann supported the idea that there is a fifth kind of taste receptor that detects a pleasant "brothy" taste associated with foods like chicken soup, tuna, kelp, cheese, and soy products, among others. Lindemann proposed that this fifth taste be called *umami*, a Japanese word first coined in 1908 by Dr. Kikunae Ikeda of Tokyo Imperial University to describe the taste. Dr. Ikeda had succeeded in isolating the substance in kelp that generated the sensation of umami—glutamate (Beyreuther et al., 2007). (L I N K) *to Chapter Two: The Biological Perspective, p. 56.* Glutamate exists not only in the foods listed earlier, but is also present in human breast milk and is the reason that the seasoning MSG—monosodium *glutamate*—adds a pleasant flavor to foods.

The five taste sensations work together, along with the sense of smell and the texture, temperature, and "heat" of foods, to produce thousands of taste sensations. Although researchers used to believe that certain tastes were located on certain places on the tongue, it is now known that all of the taste sensations are processed all over the tongue (Bartoshuk, 1993).

Have you ever noticed that when you have a cold, food tastes really bland? Everything becomes bland because you can taste only sweet, salty, bitter, sour, and umami—and because your nose is stuffed up with a cold, you don't get all the enhanced variations of those tastes that come from the sense of smell.

THE SENSE OF SCENTS: OLFACTION

Like the sense of taste, the sense of smell is a chemical sense. The ability to smell odors is called **olfaction,** or the **olfactory sense**. (It's pretty easy to remember that, because "old factories" really smell, don't they?)

People don't actually smell with their noses. The outer part of the nose serves the same purpose for odors that the pinna and ear canal serve for sounds: Both are merely ways to get the sensory information to the part of the body that will translate it into neural signals. So the external nose, like the outer ear, is just a collection device.

The part of the olfactory system that transduces odors—turns odors into signals the brain can understand—is located at the top of the nasal passages. This area of olfactory receptor cells is only about an inch square in each cavity yet contains about 10 million olfactory receptors. (See Figure 3.12.) ◉┤Watch on **MyPsychLab**

◉ **Watch** a video on olfactory and hearing senses. **www.mypsychlab.com**

Olfactory Receptor Cells   The *olfactory receptor cells* each have about a half dozen to a dozen little "hairs" that project into the cavity. These "hairs" are called *cilia*. Like taste buds, there are receptor sites on these hair cells that send signals to the brain when stimulated by the molecules of substances that are in the air moving past them.

olfaction (olfactory sense)   the sensation of smell.

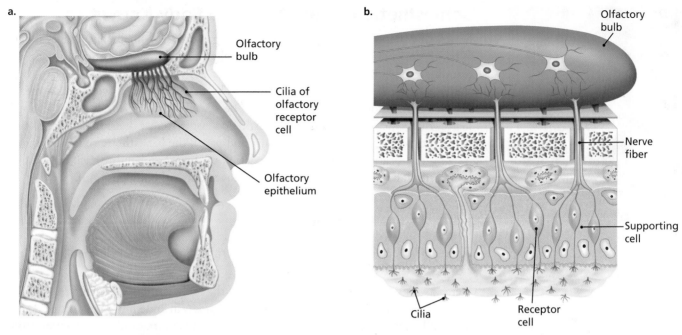

Figure 3.12 The Olfactory Receptors

(a) A cross section of the nose and mouth. This drawing shows the nerve fibers inside the nasal cavity that carry information about smell directly to the olfactory bulb just under the frontal lobe of the brain (shown in green). (b) A diagram of the cells in the nose that process smell. The olfactory bulb is on top. Notice the cilia, tiny hairlike cells that project into the nasal cavity. These are the receptors for the sense of smell.

Wait a minute—you mean that when I can smell something like a skunk, there are little particles of skunk odor IN my nose?

Yes. When a person is sniffing something, the sniffing serves to move molecules of whatever the person is trying to smell into the nose and into the nasal cavities. That's okay when it's the smell of baking bread, apple pie, flowers, and the like, but when it's skunk, rotten eggs, dead animals—well, try not to think about it too much.

Olfactory receptors are like taste buds in another way, too. Olfactory receptors also have to be replaced as they naturally die off, about every 5 to 8 weeks. Unlike the taste buds, there are more than five types of olfactory receptors. In fact, there are at least 1,000 of them.

You might remember from Chapter Two that signals from the olfactory receptors in the nasal cavity do not follow the same path as the signals from all the other senses. Vision, hearing, taste, and touch all go through lower brain centers to the area of the cortex that processes that particular sensory information. But the sense of smell has its own special place in the brain—the olfactory bulbs.

The Olfactory Bulbs The **olfactory bulbs** are located right on top of the sinus cavity on each side of the brain directly beneath the frontal lobes. (Refer back to Figure 3.12.) The olfactory receptors send their neural signals directly up to these bulbs, bypassing the thalamus, the relay center for all other senses. Ⓛ Ⓘ Ⓝ Ⓚ *to Chapter Two: The Biological Perspective, pp. 70–71.*

Remember when sensory adaptation was covered earlier in the chapter? The text stated that certain sensory receptors become less sensitive to a constant stimulus as time goes by, so that eventually a person no longer perceives the stimulus. This adaptation is why people don't continue to smell the odor of the kitchen garbage can after being home for a while—thank goodness!

◄ Wait a minute—you mean that when I can smell something like a skunk, there are little particles of skunk odor IN my nose?

olfactory bulbs areas of the brain located just above the sinus cavity and just below the frontal lobes that receive information from the olfactory receptor cells.

Her sense of touch is allowing this blind girl to "read" a Braille book with her fingers. The fingertips are extremely sensitive to fine differences in texture, allowing her to distinguish between small dots representing the different letters of the alphabet.

How exactly does pain work? Why is it that sometimes I feel pain deep ▶ inside? Are there pain receptors there, too?

somesthetic senses the body senses consisting of the skin senses, the kinesthetic sense, and the vestibular senses.

skin senses the sensations of touch, pressure, temperature, and pain.

kinesthetic sense sense of the location of body parts in relation to the ground and each other.

vestibular senses the sensations of movement, balance, and body position.

Somesthetic Senses: What the Body Knows

So far, this chapter has covered vision, hearing, taste, and smell. That leaves touch. What is thought of as the sense of touch is really several sensations, originating in several different places in—and on—the body. It's really more accurate to refer to these as the body senses, or **somesthetic senses**. The first part of that word, *soma*, means "body," as mentioned in Chapter Two. The second part, *esthetic*, means "feeling," hence, the name. There are three somesthetic sense systems, the **skin senses** (having to do with touch, pressure, temperature, and pain), the **kinesthetic sense** (having to do with the location of body parts in relation to the ground and to each other), and the **vestibular senses** (having to do with movement and body position).

PERCEPTION OF TOUCH, PRESSURE, AND TEMPERATURE

3.7   What allows people to experience the sense of touch, pain, motion, and balance?

Here's a good trivia question: What organ of the body is about 20 square feet in size? The answer is the skin. Skin is an organ. Its purposes include more than simply keeping bodily fluids in and germs out; skin also receives and transmits information from the outside world to the central nervous system (specifically, to the somatosensory cortex). ⬤ⓛⓘⓝⓚ *to Chapter Two: The Biological Perspective, pp. 73–74.* Information about light touch, deeper pressure, hot, cold, and even pain is collected by special receptors in the skin's layers.

Types of Sensory Receptors in the Skin   There are about half a dozen different receptors in the layers of the skin. (See Figure 3.13.) Some of them will respond to only one kind of sensation. For example, the *Pacinian corpuscles* are just beneath the skin and respond to changes in pressure. There are nerve endings that wrap around the ends of the hair follicles, a fact people may be well aware of when they tweeze their eyebrows, or when someone pulls their hair. These nerve endings are sensitive to both pain and touch. There are *free nerve endings* just beneath the uppermost layer of the skin that respond to changes in temperature and to pressure—and to pain.

How exactly does pain work? Why is it that sometimes I feel pain deep inside? Are there pain receptors there, too?

Yes, there are pain nerve fibers in the internal organs as well as receptors for pressure. How else would people have a stomachache or intestinal* pain? Or get that full feeling of pressure when they've eaten too much or their bladder is full?

There are actually different types of pain. There are receptors that detect pain (and pressure) in the organs, a type of pain called *visceral pain.* But pain sensations in the skin, muscles, tendons, and joints are carried on large nerve fibers and are called *somatic pain.* Somatic pain is the body's warning system that something is being, or is about to be, damaged and tends to be sharp and fast. Another type of somatic pain is carried on small nerve fibers and is slower and more of a general ache. This somatic pain acts as a kind of reminder system, keeping people from further injury by reminding them that the body has already been damaged. For example, if you hit your thumb with a hammer, the immediate pain sensation is of the first kind—sharp, fast, and bright. But later the bruised tissue simply aches, letting you know to take it easy on that thumb.

---

*Intestinal: having to do with the tubes in the body that digest food and process waste material.

People may not like pain, but the function it serves as a warning system is vitally important. There are people who are born without the ability to feel pain, rare conditions called *congenital analgesia* and *congenital insensitivity to pain with anhidrosis (CIPA)*. Children with these disorders cannot feel pain when they cut or scrape themselves, leading to an increased risk of infection when the cut goes untreated (Mogil, 1999). They fear nothing—which can be a horrifying trial for the parents and teachers of such a child. These disorders affect the neural pathways that carry pain, heat, and cold sensations. (Those with CIPA have an additional disruption in the body's heat/cold sensing perspiration system [anhidrosis], so that the person is unable to cool off the body by sweating.)

A condition called *phantom limb pain* occurs when a person who has had an arm or leg removed sometimes "feels" pain in the missing limb (Nikolajsen & Jensen, 2001; Woodhouse, 2005). As many as 50 to 80 percent of people who have had amputations experience various sensations: burning, shooting pains, or pins and needles sensations where the amputated limb used to be. Once believed to be a psychological problem, some now believe that it is caused by the traumatic injury to the nerves during amputation (Ephraim et al., 2005). ❋ Explore on MyPsychLab

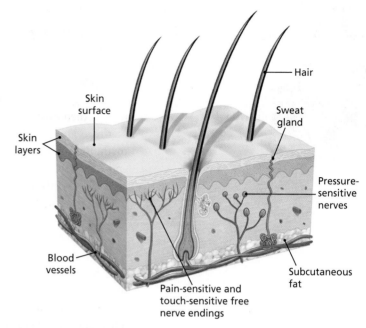

Figure 3.13 Cross Section of the Skin and Its Receptors
The skin is composed of several types of cells that process pain, pressure, and temperature. Some of these cells are wrapped around the ends of the hairs on the skin and are sensitive to touch on the hair itself, whereas others are located near the surface and still others just under the top layer of tissue.

PAIN: GATE-CONTROL THEORY

The best current explanation for how the sensation of pain works is called *gate-control theory*, first proposed by Melzack and Wall (1965) and later refined and expanded (Melzack & Wall, 1996). In this theory, the pain signals must pass through a "gate" located in the spinal cord. The activity of the gate can be closed by nonpain signals coming into the spinal cord from the body and by signals coming from the brain. The gate is not a physical structure but instead represents the relative balance in neural activity of cells in the spinal cord that receive information from the body and then send information to the brain.

Stimulation of the pain receptor cells releases a chemical called *substance P* (for pain, naturally). Substance P released into the spinal cord activates other neurons that send their messages through spinal gates (opened by the pain signal). From the spinal cord, the message goes to the brain, activating cells in the thalamus, somatosensory cortex, areas of the frontal lobes, and the limbic system in the process called transduction. The brain then interprets the pain information and sends signals that either open the spinal gates farther, causing a greater experience of pain, or close them, dampening the pain. Of course, this decision by the brain is influenced by the psychological aspects of the pain-causing stimulus. Anxiety, fear, and helplessness intensify pain, whereas laughter, distraction, and a sense of control can diminish it. (This is why people might bruise themselves and not know it if they were concentrating on something else.) Pain can also be affected by competing signals from other skin senses, which is why rubbing a sore spot can reduce the feeling of pain.

Those same psychological aspects can also influence the release of the *endorphins*, the body's natural version of morphine. ⓛⓘⓝⓚ *to Chapter Two: The Biological Perspective, pp. 56–57.* Endorphins can inhibit the transmission of pain signals in the brain, and in the spinal cord they can inhibit the release of substance P. As

❋ **Explore** the condition of Phantom limb pain. **www.mypsychlab.com**

Congenital insensitivity to pain with anhidrosis (CIPA) is a rare genetic disorder that makes 5-year-old Ashlyn unable to feel pain. She must be examined carefully for scrapes and cuts after recess at school because she cannot feel when she hurts herself, putting her at risk for infection. What are some of the problems that Ashlyn and her parents may face as she grows older?

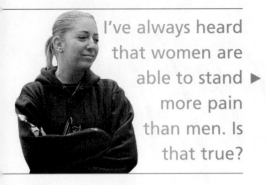

I've always heard that women are able to stand ▶ more pain than men. Is that true?

discussed in the section on neurotransmitters in Chapter Two, the release of endorphins is perhaps one explanation for "runner's high" (the pleasurable feeling a runner may experience after running a long distance) and the effectiveness of acupuncture.

I've always heard that women are able to stand more pain than men. Is that true?

The statement that women are better able to tolerate higher levels of pain than are men is a generalization that has no basis in fact—and most likely comes from the idea that women experience the pain of labor and childbirth. Some people also have heard that men are very childish about pain and do not cope well with pain, but that is also a myth. Research has shown that women apparently feel pain more intensely than do men, and they also report pain more often than men do (Chesterton et al., 2003; Faucett et al., 1994; Norrbrink et al., 2003). Men have been shown to cope better with many kinds of pain, possibly because men are often found to have a stronger belief than women that they can control their pain by their own efforts (Jackson et al., 2002).

THE KINESTHETIC SENSE

The receptors located in the skin, joints, muscles, and tendons, mentioned in the discussion of pain, are part of the body's sense of position in space—the location of the arms, legs, and so forth in relation to one another and in relation to the ground. This sense is called *kinesthesia*, from the Greek words *kinein* ("to move") and *aesthesis* ("sensation"). When you close your eyes and raise your hand above your head, you know where your hand is because the proprioceptors tell you about the changes in pressure within the muscles.

If you have ever gotten sick from traveling in a moving vehicle, you might be tempted to blame these proprioceptors. Actually, it's not the proprioceptors in the body that make people get sick. The culprits are special structures in the ear that make up the *vestibular sense*—the sense of balance.

THE VESTIBULAR SENSE

The name of this particular sense comes from a Latin word that means "entrance" or "chamber." The latter definition is probably the one that fits better here, as the structures for this sense are located in the innermost chamber of the ear. There are two kinds of vestibular organs, the otolith organs and the semicircular canals.

The *otolith organs* are tiny sacs found just above the cochlea. These sacs contain a gelatin-like fluid within which tiny crystals are suspended (much like pieces of fruit in a bowl of Jello®). The head moves and the crystals cause the fluid to vibrate, setting off some tiny hairlike receptors on the inner surface of the sac, telling the person that he or she is moving forward, backward, sideways, or up and down. (It's pretty much the way the cochlea works but with movement as the stimulus instead of sound vibrations.)

The *semicircular canals* are three somewhat circular tubes that are also filled with fluid and will stimulate hairlike receptors when rotated. There are three tubes so that there is one in each of the three planes of motion. Remember learning in geometry class about the *x*-, *y*-, and *z*-axes? Those are the three planes through which the body can rotate, and when it does, it sets off the receptors in these canals. Ever spin around and around like a top when you were a kid? When you stopped, the fluid in the horizontal canal was still rotating and making you feel dizzy because your body was telling you that you were still moving, but your eyes were telling you that you had stopped.

This tightrope-walking violinist is performing an amazing feat of coordination and muscular control. He must not only use his vestibular organs to help maintain his balance, but also his kinesthetic sense to be aware of exactly where each foot is in relation to the rope.

Motion Sickness   This disagreement between what the eyes say and what the body says is pretty much what causes *motion sickness*, the tendency to get nauseated when in a moving vehicle, especially one with an irregular movement. Normally, the vestibular sense coordinates with the other senses. But for some people, the information from the eyes may conflict a little too much with the vestibular organs, and dizziness, nausea, and disorientation are the result. This explanation of motion sickness is known as **sensory conflict theory** (Oman, 1990; Reason & Brand, 1975). Actually, people can probably blame the dizziness for the nausea—in human evolutionary history, many poisons make a person dizzy, and the most adaptive thing to do is to expel the poison. So although there isn't any poison in a case of motion sickness, the person may "expel" something anyway (Treisman, 1977).

One way some people overcome motion sickness is to focus on a distant point or object. This provides visual information to the person about how he or she is moving, bringing the sensory input into agreement with the visual input. This is also how ballerinas and ice skaters manage not to get sick when turning rapidly and repeatedly—they focus their eyes at least once on some fixed object every so many turns.

Astronauts, who travel in low gravity conditions, can get a related condition called space motion sickness (SMS). This affects about 60 percent of those who travel in space, typically for about the first week of space travel. After that time of adaptation, the astronauts are able to adapt and the symptoms diminish. Repeated exposure to some environment that causes motion sickness—whether it is space, a car, a train, or some other vehicle—is actually one of the best ways to overcome the symptoms (Hu & Stern, 1999).

sensory conflict theory   an explanation of motion sickness in which the information from the eyes conflicts with the information from the vestibular senses, resulting in dizziness, nausea, and other physical discomfort.

3.6   3.7

smell/olfaction —
- called a chemical sense because substance molecules are suspended in the air, carried to the nasal cavity, and fit into receptor sites
- nose serves as a collection device
- unique in that signals do not first travel to the thalamus before going to the brain

Chemical Senses

taste/gustation —
- made possible largely through the role of taste buds (taste receptor cells)
- five basic tastes (receptor types) —
  - sweet
  - sour
  - salty
  - bitter
  - umami
- called a chemical sense because food molecules dissolve in saliva, which then fits into receptor sites

Somesthetic Senses

skin senses — processed by the skin
- is an organ—receives and transmits information from the outside world to the somatosensory cortex of the brain
- sensitive to touch, pressure, temperature — **pain**

kinesthetic sense — processed by proprioceptive receptors in skin, joints, muscles, and tendons

vestibular sense — processed by vestibular organs
- convey information about movement and body position
- found in the inner ear —
  - **otolith organs**
  - **semicircular canals**
- responsible for motion sickness

(continued)

PRACTICE **QUIZ:** PREPARING FOR THE AP* EXAM

ANSWERS ON PAGE AK-1.

Directions: Read each of the questions or incomplete sentences below. Then choose the response that best answers the question or completes the sentence.

1. How are receptor sites on neurons similar to taste receptor cells?
   a. They line the walls of small bumps known as papillae
   b. They are only able to identify and process taste sensations
   c. They are located on the postsynaptic membrane of a neuron
   d. They are located on the tongue and on the roof of the mouth
   e. They receive molecules of substances that fit into the receptors

2. After some time has passed, you can no longer smell the odor of wet paint that you noticed when you first walked into your classroom. Which is the most likely reason for this?
   a. The smell has gone away
   b. You have adapted to the smell
   c. Your olfactory bulbs have failed
   d. Your olfactory receptor cells have died off
   e. You do not have as many cilia as other people do

3. Pain sensations in the skin, muscles, tendons, and joints that are carried on large nerve fibers are called _____.
   a. visceral pain
   b. somatic pain
   c. referred pain
   d. phantom pain
   e. indigenous pain

4. In gate-control theory, substance P _____.
   a. activates neurons that send their messages through spinal gates
   b. dampens the experience of pain
   c. consists primarily of endorphins
   d. stimulates the pain receptor cells
   e. reduces anxiety and helplessness

5. A bowl of gelatin with fruit in it will wiggle more than if it contained no fruit. Which of the following structures works in a similar manner?
   a. Taste buds
   b. Proprioceptors
   c. Otolith organs
   d. Olfactory bulbs
   e. Semicircular canals

The ABCs of Perception

3.8 What are perception and perceptual constancies?

Perception is the method by which the brain takes all the sensations people experience at any given moment and allows them to be interpreted in some meaningful fashion. Perception has some individuality to it—no two people will perceive the world in exactly the same way. Two people might be looking at a cloud, for example, and while one thinks it's shaped like a horse, the other thinks it's more like a cow. They both *see* the same cloud, but they *perceive* that cloud differently. As individual as perception might be, there are some similarities in how people perceive the world around them. The following section discusses some of the basic principles of visual perception.

THE ROLE OF ATTENTION

What would the world be like if you could pay constant attention to every noise, sight, feeling, and smell around you? Think about what it would be like to read this book while paying attention to all the sensations in your environment: On the page in front of you, you see words, but you also see the white spaces between the lines and in the margins. The book's cover feels smooth against your fingertips; the chair you're sitting in is digging into your back. You can hear the pages crinkling, the traffic outside, the noise of the dishwasher, your parents talking in the next room, your dog panting, your computer humming, your own heartbeat. You are aware of each breath you take. In a world like this, you'd be so distracted that it would be hard to get any reading done!

Luckily for all of us, we are able to use our powers of attention to focus on certain stimuli in our environment and ignore the rest. When you read a book, you don't hear the noise of the traffic outside because you are choosing not to pay attention to it. In other words, although your ears are sensing the sounds of the traffic, your brain is not perceiving those sounds.

Sometimes, we choose where to direct our attention. If your friend is talking to you while you're trying to read, you can choose to listen to your friend, or you can choose to

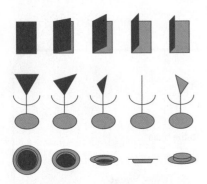

Figure 3.14 Shape Constancy

Three examples of shape constancy are shown here. The opening door is actually many different shapes, yet we still see it as basically a rectangular door. We do the same thing with a triangle and a circle—although when we look at them from different angles they cast differently shaped images on our retina, we experience them as a triangle and a circle because of shape constancy.

AP* Discuss the role of attention in behavior. ▶

perception the method by which the sensations experienced at any given moment are interpreted and organized in some meaningful fashion.

ignore her and pay attention to your book instead. Other times, however, our attention is grabbed by a particularly unusual stimulus. If you're taking the bus, you might not process the familiar noise of the bus's brakes or the usual bus-station smell, but you'll most definitely pay attention to that bright orange elephant sitting across from you!

Whether we focus our attention on an object or sensation willingly or unwillingly, the simple act of paying attention is the first step in the process of perception.

THE CONSTANCIES: SIZE, SHAPE, AND BRIGHTNESS

There's an old cartoon that shows a very large man speaking to a very small man. He's saying, "Excuse me for shouting—I thought you were much farther away." This cartoon makes use of the concept of a perceptual constancy* for size. **Size constancy** is the tendency to interpret an object as always being the same size, regardless of its distance from the viewer (or the size of the image it casts on the retina). So if an object that is normally perceived to be about 6 feet tall appears very small on the retina, it will be interpreted as being very far away.

Another perceptual constancy is the tendency to interpret the shape of an object as constant, even when it changes on the retina. This **shape constancy** is why a person still perceives a coin as a circle even if it is held at an angle that makes it appear to be an oval on the retina. Dinner plates on a table are also seen as round, even though from the angle of viewing they are oval. (See Figure 3.14.)

The third form of perceptual constancy is called **brightness constancy**, the tendency to perceive the apparent brightness of an object as the same even when the light conditions change. If a person is wearing black pants and a white shirt, for example, in broad daylight the shirt will appear to be much brighter than the pants. But if the sun is covered by thick clouds, even though the pants and shirt have less light to reflect than previously, the shirt will still appear to be just as much brighter than the pants as before—because the different amount of light reflected from each piece of clothing is still the same difference as before (Zeki, 2001).

THE GESTALT PRINCIPLES

Remember the discussion of the Gestalt theorists in Chapter One? Those scientists were studying the very same concepts that we are discussing here, the common elements of human perception. Their original focus can still be seen in certain basic principles today, such as based on the idea that people have a natural tendency to force patterns onto whatever they see. Following are some of the basic principles of this tendency to group objects and perceive whole shapes.

3.9 What are the Gestalt principles of perception?

Figure–Ground Relationships   Take a look at the drawing of the cube in Figure 3.15. Which face of the cube is in the front? Look again—do the planes and corners of the cube seem to shift as you look at it?

This is called the Necker cube. It has been around officially since 1832, when a Swiss scientist who was studying the structure of crystals first drew it in his published papers. The problem with this cube is that there are conflicting sets of depth cues, so the viewer is never really sure which plane or edge is in the back and which is in the front—the visual presentation of the cube seems to keep reversing its planes and edges.

A similar illusion can be seen in Figure 3.16. In this picture, the viewer can switch perception back and forth from two faces looking at each other to the outline of a goblet in the middle. Which is the figure in front and which is the background?

---

*Constancy: something that remains the same, the property of remaining stable and unchanging.

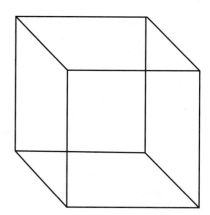

Figure 3.15 The Necker Cube
This is an example of a reversible figure. It can also be described as an ambiguous figure, since it is not clear which pattern should predominate.

AP* Describe general principles of organizing and integrating sensation to promote stable awareness of the external world.

Figure 3.16 Figure–Ground Illusion
What do you see when you look at this picture? Is it a wine goblet? Or two faces looking at each other? This is an example in which the figure and the ground seem to "switch" each time you look at the picture.

size constancy the tendency to interpret an object as always being the same actual size, regardless of its distance.

shape constancy the tendency to interpret the shape of an object as being constant, even when its shape changes on the retina.

brightness constancy the tendency to perceive the apparent brightness of an object as the same even when the light conditions change.

Figure 3.17 Gestalt Principles of Grouping

The Gestalt principles of grouping are shown here. These are the human tendency to organize isolated stimuli into groups on the basis of five characteristics: proximity, similarity, closure, continuity, and common region.

Proximity: The dots on the left can be seen as horizontal or vertical rows—neither organization dominates. But just by changing the proximity of certain dots, as in the other two examples, we experience the dots as vertical columns (middle) or horizontal rows (right).

Similarity: The similarity of color here makes you perceive these dots as forming black squares and color squares rather than two rows of black and colored dots.

Closure: Even though the lines are broken, we still see these figures as a circle and a square—an example of how we tend to "close" or "fill in" missing parts from what we know of the whole.

Continuity: Because of continuity, we are much more likely to see the figure on the left as being made up of two lines, A to B and C to D, than we are to see it as a figure made up of lines A to D and C to B or A to C and B to D.

Common Region: Similarity would suggest that people see two groups, stars and circles. But the colored backgrounds define a visible common region, and the tendency is to perceive three different groups.

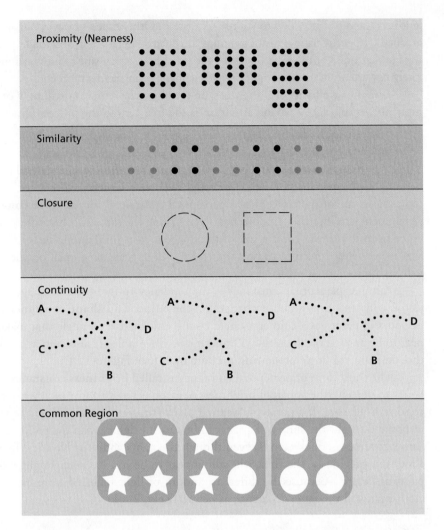

Figure–ground relationships refer to the tendency to perceive objects or figures as existing on a background. People seem to have a preference for picking out figures from backgrounds even as early as birth, and this is the first visual ability to reappear after a cataract* patient regains sight. The illusions in Figures 3.15 and 3.16 are **reversible figures**, in which the figure and the ground seem to switch back and forth.

Proximity   Another very simple rule of perception is the tendency to perceive objects that are close to one another as part of the same grouping, a principle called **proximity**, or nearness. (See Figure 3.17.)

Similarity   **Similarity** refers to the tendency to perceive things that look similar as being part of the same group. When members of a sports team wear uniforms that are all the same color, it allows people viewing the game to perceive them as one group even when they are scattered around the field or court.

Closure   **Closure** is the tendency to complete figures that are incomplete. In class, one instructor usually draws a series of curved lines, spaced an inch or so apart, in a circular pattern on the board. When students are asked what they see, they invariably say "a circle." But it isn't a circle at all—just curved lines laid out in a circular formation. The brain fills in the spaces between the arcs to perceive a circle. In the same way, a talented artist can give the impression of an entire face with just a few cleverly placed strokes of the pen or brush—the viewers fill in the details.

figure–ground the tendency to perceive objects, or figures, as existing on a background.

reversible figures visual illusions in which the figure and ground can be reversed.

proximity the tendency to perceive objects that are close to each other as part of the same grouping.

similarity the tendency to perceive things that look similar to each other as being part of the same group.

closure the tendency to complete figures that are incomplete.

---

*Cataract: a disorder in which the lens of the eye becomes cloudy.

Continuity The principle of **continuity** is easier to see than it is to explain in words. It refers to the tendency to perceive things as simply as possible with a continuous pattern rather than with a complex, broken-up pattern. Look at Figure 3.17 for an example of continuity. Isn't it much easier to see the figure on the left as two wavy lines crossing each other than as the little sections in the diagram to the right?

Contiguity **Contiguity** isn't shown in Figure 3.17 because it involves not just nearness in space but nearness in time also. Basically, contiguity is the tendency to perceive two things that happen close together in time as being related. Usually the first occurring event is seen as causing the second event. Ventriloquists* make great use of this principle. They make the vocalizations without appearing to move their own mouths but move the dummy's mouth instead. The tendency to believe that the dummy is doing the talking is due largely to contiguity.

There is one other principle of perceptual grouping that was not one of the original principles. It was added to the list (and can be seen at the bottom of Figure 3.17) by Stephen Palmer (Palmer, 1992). In *common region*, the tendency is to perceive objects that are in a common area or region as being in a group. In Figure 3.17, people could perceive the stars as one group and the circles as another on the basis of similarity. But the colored backgrounds so visibly define common regions that people instead perceive three groups—one of which has both stars and circles in it.

DEVELOPMENT OF PERCEPTION

3.10 How do infants develop perceptual abilities, including the perception of depth and its cues?

Although many of the sensory abilities of infants will take a few months to fully develop, (L I N K) *to Chapter Ten: Development Across the Life Span, pp. 399–401,* many of the perceptual abilities seem to develop rather rapidly. For example, evidence for size constancy has been found in 6-month-old infants (McKenzie et al., 1980), 4-month-olds (Day & McKenzie, 1981), and even newborns (Slater, 2001; Slater et al., 1990). In spite of its presence in newborns, researchers do not think that size constancy is fully present at birth, because in cases of people who have been blind since birth and who then have sight restored, size constancy is absent or severely limited (Gregory, 1990; Sacks, 1995). The infant may need some particular experience to maintain and further develop the size constancy aspect of perception.

Could it be that the blind people in these cases missed some kind of critical time period during which their brains needed the visual experience of seeing objects in order to develop size constancy? There are some abilities that seem to have a *critical period* for development: a time during which the infant animal or human must have a certain experience in order for that ability to develop. For example, in two classic perceptual studies, researchers Dr. Richard Held and Dr. Alan Hein of the Massachusetts Institute of Technology (Hein & Held, 1967; Held & Hein, 1963) found that kittens deprived for the first few weeks after birth of the experience of seeing their paws moving in relation to their surroundings were later unable to guide their paws to an object in plain sight—they would miss the object by reaching over it or by falling too short. Combining the image of their own paw with the location of objects in their visual experience and in relation to their bodies seems to be necessary for the proper development of this perceptual skill. The same skill develops in human infants at about 4 to 5 months of age, and it is entirely possible that there is a similar period of time for visual-motor experiences to occur.

---

*Ventriloquist: an entertainer who, through the use of misdirection and skill, makes other objects such as a dummy appear to talk.

continuity the tendency to perceive things as simply as possible with a continuous pattern rather than with a complex, broken-up pattern.

contiguity the tendency to perceive two things that happen close together in time as being related.

Watch classic video footage on Eleanor Gibson, Richard Walk, and the visual cliff. **www.mypsychlab.com**

Classic Studies in Psychology

The Visual Cliff

In the late 1950s, psychologist Eleanor Gibson was on a picnic at a local park. She was watching toddlers playing near the edge of a drop-off and began to wonder how the children knew not to step off the drop. (Most people would probably be yelling at the toddlers to get away from the cliff, but most people aren't psychologists.) This simple observation led to one of the most famous experiments in the field of developmental psychology.

Eleanor Gibson and her fellow researcher, Richard Walk, wondered if infants could perceive the world in three dimensions and thought up a way to test babies for depth perception (Gibson & Walk, 1960). They built a special table (see Figure 3.18) that had a big drop on one side. The surface of the table on both the top and the drop to the floor were covered in a patterned tablecloth, so that the different size of the patterns would be a cue for depth (remember, in size constancy, if something looks smaller, people assume it is farther away from them). The whole table was then covered by a clear glass top, so that a baby could safely be placed on or crawl across the "deep" side.

The infants tested in this study ranged from 6 months to 14 months old. They were placed on the middle of the table and then encouraged (usually by their mothers) to crawl over either the shallow side or the deep side. Most babies—81 percent—refused to crawl over the deep side, even though they could touch it with their hands and feel that it was solid. Because they were upset and seemed fearful when encouraged to crawl across the deep side, Gibson and Walk interpreted this as a very early sign of depth perception. **Watch** on **MyPsychLab**

Figure 3.18 The Visual Cliff Experiment

In the visual cliff experiment, the table has both a shallow and a "deep" side, with glass covering the entire table. When an infant looks down at the deep-appearing side, the squares in the design on the floor look smaller than the ones on the shallow side, forming a visual cue for depth. Notice that this little girl seems to be very reluctant to cross over the deep-appearing side of the table, gesturing to be picked up instead.

Glass only — Glass over patterned surface

Deep side — Shallow side

Floor pattern seen through glass

Questions for Further Discussion

1. Does the fact that 19 percent of the infants did crawl over the deep side of the visual cliff necessarily mean that those infants could not perceive the depth?

2. What other factors might explain the willingness of the 19 percent to crawl over the deep side?

3. Are there any ethical concerns in this experiment?

4. Ducks aren't bothered by the visual cliff at all—why would that be?

Another very important perceptual ability that seems to develop very early in infancy, if it is not actually present at birth, is the perception of depth. The ability to see the world in three dimensions is called **depth perception**. It's a handy ability because without it you would have a hard time judging how far away objects are. How early is depth perception developed? People who have had sight restored have almost no ability to perceive depth if they were blind from birth. Depth perception, like the constancies, seems to be present in infants at a very young age. The Classic Studies in Psychology section presents one of the most famous studies in the field of depth perception.

Of course, the youngest babies in Gibson and Walk's classic study were 6 months old, and that might be old enough to have learned depth cues. In later studies, researchers (Campos et al., 1970) were able to demonstrate depth perception in infants as young as 2 months. These researchers placed very young infants on either the deep side or the shallow side and measured their heart rate. A decreasing heart rate is associated with interest in infants, whereas an increasing rate is associated with fear. The heart rate of the infants did not alter when they were placed on the shallow side but decreased when placed on the deep side. They were interested but not afraid. The older infants in the Gibson and Walk study were old enough to have experience with falling and tumbling down, and it is probably this experience that caused them to fear the depth. Based on the reactions of the infants in the Campos study, it is very likely that the ability to perceive the world in three dimensions is more or less inborn. It is fear of depth that requires learning and experience.

There are various cues for perceiving depth in the world. Some require the use of only one eye (**monocular cues**) and some are a result of the slightly different visual patterns that exist when the visual fields* of both eyes are used (**binocular cues**).

Monocular Cues Monocular cues are often referred to as **pictorial depth cues** because artists can use these cues to give the illusion of depth to paintings and drawings. Examples of these cues are discussed next and can be seen in Figure 3.19.

1. **Linear perspective:** When looking down a long interstate highway, the two sides of the highway appear to merge together in the distance. This tendency for lines that are actually parallel to *seem* to converge** on each other is called **linear perspective**. It works in pictures because people assume that in the picture, as in real life, the converging lines indicate that the "end" of the lines are a great distance away from where the people are as they view them.

2. **Relative size:** The principle of size constancy is at work in **relative size**, when objects that people expect to be of a certain size appear to be small and are, therefore, assumed to be much farther away. Movie makers use this principle to make their small models seem gigantic but off in the distance.

3. **Overlap:** If one object seems to be blocking another object, people assume that the blocked object is behind the first one and, therefore, farther away. This cue is also known as **interposition**.

4. **Aerial (atmospheric) perspective:** The farther away an object is, the hazier the object will appear to be, a perceptual cue called **aerial (atmospheric) perspective**. This is why distant mountains often look fuzzy, and buildings far in the distance are blurrier than those that are close. At greater distances more tiny particles of dust, dirt, and other pollutants in the air can come between the object and a person's eyes, causing blurred vision.

---

*Visual field: the entire area of space visible at a given instant without moving the eyes.
**Converge: come together.

depth perception the ability to perceive the world in three dimensions.

monocular cues (pictorial depth cues) cues for perceiving depth based on one eye only.

binocular cues cues for perceiving depth based on both eyes.

linear perspective the tendency for parallel lines to appear to converge on each other.

relative size perception that occurs when objects that a person expects to be of a certain size appear to be small and are, therefore, assumed to be much farther away.

Overlap (interposition) the assumption that an object that appears to be blocking part of another object is in front of the second object and closer to the viewer.

aerial perspective the haziness that surrounds objects that are farther away from the viewer, causing the distance to be perceived as greater.

texture gradient the tendency for textured surfaces to appear to become smaller and finer as distance from the viewer increases.

motion parallax the perception of motion of objects in which close objects appear to move more quickly than objects that are farther away.

accommodation as a monocular clue, the brain's use of information about the changing thickness of the lens of the eye in response to looking at objects that are close or far away.

5. **Texture gradient:** If there are any large expanses of pebbles, rocks, or patterned roads (such as a cobblestone street) nearby, go take a look at them one day. The pebbles or bricks that are close to you are very distinctly textured, but as you look farther off into the distance, their texture becomes smaller and finer. **Texture gradient** is another trick used by artists to give the illusion of depth in a painting.

6. **Motion parallax:** The next time you're in a car, notice how the objects outside the car window seem to zip by very fast when they are close to the car, and objects in the distance, such as mountains, seem to move more slowly. This discrepancy in motion of near and far objects is called **motion parallax**.

7. **Accommodation:** A monocular cue that is not one of the pictorial cues, **accommodation** makes use of something that happens inside the eye. The lens of the human eye is flexible and held in place by a series of muscles. The discussion of the eye earlier in this chapter mentioned the process of visual accommodation as the tendency of the lens to change its shape, or thickness, in response to objects near or far away. The brain can use this information about accommodation as a cue for distance. Accommodation is also called a muscular cue.

a.

c.

b.

d.

Figure 3.19 Examples of Pictorial Depth Cues

(a) Both the lines of the trees and the sides of the road appear to come together or converge in the distance. This is an example of *linear perspective*. (b) Notice how the larger pebbles in the foreground seem to give way to smaller and smaller pebbles near the middle of the picture. *Texture gradient* causes the viewer to assume that as the texture of the pebbles gets finer, the pebbles are getting farther away. (c) In *aerial* or *atmospheric perspective*, the farther away something is the hazier it appears because of fine particles in the air between the viewer and the object. Notice that the road and farmhouse in the foreground are in sharp focus while the mountain ranges are hazy and indistinct. (d) The depth cue of *relative size* appears in this photograph. Notice that the flowers in the distance appear much smaller than those in the foreground. Relative size causes smaller objects to be perceived as farther away from the viewer.

Binocular Cues   As the name suggests, these cues require the use of two eyes.

1. **Convergence:** Another muscular cue, **convergence**, refers to the rotation of the two eyes in their sockets to focus on a single object. If the object is close, the convergence is pretty great (almost as great as crossing the eyes). If the object is far, the convergence is much less. Hold your finger up in front of your nose, and then move it away and back again. That feeling you get in the muscles of your eyes is convergence. (See Figure 3.20, left.)

2. **Binocular disparity: Binocular disparity** is a scientific way of saying that because the eyes are a few inches apart, they don't see exactly the same image. The brain interprets the images on the retina to determine distance from the eyes. If the two images are very different, the object must be pretty close. If they are almost identical, the object is far enough away to make the retinal disparity very small. You can demonstrate this cue for yourself by holding an object in front of your nose. Close one eye, note where the object is, and then open that eye and close the other. There should be quite a difference in views. But if you do the same thing with an object that is across the room, the image doesn't seem to "jump" or move nearly as much, if at all. (See Figure 3.20, right.)

In spite of all the cues for perception that exist, even the most sophisticated perceiver can still fail to perceive the world as it actually is, as the next section demonstrates.

PERCEPTUAL ILLUSIONS

You've mentioned the word illusion *several times. Exactly what are illusions, and why is it so easy to be fooled by them?*

An *illusion* is a perception that does not correspond to reality. People *think* they see something when the reality is quite different. Another way of thinking of illusions is as visual stimuli that "fool" the eye. (Illusions are different from hallucinations in that a hallucination's origin is in the brain itself—a person is seeing or hearing something that is actually not there at all. An illusion is a distorted perception of something that *is* there.)

convergence   the rotation of the two eyes in their sockets to focus on a single object, resulting in greater convergence for closer objects and lesser convergence if objects are distant.

binocular disparity   the difference in images between the two eyes, which is greater for objects that are close and smaller for distant objects.

You've mentioned the word *illusion* several ◄ times. Exactly what are illusions, and why is it so easy to be fooled by them?

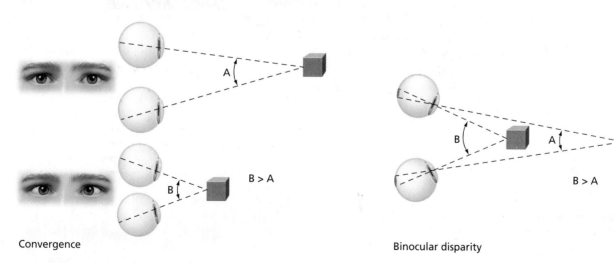

Convergence

Binocular disparity

Figure 3.20 Binocular Cues to Depth Perception

(left) Convergence is a depth cue that involves the muscles of the eyes. When objects are far away, the eye muscles are more relaxed; when objects are close, the eye muscles move together, or converge. (right) Binocular disparity. Because your eyes are separated by several centimeters, each eye sees a slightly different image of the object in front of you. In A, the object is far enough away that the difference is small. In B, while the object is closer, there is a greater difference between what each eye sees. The brain interprets this difference as the distance of the object.

Müller-Lyer illusion illusion of line length that is distorted by inward-turning or outward-turning corners on the ends of the lines, causing lines of equal length to appear to be different.

3.11 What are visual illusions, and how can they and other factors influence and alter perception?

Müller-Lyer Illusion   One of the most famous visual illusions, the **Müller-Lyer illusion**, is shown in Figure 3.21. The distortion happens when the viewer tries to determine if the two lines are exactly the same length. They are identical, but one line looks longer than the other. (It's always the line with the angles on the end facing outward.) Why is this illusion so powerful? The explanation is that most people live in a world with lots of buildings. Buildings have corners. When a person is outside a building, the corner of the building is close to that person, while the walls seem to be moving away. When the person is inside a building, the corner of the room seems to move away from the viewer while the walls are coming closer. In the illusion, the line with the angles facing inward is like the outside of the building, and the one with the angles facing outward is like the inside of the room. In their minds, people "pull" the inward-facing angles toward them like the outside corners of a building, and they make the outward-facing angles "stretch" away from them like the inside corners of the room (Enns & Coren, 1995; Gregory, 1990).

Segall and colleagues (Segall et al., 1966) found that people in Western cultures, having carpentered buildings with lots of straight lines and corners (Segall and colleagues refer to this as a "carpentered world"), are far more susceptible to this illusion than people from non-Western cultures (having round huts with few corners—an "uncarpentered world"). Gregory (1990) found that Zulus, for example, rarely see this illusion. They live in round huts arranged in circles, use curved tools and toys, and experience few straight lines and corners in their world.

The Moon Illusion   Another common illusion is the *moon illusion*, in which the moon on the horizon* appears to be much larger than the moon in the sky (Plug & Ross, 1994). One explanation for this is that the moon high in the sky is all alone, with no cues for depth surrounding it. But on the horizon, the moon appears behind trees and houses, cues for depth that make the horizon seem very far away. The moon is seen as being behind these objects and, therefore, farther away from the viewer. Because people know that objects that are farther away from them and still seem large are very large indeed, they "magnify" the moon in their minds—a misapplication of the principle of size constancy. This explanation of the moon illusion is called the *apparent distance hypothesis*. This explanation goes back to the second century A.D., first written about by the Greek-Egyptian astronomer Ptolemy and later further developed by an eleventh-century Arab astronomer, Al-Hazan (Ross & Ross, 1976).

Figure 3.21 The Müller-Lyer Illusion

(a) Which line is longer? In industrialized Western countries, people generally see the lines in part (a) in situations similar to those in part (b). According to one theory, people have become accustomed to seeing right angles in their environment and assume that the short, slanted lines are forming a right angle to the vertical line. They make that assumption because they are accustomed to seeing corners, such as the ones shown in figure (b) on the right. Consequently, in figure (b) on the left, they tend to perceive the line on the right as slightly longer than the line on the left.

a.   b.

---

*Horizon: the place where the earth apparently meets the sky.

Illusions of Motion   Sometimes people perceive an object as moving when it is really still. One example of this takes place as part of a famous experiment in conformity: the *autokinetic effect*. In this effect, a small, stationary light in a darkened room will appear to move or drift because there are no surrounding cues to indicate that the light is *not* moving. Another is the *stroboscopic motion* seen in motion pictures, in which a rapid series of still pictures will seem to be in motion. Many a student has discovered that drawing little figures on the edges of a notebook and then flipping the pages quickly will also produce this same illusion of movement.

Another movement illusion related to stroboscopic motion is the *phi phenomenon*, in which lights turned on in sequence appear to move. For example, if a light is turned on in a darkened room and then turned off, and then another light a short distance away is flashed on and off, it will appear to be one light moving across that distance. This principle is used to suggest motion in many theater marquee signs, flashing arrows indicating direction that have a series of lights going on and off in a sequence, and even in strings of decorative lighting, such as the "chasing" lights seen on houses at holiday times.

The moon illusion. When this moon is high in the night sky, it will still be the same size to the eye as it is now. Nevertheless, it is perceived to be much larger when on the horizon. In the sky, there are no objects for comparison, but on the horizon, objects such as this tree are seen as being in front of a very large moon.

FACTORS THAT INFLUENCE PERCEPTION

Human perception of the world is obviously influenced by things such as culture and misinterpretations of cues. Following are other factors that cause people to alter their perceptions.

Perceptual Sets and Expectancies   People often misunderstand what is said to them because they were expecting to hear something else. People's tendency to perceive things a certain way because their previous experiences or expectations influence them is called **perceptual set** or **perceptual expectancy**. Although expectancies can be useful in interpreting certain stimuli, they can also lead people down the wrong path. For example, look at Figure 3.22. The drawing in the middle is a little hard to identify. People who start looking at these five drawings by looking at the drawing on the far left (which is clearly a man's face) tend to see the middle drawing as a man's face. But people who start looking from the far right (where the drawing is a kneeling woman with one arm over her chest and one touching her knee) see the middle picture as a woman. What you see depends on what you expect to see.

The way in which people <u>interpret</u> what they perceive can also influence their perception. For example, people can try to understand what they perceive by using information they already have (as is the case of perceptual expectancy). But if there is no existing information that relates to the new information, they can look at each feature of what they perceive and try to put it all together into one whole.

Anyone who has ever worked on a jigsaw puzzle knows that it's a lot easier to put it together if there is a picture of the finished puzzle to act as a guide. It also helps to have worked the puzzle before—people who have done that already know what it's going to look like when it's finished. In the field of perception,

AP*   Discuss how experience and culture can influence perceptual processes.

perceptual set (perceptual expectancy) the tendency to perceive things a certain way because previous experiences or expectations influence those perceptions.

Figure 3.22 Perceptual Set
Look at the drawing in the middle. What do you see? Now look at the drawings on each end. Would you have interpreted the middle drawing differently if you had looked at the drawing of the man or the sitting woman first?

this is known as **top-down processing**—the use of preexisting knowledge to organize individual features into a unified whole. This is also a form of perceptual expectancy.

If the puzzle is one the person has never worked before or if that person has lost the top of the box with the picture on it, he or she would have to start with a small section, put it together, and keep building up the sections until the recognizable picture appears. This analysis of smaller features and building up to a complete perception is called **bottom-up processing** (Cave & Kim, 1999). In this case, there is no expectancy to help organize the perception, making bottom-up processing more difficult in some respects. Fortunately, the two types of processing are often used together in perceiving the surrounding world.

Would people of different cultures perceive objects differently because of different expectancies? Some research suggests that this is true. For example, take a look at Figure 3.23. This figure is often called the "devil's trident." Europeans and North Americans insist on making this figure three dimensional, so they have trouble looking at it—the figure is impossible if it is perceived in three dimensions. But people in less technologically oriented cultures have little difficulty with seeing or even reproducing this figure, because they see it as a two-dimensional drawing, quite literally a collection of lines and circles rather than a solid object (Deregowski, 1969). By contrast, if you give Europeans and North Americans the task of reproducing a drawing of an upside-down face, their drawings tend to be more accurate because the upside-down face has become a "collection of lines and circles." That is, they draw what they actually see in terms of light and shadow rather than what they "think" is there three dimensionally.

Figure 3.23 The Devil's Trident
At first glance, this seems to be an ordinary three-pronged figure. But a closer look reveals that the three prongs cannot be real as drawn. Follow the lines of the top prong to see what goes wrong.

top-down processing the use of pre-existing knowledge to organize individual features into a unified whole.

bottom-up processing the analysis of the smaller features to build up to a complete perception.

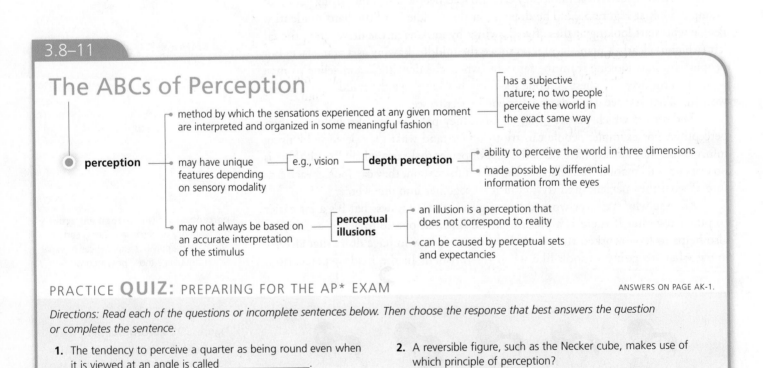

3.8–11

The ABCs of Perception

perception
- method by which the sensations experienced at any given moment are interpreted and organized in some meaningful fashion
  - has a subjective nature; no two people perceive the world in the exact same way
- may have unique features depending on sensory modality
  - e.g., vision — **depth perception**
    - ability to perceive the world in three dimensions
    - made possible by differential information from the eyes
- may not always be based on an accurate interpretation of the stimulus
  - **perceptual illusions**
    - an illusion is a perception that does not correspond to reality
    - can be caused by perceptual sets and expectancies

PRACTICE **QUIZ**: PREPARING FOR THE AP* EXAM   ANSWERS ON PAGE AK-1.

Directions: Read each of the questions or incomplete sentences below. Then choose the response that best answers the question or completes the sentence.

1. The tendency to perceive a quarter as being round even when it is viewed at an angle is called _____.
  a. contiguity
  b. shape constancy
  c. depth perception
  d. linear perspective
  e. binocular disparity

2. A reversible figure, such as the Necker cube, makes use of which principle of perception?
  a. Closure
  b. Proximity
  c. Expectancy
  d. Accommodation
  e. Figure–ground relationships

3. Which of the following is not a monocular cue for depth?

   a. Overlap   **d.** Motion parallax

   b. Convergence   **e.** Linear perspective

   c. Texture gradient

4. The first time Joe had to put together a bicycle, it took a long time. Now that he has built several bicycles, he can put together a bicycle quickly and easily. Joe's improved speed and skill can be attributed to _____.

   a. perceptual set   **d.** bottom-up processing

   b. perceptual expectancy   **e.** atmospheric perspective

   c. top-down processing

5. Tasha is waiting for her friend at the mall. She listens for the sound of her friend calling her name. She hears a word that sounds like her name and turns around, but she soon realizes that she's made a mistake: A stranger behind her was calling to his small child. Which of the following influenced Tasha's conviction that she heard her own name?

   a. Monocular cues

   b. Gestalt principles

   c. Autokinetic effect

   d. Perceptual expectancy

   e. Bottom-up processing

Applying Psychology to Everyday Life: Thinking Critically about ESP

Extrasensory perception (ESP) is usually defined as a claim of perception that occurs without the use of normal sensory channels such as sight, hearing, touch, taste, or smell. People who claim to have one or more of these abilities are commonly called "psychics." It was J. B. Rhine, a professor at Duke University, who first coined the term *ESP* in 1927 and in fact invented the field of **parapsychology**, the scientific study of ESP, ghosts, and all things that do not normally fall into the realm of ordinary psychology (Rhine, 1935). Dr. Rhine invented the Zener cards (see Figure 3.24) to test for one of the ESP abilities, telepathy.

There are supposedly several different kinds of extrasensory perception. Here's a list of the more common "abilities" that psychics are supposed to have:

1. **Telepathy.** The word literally means "distant feeling" and is commonly used to refer to the claimed ability to read another person's thoughts, or mind reading.

2. **Clairvoyance.** Literally "clear sight," this term refers to the supposed ability to "see" things that are not actually present. This ability is also claimed by many so-called psychic detectives, who believe that they can find lost objects, people, or even the bodies of murder victims by touching objects associated with the people in question.

Figure 3.24 Zener Cards

These five shapes—star, circle, cross, wavy lines, and square—are used in a test for telepathy, a form of extrasensory perception. One person (the sender) looks at each card after pulling it from a randomly shuffled deck of these five cards and thinks about the image on the card. The person being tested for telepathy, who cannot see the card, is supposed to guess what the shape is. An accuracy rate greater than chance is taken as an indication of telepathic ability.

AP* Challenge common beliefs in parapsychological phenomena.

parapsychology the study of ESP, ghosts, and other subjects that do not normally fall into the realm of ordinary psychology.

3. **Precognition.** Precognition is the supposed ability to know something in advance of its occurrence or to predict a future event. Note that precognition is often confused with clairvoyance. The difference is that in clairvoyance, what is "seen" is something that exists at the present time, whereas precognition is supposed to involve "seeing" the future.

Research has been conducted since the time of Rhine's early experiments with mixed results. Many of the earlier methodologies used in researching psychic phenomena were flawed, making their results useless (Randi, 1980, 1982). Critics and skeptics point to the lack of consistent scientific evidence and the inability to replicate experiments, both of which support the idea of ESP and other psychic abilities as fakery, fraud, and misdirection. Believers claim that ESP is a talent that does not work "on command" and is detrimentally* affected by the presence of skepticism during tests.

Is there a case for ESP, or "psi" as it is sometimes called? Here's a quote from the online *Skeptic's Dictionary* (**http://skepdic.com/esp.html**):

> *Most ESP claims do not get tested, but parapsychologists have attempted to verify the existence of ESP under controlled conditions. Some, like Charles Tart and Raymond Moody, claim success; others, such as Susan J. Blackmore, claim that years of trying to find experimental proof of ESP have failed to turn up any proof of indisputable,** repeatable psychic powers. Defenders of psi claim that the gansfeld (sic) experiments, the CIA's remote viewing experiments and attempts to influence randomizers at Princeton Engineering Anomalies Research have produced evidence of ESP. Psychologists who have thoroughly investigated parapsychological studies, like Ray Hyman and Blackmore, have concluded that where positive results have been found, the work was fraught with fraud, error, incompetence, and statistical legerdemain.† (Carroll, 2002)*

One of the most promising research techniques is the ganzfeld experiment, in which a person who is the "receiver" is placed in a room and wears special goggles (Ping-Pong balls cut in half and secured over the eyes) and earphones that produce white noise. This creates a kind of sensory deprivation. A "sender" in another room tries to mentally send images or video clips to the receiver. In one set of studies published in *Psychological Bulletin* (Bem & Honorton, 1994), these experiments seemed to produce a "hit rate" greater than that predicted by chance and were taken as evidence that some kind of mental telepathy had taken place. But later studies that examined all of the completed ganzfeld studies demonstrated that there were no consistent findings across studies, no replication, and no support for any kind of telepathy (Milton & Wiseman, 2001).

It may be that those who want very badly for there to be such a thing as extrasensory perception, like J. B. Rhine, lose the ability to think critically about the very concepts they are testing.

---

*Detrimentally: harmfully or involving damage.

**Indisputable: unquestionable, unable to be argued against.

†Legerdemain: trickery of any sort; deceit.

3 CHAPTER SUMMARY

The ABCs of Sensation

3.1 How does sensation travel through the central nervous system, and why are some sensations ignored?

- Sensation is the activation of receptors located in the eyes, ears, skin, nasal cavities, and tongue.
- Sensory receptors are specialized forms of neurons that are activated by different stimuli such as light and sound.
- A just noticeable difference is the point at which a stimulus is detectable half the time it is present.
- Weber's law of just noticeable differences states that the just noticeable difference between two stimuli is always a constant.
- Absolute thresholds are the smallest amount of energy needed for conscious detection of a stimulus at least half the time it is present.
- Subliminal stimuli are just below the level of conscious awareness but have not been shown to affect behavior in day-to-day life.
- Habituation occurs when the brain ignores a constant stimulus.
- Sensory adaptation occurs when the sensory receptors stop responding to a constant stimulus.

The Science of Seeing

3.2 What is light, and how does it travel through the various parts of the eye?

- Brightness corresponds to the amplitude of light waves, whereas color corresponds to the length of the light waves.
- Saturation is the psychological interpretation of wavelengths that are all the same (highly saturated) or varying (less saturated).
- Light enters the eye and is focused through the cornea, passes through the aqueous humor, and then through the hole in the iris muscle called the pupil.
- The lens also focuses the light on the retina, where it passes through ganglion and bipolar cells to stimulate the rods and cones.

3.3 How do the eyes see, and how do the eyes see different colors?

- Rods detect changes in brightness but do not see color and function best in low levels of light. They do not respond to different colors and are found everywhere in the retina except the center or fovea.
- Cones are sensitive to colors and work best in bright light. They are responsible for the sharpness of visual information and are found in the fovea.
- Trichromatic theory of color perception assumes three types of cones: red, green, and blue. All colors would be perceived as combinations of these three.
- Opponent-process theory of color perception assumes four primary colors of red, green, blue, and yellow. Cones are arranged in pairs, and when one member of a pair is activated, the other is not.
- Color blindness is either a total lack of color perception or color perception that is limited to yellows and blues or reds and greens only.

The Hearing Sense: Can You Hear Me Now?

3.4 What is sound, and how does it travel through the various parts of the ear?

- Sound has three aspects: pitch (frequency), loudness, and timbre (purity).
- Sound enters the ear through the visible outer structure, or pinna, and travels to the eardrum and then to the small bones of the middle ear.
- The bone called the stirrup rests on the oval window, causing the cochlea and basilar membrane to vibrate with sound.
- The organ of Corti on the basilar membrane contains the auditory receptors, which send signals to the brain about sound qualities as they vibrate.
- Place theory states that the location of the hair cells on the organ of Corti correspond to different pitches of sound. This can explain pitch above 1,000 Hz.
- Frequency theory states that the speed with which the basilar membrane vibrates corresponds to different pitches of sound. This explains pitch below 1,000 Hz.
- The volley principle states that neurons take turns firing for sounds above 400 Hz and below 4,000 Hz.

3.5 Why are some people unable to hear, and how can their hearing be improved?

- Conduction hearing impairment is caused by damage to the outer or middle ear structures, whereas nerve hearing impairment is caused by damage to the inner ear or auditory pathways in the brain.

Chemical Senses: It Tastes Good, but It Smells Terrible

3.6 How do the senses of taste and smell work, and how are they alike?

- Gustation is the sense of taste. Taste buds in the tongue receive molecules of substances, which fit into receptor sites.
- The five basic types of taste are sweet, sour, salty, bitter, and umami (brothy).
- Olfaction is the sense of smell. The olfactory receptors in the upper part of the nasal passages receive molecules of substances and create neural signals that then go to the olfactory bulbs under the frontal lobes.

Somesthetic Senses: What the Body Knows

- The somesthetic senses include the skin senses and the vestibular senses.

3.7 What allows people to experience the sense of touch, pain, motion, and balance?

- Pacinian corpuscles respond to pressure, certain nerve endings around hair follicles respond to pain and pressure, and free nerve endings respond to pain, pressure, and temperature.
- The gate-control theory of pain states that when receptors sensitive to pain are stimulated, a neurotransmitter called substance P is released into the spinal cord, activating other pain receptors by opening "gates" in the spinal column and sending the message to the brain.
- The kinesthetic senses allow the brain to know its position in space through the activity of special receptors that are responsive to pressure inside the body.

- The vestibular sense also contributes to the body's sense of spatial orientation through the activity of the otolith organs (up and down movement) and the semicircular canals (movement through arcs).
- Motion sickness is explained by sensory conflict theory, in which information from the eyes conflicts with information from the vestibular sense, causing nausea.

The ABCs of Perception

3.8 What are perception and perceptual constancies?
- Perception is the interpretation and organization of sensations.
- Size constancy is the tendency to perceive objects as always being the same size, no matter how close or far away they are.
- Shape constancy is the tendency to perceive objects as remaining the same shape even when the shape of the object changes on the retina of the eye.
- Brightness constancy is the tendency to perceive objects as a certain level of brightness, even when the light changes.

3.9 What are the Gestalt principles of perception?
- The Gestalt psychologists developed several principles of perception that involve interpreting patterns in visual stimuli. The principles are figure–ground relationships, closure, similarity, continuity, contiguity, and common region.

Classic Studies in Psychology: The Visual Cliff

3.10 How do infants develop perceptual abilities, including the perception of depth and its cues?
- Depth perception is the ability to see in three dimensions. Infants as young as 2 months can detect depth.
- Monocular cues for depth perception include linear perspective, relative size, overlap, aerial perspective, texture gradient, motion parallax, and accommodation.

- Binocular cues for depth perception include convergence and binocular overlap.

3.11 What are visual illusions, and how can they and other factors influence and alter perception?
- Illusions are perceptions that do not correspond to reality or are distortions of visual stimuli.
- The Müller-Lyer illusion involves the misperception of two lines of equal length as being different in length because of angles placed on the ends of each line.
- The moon illusion occurs when the moon appears to be larger on the horizon than high in the sky. It is explained by the apparent distance hypothesis, which involves a misinterpretation of size constancy.
- Perceptual set or expectancy refers to the tendency to perceive objects and situations in a particular way because of prior experiences.
- Top-down processing involves the use of preexisting knowledge to organize individual features into a unified whole.
- Bottom-up processing involves the analysis of smaller features, building up to a complete perception.

Applying Psychology to Everyday Life: Thinking Critically about ESP

- Extrasensory perception (ESP) is a claim of perception that occurs without the use of normal sensory channels such as sight, hearing, touch, taste, or smell.
- ESP claimed abilities include telepathy, clairvoyance, and precognition.
- Research has produced some support for ESP, but critics claim these studies were flawed. Other research has failed to find any support for the claims of ESP.

TEST YOURSELF: PREPARING FOR THE AP* EXAM

ANSWERS ON PAGE AK-1.

✔—Practice on **MyPsychLab**   **Ready for your test?** More quizzes and a customized study plan. **www.mypsychlab.com**

PART I: MULTIPLE-CHOICE QUESTIONS

Directions for Part I: Read each of the questions or incomplete sentences below. Then choose the response that best answers the question or completes the sentence.

1. You find that you have to add 1 teaspoon of sugar to a cup of coffee that already has 5 teaspoons of sugar in it to notice the difference in sweetness 50 percent of the time. If you have a cup of coffee with 10 teaspoons of sugar in it, how many teaspoons would you have to add to notice the difference in sweetness at least half of the time?
   a. 1   d. 10
   b. 2   e. 50
   c. 5

2. Which type of retinal cell forms the optic nerve?
   a. Rods   d. Bipolar cells
   b. Cones   e. Photoreceptors
   c. Ganglion cells

3. The thin membrane stretched over the opening to the inner ear is known as the _____.
   a. pinna   d. oval window
   b. stirrup   e. tympanic membrane
   c. cochlea

4. Where are the olfactory receptor cells located?
   a. Around the nostrils
   b. In the auditory passages
   c. On the roof of the mouth
   d. At the tops of the nasal passages
   e. Along the lining of the outer nose

5. Ellis turns around and around in a circle. When he stops, he feels like his head is still spinning. What is responsible for this sensation?
   a Cochlea   d. Organ of Corti
   b. Proprioceptors   e. Semicircular canals
   c. Otolith organs

6. Which Gestalt principle is at work when a ventriloquist moves a dummy's mouth while talking, making it seem like the dummy is talking?
   a. Closure   d. Continuity
   b. Similarity   e. Common region
   c. Contiguity

7. The Müller-Lyer illusion exists in cultures in which there are _____.
   a. many trees
   b. wide horizons
   c. buildings with straight lines and corners
   d. more men than women
   e. many mountains and cliffs

8. Allison opened her new jigsaw puzzle but soon realized that the puzzle pieces inside had nothing to do with the picture on the box. She completed the puzzle without knowing what the finished picture would look like. Which of the following did Allison most likely use?
   a. Precognition
   b. Perceptual set
   c. Top-down processing
   d. Bottom-up processing
   e. Perceptual expectancy

9. Which of the following people is most likely to be color blind?
   a. A man whose mother is color-blind
   b. A man whose father is color-blind
   c. A woman whose mother is color-blind
   d. A woman whose father is color-blind
   e. A man with no family history of color blindness

10. Tariq is a 4-year-old child who cannot feel pain. He hurts himself constantly, and his body cannot cool itself by sweating. Tariq is most likely suffering from _____.
    a. SMS
    b. CIPA
    c. tinnitus
    d. visceral pain
    e. congenital analgesia

PART II: FREE-RESPONSE QUESTION

Directions for Part II: Read the essay question that follows. Then, respond to the question in a clear, concise essay. Do not simply list facts. Instead, present a thorough argument based on your critical consideration of the topic. Use proper psychological terminology as necessary.

Jonah, his wife Alana, and their son Rory are on a family road trip. The trip is difficult for all of them: Jonah needs to wear glasses when he drives because he cannot see objects clearly from a distance. Alana is unable to drive because she has difficulty distinguishing red traffic lights from green traffic lights. Both Jonah and Alana complain that Rory's loud music is making their ears ring. After a few hours in the car, Rory feels nauseated and dizzy. In an essay, give detailed explanations of potential biological causes for each of the following:
   a. Jonah's poor eyesight
   b. Alana's difficulty distinguishing red from green
   c. Jonah's and Alana's ringing ears
   d. Rory's nausea and dizziness

3.1   p. 93

The ABCs of Sensation

● **sensation**
process by which information
from the outside world
enters the brain

- related to the activation of receptors in the various sense organs
- related to changes in physical stimuli

3.2–3   p. 100

● **light**

- has psychological properties
  - brightness
  - color/hue
  - saturation
- is a physical stimulus
  - is a form of electromagnetic radiation
  - processed by the eye

The Science of Seeing

● **seeing** — begins with retinal receptor cells
- rods
- cones

Pupil   Lens

Iris

Retina

Fovea

Light

Cornea

Optic nerve

Blind spot (optic disc)

Blood vessels

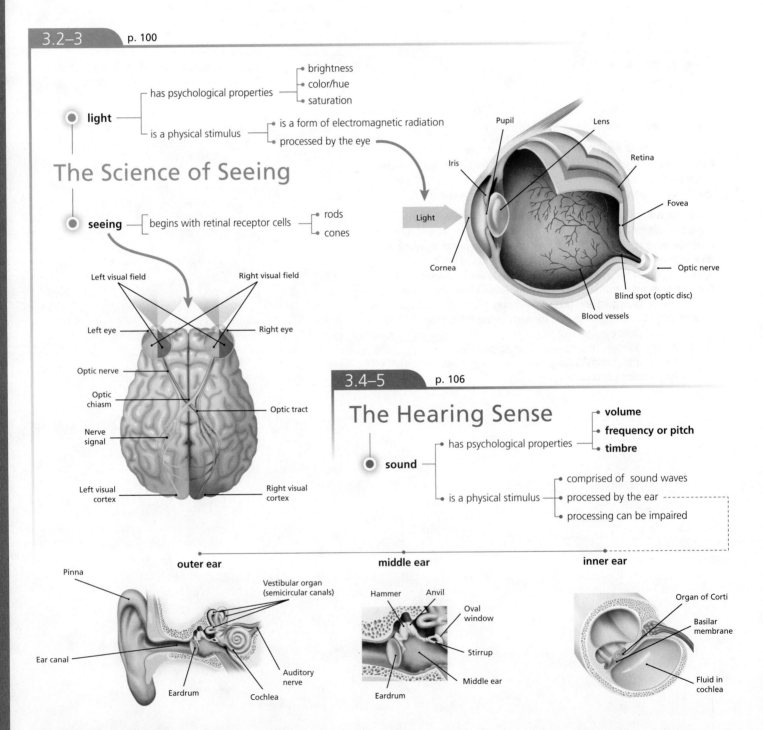

Left visual field   Right visual field

Left eye   Right eye

Optic nerve

Optic chiasm

Optic tract

Nerve signal

Left visual cortex   Right visual cortex

3.4–5   p. 106

The Hearing Sense

● **sound**

- has psychological properties
  - **volume**
  - **frequency or pitch**
  - **timbre**
- is a physical stimulus
  - comprised of sound waves
  - processed by the ear
  - processing can be impaired

outer ear   **middle ear**   **inner ear**

Pinna

Vestibular organ (semicircular canals)

Hammer   Anvil

Oval window

Organ of Corti

Basilar membrane

Ear canal

Stirrup

Eardrum   Cochlea

Auditory nerve

Middle ear

Eardrum

Fluid in cochlea

3.6   p. 113

- **smell/olfaction**
  - called a chemical sense because substance molecules are suspended in the air, carried to the nasal cavity, and fit into receptor sites
  - nose serves as a collection device
  - unique in that signals do not first travel to the thalamus before going to the brain

Olfactory bulb

Cilia of olfactory receptor cell

Olfactory epithelium

Chemical Senses

- **taste/gustation**
  - made possible largely through the role of taste buds (taste receptor cells)
  - five basic tastes (receptor types)
  - called a chemical sense because food molecules dissolve in saliva, which then fits into receptor sites

Taste pore

Taste hair

Receptor cell

Supporting cell

Outer layer of tongue

Nerve fiber

Skin surface

Skin layers

Blood vessels

Hair

Sweat gland

Pressure-sensitive nerves

Pain-sensitive and touch-sensitive free nerve endings

Subcutaneous fat

3.7   p. 113

Somesthetic Senses

- **skin senses** — processed by the skin
- **kinesthetic sense** — processed by proprioceptive receptors in skin, joints, muscles, and tendons
- **vestibular sense** — processed by vestibular organs

3.8–11   p. 124

The ABCs of Perception

- **perception**
  - method by which the sensations experienced at any given moment are interpreted and organized in some meaningful fashion
  - may have unique features depending on sensory modality
  - may not always be based on an accurate interpretation of the stimulus

4
Consciousness: Sleep, Dreams, Hypnosis, and Drugs

A Scream in the Night

Imagine: It's a quiet night. Your 2-year-old son has been asleep for a few hours, and you and your spouse have just gone to bed. As you begin to drift off, you hear a bloodcurdling scream from the child's room. Both of you leap up and run to the nursery, where you find your son, bolt upright in bed, screaming at the top of his not-so-little lungs. You try to calm him down but soon realize that he is not even awake—he is terrified, yet asleep.

That is the experience Jenny and Jim had about once a month for the first few years of their son's life. Their son, Alex, suffered from *night terrors*, a relatively rare sleep disorder that occurs more often in children than adults and more often in boys than girls. It took several months and some research to find out that they could prevent most of these episodes by making sure that Alex always got a good night's sleep. One of the primary triggers of a night terror is a night or two of sleep loss just before the night of the episode.

Why study consciousness? Consciousness, as humans experience it, is the key difference between humans and the lower animals. Waking, sleeping, dreaming, daydreaming, and other forms of conscious awareness make up the better part of the human experience. Drug use is on the rise, not only as recreation but also for many health and psychological conditions, including the treatment of children. It seems obvious that we need to understand how drugs affect our thinking and behavior in everyday life. In a very real sense, to understand consciousness is to understand what it means to be who we are.

4 Learning Objectives

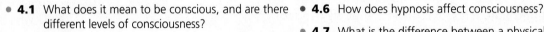

- **4.1** What does it mean to be conscious, and are there different levels of consciousness?
- **4.2** Why do people need to sleep, and how does sleep work?
- **4.3** What are the different stages of sleep, including the stage of dreaming and its importance?
- **4.4** How do sleep disorders interfere with normal sleep?
- **4.5** Why do people dream, and what do they dream about?

- **4.6** How does hypnosis affect consciousness?
- **4.7** What is the difference between a physical dependence and a psychological dependence on a drug?
- **4.8** How do stimulants and depressants affect consciousness, and what are the dangers associated with taking them, particularly alcohol?
- **4.9** What are some of the effects and dangers of using narcotics and hallucinogens, including marijuana?
- **4.10** How serious is the problem of sleep deprivation?

AP* Identify the major figures in consciousness research. ▶

What exactly is meant ▶ by the term *consciousness*? I've heard it a lot, but I'm not sure that I know everything it means.

What Is Consciousness?

4.1   What does it mean to be conscious, and are there different levels of consciousness?

What exactly is meant by the term consciousness? *I've heard it a lot, but I'm not sure that I know everything it means.*

Consciousness is one of those terms that most people think they understand until someone asks them to define it. But if you are sitting there trying to define it now, don't worry if you have trouble coming up with a definition that satisfies you. Various sorts of scientists, psychologists, neuroscientists, philosophers, and even computer scientists (who have been trying to develop an artificial intelligence for some time now) have tried to define consciousness, and so there are several definitions—one for nearly every field in which consciousness is studied. The early psychologist and functionalist William James devoted quite a bit of space in his textbook to the concept of a "stream of consciousness" in which ideas, sensations, and thoughts flow from one into another (James, 1894). Philosopher Daniel Dennett, in his 1991 book *Consciousness Explained,* asserts that there is no single stream of consciousness but rather multiple "channels," each of which is handling its own tasks (Dennett, 1991). All of these channels operate in parallel, a kind of chaos of consciousness. People must somehow organize all this conscious experience, and that organization is influenced by their particular social groups and culture.

Do animals experience consciousness in the same way as people? That is a question too complex to answer fully here, but many researchers into animal behavior, language, and cognition have some reason to propose that there is a kind of consciousness in at least some animals, although its organization would naturally not be the same as human consciousness (Block, 2005; Browne, 2004; Hurley & Nudds, 2006). In this chapter, the focus is on human consciousness, but Chapter Seven does include a discussion of animal language that touches on some of these issues. Ⓛ Ⓘ Ⓝ Ⓚ *to Chapter Seven: Cognition: Thinking, Intelligence, and Language, pp. 297–298.*

DEFINITION OF CONSCIOUSNESS

So where does that leave us in the search for a working definition of consciousness?

For our purposes, a more useful definition of consciousness might be the following: **Consciousness** is your awareness of everything that is going on around you and inside your own head at any given moment, which you use to organize your behavior (Farthing, 1992), including thoughts, sensations, and feelings. Much of people's time awake is spent in a state called **waking consciousness** in which their thoughts, feelings, and sensations are clear and organized, and they feel alert. But there are many times in daily activities and in life when people experience states of consciousness that differ from this organized waking state. These variations in consciousness are called altered states of consciousness.

ALTERED STATES OF CONSCIOUSNESS

An **altered state of consciousness** occurs when there is a shift in the quality or pattern of your mental activity (Tart, 1986). Thoughts may become fuzzy and disorganized and you may feel less alert, or your thoughts may take bizarre turns, as they so often do in dreams. You may also divide your conscious awareness, as when you drive to work or school and then wonder how you got there—one level of conscious awareness was driving, while the other was thinking about the day ahead, perhaps. This altered state of divided consciousness can be a dangerous thing, as many people who try to drive and talk on a cell phone at the same time have discovered. Driving and carrying on a conversation on a phone are both processes that should demand focused attention, and it is simply not possible to do both at once in a safe and efficient manner. Studies have shown that driving while talking on a cell phone, even a hands-free phone, puts a person at the same degree of risk as driving under the influence of alcohol (Alm & Nilsson, 1995; Briem & Hedman, 1995; Strayer & Drews, 2007; Strayer & Johnston, 2001; Strayer et al., 2006).

There are many other forms of altered states of consciousness: being under the influence of certain drugs, daydreaming, being hypnotized, or achieving a meditative state. ⓛⓘⓝⓚ *to Chapter Nine: Stress and Health, pp. 374–376.* But the most common altered state people experience is the one they spend about a third of their lives in on a nightly basis—sleep.

Altered States: Sleep

Have you ever wondered why people have to sleep? They could get so much more work done if they didn't have to sleep, and they would have more time to play and do creative things.

THE BIOLOGY OF SLEEP

4.2   Why do people need to sleep, and how does sleep work?

Sleep was once referred to as "the gentle tyrant" (Webb, 1992). People can try to stay awake, and sometimes they may go for a while without sleep, but eventually they *must* sleep. One reason for this fact is that sleep is one of the human body's *biological rhythms*, natural cycles of activity that the body must go through. Some biological rhythms are monthly, like the cycle of a woman's menstruation, whereas others are far shorter—the beat of the heart is a biological rhythm. But many biological rhythms take place on a daily basis, like the rise and fall of blood pressure and body temperature or the production of certain body chemicals (Moore-Ede, et al., 1982). The most obvious of these is the sleep–wake cycle (Baehr et al., 2000).

◄ So where does that leave us in the search for a working definition of consciousness?

AP* Describe various states of consciousness and their impact on behavior.

Sleep, according to Webb (1992), is the "gentle tyrant." As this picture shows, when the urge to sleep comes upon a person, it can be very difficult to resist—no matter where that person is at the time. Can you think of a time or place when you fell asleep without meaning to do so? What do you think were the factors in your "sleep attack"?

◄ **AP*** Discuss aspects of sleep and dreaming.

consciousness a person's awareness of everything that is going on around him or her at any given moment, which is used to organize behavior.

waking consciousness state in which thoughts, feelings, and sensations are clear, organized, and the person feels alert.

altered state of consciousness state in which there is a shift in the quality or pattern of mental activity as compared to waking consciousness.

The Rhythms of Life: Circadian Rhythms The sleep–wake cycle is a **circadian rhythm**. The term actually comes from two Latin words, *circa* ("about") and *diem* ("day"). So a circadian rhythm is a cycle that takes "about a day" to complete.

For most people, this means that they will experience several hours of sleep at least once during every 24-hour period. The sleep–wake cycle is ultimately controlled by the brain, specifically by an area within the *hypothalamus*, the tiny section of the brain that influences the glandular system. (L I N K) *to Chapter Two: The Biological Perspective, pp. 70–71.*

THE ROLE OF THE HYPOTHALAMUS: THE MIGHTY MITE

There was a big fuss over something called melatonin a few years ago—isn't melatonin supposed to make people sleep?

A lot of people were buying supplements of *melatonin* (a hormone normally secreted by the pineal gland) several years ago, hoping to sleep better and perhaps even slow the effects of aging (Folkard et al., 1993; Herxheimer & Petrie, 2001; Young, 1996). The release of melatonin is influenced by a structure deep within the hypothalamus in an area called the *suprachiasmatic* (SOO-prah-ki-AS-ma-tik) *nucleus*, the internal clock that tells people when to wake up and when to fall asleep (Quintero et al., 2003; Yamaguchi et al., 2003; Zisapel, 2001). The suprachiasmatic nucleus, or SCN, is sensitive to changes in light. As daylight fades, the SCN tells the pineal gland (located in the base of the brain) to secrete melatonin (Bondarenko, 2004; Delagrange & Guardiola-Lemaitre, 1997). As melatonin accumulates, a person will feel sleepy. As the light coming into the eyes increases (as it does in the morning), the SCN tells the pineal gland to stop secreting melatonin, allowing the body to awaken.

Melatonin supplements are often used to treat a condition called *jet lag*, in which the body's circadian rhythm has been disrupted by traveling to another time zone. It may help people who suffer from sleep problems due to shift work. Shift work sleep problems, often attributed to the custom of having workers change shifts against their natural circadian rhythms (e.g., from a day shift to a night shift, and then backwards to an evening shift), have been linked to increased accident rates, increased absence from work due to illness, and lowered productivity rates (Folkard et al., 1993; Folkard & Tucker, 2003; Folkard et al., 2005; Folkard et al., 2005). In addition to melatonin supplements, simply changing the shifts that workers take according to the natural cycle of the day (e.g., from day shift to evening shift to night shift, rather than from night shift back to day shift) has significantly reduced the problems (Czeisler et al., 1982; Folkard et al., 2006).

Melatonin is not the whole story, of course. There is ongoing discussion and research into the role of the neurotransmitter serotonin in the regulation of sleep (Joiner et al., 2006; Veasey, 2003; Yuan et al., 2005). As the day goes by, serotonin levels in the nervous system increase and seem to be associated with sleepiness. This correlation would explain why, at the end of the day, it is very hard for people to stay awake past their usual bedtime. The serotonin level may be high enough at that time to produce an intense feeling of sleepiness.

Body temperature plays a part in inducing sleep, too. The SCN, as part of the hypothalamus, controls body temperature. The higher the body temperature, the more alert people are; the lower the temperature, the sleepier they are. When people are asleep at night, their body temperature is at its lowest level. Be careful: The research on the effects of serotonin and body temperature on sleep is correlational, which means that it cannot yet be assumed that these two factors actually *cause* sleep to occur. (L I N K) *to Chapter One: The Science of Psychology, pp. 26–28.*

In studies in which volunteers spend several days without access to information about day or night, their sleep–wake cycles lengthened (Czeisler, 1995; Czeisler et al.,

> There was a big fuss over something called melatonin a few years ago—isn't melatonin supposed to make people sleep?

circadian rhythm a cycle of bodily rhythm that occurs over a 24-hour period.

1980). The daily activities of their bodies, such as sleeping, waking, waste production, blood pressure rise and fall, and so on, took place over a period of 25 hours rather than 24 hours. Based on this research, it appears that the SCN may be responsible for resetting the body's biological "clock" to a 24-hour cycle every day.

In the same studies, body temperature dropped consistently even in the absence of light (Czeisler et al., 1980). As body temperature dropped, sleep began, giving further support to the importance of body temperature in the regulation of sleep.

The Price of Not Sleeping   Although people can do without sleep for a while, they cannot do without it altogether. In one experiment, rats were placed on moving treadmills over water. They couldn't sleep normally because they would then fall into the water and be awakened, but they did drift repeatedly into **microsleeps**, or brief sidesteps into sleep lasting only seconds (Goleman, 1982; Konowal et al., 1999). People can have microsleeps, too, and if this happens while they are driving a car or a truck, it's obviously bad news (Dinges, 1995; Lyznicki et al., 1998; Thomas et al., 1998). Microsleep periods are no doubt responsible for a lot of car accidents that occur when drivers have had very little sleep.

Contrary to popular belief, sleep deprivation often affects younger people more than older people, who need less sleep. Does this young man look well rested and able to successfully complete the task of brushing his teeth?

What will missing out on one night's sleep do to a person? For most people, a missed night of sleep will result in concentration problems and the inability to do simple tasks that normally would take no thought at all, such as loading a CD into a player. More complex tasks, such as math problems, suffer less than these simple tasks (Chee & Choo, 2004; Lim et al., 2007).

Even so, **sleep deprivation**, or loss of sleep, is a serious problem, which many people have without realizing it. People stay up too late at night during the week, get up before they've really rested to go to work or school, and then try to pay off the "sleep debt" on the weekend. All of that disrupts the normal sleep–wake cycle and isn't good for anyone's health. Students, for example, may stay up all night to study for an important test the next day. In doing so, they will lose more information than they gain, as a good night's sleep is important for memory and the ability to think well. (L I N K) *to Introduction, p. I-9.* Some typical symptoms of sleep deprivation include trembling hands, inattention, staring off into space, droopy eyelids, and general discomfort (Naitoh et al., 1989), as well as emotional symptoms such as irritability and even depression. (L I N K) *to Chapter Twelve: Psychological Disorders, p. 497.* (For more information about sleep deprivation, see the Applying Psychology section at the end of this chapter.)

In one study, researchers found that air traffic controllers such as those pictured here were significantly more impaired in performance after working an eight-hour midnight shift as compared to a day or evening shift of equal length (Heslegrave & Rhodes, 1997).

Just how serious is missing a few nights' sleep? Sleep researchers conducted a study in which healthy adults between the ages of 21 and 38 were randomly placed in one of four restricted sleep conditions (Van Dongen et al., 2003). Participants began the experiment with at least 3 days of regular sleep and then were allowed to get only 4 hours, 6 hours, or 8 hours (this was the control group) of sleep each day for 14 days. A fourth group of participants was totally deprived of sleep (by being kept awake by the researchers) for 3 days in a row. Measurements of the participants' cognitive abilities and physical alertness were taken every 2 hours during the scheduled "awake" times. The results showed that even in the 6-hour sleep condition, participants' abilities to function mentally and physically were as negatively affected as if they had been entirely deprived of sleep for 2 nights. All participants in the sleep-deprived and no-sleep conditions were seriously impaired in their functioning and were relatively unaware of the seriousness of the impairment. That the participants did not seem to be aware of their problems in functioning may account for the impression many people have that a few nights of poor sleep are not that serious. The results of this study seem to indicate that even moderate sleep loss is a serious problem.

microsleeps   brief sidesteps into sleep lasting only a few seconds.

sleep deprivation   any significant loss of sleep, resulting in problems in concentration and irritability.

Okay, so we obviously need to sleep. But what does it do for us? Why do we have to sleep at all?

This tree-dwelling loris, like most nocturnal animals, has very large eyes. The adaptive theory of sleep assumes that animals in danger from predators tend to sleep at night. With its nightly activities confined safely to the trees, the loris has no need to fear predators at night and instead sleeps during the day.

These lionesses are predators and have no need to sleep at night to protect themselves. They sleep and hunt on and off during the day in perfect safety, while the animals that the lionesses prey upon sleep at night in the safety of dens or other shelter.

adaptive theory　theory of sleep proposing that animals and humans evolved sleep patterns to avoid predators by sleeping when predators are most active.

restorative theory　theory of sleep proposing that sleep is necessary to the physical health of the body and serves to replenish chemicals and repair cellular damage.

▶ *Okay, so we obviously need to sleep. But what does it do for us? Why do we have to sleep at all?*

The Adaptive Theory of Sleep　According to the **adaptive theory** of why organisms sleep, sleep is a product of evolution (Webb, 1992). Animals and humans evolved different sleep patterns to avoid predators during the predators' normal hunting times, which are generally at night. If a prey animal (one the predator will eat) is out and about at night, it is likely to be eaten. If instead it is in a safe place sleeping and conserving energy, it remains safe. If this is true, then one would expect prey animals to sleep mostly at night and for shorter periods of time than predator animals, whereas the predator animals can sleep in the daytime and as much as they want. In fact, animals like lions that have very few natural predators sleep nearly 15 hours a day, whereas animals like gazelles that are prey sleep only a total of 4 hours a day, usually in short naps.

The Restorative Theory of Sleep　The other major theory of why organisms sleep is called **restorative theory**, which states that sleep is necessary to the physical health of the body. During sleep, chemicals that were used up during the day's activities are replenished and cellular damage is repaired (Adam, 1980; Moldofsky, 1995). There is evidence that most bodily growth and repair occur during the deepest stages of sleep, when enzymes responsible for these functions are secreted in higher amounts. This may account for the fact that children in periods of rapid growth need to sleep more and also helps to explain why children who are experiencing disrupted sleep (as is the case in situations of domestic violence) suffer delays in growth (Gilmore & Skuse, 1999; Swanson, 1994).

Which of these theories is correct? The answer is that both are probably needed to understand why sleep occurs the way it does. Adaptive theory explains why people sleep *when* they do, and restorative theory explains why people *need* to sleep.

How Much Sleep Do People Need?　How much sleep is enough sleep? The answer varies from person to person because of each person's age and possibly inherited sleep needs (Feroah et al., 2004), but most adults need about 7 to 9 hours of sleep each 24-hour period in order to function well. (See Figure 4.1.) Some people are short sleepers, needing only 4 or 5 hours, whereas others are long sleepers and need more than 9 hours of sleep (McCann & Stewin, 1988).

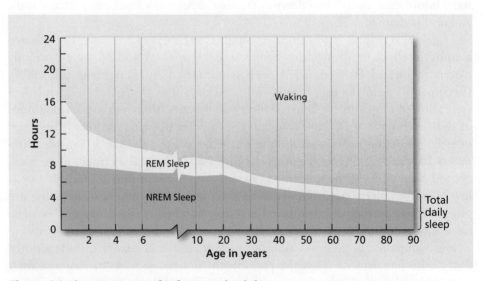

Figure 4.1 Sleep Patterns of Infants and Adults
Infants need far more sleep than older children and adults. Both REM sleep and NREM sleep decrease dramatically in the first 10 years of life, with the greatest decrease in REM sleep. Nearly 50 percent of an infant's sleep is REM, compared to only about 20 percent for a normal, healthy adult. (Roffwarg, 1966)

4.2

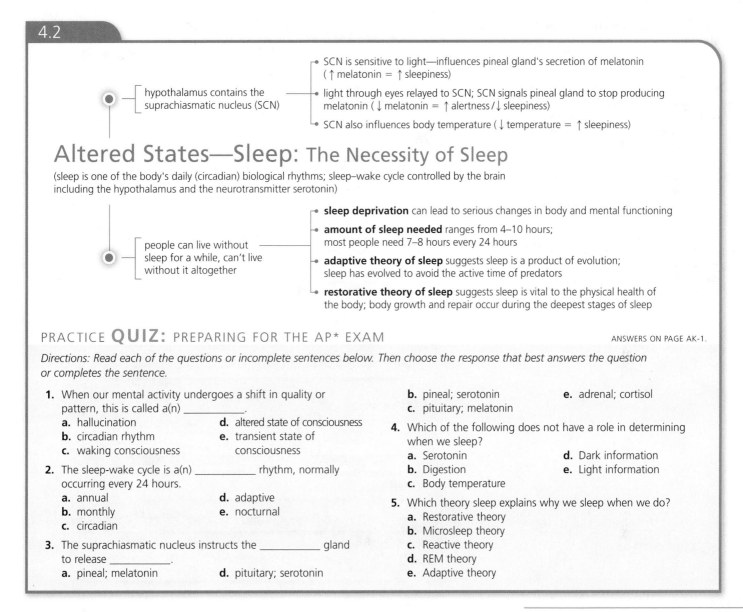

SCN is sensitive to light—influences pineal gland's secretion of melatonin
(↑ melatonin = ↑ sleepiness)

hypothalamus contains the suprachiasmatic nucleus (SCN)

light through eyes relayed to SCN; SCN signals pineal gland to stop producing melatonin (↓ melatonin = ↑ alertness / ↓ sleepiness)

SCN also influences body temperature (↓ temperature = ↑ sleepiness)

Altered States—Sleep: The Necessity of Sleep

(sleep is one of the body's daily (circadian) biological rhythms; sleep–wake cycle controlled by the brain including the hypothalamus and the neurotransmitter serotonin)

people can live without sleep for a while, can't live without it altogether

sleep deprivation can lead to serious changes in body and mental functioning

amount of sleep needed ranges from 4–10 hours; most people need 7–8 hours every 24 hours

adaptive theory of sleep suggests sleep is a product of evolution; sleep has evolved to avoid the active time of predators

restorative theory of sleep suggests sleep is vital to the physical health of the body; body growth and repair occur during the deepest stages of sleep

PRACTICE **QUIZ:** PREPARING FOR THE AP* EXAM   ANSWERS ON PAGE AK-1.

Directions: Read each of the questions or incomplete sentences below. Then choose the response that best answers the question or completes the sentence.

1. When our mental activity undergoes a shift in quality or pattern, this is called a(n) _____.
   a. hallucination
   b. circadian rhythm
   c. waking consciousness
   d. altered state of consciousness
   e. transient state of consciousness

2. The sleep-wake cycle is a(n) _____ rhythm, normally occurring every 24 hours.
   a. annual
   b. monthly
   c. circadian
   d. adaptive
   e. nocturnal

3. The suprachiasmatic nucleus instructs the _____ gland to release _____.
   a. pineal; melatonin
   d. pituitary; serotonin

   b. pineal; serotonin
   c. pituitary; melatonin
   e. adrenal; cortisol

4. Which of the following does not have a role in determining when we sleep?
   a. Serotonin
   b. Digestion
   c. Body temperature
   d. Dark information
   e. Light information

5. Which theory sleep explains why we sleep when we do?
   a. Restorative theory
   b. Microsleep theory
   c. Reactive theory
   d. REM theory
   e. Adaptive theory

THE STAGES OF SLEEP

So are there different kinds of sleep? Do you go from being awake to being asleep and dreaming—is it instant?

There are actually two kinds of sleep: **REM (rapid eye movement)** and **non-REM sleep**. REM sleep is a relatively active type of sleep when most of a person's dreaming takes place, whereas non-REM sleep is a much deeper, more restful kind of sleep. In REM sleep, the voluntary muscles are inhibited, meaning that the person in REM sleep moves very little, whereas in non-REM sleep the person's body is free to move around (including kicking one's bed partner!). There are also several different stages of sleep that people go through each night in which REM sleep and non-REM sleep occur. A machine called an electroencephalograph (EEG) allows scientists to record the brain wave activity as a person passes through the various stages of sleep and to determine what type of sleep the person has entered (Aserinsky & Kleitman, 1953). See Figure 4.2 for a look at what happens in each stage of sleep.

A person who is wide awake and mentally active will show a brain wave pattern on the EEG called *beta waves*. Beta waves are very small and very fast. As the person

◄ So are there different kinds of sleep? Do you go from being awake to being asleep and dreaming— is it instant?

◄ **AP*** Discuss aspects of sleep and dreaming.

rapid eye movement (REM) stage of sleep in which the eyes move rapidly under the eyelids and the person is typically experiencing a dream.

non-REM (NREM) sleep any of the stages of sleep that do not include REM.

Figure 4.2 **Brain Activity During Sleep**

The EEG reflects brain activity during both waking and sleep. This activity varies according to level of alertness while awake (top two segments) and the stage of sleep (middle segments). Sleep stages 3 and 4 are indicated by the presence of delta activity, which is much slower and accounts for the larger, slower waves on these graphs. REM has activity that resembles alert wakefulness but has relatively no muscle activity except rapid eye movement. The bottom segments illustrate how EEG activity differs between wakefulness, light and deep sleep, and lastly what it looks like when brain activity has ceased in cerebral death. EEG data and images in this figure are courtesy of Dr. Leslie Sherlin.

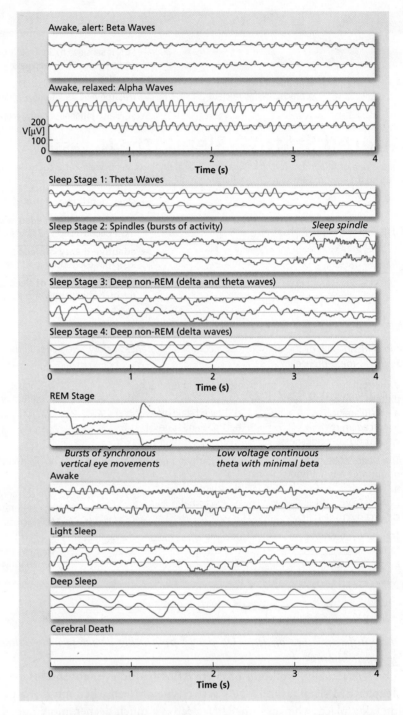

relaxes and gets drowsy, slightly larger and slower **alpha waves** appear. The alpha waves are eventually replaced by even slower and larger **theta waves**.

4.3   What are the different stages of sleep, including the stage of dreaming and its importance?

Non-REM Stage One: Light Sleep   As theta wave activity increases and alpha wave activity fades away, people are said to be entering Stage One sleep, or light sleep. Several rather interesting things can happen in this non-REM stage of sleep. If people are awakened at this point, they will probably not believe that they were actually asleep. They may also experience vivid visual events called *hypnagogic images* (Mavromatis, 1987; Mavromatis & Richardson, 1984). (The Greek word *hypnos* means "sleep.") These images are bits and

alpha waves   brain waves that indicate a state of relaxation or light sleep.

theta waves   brain waves indicating the early stages of sleep.

pieces of what may eventually become dreams but are most often seen as flashes of light. Some people have very vivid images that seem realistic. Many researchers now believe that peoples' experiences of ghostly visits, alien abductions, and near-death experiences may be most easily explained by these images (Moody & Perry, 1993). (They can also occur just as people are about to wake up and are then called *hypnopompic images.*)

A much more common occurrence is called the *hypnic jerk* (Mahowald & Schenck, 1996; Oswald, 1959). Have you ever been drifting off to sleep when your knees, legs, or sometimes your whole body gives a big "jerk"? Although experts have no solid proof of why this occurs, many believe that it has something to do with the possibility that our ancestors slept in trees: The relaxation of the muscles as one drifts into sleep causes a "falling" sensation, at which point the body jerks awake to prevent the "fall" from the hypothetical tree (Coolidge, 2006; Sagan, 1977).

Non-REM Stage Two: Sleep Spindles   As people drift further into sleep, the body temperature continues to drop. Heart rate slows, breathing becomes more shallow and irregular, and the EEG will show the first signs of *sleep spindles*, brief bursts of activity lasting only a second or two. Theta waves still predominate in this stage, but if people are awakened during this stage, they will be aware of having been asleep.

Non-REM Stage Three and Stage Four: Delta Waves Roll In   In the third stage of sleep, the slowest and largest waves make their appearance. These waves are called **delta waves**. In Stage Three, delta waves make up only about 20 to 50 percent of the brain wave pattern.

Once delta waves account for more than 50 percent of total brain activity, the person is said to have entered Stage Four sleep, the deepest stage of sleep. It is during this stage that growth hormones (often abbreviated as GH) are released from the pituitary gland and reach their peak. The body is at its lowest level of functioning. Eventually, the delta waves become the dominant brain activity for this stage of sleep. See Figure 4.3 to show movement through the sleep stages throughout one night.

People in deep sleep are very hard to awaken. If something does wake them, they may be very confused and disoriented at first. It is not unusual for people to wake up in this kind of disoriented state only to hear the crack of thunder and realize that a storm has come up. Children, who need deep sleep so that their bodies will grow, are even harder to wake up when in this state than are adults.

The fact that children do sleep so deeply may explain why certain sleep disorders are more common in childhood. In fact, many sleep disorders are more common in boys than

delta waves long, slow waves that indicate the deepest stage of sleep.

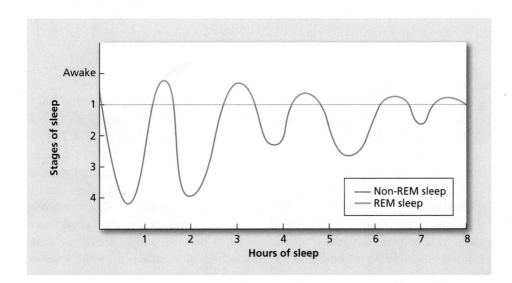

Figure 4.3 A Typical Night's Sleep
The graph shows the typical progression through the night of Stages 1–4 and REM sleep. Stages 1–4 are indicated on the *y*-axis, and REM stages are represented by the green curves on the graph. The REM periods occur about every 90 minutes throughout the night (Dement, 1974).

✳ **Explore** with the stages of sleep simulation. **www.mypsychlab.com**

in girls because boys sleep more deeply than do girls due to high levels of the male hormone testosterone (Miyatake et al., 1980; Thiedke, 2001). ✳ Explore on **MyPsychLab**

WHAT HAPPENS IN REM SLEEP?

After spending some time in Stage Four, the sleeping person will go back up through Stage Three, Stage Two, and then into a stage in which body temperature increases to near-waking levels, the eyes move rapidly under the eyelids, the heart beats much faster, and brain waves resemble beta waves—the kind of brain activity that usually signals wakefulness. The person is still asleep but in the stage known as rapid eye movement sleep (REM).

When a person in REM sleep is awakened, he or she almost always reports being in a dream state (Shafton, 1995). REM sleep is, therefore, associated with dreaming, and 90 percent of dreams actually take place in REM sleep. People do have dreams in the other non-REM (or NREM) stages, but REM dreams tend to be more vivid, more detailed, longer, and more bizarre than the dreams of NREM sleep. NREM dreams tend to be more like thoughts about daily occurrences and far shorter than REM dreams (Foulkes & Schmidt, 1983; Takeuchi et al., 2003). Fortunately, the body is unable to act upon these dreams under normal conditions because the voluntary muscles are paralyzed during REM sleep, a condition known as **REM paralysis**.

The Need for REM Sleep   Why two kinds of sleep? And why would REM sleep ever be considered restful when the body is almost awake and the brain is so active? REM sleep seems to serve a different purpose than does NREM, or deep sleep. After a very physically demanding day, people tend to spend more time in NREM deep sleep than is usual. But an emotionally stressful day leads to increased time in REM sleep (Horne & Staff, 1983). Perhaps the dreams people have in REM sleep are a way of dealing with the stresses and tensions of the day, whereas physical activity would demand more time for recovery of the body in NREM sleep. Also, if deprived of REM sleep (as would occur with the use of sleeping pills or other depressant drugs), a person will experience greatly increased amounts of REM sleep the next night, a phenomenon called **REM rebound** (Vogel, 1975, 1993).

A very early study of REM sleep deprivation (Dement, 1960) seemed to suggest that people deprived of REM sleep would become paranoid, seemingly mentally ill from lack of this one stage of sleep. This is called the *REM myth* because later studies failed to reliably produce the same results (Dement et al., 1969).

Some early research attempted to link REM sleep with the physical changes that occur during storing a memory for what one has recently learned, but the evidence today suggests that no one particular stage of sleep is the "one" in which this memory process occurs; rather, the evidence is mounting for sleep in general as necessary to the formation of memory (Ellenbogen et al., 2006; Maquet et al., 2003; Siegel, 2001; Stickgold et al., 2001; Walker, 2005).

REM sleep in early infancy differs from adult REM sleep in two ways: Babies spend nearly half of their sleep in REM as compared to 20 percent doing so in adulthood, the brain wave patterns on EEG recordings are not exactly the same in infant REM when compared to adult REM recordings, and infants can and do move around quite a bit during REM sleep (Carskadon & Dement, 2005; Davis et al., 2004; Sheldon, 2002; Tucker et al., 2006). Both differences can be explained: When infants are engaged in REM sleep, they are not dreaming but rather forming new connections between neurons (Carskadon & Dement, 2005; Davis et al., 2004; Sheldon, 2002). The infant brain is highly plastic, ⓛⓘⓝⓚ *to Chapter Two: The Biological Perspective, p. 60,* and much of brain growth and development takes place during REM sleep. As the infant's brain nears its adult size by age 5 or 6, the proportion of REM sleep has also decreased to a more adult-like ratio of REM to non-REM. For infants, to sleep is perchance to grow synapses.

While this infant is sleeping, her REM sleep (occurring about half of the time she is asleep) allows her brain to make new neural connections.

REM paralysis   the inability of the voluntary muscles to move during REM sleep.

REM rebound   increased amounts of REM sleep after being deprived of REM sleep on earlier nights.

SLEEP DISORDERS

4.4 How do sleep disorders interfere with normal sleep?

What would happen if we could act out our dreams? Would it be like sleepwalking?

Nightmares and REM Behavior Disorder Being able to act out one's dreams, especially nightmares, is a far more dangerous proposition than sleepwalking. **Nightmares** are bad dreams, and some nightmares can be utterly terrifying. Children tend to have more nightmares than adults do because they spend more of their sleep in the REM state, as discussed earlier. As they age, they have fewer nightmares because they have less opportunity to have them. But some people still suffer from nightmares as adults.

Some people have a rare disorder in which the brain mechanisms that normally inhibit the voluntary muscles fail, allowing the person to thrash around and even get up and act out nightmares. This disorder is called **REM behavior disorder**, which is a fairly serious condition (Shafton, 1995). Usually seen in men over age 60, it can happen in younger men and in women. (For more about this disorder, see Psychology in the News: Murder While Sleepwalking, later in this section.)

Stage Four Sleep Disorders Real **sleepwalking**, or **somnambulism**, occurs in about 20 percent of the population and is at least partially due to heredity (Abe et al., 1984; Kales et al., 1980). It is much more common in childhood and also occurs more frequently in boys than in girls. Although the old movies portray sleepwalkers as zombie-like and with arms outstretched, in reality a sleepwalker may do nothing more than sit up in bed. But other sleepwalking episodes may involve walking around the house, looking in the refrigerator or even eating, and getting into the car. One student said that her brother was a sleepwalker, and one morning his family found him sound asleep behind the wheel of the family car in the garage. Fortunately, he had not been able to find the keys in his sleep.

Alex, the child whose night terrors were described in the opening story of this chapter, also suffered from sleepwalking. As many somnambulists do, he grew out of this behavior by the time he became an adolescent. His parents also found that preventing sleep loss made sleepwalking a rare occurrence. When Alex did have an episode, he never recalled it the next day. This lack of memory is typical of most sleepwalking episodes. The only real precaution that the families of people who sleepwalk should take is to clear their floors of obstacles and to put not-easy-to-reach locks on the doors. And although it is not dangerous to wake sleepwalkers, they may strike out before awakening.

Night Terrors As discussed in the prologue, **night terrors** are a rare disorder, although one that is more likely in children and also likely to disappear as the child grows older (Garland & Smith, 1991). A night terror is essentially a state of panic experienced while sound asleep. People may sit up, scream, run around the room, or flail at some unseen attacker. It is not uncommon for people to feel unable to breathe as well. Considering that people suffering a night terror episode are in a deep stage of sleep and breathing

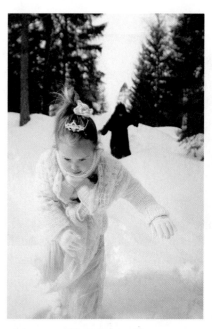

Nightmares of being chased by a monster or similar frightening creature are common, especially in childhood.

"Wait! Don't! It can be dangerous to wake them."
©The New Yorker Collection J. Dator from cartoonbank.com.
All Rights Reserved.

◄ What would happen if we could act out our dreams? Would it be like sleepwalking?

nightmares bad dreams occurring during REM sleep.

REM behavior disorder a rare disorder in which the mechanism that blocks the movement of the voluntary muscles fails, allowing the person to thrash around and even get up and act out nightmares.

sleepwalking (somnambulism) occurring during deep sleep, an episode of moving around or walking around in one's sleep.

night terrors relatively rare disorder in which the person experiences extreme fear and screams or runs around during deep sleep without waking fully.

Psychology in the News

Murder While Sleepwalking

According to a compilation of information by Dr. Lawrence Martin, Associate Professor at Case Western Reserve University and specialist in pulmonary* and sleep medicine, at least 20 cases of "murder while sleepwalking" have been recorded. The term *sleepwalking* as used in these cases most likely refers to the very real condition called REM behavior disorder rather than ordinary sleepwalking. Use of this disorder as a defense in a murder trial has sometimes been successful. Here are short descriptions of four cases and their outcomes.

Case One: In 1987, Kenneth Parks, a 23-year-old man from Toronto, Canada, got up early in the morning, got in his car, and drove 23 kilometers (about 14 miles) to the home of his wife's parents. He killed his mother-in-law, attacked his father-in-law, and then drove to the police. Once there, he told them that he thought he had killed some people. Parks had no motive and had been suffering from severe insomnia. He did have a history of sleepwalking and his defense team, which included sleep experts and psychiatrists, concluded that he was indeed unaware of his actions at the time of the crime. He was acquitted (Denno, 2002; Martin, 2004).

Case Two: Scott Falater, 43 years old, was accused of murdering his wife in 1997. A neighbor, looking over a fence, witnessed Scott holding his wife's head under water in the swimming pool. He called the police, who found the body of Yamila Falater with stab wounds.

Falater had performed a series of very deliberate and time-consuming actions in cleaning up after the murder. But Falater claimed to be sleepwalking during all of these actions. Although sleep experts for the defense stated that Falater's story was possible, the prosecution pointed to marital troubles as motive. Most damaging to his case was the witness who stated that three weeks before the murder, Falater had been discussing the case of Kenneth Parks and Parks's acquittal for murder based on a sleepwalking defense. The jury found Falater guilty of murder in the first degree and he was given a life sentence (Martin, 2004; Tresniowski, 1999).

Case Three: In 2001 Stephen Reitz claimed to be sleepwalking when he killed his married girlfriend in their hotel room and later walked to the police station to turn himself in (Krasnowski, 2004). Reitz claimed to be dreaming of attacking a male intruder in "flashbacks," although he also claimed to remember nothing of the attack. Although Reitz had no apparent motive, he did have a history of violence and abuse. In 2004, Stephen Reitz was convicted of first-degree murder.

Case Four: In 2003, Jules Lowe of Manchester, England, attacked and killed his 82-year-old father while sleepwalking. Lowe had a history of sleepwalking, was under great stress, and had no motive to kill his father. Sleep expert Dr. Irshaad Ebrahim testified that tests showed Lowe to be sleepwalking at the time of the attack. In 2005, Lowe was acquitted (Smith-Spark, 2005).

((⬤—[**Listen** on **MyPsychLab**

Questions for Further Discussion

1. Should sleepwalking be a valid defense for a crime as serious as murder? What about other kinds of crimes?

2. What kind of evidence should be required to convince a jury that a crime was committed while sleepwalking?

*Pulmonary: having to do with the lungs.

Scott Falater testifies at his trial for the murder of his wife, which he claims he committed while he was sleepwalking.

((⬤ **Listen** to the Psychology in the News podcast.
www.mypsychlab.com

shallowly, one can understand why breathing would seem difficult when they are suddenly active. Most people do not remember what happened during a night terror episode, although a few people can remember vividly the images and terror they experienced.

But that sounds like the description of a nightmare—what's the difference?

There are some very real differences between night terrors and nightmares. Nightmares are usually vividly remembered immediately upon waking. A person who has had a nightmare, unlike a person experiencing a night terror, will actually be able to come awake and immediately talk about the bad dream. Perhaps the most telling difference is that nightmares occur during REM sleep rather than deep non-REM sleep, which means that people don't move around in a nightmare as they do in a night terror experience.

For a look at some people who may have experienced very real "terror in the night," see the previous page on murders committed while the murderer was allegedly asleep. A number of other problems can occur during sleep in addition to sleepwalking, nightmares, and REM behavior disorder.

Insomnia Most people think that **insomnia** is the inability to sleep. Although that is the literal meaning of the term, in reality insomnia is the inability to get to sleep, stay asleep, or get a good quality of sleep (Kryger, Lavie, & Rosen, 1999). There are many causes of insomnia, both psychological and physiological. Some of the psychological causes are worrying, trying too hard to sleep, or having anxiety. Some of the physiological causes are too much caffeine, indigestion, or aches and pain.

There are several steps people can take to help them sleep. Obvious ones are taking no caffeinated drinks or foods that cause indigestion before bedtime, taking medication for pain, and dealing with anxieties in the daytime rather than facing them at night. That last bit of advice is easy to say but not always easy to do. Here are some other helpful hints (Kupfer & Reynolds, 1997):

1. Go to bed only when you are sleepy. If you lie in bed for 20 minutes and are still awake, get up and do something like reading or other light activity until you feel sleepy, and then go back to bed.

2. Don't do anything in your bed but sleep. Your bed should be a cue for sleeping, not studying or watching television. Using the bed as a cue for sleeping is a kind of learning called *classical conditioning,* or the pairing of cues and automatic responses. (LINK) *to Chapter Five: Learning, p. 177.*

3. Don't try too hard to get to sleep, and especially do not look at the clock and calculate how much sleep you aren't getting. That just increases the tension and makes it harder to sleep.

4. Keep to a regular schedule. Go to bed at the same time and get up at the same time, even on days that you don't have to go to work or class.

5. Don't take sleeping pills or drink alcohol or other types of drugs that slow down the nervous system (see the category Depressants later in this chapter). These drugs force you into deep sleep and do not allow you to get any REM sleep or the lighter stages. When you try to sleep without these drugs the next night, you will experience REM rebound, which will cause you to feel tired and sleepy the next day. REM rebound is one way to experience the form of insomnia in which a person sleeps but sleeps poorly.

If none of these things seem to be working, there are sleep clinics and sleep experts who can help people with insomnia. The American Academy of Sleep Medicine has an excellent Web site at **www.aasmnet.org** that has links to find sleep clinics in any area. One treatment that seems to have more success than any kind of sleep medication is the use of cognitive-behavior therapy, a type of therapy in which both rational thinking and

◄ But that sounds like the description of a nightmare— what's the difference?

This woman has insomnia. In insomnia, a person has trouble getting to sleep, staying asleep, or getting enough sleep. How will this woman feel when she wakes up in the morning?

insomnia the inability to get to sleep, stay asleep, or get a good quality of sleep.

sleep apnea disorder in which the person stops breathing for nearly half a minute or more.

narcolepsy sleep disorder in which a person falls immediately into REM sleep during the day without warning.

BILL ABBOTT

"On your application it says you have narcolepsy. What is that?"

www.CartoonStock.com

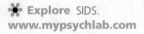

❊ Explore SIDS.
www.mypsychlab.com

controlled behavior are stressed (Bastien et al., 2004; Irwin et al., 2006; Morin et al., 2006). ⓛⓘⓝⓚ *to Chapter Thirteen: Psychological Therapies, pp. 529–531.*

Sleep Apnea Gerald was a snorer. Actually, that's an understatement. Gerald could give a jet engine some serious competition. Snoring is fairly common, occurring when the breathing passages (nose and throat) get blocked. Most people snore only when they have a cold or some other occasional problem, but some people snore every night and quite loudly, like Gerald. It is this type of snoring that is often associated with a condition called **sleep apnea**, in which the person stops breathing for nearly half a minute or more. When breathing stops, there will be a sudden silence, followed shortly by a gasping sound as the person struggles to get air into the lungs. Many people do not wake up while this is happening, but they do not get a good, restful night's sleep because of the apnea.

Apnea is a serious problem. Not only does it disturb nightly sleep, making the person excessively sleepy in the daytime, but also it can cause heart problems (Flemons, 2002). If a person suspects the presence of apnea, a visit to a physician is the first step in identifying the disorder and deciding on a treatment. With mild apnea, treatment may be a device worn on the nose at night to open the nostrils and prevent blockage. Obesity is a primary cause of apnea, especially in men, so another solution might be to lose excess weight. There are also sprays that are supposed to shrink the tissues lining the throat (much as a nasal decongestant spray shrinks the tissues of the nasal passages). Some people sleep with a device that delivers a continuous stream of air under mild pressure, called a *continuous positive airway pressure (CPAP) device*. Others undergo a simple surgery in which the *uvula* (the little flap that hangs down at the back of the throat) and some of the soft tissues surrounding it are removed.

Some very young infants also experience a kind of apnea due to immaturity of the brain stem. These infants are typically placed on monitors that sound an alarm when breathing stops, allowing caregivers to help the infant begin breathing again. Although sleep apnea in infants is often associated with sudden infant death syndrome, or SIDS, it is not a necessarily caused by it: Many infants who die of SIDS were never diagnosed with sleep apnea (Blackmon et al., 2003). ❊ Explore on MyPsychLab

Narcolepsy A disorder affecting one in every 2,000 persons, **narcolepsy** is a kind of "sleep seizure." In narcolepsy, the person may slip suddenly into REM sleep during the day (especially when the person experiences strong emotions). Another symptom is excessive daytime sleepiness that results in the person falling asleep throughout the day at inappropriate times and in inappropriate places (Overeem et al., 2001). These sleep attacks may occur many times and without warning, making the operation of a car or other machinery very dangerous for the *narcoleptic* (person who suffers from narcolepsy). The sudden REM attacks are especially dangerous because of the symptom of *cataplexy*, or a sudden loss of muscle tone. This REM paralysis may cause injuries if the person is standing when the attack occurs. The same hypnogogic images that may accompany Stage One sleep may also occur in the narcoleptic person. Table 4.1 has a more detailed list of known sleep disorders.

Table 4.1 Sleep Disorders

NAME OF DISORDER	PRIMARY SYMPTOMS
Somnambulism	Sitting, walking, or performing complex behavior while asleep
Night terrors	Extreme fear, agitation, screaming while asleep
Restless leg syndrome	Uncomfortable sensations in legs causing movement and loss of sleep
Nocturnal leg cramps	Painful cramps in calf or foot muscles
Hypersomnia	Excessive daytime sleepiness
Circadian rhythm disorders	Disturbances of the sleep–wake cycle such as jet lag and shift work
Enuresis	Urinating while asleep in bed

4.3–4

- **non-REM Stage 1:** while awake, primarily beta activity, more alpha as one relaxes, onset of sleep in Stage 1 is associated with alpha being replaced by theta
- **non-REM Stage 2:** EEG sleep spindles appear; theta activity is predominant; body temperature continues to drop, heart rate and breathing slow
- **non-REM Stages 3 & 4:** delta activity makes up 20–50% of EEG activity in Stage 3; over 50% indicates Stage 4; body is at lowest level of functioning and people are hard to awaken; sleep disorders such as sleepwalking and night terrors occur in Stage 4
- **REM sleep:** dreaming occurs; eyes move rapidly under the eyelids and EEG indicates presence of beta, but body is typically still due to sleep paralysis; REM behavior disorder occurs when body is not still or acts out dreams, usually seen in men over age 60

consist of both REM (rapid eye movement) and non-REM stages; REM is relatively active whereas non-REM is much deeper and restful; stages defined by level of brain activity as measured by the EEG (delta, theta, alpha, beta waves); sleep cycle is made up of various stages repeated 4–5 times a night

Altered States—Sleep: Stages and Disorders

sleep disorders include a variety of problems that can interfere with sleep

- **insomnia** is the inability to get to sleep, stay asleep, or get good quality sleep
- **sleep apnea** consists of loud snoring and stopped breathing
- **narcolepsy** consists of sudden onset of REM sleep during otherwise waking hours

PRACTICE **QUIZ:** PREPARING FOR THE AP* EXAM   ANSWERS ON PAGE AK-1.

Directions: Read each of the questions or incomplete sentences below. Then choose the response that best answers the question or completes the sentence.

1. During which stage of sleep is it most difficult to wake a person up?
   a. Stage One
   b. Stage Two
   c. Stage Three
   d. Stage Four
   e. All of the above

2. Which of the following is not a characteristic of REM sleep?
   a. Paralysis of voluntary muscles
   b. Increased heart rate
   c. Slower, deeper breathing
   d. Increased body temperature
   e. Vivid, detailed dreaming

3. Acting out your nightmares is a rare condition called _____.
   a. sleep apnea
   b. night terrors
   c. narcolepsy
   d. somnambulism
   e. REM behavior disorder

4. In which disorder does breathing stop for nearly half a minute or more?
   a. Sleep apnea
   b. Night terrors
   c. Sleepwalking
   d. Narcolepsy
   e. REM behavior disorder

5. Which of the following is bad advice for someone suffering from insomnia?
   a. Keep a regular schedule
   b. Do not study or work in bed
   c. Do not watch TV or read in bed
   d. Lie in bed until you fall asleep, even if it takes several hours
   e. Avoid coffee, tea, and other caffeine-containing products before bed

6. Nightmares occur in _____ sleep, whereas night terrors occur in _____ sleep.
   a. Stage One; Stage Two
   b. REM; NREM
   c. Stage Four; Stage One
   d. NREM; REM
   e. Stage Three; Stage Two

Dreams

4.5   Why do people dream, and what do they dream about?

Dreams have long been a source of curiosity. People of ancient times tried to find meaning in dreams. Some saw dreams as prophecy, some as messages from the spirits. But the real inquiry into the process of dreaming began with the publication of Freud's *The Interpretation of Dreams* (1900).

◄ **AP*** Discuss aspects of sleep and dreaming.

◄ **AP*** Identify the major figures in consciousness research.

CAST OF DREAM

THE MONSTER . . . . . . YOUR FATHER
KIND WOMAN . . . . . . YOUR MOTHER
POLICEMAN . . . . YOUR ANALYST
FIRST STRANGER . . . . YOUR BROTHER
SECOND STRANGER . . YOUR SISTER
LITTLE BOY . . . . . YOU

Dana Fradon

©The New Yorker Collection 1973 Dana Fradon
from cartoonbank.com. All Rights Reserved.

Seems like quite a stretch. Wouldn't ▶ there be lots of other possible interpretations?

Dreams are often filled with unrealistic and imaginative events and images. A common dream is that of flying. What do you think flying might represent in a dream?

FREUD'S INTERPRETATION: DREAMS AS WISH FULFILLMENT

Sigmund Freud (1856–1939) believed that the problems of his patients stemmed from conflicts and events that had been buried in their unconscious minds since childhood. These early traumas were seen as the cause of behavior problems in adulthood, in which his patients suffered from symptoms such as a type of paralysis that had no physical basis or repetitive, ritualistic* hand washing. One of the ways Freud devised to get at these early memories was to examine the dreams of his patients, believing that conflicts, events, and desires of the past would be represented in symbolic** form in the dreams. ⓛⓘⓝⓚ *to Chapter Eleven: Theories of Personality, p. 437.*

Manifest Content The *manifest content* of a dream is the actual dream itself. For example, if Chad has a dream in which he is trying to climb out of a bathtub, the manifest content of the dream is exactly that—he's trying to climb out of a bathtub.

Latent Content But, of course, Freud would no doubt find more meaning in Chad's dream than is at first evident. He believed that the true meaning of a dream was hidden, or *latent*, and only expressed in symbols. In the dream, the water in the tub might symbolize the waters of birth, and the tub itself might be his mother's womb. Chad may be dreaming about being born in Freudian terms.

Seems like quite a stretch. Wouldn't there be lots of other possible interpretations?

Yes, and today many professionals are no longer as fond of Freud's dream analysis as they once were. But there are still some people who insist that dreams have symbolic meaning. For example, dreaming about being naked in a public place is very common, and most dream analyzers interpret that to mean feeling open and exposed, or even an expression of childhood innocence. Exactly how the dream is interpreted depends on the other features of the dream and what is happening in the person's waking life.

The development of techniques for looking at the structure and activity of the brain (see ⓛⓘⓝⓚ *to Chapter Two, pp. 65–68)* has led to an explanation of why people dream that is more concrete than that of Freud.

THE ACTIVATION-SYNTHESIS HYPOTHESIS

Using brain-imaging techniques such as a PET scan (see Chapter Two), researchers have found evidence that dreams are products of activity in the pons (Hobson, 1988; Hobson & McCarley, 1977; Hobson et al., 2000). This lower area inhibits the neurotransmitters that would allow movement of the voluntary muscles while sending random signals to the areas of the cortex that interpret vision, hearing, and so on.

When signals from the pons bombard† the cortex during waking consciousness, the association areas of the cortex interpret those signals as seeing, hearing, and so on. Because those signals come from the real world, this process results in

---

*Ritualistic: referring to an action done in a particular manner each time it is repeated, according to some specific pattern.

**Symbolic: having the quality of representing something other than itself.

†Bombard: to attack or press.

an experience of reality. But when people are asleep, the signals from the brain stem are random and not necessarily attached to actual external stimuli, yet the brain must somehow interpret these random signals. It *synthesizes* (puts together) an explanation of the cortex's activation from memories and other stored information.

In this theory, called the **activation-synthesis hypothesis**, a dream is merely another kind of thinking that occurs when people sleep. It is less realistic because it comes not from the outside world of reality but from within people's memories and experiences of the past. The frontal lobes, which people normally use in daytime thinking, are more or less shut down during dreaming, which may also account for the unrealistic and often bizarre nature of dreams (Macquet & Franck, 1996).

My dreams can be really weird, but sometimes they seem pretty ordinary or even seem to mean something. Can dreams be more meaningful?

There are dream experts who suggest that dreams may have more meaning than Hobson and McCarley originally theorized. A survey questioning subjects about their dream content, for example, concluded that much of the content of dreams is meaningful, consistent over time, and fits in with past or present emotional concerns rather than being bizarre, meaningless, and random (Domhoff, 1996, 2005).

Hobson and colleagues have reworked the activation-synthesis hypothesis to reflect concerns about dream meaning, calling it the **activation-information-mode model**, or **AIM** (Hobson et al., 2000). In this newer version, information that is accessed during waking hours can have an influence on the synthesis of dreams. In other words, when the brain is "making up" a dream to explain its own activation, it uses meaningful bits and pieces of the person's experiences from the previous day or the last few days rather than just random items from memory.

WHAT DO PEOPLE DREAM ABOUT?

Calvin Hall collected over 10,000 dreams and concluded that most dreams reflect the events that occur in everyday life (Hall, 1966). Although most people dream in color, people who grew up in the era of black and white television sometimes have dreams in black and white. There are gender differences, although whether those differences are caused by hormonal/genetic influences, sociocultural influences, or a combination of influences remains to be seen. In his book *Finding Meaning in Dreams*, Dr. William Domhoff (1996) concluded that across many cultures, men more often dream of other males whereas women tend to dream about males and females equally. Men across various cultures also tend to have more physical aggression in their dreams than do women, with women more often being the victims of such aggression in their dreams. Domhoff also concluded that where there are differences in the content of dreams across cultures, the differences make sense in light of the culture's "personality." For example, American culture is considered fairly aggressive when compared to the culture of the Netherlands, and the aggressive content of the dreams in both cultures reflects this difference: There were lower levels of aggression in the dreams of those from the Netherlands when compared to the Americans' dream content.

Girls and women tend to dream about people they know, personal appearance concerns, and family and home. Boys and men tend to have more male characters in their dreams, which are also typically in outdoor or unfamiliar settings and may involve weapons, tools, cars, and roads. Men also report more sexual dreams, usually

◄ My dreams can be really weird, but sometimes they seem pretty ordinary or even seem to mean something. Can dreams be more meaningful?

activation-synthesis hypothesis explanation that states that dreams are created by the higher centers of the cortex to explain the activation by the brain stem of cortical cells during REM sleep periods.

activation-information-mode model (AIM) revised version of the activation-synthesis explanation of dreams in which information that is accessed during waking hours can have an influence on the synthesis of dreams.

with unknown and attractive partners (Domhoff, 1996; Foulkes, 1982; Van de Castle, 1994).

In dreams people run, jump, talk, and do all of the actions that they do in normal daily life. In fact, nearly 50 percent of the dreams recorded by Hall (1966) had sexual content, although later research has found lower percentages (Van de Castle, 1994). Then there are dreams of flying, falling, trying to do something and failing, all of which are very common dreams, even in other cultures (Domhoff, 1996). So is a dream of being naked in public.

4.5

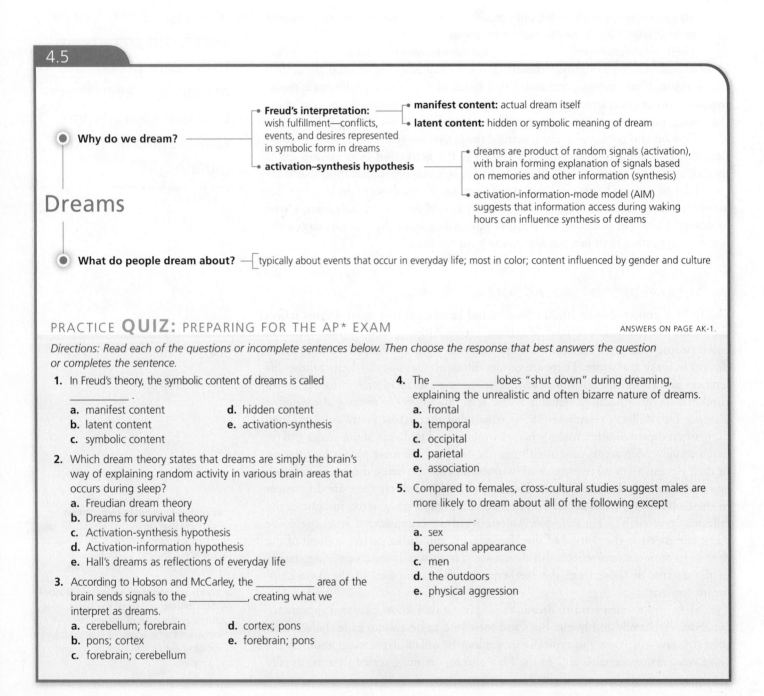

Dreams

Why do we dream?

Freud's interpretation: wish fulfillment—conflicts, events, and desires represented in symbolic form in dreams

- **manifest content:** actual dream itself
- **latent content:** hidden or symbolic meaning of dream

activation–synthesis hypothesis
- dreams are product of random signals (activation), with brain forming explanation of signals based on memories and other information (synthesis)
- activation-information-mode model (AIM) suggests that information access during waking hours can influence synthesis of dreams

What do people dream about? — typically about events that occur in everyday life; most in color; content influenced by gender and culture

PRACTICE QUIZ: PREPARING FOR THE AP* EXAM

ANSWERS ON PAGE AK-1.

Directions: Read each of the questions or incomplete sentences below. Then choose the response that best answers the question or completes the sentence.

1. In Freud's theory, the symbolic content of dreams is called _____ .
   a. manifest content
   b. latent content
   c. symbolic content
   d. hidden content
   e. activation-synthesis

2. Which dream theory states that dreams are simply the brain's way of explaining random activity in various brain areas that occurs during sleep?
   a. Freudian dream theory
   b. Dreams for survival theory
   c. Activation-synthesis hypothesis
   d. Activation-information hypothesis
   e. Hall's dreams as reflections of everyday life

3. According to Hobson and McCarley, the _____ area of the brain sends signals to the _____, creating what we interpret as dreams.
   a. cerebellum; forebrain
   b. pons; cortex
   c. forebrain; cerebellum
   d. cortex; pons
   e. forebrain; pons

4. The _____ lobes "shut down" during dreaming, explaining the unrealistic and often bizarre nature of dreams.
   a. frontal
   b. temporal
   c. occipital
   d. parietal
   e. association

5. Compared to females, cross-cultural studies suggest males are more likely to dream about all of the following except _____ .
   a. sex
   b. personal appearance
   c. men
   d. the outdoors
   e. physical aggression

Altered States: Hypnosis

Hypnosis is a state of consciousness in which a person is especially susceptible to suggestion. Although a lot of misunderstandings exist about hypnosis, it can be a useful tool when properly managed. ⊙─ Watch on MyPsychLab

STEPS IN HYPNOTIC INDUCTION

4.6 How does hypnosis affect consciousness?

There are several key steps in inducing hypnosis. According to Druckman and Bjork (1994), although every hypnotist may have a different style or use different words, these four steps are always present:

1. The hypnotist tells the person to focus on what is being said.
2. The person is told to relax and feel tired.
3. The hypnotist tells the person to "let go" and accept suggestions easily.
4. The person is told to use vivid imagination.

The real key to hypnosis seems to be a heightened state of suggestibility.* People can be hypnotized when active and alert, but only if they are willing to be hypnotized. Only 80 percent of all people can be hypnotized, and only 40 percent are good hypnotic subjects. People who fantasize a lot, who daydream and have vivid imaginations, as well as people who get "really into" whatever task they are doing are more susceptible** to hypnosis than others (Silva & Kirsch, 1992).

A test of *hypnotic susceptibility*, or the degree to which a person is a good hypnotic subject, often makes use of a series of ordered suggestions. The more suggestions in the ordered list the person responds to, the more susceptible that person is. (See Table 4.2 for an example of a susceptibility scale developed at Stanford University.)

FACT OR MYTH: WHAT CAN HYPNOSIS REALLY DO?

Is it true that people can be hypnotized into doing things that they would never do under normal conditions?

Books, movies, and television programs have often misrepresented the effects of hypnosis. Although the popular view is that the hypnotized person is acting

---

Table 4.2 **Sample Items from the Stanford Hypnotic Susceptibility Scale: Form A (SHSS:A)**

1. Postural sway	**5.** Finger lock	**9.** Hallucination (fly)
2. Eye closure	**6.** Arm rigidity (left arm)	**10.** Eye catalepsy
3. Hand lowering (left)	**7.** Hands moving together	**11.** Posthypnotic (changes chairs)
4. Immobilization (right arm)	**8.** Verbal inhibition (name)	**12.** Amnesia

Source: Hilgard, E. (1965). *Hypnotic Susceptibility*. New York: Harcourt, Brace & World.

---

*Suggestibility: being readily influenced.
**Susceptible: easily affected emotionally.

⊙ **Watch** classic video footage on hypnosis. **www.mypsychlab.com**

◄ **AP*** Describe historic and contemporary uses of hypnosis.

◄ **AP*** Explain hypnotic phenomena.

◄ Is it true that people can be hypnotized into doing things that they would never do under normal conditions?

hypnosis state of consciousness in which the person is especially susceptible to suggestion.

involuntarily, the fact is that the hypnotized person is really the one in control. In fact, the hypnotist may only be a guide into a more relaxed state, while the subject actually hypnotizes himself or herself (Kirsch & Lynn, 1995). So relax, you won't be committing any immoral acts or doing anything really objectionable under hypnosis because you are really the one in control. People cannot be hypnotized against their will. The tendency to act as though their behavior is automatic and out of their control is called the *basic suggestion effect* (Kihlstrom, 1985); it gives people an excuse to do things they might not otherwise do because the burden of responsibility for their actions falls on the hypnotist.

Hypnosis is also a controversial tool when used in therapy to help people "recover" what are thought to be repressed memories. Chapter Six has a more detailed discussion of the problems in using hypnosis for memory retrieval. (L I N K) *to Chapter Six: Memory, p. 244.* For a concise look at what hypnosis can and cannot do, see Table 4.3.

In general, hypnosis is a handy way to help people relax and control pain. These subjective experiences are very much under people's mental influence. Actual physical behavior is harder to change, and that is why hypnosis is not as effective at changing eating habits or helping people to stop smoking (Druckman & Bjork, 1994). Hypnosis is sometimes used in psychological therapy to help people cope with anxiety or deal with cravings for food or drugs. ✹ Explore on MyPsychLab

Explore hypnosis and research by Elizabeth Bowman.
www.mypsychlab.com

AP* Identify the major figures in consciousness research. ▶

THEORIES OF HYPNOSIS

There are two views of why hypnosis works. One emphasizes the role of *dissociation*, or a splitting of conscious awareness, whereas the other involves a kind of social role-playing.

Hypnosis as Dissociation: The Hidden Observer   Ernest Hilgard (1991; Hilgard & Hilgard, 1994) believed that hypnosis worked only on the immediate conscious mind of a person, while a part of that person's mind (a "hidden observer") remained aware of all that was going on. It's the same kind of dissociation that takes place when people drive somewhere familiar and then wonder how they got there. One part of the mind, the conscious part, is thinking about dinner or a date or something else, while the other part is doing the actual driving. When people

---

Table 4.3   Facts about Hypnosis

HYPNOSIS CAN:	HYPNOSIS CANNOT:
Create amnesia for whatever happens during the hypnotic session, at least for a brief time (Bowers & Woody, 1996).	Give people superhuman strength. (People may use their full strength under hypnosis, but it is no more than they had before hypnosis.)
Relieve pain by allowing a person to remove conscious attention from the pain (Holroyd, 1996).	Reliably enhance memory. (There's an increased risk of false memory retrieval because of the suggestible state hypnosis creates.)
Alter sensory perceptions. (Smell, hearing, vision, time sense, and the ability to see visual illusions can all be affected by hypnosis.)	Regress people back to childhood. (Although people may *act* like children, they do and say things children would not.)
Help people relax in situations that normally would cause them stress, such as flying on an airplane (Muhlberger et al., 2001).	Regress people to some "past life." There is no scientific evidence for past life regression (Lilienfeld et al., 2004).

Stage hypnotists often make use of people's willingness to believe that something ordinary is extraordinary. This woman was hypnotized and suspended between two chairs after the person supporting her middle stepped away. The hypnotist led the audience to believe that she could not do this unless hypnotized, but in reality anyone can do this while fully conscious.

arrive at their destination, they don't really remember the actual trip. In the same way, Hilgard believes that there is a hidden part of the mind that is very much aware of the hypnotic subject's activities and sensations, even though the "hypnotized" part of the mind is blissfully unaware of these same things.

In one study (Miller & Bowers, 1993), subjects were hypnotized and told to put their arms in ice water, although they were instructed to feel no pain. There had to be pain—most people can't even get an ice cube out of the freezer without *some* pain—but subjects reported no pain at all. The subjects who were successful at denying the pain also reported that they imagined being at the beach or in some other place that allowed them to dissociate* from the pain.

Hypnosis as Social Role-Playing: The Social-Cognitive Explanation　The other theory of why hypnosis works began with an experiment in which people who were *not* hypnotized were instructed to behave as if they were (Sarbin & Coe, 1972). These people had no trouble copying many actions previously thought to require a hypnotic state, such as being rigidly suspended between two chairs. Researchers (Sarbin & Coe, 1972) also found that people who were not familiar with hypnosis, and had no idea what the "role" of a hypnotic subject was supposed to be, could not be hypnotized.

Add to those findings the later findings of Kirsch (2000) that expectancies of the hypnotized person play a big part in how the person responds and what the person does under hypnosis. The **social-cognitive theory of hypnosis** assumes that people who are hypnotized are not in an altered state but are merely playing the role expected of them in the situation. They might believe that they are hypnotized, but in fact it is all a very good performance, so good that even the "subjects" are unaware that they are role-playing. Social roles are very powerful influences on behavior, as anyone who has ever worn a uniform can understand—the uniform stands for a particular role that becomes very easy to play (Zimbardo, 1970; Zimbardo et al., 2000). Ⓛⓘⓝⓚ *to Chapter Fourteen: Social Psychology, pp. 586–587.*

---

*Dissociate: break a connection with something.

social-cognitive theory of hypnosis theory that assumes that people who are hypnotized are not in an altered state but are merely playing the role expected of them in the situation.

4.6

Altered States: Hypnosis

(state of consciousness during which person is more susceptible to suggestion)

- can be assessed by scale of hypnotic susceptibility
- induction typically involves relaxed focus and "permission to let go"; person being hypnotized is in control and cannot be hypnotized against his or her will
- can be used in therapy—help people deal with pain, anxiety, or cravings (e.g., food, drug)
- **theories**
  - **dissociation:** one part of mind is aware of actions/activities taking place, while the "hypnotized" part is not
  - **social-cognitive theory** suggests that people assume roles based on expectations for a given situation

PRACTICE QUIZ: PREPARING FOR THE AP* EXAM

ANSWERS ON PAGE AK-1.

Directions: Read each of the questions or incomplete sentences below. Then choose the response that best answers the question or completes the sentence.

1. Which of the following is not one of the steps in inducing hypnosis?
   a. Putting the person to sleep
   b. Telling the person to relax
   c. Telling the person to use vivid imagination
   d. Telling the person to "let go"
   e. Telling the person to focus

2. The tendency to act as though your behavior is out of your control and involuntary is called (the) _____.
   a. hypnosis effect
   b. basic involuntary effect
   c. basic suggestion effect
   d. social-cognitive theory
   e. none of the above

3. Hypnosis has been successfully used to _____.
   a. reduce sensations of pain
   b. regress a person back to infancy
   c. suspend a person between chairs
   d. give a person superhuman strength
   e. recall memories accurately and completely

4. In the _____ theory of hypnosis, the person has a part of the mind that is not hypnotized and that is fully aware of the proceedings.
   a. social-cognitive
   b. dissociative
   c. role-playing
   d. expectancy
   e. alternative

AP* Discuss drug dependence, addiction, tolerance, and withdrawal.

▶

Altered States: Psychoactive Drugs

Whereas some people seek altered states of consciousness in sleep, daydreaming, meditation, or even hypnosis, others try to take a shortcut. They use drugs that alter thinking, perception, memory, or some combination of those abilities called **psychoactive drugs**. Many of the drugs discussed in the following sections are very useful and were originally developed to help people. Some allow sedation so that operations that would otherwise be impossible can be performed, whereas others help people deal with the pain of injuries or disease. Still others may be used in helping to control various conditions such as sleep disorders or attention deficits in children and adults.

The usefulness of these drugs must not blind us to the dangers of misusing or abusing them. When taken for pleasure, to get "high" or to dull psychological pain, or when taken without the supervision of a qualified medical professional, these drugs can pose serious risks to one's health and may even cause death. One danger of such drugs is their potential to create either a physical or psychological dependence, both of which can lead to a lifelong pattern of abuse as well as the risk of taking increasingly larger doses, leading to one of the clearest dangers of dependence: a drug overdose. Drug overdoses do not happen only with illegal drugs; even certain additives in so-called natural supplements can have a deadly effect. For example, in January 2003,

psychoactive drugs drugs that alter thinking, perception, and memory.

Steve Bechler, a prospective pitcher for the Baltimore Orioles, died after taking three Ephedra pills on an empty stomach (Shekelle et al., 2003). Ephedra is a substance derived from a shrub found in desert areas and has been used in supplements that claim to promote weight loss. ✳ Explore on MyPsychLab

✳ **Explore** with the simulation on psychoactive drugs. **www.mypsychlab.com**

PHYSICAL DEPENDENCE

4.7 What is the difference between a physical dependence and a psychological dependence on a drug?

Drugs that people can become physically dependent on cause the user's body to crave the drug (Abadinsky, 1989; Fleming & Barry, 1992; Pratt, 1991). After using the drug for some period of time, the body becomes unable to function normally without the drug and the person is said to be dependent or addicted, a condition commonly called **physical dependence**.

Drug Tolerance　One sign of physical dependence is the development of a *drug tolerance* (Pratt, 1991). As the person continues to use the drug, larger and larger doses of the drug are needed to achieve the same initial effects of the drug.

Withdrawal　Another sign of a physical dependence is that the user experiences symptoms of **withdrawal** when deprived of the drug. Depending on the drug, these symptoms can range from headaches, nausea, and irritability to severe pain, cramping, shaking, and dangerously elevated blood pressure. These physical sensations occur because the body is trying to adjust to the absence of the drug. Many users will take more of the drug to alleviate the symptoms of withdrawal, which makes the entire situation worse. In Chapter Five, the text will discuss the concept of *negative reinforcement*, the tendency to continue a behavior that leads to the removal of or escape from unpleasant circumstances or sensations. Negative reinforcement is a very powerful motivating factor, and scores of drug-dependent users exist as living proof of that power.

　　But not all drugs produce physical dependence, right? For example, some people say that you can't get physically dependent on marijuana. If that's true, why is it so hard for some people to quit smoking pot?

PSYCHOLOGICAL DEPENDENCE

Not all drugs cause physical dependence; some cause **psychological dependence**, or the belief that the drug is needed to continue a feeling of emotional or psychological well-being, which is a very powerful factor in continued drug use. The body may not need or crave the drug, and people may not experience the symptoms of physical withdrawal or tolerance, but they will continue to use the drug because they *think* they need it. In this case, it is the rewarding properties of using the drug that cause a dependency to develop. In Chapter Five, this is called *positive reinforcement*, or the tendency of a behavior to strengthen when followed by pleasurable consequences. Negative reinforcement is also at work here, as taking the drug will lower levels of anxiety.

　　Although not all drugs produce physical dependence, *any* drug can become a focus of psychological dependence. Indeed, because there is no withdrawal to go through and from which to recover, psychological dependencies can last forever. Some people who gave up smoking pot decades ago still say that the craving returns every now and then (Roffman et al., 1988).

　　The effect of a particular drug depends on the category to which it belongs and the particular neurotransmitter the drug affects. ⓁⒾⓃⓀ *to Chapter Two: The Biological Perspective, pp. 55–57.* This chapter will describe several of the major drug

◄ But not all drugs produce physical dependence, right? For example, some people say that you can't get physically dependent on marijuana. If that's true, why is it so hard for some people to quit smoking pot?

physical dependence　condition occurring when a person's body becomes unable to function normally without a particular drug.

withdrawal　physical symptoms that can include nausea, pain, tremors, crankiness, and high blood pressure, resulting from a lack of an addictive drug in the body systems.

psychological dependence　the feeling that a drug is needed to continue a feeling of emotional or psychological well-being.

categories: **stimulants** (drugs that increase the functioning of the nervous system), **depressants** (drugs that decrease the functioning of the nervous system), **narcotics** (painkilling depressant drugs derived from the opium poppy), and **hallucinogenics** (drugs that alter perceptions and may cause hallucinations).

AP* Identify the major psychoactive drug categories and classify specific drugs, including their psychological and physiological effects.

STIMULANTS: UP, UP, AND AWAY

Stimulants are a class of drugs that cause either the sympathetic division or the central nervous system (or both) to increase levels of functioning, at least temporarily. In simple terms, stimulants "speed up" the nervous system—the heart may beat faster or the brain may work faster, for example. Many of these drugs are called "uppers" for this reason.

4.8 How do stimulants and depressants affect consciousness, and what are the dangers associated with taking them, particularly alcohol?

Amphetamines **Amphetamines** are stimulants that are synthesized (made) in laboratories rather than being found in nature. Among the amphetamines are drugs like Benzedrine, Methedrine, and Dexedrine. Truck drivers use amphetamines to stay awake while driving long hours, and many doctors used to prescribe these drugs as diet pills for overweight people. A related compound, *methamphetamine*, is sometimes used to treat attention-deficit hyperactivity disorder or narcolepsy. "Crystal meth" is a crystalline form that can be smoked and is used by "recreational" drug users, people who do not need drugs but instead use them to gain some form of pleasure.

Black Eyed Peas singer Fergie battled crystal meth addiction earlier in her life, reporting that it was the "..hardest boyfriend I ever had to break up with" (Associated Press, 2006).

Like other stimulants, amphetamines cause the sympathetic nervous system to go into overdrive. **LINK** *to Chapter Two: The Biological Perspective, pp. 62–64.* Stimulants won't give people any extra energy, but they will cause people to burn up whatever energy reserves they do have. They also depress the appetite, which is another function of the sympathetic division. When the energy reserves are exhausted, or the drug wears off, a "crash" is inevitable.

This is why people who take amphetamines often develop a physical dependency on the drug and quickly develop a tolerance. When the "crash" or depression comes, the tendency is to take more pills to get back "up." The person taking these pills finds that it takes more and more pills to get the same stimulant effect. Doses can easily become toxic and deadly. Nausea, vomiting, high blood pressure, and strokes are possible, as is a condition called *amphetamine psychosis*. This condition causes addicts to become delusional (losing contact with what is real) and paranoid. They think people are out to "get" them. Violence is a likely outcome, both against the self and others (Kratofil et al., 1996).

Of course, amphetamines are also used to treat narcolepsy, the sleep disorder discussed earlier in this chapter. They are still used as diet pills, but only on a short-term basis and under strict medical supervision. The diet aids people buy over the counter usually contain another relatively mild stimulant, caffeine.

stimulants drugs that increase the functioning of the nervous system.

depressants drugs that decrease the functioning of the nervous system.

narcotics a class of opium-related drugs that suppress the sensation of pain by binding to and stimulating the nervous system's natural receptor sites for endorphins.

hallucinogenics drugs including hallucinogens and marijuana that produce hallucinations or increased feelings of relaxation and intoxication.

amphetamines stimulants that are synthesized (made) in laboratories rather than being found in nature.

cocaine a natural drug derived from the leaves of the coca plant.

Cocaine Unlike amphetamines, **cocaine** is a natural drug found in coca plant leaves. It produces feelings of euphoria (a feeling of great happiness), energy, power, and pleasure. It also deadens pain and suppresses the appetite. It was used rather liberally by both doctors and dentists (who used it in numbing the mouth prior to extracting a tooth, for example) near the end of the nineteenth century and the beginning of the twentieth century, until the deadly effects of its addictive qualities became known. Many patent medicines contained minute traces of cocaine, including the now famous Coca-Cola™ (this popular soft drink was originally marketed as a nerve tonic). The good news is that even in 1902, there wasn't enough cocaine in a bottle of cola to affect even a fly, and by 1929, all traces of cocaine were removed (Allen, 1994).

Cocaine is a highly dangerous drug, not just for its addictive properties. Some people have convulsions and may even die when using cocaine for the first time (Lacayo, 1995). It has devastating effects on the children born to mothers who use cocaine, causing learning disabilities, hyperactivity, delayed language development, and tremors, among other symptoms (Blatt et al., 2000; Frank et al., 2001). Laboratory animals have been known to press a lever to give themselves cocaine rather than eating or drinking, even to the point of starvation and death (Iwamoto & Martin, 1988; Ward et al., 1996).

What are the signs of physical dependency? Although cocaine users do not go through the same kind of physical withdrawal symptoms that users of heroin, alcohol, and other physically addictive drugs go through, users will experience a severe mood swing into depression (the "crash"), followed by extreme tiredness, nervousness, an inability to feel pleasure, and paranoia. The brain is the part of the body that develops the craving for cocaine because of chemical changes caused by the drug (Hurley, 1989). There are three basic signs of physical dependency:

- **Compulsive use.** If cocaine is available, the person has to use it. He or she can't say no to it.

- **Loss of control.** Once people start using it, they can't stop until it is all gone or they have exhausted themselves to the point where they can no longer function.

- **Disregard for the consequences of use.** Cocaine addicts will lie, cheat, steal, lose their jobs, damage or break up relationships, and use rent money to buy cocaine—nothing else matters to them but the drug.

As addictive as cocaine is, there is one other stimulant that comes in a very close second. The Surgeon General's Report (Centers for Disease Control and Prevention [CDC], 1992) reports that although crack cocaine (a less pure, cheaper version found on the streets) produces addiction in every person who uses it, nicotine produces addiction in 99 percent of the people who use it.

Hasn't nicotine just been the victim of a lot of bad press? After all, it's legal, unlike cocaine and heroin.

Nicotine Every year, nearly 438,000 people in the United States die from illnesses related to smoking. That's more people than those who die from accidents in motor vehicles, alcohol, cocaine, heroin and other drug abuse, AIDS, suicide, and homicide *combined* (CDC, 2002). Remember, cocaine, heroin, morphine, and many other currently controlled substances or illegal drugs once used to be legal. One has to wonder what would have been the fate of these drugs if as many people had been making money off of them at that time as do those who farm, manufacture, and distribute tobacco products today.

Nicotine is a relatively mild but nevertheless toxic stimulant, producing a slight "rush" or sense of arousal as it raises blood pressure and accelerates the heart, as well as providing a rush of sugar into the bloodstream by stimulating the release

Hasn't nicotine just been the victim ◀ of a lot of bad press? After all, it's legal, unlike cocaine and heroin.

nicotine the active ingredient in tobacco.

Sleep deprivation causes this man to struggle to wake up. Caffeine can help with alertness but may worsen his sleep deprivation when he tries to get a decent night's sleep tonight.

of adrenalin (Rezvani & Levin, 2001). As is the case with many stimulants, it also has a relaxing effect on most people and seems to reduce stress (Pormerleau & Pormerleau, 1994).

Although fewer Americans are smoking (down to about 25 percent from over 40 percent in the sixties), women and teenagers are actually smoking more than before (CDC, 2002). This is alarming news when one considers the toxic nature of nicotine: In the 1920s and 1930s it was used as an insecticide and is considered to be highly toxic and fast-acting (Gosselin et al., 1984). Although the amount of nicotine in a cigarette is low, first-time smokers often experience nausea as a result of the toxic effects after just a few puffs.

Quitting is a good idea but hard to accomplish for many people. Although there are a lucky few who can quit "cold turkey" without ever smoking again, the majority of people who quit will start smoking again, even after having quit for years.

Why is it so difficult to quit? Aside from the powerfully addictive nature of nicotine, the physical withdrawal symptoms can be as bad as those resulting from alcohol, cocaine, or heroin abuse (Epping-Jordan et al., 1998). People don't think about nicotine as being as bad as cocaine or heroin because nicotine is legal and easily obtainable, but in terms of its addictive power, it is *more powerful* than heroin or alcohol (Henningfield et al., 1990).

There are many ways to quit, but the most effective methods involve delayed smoking (Cincirpini et al., 1995). In delayed smoking, the smoker begins by delaying that first cigarette of the morning, increasing the delay by a little bit every morning. Next, the total number of cigarettes smoked each day is reduced. There are also medications that can help smokers deal with the cravings for nicotine while they try to quit, as well as nicotine-containing gums and patches (worn on the skin to deliver a measured dose of nicotine in decreasing doses). The gum and patch methods deliver nicotine in a much safer, less-addictive way, allowing the smoker to control the cravings until quitting completely (Benowitz, 1996; Henningfield, 1995; Stitzer & De Wit, 1998).

Caffeine   Although many people will never use amphetamines or take cocaine, and others will never smoke or will quit successfully, there is one stimulant that almost everyone uses, with many using it every day. Of course, this is **caffeine**, the stimulant found in coffee, tea, most sodas, chocolate, and even many over-the-counter drugs.

Caffeine is another natural substance, like cocaine and nicotine, and is found in coffee beans, tea leaves, cocoa nuts, and at least 60 other types of plants (Braun, 1996). It is a mild stimulant, helps maintain alertness, and can increase the effectiveness of some pain relievers such as aspirin. Caffeine is often added to pain relievers for that reason and is the key ingredient in medications meant to keep people awake.

For a comparison of amounts of caffeine in some beverages, see Table 4.4.

DOWN IN THE VALLEY: DEPRESSANTS

Another class of psychoactive drugs is *depressants*, drugs that slow the central nervous system.

Barbiturates or a Major Tranquilizers   Commonly known as the *major tranquilizers* (drugs that have a strong depressant effect) or sleeping pills, **barbiturates** are drugs that have a sedative (sleep-inducing) effect. The effects, depending on dosage levels,

caffeine   a mild stimulant found in coffee, tea, and several other plant-based substances.

barbiturates   depressant drugs that have a sedative effect.

Table 4.4 Average Caffeine Content of Some Beverages	
PRODUCT (8 OZ. EXCEPT AS NOTED)	CAFFEINE (MILLIGRAMS)
Brewed coffee	60–120
Decaffeinated coffee	2–4
Espresso/cappuccino (1 oz.)	30–50
Tea brewed 1 minute	9–33
Tea brewed 3 minutes	20–46
Tea brewed 5 minutes	20–50
Iced tea (8 oz./12 oz.)	15–24/22–36
Hot cocoa	3–32
Milk chocolate (1 oz.)	1–15
Dark chocolate (1 oz.)	5–35
Jolt soda (8 oz./12 oz.)	47/71
Mountain Dew (8 oz./12 oz.)	36/54
Coca-Cola (8 oz./12 oz.)	31/46
Pepsi (8 oz./12 oz.)	24/36

Source: Barone and Roberts (1996).

range from mild sedation or sleepiness to unconsciousness or coma. Overdoses can lead to death as breathing and heart action are stopped. Barbiturates are highly addictive and users can quickly develop a tolerance. Withdrawal can be as serious as convulsions, which are life threatening (Olin, 1993).

Another danger of barbiturate use is the combination of one of these drugs with alcohol, another kind of depressant drug. A person who takes a dose of barbiturates that is not deadly in and of itself may die from the interaction of that dose with alcohol. This is called a *drug interaction* and is a major contributor to many unfortunate deaths.

"Nowadays, Hal is ninety-nine per cent caffeine-free."

Benzodiazepines or the Minor Tranquilizers   The *minor tranquilizers* (drugs having a relatively mild depressant effect) are called **benzodiazepines**. These drugs are used to lower anxiety and reduce stress. They are considered safer than barbiturates and are now the drugs of choice to treat sleep problems, nervousness, and anxiety. Some of the most common are Valium, Xanax, Halcion, Ativan, and Librium. Even these minor tranquilizers can be addictive, and large doses can be dangerous, as can an interaction with alcohol or other drugs.

ALCOHOL

The most commonly used and abused depressant is **alcohol**, the chemical resulting from fermentation or distillation of various kinds of vegetable matter. Anywhere from 10 to 20 million people in the United States suffer from alcoholism. Aside from the

benzodiazepines   drugs that lower anxiety and reduce stress.

alcohol   the chemical resulting from fermentation or distillation of various kinds of vegetable matter.

Although many young adults see drinking as a rite of passage into adulthood, few may understand the dangers of "binge" drinking, or drinking four to five drinks within a limited amount of time. Inhibitions are lowered and poor decisions may be made, such as driving while intoxicated. Binge drinking, a popular activity on some college campuses, can also lead to alcoholism.

I have friends who insist that alcohol is a stimulant because they feel more uninhibited when they drink, so ▶ why is it considered a depressant?

obvious health risks to the liver, brain, and heart, alcohol is associated with loss of work time, loss of a job, and loss of economic stability.

Signs of Alcohol Abuse Many people are alcoholics but deny the fact, a common psychological defense. (L I N K) *to Chapter Nine: Stress and Health, pp. 374–375.* They believe that getting drunk, especially in college, is a ritual of adulthood. Many college students and even older adults engage in binge drinking (drinking four or five drinks within a limited amount of time, such as at "happy hour"). Binge drinking quickly leads to being drunk, and drunkenness is a major sign of alcoholism. Some other danger signs are feeling guilty about drinking, drinking in the morning, drinking to recover from drinking, drinking alone, being sensitive about how much one drinks when others mention it, drinking so much that one does and says things one later regrets, drinking enough to have blackouts or memory loss, drinking too fast, lying about drinking, and drinking enough to pass out.

The dangers of abusing alcohol cannot be stressed enough. According to the National Center for Health Statistics (National Center for Health Statistics [NCHS], 2007), the number of alcohol-induced deaths in 2003 was 20,687. This figure does *not* include deaths due to accidents and homicides, that may be related to abuse of alcohol—only those deaths that are caused by the body's inability to handle the alcohol. Of these deaths, 12,360 were attributed to liver disease caused by alcoholism. The National Institute on Alcoholism and Alcohol Abuse (National Institute on Alcoholism and Alcohol Abuse [NIAAA], 2007) has statistics from 2001–2002 showing that the rate of psychiatric disorders, including alcohol and other drug abuse as well as depression and anxiety disorders, increases from about 2.5 percent for a light drinker to 13.2 percent for a moderate drinker and around 17.1 percent for a heavy drinker. Alcohol was involved in nearly 22.5 percent of the fatal traffic crashes for drivers under 21 and 24.8 percent of the fatal crashes for those over 21 (NIAAA, 2007).

There are numerous disorders that can be caused by alcoholism in addition to liver disease. *Korsakoff's syndrome* is a form of dementia brought about by a severe vitamin B1 deficiency, caused by the alcoholic's tendency to drink rather than eat (Manzo et al., 1994). Pregnant women should not drink at all, as alcohol can damage the growing embryo, causing a condition of mental retardation and physical deformity known as fetal alcohol syndrome. (L I N K) *to Chapter Ten: Development Across the Life Span, p. 395.* Increased risk of loss of bone density (known as osteoporosis) and heart disease has also been linked to alcoholism (Abbott et al., 1994). These are just a few of the many health problems that alcohol can cause.

If you are concerned about a friend or loved one's drinking habits, there is a free and very simple online assessment at this site on the Internet: **www.alcoholscreening.org**.

I have friends who insist that alcohol is a stimulant because they feel more uninhibited when they drink, so why is it considered a depressant?

Alcohol is often confused with stimulants. Many people think this is because alcohol makes a person feel "up" and euphoric (happy). Actually, alcohol is a depressant that gives the illusion of stimulation, because the very first thing alcohol depresses is a person's natural inhibitions, or the "don'ts" of behavior. Inhibitions are all the social rules people have learned that allow them to get along with others and function in society. Inhibitions also keep people from taking off all their clothes and dancing on the table at a crowded bar—inhibitions are a good thing.

Table 4.5   Blood Alcohol Level and Behavior Associated with Amounts of Alcohol

A drink is a drink. Each contains half an ounce of alcohol.
So a drink is . . .

- 1 can of beer (12 oz. 4–5% alcohol)
- 1 glass of wine (4 oz. 12% alcohol)
- 1 shot of most liquors (1 oz. 40–50% alcohol)

At times "a drink" is really the equivalent of more than just one drink, like when you order a drink with more than one shot of alcohol in it, or you do a shot followed by a beer.

AVERAGE NUMBER OF DRINKS	BLOOD ALCOHOL LEVEL	BEHAVIOR
1–2 drinks	.05%	Feeling of well-being
		Release of inhibitions
		Judgment impaired
		Coordination and level of alertness lowered
		Increased risk of collision while driving
3–5 drinks	.10%	Reaction time significantly slowed
		Muscle control and speech impaired
		Limited night and side vision
		Loss of self-control
		Crash risk greatly increased
6–7 drinks	.15%	Consistent and major increases in reaction time
8–10 drinks	.20%	Loss of equilibrium and technical skills
		Sensory and motor capabilities depressed
		Double vision and legal blindness (20/200)
		Unfit to drive for up to 10 hours
10–14 drinks	.20% and .25%	Staggering and severe motor disturbances
10–14 drinks	.30%	Not aware of surroundings
10–14 drinks	.35%	Surgical anesthesia
		Lethal dosage for a small percentage of people
14–20 drinks	.40%	Lethal dosage for about 50% of people
		Severe circulatory/respiratory depression
		Alcohol poisoning/overdose

Source: Adapted from the *Moderate Drinking Skills Study Guide*. (2004). Eau-Claire, WI: University of Wisconsin.

Many people are unaware of exactly what constitutes a "drink." Table 4.5 explains this and show the effects of various numbers of drinks on behavior. Alcohol, as stated in Chapter Two, indirectly stimulates the release of a neurotransmitter called GABA, the brain's major depressant (Brick, 2003). GABA slows down or stops neural activity. As more GABA is released, the brain's functioning actually becomes more and more inhibited, depressed, or slowed down. The areas of the brain that are first affected by alcohol are unfortunately the areas that control social inhibitions, so alcohol (due to its simulation of GABA) has the effect of depressing the inhibitions. As the effects continue, motor skills, reaction time, and speech are all affected.

Some people might be surprised that only one drink can have a fairly strong effect. People who are not usually drinkers will feel the effects of alcohol much more quickly than those who have built up a tolerance. Women also feel the effects sooner, as their bodies process alcohol differently than men's bodies do. (Women are typically smaller, too, so alcohol has a quicker impact on women.) ◉│Watch on **MyPsychLab**

◉ **Watch** videos on alcohol and the brain as well as alcoholism. **www.mypsychlab.com**

4.9 What are some of the effects and dangers of using narcotics and hallucinogens, including marijuana?

NARCOTICS: I FEEL YOUR PAIN

Narcotics are a class of drugs that suppress the sensation of pain by binding to and stimulating the nervous system's natural receptor sites for endorphins, the neurotransmitters that naturally deaden pain sensations (Olin, 1993). Because they also slow down the action of the nervous system, drug interactions with alcohol and other depressants are possible—and deadly. All narcotics are a derivative of a particular plant-based substance—opium.

Opium **Opium**, made from the opium poppy, has pain-relieving and euphoria-inducing properties that have been known for at least 2,000 years. It was commonly used by ladies of the Victorian era in a form called *laudanum* and was still prescribed as *paregoric* for teething infants in the middle of the twentieth century. (Your own parents or grandparents may have been given paregoric as infants.) It was not until 1803 that opium was developed for use as a medication by a German physician. The new form—morphine—was hailed as "God's own medicine" (Hodgson, 2001).

Morphine **Morphine** was created by dissolving opium in an acid and then neutralizing the acid with ammonia. Morphine was thought to be a wonder drug, although its addictive qualities soon became a major concern to physicians and their patients. Morphine is still used today but in carefully controlled doses and for short periods of time.

Heroin Ironically, **heroin** was first hailed as the new wonder drug—a derivative of morphine that did not have many of the disagreeable side effects of morphine. The theory was that heroin was a purer form of the drug, and that the impurities in morphine were the substances creating the harmful side effects. It did not take long, however, for doctors and others to realize that heroin was even more powerfully addictive than morphine or opium. Although usage as a medicine ceased, it is still used by many people.

Why are morphine and heroin so addictive?

Why are morphine and ▶ heroin so addictive?

Think back to Chapter Two, which discussed the roles of endorphins in relieving pain. Opium and its derivatives, morphine and heroin, duplicate the action of endorphins so well that the nervous system slows or stops its production of the neurotransmitter. When the drug wears off, there is no protection against any kind of pain, causing the severe symptoms of withdrawal associated with these drugs. The addict who tries to quit using the drug feels such pain that the urge to use again becomes unbearable.

Methadone is also a derivative of opium but does not produce the euphoric "high" of morphine or heroin. It is used to control heroin dependency and can be taken only once a day to control the withdrawal symptoms that would otherwise follow when stopping heroin use (Kahan & Sutton, 1998). Two other drugs, buprenorphine and naltrexone, are also used to treat opiate addictions (Kakko et al., 2003; Ward et al., 1999). Eventually, as the addicted person is weaned from these drugs, the natural endorphin system starts to function more normally. This means that one does not have to take these other drugs forever.

opium substance derived from the opium poppy from which all narcotic drugs are derived.

morphine narcotic drug derived from opium, used to treat severe pain.

heroin narcotic drug derived from opium that is extremely addictive.

The "high" of drug use, whether it comes from an opiate derivative, a stimulant, or a depressant such as alcohol, often takes place in certain surroundings, with certain other people, and perhaps even using certain objects, such as the tiny spoons used by cocaine addicts. These people, settings, and objects can become cues that are associated with the drug high. When the cues are present, it may be even harder to resist using the drug because the body and mind have become conditioned, or trained, to associate drug use with the cues. This is a form of *classical conditioning.* (L)(I)(N)(K) *to Chapter Five: Learning, pp. 177–178.* This learned behavioral effect has led to nondrug treatments that make use of behavioral therapies such as *contingency management therapy*, in which patients earn vouchers for negative drug tests (Tusel et al., 1994). The vouchers can be exchanged for healthier, more desirable items like food. These behavioral therapies can include residential and outpatient approaches. (L)(I)(N)(K) *to Chapter Thirteen: Psychological Therapies, p. 527. Cognitive-behavioral interventions* work to change the way people think about the stresses in their lives and react to those stressors, working toward more effective coping without resorting to heroin.

HALLUCINOGENS: HIGHER AND HIGHER

Hallucinogens actually cause the brain to alter its interpretation of sensations (Olin, 1993) and can produce sensory distortions very similar to the disorder *synesthesia* (L)(I)(N)(K) *to Chapter Three: Sensation and Perception, p. 88,* in which sensations cross over each other—colors have sound, sounds have smells, and so on. False sensory perceptions, called *hallucinations*, are often experienced, especially with the more powerful hallucinogens. As with other stimulants, there are two basic types—those that are created in a laboratory and those that are from natural sources.

Manufactured Highs There are several drugs that were developed in the laboratory instead of being found in nature. Perhaps because these drugs are manufactured, they are often more potent than drugs found in the natural world. ✱ Explore on MyPsychLab

LSD **LSD**, or **lysergic acid diethylamide**, is synthesized from a grain fungus called *ergot*. Ergot fungus commonly grows on rye grain but can be found on other grains as well. First manufactured in 1938, LSD is one of the most potent, or powerful, hallucinogens (Lee & Shlain, 1986). It takes only a very tiny drop of LSD to achieve a "high."

People who take LSD usually do so to get that high feeling. Some people feel that LSD helps them to expand their consciousness or awareness of the world around them. Colors seem more intense, sounds more beautiful, and so on. But the fact is that LSD takes people out of the real world and dumps them into a world of the brain's creation. This is not always a pleasant experience, just as dreams are not always filled with positive emotions. "Bad trips" are quite common, and there is no way to control what kind of "trip" the brain is going to decide to take.

One of the greater dangers in using LSD is the effect it has on a person's ability to perceive reality. Real dangers and hazards in the world may go unnoticed by a person "lost" in an LSD fantasy, and people under the influence of this drug may make poor decisions, such as trying to drive while high.

PCP Another synthesized drug was found to be so dangerous that it became useful only in veterinary medicine as a tranquilizer. The drug is **PCP** (which stands for *p*henyl *c*yclohexyl *p*iperidine, a name which is often contracted as *phencyclidine*) and can have many different effects. Depending on the dosage, it can be a hallucinogen, stimulant, depressant, or an analgesic (painkilling) drug. As with LSD, PCP users can experience hallucinations, distorted sensations, and very unpleasant effects. PCP can also lead to acts of violence against others or suicide (Brecher 1988; Cami et al., 2000). Users may even physically injure themselves unintentionally because PCP causes them to feel no warning signal of pain.

✱ **Explore** other dangerous synthetic drugs. **www.mypsychlab.com**

hallucinogens drugs that cause false sensory messages, altering the perception of reality.

LSD (lysergic acid diethylamide) powerful synthetic hallucinogen.

PCP synthesized drug now used as an animal tranquilizer that can cause stimulant, depressant, narcotic, or hallucinogenic effects.

MDMA (Ecstasy) This last synthetic drug is technically an amphetamine but is capable of producing hallucinations as well. In fact, both **MDMA** (a "designer drug" known on the streets as **Ecstasy** or simply **X**) and PCP are now classified as **stimulatory hallucinogenics**, drugs that produce a mixture of psychomotor stimulant and hallucinogenic effects (Shuglin, 1986). Although many users of MDMA believe that it is relatively harmless, the fact is that it can be deadly. One of the properties of this drug is to dehydrate the body and raise body temperature, so it is very important that someone taking this drug drink enough water. But excessive drinking of water can also lead to coma and death, as excess fluid can disrupt the salt content of body tissue, making it impossible for all body parts to function properly. A person under the influence of MDMA (ecstasy) might forget to drink enough water—or might drink far too much. Adding to the risk is the possibility that Ecstasy users are also consuming alcohol, and that interaction increases the dehydration and rise in body temperature (Leccese et al., 2000).

Nonmanufactured Highs A number of substances found in nature can produce hallucinogenic effects. Although some people might refer to these substances as "natural" highs, they are still drugs and still potentially dangerous, especially when used in conjunction with driving a vehicle or performing some other task that requires a clear head and focused attention.

Mescaline **Mescaline** comes from the buttons found on the peyote cactus and has long been a part of many Native American religious and spiritual rituals. The duration of its hallucinogenic effects can last longer than those of LSD (Aghajanian & Marek, 1999). Native Americans have used mescaline in combination with sitting in a hut or other enclosed space while water is poured over very hot rocks. This sauna effect, together with the drug, may produce sensations of being out of one's own body or talking with spirits, which is the purpose of these rituals (Lyvers, 2003).

Psilocybin **Psilocybin** (sigh-luh-SIGH-bun) is another naturally occurring hallucinogen, contained in a certain kind of mushroom, often referred to as "magic mushrooms." Like mescaline, it has also been used in similar rituals by several native cultures (Aghajanian & Marek, 1999).

Is using mescaline or psilocybin addictive?

Neither mescaline nor psilocybin has been shown to create physical dependency, but as with any psychoactive drug, psychological dependency is possible (Lyvers, 2003). Eating psilocybin has been linked, however, to a psychiatric disorder called hallucinogen-persisting perception disorder (HPPD), as has the next drug: marijuana (Espiard et al., 2005).

MARIJUANA

One of the best known and most commonly abused of the hallucinogenic drugs, **marijuana** (also called *pot* or *weed*) comes from the leaves and flowers of the hemp plant called *cannabis sativa*. (*Hashish* is the concentrated substance made by scraping the resin from these leaves, and both marijuana and hashish contain *cannabinoids*.) The most psychoactive cannabinois, and the active ingredient in marijuana, is *tetrahydrocannabinol* (THC). Marijuana is best known for its ability to produce a feeling of well-being, mild intoxication, and mild sensory distortions or hallucinations (Olin, 1993; Tart, 1970).

The effects of marijuana are relatively mild compared to the other hallucinogens. In fact, an inexperienced user who doesn't know what to expect upon smoking that first marijuana cigarette may feel nothing at all. Most people do report a feeling of mild euphoria and relaxation, along with an altered time sense and mild visual distortions.

Is using mescaline or psilocybin addictive? ▶

MDMA (Ecstasy or **X)** designer drug that can have both stimulant and hallucinatory effects.

stimulatory hallucinogenics drugs that produce a mixture of psychomotor stimulant and hallucinogenic effects.

mescaline natural hallucinogen derived from the peyote cactus buttons.

psilocybin natural hallucinogen found in certain mushrooms.

marijuana mild hallucinogen (also known as *pot* or *weed*) derived from the leaves and flowers of a particular type of hemp plant.

Higher doses can lead to hallucinations, delusions, and the all-too-common paranoia. Most studies of marijuana's effects have concluded that while marijuana can create a powerful psychological dependency, it does not produce physical dependency or physical withdrawal symptoms. Newer studies, however, suggest that long-term marijuana use can produce signs of withdrawal such as irritability, memory difficulties, sleep difficulties, and increased aggression (Block & Ghoneim, 1993; Budney et al., 2001; Kouri et al., 1999; Pope et al., 2001). A recent study of the long-term effects of marijuana use has also correlated smoking marijuana with an increased risk of psychotic behavior, with a greater risk for heavier users (Moore et al., 2007).

Even at mild doses, it is not safe to operate heavy machinery or drive a car while under the influence of marijuana. The effect on a person's reaction time and perception of surroundings is too damaging to the ability to make the split-second decisions that are required in driving.

Marijuana is most commonly smoked like tobacco, but some people have been known to eat it baked into brownies or other foods. This is a kind of double duty for the doctored food, as marijuana stimulates the appetite.

Although no one has ever been known to die from an overdose of marijuana, it is not exactly a healthy habit. Research linking marijuana smoking and lung cancer is not clear due to many studies not being able to control for confounding variables, (L)(I)(N)(K) *to Chapter One: The Science of Psychology, pp. 27–28,* such as cigarette smoking, alcohol use, or other risk factors (Hall, 2009). Aside from those mentioned above, probable adverse effects from chronic non-medical marijuana use also include increased risk of motor vehicle crashes, chronic bronchitis or other lung problems, and cardiovascular disease. In adolescents that are regular users, psychosocial development, educational attainment, and mental health can be negatively impacted (Hall, 2009).

Table 4.6 summarizes the various types of drugs, their common names, and their effects on human behavior.

Cannabis is reported to relieve pain in cases of multiple sclerosis and chronic pain from nerve damage. Such use is controversial as cannabis is classified as an illegal drug in some countries.

Table 4.6   How Drugs Affect Consciousness

DRUG CLASSIFICATION	COMMON NAME	MAIN EFFECT	ADVERSE EFFECTS
Depressants			
Alcohol	Beer, wine, spirits	Relaxation	Alcoholism, health problems, depression, increased risk of accidents, death
Barbiturates (tranquilizers)	Nembutal, Seconal		Addiction, brain damage, death
Stimulants			
Amphetamines	Methamphetamine, speed, Ritalin, Dexedrine	Stimulation, excitement	Risk of addiction, stroke, fatal heart problems, psychosis
Cocaine	Cocaine, crack		Risk of addiction, stroke, fatal heart problems, psychosis
Nicotine	Tobacco		Addiction, cancer
Caffeine	Coffee, tea		Caffeinism, high blood pressure
Narcotics (Opiates)	Morphine, heroin	Euphoria	Addiction, death
Hallucinogens	Marijuana, hashish, LSD, Ecstasy	Distorted consciousness, altered perception	Possible permanent memory problems, bad "trips," suicide, overdose, and death

4.7–9

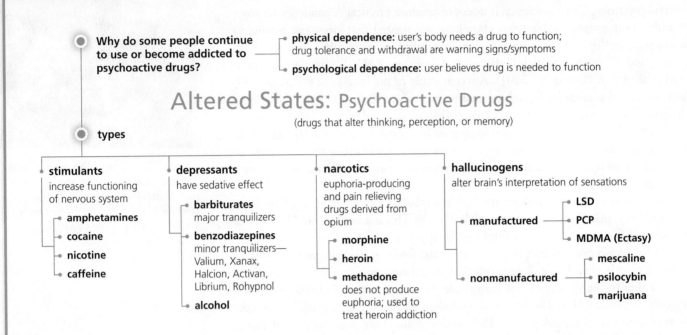

Why do some people continue to use or become addicted to psychoactive drugs?

physical dependence: user's body needs a drug to function; drug tolerance and withdrawal are warning signs/symptoms

psychological dependence: user believes drug is needed to function

Altered States: Psychoactive Drugs
(drugs that alter thinking, perception, or memory)

types

stimulants
increase functioning of nervous system
- **amphetamines**
- **cocaine**
- **nicotine**
- **caffeine**

depressants
have sedative effect
- **barbiturates**
  major tranquilizers
- **benzodiazepines**
  minor tranquilizers—Valium, Xanax, Halcion, Activan, Librium, Rohypnol
- **alcohol**

narcotics
euphoria-producing and pain relieving drugs derived from opium
- **morphine**
- **heroin**
- **methadone**
  does not produce euphoria; used to treat heroin addiction

hallucinogens
alter brain's interpretation of sensations
- **manufactured**
  - **LSD**
  - **PCP**
  - **MDMA (Ectasy)**
- **nonmanufactured**
  - **mescaline**
  - **psilocybin**
  - **marijuana**

PRACTICE QUIZ: PREPARING FOR THE AP* EXAM

ANSWERS ON PAGE AK-1.

Directions: Read each of the questions or incomplete sentences below. Then choose the response that best answers the question or completes the sentence.

1. What are two signs of physical dependence?
   a. Drug tolerance and psychological cravings
   b. Psychological cravings and withdrawal
   c. Drug tolerance and withdrawal
   d. Psychological cravings and nausea
   e. Withdrawal and nausea

2. Larger and larger doses of amphetamines can lead to a severe mental disturbance and paranoia called _____.
   a. amphetamine neurosis
   b. amphetamine psychosis
   c. amphetaminism
   d. amphetamine toxicity
   e. none of the above

3. Doris is really tired and wants a quick "pick-me-up." Which of the following would contain the highest amount of caffeine to help her feel energized?
   a. An 8-ounce cup of strong coffee
   b. A 1-ounce cup of espresso
   c. A 12-ounce can of Jolt soda
   d. A 12-ounce can of Mountain Dew soda
   e. An 8-ounce cup of tea that was brewed for five minutes

4. Several of her friends suspect that Marnie is using some sort of drug. She is very thin, stays awake for long periods of time, and is often jittery, nervous, and somewhat paranoid. If Marnie is using a drug, it is likely to be _____.
   a. alcohol
   b. marijuana
   c. sleeping pills
   d. benzodiazepine
   e. an amphetamine

5. All narcotics are derived from _____.
   a. cannabis
   b. opium
   c. mescaline
   d. morphine
   e. tobacco

6. Which of the following hallucinogens is not a synthetically created drug?
   a. Psilocybin
   b. LSD
   c. PCP
   d. MDMA
   e. All of the above

Applying Psychology to Everyday Life: Are You Sleep Deprived?

4.10 How serious is the problem of sleep deprivation?

Sleep deprivation has long been considered a fact of life for many people, especially college students. Dr. William Dement (1997), one of the most renowned sleep experts in the field, believes that people are ignorant of the detrimental effects of sleep deprivation. Here are some of the facts he points out concerning the widespread nature of sleep deprivation:

◄ **AP*** Discuss aspects of sleep and dreaming.

- 55 percent of drowsy driving fatalities occur under the age of 25.
- 56 percent of the adult population reports that daytime drowsiness is a problem.
- In a study of 1,000 people who reported no daytime drowsiness, 34 percent were actually found to be dangerously sleepy.
- In samples of undergraduates, nurses, and medical students, 80 percent were dangerously sleep deprived.

Dr. Dement cautions that drowsiness should be considered a red alert. Contrary to many people's belief that drowsiness indicates the first step in falling asleep, he states that drowsiness is the last step—if you are drowsy, you are seconds away from sleep.

In an article published by CNN on its interactive Web site (**www.cnn.com/HEALTH/9703/17/nfm/sleep.deprivation/index.html**), the National Commission on Sleep Disorders (1997) estimates that "sleep deprivation costs $150 billion a year in higher stress and reduced workplace productivity." Sleep deprivation was one of the factors indicated in such disasters as the explosion of the *Challenger*, the Exxon *Valdez* oil spill, and the Chernobyl disaster.

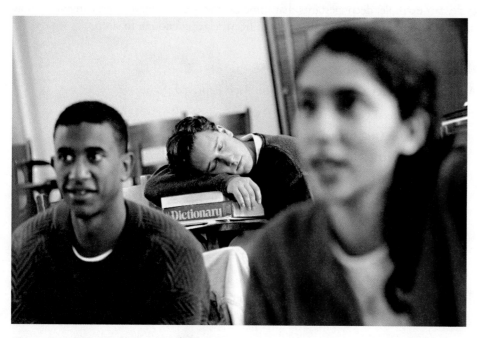

The student in the background is unable to stay awake during his class, indicating that he is seriously sleep deprived. Has this happened to you?

More disturbing facts (data taken from Williamson & Feyer, 2000):

- 30 to 40 percent of all heavy truck accidents can be attributed to driver fatigue.
- Drivers who are awake for 17 to 19 hours were more dangerous than drivers with a blood alcohol level of .05.
- 16 to 60 percent of road accidents involve sleep deprivation (the wide variation is due to the inability to confirm the cause of accidents, as the drivers are often killed).
- Sleep deprivation is linked to higher levels of stress, anxiety, depression, and unnecessary risk taking.

Clearly, sleep deprivation is a serious and all-too-common problem. In today's 24-hour-a-day society, stores are always open, services such as banking and transportation are always available, and many professionals (such as nurses, doctors, and firefighters) must work varying shifts around the clock (Knauth, 1993). As stated earlier, shift work can seriously disrupt the normal sleep–wake cycle, often causing insomnia.

CAUSES OF SLEEP DEPRIVATION

Many of the sleep disorders that were discussed in this chapter are themselves causes of sleep deprivation. Sleep apnea, narcolepsy, sleepwalking, night terrors, and a condition called "restless leg syndrome," in which a person constantly moves his or her legs that are tingly or have crawling sensations, are all causes. Yet these problems are not the sole, or most common, cause of sleep deprivation.

The most obvious cause is the refusal of many people to go to sleep at a reasonable time, so that they can get the 8 hours of sleep that most adults need in order to function well (Bonnet & Arand, 1995). People want to watch that last bit of news or get a little more work done or party into the wee hours. Another reason for sleep loss is worry. People live in stressful times, and many people worry about a variety of concerns: debts, the stock market, relationships, war, rising crime, and so on. Finally, some medications that people take, both prescription and over-the-counter drugs, interfere with the sleep–wake cycle. For example, decongestants that some people take to relieve sinus congestion may cause a racing heartbeat, preventing them from relaxing enough to sleep.

HOW CAN YOU TELL IF YOU ARE SLEEP DEPRIVED?

According to Fahey (1993), you may be sleep deprived if you:

- actually need your alarm clock to wake up.
- find getting out of bed in the morning is a struggle.
- feel tired, irritable, or stressed out for much of the day.
- have trouble concentrating or remembering.
- fall asleep watching TV, in meetings, lectures, or warm rooms.
- fall asleep after heavy meals or after a low dose of alcohol.
- fall asleep within 5 minutes of getting into bed. (A well-rested person actually takes 15 to 20 minutes to fall asleep.)

If you are interested in learning more about sleep deprivation and sleep disorders that can cause it, try searching the Internet. There are some excellent sites about sleep and sleep disorders, including many with online tests that can help people decide whether or not they have a sleep disorder. Here are a few good sites:

- The American Sleep Association **http://www.sleepassociation.org** has information on sleep health and sleep disorders.
- The National Sleep Foundation at **www.sleepfoundation.org** also has many links to information about sleep, sleep disorders, and sleep tips.

4 CHAPTER SUMMARY

What Is Consciousness?

4.1 What does it mean to be conscious, and are there different levels of consciousness?

- Consciousness is a person's awareness of everything that is going on at any given moment. Most waking hours are spent in waking consciousness.
- Altered states of consciousness are shifts in the quality or pattern of mental activity.

Altered States: Sleep

4.2 Why do people sleep, and how does sleep work?

- Sleep is a circadian rhythm, lasting 24 hours, and is a product of the activity of the hypothalamus, the hormone melatonin, the neurotransmitter serotonin, and body temperature.
- Adaptive theory states that sleep evolved as a way to conserve energy and keep animals safe from predators that hunt at night.
- Restorative theory states that sleep provides the body with an opportunity to restore chemicals that have been depleted during the day as well as the growth and repair of cell tissue.
- The average amount of sleep needed by most adults is about 7 to 9 hours within each 24-hour period.

4.3 What are the different stages of sleep, including the stage of dreaming and its importance?

- Stage One sleep is light sleep.
- Stage Two sleep is indicated by the presence of sleep spindles, bursts of activity on the EEG.
- Stage Three is highlighted by the first appearance of delta waves, the slowest and largest waves, whereas Stage Four is predominantly delta waves, and the body is at its lowest level of functioning.

4.4 How do sleep disorders interfere with normal sleep?

- Sleepwalking and sleeptalking occur in Stage Four sleep.
- Night terrors are attacks of extreme fear that the victim has while sound asleep.
- REM sleep occurs four or five times a night, replacing Stage One sleep in the sleep–wake cycle, and is accompanied by paralysis of the voluntary muscles.

- Nightmares are bad or unpleasant dreams that occur during REM sleep.
- REM behavior disorder is a rare condition in which REM paralysis fails and the person moves violently while dreaming, often acting out the elements of the dream.

Psychology in the News: Murder While Sleepwalking

- Sleepwalking has been used as a defense in numerous cases of murder. In many of these cases, the defendant has been acquitted because of the sleepwalking defense.
- Insomnia is an inability to get to sleep, stay asleep, or get enough sleep.
- Sleep apnea occurs when a person stops breathing for nearly half a minute or more, followed by gasping for breath.
- Narcolepsy is a genetic disorder in which the person suddenly and without warning collapses into REM sleep.

Dreams

4.5 Why do people dream, and what do they dream about?

- Manifest content of a dream is the actual dream and its events. Latent content of a dream is the symbolic content, according to Freud.
- Without outside sensory information to explain the activation of the brain cells in the cortex by the pons area, the association areas of the cortex synthesize a story, or dream, to explain that activation in the activation-synthesis hypothesis.
- A revision of activation-synthesis theory, the activation-information-mode model (AIM) states that information experienced during waking hours can influence the synthesis of dreams.

Altered States: Hypnosis

4.6 How does hypnosis affect conciousness?

- Hypnosis is a state of consciousness in which a person is especially susceptible to suggestion.
- The hypnotist will tell the person to relax and feel tired, to focus on what is being said, to let go of inhibitions and accept suggestions, and to use vivid imagination.
- Hypnosis cannot give increased strength, reliably enhance memory, or regress people to an earlier age or an earlier life, but it can produce amnesia, reduce pain, and alter sensory impressions.

- Hilgard believed that a person under hypnosis is in a state of dissociation, in which one part of consciousness is hypnotized and susceptible to suggestion, while another part is aware of everything that occurs.
- Other theorists believe that the hypnotized subject is merely playing a social role—that of the hypnotized person. This is called the social-cognitive theory of hypnosis.

Altered States: Psychoactive Drugs

4.7 What is the difference between a physical dependence and a psychological dependence on a drug?

- Drugs that are physically addictive cause the user's body to crave the drug. When deprived of the drug, the user will go through physical withdrawal.
- Drug tolerance occurs as the user's body becomes conditioned to the level of the drug. After a time, the user must take more and more of the drug to get the same effect.
- In psychological dependence, the user believes that he or she needs the drug to function well and maintain a sense of well-being. Any drug can produce psychological dependence.

4.8 How do stimulants and depressants affect consciousness, and what are the dangers associated with taking them, particularly alcohol?

- Stimulants are drugs that increase the activity of the nervous system, particularly the sympathetic division and the central nervous system.
- Amphetamines are synthetic drugs such as Benzedrine or Dexedrine. They help people stay awake and reduce appetite but are highly physically addictive.
- Cocaine is highly addictive and can cause convulsions and death in some first-time users.
- Nicotine is a mild stimulant and is very physically addictive.
- Caffeine is the most commonly used stimulant, found in coffee, tea, chocolate, and many sodas.
- Barbiturates, also known as major tranquilizers, have a sedative effect and are used as sleeping pills.
- The minor tranquilizers are benzodiazepines such as Valium or Xanax.
- Alcohol is the most commonly used and abused depressant.

- Alcohol can interact with other depressants.
- Excessive use of alcohol can lead to alcoholism, health problems, loss of control, and death.

4.9 What are the effects and dangers of using narcotics and hallucinogens, including marijuana?

- Narcotics are pain-relieving drugs of the depressant class that are derived from the opium poppy.
- Opium is the earliest form of this drug and is highly addictive because it directly stimulates receptor sites for endorphins. This causes natural production of endorphins to decrease.
- Morphine is a more refined version of opium but is highly addictive.
- Heroin was believed to be a purer form of morphine and, therefore, less addictive but in fact is even more powerfully addictive.
- Methadone has the ability to control the symptoms of heroin or morphine withdrawal without the euphoria, or "high," of heroin or morphine.
- Hallucinogens are stimulants that alter the brain's interpretation of sensations, creating hallucinations. Three synthetically created hallucinogens are LSD, PCP, and MDMA.
- Three naturally occurring hallucinogens are mescaline, psilocybin, and marijuana.
- Marijuana is a mild hallucinogen, producing a mild euphoria and feelings of relaxation in its users. Larger doses can lead to hallucinations and paranoia. It contains substances that are carcinogenic and impairs learning and memory.

Applying Psychology to Everyday Life: Are You Sleep Deprived?

4.10 How serious is the problem of sleep deprivation?

- Sleep deprivation is a serious disorder responsible for a large portion of traffic accidents and fatalities as well as increased stress, depression, anxiety, reduced productivity, and risk-taking behavior.
- Causes of sleep deprivation include sleep disorders such as apnea and narcolepsy, failure of people to go to sleep or stay asleep for an adequate amount of time, worrying, and the influence of some drugs.

TEST YOURSELF: PREPARING FOR THE AP* EXAM

ANSWERS ON PAGE AK-1.

✓—Practice on MyPsychLab   **Ready for your test?** More quizzes and a customized study plan. **www.mypsychlab.com**

PART I: MULTIPLE-CHOICE QUESTIONS

Directions for Part I: Read each of the questions or incomplete sentences below. Then choose the response that best answers the question or completes the sentence.

1. Most of our time awake is spent in a state called _____, in which our thoughts, feelings, and sensations are clear and organized and we feel alert.
   a. unconsciousness
   b. circadian rhythm
   c. waking consciousness
   d. working consciousness
   e. altered state of consciousness

2. When light begins to fade at the end of the day, the suprachiasmatic nucleus in the _____ signals the pineal gland to release _____.
   a. thalamus; melatonin
   b. hippocampus; melatonin
   c. hippocampus; serotonin
   d. hypothalamus; melatonin
   e. hypothalamus; serotonin

3. It might be best to say that adaptive theory explains _____, whereas restorative theory explains _____.
   a. when we sleep; why we need to sleep
   b. where we sleep; why we need to sleep
   c. why we need to sleep; where we sleep
   d. when we sleep; where we sleep
   e. why we need to sleep; when we need to sleep

4. Which of the following statements about REM sleep is false?
   a. The eyes move rapidly back and forth under the eyelids.
   b. Lack of REM sleep produces psychological disorders.
   c. Most people report that they were dreaming if awakened.
   d. The body is aroused and brain waves resemble waking beta waves.
   e. The person moves very little because muscles are inhibited.

5. Hypnosis has been shown to do all of the following except _____.
   a alter sensory perceptions
   b. help people relax during times of stress
   c. provide pain relief without medication
   d. regress people back to their early childhood experiences
   e. induce amnesia for what happens during the hypnotic state

6. Alcohol actually _____ the release of GABA, a neurotransmitter that inhibits many brain functions.
   a. depresses
   b. decreases
   c. stimulates
   d. prevents
   e. inhibits

7. Which drug was originally thought to be a more pure form of morphine with fewer side effects?
   a. Heroin
   b. Laudanum
   c. Cocaine
   d. Paregoric
   e. Methadone

8. Which of the following is not a naturally occurring substance?
   a. Nicotine
   b. Amphetamine
   c. Caffeine
   d. Cocaine
   e. Marijuana

9. Jackie used Ecstasy while she was in college, but now that she has a government job she has avoided using any recreational drugs. Although she had no problem quitting, she still finds that every now and then she gets a strong craving to use Ecstasy again. Her craving is most likely the result of _____.
   a. psychological dependence
   b. physical dependence
   c. withdrawal
   d. drug tolerance
   e. none of the above

10. Randall tells his therapist that he had a dream about riding on a train that went through a tunnel. The therapist tells Randall that his dream was most likely about a quickly approaching event that he is worried about. Randall's therapist is using the _____ theory of dreams to explain Randall's dream.
    a. adaptive
    b. Freudian
    c. Hobson/McCarley
    d. dreams-for-survival
    e. activation-synthesis

PART II: FREE-RESPONSE QUESTION

Directions for Part II: Read the essay question that follows. Then, respond to the question in a clear, concise essay. Do not simply list facts. Instead, present a thorough argument based on your critical consideration of the topic. Use proper psychological terminology as necessary.

Alpa's friends believe that Alpa has developed a physical dependence on cocaine. In an essay, explain the effects and risks of cocaine use, the signs of physical dependence, and the signs Alpa's friends may have noticed, using each of the following terms:

   a. Signs of physical dependence
   b. Stimulant

4 VISUAL SUMMARY
Consciousness: Sleep, Dreams, Hypnosis, and Drugs

4.2   p. 139

hypothalamus contains the suprachiasmatic nucleus (SCN)
- SCN is sensitive to light—influences pineal gland's secretion of melatonin (↑ melatonin = ↑ sleepiness)
- light through eyes relayed to SCN; SCN signals pineal gland to stop producing melatonin (↓ melatonin = ↑ alertness / ↓ sleepiness)
- SCN also influences body temperature (↓ temperature = ↑ sleepiness)

Altered States—Sleep: The Necessity of Sleep

(sleep is one of the body's daily (circadian) biological rhythms; sleep–wake cycle controlled by the brain including the hypothalamus and the neurotransmitter serotonin)

people can live without sleep for a while, can't live without it altogether
- **sleep deprivation**
- **amount of sleep needed**
- **adaptive theory of sleep**
- **restorative theory of sleep**

4.3–4   p. 147

consist of both REM (rapid eye movement) and non-REM stages
- **non-REM Stage 1**
- **non-REM Stage 2**
- **non-REM Stages 3 & 4**
- **REM sleep**

Altered States—Sleep: Stages and Disorders

Table 4.1 Sleep Disorders

NAME OF DISORDER	PRIMARY SYMPTOMS
Somnambulism	Sitting, walking, or performing complex behavior while asleep
Night terrors	Extreme fear, agitation, screaming while asleep
Restless leg syndrome	Uncomfortable sensations in legs causing movement and loss of sleep
Nocturnal leg cramps	Painful cramps in calf or foot muscles
Hypersomnia	Excessive daytime sleepiness
Circadian rhythm disorders	Disturbances of the sleep–wake cycle such as lag and shift work
Enuresis	Urinating while asleep in bed

people can live without sleep for a while, can't live without it altogether
- **insomnia**
- **sleep apnea**
- **narcolepsy**

"On your application it says you have narcolepsy. What is that?"

4.5   p. 150

Dreams
- **Why do we dream?**
  - **Freud's interpretation:** wish fulfillment—conflicts, events, and desires represented in symbolic form in dreams
  - **activation–synthesis hypothesis**
- **What do people dream about?** typically about events that occur in everyday life; most in color; content influenced by gender and culture

CAST OF DREAM

THE MONSTER	YOUR FATHER
KIND WOMAN	YOUR MOTHER
POLICEMAN	YOUR ANALYST
FIRST STRANGER	YOUR BROTHER
SECOND STRANGER	YOUR SISTER
LITTLE BOY	YOU

Awake, alert: Beta Waves

Awake, relaxed: Alpha Waves

200 V[µV] 100 0

Sleep Stage 1: Theta Waves

Sleep Stage 2: Spindles (bursts of activity)   *Sleep spindle*

Sleep Stage 3: Deep non-REM (delta and theta waves)

Sleep Stage 4: Deep non-REM (delta waves)

Time (s)

REM Stage

Bursts of synchronous vertical eye movements   *Low voltage continuous theta with minimal beta*

4.6 p. 154

Altered States: Hypnosis

(state of consciousness during which person is more susceptible to suggestion)

- can be assessed by scale of hypnotic susceptibility

- induction typically involves relaxed focus and "permission to let go"; person being hypnotized is in control and cannot be hypnotized against his or her will

- can be used in therapy—help people deal with pain, anxiety, or cravings (e.g., food, drug)

- **theories**
  - **dissociation:** one part of mind is aware of actions/activities taking place, while the "hypnotized" part is not
  - **social-cognitive theory** suggests that people assume roles based on expectations for a given situation

Table 4.3 Facts About Hypnosis

HYPNOSIS CAN:	HYPNOSIS CANNOT:
Create amnesia for whatever happens during the hypnotic session, at least for a brief time (Bowers & Woody, 1996).	Give people superhuman strength. (People may use their full strength under hypnosis, but it is no more than they had before hypnosis.)
Relieve pain by allowing a person to remove conscious attention from the pain (Holroyd, 1996).	Reliably enhance memory. (There's an increased risk of false memory retrieval because of the suggestible state hypnosis creates.)
Alter sensory perceptions. (Smell, hearing, vision, time sense, and the ability to see visual illusions can all be affected by hypnosis.)	Regress people back to childhood. (Although people may act like children, they do and say things children would not.)
Help people relax in situations that normally would cause them stress, such as flying on an airplane (Muhlberger et al., 2001).	Regress people to some "past life." There is no scientific evidence for past life regression (Lilienfeld et al., 2004)

Table 4.5 Blood Alcohol Level and Behavior Associated with Amounts of Alcohol

A drink is a drink. Each contains half an ounce of alcohol.
So a drink is . . .

- 1 can of beer (12 oz. 4–5% alcohol)
- 1 glass of wine (4 oz. 12% alcohol)
- 1 shot of most liquors (1 oz. 40–50% alcohol)

At times "a drink" is really the equivalent of more than just one drink, like when you order a drink with more than one shot of alcohol in it, or you do a shot followed by a beer.

AVERAGE NUMBER OF DRINKS	BLOOD ALCOHOL LEVEL	BEHAVIOR
1–2 drinks	.05%	Feeling of well-being
		Release of inhibitions
		Judgment impaired
		Coordination and level of alertness lowered
		Increased risk of collision while driving
3–5 drinks	.10%	Reaction time significantly slowed
		Muscle control and speech impaired
		Limited night and side vision
		Loss of self-control
		Crash risk greatly increased
6–7 drinks	.15%	Consistent and major increases in reaction time
8–10 drinks	.20%	Loss of equilibrium and technical skills
		Sensory and motor capabilities depressed
		Double vision and legal blindness (20/20)
		Unfit to drive for up to 10 hours
10–14 drinks	.20% and .25%	Staggering and severe motor disturbances
10–14 drinks	.30%	Not aware of surroundings
10–14 drinks	.35%	Surgical anesthesia
		Lethal dosage for a small percentage of people
14–20 drinks	.40%	Lethal dosage for about 50% of people
		Severe circulatory/respiratory depression
		Alcohol poisoning/overdose

Source: Adapted from the *Moderate Drinking Skills Study Guide.* (2004). Eau-Claire, WI: University of Wisconsin.

4.7–9 p. 166

"Nowadays, Hal is ninety-nine per cent caffeine-free."

Why do some people continue to use or become addicted to psychoactive drugs?

- **physical dependence:** user's body needs a drug to function; drug tolerance and withdrawal are warning signs/symptoms

- **psychological dependence:** user believes drug is needed to function

Altered States: Psychoactive Drugs

(drugs that alter thinking, perception, or memory)

- **types**

stimulants
increase functioning of nervous system
- **amphetamines**
- **cocaine**
- **nicotine**
- **caffeine**

depressants
have sedative effect
- **barbiturates**
  major tranquilizers
- **benzodiazepines**
  minor tranquilizers—
  Valium, Xanax, Halcion,
  Activan, Librium, Rohypnol
- **alcohol**

narcotics
euphoria-producing and
pain-relieving drugs derived
from opium
- **morphine**
- **heroin**
- **methadone**
  does not produce euphoria;
  used to treat heroin addiction

hallucinogens
alter brain's interpretation of sensations
- **manufactured**
  - **LSD**
  - **PCP**
  - **MDMA (Ectasy)**
- **nonmanufactured**
  - **mescaline**
  - **psilocybin**
  - **marijuana**

5
Learning

Why White Coats Made the Baby Scream

When Stephanie was an infant, she was constantly getting sick. This was long before the time when giving immunizations to infants had become routine, which meant that Stephanie was frequently ill and spent a lot of her infancy in the doctor's office. Antibiotics were delivered by injection. The shots were obviously painful and caused Stephanie to scream and cry.

Of course, the doctor in his white coat and the nurse in her white uniform were always present, as well as the white paper covering the examining table. It didn't take too many visits before Stephanie would scream when she saw the "white coat" people coming toward her—especially the nurse, who was usually the one who delivered the hated shot.

When she was 1 year old, her mother took her to a photography studio to have her portrait made. In those days, the photographer wore a white jacket to look more professional and took the pictures on a carpeted platform with a white sheet draped across it. Stephanie threw a fit, crying and screaming. The photographer had to take his jacket off and remove the white drape. After about an hour, she was finally calm enough to pose for the picture on a bare platform. Why did Stephanie have this reaction?

Stephanie's reaction to the photo session was a result of a special type of learning called *classical conditioning*. In this type of learning, objects or situations (such as white coats and being up on a table) can become associated or linked with other kinds of situations (such as the pain of injections). Once the association is made, similar objects or situations can cause the same response (e.g., screaming in fear) that the earlier situation caused.

Why study learning? If we had not been able to learn, we would have died out as a species long ago. Learning is the process that allows us to adapt to the changing conditions of the world around us. We can alter our actions until we find the behavior that leads us to survival and rewards, and we can eliminate actions that have been unsuccessful in the past. Without learning, there would be no buildings, no agriculture, no lifesaving medicines, and no human civilization.

5 Learning Objectives

- **5.1** What does the term *learning* really mean?
- **5.2** How was classical conditioning first studied, and what are the important elements and characteristics of classical conditioning?
- **5.3** What is a conditioned emotional response, and how do cognitive psychologists explain classical conditioning?
- **5.4** How does operant conditioning occur, and what were the contributions of Thorndike and Skinner?
- **5.5** What are the important concepts in operant conditioning?
- **5.6** What are some of the problems with using punishment?
- **5.7** What are the schedules of reinforcement?

- **5.8** How do operant stimuli control behavior, and what kind of behavior is resistant to operant conditioning?
- **5.9** What is behavior modification, and how can behavioral techniques be used to modify involuntary biological responses?
- **5.10** How do latent learning, learned helplessness, and insight relate to cognitive learning theory?
- **5.11** What occurs in observational learning, including findings from Bandura's classic Bobo doll study and the four elements of observational learning?
- **5.12** What is a real-world example of the use of conditioning?

Definition of Learning

5.1   What does the term *learning* really mean?

> **What does "relatively permanent" mean? And how does experience change what we do?** ▶

The term *learning* is one of those concepts whose meaning is crystal clear until one has to put it in actual words. "Learning is when you learn something." "Learning is learning how to do something." A more useful definition is as follows: *Learning* is any relatively permanent change in behavior brought about by experience or practice.

What does "relatively permanent" mean? And how does experience change what we do?

The "relatively permanent" part of the definition refers to the fact that when people learn anything, some part of their brain is physically changed to record what they've learned. This is actually a process of memory, for without the ability to remember what happens, people cannot learn anything. Although there is no conclusive proof as yet, research suggests strongly that once people learn something, it is always present somewhere in memory (Barsalou, 1992). They may be unable to "get" to it, but it's there. **LINK** *to Chapter Six: Memory, p. 228.*

As for the part about experience or practice, think about the last time you did something that caused you a lot of pain. Are you going to do it again? Of course not. You don't want to experience that pain again, so you change your behavior to avoid the painful consequence.* This is how children learn not to touch hot stoves. Of course, if a person does something resulting in a very pleasurable consequence, that person is more likely to do that same thing again. This is another change in behavior. Think back to the prologue. Stephanie's experience with the white coats changed her behavior when she saw the photographer in a white coat later on.

So, is any kind of change learning? Not all change is accomplished through learning. Any kind of change in the way an organism *behaves* is learning. Changes like an increase in height or the size of the brain are another kind of change controlled by a genetic blueprint. This kind of change is called *maturation*, which is not the same as learning. For example, children learn to walk *when* they do because their nervous systems, muscle strength, and sense of balance have reached the point where walking is possible for

the neighborhood Jerry Van Amerongen

An instantaneous learning experience.

---
*Consequence: an end result of some action.

them—all factors controlled by maturation, not by how much practice those children have had in trying to walk. No amount of experience or practice will help that child walk before maturation makes it possible—in spite of what some eager parents might wish.

It Makes Your Mouth Water: Classical Conditioning

5.2 How was classical conditioning first studied, and what are the important elements and characteristics of classical conditioning?

In the early 1900s, when Freud was just becoming famous in Europe and the structuralists and functionalists were arguing over consciousness in the ivy-covered halls of American universities, research scientists were unhappy with psychology's focus on mental activity. (L I N K) *to Chapter One: The Science of Psychology, pp. 6–10.* Many were looking for a way to bring some kind of objectivity and scientific research to the field.

It was not a psychologist who accomplished that goal. It was a Russian *physiologist* (a person who studies the workings of the body) named Ivan Pavlov (1849–1936) who accidentally stumbled across the basic principles of a particular kind of learning (Pavlov, 1906, 1926).

Studying the digestive system in his dogs, Pavlov had built a device that would accurately measure the amount of saliva produced by the dogs when they were fed a measured amount of food. Normally, when food is placed in the mouth of any animal, the salivary glands automatically start releasing saliva to help with chewing and digestion. This is a normal *reflex* (involuntary* response) in both animals and humans. The food causes a particular reaction, the salivation. A *stimulus* can be defined as any object, event, or experience that causes a *response*, the reaction of an organism. In the case of Pavlov's dogs, the food is the stimulus and salivation is the response. ◉⌐|**Watch** on **MyPsychLab**

PAVLOV AND THE SALIVATING DOGS

What first annoyed and then intrigued Pavlov was that his dogs began salivating when they weren't supposed to be salivating. Some dogs would start salivating when they saw the lab assistant bringing their food, others when they heard the clatter of the food bowl from the kitchen, and still others when it was the time of day they were usually fed. Pavlov spent the rest of his career studying what eventually he termed **classical conditioning**, learning to make a reflex response to a stimulus other than the original, natural stimulus that normally produces it.

ELEMENTS OF CLASSICAL CONDITIONING

Pavlov eventually identified several key elements that must be present and experienced in a particular way for conditioning to take place.

Unconditioned Stimulus   The original, naturally occurring stimulus mentioned in the preceding paragraph is called the **unconditioned stimulus (UCS)**. The term *unconditioned* means "unlearned" or "naturally occurring." This is the stimulus that ordinarily leads to the involuntary reflex response. In the case of Pavlov's dogs, the food is the unconditioned stimulus.

Unconditioned Response   The reflex response to the unconditioned stimulus is called the **unconditioned response (UCR)** for much the same reason. It is unlearned and occurs because of genetic "wiring" in the nervous system. For example, in Pavlov's experiment, the food given to the dogs is the UCS (unconditioned stimulus), and the salivation to that food is the UCR (unconditioned response).

---

*Involuntary: not under personal control or choice.

AP* Distinguish general differences between principles of classical conditioning, operant conditioning, and observational learning.

AP* Describe basic classical conditioning phenomena.

AP* Identify key contributors in the psychology of learning.

◉ **Watch** classic video footage of Pavlov. **www.mypsychlab.com**

Dr. Ivan Pavlov and students working in his laboratory. Pavlov, a Russian physiologist, was the first to study and write about the basic principles of classical conditioning.

classical conditioning learning to make an involuntary (reflex) response to a stimulus other than the original, natural stimulus that normally produces the reflex.

unconditioned stimulus (UCS) a naturally occurring stimulus that leads to an involuntary (reflex) response.

unconditioned response (UCR) an involuntary (reflex) response to a naturally occurring or unconditioned stimulus.

Conditioned Stimulus   Pavlov determined that almost any kind of stimulus could become associated with the unconditioned stimulus (UCS) if it is paired with the UCS often enough. In his original study, for example, the sight of the food dish itself became a stimulus for salivation *before* the food was given to the dogs. Every time they got food (to which they naturally salivated), they saw the dish. At this point, the dish was called a **neutral stimulus (NS)** because it had no effect on salivation. After being paired with the food so many times, the dish came to produce the same salivation response, although a somewhat weaker one, as did the food itself. When a previously neutral stimulus, through repeated pairing with the unconditioned stimulus, begins to cause the same kind of reflexive response, learning has occurred. The neutral stimulus can now be called a **conditioned stimulus (CS)**. (*Unconditioned* means "unlearned," and *conditioned* means "learned.")

Conditioned Response   The response that is given to the CS (conditioned stimulus) is not usually quite as strong as the original unconditioned response (UCR), but it is essentially the same response. However, because it comes as a response to the conditioned stimulus (CS), it is called the **conditioned response (CR)**.

PUTTING IT ALL TOGETHER: PAVLOV'S CANINE CLASSIC, OR DING, DONG, BELL

The whole idea of classical conditioning is not as complex as it sounds. What gets tough is keeping all the letters straight: NS, UCS, UCR, CS, and CR. Here is another example to help you put these terms in context: Pavlov did a classic experiment in which he paired the ringing of a bell with the presentation of food to see if the dogs would eventually salivate to the sound of the bell. Since the bell did not normally produce salivation, it was the neutral stimulus (NS) before any conditioning took place. The repeated pairing of the NS and the UCS (unconditioned stimulus) is usually called *acquisition,* because the organism is in the process of acquiring learning. Figure 5.1 is a chart of how each element of the conditioning relationship worked in Pavlov's experiment.

Notice that the responses, CR (conditioned response) and UCR (unconditioned response), are essentially the same—salivation. They simply differ in strength and what they are the response *to*. An *unconditioned* stimulus (UCS) is always followed by an *unconditioned* response (UCR), and a *conditioned* stimulus (CS) is always followed by a *conditioned* response (CR).

Is this rocket science? No, not really. Classical conditioning is actually one of the simplest forms of learning. It's so simple that it happens to people all the time without them even being aware of it. Does your mouth water when you merely *see* an advertisement for your favorite food on television? Does your stomach get upset every time you hear the high-pitched whine of the dentist's drill? These are both examples of classical conditioning.

After all the dog stories, your mouth-watering response to the TV ad probably needs no explanation, but what about the dentist's drill? Over the course of many visits, the body comes to associate that sound (CS) with the anxiety or fear (UCR) the person has felt while receiving a painful dental treatment (UCS), and so the sound produces a feeling of anxiety (CR) whether that person is in the chair or just in the outer waiting area.

Although classical conditioning happens quite easily, there are a few basic principles that Pavlov and other researchers discovered:

1. The CS must come *before* the UCS. If Pavlov rang the bell just after he gave the dogs the food, they did not become conditioned (Rescorla, 1988).
2. The CS and UCS must come very close together in time—ideally, no more than 5 seconds apart. When Pavlov tried to stretch the time between the potential CS and the UCS to several minutes, no association or link between the two was made. Too much could happen in the longer interval of time to interfere with

Classical conditioning in the real world. These children are no doubt salivating to the sound of the ice cream truck's bell, much as Pavlov's dogs were conditioned to respond. What other kinds of stimuli might make a person salivate?

Could this be you? The anxiety that many people feel while in the dentist's office is a conditioned response, with the dentist's chair and the smells of the office acting as conditioned stimuli.

neutral stimulus (NS)   stimulus that has no effect on the desired response.

conditioned stimulus (CS)   stimulus that becomes able to produce a learned reflex response by being paired with the original unconditioned stimulus.

conditioned response (CR)   learned reflex response to a conditioned stimulus.

Before Conditioning

Neutral Stimulus
(NS) Bell → No Salivation

During Conditioning

Neutral Stimulus
(NS) Bell → Unconditioned Stimulus
(UCS) Food → Unconditioned Response
(UCR) Salivation

After Conditioning

Conditioned Stimulus
(CS) Bell → Conditioned Response
(CR) Salivation

Figure 5.1 Classical Conditioning
Before conditioning takes place, the sound of the bell does not cause salivation and is a neutral stimulus, or NS. During conditioning, the sound of the bell occurs just before the presentation of the food, the UCS. The food causes salivation, the UCR. When conditioning has occurred after several pairings of the bell with the food, the bell will begin to elicit a salivation response from the dog without any food. This is learning, and the sound of the bell is now a CS and the salivation to the bell is the CR.

conditioning (Pavlov, 1926; Wasserman & Miller, 1997). Recent studies have found that the interstimulus interval (ISI, or the time between the CS and UCS) can vary depending on the nature of the conditioning task and even the organism being conditioned. In these studies, shorter ISIs (less than 500 milleseconds) have been found to be ideal for conditioning (Polewan et al., 2006).

3. The neutral stimulus must be paired with the UCS several times, often many times, before conditioning can take place (Pavlov, 1926). (As with the second "rule" regarding timing, there are exceptions to this rule that we'll get to in a bit.)

4. The CS is usually some stimulus that is distinctive* or stands out from other competing stimuli. The bell was a sound that was not normally present in the laboratory and, therefore, distinct (Pavlov, 1926; Rescorla, 1988).

That seems simple enough. But I wonder—did Pavlov's dogs salivate to the doorbell, too?

They certainly could have, if the doorbell were similar in sound to the CS bell, and if the dogs were near enough to hear the doorbell, and assuming Pavlov even *had* a doorbell.

Stimulus Generalization and Discrimination Pavlov did find that similar-sounding bells would produce the same conditioned response from his dogs. He and other researchers found that the strength of the response to the similar bells was not as strong as to the original one, but the more similar the other bell tone was to the original bell

That seems simple
enough. But I
wonder—did
◄ Pavlov's dogs
salivate to the
doorbell, too?

---

*Distinctive: separate, having a different quality from something else.

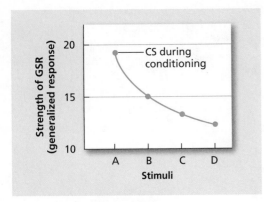

Figure 5.2 Strength of the Generalized Response (GSR)

An example of generalization. The subjects had been conditioned originally to a CS (A) of a given frequency. When tested with the original tone, and with tones B, C, and D of differing frequencies, a clear generalization effect appeared. The closer the frequency of the test tone to the frequency of tone A, the greater was the magnitude of the response to the tone. (Howland, 1937)

stimulus generalization the tendency to respond to a stimulus that is only similar to the original conditioned stimulus with the conditioned response.

stimulus discrimination the tendency to stop making a generalized response to a stimulus that is similar to the original conditioned stimulus because the similar stimulus is never paired with the unconditioned stimulus.

extinction the disappearance or weakening of a learned response following the removal or absence of the unconditioned stimulus (in classical conditioning) or the removal of a reinforcer (in operant conditioning).

reinforcer any event or object that, when following a response, increases the likelihood of that response occurring again.

spontaneous recovery the reappearance of a learned response after extinction has occurred.

tone, the more similar the strength of the response was as well (Siegel, 1969). (See Figure 5.2.) The tendency to respond to a stimulus that is only similar to the original conditioned stimulus is called **stimulus generalization**. For example, a person who reacts with anxiety to the sound of a dentist's drill might react with some slight anxiety to a similar-sounding machine, such as an electric coffee grinder or a construction worker's drill.

Of course, Pavlov did not give the dogs any food after the similar bell sounded. They only got food following the correct CS. It didn't take long for the dogs to stop responding (generalizing) to the "fake" bell sounds altogether. Because only the real CS was followed with food, they learned to tell the difference, or *discriminate*, between the "fake" bells and the real one, a process called **stimulus discrimination**. Stimulus discrimination occurs when an organism learns to respond to different stimuli in different ways. For example, although the sound of the coffee grinder might produce a little anxiety in the dental-drill-hating person, after a few uses that sound will no longer produce anxiety because it isn't associated with dental pain.

Extinction and Spontaneous Recovery What would have happened if Pavlov had stopped giving the dogs food after the real CS? Pavlov did just that, and the dogs gradually stopped salivating to the sound of the bell. When the bell (CS or conditioned stimulus) was repeatedly presented in the absence of the UCS (unconditioned stimulus or food, in this case), the salivation (CR or conditioned response) "died out" in a process called **extinction**.

Why does the removal of an unconditioned stimulus lead to extinction of the conditioned response? One theory is that the presentation of the CS alone leads to new learning. During extinction, the CS-UCS association that was learned is weakened, as the CS no longer predicts the UCS. In the case of Pavlov's dogs, through extinction they learned to not salivate to the bell as it no longer predicted that food was on its way.

The term *extinction* is a little unfortunate in that it seems to mean that the original conditioned response is totally gone, dead, never coming back, just like the dinosaurs. Remember the definition of learning is any relatively *permanent* change in behavior. The fact is that once people learn something, it's almost impossible to "unlearn" it. People can learn new things that replace it or lose their way to it in memory, but it's still there. In the case of classical conditioning, this is easily demonstrated.

After extinguishing the conditioned salivation response in his dogs, Pavlov waited a few weeks, putting the bell away. There were no more training sessions and the dogs were not exposed to the bell's ringing in that time at all. But when Pavlov took the bell back out and rang it, the dogs all began to salivate, although it was a fairly weak response and didn't last very long. This brief recovery of the conditioned response proves that the CR is still in there somewhere. It isn't dead and gone, it's just suppressed or inhibited by the lack of an association with the unconditioned stimulus of food. As time passes, this inhibition weakens, especially if the original conditioned stimulus has not been present for a while. In **spontaneous recovery** the conditioned response can briefly reappear when the original CS returns, although the response is usually weak and short-lived. See Figure 5.3 for a graph showing both extinction and spontaneous recovery. People experience classical conditioning in many ways. A person who has been hit from behind in a car accident, for example, will spend the next few weeks cringing every time another vehicle gets too close to the rear of the car. That cringing reaction is a conditioned response. The crash itself was the UCS (unconditioned stimulus) and the closeness of the other cars becomes a CS (conditioned stimulus). People who are allergic to cats sometimes sneeze when they see a *picture* of a cat. Remember the discussion of how to treat insomnia in Chapter Four (p. 145)? One of the recommendations was to avoid reading,

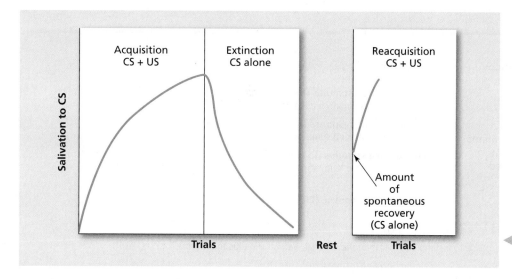

◀ AP*

AP* Interpret graphs that exhibit the results of learning experiments.

Figure 5.3 Extinction and Spontaneous Recovery

This graph shows the acquisition, extinction, spontaneous recovery, and reacquisition of a conditioned salivary response. Typically, the measure of conditioning is the number of drops of saliva elicited by the CS on each trial. Note that on the day following extinction, the first presentation of the CS elicits quite a large response.

working, watching television, or eating in bed. The bed should only be used for sleeping and will eventually become a conditioned stimulus (CS) for sleeping.

Higher-Order Conditioning Another concept in classical conditioning is **higher-order conditioning** (see Figure 5.4). This occurs when a strong conditioned stimulus is paired with a neutral stimulus. The strong CS can actually play the part of a UCS, and the previously neutral stimulus becomes a *second* conditioned stimulus.

For example, let's assume that Pavlov has conditioned his dogs to salivate at the sound of the bell. What would happen if just before Pavlov rang the bell, he snapped his fingers? The sequence would now be "snap-bell-salivation," or "NS-CS-CR" ("neutral stimulus/conditioned stimulus/conditioned response"). If this happens enough times, the finger snap will eventually also produce a salivation response. The finger snap becomes associated with the bell through the same process that the bell became associated with the food originally and is now another conditioned stimulus. Of course, the food (UCS) would have to be presented every now and then to maintain the original conditioned response to the bell. Without the UCS, the higher-order conditioning would be difficult to maintain and would gradually fade away.

higher-order conditioning occurs when a strong conditioned stimulus is paired with a neutral stimulus, causing the neutral stimulus to become a second conditioned stimulus.

Figure 5.4 Higher-Order Conditioning

In Stage 1, a strong salivation response is conditioned to occur to the sound of the bell (CS1). In Stage 2, finger snapping (CS2) is repeatedly paired with the ringing of the bell (CS1) until the dog begins to salivate to the finger snapping alone. This is called higher-order conditioning, because one CS is used to create another, "higher" CS.

5.2

discovered by Ivan Pavlov — focused on observable, measurable behavior
worked with salivating dogs

several key elements must be present and experienced

- **unconditioned stimulus (UCS):** original, naturally occurring stimulus that ordinarily leads to an involuntary response
- **unconditioned response (UCR):** involuntary response to the unconditioned stimulus
- **conditioned stimulus (CS):** previously neutral stimulus that begins to cause the same kind of involuntary response when paired repeatedly with the UCS
- **conditioned response (CR):** response that is given to the CS

Classical Conditioning (part 1)

(learning to make an involuntary response to a stimulus other than the original, natural stimulus that normally produces it)

basic principles for classical conditioning to occur

- CS must come before the UCS
- CS and UCS must come very close together in time (<5 sec)
- CS must be paired with the UCS many times
- CS must be distinct from other competing stimuli

key features

- **stimulus generalization:** response to a stimulus that is similar to the original CS
- **stimulus discrimination:** response to different stimuli in different ways
- **extinction:** presentation of the CS in the absence of the UCS leads to reduction in the CR
- **spontaneous recovery:** reappearance of a previously extinguished CR
- **higher-order conditioning:** occurs when strong CS is paired with new neutral stimulus; new previously neutral stimulus becomes a second CS

PRACTICE QUIZ: PREPARING FOR THE AP* EXAM

ANSWERS ON PAGE AK-2.

Directions: Read each of the questions or incomplete sentences below. Then choose the response that best answers the question or completes the sentence.

1. Which of the following illustrates the classical conditioning concept of acquisition?
   a. A neutral stimulus is repeatedly paired with a neutral response
   b. A conditioned stimulus is repeatedly paired with an unconditioned stimulus
   c. A neutral stimulus is repeatedly paired with an unconditioned stimulus
   d. A conditioned stimulus is repeatedly paired with a conditioned response
   e. An unconditioned stimulus is repeatedly paired with an unconditioned response

2. Ed noticed that whenever he used his electric can opener, his cat would come into the kitchen and act hungry—drooling and mewing pitiably. He reasoned that because he used the can opener to open the cat's food, the sound of the can opener had become a(n)
   a. unconditioned stimulus
   b. conditioned stimulus
   c. unconditioned response
   d. conditioned response
   e. neutral stimulus

3. Stephanie, a young child, developed a fear of white coats as a result of painful shots given to her by doctors and nurses dressed in white coats. The fact that she was not only afraid of white coats worn by doctors and nurses but also those worn by photographers is an example of _____

   a. extinction
   b. reinforcement
   c. stimulus discrimination
   d. spontaneous recovery
   e. stimulus generalization

4. Which of the following illustrates the phenomenon of spontaneous recovery?
   a. A dog, which has been conditioned to salivate at the sound of a bell, begins to salivate at the sound of all bells
   b. A dog, which has been conditioned to salivate at the sound of a bell, ceases to salivate at the bell and salivates only when food is present
   c. A dog, whose conditioned response to a bell has been extinguished, briefly displays the conditioned response to the bell
   d. A dog, whose conditioned response to a bell has been extinguished, briefly displays a new and different response to the bell
   e. A dog, which has been conditioned to salivate at the sound of a bell, begins to salivate at all times, regardless of the presence of a bell

5. The use of a strong conditioned stimulus to create a second conditioned stimulus is called _____
   a. spontaneous recovery
   b. higher-order conditioning
   c. extinction
   d. stimulus generalization
   e. secondary learning

CONDITIONED EMOTIONAL RESPONSES: RATS!

Later scientists took Pavlov's concepts and expanded them to explain not only animal behavior but also human behavior. One of the earliest of these studies showed that even an emotional response could be conditioned.

5.3   What is a conditioned emotional response, and how do cognitive psychologists explain classical conditioning?

Watson and "Little Albert"   In the first chapter of this text, John B. Watson was discussed as the founder of *behaviorism*. He firmly believed that all behavior could be explained in terms of learning, including even the *phobias* (irrational fear responses) that the Freudian camp thought were deeply rooted in the unconscious mind. His classic experiment with "Little Albert" and the white rat was a demonstration of learning a phobia (Watson & Rayner, 1920). It was also a very good example of classical conditioning.

Watson paired the presentation of the white rat to the baby with a loud, scary noise. Although the baby was not afraid of the rat, he was naturally afraid of the loud noise and started to cry. Soon, every time the baby saw the rat, he started to cry. In conditioning terms, the loud noise was the UCS, the fear of the noise the UCR, the white rat became the CS, and the fear of the rat (the phobia) was the CR. (See Figure 5.5.) (Of course, no ethics committee today would approve an experiment in which an infant experiences psychological distress like this.) ◉ Watch on MyPsychLab

The learning of phobias is a very good example of a certain type of classical conditioning, the **conditioned emotional response (CER)**. Conditioned emotional responses are some of the easiest forms of classical conditioning to accomplish, and our lives are full of them. It's easy to think of fears people might have that are conditioned or learned: a child's fear of the dentist's chair, a puppy's fear of a rolled-up newspaper, or the fear of dogs that is often shown by a person who has been attacked by a dog in the past. But other emotions can be conditioned, too.

The next time you watch television, watch the commercials closely. Advertisers often use certain objects or certain types of people in their ads to generate a specific emotional response in viewers, hoping that the emotional response will become associated with their product. Glamorous models, cute little babies, and adorable puppies are some of the examples of stimuli the advertising world uses to tug at our heartstrings, so to speak.

Other television messages are meant to elicit a fear response, such as messages about what drugs will do to your brain. In a classic public service message from the 1980s, a woman holds up an egg and says, "This is your brain." She then drops the egg into a grease-filled, smoking hot skillet and says, "This is your brain on drugs.

AP* Apply learning principles to explain emotional learning, taste aversion, superstitious behavior, and learned helplessness.

AP* Identify key contributors in the psychology of learning.

◉ **Watch** classic video footage of Pavlov. **www.mypsychlab.com**

conditioned emotional response (CER) emotional response that has become classically conditioned to occur to learned stimuli, such as a fear of dogs or the emotional reaction that occurs when seeing an attractive person.

Figure 5.5 Conditioning of "Little Albert"

After "Little Albert" had been conditioned to fear a white rat, he became afraid of other white and fuzzy things, including a white rabbit and a sealskin coat. Can you think of any emotional reactions you experience that might be classically conditioned emotional responses?

Conditioned taste aversions in nature. This moth is not poisonous to birds, but the monarch butterfly whose coloring the moth imitates is quite poisonous. Birds find their food by vision and will not eat anything that resembles the monarch.

But I thought that it took several pairings of these ▶ stimuli to bring about conditioning. How can classical conditioning happen so fast?

AP* Identify key contributors in the psychology of learning. ▶

vicarious conditioning classical conditioning of a reflex response or emotion by watching the reaction of another person.

conditioned taste aversion development of a nausea or aversive response to a particular taste because that taste was followed by a nausea reaction, occurring after only one association.

biological preparedness referring to the tendency of animals to learn certain associations, such as taste and nausea, with only one or few pairings due to the survival value of the learning.

Any questions?" This spot was supposed to cause disgust by showing the egg being cracked into a filthy-looking skillet and getting immediately fried to a crisp.

It is even possible to become classically conditioned by simply watching someone else respond to a stimulus in a process called **vicarious conditioning** (Bandura & Rosenthal, 1966). Many years ago, children received vaccination shots in school. The nurse lined the children up, and one by one they had to go forward to get a needle in the arm. When some children received their shots, they cried quite a bit. By the time the nurse got near the end of the line of children, they were all crying—many of them before she ever touched needle to skin. They had learned their fear response from watching the reactions of the other children.

OTHER CONDITIONED RESPONSES IN HUMANS

Are there any foods that you just can't eat anymore because of a bad experience with them? Believe it or not, your reaction to that food is a kind of classical conditioning.

Many experiments have shown that laboratory rats will develop a **conditioned taste aversion** for any liquid or food they swallow up to six hours before becoming nauseated. Researchers (Garcia et al., 1989; Garcia & Koelling, 1966) found that rats that were given a sweetened liquid and then injected with a drug or exposed to radiation* that caused nausea would not touch the liquid again. In a similar manner, the chemotherapy drugs that cancer patients receive also can create severe nausea, which causes those people to develop a taste aversion for any food they have eaten before going in for the chemotherapy treatment (Berteretche et al., 2004).

But I thought that it took several pairings of these stimuli to bring about conditioning. How can classical conditioning happen so fast?

Biological Preparedness Conditioned taste aversions, along with phobic reactions, are an example of something called **biological preparedness**. Most mammals find their food by smell and taste and will learn to avoid any food that smells or tastes like something they ate just before becoming ill. It's a survival mechanism, because if they kept on eating a "bad" food, they might die. The mammalian** body seems to be prepared to associate smell and taste with getting sick (Garcia & Koelling, 1966; Seligman, 1970). Although most conditioning requires repeated pairings of CS with UCS, and the CS and UCS close together in time, when the response is nausea, one pairing may be all that is necessary. Taste aversion conditioning is so effective that it has even been used by renowned psychologist Dr. John Garcia and colleagues as a tool to stop coyotes from killing ranchers' sheep and also to stop the ranchers from wiping out the coyote population entirely (Gustavson et al., 1976). Garcia and his fellow researchers laced sheep meat with lithium chloride and left it for the coyotes to find. The coyotes ate the drugged meat, got extremely sick, and avoided eating sheep for quite some time afterwards. The coyotes got to live and the ranchers got to keep their sheep.

It's interesting to note that birds, which find their food by sight, will avoid any object or insect that simply *looks* like the one that made them sick. There is a certain species of moth with coloring that mimics the monarch butterfly. The butterfly is poisonous to birds, but the moth isn't. The moths' mimicry causes birds to avoid eating them, even though they are quite edible. Whereas mammals are biologically prepared to associate taste with illness, birds are biologically prepared to associate visual characteristics with illness (Shapiro et al., 1980).

---

*Radiation: beams of energy.
**Mammalian: having to do with mammals (animals with fur or hair that feed their young with milk from milk glands).

WHY DOES CLASSICAL CONDITIONING WORK?

There are two ways to explain how one stimulus comes to "stand in" for another. One is the original explanation given by Pavlov, whereas the other is based on a cognitive explanation. Pavlov believed that the conditioned stimulus, through its association close in time with the unconditioned stimulus, came to activate the same place in the animal's brain that was originally activated by the unconditioned stimulus. He called this process **stimulus substitution**. But if a mere association in time is all that is needed, why would conditioning *fail to happen* when the CS is presented immediately *after* the UCS?

Robert Rescorla (1988) found that the CS has to provide some kind of information about the coming of the UCS in order to achieve conditioning. In other words, the CS must predict that the UCS is coming. In one study, Rescorla exposed one group of rats to a tone, and just after the tone's onset and while the tone was still able to be heard, an electric shock was administered for some of the tone presentations. Soon the rats became agitated* and reacted in fear by shivering and squealing at the onset of the tone, a kind of conditioned emotional response. But with a second group of rats, Rescorla again sounded a tone but administered the electric shock only *after* the tone *stopped*, not while the tone was being heard. That group of rats responded with fear to the *stopping* of the tone (Rescorla, 1968).

The tone for the second group of rats provided a different kind of information than the tone in the first instance. For the first group, the tone means the shock is coming, whereas for the second group, the tone means there is no shock while the tone is on. It was the particular *expectancy* created by pairing the tone or absence of tone with the shock that determined the particular response of the rats. Because this explanation involves the mental activity of consciously expecting something to occur, it is an example of an explanation for classical conditioning called the **cognitive perspective**.

---

*Agitated: excited, upset.

stimulus substitution original theory in which Pavlov stated that classical conditioning occurred because the conditioned stimulus became a substitute for the unconditioned stimulus by being paired closely together.

cognitive perspective modern theory in which classical conditioning is seen to occur because the conditioned stimulus provides information or an expectancy about the coming of the unconditioned stimulus.

◄ **AP*** Identify key contributors in the psychology of learning.

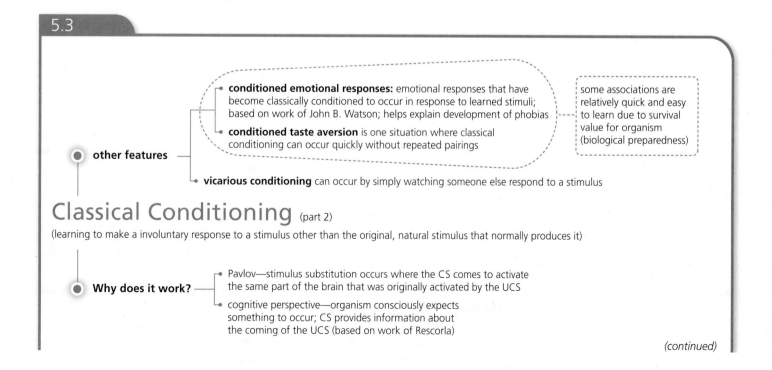

5.3

conditioned emotional responses: emotional responses that have become classically conditioned to occur in response to learned stimuli; based on work of John B. Watson; helps explain development of phobias

conditioned taste aversion is one situation where classical conditioning can occur quickly without repeated pairings

some associations are relatively quick and easy to learn due to survival value for organism (biological preparedness)

other features

vicarious conditioning can occur by simply watching someone else respond to a stimulus

Classical Conditioning (part 2)
(learning to make a involuntary response to a stimulus other than the original, natural stimulus that normally produces it)

Why does it work?
— Pavlov—stimulus substitution occurs where the CS comes to activate the same part of the brain that was originally activated by the UCS

— cognitive perspective—organism consciously expects something to occur; CS provides information about the coming of the UCS (based on work of Rescorla)

(continued)

Directions: Read each of the questions or incomplete sentences below. Then choose the response that best answers the question or completes the sentence.

1. What did John B. Watson's classic experiment with "Little Albert" demonstrate?
   a. The learning of a phobia
   b. The biological basis of fear
   c. The existence of vicarious conditioning
   d. The extinction of a conditioned response
   e. The phenomenon of biological preparedness

2. Often, people with certain types of cancer must take chemotherapy treatments. The drugs used in these treatments are powerful and usually cause strong nausea reactions. If Cindy had scrambled eggs for breakfast and then took a chemotherapy treatment later that same morning, which of the following responses is most likely to occur?
   a. Cindy will develop a strong liking for scrambled eggs.
   b. Cindy will be able to eat scrambled eggs with no nausea at all.
   c. Cindy will get nauseated the next time she tries to eat scrambled eggs.
   d. Cindy will get nauseated the next time she tries to eat any sort of food.
   e. Cindy will experience no significant effects as a result of the chemotherapy treatment.

3. A parakeet eats some cooked spaghetti noodles. Later, the bird gets very ill. According to research on biological preparedness, which of the following is most likely to occur?

   a. The parakeet will not eat shell macaroni because it smells similar to spaghetti.
   b. The parakeet will not eat shell macaroni because it tastes similar to spaghetti.
   c. The parakeet will not eat linguini noodles because they are long and thin and look similar to spaghetti.
   d. The parakeet will avoid spaghetti but eat all other types of cooked noodles.
   e. The parakeet will eat spaghetti again.

4. The fact that the conditioned stimulus must come immediately before the unconditioned stimulus, and not after, challenges which of the following theories?
   a. Stimulus substitution
   b. Cognitive perspective
   c. Behaviorism
   d. Classical conditioning
   e. The Law of Effect

5. Robert Rescorla discovered that in order for conditioning to take place, the conditioned stimulus must _____.
   a. replace the unconditioned stimulus
   b. occur at the same time as the unconditioned stimulus
   c. be removed before the unconditioned stimulus is presented
   d. have a physical resemblance to the unconditioned stimulus
   e. provide predictive information about the unconditioned stimulus

---

> *So far, all learning seems to involve reflex behavior, but I know that I am more than just reflexes. People do things on purpose, so is that kind of behavior also learned?*

What's in It for Me? Operant Conditioning

5.4 How does operant conditioning occur, and what were the contributions of Thorndike and Skinner?

There are two kinds of behavior that all organisms are capable of doing: involuntary (reflexive) and voluntary. If Inez blinks her eyes because a gnat flies close to them, that's a reflex and totally involuntary. But if she then swats at the gnat to frighten it, that's a voluntary choice. She *had* to blink, but she *chose* to swat.

Classical conditioning is the kind of learning that occurs with reflexive, involuntary behavior. The kind of learning that applies to voluntary behavior is called **operant conditioning**, which is both different from and similar to classical conditioning.

FRUSTRATING CATS: THORNDIKE'S PUZZLE BOX AND THE LAW OF EFFECT

Edward L. Thorndike (1874–1949) was one of the first researchers to explore and attempt to outline the laws of learning voluntary responses, although the field was not yet called operant conditioning. Thorndike placed a hungry cat inside a "puzzle box" from which the only escape was to press a lever located on the floor of the box. Cats definitely do *not* like being confined, as anyone who has ever tried to stuff one into a travel box will know (and probably has the scars to prove it), and there's a dish of food *outside* the box, so the cat is highly motivated to get out. Thorndike observed that the cat would move around the box, pushing and rubbing up against the walls in an effort to escape. Eventually, the

---

AP* Distinguish general differences between principles of classical conditioning, operant conditioning, and observational learning.

AP* Identify key contributors in the psychology of learning.

operant conditioning the learning of voluntary behavior through the effects of pleasant and unpleasant consequences to responses.

cat would accidentally push the lever, opening the door. Upon escaping, the cat was fed from a dish placed just outside the box. The lever is the stimulus, the pushing of the lever is the response, and the consequence is both escape (good) and food (even better).

The cat did not learn to push the lever and escape right away. After a number of trials (and many errors) in a box like this one, the cat took less and less time to push the lever that would open the door (see Figure 5.6). It's important not to assume that the cat had "figured out" the connection between the lever and freedom—Thorndike kept moving the lever to a different position, and the cat had to learn the whole process over again. The cat would simply continue to rub and push in the same general area that led to food and freedom the last time, each time getting out and fed a little more quickly.

Based on this research, Thorndike developed the **Law of Effect**: If an action is followed by a pleasurable consequence, it will tend to be repeated. If an action is followed by an unpleasant consequence, it will tend not to be repeated (Thorndike, 1911). This is the basic principle behind learning voluntary behavior. In the case of the cat in the box, pushing the lever was followed by a pleasurable consequence (getting out and getting fed), so pushing the lever became a repeated response.

So did Thorndike call this operant conditioning?

Thorndike's work began the study of voluntary learning, but the person who has had the greatest influence on the field and who gave it the name *operant conditioning* was B. F. Skinner. He is also known as behaviorism's biggest supporter. ✳⎯Explore on MyPsychLab

B. F. SKINNER: THE BEHAVIORIST'S BEHAVIORIST

B. F. Skinner (1904–1990) was the behaviorist who assumed leadership of the field after John Watson. He was even more determined than Watson that psychologists should study only measurable, observable behavior. In addition to his knowledge of Pavlovian classical conditioning, Skinner found in the work of Thorndike a way to explain all behavior as the product of learning. He even gave the learning of voluntary behavior a special name: *operant conditioning* (Skinner, 1938). Voluntary behavior is what people and animals do to *operate* in the world. When people perform a voluntary action, it is to get something they want or avoid something they don't want, right? So voluntary behavior, for Skinner, is **operant** behavior, and the learning of such behavior is operant conditioning.

The heart of operant conditioning is the effect of consequences on behavior. Thinking back to the section on classical conditioning, learning a reflex really depends on what comes *before* the response—the unconditioned stimulus and what will become the conditioned stimulus. These two stimuli are the *antecedent* stimuli (antecedent

◀ So did Thorndike call this operant conditioning?

✳ **Explore** with a simulation on operant conditioning. **www.mypsychlab.com**

◀ **AP*** Identify key contributors in the psychology of learning.

Law of Effect law stating that if an action is followed by a pleasurable consequence, it will tend to be repeated, and if followed by an unpleasant consequence, it will tend not to be repeated.

operant any behavior that is voluntary.

◀ **AP*** Interpret graphs that exhibit the results of learning experiments.

Figure 5.6 Graph of the Time to Learn in Thorndike's Experiment
This is one of the earliest "learning curves" in the history of the experimental study of conditioning. The time required by one of Thorndike's cats to escape from the puzzle box gradually decreased with trials but with obvious reversals.

AP* Predict the effects of operant conditioning. ▶

Figure 5.7 A Typical Skinner Box
This rat is learning to press the bar in the wall of the cage in order to get food (delivered a few pellets at a time in the food trough on lower left). In some cases, the light on the top left might be turned on to indicate that pressing the bar will lead to food or to warn of an impending shock delivered by the grate on the floor of the cage.

reinforcement any event or stimulus that, when following a response, increases the probability that the response will occur again.

primary reinforcer any reinforcer that is naturally reinforcing by meeting a basic biological need, such as hunger, thirst, or touch.

secondary reinforcer any reinforcer that becomes reinforcing after being paired with a primary reinforcer, such as praise, tokens, or gold stars.

means something that comes before another thing). But in operant conditioning, learning depends on what happens *after* the response—the consequence. In a way, operant conditioning could be summed up as this: "If I do this, what's in it for me?"

THE CONCEPT OF REINFORCEMENT

5.5 What are the important concepts in operant conditioning?

"What's in it for me?" represents the concept of **reinforcement**, one of Skinner's major contributions to behaviorism. The word itself means to strengthen, and Skinner defined reinforcement as anything that, when following a response, causes that response to be more likely to happen again. Typically, this means that reinforcement is a consequence that is in some way pleasurable to the organism, which relates back to Thorndike's Law of Effect. The "pleasurable consequence" is what's in it for the organism. (Keep in mind that a "pleasurable consequence" might be something like getting food when you are hungry or money when you need money, but it might also mean *avoiding* a tiresome chore, like doing the dishes, completing a homework assignment, or taking out the garbage. I'll do almost anything to get out of doing the dishes, myself!)

Going back to Thorndike's puzzle box research, what was "in it" for the cat? We can see that the escape from the box and the food that the cat received after getting out are both *reinforcement* of the lever-pushing response. Every time the cat got out of the box, it got reinforced for doing so. In Skinner's view, this reinforcement is the reason that the cat learned anything at all. In operant conditioning, reinforcement is the key to learning.

Skinner had his own research device called a "Skinner box" or "operant conditioning chamber" (see Figure 5.7). His early research often involved placing a rat into one of these chambers and training it to push down on a bar to get food.

Primary and Secondary Reinforcers The events or items that can be used to reinforce behavior are not all alike. Let's say that a friend of yours asks you to help her repaint her bedroom walls. In return for your help, she offers you $25 or a sandwich. Unless you've suffered recent brain damage, you'll most likely choose the money, right? With $25, you could buy more than one sandwich.

Now pretend that your friend offers the same deal to her 3-year-old cousin who likes to play around with paint: $25 or a sandwich. Which reward will the child more likely choose? Most children at that age have no real idea of the value of money, so the child will probably choose the sandwich. The money and the sandwich represent two basic kinds of *reinforcers*, items or events that when following a response will strengthen it. The reinforcing properties of money must be learned, but food gives immediate reward in the form of taste and satisfying hunger.

A reinforcer such as a sandwich that satisfies a basic need like hunger is called a **primary reinforcer**. Examples would be any kind of food (hunger drive), liquid (thirst drive), or touch (pleasure drive). Infants, toddlers, preschool-age children, and animals can be easily reinforced by using primary reinforcers. (It's not a good idea, however, to start thinking of reinforcers as rewards—freedom from pain is also a basic need, so pain itself can be a primary reinforcer when it is *removed*. Removal of a painful stimulus fills a basic need just as eating food when hungry fills the hunger need.)

A **secondary reinforcer** such as money, however, gets its reinforcing properties from being associated with primary reinforcers in the past. A child who is given money to spend soon realizes that the ugly green paper can be traded for toys and treats—primary reinforcers—and so money becomes reinforcing in and of itself. If a person praises a puppy while petting him (touch, a primary reinforcer), the praise alone will eventually make the puppy squirm with delight.

That sounds very familiar. Isn't this related to classical conditioning?

Secondary reinforcers do indeed get their reinforcing power from the process of classical conditioning. After all, the pleasure people feel when they eat, drink, or get a back rub is an automatic response, and any automatic response can be classically conditioned to occur to a new stimulus. In the case of money, the toys and treats are a UCS for pleasure (the UCR) and the money is present just before the treats are obtained. The money becomes a CS for pleasure, and people certainly do feel happy when they have a lot of that green stuff, don't they?

In the case of the puppy, the petting is the UCS, the pleasure at being touched and petted is the UCR. The praise, or more specifically the tone of voice, becomes the CS for pleasure. Although classical and operant conditioning often "work together," as in the creation of secondary reinforcers, they are two different processes. Table 5.1 presents a brief look at how the two types of conditioning differ from each other.

Positive and Negative Reinforcement   Reinforcers can also differ in the way they are used. Most people have no trouble at all understanding that following a response with some kind of pleasurable consequence (like a reward) will lead to an increase in the likelihood of that response being repeated. But many people have trouble understanding that the opposite is also true: Following a response with *the removal or escape* from something *unpleasant* will also increase the likelihood of that response being repeated. Remember the idea that pain can be a reinforcer if it is removed? If a person's behavior gets pain to stop, the person is much more likely to do that same thing again—which is part of the reason people can get addicted to painkilling medication.

There are really only two kinds of things people ever experience as consequences in the world: things they like (food, money, candy, sex, praise, and so on) and things they don't like (spankings, being yelled at, and experiencing any kind of pain, to name a few). There are also only two possibilities for experiencing these two kinds of consequences: Either people experience them directly (such as getting money for working or getting yelled at for misbehaving) or they don't experience them, such as losing an allowance for misbehaving or avoiding a scolding by lying about misbehavior. These four consequences are named and described in Table 5.2.

First, take a look at the left column of Table 5.2, the one labeled "Reinforcement." Getting money for working is another example of **positive reinforcement**, the reinforcement of a response by the *addition* or experience of a pleasurable consequence, such as a reward or a pat on the back. That one everyone understands. But avoiding a penal-

◀ That sounds very familiar. Isn't this related to classical conditioning?

positive reinforcement   the reinforcement of a response by the addition or experiencing of a pleasurable stimulus.

Table 5.1 Comparing Two Kinds of Conditioning

OPERANT CONDITIONING	CLASSICAL CONDITIONING
End result is an increase in the rate of an already occurring response.	End result is the creation of a new response to a stimulus that did not normally produce that response.
Responses are voluntary.	Responses are involuntary and reflexive.
Consequences are important in forming an association.	Antecedent stimuli are important in forming an association.
Reinforcement should be immediate.	CS must occur immediately before the UCS.
An expectancy develops for reinforcement to follow a correct response.	An expectancy develops for UCS to follow CS.

Table 5.2   Four Ways to Modify Behavior

	REINFORCEMENT	PUNISHMENT
Positive (Adding)	Something valued or desirable	Something unpleasant
	Positive Reinforcement	*Punishment by Application*
	Example: getting a gold star for good behavior in school	Example: getting a spanking for disobeying
Negative (Removing/ Avoiding)	Something unpleasant	Something valued or desirable
	Negative Reinforcement	*Punishment by Removal*
	Example: avoiding a ticket by stopping at a red light	Example: losing a privilege such as going out with friends

Javier Bardem receives an Academy Award for his role in No Country for Old Men. *The award, the applause of the audience, and the attention of the photographers are all positive reinforcement.*

negative reinforcement   the reinforcement of a response by the removal, escape from, or avoidance of an unpleasant stimulus.

I'm confused—I thought taking something away was a kind of punishment?

ty by turning one's homework assignment in on time is an example of negative rein-forcement. **Negative reinforcement** is the reinforcement of a response by the removal, escape from, or avoidance of an unpleasant stimulus. Because the behavior (turning in the assignment before the deadline) results in *avoiding* an unpleasant stimulus (a penal-ty), the likelihood that the person will behave that way again (turn it in on time in the future) is *increased*—just as positive reinforcement will increase a behavior's likelihood. Examples are the best way to figure out the difference between these two types of rein-forcement, so try to figure out which of the following examples would be positive rein-forcement and which would be negative reinforcement:

1. Arnie's father nags him to wash the family car. Arnie hates being nagged, so he washes the car so his father will stop nagging.
2. Trey learns that talking in a funny voice gets him lots of attention from his classmates, so now he talks that way often.
3. Allen is a server at a restaurant and always tries to smile and be pleasant be-cause that seems to lead to bigger tips.
4. An Li turns her report in to her teacher on the day it is due because papers get marked down a letter grade for every day they are late.

   Here are the answers:

1. Arnie is being negatively reinforced for washing the car because the nagging (unpleasant stimulus) stops when he does so.
2. Trey is getting positive reinforcement in the form of his classmates' attention.
3. Allen's smiling and pleasantness are positively reinforced by the customers' tips.
4. An Li is avoiding an unpleasant stimulus (the marked-down grade) by turning in her paper on time, which is an example of negative reinforcement.

TWO KINDS OF PUNISHMENT

▶ *I'm confused—I thought taking something away was a kind of punishment?*

People get confused because "negative" sounds like it ought to be something bad, like a kind of punishment. **Punishment** is actually the opposite of reinforcement. It is any event or stimulus that, when following a response, causes that response to be less likely to happen again. Punishment *weakens* responses, whereas reinforcement (no mat-ter whether it is positive or negative) *strengthens* responses. There are two ways in which punishment can happen, just as there are two ways in which reinforcement can happen.

Now take a look at the right column of Table 5.2, labeled "Punishment." **Punishment by application** occurs when something unpleasant (such as a spanking, scolding, or other unpleasant stimulus) is added to the situation or *applied*. This is the kind of punishment that most people think of when they hear the word *punishment*. This is also the kind of punishment that many child development specialists strongly recommend parents avoid using with their children because it can easily escalate into abuse (Dubowitz & Bennett, 2007; Saunders & Goddard, 1998; Straus, 2000; Straus & Stewart, 1999; Straus & Yodanis, 1994; Trocmé et al., 2001). A spanking might be *physically* harmless if it is only two or three swats with a hand, but if done in anger or with a belt or other instrument, it becomes abuse, both physical and emotional.

Punishment by removal, on the other hand, is the kind of punishment most often confused with negative reinforcement. In this type of punishment, behavior is punished by the removal of something pleasurable or desired after the behavior occurs. Have you ever been "grounded" and forced to stay at home as punishment for breaking a rule? Grounding removes your freedom to do what you want and is an example of punishment by removal. Other examples include placing a child in time-out (removing the attention of the others in the room), fining someone for disobeying the law (removing money), and punishing aggressive behavior by taking away television privileges. This type of punishment is far more acceptable to child development specialists because it involves no physical aggression and avoids many of the problems caused by more aggressive punishments.

The confusion over the difference between negative reinforcement and punishment by removal makes it worth examining the difference just a bit more. Negative reinforcement occurs when a response is followed by the *removal* of an *unpleasant* stimulus. If something unpleasant has just gone away as a consequence of that response, wouldn't that response tend to happen again and again? If the response increases, the consequence has to be a kind of *reinforcement*. The problem is that the name sounds like it should be some kind of punishment because of the word *negative*, and that's exactly the problem that many people experience when they are trying to understand negative reinforcement. They get negative reinforcement mixed up with punishment by removal, in which a *pleasant* thing is removed (like having your driver's license taken away because you caused a bad accident). Because something is removed (taken away) in both cases, people think that they will both have the effect of punishment, or weakening a response. The difference between them lies in *what* is taken away: In the case of negative reinforcement, it is an *unpleasant* thing; in the case of this particular form of punishment, it is a *pleasant* or desirable thing. For a head-to-head comparison of negative reinforcement and this particular type of punishment by removal, see Table 5.3.

You said earlier that there are some problems with punishment, and that many psychologists don't recommend using it. What are the problems?

PROBLEMS WITH PUNISHMENT

5.6 What are some of the problems with using punishment?

Although punishment can be effective in reducing or weakening a behavior, it has several drawbacks. The job of punishment is much harder than that of reinforcement. In using reinforcement, all one has to do is strengthen a response that is already there. But punishment is used to weaken a response, and getting rid of a response that is already well established is not that easy. (Ask any parent or pet owner.) Many times punishment only serves to temporarily suppress or inhibit a behavior until enough time has passed. For example, punishing a child's bad behavior doesn't always eliminate the behavior completely.

punishment any event or object that, when following a response, makes that response less likely to happen again.

punishment by application the punishment of a response by the addition or experiencing of an unpleasant stimulus.

punishment by removal the punishment of a response by the removal of a pleasurable stimulus.

This young woman's mother is applying punishment by removal as she takes the car keys away from her daughter.

You said earlier that there are some problems with punishment, and that many psychologists don't recommend using it.
◀ What are the problems?

Table 5.3   Negative Reinforcement Versus Punishment by Removal

EXAMPLE OF NEGATIVE REINFORCEMENT	EXAMPLE OF PUNISHMENT BY REMOVAL
Stopping at a red light to avoid getting in an accident.	Losing the privilege of driving because you got into too many accidents.
Submitting a homework assignment on time to avoid being penalized.	Receiving a low grade on an assignment because it was turned in late.
Obeying a parent before the parent reaches the count of "three" to avoid getting a scolding.	Being "grounded" (losing your freedom) because of disobedience.

✳ **Explore** the controversy surrounding spanking. **www.mypsychlab.com**

As time goes on, the punishment is forgotten, and the "bad" behavior may occur again in a kind of spontaneous recovery of the old (and probably pleasurable for the child) behavior.

Look back at Table 5.2 under the "Punishment" column. Punishment by application can be quite severe, and severe punishment does do one thing well: It stops the behavior immediately (Bucher & Lovaas, 1967; Carr & Lovass, 1983). It may not stop it permanently, but it does stop it. In a situation in which a child might be doing something dangerous or self-injurious, this kind of punishment is sometimes more acceptable (Duker & Seys, 1995). For example, if a child starts to run into a busy street, the parent might scream at the child to stop and then administer several rather severe swats to the child's rear. If this is not usual behavior on the part of the parent, the child will most likely never run into the street again. ✳ **Explore** on **MyPsychLab**

Other than situations of immediately stopping dangerous behavior, severe punishment has too many drawbacks to be really useful. It should also be discouraged because of its potential for leading to abuse (Dubowitz & Bennett, 2007; Gershoff, 2000; Millan et al., 1999; Trocmé et al., 2001):

- Severe punishment may cause the child (or animal) to avoid the punisher instead of the behavior being punished, so the child (or animal) learns the wrong response.
- Severe punishment may encourage lying to avoid the punishment (a kind of negative reinforcement)—again, not the response that is desired.
- Severe punishment creates fear and anxiety, emotional responses that do not promote learning (Baumrind, 1997; Gershoff, 2000; Gershoff, 2002). If the point is to teach something, this kind of consequence isn't going to help.
- Hitting provides a successful model for aggression (Gershoff, 2000; Milner, 1992).

That last point is worth a bit more discussion. In using an aggressive type of punishment, such as spanking, the adult is actually modeling (presenting a behavior to be imitated by the child). After all, the adult is using aggression to get what the adult wants from the child. Children sometimes become more likely to use aggression to get what they want when they receive this kind of punishment (Bryan & Freed, 1982; Larzelere, 1986), and the adult has lost an opportunity to model a more appropriate way to deal with parent–child disagreements. Since aggressive punishment does tend to stop the undesirable behavior, at least for a while, the parent who is punishing actually experiences a kind of negative reinforcement: "When I spank, the unpleasant behavior goes away." This may increase the tendency to use aggressive punishment over other forms of discipline and could even lead to child abuse (Dubowitz & Bennett, 2007). Finally, some children are so desperate for attention from their parents that they will actually misbehave on purpose. The punishment is a form of attention, and these children will take whatever attention they can get, even negative attention.

Punishment by removal is less objectionable to many parents and educators and is the only kind of punishment that is permitted in many public schools. But this kind of punishment also has its drawbacks—it teaches the child what *not* to do but not what the child should do. Both punishment by removal and punishment by application are usually only temporary in their effect on behavior. After some time has passed, the behavior will most likely return as the memory of the punishment gets weaker, allowing spontaneous recovery.

If punishment doesn't work very well, what can a parent do to keep a child from behaving badly?

How to Make Punishment More Effective   If you babysit, volunteer with children, or have younger siblings, you may find yourself in the role of disciplinarian. How can you maintain order in a way that's both effective and ethical? Try to remember a few simple rules:

1. **Punishment should immediately follow the behavior it is meant to punish.** If the punishment comes long after the behavior, it will not be associated with that behavior. (This is also true of reinforcement.)
2. **Punishment should be consistent.** This actually means two things. First, if you say that a certain punishment will follow a certain behavior, then you must make sure to follow through and do what you promised to do. Second, punishment for a particular behavior should stay at the same intensity or increase slightly but never decrease. For example, if a child is scolded for jumping on the bed the first time, the second time this behavior happens the child should also be punished by scolding or by a stronger penalty, such as removal of a favorite toy. But if the first misbehavior is punished by spanking and the second by only a scolding, the child learns to "gamble" with the possible punishment.
3. **Punishment of the wrong behavior should be paired, whenever possible, with reinforcement of the right behavior.** Instead of yelling at a 2-year-old for eating with her fingers, you should pull her hand gently out of her plate while saying something such as, "No, we do not eat with our fingers. We eat with our fork," and then placing the fork in the child's hand and praising her for using it. "See, you are doing such a good job with your fork. I'm so proud of you." Pairing punishment (the mild correction of pulling her hand away while saying "No, we do not eat with our fingers") with reinforcement allows caregivers to use a much milder punishment and still be effective. It also teaches the desired behavior rather than just suppressing the undesired one.

MORE CONCEPTS IN OPERANT CONDITIONING

Operant conditioning is more than just the reinforcement of simple responses. For example, have you ever tried to teach a pet to do a trick? If you have, you probably know that training animals involves more than simple reinforcement.

How do the circus trainers get their animals to do all those complicated tricks?

Shaping   When you see an animal in a circus or in a show at a zoo perform tricks, you are seeing the result of applying the rules of conditioning—both classical and operant—to animals. But the more complex tricks are a process in operant conditioning called **shaping**, in which small steps toward some ultimate goal are reinforced until the goal itself is reached.

For example, if Jody wanted to train his dog to jump through a hoop, he would have to start with some behavior that the dog is already capable of doing on its own. Then he would gradually "mold" that starting behavior into the jump—something the dog is capable of doing but not likely to do on its own. Jody would have to start with the hoop on the ground in front of Rover's face and then call the dog through the hoop, using the treat as bait. After Rover steps through the hoop (as the shortest way

If punishment doesn't work very well, what can a parent do to keep a child from ◄ **behaving badly?**

This dog has been trained to help its physically challenged owner. Operant conditioning principles can be used to train animals to do many useful tasks, including opening the refrigerator.

How do the circus ◄ trainers get their animals to do all those complicated tricks?

shaping   the reinforcement of simple steps in behavior that lead to a desired, more complex behavior.

to the treat), Jody should give Rover the treat (positive reinforcement). Then he could raise the hoop just a little, reward him for walking through it again, raise the hoop, reward him . . . until Rover is jumping through the hoop to get the treat. The goal is achieved by reinforcing each **successive approximation** (small steps one after the other that get closer and closer to the goal). This process is shaping (Skinner, 1974).

Extinction, Generalization, and Spontaneous Recovery in Operant Conditioning

Extinction in classical conditioning involves the removal of the UCS, the unconditioned stimulus that is associated with the CS during acquisition. It should come as no surprise, then, that extinction in operant conditioning involves the removal of reinforcement. Have you ever seen a child throw a temper tantrum in the checkout line because he or she wants a treat? Many exasperated* parents will cave in and give the child the treat, positively reinforcing the tantrum. The parent is also being negatively reinforced for giving in, because the obnoxious** behavior stops. The only way to get the tantrum behavior to stop is to remove the reinforcement, which means no treat, and if possible, no attention from the parent. (Not only is this hard enough to do while enduring the tantrum, but also the tantrum behavior may actually get worse before it extinguishes!)

Ignoring a child's tantrum in public is a lot harder than ignoring it at home, but it can be done. In fact, the other people in the store who witness the tantrum will most likely silently applaud a caregiver who does not give in, but will groan inwardly when they see the child's tantrum rewarded.

Just as in classical conditioning, operantly conditioned responses also can be generalized to stimuli that are only similar to the original stimulus. For example, when you were a baby, you may have referred to every man you saw as "Dada." The name "Dada" begins as a baby's response to the presence of her own father and is reinforced by his delight and attention to her. But in the beginning, she will generalize her "Dada" response to any man. As other men fail to reinforce her for this response, she'll learn to discriminate between them and her father and only call her father "Dada." In this way, the man who is actually her father becomes a **discriminative stimulus**, which is any stimulus such as a stop sign or a doorknob that provides the organism with a cue for making a certain response in order to obtain reinforcement.

Spontaneous recovery (the recurrence of a conditioned response after extinction) will also happen with operant responses. Remember the hoop-jumping dog? Anyone who has ever trained animals to do several different tricks will say that when first learning a new trick, most animals will try to get reinforcers by performing their *old* tricks. Rover might very well have tried to roll over, speak, and shake paws to get that treat before finally walking through the hoop. Operant conditioning isn't only at work in pet-training classes. It's also responsible for a number of normal human behaviors—and a few not-so-normal behaviors. Many people's superstitious actions, for example, can be explained using the principles of conditioning. Let's say you're a goalie on your school's varsity soccer team. You haven't been having a very good season, but before one game, you put on a pair of bright orange socks. During that game, you're a superstar, blocking your opponents' shots left and right. You wear your orange socks to the next game, and once again, you play brilliantly. After a while, you're wearing your orange socks to every soccer game because you've come to believe that they're lucky. Do the socks really improve your game? Almost certainly not. But this type of superstitious behavior is an example of conditioning in action. Your great athletic skills serve as reinforcement for your superstitious sock-wearing practices. Of course, if you start to play poorly while you're wearing those socks, the positive reinforcement will vanish and your superstitious behavior may face extinction.

*Exasperated: irritated or annoyed.
**Obnoxious: highly offensive or undesirable.

One way to deal with a child's temper tantrum is to ignore it. The lack of reinforcement for the tantrum behavior will eventually result in extinction.

AP* Apply learning principles to explain emotional learning, taste aversion, superstitious behavior, and learned helplessness.

successive approximations small steps in behavior, one after the other, that lead to a particular goal behavior.

discriminative stimulus any stimulus, such as a stop sign or a doorknob, that provides the organism with a cue for making a certain response in order to obtain reinforcement.

5.4–6

focused on observable, measurable behavior

Thorndike was among the first to study learning of voluntary responses — developed Law of Effect—action followed by pleasurable consequence will tend to be repeated; action followed by unpleasant consequence will tend not to be repeated

Skinner led field of behaviorism after Watson — coined term *operant conditioning*—voluntary behavior that people and animals do to operate in the world

Operant Conditioning (part 1)

(learning to make voluntary responses through the effects of positive or negative consequences)

reinforcement any event or stimulus, that when following a response increases the probability that the response will occur again

- **primary reinforcers:** satisfy basic biological needs (e.g., hunger, thirst, touch)
- **secondary reinforcers:** gain reinforcing properties through previous association with primary reinforcers
- **positive reinforcement:** addition, or experiencing, of a pleasurable stimulus
- **negative reinforcement:** removal, escape, or avoidance of unpleasant stimulus

punishment is any event or stimulus, that when following a response, decreases the probability that the response will occur again

- **punishment by application:** something unpleasant is added to the situation
- **punishment by removal:** something pleasurable is removed
- to work—must be immediate, consistent, and paired with reinforcement of actual behavior desired

other features

- some behaviors can be shaped by reinforcing small steps, each successive approximation toward ultimate goal
- as in classical conditioning, extinction, generalization, and spontaneous recovery can occur

PRACTICE QUIZ: PREPARING FOR THE AP* EXAM

ANSWERS ON PAGE AK-2.

Directions: Read each of the questions or incomplete sentences below. Then choose the response that best answers the question or completes the sentence.

1. Edward L. Thorndike's experiments with cats placed in "puzzle boxes" were directly related to the study of _____.
   a. latent learning
   b. sensory memory
   c. split-brain research
   d. operant conditioning
   e. neurotransmitter reuptake

2. Bennie is afraid of snakes. When he sees a picture of a snake, he becomes more anxious, but when he avoids looking at the picture, he becomes less anxious. It is most correct to say that Bennie's avoidance behavior is being _____.
   a. extinguished
   b. punished by application
   c. punished by removal
   d. positively reinforced
   e. negatively reinforced

3. Jessica's mother was upset to find that Jessica had used her crayons to draw flowers on her bedroom wall. Her mother took the crayons away from her and made Jessica wash the drawings off the wall. Which of the following best describes Jessica's punishment?
   a. Punishment by application
   b. Punishment by removal
   c. Punishment by both application and removal
   d. Punishment by negative reinforcement
   e. Punishment by both positive and negative reinforcement

4. Elizabeth's parents want her to put her clothes in the hamper. At first, they praise her for putting the clothes together in one pile. Then they praise her for getting the clothes on the same side of the room as the hamper. When she gets the clothes on top of the hamper, she gets praise. Finally, her parents praise her when she puts her clothes in the hamper. This process is an example of _____.
   a. a discriminative stimulus
   b. negative reinforcement
   c. punishment
   d. extinction
   e. shaping

5. Ella is teaching her parrot a new word. Every time the parrot says a sound that is close to the new word, she gives it a treat. But the parrot keeps repeating other words it has learned in the past, trying to get a treat that way. The parrot is exhibiting _____.
   a. extinction
   b. discrimination
   c. generalization
   d. spontaneous recovery
   e. biological preparedness

"Remember, every time he gives you a pellet, reinforce that behavior by pulling the lever."

©The New Yorker Collection 2005 Joe Dator from cartoonbank.com. All Rights Reserved.

partial reinforcement effect the tendency for a response that is reinforced after some, but not all, correct responses to be very resistant to extinction.

continuous reinforcement the reinforcement of each and every correct response.

fixed interval schedule of reinforcement schedule of reinforcement in which the interval of time that must pass before reinforcement becomes possible is always the same.

THE SCHEDULES OF REINFORCEMENT: WHY THE ONE-ARMED BANDIT IS SO SEDUCTIVE

The timing of reinforcement can make a tremendous difference in the speed at which learning occurs and the strength of the learned response. Skinner (1956) found that reinforcing each and every response was not necessarily the best schedule of reinforcement for long-lasting learning.

5.7 What are the schedules of reinforcement?

The Partial Reinforcement Effect Alicia's mother gives her a quarter every night she remembers to put her dirty clothes in the clothes hamper. Bianca's mother gives her a dollar at the end of the week, but only if she has put her clothes in the hamper every night. Alicia learns more quickly than does Bianca because responses that are reinforced each time they occur are more easily and quickly learned. After a time, the mothers stop giving the girls the money. Which child will stop putting her clothes in the hamper more quickly?

The answer might be surprising. It will more likely be Alicia, who has expected to get a reinforcer (the quarter) after *every single response*. As soon as the reinforcers stop, the behavior extinguishes. Bianca has expected to get a reinforcer only after *seven correct responses*. When the reinforcers stop, Bianca might continue to put the clothes in the hamper for several more days or even another whole week, hoping that the reinforcer will eventually come anyway. Bianca may have learned more slowly than Alicia, but once she learned the connection between putting her clothes in the hamper and getting that dollar, she was less likely to stop doing it—even when her mother failed to give the dollar as expected.

Bianca's behavior illustrates the **partial reinforcement effect** (Skinner, 1956): A response that is reinforced after some, but not all, correct responses will be more resistant to extinction than a response that receives **continuous reinforcement** (a reinforcer for each and every correct response). Although it may be easier to teach a new behavior using continuous reinforcement, partially reinforced behavior is not only more difficult to suppress but also more like real life. Imagine being paid for every hamburger you make or every report you turn in. In the real world, people tend to receive partial reinforcement rather than continuous reinforcement for their work.

Partial reinforcement can be accomplished according to different patterns or schedules. For example, it might be a certain interval of time that's important, such as a spectacular geyser that only erupts a few times a day. It wouldn't matter how many times you tried to catch a glimpse of the geyser if your effort didn't come at the right *time*. On the other hand, it may be the number of responses that is important, as it would be if one had to sell a certain number of raffle tickets in order to get a prize. When the timing of the response is more important, it is called an *interval schedule*. When it is the number of responses that is important, the schedule is called a *ratio schedule* because a certain number of responses is required for each reinforcer (e.g., 50 raffle tickets for each prize). The other way in which schedules of reinforcement can differ is in whether the number of responses or interval of time is *fixed* (the same in each case) or *variable* (a different number or interval is required in each case). So it is possible to have a fixed interval schedule, a variable interval schedule, a fixed ratio schedule, and a variable ratio schedule (Skinner, 1961).

Fixed Interval Schedule of Reinforcement The kind of reinforcement schedule most people are more familiar with is called a **fixed interval schedule of reinforcement**, in which a reinforcer is received after a certain, fixed interval of time has passed. If a researcher were teaching a rat to press a lever to get food pellets, she might require it to push the lever for 2 minutes to get a pellet. It wouldn't matter how many times the rat pushed the bar press, it would only get the pellet after 2 minutes had passed. If people receive a paycheck once every two weeks (provided that they show up to work in those two weeks), they are being reinforced on this kind of schedule.

As shown in the graph in the upper left corner of Figure 5.8, this schedule of reinforcement does not produce a fast rate of responding (notice that the line doesn't go "up" as fast as in the graph on the right). It only matters that at least one response is made during the specific interval of time, so speed is not that important. It might be required to press the lever during a 5-minute interval of time. It doesn't have to press the bar fast or even very many times—just once in the 5 minutes. It is the first correct response after the interval of time has passed that gets reinforced. Eventually, the rat will start pushing the lever only as the interval of time nears its end, causing the *scalloping* effect you see in the graph. The response rate goes up just before the reinforcer and then drops off immediately after, until it is almost time for the next food pellet.

Paychecks aren't the only kind of fixed schedule that people experience. When do you study the hardest? Isn't it right before a test? If you know when the test is to be given, that's like having a fixed interval of time that is predictable, and you can save your greatest studying efforts until closer to the exam. (Some students save *all* of their studying for the night before the exam, which is not exactly the best strategy.) Another example of a fixed interval schedule would be the way that most people floss and brush their teeth most rigorously* the few days before their next dental exam. In this case, they are probably hoping for negative reinforcement. The cleaner they get their teeth before the appointment, the less time they might have to spend in that chair.

So if a scheduled test is a fixed interval, then would a pop quiz be a variable interval schedule?

Variable Interval Schedule of Reinforcement   Pop quizzes are unpredictable. Students don't know exactly what day they might be given a pop quiz, so the best strategy is to study a little every night just in case there is a quiz the next day. Pop quizzes are good examples of a **variable interval schedule of reinforcement**, in which the interval of time after which the organism must respond in order to receive a reinforcer changes from one time to the next. For example, the rat might receive a food pellet every 5 minutes *on average*. Sometimes it might be two minutes, sometimes ten, but the rat must push the lever at least once after that interval to get the pellet. Because the rat can't predict how long the interval is going to be, it pushes the bar more or less continuously, producing the

Figure 5.8 Schedules of Reinforcement
These four graphs show the typical pattern of responding for both fixed and variable interval and ratio schedules of reinforcement. The responses are cumulative, which means new responses are added to those that come before, and all graphs begin after the learned pattern is well established. Slash marks mean that a reinforcement has been given. In both the fixed interval and fixed ratio graphs, there is a pause after each reinforcement as the learner briefly "rests." The "scalloped" shape of the fixed interval curve is a typical indicator of this pause, as is the stair-step shape of the fixed ratio curve. In the variable interval and ratio schedules, no such pause occurs, because the reinforcements are unpredictable. Notice that both fixed and variable interval schedules are slower (less steep) than the two ratio schedules because of the need to respond as quickly as possible in the ratio schedules.

So if a scheduled test is a fixed interval, then would a pop quiz be a variable interval schedule?

variable interval schedule of reinforcement   schedule of reinforcement in which the interval of time that must pass before reinforcement becomes possible is different for each trial or event.

*Rigorously: strictly, consistently.

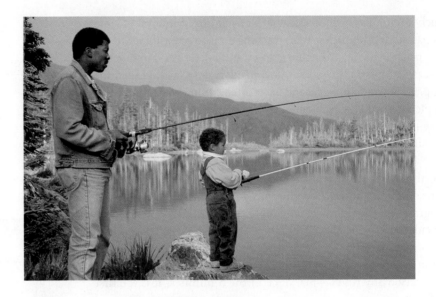

When people go fishing, they never know how long they may have to dangle the bait in the water before snagging a fish. This is an example of a variable interval schedule of reinforcement and explains why some people, such as this father and son, are reluctant to pack up and go home.

fixed ratio schedule of reinforcement schedule of reinforcement in which the number of responses required for reinforcement is always the same.

variable ratio schedule of reinforcement schedule of reinforcement in which the number of responses required for reinforcement is different for each trial or event.

In Figure 5.8 the graph on the lower right is also very fast, but it's so much smoother, like the variable interval graph on the left. Why are they similar?

smooth graph in the lower left corner of Figure 5.8. Once again, speed is not important, so the rate of responding is slow but steady.

Another example of a variable interval schedule might be the kind of fishing in which people put the pole in the water and wait—and wait, and wait, until a fish takes the bait—if they are lucky. They only have to put the pole in once, but they might refrain from taking it out for fear that just when they do, the biggest fish in the world would swim by. Dialing a busy phone number is also this kind of schedule, as people don't know *when* the call will go through, so they keep dialing and dialing.

Fixed Ratio Schedule of Reinforcement   In ratio schedules, it is the number of responses that counts. In a **fixed ratio schedule of reinforcement**, the number of responses required to receive each reinforcer will always be the same number.

Notice two things about the graph in the upper right corner of Figure 5.8. The rate of responding is very fast, especially when compared to the fixed interval schedule on the left, and there are little "breaks" in the response pattern immediately after a reinforcer is given. The rapid response rate occurs because the rat wants to get to the next reinforcer just as fast as possible, and the number of lever pushes counts. The pauses or breaks come right after a reinforcer, because the rat knows "about how many" lever pushes will be needed to get to the next reinforcer because it's always the same. Fixed schedules—both ratio and interval—are predictable, which allows rest breaks.

In human terms, anyone who does piecework, in which a certain number of items have to be completed before payment is given, is reinforced on a fixed ratio schedule. Some sandwich shops give out punch cards that get punched one time for each sandwich purchased. When the card has 10 punches, for example, the person might get a free sandwich.

Variable Ratio Schedule of Reinforcement
▶ *In Figure 5.8 the graph on the lower right is also very fast, but it's so much smoother, like the variable interval graph on the left. Why are they similar?*

A **variable ratio schedule of reinforcement** is one in which the number of responses changes from one trial to the next. In the rat example, the rat might be expected to push the bar an *average* of 20 times to get reinforcement. That means that sometimes the rat would push the lever only 10 times before a reinforcer comes, but at other times it might take 30 lever pushes or more.

The graph at the lower right of Figure 5.8 shows a curve that is just as rapid a response rate as the fixed ratio schedule because the *number* of responses still matters. But the graph is much smoother because the rat is taking no rest breaks. It can't afford to do so because it *doesn't know* how many times it may have to push that lever to get the next food pellet. It pushes as fast as it can and eats while pushing. It is the *unpredictability* of the variable schedule that makes the responses more or less continuous—just as in a variable interval schedule.

In human terms, people who shove money into the one-armed bandit, or slot machine, are being reinforced on a variable ratio schedule of reinforcement (they hope). They put their coins in (response), but they don't know how many times they will have to do this before reinforcement (the jackpot) comes. People who do this tend to sit there until they either win or run out of money. They don't dare stop because the "next one" might hit that jackpot. Buying lottery tickets is much the same thing, as is any kind of gambling. People don't know how many tickets they will have to buy, and they're afraid that if they don't buy the next one, that will be the ticket that would have won, so they keep buying and buying.

Regardless of the schedule of reinforcement one uses, there are some things that can be done to make using reinforcement of a behavior as effective as possible. One thing also concerns timing: A reinforcer should be given as immediately as possible after the desired behavior. Delaying reinforcement tends not to work well, especially when dealing with animals and small children. (Older children and adults can think about future reinforcements, such as saving up one's money to buy a highly desired item, so delayed reinforcement can work with them.) Care should also be taken to reinforce *only* the desired behavior—for example, many parents make the mistake of giving a child who has not done some chore the promised treat anyway, which completely undermines the child's learning of that chore or task.

STIMULUS CONTROL: SLOW DOWN, IT'S THE COPS

5.8 How do operant stimuli control behavior, and what kind of behavior is resistant to operant conditioning?

You see a police car in your rearview mirror and automatically slow down, even if you weren't speeding. The traffic light turns red, so you stop. When you want to get into a store, you head for the door and push or pull on the handle. All of these things—slowing down, stopping, using the door handle—are learned. But how do you know what learned response to make, and when? The police car, the stoplight, and the door handle are all cues, stimuli that tell you what behavior will get you what you want.

Discriminative Stimuli   As stated earlier, a *discriminative stimulus* is any stimulus that provides an organism with a cue for making a certain response in order to obtain reinforcement. For example, a police car is a discriminative stimulus for slowing down and a stop sign is a cue for stopping because both of these actions are usually followed by negative reinforcement—people don't get a ticket or don't get hit by another vehicle. A doorknob is a cue for where to grab the door in order to successfully open it. In fact, if a door has a knob, people always turn it, but if it has a handle, people usually push it, right? The two kinds of opening devices each bring forth a different response from people, and their reward is opening the door.

Raccoons commonly dunk their food in and out of water before eating. This "washing" behavior is controlled by instinct and difficult to change even using operant techniques.

Classic Studies in Psychology
Biological Constraints on Operant Conditioning

Raccoons are fairly intelligent animals and are sometimes used in learning experiments. In a typical experiment, a behaviorist would use shaping and reinforcement to teach a raccoon a trick. The goal might be to get the raccoon to pick up several coins and drop them into a metal container, for which the raccoon would be rewarded with food. The behaviorist starts by reinforcing the raccoon for picking up a single coin. Then the metal container is introduced and the raccoon is now required to drop the coin into the slot on the container in order to get reinforcement.

It is at this point that operant conditioning seems to fail. Instead of dropping the coin in the slot, the raccoon puts the coin in and out of the slot and rubs it against the inside of the container, then holds it firmly for a few seconds before finally letting it go. When the requirement is upped to two coins, the raccoon spends several minutes rubbing them against each other and dipping them into the container, without actually dropping them in. In spite of the fact that this dipping and rubbing behavior is not reinforced, it gets worse and worse until conditioning becomes impossible.

How can this be? If a behavior is followed by a reinforcer it should be repeated, yet this raccoon is not only failing to repeat the behavior it is being reinforced to do, but also the raccoon is doing behavior that gets no reward at all. Why has operant conditioning failed?

Keller and Marian Breland found themselves pondering that very question because the raccoon study was one of their attempts to condition an animal in this manner (Breland & Breland, 1961). The problem wasn't limited to the raccoon, either. They ran into a similar difficulty with a pig that was being trained to pick up a total of five large wooden coins and put them into a "piggy bank." Although at first successful, the pig became slower and slower at the task over a period of weeks, dropping the coin, rooting (pushing) it around with its nose, picking it up, dropping it again, and rooting some more. This behavior became so persistent that the pig actually did not get enough to eat for the day.

The Brelands concluded that the raccoon and the pig were reverting* to behavior that was instinctual for them. Instinctual behavior is genetically determined and not under the influence of learning. Apparently, even though the animals were at first able to learn the tricks, as the coins became more and more associated with food, the animals began to drift back into the instinctual patterns of behavior that they used with real food. Raccoons rub their food between their paws and dip it in and out of water. Pigs root and throw their food around before eating it. The Brelands called this tendency to revert to genetically controlled patterns **instinctive drift**.

In their 1961 paper describing these and other examples of instinctive drift, the Brelands (both trained by Skinner himself) determined that three assumptions in which most Skinnerian behaviorists believed were not actually true. The three false assumptions:

1. The animal comes to the laboratory a *tabula rasa*, or "blank slate," and can, therefore, be taught anything with the right conditioning.

2. Differences between species of animals are insignificant.

3. All responses are equally able to be conditioned to any stimulus.

As became quickly obvious in their studies with these animals, each animal comes into the world (and the laboratory) with certain genetically determined instinctive patterns of behavior already in place. These instincts differ from species to species, with the result that there are some responses that simply cannot be trained into an animal regardless of conditioning. To quote Breland and Breland (1961):

It is our reluctant conclusion that the behavior of any species cannot be adequately understood, predicted, or controlled without knowledge of its instinctive patterns, evolutionary history, and ecological niche. (p. 684)

instinctive drift tendency for an animal's behavior to revert to genetically controlled patterns.

Questions for Further Discussion

1. What other kinds of limitations do animals have in learning?

2. What kinds of behavior might people do that would be resistant to conditioning?

3. How can these research findings about animal behavior be generalized to human behavior?

---

*Reverting: to go back in action, thought, speech, and so on.

APPLYING OPERANT CONDITIONING: BEHAVIOR MODIFICATION

5.9   What is behavior modification, and how can behavioral techniques be used to modify involuntary biological responses?

AP* Suggest how behavior modification, biofeedback, coping strategies, and self-control can be used to address behavioral problems.

Operant conditioning principles such as reinforcement and the process of shaping have been used for many years to change undesirable behavior and create desirable responses in animals and humans—particularly in schoolchildren. The term **behavior modification** refers to the application of operant conditioning (and sometimes classical conditioning) to bring about such changes. You might recall your elementary school teacher offering gold stars or some other incentive* as a reward for reading a certain number of books or giving a reward like a wooden stick that could be traded in for a treat.

For example, if a teacher wants to use behavior modification to help a child learn to be more attentive during the teacher's lectures, the teacher may do the following:

1. Select a target behavior, such as making eye contact with the teacher.
2. Choose a reinforcer. This may be a gold star applied to the child's chart on the wall, for example.
3. Put the plan in action. Every time the child makes eye contact, the teacher gives the child a gold star. Inappropriate behavior (such as looking out of the window) is not reinforced with gold stars.
4. At the end of the day, the teacher gives the child a special treat or reward for having a certain number of gold stars. This special reward is decided on ahead of time and discussed with the child.

Both gold stars and wooden sticks can be considered *tokens*, secondary reinforcers that can be traded in for other kinds of reinforcers. The use of tokens to modify behavior is called a **token economy**. ⓁⒾⓃⓀ *to Chapter Thirteen: Psychological Therapies, p. 527.* In the example, the child is collecting gold stars to "buy" the special treat at the end of the day. When one thinks about it, the system of money is very much a token economy. People are rewarded for working for money, which they then trade for food, shelter, and so on.

Another tool that behaviorists can use to modify behavior is the process of *time-out*. Time-out is a form of mild punishment by removal in which a misbehaving animal, child, or adult is placed in a special area away from the attention of others. Essentially, the organism is being "removed" from any possibility of positive reinforcement in the form of attention. When used with children, time-out should be limited to 1 minute for each year of age with a maximum time-out of 10 minutes (longer than that and the child can forget why the time-out occurred).

Applied behavior analysis (ABA), is the modern term for a form of behavior modification that uses the shaping process to mold a desired behavior or

behavior modification   the use of operant conditioning techniques to bring about desired changes in behavior.

token economy   type of behavior modification in which desired behavior is rewarded with tokens.

applied behavior analysis (ABA) modern term for a form of behavior modification that uses shaping techniques to mold a desired behavior or response.

---

*Incentive: something that encourages a particular action.

((•• **Listen** to the Psychology in the News podcast. **www.mypsychlab.com**

response. It can be said to have begun with the work of Lovaas (1964) and his associates, although the basic techniques are those first outlined by Skinner. Lovaas used small pieces of candy as reinforcers to teach social skills and language to children with *autism*. (Autism is a disorder in which the person has great difficulty in communicating with others, often refusing to look at another person). ⓁⒾⓃⓀ *to Chapter Ten: Development Across the Life Span, p. 401.* People who are autistic may also fail to learn to speak at all, and they normally do not like to be touched. ((•• Listen on **MyPsychLab**

In ABA, skills are broken down to their simplest steps and then taught to the child through a system of reinforcement. Prompts (such as moving a child's face back to look at the teacher or the task) are given as needed when the child is learning a skill or refuses to cooperate. As the child begins to master a skill and receives reinforcement in the form of treats or praise, the prompts are gradually withdrawn until the child can do the skill independently. Applied behavior analysis is a growing field with many colleges and universities offering excellent degrees at both the undergraduate and graduate levels. A person graduating from one of these programs may act as a consultant* to schools or other institutions or may set up a private practice. Typical uses for ABA are dealing with children with disorders, training animals, and developing effective teaching methods for children and adults of all levels of mental abilities (Baer et al., 1968).

Other techniques for modifying behavior have been developed so that even behavior that is normally considered involuntary such as blood pressure, muscle tension, and hyperactivity can be brought under conscious control. For nearly 60 years, scientists have known how to use feedback of a person's biological information (such as heart rate) to create a state of relaxation (Margolin & Kubic, 1944). **Biofeedback** is the traditional term used to describe this kind of biological feedback of information, and through its use many problems can be relieved or controlled.

A relatively newer technique called **neurofeedback** has been used to treat a child's attention problems in the classroom. Although this technique uses the latest in technology, the basic principles behind it are much older. Neurofeedback involves trying to change brain-wave activity. In neurofeedback, the person is connected to an *electroencephalograph*, a machine that records the brain's electrical activity. Neurofeedback devices can be integrated into video-game–style programs. In one case a young boy with attention problems was able to make a car on a screen go faster or slower in response to his own changing brain activity, which reflected his mental state of relaxation or excitement (Radford, 2004). ✳ Explore on **MyPsychLab**

✳ **Explore** research on neurofeedback. **www.mypsychlab.com**

Neurofeedback has been used to treat a number of disorders and conditions in the last few years, including epilepsy (Sterman, 2000; Sterman & Lantz, 2001), anxiety disorders (Egner et al., 2002; Norris et al., 2001), depression and anger (Hammond, 2001a; Putnam, 2001), drug addiction (Trudeau, 2000), chronic fatigue syndrome (Hammond, 2001b; Mueller et al., 2001), obsessive-compulsive disorder (Hammond, 2003), autism (Jarusiewicz, 2002), and attention-deficit hyperactivity disorder (Linden et al., 1996; Monastra et al., 2002; Rossiter & La Vaque, 1995). Playing a video game to help solve problems like anxiety and attention problems? To many people, it probably sounds like a perfect world.

biofeedback using feedback about biological conditions to bring involuntary responses, such as blood pressure and relaxation, under voluntary control.

neurofeedback form of biofeedback using brain-scanning devices to provide feedback about brain activity in an effort to modify behavior.

---

*Consultant: someone who offers expert advice or services.

5.7–9

- **timing of reinforcement:** influences speed of learning, strength of learned response, and subsequent behavior pattern

schedules of reinforcement

- **continuous reinforcement:** providing reinforcer for each and every correct response
  - easier to establish new responses but more sensitive to extinction
- **partial reinforcement:** reinforcing behavior after some, but not all, correct responses
  - leads to a response that is resistant to extinction
  - schedule can be specified by the pattern/ratio of responses or by time/interval
  - both ratio and interval schedules can be either fixed or variable

Operant Conditioning (part 2)
(learning to make voluntary responses through the effects of positive or negative consequences)

behavior modification

- application of operant conditioning principles (sometimes classical conditioning) to change undesirable behaviors and create desirable behaviors in both humans and animals
- token economies, time-out, applied behavior analysis, biofeedback, and neurofeedback use these principles

PRACTICE QUIZ: PREPARING FOR THE AP* EXAM

ANSWERS ON PAGE AK-2.

Directions: Read each of the questions or incomplete sentences below. Then choose the response that best answers the question or completes the sentence.

1. Which of the following scenarios illustrates a variable interval schedule of reinforcement?
   a. Receiving a paycheck once every two weeks
   b. Holding regular, but unpredictable, fire drills in anticipation of a possible fire
   c. Earning a prize for every five books read in the library's summer reading program
   d. Receiving five additional vacation days for each year of employment at a company
   e. Brushing and flossing teeth immediately before a dental exam

2. Dr. Lazarus tells his Psychology 101 students that they can earn one extra credit point for every three reports they write summarizing an article from the professional psychology literature. What schedule of reinforcement is illustrated in this scenario?
   a. Fixed interval
   b. Variable interval
   c. Fixed ratio
   d. Variable ratio
   e. Continuous

3. Mr. Elliot told his students that if his door was open, it meant that he was available to them and would gladly answer any questions they might have. But if his door was pushed almost completely shut, it meant that he was busy and would prefer not to answer questions at that time. Which of the following best describes Mr. Elliot's open door in terms of operant conditioning?
   a. The open door provides punishment by application.
   b. The open door provides negative reinforcement.

   c. The open door facilitates a fixed interval schedule of reinforcement.
   d. The open door is a discriminative stimulus for asking questions.
   e. The open door is a discriminative stimulus for not asking questions.

4. Which of the following illustrates an instance of instinctive drift?
   a. A dog salivates in response to a ringing bell.
   b. A circus elephant is unable to learn a difficult trick from its trainer.
   c. A mouse learns to navigate a maze and receives a reward for exiting the maze.
   d. A child has difficulty learning the difference between positive and negative social behaviors.
   e. A bird associates a certain toy with food and begins to treat that toy as it would treat food.

5. An elementary school teacher gives students a sticker each time the students raise their hands before speaking in class. When a student has earned ten stickers, he or she is given an extra five minutes of recess. What process is the teacher using?
   a. Behavior modification and/or a token economy
   b. Neurofeedback
   c. Partial reinforcement
   d. Biofeedback
   e. Applied behavior analysis

AP* Describe the essential characteristics of insight learning, latent learning, and social learning.

AP* Identify key contributors in the psychology of learning.

Cognitive Learning Theory

5.10 How do latent learning, learned helplessness, and insight relate to cognitive learning theory?

In the early days of behaviorism, the original focus of Watson, Skinner, and many of their followers was on observable, measurable behavior. Anything that might be occurring inside a person or animal's head during learning was considered to be of no interest to the behaviorist because it could not be seen or directly measured. Other psychologists, however, were still interested in the mind's influence over behavior. Gestalt psychologists, for instance, were studying the way that the human mind tried to force a pattern on stimuli in the world around the person. **LINK** *to Chapter One: The Science of Psychology, pp. 8–9.* This continued interest in the mind was followed, in the 1950s and 1960s, by the comparison of the human mind to the workings of those fascinating "thinking machines," computers. Soon after, interest in *cognition*, the mental events that take place inside a person's mind while engaging in behavior, began to dominate experimental psychology. Many behavioral psychologists could no longer ignore the thoughts, feelings, and expectations that clearly existed in the mind and that seemed to influence observable behavior and eventually began to develop a cognitive learning theory to supplement the more traditional theories of learning (Kendler, 1985). Three important figures often cited as key theorists in the early days of the development of cognitive learning theory were the Gestalt psychologists Edward Tolman and Wolfgang Köhler and modern psychologist Martin Seligman.

TOLMAN'S MAZE-RUNNING RATS: LATENT LEARNING

One of Gestalt psychologist Edward Tolman's best-known experiments in learning involved teaching three groups of rats the same maze, one at a time (Tolman & Honzik, 1930). In the first group, each rat was placed in the maze and reinforced with food for making its way out the other side. The rat was then placed back in the maze, reinforced, and so on until the rat could successfully solve the maze with no errors—the typical maze-learning experiment (see Figure 5.9).

Figure 5.9 A Typical Maze

This is an example of a maze such as the one used in Tolman's experiments in latent learning. A rat is placed in the start box. The trial is over when the rat gets to the end box.

The second group of rats was treated exactly like the first, except that they never received any reinforcement upon exiting the maze. They were simply put back in again and again, until the tenth day of the experiment. On that day, the rats in the second group began to receive reinforcement for getting out of the maze. The third group of rats, serving as a control group, was also not reinforced and was not given reinforcement for the entire duration of the experiment.

A strict Skinnerian behaviorist would predict that only the first group of rats would learn the maze successfully because learning depends on reinforcing consequences. At first, this seemed to be the case. The first group of rats did indeed solve the maze after a certain number of trials, whereas the second and third groups seemed to wander aimlessly around the maze until accidentally finding their way out.

On the tenth day, however, something happened that would be difficult to explain using only Skinner's basic principles. The second group of rats, upon receiving the reinforcement for the first time, *should* have then taken as long as the first group to solve the maze. Instead, they began to solve the maze almost immediately (see Figure 5.10).

Tolman concluded that the rats in the second group, while wandering around in the first nine days of the experiment, had indeed learned where all the blind alleys, wrong turns, and correct paths were and stored this knowledge away as a kind of "mental map," or *cognitive map* of the physical layout of the maze. The rats in the second group had learned and stored that learning away mentally but had not *demonstrated* this learning because there was no reason to do so. The cognitive map had remained hidden, or latent, until the rats had a reason to demonstrate their knowledge by getting to the food. Tolman called this **latent learning**. The idea that learning could happen without reinforcement, and then later affect behavior, was not something traditional operant conditioning could explain. ✻⌐Explore on **MyPsychLab**

latent learning learning that remains hidden until its application becomes useful.

✻ **Explore** with the simulation on latent learning. **www.mypsychlab.com**

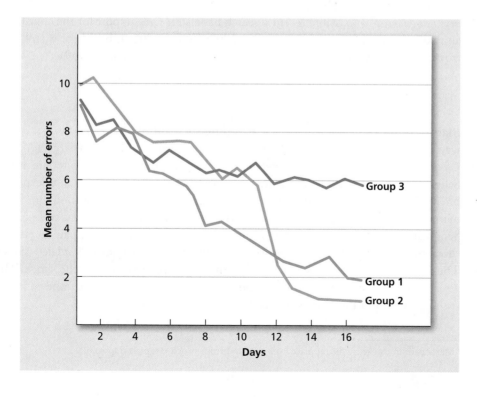

Figure 5.10 Learning Curves for Three Groups of Rats

In the results of the classic study of latent learning, Group 1 was rewarded on each day, while Group 2 was rewarded for the first time on Day 11. Group 3 was never rewarded. Note the immediate change in the behavior of Group 2 on Day 12 (Tolman & Honzik, 1930).

◀ **AP**✶ Interpret graphs that exhibit the results of learning experiments.

Another of Köhler's chimpanzees, Grande, has just solved the problem of how to get to the banana by stacking boxes. Does this meet the criteria for insight, or was it simple trial-and-error learning?

AP* Identify key contributors in the psychology of learning.

AP* Apply learning principles to explain emotional learning, taste aversion, superstitious behavior, and learned helplessness.

insight the sudden perception of relationships among various parts of a problem, allowing the solution to the problem to come quickly.

KOHLER'S SMART CHIMP: INSIGHT LEARNING

Another exploration of the cognitive elements of learning came about almost by accident. Wolfgang Köhler (1887–1967) was a Gestalt psychologist who became marooned* on an island in the Canaries (a series of islands off the coast of North Africa) when World War I broke out. Stuck at the primate research lab that had first drawn him to the island, he turned to studies of animal learning.

In one of his more famous studies (Köhler, 1925), he set up a problem for one of the chimpanzees. Sultan the chimp was faced with the problem of how to get to a banana that was placed just out of his reach outside his cage. Sultan solved this problem relatively easily, first trying to reach through the bars with his arm, then using a stick that was lying in the cage to rake the banana into the cage. As chimpanzees are natural tool users, this behavior is not surprising and is still nothing more than simple trial-and-error learning.

But then the problem was made more difficult. The banana was placed just out of reach of Sultan's extended arm with the stick in his hand. At this point there were two sticks lying around in the cage, which could be fitted together to make a single pole that would be long enough to reach the banana. Sultan first tried one stick, then the other (simple trial and error). After about an hour of trying, Sultan seemed to have a sudden flash of inspiration. He pushed one stick out of the cage as far as it would go toward the banana and then pushed the other stick behind the first one. Of course, when he tried to draw the sticks back, only the one in his hand came. He jumped up and down and was very excited, and when Köhler gave him the second stick, he sat on the floor of the cage and looked at them carefully. He then fitted one stick into the other and retrieved his banana. Köhler called Sultan's rapid "perception of relationships" **insight** and determined that insight could not be gained through trial-and-error learning alone (Köhler, 1925). Although Thorndike and other early learning theorists believed that animals could not demonstrate insight, Kohler's work seems to demonstrate that insight requires a sudden "coming together" of all the elements of a problem in a kind of "aha" moment that is not predicted by traditional animal learning studies. (LINK) *to Chapter Seven: Cognition: Thinking, Intelligence, and Language, p. 268.* More recent research has also found support for the concept of animal insight (Heinrich, 2000; Heyes, 1998; Zentall, 2000), but there is still controversy over how to interpret the results of those studies (Wynne, 1999).

SELIGMAN'S DEPRESSED DOGS: LEARNED HELPLESSNESS

Martin Seligman is now famous for founding the field of *positive psychology*, a new way of looking at the entire concept of mental health and therapy. (LINK) *to Chapter Eight: Motivation and Emotion, pp. 338–339.* But in the mid- to late 1960s Seligman, a learning theorist, and his colleagues accidentally discovered an unexpected phenomenon while doing experiments on dogs using classical conditioning (Seligman, 1975). Their original intention was to study escape and avoidance learning. Seligman and colleagues presented a tone followed by a harmless but painful electric shock to one group of dogs (Overmier & Seligman, 1967; Seligman & Maier, 1967). The dogs in this group were harnessed so that they could not escape the shock. The researchers assumed that the dogs would learn to fear the sound of the tone and later try to escape from the tone before being shocked.

---

*Marooned: in this sense, being placed on an island from which escape is impossible.

These dogs, along with another group of dogs that had not been conditioned to fear the tone, were placed into a special box consisting of a low fence that divided the box into two compartments. The dogs, which were now unharnessed, could easily see over the fence and jump over if they wished—which is precisely what the dogs that had not been conditioned did as soon as the shock occurred. Imagine the researchers' surprise when, instead of jumping over the fence when the tone sounded, the previously conditioned dogs just sat there. In fact, these dogs showed distress but didn't try to jump over the fence *even when the shock itself began.*

Why would the conditioned dogs refuse to move when shocked? The dogs that had been harnessed while being conditioned had apparently learned in the original tone/shock situation that there was nothing they could do to escape the shock. So when placed in a situation in which escape was possible, the dogs still did nothing because they had learned to be "helpless." They believed they could not escape, so they did not try.

I know some people who seem to act just like those dogs—they live in a horrible situation but won't leave. Is this the same thing?

Seligman extended this theory of **learned helplessness**, the tendency to fail to act to escape from a situation because of a history of repeated failures in the past, to explain *depression.* Depressed people seem to lack normal emotions and become somewhat apathetic, often staying in unpleasant work environments or bad marriages or relationships rather than trying to escape or better their situation. Seligman proposed that this depressive behavior is a form of learned helplessness. Depressed people may have learned in the past that they seem to have no control over what happens to them (Alloy & Clements, 1998). A sense of powerlessness and hopelessness is common to depressed people, and certainly this would seem to apply to Seligman's dogs as well.

Think about how this might apply to other situations. There are many students who feel that they are bad at math because they have had problems with it in the past. Is it possible that this belief could make them not try as hard or study as much as they should? Isn't this kind of thinking also an example of learned helplessness?

◀ I know some people who seem to act just like those dogs—they live in a horrible situation but won't leave. Is this the same thing?

Observational Learning

5.11 What occurs in observational learning, including findings from Bandura's classic Bobo doll study and the four elements of observational learning?

Another type of learning theory that departs from the traditional theories of Pavlov and Skinner and also depends on cognition is that of **observational learning**, the learning of new behavior through the observation of a model (watching someone else who is doing that behavior).

BANDURA AND THE BOBO DOLL

Bandura's classic study in observational learning involved having a preschool child in a room in which the experimenter and a model interacted with toys in the room in front of the child (Bandura, et al., 1961). In one condition, the model interacted with the toys in a nonaggressive manner, completely ignoring the presence of a "Bobo" doll (a punch-bag doll in the shape of a clown). In another condition, the model became very aggressive with the doll, kicking it and yelling at it, throwing it in the air and hitting it with a hammer.

When each child was left alone in the room and had the opportunity to play with the toys, a camera filming through a one-way mirror caught the children who were exposed to the aggressive model beating up on the Bobo doll in exact imitation

◀ **AP*** Distinguish general differences between principles of classical conditioning, operant conditioning, and observational learning.

◀ **AP*** Identify key contributors in the psychology of learning.

learned helplessness the tendency to fail to act to escape from a situation because of a history of repeated failures in the past.

observational learning learning new behavior by watching a model perform that behavior.

Albert Bandura's famous Bobo doll experiment. This doll was used to demonstrate the impact of observing an adult model performing aggressive behavior on the later aggressive behavior of children. The children in these photos are imitating the adult model's behavior even though they believe they are alone and are not being watched.

of the model. The children who saw the model ignore the doll did not act aggressively toward the toy. Obviously, the aggressive children had learned their aggressive actions from merely watching the model—with no reinforcement necessary. The fact that learning can take place without actual performance (a kind of latent learning) is called the **learning/performance distinction**.

Ah, but would that child have imitated the model if the model had been punished? Wouldn't the <u>consequences</u> of the model's behavior make a difference?

In later studies, Bandura showed a film of a model beating up the Bobo doll. In one condition, the children saw the model rewarded afterward. In another, the model was punished. When placed in the room with toys, the children in the first group beat up the doll, but the children in the second group did not. But, when Bandura told the children in the second group that he would give them a reward if they could show him what the model in the film did, each child duplicated the model's actions. Both groups had learned from watching the model, but only the children watching the successful (rewarded) model imitated the aggression with no prompting (Bandura, 1965). Apparently, consequences do matter in motivating a child (or an adult) to imitate a particular model. The tendency for some movies and television programs to make "heroes" out of violent, aggressive "bad guys" is particularly disturbing in light of these findings. In fact, Bandura began this research to investigate possible links between children's exposure to violence on television and aggressive behavior toward others.

By some accounts, the average child in the United States will have seen 8,000 murders and 100,000 acts of violence on television before he or she has started elementary school (Donnerstein et al., 1994). While there is a body of evidence stretching over nearly two decades that suggests a link between viewing violent television and an increased level of aggression in children (Bushman & Huesmann, 2001; Huesmann & Eron, 1986), this evidence is based on correlational data. ⓛⓘⓝⓚ *to Chapter One: The Science of Psychology, pp. 26–28.* Correlations do not prove that viewing violence on TV is the *cause* of the increased violence. What if naturally aggressive children just like to watch more violent shows? What if homes in which children are permitted to watch violent programs are those in which parents use aggressive punishment or in which aggressive behavior is permitted or even encouraged? ◉ Watch on MyPsychLab

Ah, but would that child have imitated the model if the model had been punished? Wouldn't the <u>consequences</u> of the model's behavior make a difference? ▶

◉ **Watch** classic video footage of Bandura and Walter's study.
www.mypsychlab.com

AP* Describe the essential characteristics of insight learning, latent learning, and social learning. ▶

learning/performance distinction
referring to the observation that learning can take place without actual performance of the learned behavior.

THE FOUR ELEMENTS OF OBSERVATIONAL LEARNING

Bandura (1986) concluded, from these studies and others, that observational learning required the presence of four elements.

Attention To learn anything through observation, the learner must first pay *attention* to the model. For example, if your grandparents host a fancy dinner party and you want to know which utensils to use at certain points during the multi-course meal, you might want to pay attention to your grandparents to see when they pick up their salad forks and soup spoons. Certain characteristics of models can make attention more likely. For example, people pay more attention to those people they perceive as similar to them and to people whom they perceive as attractive.

Memory The learner must also be able to retain the *memory* of what was done. If your friend shows you how to install and run a new computer program, you have to remember those steps in order to put the program on your own computer later on.

Imitation The learner must be capable of reproducing, or *imitating*, the actions of the model. A 2-year-old might be able to watch someone tie shoelaces and might even remember most of the steps, but the 2-year-old's chubby little fingers will not have the dexterity* necessary for actually tying the laces. A person with extremely weak ankles might be able to watch and remember how some ballet move was accomplished but will not be able to reproduce it. The mirror neurons discussed in Chapter Two may be willing, but the flesh is weak. (LINK) *to Chapter Two: The Biological Perspective, p. 82.*

Motivation Finally, the learner must have the desire or *motivation* to perform the action. Even though you are a guest at your grandparents' fancy dinner, for example, you might not care which fork or which knife is the "proper" one to use. Also, if a person expects a reward because one has been given in the past, or has been promised a future reward (like the children in the second group of Bandura's study), or has witnessed a model getting a reward (like the children in the first group), that person will be much more likely to imitate the observed behavior. Successful models are powerful figures for imitation, but rarely would we be motivated to imitate someone who fails or is punished.

(An easy way to remember the four elements of modeling is to remember the letters AMIM, which stand for the first letters of each of the four elements. This is a good example of using a strategy to improve memory. (LINK) *to Introduction, pp. I-11–I-13*)

---

*Dexterity: skill and ease in using the hands.

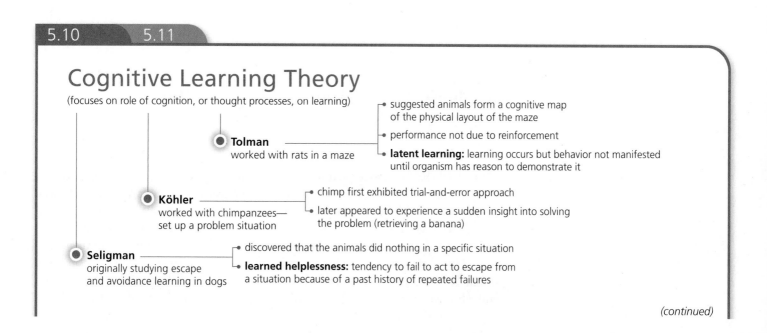

5.10   **5.11**

Cognitive Learning Theory
(focuses on role of cognition, or thought processes, on learning)

Tolman
worked with rats in a maze
- suggested animals form a cognitive map of the physical layout of the maze
- performance not due to reinforcement
- **latent learning:** learning occurs but behavior not manifested until organism has reason to demonstrate it

Köhler
worked with chimpanzees— set up a problem situation
- chimp first exhibited trial-and-error approach
- later appeared to experience a sudden insight into solving the problem (retrieving a banana)

Seligman
originally studying escape and avoidance learning in dogs
- discovered that the animals did nothing in a specific situation
- **learned helplessness:** tendency to fail to act to escape from a situation because of a past history of repeated failures

(continued)

Observational Learning

(the learning of a new behavior through the observation of a model; typically associated with classic work of Bandura and "Bobo doll" study)

- **children observing** — an adult model's aggressive or nonaggressive behaviors tended to later act in the same manner they saw modeled; no reinforcement was necessary
  - later research suggested that potential consequences can influence motivation to imitate a particular model

- **key elements for learner**
  - pay attention to the model
  - able to remember what was done
  - capable of reproducing, or imitating, the actions of the model
  - have the desire or motivation to perform the action

PRACTICE QUIZ: PREPARING FOR THE AP* EXAM

ANSWERS ON PAGE AK-2.

Directions: Read each of the questions or incomplete sentences below. Then choose the response that best answers the question or completes the sentence.

1. Attention, memory, imitation, and motivation are the four elements required for the process of _____.
   a. insight
   b. latent learning
   c. learned helplessness
   d. observational learning
   e. spontaneous recovery

2. In Edward Tolman's maze study, the fact that the group of rats receiving reinforcement only after the tenth day of the study solved the maze far more quickly than did the rats who had been reinforced from the first day can be interpreted to mean that these particular rats _____.
   a. were much smarter than the other rats
   b. had already learned the maze in the first nine days
   c. had the opportunity to cheat by watching the other rats
   d. were very hungry and, therefore, learned much more quickly
   e. were able to learn only because they had not received much reinforcement

3. Martin Seligman found many similarities between his "helpless" dogs and people suffering from _____.
   a. depression
   b. agoraphobia
   c. schizophrenia
   d. eating disorders
   e. aggressive behavior syndrome

4. Wolfgang Köhler determined that his chimpanzee's two-stick solution to the banana problem was an example of insight because it was _____.
   a. intelligent
   b. sudden and rapid
   c. the result of trial-and-error learning
   d. arrived at after a long period of time
   e. based on natural biological behaviors

5. In Albert Bandura's study with the Bobo doll, the children in the group that saw the model punished did not imitate the model at first. They would only imitate the model if given a reward for doing so. The fact that these children had obviously learned the behavior without actually performing it is an example of _____.
   a. the learning/performance distinction
   b. insight learning
   c. operant conditioning
   d. classical conditioning
   e. learned helplessness

Applying Psychology to Everyday Life: Can You Really Toilet Train Your Cat?

5.12 What is a real-world example of the use of conditioning?

(This article has been excerpted with permission of the author and cat-trainer extraordinaire, Karawynn Long. Karawynn Long is a published writer and Web designer who lives in Seattle with her family. Sadly, since this article was written, her cat, Misha has passed away. Ms. Long can be reached at her Web site **www.karawynn.net/mishacat/ toilet.html**. The italicized words in brackets are the author's "editorial" comments.)

There have been more books and articles about toilet-training cats than you'd think. In the summer of 1989, when Misha was a small kitten with big ears and enough meow for five cats, I searched out and read a half-dozen of them. And then tried it myself, and discovered there were a couple of things they all failed to mention . . . here's what worked for me and Misha.

The central idea is that the transition from litter box to toilet should be accomplished in a series of stages. [*This is shaping.*] You make a small change and then give your cat time to adjust before you make another small change. If at any time Felix gives the whole thing up and goes on the rug instead, you're pushing him too far too fast; back up a stage or two and try again, more slowly.

READY? FIRST START BY TRAINING YOURSELF . . .

The very most important thing to remember is: Lid Up, Seat Down. Post a note on the back of the door or the lid of the toilet if you think you (or your housemates or guests) might forget. And if you are accustomed to closing the bathroom door when it's empty, you'll have to break that habit too. [*In operant conditioning, this is part of "preparing the training arena."*]

Begin by moving the cat's current litter box from wherever it is to one side of the toilet. Make sure he knows where it is and uses it. Rest (this means doing nothing for a period of between a day and a week, depending on how flappable your cat is). Next put something—a stack of newspapers, a phone book, a cardboard box— under the litter box to raise it, say, about an inch. (Magazines are too slick; you don't want the litter box sliding around and making your cat feel insecure. Tape the litter box down if you need to.) Rest. Get another box or phone book and raise it a little higher. Rest. Continue this process until the bottom of the litter box is level with the top of the toilet seat. (For Misha I raised it about two inches per day.) [*Notice that this is the step-by-step process typically used in shaping.*]

At the beginning of this process, your cat could just step into the litter box; later he began jumping up into it, until at some point he probably started jumping up onto the toilet seat first and stepping into the box from there. Lift the seat on your toilet and measure the inside diameter of the top of the bowl at its widest point. Venture forth and buy a metal mixing bowl of that diameter. Do not (I discovered this the hard way) substitute a plastic bowl. A plastic bowl will not support the cat's weight and will bend, dropping into the toilet bowl and spilling litter everywhere, not to mention startling the cat.

Now you move the litter box over so that it's sitting directly over the toilet seat. (If your cat has shown reluctance over previous changes, you might want to split this into two stages, moving it halfway onto the seat and then fully over.) Take away the stack of phone books or whatever you used. Rest. [*Again, notice that everything has to be done in small steps. This is the heart of the shaping process—requiring too large a step will stop the process.*]

Here's the cool part. Take away the litter box entirely. (Ta da!) Nestle the metal mixing bowl inside the toilet bowl and lower the seat. Fill the bowl with about two inches of litter (all of this is much easier if you have the tiny granules of litter that can be scooped out and flushed).

Naturally, any humans using the toilet at this point will want to remove the metal bowl prior to their own use and replace it afterward. The next week or two the whole process is likely to be something of an annoyance; if you begin to think it's not worth it, just remember that you will never have to clean a litter box again.

Watch your cat using the bathroom in the metal bowl. Count the number of feet he gets up on the toilet seat (as opposed to down in the bowl of litter). The higher the number, the luckier you are and the easier your job is going to be . . .

. . . because next you have to teach him proper squatting posture. Catch him beginning to use the toilet as much of the time as possible and show him where his feet are supposed to go. Just lift them right out of the bowl and place them on the seat (front legs in the middle, hind legs on the outside). If he starts out with three

Misha's first attempt without the box. He scored two out of a possible four.

Misha demonstrates proper squatting posture. Note the look of firm concentration.

or, heaven forbid, all four feet in the bowl, just get the front two feet out first. Praise him all over the place every time he completes the activity in this position. [*The praise is the positive reinforcement, and should be done with each successful step.*]

(Misha is very doglike in that he craves approval and praise. If your cat is indifferent to this sort of thing, you can also reward him with small food treats and wean him from them later when the toilet behavior has "set." Just keep the treats as small and infrequent as possible—half a Pounce™ or similar treat per occasion should be plenty.) [*If treats are too frequent, it will make it difficult to phase out the reinforcer after the behavior is well learned.*]

When he is regularly using the toilet with his front feet out (and some cats naturally start from this position), begin lifting a hind foot out and placing it on the seat outside the front paws. Your cat will probably find this awkward at first and try to replace the foot in the litter. Be persistent. Move that foot four times in a row if you have to, until it stays there. Praise and/or treat.

Repeat with the other hind foot, until your cat learns to balance in that squat. Once he's getting all four feet regularly on the seat, it's all easy from here.

Which is fortunate, because the last bit is also the most unpleasant. I suggest that you postpone this stage until you have at least a weekend, and preferably several days, when you (or another responsible party) will be at home most of the time. I skipped through this part in about two days; I only hope that your cat allows you to move along that fast.

Begin reducing the litter in the bowl. Go as fast as he'll feel comfortable with, because as the litter decreases, the odor increases. You'll want to be home at this point so that you can praise him and dump out the contents of the bowl immediately after he's finished, to minimize both the smell and the possibility that your cat, in a confused attempt to minimize the smell on his own, tries to cover it up with litter that no longer exists and ends up tracking unpleasantness into the rest of the house.

By the time you're down to a token teaspoonful of litter in the bottom of the bowl, your next-door neighbors will probably be aware of the precise instant your cat has used the toilet. This is as bad as it gets. The next time you rinse out the metal bowl, put a little bit of water in the bottom. Increase the water level each time, just as you decreased the litter level. Remember—if at any point Felix looks nervous enough about the change to give the whole thing up and take his business to the corner behind the door, back up a step or two and try the thing again more slowly. [*Shaping takes a lot of patience, depending on the behavior being shaped and the learning ability of the animal—or person.*]

Once the water in the mixing bowl is a couple of inches deep and your cat is comfortable with the whole thing, you get to perform the last bit of magic. Take the mixing bowl away, leaving the bare toilet. (Lid Up, Seat Down.)

VOILA! YOUR CAT IS NOW TOILET TRAINED

Some useful books on using operant conditioning to toilet train cats:

Brotman, E. (2001). *How to Toilet Train Your Cat: The Education of Mango.* Sherman Oaks, CA: Bird Brain Press.

Kunkel, P. & Mead K. P. (1991). *How to Toilet Train Your Cat: 21 Days to a Litter-Free Home.* New York: Workman Publishing Company.

Questions for Further Discussion

1. Why would this technique probably not work with a dog?
2. Are there any safety concerns with teaching a cat in this way?
3. Are there any other difficulties that might arise when doing this training?

5 CHAPTER SUMMARY

Definition of Learning

5.1 What does the term *learning* really mean?

- Learning is any relatively permanent change in behavior brought about by experience or practice and is different from maturation that is genetically controlled.

It Makes Your Mouth Water: Classical Conditioning

5.2 How was classical conditioning first studied, and what are the important elements and characteristics of classical conditioning?

- Pavlov accidentally discovered the phenomenon in which one stimulus can, through pairing with another stimulus, come to produce a similar response. He called this classical conditioning.
- The unconditioned stimulus (UCS) is the stimulus that is naturally occurring and produces the reflex, or involuntary unconditioned response (UCR). Both are called "unconditioned" because they are not learned.
- The conditioned stimulus (CS) begins as a neutral stimulus, but when paired with the unconditioned stimulus eventually begins to elicit the reflex on its own. The reflex response to the conditioned stimulus is called the conditioned response (CR), and both stimulus and response are learned.
- Pavlov paired a sound with the presentation of food to dogs and discovered several principles for classical conditioning: The neutral stimulus (NS) and UCS must be paired several times and the CS must precede the UCS by only a few seconds.
- Other important aspects of classical conditioning include stimulus generalization, stimulus discrimination, extinction, spontaneous recovery, and higher-order conditioning.

5.3 What is a conditioned emotional response, and how do cognitive psychologists explain classical conditioning?

- Watson was able to demonstrate that an emotional disorder called a phobia could be learned through classical conditioning by exposing a baby to a white rat and a loud noise, producing conditioned fear of the rat in the baby.
- Conditioned taste aversions occur when an organism becomes nauseated some time after eating a certain food, which then becomes aversive to the organism.
- Some kinds of conditioned responses are more easily learned than others because of biological preparedness.
- Pavlov believed that the NS became a substitute for the UCS through association in time.
- The cognitive perspective asserts that the CS has to provide some kind of information or expectancy about the coming of the UCS in order for conditioning to occur.

What's in It for Me? Operant Conditioning

5.4 How does operant conditioning occur, and what were the contributions of Thorndike and Skinner?

- Thorndike developed the Law of Effect: A response followed by a pleasurable consequence will be repeated, but a response followed by an unpleasant consequence will not be repeated.

- B. F. Skinner named the learning of voluntary responses operant conditioning because voluntary responses are what we use to operate in the world around us.

5.5 What are the important concepts in operant conditioning?

- Skinner developed the concept of reinforcement, the process of strengthening a response by following it with a pleasurable, rewarding consequence.
- A primary reinforcer is something such as food or water that satisfies a basic, natural drive, whereas a secondary reinforcer is something that becomes reinforcing only after being paired with a primary reinforcer.
- In positive reinforcement, a response is followed by the presentation of a pleasurable stimulus, whereas in negative reinforcement, a response is followed by the removal or avoidance of an unpleasant stimulus.
- Shaping is the reinforcement of successive approximations to some final goal, allowing behavior to be molded from simple behavior already present in the organism.
- Extinction, generalization and discrimination, and spontaneous recovery also occur in operant conditioning.

5.6 What are some of the problems with using punishment?

- Punishment is any event or stimulus that, when following a response, makes that response less likely to happen again.
- In punishment by application, a response is followed by the application or experiencing of an unpleasant stimulus, such as a spanking.
- In punishment by removal, a response is followed by the removal of some pleasurable stimulus, such as taking away a child's toy for misbehavior.
- A person who uses aggressive punishment, such as spanking, can act as a model for aggressive behavior. This will increase aggressive behavior in the one being punished, which is an undesirable response.
- Punishment of both kinds normally has only a temporary effect on behavior.
- Punishment can be made more effective by making it immediate and consistent and by pairing punishment of the undesirable behavior with reinforcement of the desirable one.

5.7 What are the schedules of reinforcement?

- Continuous reinforcement occurs when each and every correct response is followed by a reinforcer.
- Partial reinforcement, in which only some correct responses are followed by reinforcement, is much more resistant to extinction. This is called the partial reinforcement effect.
- In a fixed ratio schedule of reinforcement, a certain number of responses is required before reinforcement is given.
- In a variable ratio schedule of reinforcement, a varying number of responses is required to obtain reinforcement.
- In a fixed interval schedule of reinforcement, at least one correct response must be made within a set interval of time to obtain reinforcement.

- In a variable interval schedule of reinforcement, reinforcement follows the first correct response made after an interval of time that changes for each reinforcement opportunity.

5.8 How do operant stimuli control behavior, and what kind of behavior is resistant to operant conditioning?

- Discriminative stimuli are cues, such as a flashing light on a police car or a sign on a door that says "Open," that provide information about what response to make in order to obtain reinforcement.

Classic Studies in Psychology: Biological Constraints on Operant Conditioning

- Instinctive behavior in animals is resistant to conditioning or modification. Although an animal may change its behavior at first through conditioning, the behavior will revert to the instinctual pattern in a process called instinctive drift.

5.9 What is behavior modification, and how can behavioral techniques be used to modify involuntary biological responses?

- Operant conditioning can be used in many settings on both animals and people to change, or modify, behavior. This use is termed *behavior modification* and includes the use of reinforcement and shaping to alter behavior.
- Token economies are a type of behavior modification in which secondary reinforcers, or tokens, are used.
- Applied behavior analysis (ABA) is the modern version of behavior modification and makes use of shaping by breaking desired behavior down into discrete steps.
- Neurofeedback is a version of biofeedback in which the person is connected to an electroencephalograph, a machine that records the brain's electrical activity.

Cognitive Learning Theory

5.10 How do latent learning, learned helplessness, and insight relate to cognitive learning theory?

- Cognitive learning theory states that learning requires cognition, or the influence of an organism's thought processes.

- Tolman found that rats that were allowed to wander in a maze but were not reinforced still showed evidence of having learned the maze once reinforcement became possible. He termed this hidden learning *latent learning*, a form of cognitive learning.
- Seligman found that dogs that had been placed in an inescapable situation failed to try to escape when it became possible to do so, remaining in the painful situation as if helpless to leave. Seligman called this phenomenon learned helplessness and found parallels between learned helplessness and depression.
- Köhler found evidence of insight, the sudden perception of the relationships among elements of a problem, in chimpanzees.

Observational Learning

5.11 What occurs in observational learning, including findings from Bandura's classic Bobo doll study and the four elements of observational learning?

- Observational learning is learning through watching others perform, or model, certain actions.
- Bandura's famous Bobo doll experiment demonstrated that young children will imitate the aggressive actions of a model even when there is no reinforcement for doing so.
- Bandura determined that four elements needed to be present for observational learning to occur: attention, memory, imitation, and motivation.

Applying Psychology to Everyday Life: Can You Really Toilet Train Your Cat?

5.12 What is a real-world example of the use of conditioning?

- Writer Karawynn Long used shaping, reinforcement, and classical conditioning to train her cat to use the toilet in her bathroom instead of a litter box.

TEST YOURSELF: PREPARING FOR THE AP* EXAM

ANSWERS ON PAGE AK-2.

✓ Practice on MyPsychLab   Ready for your test? More quizzes and a customized study plan. www.mypsychlab.com

PART I: MULTIPLE-CHOICE QUESTIONS

Directions for Part I: Read each of the questions or incomplete sentences below. Then choose the response that best answers the question or completes the sentence.

1. In your family's apartment building, any time you take a shower, someone always flushes the toilet and causes the water in your shower to turn icy cold, making you cringe. After several episodes like this, you find that you tend to cringe whenever you hear a toilet flush, no matter where you are. In this example, what is the conditioned stimulus?
   a. The cold temperature
   b. The sound of flushing
   c. The cringing reaction
   d. The sight of a toilet
   e. The presence of water

2. A child has been classically conditioned to fear a white rat. If the child also shows fear when shown a white rabbit, this is called _____.
   a. stimulus generalization
   b. discriminative stimulation
   c. successive approximation
   d. stimulus substitution
   e. secondary reinforcement

3. The fact that some kinds of stimuli (like a taste) are more easily and quickly connected to a response (like nausea) is explained by the concept of _____.
   a. biofeedback
   b. instinctive drift
   c. vicarious conditioning
   d. behavior modification
   e. biological preparedness

4. Who added the concept of reinforcement to learning theory?
   a. Watson
   b. Skinner
   c. Thorndike
   d. Pavlov
   e. Bandura

5. Which of the following is an example of a secondary reinforcer?
   a. A 10-dollar bill
   b. A glass of cold milk
   c. A piece of ripe fruit
   d. A hug from a parent
   e. An ice pack on a bruised knee

6. Liz failed her French test, so her parents told her that she could not play video games for a month. Her parents are using _____.
   a. positive reinforcement
   b. negative reinforcement
   c. punishment by removal
   d. punishment by application
   e. primary reinforcement

7. Which of the following punishments would most likely be most effective?
   a. Punishment that is aggressive and physical.
   b. Punishment applied after both right and wrong behavior.
   c. Punishment applied every other time the wrong behavior occurs.
   d. Punishment of the wrong behavior paired with reinforcement of the right behavior.
   e. Punishment that occurs several hours after the wrong behavior.

8. Sherry wants her dog to "heel" on command. At first she gives the dog a treat for coming to her when she speaks the command, "Heel!" Then she rewards the dog only when it stands at her side when she gives the command. Finally, she rewards the dog only when it is at her side and facing front. Sherry is using
   a. shaping
   b. generalization
   c. instinctive drift
   d. higher-order conditioning
   e. a fixed ratio schedule of reinforcement

9. For every 5 boxes of cookies that Lisa sells, her scout troop gets a dollar. Through what type of schedule is Lisa being reinforced?
   a. A fixed interval schedule
   b. A fixed ratio schedule
   c. A variable interval schedule
   d. A variable ratio schedule
   e. A continuous reinforcement schedule

10. Jared learns how to prepare his father's famous chili recipe by watching his father in the kitchen for many years. This kind of learning is known as _____.
    a. insight learning
    b. operant learning
    c. discovery learning
    d. conditioned learning
    e. observational learning

PART II: FREE-RESPONSE QUESTION

Directions for Part II: Read the essay question that follows. Then, respond to the question in a clear, concise essay. Do not simply list facts. Instead, present a thorough argument based on your critical consideration of the topic. Use proper psychological terminology as necessary.

Owen is a six-year-old child who frequently misbehaves at home. Owen's parents would like to use fundamental principles of learning to curb Owen's inappropriate behavior. Explain each concept that follows, and describe how Owen's parents could use that concept to improve Owen's behavior:
   a. The Law of Effect
   b. Punishment by removal
   c. Fixed interval schedule of reinforcement
   d. Applied behavior analysis
   e. Token economy
   f. Observational learning

5 VISUAL SUMMARY
Learning

5.2   p. 182

- **discovered by Ivan Pavlov** — focused on observable, measurable behavior
  worked with salivating dogs

  - **several key elements must be present and experienced**
    - unconditioned stimulus (UCS)
    - unconditioned response (UCR)
    - conditioned stimulus (CS)
    - conditioned response (CR)

Classical Conditioning (part 1)

(learning to make an involuntary response to a stimulus other than the original, natural stimulus that normally produces it)

- **basic principles for classical conditioning to occur**
  - CS must come before the UCS
  - CS and UCS must come very close together in time (<5 sec)
  - CS must be paired with the UCS many times
  - CS must be distinct from other competing stimuli

- **key features**
  - stimulus generalization
  - stimulus discrimination
  - extinction
  - spontaneous recovery
  - higher-order conditioning

Before Conditioning
Neutral Stimulus (NS) Bell → No Salivation

During Conditioning
Neutral Stimulus (NS) Bell → Unconditioned Stimulus (UCS) Food → Unconditioned Response (UCR) Salivation

After Conditioning
Conditioned Stimulus (CS) Bell → Conditioned Response (CR) Salivation

5.3   p. 185

Classical Conditioning (part 2)

(learning to make an involuntary response to a stimulus other than the original, natural stimulus that normally produces it)

- **other features**
  - conditioned emotional responses
  - conditioned taste aversion
  - vicarious conditioning

- **Why does it work?**
  - Pavlov
  - cognitive perspective

"Bathroom? Sure, it's just down the hall to the left, jog right, left, another left, straight past two more lefts, then right, and it's at the end of the third corridor on your right."

P. BYRNES.

- One-way door
-- Curtain

Start box   End box

5.10   p. 209

Cognitive Learning Theory

(focuses on role of cognition, or thought processes, on learning)

- **Tolman**
  worked with rats in a maze

- **Köhler**
  worked with chimpanzees—set up a problem situation

- **Seligman**
  originally studying escape and avoidance learning in dogs

5.4–6   p. 195

- **Thorndike** ─┐ developed
  was among the first ┘ Law of Effect
  to study learning of
  voluntary responses

- **Skinner** ─┐ coined term
  led field of ┘ *operant*
  behaviorism ┘ *conditioning*
  after Watson

Operant Conditioning (part 1)

(learning to make voluntary responses through the effects of positive or negative consequences)

"Remember, every time he gives you a pellet, reinforce that behavior by pulling the lever."

- **reinforcement** ──────────
  any event or stimulus, that when following a response
  increases the probability that the response will occur again

  - **primary reinforcers**
  - **secondary reinforcers**
  - **positive reinforcement**
  - **negative reinforcement**

- **punishment**
  is any event or stimulus, that
  when following a response decreases
  the probability that the response
  will occur again

  - **punishment by application**
  - **punishment by removal**

Fixed interval | Fixed ratio
Variable interval | Variable ratio

(Cumulative responses / Time)

5.7–9   p. 203

- **schedules of reinforcement** ──
  - **timing of reinforcement**
  - **continuous reinforcement**
  - **partial reinforcement**

Operant Conditioning (part 2)

(learning to make voluntary responses through
the effects of positive or negative consequences)

- **behavior modification**

Table 5.2 Four Ways to Modify Behavior

	REINFORCEMENT	PUNISHMENT
Positive (Adding)	Something valued or desirable	Something unpleasant
	Positive Reinforcement	*Punishment by Application*
	Example: getting a gold star for good behavior in school	Example: getting a spanking for disobeying
Negative (Removing/ Avoiding)	Something unpleasant	Something valued or desirable
	Negative Reinforcement	*Punishment by Removal*
	Example: avoiding a ticket by stopping at a red light	Example: losing a privilege such as going out with friends

5.11   p. 210

Observational Learning

(the learning of a new behavior through the observation of a model; typically associated with classic work of Bandura and "Bobo doll" study)

- **children observing** ──────
  an adult model's aggressive or
  nonaggressive behaviors tended to later act
  in the same manner they saw modeled;
  no reinforcement was necessary

  later research suggested
  that potential conse-
  quences can influence
  motivation to imitate
  a particular model

- **key elements for learner**
  - pay attention to the model
  - able to remember what was done
  - capable of reproducing, or imitating, the actions of the model
  - have the desire or motivation to perform the action

6
Memory

The Masters of Memory

Most of us, at some point in our busy days, have a little trouble remembering things. That problem doesn't seem to be shared by the people who enter the U.S. Memory Championship, held in New York every year since 1998 (PR Newswire Association, Inc., 2000). The championship has five events: First, contestants have 15 minutes to memorize 99 names and faces and 20 minutes to recite them back. Second, they must memorize an unpublished poem of 50 lines in 15 minutes. The third task is to memorize a list of random numbers, the fourth a list of random words, and finally contestants must memorize the position of all 52 cards in a shuffled deck of playing cards.

Sound impossible? Scott Hagwood can do it and has done it four times. Scott also holds the world rank of grand master. Grand masters must memorize three things: 1,000 numbers in under an hour, the exact order of 10 shuffled decks of cards (also in less than 1 hour), and one shuffled deck of cards in less than 2 minutes. In 2007, David Thomas did it—also a grand master, ranked number 35 in the world in terms of memory masters. (Also in 2007, Ben Pridmore of Derby, England, broke the "holy grail" of memory sports by memorizing a shuffled deck of 52 cards—in an astonishing 26.28 seconds! This is the equivalent, according to memory sport experts, of breaking the 4-minute mile in physical sports.)

How do they do it? Although they do spend thousands of hours in training, in the end memory masters like Scott and David simply use a strategy that has been around since the fifth century B.C. A Greek poet named Simonides discovered that he could easily remember who was sitting at a large banquet by remembering *where* each person sat—people apparently have a great memory for location (Schachter, 1996). The memory masters simply take each number or card or person and associate it with a familiar place or even an image. (LINK) *to Introduction, pp. I-11–I-13.* Retrieving such memories becomes fairly simple. In the chapter you are about to read, you will learn why this "trick" works so well.

Why study memory? Without memory, how would we be able to learn anything? The ability to learn is the key to our very survival, and we cannot learn unless we can remember what happened the last time a particular situation arose. Why study forgetting? If we can learn about the ways in which we forget information, we can apply that learning so that forgetting occurs less frequently.

6 Learning Objectives

- **6.1** What are the three processes of memory and the different models of how memory works?
- **6.2** How does sensory memory work?
- **6.3** What is short-term memory, and how does it differ from working memory?
- **6.4** How is long-term memory different from other types of memory?
- **6.5** What are the various types of long-term memory, and how is information stored in long-term memory organized?
- **6.6** What kinds of cues help people remember?
- **6.7** How do the retrieval processes of recall and recognition differ, and how reliable are our memories of events?
- **6.8** How are long-term memories formed, and what kinds of problems do people experience as a result?
- **6.9** What is false memory syndrome?
- **6.10** Why do we forget?
- **6.11** How and where are memories formed in the brain?
- **6.12** How does amnesia occur, and what is Alzheimer's disease?

AP* Outline the principles that underlie effective encoding, storage, and construction of memories.

---

memory an active system that receives information from the senses, puts that information into a usable form, and organizes it as it stores it away, and then retrieves the information from storage.

encoding the set of mental operations that people perform on sensory information to convert that information into a form that is usable in the brain's storage systems.

storage holding onto information for some period of time.

It sounds like memory encoding ▶ works just like the senses—is there a difference?

Memory

▶ 6.1   What are the three processes of memory and the different models of how memory works?

Is memory a place or a process? The answer to that question is not simple. In reading through this chapter, it becomes clear that memory is a process but that it also has a "place" in the brain as well. Perhaps the best definition of **memory** is an active system that receives information from the senses, puts that information into a usable form, organizes it as it stores it away, and then retrieves the information from storage (Baddeley, 1996, 2003).

Although there are several different models of how memory works, all of them involve the same three processes: getting the information into the memory system, storing it there, and getting it back out.

PUTTING IT IN: ENCODING

The first stage in the memory system is to get sensory information (sight, sound, etc.) into a form that the brain can use. This is called **encoding**. Encoding is the set of mental operations that people perform on sensory information to convert that information into a form that is usable in the brain's storage systems. For example, when people hear a sound, their ears turn the vibrations in the air into neural messages from the auditory nerve (*transduction*), which makes it possible for the brain to interpret that sound. ⓁⒾⓃⓀ *to Chapter Three: Sensation and Perception, p. 103.*

It sounds like memory encoding works just like the senses—is there a difference? Encoding is not limited to turning sensory information into signals for the brain. Encoding is accomplished differently in each of three different storage systems, or stages of memory. In one stage of memory storage, encoding may involve rehearsing information over and over to keep it in memory, whereas in another stage encoding involves elaborating on the meaning of the information—but let's elaborate on that later.

KEEPING IT IN: STORAGE

The next step in memory is to hold on to the information for some period of time in a process called **storage**. This period of time will actually be of different lengths, depending on the stage of memory being used. For example, in one stage of memory people hold on to information just long enough to work with it, about 20 seconds or so. In another stage of memory, people hold on to information more or less permanently.

GETTING IT OUT: RETRIEVAL

The biggest problem many people have is **retrieval**, getting the information they know they have out of storage. Have you ever handed in an essay test and *then* remembered several other things you could have said? Retrieval problems are discussed in a major section of this chapter.

Models of Memory

Exactly how does memory work? When the storage process occurs, where does that information go and why? Memory experts have proposed several different ways of looking at memory. The model that many researchers feel is the most comprehensive* and perhaps the most influential over the last several decades is the **information-processing model**, an approach that focuses on the way information is processed, or handled, through three different stages of memory. The processes of encoding, storage, and retrieval are seen as part of this model. This theory is covered in greater detail throughout the rest of this chapter, but the other newer models deserve attention as well.

LEVELS-OF-PROCESSING MODEL

The information-processing model assumes that how long a memory will be remembered depends on the stage of memory in which it is stored. Other researchers have proposed that how long a memory will be retained depends on the depth (i.e., the effort made to understand the meaning) to which the information is processed

---

*Comprehensive: all inclusive, covering everything.

retrieval getting information that is in storage into a form that can be used.

information-processing model model of memory that assumes the processing of information for memory storage is similar to the way a computer processes memory in a series of three stages.

AP* Compare and contrast various cognitive processes.

Scrabble™ player Marlon Hill (right) poses with Eric Chalkin, director of the documentary "Word Wars," a film about top-rated players of this classic word game. A game such as this requires retrieval of not only the words but also the word spellings from previously stored memories.

levels-of-processing model model of memory that assumes information that is more "deeply processed," or processed according to its meaning rather than just the sound or physical characteristics of the word or words, will be remembered more efficiently and for a longer period of time.

parallel distributed processing (PDP) model a model of memory in which memory processes are proposed to take place at the same time over a large network of neural connections.

(Cermak & Craik, 1979; Craik & Lockhart, 1972). If the word *BALL* is flashed on a screen, for example, and people are asked to report whether the word was in capital letters or lowercase, the word itself does not have to be processed very much at all—only its visual characteristics need enter into conscious attention. But if those people were to be asked to use that word in a sentence, they would have to think about what a ball is and how it can be used. They would have to process its meaning, not just its "looks," which requires more mental effort. Thinking about the meaning of something is a deeper level of processing and results in longer retention of the word, researchers have found in numerous experiments (Cermak & Craik, 1979; Craik & Tulving, 1975; Watson et al., 1999). This model of memory is called the **levels-of-processing model**.

This depth-of-processing effect even holds true for people who suffer from *schizophrenia*, a serious mental disorder in which thoughts are disorganized and often random, and attention is scattered. ⓛⓘⓝⓚ *to Chapter Twelve: Psychological Disorders, pp. 501–502.* In one study, researchers gave both schizophrenic patients and a group of healthy control participants a task in which they had to look at a list of words and decide one of two things: Does the word contain the letter *a* (shallow processing), or is the item represented by the word *living* or *nonliving* (deep processing)? Although the group of patients did not perform as well as the control group overall, both groups were able to recall the deeply processed words from the list better than the more shallowly processed words and to the same relative degree (Paul et al., 2005). If even people such as these schizophrenic patients can benefit from more meaningful processing of information, think how much such processing may help the average person.

PARALLEL DISTRIBUTED PROCESSING (PDP) MODEL

In the **parallel distributed processing (PDP) model**, memory is seen as a simultaneous* process, with the creation and storage of memories taking place across a series of mental networks "stretched" across the brain (McClelland & Rumelhart, 1988; Rumelhart et al., 1986).

Supporters of this model base their viewpoint on the way neural processing actually takes place in the brain: Neural connections appear to be organized in a parallel manner as well as in sequential** pathways in the brain (Hinton et al., 1986; Sartori & Umilta, 2000). Instead of information for a memory being processed only in a series of steps, the brain performs several different processes all running at the same time, or parallel,† to each other, while at the same time spreading that information across the entire network of neural connections. This allows people to retrieve many different aspects of a memory all at once, facilitating much faster reactions and decisions.

The PDP model has not only been influential in the field of human memory but also has been used as a model for constructing artificial intelligence in computer programming (Clark, 1991; Marcus, 2001). In the world of computers, PDP is often related to "connectionism," a movement to use artificial neural networks to explain the mental abilities of humans (Bechtel & Abrahamsen, 2002).

So which model is right?

"Which model is right?" is not the correct question. The correct question is: Which model explains the findings of researchers about how memory works? The answer to that question is that all of these models, including the information-processing model discussed next and throughout the rest of this chapter, can be used to explain some, if not all, research findings. Whether one of these models will one day become the preferred model of memory has yet to be determined. In science, newer theories may often be combined,

So which model is ▶ right?

---

*Simultaneous: all at the same time.

**Sequential: following in time or order.

†Parallel: occurring side by side without being connected directly.

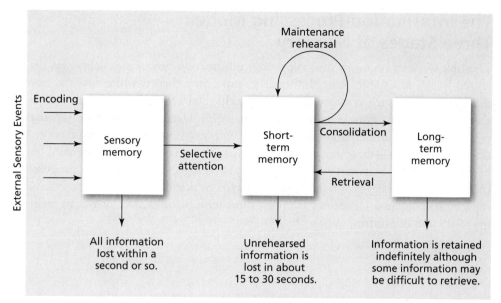

Figure 6.1 Three-Stage Process of Memory
Information enters through the sensory system, briefly registering in sensory memory. Selective attention filters the information into short-term memory, where it is held while attention (rehearsal) continues. If the information receives enough rehearsal, it will enter and be stored in long-term memory.

sometimes with each other and sometimes with older theories. They may be reworked into a new theory with more power to explain existing data. So although the information-processing model of memory (see Figure 6.1) may take "center stage" for now, it is important to remember the concepts of the levels at which information is processed and the way in which those processes may take place while reading the rest of this chapter.

6.1

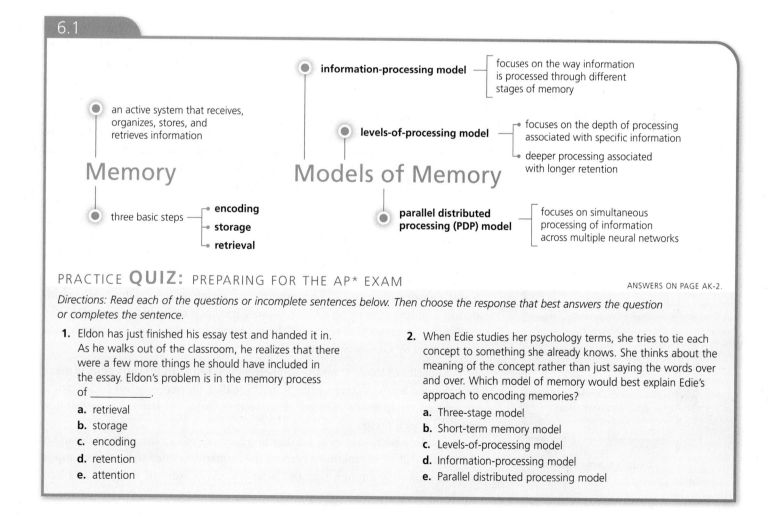

PRACTICE **QUIZ:** PREPARING FOR THE AP* EXAM

ANSWERS ON PAGE AK-2.

Directions: Read each of the questions or incomplete sentences below. Then choose the response that best answers the question or completes the sentence.

1. Eldon has just finished his essay test and handed it in. As he walks out of the classroom, he realizes that there were a few more things he should have included in the essay. Eldon's problem is in the memory process of _____.
   a. retrieval
   b. storage
   c. encoding
   d. retention
   e. attention

2. When Edie studies her psychology terms, she tries to tie each concept to something she already knows. She thinks about the meaning of the concept rather than just saying the words over and over. Which model of memory would best explain Edie's approach to encoding memories?
   a. Three-stage model
   b. Short-term memory model
   c. Levels-of-processing model
   d. Information-processing model
   e. Parallel distributed processing model

The Information-Processing Model: Three Stages of Memory

The link between cognitive psychology and information-processing theory was discussed briefly in Chapter One. Information-processing theory, which looks at how thought processes such as memory work, uses as its model for human thought the way that a computer functions (Massaro & Cowan, 1993). Data are encoded in a way that the computer can understand and use. The computer stores that information on a disk, hard drive, or—these days—a memory stick, and then the data are retrieved out of storage as needed. It was also information-processing theorists who first proposed that there are three stages or types of memory systems that differ in both duration and capacity (see Figure 6.1): sensory memory, short-term memory, and long-term memory (Atkinson & Shiffrin, 1968). ✳ Explore on MyPsychLab

> ### SENSORY MEMORY: WHY DO PEOPLE DO DOUBLE TAKES?

6.2 How does sensory memory work?

Sensory memory is the first stage of memory, the point at which information enters the nervous system through the sensory systems—eyes, ears, and so on. Think of it as a door that is open for a brief time. Looking through the door, one can see many people and objects, but only some of them will actually make it through the door itself. Sensory memory is a kind of door onto the world.

Information is encoded into sensory memory as neural messages in the nervous system. As long as those neural messages are traveling through the system, it can be said that people have a "memory" for that information that can be accessed if needed. For example, say Elaina is driving down the street, looking at the people and cars on either side of her vehicle. All of a sudden she thinks, "What? Was that man wearing a cape?" and she looks back to check. How did she know to look back? Her eyes had already moved past the possible cape-wearing person, but some part of her brain must have just processed what she saw (most likely the reticular formation, which notices new and important information). This is called a double take and can only be explained by the presence, however brief, of a memory for what she saw.

There are two kinds of sensory memory that have been studied extensively. They are the iconic (visual) and echoic (hearing) sensory memories. In the sections that follow, these and other types of memories as well as several of the experiments that have added a great deal of information to the understanding of memory will be discussed.

Iconic Sensory Memory The example of seeing the possibly cape-wearing person is an example of how visual sensory memory, or **iconic memory**, works. *Icon* is the Greek word for "image." Iconic memory was studied in several classic experiments by George Sperling (1960).

Capacity of Iconic Memory Sperling had found in his early studies that if he presented a row of letters using a machine that allowed very fast presentation, his subjects could only remember about four or five of the letters, no matter how many had been presented.

Sperling became convinced that this method was an inaccurate measure of the capacity of iconic memory because the human tendency to read from top to bottom took long enough that the letters on the bottom of the grid may have

---

sensory memory the very first stage of memory, the point at which information enters the nervous system through the sensory systems.

iconic memory visual sensory memory, lasting only a fraction of a second.

✳ **Explore** with a simulation on the information-processing model. **www.mypsychlab.com**

AP* Describe and differentiate psychological and physiological systems of memory.

AP* Identify key contributors in cognitive psychology.

Figure 6.2 Iconic Memory Test
Sample grid of letters for Sperling's test of iconic memory. To determine if the entire grid existed in iconic memory, Sperling sounded a tone associated with each row after the grid's presentation. Participants were able to recall the letters in the row for which they heard the tone. The graph shows the decrease in the number of letters recalled as the delay in presenting the tone increased.

Rows of Letters	Tone Signaling Which Row to Report
LHTY	High tone
EPNR	Medium tone
SBAX	Low tone

faded from memory by the time the person had "read" the letters at the top. He developed a method called the *partial report method*, in which he showed a grid of letters similar to those in Figure 6.2, but immediately sounded a high, medium, or low tone just after the grid was shown. Subjects were told to read off the top row of letters if they heard the high tone, the middle row for the medium tone, or the lowest row for the low tone. As they didn't hear the tone until after the grid went away, they couldn't look at just one row in advance (see Figure 6.2).

Using this method, Sperling found that subjects could accurately report any of the three rows. This meant that the entire grid was in iconic memory and available to the subjects. The capacity of iconic memory is everything that can be seen at one time.

Duration of Iconic Memory   Sperling also found that if he delayed the tone for a brief period of time, after about a second, subjects could no longer recall any better than during the whole report procedure. The icon had completely faded out of sensory memory in that brief time.

In real life, information that has just entered iconic memory will be pushed out very quickly by new information, a process called *masking* (Cowan, 1988). Research suggests that after only a quarter of a second, old information is replaced by new information.

Although it is rare, some people do have what is properly called **eidetic imagery**, or the ability to access a visual memory over a long period of time. Although the popular term *photographic memory* is often used to mean this rare ability, some people claiming to have "photographic memories" actually mean that they have very good memories. Having a very good memory and having eidetic imagery ability are two very different things. People with eidetic imagery ability might be able to look quickly at a page in a book, then by focusing on a blank wall or piece of paper, "read" the words from the image that still lingers in their sensory memory. Although it might sound like a great ability to have while in college, it actually provides little advantage when taking tests, because it's just like having an open-book test. If a student can't *understand* what's written on the pages, having the book open is useless. It is unknown why some people have this ability, but it is more common in children and tends to diminish by adolescence or young adulthood (Haber, 1979; Leask et al., 1969; Stromeyer & Psotka, 1971).

If iconic memory lasts such a brief time, what use is it to us?

Function of Iconic Memory   Iconic memory actually serves a very important function in the visual system. Chapter Three discussed the way the eyes make tiny little movements called *saccades* that keep vision from adapting to a constant visual stimulus, so that what is stared at steadily doesn't slowly disappear. Iconic memory helps the visual system to view surroundings as continuous and stable in spite of these saccadic movements. It also allows enough time for the brain stem to decide if the information is important enough to be brought into consciousness—like the possibly pants-less person.

Echoic Sensory Memory   Another type of sensory memory is **echoic memory**, or the brief memory of something a person has heard. A good example of echoic memory is the "What?" phenomenon. You might be reading or concentrating on the television, and your parent or friend walks up and says something to you. You sit there for a second or two, and then say "What? Oh—yes, I'm ready to eat now," or whatever comment is appropriate. You didn't really process the statement from the other person as he or she said it. You heard it, but your brain didn't interpret it immediately. Instead, it took several seconds for you to realize that (1) something was said, (2) it may have been important, and (3) you'd better try to remember what it was. If you realize all this within about 4 seconds (the duration of echoic memory), you will more than likely be able to "hear" an echo of the statement in your head, a kind of "instant replay."

eidetic imagery   the ability to access a visual memory for 30 seconds or more.

echoic memory   the brief memory of something a person has just heard.

If iconic memory lasts such a brief time, ◄ what use is it to us?

short-term memory (STM) the memory system in which information is held for brief periods of time while being used.

selective attention the ability to focus on only one stimulus from among all sensory input.

> If the lower centers of the brain do decide that the information is important, ▶ what happens next?

AP* Compare and contrast various cognitive processes.

AP* Describe and differentiate psychological and physiological systems of memory.

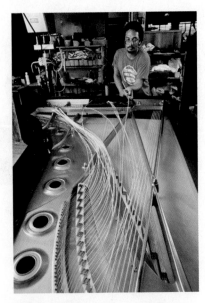

Once these piano strings have been attached to the tuning pins, the piano can be tuned. Tuning a piano requires the use of echoic sensory memory. What other occupations might find a good echoic memory to be an asset?

Echoic memory's capacity is limited to what can be heard at any one moment and is smaller than the capacity of iconic memory, although it lasts longer—about 2 to 4 seconds (Schweickert, 1993).

Echoic memory is very useful when a person wants to have meaningful conversations with others. It allows the person to remember what someone said just long enough to recognize the meaning of a phrase. As with iconic memory, it also allows people to hold on to incoming auditory information long enough for the lower brain centers to decide if the information is important enough to become conscious. It is echoic memory that allows a musician to tune a musical instrument, for example. The memory of the tuning fork's tone lingers in echoic memory long enough for the person doing the tuning to match that tone on the instrument.

If the lower centers of the brain do decide that the information is important, what happens next?

SHORT-TERM AND WORKING MEMORY

6.3 What is short-term memory, and how does it differ from working memory?

▶ Information typically moves from sensory memory to the next stage of memory, called **short-term memory (STM)**, through the process of **selective attention**, the ability to ▶ focus on only one stimulus from among all sensory input (Broadbent, 1958). When a person is thinking actively about some information, that information is said to be conscious (see Chapter Four). It can also be said to be in short-term memory, the memory system in which information is held for brief periods of time while being used.

Selective attention is responsible for the "cocktail party effect" that has been long established in studies of perception and attention (Cherry, 1953; Handel, 1989). If you've ever been at a party where there's a lot of noise and conversations going on in the background but you are able to notice when someone says your name, you have experienced this effect. The areas of the brain that are involved in selective attention were working even though you were not consciously aware of it, and when that important bit of information (your name) appeared, those areas brought the information to your conscious awareness (Hopfinger et al., 2000; Stuss et al., 2002). The only time this attention filter is not working at its peak is during deep Stage Four sleep, and it is still functioning even then (LaBerge, 1980). For example, a mother might be able to sleep through the noise of a train that passes nearby every night but immediately awakens when hearing the soft sound of her baby crying. The train sound may be louder but is not important, whereas the baby's cry is most certainly important.

When your attention is focused—in other words, when you are paying close attention to only one thing—it is relatively easy to form memories about it. For example, if you were given a list of seven numbers and told to spend a few minutes memorizing them, you most likely wouldn't have much trouble with the task. What would happen, though, if you were asked to memorize those same seven numbers while bouncing a basketball through an obstacle course? Your attention would be divided: You'd be paying attention not only to the list of numbers but to the basketball and the obstacle course. As a result, you'd most likely have a more difficult time encoding that list of numbers and storing it in your memory. Attention is the crucial tool that transforms sensations into memories, and when our attention is divided rather than focused, our memories suffer as a result.

Short-term memory tends to be encoded in auditory (sound) form. That simply means that people tend to "talk" inside their own heads. Although some images are certainly stored in STM in a kind of visual "sketchpad" (Baddeley, 1986), auditory storage accounts for much of short-term encoding. Even a dancer planning out moves in her head will not only visualize the moves but also be very likely to verbally describe the moves in her head as she plans. An artist planning a painting certainly has visual information in STM

Each person at this gathering is involved in a conversation with others, with dozens of such conversations going on at the same time all around. Yet if a person in another conversation says the name of one of the people in the crowd, that person in the crowd will likely be able to selectively attend to his or her name. This is known as the "cocktail party effect."

but may also keep up an internal dialogue that is primarily auditory. Research in which participants were asked to recall numbers and letters showed that errors were nearly always made with numbers or letters that *sounded like* the target but not with those that *looked like* the target word or number (Conrad & Hull, 1964). ◉ Watch on MyPsychLab

Some memory theorists use the term *working memory* as another way of referring to short-term memory. This is not entirely correct: Short-term memory has traditionally been thought of as a thing or a place into which information is put. **Working memory** is more correctly thought of as an active system that processes the information present in short-term memory. Working memory is thought to consist of three interrelated systems: a central executive (a kind of "CEO" or "Big Boss") that controls and coordinates the other two systems, a visual "sketchpad" of sorts, and a kind of auditory "recorder" (Baddeley, 1986; Baddeley & Hitch, 1974; Engle & Kane, 2004). The central executive acts as interpreter for both the visual and auditory information, and the visual and auditory information is itself contained in short-term memory. For example, when a person is reading a book, the sketchpad will contain images of the people and events of the particular passage being read, while the recorder "plays" the dialogue in the person's head. The central executive helps interpret the information from both systems and pulls it all together. In a sense, then, short-term memory can be seen as being a part of the working memory system (Bayliss et al., 2005; Colom et al., 2006; Kail & Hall, 2001).

As an example, let's say you run into someone familiar at the mall. You pull that person's name (perhaps with a little difficulty) from your more permanent memory and visualize that name along with the memory of the last time you saw the person, almost as if you were viewing it on a screen. At the same time, you will hear the name in your head. The central executive pulls these different types of information together and you are able to successfully greet good old Bob. *Where* you see and hear this is in short-term memory; the *process* that allows this to happen and coordinates it is working memory.

Another way to think about short-term memory is as if it were a kind of desk where you do your work. You might pull some files out of storage (permanent memory) or someone might hand you some files (sensory input). While the files are on your desk, you can see them, read them, and work with them (working memory). The

◉ **Watch** classic video footage on short-term memory. **www.mypsychlab.com**

working memory an active system that processes the information in short-term memory.

6 8 2 5

5 7 2 1 4

3 5 9 7 2 1

9 2 5 4 6 3 8

2 8 3 7 1 5 6 9

7 3 2 4 9 6 8 5 1

6 5 4 7 8 9 3 2 1 7

Figure 6.3 Digit-Span Test
Instructions for the digit-span test: Listen carefully as the instructor reads each string of numbers out loud. As soon as each string is ended (the instructor may say "go"), write down the numbers in the exact order in which they were given.

This woman must hold the phone number she is reading in short-term memory long enough to dial it on the phone next to her.

AP* Identify key contributors in cognitive psychology.

What do you mean by rehearsal? How long can short-term memories last if rehearsal is a factor?

maintenance rehearsal practice of saying some information to be remembered over and over in one's head in order to maintain it in short-term memory.

"files" are now conscious material and will stay that way as long as they are on the desk. If they are not that important or only necessary for a little while, they get "thrown out" (forgotten as you fail to pay attention to them). If they are important, they might get stored away in the filing system (permanent memory), where they are not conscious until they are once again retrieved—brought out onto the desk.

Capacity: The Magical Number Seven   George Miller (1956) wanted to know how much information humans can hold in short-term memory at any one time (or how many "files" will fit on the "desk"). He reviewed several memory studies, including some using a memory test called the *digit-span test*, in which a series of numbers is read to subjects in the study who are then asked to recall the numbers in order. Each series gets longer and longer, until the subjects cannot recall any of the numbers in order (see Figure 6.3).

What you will probably discover is that everyone you test will get past the first two sequences of numbers, but some people will make errors on the six-digit span, about half of the people you test will slip up on the seven-digit span, and very few will be able to get past the nine-digit span without errors. This led Miller to conclude that the capacity of STM is about seven items or pieces of information, plus or minus two items, or from five to nine bits of information. Miller called this the "magical number seven, plus or minus two." So the "desk" isn't really very big and can hold only so many "files."

Chunking   There is a way to "fool" STM into holding more information than is usual. (Think of it as "stacking" related files on the desk.) If the bits of information are combined into meaningful units, or chunks, more information can be held in STM. If someone were to recode the last sequence of numbers as "654-789-3217," for example, instead of 10 bits of information, there would only be three "chunks" that read like a phone number. This process of recoding, or reorganizing, the information is called *chunking*. Chances are that anyone who can easily remember more than eight or nine digits in the digit-span test is probably recoding the numbers into chunks.

Why Do You Think They Call It Short Term?   How long is the "short" of short-term memory? Research has shown that short-term memory lasts from about 12 to 30 seconds without rehearsal (Atkinson & Shiffrin, 1968; Brown, 1958; Peterson & Peterson, 1959). After that, the memory seems to rapidly "decay" or disappear.

What do you mean by rehearsal? How long can short-term memories last if rehearsal is a factor?

Most people learn that saying something they want to remember over and over again in their heads, such as repeating a phone number they need just long enough to dial it, can help them remember longer, a process called **maintenance rehearsal**. With maintenance rehearsal, a person is simply continuing to pay attention to the information to be held in memory, and since attention is how that information got into STM in the first place, it works quite well (Atkinson & Shiffrin, 1968; Rundus, 1971). With this type of rehearsal, information will stay in short-term memory until rehearsal stops. When rehearsal stops, the memory rapidly decays and is forgotten. If anything interferes with maintenance rehearsal, memories are also likely to be lost. For example, if someone is trying to count a stack of dollar bills by reciting each number out loud while counting, and someone else asks that person the time and interferes with the counting process, the person who is counting will probably forget what the last number was and have to start all over again. Short-term memory helps people keep track of things like counting.

Interference in STM can also happen if the amount of information to be held in STM exceeds its capacity (about five to nine "bits" of information, remember). Information already in STM may be "pushed out" to make room for newer information. This is why it might be possible to remember the first few names of people you meet at a party, but as more names are added, they displace the older names. A better way to remember a person's name is to associate the name with something about the person's appearance, a process that may help move the name from STM into more permanent storage. This more permanent storage is long-term memory, which is the topic of the next section.

LONG-TERM MEMORY

6.4 How is long-term memory different from other types of memory?

The third stage of memory is **long-term memory (LTM)**, the system into which all the information is placed to be kept more or less permanently. In terms of capacity, LTM seems to be unlimited (Bahrick, 1984; Barnyard & Grayson, 1996). Think about it: Would there ever really come a time when you could not fit one more piece of information into your head? When you could learn nothing more? Perhaps if humans lived much longer lives, there might be a way to "fill up" the brain's memory stores. But in practical terms, there is always room for more information (in spite of what some students may believe).

As for duration,* the name *long term* says it all. There is a physical change in the brain itself when a long-term memory is formed. This physical change is relatively permanent. That means that many of the memories people have stored away for a long, long time—even since childhood—are probably always there. That does not mean that people can always retrieve those memories. The memories may be *available* but not *accessible*, meaning that they are still there, but for various reasons (discussed later under the topic of forgetting) people cannot get to them. It's like knowing that there is a certain item on the back of the top shelf of the kitchen cabinet but having no ladder or step stool to reach it. The item is there (available), but you can't get to it (not accessible).

I once memorized a poem by repeating it over and over—that's maintenance rehearsal, right? Since I still remember most of the poem, it must be in long-term memory. Is maintenance rehearsal a good way to get information into long-term memory?

Information that is rehearsed long enough may actually find its way into long-term memory. After all, it's how most people learned their Social Security number and the letters of the alphabet (although people cheated a little on the latter by putting the alphabet to music, which makes it easier to retrieve). Most people tend to learn poems and the multiplication tables by maintenance rehearsal, otherwise known as rote learning. *Rote* is like "rotating" the information in one's head, saying it over and over again. But maintenance rehearsal is not the most efficient way of putting information into long-term storage, because to get the information back out, one has to remember it almost exactly as it went in. Try this: What is the fifteenth letter of the alphabet? Did you have to recite or sing through the alphabet song to get to that letter?

Although many long-term memories are encoded as images (think of the *Mona Lisa*), sounds, smells, and tastes (Cowan, 1988), in general LTM is encoded in meaningful form, a kind of mental storehouse of the meanings of words, concepts, and all the events that people want to keep in mind. Even the images, sounds, smells, and tastes involved in these events have some sort of meaning attached to them that gives them enough importance to be stored long term. If STM can be thought of as a

---

*Duration: how long something lasts.

long-term memory (LTM) the system of memory into which all the information is placed to be kept more or less permanently.

◀ **AP*** Describe and differentiate psychological and physiological systems of memory.

◀ **AP*** Compare and contrast various cognitive processes.

I once memorized a poem by repeating it over and over—that's maintenance rehearsal, right? Since I still remember most of the poem, it must be in long-term memory. Is maintenance rehearsal a good way to get information into ◀ long-term memory?

◀ **AP*** Describe strategies for memory improvement.

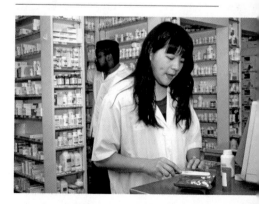

It is very important for this pharmacist to count out the number of pills in the prescription accurately. Short-term memory allows her to remember the last number she counted, but if she is interrupted, she will have to start all over again. Short-term memory is very susceptible to interference.

These students are rehearsing for a concert. They will use maintenance rehearsal (repeating the musical passages over and over) until they can play their parts perfectly. The movements of their fingers upon the strings of their instruments will be stored in long-term memory. How is this kind of long-term memory different from something like the memorized lines of one's part in a play?

I can remember a lot of stuff from my childhood. ▶ Some of it is stuff I learned in school and some of it is more personal, like the first day of school. Are these two different kinds of long-term memories?

elaborative rehearsal a method of transferring information from STM into LTM by making that information meaningful in some way.

procedural (nondeclarative) memory type of long-term memory including memory for skills, procedures, habits, and conditioned responses. These memories are not conscious but are implied to exist because they affect conscious behavior.

anterograde amnesia loss of memory from the point of injury or trauma forward, or the inability to form new long-term memories.

working "surface" or desk, then LTM can be thought of as a huge series of filing cabinets behind the desk, in which files are stored in an organized fashion, according to meaning. Files have to be placed into the cabinets in a certain organized fashion to be useful. How else could anyone ever remember any kind of information quickly if the files were not in some order? The best way to encode information into LTM in an organized fashion is to make it meaningful through *elaborative rehearsal.*

Elaborative Rehearsal   **Elaborative rehearsal** is a way of transferring information from STM into LTM by making that information meaningful in some way (Postman, 1975). The easiest way to do this is to connect new information with something that is already well known (Craik & Lockhart, 1972; Postman, 1975). For example, the French word *maison* means "house." A person could try to memorize that (using maintenance rehearsal) by saying over and over, "*Maison* means house, *maison* means house." But it would be much easier and more efficient if that person simply thought, "*Maison* sounds like masons, and masons build houses." That makes the meaning of the word tie in with something the person already knows (masons, who lay stone or bricks to build houses) and helps in remembering the French term.

As discussed in the beginning of this chapter, Craik and Lockhart (1972) theorized that information that is more "deeply processed," or processed according to its meaning rather than just the sound or physical characteristics of the word or words, will be remembered more efficiently and for a longer period of time. As the levels-of-processing approach predicts, elaborative rehearsal is a deeper kind of processing than maintenance rehearsal and so leads to better long-term storage (Craik & Tulving, 1975).

I can remember a lot of stuff from my childhood. Some of it is stuff I learned in school and some of it is more personal, like the first day of school. Are these two different kinds of long-term memories?

Types of Long-Term Information

6.5   What are the various types of long-term memory, and how is information stored in long-term memory organized?

Long-term memories include general facts and knowledge, personal facts, and even skills that can be performed. Memory for skills is called *procedural (nondeclarative) memory* because it usually involves a series of steps or procedures; memory for facts is called *declarative memory* because facts are things that are known and can be declared (stated outright). These two types of long-term memory are quite different, as the following sections will explain.

Procedural (Nondeclarative) LTM   Memories for skills that people know how to do, like tying shoes and riding a bicycle, are a kind of LTM called **procedural (nondeclarative) memory**. Procedural memories also include emotional associations, habits, and simple conditioned reflexes that may or may not be in conscious awareness, which are often very strong memories. (L I N K) *to Chapter Five: Learning, pp. 178–179.* Referring back to Chapter Two, the amygdala is the most probable location for emotional associations, such as fear, and the cerebellum in the hindbrain is responsible for storage of memories of conditioned responses, skills, and habits (Squire et al., 1993).

Evidence that separate areas of the brain control procedural memory comes from studies of people with damage to the hippocampus area of the brain. This damage causes them to have **anterograde amnesia**, in which new long-term memories cannot be formed. (This disorder is fairly accurately represented by the character of Lenny in the 2000 motion picture *Memento*.) One of the more famous anterograde amnesia patients, H. M., is discussed in detail later in this chapter on page 250.

In one study (Cohen et al., 1985), patients with this disorder were taught how to solve a particular puzzle called the Tower of Hanoi (see Figure 6.4). Although the patients were able to learn the sequence of moves necessary to solve the puzzle, when brought back into the testing room at a later time they could not remember ever having seen the puzzle before—or, for that matter, the examiner. Each trial was like the first one ever for these patients, as they were unable to store the long-term memory of having been in the room or having met the examiner previously. Yet they were able to solve the puzzle even while claiming that they had never seen it before. Their procedural memories for how to solve the puzzle were evidently formed and stored in a part of the brain separate from the part controlling the memories they could no longer form.

The patients in this study had the kind of memory problems that people with Alzheimer's disease have. Yet even people with Alzheimer's disease do not forget how to walk, talk, fasten clothing, or even tie shoes (although they do lose motor ability because the brain eventually fails to send the proper signals). These are all procedural, nondeclarative memories. They may not be able to tell someone who asks that they know how to do these things, but they can still do them. Alzheimer's disease affects the hippocampus and the frontal cortex (involved in decision making and planning) and eventually affects other areas of the brain after it has progressed nearly to the end (Kanne et al., 1998). In fact, it would be rare to find someone who has lost procedural memory. Literally, these are the kind of memories people "never forget."

Procedural memory may also be called **implicit memory** because memories for these skills, habits, and learned reflexes are not easily retrieved into conscious awareness (i.e., nondeclarative). The fact that people have the knowledge of how to tie their shoes, for example, is *implied* by the fact that they can actually tie them. But have you ever tried to tell someone how to tie shoes without using your hands to show them? The subjects in the Tower of Hanoi study provide a good example of implicit memory, as they could solve the puzzle but had no conscious knowledge of how to do so. Such knowledge is in people's memories because they use this information, but they are often not consciously aware of this knowledge (Roediger, 1990). Although procedural memories are implicit, not all implicit memories are necessarily procedural. A memory from one's early childhood of being frightened by a dog, for example, may not be a conscious memory in later childhood but may still be the cause of that older child's fear of dogs. Conscious memories for events in childhood, on the other hand, are usually considered to be a different kind of long-term memory called declarative memory.

Declarative LTM   Procedural memory is about the things that people can *do*, but **declarative memory** is about all the things that people can *know*—the facts and information that make up knowledge. People know things such as the names of the planets in the solar system, that adding two and two makes four, and that a noun is the name of a person, place, or thing. These are general facts, but people also know about the things that have happened to them personally. For example, I know what I ate for breakfast this morning and what I saw on the way to work, but I don't know what you had for breakfast or what you might have seen. There are two types of declarative long-term memories, *semantic* and *episodic* (Nyberg & Tulving, 1996).

Procedural knowledge, such as tying one's shoes, often must be learned by doing, as it is difficult to put into words. Once this child learns how to tie shoes, the knowledge will always be there to retrieve.

Figure 6.4 Tower of Hanoi
The Tower of Hanoi is a puzzle that is solved in a series of steps by moving one disk at a time. The goal is to move all of the disks from peg A to peg C; the rules are that a larger disk can not be moved on top of a smaller one and a disk can not be moved if there are other disks on top of it. Amnesia patients were able to learn the procedure for solving the puzzle but could not remember that they knew how to solve it.

implicit memory   memory that is not easily brought into conscious awareness, such as procedural memory.

declarative memory   type of long-term memory containing information that is conscious and known.

semantic memory type of declarative memory containing general knowledge, such as knowledge of language and information learned in formal education.

episodic memory type of declarative memory containing personal information not readily available to others, such as daily activities and events.

explicit memory memory that is consciously known, such as declarative memory.

One type of declarative memory is general knowledge that anyone has the ability to know. Most of this information is what is learned in school or by reading. This kind of LTM is called **semantic memory**. The word *semantic* refers to meaning, so this kind of knowledge is the awareness of the meanings of words, concepts, and terms as well as names of objects, math skills, and so on. This is also the type of knowledge that is used on game shows such as *Jeopardy* and *Who Wants to Be a Millionaire?* Semantic memories, like procedural memories, are relatively permanent. But it is possible to "lose the way to" this kind of memory, as discussed in the section on forgetting.

The other kind of factual memory is the personal knowledge that each person has of his or her daily life and personal history, a kind of autobiographical* memory. Memories of what has happened to people each day, certain birthdays, anniversaries that were particularly special, childhood events, and so on are called **episodic memory**, because they represent episodes from their lives. Unlike procedural and semantic long-term memories, episodic memories tend to be updated and revised more or less constantly. You can probably remember what you had for breakfast today, but what you had for breakfast two years ago on this date is most likely a mystery. Episodic memories that are especially *meaningful*, such as the memory of the first day of school or your first date, are more likely to be kept in LTM (although they may not be as exact as people sometimes assume they are). The updating process is a kind of survival mechanism, because although semantic and procedural memories are useful and necessary on an ongoing basis, no one really needs to remember every little detail of every day. As becomes obvious later, the ability to forget some kinds of information is very necessary.

Episodic and semantic memories are forms of declarative or **explicit memory**, memories that are easily made conscious and brought from long-term storage into short-term memory. The knowledge of semantic memories such as word meanings, science concepts, and so on can be brought out of the "filing cabinet" and placed on the "desk" where that knowledge becomes *explicit*, or obvious. The same is often true of personal, episodic memories.

But sometimes I can't remember all the names of the planets or what I had for breakfast yesterday. Doesn't that make these memories implicit instead of explicit?

The difference between implicit memories, such as how to balance on a bicycle, and explicit memories, such as naming all the planets, is that it is impossible or extremely difficult to bring implicit memories into consciousness. Explicit memories can be forgotten but always have the potential to be made conscious. When someone reminds you of what you had for breakfast the day before, for example, you will remember that you had that knowledge all along—it was just temporarily "mislaid." For a look at the connections among all these types of LTM, see Figure 6.5.

Long-Term Memory Organization As stated before, LTM has to be fairly well organized for retrieval to be so quick. Can you remember the name of your first-grade teacher? If you can, how long did it take you to pull that name out of LTM and "put it on the desk" of STM? It probably took hardly any time at all. Think of it this way: If a person who puts documents in a filing cabinet just stuffs them in any drawer with no system of organization, when a particular document is needed it requires searching through every drawer. But if documents are filed away alphabetically, and perhaps even according to type of document (deeds in one drawer,

But sometimes I can't ▶ remember all the names of the planets or what I had for breakfast yesterday. Doesn't that make these memories implicit instead of explicit?

---

*Autobiographical: the story of a person's life as told by that person.

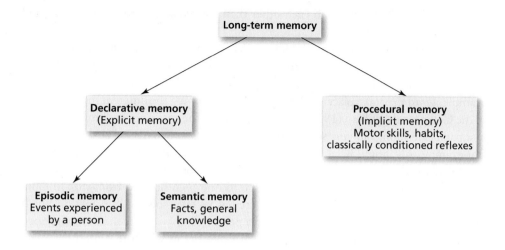

Figure 6.5 Types of Long-Term Memories
Long-term memory can be divided into declarative memories, which are factual and typically conscious (explicit) memories, and nondeclarative memories, which are skills, habits, and conditioned responses that are typically unconscious (implicit). Declarative memories are further divided into episodic memories (personal experiences) and semantic memories (general knowledge).

power of attorney forms in another, etc.), it becomes very easy to retrieve a particular document.

Research suggests that long-term memory is organized in terms of related meanings and concepts (Collins & Loftus, 1975; Collins & Quillian, 1969). In their original study, Collins and Quillian (1969) had subjects respond "true" or "false" as quickly as possible to sentences such as "a canary is a bird" and "a canary is an animal." Looking at Figure 6.6, it is apparent that information exists in a kind of network, with nodes (focal points) of related information linked to each other in a kind of hierarchy.* To verify the statement "a canary is a bird" requires moving to only one node, but "a canary is an animal" would require moving through two nodes and should take longer. This was exactly the result of the 1969 study, leading the researchers to develop the **semantic network model**, which assumes that information is stored in the brain in a connected fashion with concepts that are related to each

semantic network model model of memory organization that assumes information is stored in the brain in a connected fashion, with concepts that are related stored physically closer to each other than concepts that are not highly related.

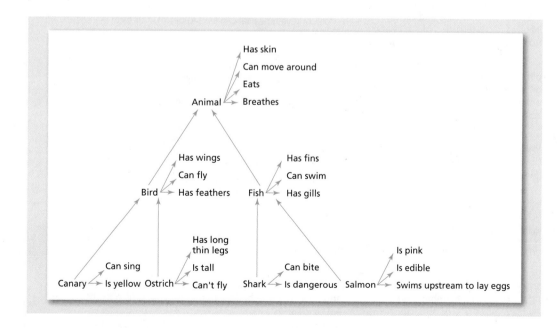

Figure 6.6 An Example of a Semantic Network
In the semantic network model of memory, concepts that are related in meaning are thought to be stored physically near each other in the brain. In this example, canary and ostrich are stored near the concept node for "bird," whereas shark and salmon are stored near "fish." But the fact that a canary is yellow is stored directly with that concept.

---

*Hierarchy: an ordered list or series.

other stored physically closer to each other than concepts that are not highly related (Collins & Quillian, 1969).

The parallel distributed processing model (Rumelhart et al., 1986) discussed earlier in this chapter can be used to explain how rapidly the different points on the networks can be accessed. Although the access of nodes within a particular category (for example, *birds*) may take place in a serial fashion, explaining the different response times in the Collins and Quillian (1969) study, access across the entire network may take place in a parallel fashion, allowing several different concepts to be targeted at the same time (for example, one might be able to think about *birds*, *cats*, and *trees* simultaneously).

Perhaps the best way to think of how information is organized in LTM is to think about the Internet. A person might go to one Web site and from that site link to many other related sites. Each related site has its own specific information but is also linked to many other related sites, and a person can have more than one site open at the same time. This may be very similar to the way in which the mind organizes the information stored in LTM. ✱ Explore on MyPsychLab

✱ **Explore** research on memory mapping. **www.mypsychlab.com**

6.2–5

The Information-Processing Model

(proposes three stages that vary both in duration and capacity; information must be processed effectively at earlier stages before long-term storage occurs)

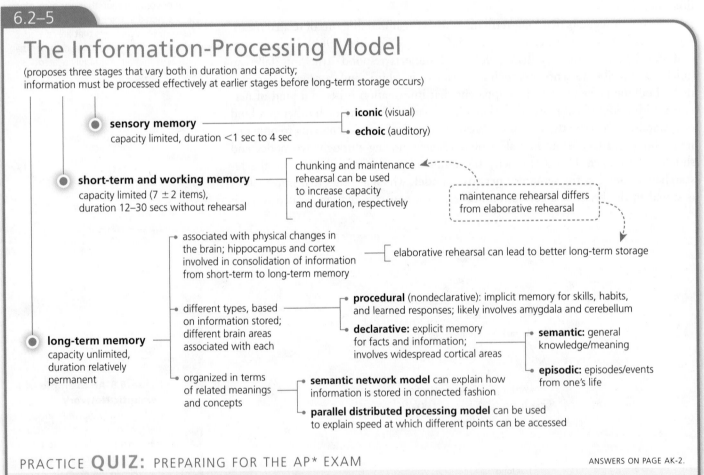

- **sensory memory**
  capacity limited, duration <1 sec to 4 sec
  - **iconic** (visual)
  - **echoic** (auditory)

- **short-term and working memory**
  capacity limited (7 ± 2 items),
  duration 12–30 secs without rehearsal
  - chunking and maintenance rehearsal can be used to increase capacity and duration, respectively

  maintenance rehearsal differs from elaborative rehearsal

- **long-term memory**
  capacity unlimited, duration relatively permanent
  - associated with physical changes in the brain; hippocampus and cortex involved in consolidation of information from short-term to long-term memory
    - elaborative rehearsal can lead to better long-term storage
  - different types, based on information stored; different brain areas associated with each
    - **procedural** (nondeclarative): implicit memory for skills, habits, and learned responses; likely involves amygdala and cerebellum
    - **declarative**: explicit memory for facts and information; involves widespread cortical areas
      - **semantic**: general knowledge/meaning
      - **episodic**: episodes/events from one's life
  - organized in terms of related meanings and concepts
    - **semantic network model** can explain how information is stored in connected fashion
    - **parallel distributed processing model** can be used to explain speed at which different points can be accessed

PRACTICE **QUIZ**: PREPARING FOR THE AP* EXAM

ANSWERS ON PAGE AK-2.

Directions: Read each of the questions or incomplete sentences below. Then choose the response that best answers the question or completes the sentence.

1. Which type of memory can a person use to keep the flow of conversation going by allowing the person to remember what was just said?
   a. Iconic memory
   b. Echoic memory
   c. Procedural memory
   d. Network memory
   e. Long-term memory

2. Fethia learned her multiplication tables by repeating them over and over until she had them memorized. Which of the following was Fethia using?
   a. Deep processing
   b. Procedural processing
   c. Imagistic rehearsal
   d. Elaborative rehearsal
   e. Maintenance rehearsal

3. The Internet, with its series of links from one site to many others, is a good analogy for the organization of

_____.

   a. sensory memory
   b. working memory
   c. episodic memory
   d. long-term memory
   e. short-term memory

4. Which of the following is an example of implicit memory?
   a. Knowing how to ride a bicycle
   b. Multiplying 2 times 4
   c. Knowing your best friend's name
   d. Thinking back on the first day of school
   e. Remembering the definition of the word *psychology*

5. According to George Miller, approximately how many pieces of information can humans hold in short-term memory at any one time?
   a. One
   b. Five
   c. Seven
   d. Ten
   e. An infinite number

Getting It Out: Retrieval of Long-Term Memories

My problem isn't so much getting information <u>into</u> my head, as finding it later. Oddly enough, most people's problems with getting information stored in LTM back out again has to do with *how* they put that information *into* LTM.

RETRIEVAL CUES

6.6 What kinds of cues help people remember?

Remember the previous discussion about maintenance rehearsal versus elaborative rehearsal? One of the main reasons that maintenance rehearsal is not a very good way to get information into LTM is that saying something over and over only gives one kind of **retrieval cue** (a stimulus for remembering), the sound of the word or phrase. When people try to remember a piece of information by thinking of what it means and how it fits in with what they already know, they are giving themselves cues for meaning in addition to sound. The more cues stored with a piece of information, the easier the retrieval of that information will be (Roediger, 2000; Roediger & Guynn, 1996). (LINK) *to Introduction, pp. I-4–I-6.*

Encoding Specificity and State-Dependent Learning: Context and Mood Effects on Memory Retrieval   Although most people would assume that cues for retrieval would have to be directly related to the concepts being studied, the fact is that almost anything in one's surroundings is capable of becoming a cue. If you usually watch a particular television show while eating peanuts, for example, the next time you eat peanuts you might find yourself thinking of the show you were watching. This connection between surroundings and remembered information is called *encoding specificity.*

Have you ever had to take a test in a different classroom than the one in which you learned the material being tested? Do you think that your performance on that test was hurt by being in a different physical context? Researchers have found strong

My problem isn't so much getting information <u>into</u> my head, as finding it later.

AP* Describe strategies for memory improvement.

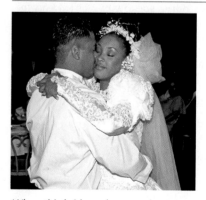

When this bride and groom dance together later on in their marriage, they will be able to recall this moment at their wedding and the happiness they felt at that time. State-dependent learning makes it easier for people to recall information stored while in a particular emotional state (such as the happiness of this couple) if the recall occurs in a similar emotional state.

retrieval cue a stimulus for remembering.

evidence for the concept of **encoding specificity**, the tendency for memory of any kind of information to be improved if the physical surroundings available when the memory is first formed are also available when the memory is being retrieved (Reder et al., 1974; Tulving & Thomson, 1973). For example, encoding specificity would predict that the best place to take one's chemistry test is in the same room in which you learned the material. Also, it's very common to walk into a room and know that there was something you wanted, but in order to remember it, you have to go back to the room you started in to use your surroundings as a cue for remembering.

In one study, researchers had students who were learning to scuba dive in a pool also learn lists of words while they were either out of the pool or in the pool under the water (Godden & Baddeley, 1975). Subjects were then asked to remember the two lists in each of the two conditions. Words that were learned while out of the pool were remembered significantly better when the subjects were out of the pool, and words that were learned underwater were more easily retrieved if the subjects were underwater while trying to remember (see Figure 6.7).

Physical surroundings at the time of encoding a memory are not the only kinds of cues that can help in retrieval. In *state-dependent learning*, memories formed during a particular physiological or psychological state will be easier to remember while in a similar state. For example, when you are fighting with someone, it's much easier to remember all of the bad things that person has done than to remember the good times. In one study (Eich & Metcalfe, 1989), researchers had subjects try to remember words that they had read while listening to music. Subjects read one list of words while listening to sad music (influencing their mood to be sad) and another list of words while listening to happy music. When it came time to recall the lists, the researchers again manipulated the mood of the subjects. The words that were read while subjects were in a happy mood were remembered better if the manipulated mood was also happy but far less well if the mood was sad. The reverse was also true.

encoding specificity the tendency for memory of information to be improved if related information (such as surroundings or physiological state) available when the memory is first formed is also available when the memory is being retrieved.

Figure 6.7 Recall of Target Words in Two Contexts
The retrieval of words learned while underwater was higher when the retrieval also took place underwater. Similarly, words learned while out of the water (on land) were retrieved at a higher rate out of the water. Reproduced with permission from the *British Journal of Psychology*, © The British Psychology Society.

6.7 How do the retrieval processes of recall and recognition differ, and how reliable are our memories of events?

Why do multiple-
◀ choice tests
seem so much
easier than
essay tests?

Why do multiple-choice tests seem so much easier than essay tests?

There are two kinds of retrieval of memories, recall and recognition. It is the difference between these two retrieval methods that makes some kinds of exams seem harder than others. In **recall**, memories are retrieved with few or no external cues, such as filling in the blanks on an application form. **Recognition**, on the other hand, involves looking at or hearing information and matching it to what is already in memory. A word-search puzzle, in which the words are already written down in the grid and simply need to be circled, is an example of recognition. The following section takes a closer look at these two important processes.

RECALL: HMM . . . LET ME THINK

When someone is asked a question such as "Where were you born?" the question acts as the cue for retrieval of the answer. This is an example of recall, as are essay question, short-answer, and fill-in-the-blank tests that are used to measure a person's memory for information (Borges et al., 1977; Gillund & Shiffrin, 1984; Raaijmakers & Shiffrin, 1992).

Retrieval Failure: It's Right on the Tip of My Tongue   Whenever people find themselves struggling for an answer, recall has failed (at least temporarily). Sometimes the answer seems so very close to the surface of conscious thought that it feels like it's "on the tip of the tongue." (If people could just get their tongues out there far enough, they could read it). This is sometimes called the *tip of the tongue (TOT)* phenomenon (Brown & McNeill, 1966; Burke et al., 1991). Although people may be able to say how long the word is or name letters that start or even end the word, they cannot retrieve the sound or actual spelling of the word to allow it to be pulled into the auditory "recorder" of STM so that it can be fully retrieved.

How can a person overcome TOT? The best solution is the one "everyone" seems to know: Forget about it. When you "forget about it," the brain apparently continues to work on retrieval. Some time later (perhaps when you run across a similar-sounding word in your surroundings), the word or name will just "pop out." This can make for interesting conversations, because when that particular word does "pop out," it usually has little to do with the current conversation.

The Serial Position Effect   Another interesting feature of recall is that it is often subject to a kind of "prejudice" of memory retrieval, in which information at the beginning and the end of a list, such as a poem or song, tends to be remembered more easily and accurately. This is called the **serial position effect** (Murdock, 1962).

A good demonstration of this phenomenon involves instructing people to listen to and try to remember words that are read to them that are spaced about 4 or 5 seconds apart. People typically use maintenance rehearsal by repeating each word in their heads. They are then asked to write as many of the words down as they can remember. If the frequency of recall for each word in the list is graphed, it will nearly always look like the graph in Figure 6.8.

Words at the very beginning of the list tend to be remembered better than those in the middle of the list. This effect is called the **primacy effect** and is due to the fact that the first few words, when the listener has nothing already in STM to interfere with their rehearsal, will receive far more rehearsal time than the words in the middle, which are constantly being replaced by the next word on the list (Craik, 1970; Murdock, 1962). In fact, the first words may actually move into LTM if they are

recall   type of memory retrieval in which the information to be retrieved must be "pulled" from memory with very few external cues.

recognition   the ability to match a piece of information or a stimulus to a stored image or fact.

serial position effect   tendency of information at the beginning and end of a body of information to be remembered more accurately than information in the middle of the body of information.

primacy effect   tendency to remember information at the beginning of a body of information better than the information that follows.

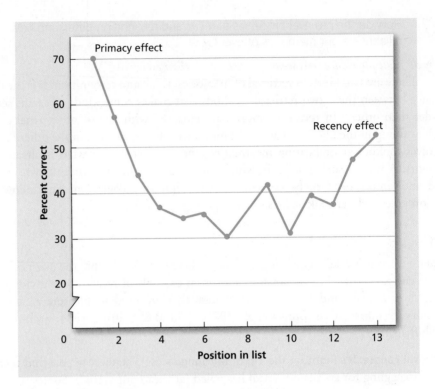

Figure 6.8 Serial Position Effect
In the serial position effect, information at the beginning of a list will be recalled at a higher rate than information in the middle of the list (primacy effect), because the beginning information receives more rehearsal and may enter LTM. Information at the end of a list is also retrieved at a higher rate (recency effect), because the end of the list is still in STM, with no information coming after it to interfere with retrieval.

recency effect   tendency to remember information at the end of a body of information better than the information at the beginning of it.

These people are waiting to interview for a job. The person who is interviewed first and the one who is interviewed last have the greatest chance of being remembered when the time comes for the employer to choose. The serial position effect will cause the impression made by the interviewees who come in the "middle" to be less memorable.

rehearsed long enough, because rote memorization, although not the best way to remember something, can lead to long-term storage.

At the end of the graph there is another increase in recall. This is the **recency effect**; it is usually attributed to the fact that the last word or two was *just heard* and is still in short-term memory for easy retrieval, with no new words entering to "push" the most recent word or words out of memory (Bjork & Whitten, 1974; Murdock, 1962). The serial position effect works with many different kinds of information. In fact, business schools often teach their students that they should try not to be "in the middle" for job interviews. Going first or last in the interview process is much more likely to make a person's interview more memorable.

The serial position effect is often used to demonstrate that there are indeed two memory systems, STM and LTM. Memory researchers point to the primacy effect as a result of LTM storage and the recency effect as a result of STM. But the serial position effect can also apply to LTM exclusively (Baddeley & Hitch, 1974; Roediger & Crowder, 1976). Think about the presidents of the United States. How many of them can you remember? Everyone remembers Washington because he was *first*. After Washington, though, it becomes a struggle for many people to remember who came next. Even if a person can get the first several, the middle presidents are almost impossible to remember. But everyone remembers who is president right now and who was president before him, and so on, up until about the time of childhood (Roediger & Crowder, 1976). In this case, the primacy effect is most likely caused by Washington's importance in history, whereas the recency effect is more likely an effect of the importance of recent events. (Lincoln is the exception to the rule, as most people always remember him because of his importance during the Civil War.)

Can knowledge of the serial position effect be of help to students trying to remember the information they need for their classes? Yes—students can take advantage of the recency effect by skimming back over their notes just before an exam. Knowing that the middle of a list of information is more likely to be forgotten means that students should pay more attention to that middle, and breaking the study sessions up into smaller segments helps reduce the amount of "middle to muddle." (Students can also use *mnemonic strategies* to help offset this memory problem, as well as others. ⓛⓘⓝⓚ *to Introduction, p. I-11.*)

RECOGNITION: HEY, DON'T I KNOW YOU FROM SOMEWHERE?

The other form of memory retrieval is *recognition,* the ability to match a piece of information or a stimulus to a stored image or fact (Borges et al., 1977; Gillund & Shiffrin, 1984; Raaijmakers & Shiffrin, 1992). Recognition is usually much easier than recall because the cue is the actual object, word, sound, and so on, that one is simply trying to detect as familiar and known. Examples of tests that use recognition are multiple-choice, matching, and true–false tests. The answer is right there and simply has to be matched to the information already in memory.

Recognition tends to be very accurate for images, especially human faces. In one study, over 2,500 photographs were shown to participants at the rate of one every 10 seconds. Participants were then shown pairs of photographs in which one member of each pair was one of the previously seen photographs. Accuracy for identifying the previous photos was between 85 to 95 percent (Standing et al., 1970). This is most likely why many people are good at recognizing a person's face but not as good at being able to come up with the name to go with it.

False Positives Recognition isn't foolproof, however. Sometimes there is just enough similarity between a stimulus that is not already in memory and one that is in memory so that a **false positive** occurs (Muter, 1978). A false positive occurs when a person thinks that he or she has recognized something or someone but in fact does not have that something or someone in memory.

False positives can become disastrous in certain situations. In one case, in a series of armed robberies in Delaware, word had leaked out that the suspect sought by police might be a priest. When police put Father Bernard Pagano in a lineup for witnesses to identify, he was the only one in the lineup wearing a priest's collar. Seven eyewitnesses identified him as the man who had robbed them. Fortunately for Father Pagano, the real robber confessed to the crimes halfway through Pagano's trial (Loftus, 1987). Eyewitness recognition can be especially prone to false positives, although most people seem to think that "seeing is believing." For more about the problems with eyewitnesses, see the box Classic Studies in Psychology.

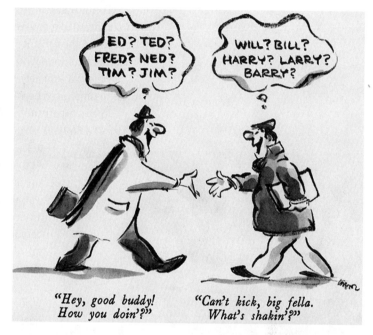

"Hey, good buddy! How you doin'?"

"Can't kick, big fella. What's shakin'?"

AUTOMATIC ENCODING: FLASHBULB MEMORIES

Although some long-term memories need extensive maintenance rehearsal or effortful encoding in the form of elaborative rehearsal to enter from STM into LTM, many other kinds of long-term memories seem to enter permanent storage with little or no effort at all, in a kind of **automatic encoding** (Mandler, 1967; Schneider et al., 1984). People unconsciously notice and seem able to remember a lot of things, such as the passage of time, knowledge of physical space, and frequency of events. For example, a person might make no effort to remember how many times cars have passed down the street but when asked can give an answer of "often," "more than usual," or "hardly any."

AP* Outline the principles that underlie effective encoding, storage, and construction of memories.

false positive error of recognition in which people think that they recognize some stimulus that is not actually in memory.

automatic encoding tendency of certain kinds of information to enter long-term memory with little or no effortful encoding.

Classic Studies in Psychology
Elizabeth Loftus and Eyewitnesses

Elizabeth Loftus is Professor of Psychology and Adjunct Professor of Law at the University of California in Irvine. For over 30 years, Dr. Loftus has been one of the world's leading researchers in the area of memory. Her focus has been on the accuracy of recall of memories—or rather, the inaccuracies of memory retrieval. She has been an expert witness at more than 200 trials, including that of Ted Bundy, the serial killer who was finally executed in Florida (Neimark, 1996).

Loftus and many others have demonstrated time and again that memory is not an unchanging, stable process but rather is a constantly changing one. People continually update and revise their memories of events without being aware that they are doing so, and they incorporate information gained after the actual event, whether correct or incorrect.

Here is a summary of one of Loftus's classic studies concerning the ways in which eyewitness testimony can be influenced by information given after the event in question (Loftus, 1975).

In this experiment, Loftus showed subjects a 3-minute video clip taken from the movie *Diary of a Student Revolution*. In this clip, eight demonstrators run into a classroom and eventually leave after interrupting the professor's lecture in a noisy confrontation. At the end of the video, two questionnaires were distributed containing one key question and 90 "filler" questions. The key question for half of the subjects was, "Was the leader of the four demonstrators who entered the classroom a male?" The other half was asked, "Was the leader of the twelve demonstrators who entered the classroom a male?" One week later, a new set of questions was given to all subjects in which the key question was, "How many demonstrators did you see entering the classroom?" Subjects who were previously asked the question incorrectly giving the number as "four" stated an average recall of 6.4 people, whereas those who read the question incorrectly giving the number as "twelve" recalled an average of 8.9 people. Loftus concluded that subjects were trying to compromise the memory of what they had actually seen—eight demonstrators—with later information. This study, along with the Father Pagano story and many others, clearly demonstrates the heart of Loftus's research: What people see and hear about an event after the fact can easily affect the accuracy of their memories of that event.

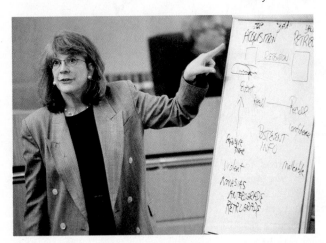

Dr. Elizabeth Loftus is an internationally known expert on the accuracy of eyewitness testimony. She is often called on to testify in court cases.

Questions for Further Discussion

1. How might police officers taking statements about a crime avoid getting inaccurate information from eyewitnesses?

2. How might Loftus's research apply to situations in which a therapist is trying to help a client recover memories that may have been repressed? What should that therapist avoid doing?

A special kind of automatic encoding takes place when an unexpected event or episode in a person's life has strong emotional associations, such as fear, horror, or joy. Memories of highly emotional events can often seem vivid and detailed, as if the person's mind took a "flash picture" of the moment in time. These kinds of memories are called **flashbulb memories** (Neisser, 1982; Neisser & Harsch, 1992; Winningham et al., 2000).

Many people share certain flashbulb memories. People of the "baby boomer" generation remember exactly where they were when the news came that President John F. Kennedy had been shot. Younger generations may remember the explosion of the space shuttle *Columbia* and the horrific events of September 11, 2001. But personal flashbulb

flashbulb memories type of automatic encoding that occurs because an unexpected event has strong emotional associations for the person remembering it.

memories also exist. These memories tend to be major emotional events, such as the first date, an embarrassing event, or a particularly memorable birthday party.

Why do flashbulb memories seem so vivid and exact? The answer lies in the emotions felt at the time of the event. Emotional reactions stimulate the release of hormones that have been shown to enhance the formation of long-term memories (McEwen, 2000). But is this kind of memory really all that accurate? Although some researchers have found evidence for a high degree of accuracy in flashbulb memories of *major events*, such as the election of President Barack Obama in November 2008 or the death of pop legend Michael Jackson in June 2009, others have found that while flashbulb memories are often convincingly real, they are just as subject to decay and alterations over time as other kinds of memories (Neisser & Harsch, 1992). Apparently, no memories are completely accurate after the passage of time. The next section will discuss some of the reasons for faulty memories.

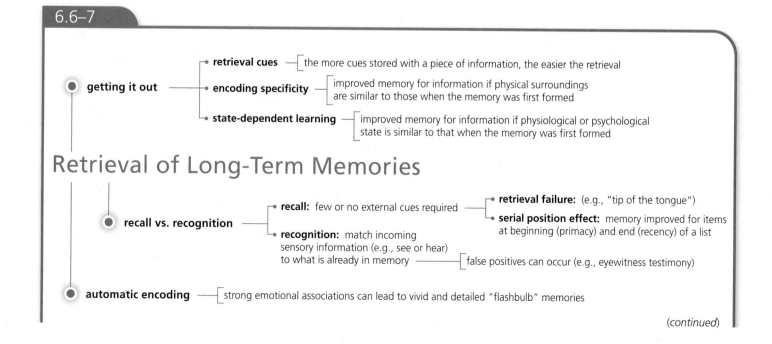

6.6–7

getting it out
- **retrieval cues** — the more cues stored with a piece of information, the easier the retrieval
- **encoding specificity** — improved memory for information if physical surroundings are similar to those when the memory was first formed
- **state-dependent learning** — improved memory for information if physiological or psychological state is similar to that when the memory was first formed

Retrieval of Long-Term Memories

recall vs. recognition
- **recall:** few or no external cues required
  - **retrieval failure:** (e.g., "tip of the tongue")
  - **serial position effect:** memory improved for items at beginning (primacy) and end (recency) of a list
- **recognition:** match incoming sensory information (e.g., see or hear) to what is already in memory — false positives can occur (e.g., eyewitness testimony)

automatic encoding — strong emotional associations can lead to vivid and detailed "flashbulb" memories

(continued)

PRACTICE QUIZ: PREPARING FOR THE AP* EXAM

ANSWERS ON PAGE AK-2.

Directions: Read each of the questions or incomplete sentences below. Then choose the response that best answers the question or completes the sentence.

1. To ensure good retrieval of the math concepts you learned in class, the best place to take your math final exam is _____.

   a. any classroom, as long as your math teacher is present
   b. a special testing room that is used for all school exams
   c. the math classroom, in the same seat where you sat all year
   d. an empty classroom with white walls, to prevent distractions
   e. an auditorium with comfortable chairs that reduce physical stress

2. Sarah can remember the names of the first two people she was introduced to at Ted's birthday party, and she can remember the name of the last person she met, but the names of the dozen or so people in between are gone. This is an example of _____.

   a. the cocktail party effect
   b. the serial position effect
   c. the state-dependent effect
   d. the tip-of-the-tongue effect
   e. the encoding specificity effect

3. If you read a book when you are feeling sad, when are you more likely to remember the details of the book?

   a. When you are feeling sad
   b. When you are feeling happy
   c. When you are focusing hard
   d. When you are not paying attention
   e. At any time, regardless of your circumstances

4. Dr. Elizabeth Loftus is most famous for her study of_____.

   a. the three-stage model of memory
   b. flashbulb memories
   c. levels of processing
   d. eyewitness memories
   e. the semantic network model of memory

5. Which of the following statements about flashbulb memories is correct?

   a. Flashbulb memories form during major emotional events.
   b. Flashbulb memories are more accurate than other memories.
   c. Flashbulb memories can only be formed during adulthood.
   d. Flashbulb memories are rarely encoded into long-term memory.
   e. Flashbulb memories cannot be forgotten like other memories can.

The Reconstructive Nature of Long-Term Memory Retrieval: How Reliable Are Memories?

> I think my memory is pretty good, but my brother and I often have arguments about things that happened when we were kids. Why don't we have the same exact memories? We were both there!

I think my memory is pretty good, but my brother and I often have arguments about things that happened when we were kids. Why don't we have the same exact memories? We were both there!

People tend to assume that their memories are accurate when, in fact, memories are revised, edited, and altered on an almost continuous basis. The reason for the changes that occur in memory has to do with the way in which memories are formed as well as how they are retrieved.

CONSTRUCTIVE PROCESSING OF MEMORIES

6.8 How are long-term memories formed, and what kinds of problems do people experience as a result?

Many people have the idea that when they recall a memory, they are recalling it as if it were an "instant replay." As new memories are created in LTM, old memories can get "lost," but they are more likely to be changed or altered in some way (Baddeley, 1988). In reality, memories (including those very vivid flashbulb memories) are never quite accurate, and the more time that passes, the more inaccuracies creep in. Psychologist John Kihlstrom, when talking about the early twentieth-century memory schema theorist Sir Frederic Bartlett's (1932) book on the constructive nature of memory, essentially says that ". . . remembering is more like making up a story than it is like reading one printed in a book. For Bartlett, every memory is a blend of knowledge and inference. Remembering is problem-solving activity, where the problem is to give a coherent* account of some past event, and the memory is the solution to that problem" (Kihlstrom, 2002, p. 3).

---

*Coherent: understandable.

Think about the example of the filing system used to talk about long-term memory. What if different parts of each file (the sound, the image, the meaning, and so on) are stored in different areas of the filing system? When a person wants to retrieve that piece of information, files have to be pulled out of several places and put back together into the original item. Isn't it very likely that some pieces of the original item will not be retrieved—in fact some may never have been properly stored in the first place—and that some information gets added in that was not originally part of the file?

Loftus, along with other researchers (Hyman, 1993; Hyman & Loftus, 1998, 2002), has provided ample evidence for the **constructive processing** view of memory retrieval. In this view, memories are literally "built" from the pieces stored away at encoding. Each time a memory is retrieved, it may be altered or revised in some way to include new information, or details that were there at encoding and may be left out of the new retrieval.

These men may engage in "Monday morning quarterbacking" as they apply hindsight to their memories of this game. Their memories of the game may be altered by information they get afterward from the television, newspapers, or their friends.

An example of how memories are reconstructed occurs when people, upon learning the details of a particular event, revise their memories to reflect their feeling that they "knew it all along." They will discard any incorrect information they actually had and replace it with more accurate information gained after the fact. This tendency of people to falsely believe that they would have accurately predicted an outcome without having been told about it in advance is called **hindsight bias** (Bahrick et al., 1996; Hoffrage et al., 2000). People who have ever done some "Monday morning quarterbacking" by saying that they knew all along who would win the game have fallen victim to hindsight bias.

MEMORY RETRIEVAL PROBLEMS

Some people may say that they have "total recall." What they usually mean is that they feel that their memories are more accurate than those of other people. As should be obvious by now, true total recall is not a very likely ability for anyone to have. Here are some reasons why people have trouble recalling information accurately.

The Misinformation Effect   Police investigators try to keep eye witnesses to crimes or accidents from talking with each other sometimes. The reason is that if one person tells the other about something she has seen, the other person may later "remember" that same detail, even though he did not actually see it at the time. Such false memories are created by a person being exposed to information after the event. That misleading information can become part of the actual memory, affecting its accuracy (Loftus et al., 1978). This is called the **misinformation effect**. Elizabeth Loftus, in addition to her studies concerning eyewitness testimony, has also done several similar studies that demonstrate the misinformation effect. In one study, subjects viewed a slide presentation of a traffic accident. The actual slide presentation contained a stop sign, but in a written summary of the presentation, the sign was referred to as a yield sign. Subjects who were given this misleading information after viewing the slides were far less accurate in their memories for the kind of sign present than were subjects given no such information. One of the interesting points to be made by this study is that information that comes not only after the original event but also in an entirely different format (i.e., written instead of visual) can cause memories of the event to be incorrectly reconstructed.

constructive processing   referring to the retrieval of memories in which those memories are altered, revised, or influenced by newer information.

hindsight bias   the tendency to falsely believe, through revision of older memories to include newer information, that one could have correctly predicted the outcome of an event.

misinformation effect   the tendency of misleading information presented after an event to alter the memories of the event itself.

Reliability of Memory Retrieval

6.9　What is false memory syndrome?

If memory is edited and changed when people are in a state of waking consciousness, alert and making an effort to retrieve information, how much more might memory be changed when people are in an altered state of conscious, such as hypnosis? *False memory syndrome* refers to the creation of inaccurate or false memories through the suggestion of others, often while the person is under hypnosis (Hochman, 1994).

In her 1996 paper, Dr. Elizabeth Bowman has summarized some of the findings about pseudomemories, or false memories, associated with hypnosis. For example, research has shown that, although hypnosis may make it easier to recall some real memories, it also makes it easier to create false memories. Hypnosis also has been found to increase the confidence people have in their memories regardless of whether those memories are real or false. False memories have been accidentally created by therapists' suggestions during hypnotic therapy sessions (especially those that involve age regression). (L I N K) *to Chapter Four: Consciousness: Sleep, Dreams, Hypnosis, and Drugs, pp. 151–152.* For more information on false memory syndrome, visit the Web site at **www.fmsfonline.org.**

There is some recent evidence that false memories are created in the brain in much the same way as real memories are formed, especially when visual images are involved (Gonsalves et al., 2004). Researchers, using fMRI, looked at brain activity of people who were looking at real visual images and then were asked to imagine looking at visual images. They found that these same people were often unable to later distinguish between the images they had really seen and the imagined images when asked to remember which images were real or imagined. This might explain why asking people if they saw a particular person at a crime scene (causing them to imagine the image of that person) might affect the memories those people have of the crime when questioned some time later—the person they were asked to think about may be falsely remembered as having been present.

Clearly, memories obtained through hypnosis should not be considered accurate without solid evidence from other sources.

So can we trust any of our memories at all?

There is evidence to suggest that false memories cannot be created for just any kind of memory. The *memories* must at least be plausible, according to the research of cognitive psychologist and memory expert Kathy Pezdek, who with her colleagues has done several studies demonstrating the resistance of children to the creation of implausible false memories (Hyman et al., 1998; Pezdek et al., 1997; Pezdek & Hodge, 1999).

In the 1999 study, Pezdek and Hodge asked children to read five different summaries of childhood events. Two of these events were false, but only one of the two false events was plausible (e.g., getting lost). Although the children were all told that all of the events happened to them as small children, the results indicated that the plausible false events were significantly more likely to be remembered as false memories than were the implausible false events. A second experiment (Pezdek & Hodge, 1999) found similar results: Children were significantly less likely to form a false memory for an implausible false event than for a plausible false event.

So can we trust any of our memories at all? ▶

The idea that only plausible events can become false memories runs contrary to the earlier work of Loftus and colleagues and to research concerning some very implausible false memories that have been successfully implanted, such as a memory for alien abductions (Mack, 1994). Loftus and colleagues (Mazzoni et al., 2001) conducted several experiments in which they found that implausible events could be made more plausible by having the experimenters provide false feedback to the participants, who read articles telling of the implausible events as if they had actually happened to other people. The false feedback involved telling the participants that their responses to a questionnaire about fears were typical of people who had been through one of the false events (much as a well-meaning therapist might suggest to a client that certain anxieties and feelings are typical of someone who has been abused). These manipulations were so successful that participants not only developed false memories for the events but also even contradicted their own earlier statements in which they denied having these experiences in childhood. The researchers concluded that there are two steps that must occur before people will be likely to interpret their thoughts and fantasies about false events as true memories:

1. The event must be made to seem as plausible as possible.

2. Individuals are given information that helps them believe that the event could have happened to them personally.

As this girl observes the activity below, she is storing some of the things she sees into memory while ignoring others. If she were to witness a crime, how would investigators know if her memories of the events were accurate or not? Would hypnotizing her to help her remember be effective? Why or why not?

6.8–9

The Reconstructive Nature of Long-Term Memory

- **constructive processing of memories**
  - memories are rarely completely accurate and become less accurate over time
  - Loftus and others have suggested that memory retrieval is a constructive process; memories are "built" at time of retrieval

- **memory retrieval problems**
  - **misinformation effect:** incorporation of inaccurate information into actual memory
  - **reliability of memory retrieval:** false memories can result from change in both waking, conscious states and in altered states (e.g., hypnosis)
    - influenced by plausibility of event and individual receiving collaborative feedback that makes it easier to believe

PRACTICE QUIZ: PREPARING FOR THE AP* EXAM

ANSWERS ON PAGE AK-2.

Directions: Read each of the questions or incomplete sentences below. Then choose the response that best answers the question or completes the sentence.

1. Which of the following phenomena most strongly supports the constructive processing view of memory retrieval?
   a. Hindsight bias
   b. Eidetic imagery
   c. The recency effect
   d. Flashbulb memories
   e. Anterograde amnesia

2. In Elizabeth Loftus's 1978 study, subjects viewed a slide presentation of an accident. Later, some of the subjects were asked a question about a yield sign when the actual slides contained pictures of a stop sign. When these same subjects were later asked about what kind of sign was at the accident, they were very likely to be confused in this situation. This is an example of the _____.
   a. instant replay effect
   b. hindsight bias effect
   c. misinformation effect
   d. levels-of-processing effect
   e. constructive processing effect

(continued)

3. Which statement about memory retrieval while under hypnosis is accurate?

 a. Hypnosis makes it harder to recall memories in general

 b. Memories retrieved under hypnosis are more accurate than other memories

 c. Because hypnosis is impossible, no memories can truly be retrieved through hypnosis

 d. Age regression through hypnosis can increase the accuracy of recall of early childhood memories

 e. People recalling memories under hypnosis are more confident in their memories, regardless of accuracy

4. Psychologist Kathy Pezdek and her colleagues found that for a person to interpret thoughts and fantasies about false events as true memories, _____.

 a. the person must believe in repression

 b. the person must be a child or teenager

 c. the person must hear about the event more than once

 d. the event must seem as plausible as possible

 e. the event must be described in extensive detail

5. Lavelle and his friend Gerald are having a disagreement about the upcoming football game. Lavelle thinks the home team will win, while Gerald is convinced the visitors will win. They decide to place a friendly bet, and the loser will have to buy the winner a t-shirt from his favorite team. Lavelle ends up winning the bet and as Gerald is buying Lavelle his winning t-shirt, he says to the store clerk "I knew they were going to lose this week. How could I make that bet?" Gerald has fallen victim to the _____.

 a. hindsight bias

 b. misinformation effect

 c. Loftus phenomenon

 d. constructive error

 e. reconstructive attribution error

What Were We Talking About? Forgetting

Why do we forget things? And why do we forget some things but not others?

Why do we forget things? And why do we forget some things but not others?

6.10 Why do we forget?

Think for a minute: What would it be like if people didn't forget anything? At first, the answer seems to be that such a phenomenal memory would be great, right? Anything people learned would always be there. But what if people *couldn't* forget? That is exactly the problem experienced in the case of A. R. Luria's (1968) famous *mnemonist*, Mr. S. (A mnemonist is a memory expert or someone with exceptional memory ability.) Mr. S. was a performing mnemonist, astonishing his audiences with lists of numbers that he memorized in minutes. But Mr. S. found that he *was unable to forget* the lists. He also could not easily separate important memories from trivial ones, and each time he looked at an object or read a word, images stimulated by that object or word would flood his mind. He eventually invented a way to "forget" things—by writing them on a piece of paper and then burning the paper (Luria, 1968).

The ability to forget seems necessary to one's sanity if the experience of Mr. S. is any indicator. But how fast do people forget things? Are there some things that are harder or easier to forget? ✳ Explore on MyPsychLab

✳ **Explore** with a simulation about forgetting. **www.mypsychlab.com**

AP✳ Identify key contributors in cognitive psychology.

▶ EBBINGHAUS AND THE FORGETTING CURVE

Hermann Ebbinghaus (1913) was one of the first researchers to study forgetting. Because he did not want any verbal associations to aid him in remembering, he created several lists of "nonsense syllables," pronounceable but meaningless (such as GEX and WOL). He memorized a list, waited a specific amount of time, and then tried to retrieve the list, graphing his results each time. The result has become a familiar graph: the **curve of forgetting**. This graph clearly shows that forgetting happens quickly within the first hour after learning the lists and then tapers off gradually. (See Figure 6.9.) In other words, forgetting is greatest just after learning. This curve can be applied to other types of information as well. Although meaningful material is forgotten much more slowly and much less com-

curve of forgetting a graph showing a distinct pattern in which forgetting is very fast within the first hour after learning a list and then tapers off gradually.

Figure 6.9 Curve of Forgetting
Ebbinghaus found that his recall of words from his memorized word lists was greatest immediately after learning the list but rapidly decreased within the first hour. After the first hour, forgetting leveled off.

pletely, the pattern obtained when testing for forgetting is similar (Conway et al., 1992).

Distributed Practice   In his early studies, Ebbinghaus (1885) found that it is also important not to try to "cram" information you want to remember into your brain. Research has found that spacing out one's study sessions, or **distributed practice**, will produce far better retrieval of information studied in this way than does *massed practice*, or the attempt to study a body of material all at once. For example, studying your psychology material for 3 hours may make you feel that you've done some really hard work, and you have. Unfortunately, you won't remember as much of what you studied as you would if you had shorter study times of 30 minutes to an hour followed by short breaks (Cepeda et al., 2006; Dempster & Farris, 1990; Donovan & Radosevich, 1999; Simon & Bjork, 2001).

ENCODING FAILURE

There are several reasons why people forget things. One of the simplest is that some things never get encoded in the first place. Your friend, for example, may have said something to you as he walked out the door, and you may have heard him, but if you weren't paying attention to what he said, it would not get past sensory memory. This isn't forgetting so much as it is **encoding failure**, the failure to process information into memory. Researchers (Nickerson & Adams, 1979) developed a test of encoding failure using images of pennies. Look at Figure 6.10. Which view of a penny is the correct one? People see pennies nearly every day, but how many people actually look at what's on the penny and try to remember it?

distributed practice spacing the study of material to be remembered by including breaks between study periods.

encoding failure failure to process information into memory.

AP* Describe and differentiate psychological and physiological systems of memory.

Figure 6.10 Which Penny Is Real?
Most people do not really look at the face of a penny. Which of these pennies represents an actual penny? The answer can be found on the next page.

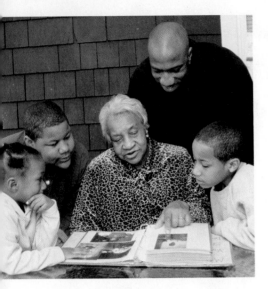

The fact that this woman can remember the things shown in the pictures even after many years makes it unlikely that the memory trace decay theory can explain all forgetting in long-term memory.

memory trace physical change in the brain that occurs when a memory is formed.

decay loss of memory due to the passage of time, during which the memory trace is not used.

disuse another name for decay, assuming that memories that are not used will eventually decay and disappear.

proactive interference memory retrieval problem that occurs when older information prevents or interferes with the retrieval of newer information.

The answer to **Figure 6.10** on page 247 is A.

Figure 6.11 Proactive and Retroactive Interference
If a student were to study for a French exam and then a Spanish exam, interference could occur in two directions. When taking the Spanish exam, the French information studied first may proactively interfere with retrieval of the Spanish information. But when taking the French exam, the more recently studied Spanish information may retroactively interfere with the retrieval of the French information.

MEMORY TRACE DECAY THEORY

One of the older theories of forgetting involves the concept of a **memory trace**. A memory trace is some physical change in the brain, perhaps in a neuron or in the activity between neurons, which occurs when a memory is formed (Brown, 1958; Peterson & Peterson, 1959). Over time, if these traces are not used, they may **decay**, fading into nothing. It would be similar to what happens when a number of people walk across a particular patch of grass, causing a path to appear in which the grass is trampled down and perhaps turning brown. But if people stop using the path, the grass grows back and the path disappears.

Forgetting in sensory memory and short-term memory seems easy to explain as decay: Information that is not brought to attention in sensory memory or continuously rehearsed in STM will fade away. But is decay a good explanation for forgetting from long-term memory? When referring to LTM, decay theory is usually called **disuse**, and the phrase "use it or lose it" takes on great meaning (Bjork & Bjork, 1992). Although the fading of information from LTM through disuse sounds logical, there are many times when people can recall memories they had assumed were long forgotten. There must be other factors involved in the forgetting of long-term memories.

INTERFERENCE THEORY

A possible explanation of LTM forgetting is that although most long-term memories may be stored more or less permanently in the brain, those memories may not always be accessible to attempted retrieval because other information interferes (Anderson & Neely, 1995). (And even memories that are accessible are subject to constructive processing, which can lead to inaccurate recall.) An analogy might be this: The can of paint that Phillip wants may very well be on some shelf in his storeroom, but there's so much other junk in its way that he can't see it and can't get to it. In the case of LTM, interference can come from two different "directions."

Proactive Interference Have you ever switched from a sport you've been playing for years, like soccer, to a new sport like field hockey? If the answer is yes, you may have found that you had some trouble picking up the new sport. You may have tried to kick the field hockey ball instead of hitting it with your stick—after all, while kicking the ball isn't allowed in field hockey, it's basically required in soccer. The reason why you accidentally kicked that field hockey ball is called **proactive interference**: the tendency for older or previously learned material to interfere with the retrieval of newer, more recently learned material. (See Figure 6.11.)

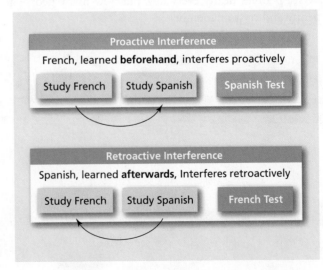

Table 6.1 Reasons for Forgetting

REASON	DESCRIPTION
Encoding Failure	The information is not attended to and fails to be encoded.
Decay or Disuse	Information that is not accessed decays from the storage system over time.
Proactive Interference	Older information already in memory interferes with the retrieval of newer information.
Retroactive Interference	Newer information interferes with the retrieval of older information.

Another example of proactive interference often occurs when someone gets a new cell phone. People in this situation often find themselves remembering their old cell phone number or some of its digits instead of the new cell phone number when they are trying to give the new number to friends.

Retroactive Interference   When newer information interferes with the retrieval of older information, this is called **retroactive interference**. (See Figure 6.11.) What happens when you decide to quit the field hockey team and start playing soccer again? You might find yourself swinging an imaginary stick to hit the soccer ball because the newer skill retroactively interferes with remembering the old skill.

How might interference work in each of the following cases?

1. Moving from the United States to England, where people drive on the left instead of the right side of the road.
2. Trying to program your old DVD player after having a new one for a year.
3. Moving from one computer operating system to a different one.

The different ways that forgetting occurs are summarized in Table 6.1.

retroactive interference memory retrieval problem that occurs when newer information prevents or interferes with the retrieval of older information.

Memory and the Brain: The Physical Aspects of Memory

6.11 How and where are memories formed in the brain?

Researchers have evidence that memories involve specific areas of the brain and that these areas are different for different types of memory. For example, procedural memories seem to be stored in the cerebellum (Boyd & Winstein, 2004; Daum & Schugens, 1996). Research involving PET scanning techniques strongly suggest that short-term memories are stored in the prefrontal cortex (the very front of the frontal lobe) and the temporal lobe (Goldman-Rakic, 1998; Rao et al., 1997).

As for semantic and episodic long-term memories, evidence suggests that these memories are also stored in the frontal and temporal lobes but not in exactly the same places nor in the same location as short-term memories (Weis et al., 2004). In Chapter

All that explains is the ▶
"where" of memory.
Did scientists ever find
out the "what" or the
exact physical change
that happens in the
brain when memories
are stored?

Two the role of the amygdala was discussed as the place in the brain where our memories of fear are stored.

All that explains is the "where" of memory. Did scientists ever find out the "what" or the exact physical change that happens in the brain when memories are stored?

NEURAL ACTIVITY AND STRUCTURE IN MEMORY FORMATION

Several studies have offered evidence that a memory is not simply one physical change but many: changes in the number of receptor sites, changes in the sensitivity of the synapse through repeated stimulation (called *long-term potentiation*), and changes in the dendrites and in the proteins within the neurons (Alkon, 1989; Kandel & Schwartz, 1982; Squire & Kandel, 1999). All of these changes serve to increase the neural connections and make connections that already exist more sensitive to stimulation. These changes that take place as a memory is forming are called **consolidation**. Although people may learn quickly, the memory of what has been learned takes some time to form completely.

THE HIPPOCAMPUS AND MEMORY

In the discussion of the *hippocampus* (a part of the limbic system) in Chapter Two (p. 71), it was identified as the part of the brain that is responsible for the formation of new long-term memories. One of the clearest pieces of evidence of this function comes from the study of a man known as H. M. (Milner et al., 1968).

H. M. was about 17 when he began to suffer from severe epileptic seizures. A few years later, the majority of H. M.'s hippocampi were removed (along with the amygdala and portions of the parahippocampal region in each hemisphere) in an attempt to remove what the surgeon believed was the source of the seizures. The last thing H. M. could remember was being rolled on the gurney to the operating room, and that was the last memory he was ever able to form. The hippocampus was not the source of his problem, but it was apparently the source of his ability to store any new factual information he encountered, because without either hippocampus, he was completely unable to remember anything new. Consolidation had become impossible. He had a magazine that he carried around, reading and rereading the stories, because each time he did so the stories were completely new to him. As with most amnesiacs of this type (although H. M.'s case was quite severe), his procedural memory was still intact. It was only new declarative memory—both semantic and episodic—that was lost.

The man that most of the world has only known as H.M., Henry Molaison, died in December 2008. His experience and his brain will continue to educate students and neuroscientists as he agreed many years ago that his brain would be donated for further scientific study upon his death. It has now been sliced into almost 2400 slices, each about the width of a human hair, in preparation for further study. You can learn more about the H.M. Project at the web site of the The Brain Observatory, housed at the University of California San Diego, http://thebrainobservatory.ucsd.edu.

WHEN MEMORY FAILS: ORGANIC AMNESIA

6.12 How does amnesia occur, and what is Alzheimer's disease?

There are two forms of severe loss of memory disorders caused by problems in the functioning of the memory areas of the brain. These problems can result from concussions, brain injuries brought about by trauma, alcoholism (Korsakoff's syndrome), or disorders of the aging brain. ◉ Watch on MyPsychLab

Retrograde Amnesia　　If the hippocampus is that important to the formation of declarative memories, what would happen if it got temporarily "disconnected"? People

◉ **Watch** video footage about Alzheimer's and dementia.
www.mypsychlab.com

consolidation the changes that take place in the structure and functioning of neurons when a memory is formed.

who are in accidents in which they received a head injury often are unable to recall the accident itself. Sometimes they cannot remember the last several hours or even days before the accident. This type of amnesia (literally, "without memory") is called **retrograde amnesia**, which is loss of memory from the point of injury backwards (Hodges, 1994). What apparently happens in this kind of memory loss is that the consolidation process, which was busy making the physical changes to allow new memories to be stored, gets disrupted and loses everything that was not already nearly "finished."

Think about this: You are working on your computer, trying to finish a history paper that is due tomorrow. Your computer saves the document every 10 minutes, but you are working so furiously that you've written a lot in the last 10 minutes. Then the power goes out—horrors! When the power comes back on, you find that while all the files you had already saved are still intact,* your history paper is missing that last 10 minutes' worth of work. This is similar to what happens when someone's consolidation process is disrupted. All memories that were in the process of being stored but not yet permanent are lost.

One of the therapies for severe depression is *ECT*, or *electroconvulsive therapy*. (LINK) *to Chapter Thirteen: Psychological Therapies, p. 544.* In one study with depressed patients who were being treated with ECT (Squire et al., 1975), patients were tested for their memory of certain television programs both before and after the treatment. Before treatment, recent programs were recalled in more detail and more often than older ones. But after treatment, these patients seemed to forget the *last three years of programs,* remembering only the older ones. Not only does this indicate that memories are lost when consolidation is interrupted (as it is by the seizure caused by the treatment) but also that consolidation may take not just days or months but sometimes years to be completed.

Anterograde Amnesia   Concussions can also cause a more temporary version of the kind of amnesia experienced by H. M.; this kind of amnesia is called *anterograde amnesia*, or the loss of memories from the point of injury or illness forward (Squire & Slater, 1978). People with this kind of amnesia, like H. M., have difficulty remembering anything new. This is also the kind of amnesia most often seen in people with *senile dementia*, a mental disorder in which severe forgetfulness, mental confusion, and mood swings are the primary symptoms. (Dementia patients also may suffer from retrograde amnesia in addition to anterograde amnesia.) If retrograde amnesia is like losing a document in the computer because of a power loss, anterograde amnesia is like discovering that your hard drive has become defective—you can read data that are already on the hard drive, but you can't store any new information. As long as you are looking at the data in your open computer window (i. e., attending to it), you can access it, but as soon as you close that window (stop thinking about it), the information is lost, because it was never transferred to the hard drive (long-term memory).

This is the reason that elderly people with a dementia such as Alzheimer's will sometimes take several doses of medicine because they cannot remember having already taken a dose. It also makes for some very repetitive conversations, such as being told the same story or asked the same question numerous times in the space of a 20-minute conversation. For more about Alzheimer's disease, see Applying Psychology to Everyday Life on page 253.

I've tried to remember things from when I was a baby, but I don't seem to be able to recall much. Is this some kind of amnesia, too?

Infantile Amnesia   What is the earliest memory you have? Chances are you cannot remember much that happened to you before age 3. When a person does claim to "remember" some event from infancy, a little investigation usually reveals that the

Colorado Avalanche defenseman Steve Moore makes his first public appearance after suffering major injuries in a hockey game in 2004. In addition to a broken neck, Moore suffered a concussion and developed amnesia. From which type of amnesia did he most likely suffer?

I've tried to remember things from when I was a baby, but I don't seem to be able to recall much. ◄ Is this some kind of amnesia, too?

retrograde amnesia loss of memory from the point of some injury or trauma backwards, or loss of memory for the past.

---

*Intact: whole or complete.

infantile amnesia the inability to retrieve memories from much before age 3.

autobiographical memory the memory for events and facts related to one's personal life story.

"memory" is really based on what family members have told the person about that event and is not a genuine memory at all. This type of "manufactured" memory often has the quality of watching yourself in the memory as if it were a movie and you were an actor. In a genuine memory, you would remember the event through your own eyes—as if you were the camera.

Why can't people remember events from the first two or three years of life? One explanation of **infantile amnesia** involves the type of memory that exists in the first few years of life, when a child is still considered an infant. Early memories tend to be implicit and, as stated earlier in this chapter, implicit memories are difficult to bring to consciousness. Explicit memory, which is the more verbal and conscious form of memory, does not really develop until after about age 2, when the hippocampus is more fully developed and language skills blossom (Carver & Bauer, 2001).

Katherine Nelson (1993) also gives credit to the social relationships that small children have with others. As children are able to talk about shared memories with adults, they begin to develop their **autobiographical memory**, or the memory for events and facts related to one's personal life story. ✱ Explore on **MyPsychLab**

✱ **Explore** the topic of amnesia.
www.mypsychlab.com

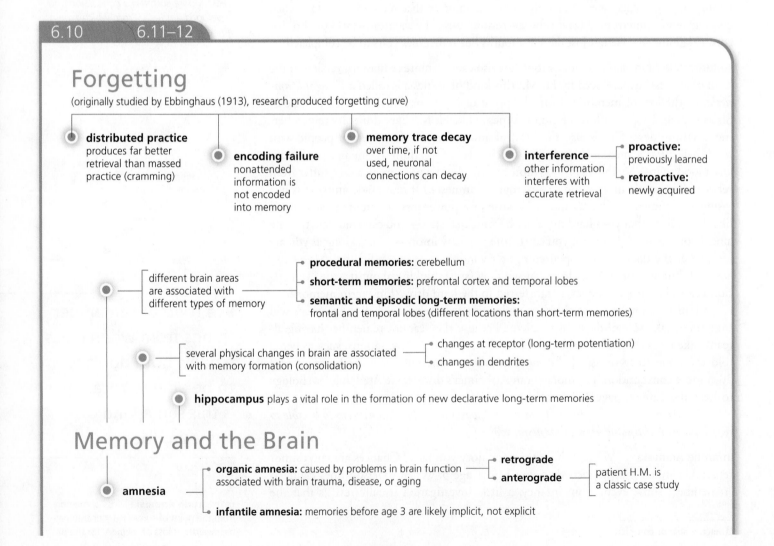

6.10　　6.11–12

Forgetting

(originally studied by Ebbinghaus (1913), research produced forgetting curve)

- **distributed practice** produces far better retrieval than massed practice (cramming)
- **encoding failure** nonattended information is not encoded into memory
- **memory trace decay** over time, if not used, neuronal connections can decay
- **interference** other information interferes with accurate retrieval
  - **proactive:** previously learned
  - **retroactive:** newly acquired

- different brain areas are associated with different types of memory
  - **procedural memories:** cerebellum
  - **short-term memories:** prefrontal cortex and temporal lobes
  - **semantic and episodic long-term memories:** frontal and temporal lobes (different locations than short-term memories)

- several physical changes in brain are associated with memory formation (consolidation)
  - changes at receptor (long-term potentiation)
  - changes in dendrites

- **hippocampus** plays a vital role in the formation of new declarative long-term memories

Memory and the Brain

- **amnesia**
  - **organic amnesia:** caused by problems in brain function associated with brain trauma, disease, or aging
    - **retrograde**
    - **anterograde** — patient H.M. is a classic case study
  - **infantile amnesia:** memories before age 3 are likely implicit, not explicit

Directions: Read each of the questions or incomplete sentences below. Then choose the response that best answers the question or completes the sentence.

1. Salvatore was introduced to a number of new people on his first day at his new job. According to Hermann Ebbinghaus, when will Salvatore experience the most rapid rate of forgetting his new colleagues' names?
   a. Within seconds of learning the names
   b. Within the first hour after learning the names
   c. One day after learning the names
   d. Two days after learning the names
   e. One week after learning the names

2. Sarah did not pay attention to Jamal when he was speaking. As a result, Sarah "forgot" what Jamal said. Sarah's experience is an example of _____.
   a. encoding failure
   b. memory trace decay
   c. proactive interference
   d. retroactive interference
   e. retrograde amnesia

3. Brian went from the United States, where he grew up, to England. The first week he was there, he had a terrible time remembering to drive on the left side of the road. His problem was most likely due to _____.
   a. disuse
   b. encoding failure
   c. distributed practice
   d. proactive interference
   e. retroactive interference

4. Katherine is trying to hold the name of the students she just met in her psychology class in short-term memory. According to studies, where in the brain will these short-term memories be stored?
   a. The medulla and the brainstem
   b. The amygdala and the central sulcus
   c. The cerebellum and the reticular formation
   d. The hippocampus and the pons
   e. The prefrontal cortex and the temporal lobe

5. The case of H. M., a famous amnesiac, helped researchers discover a connection between the formation of new long-term declarative memories and the _____.
   a. medulla
   b. amygdala
   c. cerebellum
   d. hippocampus
   e. prefrontal cortex

Applying Psychology to Everyday Life: Current Research in Alzheimer's Disease

Listen on **MyPsychLab**

Listen to the Psychology in the News podcast. **www.mypsychlab.com**

Nearly 4 million Americans have Alzheimer's disease, including the late former President Ronald Reagan. It is the most common type of dementia found in adults and the elderly. It has also become the third leading cause of death in late adulthood, with only heart disease and cancer responsible for more deaths (Antuono et al., 2001).

Symptoms usually begin with changes in memory, which may be rather mild at first but which become more severe over time, causing the person to become more and more forgetful about everyday tasks, such as remembering to turn off the stove. Eventually more dangerous forgetting occurs, such as taking extra doses of medication or leaving something cooking on the stove unattended. The person with this disorder repeats things in conversation, thoughts become disorganized, and messages get garbled. As Alzheimer's progresses, the ability to do simple calculations such as balancing a checkbook is lost, along with remembering how to do simple tasks such as bathing or getting dressed. It is a costly disease to care for, and caregivers often face severe emotional and financial burdens in caring for a loved one who is slowly becoming a stranger.

What can be done? There is at present no cure, but in recent years several new medications have been developed that seem to slow the progress of the disease, and new research into the cause gives hope that a cure may one day be a reality. One common treatment is to place the person on a drug such as Aricept®, which blocks the breakdown of acetylcholine, the neurotransmitter involved in the formation of memories.

To track the cell death that occurs in Alzheimer's disease, researchers used MRI technology to scan both patients with Alzheimer's disease and normal elderly. Using supercomputers, the UCLA team created color-coded maps that revealed the degenerative sequence of the disease through novel brain mapping methods. The wave of gray matter loss was strongly related to the progressive decline in cognitive functioning that is a key feature of the disease. Other researchers have used PET scans as in the image above to illustrate differences in brain activity between individuals with and without Alzheimer's disease.

Other drugs to reduce the agitation,* restlessness, and hallucinations that can come with the disease may be administered. There is some evidence that taking an herbal supplement, gingko biloba, may help the memory problems of some Alzheimer's victims, although this supplement has been shown not to affect the functioning of normal memory (Le Bars et al., 2002). A new drug, memantine, stimulates the proteins responsible for nerve growth and repair and is being tested for effectiveness with Alzheimer's disease (Reiseberg et al., 2003).

Finally, clinical trials are underway to test the effects of statins, drugs that lower cholesterol, on Alzheimer's. A gene that is involved in cholesterol production is also a known risk factor for late-onset Alzheimer's (Zamrini et al., 2004). People taking statins may have a lower than usual risk of Alzheimer's disease.

Questions for Further Discussion

1. What might be some dangers associated with taking an over-the-counter herbal remedy, such as gingko biloba, to treat Alzheimer's or any other medical condition?

2. People are now living much longer than their ancestors, and it is no longer unusual to hear of people who are well over 100 years of age. How might this extension of life expectancy be related to an increased rate of Alzheimer's disease?

3. What kinds of social programs or interventions could help people who are taking care of a relative with Alzheimer's?

———————————————

*Agitation: excitement or upset.

CHAPTER SUMMARY

Memory

6.1 What are the three processes of memory and the different models of how memory works?

- Memory can be defined as an active system that receives information from the senses, organizes and alters it as it stores it away, and then retrieves the information from storage.
- The three processes are encoding, storage, and retrieval.

Models of Memory

- In the levels-of-processing model of memory, information that gets more deeply processed is more likely to be remembered.
- In the parallel distributed processing model of memory, information is simultaneously stored across an interconnected neural network that stretches across the brain.

The Information-Processing Model: Three Stages of Memory

6.2 How does sensory memory work?

- Iconic memory is the visual sensory memory, in which an afterimage or icon will be held in neural form for about one-fourth to one-half second.
- Echoic memory is the auditory form of sensory memory and takes the form of an echo that lasts for up to 4 seconds.

6.3 What is short-term memory, and how does it differ from working memory?

- Short-term memory is where information is held while it is conscious and being used. It holds about seven plus or minus two chunks of information and lasts about 30 seconds without rehearsal.

- Working memory is an active system responsible for processing the information in STM.
- STM is easily lost through decay or interference.

6.4 How is long-term memory different from other types of memory?

- Long-term memory is the system in which memories that are to be kept more or less permanently are stored and is unlimited in capacity and relatively permanent in duration.
- Information that is more deeply processed, or processed according to meaning, will be retained and retrieved more efficiently.

6.5 What are the various types of long-term memory, and how is information stored in long-term memory organized?

- Procedural memories are memories for skills, habits, and conditioned responses. Declarative memories are memories for general facts and personal experiences and include both semantic memories and episodic memories.
- Implicit memories are difficult to bring into conscious awareness, whereas explicit memories are those that a person is aware of possessing.
- LTM is organized in the form of semantic networks, or nodes of related information spreading out from a central piece of knowledge.

Getting It Out: Retrieval of Long-Term Memories

6.6 What kinds of cues help people remember?

- Retrieval cues are words, meanings, sounds, and other stimuli that are encoded at the same time as a new memory.
- Encoding specificity occurs when physical surroundings become encoded as retrieval cues for specific memories.
- State-dependent learning occurs when physiological or psychological states become encoded as retrieval cues for memories formed while in those states.

6.7 How do the retrieval processes of recall and recognition differ, and how reliable are our memories of events?

- Recall is a type of memory retrieval in which the information to be retrieved must be "pulled" out of memory with few or no cues, whereas recognition involves matching information with stored images or facts.
- The serial position effect, or primacy or recency effect, occurs when the first items and the last items in a list of information are recalled more efficiently than items in the middle of the list.

Classic Studies in Psychology: Elizabeth Loftus and Eyewitnesses

- Loftus and others have found that people constantly update and revise their memories of events. Part of this revision may include adding information acquired later to a previous memory. That later information may also be in error, further contaminating the earlier memory.
- Automatic encoding of some kinds of information requires very little effort to place information into long-term memory.
- Memory for particularly emotional or traumatic events can lead to the formation of flashbulb memories, memories that seem as vivid and detailed as if the person were looking at a snapshot of the event but that are no more accurate than any other memories.

The Reconstructive Nature of Long-Term Memory Retrieval: How Reliable Are Memories?

6.8 How are long-term memories formed, and what kinds of problems do people experience as a result?

- Memories are reconstructed from the various bits and pieces of information that have been stored away in different places at the time of encoding in a process called constructive processing.
- Hindsight bias occurs when people falsely believe that they knew the outcome of some event because they have included knowledge of the event's true outcome into their memories of the event itself.
- The misinformation effect refers to the tendency of people who are asked misleading questions or given misleading information to incorporate that information into their memories for a particular event.

6.9 What is false memory syndrome?

- Rather than improving memory retrieval, hypnosis makes the creation of false memories more likely.
- False memory syndrome is the creation of false or inaccurate memories through suggestion, especially while hypnotized.
- Pezdek and colleagues assert that false memories are more likely to be formed for plausible false events than for implausible ones.

What Were We Talking About? Forgetting

6.10 Why do we forget?

- Ebbinghaus found that information is mostly lost within 1 hour after learning and then gradually fades away. This is known as the curve of forgetting.
- Some "forgetting" is actually a failure to encode information.
- Memory trace decay theory assumes the presence of a physical memory trace that decays with disuse over time.
- Forgetting in LTM is most likely due to proactive or retroactive interference.

Memory and the Brain: The Physical Aspects of Memory

- Evidence suggests that procedural memories are stored in the cerebellum, whereas short-term memories are stored in the prefrontal and temporal lobes of the cortex.
- Semantic and episodic memories may be stored in the frontal and temporal lobes as well but in different locations than short-term memory, whereas memory for fear of objects is most likely stored in the amygdala.

6.11 How and where are memories formed in the brain?

- Consolidation consists of the physical changes in neurons that take place during the formation of a memory.
- The hippocampus appears to be responsible for the storage of new declarative long-term memories. If it is removed, the ability to store any new factual information is completely lost.

6.12 How does amnesia occur, and what is Alzheimer's disease?

- In retrograde amnesia, memory for the past (prior to the injury) is lost, which can be a loss of only minutes or a loss of several years.

- ECT, or electroconvulsive therapy, can disrupt consolidation and cause retrograde amnesia.

- In anterograde amnesia, memory for anything new becomes impossible, although old memories may still be retrievable.

- Most people cannot remember events that occurred before age 2 or 3. This is called infantile amnesia and is most likely due to the implicit nature of infant memory.

Applying Psychology to Everyday Life: Current Research in Alzheimer's Disease

- The primary memory difficulty in Alzheimer's is anterograde amnesia, although retrograde amnesia can also occur as the disease progresses.

- There are various drugs in use or in development for use in slowing or stopping the progression of Alzheimer's disease.

TEST YOURSELF PREPARING FOR THE AP* EXAM

ANSWERS ON PAGE AK-2.

✓•┌Practice on MyPsychLab   **Ready for your test?** More quizzes and a customized study plan. **www.mypsychlab.com**

PART I: MULTIPLE-CHOICE QUESTIONS

Directions for Part I: Read each of the questions or incomplete sentences below. Then choose the response that best answers the question or completes the sentence.

1. In which model of memory are memories simultaneously created and stored across a series of mental networks that are "stretched" across the brain?
   a. Dual processing model
   b. Levels-of-processing model
   c. Information-processing model
   d. Parallel distributed processing model
   e. Transfer-appropriate processing model

2. In which form are short-term memories primarily encoded?
   a. Auditory
   b. Visual
   c. Tactile
   d. Gustatory
   e. Olfactory

3. If you wanted to memorize a string of 20 numbers, which of the following would most likely help you encode those numbers in short-term memory?
   a. Chunking
   b. Rote rehearsal
   c. Divided attention
   d. Encoding specificity
   e. State-dependent cues

4. Which of the following descriptions would best help a person remember the word *frog*?
   a. It has four letters
   b. It contains one vowel
   c. It is often found in a pond
   d. It begins with an *f* sound
   e. It rhymes with the word *slog*

5. Which type of long-term memory is revised and updated more or less constantly?
   a. Implicit
   b. Semantic
   c. Episodic
   d. Procedural
   e. Nondeclarative

6. According to the semantic network model of memory, which of the following questions would take longest to answer?
   a. Is a parrot a bird?
   b. Is a cricket an insect?
   c. Is a dog a mammal?
   d. Is a salmon a fish?
   e. Is a spider an animal?

7. A person who learns the name of a tropical fish while underwater is most likely to remember the name of that fish _____.
   a. when she is underwater again
   b. when she sees a photo of the fish
   c. when she feels happy and calm
   d. when she takes an exam about fish
   e. when she is in a quiet, empty room

8. What did Hermann Ebbinghaus discover about forgetting?
   a. Forgetting occurs rapidly as time goes by
   b. Forgetting occurs gradually at first but increases in speed
   c. Forgetting occurs quickly at first but slows down over time
   d. Forgetting occurs most quickly one day after learning information
   e. Forgetting occurs most frequently in the middle of learning a list of information

9. The main type of memory problem that people with dementia, including Alzheimer's, typically have is called _____.
  a. psychogenic amnesia
  b. retrograde amnesia
  c. retroactive amnesia
  d. infantile amnesia
  e. anterograde amnesia

10. For years, Pauline has used the same computer operating system. When she gets a new computer, she discovers that it has a new operating system. However, Pauline keeps looking for the old system's programs and trying to use the old system's shortcuts. Pauline's learning process is being inhibited by
  a. encoding failure
  b. memory trace decay
  c. proactive interference
  d. retroactive interference
  e. the misinformation effect

PART II: FREE-RESPONSE QUESTION

Directions for Part II: Read the essay question that follows. Then, respond to the question in a clear, concise essay. Do not simply list facts. Instead, present a thorough argument based on your critical consideration of the topic. Use proper psychological terminology as necessary.

Lisa is studying for her U.S. History test. In order to do well on the test, she will need to memorize dates of important events, answer multiple-choice questions about historical figures, and write an essay about the Civil War. If you were Lisa's tutor, what advice would you give her to help her encode, store, and retrieve the information she needs for the test? Describe your advice in a detailed, well-organized essay that addresses each of the following topics:

  a. levels of processing
  b. maintenance rehearsal versus elaborative rehearsal
  c. retrieval cues
  d. recognition versus recall
  e. serial position effect

6 VISUAL SUMMARY
Memory

6.1   p. 223

Memory — an active system that receives, organizes, stores, and retrieves information

Memory → three basic steps
- **encoding**
- **storage**
- **retrieval**

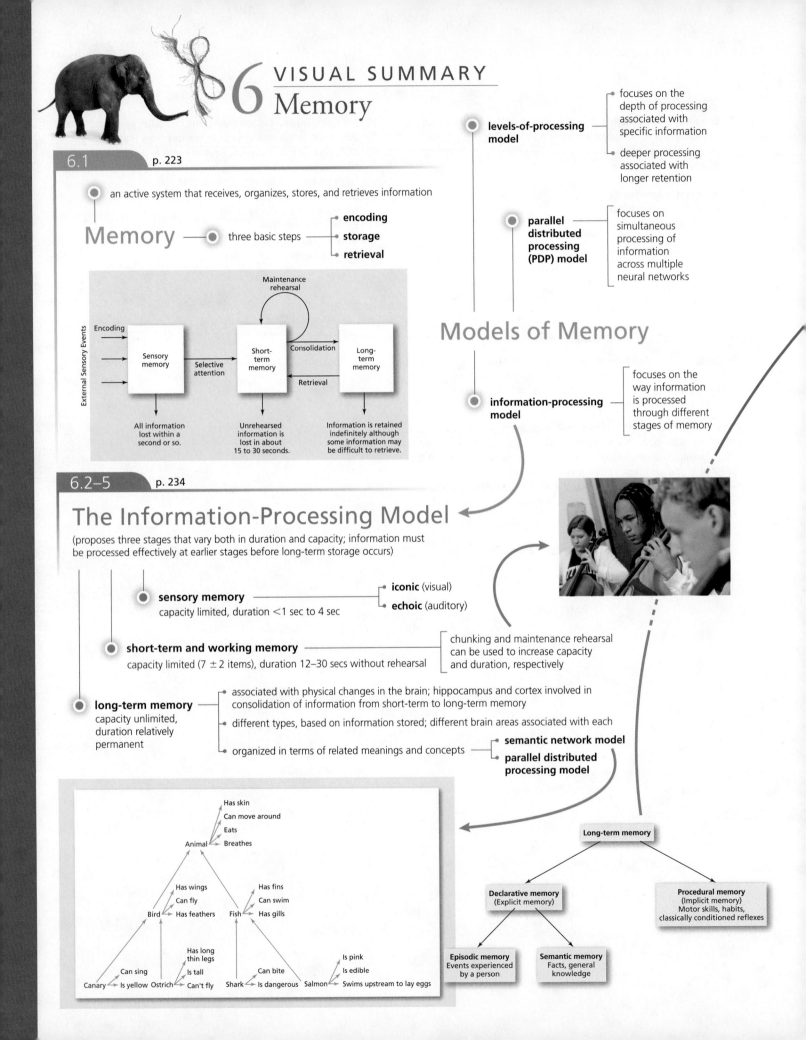

Maintenance rehearsal

External Sensory Events

Encoding →

Sensory memory → Selective attention → Short-term memory → Consolidation / Retrieval → Long-term memory

All information lost within a second or so.

Unrehearsed information is lost in about 15 to 30 seconds.

Information is retained indefinitely although some information may be difficult to retrieve.

Models of Memory

levels-of-processing model
- focuses on the depth of processing associated with specific information
- deeper processing associated with longer retention

parallel distributed processing (PDP) model
- focuses on simultaneous processing of information across multiple neural networks

information-processing model
- focuses on the way information is processed through different stages of memory

6.2–5   p. 234

The Information-Processing Model

(proposes three stages that vary both in duration and capacity; information must be processed effectively at earlier stages before long-term storage occurs)

sensory memory
capacity limited, duration <1 sec to 4 sec
- **iconic** (visual)
- **echoic** (auditory)

short-term and working memory
capacity limited (7 ± 2 items), duration 12–30 secs without rehearsal
— chunking and maintenance rehearsal can be used to increase capacity and duration, respectively

long-term memory
capacity unlimited, duration relatively permanent
- associated with physical changes in the brain; hippocampus and cortex involved in consolidation of information from short-term to long-term memory
- different types, based on information stored; different brain areas associated with each
- organized in terms of related meanings and concepts
  - **semantic network model**
  - **parallel distributed processing model**

Has skin
Can move around
Eats
Animal — Breathes

Has wings
Can fly
Bird — Has feathers

Has fins
Can swim
Fish — Has gills

Has long thin legs
Can sing
Canary — Is yellow
Ostrich — Is tall / Can't fly

Can bite
Shark — Is dangerous

Is pink
Is edible
Salmon — Swims upstream to lay eggs

Long-term memory

Declarative memory (Explicit memory)

Procedural memory (Implicit memory) Motor skills, habits, classically conditioned reflexes

Episodic memory Events experienced by a person

Semantic memory Facts, general knowledge

6.6–7 p. 241

- **getting it out**
  - retrieval cues
  - encoding specificity
  - state-dependent learning

Retrieval of Long-Term Memories

"Hey, good buddy! How you doin'?"

"Can't kick, big fella. What's shakin'?"

- **automatic encoding** — strong emotional associations can lead to vivid and detailed "flashbulb" memories

- **recall vs. recognition**
  - **recall:** few or no external cues required
  - **recognition:** match incoming sensory information (e.g., see or hear) to what is already in memory

6.8–9 p. 245

The Reconstructive Nature of Long-Term Memory

- **memory retrieval problems**
  - **misinformation effect**
  - **reliability of memory retrieval**

- **constructive processing of memories**
  - memories are rarely completely accurate and become less accurate over time
  - Loftus and others have suggested that memory retrieval is a constructive process; memories are "built" at time of retrieval

6.10 p. 252

Forgetting

(originally studied by Ebbinghaus (1913), research produced forgetting curve)

- **distributed practice**
  produces far better retrieval than massed practice (cramming)

- **encoding failure**
  nonattended information is not encoded into memory

- **memory trace decay**
  over time, if not used neuronal connections can decay

- **interference**
  other information interferes with accurate retrieval

Table 6.1 Reasons for Forgetting

REASONS	DESCRIPTION
Encoding Failure	The information is not attended to and fails to be encoded.
Decay or Disuse	Information that is not accessed decays from the storage system over time.
Proactive Interference	Older information already in memory interferes with the retrieval of newer information.
Retroactive Interference	Newer information interferes with the retrieval of older information.

6.11–12 p. 252

- different brain areas are associated with different types of memory
  - **procedural memories**
  - **short-term memories**
  - **semantic and episodic long-term memories**

- several physical changes in brain are associated with memory formation (consolidation)
  - changes at receptor (long-term potentiation)
  - changes in dendrites

- **hippocampus** plays a vital role in the formation of new declarative long-term memories

Memory and the Brain

Proactive Interference
French, learned **beforehand**, interferes proactively
Study French | Study Spanish | Spanish Test

Retroactive Interference
Spanish, learned **afterwards**, Interferes retroactively
Study French | Study Spanish | French Test

- **amnesia**
  - **retrograde amnesia**
  - **anterograde amnesia**

7

Cognition: Thinking, Intelligence, and Language

The Life of Alex

On September 6, 2007, Alex the African gray parrot died. Alex was not an ordinary pet; he was made famous by the groundbreaking work of Dr. Irene Pepperberg and her colleagues in cognition and communication research. Although most people know that parrots can learn to mimic words and sounds made by humans—and even machines—Alex could use language in a very different way. He could identify over 50 different objects, seven colors, and five shapes by naming them out loud. Alex could even count up to six objects. He could verbally identify which of two objects was the bigger or the smaller, sort over 100 objects into categories, and say whether two objects were the same kind of object or different objects—hardly simple imitation.

But does this constitute a real use of language? Is Alex the parrot really thinking much like a very young child would think about these objects? Many cognitive theorists seem to think so (Pepperberg, 2005, 2007), although some caution against interpreting Alex's behavior in human terms and motivations (Premack, 2004). The researchers taught Alex by modeling competitive behavior—for example, one researcher might offer another a toy if he could correctly name it, and the second researcher would be "rewarded" by getting to play with the toy. Through modeling and shaping of Alex's words, the parrot was able to learn concepts similar to that of a very young child. Since Alex's death, Pepperberg and her colleagues have continued to work with their two other African gray parrots, Griffin and Arthur (affectionately known as "Wart"), and are even teaching the parrots to "surf the Web" after a fashion by linking simple actions to different recorded sites on a television monitor.

As reported, Alex's last words to Pepperberg were, "You be good, see you tomorrow. I love you."

Why study the nature of thought? To fully understand how we do any of the things we do (such as learning, remembering, and behaving), we need to understand how we think. How do we organize our thoughts? How do we communicate those thoughts to others? What do we mean by intelligence? Why are some people able to learn so much faster than others?

a rose is a rose   a x   (R+r)*cos(t) – (r+O)*c

7 Learning Objectives

- **7.1** How are mental images and concepts involved in the process of thinking?
- **7.2** What are the methods people use to solve problems and make decisions, and can a machine be made to think like a person?
- **7.3** Why does problem solving sometimes fail, and what is meant by creative thinking?
- **7.4** How do psychologists define intelligence, and how do various theories of intelligence differ?
- **7.5** How is intelligence measured, and how are intelligence tests constructed?
- **7.6** What is mental retardation, and what are its causes?

- **7.7** What defines giftedness, and does being intellectually gifted guarantee success in life?
- **7.8** What is the influence of heredity and environment on the development of intelligence?
- **7.9** How is language defined, and what are its different elements and structure?
- **7.10** Does language influence the way people think, and are animals capable of learning language?
- **7.11** What are some ways to improve thinking?

---

thinking (cognition) mental activity that goes on in the brain when a person is organizing and attempting to understand information and communicating information to others.

mental images mental representations that stand for objects or events and have a picture-like quality.

AP* Compare and contrast various cognitive processes. ▶

So more windows means more time to count them in your head? I guess mentally "walking" through a bigger house in your head would take longer than "walking" through a smaller one.

How People Think

What does it mean to think? People are thinking all the time and talking about thinking as well: "What do you think?" "Let me think about that." "I don't think so." What does it mean to think? **Thinking**, or **cognition** (from a Latin word meaning "to know"), can be defined as mental activity that goes on in the brain when a person is processing information—organizing it, understanding it, and communicating it to others. Thinking includes memory, but it is much more. When people think, they are not only aware of the information in the brain but also are making decisions about it, comparing it to other information, and using it to solve problems.

Thinking also includes more than just a kind of verbal "stream of consciousness." When people think, they often have images as well as words in their minds.

7.1 How are mental images and concepts involved in the process of thinking?

MENTAL IMAGERY

As stated in Chapter Six, short-term memories are encoded in the form of sounds and also as visual images, forming a mental picture of the world. Thus, **mental images** (representations that stand in for objects or events and have a picture-like quality) are one of several tools used in the thought process.

Here's an interesting demonstration of the use of mental images. Get several people together and ask them to tell you *as fast as they can* how many windows are in the place where they live. Usually you'll find that the first people to shout out an answer have fewer windows in their houses than the ones who take longer to respond. You'll also notice that most of them look up, as if looking at some image that only they can see. If asked, they'll say that to determine the number of windows, they pictured where they live and simply counted windows as they "walked through" the image.

So more windows means more time to count them in your head? I guess mentally "walking" through a bigger house in your head would take longer than "walking" through a smaller one. ▶

That's what researchers think, too. They have found that it does take longer to view a mental image that is larger or covers more distance than a smaller, more compact one (Kosslyn et al., 2001; Ochsner & Kosslyn, 1994). In one study (Kosslyn et al., 1978), participants were asked to look at a map of an imaginary island (see Figure 7.1). On this map were several landmarks, such as a hut, a lake, and a grassy area. After viewing the map and memorizing it, participants were asked to imagine a specific place on the island, such as the hut, and then to "look" for another place, like the lake. When they mentally "reached" the second place, they pushed a button that recorded reaction time. The greater the physical distance on the map between the two locations, the longer it took participants to scan the image for the second location. The participants were apparently looking at their mental image and scanning it just as if it were a real, physical map.

Mental imagery is something people use every day. It helps them remember where they parked the car, find furniture that fits the space they have for it, and relax by creating daydreams. It allows people to find their way home and to other places by using their learned "mental maps" of how to get to familiar locations. (L)(I)(N)(K) *to Chapter Five: Learning, p. 205.* As discussed in the Introduction to this text, mental imagery is also a very useful tool for remembering other ideas and concepts, such as remembering your grocery list by linking the items on it to a series of standard images (Paivio, 1971, 1986; Thomas, 2001). (L)(I)(N)(K) *to Introduction, pp. I-11 to I-12.*

People are even able to mentally rotate, or turn, images (Shepherd & Metzler, 1971). Kosslyn (1983) asked subjects questions such as the following: "Do frogs have lips and a stubby tail?" He found that most people reported visualizing a frog, starting with the face ("no lips") and mentally rotating the image to look for the stubby tail ("yes, there it is").

In the brain, the process of creating a mental image is almost the opposite of seeing an actual image. With an actual image, the information goes from the eyes to the visual cortex of the occipital lobe and is processed, or interpreted, by other areas of the cortex that compare the new information to information already in memory. (L)(I)(N)(K) *to Chapter Two: The Biological Perspective, p. 73.* In creating a mental image, other areas of the cortex associated with stored knowledge send information to the visual cortex, where the image is perceived in the "mind's eye" (Kosslyn et al., 1993; Sparing et al., 2002). PET scans show areas of the visual cortex being activated during the process of forming an image, providing evidence for the role of the visual cortex in mental imagery (Kosslyn et al., 1993, 1999, 2001).

CONCEPTS

Images are not the only way we think, are they?

Mental images are only one form of mental representation. Another aspect of thought processes is the use of concepts. **Concepts** are ideas that represent a class or category of objects, events, or activities. People use concepts to think about objects or events without having to think about all the specific examples of the category. For example, a person can think about "fruit" without thinking about every kind of fruit there is in the world, which would take far more effort and time. This ability to think in terms of concepts allows us to communicate with each other: If I mention a bird to you, you know what I am referring to, even if we aren't actually thinking of the same *type* of bird.

Concepts not only contain the important features of the objects or events people want to think about, but also they allow the identification of new objects and events that may fit the concept. For example, dogs come in all shapes, sizes, colors, and lengths of fur. Yet most people have no trouble recognizing dogs as dogs, even

Figure 7.1 Kosslyn's Fictional Island
In Kosslyn's 1978 study, participants were asked to push a button when they had imagined themselves moving from one place on the island to another. As the graph below the picture shows, participants took longer times to complete the task when the locations on the image were farther apart. *Source:* Kosslyn et al. (1978).

Images are not the only way we think, are they?

concepts ideas that represent a class or category of objects, events, or activities.

Both of these animals are dogs. They both have fur, four legs, a tail—but the similarities end there. With so many variations in the animals we call "dogs," what is the prototype for "dog"?

> But what about things that don't easily fit the rules or features? ▶ What if a thing has some, but not all, features of a concept?

superordinate concept   the most general form of a type of concept, such as "animal" or "fruit."

basic level type   an example of a type of concept around which other similar concepts are organized, such as "dog," "cat," or "pear."

subordinate concept   the most specific category of a concept, such as one's pet dog or a pear in one's hand.

formal concepts   concepts that are defined by specific rules or features.

natural concepts   concepts people form as a result of their experiences in the real world.

though they may never before have seen that particular breed of dog. Friends of the author have a dog called a briard, which is a kind of sheepdog. In spite of the fact that this dog is easily the size of a small pony, the author had no trouble recognizing it as a dog, albeit a huge and extremely shaggy one.

Concepts can represent many different levels of objects or events. Concepts can be of a very general form, such as "fruit," called a **superordinate* concept**. The concept "apple" is more specific but can still be a **basic level type**. "Pear," "orange," and "watermelon" would also be basic level. A "Granny Smith apple" would be a **subordinate** concept**, or one that is the most specific example (Mandler, 2000, 2003; Rosch et al., 1976). As discussed in Chapter Six, concepts are thought to form a network of associations based on these levels. (See Figure 6.6, on p. 233.)

Concepts can have very strict definitions, such as the concept of a square as a shape with four equal sides. Concepts defined by specific rules or features are called **formal concepts** and are pretty rigid. To be a square, for example, an object must be a two-dimensional figure with four equal sides and four angles adding up to 360 degrees. If an object has those features, it is not only a square, but also it cannot be anything BUT a square. Science and mathematics are full of formal concepts: Acid, limestone, asteroid, and wavelength are a few scientific formal concepts; in geometry, there are triangles, squares, rectangles, polygons, and lines. In psychology, there are double-blind experiments, sleep stages, and conditioned stimuli, to name a few. Each of these concepts must fit very specific features to be considered true examples.

But what about things that don't easily fit the rules or features? What if a thing has some, but not all, features of a concept? In everyday life, people are surrounded by objects, events, and activities that are not as clearly defined as the concepts of science and mathematics. What is a vehicle? Cars and trucks leap immediately to mind, but what about a bobsled? How about a raft? Those last two objects aren't quite as easy to classify as vehicles immediately, but they fit some of the rules for "vehicle." These are examples of **natural concepts**, concepts people form not as a result of the application of a strict set of rules, but rather as the result of their experiences with these concepts in the real world (Ahn, 1998; Barton & Komatsu, 1989; Gelman, 1988; Rosch, 1973). Whereas formal concepts are well defined, natural concepts are "fuzzy" (Hampton, 1998). Is a whale a fish or a mammal? Is a platypus a mammal or a bird? People may know that whales are technically mammals, but whales also share a lot of fish-defining characteristics. Mammals have fur; birds lay eggs and have beaks. The duck-billed platypus has and does all three (has fur, lays eggs, and has a beak), yet it is classified as a mammal, not a bird.

Natural concepts are important in helping people understand their surroundings in a less structured manner than the formal concepts that are taught in school, and they form the basis for interpreting those surroundings and the events that may occur in everyday life.

Prototypes   When someone says "fruit," what's the first image that comes to mind? More than likely, it's a specific kind of fruit like an apple, pear, or orange. It's less likely that someone's first impulse will be to say "guava" or "papaya," or even "banana,"

---

*Superordinate: ranked highest in status or standing.
**Subordinate: ranked lowest in status or standing.

A duck-billed platypus is classified as a mammal yet shares features with birds, such as webbed feet and a bill and also lays eggs. The platypus is an example of a "fuzzy" natural concept. Courtesy of Dave Watts, Nature Picture Library.

unless that person comes from a tropical area. In the United States, apples are a good example of a **prototype**, a concept that closely matches the defining characteristics of the concept (Mervis & Rosch, 1981; Rosch, 1977). Fruit is sweet, grows on trees, has seeds, and is usually round—all very apple-like qualities. Coconuts are sweet and they also grow on trees, but many people in the Northern Hemisphere have never actually seen a coconut tree. They have more likely seen countless apple trees. So people who do have very different experiences with fruit, for instance, will have different prototypes, which are the most basic examples of concepts.

What about people who live in a tropical area? Would their prototype for fruit be different? And would people's prototypes be different in different cultures? More than likely, prototypes develop according to the exposure a person has to objects in that category. So someone who grew up in an area where there are many coconut trees might think of coconuts as more prototypical than apples, whereas someone growing up in the northwestern United States would more likely see apples as a prototypical fruit (Aitchison, 1992). Research suggests that what a person knows about a particular type of object does affect the person's prototype for the category (Lynch et al., 2000; Shafto & Coley, 2003). For example, people who are not that knowledgeable about trees tend to pick a tree that is found where they live as the prototypical tree (such as an oak tree), whereas experts in tree identification tend to select trees that have more ideal characteristics (tall, for example) rather than one specific type of tree. For nonexperts, familiarity was important in selecting a prototype, but for the experts central characteristics more representative of trees in general were the standard (Lynch et al., 2000).

Culture also matters in the formation of prototypes. Research on concept prototypes across various cultures found greater differences and variations in prototypes between cultures that were dissimilar, such as Taiwan and American, than between cultures that are more similar, such as Hispanic Americans and non–Hispanic Americans living in Florida (Lin et al., 1990; Lin & Schwanenflugel, 1995; Schwanenflugel & Rey, 1986).

How do prototypes affect thinking? People tend to look at potential examples of a concept and compare them to the prototype to see how well they match—which is why it takes most people much longer to think about olives and tomatoes as fruit because they aren't sweet, one of the major characteristics of the prototype of fruit (Rosch & Mervis, 1975). Table 7.1 presents some prototypical examples of the concepts "vehicle" and "fruit" as well as less typical examples.

What about people who live in a tropical area?
◄ Would their prototype for fruit be different? And would people's prototypes be different in different cultures?

prototype an example of a concept that closely matches the defining characteristics of a concept.

Table 7.1   From Prototypes to Atypical Examples (Most Typical to Least Typical)

VEHICLES	FRUITS
Car	Orange
Bus	Apple
Train	Peach
Bicycle	Grape
Airplane	Strawberry
Boat	Grapefruit
Wheelchair	Watermelon
Sled	Date
Skates	Tomato
Elevator	Olive

Source: Adapted from Rosch & Mervis (1975), p. 576.

No matter what type, concepts are one of the ways people deal with all the information that bombards* their senses every day and allows them to organize their perceptions of the world around them. This organization may take the form of *schemas*, generalizations about objects, places, events, and people (for example, one's schema for "library" would no doubt include books and bookshelves), or *scripts*, a kind of schema that involves a familiar sequence of activities (for example, "going to a movie" would include traveling there, getting the ticket, buying snacks, finding the right theater, etc.). Concepts not only help people think, but also they are an important tool in *problem solving*, a type of thinking that people engage in every day and in many different situations.

PROBLEM SOLVING AND DECISION MAKING

Problem solving is certainly a big part of any college student's life. Is there any one "best" way to go about solving a problem? Put a coin in a bottle and then cork the opening. How can you get the coin out of the bottle without pulling out the cork or breaking the bottle? (For the solution, see p. 268.)

As stated earlier, images and concepts are mental tools that can be used to solve problems. For the preceding problem, you are probably trying to create an image of the bottle with a coin in it. **Problem solving** occurs when a goal must be reached by thinking and behaving in certain ways. Problems range from figuring out how to cut a recipe in half to understanding complex mathematical proofs to deciding what to major in at college. There are several different ways in which people can think in order to solve problems.

Problem solving is certainly a big part of any college student's life. Is there any one "best" way to ▶ go about solving a problem?

AP* Identify problem-solving strategies as well as factors that influence their effectiveness.

▶

problem solving process of cognition that occurs when a goal must be reached by thinking and behaving in certain ways.

---

*Bombards: attacks again and again.

7.2 What are the methods people use to solve problems and make decisions, and can a machine be made to think like a person?

Trial and Error (Mechanical Solutions)   One method is to use **trial and error**, also known as a **mechanical solution**. Trial and error refers to trying one solution after another until finding one that works. For example, if Shelana has forgotten the PIN number for her online banking Web site, she can try one combination after another until she finds the one that works, if she has only a few such PINs that she normally uses. Mechanical solutions can also involve solving by *rote*, or a learned set of rules. This is how word problems were solved in grade school, for example. One type of rote solution is to use an algorithm.

Algorithms   **Algorithms** are specific, step-by-step procedures for solving certain types of problems. Algorithms will always result in a correct solution, if there is a correct solution to be found, and you have enough time to find it. Mathematical formulas are algorithms. When librarians organize books on bookshelves, they also use an algorithm: Place books in alphabetical order within each category, for example. Many puzzles, like a Rubik's Cube®, have a set of steps that, if followed exactly, will always result in solving the puzzle. But algorithms aren't always practical to use. For example, if Shelana didn't have a clue what those four numbers might be, she *might* be able to figure out her forgotten PIN number by trying *all possible combinations* of four digits, 0 through 9. She would eventually find the right four-digit combination—but it might take years! Computers, however, can run searches like this one very quickly, so the systematic search algorithm is a useful part of some computer programs.

Heuristics   Unfortunately, humans aren't as fast as computers and need some other way to narrow down the possible solutions to only a few. One way to do this is to use a heuristic. A **heuristic**, or "rule of thumb," is a simple rule that is intended to apply to many situations. Whereas an algorithm is very specific and will always lead to a solution, a heuristic is an educated guess based on prior experiences that helps narrow down the possible solutions for a problem. For example, if a student is typing a paper in a word-processing program and wants to know how to format the page, he or she could try to read an entire manual on the word-processing program. That would take a while. Instead, the student could type "format" into the help feature's search program or click on the word "Format" on the tool bar. Doing either action greatly reduces the amount of information the student will have to look at to get an answer. Using the help feature or clicking on the appropriate tool bar word will also work for similar problems.

Will using a rule of thumb always work, like algorithms? Using a heuristic is faster than using an algorithm in many cases, but unlike algorithms, heuristics will *not* always lead to the correct solution. What you gain in speed is sometimes lost in accuracy. For example, one kind of heuristic (called a *representative heuristic*) for categorizing objects simply assumes that any object (or person) that shares characteristics with the members of a particular category is also a member of that category. This is a handy tool when it comes to classifying plants but doesn't work as well when applied to people. Are all people with dark skin from Africa? Does everyone with red hair also have a bad temper? Are all blue-eyed blondes from Sweden? See the point? The representative heuristic can be used—or misused—to create and sustain stereotypes (Kahneman & Tversky, 1973; Kahneman et al., 1982).

A useful heuristic that works much of the time is to work backward from the goal. For example, if you want to know the shortest way to get to the new bookstore in town, you already know the goal, which is finding the bookstore. There are

This child tries one piece after another until finding the piece that fits. This is an example of trial-and-error learning.

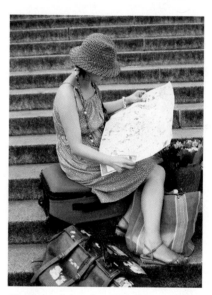

One rule of thumb, or heuristic, involves breaking down a goal into subgoals. This woman is consulting the map to see which of several possible paths she needs to take to get to her goal destination.

trial and error (mechanical solution) problem-solving method in which one possible solution after another is tried until a successful one is found.

algorithms very specific, step-by-step procedures for solving certain types of problems.

heuristic an educated guess based on prior experiences that helps narrow down the possible solutions for a problem. Also known as a "rule of thumb."

probably several ways to get there from your house, and some are shorter than others. Assuming you have the address of the store, the best way to determine the shortest route is to look up the location of the store on a map of the city and then trace a route back to where you live.

What if my problem is writing a term paper? Starting at the end isn't going to help me much! Sometimes it's better to break a goal down into subgoals, so that as each subgoal is achieved, the final solution is that much closer. Writing a term paper, for example, can seem overwhelming until it is broken down into steps: choose a topic, research the topic, organize what has been gathered, write one section at a time, and so on. Other examples of heuristics include making diagrams to help organize the information concerning the problem or testing possible solutions to the problem one by one and eliminating those that do not work.

Another kind of heuristic is **means–end analysis**, in which a person determines the difference between the current situation and the goal and then tries to reduce that difference by various means (methods). For example, Katrina wanted a certain kind of invitation for her graduation party, but buying it already made was very expensive and well over her budget. She ordered one sample of the invitation and examined it carefully. It had a pocket inside that held the response cards for people to send back to Katrina, a decorative graduation cap tied onto the outside of the card with fancy ribbon, and a blue envelope. Her goal was to make 30 of these invitations by hand. Her subgoals were to find the paper, take the invitation carefully apart to see how to put one together, buy the decorative graduation caps, find and buy the right size envelopes for mailing, and assemble the invitations. What might have seemed an impossible task became doable once it was broken down into smaller subgoals.

Insight

Sometimes I have to find answers to problems one step at a time, but in other cases the answer seems to just "pop" into my head all of a sudden. Why do some answers come so easily to mind? When the solution to a problem seems to come suddenly to mind, it is called *insight*. Chapter Five (p. 206) contained a discussion of Köhler's (1925) work with Sultan the chimpanzee, which demonstrated that even some animals can solve problems by means of a sudden insight. In humans, insight often takes the form of an "aha!" moment—the solution seems to come in a flash. A person may realize that this problem is similar to another one that he or she already knew how to solve or might see that an object can be used for a different purpose than its original one, like using a dime as a screwdriver.

Remember the problem of the bottleneck discussed earlier in this chapter? The task was to get the coin out of the bottle without removing the cork or breaking the bottle. The answer is simple: *Push the cork into the bottle and shake out the coin. Aha!*

Insight is not really a magical process, although it can seem like magic. What usually happens is that the mind simply reorganizes a problem, sometimes while the person is thinking about something else (Durso et al., 1994).

Here's a problem that can be solved with insight: Marsha and Marjorie were born on the same day of the same month of the same year to the same mother and the same father yet they are not twins. How is that possible? Think about it and then look for the answer on p. 270.

In summary, thinking is a complex process involving the use of mental imagery and various types of concepts to organize the events of daily life. Problem solving is a

---

> What if my problem is writing a term paper? ▶ Starting at the end isn't going to help me much!

> Sometimes I have to find answers to problems one step at a time, but in other cases the answer seems to ▶ just "pop" into my head all of a sudden. Why do some answers come so easily to mind?

means–end analysis   heuristic in which the difference between the starting situation and the goal is determined and then steps are taken to reduce that difference.

special type of thinking that involves the use of many tools, such as trial-and-error thinking, algorithms, and heuristics, to solve different types of problems.

For a look at how some scientists are trying to develop machines that can think in a similar fashion to a human, see the following special section.

artificial intelligence (AI) the creation of a machine that can think like a human.

Psychology in the News

Artificial Intelligence (AI)

Many people might think that interest in **artificial intelligence (AI)**, or the creation of a machine that can think like a human, is a relatively recent phenomenon. But the idea of a mechanical "man" or robot is ancient. In Greek mythology, the god Hephaestus created a bronze man called Talos 1, the guardian of Crete. In a sense, Mary Shelley's *Frankenstein* (1818/1969) was an artificially created being as well. The first use of the term *robot* was in Karel Capek's famous play "*R. U. R.*" (*Rossum's Universal Robots*) in 1923 (Capek & Capek, 1923), and robots became a standard feature of many science fiction novels and short stories in the 1950s, in particular in the major works of Isaac Asimov. His most famous robotic novel, *I, Robot* (1950, 2008), was made into a major motion picture in 2004.

It was John McCarthy (1959) who first coined the term *artificial intelligence* at a conference devoted to the subject. Today artificial intelligence is represented in computer programs such as Deep Blue, a chess program that allowed a computer to beat the world chess champion, Garry Kasparov, in 1997 (Kasparov had beaten Deep Blue in 1996, four games to two). In 2003, Kasparov played Deep Blue's "descendent," Deep Junior, and managed only a draw. Deep Junior, unlike Deep Blue, was programmed to consider only the strongest possible positions in detail (Knight, 2003). Interestingly, Deep Blue was programmed to use heuristics, the same kind of decision-making processes that humans use when playing chess. Deep Junior used algorithms (the more typical way in which computers are programmed).

Will Smith faces an army of robots on the set of the movie I, Robot, *which was loosely based on Isaac Asimov's famous book.*

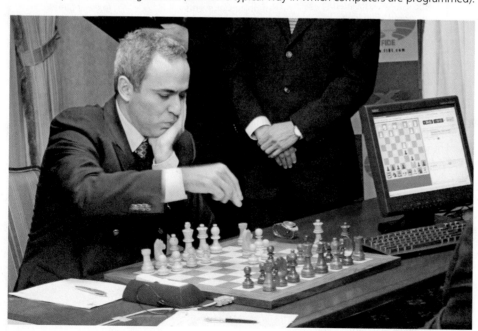

Chess genius Garry Kasparov plays against the artificial intelligence program Deep Junior. The outcome was a draw.

Deep Junior was able to play Kasparov to a draw using strategies that were less like human thinking than Deep Blue's strategies.

Should scientists be trying to create artificial intelligence that mimics human thought processes? That is one of the arguments among researchers in the field of AI (Hoffmann, 1998; Weizenbaum, 1976). Scientists will no doubt continue to try to refine robotic machines that can be used to go where humans cannot safely go, such as the depths of the oceans and the farthest reaches of our solar system. Will those machines think like machines, think like humans, or use a blend of machine and human cognitive processes? Only the future knows. ((•─Listen on **MyPsychLab**

((•● **Listen** to the Psychology in the News podcast. **www.mypsychlab.com**

Questions for Further Thought

1. How might having hands and feet make a robot more useful for certain tasks?

2. What are some of the concerns that might arise if human-shaped robots become a reality?

3. In what other areas of life might robots become useful?

4. Should a robot be able to function without human supervision or control?

Answer to insight problem on p. 268: *Marsha and Marjorie are two of a set of triplets. Gotcha!*

7.1–2

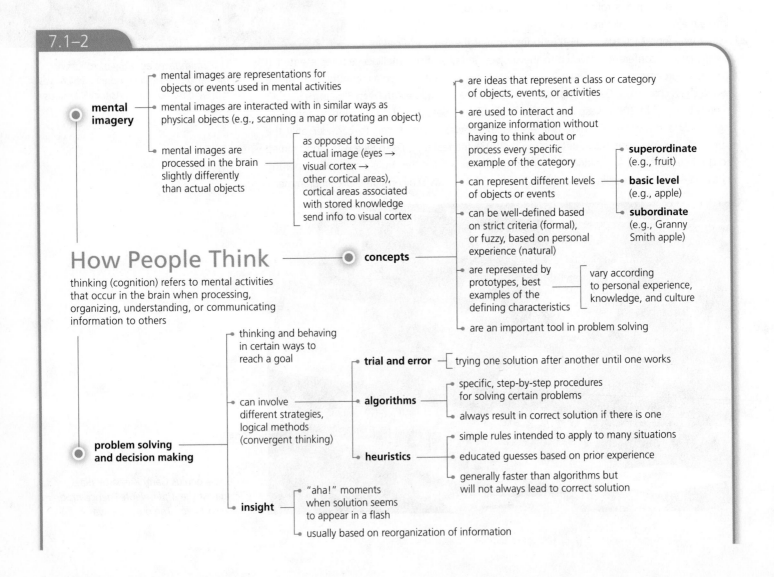

PROBLEMS WITH PROBLEM SOLVING

7.3 Why does problem solving sometimes fail, and what is meant by creative thinking?

◀ **AP*** Identify problem-solving strategies as well as factors that influence their effectiveness.

functional fixedness a block to problem solving that comes from thinking about objects in terms of only their typical functions.

Using insight to solve a problem is not always foolproof. Sometimes a solution to a problem remains just "out of reach" because the elements of the problem are not arranged properly or because people get stuck in certain ways of thinking that act as barriers to solving problems. Such ways of thinking occur more or less automatically, influencing attempts to solve problems without any conscious awareness of that influence. Here's a classic example:

Two strings are hanging from a ceiling but are too far apart to allow a person to hold one and walk to the other. (See Figure 7.2.) Nearby is a table with a pair of pliers on it. The goal is to tie the two pieces of string together. How? For the solution to this problem, see page 274.

People can become aware of automatic tendencies to try to solve problems in ways that are not going to lead to solutions and in becoming aware can abandon the "old" ways for more appropriate problem-solving methods. Three of the most common barriers* to successful problem solving are functional fixedness, mental sets, and confirmation bias.

Functional Fixedness One problem-solving difficulty involves thinking about objects only in terms of their typical uses, which is a phenomenon called **functional fixedness** (literally, "fixed on the function"). Have you ever searched high and

The string problem: How do you tie the two strings together if you cannot reach them both at the same time?

Figure 7.2 The String Problem

---

*Barrier: something that blocks one's path; an obstacle preventing a solution.

mental set the tendency for people to persist in using problem-solving patterns that have worked for them in the past.

confirmation bias the tendency to search for evidence that fits one's beliefs while ignoring any evidence that does not fit those beliefs.

creativity the process of solving problems by combining ideas or behavior in new ways.

low for a screwdriver to fix something around the house? All the while there are several objects close at hand that could be used to tighten a screw: a butter knife, a key, or even a dime in your pocket. Because the tendency is to think of those objects in terms of cooking, unlocking, and spending, we sometimes ignore the less obvious possible uses. The string problem is an example of functional fixedness. The pair of pliers is often seen as useless until the person realizes it can be used as a weight. (See page 274.)

Alton Brown, renowned chef and star of the Food Network's *Good Eats* cooking show, is a big fan of what he calls "multitaskers," kitchen items that can be used for more than one purpose. For example, a cigar-cutter can become a tool for cutting carrots, green onions, and garlic. Obviously, Chef Brown is not a frequent victim of functional fixedness.

Mental Sets   Functional fixedness is actually a kind of **mental set**, which is defined as the tendency for people to persist in using problem-solving patterns that have worked for them in the past. Solutions that have worked in the past tend to be the ones people try first, and people are often hesitant or even unable to think of other possibilities. Look at the accompanying figure.

Can you draw four straight lines so that they pass through all nine dots *without lifting your pencil from the page and without touching any dot more than once*?

People are taught from the earliest grades to stay within the lines, right? That tried-and-true method will not help in solving the dot problem. The solution involves drawing the lines beyond the actual dots, as seen in Figure 7.3 on page 278.

Confirmation Bias   Another barrier to logical thinking, called **confirmation bias**, is the tendency to search for evidence that fits one's beliefs while ignoring any evidence to the contrary. This is similar to a mental set, except that what is "set" is a belief rather than a method of solving problems. For example, believers in ESP tend to remember the few studies that seem to support their beliefs and psychic predictions that worked out while at the same time "forgetting" the cases in which studies found no proof or psychics made predictions that failed to come true. They remember only that which confirms their bias toward a belief in the existence of ESP.

CREATIVITY

So far, we've only talked about logic and pretty straightforward thinking. How do people come up ▶ with totally new ideas, things no one has thought of before?

So far, we've only talked about logic and pretty straightforward thinking. How do people come up with totally new ideas, things no one has thought of before? Not every problem can be answered by using information already at hand and the rules of logic in applying that information. Sometimes a problem requires coming up with entirely new ways of looking at the problem or unusual, inventive solutions. This kind of thinking is called **creativity**: solving problems by combining ideas or behavior in new ways (Csikszentmihalyi, 1996).

Divergent and Convergent Thinking   The logical method for problem solving that has been discussed so far is based on a type of thinking called **convergent thinking**. In convergent thinking, a problem is seen as having only one answer and all lines of thinking will eventually lead to (converge on) that single answer by using previous knowledge and logic (Ciardiello, 1998). For example, the question "In what ways are a pencil and a pen alike?" can be answered by listing the features that the two items have in common: Both can be used to write, have similar shapes, and so on, in a simple comparison process. Convergent thinking works well for routine problem solving but may be of little use when a more creative solution is needed.

Divergent thinking is the reverse of convergent thinking. Here a person starts at one point and comes up with many different, or divergent, ideas or possibilities based on that point (Finke, 1995). For example, if someone were to ask the question, "What is a pencil used for?" the convergent answer would be "to write." But if the question is put this way: "How many different uses can you think of for a pencil?" the answers multiply: "writing, poking holes, a weight for the tail of a kite, a weapon."

What are the characteristics of a creative, divergent thinker? Theorists in the field of creative thinking have found through examining the habits of highly creative people that the most productive periods of divergent thinking for those people tend to occur when they are doing some task or activity that is more or less automatic, such as walking or swimming (Csikszentmihalyi, 1996; Gardner, 1993a; Goleman, 1995). These automatic tasks take up some attention processes, leaving the remainder to devote to creative thinking. The fact that all of one's attention is not focused on the problem is actually a benefit, because divergent thinkers often make links and connections at a level of consciousness just below alert awareness, so that ideas can flow freely without being censored* by the higher mental processes (Goleman, 1995). In other words, having part of one's attention devoted to walking, for example, allows the rest of the mind to "sneak up on" more creative solutions and ideas.

Divergent thinkers will obviously be less prone to some of the barriers to problem solving, such as functional fixedness. For example, what would most people do if it suddenly started to rain while they are stuck in class with no umbrella? How many people would think of using a see-through vinyl tote bag as a makeshift umbrella?

Creative, divergent thinking is often a neglected topic in the education of young people. Although some people are naturally more creative, it is possible to develop one's creative ability. The ability to be creative is important—coming up with topics for a research paper, for example, is something that many students have trouble doing. Cross-cultural research (Basadur et al., 2002; Colligan, 1983) has found

◄ **AP*** List the characteristics of creative thought and creative thinkers.

◄ **AP*** Compare and contrast various cognitive processes.

Pablo Picasso was one of the most creative artists of his time. Here he is seen drawing an abstract of a woman in the air with a flashlight, using multiple exposures of the camera. What does his ability to "hold" the light image in his head long enough to complete the abstract tell us about his mental imagery?

Cynthia Breazeal is a researcher at the Artificial Intelligence Lab at MIT. Here she is pictured with the robot she designed called Kismet. Designed to help with the study of infant emotional expressions, Kismet can display several "moods" on its face as emotional expressions. This is divergent thinking at its best—a "baby" that won't cry, wet, or demand to be fed.

convergent thinking type of thinking in which a problem is seen as having only one answer, and all lines of thinking will eventually lead to that single answer, using previous knowledge and logic.

divergent thinking type of thinking in which a person starts from one point and comes up with many different ideas or possibilities based on that point.

---

*Censored: blocked from conscious awareness as unacceptable thoughts.

Table 7.2   Stimulating Divergent Thinking

Brainstorming	Generate as many ideas as possible in a short period of time, without judging each idea's merits until all ideas are recorded.
Keeping a Journal	Carry a journal to write down ideas as they occur or a recorder to capture those same ideas and thoughts.
Freewriting	Write down or record everything that comes to mind about a topic without revising or proofreading until all of the information is written or recorded in some way. Organize it later.
Mind or Subject Mapping	Start with a central idea and draw a "map" with lines from the center to other related ideas, forming a visual map of the concepts and their connections.

The solution to the string problem is to use the pliers as a pendulum to swing the second string closer to you.

✻ **Explore** with the simulation on obstacles and problem solving.
www.mypsychlab.com

that divergent thinking and problem-solving skills cannot be easily taught in cultures such as that of Japan and the Omaha Native Americans. In these cultures creativity in many areas is not normally prized and the preference is to hold to well-established traditions, such as that of traditional dances that have not varied for centuries. See Table 7.2 for some ways to become a more divergent thinker.

Many people have the idea that creative people are also a little different from other people. There are artists and musicians, for example, who actually encourage others to see them as eccentric. But the fact is that creative people are actually pretty normal. According to Csikszentmihalyi (1997),

1. Creative people usually have a broad range of knowledge about a lot of subjects and are good at using mental imagery.
2. Creative people aren't afraid to be different—they are more open to new experiences than many people, and they tend to have more vivid dreams and daydreams than others do.
3. Creative people value their independence.
4. Creative people are often unconventional in their work but not otherwise.

✻ Explore on **MyPsychLab**

7.3

problems with problem solving
- solutions to problems are not always apparent
- problems can be caused by three common barriers

  - **functional fixedness:** only thinking about objects in terms of their typical uses
  - **mental set:** a tendency to persist in using problem-solving patterns that have worked in the past
  - **confirmation bias:** a tendency to search for evidence that fits your beliefs while ignoring evidence to the contrary

Problem Solving and Decision Making

creativity
- consists of new ways of combining ideas or behavior
- typically the result of divergent thinking
  - less prone to common barriers of problem solving
  - can be stimulated (see Table 7.2)

Directions: Read each of the questions or incomplete sentences below. Then choose the response that best answers the question or completes the sentence.

1. Al goes out one frosty morning to find that his car is covered with a layer of thick frost. He needs to get to work and looks for his ice scraper. Unable to find it, he thinks a moment, goes into the house, and returns with a hard plastic spatula from the kitchen. In using the spatula as a makeshift ice scraper, what has Al overcome?
   a. Creativity bias
   b. Confirmation bias
   c. Functional fixedness
   d. Convergent thinking
   e. Confirmation fixedness

2. Randall believes that aliens crashed in the western United States in the 1950s. When looking for information about this on the Internet, he ignores any sites that are skeptical of his belief and only visits and talks with his friends about the sites that support his belief. What is this an example of?
   a. Creativity bias
   b. Confirmation bias
   c. Functional fixedness
   d. Convergent thinking
   e. Confirmation fixedness

3. What type of thinking occurs when a problem is seen as having only one answer, with all lines of thinking leading to that answer?
   a. Creative
   b. Divergent
   c. Mental set
   d. Convergent
   e. Subject mapping

4. Which of the following statements about creative people is true?
   a. They are not afraid to be different
   b. They value their dependence on others
   c. They are not very good at mental imagery
   d. They are often very conventional in their work
   e. They have a narrow range of knowledge about a lot of subjects

Intelligence

Think back to Alex the parrot in the opening story. Whether you accept Alex's verbal abilities as true language or not, one thing is clear: Alex is one smart bird. But what do we mean when we say he is "smart"? Is "smart" in a bird the same thing we mean when we say a human is smart? What exactly do we mean by the term *intelligence?*

DEFINITION

7.4 How do psychologists define intelligence, and how do various theories of intelligence differ?

Is intelligence merely a score on some test, or is it practical knowledge of how to get along in the world? Is it making good grades or being a financial success or a social success? Ask a dozen people and you will probably get a dozen different answers. Psychologists have come up with a workable definition that combines many of the ideas just listed: They define **intelligence** as the ability to learn from one's experiences, acquire knowledge, and use resources effectively in adapting to new situations or solving problems (Sternberg & Kaufman, 1998; Wechsler, 1975). These are the characteristics that people need to be able to survive in their culture. ◉⃞**Watch** on **MyPsychLab**

THEORIES OF INTELLIGENCE

Although we have defined intelligence in a general way, there are differing opinions of the specific knowledge and abilities that make up the concept of intelligence. It is these differing opinions as to the nature and number of intelligence-related abilities that are discussed in the following different views of intelligence.

Spearman's G Factor   Spearman (1904) saw intelligence as two different abilities. The ability to reason and solve problems was labeled **g factor** for *general intelligence*, whereas task-specific abilities in certain areas such as music, business, or art are labeled **s factor** for *specific intelligence*. A traditional IQ test would most likely measure g factor, but Spearman believed that superiority in one type of intelligence predicts

◀ **AP*** Define intelligence and list characteristics of how psychologists measure intelligence.

◀ **AP*** Compare and contrast historic and contemporary theories of intelligence.

◀ **AP*** Identify key contributors in intelligence research and testing.

◉ **Watch** classic video footage on experiments with ape intelligence.
www.mypsychlab.com

intelligence   the ability to learn from one's experiences, acquire knowledge, and use resources effectively in adapting to new situations or solving problems.

g factor   the ability to reason and solve problems, or general intelligence.

s factor   the ability to excel in certain areas, or specific intelligence.

Table 7.3   Gardner's Nine Intelligences

TYPE OF INTELLIGENCE	DESCRIPTION	SAMPLE OCCUPATION
Verbal/linguistic	Ability to use language	Writers, speakers
Musical	Ability to compose and/or perform music	Musicians, even those who do not read musical notes but can perform and compose
Logical/mathematical	Ability to think logically and to solve mathematical problems	Scientists, engineers
Visual/spatial	Ability to understand how objects are oriented in space	Pilots, astronauts, artists, navigators
Movement	Ability to control one's body motions	Dancers, athletes
Interpersonal	Sensitivity to others and understanding motivation of others	Psychologists, managers
Intrapersonal	Understanding of one's emotions and how they guide actions	Various people-oriented careers
Naturalist	Ability to recognize the patterns found in nature	Farmers, landscapers, biologists, botanists
Existentialist	Ability to see the "big picture" of the human world by asking questions about life, death, and the ultimate reality of human existence	Various careers, philosophical thinkers

This child is displaying only one of the many forms that intelligence can take, according to Gardner's multiple intelligences theory.

triarchic theory of intelligence
Sternberg's theory that there are three kinds of intelligence: analytical, creative, and practical.

superiority overall. Although his early research found some support for specific intelligences, other researchers (Guilford, 1967; Thurstone, 1938) felt that Spearman had oversimplified the concept of intelligence. Intelligence began to be viewed as composed of numerous factors. In fact, Guilford (1967) proposed that there were 120 types of intelligence.

Gardner's Multiple Intelligences   One of the later theorists to propose the existence of several kinds of intelligence was Gardner (1993b, 1999a). Although many people use the terms *reason, logic,* and *knowledge* as if they are the same ability, Gardner believes that they are different aspects of intelligence, along with several other abilities. He originally listed seven different kinds of intelligence but later added an eighth type and then a ninth (Gardner, 1998, 1999b). The nine types of intelligence are described in Table 7.3.

The idea of multiple intelligences has great appeal, especially for educators. However, some argue that there are few scientific studies providing evidence for the concept of multiple intelligences (Waterhouse, 2006a, 2006b), while others claim that the evidence does exist (Gardner & Moran, 2006). Some critics propose that such intelligences are no more than different abilities and that those abilities are not necessarily the same thing as what is typically meant by *intelligence* (Hunt, 2001).

Sternberg's Triarchic Theory   Sternberg (1988, 1997) has theorized that there are three kinds of intelligence. Called the **triarchic theory of intelligence** (*triarchic* means "three"), this theory is similar to Aristotle's theory that intelligence is composed of theoretical, productive, and practical aspects.

In Sternberg's theory, the three aspects are *analytical, creative*, and *practical intelligence*. **Analytical intelligence** refers to the ability to break problems down into component parts, or analysis, for problem solving. This is the type of intelligence that is measured by intelligence tests and academic achievement tests, or "book smarts" as some people like to call it. **Creative intelligence** is the ability to deal with new and different concepts and to come up with new ways of solving problems (divergent thinking, in other words). **Practical intelligence** is best described as "street smarts," or the ability to use information to get along in life. People with a high degree of practical intelligence know how to be tactful, how to manipulate situations to their advantage, and how to use inside information to increase their odds of success.

How might these three types of intelligence be illustrated? All three might come into play when planning and completing an experiment. For example:

- *Analytical:* Being able to run a statistical analysis on data from the experiment.
- *Creative:* Being able to design the experiment in the first place.
- *Practical:* Being able to get funding for the experiment from donors.

Practical intelligence has become a topic of much interest and research. Sternberg (1996, 1997a, b) has found that practical intelligence predicts success in life but has a surprisingly low relationship to academic (analytical) intelligence. In fact, the higher one's degree of practical intelligence, the less likely that person is to succeed in a university or other academic setting.

MEASURING INTELLIGENCE

7.5 How is intelligence measured, and how are intelligence tests constructed?

The history of intelligence testing spans the twentieth century and has at times been marked by controversies and misuse. A full history of how intelligence testing developed would take at least an entire chapter, so this section will discuss only some of the better-known forms of testing and how they came to be.

It doesn't sound like intelligence would be easy to measure on a test—how do IQ tests work, anyway?

The measurement of intelligence by some kind of test is a concept that is less than a century old. It began when educators in France realized that some students needed more help with learning than others did. They thought that if a way could be found to identify these students, they could be given a different kind of education than the more capable students.

Binet's Mental Ability Test   In those early days, a French psychologist named Alfred Binet was asked by the French Ministry of Education to design a formal test of intelligence that would help identify children who were unable to learn as quickly or as well as others, so that they could be given remedial education. Eventually, he and colleague Théodore Simon came up with a test that not only distinguished between fast and slow learners but also between children of different age groups as well (Binet & Simon, 1916). They noticed that the fast learners seemed to give answers to questions that older children might give, whereas the slow learners gave answers that were more typical of a younger child. Binet decided that the key element to be tested was a child's *mental age*, or the average age at which children could successfully answer a particular level of questions.

Stanford-Binet and IQ   Terman (1916), a researcher at Stanford University, adopted German psychologist William Stern's method for comparing mental age and *chronological age* (number of years since birth) for use with the translated and revised

Sternberg's practical intelligence is a form of "street smarts" that includes the ability to adapt to one's environment and solve practical problems. These girls are giving their younger brother a drink of water by using a folded leaf as an impromptu cup.

It doesn't sound like intelligence would be easy to measure on a test—how do IQ tests work, anyway?

AP* Explain how psychologists design tests.

AP* Identify key contributors in intelligence research and testing.

analytical intelligence   the ability to break problems down into component parts, or analysis, for problem solving.

creative intelligence   the ability to deal with new and different concepts and to come up with new ways of solving problems.

practical intelligence   the ability to use information to get along in life and become successful.

intelligence quotient (IQ) a number representing a measure of intelligence, resulting from the division of one's mental age by one's chronological age and then multiplying that quotient by 100.

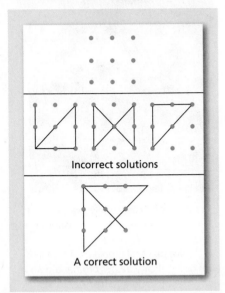

Figure 7.3 The Solution to the Dot Problem
When people try to solve this problem, a mental set causes them to think of the dots as representing a box, and they try to draw the line while staying in the box. The only way to connect all nine dots without lifting the pencil from the paper is to draw the lines so they extend out of the box of dots—literally "thinking outside the box."

Binet test. Stern's (1912) formula was to divide the mental age (MA) by the chronological age (CA) and multiply the result by 100 to get rid of any decimal points. The resulting score is called an **intelligence quotient**, or **IQ**. (A quotient is a number that results from dividing one number by another.)

$$IQ = MA/CA \times 100$$

For example, if a child who is 10 years old takes the test and scores a mental age of 15 (is able to answer the level of questions typical of a 15-year-old), the IQ would look like this:

$$IQ = 15/10 \times 100 = 150$$

The quotient had the advantage of allowing testers to compare the intelligence levels of people of different age groups. Today, the *Stanford-Binet Intelligence Scales, Fifth Edition (SB5)* (Roid, 2003) uses age-group comparison norms like the Wechsler tests and is often used by educators to make decisions about the placement of students into special educational programs. Most children are given this test in the second grade, or age 7 or 8. See Table 7.4 for descriptions of some items similar to those from the SB5.

The Wechsler Tests Although the Stanford-Binet Test is now in its fifth edition and includes different questions for people of different age groups, it is not the only IQ test that is popular today. David Wechsler (1981, 1990, 1991) was the first to devise a series of tests designed for specific age groups (also given to an individual, not just groups, as was the original Stanford-Binet). Dissatisfied with the fact that the Stanford-Binet was designed for children but being administered to adults, he developed an IQ test specifically for adults. He later designed tests specifically for older school-age children and preschool children as well as those in the early grades. The Wechsler Adult Intelligence Scale (WAIS-IV), Wechsler Intelligence Scale for Children (WISC-IV), and the Wechsler Preschool and Primary Scale of Intelligence (WPPSI-III) are the three versions of this test, and in the United States these tests are now used more frequently than the Stanford-Binet. These tests differ from the Stanford-Binet and

Table 7.4 Paraphrased Items from the Stanford-Binet Intelligence Test

AGE*	TYPE OF ITEM	DESCRIPTION OF ITEM
2	Board with three differently shaped holes	Child can place correct shape into matching hole on board.
4	Building block bridge	Child can build a simple bridge out of blocks after being shown a model.
7	Similarities	Child can answer such questions as "In what way are a ship and a car alike?"
9	Digit reversal	Child can repeat four digits backwards.
Average adult	Vocabulary	Child can define 20 words from a list.

*Age at which item typically is successfully completed.
Source: Roid, G. H. (2003).

Table 7.5 Paraphrased Sample Items from the Wechsler Adult Intelligence Scale (WAIS–III)

VERBAL SCALE

Information	What is steam made of? What is pepper? Who wrote *Tom Sawyer*?
Comprehension	Why is copper often used in electrical wire? What is the advantage of keeping money in a bank?
Arithmetic	Three women divided eighteen golf balls equally among themselves. How many golf balls did each person receive?
	If two buttons cost $.15, what will be the cost of a dozen buttons?
Similarities	In what way are a circle and a triangle alike? In what way are a saw and a hammer alike?
Vocabulary	What is a hippopotamus? What does "resemble" mean?

PERFORMANCE SCALE

Picture Arrangement	A story is told in three or more cartoon panels placed in the incorrect order; put them together to tell the story.
Picture Completion	Point out what's missing from each picture.
Block Design	After looking at a pattern or design, try to arrange small cubes in the same pattern.
Object Assembly	Given pieces with part of a picture on each, put them together to form objects such as a hand or a profile.
Digit Symbol	Learn a different symbol for each number and then fill in the blank under the number with the correct symbol. (This test is timed.)

Simulated items similar to those in the *Wechsler Adult Intelligence Scale*, Third Edition (1997).

traditionally had a verbal and a performance (nonverbal) scale, as well as providing an overall score of intelligence. While still using both verbal and nonverbal items, the WISC-IV and WAIS-IV currently provide an overall score of intelligence and index scores related to verbal comprehension, perceptual reasoning, working memory, and processing speed. Table 7.5 has sample verbal and performance items from the WAIS-III, the previous version of the WAIS.

Test Construction: Good Test, Bad Test?   All tests are not equally good tests. Some tests may fail to give the same results on different occasions for the same person when that person has not changed—making the test useless. These would be considered unreliable tests. **Reliability** of a test refers to the test producing consistent results each time it is given to the same individual or group of people. For example, if Nicholas takes a personality test today and then again in a month or so, the results should be very similar if the personality test is reliable. Other tests might be easy to use and even reliable, but if they don't actually measure what they are supposed to measure, they are also useless. These tests are thought of as "invalid" (untrue) tests. **Validity** is the degree to which a test actually measures what it's supposed to measure. And what does a test score mean? To what, or whom, is it compared?

reliability the tendency of a test to produce the same scores again and again each time it is given to the same people.

validity the degree to which a test actually measures what it's supposed to measure.

deviation IQ scores a type of intelligence measure that assumes that IQ is normally distributed around a mean of 100 with a standard deviation of about 15.

AP* Interpret the meaning of scores in terms of the normal curve. ▶

Take the hypothetical example of Professor Stumpwater, who for reasons best known only to him believes that intelligence is related to a person's golf scores. Let's say that he develops an adult intelligence test based on golf scores. What do we need to look at to determine if his test is a good one?

Standardization of Tests   First of all, we would want to look at how he tried to standardize his test. *Standardization* refers to the process of giving the test to a large group of people that represents the kind of people for whom the test is designed. Standardization groups are chosen randomly from the population for whom the test is intended and, like all samples, must be representative of that population. ⓛⓘⓝⓚ *to Appendix A: Statistics.* If a test is designed for children, for example, then a large sample of randomly selected children would be given the test. All test subjects would take the test under the same conditions. In the professor's case, this would mean that he would have to allow his sample members to play the same number of rounds of golf on the same course under the same weather conditions, and so on.

Norms   The scores from the standardization group would be called the *norms*, the standards against which all others who take the test would be compared. Most tests of intelligence follow a *normal curve*, or a distribution in which the scores are the most frequent around the *mean*, or average, and become less and less frequent the farther from the mean they occur (see Figure 7.4). ⓛⓘⓝⓚ *to Appendix A: Statistics.*

On the Wechsler IQ test, the percentages under each section of the normal curve represent the percentage of scores falling within that section for each *standard deviation (SD)* from the mean on the Wechsler IQ test. The standard deviation is the average variation of scores from the mean. ⓛⓘⓝⓚ *to Appendix A: Statistics.*

In the case of the professor's golf test, he might find that a certain golf score is the average, which he would interpret as average intelligence. People who scored extremely well on the golf test would be compared to the average, as well as people with unusually poor scores.

The normal curve allows IQ scores to be more accurately estimated. The old IQ scoring method using the simple formula devised by Stern produces raw ratio IQ scores that start to become meaningless as the person's chronological age passes 16 years. (Once a person becomes an adult, the idea of questions that are geared for a particular age group loses its power. For example, what kind of differences would there be between questions designed for a 30-year-old versus a 40-year-old?) Test designers replaced the old ratio IQ of the earlier versions of IQ tests with **deviation IQ scores**, which are based on the normal curve distribution (Eysenck, 1994): IQ is as-

Figure 7.4 The Normal Curve
On the Wechsler IQ test, the percentages under each section of the normal curve represent the percentage of scores falling within that section for each *standard deviation (SD)* from the mean. ⓛⓘⓝⓚ *to Appendix A: Statistics.*

sumed to be normally distributed with a mean IQ of 100 and a typical standard deviation of about 15 (the standard deviation can vary according to the particular test). An IQ of 130, for example, would be two standard deviations above the mean, whereas an IQ of 70 would be two standard deviations below the mean, and in each case the person's score is being compared to the population's average score.

With respect to validity and reliability, the professor's test fares poorly. If the results of the professor's test were compared with other established intelligence tests, there would probably be no relationship at all. Golf scores have nothing to do with intelligence, so the test is not a valid, or true, measure of intelligence.

On the other hand, his test might work well for some people and poorly for others on the question of reliability. Some people who are good and regular golfers tend to score about the same for each game that they play, so for them, the golf score IQ would be fairly reliable. But others, especially those who do not play golf or play infrequently, would have widely varying scores from game to game. For those people, the test would be very unreliable, and if a test is unreliable for some, it's not a good test.

A test can fail in validity but still be reliable. If for some reason Professor Stumpwater chose to use height as a measure of intelligence, an adult's score on Stumpwater's "test" would always be the same, as height does not change by very much after the late teens. But the opposite is not true. If a test is unreliable, how can it accurately measure what it is supposed to measure? For example, adult intelligence remains fairly constant. If a test meant to measure that intelligence gave different scores at different times, it's obviously not a valid measure of intelligence.

Just because an IQ test gives the same score every time a person takes it doesn't mean that the score is actually measuring real intelligence, right? That's right—think about the definition of intelligence for a moment: the ability to learn from one's experiences, acquire knowledge, and use resources effectively in adapting to new situations or solving problems. How can anyone define what "effective use of resources" might be? Does everyone have access to the same resources? Is everyone's "world" necessarily perceived as being the same? Intelligence tests are useful measuring devices but should not necessarily be assumed to be measures of all types of intelligent behavior, or even good measures for all groups of people, as the next section discusses. ✴ Explore on MyPsychLab

IQ Tests and Cultural Bias   The problem with trying to measure intelligence with a test that is based on an understanding of the world and its resources is that not everyone comes from the same "world." People raised in a different culture, or even a different economic situation, from the one in which the designer of an IQ test is raised are not likely to perform well on such a test—not mention the difficulties of taking a test that is written in an unfamiliar language or dialect. In the early days of immigration, people from non-English-speaking countries would score very poorly on intelligence tests, in some cases being denied entry to the United States on the basis of such tests (Allen, 2006).

It is very difficult to design an intelligence test that is completely free of *cultural bias*, a term referring to the tendency of IQ tests to reflect, in language, dialect, and content, the culture of the person or persons who designed the test. A person who comes from the same culture (or even socioeconomic background) as the test designer may have an unfair advantage over a person who is from a different cultural or socioeconomic background (Helms, 1992). If people raised in an Asian culture are

Just because an IQ test gives the same score every time a person takes it ◀ doesn't mean that the score is actually measuring real intelligence, right?

✴ **Explore** with a simulation on the the normal curve. **www.mypsychlab.com**

◀ **AP*** Discuss how culture influences the definition of intelligence.

◀ **AP*** Debate the appropriate testing practices, particularly in relation to culture-fair test uses.

given a test designed within a traditional Western culture, many items on the test might make no sense to them. For example, one kind of question might be: Which one of the five is least like the other four?

DOG - CAR - CAT - BIRD - FISH

The answer is supposed to be "car," which is the only one of the five that is not alive. But a Japanese child, living in a culture that relies on the sea for so much of its food and culture, might choose "fish," because none of the others are found in the ocean. That child's test score would be lower but not because the child is not intelligent.

In 1971, Adrian Dove designed an intelligence test to highlight the problem of cultural bias. Dove, an African American sociologist, created the Dove Counterbalance General Intelligence Test (later known as the Chitling Test) in an attempt to demonstrate that a significant language/dialect barrier exists among children of different backgrounds. Look at Table 7.6 and take a sample of the test.

A person who is not from the African American culture of the southeastern United States will probably score very poorly on this test. African American people from different geographical regions don't always do well on this test either. The point is simply this: Tests such as these are created by people who are from a particular culture and background. Test questions and answers that the creators might think are common knowledge may relate to their own experiences and not to people of other cultures, backgrounds, or socioeconomic levels.

Table 7.6   Sample of the Dove Counterbalance General Intelligence Test

1. A "handkerchief head" is:

   a. a cool cat,   d. a hoddi,

   b. a porter,   e. a preacher.

   c. an Uncle Tom,

2. Cheap chitlings (not the kind you purchase at a frozen food counter) will taste rubbery unless they are cooked long enough. How soon can you quit cooking them to eat and enjoy them?

   a. 45 minutes,

   b. 2 hours,

   c. 24 hours,

   d. 1 week (on a low flame),

   e. 1 hour.

3. What are the "Dixie Hummingbirds"?

   a. part of the KKK,

   b. a swamp disease,

   c. a modern gospel group,

   d. a Mississippi Negro paramilitary group,

   e. deacons.

4. "Money don't get everything it's true"

   a. but I don't have none and I'm so blue,

   b. but what it don't get I can't use,

   c. so make do with what you've got,

   d. but I don't know that and neither do you.

   The answers are as follows:

   1. c.   2. c.   3. c.   4. b.

Source: Dove, A. (1971).

Attempts have been made to create intelligence tests that are as free of cultural influences as is humanly possible. Many test designers have come to the conclusion that it may be impossible to create a test that is completely free of cultural bias (Carpenter et al., 1990). Instead, they are striving to create tests that are at least *culturally fair*. These tests use questions that do not create a disadvantage for people whose culture differs from that of the majority. Many items on a "culture-fair" test require the use of nonverbal abilities, such as rotating objects, rather than items about verbal knowledge that might be culturally specific.

If intelligence tests are so flawed, why do people still use them? The one thing that IQ tests do well is predict academic success for those who score at the higher and lower ends of the normal curve. (For those who score in the average range of IQ, the predictive value is less clear.) The kinds of tests students are given in school are often similar to intelligence tests, and so people who do well on IQ tests typically do well on other kinds of academically oriented tests as well, such as the Scholastic Assessment Test (SAT), the American College Test (ACT), the Graduate Record Exam (GRE), and actual college examinations. These achievement tests are very similar to IQ tests but are administered to groups of people rather than to individuals. ❋ Explore on MyPsychLab

◀ **AP*** Debate the appropriate testing practices, particularly in relation to culture-fair test uses.

If intelligence tests are so ◀ flawed, why do people still use them?

❋ **Explore** intelligence tests and testing. **www.mypsychlab.com**

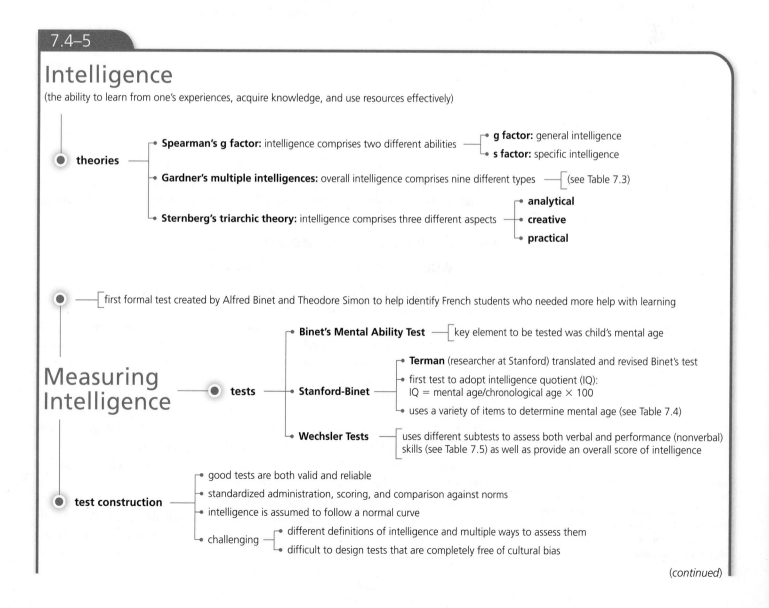

7.4–5

Intelligence
(the ability to learn from one's experiences, acquire knowledge, and use resources effectively)

theories
- **Spearman's g factor:** intelligence comprises two different abilities
  - **g factor:** general intelligence
  - **s factor:** specific intelligence
- **Gardner's multiple intelligences:** overall intelligence comprises nine different types — (see Table 7.3)
- **Sternberg's triarchic theory:** intelligence comprises three different aspects
  - **analytical**
  - **creative**
  - **practical**

Measuring Intelligence

first formal test created by Alfred Binet and Theodore Simon to help identify French students who needed more help with learning

tests
- **Binet's Mental Ability Test** — key element to be tested was child's mental age
- **Stanford-Binet**
  - **Terman** (researcher at Stanford) translated and revised Binet's test
  - first test to adopt intelligence quotient (IQ): IQ = mental age/chronological age × 100
  - uses a variety of items to determine mental age (see Table 7.4)
- **Wechsler Tests** — uses different subtests to assess both verbal and performance (nonverbal) skills (see Table 7.5) as well as provide an overall score of intelligence

test construction
- good tests are both valid and reliable
- standardized administration, scoring, and comparison against norms
- intelligence is assumed to follow a normal curve
- challenging
  - different definitions of intelligence and multiple ways to assess them
  - difficult to design tests that are completely free of cultural bias

(continued)

Directions: Read each of the questions or incomplete sentences below. Then choose the response that best answers the question or completes the sentence.

1. According to Spearman, what would a traditional IQ test most likely measure?
   a. General intelligence
   b. Spatial intelligence
   c. Specific intelligence
   d. Practical intelligence
   e. Emotional intelligence

2. In Gardner's view, astronauts, navigators, and artists would have high levels of which type of intelligence?
   a. Naturalist
   b. Visual/spatial
   c. Interpersonal
   d. Intrapersonal
   e. Verbal/linguistic

3. Adrian Dove designed the Dove Counterbalance General Intelligence Test to highlight what intelligence testing problem?
   a. Unreliability
   b. Ineffective resources
   c. Standardization
   d. Norm deviations
   e. Cultural bias

4. Darla is 4 years old. The intelligence test that would most likely be used to measure her intelligence is the

   _____.
   a. Binet's Mental Ability Test
   b. Wechsler Intelligence Scale for Children
   c. Wechsler Adult Intelligence Scale
   d. Dove Counterbalance General Intelligence Test
   e. Wechsler Preschool and Primary Scale of Intelligence

5. Professor Beckett designed an IQ test. To standardize this test, the professor should be careful to do which of the following?
   a. Use only a small sample to prevent possible cheating on the test
   b. Test each member of the sample under different conditions
   c. Adjust the test questions each time the test is administered
   d. Make sure that the standardization sample is representative of the population for whom the test is intended
   e. Select only university professors to take the test so they can critique the questions on the test

---

AP* Describe relevant labels related to intelligence testing. ▶

INDIVIDUAL DIFFERENCES IN INTELLIGENCE

Another use of IQ tests is to identify people who differ from those of average intelligence by a great degree. Although one such group is composed of those who are sometimes called "geniuses" (who fall at the extreme high end of the normal curve for intelligence), the other group is made up of people who, for various reasons, are considered intellectually delayed and whose IQ scores fall well below the mean on the normal curve.

Mental Retardation (Developmental Delay)

7.6   What is mental retardation, and what are its causes?

Mental retardation is defined in several ways. First, the person's IQ score must fall below 70, or two standard deviations below the mean on the normal curve. Second, the person's *adaptive behavior* (skills that allow people to live independently, such as being able to work at a job, the ability to communicate well with others, and grooming skills such as being able to get dressed, eat, and bathe with little or no help) is severely below a level appropriate for the person's age. Finally, these limitations must be present before the age of 18 years. Mental retardation occurs in about 3 percent of the population (American Psychiatric Association, 2000; The Arc, 1982) and affects an estimated 6.2 to 7.5 million people (American Association on Mental Retardation, 2002). Although the term *mental retardation* is still commonly used to refer to the condition, another term that has been used for individuals with these characteristics is **developmentally delayed**, meaning that their behavioral and cognitive skills exist at an earlier developmental stage than the skills of others who are the same chronological age (Smith & Mitchell, 2001). The DSM-IV-TR (American Psychiatric Association, 2000) still uses the term mental retardation but the American Association on Intellectual and Developmental Disabilities (AAIDD) is now using the term *intellectual*

developmentally delayed condition in which a person's behavioral and cognitive skills exist at an earlier developmental stage than the skills of others who are the same chronological age. A more acceptable term for mental retardation.

This middle-aged man, named Jack, lives in a small town in Arkansas and serves as a deacon in the local church. He is loved and respected and leads what, for him, is a full and happy life. Jack has Down syndrome and he has managed to find his place in the world.

disability (AAIDD, 2009). This new term is also being considered for use in the next edition of the DSM, the DSM-V (American Psychiatric Association, 2009).

So how would a professional go about deciding whether or not a child is developmentally delayed? Is the IQ test the primary method?

As indicated above, the diagnosis of mental retardation/developmental delay, according to the DSM-IV (American Psychiatric Association, 2000), is based not only on IQ tests scores but also on the strengths and weaknesses of the person in adaptive functioning and the onset of impairments in intellectual functioning and adaptive behavior is before 18 years of age (American Psychiatric Association, 2000). The recent recommendations from the AAIDD also require deficits in more than one area. According to their definition, intellectual disability refers to significant limitations not only in intellectual functioning but also in adaptive behavior that may be conceptual, social, or practical in nature (AAIDD, 2009).

Classifications Developmental delay can vary from mild to extremely severe. Even with their flaws, IQ test scores are still used to classify the various levels of delay, as can be seen in Table 7.7.

Causes What causes developmental delay? There are unhealthy living conditions that can affect brain development. Examples of such conditions are lead poisoning from eating paint chips (Lanphear et al., 2000), exposure to PCBs (Darvill et al., 2000), prenatal exposure to mercury (Grandjean et al., 1997) as well as other toxicants (Ericksson et al., 2001; Eskenazi et al., 1999; Schroeder, 2000), poor nutrition resulting in inadequate development of the brain, or a lack of mental stimulation in one's surroundings during the formative years of infancy and childhood (Shah, 1991). Such environmental conditions are said to produce familial retardation (Schroeder, 2000), a delay related to living in poverty conditions and one that usually produces relatively mild retardation.

The three most common biological causes of developmental delay are Down syndrome (ⓁⓘⓃⓀ *to Chapter Ten: Development Across the Life Span, p. 391*), fetal alcohol syndrome, and fragile X syndrome. *Fetal alcohol syndrome* is a condition that results from exposing a developing embryo to alcohol, and intelligence levels range from below average to developmentally delayed (Olson & Burgess, 1997).

◄ So how would a professional go about deciding whether or not a child is developmentally delayed? Is the IQ test the primary method?

Table 7.7   Classifications of Developmental Delay

CLASSIFICATION	RANGE OF IQ SCORES	ADAPTIVE LIMITATIONS	PERCENTAGE OF DEVELOPMENTALLY DELAYED POPULATION
Mild	55–70	Can reach sixth-grade skill level. Capable with training of living independently and being self-supporting. (This category makes up the vast majority of those with developmental delays.)	90%
Moderate	40–55	Can reach second-grade skill level. Can work and live in sheltered environments with supervision.	6%
Severe	25–40	Can learn to talk and perform basic self-care but needs constant supervision.	3%
Profound	Below 25	Very limited ability to learn, may only be able to learn very simple tasks, poor language skills and limited self-care.	1%

Source: Table based on classifications in DSM-IV-TR (American Psychiatric Association, 2000).

In *fragile X syndrome*, a male has a defect in a gene on the X chromosome of the twenty-third pair, leading to a deficiency in a protein needed for brain development. Depending on the severity of the damage to this gene, symptoms of fragile X syndrome can range from mild to severe or profound developmental delay (Dykens et al., 1994; Valverde et al., 2007).

There are many other causes of developmental delay (Murphy et al., 1998). Lack of oxygen at birth, damage to the fetus in the womb from diseases, infections, or drug use by the mother, and even diseases and accidents during childhood can lead to developmental delay.

One thing should always be remembered: Developmental delay affects a person's <u>intellectual</u> capabilities and adaptive behaviors. Developmentally delayed people are just as responsive to love and affection as anyone else and need to be loved and to have friends just as all people do. Intelligence is only one characteristic; warmth, friendliness, caring, and compassion also count for a great deal and should not be underrated.

Giftedness

7.7   What defines giftedness, and does being intellectually gifted guarantee success in life?

At the other end of the intelligence scale* are those who fall on the upper end of the normal curve (see Figure 7.4, p. 280) above an IQ of 130 (about 2 percent of the population). The term applied to these people is **gifted**, and if the IQ falls above 140 to

gifted   the 2 percent of the population falling on the upper end of the normal curve and typically possessing an IQ of 130 or above.

*Scale: a graded series of tests or performances used in rating individual intelligence or achievement.

145 (less than half of 1 percent of the population), the term is often *genius*. Some people use the term *genius* only for people with extremely high IQs or with other qualities that are extreme, such as creativity (Kamphaus, 1993).

I've heard that geniuses are sometimes a little "nutty" and odd. Are geniuses, especially the really high IQ ones, "not playing with a full deck," as the saying goes? People have long held many false beliefs about people who are very, very intelligent. One common phrase around the turn of the twentieth century was "early ripe, early rot," which meant that people expected young geniuses to lose their genius early in life (Shurkin, 1992). Other beliefs were that gifted people are weird and socially awkward, physically weak, and more likely to suffer from mental illnesses. From these beliefs comes the "mad scientist" of the cinema (think "Dr. Evil" of *Austin Powers*) and the "evil genius" of literature—Dr. Frankenstein, Dr. Jekyll, and Superman's archenemy,* Lex Luthor, to name a few.

These beliefs were shattered by a groundbreaking study that was initiated in 1921 by Lewis M. Terman, a psychologist at Stanford University. Terman (1925) selected 1,528 children to participate in a longitudinal study. ⒧ⒾⓃⓀ *to Chapter Ten: Development Across the Life Span, pp. 386–387.* These children, 857 boys and 671 girls, had IQs (as measured by the Stanford-Binet) ranging from 130 to 200. For more on Terman's famous study, see Classic Studies in Psychology.

The early findings of this major study (Terman & Oden, 1947) demonstrated that the gifted were socially well adjusted and often skilled leaders. They were also above average in height, weight, and physical attractiveness, putting an end to the myth of the weakling genius. Terman was able to demonstrate not only that his gifted children were *not* more susceptible to mental illness than the general population, but he was also able to show that they were actually more resistant to mental illnesses than those of average intelligence. Only those with the highest IQs (180 and above) were found to have some social and behavioral adjustment problems *as children* (Janos, 1987).

Terman's "Termites," as they came to be called, were also typically successful as adults. They earned more academic degrees and had higher occupational and financial success than their average peers (at least, the men in the study had occupational success—women at this time did not typically have careers outside the home). Researchers Zuo and Cramond (2001) examined some of Terman's gifted people to see if their identity formation as adolescents was related to later occupational success. ⒧ⒾⓃⓀ *to Chapter Ten: Development Across the Life Span, p. 419.* They found that most of the more successful "Termites" had in fact successfully achieved a consistent sense of self, whereas those who were less successful had not done so.

◄ I've heard that geniuses are sometimes a little "nutty" and odd. Are geniuses, especially the really high IQ ones, "not playing with a full deck," as the saying goes?

◄ **AP** * Identify key contributors in intelligence research and testing.

---

*Archenemy: a main enemy; the most important enemy.

A book by Joan Freeman called *Gifted Children Grown Up* (Freeman, 2001) describes the results of a similar longitudinal study of 210 gifted and nongifted children in Great Britain. One of the more interesting finds from this study is that gifted children who are "pushed" to achieve at younger and younger ages, sitting for exams long before their peers would do so, often grow up to be disappointed, somewhat unhappy adults. Freeman (2001) points to differing life conditions for the gifted as a major factor in their success, adjustment, and well-being: Some lived in poverty and some in wealth, for example. Yet another longitudinal study (Torrance, 1993) found that in both gifted students and gifted adults there is more to success in life than intelligence and high academic achievement. In that study, liking one's work, having a sense of purpose in life, a high energy level, and persistence were also very important factors. If the picture of the genius as mentally unstable is a myth, so, too, is the belief that being gifted will always lead to success, as even Terman found in his original study.

Classic Studies in Psychology

Terman's "Termites"

Terman's (1925) longitudinal study is still going on today, although many of his original subjects have passed away and those who remain are in their eighties. Terman himself died in 1956, but several other researchers (including Robert Sears, one of the original "Termites") have kept track of the remaining "Termites" over the years (Holahan & Sears, 1996).

As adults, the "Termites" were relatively successful, with a median income in the 1950s of $10,556, compared to the national median at that time of $5,800 a year. Most of them had graduated from college, many earning advanced degrees. Their occupations included doctors, lawyers, business executives, university professors, scientists, and even one famous science fiction writer and an Oscar-winning director (Edward Dmytryk, director of *The Caine Mutiny in 1954*, among others).

By 2000, only about 200 "Termites" were still living. Although the study was marred by several flaws, it still remains one of the most important and rich sources of data on an entire generation. Terman's study was actually the first truly longitudinal study (to Chapter Ten: *Development Across the Life Span, pp. 386–387*) ever to be accomplished, and scientists have gotten data about the effects of phenomena such as World War II and the influence of personality traits on how long one lives from the questionnaires filled out by the participants over the years.

Terman and Oden (1959) compared the 100 most successful men in the group to the 100 least successful by defining "successful" as holding jobs that related to or used their intellectual skills. The more successful men earned more money, had careers with more prestige, and were healthier and less likely to be divorced or alcoholics than the less successful men. The IQ scores were relatively equal between the two groups, so the differences in success in life had to be caused by some other factor or factors. Terman and Oden found that the successful adults were different from the others in three ways: They were more goal oriented, more persistent in pursuing those goals, and more self-confident than the less successful "Termites."

What were the flaws in this study? Terman acquired his participants by getting recommendations from teachers and principals, not through random selection, so that there was room for bias in the pool of participants from the start. It is quite possible that the teachers and principals were less likely, especially in 1921, to recommend students who were "troublemakers" or different from the majority. Consequently, Terman's original group consisted of almost entirely white, urban, and middle-class children, with the majority (856 out of 1,528) being male. There were two African Americans, six Japanese Americans, and one Native American.

Stanford University psychologist Lewis Terman is pictured at his desk in 1942. Terman spent a good portion of his career researching children with high IQ scores and was the first to use the term gifted to describe these children.

Another flaw is the way Terman interfered in the lives of his "children." In any good research study, the investigator should avoid becoming personally involved in the lives of the participants in the study to reduce the possibility of biasing the results. Terman seemed to find it nearly impossible to remain objective (Leslie, 2000). He became like a surrogate father to many of them, even going so far as to write a letter urging authorities to give Edward Dmytryk every consideration as they tried to determine whether 14-year-old runaway Edward was indeed being abused by his father or just telling a tall tale. Terman's letter did the trick, and Edward went to a good foster home and grew up to become a famous Hollywood director of 23 films. In another incident, one of Terman's Japanese American participants and family were in danger of being sent to an internment camp (essentially a prison camp) during World War II. They wrote to Terman and he again wrote a letter, this time to the government, vouching for the family's loyalty and arguing that they should not be interned. They were not interned. These are just two of the many ways in which Terman not only observed his participants but also influenced the course of their lives above and beyond their own intelligence levels.

Flawed as it may have been, Terman's groundbreaking study did accomplish his original goal of putting to rest the myths that existed about genius in the early part of the twentieth century. Gifted children and adults are no more prone to mental illnesses or odd behavior than any other group, and they also have their share of failures as well as successes. Genius is obviously not the only factor that influences success in life—personality and experiences are strong factors as well. For example, the homes of the children in the top 2 percent of Terman's group had an average of 450 books in their libraries, a sign that the parents of these children valued books and learning, and these parents were also more likely to be teachers, professionals, doctors, and lawyers. The experiences of these gifted children growing up would have been vastly different from those in homes with less emphasis on reading and lower occupational levels for the parents.

Questions for Further Discussion

1. In Terman and Oden's 1959 study of the successful and unsuccessful "Termites," what might be the problems associated with the definition of "successful" in the study?

2. Thinking back to the discussion of research ethics in Chapter One (pp. 35–36), what ethical violations may Terman have committed while involved in this study?

3. If gifted children thrive when growing up in more economically sound and educationally focused environments, what should the educational system strive to do to nourish the gifted? Should the government get involved in programs for the gifted?

Emotional Intelligence   What about people who have a lot of "book smarts" but not much common sense? There are people like that, who never seem to get ahead in life, in spite of having all that so-called intelligence. It is true that not everyone who is intellectually able is going to be a success in life (Mehrabian, 2000). Sometimes the people who are most successful are those who didn't do all that well in the regular academic setting.

One of the early explanations for why people who succeed in life did poorly in school and those who did well in school did not excel in the "real" world was that success relies on a certain degree of **emotional intelligence**, the awareness of and ability to manage one's own emotions as well as the ability to be self-motivated, to feel what others feel, and to be socially skilled (Persaud, 2001).

The concept of emotional intelligence was first introduced by Salovey and Mayer (1990) and later expanded upon by Goleman (1995). Goleman proposed that emotional intelligence is a more powerful influence on success in life than more traditional views of intelligence. One who is emotionally intelligent possesses self-control of emotions such as anger, impulsiveness, and anxiety. Empathy, the ability to

emotional intelligence the awareness of and ability to manage one's own emotions as well as the ability to be self-motivated, able to feel what others feel, and socially skilled.

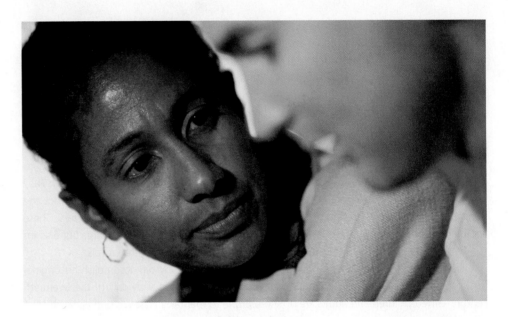

Emotional intelligence includes empathy, which is the ability to feel what others are feeling. This doctor is not only able to listen to her patient's problems but also is able to show by her facial expression, body language, and gestures that she understands how the patient feels.

> That all sounds very nice, but how can anything ▶ like this be measured?

understand what others feel, is also a component, as are an awareness of one's own emotions, sensitivity, persistence even in the face of frustrations, and the ability to motivate oneself (Salovey & Mayer, 1990).

That all sounds very nice, but how can anything like this be measured? Is there research to support this idea? In one study, researchers asked 321 participants to read passages written by nonparticipants and try to guess what the nonparticipants were feeling while they were writing (Mayer & Geher, 1996). The assumption was that people who were good at connecting thoughts to feelings would also have a high degree of empathy and emotional intelligence. The participants who more correctly judged the writers' emotional experiences (assessed by both how well each participant's emotional judgments agreed with a group consensus and the nonparticipant's actual report of feelings) also scored higher on the empathy measure and lower on the defensiveness measure. These same participants also had higher SAT scores (self-reported), leading Mayer and colleagues to conclude not only that emotional intelligence is a valid and measurable concept but also that general intelligence and emotional intelligence may be related: Those who are high in emotional intelligence are also smarter in the traditional sense (Mayer et al., 2000).

Although his own work and that of his colleagues provide empirical support for the concept of emotional intelligence, Mayer (1999) has criticized the presentation of emotional intelligence in popular magazines and best-selling (but nonscientific) books by stating in an online article for the American Psychological Association,

> . . . *the popular literature's implication—that highly emotionally intelligent people possess an unqualified advantage in life—appears overly enthusiastic at present and unsubstantiated by reasonable scientific standards.*

THE NATURE/NURTURE CONTROVERSY REGARDING INTELLIGENCE: GENETIC INFLUENCES

7.8 What is the influence of heredity and environment on the development of intelligence?

Are people born with all of the "smarts" they will ever have, or does experience and learning count for something in the development of intellect? The influence of nature (heredity or genes) and nurture (environment) on personality traits has long been

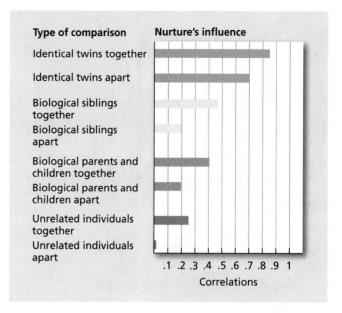

Figure 7.5 **Correlations Between IQ Scores of Persons with Various Relationships**
In the graph on the left, the degree of genetic relatedness seems to determine the agreement (correlation) between IQ scores of the various comparisons. For example, identical twins, who share 100 percent of their genes, are more similar in IQ than fraternal twins, who share only about 50 percent of their genes, even when raised in the same environment. In the graph on the right, identical twins are still more similar to each other in IQ than are other types of comparisons, but being raised in the same environment increases the similarity considerably.

debated in the field of human development, and intelligence is one of the traits that has been examined closely. Ⓛ Ⓘ Ⓝ Ⓚ *to Chapter Ten: Development Across the Life Span, pp. 387–388.*

Twin Studies   The problem with trying to separate the role of genes from that of environment is that controlled, perfect experiments are neither practical nor ethical. Instead, researchers find out what they can from *natural experiments,* circumstances existing in nature that can be examined to understand some phenomenon. *Twin studies* are an example of such circumstances.

Identical twins are those who originally came from one fertilized egg and, therefore, share the same genetic inheritance. Any differences between them on a certain trait, then, should be caused by environmental factors. Fraternal twins come from two different eggs, each fertilized by a different sperm, and share only the amount of genetic material that any two siblings would share. Ⓛ Ⓘ Ⓝ Ⓚ *to Chapter Ten: Development Across the Life Span, p. 391.* By comparing the IQs of these two types of twins reared together (similar environments) and reared apart (different environments), as well as persons of other degrees of relatedness, researchers can get a general, if not exact, idea of how much influence heredity has over the trait of intelligence (see Figure 7.5). As can be easily seen from the chart, the greater the degree of genetic relatedness, the stronger the correlation is between the IQ scores of those persons. The fact that genetically identical twins show a correlation of 0.86 means that the environment must play a part in determining some aspects of intelligence as measured by IQ tests. If heredity alone were responsible, the correlation between genetically identical twins should be 1.00. At this time, researchers have determined that the estimated *heritability* (proportion of change in IQ within a population that is caused by hereditary factors) for intelligence is about 0.50 or 50 percent (Plomin & DeFries, 1998).

Wait a minute—if identical twins have a correlation of 0.86, wouldn't that mean that intelligence is 86 percent inherited? Although the correlation between identical twins is higher than the estimated heritability of 0.50, that similarity is not entirely due to the twin's genetic similarity. Twins who are raised in the same household obviously share very similar environments as well. Even twins who are reared apart are usually placed in homes that are similar in socioeconomic and ethnic background—more similar than one might think. So when twins who are genetically similar are raised in similar environments, their IQ scores are also going to be similar.

◄ Wait a minute—if identical twins have a correlation of 0.86, wouldn't that mean that intelligence is 86 percent inherited?

"I told my parents that if grades were so important they should have paid for a smarter egg donor."

Although The Bell Curve *stated that Japanese Americans are genetically superior in intelligence, the book's authors overlook the influence of cultural values. Japanese American parents put much time and effort into helping their children with schoolwork.*

Heritability is worth a little more explanation because findings show that genes have significant influence on human behavior. A trait like height is one that is highly heritable; in a group of people who are all nearly equal in nourishment, for example, differences between them in height will be caused almost entirely by differences in their genes. But something like table manners is very low in heritability; table manners are a result of experience and upbringing, not genetics (Dickens & Flynn, 2001).

One of the things that people need to understand about heritability is that estimates of heritability apply only to changes in IQ within a *group* of people, *not to the individual people themselves.* Each individual is far too different in experiences, education, and other nongenetic factors to predict exactly how a particular set of genes will interact with those factors in that one person. Only differences among people *in general* can be investigated for the influence of genes (Dickens & Flynn, 2001). Genes always interact with environmental factors, and in some cases extreme environments can modify even very heritable traits, as would happen in the case of a severely malnourished child's growth pattern.

The Bell Curve and Misinterpretation of Statistics One of the other factors that has been examined for possible heritable differences in performance on IQ tests is the concept of race. (The term *race* is used in most of these investigations as a way to group people with common skin colors or facial features, and one should always be mindful of how suspect that kind of classification is. Cultural background, educational experiences, and socioeconomic factors typically have far more to do with similarities in group performances than does the color of one's skin.) In 1994, Herrnstein and Murray published the controversial book *The Bell Curve*, in which they cite large amounts of statistical studies (never published in scientific journals prior to the book) that led them to make the claim that IQ is largely inherited. These authors go further by also implying that people from lower economic levels are poor because they are unintelligent.

In their book, Herrnstein and Murray made several statistical errors and ignored the effects of environment and culture. First, they assumed that IQ tests actually do measure intelligence. As discussed earlier, IQ tests are not free of cultural or socioeconomic bias. So all they really found was a correlation between race and *IQ*, not race and *intelligence*. Second, they assumed that intelligence itself is very heavily influenced by genetics, with a heritability factor of about 0.80. The current estimate of the heritability of intelligence is about 0.50 (Plomin & DeFries, 1998).

Herrnstein and Murray also failed to understand that heritability only applies to differences that can be found *within* a group of people as opposed to those *between* groups of people or individuals (Gould, 1981). Heritability estimates can only be made truly from a group that was exposed to a similar environment.

One of their findings was that Japanese Americans are at the top of the IQ ladder, a finding that they attribute to racial and genetic characteristics. They seem to ignore the cultural influence of intense focus on education and achievement by Japanese American parents (Neisser et al., 1996). Scientists (Beardsley, 1995; Kamin, 1995) have concluded that, despite the claims of *The Bell Curve*, there is no real scientific evidence for genetic differences in intelligence *between* different racial groups. A series of studies, using blood-group testing for racial grouping (different racial groups have different rates of certain blood groups, allowing a statistical estimation of ancestry), found no significant relationship between ethnicity and IQ (Neisser et al., 1996).

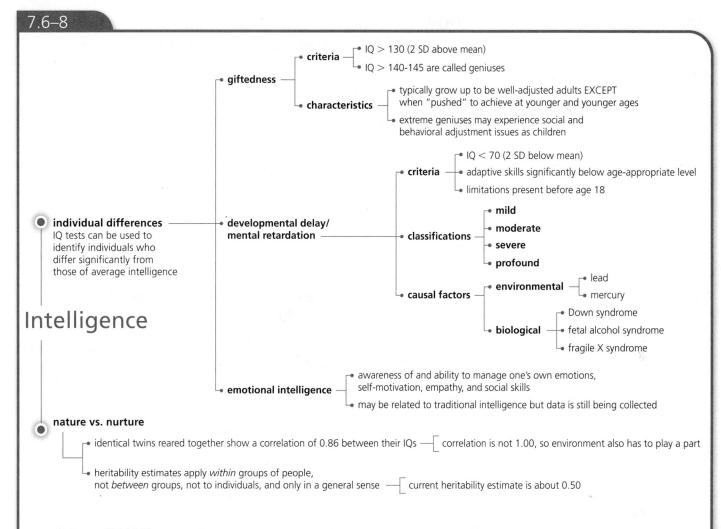

Intelligence

individual differences
IQ tests can be used to identify individuals who differ significantly from those of average intelligence

giftedness
- **criteria**
  - IQ > 130 (2 SD above mean)
  - IQ > 140-145 are called geniuses
- **characteristics**
  - typically grow up to be well-adjusted adults EXCEPT when "pushed" to achieve at younger and younger ages
  - extreme geniuses may experience social and behavioral adjustment issues as children

developmental delay/ mental retardation
- **criteria**
  - IQ < 70 (2 SD below mean)
  - adaptive skills significantly below age-appropriate level
  - limitations present before age 18
- **classifications**
  - **mild**
  - **moderate**
  - **severe**
  - **profound**
- **causal factors**
  - **environmental**
    - lead
    - mercury
  - **biological**
    - Down syndrome
    - fetal alcohol syndrome
    - fragile X syndrome

emotional intelligence
- awareness of and ability to manage one's own emotions, self-motivation, empathy, and social skills
- may be related to traditional intelligence but data is still being collected

nature vs. nurture
- identical twins reared together show a correlation of 0.86 between their IQs — correlation is not 1.00, so environment also has to play a part
- heritability estimates apply *within* groups of people, not *between* groups, not to individuals, and only in a general sense — current heritability estimate is about 0.50

PRACTICE **QUIZ:** PREPARING FOR THE AP* EXAM   ANSWERS ON PAGE AK-2.

Directions: Read each of the questions or incomplete sentences below. Then choose the response that best answers the question or completes the sentence.

1. Jared is 35 years old, but his cognitive abilities have never gone beyond the level of a second-grade child. At what level of developmental delay would Jared be classified?
   a. Mild
   b. Moderate
   c. Severe
   d. Profound
   e. Adaptive

2. A male with a defective chromosome leading to severe protein deficiency and poor brain development probably suffers from _____.
   a. Down syndrome
   b. fetal alcohol syndrome
   c. hydrocephaly
   d. fragile X syndrome
   e. familial retardation

3. Elizabeth was tested while in grade school and was found to have an IQ of 134. Elizabeths intelligen ce level can be labeled as _____.
   a. average
   b. somewhat above normal
   c. moderate
   d. genius
   e. gifted

4. Which of the following statements about Terman's "Termites" is not true?
   a. The successful men earned more money
   b. The successful men were more likely to be divorced
   c. The unsuccessful men were less healthy
   d. The unsuccessful men held jobs of lower prestige
   e. The successful men had a consistent sense of self

Language

7.9 How is language defined, and what are its different elements and structure?

Language is a system for combining symbols (such as words) so that an infinite* number of meaningful statements can be made for the purpose of communicating with others. Language allows people not only to communicate with one another but also to represent their own internal mental activity. In other words, language is a very important part of how people think.

THE LEVELS OF LANGUAGE ANALYSIS

The structures of languages all over the world share common characteristics. Languages involve word order, word meanings, the rules for making words into other words, the sounds that exist within a language, the rules for practical communication with others, and the meanings of sentences and phrases.

Grammar **Grammar** is the system of rules governing the structure and use of a language. According to famed linguist Noam Chomsky (Chomsky, 2006; Chomsky et al., 2002), humans have an innate ability to understand and produce language through a device he calls the *language acquisition device,* or *LAD.* While humans may learn the *specific* language (English, Spanish, Mandarin, etc.) through the processes of imitation, reinforcement, and shaping, ⓁⒾⓃⓀ *to Chapter Five: Learning, p. 193,* the complexities of the grammar of a language are, according to Chomsky, to some degree "wired in" to the developing brain. The LAD "listens" to the language input of the infant's world and then begins to produce language sounds and eventually words and sentences in a pattern found across cultures. This pattern is discussed in greater detail in Chapter Ten. ⓁⒾⓃⓀ *to Chapter Ten: Development Across the Life Span, pp. 405–406.* Grammar includes rules for the order of words known as syntax, morphology (the study of the formation of words), phonemes (the basic sounds of language), and pragmatics (the practical social expectations and uses of language).

Syntax **Syntax** is a system of rules for combining words and phrases to form grammatically correct sentences. Syntax is quite important, as just a simple mix-up can cause sentences to be completely misunderstood. For example, "John kidnapped the boy" has a different meaning from "John, the kidnapped boy," although all four words are the same (Lasnik, 1990). Another example of the importance of syntax can be found in the lobby of a Moscow hotel across from a monastery: "You are welcome to visit the cemetery where famous composers, artists, and writers are buried daily except Thursday." So if people want to watch famous composers, artists, and writers being buried, they should not go to this monastery on Thursday.

Morphemes **Morphemes** are the smallest units of meaning within a language. For example, the word *playing* consists of two morphemes, *play* and *ing.* Morphemes themselves are governed by **semantics**, rules for determining the meaning of words and sentences. Sentences, for example, can have the same semantic meaning while having different syntax: "Johnny hit the ball" and "the ball was hit by Johnny."

Phonemes **Phonemes** are the basic units of sound in a language. The *a* in the word *car* is a very different phoneme from the *a* in the word *day,* even though it is the same letter of the alphabet. The difference is in how we say the sound of the *a* in each word. Phonemes are more than just the different ways in which we pronounce single letters, too. *Th, sh,* and *au* are also phonemes. Phonemes for different languages are also

language a system for combining symbols (such as words) so that an unlimited number of meaningful statements can be made for the purpose of communicating with others.

grammar the system of rules governing the structure and use of a language.

syntax the system of rules for combining words and phrases to form grammatically correct sentences.

morphemes the smallest units of meaning within a language.

semantics the rules for determining the meaning of words and sentences.

phonemes the basic units of sound in language.

---

*Infinite: unlimited, without end.

different, and one of the biggest problems for people who are trying to learn another language is the inability to both hear and pronounce the phonemes of that other language. Although infants are born with the ability to recognize all phonemes (Werker & Lalonde, 1988), after about nine months, that ability has deteriorated and the infant recognizes only the phonemes of the language to which the infant is exposed (Boyson-Bardies et al., 1989).

Pragmatics   The **pragmatics** of language has do with the practical aspects of communicating with others, or the social "niceties" of language. Simply put, pragmatics involves knowing things like how to take turns in a conversation, the use of gestures to emphasize a point or indicate a need for more information, and the different ways in which one speaks to different people (Yule, 1996). For example, adults speak to small children differently than they do to other adults by using simpler words. Both adults and children use higher-pitched voices and many repeated phrases when talking to infants. Part of the pragmatics of language includes knowing just what rhythm and emphasis to use when communicating with others, called *intonation*. When speaking to infants, adults and children are changing the inflection when they use the higher pitch and stress certain words differently than others. Some languages, such as Japanese, are highly sensitive to intonation, meaning that changing the stress or pitch of certain words or syllables of a particular word can change its meaning entirely (Beckman & Pierrehumbert, 1986). For example, the Japanese name "Yoshiko" should be pronounced with the accent or stress on the first syllable: YO-she-koh. This pronunciation of the name means "woman-child." But if the stress is placed on the second syllable (yo-SHE-ko), the name means "woman who urinates."

Pragmatics involves the practical aspects of communicating. This young mother is talking and then pausing for the infant's response. In this way, the infant is learning about taking turns, an important aspect of language development. What kinds of games do adults play with infants that also aid the development of language?

THE RELATIONSHIP BETWEEN LANGUAGE AND THOUGHT

7.10   Does language influence the way people think, and are animals capable of learning language?

As with the controversy of nature versus nurture, researchers have long debated the relationship between language and thought. Does language actually influence thought, or does thinking influence language?

Two very influential developmental psychologists, Jean Piaget and Lev Vygotsky, often debated the relationship of language and thought (Duncan, 1995). Piaget (1926, 1962) theorized that concepts preceded and aided the development of language. For example, a child would have to have a concept or mental schema for "mother" before being able to learn the word "mama." In a sense, concepts become the "pegs" upon which words are "hung." Piaget also noticed that preschool children seemed to spend a great deal of time talking to themselves—even when playing with another child. Each child would be talking about something totally unrelated to the speech of the other, in a process Piaget called *collective monologue.* Piaget believed that this kind of nonsocial speech was very egocentric (from the child's point of view only, with no regard for the listener), and that as the child became more socially involved and less egocentric, these nonsocial speech patterns would reduce.

Vygotsky, however, believed almost the opposite. He theorized that language actually helped develop concepts and that language could also help the child learn to control behavior—including social behavior (Vygotsky, 1962, 1978, 1987). For Vygotsky, the word helped form the concept: Once a child had learned the word "mama," the various elements of "mama-ness"—*warm, soft, food, safety,* and so on— could come together around that word. Vygotsky also believed that the "egocentric" speech of the preschool child was actually a way for the child to form thoughts and control actions. This "private speech" was a way for children to plan their behavior

pragmatics aspects of language involving the practical ways of communicating with others, or the social "niceties" of language.

and organize actions so that their goals could be obtained. Since socializing with other children would demand much more self-control and behavioral regulation on the part of the preschool child, Vygotsky believed that private speech would actually *increase* as children became more socially active in the preschool years. This was, of course, the opposite of Piaget's assumption, and the evidence seems to bear out Vygotsky's view: Children, especially bright children, do tend to use more private speech when learning how to socialize with other children or when working on a difficult task (Berk, 1992; Berk & Spuhl, 1995; Bivens & Berk, 1990).

Linguistic Relativity Hypothesis   The hypothesis that language shapes and influences thoughts was accepted by many theorists, with a few notable exceptions, such as Piaget. One of the best-known versions of this view is the Sapir-Whorf hypothesis (named for the two theorists who developed it, Edward Sapir and his student, Benjamin Lee Whorf). This hypothesis assumes that the thought processes and concepts within any culture are determined by the words of the culture (Sapir, 1921; Whorf, 1956). It has come to be known as the **linguistic relativity hypothesis**, meaning that thought processes and concepts are controlled by (relative to) language. That is, the words people use determine much of the way in which they think about the world around them.

One of the most famous examples used by Whorf to support this idea was that of the Inuits, Native Americans living in the Arctic. Supposedly, the Inuits have many more words for *snow* than do people in other cultures. One estimate was 23 different words, whereas other estimates have ranged in the hundreds. Unfortunately, this anecdotal evidence has turned out to be false, being more myth than reality (Pullum, 1991). In fact, English speakers also have many different words for snow (sleet, slush, powder, dusting, and yellow, to name a few).

Is there evidence for the linguistic relativity hypothesis? Neither Sapir nor Whorf provided any scientific studies that would support their proposition. There have been numerous studies by other researchers, however. For example, in one study researchers assumed that a language's color names would influence the ability of the people who grew up with that language to distinguish among and perceive colors. The study found that basic color terms did directly influence color recognition memory (Lucy & Shweder, 1979). But an earlier series of studies of the perception of colors (Rosch-Heider, 1972; Rosch-Heider & Olivier, 1972) had already found just the opposite effect: Members of the Dani tribe, who have only two names for colors, were no different in their ability to perceive all of the colors than were the English speakers in the study. More recent studies (Davies et al., 1998a, 1998b; Laws et al., 1995; Pinker & Bloom, 1990) support Rosch-Heider's findings and the idea of a **cognitive universalism** (concepts are universal and influence the development of language) rather than linguistic relativity.

Other research suggests that although the linguistic relativity hypothesis may not work for fine perceptual discriminations such as those in the Rosch-Heider studies, it may be an appropriate explanation for concepts of a higher level. In one study, researchers showed pictures of two animals to preschool children (Gelman & Markman, 1986). The pictures were of a flamingo and a bat. The children were told that the flamingo feeds its baby mashed-up food but the bat feeds its baby milk. Then they were shown a picture of a blackbird (which looked more like the bat than the flamingo). Half of the children were told that the blackbird was a bird, while the other children were not. When asked how the blackbird fed its baby, the children who had been given the bird label were more likely to say that it fed its baby mashed-up food than were the children who were not given the label, indicating that the preschoolers were making inferences about feeding habits based on category membership rather than perceptual similarity—the word *bird* helped the children who were given that label to place the blackbird in its proper higher-level category.

linguistic relativity hypothesis the theory that thought processes and concepts are controlled by language.

cognitive universalism theory that concepts are universal and influence the development of language.

Psychologists cannot deny the influence of language on problem solving, cognition, and memory. Sometimes a problem can simply be worded differently to have the solution become obvious, and memory (LINK to Chapter Six: Memory, p. 232) is certainly stored in terms of the semantics of language. Language can definitely influence the perception of others as well—"computer geek" and "software engineer" might be used to describe the same person, but one phrase is obviously less flattering and the image brought to mind is different for the two terms. In the end, trying to determine whether language influences thoughts or thoughts influence language may be like trying to determine which came first, the chicken or the egg.

Animal Studies in Language

I've heard that chimpanzees can be taught to use sign language. Is this for real, or are the chimps just performing tricks like the animals in the circus or the zoo? There are really two questions about animals and language. The first is "can animals communicate?" and the second is "can animals use language?" The answer to the first question is a definite "yes." Animals communicate in many ways. They use sounds such as the rattle of a rattlesnake or the warning growl of an angry dog. There are also physical behaviors, such as the "dance" of honeybees that tells the other bees where a source of pollen is (Gould & Gould, 1994). But the answer to the second question is more complicated, because language is defined as the use of symbols, and symbols are things that stand for something else. Words are symbols, and gestures can be symbols. But the gestures used by animals are instinctual, meaning they are controlled by the animal's genetic makeup. The honeybee doing the "dance" is controlled completely by instinct, as is the growling dog. In human language, symbols are used quite deliberately and voluntarily, not by instinct, and abstract symbols have no meaning until people assign meaning to them. (Although Chomsky's innate language acquisition device might lead some to think that language for humans is instinctual, it should be noted that the infant's production of speech sounds becomes quite deliberate within a short period of time.)

Can animals be taught to use symbols that are abstract? There have been attempts to teach animals how to use sign language (as animals lack the vocal structure to form spoken words), but many of these attempts were simply not "good science." The most successful of these experiments (which is not without its critics as well) has been with Kanzi, a bonobo chimpanzee trained to press abstract symbols on a computer keyboard (Savage-Rumbaugh & Lewin, 1994). Kanzi actually was not the original subject of the study—his mother, Matata, was the chimp being trained. She did not learn many of the symbols, but Kanzi watched his mother use the keyboard and appeared to learn how to use the symbols through that observation. At last count, Kanzi could understand about 150 spoken English words. Trainers who speak to him are not in his view, so he is not responding to physical cues or symbols. He has managed to follow correctly complex instructions up to the level of a $2\frac{1}{2}$-year-old child (Savage-Rumbaugh et al., 1998). The most recent studies with Kanzi have him making sounds that seem to have consistent meaning across different situations (Tagliatatela et al., 2003). Nearly 100 videotaped hours of Kanzi engaged in day-to-day activites were analyzed for these sounds. The researchers were able to identify four sounds that seemed to represent banana, grapes, juice, and the word *yes*. (However, remember that four sounds do not come close to making an entire language.)

I've heard that chimpanzees can be taught to use sign language. Is this for real, or are the chimps just performing tricks like the animals in the circus or the zoo?

Kanzi looks at the keyboard used in teaching language to chimpanzees. Kanzi's language abilities were learned through watching researchers train his mother rather than directly—much as a human infant learns through listening to the speech of adults.

Other studies, with dolphins (Herman et al., 1993) and with parrots such as Alex in the opening story (Pepperberg, 1998, 2007), have also met with some success. Is it real language? The answer seems to be a qualified "yes." The qualification is that none of the animals that have achieved success so far can compare to the level of language development of a 3-year-old human child (Pinker, 1995). However, linguists still debate whether these animals are truly learning language if they are not also learning how to use syntax—combining words into grammatically correct sentences as well as being able to understand the differences between sentences such as "The girl kissed the boy" and "The boy kissed the girl." As yet, there is no evidence that any of the animals trained in language have been able to master syntax (Demers, 1988; Johnson, 1995; Pinker, 1995). ✳ Explore on MyPsychLab

✳ **Explore** animal studies and language. **www.mypsychlab.com**

7.9–10

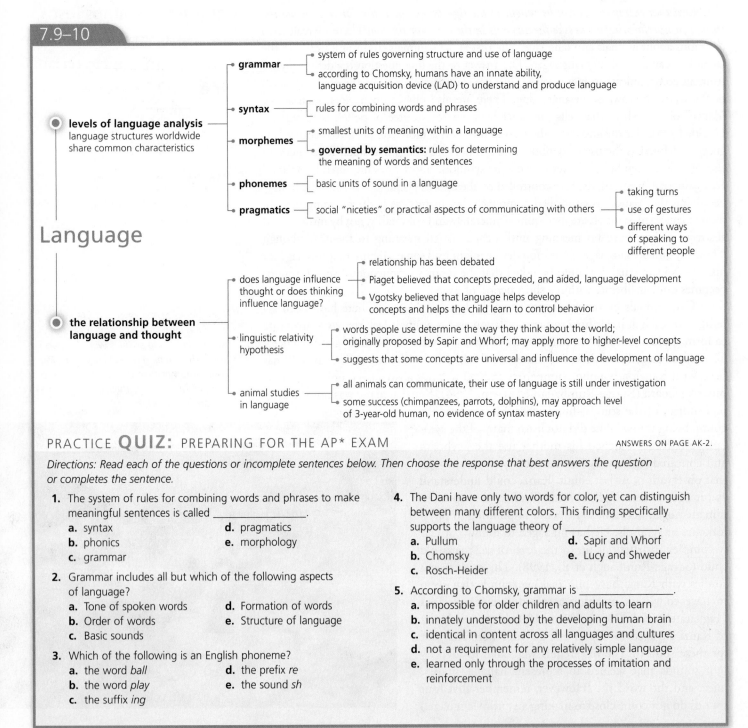

Language

levels of language analysis
language structures worldwide share common characteristics

- **grammar**
  - system of rules governing structure and use of language
  - according to Chomsky, humans have an innate ability, language acquisition device (LAD) to understand and produce language
- **syntax** — rules for combining words and phrases
- **morphemes**
  - smallest units of meaning within a language
  - **governed by semantics:** rules for determining the meaning of words and sentences
- **phonemes** — basic units of sound in a language
- **pragmatics** — social "niceties" or practical aspects of communicating with others
  - taking turns
  - use of gestures
  - different ways of speaking to different people

the relationship between language and thought

- does language influence thought or does thinking influence language?
  - relationship has been debated
  - Piaget believed that concepts preceded, and aided, language development
  - Vgotsky believed that language helps develop concepts and helps the child learn to control behavior
- linguistic relativity hypothesis
  - words people use determine the way they think about the world; originally proposed by Sapir and Whorf; may apply more to higher-level concepts
  - suggests that some concepts are universal and influence the development of language
- animal studies in language
  - all animals can communicate, their use of language is still under investigation
  - some success (chimpanzees, parrots, dolphins), may approach level of 3-year-old human, no evidence of syntax mastery

PRACTICE **QUIZ:** PREPARING FOR THE AP* EXAM

ANSWERS ON PAGE AK-2.

Directions: Read each of the questions or incomplete sentences below. Then choose the response that best answers the question or completes the sentence.

1. The system of rules for combining words and phrases to make meaningful sentences is called _____.
   a. syntax
   b. phonics
   c. grammar
   d. pragmatics
   e. morphology

2. Grammar includes all but which of the following aspects of language?
   a. Tone of spoken words
   b. Order of words
   c. Basic sounds
   d. Formation of words
   e. Structure of language

3. Which of the following is an English phoneme?
   a. the word *ball*
   b. the word *play*
   c. the suffix *ing*
   d. the prefix *re*
   e. the sound *sh*

4. The Dani have only two words for color, yet can distinguish between many different colors. This finding specifically supports the language theory of _____.
   a. Pullum
   b. Chomsky
   c. Rosch-Heider
   d. Sapir and Whorf
   e. Lucy and Shweder

5. According to Chomsky, grammar is _____.
   a. impossible for older children and adults to learn
   b. innately understood by the developing human brain
   c. identical in content across all languages and cultures
   d. not a requirement for any relatively simple language
   e. learned only through the processes of imitation and reinforcement

Applying Psychology to Everyday Life: Mental Exercises for Better Cognitive Health

7.11 What are some ways to improve thinking?

The brain is not a muscle, but it needs exercise to stay fit, just as muscles do. Research has shown that people who regularly work crossword puzzles, take classes, read, and stay mentally active are less likely to develop senile dementia than those who do not (Ball et al., 2002; Cabeza et al., 2002; Wilson et al., 2002). Neuroscientists researching Alzheimer's disease ((L)(I)(N)(K) *to Chapter Six: Memory, pp. 253–254*) have found that this kind of "brain exercise" may help to improve the brain's ability to develop extra neural connections—new neurons and the axons and dendrites that connect them, an ability called **cognitive reserve** (Scarmeas et al., 2003).

Cognitive reserve may explain why up to two-thirds of the autopsies of elderly women in one study showed that they had signs of advanced Alzheimer's disease at the time of death, in spite of the fact that these women had shown no signs of dementia or cognitive impairment before they died (Katzman et al., 1989). The theory is that having extra neurons and neural connections compensates for the neurons that are being damaged by the Alzheimer's progression. Since it is difficult to know who might develop Alzheimer's or one of the many other forms of dementia, building up a cognitive reserve is a good idea.

How can you increase your cognitive reserve? Cognitive reserve is greater in people who finish higher levels of education—the intellectual challenges help form new neural connections, especially early in life (see, aren't you glad you're reading this while you're in college?). Those who are socially as well as intellectually active are also building up their cognitive reserves (Scarmeas et al., 2001, 2003). And believe it or not, you really are what you eat: Studies have shown that those who follow a "Mediterranean diet"—one high in vegetables, fruits, whole grains, and legumes and low in saturated fats—are less at risk for developing Alzheimer's disease, perhaps because of the increased health of the blood supply to the brain related to this kind of healthy eating (Scarmeas et al., 2006, 2007).

In addition to challenging one's brain, socializing, and eating right, there are any number of mental "gymnastics" available to people wishing to improve their cognitive health. The following are a few of the mental exercises taken from *Brain Fitness,* by Monique LePoncin, the founder of the French National Institute for Research on the Prevention of Cerebral Aging (LePoncin, 1990). The exercises that follow are based on the various mental abilities, such as memory and perception, that have been researched in human thought processes. Many of these can be done while traveling to or from work, shopping, or doing other errands, during breaks, or even when in the bathroom.

PERCEPTIVE ABILITY EXERCISES

1. For sight, try to look at an object such as a photograph or a person you pass on the street. Draw it (or him or her) immediately to exercise short-term memory. At the end of the week, redraw the seven things you have observed during the seven days—an exercise of long-term memory.

2. For smell and taste (which do decline with age), try to identify the ingredients in whatever food you are eating at a friend's house or in a restaurant. Concentrate on the herbs and spices, and ask the host or wait staff to confirm your guesses.

3. For memory, try to memorize the dishes on your favorite restaurant's menu. If you want a greater challenge, memorize the prices, too. At the end of the day, try to write as many of the dishes and prices down as you can.

cognitive reserve The ability of the brain to build and maintain new neurons and the connections between them.

4. For hearing as well as memory, try to recognize callers on the phone by voice alone, before they identify themselves. (No fair looking at the caller ID!) Memorize the phone numbers and then write down both the people and the numbers of those with whom you spoke at the end of the day. Repeat at the end of the week for the entire week.

5. Another exercise for smell as well as touch is to try to identify objects with your eyes closed.

6. Visuospatial abilities are used to estimate distances, areas, and volumes (handy when packing a suitcase or storing items away in a box). When you walk into a room, try to determine how many people are on your right and on your left, as well as where the objects in the room are, as quickly as you can. Draw maps of the places you have visited when you return home, and draw them again the next day.

7. Working jigsaw puzzles as quickly as possible will exercise your ability to build a logical whole from different elements.

8. Exercising logical thinking can be accomplished by using memory systems to remember the items you need to buy in the store rather than using a list. Any of the systems mentioned in the Introduction (Ⓛⓘⓝⓚ *to Introduction, pp. I-11 to I-12*) will work. Play card games and board games that use strategy like bridge, chess, or checkers, and do word games like crosswords, anagrams, and word searches. Don't play the same games all the time; mix them up for variety.

9. Exercise your verbal abilities by listening to the news and writing down the main points at some later time in the day. When reading a chapter of a book, try to imagine having to summarize it as briefly as possible to someone who has not read it. Do the same thing for the whole book when finished.

Questions for Further Discussion

1. What other kinds of mental activities might help to keep the brain fit?

2. Should doctors suggest mental fitness exercises to their patients?

3. What media sources (e.g., television, magazines) exist that help to promote mental fitness?

---

7 | CHAPTER SUMMARY

How People Think

- Thinking (cognition) is mental activity that occurs in the brain when information is being organized, stored, communicated, or processed.

7.1 How are mental images and concepts involved in the process of thinking?

- Mental images represent objects or events and have a picture-like quality.

- Concepts are ideas that represent a class or category of events, objects, or activities.

- Prototypes are examples of a concept that more closely match the defining characteristics of that concept.

7.2 What are the methods people use to solve problems and make decisions, and can a machine be made to think like a person?

- Problem solving consists of thinking and behaving in certain ways to reach a goal.

- Mechanical solutions include trial-and-error learning and rote solutions.
- Algorithms are a type of rote solution in which one follows step-by-step procedures for solving certain types of problems.
- A heuristic or "rule of thumb" is a strategy that narrows down the possible solutions for a problem.
- Insight is the sudden perception of a solution to a problem.

Psychology in the News: Artificial Intelligence (AI)

- Artificial intelligence refers to the attempt to create a machine that thinks like a human being.
- Although some computers have been designed that can play chess and perform in similar ways to a human, the true flexibility of human thought processes has yet to be developed in a machine.

7.3 Why does problem solving sometimes fail, and what is meant by creative thinking?

- Functional fixedness is the tendency to perceive objects as having only the use for which they were originally intended and, therefore, failing to see them as possible tools for solving other problems.
- Confirmation bias is the tendency to search for evidence that confirms one's beliefs, ignoring any evidence to the contrary.
- Divergent thinking involves coming up with as many different answers as possible. This is a kind of creativity (combining ideas or behavior in new ways).
- Creative people are usually good at mental imagery and have knowledge on a wide range of topics, are unafraid to be different, value their independence, and are often unconventional in their work but not in other areas.

Intelligence

7.4 How do psychologists define intelligence, and how do various theories of intelligence differ?

- Intelligence is the ability to understand the world, think rationally or logically, and use resources effectively when faced with challenges or problems.
- Spearman proposed general intelligence, or g factor, as the ability to reason and solve problems, whereas specific intelligence, or s factor, includes task-specific abilities in certain areas such as music, business, or art.
- Gardner proposed nine different types of intelligence, ranging from verbal, linguistic, and mathematical to interpersonal and intrapersonal intelligence.
- Sternberg proposed three types of intelligence: analytical, creative, and practical.
- Emotional intelligence is viewed as a powerful influence on success in life.

7.5 How is intelligence measured, and how are intelligence tests constructed?

- The Stanford-Binet Intelligence Test yields an IQ score that was once determined by dividing the mental age of the person by the chronological age and multiplying that quotient by 100 but now involves comparing a person's score to a standardized norm.

- The Wechsler Intelligence Tests yield four index scores derived from both verbal and nonverbal subtests and an overall score of intelligence.
- Standardization, validity, and reliability are all important factors in the construction of an intelligence test.
- Deviation IQs are based on the normal curve, defining different levels of intelligence based on the deviation of scores from a common mean.
- IQ tests are often criticized for being culturally biased.

7.6 What is mental retardation, and what are its causes?

- Mental retardation or developmental delay is a condition in which IQ falls below 70 and adaptive behavior is severely deficient for a person of a particular chronological age.
- The four levels of delay are mild (55–70 IQ), moderate (40–55 IQ), severe (25–40 IQ), and profound (below 25 IQ).
- Causes of developmental delay include deprived environments as well as chromosome and genetic disorders and dietary deficiencies.

7.7 What defines giftedness, and does being intellectually gifted guarantee success in life?

- Gifted persons are defined as those having IQ scores at the upper end of the normal curve (130 or above).

Classic Studies in Psychology: Terman's "Termites"

- Terman conducted a longitudinal study that demonstrated that gifted children grow up to be successful adults for the most part.
- Terman's study has been criticized for a lack of objectivity because Terman became too involved in the lives of several of his participants, even to the point of intervening on their behalf.

7.8 What is the influence of heredity and environment on the development of intelligence?

- Stronger correlations are found between IQ scores as genetic relatedness increases. Heritability of IQ is estimated at 0.50.
- In 1994, Herrnstein and Murray published *The Bell Curve* in which they made widely criticized claims about the heritability of intelligence.

Language

7.9 How is language defined, and what are its different elements and structure?

- Language is a system for combining symbols so that an infinite number of meaningful statements can be created and communicated to others.
- Grammar is the system of rules by which language is governed and includes the rules for using phonemes, morphemes, and syntax. Pragmatics refers to practical aspects of language.

7.10 Does language influence the way people think, and are animals capable of learning language?

- Sapir and Whorf originally proposed that language controls and helps the development of thought processes and concepts, an idea that is known as the linguistic relativity hypothesis.
- Other researchers have found evidence that concepts are universal and directly influence the development of language, called the cognitive universalism viewpoint.

- Studies with chimpanzees, parrots, and dolphins have been somewhat successful in demonstrating that animals can develop a basic kind of language, including some abstract ideas.
- Controversy exists over the lack of evidence that animals can learn syntax, which some feel means that animals are not truly learning and using language.

Applying Psychology to Everyday Life: Mental Exercises for Better Cognitive Health

7.11 What are some ways to improve thinking?

- Mental activity that requires creativity and the use of memory abilities, such as working crossword puzzles and reading books, can help to keep the brain fit.

TEST YOURSELF: PREPARING FOR THE AP* EXAM

ANSWERS ON PAGE AK-2.

✓●—|Practice on **MyPsychLab**　**Ready for your test?** More quizzes and a customized study plan. **www.mypsychlab.com**

PART I: MULTIPLE-CHOICE QUESTIONS

Directions for Part I: Read each of the questions or incomplete sentences below. Then choose the response that best answers the question or completes the sentence.

1. Algorithms are a type of _____.
   a. heuristic
   b. mental set
   c. rule of thumb
   d. mechanical solution
   e. means-end analysis

2. Which heuristic can be used to create and maintain stereotypes?
   a. Insight
   b. Availability
   c. Representative
   d. Means-end analysis
   e. Working backward from a goal

3. When people persist in trying to solve a problem the same way they have always gone about solving problems, they have developed _____.
   a. a mental set
   b. functional fixedness
   c. confirmation bias
   d. transformation bias
   e. emotional intelligence

4. Which of the following questions would be most likely to produce divergent thinking?
   a. What is a stapler?
   b. How do you spell *stapler*?
   c. What is a stapler's main use?
   d. What does a stapler look like?
   e. How many uses can you think of for a stapler?

5. According to Sternberg, "street smarts" is another way of talking about which kind of intelligence?
   a. Analytical　　　　d. Emotional
   b. Creative　　　　　e. Interpersonal
   c. Practical

6. Which of the following makes the Weschler tests different from the Stanford-Binet?
   a. The Stanford-Binet is designed only for adults.
   b. The Stanford-Binet has both a verbal and a performance component.
   c. The Weschler tests are administered to individuals.
   d. The Weschler tests are designed only for children.
   e. Different Weschler tests exist for preschoolers, older children, and adults.

7. A test that gives similar scores for a person each time the person takes it is considered to be _____.
   a. valid
   b. reliable
   c. flawless
   d. unbiased
   e. standardized

8. Denny is mildly retarded. His mother drank heavily while pregnant with him. Denny most likely suffers from _____.
   a. cretinism
   b. Down syndrome
   c. fragile X syndrome
   d. familial retardation
   e. fetal alcohol syndrome

9. The current estimate of heritability of intelligence is _____.
   a. 0.99
   b. 0.90
   c. 0.86
   d. 0.50
   e. 0.34

10. The linguistic relativity hypothesis states that _____.
   a. language shapes thoughts
   b. thoughts shape language
   c. thought is impossible without language
   d. language and thought influence each other
   e. language and thought develop independently

PART II: FREE-RESPONSE QUESTION

Directions for Part II: Read the essay question that follows. Then, respond to the question in a clear, concise essay. Do not simply list facts. Instead, present a thorough argument based on your critical consideration of the topic. Use proper psychological terminology as necessary.

Prashant, a student who has recently moved to the United States from India, takes an IQ test. In a well-organized essay, explain how each of the following factors could potentially contribute to Prashant's score on the test:

   a. Mental sets
   b. Divergent thinking
   c. Test validity
   d. Cultural bias
   e. Fragile X syndrome

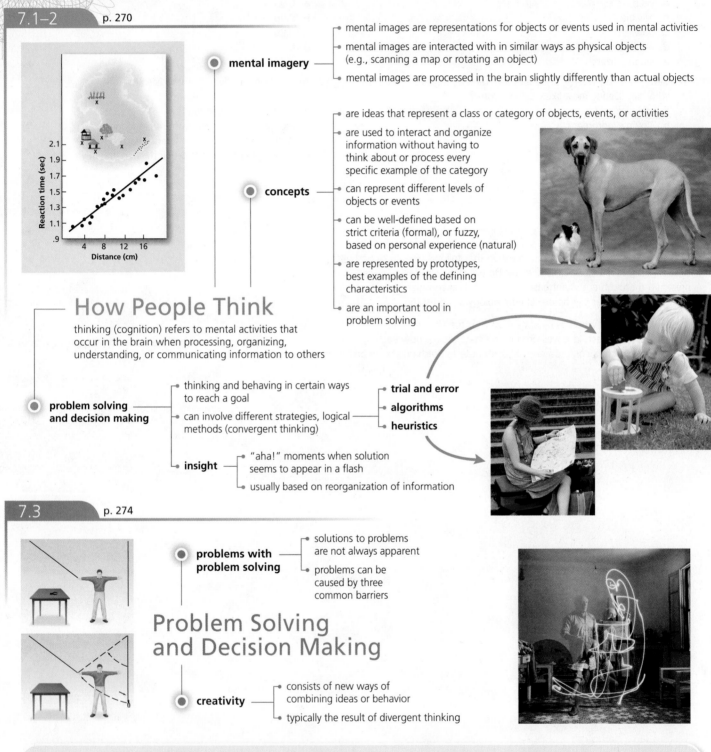

7.1–2   p. 270

mental imagery
- mental images are representations for objects or events used in mental activities
- mental images are interacted with in similar ways as physical objects (e.g., scanning a map or rotating an object)
- mental images are processed in the brain slightly differently than actual objects

concepts
- are ideas that represent a class or category of objects, events, or activities
- are used to interact and organize information without having to think about or process every specific example of the category
- can represent different levels of objects or events
- can be well-defined based on strict criteria (formal), or fuzzy, based on personal experience (natural)
- are represented by prototypes, best examples of the defining characteristics
- are an important tool in problem solving

How People Think

thinking (cognition) refers to mental activities that occur in the brain when processing, organizing, understanding, or communicating information to others

problem solving and decision making
- thinking and behaving in certain ways to reach a goal
- can involve different strategies, logical methods (convergent thinking)
  - trial and error
  - algorithms
  - heuristics

insight
- "aha!" moments when solution seems to appear in a flash
- usually based on reorganization of information

7.3   p. 274

problems with problem solving
- solutions to problems are not always apparent
- problems can be caused by three common barriers

Problem Solving and Decision Making

creativity
- consists of new ways of combining ideas or behavior
- typically the result of divergent thinking

Table 7.2 Stimulating Divergent Thinking	
Brainstorming	Generating as many ideas as possible in a short period of time, without judging each idea's merits until all ideas are recorded.
Keeping a Journal	Carry a journal to write down ideas as they occur or a recorder to capture those same ideas and thoughts.
Freewriting	Write down or record everything that comes to mind about a topic without revising or proofreading until all of the information is written or recorded in some way. Organize it later.
Mind or Subject Mapping	Start with a central idea and draw a "map" with lines from the center to other related ideas, forming a visual map of the concepts and their connections.

7.4–5   p. 283

Intelligence
(the ability to learn from one's experiences, acquire knowledge, and use resources effectively)

- **theories**
  - **Spearman's g factor:** intelligence comprises two different abilities
  - **Gardner's multiple intelligences:** overall intelligence comprises nine different types
  - **Sternberg's triarchic theory:** intelligence comprises three different aspects

first formal test created by Alfred Binet and Theodore Simon to help identify French students who needed more help with learning

Measuring Intelligence
- **tests**
  - **Binet's Mental Ability Test**
  - **Stanford-Binet**
  - **Wechsler Tests**
- **test construction**
  - good tests are both valid and reliable
  - standardized administration, scoring, and comparison against norms
  - intelligence is assumed to follow a normal curve
  - challenging

7.6–8   p. 293

- **individual differences**
  IQ tests can be used to identify individuals who differ significantly from those of average intelligence
  - **giftedness**
    - criteria
    - characteristics
  - **developmental delay/mental retardation**
    - criteria
    - classifications
    - causal factors
  - **emotional intelligence**

Intelligence
- **nature vs. nurture**
  - identical twins reared together show a correlation of 0.86 between their IQs
  - heritability estimates apply *within* groups of people, not *between* groups, not to individuals, and only in a general sense

7.9–10   p. 298

- **levels of language analysis**
  language structures worldwide share common characteristics
  - grammar
  - syntax
  - morphemes
  - phonemes
  - pragmatics

Language

- **the relationship between language and thought**
  - does language influence thought or does thinking influence language?
  - linguistic relativity hypothesis
  - animal studies in language

8
Motivation and Emotion

Walking Tall

Debi R. was a relatively healthy woman in her early fifties when her back began to bother her. Her doctor recommended surgery to relieve two bad disks in her back. Her disks had begun to slip out of place, causing the pain in her back.

After the surgery, the pain was still there. The surgeon operated again the next day, saying that another disk had ruptured. When Debi began to recover, she found that she could not move her legs or feel her feet—she was partially paralyzed. Several months later the truth was revealed that the doctor had operated on the wrong side of her disks the first time and then made matters worse by operating again while her tissues were still swollen. Debi was told that she might never walk again.

That was over a year ago. Today Debi still has pain but can walk with only a cane to aid in her balance. She still has numbness in her feet, but she is no longer confined to a wheelchair. How did she do it? She refused to accept the predictions of the doctors, and she worked extremely hard to achieve the goal of walking again. She did everything the therapists told her to do, and when the therapy was stopped, she continued on her own. She is finally at the point where she can walk for short distances with no help at all.

Debi was able to overcome her disability because she was highly *motivated* to do so. She also overcame her fears about not being able to walk and manages her feelings about the pain and the unfairness of what happened to her so that her outlook on life remains sunny and joyful. Each day brings a new hope that more progress will be made. Debi isn't even close to giving up.

Why study motivation and emotion? The study of motivation not only helps us understand why we eat and drink the way we do but also why some people are more driven to achieve than others. Emotions are a part of everything we do, affecting our relationships with others and our own health, as well as influencing important decisions. In this chapter, we will explore the motives behind our actions and the origins and influences of emotions.

8 Learning Objectives

- **8.1** How do psychologists define motivation, and what are the key elements of the early instinct and drive-reduction approaches to motivation?

- **8.2** What are the characteristics of the three types of needs?

- **8.3** What are the key elements of the arousal and incentive approaches to motivation?

- **8.4** How do Maslow's humanistic approach and self-determination theory explain motivation?

- **8.5** What happens in the body to cause hunger, and how do social factors influence a person's experience of hunger?

- **8.6** What are some problems in eating behavior, and how are they affected by biology and culture?

- **8.7** What are the three elements of emotion?

- **8.8** How do the James-Lange and Cannon-Bard theories of emotion differ?

- **8.9** What are the key elements in cognitive arousal theory, the facial feedback hypothesis, and the cognitive-mediational theory of emotion?

- **8.10** What is the positive psychology movement?

Approaches to Understanding Motivation

▶ **8.1** How do psychologists define motivation, and what are the key elements of the early instinct and drive-reduction approaches to motivation?

Motivation is the process by which activities are started, directed, and continued so that physical or psychological needs or wants are met (Petri, 1996). The word itself comes from the Latin word *movere*, which means "to move." Motivation is what "moves" people to do the things they do. For example, when a person is relaxing in front of the television and begins to feel hungry, the physical need for food might cause the person to get up, go into the kitchen, and search for something to eat. If the hunger is great enough, the person might even cook something. The physical need of hunger caused the action (getting up), directed it (going to the kitchen), and sustained the search (finding or preparing something to eat). Hunger is only one example, of course. Loneliness may lead to calling a friend or going to a place where there are people. The desire to get ahead in life motivates many people to go to college. Just getting out of bed in the morning is motivated by the need to keep a roof over one's head and food on the table by going to work.

There are different types of motivation. Sometimes people are driven to do something because of an external reward of some sort (or the avoidance of an unpleasant consequence), as when someone goes to work at a job to make money and avoid losing possessions such as a house or a car ⓛⓘⓝⓚ *to Chapter Five: Learning, p. 190.* When the motivation is external (coming from outside the self), it is called **extrinsic motivation**. In extrinsic motivation, a person performs an action because it leads to an outcome that is separate from the person (Ryan & Deci, 2000). Other examples would be giving a child money for every "A" on a report card, offering a bonus to an employee for increased performance, or tipping a server in a restaurant for good service. The child, employee, and server are motivated to work for the external or extrinsic rewards. In contrast, **intrinsic motivation** is the type of motivation in which a person performs an action because the act itself is rewarding or satisfying in some internal manner. You might remember that in the Classic Studies in Psychology section in Chapter One (p. 30), psychologist Teresa Amabile (Amabile et al., 1976)

motivation the process by which activities are started, directed, and continued so that physical or psychological needs or wants are met.

extrinsic motivation type of motivation in which a person performs an action because it leads to an outcome that is separate from or external to the person.

intrinsic motivation type of motivation in which a person performs an action because the act itself is rewarding or satisfying in some internal manner.

found that children's creativity was affected by the kind of motivation for which they worked: Extrinsic motivation decreased the degree of creativity shown in the experimental group's artwork when compared to the creativity levels of the children in the intrinsically motivated control group.

INSTINCT APPROACHES

One of the earliest approaches to motivation focused on the biologically determined and innate patterns of behavior that exist in both people and animals called **instincts**. Just as animals are governed by their instincts to do things such as migrating, nest building, mating, and protecting their territory, early researchers proposed that human beings may also be governed by similar instincts (James, 1890; McDougall, 1908). According to these **instinct approach** theorists, in humans the instinct to reproduce is responsible for sexual behavior, and the instinct for territorial protection may be related to aggressive behavior.

William McDougall (1908) proposed a total of 18 instincts for humans, including curiosity, flight (running away), pugnacity (aggressiveness), and acquisition (gathering possessions). As the years progressed, psychologists added more and more instincts to the list until there were thousands of proposed instincts. However, none of these early theorists did much more than give names to these instincts. Although there were plenty of descriptions, such as "submissive people possess the instinct of submission," there was no attempt to explain why these instincts exist in humans, if they exist at all (Petri, 1996).

Freud's psychoanalytic theory still includes the concept of instincts that reside in the id (the part of the personality containing all the basic human needs and drives). Ⓛⓘⓝⓚ *to Chapter Eleven: Theories of Personality, p. 438.* Even so, instinct approaches have faded away because, although they could describe human behavior, they could not explain it. But these approaches did accomplish one important thing by forcing psychologists to realize that some human behavior is controlled by hereditary factors. This idea remains central in the study of human behavior today.

instincts the biologically determined and innate patterns of behavior that exist in both people and animals.

instinct approach approach to motivation that assumes people are governed by instincts similar to those of animals.

(left) The human body needs water, especially when a person is working hard or under stress, as this man appears to be. Thirst is a survival need of the body, making it a primary drive, according to drive-reduction theory. What other kinds of needs might be primary drives?

(right) Some people are driven to do strenuous, challenging activities even when there is no physical need to do so. When a drive is acquired through learning, it is called an acquired or secondary drive. Fulfilling an acquired drive provides secondary reinforcement. What might this rock climber find reinforcing about scaling this steep cliff?

AP* Compare and contrast
motivational theories.

AP* Identify key contributors
in the psychology of motivation
and emotion.

AP* Discuss the biological
underpinnings of motivation.

Watch classic video footage
on drive theory with Carl Rogers.
www.mypsychlab.com

DRIVE-REDUCTION APPROACHES

The next approach to gain support involved the concepts of needs and drives. A **need** is a requirement of some material (such as food or water) that is essential for survival of the organism. When an organism has a need, it leads to a psychological tension as well as a physical arousal that motivates the organism to act in order to fulfill the need and reduce the tension. This tension is called a **drive** (Hull, 1943). ⊙ Watch on MyPsychLab

Drive-reduction theory proposes just this connection between internal physiological states and outward behavior. In this theory, there are two kinds of drives. **Primary drives** are those that involve survival needs of the body such as hunger and thirst, whereas **acquired (secondary) drives** are those that are learned through experience or conditioning, such as the need for money or social approval, or the need of recent ex-smokers to have something to put in their mouths. If this sounds familiar, it should. The concepts of primary and secondary reinforcers from Chapter Five are related to these drives. Primary reinforcers satisfy primary drives, and secondary reinforcers statisfy acquired, or secondary, drives. ⓛⓘⓝⓚ *to Chapter Five: Learning, p. 188.*

This theory also includes the concept of **homeostasis**, or the tendency of the body to maintain a steady state. One could think of homeostasis as the body's version of a thermostat—thermostats keep the temperature of a house at a constant level, and homeostasis does the same thing for the body's functions. When there is a primary drive need, the body is in a state of imbalance. This stimulates behavior that brings the body back into balance, or homeostasis. For example, if Jarrod's body needs food, he feels hunger and the state of tension/arousal associated with that need. He will then seek to restore his homeostasis by eating something, which is the behavior stimulated to reduce the hunger drive (see Figure 8.1).

Although drive-reduction theory works well to explain the actions people take to reduce tension created by needs, it does not explain all human motivation. Why do people eat when they are not really hungry? People don't always seek to reduce their inner arousal either—sometimes they seek to increase it. Bungee-jumping, parachuting as a recreation, rock climbing, and watching horror movies are all activities that increase the inner state of tension and arousal, and many people love doing these activities. Why would people do such things if they don't reduce some need or restore homeostasis? The answer is complex: There are different types of needs, different effects of arousal, different incentives, and different levels of importance attached to many forms of behavior. The following theories explore some of these factors in motivation.

need a requirement of some material (such as food or water) that is essential for survival of the organism.

drive a psychological tension and physical arousal arising when there is a need that motivates the organism to act in order to fulfill the need and reduce the tension.

drive-reduction theory approach to motivation that assumes behavior arises from physiological needs that cause internal drives to push the organism to satisfy the need and reduce tension and arousal.

primary drives those drives that involve needs of the body such as hunger and thirst.

acquired (secondary) drives those drives that are learned through experience or conditioning, such as the need for money or social approval.

homeostasis the tendency of the body to maintain a steady state.

Figure 8.1 Homeostasis

In homeostasis, the body maintains balance in the body's physical states. For example, this diagram shows how increased hunger (a state of imbalance) prompts a person to eat. Eating increases the level of glucose (blood sugar), causing the feelings of hunger to reduce. After a period without eating, the glucose levels become low enough to stimulate the hunger drive once again, and the entire cycle is repeated.

Different Strokes for Different Folks: Needs   Obviously, motivation is about needs. Drive-reduction theory talks about needs, and other theories of motivation include the concept of needs. In many of these theories, most needs are the result of some inner physical drive (such as hunger or thirst) that demands to be satisfied. Harvard University psychologist David C. McClelland (1961, 1987) proposed a theory of motivation that highlights the importance of three psychological needs not typically considered by the other theories: achievement, affiliation, and power.

8.2   What are the characteristics of the three types of needs?

Need for Achievement: How to Succeed by Excelling at Everything   The **need for achievement** (abbreviated as **nAch** in McClelland's writings) involves a strong desire to succeed in attaining goals, not only realistic ones but also challenging ones. People who are high in nAch look for careers and hobbies that allow others to evaluate them because these high achievers also need to have feedback about their performance in addition to the achievement of reaching the goal. Although many of these people do become wealthy, famous, and publicly successful, others fulfill their need to achieve in ways that lead only to their own personal success, not material riches—they just want the challenge.

Achievement motivation appears to be strongly related to success in school, occupational success, and the quality and amount of what a person produces (Collins et al., 2004; Gillespie et al., 2002; Spangler, 1992). The chapter-opening story about Debi R. is a good example of the need for achievement. Debi's desire to overcome her physical difficulties and walk once again had nothing to do with becoming successful or wealthy, but she certainly showed a strong desire to achieve a challenging goal.

Need for Affiliation: Popularity Rules   Another psychological need is for friendly social interactions and relationships with others. Called the **need for affiliation (nAff)**, people high in this need seek to be liked by others and to be held in high regard by those around them. This makes high affiliation people good team players, whereas a person high in achievement just might run over a few team members on the way to the top. ✳ Explore on MyPsychLab

Need for Power: The One Who Dies with the Most Toys Wins   The final psychological need proposed by McClelland is the **need for power (nPow)**. Power is not about reaching a goal but about having control over other people. People high in this need would want to have influence over others and make an impact on them. They want their ideas to be the ones that are used, regardless of whether or not their ideas will lead to success. Status and prestige are important, so these people wear expensive clothes, live in expensive houses, drive fancy cars, and dine in the best restaurants. Whereas someone who is a high achiever may not need a lot of money to validate the achievement, someone who is high in the need for power typically sees the money (and cars, houses, jewelry, and other "toys") as the achievement. The subtitle for this section is a saying from a popular bumper sticker but is really a comment on the more negative aspect of the need for power. For the person high in the need for power, it's all about who has the most expensive "toys" in the end.

Personality and nAch: Carol Dweck's Self-Theory of Motivation
How do people get to be high achievers? According to motivation and personality psychologist Carol Dweck (1999), the need for achievement is closely linked to personality factors, including a person's view of how *self* can affect the understanding of how much a person's actions can influence his or her success. (Dweck defines

need for achievement (nAch) a need that involves a strong desire to succeed in attaining goals, not only realistic ones but also challenging ones.

need for affiliation (nAff) the need for friendly social interactions and relationships with others.

need for power (nPow) the need to have control or influence over others.

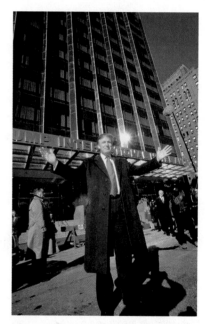

Donald Trump stands triumphant at the opening of his Trump International Hotel and Tower in New York. Many people who are as wealthy as "The Donald" continue to buy new houses, businesses, clothing, and cars (among other things) even though they do not need them. This is an example of the need for power at work. How might this need for power be expressed in a person's relationships with others, such as a spouse, employee, or friend?

✳ **Explore** the need for affiliation. **www.mypsychlab.com**

How do people get to be high achievers?

self as the beliefs one holds about one's abilities and relationships to others.) This concept is related to the much older notion of *locus of control*, in which people who assume that they have control over what happens in their lives are considered to be *internal* in locus of control, and those who feel that their lives are controlled by powerful others, luck, or fate are considered to be *external* in locus of control (MacDonald, 1970; Rotter, 1966).

Dweck has amassed a large body of empirical research, particularly in the field of education, to support the idea that people's "theories" about their own selves can affect their level of achievement motivation and their willingness to keep trying to achieve success in the face of failure (Dweck, 1986; Dweck & Elliott, 1983; Dweck & Leggett, 1988; Elliott & Dweck, 1988). According to this research, people can form one of two belief systems about intelligence, which in turn affects their motivation to achieve. Those who believe intelligence is fixed and unchangeable often demonstrate an external locus of control, leading them to give up easily or avoid situations in which they might fail—often ensuring their own failure in the process. They are prone to developing learned helplessness, the tendency to stop trying to achieve a goal because past failure has led them to believe that they cannot succeed. Ⓛ Ⓘ Ⓝ Ⓚ *to Chapter Five: Learning, p. 206.* Their goals involve trying to "look smart" and outperform others ("See, at least I did better than she did"). For example, a student faced with a big exam may avoid coming to class that day, even though that might mean getting an even lower score on a makeup exam.

This does not mean that students with this view of intelligence are always unsuccessful. In fact, Dweck's research (1999) suggests that students who have had a long history of successes may be most at risk for developing a learned helplessness after a big failure precisely because their previous successes have led them to believe in their own fixed intelligence. For example, a child who had never earned anything less than an "A" in school who then receives his first "C" might become depressed and refuse to do any more homework, ensuring future failure.

The other type of person believes that intelligence is changeable and can be shaped by experiences and effort in small increases, or increments. These people tend to show an internal locus of control, believing that their own actions and efforts will improve their intelligence. They work at developing new strategies and get involved in new tasks, with the goal of increasing their "smarts." They are motivated to master tasks and don't allow failure to destroy their confidence in themselves or prevent them from trying again and again, using new strategies each time.

Based on this and other research, Dweck recommends that parents and teachers encourage children to value the learning process more than "looking smart" by always having the right answer (and only responding when sure of that answer, for example). Errors should not be viewed as failures but as a way to improve future performance on the road to mastering whatever the goal in question is. Essentially, this means praising efforts and the methods that children use to make those efforts, not just successes or ability. Instead of saying, "You're right, how smart you are," the parent or teacher should say something such as, "You are really thinking hard," or "That was a very clever way to think about this problem." In the past, teachers and parents have been told that praise is good and criticism is bad—it might damage a child's self-esteem. Dweck believes that constructive criticism, when linked with praise of effort and the use of strategies, will be a better influence on the child's self-esteem than endless praise that can become meaningless when given indiscriminately.

Many people are driven by a need to attain both realistic and challenging goals. This young girl seems eager to provide an answer to the teacher's question, and the teacher's positive feedback will help foster the girl's need for achievement.

8.1–2

types ─┬─ **intrinsic:** actions are rewarding or satisfying in and of themselves
└─ **extrinsic:** actions are performed because they lead to some sort of external outcome

Motivation
(process by which activities are started, directed, and continued so that physical or psychological needs or wants are met)

instinct ─┬─ biologically determined/innate patterns of behavior
└─ old approach: instincts are mainly descriptions, not explanations; idea that some behavior is hereditary remains an important focus

drive reduction ─┬─ **need:** requirement for something essential for survival; existence of need leads to psychological tension (drive) and physical arousal; satisfying need reduces drive/tension
├─ **primary drives** involve survival needs (e.g., hunger, thirst) and maintaining homeostasis
└─ **secondary (acquired) drives** are learned through experience or conditioning (e.g., money, social approval)

psychological needs ─┬─ psychological needs have been highlighted in some theories (e.g., McClelland) ─┬─ need for **achievement**
│ ├─ need for **affiliation**
│ └─ need for **power**
└─ Dweck suggests that the need for achievement is linked to a person's view of self (locus of control)

Approaches to Understanding Motivation (part 1)

PRACTICE **QUIZ:** PREPARING FOR THE AP* EXAM

ANSWERS ON PAGE AK-2.

Directions: Read each of the questions or incomplete sentences below. Then choose the response that best answers the question or completes the sentence.

1. The process by which activities are started, directed, and sustained to meet a person's physical or psychological needs or wants is called _____.
   a. drive
   b. instinct
   c. incentive
   d. motivation
   e. homeostasis

2. Liz picked out "her" desk on the first day of class. But in the second class period, someone else was sitting in her chosen seat. Liz's territorial attitude about that desk and her negative feelings toward the "interloper" sitting there is best explained by which of the following?
   a. Instinct approach
   b. Intrinsic motivation
   c. Extrinsic motivation
   d. Drive-reduction theory
   e. Need for achievement

3. People who want to be liked by others and who are good team players are high in the need for _____.
   a. power
   b. emotion
   c. affiliation
   d. aggression
   e. achievement

4. Ronnie believes that people are just born smart or not smart, and he thinks of himself as "not smart." As a result, Ronnie doesn't really try all that hard to succeed in school. Dweck would say that Ronnie's achievement motivation is being affected by his _____.
   a. need for homeostasis
   b. need to reduce his drives
   c. centralized locus of control
   d. internal locus of control
   e. external locus of control

5. Which of the following is a primary drive?
   a. The need for love
   b. The need for food
   c. The need for money
   d. The need for creativity
   e. the need for friendship

AROUSAL APPROACHES

8.3 What are the key elements of the arousal and incentive approaches to motivation?

◀ **AP*** Compare and contrast motivational theories.

Another explanation for human motivation involves the recognition of yet another type of need, the need for stimulation. A **stimulus motive** is one that appears to be unlearned but causes an increase in stimulation. Examples would be curiosity, playing, and exploration.

stimulus motive a motive that appears to be unlearned but causes an increase in stimulation, such as curiosity.

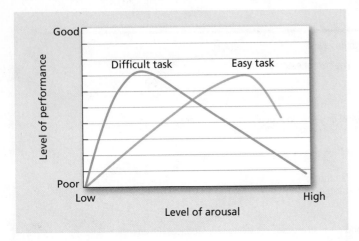

Figure 8.2 Arousal and Performance
The optimal level of arousal for task performance depends on the difficulty of the task. We generally perform easy tasks well if we are at a high-moderate level of arousal (green) and accomplish difficult tasks well if we are at a low-moderate level (red).

If people are supposed ▶ to be seeking a level of arousal somewhere around the middle, why do some people love to do things like bungee-jumping?

In **arousal theory**, people are said to have an optimal (best or ideal) level of tension. Task performances, for example, may suffer if the level of arousal is too high (such as severe test anxiety) or even if the level of arousal is too low (such as boredom). For many kinds of tasks, a moderate level of arousal seems to be best. This relationship between task performance and arousal is called the **Yerkes-Dodson law** (Teigen, 1994; Yerkes & Dodson, 1908). However, this effect is modified by the difficulty level of the task: Easy tasks demand a somewhat "high-moderate" level for optimal performance, whereas difficult tasks require a "low-moderate" level. Figure 8.2 shows this relationship in graphic form.

Maintaining an optimal level of arousal, then, may involve reducing tension or creating it (Hebb, 1955). For example, husbands or wives who are underaroused may pick a fight with their spouse. Students who experience test anxiety (a high level of arousal) may seek out ways to reduce that anxiety in order to improve test performance. Students who are not anxious at all may not be motivated to study well, lowering their test performance. Many arousal theorists believe that the optimal level of arousal for most people under normal circumstances is somewhere in the middle, neither too high nor too low.

If people are supposed to be seeking a level of arousal somewhere around the middle, why do some people love to do things like bungee-jumping?

Even though the average person might require a moderate level of arousal to feel content, there are some people who need less arousal and some who need more. The person who needs more arousal is called a **sensation seeker** (Zuckerman, 1979, 1994). Sensation seekers seem to need more complex and varied sensory experiences than do other people. The need does not always have to involve danger. For example, students who travel to other countries to study tend to score higher on scales of sensation seeking than do students who stay at home (Schroth & McCormack, 2000). Sensation seeking may be related to temperament, as discussed in Chapter Ten: Development Across the Life Span (pp. 411–412). Table 8.1 has some sample items from a typical sensation-seeking scale.

In one study (Putnam & Stifter, 2002), researchers found evidence of "sensation-seeking" behavior in children as young as age 2. In this study, 90 children

arousal theory theory of motivation in which people are said to have an optimal (best or ideal) level of tension that they seek to maintain by increasing or decreasing stimulation.

Yerkes-Dodson law law stating performance is related to arousal; moderate levels of arousal lead to better performance than do levels of arousal that are too low or too high. This effect varies with the difficulty of the task: Easy tasks require a high-moderate level whereas more difficult tasks require a low-moderate level.

sensation seeker someone who needs more arousal than the average person.

Table 8.1	Sample Items from the Zuckerman-Kuhlman Personality Questionnaire	
SCALE ITEM		**SENSATION SEEKING**
I sometimes do "crazy" things just for fun.		High
I prefer friends who are excitingly unpredictable.		High
I am an impulsive person.		High
Before I begin a complicated job, I make careful plans.		Low
I usually think about what I am going to do before doing it.		Low

Source: Adapted from Zuckerman, M. (2002).

were studied at the ages of 6, 12, 24, and 25 months. In a test of the youngest participants, the babies were shown two sets of toys: a block, a plate, and a cup; or a flashing light, a toy beeper, and a wind-up dragon. The first set was considered a low-intensity stimulus whereas the second set was labeled a high-intensity stimulus. The infants who reached out for the toys more quickly, and reached for the high-intensity toys in particular, were labeled "approach motivated."

The same children at age 2 were given an opportunity to explore a black box with a hole in one side. The children who were labeled "low approach motivated" at 6 and 12 months were unwilling to put their hands into the hole to see what might be in the box, whereas the "high-approach-motivated" children not only put their hands in but also in some cases tried to climb into the box.

Is sensation seeking something people have when they are born? Although it is tempting to think of 6-month-old children as having little in the way of experiences that could shape their personalities, the fact is that the first six months of life is full of experiences that might affect children's choices in the future. For example, a very young infant might, while being carried, stick a hand into some place that ends up causing pain. This experience might affect that infant's willingness in the future to put his or her hand in something else through the simple learning process of operant conditioning. (LINK) *to Chapter Five: Learning, pp. 186–187.* Determining the origins of sensation seeking will have to wait for further research.

This daring preschool boy has climbed high into this massive tree and looks as though he might try to climb higher still.

INCENTIVE APPROACHES

Last Thanksgiving, I had eaten about all I could. Then my aunt brought out a piece of her wonderful pumpkin pie and I couldn't resist—I ate it, even though I was not at all hungry. What makes us do things even when we don't have the drive or need to do them? It's true that sometimes there is no physical need present, yet people still eat, drink, or react as if they did have a need. Even though that piece of pie was not necessary to reduce a hunger drive, it was very rewarding, wasn't it? And on past occasions, that pie was also delicious and rewarding, so there is anticipation of that reward now. The pie, in all its glorious promise of flavor and sweetness, becomes an incentive to eat. **Incentives** are things that attract or lure people into action. In fact, the dictionary (Merriam-Webster, 2003) lists *incentive* as meaning the same thing as *motive*.

In **incentive approaches**, behavior is explained in terms of the external stimulus and its rewarding properties. These rewarding properties exist independently of any need or level of arousal and can cause people to act only upon the incentive. Thus, incentive theory is actually based, at least in part, on the principles of learning that were discussed in Chapter Five. (LINK) *to Chapter Five: Learning, pp. 188–190.*

One of the earliest incentive approaches clearly demonstrates the relationship to learning, particularly the early cognitive learning theories found in the work of Edward Tolman (1932). **Expectancy-value theories** are a class of incentive theories based on the work of Tolman and others (Lewin, 1936; Rotter, 1954). In general, these theories assume that the actions of humans cannot be predicted or fully understood without understanding the beliefs, values, and the importance that people attach to those beliefs and values at any given moment in time. Tolman's work with animals (the latent learning studies with rats discussed in Chapter Five, p. 204) demonstrated that organisms are capable of remembering what had happened in the past, anticipating future events, and adjusting their own actions according to those cognitive *expectancies* (a set of beliefs about what will happen in the future based on

Last Thanksgiving, I had eaten about all I could. Then my aunt brought out a piece of her wonderful pumpkin pie and I couldn't resist—I ate it, even though I was not at all hungry. What makes us do things even when we don't have the drive or need to do them?

AP* Identify and apply basic motivational concepts to understand the behavior of humans and other animals.

incentives things that attract or lure people into action.

incentive approaches theories of motivation in which behavior is explained as a response to the external stimulus and its rewarding properties.

expectancy-value theories incentive theories that assume the actions of humans cannot be predicted or fully understood without understanding the beliefs, values, and the importance that a person attaches to those beliefs and values at any given moment in time.

past experiences). Kurt Lewin (1936) applied these concepts to the estimated likelihood of future success or failure in his field theory of decision making. Julian Rotter's (1954) social learning theory included expectancy as one of the three factors that predict people's behavior—if Terry's past experiences with writing papers, for example, have led to an expectancy of failing to get a high grade, Terry is unlikely to take on the task of an extra term paper to earn bonus points.

By itself, the incentive approach does not explain the motivation behind all behavior. Many theorists today see motivation as a result of both the "push" of internal needs or drives and the "pull" of a rewarding external stimulus. For example, sometimes a person may actually be hungry (the push) but choose to satisfy that drive by selecting a candy bar instead of a rice cake. The candy bar has more appeal to most people and it, therefore, has more "pull" than the rice cake. (Frankly, to most people, just about anything has more pull than a rice cake.)

HUMANISTIC APPROACHES: MASLOW'S HIERARCHY OF NEEDS

8.4 How do Maslow's humanistic approach and self-determination theory explain motivation?

A final approach to the study of motivation is based on the work of Abraham Maslow (1943, 1987). Maslow was one of the early humanistic psychologists who rejected the dominant theories of psychoanalysis and behaviorism in favor of a more positive view of human behavior. (L)(I)(N)(K) *to Chapter One: The Science of Psychology, p. 14.* Maslow proposed that there are several levels of needs that a person must strive to meet before achieving the highest level of personality fulfillment. According to Maslow, **self-actualization** is the point that is seldom reached at which people have satisfied the lower needs and achieved their full human potential.

These needs include both deficiency needs and growth needs. Deficiency needs are needs of the body, such as the need for food or water, whereas growth needs are for desires like having friends or feeling good about oneself. For a person to achieve self-actualization, which is the highest level of growth needs, the primary, basic needs must first be fulfilled. Figure 8.3 shows the typical way to represent Maslow's series of needs as a pyramid with the most basic needs for survival at the bottom and the highest needs at the top. This type of ranking is called a hierarchy.*

The lowest level of the pyramid consists of physiological needs such as food, water, and rest. Once those needs are met, safety becomes important and involves feeling secure. Belongingness and love are the needs for friends and companions as well as to be accepted by others, and self-esteem is the need to feel that one has accomplished something good or earned the esteem of others. Although Maslow's original hierarchy included only one more level of self-actualization needs, Maslow later inserted two other needs just below this level (Maslow, 1971; Maslow & Lowery, 1998). Just above the esteem needs on the hierarchy come the cognitive needs, or the need to know and understand the world. This need is typical of an academic person who learns for the sake of gathering knowledge, and all people have a natural curiosity. Above the cognitive needs are the aesthetic needs, which include the need for order and beauty and are typical of artistic people. (It should be noted that all people also seem to like to express themselves artistically—even if it's only graffiti on a wall.) Once all these needs are met, it is possible to be concerned about self-actualization needs, or needs that help a person reach his or her full potential and capabilities as a human being. As you can see in Figure 8.3, Maslow also added a higher need called

AP* Identify key contributors in the psychology of motivation and emotion.

self-actualization according to Maslow, the point that is seldom reached at which people have sufficiently satisfied the lower needs and achieved their full human potential.

_____

*Hierarchy: a graded or ranked series.

transcendence above the self-actualization needs (Maslow, 1971). Transcendence involves helping others to achieve their full potential. This aspect of Maslow's hierarchy is very similar to a stage in another theorist's work. Erik Erikson theorized a stage in personality development called generativity, in which people focus on helping the next generation through earlier crises of personality development. ⓁⒾⓃⓀ *to Chapter Ten: Development Across the Life Span, pp. 422–423.*

People move up the pyramid as they go through life, gaining wisdom and the knowledge of how to handle many different situations. But a shift in life's circumstances can result in a shift down to a lower need. For example, someone might be near the top, fulfilling the need for growth in ways that lead to self-actualization (appreciation of beauty, need for truth and justice, and helping others to grow, for example). But if that person loses her job and cannot find another one for quite some time, her money will start running out. She might take a job that is not good for her self-esteem out of love for her family and the need to provide a safe place for them to live (by being able to make the house payments) and food for them to eat. She would be starting at the level of love and working her way back up. Moving up and down and then back up can occur frequently—even from one hour to the next. Times in a person's life in which self-actualization is achieved, at least temporarily, are called **peak experiences**. For Maslow, the process of growth and self-actualization is the striving to make peak experiences happen again and again. ✳ Explore on MyPsychLab

Here's an example that might help in understanding this hierarchy. In the movie *Castaway*, Tom Hanks's character is stranded on a deserted island. His first concern is to find something to eat and fresh water to drink—without those two things, he cannot survive. Even while he is building a crude shelter, he is still thinking about how to obtain food. Once he has those needs met, however, he gets lonely. He finds a volleyball, paints a handprint and then a crude face on it, and names it "Wilson." He talks to the volleyball as if it were a person, at first as a kind of way to talk out the things he needs to do and later as a way of staying relatively sane. The need for companionship is *that* strong.

Maslow's theory has had a powerful influence on the field of management (Heil et al., 1998). Douglas McGregor, in his explanations of two different styles of management (McGregor, 1960), relates the older and less productive "Theory X" (workers are unmotivated and need to be managed and directed) to Maslow's lower needs and the newer, more productive style of management called "Theory Y" (workers want to work and want that work to be meaningful)

peak experiences according to Maslow, times in a person's life during which self-actualization is temporarily achieved.

✳ **Explore** with Maslow's Hierarchy of Needs simulation.
www.mypsychlab.com

Figure 8.3 Maslow's Hierarchy of Needs

Maslow proposed that human beings must fulfill the more basic needs, such as physical and security needs, before being able to fulfill the higher needs of self-actualization and transcendence.

Transcendence needs: to help others achieve self-actualization

Self-actualization needs: to find self-fulfillment and realize one's potential

Aesthetic needs: to appreciate symmetry, order, and beauty

Cognitive needs: to know, understand, and explore

Esteem needs: to achieve, be competent, gain approval and recognition

Belongingness and love needs: to be with others, be accepted, and belong

Safety needs: to feel secure and safe, out of danger

Physiological needs: to satisfy hunger, thirst, fatigue, etc.

to the higher needs. ⓁⓘⓃⓀ *to Appendix B: Applied Psychology.* In spite of this influence, Maslow's theory is not without its critics. There are several problems that others have highlighted, and the most serious is that there is little scientific support (Drenth et al., 1984). Like Sigmund Freud, Maslow developed his theory based on his own personal observations of people rather than any empirically gathered observations or research. Although many people report that while they were starving, they could think of nothing but food, there is anecdotal evidence in the lives of many people, some of them quite well known, that the lower needs do not have to be satisfied before moving on to a higher need (Drenth et al., 1984). For example, artists and scientists throughout history have been known to deny their own physical needs while producing great works (a self-actualization need). Abraham Lincoln and Edgar Allan Poe both suffered from a severe mood disorder called bipolar disorder, ⓁⓘⓃⓀ *to Chapter Twelve: Psychological Disorders, pp. 498–499,* which causes the sufferer to have severe periods of depression and insecurity. This should have placed them on the lowest levels of the hierarchy, yet Lincoln and Poe are responsible for some of the most memorable deeds and works in history (Fieve, 1997).

Does this theory apply universally?

Maslow's work was based on his studies of Americans. Cross-cultural research suggests that the order of needs on the hierarchy does not always hold true for other cultures, particularly those cultures with a stronger tendency than the culture of the United States to avoid uncertainty, such as Greece and Japan. In those countries security needs are much stronger than self-actualization needs in determining motivation (Hofstede, 1980; Hofstede et al., 2002). This means that people in those cultures value job security more than they do job satisfaction (holding an interesting or challenging job). In countries such as Sweden and Norway that stress the quality of life as being of greater importance than what a person produces, social needs may be more important than self-actualization needs (Hofstede et al., 2002). ⓁⓘⓃⓀ *to Chapter Eleven: Theories of Personality, pp. 457–458.*

Other theorists have developed and refined Maslow's hierarchy. Clayton Alderfer developed one of the more popular versions of this refinement. In his theory, the hierarchy has only three levels: *existence needs,* which include the physiological needs and basic safety needs that provide for the person's continued existence; *relatedness needs,* which include some safety issues as well as belongingness and self-esteem needs and are related to social relationships; and *growth needs,* which include some self-esteem issues and the self-actualization needs that help people develop their full potential as human beings (Alderfer, 1972).

Alderfer believed that more than one need could be active at a time and that progression up and down the hierarchy is common as one type of need assumes greater importance at a particular time in a person's life than other needs. This makes Alderfer's hierarchy of needs less rigid and more in line with observations about life's "ups and downs."

SELF-DETERMINATION THEORY (SDT)

Another theory of motivation that is similar to Maslow's hierarchy of needs is the **self-determination theory (SDT)** of Ryan and Deci (2000). In this theory, there are three inborn and universal needs that help people gain a complete sense of self and whole, healthy relationships with others. The three needs are *autonomy,* or the need to be in control of one's own behavior and goals (i.e., self-determination); *competence,* or the need to be able to master the challenging tasks of one's life; and *relatedness,* or the need to feel a sense of belonging, intimacy, and security in relationships with others. These

Does this theory apply ► universally?

In the movie Castaway, *the character played by actor Tom Hanks feels the need for a companion so badly that he names this volleyball "Wilson." He comes to think of "Wilson" as such a good friend that he almost fails in his attempt to escape the island on which he is stranded to "rescue" the ball when it falls off his makeshift raft.*

self-determination theory (SDT) theory of human motivation in which the social context of an action has an effect on the type of motivation existing for the action.

needs are common in several theories of personality; the relatedness need is, of course, similar to Maslow's belongingness and love needs, and both autonomy and competence are important aspects of Erikson's theory of psychosocial personality development (Erikson, 1950, 1980). Ⓛ Ⓘ Ⓝ Ⓚ *to Chapter Ten: Development Across the Life Span, pp. 411–412.*

Ryan, Deci, and their colleagues (Deci et al., 1994; Ryan & Deci, 2000) believe that satisfying these needs can best be accomplished if the person has a supportive environment in which to develop goals and relationships with others. Such satisfaction will not only foster healthy psychological growth but also increase the individual's intrinsic motivation (actions are performed because the act is internally rewarding or satisfying). Evidence suggests that intrinsic motivation is increased or enhanced when a person not only feels competence (through experiencing positive feedback from others and succeeding at what are perceived to be challenging tasks) but also a sense of autonomy or the knowledge that his or her actions are self-determined rather than controlled by others (deCharms, 1968; Deci & Ryan, 1985).

Previous research has found a negative impact on intrinsic motivation when an external reward is given for the performance (Deci et al., 1999), but a more recent paper discusses the results of other studies that find negative effects only for tasks that are not interesting in and of themselves (Cameron et al., 2001). When the task itself is interesting to the person (as might be an assignment that an instructor or manager has explained in terms of its importance and future value), external rewards may increase intrinsic motivation, at least in the short term. Although this recent finding is intriguing, further research is needed to determine if the long-term effects of extrinsic rewards on intrinsic motivation are consistently negative, as the bulk of the research has shown up to now.

But don't we sometimes do things for both kinds of motives? There are usually elements of both intrinsic and extrinsic motives in many of the things people do. Most teachers, for example, work for money to pay bills (the extrinsic motive) but may also feel that they are helping young children to become better adults in the future, which makes the teachers feel good about themselves (the intrinsic motive).

"That is the correct answer, Bill, but I'm afraid you don't win anything for it."
©The New Yorker Collection 1986 Lee Lorenz from cartoonbank.com. All Rights Reserved.

◄ But don't we sometimes do things for both kinds of motives?

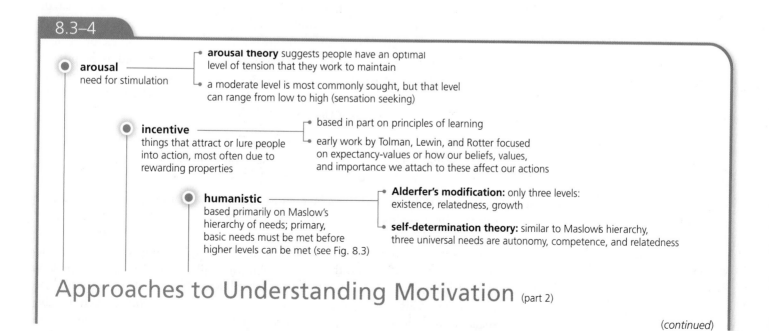

Approaches to Understanding Motivation (part 2)

8.3–4

- **arousal** — need for stimulation
  - **arousal theory** suggests people have an optimal level of tension that they work to maintain
  - a moderate level is most commonly sought, but that level can range from low to high (sensation seeking)
- **incentive** — things that attract or lure people into action, most often due to rewarding properties
  - based in part on principles of learning
  - early work by Tolman, Lewin, and Rotter focused on expectancy-values or how our beliefs, values, and importance we attach to these affect our actions
- **humanistic** — based primarily on Maslow's hierarchy of needs; primary, basic needs must be met before higher levels can be met (see Fig. 8.3)
  - **Alderfer's modification:** only three levels: existence, relatedness, growth
  - **self-determination theory:** similar to Maslow's hierarchy, three universal needs are autonomy, competence, and relatedness

(continued)

Directions: Read each of the questions or incomplete sentences below. Then choose the response that best answers the question or completes the sentence.

1. Which approach to motivation claims that people have an optimal level of tension?
   a. Arousal
   b. Incentive
   c. Humanistic
   d. Drive-reduction
   e. Self-determination

2. In which of the following approaches to motivation is behavior explained in terms of external stimuli and their rewarding properties?
   a. Arousal
   b. Incentive
   c. Humanistic
   d. Drive-reduction
   e. Self-determination

3. What are the most basic needs in Maslow's hierarchy?
   a. Love
   b. Safety
   c. Esteem
   d. Cognitive
   e. Physiological

4. Jamal gets a new toy for every good grade on his report card in first grade. Jamal is receiving _____.
   a. need motivation
   b. intrinsic rewards
   c. self-actualization
   d. intrinsic motivation
   e. extrinsic motivation

5. Which of the following is an example of fulfillment of an esteem need?
   a. Eating a hamburger
   b. Looking at a work of art
   c. Graduating from college
   d. Finding a romantic partner
   e. Purchasing a smoke detector

AP* Describe classic research findings in specific motivation systems. ▶

AP* Identify key contributors in the psychology of motivation and emotion. ▶

What, Hungry Again? Why People Eat

Satisfying hunger is one of Maslow's most basic needs. The eating habits of people today have become a major concern and a frequent topic of news programs, talk shows, and scientific research. There are countless pills, supplements, and treatments to help people eat less and others to help people eat more. Eating is not only a basic survival behavior that reduces a primary drive; it is also a form of entertainment for many, and the attractive presentations and social environment of many eating experiences are a powerful incentive.

PHYSIOLOGICAL COMPONENTS OF HUNGER

Why do we eat? ▶
What causes us to feel hungry in the first place?

Why do we eat? What causes us to feel hungry in the first place? There are actually several factors involved in the hunger drive. Cannon (Cannon & Washburn, 1912) believed that stomach contractions, or "hunger pangs," caused hunger and that the presence of food in the stomach would stop the contractions and appease the hunger drive. Oddly enough, having an empty stomach is not the deciding factor in many cases. Although the stomach does have sensory receptors that respond to the pressure of the stretching stomach muscles as food is piled in and that send signals to the brain indicating that the stomach is full (Geliebter, 1988), people who have had their stomachs removed still get hungry (Janowitz, 1967).

8.5   What happens in the body to cause hunger, and how do social factors influence a person's experience of hunger?

insulin a hormone secreted by the pancreas to control the levels of fats, proteins, and carbohydrates in the body by reducing the level of glucose in the bloodstream.

glucagons hormones that are secreted by the pancreas to control the levels of fats, proteins, and carbohydrates in the body by increasing the level of glucose in the bloodstream.

One factor in hunger seems to be the insulin response that occurs after we begin to eat. **Insulin** and **glucagons** are hormones that are secreted by the pancreas to control the levels of fats, proteins, and carbohydrates in the whole body, including glucose (blood sugar). Insulin reduces the level of glucose in the bloodstream, for example, whereas glucagons increase the level. Insulin, normally released in greater amounts after eating has begun, causes a feeling of more hunger because of the drop in blood sugar levels. Carbohydrates, especially those that are highly refined (such as table sugar, white flour, and white potatoes), cause the insulin level to spike even more than other foods do because there is such a large amount of glucose released by these foods at one time. High blood sugar leads to more insulin released, which leads to a low blood sugar level, increased appetite, and the tendency to overeat. That is the basic principle behind many of the newest diets that promote low-carbohydrate intake. The proponents of these new diets argue that if people control the carbohydrates, they can control the insulin reaction and prevent hunger cravings later on.

The Role of the Hypothalamus The stomach and the pancreas are only two of the factors in hunger. In Chapter Two the role of the hypothalamus in controlling many kinds of motivational stimuli, including hunger, was seen as a result of its influence on the pituitary. But the hypothalamus itself has two separate areas, controlled by the levels of glucose and insulin in the body, which appear to control eating behavior.

The *ventromedial hypothalamus (VMH)* may be involved in stopping the eating response when glucose levels go up (Neary et al., 2004). In one study, rats whose VMH areas (located toward the bottom and center of the hypothalamus) were damaged would no longer stop eating—they ate and ate until they were quite overweight (Hetherington & Ranson, 1940). (See Figure 8.4 for a picture of a rat with this kind of damage.) However, they did not eat everything in sight. They actually got rather picky, only overeating on food that appealed to them (Ferguson & Keesey, 1975; Parkinson & Weingarten, 1990). In fact, if all the food available to them was unappealing, they did not become obese and in some cases even lost weight.

Another part of the hypothalamus, located on the side and called the *lateral hypothalamus (LH)*, seems to influence the onset of eating when insulin levels go up (Neary et al., 2004). Damage to this area caused rats to stop eating to the point of starvation. They would eat only if force-fed and still lost weight under those conditions (Anand & Brobeck, 1951; Hoebel & Teitelbaum, 1966).

Weight Set Point and Basal Metabolic Rate Obviously, the role of the hypothalamus in eating behavior is complex. Some researchers (Leibel et al., 1995; Nisbett, 1972) believe that the hypothalamus affects the particular level of weight that the body tries to maintain, called the **weight set point**. Injury to the hypothalamus does raise or lower the weight set point rather dramatically, causing either drastic weight loss or weight gain.

Metabolism, the speed at which the body burns available energy, and exercise also play a part in the weight set point. Some people are no doubt genetically wired to have faster metabolisms, and those people can eat large amounts of food without gaining weight. Others have slower metabolisms and may eat a normal or even less than normal amount of food and still gain weight or have difficulty losing it (Bouchard et al., 1990). (Some people swear they can gain weight just by *looking* at a piece of cake!) Regular, moderate exercise also helps offset the slowing of metabolism and the accompanying increase in the weight set point (Tremblay et al., 1999).

The rate at which the body burns energy when a person is resting is called the **basal metabolic rate (BMR)** and is directly tied to the set point. If a person's BMR decreases (as it does in adulthood and with decreased activity levels), that person's weight set point increases if the same number of calories is consumed. Table 8.2 shows the changes in BMR of a typical woman and man as age increases from 10 years to 80 years. Notice that the BMR decreases more dramatically as the age of the person increases. Adolescents typically have a very high BMR and activity level and, therefore, a lower weight set point, meaning they can eat far more than an adult of the same size and not gain weight. But when that adolescent becomes an adult, the BMR begins to

Figure 8.4 Obese Laboratory Rat
This rat has reached a high level of obesity because its ventromedial hypothalamus has been deliberately damaged in the laboratory. The result is a rat that no longer receives signals of being satiated, and so the rat continues to eat and eat and eat.

weight set point the particular level of weight that the body tries to maintain.

basal metabolic rate (BMR) the rate at which the body burns energy when the organism is resting.

Table 8.2 Average Basal Metabolic Rates for a Female and Male

AGE RANGE	AGES 10–18	AGES 19–30	AGES 31–60	AGES 61–80
Female (5½ ft.)	1,770*	1,720	1,623	1,506
Male (6 ft.)	2,140	2,071	1,934	1,770

*Numbers in the table represent the number of calories a person needs to consume each day to maintain body weight (without exercise).

decline. Adults should reduce the number of calories they consume, but the tendency is to eat more and move less as income levels and job demands increase. Even if the eating habits of the teenage years are simply maintained, excessive weight gain is not far behind. (In some people, the excessive weight gain may be mostly "behind.")

If you would like to calculate your own BMR, there are numerous Internet sites that allow a person to enter data such as height, age, weight, and activity level. The BMR is then automatically calculated according to a standard formula. Simply type "basal metabolic rate calculator" into your Web search engine to find these sites.

SOCIAL COMPONENTS OF HUNGER

People often eat when they are not really hungry. There are all sorts of social cues that tell people to eat, such as the convention of eating breakfast, lunch, and dinner at certain times. A large part of that "convention" is actually the result of classical conditioning. **LINK** *to Chapter Five: Learning, pp. 177–179.* The body becomes conditioned to respond with the hunger reflex at certain times of the day; through association with the act of eating, those times of the day have become conditioned stimuli for hunger. Sometimes a person who has just eaten a late breakfast will still "feel" hungry at noon, simply because the clock says it's time to eat. People also respond to the appeal of food. How many times has someone finished a huge meal only to be tempted by that luscious-looking dessert on the dessert cart?

Food can also be used in times of stress as a comforting routine, an immediate escape from whatever is unpleasant (Dallman et al., 2003). Rodin (1981, 1985) found that the insulin levels that create hunger may actually increase *before* food is eaten (similar to the way Pavlov's dogs began salivating before they received their food). Like getting hungry at a certain time of day, this physiological phenomenon may also be due to classical conditioning: In the past, eating foods with certain visual and sensory characteristics led to an insulin spike, and this pairing occurred so frequently that now just looking at or smelling the food produces the spike before the food is consumed (Stockhorst, 1999). This may explain why some people (who are called "externals" because of their tendency to focus on the external features of food rather than internal hunger) are far more responsive to these external signals—they produce far more insulin in response to the *anticipation* of eating than do nonexternals, or people who are less affected by external cues (Rodin, 1985).

Cultural factors and gender also play a part in determining hunger and eating habits. In one study, a questionnaire about eating habits was given to both men and women from the United States and Japan. Although no significant differences in what initiates eating existed for men in either culture, women in the United States were found to be much more likely to start eating for emotional reasons, such as depression. Japanese women were more likely to eat because of hunger signals or social

(top) Cultural factors play an important part in why people eat. Women in Japan have been found to be motivated to eat by hunger and social demands, as this woman and her family are doing.

(bottom) Women in the United States may eat because they are depressed or for other emotional reasons, rather than just to appease hunger or in a social situation. Obviously, this woman does not need the social trappings of a bowl, dining table, and the company of others to motivate her eating habits—unless you count the cat.

demands (Hawks et al., 2003). In this same study, both men and women from the United States were more likely to eat while watching television or movies than were Japanese men and women. Both culture and gender must be taken into account when studying why and under what circumstances people eat.

MALADAPTIVE EATING PROBLEMS

8.6 What are some problems in eating behavior, and how are they affected by biology and culture?

◄ **AP*** Describe classic research findings in specific motivation systems.

It would be nice if people all over the world ate just the amount of food that they needed and were able to maintain a healthy, normal weight. Unfortunately, that is not the case for many people. Some people weigh far more than they should, whereas others weigh far less. Why do some people get so fat? Is it just overeating?

Obesity   There are several factors that create *obesity*, a condition in which the body weight of a person is 20 percent or more over the ideal body weight for that person's height. Actual definitions of obesity vary. Some definitions consider 20 to 30 percent to be overweight and limit obesity to 30 percent. Others state that men are obese at 20 percent over the ideal weight and women at 30 percent. However it is defined, a significant factor in obesity is heredity. There appear to be several sets of genes, some on different chromosomes, which influence a person's likelihood of becoming obese (Barsh et al., 2000). If there is a history of obesity in a particular family, each family member has a risk of becoming obese that is double or triple the risk of people who do not have a family history of obesity (Bouchard, 1997).

Another factor is certainly overeating. Around the world, as developing countries get stronger economies and their food supplies become stable, the rates of obesity increase dramatically and quickly (Barsh et al., 2000). Foods become more varied and enticing* as well, and an increase in variety is associated with an increase in eating beyond the physiological need to eat (Raynor & Epstein, 2001). In industrialized societies when workers spend more hours in the workplace, there is less time available for preparing meals at home and more incentive to dine out (Chou et al., 2004). When the "dining out" choices include fast food and soft drinks, as is so often the case, obesity rates increase. In sum, as cultures become more industrialized and follow Western cultural lifestyles, negative aspects such as obesity of those lifestyles also increase. Over the last 20 years, rates of obesity in developing countries have tripled. Specifically, it is the developing countries that have been imitating the Western lifestyle of lower exercise rates and overeating foods that are cheap but high in fat and calories, countries such as China, the Middle East, Southeast Asia, and the Pacific Islands. In children from these countries, 10 to 25 percent are overweight and another 2 to 10 percent are obese (Hossain et al., 2007).

As mentioned earlier, metabolism slows down as people age. Aside from not changing the eating habits of their youth, as they earn more income people also often increase the amount of food they consume, thereby assuring a weight gain that may lead to obesity. At about 31 percent, the United States has the highest rate of obesity in the world (Friedman, 2000, 2003; Marik, 2000; Mokdad et al., 2001).

In recent years, a hormone called *leptin* has been identified as one of the factors that controls appetite, which may also play an important role in obesity. The role of leptin is discussed in Psychology in the News, which follows.

*Enticing: attractive; desirable.

YOUR LOST WEIGHT

"Ready to head back?"

©The New Yorker Collection 2003 Robert Leighton from cartoonbank.com. All Rights Reserved.

Why are some ▶ people naturally so slender, whereas others seem likely to get fat?

This family is becoming more typical in the United States as obesity rates continue to rise. How much of the excess weight on each of these family members is caused by poor choices in diet and lack of exercise, and how much might be caused by inherited biological factors, such as a resistance to the hormone leptin?

((•● **Listen** to the Psychology in the News podcast.
www.mypsychlab.com

leptin   a hormone that, when released into the bloodstream, signals the hypothalamus that the body has had enough food and reduces the appetite while increasing the feeling of being full.

Psychology in the News

The Biology of Obesity

Why are some people naturally so slender, whereas others seem likely to get fat? Scientists now believe that a hormone called **leptin** plays a key role in appetite control. Leptin is a protein that is secreted as a *hormone* (a chemical that travels by way of the blood to all parts of the body) by the fatty tissues of the body. When released into the bloodstream, leptin signals the hypothalamus that the body has had enough food, reducing appetite and increasing the feeling of being full, or satiated (Friedman & Halaas, 1998).

Leptin enters the bloodstream from the fat cells, traveling to the hypothalamus in the brain where it binds to receptors and causes the hypothalamus to signal the body to either stop eating or to eat more. High levels of leptin, which are produced when enough food is consumed, cause the appetite to decrease, whereas low levels of leptin signal a condition of starvation and lead to increased appetite and the urge to eat (Brunner et al., 1997). This is the normal feedback loop for appetite control in the brain.

Having found this link, scientists experimented on obese mice by giving them a high dosage of the hormone, which should lead to a decrease in appetite and weight loss. Although at first the results seemed promising, more recent studies have found that certain strains of obese mice do not lose weight when leptin levels are increased, suggesting a resistance to leptin—their bodies can respond only to certain levels of leptin, and when the levels go too high, the body stops responding, allowing appetite to remain out of control (Friedman, 2003).

To make matters worse, the genes that once helped people survive famine and times of want may be the very genes that are now responsible for the rise in obesity (Friedman, 2003). Essentially, humans once lived in two major groupings: the hunter-gatherers, who had to take food as they could get it and often faced very lean times; and the herder-farmers, who lived in areas where cultivating food and raising domesticated animals were possible. The hunter-gatherer population would benefit more from genes that allowed their bodies to store energy very efficiently against the lean times.

What aided the hunter-gatherer population in ancient times, then, may be what is causing people descended from that population to store excess amounts of energy—the obese are storing up for a famine that does not come: "Obesity is not a personal failing. In trying to lose weight, the obese are fighting a difficult battle—a battle against biology, a battle that only the intrepid take on and one in which only a few prevail" (Friedman, 2003, p. 856.)

Questions for Further Discussion

1. What might the research with leptin-resistant mice imply for some obese people?

2. Many obese people face discrimination in various forms. If obesity is, at least in part, controlled by hormonal and genetic factors, how might the attitudes of others toward the obese change?

((•●─Listen on **MyPsychLab**

Anorexia Nervosa   Jennifer is an attractive 20-year-old overachiever who rigidly maintains her weight with diet, exercise, and self-discipline. Although she is thin, she still is dissatisfied with her weight and appearance (she looks in the mirror and sees a fat person) and strives to lose more. Jennifer is 5 feet, 6 inches tall and weighs only 85 pounds (Rideout, 2005). Why does Jennifer think she needs to lose more weight?

Anorexia Nervosa, often called anorexia, is a condition in which a person (typically young and female) reduces eating to the point that a weight loss of 15 percent below expected body weight or more is the result. At a weight loss of 40 percent below expected body weight, hospitalization is necessary. Hormone secretion becomes abnormal, especially in the thyroid and adrenal glands. The heart muscles become weak and heart rhythms may alter. Other physical effects of anorexia include diarrhea, loss of muscle tissue, loss of sleep, and low blood pressure.

Some individuals with anorexia will eat in front of others but then force themselves to throw up or take large doses of laxatives. They are often obsessed with exercising and with food—cooking elaborate meals for others while eating nothing themselves. They have extremely distorted body images, seeing fat where others see only skin and bones.

What causes anorexia is not yet fully understood. Some theories involve biological explanations. Others point to psychological factors such as a rejection of sexual maturity (anorexia usually begins in the early teens and often causes menstruation to cease), sexual abuse, perfectionism with a desire to control as many aspects of one's life as possible, and family dysfunction (Abraham & Llewellyn-Jones, 2001; Mitchell, 1985).

What can be done to treat anorexia? If the anorexic weight loss is severe (40 percent or more below expected normal weight), dehydration, severe chemical imbalances, and possibly organ damage may result. Hospitalization should occur before this dangerous point is reached. In the hospital the individual's physical needs will be treated, even to the point of force-feeding in extreme cases. Anorexia Nervosa is classified as a clinical (mental) disorder in the *Diagnostic and Statistical Manual of Mental Disorders, Fourth Edition, Text Revision* or *DSM-IV-TR* (American Psychiatric Association, 2000), which is a listing of disorders and their symptoms used by psychological professionals to make a diagnosis. (L)(I)(N)(K) *to Chapter Twelve: Psychological Disorders, pp. 481–482.* As a result, psychological counseling will also be part of the hospital treatment, which may last from two to four months. Those individuals with anorexia who are not so severely malnourished as to be in immediate danger can be treated outside of the hospital setting, typically receiving supportive psychotherapy, behavioral therapy, and perhaps group therapy. Family therapy is nearly always indicated in cases in which the family of the person with anorexia is contributing in some way to the behavior. (L)(I)(N)(K) *to Chapter Thirteen: Psychological Therapies, p. 532.* (The author was recently told of a mother and daughter who were both developing anorexia, with the mother encouraging the behavior in her daughter.) The prognosis for full recovery is not as hopeful as it should be because only 40 to 60 percent of all individuals with anorexia who receive treatment will make a recovery. For some persons with anorexia who do gain weight, the damage to the heart and other body systems may still be so great that an early death is a possibility (Neumarker, 1997).

The following Web sites provide access to information, help, and professional referrals for people with anorexia and other eating disorders:

- **http://www.nationaleatingdisorders.org/** (information about eating disorders and professional referrals)
- **http://www.womenshealth.gov/FAQ/anorexia-nervosa.cfm** (information and links to other organizations)
- **http://www.nami.org/Content/ContentGroups/Helpline1/Anorexia_Nervosa.htm**

Bulimia Nervosa   In her late twenties, Carrie is the expected weight for her height but obsesses about food. She alternates between starving herself and then gorging on large amounts of food. After gorging, she makes herself throw up to rid her body of the food she has just eaten. Typically, she gorges on fattening, sugary foods such as cookies, ice cream, and breads (Rideout, 2005). Why does Carrie eat like this?

The "thin is in" mentality that dominates the field of fashion design models is a major contributor to the Western cultural concept of very thin women as beautiful and desirable. Many of today's fashion models are a far cry from the days of sex symbol Marilyn Monroe, who was rumored to be a size 12.

anorexia nervosa a condition in which a person reduces eating to the point that a weight loss of 15 percent below the ideal body weight or more occurs.

Bulimia Nervosa, often called bulimia, is a condition in which a person develops a cycle of "binging" or overeating enormous amounts of food at one sitting, and then using inappropriate methods for avoiding weight gain (American Psychiatric Association, 2000). Most individuals with bulimia engage in "purging" behaviors, such as deliberately vomiting after the binge or misuse of laxatives, but may not, using other inappropriate methods to avoid weight gain such as fasting the day or two after the binge or engaging in excessive exercise (American Psychiatric Association, 2000). There are some similarities to anorexia: The victims are usually female, are obsessed with their appearance, diet excessively, and believe themselves to be fat even when they are quite obviously not fat. But individuals with bulimia are typically a little older than those with anorexia at the onset of the disorder—early twenties rather than early puberty. Like Carrie, individuals with bulimia often maintain a normal weight, making it difficult to detect. The most obvious difference is that the person with bulimia will eat, and eat to excess, binging on huge amounts of food—as much as 50,000 calories in one sitting (Humphries, 1987). A typical binge may include a gallon of ice cream, a package of cookies, and a gallon of milk—all consumed as quickly as possible.

But wait a minute—if individuals with bulimia are so concerned about gaining weight, why do they binge at all? Individuals with bulimia have very distorted views of how much food is too much food, and eating one cookie while trying to control weight can lead to a binge—after all, since the diet is completely blown, why not go all out?

One might think that bulimia is not as damaging to the health as anorexia. After all, the person with bulimia is in no danger of starving to death. But bulimia comes with many serious health consequences: severe tooth decay and erosion of the lining of the esophagus from the acidity of the vomiting, enlarged salivary glands, potassium, calcium, and sodium imbalances that can be very dangerous, damage to the intestinal tract from overuse of laxatives, heart problems, fatigue, and seizures (Berg, 1999).

As with anorexia, there have been many proposed causes. Several research studies indicate a genetic component for both bulimia and anorexia (Fumeron et al., 2001; Strober et al., 2000; Vink et al., 2001). Psychological issues of control have also been cited, but biological evidence suggests that brain chemistry, and in particular the neurotransmitter *serotonin*, is involved in both bulimia and anorexia (Fumeron et al., 2001; Jimerson et al., 1997). Other studies point to the role of leptin, a hormone that has also been implicated in obesity and discussed in the previous Psychology in the News section (Ferron et al., 1997).

Treatment of bulimia, which like anorexia is listed as a clinical (mental) disorder in the *DSM-IV-TR* (American Psychiatric Association, 2000), can involve many of the same measures taken to treat anorexia: hospitalization, drugs that affect serotonin levels, and psychotherapy. The prognosis for the individual's recovery is somewhat more hopeful than that of someone with anorexia. Cognitive therapy, which involves helping clients to understand how illogical and irrational their thought patterns have become, has been successful in treating bulimia (DeAngelis, 2002). A cognitive therapist is very direct, forcing clients to see how their beliefs do not stand up when considered in "the light of day" and helping them form new and more constructive ways of thinking about themselves and their behavior. (LINK) *to Chapter Thirteen: Psychological Therapies, pp. 528–531.* Table 8.3 lists just a few of the more visible signs and symptoms of eating disorders.

Culture and Eating Disorders   Although many researchers have believed eating disorders, especially anorexia, to be culture-bound syndromes that only show up in cultures obsessed with being thin (as many Western cultures are), eating disorders are also found in other cultures (Miller & Pumariega, 1999). What differs between

> But wait a minute—if individuals with bulimia ▶ are so concerned about gaining weight, why do they binge at all?

bulimia nervosa   a condition in which a person develops a cycle of "binging," or overeating enormous amounts of food at one sitting, and then using unhealthy methods to avoid weight gain.

Western and non-Western cultures is the rate at which such disorders appear. For example, Chinese and Chinese American women are far less likely to suffer from eating disorders than are non-Hispanic white women (Pan, 2000). Why wouldn't Chinese American women be more likely to have eating disorders after being exposed to the Western cultural obsession with thinness? Pan (2000) assumes that whatever Chinese cultural factors "protect" Chinese women from developing eating disorders may also still have a powerful influence on Chinese American women.

One problem with looking at anorexia and bulimia in other cultures is that the behavior of starving oneself may be seen in other cultures as having an entirely different purpose than in Western cultures. One key component of anorexia, for example, is a fear of being fat, a fear that is missing in many other cultures. Yet women in those cultures have starved themselves for other socially recognized reasons: religious fasting or unusual ideas about nutrition (Castillo, 1997).

Anorexia and bulimia have also been thought to occur only rarely in African American women, but that characterization seems to be changing. Researchers are seeing an increase in anorexia and bulimia among young African American women of all socioeconomic levels (Crago et al., 1996; Mintz & Betz, 1998; Pumariega & Gustavson, 1994). If clinicians and doctors are not aware that these disorders can affect more than the typical white, young, middle-class to upper-middle-class woman, important signs and symptoms of eating disorders in nonwhite or non-Western people may allow these disorders to go untreated until it is too late.

Table 8.3 Possible Signs of Eating Disorders

Dramatic weight loss in a relatively short period of time
Obsession with calories and fat content of food
Hiding food in strange places
Hair loss, pale appearance to the skin
Bruised or callused knuckles, bloodshot eyes with light bruising under the eyes
Frequent trips to the bathroom following meals
Obsession with continuous exercise
Wearing baggy clothes to hide body shape or weight loss
Reading books about weight loss and eating disorders
Complaints of often feeling cold

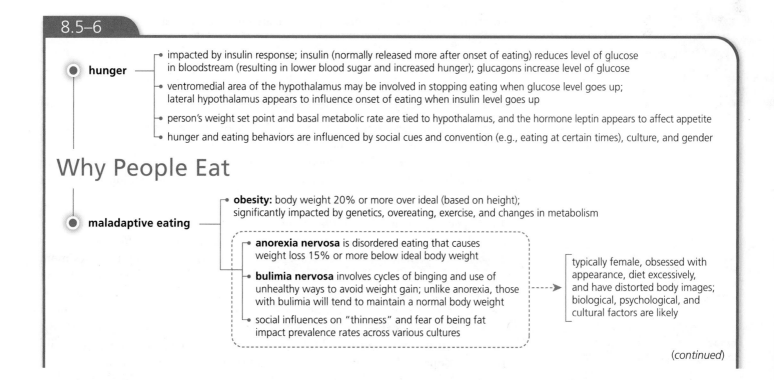

8.5–6

hunger
- impacted by insulin response; insulin (normally released more after onset of eating) reduces level of glucose in bloodstream (resulting in lower blood sugar and increased hunger); glucagons increase level of glucose
- ventromedial area of the hypothalamus may be involved in stopping eating when glucose level goes up; lateral hypothalamus appears to influence onset of eating when insulin level goes up
- person's weight set point and basal metabolic rate are tied to hypothalamus, and the hormone leptin appears to affect appetite
- hunger and eating behaviors are influenced by social cues and convention (e.g., eating at certain times), culture, and gender

Why People Eat

maladaptive eating
- **obesity:** body weight 20% or more over ideal (based on height); significantly impacted by genetics, overeating, exercise, and changes in metabolism
- **anorexia nervosa** is disordered eating that causes weight loss 15% or more below ideal body weight
- **bulimia nervosa** involves cycles of binging and use of unhealthy ways to avoid weight gain; unlike anorexia, those with bulimia will tend to maintain a normal body weight
- social influences on "thinness" and fear of being fat impact prevalence rates across various cultures

typically female, obsessed with appearance, diet excessively, and have distorted body images; biological, psychological, and cultural factors are likely

(continued)

PRACTICE **QUIZ:** PREPARING FOR THE AP* EXAM

ANSWERS ON PAGE AK-2.

Directions: Read each of the questions or incomplete sentences below. Then choose the response that best answers the question or completes the sentence.

1. Which of the following is not one of the physiological factors in hunger?
   - **a.** Insulin
   - **b.** Stomach
   - **c.** Pancreas
   - **d.** Hypothalamus
   - **e.** Corpus callosum

2. If calorie intake stays the same as the basal metabolic rate decreases, the weight set point _____.
   - **a.** decreases
   - **b.** increases
   - **c.** stays the same
   - **d.** wavers up and down
   - **e.** increases at first, then decreases

3. Which of the following is a social cue for hunger?
   - **a.** Eating a late breakfast
   - **b.** Feeling your stomach ache
   - **c.** Noticing that it is time for dinner
   - **d.** Producing higher insulin levels
   - **e.** Hearing your stomach rumble

4. One of the main differences between anorexia and bulimia is that individuals suffering from anorexia _____.
   - **a.** weigh 15 percent or more below expected body weight
   - **b.** have a negative self-image
   - **c.** are obsessed with body weight
   - **d.** can suffer from heart problems
   - **e.** tend to be female

5. Bulimia, unlike anorexia, _____.
   - **a.** involves starvation
   - **b.** is not physically harmful
   - **c.** produces an obsession with food
   - **d.** involves a cycle of binging and possibly purging
   - **e.** is most prevalent in early puberty

What part does the way we feel about things play in all of our daily activities—what exactly causes feelings? ▶

AP* Identify key contributors in the psychology of motivation and emotion. ▶

emotion the "feeling" aspect of consciousness, characterized by a certain physical arousal, a certain behavior that reveals the emotion to the outside world, and an inner awareness of feelings.

The first section of this chapter has looked at the motives that drive human behavior. But people do more than just behave—there are feelings that accompany every human action. The second section of the chapter explores the world of human emotions and how those emotions are connected to both thinking and actions.

Emotion

What part does the way we feel about things play in all of our daily activities—what exactly causes feelings? Human beings are full of feelings, or emotions, and although emotions may be internal processes, there are outward physical signs of what people are feeling.

THE THREE ELEMENTS OF EMOTION

8.7   What are the three elements of emotion?

The Latin word meaning "to move" is the source of both words used in this chapter over and over again—*motive* and *emotion*. **Emotion** can be defined as the "feeling" aspect of consciousness, characterized by three elements: a certain physical arousal, a certain behavior that reveals the feeling to the outside world, and an inner awareness of feelings.

The Physiology of Emotion   Physically, when a person experiences an emotion, an arousal is created by the sympathetic nervous system. **LINK** *to Chapter Two: The Biological Perspective, pp. 62–64.* The heart rate increases, breathing becomes more rapid, the pupils dilate, and the mouth may become dry. Think about the last time you were angry and then about the last time you were frightened. Weren't the physical symptoms pretty similar? Although facial expressions do differ among various emotional responses (Ekman, 1980; Ekman et al., 1969; Ekman & Friesen, 1978), emotions are difficult to distinguish from one another on the basis of outward bodily reactions alone. In fact, it is quite easy to mistake a person who is actually afraid or angry as being aroused if the person's face is not clearly visible, which can lead to much miscommunication and misunderstanding. However, in the laboratory using devices to measure the heart rate, blood pressure, and skin temperature, researchers have found that some emotions may be associated with different physiological reactions: Fear is associated with a decrease in skin temperature, whereas anger is associated with an increase in skin temperature and a greater increase in blood pressure, (Levenson, 1992; Levenson et al., 1992).

Which parts of the brain are involved in various aspects of emotion? As discussed in Chapter Two, the *amygdala*, a small area located within the limbic system on each side of the brain, is associated with fear in both humans and animals (Davis & Whalen, 2001; Fanselow & Gale, 2003) and is also involved in the facial expressions of human emotions (Morris et al., 1998). When the amygdala is damaged in rats, they cannot be classically conditioned to fear new objects—they apparently cannot remember to be afraid (Davidson et al., 2000; Fanselow & Gale, 2003). In humans, damage to the amygdala has been associated with similar effects (LaBar et al., 1995) and with impairment of the ability to determine emotions from looking at the facial expressions of others (Adolphs & Tranel, 2003).

While emotions involve both cortical and subcortical areas of the brain, research suggests that emotions may work differently depending on which side of the brain is involved. One area of investigation has been the frontal lobes. Researchers have found that positive emotions are associated with the left frontal lobe of the brain whereas negative feelings such as sadness, anxiety, and depression seem to be a function of the right frontal lobe (Davidson, 2003; Geschwind & Iacoboni, 2007; Heilman, 2002). In studies where the electrical activity of the brain has been tracked using an electroencephalograph (EEG), (LINK) *to Chapter Two: The Biological Perspective, pp. 66–67*, left frontal lobe activation has been associated with pleasant emotions while right frontal lobe activity has been associated with negative emotional states (Davidson, 2003). Furthermore, increased left frontal lobe activity has been found in individuals trained in meditation, and for the participants in this study, greater left frontal lobe activity was accompanied by a reduction in their anxiety as well as a boost in their immune system (Davidson et al., 2003).

The ability to interpret the facial expressions of others as a particular emotion also seems to be a function of one side of the brain more than the other. Researchers have found that when people are asked to identify the emotion on another person's face, the right hemisphere is more active than the left, particularly in women (Voyer & Rodgers, 2002). This difference begins weakly in childhood but increases in adulthood, with children being less able to identify negative emotions as well as positive emotions when compared to adults (Barth & Boles, 1999; Lane et al., 1995). This finding is consistent with early research that assigns the recognition of faces to the right hemisphere (Berent, 1977; Ellis, 1983).

The Behavior of Emotion: Emotional Expression   How do people behave when in the grip of an emotion? There are facial expressions, body movements, and actions that indicate to others how a person feels. Frowns, smiles, and sad expressions combine with hand gestures, the turning of one's body, and spoken words to produce an understanding of emotion. People fight, run, kiss, and yell, along with countless other actions stemming from the emotions they feel.

Facial expressions can vary across different cultures, although some aspects of facial expression seem to be universal. (See Figure 8.5 for some examples of universal facial expressions.) Charles Darwin (1898) was one of the first to theorize that emotions were a product of evolution and, therefore, universal—all human beings, no matter what their culture, would show the same facial expression because the facial muscles evolved to communicate specific information to onlookers. For example, an angry face would signal to onlookers that they should act submissively or expect a

◄ **AP** Describe how cultural influences shape emotional expression.

◄ **AP** Identify key contributors in the psychology of motivation and emotion.

Figure 8.5 Facial Expressions of Emotion
Facial expressions appear to be universal. For example, these faces are interpreted as showing (a) anger, (b) fear, (c) disgust, (d) happiness, (e) surprise, and (f) sadness by people of cultures all over the world. Although the situations that cause these emotions may differ from culture to culture, the expression of particular emotions remains strikingly the same.

* **Explore** with the simulation on facial expressions of emotion.
www.mypsychlab.com

AP* Identify key contributors in the psychology of motivation and emotion.

display rules learned ways of controlling displays of emotion in social settings.

fight. Although Darwin's ideas were not in line with the behaviorist movement of the early and middle twentieth century, which promoted environment rather than heredity as the cause of behavior, other researchers have since found evidence that there is a universal nature to at least seven basic emotions, giving more support to the evolutionary perspective within psychology (Ekman, 1973; Ekman & Friesen, 1969, 1971). ⓛⓘⓝⓚ *to Chapter One: The Science of Psychology, pp. 16–17.* Even children who are blind from birth can produce the appropriate facial expressions for any given situation without ever having witnessed those expressions on others, which strongly supports the idea that emotional expressions have their basis in biology rather than in learning (Charlesworth & Kreutzer, 1973; Fulcher, 1942). * **Explore** on MyPsychLab

In their research, Ekman and Friesen found that people of many different cultures (Japanese, Europeans, Americans, and even the Fore tribe of New Guinea) can consistently recognize at least seven facial expressions: anger, fear, disgust, happiness, surprise, sadness, and contempt (Ekman & Friesen, 1969, 1971). Although the emotions and the related facial expressions appear to be universal, exactly when, where, and how an emotion is expressed may be determined by the culture. **Display rules** that can vary from culture to culture (Ekman, 1973; Ekman & Friesen, 1969) are learned ways of controlling displays of emotion in social settings. For example, Japanese people have strict social rules about showing emotion in public situations—they simply do not show emotion, remaining cool, calm, and collected, at least on the *outside*. But if in a more private situation, as a parent scolding a child within the home, the adult's facial expression would easily be recognized as "angry" by people of any culture. The emotion is universal and the way it is expressed on the face is universal, but whether it is expressed or displayed depends on the learned cultural rules for displaying emotion.

Display rules are different between cultures that are individualistic (placing the importance of the individual above the social group) and those that are collectivistic (placing the importance of the social group above that of the individual). Whereas the culture of the United States is individualistic, for example, the culture of Japan is collectivistic. At least part of the difference between the two types of display rules may be due to these cultural differences (Edelmann & Iwawaki, 1987; Hofstede, 1980; Hofstede et al., 2002). **LINK** *to Chapter Eleven: Theories of Personality, pp. 457–458.*

Display rules are also different for males and females. Researchers looking at the display rules of boys and girls found that boys are reluctant to talk about feelings in a social setting, whereas girls are expected and encouraged to do so (Polce-Lynch et al., 1998). With adults, researchers looking at the expression of anger in the workplace found that women are generally less willing than men to express negative emotions, although factors such as status complicate the findings somewhat (Domagalski & Steelman, 2007).

Subjective Experience: Labeling Emotion   The third element of emotion is interpreting the subjective feeling by giving it a label: anger, fear, disgust, happiness, sadness, shame, interest, and so on. Another way of labeling this element is to call it the "cognitive element," because the labeling process is a matter of retrieving memories of previous similar experiences, perceiving the context of the emotion, and coming up with a solution—a label.

The label a person applies to a subjective feeling is at least in part a learned response influenced by that person's language and culture. Such labels may differ in people of different cultural backgrounds. For example, researchers in one study (Tsai et al., 2004) found that Chinese Americans who were still firmly rooted in their original Chinese culture were far more likely to use labels to describe their emotions that referred to bodily sensations (such as "dizzy") or social relationships (such as "friendship") than were more "Americanized" Chinese Americans and European Americans, who tended to use more directly emotional words (such as "liking" or "love").

In another study, even the subjective feeling of happiness showed cultural differences (Kitayama & Markus, 1994). In this study, Japanese students and students from the United States were found to associate a general positive emotional state with entirely different circumstances. In the case of the Japanese students, the positive state was more associated with friendly or socially engaged feelings. The students from the United States associated their positive emotional state more with feelings that were socially disengaged, such as pride. This finding is a further reflection of the differences between cultures that are either collectivistic or individualistic.

So which of the three elements is the most important?

In the early days of psychology, it was assumed that feeling a particular emotion led first to a physical reaction and then to a behavioral one. Seeing a snarling dog in one's path causes the feeling of fear, which stimulates the body to arousal, followed by the behavioral act of running. People are aroused because they are afraid. (See Figure 8.6.)

So which of the three elements is the most important?

	Stimulus	First response	Second response
Common sense theory "I'm shaking because I'm afraid."	Snarling dog	FEAR Conscious fear	ANS arousal

Figure 8.6 Common Sense Theory of Emotion

In the common sense theory of emotion, a stimulus (snarling dog) leads to an emotion of fear, which then leads to bodily arousal (in this case, indicated by shaking) through the autonomic nervous system (ANS).

AP* Compare and contrast major theories of emotion.

AP* Identify key contributors in the psychology of motivation and emotion.

8.8 How do the James-Lange and Cannon-Bard theories of emotion differ?

James-Lange   William James (1884, 1890, 1894), who was also the founder of the functionalist perspective in the early history of psychology ⓛⓘⓝⓚ *to Chapter One: The Science of Psychology, pp. 7–8,* disagreed with this early viewpoint. He believed that the order of the components of emotions was quite different. At nearly the same time, a physiologist and psychologist in Denmark, Carl Lange (1885), came up with an explanation of emotion so similar to that of James that the two names are used together to refer to the theory—the **James-Lange theory of emotion**. (See Figure 8.7.)

	Stimulus	First response	Second response
James-Lange theory "I'm afraid because I'm shaking."	Snarling dog	ANS arousal, changes in body	*FEAR* Conscious fear

Figure 8.7 James-Lange Theory of Emotion

In the James-Lange theory of emotion, a stimulus leads to bodily arousal first, which is then interpreted as an emotion.

In this theory, a stimulus of some sort (for example, the large snarling dog) produces a physiological reaction. This reaction, which is the arousal of the "fight-or-flight" sympathetic nervous system (wanting to run), produces bodily sensations such as increased heart rate, dry mouth, and rapid breathing. James and Lange believed that the physical arousal led to the labeling of the emotion (*fear*). Simply put, "I am afraid because I am aroused," "I am embarrassed because my face is red," "I am nervous because my stomach is fluttering," and "I am in love because my heart rate increases when I look at her or him."

What about people who have spinal cord injuries that prevent the sympathetic nervous system from functioning? Although James-Lange would predict that these people should show decreased emotion because the arousal that causes emotion is no longer there, this does not in fact happen. Several studies of people with spinal cord injuries report that these people are capable of experiencing the same emotions after their injury as before, sometimes even more intensely (Bermond et al., 1991; Chwalisz et al., 1988).

Cannon-Bard   Physiologists Walter Cannon (1927) and Philip Bard (1934) theorized that the emotion and the physiological arousal occur more or less at the same time. Cannon, an expert in sympathetic arousal mechanisms, did not feel that the physical changes caused by different emotions were distinct enough to allow them to be perceived as different emotions. Bard expanded on this idea by stating that the sensory information that comes into the brain is sent simultaneously (by the thalamus) to both the cortex and the organs of the sympathetic nervous system. The fear and the bodily reactions are, therefore, experienced at the same time—not one after the other. "I'm afraid and running and aroused!" (See Figure 8.8.)

James-Lange theory of emotion theory in which a physiological reaction leads to the labeling of an emotion.

Figure 8.8 Cannon-Bard Theory of Emotion

In the Cannon-Bard theory of emotion, a stimulus leads to activity in the brain, which then sends signals to arouse the body and interpret the emotion at the same time.

	Stimulus	First response	Second response
Cannon-Bard theory "I'm shaking and feeling afraid at the same time."	Snarling dog	Subcortical brain activity	ANS arousal, changes in body / *FEAR* Conscious fear

This theory, known as the **Cannon-Bard theory of emotion**, also had its critics. Lashley (1938) stated that the thalamus would have to be pretty sophisticated to make sense of all the possible human emotions and relay them to the proper areas of the cortex and body. It would seem that other areas of the brain must be involved in processing emotional reactions. The studies of people with spinal cord injuries, which seem to suggest that emotions can be experienced without feedback from the sympathetic organs to the cortex and were cited as a criticism of the James-Lange theory, seem at first to support the Cannon-Bard version of emotions: People do not need feedback from those organs to experience emotion. However, there is an alternate pathway that does provide feedback from these organs to the cortex; this is the *vagus nerve*, one of the cranial nerves (LeDoux, 1994). The existence of this feedback pathway makes the case for Cannon-Bard a little less convincing.

8.9 What are the key elements in cognitive arousal theory, the facial feedback hypothesis, and the cognitive-mediational theory of emotion?

Schachter-Singer and Cognitive Arousal Theory   The early theories talked about the emotion and the physical reaction, but what about the mental interpretation of those components? In their **cognitive arousal theory**, Schachter and Singer (1962) proposed that two things have to happen before emotion occurs: the physical arousal and a labeling of the arousal based on cues from the surrounding environment. These two things happen at the same time, resulting in the labeling of the emotion. (See Figure 8.9.)

| Stimulus | First response | Second response |

Schachter's cognitive arousal theory

"This snarling dog is dangerous and that makes me feel afraid."

Snarling dog

Cognitive appraisal

ANS arousal, changes in body

FEAR

Conscious fear

For example, if a person comes across a snarling dog while taking a walk, the physical arousal (heart racing, eyes opening wide) is accompanied by the thought (cognition) that this must be fear. Then and only then will the person experience the fear emotion. In other words, "I am aroused in the presence of a scary dog; therefore, I must be afraid." Evidence for this theory was found in what is now a classic experiment, described in the accompanying Classic Studies in Psychology.

Classic Studies in Psychology

The Angry/Happy Man

In 1962, Stanley Schachter and Jerome Singer designed an experiment to test their theory that emotions are determined by an interaction between the physiological state of arousal and the label, or cognitive interpretation, that a person places on the arousal. Male student volunteers were told that they were going to answer a questionnaire about their reactions to a new vitamin called Suproxin. In reality, they were all injected with a drug called epinephrine, which causes physical arousal in the form of increased heart rate, rapid breathing, and a reddened face—all responses that happen during a strong emotional reaction.

Cannon-Bard theory of emotion
theory in which the physiological reaction and the emotion are assumed to occur at the same time.

cognitive arousal theory   theory of emotion in which both the physical arousal and the labeling of that arousal based on cues from the environment must occur before the emotion is experienced.

Figure 8.9 Schachter's Cognitive Arousal Theory of Emotion
Schachter's cognitive arousal theory is similar to the James-Lange theory but adds the element of cognitive labeling of the arousal. In this theory, a stimulus leads to both bodily arousal and the labeling of that arousal (based on the surrounding context), which leads to the experience and labeling of the emotional reaction.

Each student then participated in one of two conditions. In one condition, a confederate* posing as one of the participants started complaining about the experimenter, tearing up his questionnaire and storming out. In the other condition, there was one man who acted more like he was very happy, almost giddy and playing with some of the objects in the room. The "angry" man and the "happy" man in both conditions deliberately behaved in the two different ways as part of the experiment.

After both conditions had played out, participants in each of the two conditions were asked to describe their own emotions. The participants who had been exposed to the "angry" man interpreted their arousal symptoms as anger, whereas those exposed to the "happy" man interpreted their arousal as happiness. In all cases, the actual cause of arousal was the epinephrine and the physical symptoms of arousal were identical. The only difference between the two groups of participants was their exposure to the two different contexts. Schachter and Singer's theory would have predicted exactly these results: Physiological arousal has to be interpreted cognitively before it is experienced as a specific emotion.

Although this classic experiment stimulated a lot of research, much of that research has failed to find much support for the cognitive arousal theory of emotion (Reisenzein, 1983, 1994). But this theory did serve to draw attention to the important role that cognition plays in determining emotions. The role of cognition in emotion has been revisited in some more modern theories of emotion, as you will see in the following discussions.

Questions for Further Discussion

1. How might observing the emotions of others under more normal circumstances (i.e., not in a drugged state) affect a person's own emotional state?

2. According to Schachter and Singer's theory, for your first date with a person, should you choose a happy movie or a sad one?

3. In this experiment, what was the independent variable manipulated by the experimenters? What was the dependent variable?

4. This experiment used deception, as the participants were not told the true nature of the injection they received. What kind of ethical problems might have arisen from this deception? What problems would the experimenters have had in getting this study approved by an ethics committee today?

---

facial feedback hypothesis theory of emotion that assumes that facial expressions provide feedback to the brain concerning the emotion being expressed, which in turn causes and intensifies the emotion.

Does that mean that I don't smile because I'm happy—I'm happy because I smile?

The Facial Feedback Hypothesis: Smile, You'll Feel Better   In his (1898) book *The Expression of the Emotions in Man and Animals*, Charles Darwin stated that facial expressions evolved as a way of communicating intentions, such as threat or fear, and that these expressions are universal within a species rather than specific to a culture. He also believed (as in the James-Lange theory) that when such emotions are expressed freely on the face, the emotion itself intensifies—meaning that the more one smiles, the happier one feels.

Modern psychologists have proposed a theory of emotion that is consistent with much of Darwin's original thinking. Called the **facial feedback hypothesis**, this explanation assumes that facial expressions provide feedback to the brain concerning the emotion being expressed, which in turn not only intensifies the emotion but also actually *causes* the emotion (Buck, 1980; Ekman, 1980; Ekman & Friesen, 1978; Keillor et al., 2002). (See Figure 8.10.)

Does that mean that I don't smile because I'm happy—I'm happy because I smile?

As the old song goes, "put on a happy face" and yes, you'll feel happier, according to the facial feedback hypothesis. One fairly recent study does cast some doubt on the validity of this hypothesis, however. If the facial feedback hypothe-

---

*Confederate: someone who is cooperating with another person on some task.

	Stimulus	First response	Second response
Facial feedback theory		ANS arousal in face → Facial expression → Cognitive interpretation of face motions	**FEAR**

Figure 8.10 Facial Feedback Theory of Emotion

In the facial feedback theory of emotion, a stimulus such as this snarling dog causes arousal and a facial expression. The facial expression then provides feedback to the brain about the emotion. The brain then interprets the emotion and may also intensify it.

sis is correct, then people who have facial paralysis on both sides of the face should be unable to experience emotions in a normal way. But a case study conducted on just such a person revealed that although she was unable to express emotions on her paralyzed face, she could respond emotionally to slides meant to stimulate emotional reactions, just as anyone else would (Keillor et al., 2002). Clearly, the question of how much the actual facial expression determines the emotional experience has yet to be fully answered.

For more about the psychology of happiness, see the section Applying Psychology to Everyday Life at the end of this chapter.

Lazarus and the Cognitive-Mediational Theory   As mentioned in the Classic Studies in Psychology section, Schachter and Singer's (1962) study stressed the importance of cognition, or thinking, in the determination of emotions. One of the more modern versions of cognitive emotion theories is Lazarus's **cognitive-mediational theory** of emotion (1991). In this theory, the most important aspect of any emotional experience is how the person interprets, or appraises, the stimulus that causes the emotional reaction. To *mediate* means to "come between" and in this theory, the cognitive appraisal mediates by coming between the stimulus and the emotional response to that stimulus.

For example, remember the person who encountered a snarling dog while walking through the neighborhood? According to Lazarus, the appraisal of the situation would come *before* both the physical arousal and the experience of emotion. If the dog is behind a sturdy fence, the appraisal would be something like "no threat." The most likely emotion would be annoyance, and the physical arousal would be minimal. But if the dog is not confined, the appraisal would more likely be "danger—threatening animal!" which would be followed by an increase in arousal and the emotional experience of fear. In other words, it's the *interpretation* of the arousal that results in the emotion of fear, not the labeling as in the Schachter-Singer model, and the interpretation comes first. (See Figure 8.11.)

Not everyone agrees with this theory, of course. Some researchers believe that emotional reactions to situations are so fast that they are almost instantaneous, which would leave little time for a cognitive appraisal to occur first (Zajonc, 1998). Others (Kilhstrom et al., 2000) have found that the human brain can respond to a physical threat before conscious thought enters the picture. The simple spinal cord reflex of pain withdrawal discussed in Chapter Two is an example of this—the reflex occurs so quickly that the brain itself is not involved, and the experience of pain is consciously felt *after* the injured body part is jerked away from the painful stimulus. ⓛⓘⓝⓚ *to Chapter Two: The Biological Perspective, pp. 59–60.*

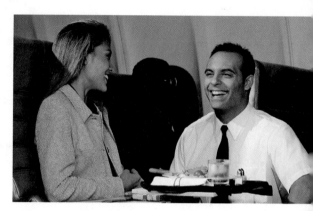

The facial feedback hypothesis assumes that changing your own facial expression can change the way you feel. Smiling makes people feel happy, and frowning makes people feel sad. This effect seems to have an impact on the people around us as well. If this is true, this smiling woman may make the airline steward handing her the food feel good, too. Is it hard for you to stay in a bad mood when the people around you are smiling and laughing?

cognitive-mediational theory   theory of emotion in which a stimulus must be interpreted (appraised) by a person in order to result in a physical response and an emotional reaction.

Figure 8.11 Lazarus's Theory of Emotion

In Lazarus's cognitive-mediational theory of emotion, a stimulus causes an immediate appraisal (e.g., "The dog is snarling and not behind a fence, so this is dangerous"). The cognitive appraisal results in an emotional response, which is then followed by the appropriate bodily response.

	Stimulus	First response	Second response
Lazarus's Cognitive-mediational theory		Appraisal of threat → **FEAR**	Bodily response

Which theory is right?

Which theory is right? Human emotions are so incredibly complex that it might not be out of place to say that all of the theories are correct to at least some degree. In certain situations, the cognitive appraisal might have time to mediate the emotion that is experienced (such as falling in love), whereas in other situations, the need to act first, think and feel later is more important. (See Figure 8.12.)

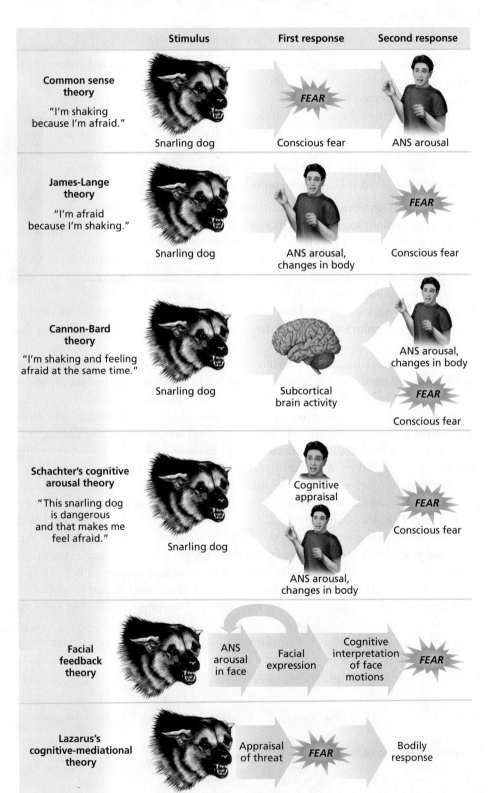

Figure 8.12 Comparison of Theories of Emotion

These figures represent the six different theories of emotion as discussed in the text.

physiological arousal is created by the sympathetic nervous system and is associated with brain activity in specific areas (e.g., the amygdala) and right or left hemisphere activity

emotional expressions can vary across cultures but some expressions seem to be universal; display rules also vary across cultures and according to gender

subjective labeling of emotion is largely a learned response, influenced by both language and culture

Emotion

is "feeling" aspect of consciousness, characterized by physiological arousal, specific expressive behavior, and inner awareness of feelings

Lazarus's **cognitive-mediational theory** places the emphasis on the cognitive appraisal and interpretation of the stimulus that causes the emotional reaction

based on ideas from Darwin, the **facial feedback hypothesis** suggests that facial expressions (and other behaviors) provide feedback to the brain that can intensify or cause a specific emotion

James-Lange theory suggests that specific stimuli result in physical arousal and leads to labeling of the emotion

Cannon-Bard theory suggests that emotion and physiological arousal occur simultaneously

cognitive arousal theory (Schacter and Singer) suggests that physiological arousal and the actual interpretation of that arousal based on cues from the environment must occur before the emotion itself is experienced

Various Theories of Emotion

have been suggested, each with a slightly different focus and interpretation (see Fig. 8.12)

PRACTICE **QUIZ:** PREPARING FOR THE AP* EXAM

ANSWERS ON PAGE AK-2.

Directions: Read each of the questions or incomplete sentences below. Then choose the response that best answers the question or completes the sentence.

1. What are the three elements of emotion?
   a. Attention, behavior, and cognition
   b. Attention, behavior, and motivation
   c. Physical arousal, behavior, and cognition
   d. Physical arousal, attention, and behavior
   e. Physical arousal, cognition, and motivation

2. Which theory of emotion is based on the assumption that the thalamus sends sensory information to the cortex and the organs of the sympathetic nervous system at the same time?
   a. James-Lange
   b. Cannon-Bard
   c. Schachter-Singer
   d. Facial feedback
   e. Cognitive-mediational

3. Giuliana, a generally happy person, is enrolled in a psychology experiment. She is injected with epinephrine and then shown a movie clip of two people fighting. Immediately after watching the clip, Giuliana is most likely to feel _____.
   a. angry
   b. happy
   c. scared
   d. relaxed
   e. confused

4. Ming comes home from school one day in a very foul mood, due to a fight he had with his girlfriend. His mother, hoping to improve his mood, starts telling him jokes. Ming resists laughing, but he can't help but smiling at the jokes his mother is telling him, and soon his mood begins to improve. Which theory of emotion best explains Ming's change in mood?
   a. James-Lange
   b. Cannon-Bard
   c. Schachter-Singer
   d. Facial feedback
   e. Cognitive-mediational

5. In which theory of emotion is the most important aspect of an emotional experience the interpretation, or appraisal, of the stimulus?
   a. James-Lange
   b. Cannon-Bard
   c. Schachter-Singer
   d. Facial feedback
   e. Cognitive-mediational

positive psychology movement
a viewpoint that recommends shifting the focus of psychology away from the negative aspects to a more positive focus on strengths, well-being, and the pursuit of happiness.

Applying Psychology to Everyday Life: A How-To of Happiness?

8.10   What is the positive psychology movement?

One emotion that is probably nearest and dearest to most people is happiness, a state of well-being and contentment that is much to be desired. Social psychologist David G. Myers is widely recognized as a leader in the field of research into happiness. He is also one of the supporters of the **positive psychology movement**, a perspective that recommends shifting the focus of psychology away from the negative (abuse, anxiety, depression, all the things that can go wrong) to a more positive focus on strengths, well-being, and the pursuit of happiness (Myers, 1993).

According to Myers and others (Lyubomirsky, 2001; Myers, 1993; Schwartz et al., 2002), happiness is the key to many things: the perception of the world as a safer place, healthier and more satisfying lives, and even the ability to make decisions more easily. Happy people are also more likely to help others (Pizarro & Salovey, 2002; Salovey et al., 2000).

So how can people become happier? In his popular book, *The Pursuit of Happiness*, Myers (1993) lists 10 suggestions for becoming happier that are based on his many years of research:

1. **Realize that enduring happiness doesn't come from success.** Money, power, and fame do not guarantee happiness. If people don't have wealth, they may be in miserable, unhappy circumstances, but the reverse is not necessarily true: Money really doesn't buy happiness. Psychiatrists and clinical psychologists often have very wealthy, successful people as clients.

2. **Take control of your time.** People who feel in control of their lives by good time-management skills are also happier people. Setting goals and breaking those goals down into steps can help a person see progress on a daily basis. Make lists and cross off items as they are finished.

3. **Act happy.** Put on a happy face. When people smile, it releases chemicals that make them feel better, and when they frown, the opposite occurs. Think happy, talk happy, act happy, and you will be happier.

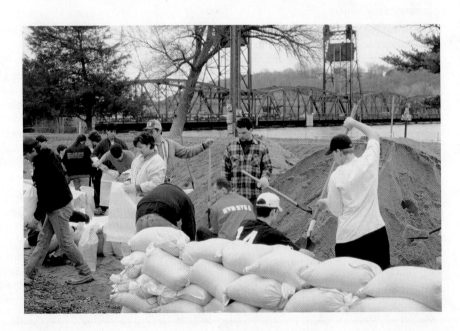

In the pursuit of happiness, many people find that helping others increases their own happiness. These volunteers are experiencing that kind of happiness as they fill sandbags to help control the flooding of a nearby river.

4. **Seek work and leisure activities that engage your skills.** Doing things that are challenging without being overwhelming can result in more happiness in both work and leisure activities. There can be more happiness in tending one's garden than in taking a world tour.

5. **Join the "movement" movement.** Exercise, particularly aerobic exercise, will not only help you to feel better and look better physically, but also it relieves depression and anxiety. Get moving and get happier.

6. **Give your body the sleep it wants.** Sleep deprivation is bad for the mind, the body, and the mood. Sleep-deprived people are crabby, whereas people who have time to sleep and rest adequately are typically happier.

7. **Give priority to close relationships.** A good social support system just can't be beat. Friends offer support and help to get you through the bad times. Take time to nurture friendships and relationships.

8. **Focus beyond the self.** Not only do happy people help other people more readily, but also they are happier for doing so. Helping others makes people feel good.

9. **Keep a gratitude journal.** Writing down the positive things that you have, such as a good thing that happened today, the friends you saw, and things that you did and enjoyed, also boosts a sense of well-being. Stop and smell the roses.

10. **Nurture your spiritual self.** People with a strong sense of faith also tend to be happier. Communities based on shared belief systems about faith provide a good support system. These communities can also give a person a sense of purpose and provide hope during times of stress. People involved in such communities also tend to help others, too (see number 8).

8 CHAPTER SUMMARY

Approaches to Understanding Motivation

8.1 How do psychologists define motivation, and what are the key elements of the early instinct and drive-reduction approaches to motivation?

- Motivation is the process by which activities are started, directed, and sustained so that physical and psychological needs are fulfilled.

- Instinct approaches proposed that some human actions may be motivated by instincts, which are innate patterns of behavior found in both people and animals.

- Drive-reduction approaches state that when an organism has a need (such as hunger), the need leads to psychological tension that motivates the organism to act, fulfilling the need and reducing the tension.

- Primary drives involve needs of the body whereas acquired (secondary) drives are those learned through experience. Homeostasis is the tendency of the body to maintain a steady state.

8.2 What are the characteristics of the three types of needs?

- The need for achievement is a strong desire to succeed in achieving one's goals, both realistic and challenging.

- The self-theory of emotion links the need for achievement to the concept of locus of control. A belief in control over one's life leads to more attempts to achieve, even in the face of failure. Those who believe that they have little control over what happens to them are more likely to develop learned helplessness.

- The need for affiliation is the desire to have friendly social interactions and relationships with others as well as the desire to be held in high regard by others.

- The need for power concerns having control over others, influencing them and having an impact on them. Status and prestige are important to people high in this need.

8.3 What are the key elements of the arousal and incentive approaches to motivation?

- In arousal theory, a person has an optimal level of arousal to maintain. People who need more arousal than others are called sensation seekers.

- In the incentive approach, an external stimulus may be so rewarding that it motivates a person to act toward that stimulus even in the absence of a drive.

8.4 How do Maslow's humanistic approach and self-determination theory explain motivation?

• Maslow proposed a hierarchy of needs, beginning with basic physiological needs and ending with transcendence needs. The more basic needs must be met before the higher needs can be fulfilled.

• Self-determination theory (SDT) is a model of motivation in which three basic needs are seen as necessary to an individual's successful development: autonomy, competence, and relatedness.

• Intrinsic motivation occurs when people act because the act itself is satisfying or rewarding, whereas extrinsic motivation occurs when people receive an external reward (such as money) for the act.

What, Hungry Again? Why People Eat

8.5 What happens in the body to cause hunger, and how do social factors influence a person's experience of hunger?

• The physiological components of hunger include signals from the stomach and the hypothalamus, and the increased secretion of insulin.

• When the basal metabolic rate slows down, the weight set point increases and makes weight gain more likely.

• The social components of hunger include social cues for when meals are to be eaten, cultural customs and food preferences, and the use of food as a comfort device or escape from unpleasantness.

• Some people may be externals who respond to the anticipation of eating by producing an insulin response, increasing the risk of obesity.

8.6 What are some problems in eating behavior, and how are they affected by biology and culture?

• Maladaptive eating problems include obesity, anorexia, and bulimia.

• Genetics may play a part in anorexia and bulimia, as well as insensitivity to leptin, a hormone that controls appetite.

Psychology in the News: The Biology of Obesity

• Scientists studying obesity have researched the role of leptin, a hormone that controls the feeling of being full.

Emotion

8.7 What are the three elements of emotion?

• Emotion is the "feeling" aspect of consciousness and includes physical, behavioral, and subjective (cognitive) elements.

8.8 How do the James-Lange and Cannon-Bard theories of emotion differ?

• The James-Lange theory states that a stimulus creates a physiological response that then leads to the labeling of the emotion.

• The Cannon-Bard theory asserts that the physiological reaction and the emotion are simultaneous, as the thalamus sends sensory information to both the cortex of the brain and the organs of the sympathetic nervous system.

8.9 What are the key elements in cognitive arousal theory, the facial feedback hypothesis, and the cognitive-mediational theory of emotion?

• In Schachter and Singer's cognitive arousal theory, both the physiological arousal and the actual interpretation of that arousal must occur before the emotion itself is experienced. This interpretation is based on cues from the environment.

Classic Studies in Psychology: The Angry/Happy Man

• In the facial feedback hypothesis, facial expressions provide feedback to the brain about the emotion being expressed on the face, intensifying the emotion.

• In the cognitive-mediational theory of emotion, the cognitive component of emotion (the interpretation) precedes both the physiological reaction and the emotion itself.

• Those participants who were exposed to the "angry" man interpreted their physical arousal as anger, whereas those who were exposed to the "happy" man interpreted their physical arousal as happiness.

Applying Psychology to Everyday Life: A How-To of Happiness?

8.10 What is the positive psychology movement?

• The positive psychology movement is a perspective that recommends shifting the focus of psychology away from negative aspects such as abuse, anxiety, depression, and all the things that can go wrong to a more positive focus on strengths, well-being, and the pursuit of happiness.

• David Myers has determined 10 things people can do to improve and increase happiness.

TEST YOURSELF: PREPARING FOR THE AP* EXAM

ANSWERS ON PAGE AK-2.

✓●─Practice on MyPsychLab   **Ready for your test?** More quizzes and a customized study plan. **www.mypsychlab.com**

PART I: MULTIPLE-CHOICE QUESTIONS

Directions for Part I: Read each of the questions or incomplete sentences below. Then choose the response that best answers the question or completes the sentence.

1. Which of the following was the approach to motivation that forced psychologists to consider the hereditary factors in motivation?
   a. Instinct
   b. Arousal
   c. Incentive
   d. Drive-reduction
   e. Self-determination

2. The need for money is an example of a(n) _____.
   a. innate drive
   b. primary drive
   c. acquired drive
   d. instinctive drive
   e. physiological drive

3. Jocelyn needs to be the one whose ideas are always used and craves prestige among others. When others contribute to a project, she either takes credit for their ideas, or immediately shoots down their thoughts. Jocelyn is high in the need for _____.
   a. aggression
   b. emotion
   c. affiliation
   d. power
   e. achievement

4. Evidence from a study with 2-year-olds who were given an opportunity to explore a black box with a hole in it suggests that sensation seeking may be _____.
   a. risky
   b. innate
   c. learned
   d. abnormal
   e. acquired over time

5. Shontia works at a day care center. The pay is low and the hours are long, but she loves being around children and has no desire to look for a higher-paying job. Shontia appears to have a(n) _____.
   a. intrinsic motive
   b. extrinsic motive
   c. stimulus motive
   d. external motive
   e. self-actualization motive

6. Which substance is released by the pancreas when we eat, lowering blood sugar and increasing feelings of hunger?
   a. Glucose
   b. Insulin
   c. Thyroxin
   d. Adrenaline
   e. Epinephrine

7. Which theory of emotion would predict that people with spinal cord injuries, which prevent them from experiencing sympathetic arousal, would show decreased emotion?
   a. James-Lange
   b. Cannon-Bard
   c. Schachter-Singer
   d. Facial feedback
   e. Cognitive-mediational

8. In Schachter and Singer's classic study, participants were physically aroused by _____.
   a. exercising
   b. receiving epinephrine
   c. watching an exciting film
   d. exposure to a "happy" man
   e. exposure to an "angry" man

9. Which theory of emotion owes most to Charles Darwin's work?
   a. James-Lange
   b. Cannon-Bard
   c. Schachter-Singer
   d. Facial feedback
   e. Cognitive-mediational

10. Researchers have found that the human brain _____.
    a. is not involved in the creation of emotions
    b. is important in the spinal cord pain withdrawal reflex
    c. has no role in labeling subjective experiences as emotions
    d. is the only organ involved in the experiencing of an emotion
    e. can respond to a threat before it becomes conscious of the threat

PART II: FREE-RESPONSE QUESTION

Directions for Part II: Read the essay question that follows. Then, respond to the question in a clear, concise essay. Do not simply list facts. Instead, present a thorough argument based on your critical consideration of the topic. Use proper psychological terminology as necessary.

You are hiking in the desert when you see a large, poisonous snake poised to attack you, and you feel afraid. In a well-organized essay, describe how each of the following theories would explain your emotional response to this situation:
   a. Common sense theory
   b. James-Lange theory
   c. Cannon-Bard theory
   d. Schacter-Singer cognitive arousal theory
   e. Cognitive-mediational theory

8.1–2   p. 313

- **types** ⎯
  - **intrinsic:** actions are rewarding or satisfying in and of themselves
  - **extrinsic:** actions are performed because they lead to some sort of external outcome

Motivation

(process by which activities are started, directed, and continued so that physical or psychological needs or wants are met)

| Increased hunger | Eat | Raised glucose |
| Lowered glucose | Don't eat | Diminished hunger |

- **drive reduction** ⎯
  - **need**
  - **primary drives**
  - **secondary (acquired) drives**

- **instinct** ⎯
  - biologically determined/innate patterns of behavior
  - old approach: instincts are mainly descriptions, not explanations; idea that some behavior is hereditary remains an important focus

- **psychological needs** ⎯
  - psychological needs have been highlighted in some theories (e.g., McClelland)
  - Dweck suggests that the need for achievement is linked to a person's view of self (locus of control)

8.3–4   p. 319

Approaches to Understanding Motivation

- **arousal**
  need for stimulation
  - **arousal theory** suggests people have an optimal level of tension that they work to maintain
  - a moderate level is most commonly sought, but that level can range from low to high (sensation seeking)

Graph — Level of performance (Poor to Good) vs. Level of arousal (Low to High): Difficult task, Easy task

- **incentive** ⎯
  things that attract or lure people into action, most often due to rewarding properties
  - based in part on principles of learning
  - early work by Tolman, Lewin, and Rotter focused on expectancy-values or how our beliefs, values, and importance we attach to these affect our actions

- **humanistic** ⎯
  based primarily on Maslow's hierarchy of needs; primary, basic needs must be met before higher levels can be met
  - **Alderfer's modification**
  - **self-determination theory**

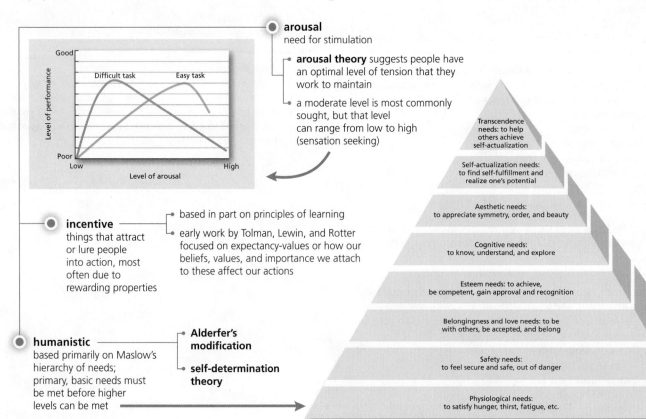

Pyramid (top to bottom):
- Transcendence needs: to help others achieve self-actualization
- Self-actualization needs: to find self-fulfillment and realize one's potential
- Aesthetic needs: to appreciate symmetry, order, and beauty
- Cognitive needs: to know, understand, and explore
- Esteem needs: to achieve, be competent, gain approval and recognition
- Belongingness and love needs: to be with others, be accepted, and belong
- Safety needs: to feel secure and safe, out of danger
- Physiological needs: to satisfy hunger, thirst, fatigue, etc.

8.5–6   p. 327

hunger
- impacted by insulin response; insulin (normally released more after onset of eating) reduces level of glucose in bloodstream (resulting in lower blood sugar and increased hunger); glucagons increase level of glucose
- ventromedial area of the hypothalamus may be involved in stopping eating when glucose level goes up; lateral hypothalamus appears to influence onset of eating when insulin level goes up
- person's weight set point and basal metabolic rate are tied to hypothalamus, and the hormone leptin appears to affect appetite
- hunger and eating behaviors are influenced by social cues and convention (e.g., eating at certain times), culture, and gender

Why People Eat → **maladaptive eating**

- **obesity:** body weight 20% or more over ideal (based on height);
  - **anorexia nervosa**
  - **bulimia nervosa**
- social influences on "thinness" and fear of being fat impact prevalence rates across various cultures

YOUR LOST WEIGHT

"Ready to head back?"

Table 8.3 Possible Signs of Eating Disorders

Dramatic weight loss in a relatively short period of time
Obsession of calories and fat content of food
Hiding food in strange places
Hair loss, pale appearance to the skin
Bruised or callused knuckles, bloodshot eyes with light bruising under the eyes
Frequent trips to the bathroom following meals
Obsession with continuous exercise
Wearing baggy clothes to hide body shape or weight loss
Reading books about weight loss and eating disorders
Complaints of often feeling cold

8.7–9   p. 337

- physiological arousal is created by the sympathetic nervous system and is associated with brain activity in specific areas (e.g., the amygdala) and right or left hemisphere activity

- emotional expressions can vary across cultures but some expressions seem to be universal; display rules also vary across cultures and according to gender

- subjective labeling of emotion is largely a learned response, influenced by both language and culture

Emotion

(is "feeling" aspect of consciousness, characterized by physiological arousal, specific expressive behavior, and inner awareness of feelings)

- Lazarus's **cognitive-mediational theory**
- based on ideas from Darwin, the **facial feedback hypothesis**
- **James-Lange theory**
- **Cannon-Bard theory**
- **cognitive arousal theory** (Schacter and Singer)

Various Theories of Emotion →

have been suggested, each with a slightly different focus and interpretation

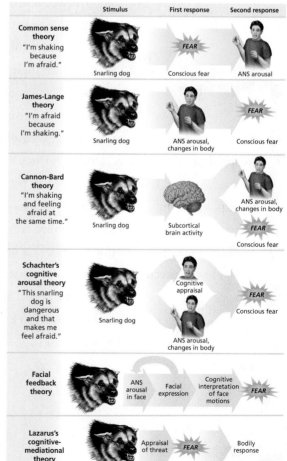

Theory	Stimulus	First response	Second response
Common sense theory "I'm shaking because I'm afraid."	Snarling dog	FEAR — Conscious fear	ANS arousal
James-Lange theory "I'm afraid because I'm shaking."	Snarling dog	ANS arousal, changes in body	FEAR — Conscious fear
Cannon-Bard theory "I'm shaking and feeling afraid at the same time."	Snarling dog	Subcortical brain activity	ANS arousal, changes in body / FEAR — Conscious fear
Schachter's cognitive arousal theory "This snarling dog is dangerous and that makes me feel afraid."	Snarling dog	Cognitive appraisal / ANS arousal, changes in body	FEAR — Conscious fear
Facial feedback theory	(Snarling dog)	ANS arousal in face → Facial expression → Cognitive interpretation of face motions	FEAR
Lazarus's cognitive-mediational theory	(Snarling dog)	Appraisal of threat → FEAR	Bodily response

9

Stress and Health

Body, Mind, Friends, Family, and Your Health

Have you ever wondered why you seem to get that nasty cold just as your final exams are coming up? Or why some people seem to be able to get over being ill faster than others can? And why is it that telling a friend about your frustrations and problems seems to make those problems easier to handle? In one case of two children raised in the same home, why will one get sick only once a year, and then only for one day, while the other will get sick several times a year and take days to get over it? Just why is it that your health (or lack of it) and things like friendships, personality, and stressful situations seem to be related?

In the last two decades, people have become more aware of health issues and their relationship to what we do, what we eat, who we see, and how we think. A relatively new branch of psychology has begun to explore these relationships. **Health psychology** focuses on how our physical activities, psychological traits, and social relationships affect our overall health and rate of illnesses. Psychologists who specialize in this field are typically clinical or counseling psychologists and may work with medical doctors in a hospital or clinic setting, although there are health psychologists who are primarily engaged in teaching and research. Some health psychologists focus on health and wellness issues in the workplace or public health issues such as disease prevention through immunizations or nutrition education. Others are more concerned with health care programs that service all levels of the socioeconomic layers of society (Marks et al., 2005).

Health psychologists seek to understand how behavior (such as use of drugs or the type of food one eats) can affect a person's ability to fight off illnesses—or increase the likelihood of getting sick. They want to know how to prevent illness, and how factors like poverty, wealth, religion, social support, personality, and even one's ethnicity can affect health.

Why study health and stress? How are they related? Stress is not a rare experience but something that all people experience in varying degrees every day. This chapter will explore the sources of stress in daily life, the factors that can make the experience of stress easier or more difficult, and how stress influences our physical and mental health, as well as ways to cope with the stresses of everyday life and extraordinary experiences.

9 Learning Objectives

- **9.1** How do psychologists define stress?
- **9.2** What kinds of external events can cause stress?
- **9.3** What are some psychological factors in stress?
- **9,4** How does stress affect the physical functioning of the body and its immune system?
- **9.5** How do cognitive factors and personality differences affect the experience of stress?
- **9.6** What social factors influence stress reactions?
- **9.7** What are some ways in which people cope with stress reactions?
- **9.8** How is coping with stress affected by culture and religion?
- **9.9** What are some ways to promote wellness?

AP* Discuss theories of stress and the effects of stress on psychological and physical well-being. ▶

Stress and Stressors

Life is really about change. Every day, each person faces some kind of challenge, big or small. Just deciding what to wear to school can be a challenge for some people, whereas others find the morning commute the most challenging part of the day. There are decisions to be made and changes that will require adapting plans already made. Sometimes there are actual threats to well-being—an accident, a fight with friends, a failed exam, or a parent's job loss to name a few. All of these challenges, threats, and changes require people to respond in some way.

DEFINITION OF STRESS

9.1 How do psychologists define stress?

Stress is the term used to describe the physical, emotional, cognitive, and behavioral responses to events that are appraised* as threatening or challenging.

Stress can show itself in many ways. Physical problems can include unusual fatigue, sleeping problems, frequent colds, and even chest pains and nausea. People under stress may behave differently, too: pacing, eating too much, crying a lot, or physically striking out at others. Emotionally, people under stress experience anxiety, depression, fear, and irritability, as well as anger and frustration. Mental symptoms of stress include problems in concentration, memory, and decision making, and people under stress often lose their sense of humor.

I feel like that most of the time!

Most people experience some degree of stress on a daily basis, and students are even more likely to face situations and events that require them to make changes and adapt their behavior: Assigned readings, papers, studying for tests, juggling part-time jobs, relationships, and dealing with deadlines are all examples of things that can cause a person to experience stress. Some people feel the effects of stress more than others because what is appraised as a threat by one person might be appraised as an opportunity by another. (For example, think of how you and your friends might respond differently to the opportunity to write a 10-page paper for extra credit in the last three weeks of the semester.) Stress-causing events are called **stressors**; they can come from within a person or from an external source and range from relatively mild to severe.

I feel like that most of the time! ▶

health psychology area of psychology focusing on how physical activities, psychological traits, and social relationships affect overall health and rate of illnesses.

stress the term used to describe the physical, emotional, cognitive, and behavioral responses to events that are appraised as threatening or challenging.

stressors events that cause a stress reaction.

---

*Appraised: in this sense, evaluated or judged in terms of importance or significance.

WHAT ARE STRESSORS?

Events that can become stressors range from being stuck behind a person in the 10-items-or-less lane of the grocery store who has twice that amount to dealing with the rubble left after a tornado or a hurricane destroys one's home. Stressors can range from the deadly serious (hurricanes, fires, crashes, combat) to the merely irritating and annoying (delays, rude people, losing one's car keys). Stressors can even be imaginary, as when a student puts off opening a report card, imagining that it will be full of failing grades, or when a parent imagines the worst happening to a teenage child who isn't yet home from an evening out.

Taking a test is just one of many possible stressors in a student's life. What aspects of school life have you found to be stressful? Do other students experience the same degree of stress in response to the same stressors?

Actually, there are two kinds of stressors: those that cause **distress**, which occurs when people experience unpleasant stressors, and those that cause *eustress*, which results from positive events that still make demands on a person to adapt or change. Starting college, getting married, and earning a job promotion, may all be positive events for most people, but they all require a great deal of change in people's habits, duties, and even lifestyle, thereby creating stress. Hans Selye (1936) originally coined the term *eustress* to describe the stress experienced when positive events require the body to adapt.

In an update of Selye's original definition, researchers now define **eustress** as the optimal amount of stress that people need to promote health and well-being. The arousal theory of Chapter Eight is based on the idea that a certain level of stress, or arousal, is actually necessary for people to feel content (Zuckerman, 1994). ⒧ⒾⓃⓀ *to Chapter Eight: Motivation and Emotion, p. 314.* That arousal can be viewed in terms of eustress. Many students are aware that experiencing a little anxiety or stress is helpful to them because it motivates them to study, for example. Without the eustress created by the impending exam, many students might not study very much or at all.

What about the student who is so stressed out that everything he's studied just flies right out of his head? Obviously, a high level of anxiety concerning an impending exam that actually interferes with the ability to study or to retrieve the information at exam time is not eustress but is, in fact, distress. The difference is not only in the degree of anxiety but also in how the person interprets the exam situation. A number of events, great and small, good and bad, can cause us to feel "stressed out." The next section looks at how life's big deals and little hassles contribute to our overall stress experience.

◀ **AP*** Identify key contributors in the psychology of motivation and emotion.

ENVIRONMENTAL STRESSORS: LIFE'S UPS AND DOWNS

9.2 What kinds of external events can cause stress?

Catastrophes Losing one's home in a tornado is an example of a stressor called a **catastrophe**, an unpredictable event that happens on a large scale and creates tremendous amounts of stress and feelings of threat. Wars, hurricanes, floods, fires, airplane crashes, and other disasters are catastrophes. The terrorist-driven destruction of the World Trade Center in New York City on September 11, 2001, is a prime example of a catastrophe. In one study, nearly 8 percent of the people living in the area near the attacks developed a severe stress disorder, and nearly 10 percent reported symptoms of depression even as late as two months after the attack (Galea et al., 2002). Another example of a catastrophe was the devastation caused by Hurricane Katrina on August 29, 2005. A Category 3 hurricane, Katrina laid waste to the north-central coastal area of the Gulf of Mexico. In New Orleans, the damage from Katrina was increased by the failure of the levees to hold back flood waters. Eighty percent of the city and many neighboring areas were flooded for weeks (Swenson & Marshall, 2005).

distress the effect of unpleasant and undesirable stressors.

eustress the effect of positive events, or the optimal amount of stress that people need to promote health and well-being.

catastrophe an unpredictable, large-scale event that creates a tremendous need to adapt and adjust as well as overwhelming feelings of threat.

Acute Stress Disorder (ASD) and Post-Traumatic Stress Disorder (PTSD) The severe stress disorder suffered by people after 9/11 and Hurricane Katrina is a type of anxiety disorder called **acute stress disorder (ASD)**. Symptoms of ASD occur within 4 weeks of the traumatic event and include anxiety, dissociative symptoms (such as emotional numbness/lack of responsiveness, not being aware of surroundings, dissociative amnesia), recurring nightmares, sleep disturbances, problems in concentration, and moments in which people seem to "relive" the event in dreams and flashbacks for as long as one month following the event. One recently published study gathered survey information from Katrina evacuees at a major emergency shelter and found that 62 percent of those sampled met the criteria for having acute stress disorder (Mills et al., 2007). When the symptoms associated with ASD last for more than one month, the disorder is then called **post-traumatic stress disorder (PTSD)**. In that same study (Mills et al., 2007), researchers concluded that it was likely that anywhere from 38 to 49 percent of all the evacuees sampled were at risk of developing PTSD that would still be present two years after the disaster. Furthermore, whereas the onset of ASD occurs within 4 weeks of the traumatic event, the symptoms of PTSD may not occur until 6 months or later after the event (American Psychiatric Association, 2000). Treatment of these stress disorders may involve psychotherapy and the use of drugs to control anxiety. (L I N K) *to Chapter Thirteen: Psychological Therapies, pp. 541–542.*

Women seem to be more vulnerable to PTSD than men. Researchers have found that women have almost twice the risk of developing PTSD than do men and that the likelihood increases if the traumatic experience took place before the woman was 15 years old (Breslau et al., 1997, 1999). Children may also suffer different effects from stress than do adults. Severe PTSD has been linked to a decrease in the size of the hippocampus in children with the disorder (Carrion et al., 2007). The hippocampus is important in the formation of new long-term declarative memories ((L I N K) *to Chapter Six: Memory, p. 250*), and this may have a detrimental effect on learning and the effectiveness of treatments for these children. The rate of PTSD (self-reported) among combat-exposed military personnel has tripled since 2001 (Smith et al., 2008), so the problems associated with this long-term stress disorder are not going away any time soon. ◉ Watch on **MyPsychLab**

Major Life Changes Thankfully, most people do not have to face the extreme stress of a catastrophe. But stress is present even in relatively ordinary life experiences and does not have to come from only negative events, such as job loss. Sometimes there are big events, such as marriage or going to college, that also require a person to make adjustments and changes—and adjustments and changes are really the core of stress, according to early researchers in the field (Holmes & Rahe, 1967).

The Social Readjustment Rating Scale (SRRS) Holmes and Rahe (1967) believed that any life event that required people to change, adapt, or adjust their lifestyles would result in stress. Like Selye, they assume that both negative events (such as getting fired) and positive events (such as getting a promotion) demand that a person adjust in some way, and so both kinds of events are associated with stress. Holmes and Rahe devised a way to measure the amount of stress in a person's life by having that person add up the total "life change units" associated with each major event in their **Social Readjustment Rating Scale (SRRS)** (see Table 9.1). The researchers sampled 394 people, giving them a list of events, such as divorce, pregnancy, or taking a vacation. The people in the sample were told that, on a scale of 0 (no changes required of the person experiencing the event) to 100 (extreme changes required), marriage represented 50 "life change units." This gave those being sampled a "yardstick" of sorts, by which they could

◉ **Watch** video footage on post-traumatic stress disorder.
www.mypsychlab.com

acute stress disorder (ASD) a disorder resulting from exposure to a major stressor, with symptoms of anxiety, dissociation, recurring nightmares, sleep disturbances, problems in concentration, and moments in which people seem to "relive" the event in dreams and flashbacks for as long as one month following the event.

post-traumatic stress disorder (PTSD) a disorder resulting from exposure to a major stressor, with symptoms of anxiety, nightmares, poor sleep, reliving the event, and concentration problems, lasting for more than one month.

Social Readjustment Rating Scale (SRRS) assessment that measures the amount of stress in a person's life over a one-year period resulting from major life events.

Table 9.1 **Sample Items from the Social Readjustment Rating Scale (SRRS)**

MAJOR LIFE EVENT	LIFE CHANGE UNITS
Death of spouse	100
Divorce	75
Marital separation	65
Jail term	63
Death of a close family member	63
Personal injury or illness	53
Marriage	50
Dismissal from work	47
Marital reconciliation	45
Pregnancy	40
Death of close friend	37
Change to different line of work	36
Change in number of arguments with spouse	36
Major mortgage	31
Foreclosure of mortgage or loan	30
Begin or end school	26
Change in living conditions	25
Change in work hours or conditions	20
Change in residence/schools/recreation	19
Change in social activities	18
Small mortgage or loan	17
Vacation	13
Christmas	12
Minor violations of the law	11

Source: Adapted and abridged from Holmes & Rahe (1967).

assign a number to each event, and these numbers became the life change units associated with each event on the SRRS.

When an individual adds up the points for each event that has happened to him or her within the past 12 months (and counting points for repeat events as well), the resulting score can provide a good estimate of the degree of stress being experienced by that person. The researchers found that certain ranges of scores on the SRRS could be associated with increased risk of illness or accidents. (Warning: Table 9.1 is *not* a complete listing of the original 43 events and associated life change units and should not be used to calculate a stress "score"! If you would like to calculate your SRRS score, try this free site: **http://www.stresstips.com/lifeevents.htm**.)

Scores of 150 or below were not associated with any significant problems, but scores between 150 and 199 were considered a "mild life crisis" and associated with a 33 percent increase in the risk of that person experiencing an illness or accident in the near future (when compared to persons not experiencing any crisis). Scores between 200 and 299 were labeled "moderate life crisis" and associated with a 50 percent increase in risk, whereas scores over 300 were considered a "major life crisis" and represented an 80 percent increase in risk (Holmes & Masuda, 1973). Simply put, if a person's score is 300 or above, that person has a very high chance of becoming ill or having an accident in the near future. Illness includes not only physical conditions such as high blood pressure, ulcers, or migraine headaches but mental illness as well. In one study, researchers found that stressful life events of the kind listed in the SRRS were excellent predictors of the onset of episodes of major depression (Kendler & Prescott, 1999).

The SRRS was later revised (Miller & Rahe, 1997) to reflect changes in the ratings of the events in the 30 intervening years. Miller and Rahe found that overall stress associated with many of the items on the original list had increased by about 45 percent from the original 1967 ratings.

How can stress cause a person to have an accident? Many studies conducted on the relationship between stress and accidents in the workplace have shown that people under a lot of stress tend to be more distracted and less cautious and, therefore, place themselves at a greater risk for having an accident (Hansen, 1988; Sherry, 1991; Sherry et al., 2003).

The SRRS as it was originally designed seems more appropriate for adults who are already established in their careers. There are variations of the SRRS that use as life events some of those things more likely to be experienced by teenagers and young adults. One of these variations is the **College Undergraduate Stress Scale (CUSS)** that is represented in part in Table 9.2 (Renner & Mackin, 1998). This scale looks quite different from Holmes and Rahe's original scale because the stressful events listed and rated include those that would be more common or more likely to happen to a student.

I notice that Table 9.2 has "falling asleep in class" as its last item. How can falling asleep in class be stressful? It's what happens when the teacher catches you that's stressful, isn't it? Ah, but if you fall asleep in class, even if the teacher doesn't catch on, you'll

> I notice that Table 9.2 has "falling asleep in class" as its last item. How can falling asleep in class be stressful? It's what happens when the teacher catches you that's stressful, isn't it?

College Undergraduate Stress Scale (CUSS) assessment that measures the amount of stress in a college student's life over a one-year period resulting from major life events.

Table 9.2 Sample Items from the College Undergraduate Stress Scale (CUSS)

EVENT	RATING
Death of a close friend	97
Finals week	90
Oversleeping for an exam	89
Flunking a class	89
Financial difficulties	84
Writing a major term paper	83
Two exams in one day	80
Getting married	76
Difficulties with parents	73
Talking in front of a class	72
Difficulties with a roommate	66
A class you hate	62
Maintaining a steady dating relationship	55
Peer pressures	53
Being away from home for the first time	53
Getting straight A's	51
Falling asleep in class	40

Source: Adapted from Renner & Mackin (1998).

miss everything that happened in class that day. You might then have to borrow a friend's notes, copy out the notes yourself, try to read your friend's handwriting, and so on—all stressful situations. Actually, all the events listed on both the SRRS and the CUSS are stressful not just because some of them are emotionally intense but also because there are so many little details, changes, adjustments, adaptations, frustrations, and delays that are caused by the events themselves. The death of a spouse, for example, rates 100 life change units because it requires the greatest amount of adjustment in a person's life. A lot of those adjustments are going to be the little details: planning the funeral, deciding what to do with the spouse's clothes and belongings, getting the notice in the obituaries, answering all of the condolence cards with a thank-you card, dealing with insurance and changing names on policies, and on and on and on. In other words, major life events create a whole host of hassles.

Hassles Although it's easy to think about big disasters and major changes in life as sources of stress, the bulk of the stress we experience daily actually comes from little frustrations, delays, irritations, minor disagreements, and similar annoyances. These daily annoyances are called **hassles** (Lazarus, 1993; Lazarus & Folkman, 1984). Experiencing major changes in one's life is like throwing a rock into a pond: There will be a big splash, but the rock itself is gone. What is left behind are all the ripples in the water that came from the impact of the rock. Those "ripples" are the hassles that arise from the big event.

Lazarus and Folkman (1984) developed a "hassles" scale that has items such as "misplacing or losing things" and "troublesome neighbors." A person taking the test for hassles would rate each item in the scale in terms of how much of a hassle that particular item was for the person. The ratings range between 0 (no hassle or didn't occur) to 3 (extremely severe hassle). Whereas the major life events of Holmes and Rahe's scale (1967) may have a long-term effect on a person's chronic physical and mental health, the day-to-day minor annoyances, delays, and irritations that affect immediate health and well-being are far better predictors of short-term illnesses such as headaches, colds, backaches, and similar symptoms (Burks & Martin, 1985; DeLongis et al., 1988; Dunn et al., 2006). In one study, researchers found that among 261 participants who experienced headaches, scores on a scale measuring the number and severity of daily hassles were significantly better predictors of headaches than were scores on a life events scale (Fernandez & Sheffield, 1996). The researchers also found that it was not so much the number of daily hassles that predicted headaches but rather the perceived severity of the hassles.

A recent study has indicated that hassles may also come from quite different sources depending on a person's developmental stage (Ellis et al., 2001). In this study, researchers surveyed 270 randomly selected people from ages 3–75. The participants were asked to check off a list of daily hassles and pleasures associated with having "bad days" and "good days," respectively, as well as ranking the hassles in terms of frequency and severity of impact. For children ages 3–5, getting teased was the biggest daily hassle. For children in the 6–10 age group, the biggest hassle was getting bad grades. Children 11–15 years old reported feeling pressured to use drugs, whereas older adolescents (ages 16–22) cited trouble at school or work. Adults found fighting among family members the greatest source of stress, whereas the elderly people in the study cited a lack of money.

hassles the daily annoyances of everyday life.

Children in the preschool age range find teasing by their peers to be the biggest daily hassle they experience. This boy is obviously upset by the teasing of the other children, who are making fun of his glasses. What other hassles might a child in this age range experience?

In that same study, the researchers were somewhat surprised to find that elderly people were much more strongly affected by such hassles as going shopping, doctor's appointments, and bad weather than the children and younger adults. It may be that while a young person may view going shopping as an opportunity to socialize, older adults find it threatening: Physically, they are less able to get to a place to shop and may have to rely on others to drive them and help them get around and, thus, may take much more time for shopping and doing errands than a younger person would. Mentally, shopping could be seen as threatening because of a lack of financial resources to pay for needed items. Even the need to make decisions might be seen as unpleasant to an older person. ❀⌐Explore on MyPsychLab

✱ **Explore** with a simulation on how stressed are you? **www.mypsychlab.com**

9.1–2

- stress is the physical, emotional, cognitive, and behavioral response to events that are appraised as threatening or challenging; first studied systematically by Hans Selye
  - can include physical fatigue, recurring illness, over/under eating, smoking/drinking more than usual, mood swings, irritability, depression, anger, memory and concentration problems

- stress-causing events are called stressors; can come from external or internal sources; range from mild to severe
  - negative events cause distress; positive events cause eustress, the optimal level of stress required to facilitate healthy adaptation and well-being
  - external stress-causing events may include catastrophes, major life changes, and daily hassles (differ according to developmental stage)
  - can be assessed systematically (e.g., Social Readjustment Rating Scale, College Undergraduate Stress Scale)

- prolonged or acute stress can cause stress-related disorders that have symptoms including anxiety, dissociation, recurring nightmares, sleep problems, problems concentrating, and "reliving" the experience through flashbacks or dreams
  - **acute stress disorder (ASD):** symptoms present for < 1 month
  - **post-traumatic stress disorder (PTSD):** symptoms persist > 1 month

Stress and Stressors (part 1)

PRACTICE **QUIZ:** PREPARING FOR THE AP* EXAM
ANSWERS ON PAGE AK-2.

Directions: Read each of the questions or incomplete sentences below. Then choose the response that best answers the question or completes the sentence.

1. The optimal amount of stress that people need to promote their health and sense of well-being is called _____.
   a. eustress
   b. distress
   c. acute stress
   d. intense stress
   e. constructive stress

2. Anxiety, recurring nightmares, sleep disturbances, and concentration problems that last for more than one month after a major stressor may be symptoms of _____.
   a. acute stress disorder
   b. general stress disorder
   c. catastrophic stress disorder
   d. social readjustment disorder
   e. post-traumatic stress disorder

3. Which of the following events is considered the most stressful, according to the Social Readjustment Rating Scale (SRRS)?
   a. The death of a spouse
   b. Divorce
   c. The death of a close family member
   d. The death of a close friend
   e. Becoming a new parent

4. Which of the following experiences is a better predictor of stress-related headaches?
   a. Having a parent die
   b. Becoming pregnant
   c. Living through an earthquake
   d. Misplacing important documents
   e. Coming home after fighting in a war

5. In children, severe post-traumatic stress disorder has been linked to _____.
   a. an increase in hippocampus size
   b. a decrease in hippocampus size
   c. an increase in amygdala size
   d. a decrease in amygdala size
   e. an increase in prefrontal cortex size

PSYCHOLOGICAL STRESSORS: STRESS AND THE MIND

Although several specific stressors (such as marriage, school problems, etc.) have already been mentioned, the psychological reasons why people find these events stressful fall into several categories.

9.3 What are some psychological factors in stress?

Pressure   When there are urgent demands or expectations for a person's behavior coming from an outside source, that person is experiencing **pressure**. Pressure occurs when people feel that they must work harder, faster, or do more, as in meeting a deadline or studying for final exams.

Time pressure is one of the most common forms of pressure. Although some people claim to "work well under pressure," the truth is that pressure can have a negative impact on a person's ability to be creative. Psychologist Teresa Amabile has gathered research within actual work settings strongly indicating that when time pressure is applied to workers who are trying to come up with creative, innovative ideas, creativity levels decrease dramatically—even though the workers may think they have been quite productive because of the effort they have made (Amabile et al., 2002).

Uncontrollability   Another factor that increases a person's experience of stress is the degree of control that the person has over a particular event or situation. The less control a person has, the greater the degree of stress. Researchers in both clinical interviews and experimental studies have found that lack of control in a situation actually increases post-traumatic stress disorder symptoms (Breier et al., 1987).

In two studies carried out in a nursing home with the elderly residents as the participants, researchers Rodin and Langer (Langer & Rodin, 1976; Rodin & Langer, 1977) gave each of the residents a houseplant. Decisions about watering and how much sun each plant should have were up to each resident. These residents, who comprised the experimental group, were also given choices such as whether they wanted to see a weekly movie, on which of the two evenings that the movie was shown did they want to attend, and in what area or room they would like to see their visitors. Participants in the control group, although also given plants, were told that the nurses would take care of the plants and were not encouraged to make decisions for themselves. The follow-up study took place a year and a half later. Using participation in activities, measures of happiness, and other assessments, the researchers found that those who had more control over their lives and who had been given more responsibility were more vigorous, active, and sociable than those in the control group.

The stress-increasing effects of lack of control explain the relationship between unpredictability and stress as well. When potentially stressful situations are unpredictable, as in police work, the degree of stress experienced is increased. An unpredictable situation is one that is not controllable, which may at least partially explain the increase in stress. In one study, rats were either given an electric shock after a warning tone or given a shock with no warning. The rats receiving the unpredictable shocks developed severe stomach ulcers (Weiss, 1972).

Frustration   **Frustration** occurs when people are blocked or prevented from achieving a desired goal or fulfilling a perceived need. As a stressor, frustration can be *external*: you're stuck in traffic on the way to an important event; you're cut from a sports team or a musical group; your wallet is stolen. Losses, rejections, failures, and delays are all sources of external frustration.

Obviously, some frustrations are minor and others are more serious. The seriousness of a frustration is affected by how important the goal or need actually is. A person who is delayed in traffic while driving to the mall to do some shopping just

pressure   the psychological experience produced by urgent demands or expectations for a person's behavior that come from an outside source.

frustration   the psychological experience produced by the blocking of a desired goal or fulfillment of a perceived need.

"I suppose this puts my new bike on the back burner?"

©The New Yorker Collection 2005 Bob Zahn from cartoonbank.com. All Rights Reserved.

for fun will be less frustrated than a person who is trying to get to the mall before it closes to get that last-minute forgotten and important birthday gift.

Internal frustrations, also known as *personal frustrations*, occur when the goal or need cannot be attained because of internal or personal characteristics. For example, someone who wants to be an astronaut might find that severe motion sickness prevents him or her from such a goal. If a man wants to be a professional basketball player but is only 5 feet tall and weighs only 85 pounds, he may find that he cannot achieve that goal because of his physical characteristics. A person wanting to be an engineer but who has no math skills would find it difficult to attain that goal.

There are several typical responses that people make when frustrated. The first is *persistence*, or the continuation of efforts to get around whatever is causing the frustration. Persistence may involve making more intense efforts or changing the style of response. For example, anyone who has ever put coins into a drink machine only to find that the drink does not come out has probably (1) pushed the button again, more forcefully, and (2) pushed several other buttons in an effort to get some kind of response from the machine. If neither of these strategies works, many people may hit or kick the machine itself in an act of aggression.

Aggression, or actions meant to harm or destroy, is unfortunately another typical reaction to frustration. Early psychologists in the field of behaviorism proposed a connection between frustration and aggression, calling it the *frustration–aggression hypothesis* (Dollard et al., 1939; Miller et al., 1941). (L I N K) *to Chapter Fourteen: Social Psychology, p. 585.* Although they believed that some form of frustration nearly always precedes aggression, that does not mean that frustration *always* leads to aggression. In fact, aggression is a frequent and persistent response to frustration, but it is seldom the first response. In a reformulation of the frustration–aggression hypothesis, Berkowitz (1993) stated that frustration creates an internal "readiness to aggress" but that aggression will not follow unless certain external cues are also present. For example, if the human source of a person's frustration is far larger and stronger in appearance than the frustrated person, aggression is an unlikely outcome!

So what happens if aggression isn't an option? What can you do? One could try to reason with the person who is the source of frustration. Reasoning with someone is a form of persistence. Trying to "get around" the problem is another way in which people can deal with frustration. Another possibility is to take out one's frustrations on less threatening, more available targets, in a process called **displaced aggression**. Displaced aggression is a form of **displacement**, one of the psychological defense mechanisms discussed a little later in this chapter. Anyone who has ever been frustrated by things that occurred at work or school and then later yelled at another person (such as a spouse, parent, child, etc.) has experienced displaced aggression. The person one really wants to strike out at is one's boss, the teacher, or whoever or whatever caused the frustration in the first place. That could be dangerous, so the aggression is reserved for another less threatening or weaker target. For example, unemployment and financial difficulties are extremely frustrating, as they block a person's ability to maintain a certain standard of living and acquire possessions. In one study, male unemployment and single parenthood were the two factors most highly correlated to rates of child abuse (Gillham et al., 1998). Unemployment is also one of the factors correlated most highly with the murder of abused women, creating four times the risk of murder for women in abusive relationships (Campbell & Wolf, 2003). Both studies are examples of displaced aggression toward the weaker targets of children and women. Such targets often become *scapegoats*, or habitual targets of displaced aggression. Scapegoats are often pets, children, spouses, and even minority groups (who are seen as having less power).

So what happens if aggression isn't an option? What can you do? ▶

aggression actions meant to harm or destroy.

displaced aggression taking out one's frustrations on some less threatening or more available target, a form of displacement.

displacement psychological defense mechanism in which emotional reactions and behavioral responses are shifted to targets that are more available or less threatening than the original target.

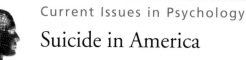

Another possible reaction to frustration is **escape or withdrawal**. Escape or withdrawal can take the form of leaving, dropping out of school, quitting a job, or ending a relationship. Some people manage a psychological escape or withdrawal into apathy (ceasing to care about or act upon the situation), fantasy (which is only a temporary escape), or the use of drugs. Obviously the latter reaction can lead to even more problems.

A far more drastic and permanent form of escape is suicide, the taking of one's own life. People who hear about someone's suicide are nearly always mystified by that choice. How can things be so bad that death seems the only option? For current facts about suicide, its causes, and what can be done to prevent it, see the Current Issues in Psychology section that follows. ((•─Listen on **MyPsychLab**

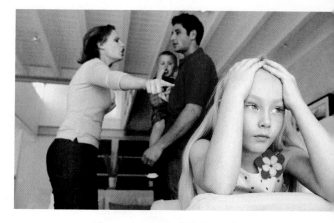

These parents are fighting in front of their obviously distressed daughter. In some instances, a child who experiences this kind of frustration might act out aggressively toward a sibling or a pet in a form of displaced aggression.

((•─ **Listen** to the Psychology in the News podcast. **www.mypsychlab.com**

escape or withdrawal leaving the presence of a stressor, either literally or by a psychological withdrawal into fantasy, drug abuse, or apathy.

Current Issues in Psychology

Suicide in America

Here are the facts:

- In 1996, among teenagers and young adults suicide took more lives than cancer, heart disease, AIDS, birth defects, strokes, pneumonia, the flu, and chronic lung diseases *combined*.
- More people die from suicide than from homicide, and the most common method of committing suicide is with a firearm.
- From 1980 to 1996 the rate of suicides among children 10 to 14 years of age increased by 100 percent. Suicide is the third leading cause of death among adolescents (Centers for Disease Control and Prevention [CDC], 2006), and in 2004 was the eleventh leading cause of death for all ages (CDC, 2005).
- Rates of suicide increase with age and are highest for those over 65.
- Women are about three times more likely than men to attempt suicide, but men are nearly four times more likely to complete the attempt (CDC, 2005).
- Suicide rates in both completed and attempted suicides among adolescents vary according to ethnicity as well as gender, with suicide *deaths* highest among male American Indian/Alaska natives, and suicide *attempts* highest among female American Indian/Alaska natives (Goldston et al., 2008). The lowest rates of deaths were African American females, and the lowest rates of attempts were among African American and white males.
- Among American Indian/Alaska natives, for young adults suicide is the second leading cause of death (CDC, 2005).

Except where noted, all of these facts are taken from *The Surgeon General's Call to Action to Prevent Suicide,* published in 1999 by the Office of the Surgeon General of the United States (Satcher, 1999). Many of these facts might come as a surprise.

What are the signs of impending suicide? Sometimes there are none, but depression is one of the most common mental disorders associated with suicide, and depression does have signs:

- feelings of hopelessness or emptiness
- lack of energy or fatigue
- *anhedonia,* or the inability to feel pleasure or enjoyment
- irritability
- sleeping problems, either too much sleep or too little
- eating more or less than usual
- physical symptoms that persist, such as headaches, stomachaches, or pain

People who are depressed and intend to commit suicide usually do talk about it, and this communication should always be taken seriously. There is a long-standing belief that "people who talk about it just want attention and won't really follow through," but this is not at all true. Talking about committing suicide is a kind of "dress rehearsal," and people who intend

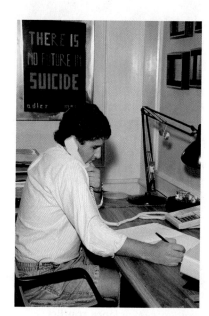

Suicide prevention hotline centers are designed to provide help and support to people who are on the verge of committing suicide. Volunteers, such as the one pictured here, act as concerned listeners for the depressed people who call in to the hotline centers.

to commit suicide may clear out desks and lockers, settle their finances, write out wills, and even seem in relatively good spirits because they have made the decision to "end it" and are looking forward to the escape (Satcher, 2001).

What can be done to prevent suicides? Here are some guidelines from the American Foundation for Suicide Prevention (**http://www.afsp.org**):

- Listen with a sincere attitude of concern.
- Avoid giving unasked-for advice.
- Ask them if they have experienced feeling like this before and how they managed to cope with it then.
- Share a time when you felt the same way and assure them that things can and will change.
- Ask them if they are feeling suicidal.
- Stay with them; do something together.
- If you have immediate concern, call the police for emergency intervention.
- Give them the number for the National Suicide Prevention Lifeline and make sure they call: it is toll-free, confidential, and available 24 hours a day, 7 days a week: 1-800-273-TALK (8255).

Above all, a person who tries to prevent a suicide and fails should not feel responsible. In the end, if a person committed to the act of suicide succeeds, there was nothing that any bystander really could have done to prevent it.

Questions for Further Thought

1. How might a parent's suicide affect the children left behind?
2. How might a teenager's suicide affect parents and siblings?
3. What are the financial implications for those left behind?

This couple has just purchased their first house, a rite of passage for many young couples. The decision to become a home owner, with the "pulls" of privacy and earning equity and the "pushes" of mortgage payments and upkeep, is often an approach–avoidance conflict.

approach–approach conflict conflict occurring when a person must choose between two desirable goals.

avoidance–avoidance conflict conflict occurring when a person must choose between two undesirable goals.

approach–avoidance conflict conflict occurring when a person must choose or not choose a goal that has both positive and negative aspects.

Conflict

Approach–Approach Conflict. In an **approach–approach conflict**, a person experiences desire for two goals, each of which is attractive. Typically, this type of conflict, often called a "win-win situation," is relatively easy to resolve and does not involve a great deal of stress. Because both goals are desirable, the only stress involved is having to choose between them, acquiring one and losing the other. An example of this might be the need to choose between the chocolate cake or key lime pie for dessert or from among several good choices for a date to the prom. "Six on one hand, half a dozen on the other" is a phrase that sums up this conflict nicely.

Avoidance–Avoidance Conflict. **Avoidance–avoidance conflicts** are much more stressful. In this conflict, the choice is between two or more goals or events that are unpleasant. This type of conflict is so common that there are numerous phrases to symbolize it, for example, "caught between a rock and a hard place," "between the devil and the deep blue sea," "out of the frying pan into the fire," and "lose-lose situation." Because neither alternative is pleasant, many people avoid making a choice by delaying decisions (Tversky & Shafir, 1992). For example, given the choice of risky back surgery or living with the pain, some people would wait, hoping that the pain would go away on its own and relieve them of the need to make a choice. People who are fearful of dental procedures might face the conflict of suffering the pain of a toothache or going to the dentist.

Approach–Avoidance Conflict. **Approach–avoidance conflicts** are a little different in that they only involve one goal or event. That goal or event may have both positive and negative aspects that make the goal appealing and unappealing at the same time. For example, leaving home and going to college has its attractive features (becoming independent, making new friends, gaining knowledge and expertise) and its negative aspects (missing old friends and family members, taking exams). This is perhaps the most stressful of all of the types of conflict, causing many people to vacillate* or be unable to decide for or against the goal or event. The author experienced a very stressful approach–avoidance conflict when deciding to write this textbook: On the one hand, there would be money, prestige, and the challenge of doing something new. On the other hand, a tremendous amount of effort and time would be required to write the text, which would take time and energy away from other areas of life.

What if I have to choose between two things, and each of them has good points and bad points?

Multiple Approach–Avoidance Conflicts. When the choice is between two goals that have both positive and negative elements to each goal, it is called a **double approach–avoidance conflict**. For example, what if a person had the choice of buying a house out in the country or in the city? The house in the country has its attractions: privacy, fresh air, and quiet. But there would be a long commute to one's job in the city. A house in the city would make getting to work a lot easier, but then there are the negative aspects of pollution, noise, and crowded city streets. Each choice has both good and bad points. This type of conflict also tends to lead to vacillation. Other examples of this type of conflict might be trying to decide which of two people one wants to date or which of two summer jobs one should choose.

It is fairly common to face **multiple approach–avoidance conflicts** in daily life. In a multiple approach–avoidance conflict, one would have more than two goals or options to consider, making the decision even more difficult and stressful. For many students, deciding on a post-graduation path is actually this type of conflict.

double approach–avoidance conflict conflict in which the person must decide between two goals, with each goal possessing both positive and negative aspects.

multiple approach–avoidance conflict conflict in which the person must decide between more than two goals, with each goal possessing both positive and negative aspects.

◄ What if I have to choose between two things, and each of them has good points and bad points?

---

*Vacillate: to go back and forth between one decision and another.

9.3

- **pressure**
  urgent demands or expectations and uncontrollability

  - **frustration**
    due to external (losses, rejections, failures, delays) or internal (personal characteristics) factors; can result in several typical responses
    - **persistence**
    - **aggression**
    - **escape/withdrawal** (**suicide** is a drastic form of escape)

  - **conflict**
    - **approach–approach conflict** does not involve a great deal of stress; person experiences attraction to two or more desires or goals
    - **avoidance–avoidance conflict** is more stressful; choice between two or more undesirable situations
    - **approach–avoidance conflict** can be most stressful; single goal or event has both positive and negative aspects
    - **multiple approach–avoidance conflicts** are fairly common in daily life (e.g., **double approach–avoidance**) due to life decisions affecting two or more goals

Stress and Stressors (part 2)
(psychological stressors are often related to external events)

(continued)

Directions: Read each of the questions or incomplete sentences below. Then choose the response that best answers the question or completes the sentence.

1. When people have to work harder, do more work, or work faster, they are experiencing _____.
   a. pressure
   b. conflict
   c. frustration
   d. aggression
   e. uncontrollability

2. Eduardo is on his way to an important job interview when he gets stuck in terrible traffic on the highway. Which type of frustration is Eduardo likely to experience?
   a. External
   b. Internal
   c. Personal
   d. Displaced
   e. Uncontrollable

3. Mima is knitting a scarf, but she keeps making mistakes, and she becomes frustrated. Which of the following is most likely Mima's first response to frustration?
   a. Deciding to make a hat instead
   b. Yelling and tearing the scarf apart
   c. Taking out the frustration on a friend
   d. Continuing to attempt to fix the scarf
   e. Giving up and throwing the scarf away

4. Which of the following is a condition in which a person loses the ability to experience pleasure or enjoyment?
   a. Irritability
   b. Withdrawal
   c. Anhedonia
   d. Neural numbness
   e. Learned helplessness

5. Jasmine has just been offered an opportunity to be a camp counselor in a rural area of Kansas. She really needs a summer job in order to make money, but the camp is far away from her family, her friends, and the excitement of the city. Jasmine cannot decide whether to accept the job. Which type of conflict is Jasmine facing?
   a. Approach–approach
   b. Avoidance–avoidance
   c. Approach–avoidance
   d. Avoidance–approach
   e. Multiple approach–avoidance

Physiological Factors: Stress and Health

9.4 How does stress affect the physical functioning of the body and its immune system?

Chapter Two discussed in detail the function of the *autonomic nervous system* (ANS), the part of the human nervous system that is responsible for all automatic, involuntary, and life-sustaining activities. The ANS consists of two divisions, the *parasympathetic* and the *sympathetic*. It is the sympathetic nervous system (the "fight-or-flight" system) that reacts when the human body is subjected to stress: Heart rate increases, digestion slows or shuts down, and energy is sent to the muscles to help deal with whatever action the stressful situation requires. The parasympathetic system returns the body to normal, day-to-day functioning after the stress is ended. If the stress is great enough and lasts long enough, the parasympathetic system may shut the body down, causing a collapse into what some people might call "nervous exhaustion." Both systems figure prominently in a classic theory of the body's physiological reactions to stress, the general adaptation syndrome.

THE GENERAL ADAPTATION SYNDROME

Psychologist Hans Selye was the founder of the field of research concerning stress and its effects on the human body. He studied the sequence of physiological reactions that the body goes through when adapting to a stressor. This sequence (see Figure 9.1) is called the **general adaptation syndrome (GAS)** and consists of three stages (Selye, 1956):

- **Alarm:** When the body first reacts to a stressor, the sympathetic nervous system is activated. The adrenal glands release hormones that increase heart rate, blood pressure, and the supply of blood sugar, resulting in a burst of energy. Reactions such as fever, nausea, and headache are common.

- **Resistance:** As the stress continues, the body settles into sympathetic division activity, continuing to release the stress hormones that help the body fight off, or resist, the stressor. The early symptoms of alarm lessen and the person or animal may actually feel better. This stage will continue until the stressor ends or

AP* Identify key contributors in the psychology of motivation and emotion.

general adaptation syndrome (GAS) the three stages of the body's physiological reaction to stress, including alarm, resistance, and exhaustion.

Alarm Stage   **Resistance Stage**   **Exhaustion Stage**

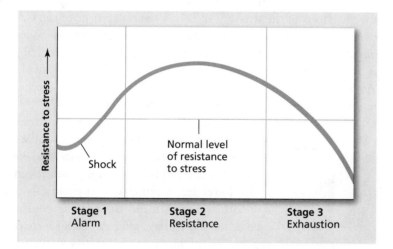

Sympathetic nervous system is activated by adrenal glands

Forehead, neck, shoulder, arm, and leg muscles contract

Pupils enlarge

Breathing is frequent and shallow

Blood pressure remains high

Liver runs out of sugar

Sugar is released into the bloodstream for energy

Accelerated heart rate increases blood flow to muscles; blood pressure increases

Hormones from adrenal glands are released into bloodstream

Prolonged muscle tension causes fatigue

Resistance to stress

Shock

Normal level of resistance to stress

Stage 1 Alarm   **Stage 2** Resistance   **Stage 3** Exhaustion

Figure 9.1 General Adaptation Syndrome
The diagram at the top shows some of the physical reactions to stress in each of the three stages of the general adaptation syndrome. The diagram at the bottom shows the relationship of each of the three stages to the individual's ability to resist a stressor. In the alarm stage, resistance drops at first as the sympathetic system quickly activates. But resistance then rapidly increases as the body mobilizes its defense systems. In the resistance stage, the body is working at a much increased level of resistance, using resources until the stress ends or the resources run out. In the exhaustion stage, the body is no longer able to resist as resources have been depleted, and at this point disease and even death are possible.

the organism has used up all of its resources. Researchers have found that one of the hormones released under stress, noradrenaline, actually seems to affect the brain's processing of pain, so that when under stress a person may experience a kind of analgesia (insensitivity to pain) if, for example, the person hits an arm or a shin (Delaney et al., 2007).

• **Exhaustion:** When the body's resources are gone, exhaustion occurs. Exhaustion can lead to the formation of stress-related diseases (i.e., high blood pressure or a weakened immune system) or the death of the organism if outside help is unavailable (Stein-Behrens et al., 1994). When the stressor ends, the parasympathetic division activates and the body attempts to replenish its resources.

Alarm and resistance are stages that people experience many times throughout life, allowing people to adapt to life's demands (Selye, 1976). It is the prolonged secretion of the stress hormones during the exhaustion stage that can lead to the most harmful effects of stress. It was this aspect of Selye's work that convinced other researchers of the connection between stress and certain "diseases of adaptation" as Selye termed them. The most common of these diseases are ulcers and high blood pressure.

immune system the system of cells, organs, and chemicals of the body that responds to attacks from diseases, infections, and injuries.

psychoneuroimmunology the study of the effects of psychological factors such as stress, emotions, thoughts, and behavior on the immune system.

IMMUNE SYSTEM AND STRESS

As Selye first discovered, the **immune system** (the system of cells, organs, and chemicals in the body that responds to attacks on the body from diseases and injuries) is affected by stress. The field of **psychoneuroimmunology** concerns the study of the effects of psychological factors such as stress, emotions, thinking, and behavior on the immune system (Cohen & Herbert, 1996; Kiecolt-Glaser et al., 1995, 1996, 2002). Researchers in this field have found that stress triggers the same response in the immune system that infection triggers (Maier & Watkins, 1998). Certain enzymes and other chemicals (including antibodies) are created by immune cells when the immune cells, or white blood cells, encounter an infection in the body. The white blood cells surround the bacteria or other infectious material and release the chemicals and enzymes into the bloodstream. From there, these chemicals activate receptor sites on the *vagus nerve*, the longest nerve that connects the body to the brain. It is the activation of these receptor sites that signals the brain that the body is sick, causing the brain to respond by further activation of the immune system.

Stress activates this same system but starts in the brain rather than in the bloodstream. The same chemical changes that occur in the brain when it has been alerted by the vagus nerve to infection in the body occurred in laboratory animals when they were kept isolated from other animals or given electric shocks (Maier & Watkins, 1998). This has the effect of "priming" the immune system, allowing it to more successfully resist the effects of the stress, as in Selye's resistance stage of the GAS.

So stress actually increases the activity of the immune system? But then how does stress end up causing those diseases, like high blood pressure? The positive effects of stress on the immune system only seem to work when the stress is not a continual, chronic condition. As stress continues, the body's resources begin to fail in the exhaustion phase of the general adaptation to stress (Kiecolt-Glaser et al., 1987, 1995, 1996; Prigerson et al., 1997). In one study, students who were undergoing a stressful series of exams were compared to a group of similar students relaxing during a time of no classes and no exams (Deinzer et al., 2000). The exam group tested significantly lower for immune system chemicals that help fight off disease than did the relaxing control group, even as long as 14 days after the exams were over. The suppression of immune system functioning by stress apparently can continue even after the stress itself is over.

One reason that the early stress reaction is helpful but prolonged stress is not might be that the stress reaction, in evolutionary terms, is really only meant for a short-term response, such as running from a predator (Sapolsky, 2004). That level of intense bodily and hormonal activity isn't really meant to go on and on, as it does for human beings in the modern, stress-filled life we now know. Humans experience the stress reaction over prolonged periods of time and in situations that are not necessarily life threatening, leading to a breakdown in the immune system. (See Figure 9.2.) ✴ Explore on MyPsychLab

Heart Disease Of course, anything that can weaken the immune system can have a negative effect on other bodily systems. The sympathetic system (active during stress) cannot work at the same time as the parasympathetic system, and vice versa. It is the parasympathetic system, remember, that is responsible for normal, day-to-day

> So stress actually increases the activity of the immune system? But then how does stress end up causing those diseases, like high blood pressure?

✴ **Explore** with the simulation on stress and the immune system.
www.mypsychlab.com

Figure 9.2 Stress Duration and Illness

In this graph, the risk of getting a cold virus increases greatly as the months of exposure to a stressor increase. Although a stress reaction can be useful in its early phase, prolonged stress has a negative impact on the immune system, leaving the body vulnerable to illnesses such as a cold.
Source: Cohen et al. (1998).

functioning of the body, including repairs and "system maintenance," so to speak. For example, stress has been shown to put people at a higher risk for heart attacks and strokes at least in part because the liver, which is activated during parasympathetic functioning, does not have a chance to clear the fat and cholesterol from the bloodstream, leading to clogged arteries and eventually the possibility of heart attacks. In one recent study, middle-aged men were questioned about stress, diet, and lifestyle factors and were examined for biological risk factors for heart disease: obesity, high blood sugar, high triglycerides (a type of fatty acid found in the blood), and low levels of HDL or "good" cholesterol. (See Figure 9.3.) Stress and the production of stress hormones were found to be strongly linked to all four factors: The more stress the workers were exposed to in their work environment and home life, the more likely they were to exhibit these risk factors (Brunner et al., 2002).

Other studies have produced similar findings. One study looked at the heart health of people who suffered acute stress reactions after the 9/11 terrorist attacks and found a 53 percent increase in heart ailments over the three years following the attacks (Holman et al., 2008), whereas another large-scale study found that work stress is highly associated with an increased risk of coronary heart disease due to negative effects of stress on the autonomic nervous system and glandular activity (Chandola et al., 2008). Prolonged stress is simply not good for the heart.

Stress can also lead to certain unhealthy behaviors, such as drinking alcohol; smoking; eating all the wrong, high-fat, high-calorie "comfort" foods; and avoiding exercise—all factors associated with poor health.

Cancer   Cancer is not one disease but rather a collection of diseases that can affect any part of the body. Unlike normal cells, which divide and reproduce according to genetic instructions and stop dividing according to those same instructions, cancer cells divide without stopping. The resulting tumors affect the normal functioning of the organs and systems they invade, causing organs to fail and eventually killing the organism. People, animals, and plants can have cancer.

Although stress itself cannot give a person cancer, stress can have a suppressing effect on the immune system, making the unchecked growth of cancer more likely. In particular, an immune system cell called a **natural killer cell** has as its main functions the suppression of viruses and the destruction of tumor cells (Herberman & Ortaldo, 1981). Stress has been shown to depress the release of natural killer cells, making it more difficult for the body's systems to fight cancerous growths (Zorilla et al., 2001).

natural killer cell   immune system cell responsible for suppressing viruses and destroying tumor cells.

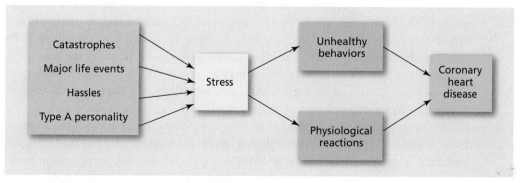

Figure 9.3 Stress and Coronary Heart Disease
The box on the left represents various sources of stress (Type A personality refers to someone who is ambitious, always working, and usually hostile). In addition to the physical reactions that accompany the stress reaction, an individual under stress may be more likely to engage in unhealthy behavior such as overeating, drinking alcohol or taking other kinds of drugs, avoiding exercise, and acting out in anger or frustration. This kind of behavior also contributes to an increased risk of coronary heart disease.

The hormone adrenaline is released under stress and has been found to interfere with a protein that normally would suppress the growth of cancer cells (Sastry et al., 2007). In other research, stress has been linked to the accumulation of genetic errors that can lead to the formation of cancer cells and tumors: Stress causes the release of hormones such as adrenaline and noradrenaline that, over time, can cause mistakes (such as damage to the telomeres, structures at the ends of chromosomes that control the number of times a cell can reproduce) in the instructions given by the genes to the cells of the body. As these mistakes "pile up" over the years, cells can begin to grow out of control, causing the growth of tumors and possibly cancer (Kiecolt-Glaser et al., 2002).

Other Health Issues   Heart disease and cancer are not the only diseases affected by stress. Studies have shown that children in families experiencing ongoing stress are more likely to develop fevers with illness than are other children (Wyman et al., 2007). (Oddly enough, this same study showed that in children stress actually seems to improve the function of their natural killer cells, just the opposite effect that is seen in adults.) A review of research and scientific literature (Cohen et al., 2007) found stress to be a contributing factor in many human diseases, including not only heart disease but also depression and HIV/AIDS.

The physical effects of stress on the body and the immune system are only part of the picture of the influence of stress in daily life. The next section looks at how cognitive factors such as how one interprets a stressful event and psychological factors such as one's personality type can affect the impact of stress.

THE INFLUENCE OF COGNITION AND PERSONALITY ON STRESS

9.5 How do cognitive factors and personality differences affect the experience of stress?

Cognitive Factors in Stress: Lazarus's Cognitive Appraisal Approach   Cognitive psychologist Richard Lazarus developed a cognitive view of stress called the *cognitive–mediational theory* of emotions, in which the way people think about and appraise a stressor is a major factor in how stressful that particular stressor becomes (Lazarus, 1991, 1999; Lazarus & Folkman, 1984). (L I N K) *to Chapter Eight: Motivation and Emotion, p. 335.* According to Lazarus, there is a two-step process in assessing the degree of threat or harm of a stressor and how one should react to that stressor. (See Figure 9.4.)

Primary Appraisal   The first step in appraising a stressor is called **primary appraisal**, which involves estimating the severity of the stressor and classifying it as a threat (something that could be harmful in the future), a challenge (something to be met and defeated), or a harm or loss that has already occurred. If the stressor is appraised as a threat, negative emotions may arise that inhibit the person's ability to cope with the threat. For example, a student who has not read the text or taken good notes will certainly appraise an upcoming exam as threatening. If the stressor is seen as a challenge, however, it is possible to plan to meet that challenge, which is a more positive and less-stressful approach. For example, the student who has studied, read, and feels prepared is much more likely to appraise the upcoming exam as an opportunity to do well.

Perceiving a stressor as a challenge instead of a threat makes coping with the stressor or the harm it may already have caused more likely to be successful, whereas perceiving it as an embarrassment or imagining failure or rejection is more likely to lead to increased stress reactions, negative emotions, and an inability to cope well (Folkman, 1997; Lazarus, 1993). Think positive!

primary appraisal the first step in assessing stress, which involves estimating the severity of a stressor and classifying it as either a threat or a challenge.

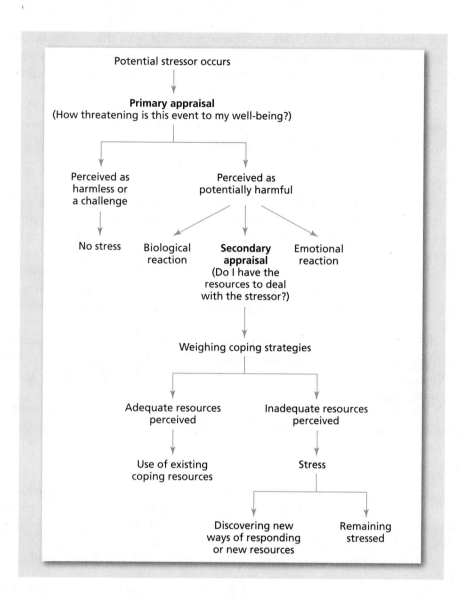

Figure 9.4 Responses to a Stressor

Lazarus's Cognitive Appraisal Approach. According to this approach, there are two steps in cognitively determining the degree of stress created by a potential stressor. Primary appraisal involves determining if the potential stressor is a threat. If it is perceived as a threat, secondary appraisal occurs in addition to the bodily and emotional reactions. Secondary appraisal involves determining the resources one has to deal with the stress, such as time, money, physical ability, and so on. Inadequate resources lead to increased feelings of stress and the possibility of developing new resources to deal with the stress.

Secondary Appraisal   In **secondary appraisal**, people who have identified a threat or harmful effect must estimate the resources that they have available for coping with the stressor. Resources might include social support, money, time, energy, ability, or any number of potential resources, depending on the threat. If resources are perceived as adequate or abundant, the degree of stress will be considerably less than if resources are missing or lacking. Using the example of the student and the upcoming exam, a student who feels that she has the time to study and the ability to understand the material in that time will feel much less distress than the student who has little time to study and doesn't feel that she understood much of the lectures covered on the exam.

As another example, let's say that a person has just been fired from a job. That's a fairly big stressor in most situations, but the degree of stress experienced and the coping abilities of that person will depend on both primary appraisal and secondary appraisal. In most cases, primary appraisal might go something like this: "I've lost my job! I need a job, so this is bad, very bad!" ("This is a threat!") The secondary appraisal might result in the following: "I don't have much money in savings, and the job market for my skills is pretty bad right now. I don't have anyone I can borrow money from or live with while I'm looking for more work. I'm going

secondary appraisal   the second step in assessing a threat, which involves estimating the resources available to the person for coping with the stressor.

Type A personality person who is ambitious, time conscious, extremely hardworking, and tends to have high levels of hostility and anger as well as being easily annoyed.

Type B personality person who is relaxed and laid-back, less driven and competitive than Type A, and slow to anger.

to lose everything!" ("I don't have the resources to deal with this!") Contrast that person's situation with this person's situation: "I've been let go, but that's not so bad. I wanted to look for a new job anyhow." ("This is a challenge.") The secondary appraisal might be: "I have some money in savings, and I can live with my brother for a while if nothing turns up quickly—I should be fine." ("I have the resources to deal with this.") Which person is going to experience more stress and have more health problems as a consequence?

PERSONALITY FACTORS IN STRESS

Of course, how one cognitively assesses a stressor has a lot to do with one's personality. People with certain kinds of personality traits—such as aggressiveness or a naturally high level of anxiety, for example—seem to create more stress for themselves than may exist in the actual stressor. Even as long ago as the early 1930s, psychologists have had evidence that personality characteristics are a major factor in predicting health. A longitudinal study begun in 1932 (Lehr & Thomae, 1987) found that personality was almost as important to longevity (how long people live) as genetic, physical, and lifestyle factors. Other researchers have found that people who live to be very old— into their nineties and even over 100 years—tend to be relaxed, easygoing, cheerful, and active. People who have opposite personality traits such as aggressiveness, stubbornness, inflexibility, and tenseness typically do not live as long as the average life expectancy (Levy et al., 2002).

Those personality traits are some of the factors associated with two personality types that have been related to how people deal with stress and the influence of certain personality characteristics on coronary heart disease.

Type A and Type B In 1974, medical doctors Meyer Friedman and Ray Rosenman published a book titled *Type A Behavior and Your Heart.* The book was the result of studies spanning three decades of research into the influence of certain personality characteristics and coronary heart disease (Friedman & Kasanin, 1943; Friedman & Rosenman, 1959; Rosenman et al., 1975). Since then, numerous researchers have explored the link between what Friedman called Type A and Type B personalities.

Type A people are workaholics—they are very competitive, ambitious, hate to waste time, and are easily annoyed. There is a constant sense of pressure and a strong tendency to try to do several things at once. Often successful but frequently unsatisfied, they always seem to want to go faster and do more, and they get easily upset over small things. A typical Type A finds it difficult to relax and do nothing— Type A people take work with them on vacation, a laptop to the beach, and do business over the phone in the car.

In 1961, the *Western Collaborative Group Study* (Rosenman et al., 1975) assessed 3,500 men and followed them for eight years. For example, participants were asked to agree or disagree with statements such as "I can relax without guilt," in which strong agreement indicates a Type B personality. The results were that Type A men were three times more likely to develop heart disease than Type B men. **Type B** people are not that competitive or driven, tend to be

"He always times 60 Minutes."

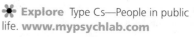

easygoing and slow to anger, and seem relaxed and at peace. Type B people are more likely to take a book to the beach to cover up their face than to actually read the book. (See Figure 9.5.)

The *Framingham Heart Study* found that the risk of coronary heart disease for women who work and are also Type A is four times that of Type B working women (Eaker & Castelli, 1988). Other research has narrowed the key factors in Type A personality and heart disease to one characteristic: hostility* (Frederickson et al., 1999; Matthews et al., 2004; Williams, 1999; Williams et al., 1980). Williams and his colleagues used the *Minnesota Multiphasic Personality Inventory*, a personality test that looks for certain characteristics that include the level of hostility. (L)(I)(N)(K) *to Chapter Eleven: Theories of Personality, p. 463.* In this study, 424 patients who had undergone exploratory surgery for coronary heart disease were examined, and the presence of heart disease was related both to being Type A and to being hostile, with hostility being the more significant factor in the hardening of the arteries to the heart (Williams et al., 1980).

There are numerous studies supporting the link between hostility and increased risk of coronary heart disease. A study of hostility levels and risk factors for heart disease in over 4,000 young adults found that increases in hostility over a five-year follow-up study were associated with a rise in high blood pressure, one of the major risk factors of heart disease (Markovitz et al., 1997). Another study of anger in young men and their risk for premature heart disease found that over a period of slightly more than three decades, the young men who had exhibited high levels of hostility in their youth were far more likely to develop premature cardiovascular disease, particularly heart attacks, than were those men who had lower levels of anger and hostility (Chang et al., 2002). Similar studies found that hostility in college-aged male and females was significantly related to increased risk of heart disease, particularly if levels of hostility rose in middle age (Brondolo et al., 2003; Siegler et al., 2003).

Even children may not escape the hostility–heart disease link. A recent study has found that children and adolescents who scored high on assessments of hostility were more likely to show physical changes such as obesity, resistance to insulin, high blood pressure, and elevated levels of triglycerides three years after the initial measurements of hostility had been made (Raikkonen et al., 2003).

What about people who don't blow their top but try to keep everything in instead? Wouldn't that be bad for a person's health?

Type C   A third personality type was identified by researchers Temoshok and Dreher (1992) as being associated with a higher incidence of cancer. **Type C** people tend to be very pleasant and try to keep the peace but find it difficult to express emotions, especially negative ones. They tend to internalize their anger and often experience a sense of despair over the loss of a loved one or a loss of hope. They are often lonely. These personality characteristics are strongly associated with cancer, and people who have cancer and this personality type often have thicker cancerous tumors as well (Eysenck, 1994; Temoshok, L., & Dreher, H. (1992). *The Type C connection: The behavioral links to cancer and your health.* New York: Random House). Just as the stress of hostility puts the cardiovascular systems of Type A people at greater risk, the internalized negative emotions of the Type C personality may increase the levels of harmful stress hormones, weaken the immune system, and slow recovery. ✻ Explore on MyPsychLab

Figure 9.5 Personality and Coronary Heart Disease
The two bars on the left represent men with Type A personalities. Notice that within the Type A men, there are more than twice as many who suffer from coronary heart disease as those who are healthy. The two bars on the right represent men with Type B personalities. Far more Type B personalities are healthy than Type A personalities, and there are far fewer Type B personalities with coronary heart disease when compared to Type A personalities. Source: Miller et al., (1991, 1996).

What about people who don't blow their top but try to keep everything in instead? Wouldn't that be bad for a person's health?

✻ Explore Type Cs—People in public life. www.mypsychlab.com

Type C personality pleasant but repressed person, who tends to internalize his or her anger and anxiety and who finds expressing emotions difficult.

---

*Hostility: feelings of conflict, anger, and ill will that are long lasting.

The Hardy Personality   Not all Type A people are prone to heart disease. There are some people who actually seem to thrive on stress instead of letting stress wear them down. These people have what is called the **hardy personality**, a term first coined by psychologist Suzanne Kobasa (1979). Hardy people (call them "Type H") differ from ordinary, hostile Type A people and others who suffer more ill effects due to stress in three ways:

- Hardy people have a deep sense of *commitment* to their values, beliefs, sense of identity, work, and family life.
- Hardy people also feel that they are in *control* of their lives and what happens to them.
- Hardy people tend to interpret events in primary appraisal differently than people who are not hardy. When things go wrong, they do not see a frightening problem to be avoided but instead a *challenge* to be met and answered.

Why would those three characteristics (often known as the three "C's" of hardiness) lessen the negative impact of stress? Commitment makes a person more willing to make sacrifices and deal with hardships than if commitment were lacking. Think about it: Have you ever been forced to participate in an activity that you hated? Every little frustration and snag was very stressful, right? Now think about doing something you love to do. The frustrations and snags that inevitably come with any endeavor just don't seem quite as bad when you are doing something you really want to do, do they?

As for control, uncontrollability is one of the major factors cited as increasing stress, as was discussed earlier in this chapter. Seeing events as challenges rather than problems also changes the level of stress experienced, a difference similar to that felt when riding a roller coaster: If riding the coaster is your own idea, it's fun; if someone makes you ride it, it's not fun.

The four personality types discussed so far could be summed up this way: If life gives you lemons,

- Type A people get enraged and throw the lemons back, having a minor heart attack while doing so.
- Type C people don't say anything but fume inside where no one can see.
- Type B people gather all the lemons and make lemonade.
- Hardy people gather the lemons, make lemonade, sell it, turn it into a franchise business, and make millions.

Explanatory Style: Optimists and Pessimists   In addition to personality type, there are other personal factors that have an influence on people's reactions to stressors. One of these factors is the attitude that people have toward the things that happen to them in life.

Optimists are people who always tend to look for positive outcomes. For an optimist, a glass is half full, whereas for a pessimist, the glass is half empty. **Pessimists** seem to expect the worst to happen. Researchers have found that optimism is associated with longer life and increased immune system functioning. Mayo Clinic researchers conducted a longitudinal study of optimists and pessimists (as assessed by a scale) over a period of 30 years (Maruta et al., 2002). The results for pessimists were not good: They had a much higher death rate than did the optimists, and those that were still living in 1994 had more problems with physical and emotional health, more pain, less ability to take part in social activities, and less energy than optimists. The optimists had a 50 percent lower risk of premature death and were more calm, peaceful, and happy than the pessimists (Maruta et al., 2002). An earlier study linked being optimistic to

Type Z behavior
©The New Yorker Collection 1987 Donald Reilly from cartoonbank.com. All Rights Reserved.

hardy personality   a person who seems to thrive on stress but lacks the anger and hostility of the Type A personality.

optimists   people who expect positive outcomes.

pessimists   people who expect negative outcomes.

higher levels of helper T cells (immune system cells that direct and increase the functioning of the immune system) and higher levels of natural killer cells, the body's antivirus, anticancer cells (Segerstrom et al., 1998).

Martin Seligman is a social learning psychologist who developed the concept of *learned helplessness,* ⓛⓘⓝⓚ *to Chapter Five: Learning, p. 207,* and began the positive psychology movement. Seligman (2002) has outlined four ways in which optimism may affect how long a person lives:

1. Optimists are less likely to develop learned helplessness, the tendency to stop trying to achieve a goal that has been blocked in the past.

2. Optimists are more likely than pessimists to take care of their health by preventive measures (such as going to the doctor regularly and eating right) because they believe that their actions make a difference in what happens to them. (Remember, this is a characteristic of hardy people as well.)

3. Optimists are far less likely than pessimists to become depressed, and depression is associated with mortality because of the effect of depression on the immune system.

4. Optimists have more effectively functioning immune systems than pessimists, perhaps because they experience less psychological stress.

Seligman (1998) has also found that optimists are more successful in their life endeavors than pessimists. Optimistic politicians win more elections, optimistic students get better grades, and optimistic athletes win more contests.

Whoa—optimistic students get better grades? How do I become an optimist? Sign me up! Optimism is mostly a matter of controlling mood or emotional reactions to situations. Psychiatrist Dr. Susan Vaughan (2000) has some good advice for optimistic people who want to keep a positive outlook:

- **Alternative thinking:** Optimists tend to take bad things that happen less personally, coming up with alternative explanations for why the bad thing happened. For example, optimists tend to attribute poor exam grades to the difficulty of that particular material or to not having enough time to study. They appraise it as a challenge and assume that they will perform more successfully in the future.

- **Downward social comparison:** Many people make themselves feel better by comparing their performance to that of less competent others, making them feel better and protecting self-esteem. Optimists use *downward social comparison* frequently.

- **Relaxation:** Optimists use relaxation as a way to improve mood, such as exercising, meditating, or reading a good book.

How to Become an Optimistic Thinker   The way to become an optimist is to monitor one's own thinking. Recognition of negative thoughts is the first step, followed by disputing those same negative thoughts (Seligman, 2002). The problem is that most people don't really think about their thoughts or characterize them as negative or pessimistic, which means that the damaging effects of such thinking are left uncontrolled. Here's a plan to follow to become an optimistic thinker:

1. When a bad mood strikes, stop and think about what just went through your head.

2. When you've recognized the negative statements, treat them as if they came from someone else—someone who is trying to make your life miserable. Think about the damage the statement is doing to you.

3. Argue with those thoughts. Challenge each negative statement and replace it with a more positive statement.

Whoa—optimistic
◀ students get
better grades?
How do I become
an optimist?
Sign me up!

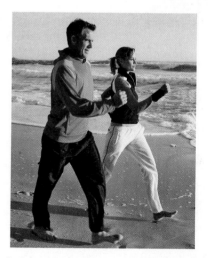

Regular exercise increases the functioning of the immune system and helps give people a sense of control over their health. Having a sense of control decreases feelings of stress, which also helps the immune system to function well.

Example:

1. "I'll never get this term paper finished, it's too hard and there's so much going on that it's impossible!" What words in this statement makes it pessimistic? "Never" is a long time. Why is it too hard? Is it really impossible, or just difficult? Is it just one part of the paper that seems so hard, or is it the whole thing?

2. That statement isn't going to help me at all, it just makes me feel worse and that makes me unmotivated to work on the paper.

3. I can finish the term paper. I'm just going to have to devote more time to working on it. I can make a timetable for finishing the different parts of the paper and stop spending so much time watching television and escaping into other activities that can wait until the paper is finished. I've been in situations like this before and managed, so I can manage now, too.

Notice that the third way of thinking is much more positive and hopeful. It includes ways to get around what seemed too hard or impossible in the negative statement. Essentially, the last step in becoming a more optimistic thinker is to learn to argue with yourself and correct distorted or faulty thinking.

How can I recognize distorted thinking when it's my own thoughts in the first place? Recognizing faulty thinking can be difficult at first. The following questions may help people to hone in on negative thinking:

1. In thinking about the thoughts you have had in the last few hours, how many of them were negative thoughts? How could you change those thoughts to be more positive?

2. When thinking about people you know who make a lot of negative self-statements or who are always minimizing their efforts or putting themselves down, how does their behavior make you feel? How do you think their behavior makes them feel?

> **How can I recognize distorted thinking when it's my own thoughts in the first place?** ▶

9.4–5

the **autonomic nervous system (ANS)** figures prominently in the body's physiological reactions to stress

Physiological Factors

Hans Selye identified the **general adaption syndrome (GAS)**, the sequence of physiological reactions the body goes through when adapting to a stressor

- **alarm:** sympathetic nervous system is first activated
- **resistance:** continued activation of sympathetic activity until organism's resources are depleted
- **exhaustion:** prolonged stress response coupled with depleted resources can lead to stress-related diseases or death of the organism; if stressor is stopped, parasympathetic division is activated and body attempts to replenish resources

the field of **psychoneuroimmunology** focuses on the effects of stress on the immune system

- stress-related responses similar to those triggered by infection —increase in white blood cell count, enzymes, and antibodies
- body is engineered for short-term, acute stress; prolonged stress/depletion of resources results in reduced functioning of immune system

Lazarus's cognitive–mediational theory of emotions suggests an individual's appraisal of a stressor is a major factor in determining how stressful that stressor becomes

- **primary appraisal** involves estimating severity of the stressor and classifying it as a threat, challenge, or loss already occurred
- **secondary appraisal** involves estimation of resources available to cope with stressor

result of appraisal determines level of stress and emotional reaction

Cognitive and Personality Factors

personality differences affect how one assesses a stressor, the coping strategies used, and possible health outcomes

- **Type A:** workaholic, competitive, ambitious, hate to waste time, easily annoyed; more likely to have health issues (e.g., heart disease), especially the more hostile an individual is

- **Type B:** more easygoing, slower to anger, not as competitive or driven; less likely to have health issues

- **Type C:** tend to be pleasant and at peace but find it difficult to express emotions, especially negative ones; associated with cancer

- **"Type H":** hardy personality, appear to be like Type A but less prone to heart disease; appear to thrive on stress due to three factors: sense of commitment, control, and seeing stressors as a challenge

explanatory style optimists tend to look for positive outcomes, whereas pessimists seem to expect the worst

- Seligman (originally studied concept of learned helplessness) began the positive psychology movement; has suggested that optimism leads to longer life and greater success in life endeavors

- optimism is associated with controlling mood or emotional reactions; can be a learned skill through alternative thinking, downward social comparison, relaxation, and correcting faulty thinking

PRACTICE QUIZ: PREPARING FOR THE AP* EXAM

ANSWERS ON PAGE AK-2.

Directions: Read each of the questions or incomplete sentences below. Then choose the response that best answers the question or completes the sentence.

1. In which stage of the general adaptation syndrome may a person actually start to feel better?
   a. Onset
   b. Alarm
   c. Resistance
   d. Exhaustion
   e. Termination

2. How does the activation of the immune system response by stress differ from the activation of that same system by illness?
   a. Stress increases the release of natural killer cells.
   b. Stress activates a different immune response than illness does.
   c. Stress activates the same system, but starts in the brain rather than the bloodstream.
   d. Stress creates certain chemicals that are not produced as a result of illness.
   e. Stress causes illnesses that are ultimately untreatable by the immune system.

3. According to researcher Richard Lazarus, secondary appraisal involves _____.
   a. estimating the severity of the stressor
   b. deciding whether the stressor is a problem
   c. classifying the stressor as a threat or challenge
   d. estimating the resources available for coping with the stressor
   e. developing negative emotions in response to the stressor's threats

4. Which of the following people is most at risk for coronary heart disease?
   a. A workaholic who has a hostile personality
   b. An easygoing person who can relax without guilt
   c. A diligent worker who views life as a challenge to be overcome
   d. An outwardly pleasant person who stores negative emotions inside
   e. A busy, ambitious person who is deeply committed to doing good work

5. Which of the following statements about optimists is true?
   a. Optimists are more likely than pessimists to develop coronary heart disease.
   b. Optimists are less likely than pessimists to go to the doctor regularly.
   c. Optimists are more likely than pessimists to develop learned helplessness.
   d. Optimists are more likely than pessimists to have a Type C personality.
   e. Optimists are less likely than pessimists to experience premature death.

SOCIAL FACTORS IN STRESS: PEOPLE WHO NEED PEOPLE

9.6 What social factors influence stress reactions?

As stated earlier, much of the stress in everyday life comes from having to deal with other people and with the rules of social interaction. Overcrowding, for example, is a common source of stress and may be one reason for the increasing rise of *road rage*, or the tendency for drivers to become excessively enraged by ordinary traffic frustrations, sometimes resulting in serious injuries, assaults, and even death (AAA Foundation for Traffic Safety, 1997). Two of the more prominent social factors in creating stressful living conditions are both economically based: poverty and job stress.

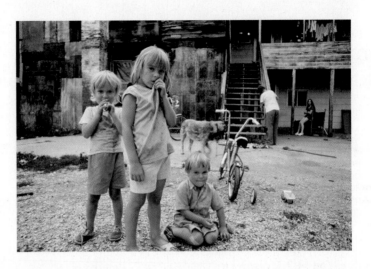

Poverty can lead to many conditions that increase the degree of stress experienced by both adults and children. These children, for example, may face an increased risk of malnutrition, illness, and exposure to violence because of the conditions under which they must live.

Poverty   Living in poverty is stressful for many reasons. Lack of sufficient money to provide the basic necessities of life can lead to many stressors for both adults and children: overcrowding, lack of medical care, increased rates of disabilities due to poor prenatal care, noisy environments, increased rates of illness (such as asthma in childhood) and violence, and substance abuse (Aligne et al., 2000; Bracey, 1997; Leroy & Symes, 2001; Park et al., 2002; Renchler, 1993; Rouse, 1998; Schmitz et al., 2001).

Job Stress   Even if a person has a job and is making an adequate salary, there are stresses associated with the workplace that add to daily stressors. Some of the typical sources of stress in the workplace include the workload, a lack of variety or meaningfulness in work, lack of control over decisions, long hours, poor physical work conditions, and lack of job security (Murphy, 1995). ◉ Watch on **MyPsychLab**

◉ **Watch** videos on rude atmosphere in the workplace. **www.mypsychlab.com**

Stress at work can result in the same symptoms as stress from any other source: headaches, high blood pressure, indigestion, and other physical symptoms; anxiety, irritability, anger, depression, and other psychological symptoms; and behavioral symptoms such as overeating, drug use, poor job performance, or changes in family relationships (Anschuetz, 1999).

There are times when I feel like I've just had it with school and all the work the teachers pile on—is that something like workplace stress?

There are times when I feel like I've just had it with school and ▶ all the work the teachers pile on—is that something like workplace stress?

Burnout   One of the more serious effects of workplace stress is a condition called burnout. **Burnout** can be defined as negative changes in thoughts, emotions, and behavior as a result of prolonged stress or frustration (Miller & Smith, 1993). Symptoms of burnout are extreme dissatisfaction, pessimism, lowered job satisfaction, and a desire to quit. Although burnout is most commonly associated with job stress, students can also suffer from burnout when the stresses of school life—term papers, exams, assignments and the like—become overwhelming. The emotional exhaustion associated with burnout can be lessened when a person at risk of burnout is a member, within the work environment, of a social group that provides support and also the motivation to continue to perform despite being exhausted (Halbesleben & Bowler, 2007). ✳ Explore on **MyPsychLab**

✳ **Explore** burnout.
www.mypsychlab.com

burnout   negative changes in thoughts, emotions, and behavior as a result of prolonged stress or frustration.

acculturative stress   stress resulting from the need to change and adapt a person's ways to the majority culture.

How Culture Affects Stress   When a person from one culture must live in another culture, that person may experience a great deal of stress. *Acculturation* means the process of adapting to a new or different culture, often the dominant culture (Sodowsky et al., 1991). The stress resulting from the need to change and adapt to the dominant or majority culture is called **acculturative stress** (Berry & Kim, 1998; Berry & Sam, 1997).

The method that a minority person chooses to enter into the majority culture can also have an impact on the degree of stress that person will experience (Berry & Kim, 1988). One method is *integration*, in which the individual tries to maintain a sense of the original cultural identity while also trying to form a positive relationship with members of the dominant culture. For example, an integrated person will maintain a lot of original cultural traditions within the home and with immediate family members but will dress like the majority culture and adopt some of those characteristics as well. For people who choose integration, acculturative stress is usually low (Ward & Rana-Deuba, 1999).

In *assimilation*, the minority person gives up the old cultural identity and completely adopts the majority culture's ways. In the early days of the United States, many immigrants were assimilated into the mainstream American culture, even changing their names to sound more "American." Assimilation leads to moderate levels of stress, most likely due to the loss of cultural patterns and rejection by other members of the minority culture who have not chosen assimilation (LaFromboise et al., 1993; Lay & Nguyen, 1998).

Separation is a pattern in which the minority person rejects the majority culture's ways and tries to maintain the original cultural identity. Members of the minority culture refuse to learn the language of the dominant culture, and they live where others from their culture live, socializing only with others from their original culture. Separation results in a fairly high degree of stress, and that stress will be even higher if the separation is forced (by discrimination from the majority group) rather than voluntary (self-imposed withdrawal from the majority culture).

The greatest acculturative stress will most likely be experienced by people who have chosen to be *marginalized*, neither maintaining contact with the original culture nor joining the majority culture. They essentially live on the "margins" of both cultures without feeling or becoming part of either culture. Marginalized individuals do not have the security of the familiar culture of origin or the acceptance of the majority culture and may suffer a loss of identity and feel alienated from others (Roysircai-Sodowsky & Maestas, 2000). Obviously, marginalized people have little in the way of a social support system to help them deal with both everyday stresses and major life changes.

I hear the term "social support system" all the time now. Exactly what is it?

The Positive Benefits of Social Support A **social support system** is the network of friends, family members, neighbors, coworkers, and others who can offer help to a person in need. That help can take the form of advice, physical or monetary support, information, emotional support, love and affection, or companionship. Research has consistently shown that having a good social support system is of critical importance in a person's ability to cope with stressors: People with good social support systems are less likely to die from illnesses or injuries than those without such support (Kulik & Mahler, 1989, 1993). Marriage, itself a form of social support, is a good predictor of healthy aging and longevity (Gardner & Oswald, 2004; Vaillant, 2002). Social support has been found to have a positive effect on the immune system (Holt-Lunstad et al., 2003) and improves the mental health and physical functioning of people who have *lupus*, a chronic inflammatory disease that can affect nearly any part of the body (Sutcliffe et al., 1999; Ward et al., 1999) as well as those with cancer and HIV (Carver & Antoni, 2004; Gonzalez et al., 2004).

Social support can make a stressor seem less threatening because people with such support know that there is help available. Having people to talk to about one's problems reduces the physical symptoms of stress—talking about frightening or frustrating events with others can help people think more realistically about the

AP* Articulate the impact of social and cultural categories on self-concept and relations with others.

This Buddhist group is celebrating Songkran, the New Year, by performing their cultural ritual of pouring water over their elder's palms. Although they are wearing clothing typical of people living in Los Angeles, California, where the ceremony is taking place, they still maintain some of their old cultural traditions.

I hear the term "social support system" all the time now. Exactly what is it?

social support system the network of family, friends, neighbors, coworkers, and others who can offer support, comfort, or aid to a person in need.

threat, for example, and talking with people who have had similar experiences can help put the event into perspective. **(LINK)** *to Chapter Thirteen: Psychological Therapies, pp. 531–534.* The negative emotions of loneliness and depression, which are less likely to occur with someone who has social support, can adversely affect one's ability to cope (Beehr et al., 2000; Weisse, 1992). Positive emotions, on the other hand, have a decidedly beneficial effect on health, helping people recover from stressful experiences more quickly and effectively (Tugade & Fredrickson, 2004). Positive emotions are more likely to occur in the presence of friends and family.

How people think about a stressor is also a powerful influence on their ability to cope, as the next section will discuss.

Coping with illness is always made easier when one has social support. Here, a man recovering in the hospital is visited by a volunteer and her dog. Animals are also a good source of social support, and people who have animals have been shown to recover from illnesses and stressors more quickly (Allen et al., 2002).

9.6

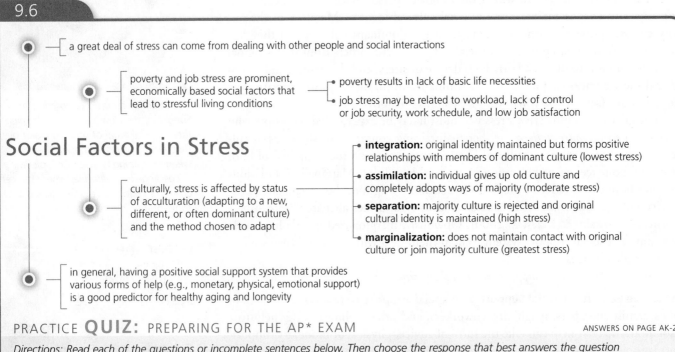

- a great deal of stress can come from dealing with other people and social interactions

- poverty and job stress are prominent, economically based social factors that lead to stressful living conditions
  - poverty results in lack of basic life necessities
  - job stress may be related to workload, lack of control or job security, work schedule, and low job satisfaction

Social Factors in Stress

- culturally, stress is affected by status of acculturation (adapting to a new, different, or often dominant culture) and the method chosen to adapt
  - **integration:** original identity maintained but forms positive relationships with members of dominant culture (lowest stress)
  - **assimilation:** individual gives up old culture and completely adopts ways of majority (moderate stress)
  - **separation:** majority culture is rejected and original cultural identity is maintained (high stress)
  - **marginalization:** does not maintain contact with original culture or join majority culture (greatest stress)

- in general, having a positive social support system that provides various forms of help (e.g., monetary, physical, emotional support) is a good predictor for healthy aging and longevity

PRACTICE **QUIZ:** PREPARING FOR THE AP* EXAM

ANSWERS ON PAGE AK-2.

Directions: Read each of the questions or incomplete sentences below. Then choose the response that best answers the question or completes the sentence.

1. Larysa moved from Ukraine to the United States. She learned to speak and write English, changed her last name so it would sound more "American," and no longer maintains any of her old culture's customs. Which method of entering the majority culture has Larysa used?
   a. Integration   **d.** Withdrawal
   b. Assimilation   **e.** Marginalization
   c. Separation

2. Which of the following people is most likely to experience job stress?
   a. A worker who must handle a variety of tasks each day
   b. A worker who controls his or her own daily schedule
   c. A worker who is well compensated for any overtime work
   d. A worker who has no contract and may be fired at any time
   e. a worker who is not well paid but finds the work meaningful

3. Negative changes in thoughts, emotions, and behavior as a result of prolonged stress and frustration are known as _____.
   a. burnout
   b. job stress
   c. exhaustion
   d. marginalization
   e. acculturative stress

4. Which of the following statements about social support systems is true?
   a. Social support systems have no impact on ability to cope with stressors.
   b. Social support systems can improve a person's overall health and longevity.
   c. Social support systems cannot successfully combat loneliness and depression.

d. Social support systems can change any stressor from a threat to a challenge.

e. Social support systems can improve minor health problems but not chronic conditions.

5. The process of adapting to a new or different culture, often the dominant culture, is known as_____.

a. socialization
b. general adaptation
c. acculturation
d. cultural appraisal
e. cultural readjustment

Coping with Stress

I have school and sports and friendships to worry about, so I feel pretty stressed out—how do people deal with all the stress they face every day? So far, this chapter has talked about what stress is and the factors that can magnify the effects of stress, as well as the effects of stress on a person's physical health. Part of dealing with stress is in knowing those kinds of things so that changes can be made in the factors that are controllable. **Coping strategies** are actions that people can take to master, tolerate, reduce, or minimize the effects of stressors, and they can include both behavioral strategies and psychological strategies.

9.7 What are some ways in which people cope with stress reactions?

PROBLEM-FOCUSED COPING

One type of coping strategy is to work on eliminating or changing the stressor itself. When people try to eliminate the source of a stress or reduce its impact through their own actions, it is called **problem-focused coping** (Folkman & Lazarus, 1980; Lazarus, 1993). For example, a student might have a problem understanding a particular teacher. The teacher is knowledgeable but has trouble explaining the concepts of the course in a way that this student can understand. Problem-focused coping might include talking to the teacher after class, asking fellow students to clarify the concepts, getting a tutor, or forming a study group with other students who are also having difficulty to pool the group's resources.

EMOTION-FOCUSED COPING

Problem-focused coping can work quite well but is not the only method people can use. Most people use both problem-focused coping and **emotion-focused coping** to successfully deal with controllable stressful events (Eschenbeck et al., 2008; Folkman & Lazarus, 1980; Lazarus, 1993; Stowell et al., 2001). Emotion-focused coping is a strategy that involves changing the way a person feels or emotionally reacts to a stressor. This reduces the emotional impact of the stressor and makes it possible to deal with the problem more effectively. For example, the student who is faced with a teacher who isn't easy to understand might share his concerns with a friend, talking it through until he is calm enough to tackle the problem in a more direct manner. Emotion-focused coping also works for stressors that are uncontrollable and for which problem-focused coping is not possible. Someone using emotion-focused coping may decide to view the stressor as a challenge rather than a threat, decide that the problem is a minor one, write down concerns in a journal, or even ignore the problem altogether.

Ignore it? But won't that just make matters worse?

True, ignoring a problem is not a good strategy when there is something a person can actively do about solving the problem. But when it is not possible to change or eliminate the stressor, or when worrying about the stressor can be a problem itself, ignoring the problem is not a bad idea. Researchers working with people who had suffered heart attacks found that those people who worried about a future attack were

◀ I have school and sports and friendships to worry about, so I feel pretty stressed out— how do people deal with all the stress they face every day?

coping strategies actions that people can take to master, tolerate, reduce, or minimize the effects of stressors.

problem-focused coping coping strategies that try to eliminate the source of a stress or reduce its impact through direct actions.

emotion-focused coping coping strategies that change the impact of a stressor by changing the emotional reaction to the stressor.

◀ Ignore it? But won't that just make matters worse?

more likely to suffer from symptoms of post-traumatic stress, such as nightmares and poor sleep (both factors that increase the risk of a future heart attack), than were the people who tried to ignore their worries (Ginzburg et al., 2003).

Using humor can also be a form of emotion-focused coping, as the old saying "laughter is the best medicine" suggests. A recent study on the effects of laughter found that laughter actually boosted the action of the immune system by increasing the work of natural killer cells (cells that attack viruses in the body). In this study, participants were shown a humor video for one hour. Blood samples were taken 10 minutes before the viewing, 30 minutes into the viewing, 30 minutes after viewing, and 12 hours after viewing the humor video. There were significant increases in natural killer cell activity and nearly half a dozen other immune system cells and systems, with some effects lasting the full 12 hours after the video ended (Berk et al., 2001).

Emotion-focused coping is highly related to several forms of psychological defenses first proposed by Sigmund Freud, as the next section discusses.

PSYCHOLOGICAL DEFENSE MECHANISMS

In Freud's writings on psychoanalysis, he stated that when people experience anxiety (stress) from conflicts between the demands of the body's needs and desires and society's rules for proper behavior, there are certain unconscious* distortions of thought that can protect their sense of self from that anxiety (Freud, 1915). (LINK) *to Chapter Eleven: Theories of Personality, p. 439.* These unconscious distortions of the perception of reality are called **psychological defense mechanisms** and were further explained by Freud's daughter, Anna Freud (1946). Although Freudian theory has fallen in and out of favor over the last century, the concept of these defense mechanisms has remained quite useful in clinical psychology as a way of describing people's defensive behavior and irrational thinking.

Table 9.3 lists, defines, and gives examples of some of the more common defense mechanisms. It may have become obvious that nearly all of these resemble emotion-focused coping strategies, although their existence can easily lead to more problems, as many of Freud's patients discovered.

Unlike much of the rest of Freud's psychoanalytic theory, research in cognitive psychology has uncovered some scientific support for the concept of unconscious coping mechanisms at work when people experience stress (Cramer, 2000). Although many psychologists in the 1970s and early 1980s rejected the idea of the unconscious mind's influence on conscious behavior, recent studies in cognitive perception have found support for the influence of experiences for which there is no conscious memory on task performance (Dehaene et al., 2001; Greenwald et al., 1996; Kihlstrom, 1987). These studies deal with the phenomenon of implicit memory. (LINK) *to Chapter Six: Memory, p. 231.* Implicit memory, is a form of long-term memory in which habits, skills, conditioned responses, emotional associations, and other well-learned procedures are stored. These memories affect conscious behavior, as in being able to balance on a bicycle, but are not stored in conscious awareness and cannot easily be brought into conscious awareness.

MEDITATION AS A COPING MECHANISM

Meditation is a mental series of exercises meant to refocus attention and achieve a trancelike state of consciousness. (LINK) *to Chapter Four: Consciousness, Sleep, Dreams, Hypnosis, and Drugs, p. 135.* Meditation can produce a state of relaxation that can aid in coping with the physiological reactions to a stressful situation.

These life-size models of Marge and Homer Simpson were created for the 350th episode of The Simpsons in April of 2005. A large part of the success of such comedies can be attributed to the human need to laugh—laughter helps us cope with many of life's stresses.

This man is practicing Zen yoga meditation. Meditation increases relaxation and helps to lower blood pressure and muscle tension.

psychological defense mechanisms unconscious distortions of a person's perception of reality that reduce stress and anxiety.

meditation mental series of exercises meant to refocus attention and achieve a trancelike state of consciousness.

---

*Unconscious: in Freud's theory, the part of the mind that holds conflicts, urges, and thoughts of which the person is not aware.

Table 9.3 The Psychological Defense Mechanisms

DEFENSE MECHANISM AND DEFINITION	EXAMPLE
Denial: refusal to recognize or acknowledge a threatening situation.	Ben is failing his classes and denies struggling academically.
Repression: "pushing" threatening or conflicting events or situations out of conscious memory.	Elise, who was badly injured in a fire as a child, cannot remember the fire at all.
Rationalization: making up acceptable excuses for unacceptable behavior.	"If I don't have breakfast, I can have that piece of cake later on without hurting my diet."
Projection: placing one's own unacceptable thoughts onto others, as if the thoughts belonged to them and not to oneself.	Keisha is attracted to her friend's boyfriend but denies this and believes the boyfriend is attracted to her.
Reaction formation: forming an emotional reaction or attitude that is the opposite of one's threatening or unacceptable actual thoughts.	Seven-year-old Darnell likes his female classmate, Annie, but he makes fun of her and acts rudely in her presence.
Displacement: expressing feelings that would be threatening if directed at the real target onto a less threatening substitute target.	Sandra gets reprimanded by her teacher and goes home to angrily pick a fight with her brother.
Regression: falling back on childlike patterns as a way of coping with stressful situations.	Four-year-old Jeff starts wetting his bed after his parents bring home a new baby.
Identification: trying to become like someone else to deal with one's anxiety.	Marie really admires Suzy, the most popular girl in school, and tries to copy her behavior and dress.
Compensation (substitution): trying to make up for areas in which a lack is perceived by becoming superior in some other area.	Reggie is not good at athletics, so he puts all of his energies into becoming an academic scholar.
Sublimation: turning socially unacceptable urges into socially acceptable behavior.	Alain, who is very aggressive, becomes a professional hockey player.

Concentrative Meditation   Have you ever found yourself staring out into space, or at some little spot on the wall or table, only to realize that your mind has been a complete blank for the last several minutes?

The state just described is really nothing more than **concentrative meditation**, the form of meditation best known to the general public. In concentrative meditation, the goal is to focus the mind on some repetitive or unchanging stimulus (such as a spot or the sound of one's own heart beating) so that the mind can forget daily hassles and problems and the body can relax. In fact, Herbert Benson (Benson, 1975; Benson et al., 1974a, 1974b) found that meditation produces a state of relaxation in which blood pressure is lowered, alpha waves (brain waves associated with relaxation) are increased, and the amount of melatonin secreted at night (the hormone that helps induce sleep) is increased.

Some people say that if you meditate for only 20 minutes a day, you don't have to sleep at night. That would be nice—think how much more could be accomplished with those extra hours. Unfortunately, although certain meditation groups do make

denial psychological defense mechanism in which the person refuses to acknowledge or recognize a threatening situation.

repression psychological defense mechanism in which the person refuses to consciously remember a threatening or unacceptable event, instead pushing those events into the unconscious mind.

rationalization psychological defense mechanism in which a person invents acceptable excuses for unacceptable behavior.

projection psychological defense mechanism in which unacceptable or threatening impulses or feelings are seen as originating with someone else, usually the target of the impulses or feelings.

reaction formation psychological defense mechanism in which a person forms an opposite emotional or behavioral reaction to the way he or she really feels to keep those true feelings hidden from self and others.

displacement redirecting feelings from a threatening target to a less threatening one.

regression · psychological defense mechanism in which a person falls back on childlike patterns of responding in reaction to stressful situations.

identification defense mechanism in which a person tries to become like someone else to deal with anxiety.

compensation (substitution) defense mechanism in which a person makes up for inferiorities in one area by becoming superior in another area.

sublimation channeling socially unacceptable impulses and urges into socially acceptable behavior.

concentrative meditation form of meditation in which a person focuses the mind on some repetitive or unchanging stimulus so that the mind can be cleared of disturbing thoughts and the body can experience relaxation.

some rather wild claims for meditation, research has shown none of them to be true (Murphy & Donavan, 1997). What research does show is that concentrative meditation is a good way to relax and lower blood pressure in adolescents and adults, men and women, and both whites and African Americans (Barnes et al., 1997; Rainforth et al., 2007; Schneider et al., 1995; Wenneberg et al., 1997). It isn't the only way, as reading a good book or taking a warm bath also produces relaxation. Even simply resting for the same amount of time as one might meditate can be just as relaxing. The advantage of meditation is that people can do it almost anywhere, even in the classroom just before a big test. (It would be a little difficult to take a warm bath then.)

Other research has suggested that concentrative meditation can reduce the levels of chronic pain (Kabat-Zinn et al., 1986), reduce the symptoms of anxiety, depression, and hostility (Kabat-Zinn et al., 1985), and reduce stress levels in cancer patients (Speca et al., 2000). Reducing stress levels in cancer patients through meditation will increase the likelihood of recovery and reduce the incidence of recurrence.

Receptive Meditation   Another kind of meditation is less well known and not as easily achieved. It is called **receptive meditation** and involves trying to expand consciousness outward. The best description of what this is like is to think about a time when you were overawed by nature. Perhaps you were standing at the ocean's edge on a starry night and became suddenly aware of how vast the universe really is. Or perhaps you were walking in the woods and listening to all the little sounds of the birds and animals surrounding you. Your attention was focused outward rather than inward, and this is similar to the state that this type of meditation tries to achieve.

The Effects of Meditation   Regardless of which form of meditation people choose to try, the effects are similar (Murphy & Donavan, 1997). Meditation for only 20 minutes can produce lowered blood pressure in people with hypertension (high blood pressure). It can calm anxiety, help people get to sleep, and help people deal with stress.

9.8   How is coping with stress affected by culture and religion?

HOW CULTURE AFFECTS COPING

Imagine this scene: You are driving out in the country when you come upon an elderly man working on a large wooden box, polishing it with great care. You stop to talk to the man and find out that the box is his own coffin, and he spends his days getting it ready, tending to it with great care. He isn't frightened of dying and doesn't feel strange about polishing his own coffin. How would you react?

If you were from the same rural area of Vietnam as the elderly man, you would probably think nothing strange is going on. For elderly people in the Vietnamese culture, thoughts of death and the things that go along with dying, such as a coffin, are not as stressful as they are to people from Western cultures. In fact, *stress* isn't all that common a term in Vietnamese society compared to Western societies (Phan & Silove, 1999).

In the case of people living in Vietnam and even Vietnamese immigrants to other countries, mental illness is explained by an imbalance between the male and female elements of a person, or by a loss of soul, evil spirits, or a weakening of the nerves. Coping with stress in Vietnamese culture may include rituals, consulting a fortune-teller, or eating certain foods (Phan & Silove, 1999).

Obviously, culture is an important factor in the kinds of coping strategies an individual may adopt and even in determining the degree of stress that is experienced. Mental health professionals should make an effort to include an assessment of a person's cultural background as well as immediate circumstances when dealing with adjustment problems due to stress.

receptive meditation form of meditation in which a person attempts to become aware of everything in immediate conscious experience, or an expansion of consciousness.

HOW RELIGION AFFECTS COPING

A belief in a higher power can also be a source of great comfort in times of stress. There are several ways that religious beliefs can affect the degree of stress people experience and the ability to cope with that stress (Hill & Butter, 1995; Pargament, 1997).

First, most people who hold strong religious beliefs belong to a religious organization and attend regular religious functions, such as services at a synagogue, mosque, temple, or church. This membership can be a vital part of a person's social support system. People do not feel alone in their struggle, both literally because of the people who surround them in their religious community and spiritually because of the intangible presence of their deity (Koenig et al., 1999).

Another way that religion helps people cope involves the rituals and rites that help people feel better about personal weaknesses, failures, or feelings of inadequacy (Koenig et al., 2001). These include rituals such as confession of sins or prayer services during times of stress. Finally, religious beliefs can give meaning to things that otherwise seem to have no meaning or purpose, such as viewing death as a pathway to a paradise, or the destruction of one's home in a natural disaster as a reminder to place less attachment on material things.

Many religions also encourage healthy behavior and eating habits through their prohibitions on such activities as overeating, drinking alcohol, smoking, drug use, and sexual activity outside marriage. Some research even suggests that people with religious commitments live longer than those who have no such beliefs, although this is correlational research and should not be interpreted as concluding that religious belief causes longer life expectancies (Hummer et al., 1999; Koenig et al., 1999; Strawbridge et al., 1997; Thoresen & Harris, 2002).

These Peruvian villagers in a cemetery are honoring their loved ones who have passed away. The Day of the Dead is not only a celebration of the lives of those who have passed on but also a celebration for the living, who use this holiday to gain a sense of control over one of life's most uncontrollable events—death itself. What rituals or ceremonies do people of other cultures use to cope with death?

9.7–8

coping strategies
are behavioral and psychological actions taken to master, tolerate, reduce, or minimize the effect of stressors

problem-focused coping
involves working to change or eliminate the stressor itself

emotion-focused coping
involves changing the way a person feels or emotionally reacts to a stressor —

several unconscious psychological defense mechanisms were proposed by Freud (see Table 9.3); originally psychoanalytical in nature, still useful to describe some thinking and behavior

various methods and behaviors exist to help individuals in dealing with stress

• meditation, in its various forms, helps to promote relaxation, calm anxiety, improve sleep, and lower blood pressure

• an individual's culture and/or religious beliefs can affect the appraisal of events as more or less stressful, the coping strategies adopted, and support systems that can offer assistance

Coping with Stress

(continued)

Directions: Read each of the questions or incomplete sentences below. Then choose the response that best answers the question or completes the sentence.

1. Which of the following is an example of problem-focused coping?
   a. Ignoring an argument with a friend and focusing on other things
   b. Writing thoughts about an argument with a friend in a private journal
   c. Venting to mutual acquaintances about an argument with a friend
   d. Making excuses for behavior that led to an argument with a friend
   e. Attempting to settle an argument with a friend by apologizing

2. Clarissa feels anxious because she is having trouble making new friends. She knows that another girl in her class, Patrice, is very social and has lots of friends. Clarissa begins copying Patrice's mannerisms and interests. Clarissa is engaging in _____.
   a. repression
   b. projection
   c. displacement
   d. identification
   e. compensation

3. Ellie sucks her thumb when she is under stress. Ellie is engaging in
   a. reaction formation
   b. displacement
   c. regression
   d. projection
   e. sublimation

4. Kareem is relaxing in a chair with his eyes closed. As he sits quietly, he is focusing on the sound of his own breathing and clearing his mind of other thoughts. Kareem is practicing _____.
   a. sensory deprivation
   b. receptive meditation
   c. implosive meditation
   d. coping-based meditation
   e. concentrative meditation

5. Max is the school's star basketball player, but during one game, he misses every shot he takes, and his coach pulls him out of the game. Matt says that his baby sister kept him from getting a good night's sleep and the coach didn't let him practice enough the day before. Max is most likely engaging in_____.
   a. denial
   b. rationalization
   c. regression
   d. identification
   e. compensation

Applying Psychology to Everyday Life: Focus on Wellness

9.9 What are some ways to promote wellness?

Wellness can be defined as the practice of behaviors and lifestyle choices that promote both physical and mental health. Here are some helpful hints on how to promote wellness in one's own life:

- **Exercise.** No one likes to admit it, but exercise is the best way to become healthier. Exercise makes the heart healthier, raises the body's metabolic rate to help maintain a healthy weight, raises good cholesterol and lowers bad cholesterol, strengthens bones, improves sleep quality, reduces tiredness, increases natural killer cell activity to help ward off viruses and cancer, and is a great way to reduce the effects of stress (Fiatarone et al., 1993; Manson et al., 2002). In fact exercise has been found to help menopausal women (women who have ceased being able to conceive a child) to reduce the anxiety and depression that may accompany the physical and chemical changes of menopause (Nelson et al., 2008). Aerobic exercise has also been found to reduce feelings of tiredness and increase energy in young adults who, because of a sedentary lifestyle, have been diagnosed with persistent fatigue (Puetz et al., 2008).

- **Get involved with others.** The benefits of social support have already been highlighted in this chapter. Make some new friends or join a social organization. Make it a point to do things with other people. Have friends over to dinner or go out shopping with others.

- **Get some sleep.** Most people in the busy, hectic modern world simply do not get enough sleep. As discussed in Chapter Four, sleep serves to restore the body physically and provides a way to manage stress during dreaming. Try to get at least seven to eight hours of sleep each night, including weekends. Try to go to bed and get up at the same time every day to maintain your sleep–wake cycle. Sleep deprivation can lead to a lower production of natural killer cells, which are a necessary and vital part of the immune system (Irwin et al., 1994, 1996).

- **Eat healthy foods.** It's also very easy to eat all the wrong things in today's world. Fortunately, even fast-food restaurants are offering more salads and grilled items to promote healthier eating. Eat breakfast every day, making sure to include a good amount of protein in that meal. Protein in the morning helps improve concentration and alertness, and eating breakfast helps you to avoid overeating at lunch or dinner. Eating breakfast has even been shown to decrease the risk of stroke, obesity, and diabetes (Pereira et al., 2003). Be sure to include some healthy snacks at least twice a day.

- **Have some fun.** Playing is important! Schedule some time to just relax, play a game with a friend, read a book, or do something fun. Playing helps prevent burnout.

- **Manage your time.** One of the things that can create a lot of stress is feeling overwhelmed when there are lots of tasks to do. Make a list of the tasks you need to accomplish, putting the most important and urgent ones first. Check each item off the list as you finish it. This gives you a sense of control over your day's activities and rewards you with a sense of accomplishment each time you can check off an item.

- **Take a deep breath.** When feeling stressed, take a moment to cope. Take some deep breaths to help calm yourself and relax tension. If you're so stressed that you feel like crying, find a quiet, private place and cry—crying can relieve stress.

Playing a game, especially one that involves having fun with your friends, is a great way to maintain a sense of wellness and stay physically healthy—especially if the game involves exercise!

9 CHAPTER SUMMARY

Stress and Stressors

9.1 How do psychologists define stress?

- Stress is the physical, emotional, and behavioral responses that occur when events are identified as threatening or challenging.

- Stress that has a negative impact is called distress. Eustress is the optimal amount of stress that people need to function well.

9.2 What kinds of external events can cause stress?

- Catastrophes are events such as floods or crashes that can result in high levels of stress, including acute stress disorder and post-traumatic stress disorder.

- Major life changes create stress by requiring adjustments. Major life changes have an impact on chronic health problems and risk of accidents.

- Hassles are the daily frustrations and irritations experienced by people that have an impact on day-to-day health.

9.3 What are some psychological factors in stress?

- Four sources of stress are pressure, uncontrollability, frustration, and conflict.

- Frustration, which can be internal or external, may result in persistence, aggression, displaced aggression, or withdrawal.

Current Issues in Psychology: Suicide in America

- Suicidal behavior is highly linked to depression. People who talk about suicide should be taken seriously and need help.

- There are four types of conflicts: approach–approach, avoidance–avoidance, approach–avoidance, and multiple approach–avoidance.

Physiological Factors: Stress and Health

- The autonomic nervous system consists of the sympathetic system, which responds to stressful events, and the parasympathetic system, which restores the body to normal functioning after the stress has ceased.

9.4 How does stress affect the physical functioning of the body and its immune system?

- The general adaptation syndrome is the body's reaction to stress and includes three stages of reaction: alarm, resistance, and exhaustion.

- Stress causes the immune system to react as though an illness or invading organism has been detected, increasing the functioning of the immune system.

- As the stress continues or increases, the immune system can begin to fail.

9.5 How do cognitive factors and personality differences affect the experience of stress?

- The cognitive appraisal approach states that how people think about a stressor determines, at least in part, how stressful that stressor will become.

- The first step in appraising a stressor is called primary appraisal, in which the person determines whether an event is threatening, challenging, or of no consequence. Threatening events are more stressful than those seen as challenging.

- The second step is secondary appraisal, in which the person assesses the resources available to deal with the stressor, such as time, money, and social support.

- Type A personalities are ambitious, time conscious, hostile, and angry workaholics who are at increased risk of coronary heart disease, primarily due to their anger and hostility.

- Type B personalities are relaxed and easygoing and have one-third the risk of coronary heart disease as do Type A personalities, if male, and one-fourth the risk if female and working outside the home.

- Type C personalities are pleasant but repressed, internalizing their negative emotions.

- Hardy people are hard workers who lack the anger and hostility of the Type A personality, instead seeming to thrive on stress.

- Optimists look for positive outcomes and experience far less stress than pessimists, who take a more negative view.

9.6 What social factors influence stress reactions?

- Several social factors can be a source of stress or increase the effects of stress: poverty, stresses on the job or in the workplace, and entering a majority culture that is different from one's culture of origin.

- Burnout is a condition that occurs when job stress is so great that the person develops negative thoughts, emotions, and behavior as well as an extreme dissatisfaction with the job and a desire to quit.

- The four methods of acculturation are integration, assimilation, separation, and marginalization.

- Social support systems are important in helping people cope with stress.

Coping with Stress

9.7 What are some ways in which people cope with stress reactions?

- Problem-focused coping is used when the problem can be eliminated or changed so that it is no longer stressful or so that the impact of the stressor is reduced.

- Emotion-focused coping is often used with problem-focused coping and involves changing one's emotional reactions to a stressor.

- Psychological defense mechanisms are unconscious distortions of perceived reality and can be a form of emotion-focused coping.

- Meditation can produce a state of relaxation and reduce the physical reactions common to stressful situations.

- Concentrative meditation involves focusing inward on some repetitive stimulus, such as one's breathing. Receptive meditation involves focusing outward to expand conscious awareness.

9.8 How is coping with stress affected by culture and religion?

- Different cultures perceive stressors differently, and coping strategies will also vary from culture to culture.

- People with religious beliefs also have been found to cope better with stressful events.

Applying Psychology to Everyday Life: Focus on Wellness

9.9 What are some ways to promote wellness?

- Factors that promote wellness include exercise, social activities, getting enough sleep, eating healthy foods, having fun, managing one's time, and practicing good coping skills.

TEST YOURSELF: PREPARING FOR THE AP* EXAM

ANSWERS ON PAGE AK-3.

✔●┤**Practice** on **MyPsychLab**   **Ready for your test?** More quizzes and a customized study plan. **www.mypsychlab.com**

PART I: MULTIPLE-CHOICE QUESTIONS

Directions for Part I: Read each of the questions or incomplete sentences below. Then choose the response that best answers the question or completes the sentence.

1. Which of the following is a mental symptom of stress?
   a. Anxiety
   b. Overeating
   c. Frequent colds
   d. Memory problems
   e. High blood pressure

2. After being in a car accident, Yoshiko suffered from nightmares and other sleeping problems, and she could not concentrate on her work. After about two weeks, these symptoms disappeared and she was able to work and sleep normally again. Yoshiko was suffering from _____.
   a. shell shock   b. acute stress disorder

   c. mild stress reaction
   d. mild anxiety
   e. post-traumatic stress disorder

3. For which of the following groups of people would going shopping or experiencing bad weather be most stressful?
   a. Children
   b. Adolescents
   c. Young adults
   d. Middle-aged adults
   e. Elderly people

4. Rachel's teacher gives her a negative evaluation, making Rachel feel upset. When Rachel arrives at home, she yells at her family members. Rachel is displaying _____.
   a. regression   b. sublimation
   c. displacement   d. compensation
   e. rationalization

5. Trying to decide between two of your favorite foods is an example of a(n) _____.
   a. approach–approach conflict
   b. avoidance–avoidance conflict
   c. approach–avoidance conflict
   d. multiple approach–approach conflict
   e. multiple approach–avoidance conflict

6. In which stage of the general adaptation syndrome is death a possible outcome?
   a. Onset
   b. Alarm
   c. Resistance
   d. Reaction
   e. Exhaustion

7. Tad seems to thrive on stress and feels very much in control of his life. His personality would most likely be labeled _____.
   a. Type A
   b. Type B
   c. Type C
   d. hardy
   e. pessimistic

8. Acculturative stress is likely to be the lowest for people who choose to enter the majority culture through the process of _____.
   a. separation
   b. integration
   c. assimilation
   d. marginalization
   e. forced adaptation

9. Shaun is having trouble in algebra. He goes to the school's academic help center for tutoring and spends extra time working on algebra problems at home. Shaun's method of coping is _____.
   a. internal
   b. meditative
   c. defense focused
   d. problem focused
   e. emotion focused

10. Which of the following activities is least likely to promote optimism?
   a. Reading a good book
   b. Working out at the gym
   c. Experimenting with meditation
   d. Comparing oneself to successful people
   e. Blaming poor performance on outside circumstances

PART II: FREE-RESPONSE QUESTION

Directions for Part II: Read the essay question that follows. Then, respond to the question in a clear, concise essay. Do not simply list facts. Instead, present a thorough argument based on your critical consideration of the topic. Use proper psychological terminology as necessary.

In a detailed, well-organized essay, describe the five types of conflict and give a real-life example of each. Then, explain which types of conflict are most likely to produce the greatest stress, and give examples of ways in which that stress might be reduced.

stress is the physical, emotional, cognitive, and behavioral response to events that are appraised as threatening or challenging; first studied systematically by Hans Selye

can include physical fatigue, recurring illness, over/under eating, smoking/drinking more than usual, mood swings, irritability, depression, anger, memory and concentration problems

stress-causing events are called stressors; can come from external or internal sources; range from mild to severe

negative events cause distress; positive events cause eustress, the optimal level of stress required to facilitate healthy adaptation and well-being

external stress-causing events may include catastrophes, major life changes, and daily hassles (differ according to developmental stage)

can be assessed systematically (e.g., Social Readjustment Rating Scale, College Undergraduate Stress Scale)

Table 9.2	Sample Items from the College Undergraduate Stress Scale (CUSS)	
EVENT		**RATING**
Death of a close friend		97
Finals week		90
Oversleeping for an exam		89
Flunking a class		89
Financial difficulties		84
Writing a major term paper		83
Two exams in one day		80
Getting married		76
Difficulties with parents		73
Talking in front of a class		72
Difficulties with a roommate		66
A class you hate		62
Maintaining a steady dating relationship		55
Peer pressures		53
Being away from home for the first time		53
Getting straight A's		51
Falling asleep in class		40

Source: Adapted from Renner & Mackin (1998).

Stress and Stressors (part 1)

prolonged or acute stress can cause stress-related disorders that have symptoms including anxiety, recurring nightmares, sleep problems, problems concentrating, and "reliving" the experience through flashbacks or dreams

acute stress disorder (ASD): symptoms present for < 1 month

post-traumatic stress disorder (PTSD): symptoms persist > 1 month

pressure
urgent demands or expectations and uncontrollability

frustration
due to external (losses, rejections, failures, delays) or internal (personal characteristics) factors; can result in several typical responses

- **persistence**
- **aggression**
- **escape/withdrawal** (**suicide** is a drastic form of escape)

Stress and Stressors (part 2)
(psychological stressors are often related to external events)

conflict

- **approach–approach conflict**
- **avoidance–avoidance conflict**
- **approach–avoidance conflict**
- **multiple approach–avoidance conflicts**

the **autonomic nervous system (ANS)** figures prominently in the body's physiological reactions to stress

Hans Selye identified the **general adaption syndrome (GAS)**, the sequence of physiological reactions the body goes through when adapting to a stressor

- **alarm**
- **resistance**
- **exhaustion**

the field of **psychoneuroimmunology** focuses on the effects of stress on the immune system

Physiological Factors

Alarm Stage
Sympathetic nervous system is activated by adrenal glands

Forehead, neck, shoulder, arm, and leg muscles contract

Pupils enlarge

Sugar is released into the bloodstream for energy

Resistance Stage

Breathing is frequent and shallow

Blood pressure remains high

Accelerated heart rate increases blood flow to muscles; blood pressure increases

Hormones from adrenal glands are released into bloodstream

Exhaustion Stage

Liver runs out of sugar

Prolonged muscle tension causes fatigue

stress-related responses similar to those triggered by infection—increase in white blood cell count, enzymes, and antibodies

body is engineered for short-term, acute stress; prolonged stress/depletion of resources results in reduced functioning of immune system

9.5 — pp. 368–369

- **Lazarus's cognitive–mediational theory of emotions**
  suggests an individual's appraisal of a stressor is a major factor in determining how stressful that stressor becomes
  - **primary appraisal**
  - **secondary appraisal**

  - **personality differences**
    affect how one assesses a stressor, the coping strategies used, and possible health outcomes

Cognitive and Personality Factors

- Type A
- Type B
- Type C
- "Type H"

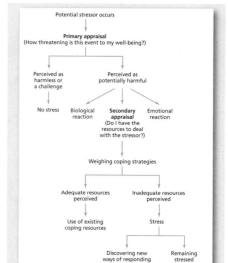

TYPE Z BEHAVIOR

- **explanatory style**
  optimists tend to look for positive outcomes, whereas pessimists seem to expect the worst

  - Seligman (originally studied concept of learned helplessness) began the positive psychology movement; has suggested that optimism leads to longer life and greater success in life endeavors

  - optimism is associated with controlling mood or emotional reactions; can be a learned skill through alternative thinking, downward social comparison, relaxation, and correcting faulty thinking

Potential stressor occurs

Primary appraisal
(How threatening is this event to my well-being?)

Perceived as harmless or a challenge / Perceived as potentially harmful

No stress — Biological reaction — **Secondary appraisal** (Do I have the resources to deal with the stressor?) — Emotional reaction

Weighing coping strategies

Adequate resources perceived / Inadequate resources perceived

Use of existing coping resources / Stress

Discovering new ways of responding or new resources / Remaining stressed

Percentage of subjects — 75 — 50 — 25 — Type As — Type Bs

■ Men with coronary heart disease
■ Healthy men

9.6 — p. 372

- a great deal of stress can come from dealing with other people and social interactions

  - poverty and job stress are prominent, economically based social factors that lead to stressful living conditions
    - poverty results in lack of basic life necessities
    - job stress may be related to workload, lack of control or job security, work schedule, and low job satisfaction

Social Factors in Stress

- culturally, stress is affected by status of acculturation (adapting to a new, different, or often dominant culture) and the method chosen to adapt
  - **integration**
  - **assimilation**
  - **separation**
  - **marginalization**

- in general, having a positive social support system that provides various forms of help (e.g., monetary, physical, emotional support) is a good predictor for healthy aging and longevity

9.7–8 — p. 377

- **coping strategies**
  are behavioral and psychological actions taken to master, tolerate, reduce, or minimize the effect of stressors

  - **problem-focused coping**
    involves working to change or eliminate the stressor itself

    - **emotion-focused coping**
      involves changing the way a person feels or emotionally reacts to a stressor
      - several unconscious psychological defense mechanisms were proposed by Freud (see Table 9.3); originally psychoanalytical in nature, still useful to describe some thinking and behavior

Coping with Stress

- various methods and behaviors exist to help individuals in dealing with stress
  - meditation, in its various forms, helps to promote relaxation, calm anxiety, improve sleep, and lower blood pressure
  - an individual's culture and/or religious beliefs can affect the appraisal of events as more or less stressful, the coping strategies adopted, and support systems that can offer assistance

10

Development Across the Life Span

Home Alone at Two: A Lesson in Survival Instincts

Don was separated from his wife, Lisa. She had custody of their 2-year-old daughter, and he had been trying to reach her to check on the little girl. Finally, he contacted the police and found out that his wife had been in jail for nearly three weeks, arrested on an aggravated battery charge. Lisa told him that their daughter was with neighbors, but after knocking on door after door without success, Don finally got the apartment manager to let him into his wife's apartment. There was his precious little child, covered in dirt and dried ketchup. She grabbed him and didn't let go.

The 2-year-old child had survived alone in the apartment for 19 days by eating mustard, ketchup, dried spaghetti, and a few other items she was able to find in the bottom sections of the refrigerator and cupboards of the kitchen and by drinking water from the bathroom sink. When her father found her, she was naked and covered in dried food. Although malnourished, she had managed to find enough to eat to survive until rescued by her father, who was amazed at her relatively good condition.

The day after arriving at the hospital to be treated for malnutrition and dehydration, the plucky little girl was sitting up in her hospital bed, laughing and playing with the nurses.

This true story, which occurred in September 2003, not only shows the power of the drive to survive in human beings but also the adaptive nature of children, even young children, to explore their environment and find ways to cope with adversity.

Why study human development? Understanding how we come to be the people we are is a critical step in understanding ourselves as we are today as well as who we may become as we grow older. From the moment of conception, we are each headed down a pathway of change, influenced by our biology, environment, and social interactions, to a destination that is the same for all of us. The twists and turns of the pathway are what make each of us unique individuals. In this chapter, we'll look at the influences that help determine our developmental pathway through life.

Learning Objectives

10.1 What are some of the special research methods used to study development?

10.2 What is the relationship between heredity and environmental factors in determining development?

10.3 How do chromosomes, genes, and DNA determine a person's characteristics or disorders, and what causes multiple births?

10.4 What happens during the germinal, embryonic, and fetal periods of pregnancy and what are some hazards in prenatal development?

10.5 What kind of physical changes take place in infancy and childhood?

10.6 What are two ways of looking at cognitive development, and how does language develop?

10.7 How do infants and children develop personalities and form relationships with others, and what are Erikson's stages of psychosocial development for children?

10.8 What is gender, and how can biology and learning influence gender role development?

10.9 What are the physical, cognitive, and personality changes that occur in adolescense, including concepts of morality and Erikson's for identity?

10.10 What are the physical, cognitive, and personality changes that occur during adulthood and aging, including Erikson's last three psychosocial stages, and patterns of parenting?

10.11 How do psychologists explain why aging occurs, and what are the stages of death and dying?

10.12 How does attention-deficit hyperactivity disorder affect adults?

Issues in Studying Human Development

What is development? In the context of life, **human development** is the scientific study of the changes that occur in people as they age, from conception until death. This chapter will touch on almost all of the topics covered in the other chapters of this text, such as personality, cognition, biological processes, and social interactions. But in this chapter, all of those topics will be studied in the context of changes that occur as a result of the process of human development.

10.1 What are some of the special research methods used to study development?

As briefly discussed in Chapter One, research in development is affected by the problem of age. In any experiment, the participants who are exposed to the independent variable (the variable in an experiment that is deliberately manipulated by the experimenter) should be randomly assigned to the different experimental conditions. The problem in developmental research is that the age of the people in the study should always be an independent variable, but people cannot be randomly assigned to different age-groups.

There are some special designs that are used in researching age-related changes: the **longitudinal design**, in which one group of people is followed and assessed at different times as the group ages; the **cross-sectional design**, in which several different age groups are studied at one time; and the **cross-sequential design**, which is a combination of the longitudinal and cross-sectional designs (Baltes et al., 1988).

The longitudinal design has the advantage of looking at real age-related changes as those changes occur in the same individuals. Disadvantages of this method are the lengthy amount of time, money, and effort involved in following participants over the years as well as the loss of participants when they move away, lose interest, or die. The cross-sectional design has the advantages of being quick, relatively inexpensive, and easier to accomplish than the longitudinal design. The main disadvantage is that one

human development the scientific study of the changes that occur in people as they age from conception until death.

longitudinal design research design in which one participant or group of participants is studied over a long period of time.

cross-sectional design research design in which several different age-groups of participants are studied at one particular point in time.

cross-sequential design research design in which participants are first studied by means of a cross-sectional design but are also followed and assessed for a period of time.

Table 10.1   A Comparison of Three Developmental Research Designs

CROSS-SECTIONAL DESIGN		
Different participants of various ages are compared at one point in time to determine age-related *differences*.	**Group One:** 20-year-old participants	Research done in 2010
	Group Two: 40-year-old participants	
	Group Three: 60-year-old participants	
LONGITUDINAL DESIGN		
The **same** participants are studied at various ages to determine age-related *changes*.	**Study One:** 20-year-old participants	Research done in 1970
	Study Two: Same participants were 40 years old	Research done in 1990
	Study Three: Same participants are now 60 years old	Research done in 2010
CROSS-SEQUENTIAL DESIGN		
Different participants of various ages are compared at several points in time, to determine both age-related *differences* and age-related *changes*.	**Study One:** Group One: 20-year-old participants	Research done in 2005
	Group Two: 40-year-old participants	
	Study Two: Group One: participants are now 25	Research done in 2010
	Group Two: participants are now 45	

is no longer comparing an individual to that same individual as he or she ages; instead, individuals of different ages are being compared to one another. Differences between age-groups are often a problem in developmental research. For example, if comparing the IQ scores of 30-year-olds to 80-year-olds to see how aging affects intelligence, questions arise concerning the differing experiences those two age-groups have had in educational opportunities that might affect IQ scores in addition to any effects of aging. Table 10.1 shows a comparison between examples of a *longitudinal design*, a *cross-sectional design*, and a *cross-sequential design*.

In studying human development, developmental psychologists have outlined many theories of how these age-related changes occur. There are some areas of controversy, however, and one of these is the issue of nature versus nurture.

NATURE VERSUS NURTURE

10.2 What is the relationship between heredity and environmental factors in determining development?

Nature refers to heredity, the influence of inherited characteristics on personality, physical growth, intellectual growth, and social interactions. **Nurture** refers to the influence of the environment on all of those same things and includes parenting styles, physical surroundings, economic factors, and anything that can have an influence on development that does not come from within the person.

So, is a person like Hitler born that way, or did something happen to make him the person he was? How much of a person's personality and behavior are determined by nature and how much are determined by nurture? This is a key question, and the answer is quite complicated. It is also quite important: Was someone like Hitler the result of bad genes? Or was it bad parenting or life-altering experiences in childhood? Or was it a unique combination of both hereditary and environmental influences? After many years of scientific research, most developmental psychologists now agree that the last possibility is the most likely explanation for most of human development: All that

nature the influence of our inherited characteristics on our personality, physical growth, intellectual growth, and social interactions.

nurture the influence of the environment on personality, physical growth, intellectual growth, and social interactions.

AP* Discuss the interaction of nature and nurture in the determination of behavior.

So, is a person like Hitler born that way, or did something happen to make him the person he was?

people are and all that people become is the product of an interaction between nature and nurture (Ridley, 1999). This does not mean that the controversy no longer exists; for example, intelligence is still a "hot topic" with regard to how much is inherited and how much is learned. There are researchers and theorists who assume a large genetic influence (Bouchard & Segal, 1985; Herrnstein & Murray, 1994; Jensen, 1969; Johnson et al., 2007; Kristensen & Bjerkedal, 2007) and those who believe that culture, economics, nutrition in early childhood, and educational opportunities have a greater impact (Gardner et al., 1996; Gould, 1996; Rose et al., 1984; Wahlsten, 1997).

Behavioral genetics is a relatively new field in the investigation of the origins of behavior in which researchers try to determine how much of behavior is the result of genetic inheritance and how much is due to a person's experiences. For more on behavioral genetics and links to other sites, go to **www.ornl.gov/sci/techresources/Human_Genome/elsi/behavior.shtml.**

Genetic researchers work with samples of DNA to examine the basic building blocks of life.

Prenatal Development

Any study of the human life span must begin with looking at the complex material contained in the cells of the body that carries the instructions for life itself. After discussing the basic building blocks of life, this text will discuss how the processes of conception and the development of the infant within the womb take place.

CHROMOSOMES, GENES, AND DNA

10.3 How do chromosomes, genes, and DNA determine a person's characteristics or disorders, and what causes multiple births?

Genetics is the science of heredity. Understanding how genes transmit human characteristics and traits involves defining a few basic terms.

DNA (deoxyribonucleic acid) is a very special kind of molecule (the smallest particle of a substance that still has all the properties of that substance). DNA consists of two sugar/phosphate strands, each linked together by certain chemical elements called *amines* or *bases* arranged in a particular pattern. See Figure 10.1 for a representation of DNA. Because of DNA's unique shape, each molecule of DNA is linked end to end with the others, forming a very long strand. Sections of this DNA strand are linked by amines, which are organic structures that contain the genetic codes for building the proteins that make up organic life (hair coloring, muscle, and skin, for example) and that control the life of each cell. Each section of DNA containing a certain sequence (ordering) of these amines is called a **gene**. These genes are located on rod-shaped structures called **chromosomes**, which are found in the nucleus of a cell.

Humans have a total of 46 chromosomes in each cell of their bodies (with the exception of the egg and the sperm). Twenty-three of these chromosomes come from the mother's egg and the other 23 from the father's sperm. Most characteristics are determined by 22 such pairs, called the *autosomes*. The last pair determines the sex of the person. These two chromosomes are called the *sex chromosomes*.

Figure 10.1 DNA Molecule
In this model of a DNA molecule, the two strands making up the sides of the "twisted ladder" are composed of sugars and phosphates. The "rungs" of the ladder that link the two strands are amines. Amines contain the genetic codes for building the proteins that make up organic life.

Frank and Ernest

I HATE BEING A DNA MOLECULE. THERE'S SO MUCH TO REMEMBER!

©1986 Thaves. Reprinted with permission. Newspaper dist. by NEA, Inc.

© Thaves. Reprinted by permission.

DOMINANT AND RECESSIVE GENES

The 46 chromosomes can be arranged in pairs, with one member of each pair coming from the mother and the other member from the father. Think about just one of these pairs for the moment.

In this particular pair of chromosomes, assume that there is a gene for hair color on each chromosome. The observable color of the person's hair will be determined by those two genes, one gene from each parent. If both genes are for brown hair, the person will obviously have brown hair, right? And if both are for blond hair, the person's hair will be blond.

But what if one gene is for brown hair and the other is for blond hair? The answer lies in the nature of each gene. Some genes that are more active in influencing the trait are called **dominant**. A dominant gene will always be expressed in the observable trait, in this case the hair color. A person with a dominant brown hair color gene will have brown hair, no matter what the other gene is, because brown is the most dominant of all the hair colors.

Some genes are less active in influencing the trait and will only be expressed in the observable trait if they are paired with another less active gene. These genes tend to recede, or fade, into the background when paired with a more dominant gene, so they are called **recessive**. Blond hair color is the most recessive color and will only show up in a person's hair color if that person has a blond hair color gene from each parent.

What about red hair? And how come some people have mixed hair color, like a strawberry blond? In reality, the patterns of genetic transmission of traits are usually more complicated. Almost all traits are controlled by more than one pair of genes in a process called *polygenic inheritance.* (*Polygenic* means "many genes.") Sometimes certain kinds of genes tend to group themselves with certain other genes, like the genes for blond hair and blue eyes. Other genes are so equally dominant or equally recessive that they combine their traits in the organism. For example, genes for blond hair and red hair are recessive. When a child inherits one of each from his or her parents, instead of one or the other controlling the child's hair color, they may blend together to form a strawberry-blond mix. Figure 10.2 illustrates a typical pattern of inheritance for dominant and recessive genes.

GENETIC AND CHROMOSOME PROBLEMS

Several genetic disorders are carried by recessive genes. Diseases carried by recessive genes are inherited when a child inherits two recessive genes, one from each parent. Examples of disorders inherited in this manner are cystic fibrosis (a disease of the respiratory and digestive tracts), sickle cell anemia (a blood disorder), Tay-Sachs disorder (a fatal neurological disorder), and Phenylketonuria (PKU; a problem with digesting a particular amino acid, phenylalanine).

But what if one gene is for brown hair and the other is for blond hair? ◄

What about red hair? And how come some people have mixed hair color, like a strawberry blond? ◄

genetics   the science of inherited traits.

DNA (deoxyribonucleic acid)   special molecule that contains the genetic material of the organism.

gene   section of DNA having the same arrangement of chemical elements.

chromosome   tightly wound strand of genetic material or DNA.

dominant   referring to a gene that actively controls the expression of a trait.

recessive   referring to a gene that only influences the expression of a trait when paired with an identical gene.

Mother — Does not carry recessive PKU gene — PP
Father — Does not carry recessive PKU gene — PP

Mother contributes either P or P   **Father contributes either P or P**

PP — Normal   PP — Normal   PP — Normal   PP — Normal

Result: No child can inherit PKU

a.

Mother — Carries recessive PKU gene — Pp
Father — Does not carry recessive PKU gene — PP

Mother contributes either P or p   **Father contributes either P or P**

PP — Normal   PP — Normal   pP — Carrier   pP — Carrier

Result: No child will be afflicted with PKU, although two in four will carry the recessive gene

b.

Mother — Carries recessive PKU gene — Pp
Father — Carries recessive PKU gene — Pp

Mother contributes either P or p   **Father contributes either P or p**

PP — Normal   Pp — Carrier   pP — Carrier   pp — Afflicted with PKU

Result: One in four children will inherit two dominant genes and will not have PKU; two in four will inherit one recessive gene and not be afflicted with PKU but will carry the recessive gene; and one in four will have PKU

c.

Figure 10.2 Dominant and Recessive Genes and PKU

This figure shows the variation of parents carrying zero, one, or two recessive genes and the result of this in their offspring.
a. With neither parent carrying a recessive PKU gene, PKU cannot exist in any of their offspring.
b. If only one parent carries the PKU gene, their children might be carriers, but will not have PKU.
c. Only if both parents are carriers of PKU will a child have the 1 in 4 possibility of having PKU.

Sometimes the chromosome itself is the problem. Although each egg and each sperm are only supposed to have 23 chromosomes, in the creation of these cells a chromosome can end up in the wrong cell, leaving one cell with only 22 and the other with 24. If either of these cells survives to "mate," the missing or extra chromosome can cause mild to severe problems in development (American Academy of Pediatrics, 1995; Barnes & Carey, 2002; Gardner & Sutherland, 1996).

Examples of chromosome disorders include *Down syndrome*, a disorder in which there is an extra chromosome in what would normally be the twenty-first pair. Symptoms include almond-shaped, wide-set eyes and mental retardation (Barnes & Carey, 2002; Hernandez & Fisher, 1996). Other chromosome disorders occur when there is an extra sex chromosome in the twenty-third pair, such as *Klinefelter's syndrome*, in which the twenty-third set of sex chromosomes is XXY, with the extra X producing a male with reduced masculine characteristics, enlarged breasts, obesity, and excessive height (Bock, 1993), and *Turner's syndrome*, in which the twenty-third pair is actually missing an X, so that the result is a lone X chromosome (Ranke & Saenger, 2001). These females tend to be very short, infertile, and sexually underdeveloped (American Academy of Pediatrics, 1995; Rovet, 1993).

FROM CONCEPTION TO BIRTH

Conception is the moment at which a female becomes pregnant. From conception to the actual birth of the baby is a period of approximately nine months, during which a single cell becomes a complete infant. It is also during this time that many things can have a positive or negative influence on the developing infant.

THE ZYGOTE AND TWINNING

When an egg (also called an **ovum**) and a sperm unite in the process of **fertilization**, the resulting single cell will have a total of 46 chromosomes and is called a **zygote**. Normally, the zygote will begin to divide, first into two cells, then four, then eight, and so on, with each new cell also having 46 chromosomes, because the DNA molecules produce duplicates of themselves before each division. (This division process is called *mitosis*.) Eventually, the mass of cells becomes a baby. Sometimes this division process doesn't work exactly this way, and twins or multiples are the result.

There are actually two kinds of twins. Twins who are commonly referred to as "identical" are **monozygotic twins**, meaning that the two babies come from one (mono) fertilized egg (zygote). Early in the division process, the mass of cells splits completely—no one knows exactly why—into two separate masses, each of which will develop into a separate infant. The infants will be the same sex and have identical features because they each possess the same set of 46 chromosomes. The other type of twin is more an accident of timing and is more common in women who are older and who are from certain ethnic groups (Allen & Parisi, 1990; Bonnelykke, 1990; Imaizumi, 1998). A woman's body may either release more than one egg at a time or release an egg after a woman has already conceived once. If two eggs are fertilized, the woman may give birth to fraternal or **dizygotic twins** (two zygotes), or possibly triplets or some other multiple number of babies (Bryan & Hallett, 2001). This is also more likely to happen to women who are taking fertility drugs to help them get pregnant. (See Figure 10.3.)

Twins are important because they provide developmental psychologists with another way to look at the contribution of nature and nurture to human development. Researchers may seek out identical twins who have been separated at birth, looking at all the

Down syndrome is a form of developmental delay caused by an extra chromosome 21.

AP* Explain the process of conception and gestation, including factors that influence successful fetal development.

conception the moment at which a female becomes pregnant.
ovum the female sex cell, or egg.

fertilization the union of the ovum and sperm.

zygote cell resulting from the uniting of the ovum and sperm.

monozygotic twins identical twins formed when one zygote splits into two separate masses of cells, each of which develops into a separate embryo.

dizygotic twins often called fraternal twins, occurring when two eggs each get fertilized by two different sperm, resulting in two zygotes in the uterus at the same time.

Figure 10.3 Monozygotic and Dizygotic Twins
Because identical twins come from one fertilized egg (zygote), they are called monozygotic. Fraternal twins, who come from two different fertilized eggs, are called dizygotic.

Identical twins

1 Accounting for about 1 in 250 births, these are created when a single egg is fertilized by one sperm.

2 The egg splits into halves. Each develops into a fetus with the same genetic composition.

Fraternal twins

1 Twice as common as identicals, fraternals arise when two eggs are released at once.

2 If both are fertilized by separate sperm, two fetuses form. Genetically they are just ordinary siblings.

ways those twins are alike in spite of being raised in different environments. (L)(I)(N)(K) *to Chapter Eleven: Theories of Personality, p. 456.*

Sometimes in the twinning process, the mass of cells does not completely split apart. When this occurs, *conjoined twins* will will result, and they will be joined at the point where the two cell masses remained "stuck." This joining may involve only soft tissues or may involve the sharing of certain body parts, like the case of Brittany and Abby, which is discussed in the Psychology in the News section that follows.

Abby and Brittany Hensel are conjoined twins who share one body from the waist down but are two distinctly different individuals.

Psychology in the News

Abby and Brittany Hensel, Together for Life

Brittany loves milk. Her twin sister, Abigail (Abby), despises milk and would rather drink orange juice. Abby likes blue, Brittany likes pink. Abby likes oyster crackers in her soup but Brittany hates them. Brittany likes a full course meal, Abby prefers pasta. Both are good with academics: Abby prefers math and Brittany prefers to do the reading. They are thinking of pursuing careers in education when they start college.

Abby and Brittany sound like many other siblings, each with separate likes and dislikes as well as different interests. But Abby and Brittany are not separate and can never truly be separate, for they have two separate heads yet share one lower body. No more than four sets of surviving conjoined twins in recorded history have this condition. In the case of Abby and Brittany Hensel, they each have their own heart, stomach and pair of lungs. Their spines are joined at the pelvis, and below the waist they have only one set of organs. Each controls one arm and one leg on one side of the body, yet they somehow manage to move as one (Miller & Doman, 1996).

The girls ride a bicycle, swim, and put on makeup just like any other girls their age. Yet every action they undertake has to be a miracle of coordination, and they do it without even seeming to think about it. If Brittany coughs, *Abby's* hand may reflexively go up to cover Brittany's mouth. When Brittany is sick, she can't take the medicine for it (her stomach is sensitive) but Abby can take it for her (her stomach isn't sensitive).

In 2002, the girls received surgery to correct a severe curve in each of their spines, the result of their unusual joining of spinal columns (Kaveny, 2001). They each gained about two inches in height and find that to be an advantage on the soccer field. Now 20 years old, they are healthy and seem to be both happy and well adjusted, surrounded by a loving mother, father, younger brother, and sister.

Questions for Further Discussion

1. What kinds of difficulties might Abby and Brittany have in adolescence?

2. How would being conjoined affect career decisions?

3. How can conjoined twins have different personalities?

4. If they decide to have a child (which is physically possible), who will claim the child, or will they both be the baby's mother?

10.1–3

Issues in Studying Human Development

(scientific study of changes that occur in people as they age)

- **topics of interest**
  - **personality**
  - **cognition**
  - **biological processes**
  - **social interactions**

- **research designs**
  - **longitudinal:** one group of people is followed and assessed at different times as they age
  - **cross-sectional:** several different age groups are studied at one time
  - **cross-sequential:** combination of longitudinal and cross-sectional designs

Issues in Studying Human Development

(nature vs. nurture debate)

- **nature** refers to heredity and the influence of inherited characteristics on personality, growth, intellect, social skills, etc.; behavioral genetics is a relatively new field that attempts to identify genetic basis of behavior

- **nurture** refers to influence of the environment on inherited traits including parenting styles, socioeconomic status, physical surroundings, etc.

- most developmental psychologists agree that most likely explanation for most human development is based on the interaction between nature and nurture

- **chromosomes, genes, and DNA**
  - **genetics** is the science of heredity
  - **deoxyribonucleic acid (DNA):** contains genetic codes and chromosomes
    - aside from egg and sperm, humans have 46 chromosomes in each cell of the body
    - individual gets 23 chromosomes from mother's egg and 23 from father's sperm
    - most characteristics are determined by 22 such pairs (autosomes); the last pair determines sex of the person (sex chromosomes)
  - **dominant and recessive genes**
    - specific physical and behavioral traits are dependent upon pairing of genes; more active genes are dominant; others are recessive (see Fig. 10.2)
    - most traits are polygenic
  - **gene and chromosome problems**
    - genetic disorders carried by recessive genes are expressed when a child gets two recessive genes
    - issue may also occur if chromosomes have an extra or a missing pair

Prenatal Development

- **from conception to birth**
  conception is moment at which female becomes pregnant; conception to birth is approximately 9 months in humans
  - **the zygote and twinning**
    - egg and sperm unite through process of fertilization, resulting in a single cell (zygote) that has 46 chromosomes
    - through mitosis, zygote begins to divide into two cells, then four, etc., until baby is formed
    - alterations in mitosis can result in twins or multiples

---

PRACTICE **QUIZ:** PREPARING FOR THE AP* EXAM

ANSWERS ON PAGE AK-3.

Directions: Read each of the questions or incomplete sentences below. Then choose the response that best answers the question or completes the sentence.

1. In what type of research design are several different age groups of participants studied at one time?
   a. Case study
   b. Longitudinal
   c. Cross-sectional
   d. Cross-sequential
   e. Cross-longitudinal

2. Brandon has blue eyes, even though both his mother and father have brown eyes. What do we know about Brandon's parents?
   a. Neither of his parents has a blue eye color gene.
   b. At least one of his parents has a recessive blue eye color gene.
   c. Each of his parents must have one recessive blue eye color gene.
   d. Each of his parents must have one dominant blue eye color gene.
   e. Nothing can be determined about Brandon's parents from this information.

3. Which of the following is a disorder caused by having an extra chromosome?
   a. PKU
   b. Tay-Sachs
   c. cystic fibrosis
   d. Down syndrome
   e. Turner's syndrome

4. A newly fertilized egg cell is called a(n) _____.
   a. fetus
   b. zygote
   c. ovum
   d. blastocyst
   e. chromosome

5. Which of the following statements about fraternal twins is accurate?
   a. Fraternal twins are most often the same sex.
   b. Fraternal twins are also called monozygotic twins.
   c. Fraternal twins are created from one fertilized egg.
   d. Fraternal twins are half as common as identical twins.
   e. Fraternal twins are genetically like non-twin siblings.

germinal period first two weeks after fertilization, during which the zygote moves down to the uterus and begins to implant in the lining.

AP* Explain the process of conception and gestation, including factors that influence successful fetal development. ▶

How does a mass of cells become a baby, with eyes, nose, hands, feet, and so on? How do all those different things come from the same original single cell? ▶

THE GERMINAL PERIOD

10.4 What happens during the germinal, embryonic, and fetal periods of pregnancy and what are some hazards in prenatal development?

Once fertilization has taken place, the zygote begins dividing and moving down to the *uterus*, the muscular organ that will contain and protect the developing infant. This process takes about a week, followed by about week during which the mass of cells, now forming a hollow ball, firmly attaches itself to the wall of the uterus. This two-week period is called the **germinal period** of pregnancy. The *placenta* also begins to form during this period. The placenta is a specialized organ that provides nourishment and filters away waste products from the developing baby. The *umbilical cord* also begins to develop at this time, connecting the organism to the placenta.

How does a mass of cells become a baby, with eyes, nose, hands, feet, and so on? How do all those different things come from the same original single cell? During the germinal period, the cells begin to differentiate, or develop into specialized cells, in preparation for becoming all the various kinds of cells that make up the human body—skin cells, heart cells, and so on. Perhaps the most important of these cells are the *stem cells*, which stay in a somewhat immature state until needed to become specific kinds of cells. Researchers are currently looking into ways to use stem cells found in the

The three periods of pregnancy are the germinal period, lasting about two weeks, the embryonic period, from about two to eight weeks, and the fetal period, which lasts from eight weeks until the end of pregnancy.

umbilical cord to grow new organs and tissues for transplant or to repair neurological damage (Chen & Ende, 2000; Holden & Vogel, 2002; Lu & Ende, 1997). ⓁⒾⓃⓀ *to Chapter Two: The Biological Perspective, pp. 60–61.*

The Embryonic Period   Once firmly attached to the uterus, the developing organism is called an **embryo**. The **embryonic period** will last from two weeks after conception to eight weeks, and during this time the cells will continue to specialize and become the various organs and structures of a human infant. By the end of eight weeks after conception, the embryo is about 1 inch long and has primitive eyes, nose, lips, teeth, little arms and legs, and a beating heart. Although no organ is fully developed or completely functional at this time, nearly all are "there."

Critical Periods   As soon as the embryo begins to receive nourishment from the mother through the placenta, it becomes vulnerable to hazards such as diseases of the mother, drugs, and other toxins that can pass from the mother through the placenta to the developing infant. (Since the developing organism in the germinal stage is not yet connected to the mother's system, the organism is not usually vulnerable to outside influences in that stage.) It is during the embryonic period that we most clearly see **critical periods**, times during which some environmental influence can have an impact—often devastating—on the development of the infant. The structural development of the arms and legs, for example, is only affected during the time that they are developing ($3\frac{1}{2}$ to 8 weeks), whereas the heart's structure is most affected very early in this period ($2\frac{1}{2}$ to $6\frac{1}{2}$ weeks). Other physical and structural problems can occur with the central nervous system (2 to 5 weeks), eyes ($3\frac{1}{2}$ to $8\frac{1}{2}$ weeks), and the teeth and roof of the mouth (about 7 to 12 weeks).

Prenatal Hazards: Teratogens   Any substance such as a drug, chemical, virus, or other factor that can cause a birth defect is called a **teratogen**. Table 10.2 shows some common teratogens and their possible negative effects on the developing embryo.

embryo   name for the developing organism from two weeks to eight weeks after fertilization.

embryonic period   the period from two to eight weeks after fertilization, during which the major organs and structures of the organism develop.

critical periods   times during which certain environmental influences can have an impact on the development of the infant.

teratogen   any factor that can cause a birth defect.

Table 10.2   Common Teratogens

TERATOGENIC AGENT	EFFECT ON DEVELOPMENT
Rubella	Blindness, deafness, heart defects, brain damage
Marijuana	Irritability, nervousness, tremors; infant is easily disturbed, startled
Cocaine	Decreased height, low birth weight, respiratory problems, seizures, learning difficulties; infant is difficult to soothe
Alcohol	Fetal alcohol syndrome (mental retardation, delayed growth, facial malformation), learning difficulties, smaller than normal head size
Nicotine	Miscarriage, low birth weight, stillbirth, short stature, mental retardation, learning disabilities
Mercury	Mental retardation, blindness
Syphilis	Mental retardation, deafness, meningitis
Caffeine	Miscarriage, low birth weight
Radiation	Higher incidence of cancers, physical deformities
High Water Temperatures	Increased chance of neural tube defects

Source: Shepard, T. H. (2001).

This pregnant woman is getting a sonogram. Sonograms allow doctors to see any physical deformities and make accurate measurements of gestational age without risk to the mother or the fetus.

fetal period the time from about eight weeks after conception until the birth of the child.

fetus name for the developing organism from eight weeks after fertilization to the birth of the baby.

The Fetal Period: Grow, Baby, Grow The **fetal period** is the time from about eight weeks after conception until the birth of the child (now called a **fetus**) and is a period of tremendous growth. The fetus's length increases by about 20 times and its weight increases from about 1 ounce at 2 months to a little over 7 pounds. The organs, while accomplishing most of their differentiation in the embryonic period, continue to develop and become functional. At this time, teratogens will more likely affect the physical functioning (physiology) of the organs rather than their structure. The functioning of the central nervous system, for example, is vulnerable throughout the fetal period, as are the eyes and the external sexual organs.

Muscles begin to contract in the third month. In the fourth month, the mother will begin to feel this movement as a tiny "flutter" or "quickening" at first, and by the fifth month, the flutter will become a "kick." The last few months continue the development of fat and the growth of the body, until about the end of the thirty-eighth week. At that time, the fetus is pushed out of the mother's body in the process of labor and childbirth and becomes a baby. Babies born before 38 weeks are called *preterm* and may need life support to survive. This is especially true if the baby weighs less than about $5\frac{1}{2}$ pounds at birth.

The most likely time for a *miscarriage*, or *spontaneous abortion*, is in the first three months, as the organs are forming and first becoming functional (Speroff et al., 1999). Some 15 to 20 percent of all pregnancies end in miscarriage, many so early that the mother may not have even known she was pregnant (Hill, 1998; Medical Economics Staff, 1994). When a miscarriage occurs, it is most likely caused by a genetic defect in the way the embryo or fetus is developing that will not allow the infant to survive. In other words, there isn't anything that the mother did wrong or that could have been done to prevent the miscarriage.

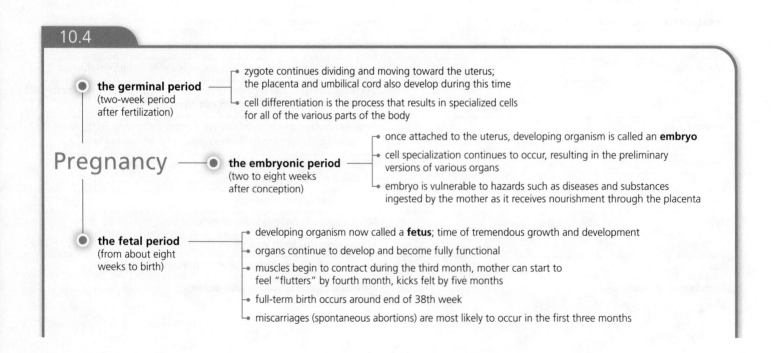

10.4

Pregnancy

the germinal period (two-week period after fertilization)
- zygote continues dividing and moving toward the uterus; the placenta and umbilical cord also develop during this time
- cell differentiation is the process that results in specialized cells for all of the various parts of the body

the embryonic period (two to eight weeks after conception)
- once attached to the uterus, developing organism is called an **embryo**
- cell specialization continues to occur, resulting in the preliminary versions of various organs
- embryo is vulnerable to hazards such as diseases and substances ingested by the mother as it receives nourishment through the placenta

the fetal period (from about eight weeks to birth)
- developing organism now called a **fetus**; time of tremendous growth and development
- organs continue to develop and become fully functional
- muscles begin to contract during the third month, mother can start to feel "flutters" by fourth month, kicks felt by five months
- full-term birth occurs around end of 38th week
- miscarriages (spontaneous abortions) are most likely to occur in the first three months

PRACTICE **QUIZ:** PREPARING FOR THE AP* EXAM   ANSWERS ON PAGE AK-3.

Directions: Read each of the questions or incomplete sentences below. Then choose the response that best answers the question or completes the sentence.

1. The first two weeks of pregnancy are called the _____.
   a. fetal period
   b. germinal period
   c. embryonic period
   d. gestational period
   e. fertilization period

2. Which of the following does not happen during the germinal period?
   a. A dividing mass of cells travels to the uterus.
   b. The cells begin to differentiate into specialized human cells.
   c. A mass of cells forms a hollow ball and attaches itself to the uterus.
   d. Developing organs can be affected by toxins passing through the placenta.
   e. The umbilical cord that connects the organism to the placenta begins to form.

3. The period of pregnancy that contains the clearest examples of critical periods is the _____.
   a. fetal period
   b. germinal period
   c. embryonic period
   d. gestational period
   e. fertilization period

4. Mental retardation and blindness are possible outcomes when a developing baby is affected by which of the following agents?
   a. Alcohol
   b. Caffeine
   c. Rubella
   d. Radiation
   e. Mercury

5. As a group, substances or agents that can cause birth defects are known as _____.
   a. drugs
   b. viruses
   c. chemicals
   d. teratogens
   e. critical periods

Infancy and Childhood Development

What can babies do? Aren't they pretty much unaware of what's going on around them at first? Surprisingly, babies can do a lot more than researchers used to believe they could. A lot of the early research on infants just after birth was done on babies who were still very drowsy from the general anesthesia that used to be given to their mothers during the labor process. Drowsy babies don't tend to respond well, as one might imagine. In the next few sections, it becomes obvious that infants accomplish a great deal throughout infancy, even in the first few days of life on the outside.

PHYSICAL DEVELOPMENT

10.5 What kind of physical changes take place in infancy and childhood?

Immediately after birth, several things start to happen. The respiratory system begins to function, filling the lungs with air and putting oxygen into the blood. The blood now circulates only within the infant's system because the umbilical cord has been cut. Body temperature is now regulated by the infant's own activity and body fat (which acts as insulation) rather than by the amniotic fluid. The digestive system probably takes the longest to adjust to life outside the womb. This is another reason for the excess body fat. It provides fuel until the infant is able to take in enough nourishment on its own. That is why most babies lose a little weight in the first week after birth.

Reflexes   Babies come into this world able to interact with it. Infants have a set of *innate* (existing from birth) involuntary* behavior patterns called *reflexes*. Until an infant is capable of learning more complex means of interaction, reflexes help the infant to survive. Figure 10.4 shows five infant reflexes. Pediatricians use these and other reflexes to determine whether or not an infant's nervous system is working properly.

Baby, Can You See Me? Baby, Can You Hear Me? Sensory Development
I've heard that babies can't see or hear very much at birth. Is that true? Although most infant sensory abilities are fairly well developed at birth, some require a bit more time to reach "full power." The sense of touch is the most well developed, which makes

◀ What can babies do? Aren't they pretty much unaware of what's going on around them at first?

◀ I've heard that babies can't see or hear very much at birth. Is that true?

---

*Involuntary: in this sense, not under conscious, deliberate control.

a.

b.

c.

d.

e.

Figure 10.4 Five Infant Reflexes

Shown here are (a) grasping reflex, (b) startle reflex (also known as the Moro reflex), (c) rooting reflex (when you touch a baby's cheek it will turn towards your hand, open its mouth, and search for the nipple), (d) stepping reflex, and (e) sucking reflex. These infant reflexes can be used to check on the health of an infant's nervous system. If a reflex is absent or abnormal, it may indicate brain damage or some other neurological problem.

perfect sense when one realizes how much skin-to-womb contact the baby has had in the last months of pregnancy. The sense of smell is also highly developed. Breast-fed babies can actually tell the difference between their own mother's milk scent and another woman's milk scent within a few days after birth.

Taste is also nearly fully developed. At birth, infants show a preference for sweets (and human breast milk is very sweet) and by four months have developed a preference for salty tastes (which may come from exposure to the salty taste of their mother's skin). Sour and bitter, two other taste sensations, produce spitting up and the making of horrible faces (Ganchrow et al., 1983).

Hearing is functional before birth but may take a little while to reach its full potential after birth. The fluids of the womb must clear out completely. From birth, newborns seem most responsive to high pitches, as in a woman's voice, and low pitches, as in a male's voice.

The least functional sense at birth is vision. As stated in Chapter Three, the eye is quite a complex organ. Ⓛ Ⓘ Ⓝ Ⓚ *to Chapter Three: Sensation and Perception, pp. 94–95.* The rods, which see in black and white and have little visual acuity, are fairly well developed at birth, but the cones, which see color and provide sharpness of vision, will take about another six months to fully develop. So the newborn has relatively poor color perception when compared to sharply contrasting lights and darks until about two months of age (Adams, 1987) and has fairly "fuzzy" vision, much as a nearsighted person would have. The lens of the newborn stays fixed until the muscles that hold it in place mature. Until then the newborn is unable to shift what little focus it has from close to far. Thus, newborns actually have a fixed distance for clear vision of about 7 to 10 inches, which is the distance from the baby's face to the mother's face while nursing (Slater, 2000).

Newborns also have visual preferences at birth, as discovered by researchers using measures of the time that infants spent looking at certain visual stimuli (Fantz, 1961). They found that infants prefer to look at complex patterns rather than simple ones, three dimensions rather than two, and that the most preferred visual stimulus was a human face. The fact that infants prefer human voices and human faces (De-Casper & Fifer, 1980; DeCasper & Spence, 1986; Fantz, 1964; Maurer & Young, 1983) makes it easier for them to form relationships with their caregivers and to develop language later on. ✳ Explore on MyPsychLab

✳ **Explore** with the simulation on newborn reflexes and cognitive development. **www.mypsychlab.com**

◄ **AP**✳ Discuss maturation of motor skills.

From Crawling to a Blur of Motion: Motor Development   Infants manage a tremendous amount of development in motor skills from birth to about 2 years of age. Figure 10.5 shows some of the major physical milestones of infancy. When looking at the age ranges listed, remember that even these ranges are averages based on large samples of infants. An infant may reach these milestones earlier or later than the average and still be considered to be developing normally.

Figure 10.5 Six Motor Milestones
Shown here are (a) raising head and chest—2 to 4 months, (b) rolling over—2 to 5 months, (c) sitting up with support—4 to 6 months, (d) sitting up without support—6 to 7 months, (e) crawling—7 to 8 months, and (f) walking—8 to 18 months. The motor milestones develop as the infant gains greater voluntary control over the muscles in its body, typically from the top of the body downward. This pattern is seen in the early control of the neck muscles and the much later development of control of the legs and feet.

a.

b.

c.

d.

e.

f.

An infant's normal development is related to many factors such as nutrition, care, and health. One important way to protect an infant's health is to make sure that immunizations against various illnesses are given at the appropriate times. The following section discusses a serious issue concerning immunizations and their importance to the developing child.

Current Issues in Psychology

The Facts and Myths About Immunizations

In the last few decades, parents of young children have begun to resist getting their infants and young children immunized against childhood diseases such as MMR—measles, mumps, and rubella (German measles). This alarming trend is probably due to a number of factors. First, the parents of these children have grown up in an era in which immunizations during infancy were common, making them unaware of the seriousness of the childhood diseases those immunizations prevent. They have not seen the serious consequences that can result from outbreaks of such diseases: blindness, deafness, mental retardation, and even death (Centers for Disease Control and Prevention, 1999).

Second, many of these parents have become influenced by misinformation that has been placed on the Internet and handed out by concerned but uninformed people that highlights the dangers of immunization (Stratton et al., 2001a, 2001b).

What are some of the myths parents now believe, and what are the facts?

Myth: Children who are given an immunization can get the disease itself.

Fact: Most vaccines are made from dead viruses, and it is impossible to get the disease in this way. Vaccines that use very weak live viruses (like the chicken pox vaccine) might cause a child to develop a mild version of the disease, but the risk is very small and the full-blown disease is far more serious and deadly (Centers for Disease Control and Prevention, 2004; National Institutes of Health, 1998; Offit & Bell, 1998).

Myth: If all the other children in a school are immunized, there's no harm in not immunizing one's own child.

Fact: If one parent is thinking like this, then others are also, and this can lead to an epidemic. One such epidemic of measles happened between 1989 and 1991 in the United States, causing rates of death due to measles to increase by a large number during that period, as well as increases in rates of brain damage due to high fevers (Centers for Disease Control and Prevention, 1999, 2000, 2004; National Institutes of Health, 1998; Offit & Bell, 1998). Whereas one in 3 million children who receives the measles, mumps, and rubella (MMR) vaccine might experience a reaction serious enough to cause death, one in 500 children who contract the measles will die.

Myth: The vaccine isn't 100 percent effective, so why subject a child to a painful injection?

Fact: Vaccines are one of the most effective weapons we have against disease. They work in 85 percent to 99 percent of cases and greatly reduce your child's risk of serious illness, particularly when more and more people use them (Centers for Disease Control and Prevention, 2000).

Myth: Immunizations cause bad reactions.

Fact: The most common reactions to vaccines are minor, including redness and swelling where the shot was given, fever, and rash. In rare cases immunizations can trigger seizures or severe allergic reactions, but the risk of these is much lower than that of catching the disease if a child is not immunized (Offit & Bell, 1998).

One of the most important things parents can do for the continued health and safety of their infant is to have the baby immunized, following an approved schedule for each type of vaccine. Immunizations today are safe and effective and prevent dangerous and often deadly childhood diseases, such as rubella.

Myth: Immunization is not needed because these diseases have been eliminated.

Fact: Even though these diseases are rare or nonexistent in the United States, they still flourish in other parts of the world. Children must continue to be vaccinated against them because it is easy to come into contact with illnesses through travel (Centers for Disease Control and Prevention, 1994).

Myth: The MMR vaccine causes autism in children.

Fact: Autism is a complex neurological disorder in which the more visible symptoms used for diagnosis, such as language delays and difficulties in speaking, do not appear until 2 to 3 years of age. The MMR vaccine is typically given at about 1 year old or shortly after and so seems to be followed by the "onset" of autism. But early signs of autism can now be observed long before the MMR vaccine (Mars et al., 1998), and studies have consistently failed to show any link between the vaccine and autism (Gilberg & Coleman, 2000; Madsen et al., 2002; Taylor et al., 1999; Thompson et al., 2007). The timing between the vaccine and the first easily visible signs of autism is simply a coincidence. ((•—[Listen on **MyPsychLab**

((•● **Listen** to the Psychology in the News podcast. **www.mypsychlab.com**

Questions for Further Discussion

1. What advice would you give someone who is having a baby concerning vaccinations?

2. Should children who are not vaccinated be allowed to attend public schools?

3. What can be done to encourage parents to have their children immunized?

COGNITIVE DEVELOPMENT

By the time the average infant has reached the age of 1 year, it has tripled its birth weight and added about another foot to its height. The brain triples its weight in the first two years, reaching about 75 percent of its adult weight. By age 5, the brain is at 90 percent of its adult weight. This increase makes possible a tremendous amount of major advances in **cognitive development**, including the development of thinking, problem solving, and memory.

10.6 What are two ways of looking at cognitive development, and how does language develop?

◀ **AP*** Explain the maturation of cognitive abilities.

◀ **AP*** Identify key contributors in developmental psychology.

Piaget's Theory: Four Stages of Cognitive Development   One of the three ways of examining the development of cognition is found in the work of Jean Piaget. Early researcher Jean Piaget developed his theory from detailed observations of infants and children, most especially his own three children. Piaget made significant contributions to the understanding of how children think about the world around them and shifted the view of children's thinking from that of "little adults" to something quite different from adult thinking. Piaget believed that children form mental concepts or **schemes** as they experience new situations and events. For example, if Sandy points to a picture of an apple and tells her child, "that's an apple," the child forms a scheme for "apple" that looks something like that picture. Piaget also believed that children first try to understand new things in terms of schemes they already possess, a process called *assimilation*. The child might see an orange and say "apple" because both objects are round. When corrected, the child might alter the scheme for apple to include "round" and "red." The process of altering or adjusting old schemes to fit new information and experiences is *accommodation* (Piaget, 1952, 1962, 1983).

Piaget also proposed that there are four distinct stages of cognitive development that occur from infancy to adolescence, as shown in Table 10.3 (Piaget, 1952, 1962, 1983).

cognitive development the development of thinking, problem solving, and memory.

scheme in this case, a mental concept formed through experiences with objects and events.

Table 10.3　Piaget's Stages of Cognitive Development

STAGE		COGNITIVE DEVELOPMENT
Sensorimotor	Birth to 2 years old	Children explore the world using their senses and ability to move. They develop object permanence and the understanding that concepts and mental images represent objects, people, and events.
Preoperational	2 to 7 years old	Young children can mentally represent and refer to objects and events with words or pictures and they can pretend. However, they can't conserve, logically reason, or simultaneously consider many characteristics of an object.
Concrete Operations	7 to 12 years old	Children at this stage are able to conserve, reverse their thinking, and classify objects in terms of their many characteristics. They can also think logically and understand analogies but only about concrete events.
Formal Operations	12 years old to adulthood	People at this stage can use abstract reasoning about hypothetical events or situations, think about logical possibilities, use abstract analogies, and systematically examine and test hypotheses. Not everyone can eventually reason in all these ways.

◉ **Watch** classic video footage on sensorimotor development with Jean Piaget. **www.mypsychlab.com**

Why is it so easy for children to believe in Santa Claus and the Tooth Fairy when they're little? ▶

sensorimotor stage Piaget's first stage of cognitive development in which the infant uses its senses and motor abilities to interact with objects in the environment.

object permanence the knowledge that an object exists even when it is not in sight.

preoperational stage Piaget's second stage of cognitive development in which the preschool child learns to use language as a means of exploring the world.

◉ **Watch** on **MyPsychLab**

The Sensorimotor Stage　The **sensorimotor stage** is the first of Piaget's stages. It concerns infants from birth to age 2. In this stage, infants use their senses and motor abilities to learn about the world around them. At first, infants only have the involuntary reflexes present at birth to interact with objects and people. As their sensory and motor development progresses, they begin to interact deliberately with objects by grasping, pushing, tasting, and so on. Infants move from simple repetitive actions, such as grabbing their toes, to complex patterns, such as trying to put a shape into a sorting box.

By the end of the sensorimotor stage, infants have fully developed a sense of **object permanence**, the knowledge that an object exists even when it is not in sight. For example, the game of "peek-a-boo" is important in teaching infants that Mommy's smiling face is always going to be behind her hands. This is a critical step in developing language (and eventually abstract thought), as words themselves are symbols of things that may not be present. Symbolic thought, which is the ability to represent objects in one's thoughts with symbols such as words, becomes possible by the end of this stage, with children at 2 years old capable of thinking in simple symbols and planning out actions.

Why is it so easy for children to believe in Santa Claus and the Tooth Fairy when they're little?

The Preoperational Stage　The **preoperational stage** (ages 2–7) is a time of developing language and concepts. Children, who can now move freely about in their world, no longer have to rely only on senses and motor skills but now can ask questions and explore their surroundings more fully. Pretending and make-believe play become possible because children at this stage can understand, through symbolic thinking, that a line of wooden blocks can "stand in" for a train. They are limited, however, in several ways. They are not yet capable of logical thought—they can use simple mental concepts but are not able to use those concepts in a more rational, logical sense. They believe that anything that moves is alive, a quality called *animism*. They tend to believe that what they see is literally true, so when children of this age see Santa Claus in a book, on television, or at the mall, Santa Claus becomes real to them. It doesn't occur to them to think about how Santa might get to every child's house in one night or why those toys are the same ones they saw in the store just last week. They may be able to count up to 10 or 20, but

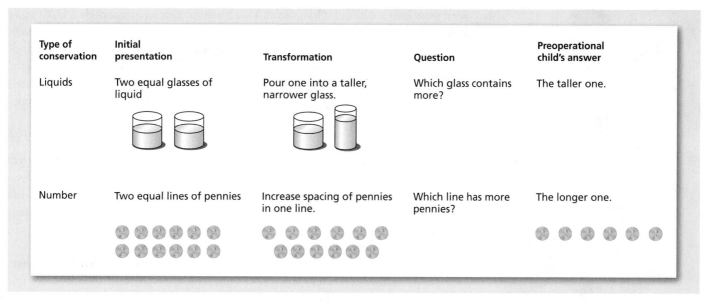

Type of conservation	Initial presentation	Transformation	Question	Preoperational child's answer
Liquids	Two equal glasses of liquid	Pour one into a taller, narrower glass.	Which glass contains more?	The taller one.
Number	Two equal lines of pennies	Increase spacing of pennies in one line.	Which line has more pennies?	The longer one.

Figure 10.6 Conservation Experiment

A typical conservation task consists of pouring equal amounts of water into two glasses of the same size and shape. When the water from one of these glasses is poured into a taller, narrower glass, children who cannot yet conserve tend to focus (centrate) on the height of the water in the second glass, assuming that the second glass now has more water than the first one. In the second example, pennies are laid out in two equal lines. When the pennies in the top line are spaced out, the child who cannot yet conserve will centrate on the top line and assume that there are actually more pennies in that line.

they won't see that in the bottom example in Figure 10.6 both rows have the same number of coins, because they focus on the longer *appearance* of the top row of coins.

Another limitation is **egocentrism**, the inability to see the world through anyone else's eyes except one's own. For the preoperational child, everyone else must see what the child sees, and what is important to the child must be important to everyone else. For example, 2-year-old Vicki, after climbing out of her crib for the third time, was told by her mother, "I don't want to see you in that living room again tonight!" So Vicki's next appearance was made with her hands over her eyes—if she couldn't see her mother, her mother couldn't see *her*. Egocentrism is not the same as being egotistical or selfish—it would also be egocentric, but completely unselfish, if 4-year-old Kenny wants to give his grandmother an action figure for her birthday because that's what *he* would want.

Remember that children in this stage are also overwhelmed by appearances, as in the coin example. A child who complains that his piece of pie is smaller than his brother's may be quite happy once his original piece is cut into two pieces—now he thinks he has "more" than his brother. He has focused only on the number of pieces, not the actual amount of the pie. Focusing only on one feature of some object rather than taking all features into consideration is called **centration**. In the coin example in Figure 10.6, children of this stage will focus (or center) on the length of the top line of coins only and ignore the number of coins. Centration is one of the reasons that children in this stage often fail to understand that changing the way something looks does not change its substance. The ability to understand that altering the appearance of something does not change its amount (as in the coin example), its volume, or its mass is called **conservation**.

Preoperational children fail at conservation not only because they centrate (focusing on just one feature, such as the number of pieces of pie) but also because they are unable to "mentally reverse" actions. This feature of preoperational thinking is called **irreversibility**. For example, if a preoperational child sees liquid poured from a short,

egocentrism the inability to see the world through anyone else's eyes.

centration in Piaget's theory, the tendency of a young child to focus only on one feature of an object while ignoring other relevant features.

conservation in Piaget's theory, the ability to understand that simply changing the appearance of an object does not change the object's nature.

irreversibility in Piaget's theory, the inability of the young child to mentally reverse an action.

This concrete operational child has begun to think logically and is able to solve many kinds of problems that were not possible for her to solve while in the preoperational stage.

concrete operations stage third stage of cognitive development in which the school-age child becomes capable of logical thought processes but is not yet capable of abstract thinking.

formal operations stage Piaget's last stage of cognitive development, in which the adolescent becomes capable of abstract thinking.

wide glass into a tall, thin glass, the child will assume that the second glass holds more liquid. This failure to "conserve" (save) the volume of liquid as it takes on a different shape in the tall, thin glass is not only caused by the child's centration on the height of the liquid in the second glass but also by the inability of the child to imagine pouring the liquid back into the first glass and having it be the same amount again. Similar "reasoning" causes children of this age to assume that a ball of clay, when rolled out into a "rope" of clay, is now greater in mass.

Concrete Operations　　　In the **concrete operations stage** (ages 7–12), children finally become capable of conservation and reversible thinking. Centration no longer occurs as children become capable of considering all the relevant features of any given object. They begin to think more logically about beliefs such as Santa Claus and ask questions, eventually coming to their own more rational conclusions about the fantasies of early childhood. They are in school, learning all sorts of science and math, and are convinced that they know more than their parents at this point.

The major limitation of this stage is the inability to deal effectively with *abstract concepts*. Abstract concepts are those that do not have some physical, *concrete*, touchable reality. For example, "freedom" is an abstract concept. People can define it, they can get a good sense of what it means, but there is no "thing" that they can point to and say, "This is freedom." *Concrete concepts*, which are the kind of concepts understood by children of this age, are about objects, written rules, and real things. Children need to be able to see it, touch it, or at least see it in their heads to be able to understand it.

Formal Operations　　　In the last of Piaget's stages, **formal operations** (age 12 to adulthood), abstract thinking becomes possible. Teenagers not only understand concepts that have no physical reality, but also they get deeply involved in hypothetical thinking, or thinking about possibilities and even impossibilities. "What if everyone just got along?" "If women were in charge of countries, would there be fewer wars?"

Piaget did not believe that everyone would necessarily reach formal operations. Studies show that only about half of all adults in the United States reach formal operations (Sutherland, 1992). Adults who do not achieve formal operations tend to use a more practical, down-to-earth kind of intelligence that suits their particular lifestyle. Successful college students, however, need formal operational thinking to succeed in their college careers, as most college classes require critical thinking, problem-solving abilities, and abstract thinking based on formal operational skills (Powers, 1984).

Piaget saw children as active explorers of their surroundings, engaged in the discovery of the properties of objects and organisms within those surroundings. Educators have put Piaget's ideas into practice by allowing children to learn at their own pace, by "hands-on" experience with objects, and by teaching concepts to children that are at an appropriate cognitive level (Brooks & Brooks, 1993). But Piaget's theory has also been criticized on several points. Some researchers believe that the idea of distinct stages of cognitive development is not completely correct and that changes in thought are more continuous and gradual rather than jumping from one stage to another (Courage & Howe, 2002; Feldman, 2003; Schwitzgebel, 1999; Siegler, 1996). Others point out that preschoolers are not as egocentric as Piaget seemed to believe (Flavell, 1999) and that object permanence exists much earlier than Piaget thought (Aguiar & Baillargeon, 2003; Baillargeon, 1986).

Piaget seemed to focus on the child's cognitive development as if the other people in the child's world were not all that necessary to the acquisition of knowledge and the development of skills. It is true, after all, that children are able to grasp many ideas and concepts through their own thought processes and interactions with objects, discovering basic principles and characteristics of objects in individual play. In contrast, psychologist Lev Vygotsky emphasized that other people, acting as teachers and mentors, were a crucial part of the cognitive development of the child (Duncan, 1995).

Vygotsky's Theory: The Importance of Being There   Russian psychologist Lev Vygotsky developed a theory of how children think that did not match the prevailing political ideas in Russia. After his death from tuberculosis in 1934, his ideas were suppressed by the government but kept alive by his students and later republished. Vygotsky's pioneering work in developmental psychology has had a profound influence on school education in Russia, and interest in his theories continues to grow throughout the world (Bodrova & Leong, 1996). Vygotsky wrote about children's cognitive development but differed from Piaget in his emphasis on the role of others in cognitive development (Vygotsky, 1934/1962, 1978, 1987). Whereas Piaget stressed the importance of the child's interaction with objects as a primary factor in cognitive development, Vygotsky stressed the importance of social interactions with other people, typically more highly skilled children and adults. Vygotsky believed that children develop cognitively when someone else helps them by asking leading questions and providing examples of concepts in a process called **scaffolding**. In scaffolding, the more highly skilled person gives the learner more help at the beginning of the learning process and then begins to withdraw help as the learner's skills improve (Rogoff, 1994).

Vygotsky also proposed that each developing child has a **zone of proximal development (ZPD)**, which is the difference between what a child can do alone versus what a child can do with the help of a teacher. For example, if little Jenny can do math problems up to the fourth-grade level on her own but with the help of a teacher can successfully work problems at a sixth-grade level, her ZPD is two years. Suzi might be the same age as Jenny (and might even score the same on a traditional IQ test), but if Suzi can only work math problems at a fifth-grade level with the help of the teacher, Suzi's ZPD is not as great as Jenny's. This might be a better way of thinking about intelligence: It isn't what you know (as measured by traditional tests), it's what you *can do*.

Other researchers have applied Vygotsky's social focus on learning to the development of a child's memory for personal (autobiographical) events, finding evidence that children learn the culturally determined structures and purposes of personal stories from the early conversations they have with their parents. This process begins with the parent telling the story to the very young child, followed by the child repeating elements of the story as the child's verbal abilities grow. The child reaches the final stage at around age 5 or 6 when the child creates the personal story entirely—an excellent example of scaffolding (Fivush et al., 1996; Fivush & Nelson, 2004; Nelson, 1993). Vygotsky's ideas have been put into practice in education through the use of cooperative learning, in which children work together in groups to achieve a common goal, and in reciprocal teaching, in which teachers lead students through the basic strategies of reading until the students themselves become capable of teaching the strategies to others.

Stages of Language Development   The development of language is a very important milestone in the cognitive development of a child because language allows children to think in words rather than just images, to ask questions, to communicate their needs and wants to others, and to form concepts (L. Bloom, 1974; P. Bloom, 2000). Early views of language development were based on Skinnerian principles of reinforcement. However, Noam Chomsky argued strongly against this. He proposed a LAD (language acquisition device), an innate "program" that contained a schema for human language. The children matched the language they heard against this schema and, thus, language developed in a well-researched sequence (Chomsky, 1957, 1964, 1981, 1986).

Newer theories of language development are focusing on environmental influences on language such as *child-directed speech* (the way adults and older children talk

◀ **AP*** Identify key contributors in developmental psychology.

This boy is helping his younger sister learn to read a book. Vygotsky's view of cognitive development states that the help of skilled others aids in making cognitive advances such as this one.

◀ **AP*** Identify key contributors in developmental psychology.

scaffolding   process in which a more skilled learner gives help to a less skilled learner, reducing the amount of help as the less skilled learner becomes more capable.

zone of proximal development (ZPD)   Vygotsky's concept of the difference between what a child can do alone and what that child can do with the help of a teacher.

to infants and very young children, with higher pitched, repetitious, sing-song speech patterns). Infants and toddlers attend more closely to this kind of speech, which creates a learning opportunity in the dialogue between caregiver and infant (Dominey & Dodane, 2004; Fernald, 1984, 1992; Küntay & Slobin, 2002). Other researchers are looking at the infant's use of gestures and signs (Behne et al. 2005; Lizskowski et al., 2006; Moll & Tomasello, 2007; Tomasello et al., 2007).

Infants also seem to understand far more than they can produce, a phenomenon known as the *receptive-productive lag* (Stevenson et al., 1988). They may be able to only produce one or two words, but they understand much longer sentences from their parents and others.

There are several stages of language development that all children experience, no matter what culture they live in or what language they will learn to speak (Brown, 1973):

1. **Cooing:** At around 2 months of age, babies begin to make vowel-like sounds.

2. **Babbling:** At about 6 months, infants add consonant sounds to the vowels to make a babbling sound, which at times can almost sound like real speech. Deaf children actually decrease their babbling after 6 months while increasing their use of primitive hand signs and gestures (Petitto & Marentette, 1991; Petitto et al., 2001).

3. **One-word speech:** Somewhere just before or around age 1, most children begin to say actual words. These words are typically nouns and may seem to represent an entire phrase of meaning. They are called *holophrases* (whole phrases in one word) for that reason. For example, a child might say "Milk!" and mean "I want some milk!" or "I drank my milk!"

4. **Telegraphic speech:** At around a year and a half, toddlers begin to string words together to form short, simple sentences using nouns, verbs, and adjectives. "Baby eat," "Mommy go," "Doggie go bye-bye" are examples of telegraphic speech. Only the words that carry the meaning of the sentence are used.

5. **Whole sentences:** As children move through the preschool years, they learn to use grammatical terms and increase the number of words in their sentences, until by age 6 or so they are nearly as fluent as an adult, although the number of words they know is still limited when compared to adult vocabulary.

This infant has already learned some of the basics of language, including the use of gestures to indicate meaning and enhance communication.

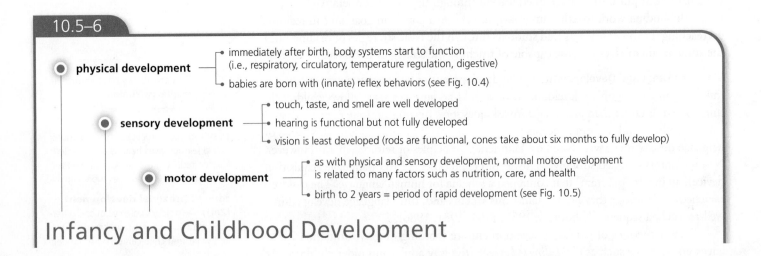

10.5–6

physical development
- immediately after birth, body systems start to function (i.e., respiratory, circulatory, temperature regulation, digestive)
- babies are born with (innate) reflex behaviors (see Fig. 10.4)

sensory development
- touch, taste, and smell are well developed
- hearing is functional but not fully developed
- vision is least developed (rods are functional, cones take about six months to fully develop)

motor development
- as with physical and sensory development, normal motor development is related to many factors such as nutrition, care, and health
- birth to 2 years = period of rapid development (see Fig. 10.5)

Infancy and Childhood Development

Piaget's theory
- suggests children form mental concepts or schemes as they experience new situations and events — understand new things in terms of schemes they already possess (assimilation) or through altering or adjusting old schemes to fit new information (accommodation)
- proposes four distinct stages of cognitive development that span infancy to adolescence —
  - • **sensorimotor**
  - • **preoperational**
  - • **concrete operations**
  - • **formal operations**
  - ----▶ see Table 10.3

Vygotsky's theory
- stresses the importance of social interactions with others, typically more highly skilled children and adults
- children's cognitive development occurs when someone helps them by asking leading questions and providing examples of concepts (scaffolding)
- each child has a zone of proximal development—difference between what they can do alone vs. with aid of a teacher

Infancy and Childhood Development: Cognitive Development

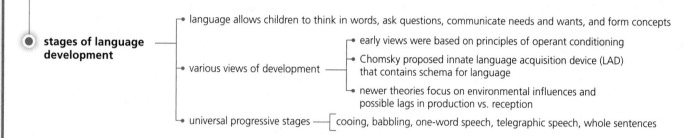

stages of language development
- language allows children to think in words, ask questions, communicate needs and wants, and form concepts
- various views of development —
  - • early views were based on principles of operant conditioning
  - • Chomsky proposed innate language acquisition device (LAD) that contains schema for language
  - • newer theories focus on environmental influences and possible lags in production vs. reception
- universal progressive stages — cooing, babbling, one-word speech, telegraphic speech, whole sentences

PRACTICE QUIZ: PREPARING FOR THE AP* EXAM

ANSWERS ON PAGE AK-3.

Directions: Read each of the questions or incomplete sentences below. Then choose the response that best answers the question or completes the sentence.

1. Which sense is least functional at birth?
   a. Touch
   b. Taste
   c. Smell
   d. Vision
   e. Hearing

2. Which of the following motor milestones is the earliest to occur in infants?
   a. Standing
   b. Crawling
   c. Rolling over
   d. Sitting without support
   e. Raising the head and chest

3. In which of Piaget's stages would a child who has just developed object permanence be categorized?
   a. Sensorimotor
   b. Preoperational
   c. Postoperational
   d. Concrete operational
   e. Formal operational

4. Which term did Vygotsky define as the difference between what a child can do alone and what the child can do with help?
   a. Scaffolding
   b. Habituation
   c. Egocentrism
   d. Receptive-productive lag
   e. Zone of proximal development

5. "Daddy go bye-bye" is an example of _____.
   a. cooing
   b. babbling
   c. a holophrase
   d. a whole sentence
   e. telegraphic speech

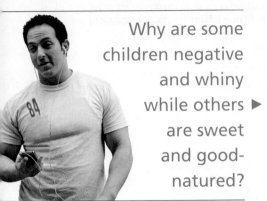

10.7 How do infants and children develop personalities and form relationships with others, and what are Erikson's stages of psychosocial development for children?

The psychological and social development of infants and children involves the development of personality, relationships, and a sense of being male or female. Although these processes begin in infancy, they will continue in many respects well into adulthood.

Why are some children negative and whiny while others are sweet and good-natured?

Temperament   One of the first ways in which infants demonstrate that they have different personalities (long-lasting characteristics that make each person different from other persons) is in their **temperament**, the behavioral and emotional characteristics that are fairly well established at birth. Researchers (Chess & Thomas, 1986; Thomas & Chess, 1977) have been able to identify three basic temperament styles of infants:

1. **Easy:** "Easy" babies are regular in their schedules of waking, sleeping, and eating and are adaptable to change. Easy babies are happy babies and when distressed are easily soothed.
2. **Difficult:** "Difficult" babies are almost the opposite of easy ones. Difficult babies tend to be irregular in their schedules and are very unhappy about change of any kind. They are loud, active, and tend to be crabby rather than happy.
3. **Slow to warm up:** This kind of temperament is associated with infants who are less grumpy, quieter, and more regular than difficult children but who are slow to adapt to change. If change is introduced gradually, these babies will "warm up" to new people and new situations.

Of course, not all babies will fall neatly into one of these three patterns—some children may be a mix of two or even all three patterns of behavior, as Chess and Thomas (1986) discovered. Even so, longitudinal research strongly suggests that these temperament styles last well into adulthood (Kagan, 1998; Kagan et al., 2007; Korn, 1984; Scarpa et al., 1995), although they are somewhat influenced by the environment in which the infant is raised. For example, a "difficult" infant who is raised by parents who are themselves very loud and active may not be perceived as difficult by the parents, whereas a child who is slow to warm up might be perceived as difficult if the parents themselves like lots of change and noise. The first infant is in a situation in which the "goodness of fit" of the infant's temperament to the parents' temperament is very close, but the parents of the second infant are a poor fit in temperament for that less active child (Chess & Thomas, 1986).

How does a baby's temperament affect the way the parents deal with the baby? Parents of babies with easy temperaments can make plans for shopping or dinner around the infant's schedule. Planning around the varying sleeping and eating behaviors of a difficult infant is much trickier (Bates, 1989; Sheeber & Johnson, 1992). As children grow, their temperament and how well it matches a parent's own temperament becomes an issue in discipline and in the formation of emotional bonds to the parents or other caregivers (Cameron et al., 1989; Goldsmith & Campos, 1982; Skolnick, 1986).

Attachment   The emotional bond that forms between an infant and a primary caregiver is called **attachment**. Attachment is a very important development in the social and emotional life of the infant, usually forming within the first six months of the infant's life and showing up in a number of ways during the second six months,

---

Why are some children negative and whiny while others are sweet and good-natured? ▶

AP* Describe the influence of temperament and other social factors on attachment and appropriate socialization. ▶

AP* Identify key contributors in developmental psychology. ▶

How does a baby's temperament affect ▶ the way the parents deal with the baby?

temperament the behavioral characteristics that are fairly well established at birth, such as easy, difficult, and slow to warm up.

attachment the emotional bond between an infant and the primary caregiver.

such as wariness of strangers and fear of being separated from the caregiver. Although attachment to the mother is usually the primary attachment, infants can attach to fathers and to other caregivers as well.

Mary Ainsworth (Ainsworth, 1985; Ainsworth et al., 1978) came up with a special experimental design to measure the attachment of an infant to the caregiver called the *Strange Situation* (exposing an infant to a series of leave-takings and returns of the mother and a stranger). Through this measurement technique, Ainsworth and another colleague identified four attachment styles:

1. **Secure:** Infants labeled as secure were willing to get down from their mother's lap when they first entered the room with their mothers. They explored happily, looking back at their mothers and returning to them every now and then (sort of like "touching base"). When the stranger came in, these infants were wary but calm as long as their mother was nearby. When the mother left, the infants got upset. When the mother returned, the infants approached her, were easily soothed, and were glad to have her back.

2. **Avoidant:** In contrast, avoidant babies, although somewhat willing to explore, did not "touch base." They did not look at the stranger or the mother and reacted very little to her absence or her return, seeming to have no interest or concern.

3. **Ambivalent:** The word *ambivalent* means to have mixed feelings about something. Ambivalent babies in Ainsworth's study were clinging and unwilling to explore, very upset by the stranger regardless of the mother's presence, protested mightily when the mother left, and were hard to soothe. When the mother returned, these babies would demand to be picked up, but at the same time push the mother away or kick her in a mixed reaction to her return.

4. **Disorganized-disoriented:** In subsequent studies, other researchers (Main & Hesse, 1990; Main & Solomon, 1990) found that some babies seemed unable to decide just how they should react to the mother's return. These disorganized-disoriented infants would approach her but with their eyes turned away from her, as if afraid to make eye contact. In general, these infants seemed fearful and showed a dazed and depressed look on their faces.

It should come as no surprise that the mothers of each of the four types of infants also behaved differently from one another. Mothers of secure infants were loving, warm, sensitive to their infant's needs, and responsive to the infant's attempts at communication. Mothers of avoidant babies were unresponsive, insensitive, and coldly rejecting. Mothers of ambivalent babies tried to be responsive but were inconsistent and insensitive to the baby's actions, often talking to the infant about something totally unrelated to what the infant was doing at the time. Mothers of disorganized-disoriented babies were found to be abusive or neglectful in interactions with the infants.

Attachment is not necessarily the result of the behavior of the mother alone, however. The temperament of the infant may play an important part in determining the reactions of the mothers (Goldsmith & Campos, 1982; Skolnick, 1986). For example, an infant with a difficult temperament is hard to soothe. A mother with this kind of infant might come to avoid unnecessary contact with the infant, as did the mothers of the avoidant babies in Ainsworth's studies.

Critics of Ainsworth's Strange Situation research focus on the artificial nature of the design and wonder if infants and mothers would behave differently in the more familiar surroundings of home, even though Ainsworth's experimental observers also observed the infants and mothers in the home prior to the Strange Situation (Ainsworth, 1985). Other research has found results supporting Ainsworth's findings

◄ **AP*** Identify key contributors in developmental psychology.

This toddler shows reluctance to explore his environment, instead clinging to his father's legs. Such clinging behavior, if common, can be a sign of an ambivalent attachment.

in home-based assessments of attachment (Blanchard & Main, 1979). Other studies have also found support for the concept of attachment styles and stability of attachment over the first six years of life (Lutkenhaus et al., 1985; Main & Cassidy, 1988; Owen et al., 1984; Wartner et al., 1994). Even adult relationships can be seen as influenced by the attachment style of the adult—those who are avoidant tend to have numerous shallow and brief relationships with different partners, whereas those who are ambivalent tend to have repeated break-ups and make-ups with the same person (Bartholomew, 1990; Hazan & Shaver, 1987).

As day care has become more widely acceptable and common, many parents have been concerned about the effect of day care on attachment. Psychologist Jay Belsky and colleagues (Belsky, 2005; Belsky & Johnson, 2005; Belsky et al., 2007) have studied the attachment of infants in day care and concluded that although higher quality of day care (small child-to-caregiver ratio, low turnover in caregivers, and caregivers educated in child care techniques and theory) is important, especially for cognitive development, positive development including attachment was more clearly related to the quality of parenting the infants and toddlers received at home.

Although there are some cultural differences in attachment, such as the finding that mothers in the United States tend to wait for a child to express a need before trying to fulfill that need, whereas Japanese mothers prefer to anticipate the child's needs (Rothbaum et al., 2000), attachment does not seem to suffer in spite of the differences in sensitivity. Evidence that similar attachment styles are found in other cultures demonstrates the need to consider attachment as an important first step in forming relationships with others, one which may set the stage for all relationships that follow (Hu & Meng, 1996; Juffer & Rosenboom, 1997; Keromoian & Leiderman, 1986).

AP* Identify key contributors in developmental psychology. ▶

Classic Studies in Psychology

Harlow and Contact Comfort

As psychologists began to study the development of attachment, they at first assumed that attachment to the mother occurred because the mother was associated with satisfaction of primary drives such as hunger and thirst. The mother is always present when the food (a primary reinforcer) is presented, so the mother becomes a secondary reinforcer capable of producing pleasurable feelings. **LINK** to *Chapter Five: Learning, p. 188.*

Psychologist Harry Harlow felt that attachment had to be influenced by more than just the provision of food. He conducted a number of studies of attachment using infant Rhesus monkeys (Harlow, 1958). Noticing that the monkeys in his lab liked to cling to the soft cloth pad used to line their cages, Harlow designed a study to examine the importance of what he termed *contact comfort,* the seeming attachment of the monkeys to something soft to the touch.

He isolated eight baby Rhesus monkeys shortly after their birth, placing each in a cage with two surrogate (substitute) "mothers." The surrogates were actually a block of wood covered in soft padding and terry cloth and a wire form, both heated from within. For half of the monkeys, the wire "mother" held the bottle from which they fed, while for the other half the soft "mother" held the bottle. Harlow then recorded the time each monkey spent with each "mother." If time spent with the surrogate is taken as an indicator of attachment, then learning theory would predict that the monkeys would spend more time with whichever surrogate was being used to feed them. ◉ **Watch** on **MyPsychLab**

◉ **Watch** classic video footage on nature and the development of affection with Harry Harlow.
www.mypsychlab.com

The results? Regardless of which surrogate was feeding them, the monkeys all spent significantly more time with the soft, cloth-covered surrogate. In fact, all monkeys spent very little time with the wire surrogate, even if this was the one with the bottle. Harlow and his colleagues concluded that "contact comfort was an important basic affectional or love variable" (Harlow, 1958, p. 574).

Harlow's work represents one of the earliest investigations into the importance of touch in the attachment process and remains an important study in human development.

Questions for Further Discussion

1. Even though the cloth surrogate was warm and soft and seemed to provide contact comfort, do you think that the monkeys raised in this way would behave normally when placed into contact with other monkeys? How might they react?

2. What might be the implications of Harlow's work for human mothers who feed their infants with bottles rather than breast-feeding?

The wire surrogate "mother" provides the food for this infant rhesus monkey. But the infant spends all its time with the soft, cloth-covered surrogate. According to Harlow, this demonstrates the importance of contact comfort in attachment.

Erikson's Theory

I've heard that you shouldn't pick a baby up every time it cries—that if you do, it might spoil the baby. Unfortunately, a lot of people have not only heard this advice but also acted on it by frequently ignoring an infant's crying, which turns out to be a very bad thing for babies. When a baby under 6 months of age cries, it is an instinctive reaction meant to get the caregiver to tend to the baby's needs—hunger, thirst, pain, and even loneliness. Research has shown that babies whose cries are tended to consistently (that is, the infant is fed when hungry, changed when wet, and so on) in the early months are more securely attached as late as age 1 than those infants whose caregivers frequently allow the infants to cry when there is a need for attention—hunger, pain, or wetness, for example (Brazelton, 1992; Heinicke et al., 2000). Erikson, a psychodynamic theorist who emphasized the importance of social relationships in the development of personality, would certainly disagree with letting a baby "cry it out," although allowing an infant who has been fed, changed, burped, and checked to cry on occasion will not damage attachment.

Erikson, who trained as a Freudian psychoanalyst but became convinced that social interactions were more important in development than Freud's emphasis on sexual development, believed that development occurred in a series of eight stages, with the first four of these stages occurring in infancy and childhood (Erikson, 1950; Erikson & Erikson, 1997). (Freud's stages of psychosexual development are covered in detail in a later chapter.) Ⓛ Ⓘ Ⓝ Ⓚ *to Chapter Eleven: Theories of Personality, pp. 440–443.* Each stage is an emotional *crisis*, or a kind of turning point, in personality, and the crisis in each stage must be successfully met for normal, healthy psychological development.

Erikson focused on the relationship of the infant and the child to significant others in the immediate surroundings—parents and then later teachers and even peers. Table 10.4 summarizes the conflict in each of Erikson's eight stages and some of the implications for future development (Erikson, 1950; Erikson & Erikson, 1997). For now, look at the first four stages in particular.

◀ I've heard that you shouldn't pick a baby up every time it cries—that if you do, it might spoil the baby.

◀ **AP**✳ Identify key contributors to personality theory.

◀ **AP**✳ Identify key contributors in developmental psychology.

Table 10.4 Erikson's Psychosocial Stages of Development

STAGE	DEVELOPMENTAL CRISIS	SUCCESSFUL DEALING WITH CRISIS	UNSUCCESSFUL DEALING WITH CRISIS
1. Infant Birth to 1 year old	**Trust Versus Mistrust** Babies learn to trust or mistrust others based on whether or not their needs—such as food and comfort—are met.	If babies' needs are met, they learn to trust people and expect life to be pleasant.	If babies' needs are not met, they learn not to trust.
2. Toddler 1 to 3 years old	**Autonomy Versus Shame and Doubt** Toddlers realize that they can direct their own behavior.	If toddlers are successful in directing their own behavior, they learn to be independent.	If toddlers' attempts at being independent are blocked, they learn self-doubt and shame for being unsuccessful.
3. Preschool Age 3 to 5 years old	**Initiative Versus Guilt** Preschoolers are challenged to control their own behavior, such as controlling their exuberance when they are in a restaurant.	If preschoolers succeed in taking responsibility, they feel capable and develop initiative.	If preschoolers fail in taking responsibility, they feel irresponsible, anxious, and guilty.
4. Elementary School Age 5 to 12 years old	**Industry Versus Inferiority** School-aged children are faced with learning new social and academic skills. Social comparison is a primary source of information.	When children succeed at learning new skills, they develop a sense of industry, a feeling of competence and self-esteem arising from their work and effort.	If children fail to develop new abilities, they feel incompetent, inadequate, and inferior.
5. Adolescence 13 to early twenties	**Identity Versus Role Confusion** Adolescents are faced with deciding who or what they want to be in terms of occupation, beliefs, attitudes, and behavior patterns.	Adolescents who succeed in defining who they are and finding a role for themselves develop a strong sense of identity.	Adolescents who fail to define their identity become confused and withdraw or want to inconspicuously blend in with the crowd.
6. Early Adulthood Twenties and thirties	**Intimacy Versus Isolation** The task facing those in early adulthood is to be able to share who they are with another person in a close, committed relationship.	People who succeed in this task will have satisfying intimate relationships.	Adults who fail at this task will be isolated from other people and may suffer from loneliness.
7. Middle Adulthood Forties and fifties	**Generativity Versus Stagnation** The challenge is to be creative, productive, and nurturant of the next generation.	Adults who succeed in this challenge will be creative, productive, and nurturant, thereby benefiting themselves, their family, community, country, and future generations.	Adults who fail will be passive, and self-centered, feel that they have done nothing for the next generation, and feel that the world is no better off for their being alive.
8. Late Adulthood Sixties and beyond	**Ego Integrity Versus Despair** The issue is whether a person will reach wisdom, spiritual tranquility, a sense of wholeness, and acceptance of his or her life.	Elderly people who succeed in addressing this issue will enjoy life and not fear death.	Elderly people who fail will feel that their life is empty and will fear death.

10.7

- **psychosocial development** — involves development of personality, relationships, and a sense of being male or female; process begins in infancy and continues into adulthood

- **important early concepts** —
  - infants demonstrate personality through their temperament (e.g., easy, difficult, slow to warm up), which can also affect and is affected by parenting and the environment
  - attachment (emotional bond between infant and a primary caregiver) is very important; different attachment styles have been identified by Ainsworth and others (e.g., secure, avoidant, ambivalent, disorganized-disoriented) that appear to be similar, but not identical, across different cultures

- **Erikson's theory** —
  - suggests development occurs in a series of eight stages (see Table 10.4)
  - at each stage an emotional crisis must be successfully met for normal development to occur

Infancy and Childhood Development: Psychosocial Development

PRACTICE QUIZ: PREPARING FOR THE AP* EXAM

ANSWERS ON PAGE AK-3.

Directions: Read each of the questions or incomplete sentences below. Then choose the response that best answers the question or completes the sentence.

1. According to Thomas and Chess, a child who is very irregular in their schedules, resists change, and is negative and loud is a(n) _____.
   a. easy child
   b. difficult child
   c. anxious child
   d. ambivalent child
   e. slow-to-warm-up child

2. According to Ainsworth, what kind of attachment is shown by a baby who explores the room, gets upset when the mother leaves but is easily soothed, and is happy to see the mother when she returns?
   a. Secure
   b. Avoidant
   c. Ambivalent
   d. Difficult
   e. Disorganized-disoriented

3. With which type of attachment are abusive and/or neglectful mothers associated?
   a. Secure
   b. Avoidant
   c. Ambivalent
   d. Difficult
   e. Disorganized-disoriented

4. In which of Erikson's developmental stages does a child learn self-control and begin to feel more capable?
   a. Trust versus mistrust
   b. Autonomy versus shame and doubt
   c. Initiative versus guilt
   d. Industry versus inferiority
   e. Identity versus role confusion

5. According to Harlow's 1958 research, which of the following surrogate mothers would infant monkeys most likely prefer?
   a. A cold wire surrogate with a milk bottle.
   b. A warm wire surrogate with a milk bottle.
   c. A cold wire surrogate without a milk bottle.
   d. A warm wire surrogate without a milk bottle.
   e. A warm cloth surrogate without a milk bottle.

How Sex and Gender Influence Development

◀ **AP*** Describe how sex and gender influence socialization and other aspects of development.

10.8 What is gender, and how can biology and learning influence gender role development?

Whereas sex can be defined as the physical characteristics of being male or female, **gender** is defined as the psychological aspects of being masculine or feminine. The expectations of one's culture, the development of one's personality, and one's sense of identity are all affected by the concept of gender.

gender the psychological aspects of being male or female.

gender roles the culture's expectations for masculine or feminine behavior, including attitudes, actions, and personality traits associated with being male or female in that culture.

gender typing the process of acquiring gender role characteristics.

gender identity the individual's sense of being male or female.

Was their early tomboy nature due to the influence of the male hormones? ▶

In studies in which infant girls were exposed to androgens (male hormones) while in their mother's womb, the girls became "tomboys" as children, preferring to play with typically masculine toys and participate in male-dominated play activities. Yet when these same girls grew into puberty and adulthood, they became more feminine in their behavior. What do these findings mean for the nature/nurture controversy?

GENDER ROLES AND GENDER TYPING

Gender roles are the culture's expectations for behavior of a person who is perceived as male or female, including attitudes, actions, and personality traits associated with a particular gender within that culture (Tobach, 2001; Unger, 1979). **Gender typing** is the process by which people learn their culture's preferences and expectations for proper "masculine" and "feminine" behavior. The process of developing a person's **gender identity** (a sense of being male or female) is influenced by both biological and environmental factors (in the form of parenting and other child-rearing behaviors), although which type of factor has greater influence is still controversial.

Biological Influences What are the biological influences on gender? Aside from the obvious external sexual characteristics of the genitals, there are also hormonal differences between men and women. Some researchers believe that exposure to these hormones during fetal development not only causes the formation of the sexual organs but also predisposes the infant to behavior that is typically associated with one gender or the other. There have been several studies of infant girls who were exposed to androgens before birth (for example, some drugs to prevent miscarriages are male hormones). In these studies, the girls were found to be tomboys during early childhood—preferring to play with typically "boy" toys, wrestling and playing rough, and playing with boys rather than with other girls (Berenbaum & Snyder, 1995; Money & Mathews, 1982; Money & Norman, 1987). However, when these girls grew up, they became more typically "female" in their desire for marriage and motherhood, which many of these same researchers took as evidence that upbringing won out over the hormonal influences.

Was their early tomboy nature due to the influence of the male hormones? This is difficult to prove, as the parents of these girls were told about their infants' exposure to male hormones during the pregnancy and may have formed assumptions about the effects of such masculinizing hormones on their children. It is entirely possible that these girls were simply allowed, or even encouraged, to be more "masculine" as small children because the parents were expecting them to be masculine. As these same girls grew older, they were exposed to the gender role expectations of teachers, friends, and the media, which may have influenced them to become more like the feminine gender stereotype in contrast to their earlier "masculine" style of behavior.

Environmental Influences Even if the girls who were exposed to androgens prenatally were initially influenced by these hormones, it seems fairly clear that their later "reversion" to more feminine ways was at least somewhat influenced by the pressures of society. In most cultures, there are certain roles that males and females are expected to play (gender roles, in other words), and the pressure that can be brought to bear on a person who does not conform to these expectations can be tremendous. In most Western cultures, the pressure to be masculine is even greater for males than the pressure to be feminine is for girls. The term *tomboy* is not generally viewed as an insult, but there are no terms for a boy who acts in a feminine manner that are not insulting—*sissy,* for example, is not a nice term at all. And although studies of parents' influence on their children's gender typing show that both parents have an impact, they also show that the fathers are almost always more concerned about their sons showing male gender behavior than their daughters showing female gender behavior (Lytton & Romney, 1991).

Culture and Gender A person's culture is also an environmental influence. Although older cross-cultural studies suggested that cultural differences had little effect on gender roles (Best & Williams, 2001), more recent research suggests that in the past few decades a change has occurred in cultures that are of different "personalities." Cultures that are more individualistic and have fairly high standards of living are becoming more nontraditional, especially for women in those cultures, whereas the more traditional views seem to be held by collectivistic cultures that have less wealth, although even in the latter, women were more likely to be less traditional than men (Gibbons et al., 1991). Other studies have found that the most nontraditional ideas about gender roles and gender behavior are found in countries such as the Netherlands, Germany, Italy, and England, whereas the most traditional ideas predominate in African and Asian countries such as Nigeria, Pakistan, and Japan (Best & Williams, 2001). The United States, often seen as very nontraditional by researchers, actually was somewhere in the middle in these studies, perhaps due to the large variation in subcultures that exists within this multicultural country. Environment, even in the form of culture, seems to play at least a partial and perhaps dominant role in gender behavior.

Several studies over the years have found differences in male and female brain activity: When doing language tasks, women use an area of the right hemisphere that is not as active in men, leading some to speculate that this is why women seem to recover faster than men from left-hemisphere strokes that affect language (Jaeger et al., 1998; Skrandies et al., 1999). Whereas men use the right side of the brain for emotional expression and the left side for visual/spatial perception, women seem to use both sides (Argyle, 1986; Fischer, 1993; Jaeger et al., 1998; Kimura, 2002; Pittam et al., 1995; Skrandies et al., 1999). There are physical differences in male and female brains from birth with the male hypothalamus being somewhat larger than that of females in rats and humans (Kimura, 2002). Even in these biological differences, the influence of the environment in the form of parenting and cultural expectations cannot be ruled out as potential causes. For example, in Western cultures, girls are encouraged to express and use their emotions while boys are encouraged to hide emotions and be calm, which might contribute to the different emphasis placed on each hemisphere for the two sexes (Argyle, 1986; Fischer, 1993; Pittam et al., 1995). Psychologist Eleanor Maccoby (1998) believes that the biological differences between males and females help to create different contexts in which boys and girls are raised; the aggressive nature of boys, for example, causes them to engage in more rough-and-tumble play and competitive games than girls. One thing is clear: The issue of differences between men and women is one that will be discussed, debated, and researched for some time to come. ◉⌐**Watch** on **MyPsychLab**

Although Asian cultures are often more traditional in the roles that men and women play within society, even in these cultures gender roles are becoming more flexible, as this male preschool teacher in a Chinese classroom demonstrates. Why might gender roles in these traditional countries be changing?

◉ **Watch** a video about gender versus sex. **www.mypsychlab.com**

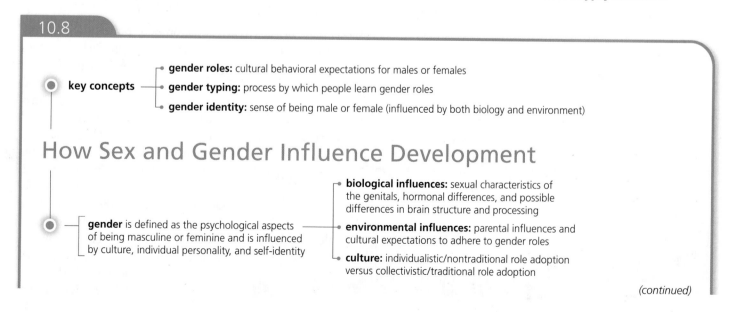

10.8

◉ **key concepts** —
- **gender roles:** cultural behavioral expectations for males or females
- **gender typing:** process by which people learn gender roles
- **gender identity:** sense of being male or female (influenced by both biology and environment)

How Sex and Gender Influence Development

◉ **gender** is defined as the psychological aspects of being masculine or feminine and is influenced by culture, individual personality, and self-identity —
- **biological influences:** sexual characteristics of the genitals, hormonal differences, and possible differences in brain structure and processing
- **environmental influences:** parental influences and cultural expectations to adhere to gender roles
- **culture:** individualistic/nontraditional role adoption versus collectivistic/traditional role adoption

(continued)

PRACTICE **QUIZ:** PREPARING FOR THE AP* EXAM

ANSWERS ON PAGE AK-3.

Directions: Read each of the questions or incomplete sentences below. Then choose the response that best answers the question or completes the sentence.

1. The development of a person's sense of being male or female is called _____.
   a. gender role
   b. gender typing
   c. gender identity
   d. gender stereotyping
   e. gender schema theory

2. Several studies have revealed that girls who are exposed to _____ before birth had a greater likelihood of being "tomboys" during early childhood.
   a. progesterone
   b. estrogen
   c. endorphins
   d. androgens
   e. teratogens

3. In which of the following types of cultures are nontraditional gender roles most likely to thrive?
   a. Poor
   b. Eastern
   c. Historic
   d. Collectivistic
   e. Individualistic

4. Which of the following statements about gender is most accurate?
   a. A person's gender is determined by his or her sex.
   b. A person's gender is determined by cultural expectations.
   c. A person's gender is determined by biological characteristics.
   d. A person's gender is determined by environmental influences.
   e. A person's gender is determined by a combination of biological and environmental factors.

5. The process by which people learn their culture's expectations for "masculine" and "feminine" behavior is known as

   _____.
   a. gender role
   b. gender typing
   c. gender identity
   d. gender stereotyping
   e. gender schema theory

---

adolescence the period of life from about age 13 to the early twenties, during which a young person is no longer physically a child but is not yet an independent, self-supporting adult.

puberty the physical changes that occur in the body as sexual development reaches its peak.

Isn't adolescence just ▶
the physical changes that
happen to your body?

AP* Discuss maturational ▶
challenges in adolescence.

Adolescence

Adolescence is the period of life from about age 13 to the early twenties, during which a young person is no longer physically a child but is not yet an independent, self-supporting adult. Although in the past, adolescence was always defined as the "teens," from ages 13 to 19, adolescence isn't necessarily determined by chronological age. It also concerns how a person deals with life issues such as work, family, and relationships. So although there is a clear age of onset, the end of adolescence may come earlier or later for different individuals.

PHYSICAL DEVELOPMENT

Isn't adolescence just the physical changes that happen to your body?

Puberty

10.9 What are the physical, cognitive, and personality changes that occur in adolescence, including concepts of morality and Erikson's search for identity?

The clearest sign of the beginning of adolescence is the onset of **puberty**, the physical changes in both *primary sex characteristics* (growth of the actual sex organs such as the penis or the uterus) and *secondary sex characteristics* (changes in the body such as the development of breasts and body hair) that occur in the body as sexual development reaches its peak. Puberty occurs as the result of a complex series of glandular activities, stimulated by the "master gland" or the pituitary gland, when the proper genetically determined age is reached. Certain psychosocial and environmental factors such as stress, exercise, and nutrition may also have an impact on the timing of puberty (Ellis et al., 1999; Graber et al., 1995). The thyroid gland increases the rate of growth, and the adrenal glands and sex glands stimulate the growth of characteristics such as body hair, muscle tissue in males, and the menstrual cycle in girls, for example (Grumbach & Kaplan, 1990; Grumbach & Styne, 1998).

Puberty often begins about two years after the beginning of the *growth spurt*, the rapid period of growth that takes place at around age 10 for girls and around age 12 for boys.

In addition to an increase in height, physical characteristics related to being male or female undergo rapid and dramatic change. In fact, the rate of growth and development in puberty approaches that of development in the womb. For females, breast tissue begins to enlarge, hips begin to widen, the uterus grows, and eventually the menstrual cycle begins. For boys, the penis and testicles increase in size, muscles become more defined, and the voice begins to deepen. For both sexes, oily secretions increase (causing pimples and even acne in many teens), hair grows on the pubic area and under the arms, and body odor becomes more noticeable. After about four years, the changes of puberty are relatively complete.

COGNITIVE DEVELOPMENT

If I'm remembering correctly, teenagers should be in Piaget's formal operations stage. So why don't many teenagers think just like adults? The cognitive development of adolescents is less visible than the physical development but still represents a major change in the way adolescents think about themselves, their peers and relationships, and the world around them.

Piaget's Formal Operations Revisited   Adolescents, especially those who receive a formal high school education, move into Piaget's final stage of formal operations, in which abstract thinking becomes possible. This cognitive advance is primarily due to the final development of the frontal lobes of the brain, the part of the brain that is responsible for organizing, understanding, and decision making (Giedd et al., 1999; Sowell et al., 1999). Teenagers begin to think about hypothetical situations, leading to a picture of what an "ideal" world would be like. (It should be noted that although adolescents have reached the formal operational stage, not all adolescents—or adults—use their formal operational thought processes equally well. In a sense, they've graduated to "bigger and better" mental tools but don't necessarily know how to use those tools effectively. A more formal educational process or demanding life experiences help adolescents and adults become skilled "tool users.")

As discussed earlier, Piaget's concept of stages has been criticized as being too simplistic. The evidence now points to gradual, continuous cognitive development (Feldman, 2003; Siegler, 1996). Even so, Piaget's theory has had a tremendous impact in the education of children and in stimulating research about children's cognitive development (Satterly, 1987). Children in varying cultures usually come to understand the world in the way that Piaget described, although the age at which this understanding comes varies from one child to another.

Although headed into an adult style of thinking, adolescents are not yet completely free of egocentric thought. At this time in life, however, their egocentrism shows up in their preoccupation* with their own thoughts. They do a lot of introspection (turning inward) and may become convinced that their thoughts are as important to others as they are to themselves. Two ways in which this adolescent egocentrism emerges are the personal fable and the imaginary audience (Elkind, 1985; Lapsley et al., 1986; Vartanian, 2000).

In the **personal fable**, adolescents have spent so much time thinking about their own thoughts and feelings that they become convinced that they are special, one of a kind, and that no one else has ever had these thoughts and feelings before them. "You just don't understand me, I'm different from you" is a common feeling of teens. The personal fable is not without a dangerous side. Because they feel unique, teenagers may feel that they are somehow protected from the dangers of the world and so do not take the precautions that they should. "It can't happen to me, I'm special" is a risky but common thought.

---

*Preoccupation: extreme or excessive concern with something.

◀ If I'm remembering correctly, teenagers should be in Piaget's formal operations stage. So why don't many teenagers think just like adults?

personal fable   type of thought common to adolescents in which young people believe themselves to be unique and protected from harm.

Figure 10.7 Example of a Moral Dilemma *Source:* Kohlberg, 1969, p. 379.

> **Example of a Moral Dilemma**
>
> A woman in Europe was dying from a rare disease. Her only hope was a drug that a local druggist had discovered. The druggist was charging ten times more than it cost him to make it. Heinz, the husband of the dying woman, had desperately tried to borrow money to buy the drug, but he could borrow only half of the amount he needed. He went to the druggist, told him that his wife was dying, and asked to let him pay the druggist later or to sell the drug at a lower cost. The druggist refused, saying that he had discovered the drug and he was going to make money from it. Later, Heinz broke into the druggist's store to steal the drug for his wife. Should Heinz have done that? Why?

imaginary audience type of thought common to adolescents in which young people believe that other people are just as concerned about the adolescent's thoughts and characteristics as they themselves are.

preconventional morality first level of Kohlberg's stages of moral development in which the child's behavior is governed by the consequences of the behavior.

conventional morality second level of Kohlberg's stages of moral development in which the child's behavior is governed by conforming to the society's norms of behavior.

postconventional morality third level of Kohlberg's stages of moral development in which the person's behavior is governed by moral principles that have been decided on by the individual and that may be in disagreement with accepted social norms.

AP* Compare and contrast models of moral development. ▶

AP* Identify key contributors in developmental psychology. ▶

✳ **Explore** Carol Gilligan's three stages of morality for women.
www.mypsychlab.com

The **imaginary audience** shows up as extreme self-consciousness in adolescents. They become convinced that *everyone is looking at them* and that they are always the center of everyone else's world, just as they are the center of their own. This explains the intense self-consciousness that many adolescents experience concerning what others think about how the adolescent looks or behaves.

Moral Development Another important aspect in the cognitive advances that occur in adolescence concerns the teenager's understanding of "right" and "wrong." Harvard University professor Lawrence Kohlberg was a developmental psychologist who, influenced by Piaget and others, outlined a theory of the development of moral thinking through looking at how people of various ages responded to stories about people caught up in moral dilemmas (see Figure 10.7 for a typical story). Kohlberg (1973) proposed three levels of moral development, or the knowledge of right and wrong behavior. These levels are summarized in Table 10.5, along with an example of each type of thinking. Although these stages are associated with certain age groups, adolescents and adults can be found at all three levels. For example, a juvenile delinquent tends to be preconventional in moral thinking.

Kohlberg's theory has been criticized as being male oriented, especially since he used only males in his studies (Gilligan, 1982). Carol Gilligan (1982) proposed that men and women have different perspectives on morality: Men tend to judge as moral the actions that lead to a fair or just end, whereas women tend to judge as moral the actions that are nonviolent and hurt the fewest people. Researchers, however, have not found consistent support for gender differences in moral thinking (Walker, 1991). Another criticism is that Kohlberg's assessment of moral development involves asking people what they think should be done in hypothetical moral dilemmas. What people say they will do and what people actually do when faced with a real dilemmas are often two different things. ✳ Explore on MyPsychLab

Table 10.5 Kohlberg's Three Levels of Morality

LEVEL OF MORALITY	HOW RULES ARE UNDERSTOOD	EXAMPLE
Preconventional morality (typically very young children)	The consequences determine morality; behavior that is rewarded is right; that which is punished is wrong.	A child who steals a toy from another child and does not get caught does not see that action as wrong.
Conventional* morality (older children, adolescents, and most adults)	Conformity to social norms is right; nonconformity is wrong.	A child criticizes his or her parent for speeding because speeding is against the posted laws.
Postconventional morality (about 20 percent of the adult population)	Moral principles determined by the person are used to determine right and wrong and may disagree with societal norms.	A reporter who wrote a controversial story goes to jail rather than reveal the source's identity.

*The term *conventional* refers to general standards or norms of behavior for a particular society, which will differ from one social group or culture to another.

PSYCHOSOCIAL DEVELOPMENT

The development of personality and social relationships in adolescence primarily concerns the search for a consistent sense of self or personal identity.

Erikson's Identity Versus Role Confusion   The psychosocial crisis that must be faced by the adolescent, according to Erikson, is that of **identity versus role confusion** (see Table 10.6 on page 425). In this stage, the teenager must choose from among many options for values in life and beliefs concerning things such as political issues, career options, and marriage (Feldman, 2003). From those options, a consistent sense of self must be found. Erikson believed that teens who have successfully resolved the conflicts of the earlier four stages are much better "equipped" to resist peer pressure to engage in unhealthy or illegal activities and find their own identity during the adolescent years. Those teens who are not as successful come into the adolescent years with a lack of trust in others, feelings of guilt and shame, low self-esteem, and dependency on others. Peer pressure is quite effective on teenagers who desperately want to "fit in" and have an identity of some sort and who feel that others will not want to be with them unless they conform to the expectations and demands of the peer group. They play the part of the model child for the parents, the good student for the teachers, and the "cool" juvenile delinquent to their friends and will be confused about which of the many roles they play are really their own identity.

Parent/Teen Conflict   Even for the majority of adolescents who end up successfully finding a consistent sense of self, there will be conflicts with parents. Many researchers believe that a certain amount of "rebellion" and conflict is a necessary step in breaking away from childhood dependence on the parents and becoming a self-sufficient* adult. Although many people think that these conflicts are intense and concern very serious behavior, the reality is that most parent/teen conflict is over trivial issues—hair, clothing, taste in music, and so on. On the really big moral issues, most parents and teens would be quite surprised to realize that they are in agreement. ◉⌐**Watch** on **MyPsychLab**

Actresses Lindsay Lohan, Amanda Seyfried, Lacey Chabert, and Rachel McAdams on the set of Mark S. Waters's comedy movie Mean Girls. This movie portrays the ins and outs of peer pressure and the desire to fit in that many adolescents face.

identity versus role confusion   fifth stage of personality development in which the adolescent must find a consistent sense of self.

◉ **Watch** a video on adolescent behavior including egocentrism, teen drinking, and teen pregnancy. **www.mypsychlab.com**

---

*Self-sufficient: able to function without outside aid; capable of providing for one's own needs.

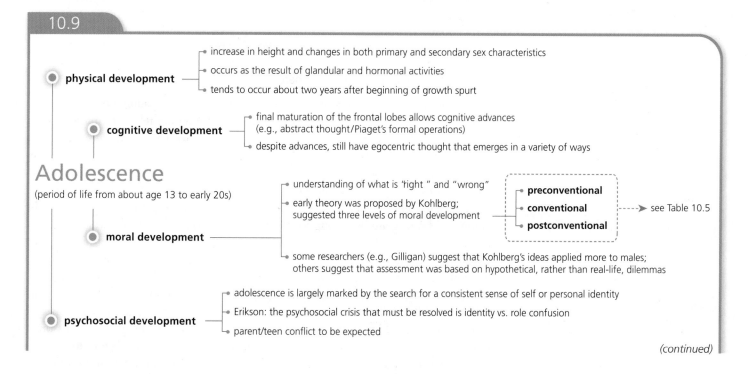

10.9

physical development
- increase in height and changes in both primary and secondary sex characteristics
- occurs as the result of glandular and hormonal activities
- tends to occur about two years after beginning of growth spurt

cognitive development
- final maturation of the frontal lobes allows cognitive advances (e.g., abstract thought/Piaget's formal operations)
- despite advances, still have egocentric thought that emerges in a variety of ways

Adolescence
(period of life from about age 13 to early 20s)

moral development
- understanding of what is "right" and "wrong"
- early theory was proposed by Kohlberg; suggested three levels of moral development
  - preconventional
  - conventional
  - postconventional   ⤑ see Table 10.5
- some researchers (e.g., Gilligan) suggest that Kohlberg's ideas applied more to males; others suggest that assessment was based on hypothetical, rather than real-life, dilemmas

psychosocial development
- adolescence is largely marked by the search for a consistent sense of self or personal identity
- Erikson: the psychosocial crisis that must be resolved is identity vs. role confusion
- parent/teen conflict to be expected

(continued)

Directions: Read each of the questions or incomplete sentences below. Then choose the response that best answers the question or completes the sentence.

1. Which of the following terms refers to the feeling of being unique and protected from harm?
   a. Personal fable
   b. Moral dilemma
   c. Role confusion
   d. Parent/teen conflict
   e. Imaginary audience

2. According to Kohlberg, at which level of morality are most adolescents?
   a. Preliminary
   b. Preconventional
   c. Conventional
   d. Postconventional
   e. Unconventional

3. What, according to Erikson, is the task of the adolescent?
   a. To learn to trust others
   b. To develop a sense of industry
   c. To develop a sense of initiative
   d. To find a consistent sense of self
   e. To find intimacy with another person

4. Most conflicts between adolescents and their parents or caregivers are created by _____.
   a. issues of morality
   b. issues of independence
   c. issues of substance abuse
   d. issues of trivial importance
   e. issues of personal responsibility

5. How is Carol Gilligan's theory of morality different from Lawrence Kohlberg's theory of morality?
   a. Gilligan proposes that all people share a single basic moral perspective.
   b. Gilligan proposes that everyone is capable of postconventional morality.
   c. Gilligan proposes that morality is only hypothetical and not measurable.
   d. Gilligan proposes that young children are more moral than older people.
   e. Gilligan proposes that men and women have different moral perspectives.

Adulthood

PHYSICAL DEVELOPMENT: USE IT OR LOSE IT

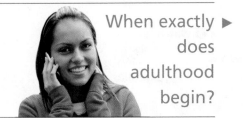

When exactly ▶ does adulthood begin?

AP* Predict the physical and cognitive changes that emerge as people age.

When exactly does adulthood begin? Adulthood can be thought of as the period of life from the early twenties until old age and death. Exactly when adulthood begins is not always easy to determine. In some cultures, adulthood is reached soon after puberty (Bledsoe & Cohen, 1993; Ocholla-Ayayo et al., 1993). Some people feel that it begins after graduation from high school, whereas others would say adulthood doesn't begin until after graduation from college. Others define it as the point when a person becomes totally self-sufficient with a job and a home separate from his or her parents. In that case, some people are not adults until their late thirties.

▶ **10.10** What are the physical, cognitive, and personality changes that occur during adulthood and aging, including Erikson's last three psychosocial stages, and patterns of parenting?

Adulthood can also be divided into at least three periods: young adulthood, middle age, and late adulthood. Physical changes in young adulthood are relatively minimal. The good news is that the twenties are a time of peak physical health, sharp senses, fewer insecurities, and mature cognitive abilities. The bad news is that even in the early twenties, the signs of aging are already beginning. Oil glands in the neck and around the eyes begin to malfunction, contributing to wrinkles in those areas near the end of the twenties and beginning of the thirties. The thirties may not bring noticeable changes, but vision and hearing are beginning to decline and by around age 40, bifocal lenses may become necessary as the lens of the eye hardens, becoming unable to change its shape to shift focus. Hearing loss may begin in the forties and fifties but often does not become noticeable until the sixties or seventies, when hearing aids may become necessary.

In the forties, while most adults are able to experience some security and stability without the worries and concerns of adolescence and young adulthood, physical aging continues: Skin begins to show more wrinkles, hair turns gray (or falls out), vision and hearing decline further, and physical strength may begin to decline (Frontera et al., 1991). In the fifties, these changes continue. Throughout middle age, weight may increase as the rate at which the body functions slows down but eating increases and less time is spent exercising. Height begins to decrease, with about half an inch of height lost for every 10 years past age 40, although people with the bone-loss disease osteoporosis may lose up to 8 inches or more (Cummings & Melton, 2002). Although sexual functioning usually does not decline in middle age, opportunities for sexual activity may be fewer than in the days of young adulthood (Hodson & Skeen, 1994; Williams, 1995). Children, mortgages, and career worries can put a damper on middle-age romance.

Menopause For women, the forties are a time of great physical changes. At this time in life a woman's reproductive organs begin functioning inconsistently, as levels of the female hormone estrogen decline in preparation for the end of reproduction. The uterus slowly begins to get smaller in size, menstrual cycles become irregular, and some women begin to experience "hot flashes," a sudden sensation of heat and sweating that may keep them up at night. Interestingly, in some cultures, particularly those in which the diet contains high amounts of soy products, hot flashes are almost nonexistent (Cassidy et al., 1994; Lock, 1994). These changes are called the *climacteric*, and the period of five to ten years over which these changes occur is called *perimenopause*. At an average age of 51, most women will cease ovulation altogether, ending their reproductive years. The cessation of ovulation and the menstrual cycle is called **menopause** (Mishell, 2001). Many women look forward to the freedom from monthly menstruation and fear of unplanned pregnancies (Adler et al., 2000; Hvas, 2001; Leon et al., 2007).

Do men go through anything like menopause? Men also go through a time of sexual changes, but it is much more gradual and less dramatic than menopause. In males, **andropause** (Carruthers, 2001) usually begins in the forties with a decline in several hormones, primarily testosterone (the major male hormone). Physical symptoms are also less dramatic but no less troubling: fatigue, irritability, possible problems in sexual functioning, and reduced sperm count. Males, however, rarely lose all reproductive ability.

Effects of Aging on Health It is in middle age that many health problems first occur, although their true cause may have begun in the young adulthood years. The wear and tear that some young adults' risky lifestyles cause on their bodies will not become obvious until those people reach their forties and fifties.

Some of the common health problems that may show up in middle age are high blood pressure, skin cancer, heart problems, arthritis, and obesity. High blood pressure can be caused by lifestyle factors such as obesity and stress but may also be related to hereditary factors (Rudd & Osterberg, 2002). Sleep problems, such as loud snoring and sleep apnea (in which breathing stops for 10 seconds or more), may also take their toll on physical health. There is some evidence that high blood pressure and apnea are linked, although the link may be as simple as the common cause of obesity (Nieto et al., 2000). The most common causes of death in middle age are heart disease, cancer, and stroke—in that order (McGinnis & Foege, 1993).

COGNITIVE DEVELOPMENT

Intellectual abilities do not decline overall, although speed of processing (or reaction time) does slow down. Compared to a younger adult, a middle-aged person may take a little longer to solve a problem. However, a middle-aged person also has more life experience and knowledge to bring to bear on a problem, which counters the lack of

"Elsie is still waiting for postmenopausal zest to kick in."

©The New Yorker Collection 1993 George Booth from cartoonbank.com. All Rights Reserved.

◀ Do men go through anything like menopause?

menopause the cessation of ovulation and menstrual cycles and the end of a woman's reproductive capability.

andropause gradual changes in the sexual hormones and reproductive system of middle-aged males.

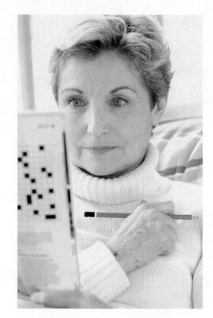

This middle-aged woman works on a crossword puzzle. Mental exercises such as this are one way to keep the brain healthy and fit. What might be some other ways to exercise one's brain?

speed. In one study (Salthouse, 1984), for example, older typists were found to outperform younger typists, even though they typed more slowly than the younger subjects. The older typists, because of years of practice, had developed a skill of looking farther ahead in the document they were typing, so that they could type more continuously without looking back at the document. This allowed them to complete their typing more quickly than the younger typists.

Changes in Memory　Changes in memory ability are probably the most noticeable changes in middle-aged cognition. People find themselves having a hard time remembering a particular word or someone's name. This difficulty in retrieval is probably not evidence of a physical decline (or the beginning of Alzheimer's disease) but is more likely caused by the stresses a middle-aged person experiences and the sheer amount of information that a person of middle years must try to keep straight (Craik, 1994; Launer et al., 1995; Sands & Meredith, 1992).

How to Keep Your Brain Young　People who exercise their mental abilities have been found to be far less likely to develop memory problems and even senile dementias such as Alzheimer's in old age (Ball et al., 2002; Colcombe et al., 2003; Fiatarone, 1996). "Use it or lose it" is the phrase to remember. Working challenging crossword puzzles, for example, can be a major factor in maintaining a healthy level of cognitive functioning. Reading, having an active social life, going to plays, taking classes, and staying physically active can all have a positive impact on the continued well-being of the brain (Bosworth & Schaie, 1997; Cabeza et al., 2002; Singh-Manoux et al., 2003).

PSYCHOSOCIAL DEVELOPMENT

In adulthood, concerns involve career, relationships, family, and approaching old age. The late teens and early twenties may be college years for many, although other young people go to work directly from high school. The task of choosing and entering a career is very serious and a task that many young adults have difficulty accomplishing. A college student may change majors more than once during the first few years of college, and even after obtaining a bachelor's degree many may either get a job in an unrelated field or go on to a different type of career choice in graduate school. Those who are working may also change careers several times (perhaps as many as five to seven times) and may experience periods of unemployment while between jobs.

Erikson's Intimacy Versus Isolation: Forming Relationships　In young adulthood, Erikson saw the primary task to be finding a mate. True **intimacy** is an emotional and psychological closeness that is based on the ability to trust, share, and care (an ability developed during the earlier stages such as trust versus mistrust), while still maintaining one's sense of self. ⓛⓘⓝⓚ *to Chapter Fourteen: Social Psychology, p. 583.* Young adults who have difficulty trusting others and who are unsure of their own identities may find *isolation* instead of intimacy—loneliness, shallow relationships with others, and even a fear of real intimacy. For example, many marriages end in divorce within a few years, with one partner leaving the relationship—and even the responsibilities of parenting—to explore personal concerns and those unfinished issues of identity. Table 10.6 summarizes the last four stages in Erikson's theory.

Erikson's Generativity Versus Stagnation: Parenting　In middle adulthood, persons who have found intimacy can now focus outward on others. (See Table 10.6.) Erikson saw this as parenting the next generation and helping them through their crises, a

AP* Characterize the development of decisions related to intimacy as people mature. ▶

intimacy　an emotional and psychological closeness that is based on the ability to trust, share, and care, while still maintaining a sense of self.

Table 10.6 Erikson's Psychosocial Adolescent and Adult Stages

STAGE	DEVELOPMENTAL CRISIS	SUCCESSFUL DEALING WITH CRISIS	UNSUCCESSFUL DEALING WITH CRISIS
5. Adolescence 13 to early twenties	**Identity Versus Role Confusion** Adolescents are faced with deciding who or what they want to be in terms of occupation, beliefs, attitudes, and behavior patterns.	Adolescents who succeed in defining who they are and find a role for themselves develop a strong sense of identity.	Adolescents who fail to define their identity become confused and withdraw or want to inconspicuously blend in with the crowd.
6. Early Adulthood Twenties and thirties	**Intimacy Versus Isolation** The task facing those in early adulthood is to be able to share who they are with another person in a close, committed relationship.	People who succeed in this task will have satisfying intimate relationships.	Adults who fail at this task will be isolated from other people and may suffer from loneliness.
7. Middle Adulthood Forties and fifties	**Generativity Versus Stagnation** The challenge is to be creative, productive, and nurturant of the next generation.	Adults who succeed in this challenge will be creative, productive, and nurturant, thereby benefiting themselves, their family, community, country, and future generations.	Adults who fail will be passive, and self-centered, feel that they have done nothing for the next generation, and feel that the world is no better off for their being alive.
8. Late Adulthood Sixties and beyond	**Ego Integrity Versus Despair** The issue is whether a person will reach wisdom, spiritual tranquility, a sense of wholeness, and acceptance of his or her life.	Elderly people who succeed in addressing this issue will enjoy life and not fear death.	Elderly people who fail will feel that their life is empty and will fear death.

Source: Erikson, 1950/1963, 1968.

process he called **generativity**. Educators, supervisors, health care professionals, doctors, and community volunteers might be examples of positions that allow a person to be generative. Other ways of being generative include engaging in careers or some major life work that can become one's legacy to the generations to come. Those who are unable to focus outward and are still dealing with issues of intimacy or even identity are said to be *stagnated*. People who frequently hand the care of their children over to grandparents or other relatives so that they can go out and "have fun" may be unable to focus on anyone else's needs but their own.

What kind of parent is the best parent—one who's really strict or one who's pretty easy going?

Parenting Styles Parenting children is a very important part of most people's middle adulthood. Diana Baumrind (1967) outlined three basic styles of parenting, each of which may be related to certain personality traits in the child raised by that style of parenting. ✴—[Explore on MyPsychLab

Authoritarian parenting tends to be overly concerned with rules. This type of parent is stern, rigid, demanding perfection, controlling, uncompromising,* and has

---

*Uncompromising: not making or accepting any viewpoint other than one's own, allowing no other viewpoints.

◀ What kind of parent is the best parent—one who's really strict or one who's pretty easy going?

◀ **AP*** Identify key contributors in developmental psychology.

✴ **Explore** with a simulation on Baumrind's parenting styles.
www.mypsychlab.com

generativity providing guidance to one's children or the next generation, or contributing to the well-being of the next generation through career or volunteer work.

authoritarian parenting style of parenting in which parent is rigid and overly strict, showing little warmth to the child.

permissive parenting style of parenting in which parent makes few, if any demands on a child's behavior.

permissive neglectful permissive parenting in which parents are uninvolved with child or child's behavior.

permissive indulgent permissive parenting in which parents are so involved that children are allowed to behave without set limits.

authoritative parenting style of parenting in which parents combine warmth and affection with firm limits on a child's behavior.

ego integrity sense of wholeness that comes from having lived a full life and the ability to let go of regrets; the final completion of the ego.

a tendency to use physical punishment. The parent who does the punishment often shows little warmth or affection to the child—which may be from a desire to appear stern more than from an actual lack of love. Children raised in this way are often insecure, timid, withdrawn, and resentful. As teenagers, they will very often rebel against parental authority in very negative and self-destructive ways (Baumrind, 1991, 2005).

Permissive parenting occurs when parents put very few demands on their children for behavior. **Permissive neglectful** parents simply aren't involved with their children, ignoring them and allowing them to do whatever they want, until it interferes with what the parent wants. At that point, this relationship may become an abusive one. **Permissive indulgent** parents seem to be too involved with their children, allowing their "little angels" to behave in any way they wish, refusing to set limits on the child's behavior or to require any kind of rules for fear of having a negative impact on the child's natural development or that the child will not love them if they set and enforce limits. Children from both kinds of permissive parenting tend to be selfish, immature, dependent, lacking in social skills, and unpopular with peers.

Authoritative parenting involves combining firm limits on behavior with love, warmth, affection, respect, and a willingness to listen to the child's point of view. Authoritative parents are more democratic, allowing the child to have some input into the formation of rules but still maintaining the role of final decision maker. Punishment tends to be nonphysical, such as restrictions, time-out, or loss of privileges. Authoritative parents set limits that are clear and understandable, and when a child crosses the limits, they allow an explanation and then agree upon the right way to handle the situation.

Erikson's Ego Integrity Versus Despair: Dealing With Mortality As people enter the stage known as late adulthood, life becomes more urgent as the realities of physical aging and the approaching end of life become harder and harder to ignore. (See Table 10.6.) Erikson (1980) believed that at this time, people look back on the life they have lived in a process called a *life review*. In the life review people must deal with mistakes, regrets, and unfinished business. If people can look back and feel that their lives were relatively full and come to terms with regrets and losses, then a feeling of **integrity** or wholeness results. Integrity is the final completion of the identity, or ego. If people have many regrets and lots of unfinished business, they feel *despair*, a sense of deep regret over things that will never be accomplished because time has run out.

10.10

physical development

young adulthood — few changes; the 20s are typically associated with peak physical and cognitive health

middle age
- hearing and vision begin to decline; weight increase is typical; height starts to decrease
- women experience menopause; men experience less dramatic change called andropause
- health problems related to genetics and lifestyle when younger start to appear

late adulthood
- further decline in hearing; may need hearing aids
- physical strength declines
- people with osteoporosis may lose up to 8 inches in height

Adulthood

(period of life from early 20s until old age and death; age of onset can vary by culture)

cognitive development
- cognitive skills often highest in 20s; processing and reaction time slow in middle age but are often compensated by greater life and situational knowledge
- memory issues begin in middle age, likely due to stress and information overload
- mental abilities aided by active cognitive engagement (challenging crossword puzzles, reading, etc.) and physical activity

psychosocial development
- typical life concerns involve career, relationships, family, and approaching old age
- Erikson's stages (see Table 10.6)

PRACTICE QUIZ: PREPARING FOR THE AP* EXAM

ANSWERS ON PAGE AK-3.

Directions: Read each of the questions or incomplete sentences below. Then choose the response that best answers the question or completes the sentence.

1. The period of five to ten years during which a woman's reproductive system begins to decline is called _____.
   a. ovulation
   b. climacteric
   c. menopause
   d. andropause
   e. perimenopause

2. Which of the following people is least likely to maintain a healthy level of cognitive functioning during the aging process?
   a. A person who goes out to plays and concerts
   b. A person who is a crossword puzzle enthusiast
   c. A person who takes long runs and bike rides
   d. A person who sits at home and reads novels
   e. A person who stays indoors and naps regularly

3. According to Baumrind, which type of parenting may lead to an abusive relationship?
   a. Authoritarian
   b. Authoritative
   c. Permissive neglectful
   d. Permissive indulgent
   e. Permissive authoritarian

4. Cate is a mother of an eight-year-old boy. Cate allows her son to help set the household rules, but she enforces those rules with punishments like time-outs when necessary. Cate is firm but loving, and does not let him get away with bad behavior. Cate's parenting style can best be described as _____.
   a. authoritarian
   b. authoritative
   c. permissive neglectful
   d. permissive indulgent
   e. permissive authoritarian

5. According to Erikson, someone who fails to deal with the developmental crisis of middle adulthood will _____.
   a. be passive and self-centered
   b. want to blend in with the crowd
   c. be lonely and isolated from others
   d. fear death and regret an empty life
   e. become irresponsible and anxious

6. According to Erikson, the developmental crisis of late adulthood is _____.
   a. initiative versus guilt
   b. intimacy versus isolation
   c. industry versus inferiority
   d. generativity versus stagnation
   e. ego integrity versus despair

7. A sense of completeness of one's ego, or identity, is called _____.
   a. despair
   b. integrity
   c. life review
   d. intelligence
   e. generativity

THEORIES OF PHYSICAL AND PSYCHOLOGICAL AGING

10.11 How do psychologists explain why aging occurs, and what are the stages of death and dying?

Why do people age? What makes us go through so many physical changes? There are a number of theories of why people physically age. Some theories of physical aging point to biological changes in cellular structure, whereas others focus on the influence of external stresses on body tissues and functioning.

Cellular Clock Theory One of the biologically based theories is the *cellular clock theory* (Hayflick, 1977). In this theory, cells are limited in the number of times they can reproduce to repair damage. Evidence for this theory is the existence of *telomeres*, structures on the ends of chromosomes that shorten each time a cell reproduces

◄ Why do people age? What makes us go through so many physical changes?

activity theory theory of adjustment to aging that assumes older people are happier if they remain active in some way, such as volunteering or developing a hobby.

(Martin & Buckwalter, 2001). When telomeres are too short, cells cannot reproduce and damage accumulates, resulting in the effects of aging.

Wear-and-Tear Theory   The theory that points to outside influences such as stress, physical exertion, and bodily damage is known as the *wear-and-tear theory of aging*. In this theory, the body's organs and cell tissues simply wear out with repeated use and abuse. Damaged tissues accumulate and produce the effects of aging. *Collagen*, for example, is a natural elastic tissue that allows the skin to be flexible. As people age, the collagen "wears out," becoming less and less "stretchy" and allowing skin to sag and wrinkle (Cua et al., 1990; Kligman & Balin, 1989).

Free Radical Theory   The *free radical theory* is actually the latest version of the wear-and-tear theory in that it gives a biological explanation for the damage done to cells over time. *Free radicals* are oxygen molecules that have an unstable electron (negative particle). They bounce around the cell, stealing electrons from other molecules and increasing the damage to structures inside the cell. As people get older, more and more free radicals do more and more damage, producing the effects of aging (Hauck & Bartke, 2001; Knight, 1998).

> *I've heard that most older people just want to be left alone and have some peace and quiet. Is that true?*

I've heard that most older people just want to be left alone and have some peace and quiet. Is that true? ▶

Activity Theory   **Activity theory** (Havighurst et al., 1968) proposes that an elderly person adjusts more positively to aging when remaining active in some way. Even if a career must end, there are other ways to stay active and involved in life. Elderly people who volunteer at hospitals or schools, those who take up new hobbies or throw themselves full time into old ones, and those who maintain their friendships with others and continue to have social activities have been shown to be happier and live longer than those who withdraw themselves from activity. Contrary to the view of the elderly as voluntarily withdrawing from activities, the withdrawal of many elderly people is not voluntary at all. Others simply stop inviting elderly people to social activities and including them in their lives.

STAGES OF DEATH AND DYING

There are several ways of looking at the process of dying. One of the more well-known theories is that of Elisabeth Kübler-Ross (Kübler-Ross, 1997), who conducted extensive interviews with dying persons and their caregivers.

Elisabeth Kübler-Ross theorized that people go through five stages of reaction when faced with death (Backer et al., 1994; Kübler-Ross, 1997). These stages are *denial*, in which people refuse to believe that the diagnosis of death is real; *anger*, which is really anger at death itself and the feelings of helplessness to change things; *bargaining*, in which the dying person tries to make a deal with doctors or even with God; *depression*, which is sadness from losses already experienced (e.g., loss of a job or one's dignity) and those yet to come (e.g., not being able to see a child grow up); and finally *acceptance*, when the person has accepted the inevitable* and quietly awaits death.

Obviously, some people do not have time to go through all of these stages or even go through them in the listed order (Schneidman, 1983, 1994). Some theorists do not agree with the stage idea, seeing the process of dying as a series of ups and downs, with hope on the rise at times and then falling, to be replaced by a rise in despair or disbelief (Schneidman, 1983, 1994; Weisman, 1972). Still others question the idea of common reactions among dying people, stating that the particular disease or condition and its treatment, the per-

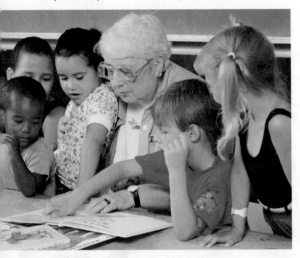

One way to age successfully and maintain psychological health is to remain active and involved in life. This woman is volunteering in a grade school classroom as a teacher's aide. This not only allows her to feel useful but also helps her to stay mentally alert and socially involved.

---

*Inevitable: something that cannot be avoided or escaped.

10.11

Adulthood: Aging

- **theories on aging**
  vary focus from biological changes to influence on external stressors
  - **cellular clock theory**
  - **wear-and-tear theory**
  - **free radical theory**

- **activity theory**
  positive psychological adjustment associated with continued activity and involvement

- **stages of death and dying**
  (based on work of Kübler-Ross)
  - **denial**
  - **anger**
  - **bargaining**
  - **depression**
  - **acceptance**

PRACTICE QUIZ: PREPARING FOR THE AP* EXAM

ANSWERS ON PAGE AK-3.

Directions: Read each of the questions or incomplete sentences below. Then choose the response that best answers the question or completes the sentence.

1. According to research, if an older person wants to adjust more positively to aging, he or she should _____.
   a. remain active in some way
   b. quietly withdraw from social life
   c. limit his or her range of activities
   d. disengage from busy family duties
   e. accept the inevitability of death

2. In which theory of aging do shortened telomeres become the major result of aging cells?
   a. Activity theory
   b. Free radical theory
   c. Wear-and-tear theory
   d. Cellular clock theory
   e. Hormonal imbalance theory

3. Paulo is an elderly cancer patient whose doctor informs him that he only has a few months left to live. Paulo promises to do everything the doctor says if only the doctor will promise that Paulo can live a little longer. In which stage of reaction to death is Paulo?
   a. Denial
   b. Anger
   c. Bargaining
   d. Depression
   e. Acceptance

---

son's personality before the terminal diagnosis, and other life history factors make the process of dying unique and unpredictable (Kastenbaum & Costa, 1977). The danger in holding too strictly to a stage theory is that people may feel there is a "right" way to face death and a "wrong" way, when in fact each person's dying process is unique.

Applying Psychology to Everyday Life: ADHD—Not Just for Children

10.12 How does attention-deficit hyperactivity disorder affect adults?

Attention-deficit hyperactivity disorder, or *ADHD*, has long been recognized and treated in children, but it is only in the last few decades that professionals have come to understand that ADHD can and often does persist into adulthood (Barkley et al., 2001; Goldstein, 1997; Murphy & LeVert, 1995; Nadeau, 1995). The causes of ADHD are not clear, but there is research pointing to a biological basis, and hereditary factors are a large part of that biological influence (Barkley, 1998; Faraone et al., 1993, 2000). Other contributing factors may include prenatal influences (see the section on teratogens earlier in this chapter), prematurity, high levels of lead in the body, and even prefrontal brain damage. Far from outgrowing this condition, from 30 to 50 percent of all children diagnosed with ADHD will continue to have attentional and behavioral problems as adults that may negatively affect both their professional and personal lives (Barkley et al., 2001; Searight et al., 2000), which could be relieved with treatment.

What are the symptoms of adult ADHD? Although hyperactivity tends to decrease, they are essentially the same as many of the symptoms of children with ADHD but concern issues of work, financial responsibility, and adult activities rather than school and discipline issues that are often seen in children. These symptoms in adults may also be more difficult to separate from other disorders with similar symptoms, such as depression and substance abuse disorders (Searight et al., 2000). Here are a few of the symptoms (Barkley et al., 2001; Wender et al., 2001):

- Failing to pay attention to details or making careless mistakes at work.

- Feeling restless, fidgeting with hands or feet, feeling "driven by a motor."

- Failing to listen when spoken to directly, talking excessively, being chronically late.

- Being impulsive and impatient, blurting out answers before questions are completed.

- Losing things needed for tasks, being disorganized, failing to follow through in work, being easily distracted, interrupting others.

The implications for adult life are serious. Adults with ADHD may also suffer from substance abuse disorders such as alcoholism, low self-esteem, anxiety, depression, mood swings, and problems in personal relationships (Hechtman et al., 1984; Wender et al., 2001). Employment may be endangered by what is seen as irresponsible and even disrespectful behavior in the workplace.

Attention-deficit hyperactivity disorder is often thought of as a disorder of childhood, but many adults may also have difficulties staying organized and on task.

What are the treatments for adults with ADHD? Obviously, diagnosis must be the first goal. People who suspect that they might have adult ADHD should consult a medical expert such as a psychiatrist or psychologist who has experience with ADHD. Adults should educate themselves about this disorder and its symptoms so that they can better recognize those symptoms in their own behavior and try to correct or control the behavior.

Medication, just as in some cases of ADHD in children, can also help adults with ADHD, but in addition to treatment with stimulants, treatment of adults with ADHD may include antidepressants as well (Searight et al., 2000). Although children are seldom encouraged to join a support group for their problem, this is an excellent idea for adults with ADHD. Cognitive-behavioral skills training (therapy that focuses on teaching individuals to think about themselves and their lives in a more rational manner, in addition to interpersonal skills), marital counseling, vocational counseling, other forms of psychotherapy, and perhaps changing occupations to ones that more appropriately fit the personality and energy level of the ADHD adult can also be of great value (Goldstein, 1997; Murphy & LeVert, 1995; Nadeau, 1995; Silver, 2000).

Questions for Further Discussion

1. What kinds of symptoms and behavior might show up in a high scholol or college student with ADHD?

2. What might be appropriate careers for someone with ADHD? What might be careers for which the ADHD adult would not be well suited?

10 CHAPTER SUMMARY

Issues in Studying Human Development

10.1 What are some of the special research methods used to study development?

- Three special research methods used in developmental research are the longitudinal design, the cross-sectional design, and the cross-sequential design.

10.2 What is the relationship between heredity and environmental factors in determining development?

- Behavioral genetics is a field investigating the relative contributions to development of heredity (nature) and environment (nurture). Most developmental psychologists agree that development is a product of an interaction between nature and nurture.

Prenatal Development

10.3 How do chromosomes, genes, and DNA determine a person's characteristics or disorders, and what causes multiple births?

- Dominant genes control the expression of a trait, whereas recessive gene traits are only expressed when paired with another recessive gene for the same trait. Almost all traits are the result of combinations of genes working together in a process called polygenic inheritance.
- Chromosome disorders include Down syndrome, Klinefelter's syndrome, and Turner's syndrome, whereas genetic disorders include PKU, cystic fibrosis, sickle cell anemia, and Tay-Sachs disease.
- The fertilized egg cell is called a zygote and divides into many cells, eventually forming the baby.
- Monozygotic twins are formed when the zygote splits into two separate masses of cells, each of which will develop into a baby identical to the other. When the two masses do not fully separate, conjoined twins occur.
- Dizygotic twins are formed when the mother's body releases multiple eggs and at least two are fertilized, or when another ovulation occurs even though the mother has already become pregnant.

Psychology in the News: Abby and Brittany Hensel, Together for Life

- Conjoined twins Abby and Brittany Hensel are relatively healthy, well adjusted, and participate fully in many normal activities for young people of their age.

10.4 What happens during the germinal, embryonic, and fetal periods of pregnancy and what are some hazards in prenatal development?

- The germinal period is the first two weeks of pregnancy in which the dividing mass of cells (blastocyst) moves down the fallopian tube into the uterus.
- The embryonic period begins at two weeks after conception and ends at eight weeks. The vital organs and structures of the baby form during this period, making it a critical one for teratogens to adversely affect the development of those organs and structures.
- The fetal period is from the beginning of the ninth week until the birth of the baby. During the fetal period, tremendous growth occurs, length and weight increase, and organs continue to become fully functional.

Infancy and Childhood Development

10.5 What kind of physical changes take place in infancy and childhood?

- Four critical areas of adjustment for the newborn are respiration, digestion, circulation, and temperature regulation.

- Infants are born with reflexes that help the infant survive until more complex learning is possible. These reflexes include sucking, rooting, Moro (startle), grasping, and Babinski.
- The senses, except for vision, are fairly well developed at birth. Vision is blurry and lacking in full color perception until about 6 months of age. Gross and fine motor skills develop at a fast pace during infancy and early childhood.

Current Issues in Psychology: The Facts and Myths About Immunizations

- Immunizations are far less dangerous than the diseases they are designed to prevent and are one of the most effective weapons in the fight against infectious diseases.

10.6 What are two ways of looking at cognitive development, and how does language develop?

- Piaget's stages include the sensorimotor stage of sensory and physical interaction with the world, preoperational thought in which language becomes a tool of exploration, concrete operations in which logical thought becomes possible, and formal operations in which abstract concepts are understood and hypothetical thinking develops.
- Vygotsky believed that children learn best when being helped by a more highly skilled peer or adult in a process called scaffolding. The zone of proximal development is the difference between the mental age of tasks the child performs without help and those the child can perform with help.
- The stages of language development are cooing, babbling, one-word speech (holophrases), and telegraphic speech. Although some language is learned through imitation and reinforcement, infants may possess a language acquisition device that governs the learning of language during infancy and early childhood.

10.7 How do infants and children develop personalities and form relationships with others, and what are Erikson's stages of psychosocial development for children?

- The three basic infant temperaments are easy (regular, adaptable, and happy), difficult (irregular, nonadaptable, and irritable), and slow to warm up (need to adjust gradually to change).
- The four types of attachment are secure, avoidant (unattached), ambivalent (insecurely attached), and disorganized-disoriented (insecurely attached and sometimes abused or neglected).
- In trust versus mistrust, the infant must gain a sense of predictability and trust in caregivers or risk developing a mistrustful nature; in autonomy versus shame and doubt the toddler needs to become physically independent.
- In initiative versus guilt the preschool child is developing emotional and psychological independence; in industry versus inferiority school-age children are gaining competence and developing self-esteem.

Classic Studies in Psychology: Harlow and Contact Comfort

- Harlow's classic research with infant Rhesus monkeys demonstrated the importance of contact comfort in the attachment process, contradicting the earlier view that attachment was merely a function of associating the mother with the delivery of food.

How Sex and Gender Influence Development

10.8 What is gender, and how can biology and learning influence gender role development?

- Gender is the psychological aspects of being male or female.
- Gender roles are the culture's expectations for male and female behavior and personality.
- Gender typing is the process by which people in a culture learn the appropriate gender role behavior.
- Gender identity is a person's sense of being male or female.
- There are both biological influences, in the form of hormones and chromosomes, and environmental influences, in the form of parenting, surroundings, and culture, on the formation of gender identity.

Adolescence

- Adolescence is the period of life from about age 13 to the early twenties during which physical development reaches completion.

10.9 What are the physical, cognitive, and personality changes that occur in adolescence, including concepts of morality and Erikson's search for identity?

- Puberty is a period of about four years during which the sexual organs and systems fully mature and during which secondary sex characteristics such as body hair, breasts, menstruation, deepening voices, and the growth spurt occur.
- Adolescents engage in two kinds of egocentric thinking called the imaginary audience and the personal fable.
- Kohlberg proposed three levels of moral development: preconventional morality, conventional morality, and postconventional morality. Gilligan suggested that Kohlberg's ideas applied more to males.
- In Erikson's identity versus role confusion crisis the job of the adolescent is to achieve a consistent sense of self from among all the roles, values, and futures open to him or her.

Adulthood

10.10 What are the physical, cognitive, and personality changes that occur during adulthood and aging, including Erikson's last three psychosocial stages, and patterns of parenting?

- Adulthood begins in the early twenties and ends with death in old age. It can be divided into young adulthood, middle adulthood, and late adulthood.
- The twenties are the peak of physical health; in the thirties the signs of aging become more visible, and in the forties visual problems may occur, weight may increase, strength may decrease, and height begins to decrease.
- Women experience a physical decline in the reproductive system called the climacteric, ending at about age 50 with menopause, when a woman's estrogen levels are at zero and her reproductive capabilities

are at an end. Men go through andropause, a less dramatic change in testosterone and other male hormones, beginning in the forties.

- Many health problems such as high blood pressure, skin cancers, and arthritis begin in middle age, with the most common causes of death in middle age being heart disease, cancer, and stroke.
- Reaction times slow down, but intelligence and memory remain relatively stable.
- Erikson's crisis of young adulthood is intimacy versus isolation, in which the young adult must establish an intimate relationship, usually with a mate.
- The crisis of middle adulthood is generativity versus stagnation, in which the task of the middle-aged adult is to help the next generation through its crises, either by parenting, mentoring, or a career that leaves some legacy to the next generation.
- Baumrind proposed three parenting styles: authoritarian (rigid and uncompromising), authoritative (consistent and strict but warm and flexible), and permissive (either indifferent and unconcerned with the daily activities of the child or indulgent and unwilling to set limits on the child).
- Erikson's final crisis is integrity versus despair, in which an older adult must come to terms with mortality.

10.11 How do psychologists explain why aging occurs, and what are the stages of death and dying?

- Research strongly indicates that remaining active and involved results in the most positive adjustment to aging.
- The cellular clock theory is based on the idea that cells only have so many times that they can reproduce; once that limit is reached, damaged cells begin to accumulate.
- The wear-and-tear theory of physical aging states that as time goes by, repeated use and abuse of the body's tissues cause it to be unable to repair all the damage.
- The free radical theory states that oxygen molecules with an unstable electron move around the cell, damaging cell structures as they go.
- The five stages of reaction to death and dying are denial, anger, bargaining, depression, and acceptance.

Applying Psychology to Everyday Life: ADHD—Not Just for Children

10.12 How does attention-deficit hyperactivity disorder affect adults?

- Many children with ADHD grow up to be adults with ADHD, affecting their work, relationships, and emotional well-being. ADHD in adults can be treated with medication and/or therapy.

TEST YOURSELF: PREPARING FOR THE AP* EXAM

ANSWERS ON PAGE AK-3.

✓ **Practice** on **MyPsychLab**   **Ready for your test?** More quizzes and a customized study plan. **www.mypsychlab.com**

PART I: MULTIPLE-CHOICE QUESTIONS

Directions for Part I: Read each of the questions or incomplete sentences below. Then choose the response that best answers the question or completes the sentence.

1. Which of the following represents dizygotic twins?
   a. One egg is fertilized by two different sperm
   b. One egg splits and is then fertilized by two different sperm
   c. One egg is fertilized by one sperm and then splits
   d. Two eggs are fertilized by two different sperm
   e. Two eggs are fertilized by the same sperm

2. The specialized organ that provides nourishment for the growing baby and filters away waste products is called the _____.
   a. uterus   d. umbilical cord
   b. embryo   e. fallopian tube
   c. placenta

3. Which reflex involves the baby moving its head toward any touch of her cheek?
   a. Sucking
   b. Startle
   c. Rooting
   d. Grasping
   e. Stepping

4. Which of the newborn's senses is the most fully developed at birth?
   a. Hearing
   b. Vision
   c. Smell
   d. Taste
   e. Touch

5. In which of Piaget's stages does the child become capable of understanding conservation?
   a. Sensorimotor
   b. Preoperational
   c. Formal operations
   d. Concrete operations
   e. Abstract operations

6. According to Vygotsky, giving a child help in the form of asking leading questions and providing examples is called _____.
   a. scaffolding
   b. habituation
   c. private speech
   d. child-directed speech
   e. the zone of proximal development

7. Kashif, a toddler, holds his empty cup up to his mother and says, "Milk!" His use of the word is correctly labeled _____.
   a. cooing
   b. babbling
   c. a holophrase
   d. a whole sentence
   e. telegraphic speech

8. Samantha refuses to go to school because her chin has a "huge" pimple on it and she is afraid that everyone will point and laugh at her. Samantha is a victim of _____.
   a. the imaginary audience
   b. the personal fable
   c. abstract egocentrism
   d. formal operations
   e. ego integrity

9. Rebellion during the teenage years is most likely the outcome of which type of parenting?
   a. Passive
   b. Authoritarian
   c. Authoritative
   d. Permissive neglectful
   e. Permissive indulgent

10. Collagen, an elastic tissue that becomes less elastic as we get older, is a good example of which theory of aging?
    a. Active   d. Free radical
    b. Wear-and-tear   e. Integrity versus despair
    c. Cellular clock

PART II: FREE-RESPONSE QUESTION

Directions for Part II: Read the essay question that follows. Then, respond to the question in a clear, concise essay. Do not simply list facts. Instead, present a thorough argument based on your critical consideration of the topic. Use proper psychological terminology as necessary.

Tisha and Ken are a married couple preparing for their first child. They are wondering to what degree their child's appearance, health, personality, and other characteristics will be determined by biology or by environmental factors such as parenting styles and cultural expectations. In a detailed, well-organized essay, discuss three ways in which the child's development will most likely be influenced by biological factors and three ways in which the child's development will most likely be influenced by environmental factors.

10 VISUAL SUMMARY
Development Across the Life Span

10.1–3 — p. 393

Issues in Studying Human Development
(scientific study of changes that occur in people as they age)

- **topics of interest**
  - personality
  - cognition
  - biological processes
  - social interactions
- **research designs**
  - longitudinal
  - cross-sectional
  - cross-sequential

Issues in Studying Human Development
(nature vs. nurture debate)

- **heredity**   **environment**
- most developmental psychologists agree that most likely explanation for most human development is based on the interaction between nature and nurture

Prenatal Development

- **chromosomes, genes, and DNA**
  - **genetics** is the science of heredity
  - **deoxyribonucleic acid (DNA):** contains genetic codes and chromosomes
  - **dominant and recessive genes**
  - **gene and chromosome problems**
- **from conception to birth**
  conception is moment at which female becomes pregnant; conception to birth is approximately 9 months in humans
  - the zygote and twinning

Mother contributes either P or p   Father contributes either P or p

Normal   Carrier   Carrier   Afflicted with PKU

Mother   Father

Carries recessive PKU gene   Carries recessive PKU gene

10.4 — p. 396

Pregnancy

- **the germinal period** (two-week period after fertilization)
  - zygote continues dividing and moving toward the uterus; the placenta and umbilical cord also develop during this time
  - cell differentiation is the process that results in specialized cells for all of the various parts of the body
- **the embryonic period** (two to eight weeks after conception)
  - once attached to the uterus, developing organism is called an **embryo**
  - cell specialization continues to occur, resulting in the preliminary versions of various organs
  - embryo is vulnerable to hazards such as diseases and substances ingested by the mother as it receives nourishment through the placenta
- **the fetal period** (from about eight weeks to birth)
  - developing organism now called a **fetus**; time of tremendous growth and development
  - organs continue to develop and become fully functional
  - muscles begin to contract during the third month, mother can start to feel "flutters" by fourth month, kicks felt by five months
  - full-term birth occurs around end of 38th week
  - miscarriages (spontaneous abortions) are most likely to occur in the first three months

---

10.5–6 — pp. 406–407

Infancy and Childhood Development

- **physical development**
  - immediately after birth, body systems start to function (i.e., respiratory, circulatory, temperature regulation, digestive)
  - babies are born with (innate) reflex behaviors (see Fig. 10.4)
- **sensory development**
  - touch, taste, and smell are well developed
  - hearing is functional but not fully developed
  - vision is least developed (rods are functional, cones take about six months to fully develop)
- **motor development**
  - as with physical and sensory development, normal motor development is related to many factors such as nutrition, care, and health
  - birth to two years = period of rapid development (see Fig. 10.5)

- **Piaget's theory**
  - suggests children form mental concepts or schemes as they experience new situations and events
  - proposes four distinct stages of cognitive development that span infancy to adolescence
- **Vygotsky's theory**
  - stresses the importance of social interactions with others, typically more highly skilled children and adults
  - children's cognitive development occurs when someone helps them by asking leading questions and providing examples of concepts (scaffolding)
  - each child has a zone of proximal development—difference between what they can do alone vs. with aid of a teacher

Infancy and Childhood Development: Cognitive Development

Table 10.3	Piaget's Stages of Cognitive Development	
STAGE		**COGNITIVE DEVELOPMENT**
Sensorimotor	Birth to 2 years old	Children explore the world using their senses and ability to move. They develop object permanence and the understanding that concepts and mental images represent objects, people, and events.
Preoperational	2 to 7 years old	Young children can mentally represent and refer to objects and events with words or pictures and they can pretend. However, they can't conserve, logically reason, or simultaneously consider many characteristics of an object.
Concrete Operations	7 to 12 years old	Children at this stage are able to conserve, reverse their thinking, and classify objects in terms of their many characteristics. They can also think logically and understand analogies but only about concrete events.
Formal Operations	12 years old	People at this stage can use abstract reasoning about hypothetical events or situations, think about logical possibilities, use abstract analogies, and systematically examine and test hypotheses. Not everyone can eventually reason in all these ways.

- **stages of language development**
  - language allows children to think in words, ask questions, communicate needs and wants, and form concepts
  - various views of development
  - universal progressive stages

10.7 p. 413

involves development of personality, relationships, and a sense of being male or female; process begins in infancy and continues into adulthood

- **important early concepts**
  - infants demonstrate personality through their temperament (e.g., easy, difficult, slow to warm up), which can also affect and is affected by parenting and the environment
  - attachment (emotional bond between infant and a primary caregiver) is very important; different attachment styles have been identified by Ainsworth and others (e.g., secure, avoidant, ambivalent, disorganized-disoriented) that appear to be similar, but not identical, across different cultures

- **Erikson's theory**
  - suggests development occurs in a series of eight stages (see Table 10.4)
  - at each stage an emotional crisis must be successfully met for normal development to occur

Infancy and Childhood Development:
Psychosocial Development

Table 10.4   Erikson's Psychosocial Stages of Development

STAGE	DEVELOPMENTAL CRISIS	SUCCESSFUL DEALING WITH CRISIS	UNSUCCESSFUL DEALING WITH CRISIS
1. Infant Birth to 1 year old	**Trust Versus Mistrust** Babies learn to trust or mistrust others based on whether or not their needs—such as food and comfort—are met.	If babies' needs are met, they learn to trust people and expect life to be pleasant.	If babies' needs are not met, they learn not to trust.
2. Toddler 1 to 3 years old	**Autonomy Versus Shame and Doubt** Toddlers realize that they can direct their own behavior.	If toddlers are successful in directing their own behavior, they learn to be independent.	If toddlers' attempts at being independent are blocked, they learn self-doubt and shame for being unsuccessful.
3. Preschool Age 3 to 5 years old	**Initiative Versus Guilt** Preschoolers are challenged to control their own behavior, such as controlling their exuberance when they are in a restaurant.	If preschoolers succeed in taking responsibility, they feel capable and develop initiative.	If preschoolers fail in taking responsibility, they feel irresponsible, anxious, and guilty.
4. Elementary School Age 5 to 12 years old	School-aged children are faced with learning new social and academic skills. Social comparison is a primary source of information.	When children succeed at learning new skills, they develop a sense of industry, a feeling of competence and self-esteem arising from their work and effort.	If children fail to develop new abilities, they feel incompetent, inadequate, and inferior.
5. Adolescence 13 to early twenties	**Identity Versus Role Confusion** Adolescents are faced with deciding who or what they want to be in terms of occupation, beliefs, attitudes, and behavior patterns.	Adolescents who succeed in defining who they are and finding a role for themselves develop a strong sense of identity.	Adolescents who fail to define their identity become confused and withdraw or want to inconspicuously blend in with the crowd.
6. Early Adulthood Twenties and thirties	**Intimacy Versus Isolation** The task facing those in early adulthood is to be able to share who they are with another person in a close, committed relationship.	People who succeed in this task will have satisfying intimate relationships.	Adults who fail at this task will be isolated from other people and may suffer from loneliness.
7. Middle Adulthood Forties and fifties	**Generativity Versus Stagnation** The challenge is to be creative, productive, and nurturant of the next generation.	Adults who succeed in this challenge will be creative, productive, and nurturant, thereby benefiting themselves, their family, community, country, and future generations.	Adults who fail will be passive, and self-centered, feel that they have done nothing for the next generation, and feel that the world is no better off for their being alive.
8. Late Adulthood Sixties and beyond	**Ego Integrity Versus Despair** The issue is whether a person will reach wisdom, spiritual tranquility, a sense of wholeness, and acceptance of his or her life.	Elderly people who succeed in addressing this issue will enjoy life and not fear death.	Elderly people who fail will feel that their life is empty and will fear death.

10.8 p. 415

How Sex and Gender Influence Development

- **key concepts**
  - **gender roles:** cultural behavioral expectations for males or females
  - **biological processes:** process by which people learn gender roles
  - **social interactions:** sense of being male or female (influenced by both biology and environment)

gender is defined as the psychological aspects of being masculine or feminine and is influenced by culture, individual personality, and self-identity

- **biological influences:** sexual characteristics of the genitals, hormonal differences, and possible differences in brain structure and processing
- **environmental influences:** parental influences and cultural expectations to adhere to gender roles
- **culture:** individualistic/nontraditional role adoption versus collectivistic/traditional role adoption

10.9 p. 419

Adolescence
(period of life from about age 13 to early 20s)

- **physical development**
  - increase in height and changes in both primary and secondary sex characteristics
  - occurs as the result of glandular and hormonal activities
  - tends to occur about two years after beginning of growth spurt

- **cognitive development**
  - final maturation of the frontal lobes allows cognitive advances (e.g., abstract thought/Piaget's formal operations)
  - despite advances, still have egocentric thought that emerges in a variety of ways

- **moral development**
  - understanding of what is "right" and "wrong"
  - early theory was proposed by Kohlberg; suggested three levels of moral development
  - other researchers (e.g., Gilligan) suggest that Kohlberg's ideas applied more to males; others suggest that assessment was based on hypothetical, rather than real-life, dilemmas

- **psychosocial development**
  - adolescence is largely marked by the search for a consistent sense of self or personal identity
  - Erikson: the psychosocial crisis that must be resolved is identity vs. role confusion
  - parent/teen conflict to be expected

IT'S FUNNY, BUT GIRLS ARE A LOT MORE INTERESTING THIS YEAR THAN THEY WERE LAST YEAR

THEY'RE MORE INTERESTING TO ME TOO

I WONDER WHAT THEY DID TO THEMSELVES

10.10 p. 424

Adulthood
(period of life from early 20s until old age and death; age of onset can vary by culture)

- **physical development**
  - young adulthood
  - middle age
  - late adulthood

- **cognitive development**
  - cognitive skills often highest in 20s; processing and reaction time slow in middle age but are often compensated by greater life and situational knowledge
  - memory issues begin in middle age, likely due to stress and information overload
  - mental abilities aided by active cognitive engagement (challenging crossword puzzles, reading, etc.) and physical activity

- **psychosocial development**
  - typical life concerns involve career, relationships, family, and approaching old age
  - Erikson's stages (see Table 10.6)

10.11 p. 427

"Elise is still waiting for postmenopausal zest to kick in."

Adulthood: Aging

- **theories on aging**
  vary focus from biological changes to influence on external stressors
  - **cellular clock theory**
  - **wear-and-tear theory**

- **activity theory**
  - positive psychological adjustment associated with continued activity and involvement

- **stages of death and dying**
  (based on work of Kübler-Ross)
  - **denial**
  - **anger**
  - **bargaining**
  - **depression**
  - **acceptance**

11
Theories of Personality

Not-So-Identical Twins

Many people have heard the story of the "Jim" twins, James Arthur Springer and James Edward Lewis, identical twins separated at the age of 1 month. At age 39 Springer and Lewis were the first set of twins studied by University of Minnesota psychologist Thomas Bouchard, who examined the differences and similarities between identical and fraternal twins raised apart from each other (Bouchard et al., 1990).

The two "Jims" shared interests in mechanical drawing and carpentry, a love of math and a dread of spelling in high school, and smoked and drank the same amount. It is understandable that many researchers attribute these similarities to the shared genetic material of the "Jim" twins. But Springer and Lewis were both raised in Ohio by parents from relatively similar socioeconomic backgrounds—how much of their similarity to each other might be due to those conditions? And how would genetics explain that they both divorced women named Linda before marrying women named Betty? Are there genes for "divorce Linda, marry Betty?" Obviously not.

Then there's the case of Oskar and Jack. Like the "Jim" twins, they also exhibited a number of similarities in personality and behavior. No one would accuse Oskar and Jack of being raised in similar environments, however. Born in Trinidad at the time Hitler was rising to power, Jack Yufe was raised by their Jewish father in Trinidad as a Jew, while their mother took Oskar Stohr to occupied Czechoslovakia, where he attended a Nazi-run school and was at one time a Hitler youth. In terms of environment, Oskar and Jack were not-so-identical twins.

If the researchers in the twin study had dug a little deeper, they would also have found countless differences between the twins in the study. To automatically assume that similarities between identical twins are all caused by genetic influences and that differences are caused by environmental influences is bad science. The fact is that any two randomly selected people will find that they have countless things in common, none of which is likely to be caused by hereditary factors.

Why study personality? Personality is the sum total of who you are—your attitudes and reactions, both physical and emotional. It's what makes each person different from every other person in the world. How can any study of human behavior not include the study of who we are and how we got to be that way?

chapter outline

THEORIES OF PERSONALITY

THE MAN AND THE COUCH: SIGMUND FREUD
AND THE PSYCHODYNAMIC PERSPECTIVE

THE BEHAVIORIST AND SOCIAL COGNITIVE VIEW OF PERSONALITY

THE THIRD FORCE: HUMANISM AND PERSONALITY

TRAIT THEORIES: WHO ARE YOU?

THE BIOLOGY OF PERSONALITY: BEHAVIORAL GENETICS

CLASSIC STUDIES IN PSYCHOLOGY:
Geert Hofstede's Four Dimensions of Cultural Personality

ASSESSMENT OF PERSONALITY

APPLYING PSYCHOLOGY TO EVERYDAY LIFE:
Personality Testing on the Internet

11 Learning Objectives

- **11.1** What is personality, and how do the various perspectives in psychology view personality?

- **11.2** How did Freud's historical view of the mind and personality form a basis for psychodynamic theory?

- **11.3** How did Jung, Adler, Horney, and Erikson modify Freud's theory?

- **11.4** How does modern psychoanalytic theory differ from that of Freud?

- **11.5** How do behaviorists and social cognitive theorists explain personality?

- **11.6** How do humanists such as Carl Rogers explain personality?

- **11.7** What are the history and current views of the trait perspective?

- **11.8** What part do biology, heredity, and culture play in personality?

- **11.9** What are the advantages and disadvantages of the following measures of personality: interviews, projective tests, behavioral assessment, personality inventories, and online personality tests?

Theories of Personality

AP* Compare and contrast the major theories and approaches to explaining personality.

▶ **11.1** What is personality, and how do the various perspectives in psychology view personality?

Personality is the unique way in which each individual thinks, acts, and feels throughout life. Personality should not be confused with **character**, which refers to value judgments made about a person's morals or ethical behavior; nor should it be confused with **temperament**, the enduring characteristics with which each person is born, such as irritability or adaptability. Temperament is based in one's biology, either through genetic influences, prenatal influences, or a combination of those influences, and forms the basis upon which one's larger personality is built. Both character and temperament are vital parts of personality, however.

Personality is an area of the still relatively young field of psychology in which there are several ways in which the characteristic behavior of human beings can be explained. One reason that there is not yet one single explanation of personality that all can agree on is that personality is still difficult to measure precisely and scientifically. At present, there are four main perspectives, or viewpoints, in personality theory:

- The *psychodynamic perspective* had its beginnings in the work of Sigmund Freud and still exists today. It focuses on the role of the unconscious mind in the development of personality. This perspective is also heavily focused on biological causes of personality differences.

- The *behaviorist perspective* is based on the theories of learning as discussed in Chapter Five. This approach focuses on the effect of the environment on behavior.

- The *humanistic perspective* first arose as a reaction against the psychoanalytic and behaviorist perspectives and focuses on the role of each person's conscious life experiences and choices in personality development.

- The *trait perspective* differs from the other three in its basic goals: The psychoanalytic, behaviorist, and humanistic perspectives all seek to explain the process that causes personality to form into its unique characteristics, whereas trait theorists are more concerned with the end result—the characteristics themselves. Although some trait theorists assume that traits are biologically determined, others make no such assumption.

personality the unique and relatively stable ways in which people think, feel, and behave.

character value judgments of a person's moral and ethical behavior.

temperament the enduring characteristics with which each person is born.

The Man and the Couch: Sigmund Freud and the Psychodynamic Perspective

FREUD'S CULTURAL BACKGROUND

It's hard to understand how Freud developed his ideas about personality without knowledge of the world in which he and his patients lived. Born in the Austro-Hungarian Empire in 1856, Freud's family moved to Vienna when he was only 4 years old. He lived there until 1938, when Germany occupied Austria, and Freud, of Jewish background, moved to England to escape the Nazis. During this time period, Europe was in what is commonly known as the Victorian Age, named for Queen Victoria of Great Britain. The Victorian Age, as discussed in Chapter One, was a time of sexual repression. People growing up in this period were told by their church that sex should take place only in the context of marriage and then only to make babies. To enjoy sexual intercourse was considered a sin. Freud's focus on sexual explanations for abnormal behavior seems more understandable in light of this cultural background.

Freud came to believe that there were layers of consciousness in the mind. His belief in the influence of the unconscious mind on conscious behavior, published in *The Psychopathology of Everyday Life* (Freud, 1901), shocked the Victorian world.

Sigmund Freud (1856–1939), founder of the psychodynamic movement in psychology.

11.2 How did Freud's historical view of the mind and personality form a basis for psychodynamic theory?

AP* Identify key contributors to personality theory.

AP* Identify key contributors in developmental psychology.

AP* Identify major figures in psychological treatment.

THE UNCONSCIOUS MIND

Freud believed that the mind was divided into three parts: the preconscious, conscious, and unconscious minds (Freud, 1904). (See Figure 11.1.) While no one really disagreed with the idea of a conscious mind in which one's current awareness exists, or even of a preconscious mind containing memories, information, and events of which one can easily become aware, the **unconscious mind** (also called "the unconscious") was the real departure for the professionals of Freud's day. Freud theorized that there is a part of the mind that remains hidden at all times, surfacing only in symbolic form in dreams and in some of the behavior people engage in without knowing why they have done so. Even when a person makes a determined effort to bring a memory out of the unconscious mind, it will not appear directly, according to Freud. Freud believed that the unconscious mind was the most important determining factor in human behavior and personality.

THE DIVISIONS OF THE PERSONALITY

Freud believed, based on observations of his patients, that personality itself could be divided into three parts, each existing at one or more levels of conscious awareness (see Figure 11.1). The way these three parts of the personality develop and interact with one another became the heart of his theory (Freud, 1923, 1933, 1940).

unconscious mind level of the mind in which thoughts, feelings, memories, and other information are kept that are not easily or voluntarily brought into consciousness.

---

*Virtuous: morally excellent.

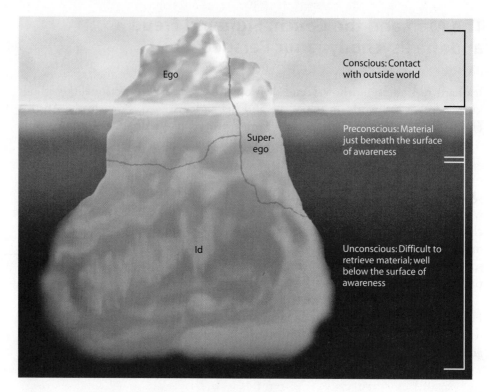

Figure 11.1 **Freud's Conception of the Personality**

This iceberg represents the three levels of the mind. The part of the iceberg visible above the surface is the conscious mind. Just below the surface is the preconscious mind, everything that is not yet part of the conscious mind. Hidden deep below the surface is the unconscious mind, feelings, memories, thoughts, and urges that cannot be easily brought into consciousness. While two of the three parts of the personality (ego and superego) exist at all three levels of awareness, the id is completely in the unconscious mind.

Id: If It Feels Good, Do It   The first and most primitive part of the personality, present in the infant, is the **id**. *Id* is a Latin word that means "it." The id is a completely unconscious, pleasure-seeking, amoral part of the personality that exists at birth, containing all of the basic biological drives: hunger, thirst, self-preservation, and sex, for example.

People do seem to be pleasure-seeking creatures, and even infants seek pleasure from sucking and chewing on anything they can get into their mouths. In fact, thinking about what infants are like when they are just born provides a good picture of the id. Infants are demanding, irrational, illogical, and impulsive. They want their needs satisfied immediately, and they don't care about anyone else's needs or desires. (A word of caution: The fact that infant behavior seems to fit Freud's concept of the id is not proof that the id exists. It simply means that Freud came up with the concept of the id to fit what he already knew about infants.)

Freud called this need for satisfaction the **pleasure principle**, which can be defined as the desire for immediate gratification of needs with no regard for the consequences. The pleasure principle can be summed up simply as "if it feels good, do it."

Ego: The Executive Director   People normally try to satisfy an infant's needs as quickly as possible. Infants are fed when hungry, changed when wet, and tended to whenever

id part of the personality present at birth and completely unconscious.

pleasure principle principle by which the id functions; the immediate satisfaction of needs without regard for the consequences.

they cry. But as infants begin to grow, adults start denying them their every wish. There will be things they cannot touch or hold, and they must learn to wait for certain things, such as food. Freud would say that reality has reared its ugly head, and the id simply cannot deal with the reality of having to wait or not getting what it wants. Worse still would be the possibility of punishment as a result of the id's unrestrained actions.

According to Freud, to deal with reality, a second part of the personality develops called the **ego**. The ego, from the Latin word for "I," is mostly conscious and is far more rational, logical, and cunning than the id. The ego works on the **reality principle**, which is the need to satisfy the demands of the id only in ways that will not lead to negative consequences. This means that sometimes the ego decides to deny the id its desires because the consequences would be painful or too unpleasant.

For example, while an infant might reach out and take an object despite a parent's protests, a toddler with the developing ego will avoid taking the object when the parent says, "No!" to avoid punishment—but may go back for the object when the parent is not looking. A simpler way of stating the reality principle, then, is "if it feels good, do it, but only if you can get away with it."

Superego: The Moral Watchdog

If everyone acted on the pleasure principle, the world would be pretty scary. How does knowing right from wrong come into Freud's theory? Freud called the third and final part of the personality, the moral center of personality, the **superego**. The superego (also Latin, meaning "over the self") develops as a preschool-aged child learns the rules, customs, and expectations of society. The super ego contains the **conscience**, the part of the personality that makes people feel pride when they do the right thing and guilt, or *moral anxiety*, when they do the wrong thing. It is not until the conscience develops that children have a sense of right and wrong. (Note that the term *conscience* is a different word from *conscious*. They may look and sound similar, but they represent totally different concepts.) ✽⎡Explore on MyPsychLab

The Angel, the Devil, and Me: How the Three Parts of the Personality Work Together

Anyone who has ever watched cartoons while growing up has probably seen these three parts of the personality shown in animated form—the id is usually a little devil, the superego an angel, and the ego is the person or animal caught in the middle, trying to decide what action to take. Images such as these appear often in animated films, with one of the more recent examples in *The Emperor's New Groove* when a character argues with his angel and devil over disposing of the emperor.

So, the id makes demands, the superego puts restrictions on how those demands can be met, and the ego has to come up with a plan that will quiet the id but satisfy the superego. Sometimes the id or the superego does not get its way, resulting in a great deal of anxiety for the ego itself. This constant state of conflict is Freud's view of how personality works; it is only when the anxiety created by this conflict gets out of hand that disordered behavior arises.

The *psychological defense mechanisms* are ways of dealing with stress through unconsciously distorting one's perception of reality. These defense mechanisms were mainly outlined and studied by Freud's daughter, Anna Freud, who was a psychoanalyst (Benjafield, 1996; A. Freud, 1946). In order for the three parts of the personality to function, the constant conflict among them must be managed, and Freud assumed that the defense mechanisms were one of the most important tools for dealing with the anxiety caused by this conflict. A list of the defense mechanisms, their definitions, and examples of each appears in Table 9.3 in Chapter Nine. ⦿⦿⦿ *to Chapter Nine: Stress and Health, p. 375.*

---

ego part of the personality that develops out of a need to deal with reality, mostly conscious, rational, and logical.

reality principle principle by which the ego functions; the satisfaction of the demands of the id only when negative consequences will not result.

superego part of the personality that acts as a moral center.

conscience part of the superego that produces pride or guilt, depending on how acceptable behavior is.

◀ If everyone acted on the pleasure principle, the world would be pretty scary. How does knowing right from wrong come into Freud's theory?

✽ **Explore** The Id, Ego and Superego.
www.mypsychlab.com

11.1

- **personality**
  unique way in which each individual thinks, acts, and feels throughout life

- **perspectives/theories**
  different ways of viewing and explaining personality
  - **psychodynamic:** based on work of Freud; primary focus is on role of unconscious mind
  - **behavioral and social cognitive views:** focus on the effect of the environment on behavior; based on theories of learning
  - **humanistic:** focuses on conscious life experiences and choices
  - **trait:** focuses on characteristics themselves, not roots of personality

- **psychodynamic perspective**
  basic aspects
  - mind made up of different levels of awareness—conscious, preconscious, and unconscious
  - personality stems from interplay and conflict between demands made by the id, restrictions set forth by the superego, and direction by the ego
  - disordered behavior is product of constant conflict and anxiety; ego uses unconscious defense mechanisms as ways to manage anxiety/conflict among three parts of personality (see Table 9.3)

Theories of Personality

PRACTICE QUIZ: PREPARING FOR THE AP* EXAM

ANSWERS ON PAGE AK-3.

Directions: Read each of the questions or incomplete sentences below. Then choose the response that best answers the question or completes the sentence.

1. Although Chien's parents have told him that he attended his grandmother's funeral when he was 9 years old, he has no memory of the funeral. Freud would most likely argue that Chien's memory of the funeral is in the _____.
   a. ego
   b. superego
   c. conscious mind
   d. unconscious mind
   e. preconscious mind

2. Which of Freud's parts of the personality is most like a director?
   a. Id
   b. Ego
   c. Superego
   d. Conscience
   e. Unconscious

3. According to Freud, which part of the personality makes the person feel pride when doing the right thing?
   a. Id
   b. Ego
   c. Conscience
   d. Unconscious
   e. Preconscious

4. The enduring characteristics with which people are born, such as irritability or adaptability, are known collectively as _____.
   a. ethics
   b. morality
   c. character
   d. personality
   e. temperament

5. Which of the following operates on the pleasure principle?
   a. Id
   b. Ego
   c. Superego
   d. Conscience
   e. Unconscious

> So the id exists at birth, but the other two parts of the personality develop later—how much later? When is personality finished?

STAGES OF PERSONALITY DEVELOPMENT

So the id exists at birth, but the other two parts of the personality develop later—how much later? When is personality finished?

For Freud, the three parts of the personality develop in a series of stages. He believed that at each stage, a different *erogenous zone*, or area of the body that produces pleasurable feelings, becomes important and can become the source of conflicts. Conflicts that are not fully resolved can result in **fixation**, or getting "stuck" to some degree in a stage of development. The child may grow into an adult but will still carry emotional and psychological "baggage" from that earlier fixated stage.

Because Freud believed that the personality, or *psyche*, develops as a result of sexual development, he called these the **psychosexual stages** of personality development.

fixation disorder in which the person does not fully resolve the conflict in a particular psychosexual stage, resulting in personality traits and behavior associated with that earlier stage.

psychosexual stages five stages of personality development proposed by Freud and tied to the sexual development of the child.

oral stage first stage occurring in the first year of life in which the mouth is the erogenous zone and weaning is the primary conflict.

anal stage second stage occurring from about 1 to 3 years of age, in which the anus is the erogenous zone and toilet training is the source of conflict.

anal expulsive personality a person fixated in the anal stage who is messy, destructive, and hostile.

anal retentive personality a person fixated in the anal stage who is neat, fussy, stingy, and stubborn.

phallic stage third stage occurring from about 3 to 6 years of age, in which the child discovers sexual feelings.

Oral Stage: Weaning and Oral Fixation   The first stage is called the **oral stage** because the erogenous zone is the mouth. This stage occurs from the birth of the infant to about 1 or $1\frac{1}{2}$ years and is dominated by the id. The conflict that can arise here, according to Freud, will be over weaning (taking the mother's breast away from the child, who will now drink from a cup). Weaning that occurs too soon or too late can result in too little or too much satisfaction of the child's oral needs, resulting in the activities and personality traits associated with an orally fixated adult personality: overeating, drinking too much, talking too much, nail biting, gum chewing, and a tendency to be either too dependent and optimistic (when the oral needs are overindulged) or too aggressive and pessimistic (when the oral needs are underindulged).

Anal Stage: Toilet Training and Anal Fixation   As the child becomes a toddler (1 or $1\frac{1}{2}$ years to 3 years), Freud believed that the erogenous zone moves from the mouth to the anus. This stage is, therefore, called the **anal stage**.

Freud thought that the main area of conflict here is toilet training, the demand that the child use the toilet at a particular time and in a particular way. This invasion of reality is part of the process that stimulates the development of the ego during this stage. Fixation in the anal stage, from toilet training that is too harsh, can take one of two forms. The child who rebels openly against the demands of the parents and other adults will refuse to go in the toilet, instead defecating where and when he or she feels like doing it. According to Freud, this translates in the adult as a person who sees messiness as a statement of personal control and who is somewhat destructive and hostile. These **anal expulsive personalities** are what most people would call "slobs." Some children, however, are terrified of making a mess and rebel passively—refusing to go at all or retaining the feces. No mess, no punishment. As adults, they are stingy, stubborn, and excessively neat. This type is called the **anal retentive personality**.

Phallic Stage   As the child grows older (3 to 6 years), the erogenous zone finally shifts to the genitals. Children have discovered the differences between the sexes by now, and this awakening of sexual curiosity and interest in the genitals is the beginning of what Freud termed the **phallic stage**. (The word *phallic* comes

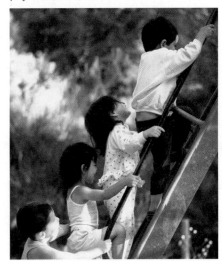

Oedipus complex situation occurring in the phallic stage in which a child develops a sexual attraction to the opposite-sex parent and jealousy of the same-sex parent.

identification defense mechanism in which a person tries to become like someone else to deal with anxiety.

latency fourth stage occurring during the school years, in which the sexual feelings of the child are repressed while the child develops in other ways.

from the Greek word *phallos* and means "penis.") Freud believed that when boys realized that the little girl down the street had no penis they developed a fear of losing the penis called *castration anxiety,* while girls developed *penis envy* because they were missing a penis. If this seems an odd focus on male anatomy, remember the era—the Western world at that time was very male oriented and male dominated. Fortunately, nearly all psychoanalysts have long since abandoned the concept of penis envy (Horney, 1939, 1973; Slipp, 1993). The conflict in the phallic stage centers on the awakening sexual feelings of the child. Freud essentially believed that boys develop both sexual attraction to their mothers and jealousy of their fathers during this stage, a phenomenon called the **Oedipus complex**. (Oedipus was a king in a Greek tragedy who unknowingly killed his father and married his mother.)

The sexual attraction is not that of an adult male for a female but more of a sexual curiosity that becomes mixed up with the boy's feelings of love and affection for his mother. Of course, his jealousy of his father leads to feelings of anxiety and fears that his father, a powerful authority figure, might get angry and do something terrible. To deal with this anxiety, two things must occur by the time the phallic stage ends. The boy will *repress* his sexual feelings for his mother and *identify* with his father. **Identification**, as discussed in Chapter Nine, is a defense mechanism used to combat anxiety. The boy tries to be just like his father in every way, taking on the father's behavior, mannerisms, values, and moral beliefs as his own, so that Daddy won't be able to get angry with the boy. Girls go through a similar process, with their father the target of their affections and their mother as the rival. The result of identification is the development of the superego, the internalized moral values of the same-sex parent.

What happens when things go wrong? Freud argued that if a child does not have a same-sex parent with whom to identify, or if the opposite-sex parent encourages the sexual attraction, fixation can occur. Fixation in the phallic stage usually involves immature sexual attitudes and excessive vanity as an adult. Men with this fixation may be "mama's boys" who never quite grow up, and women may look for much older father figures to marry.

Now the child is about 6 years old and, if passage through the first three stages was successfully accomplished, has all three parts of the personality in place. What next? The personality may be in place, but the place it is in is only 6 years old. Freud named two more periods, one a kind of "holding pattern" and the other the final coming to terms with one's own sexuality.

Latency Stage: Boys Have Cooties and Girls are Yucky   Remember that by the end of the phallic stage, children have pushed their sexual feelings into the unconscious in another defensive reaction, repression. From age 6 to the onset of puberty, children will remain in this stage of hidden, or *latent,* sexual feelings, so this stage is called **latency**. In this stage, children grow and develop intellectually, physically, and socially but not sexually. This is the age at which boys play with other boys, girls play only with girls, and each thinks the opposite sex is pretty awful.

Genital Stage   When puberty does begin, the sexual feelings that were once repressed can no longer be ignored. Bodies are changing and sexual urges are once more allowed into consciousness. Since Freud tied personality development into sexual development, the genital stage represented the final process in Freud's personality theory as well as the entry into adult social and sexual behavior. Table 11.1 summarizes the stages of the psychosexual theory of personality development. ✱⌐Explore on **MyPsychLab**

✱ **Explore** Freud's psychosexual stages of personality development. **www.mypsychlab.com**

Table 11.1 Freud's Psychosexual Stages

STAGE	AGE	FOCUS OF PLEASURE	FOCUS OF CONFLICTS	DIFFICULTIES AT THIS STAGE AFFECT LATER . . .
Oral	Birth to $1\frac{1}{2}$ years old	Oral activities (such as sucking, feeding, and making noises with the mouth)	Weaning	• Ability to form interpersonal attachments • Basic feelings about the world • Tendency to use oral forms of aggression, such as sarcasm • Optimism or pessimism • Tendency to take charge or be passive
Anal	$1\frac{1}{2}$ to 3 years old	Bowel and bladder control	Toilet training	• Sense of competence and control • Stubbornness or willingness to go along with others • Neatness or messiness • Punctuality or tardiness
Phallic	3 to 6 years old	Genitals	Sexual awareness	• Development of conscience through identification with same-sex parent • Pride or humility
Latency	6 years old to puberty	Social skills (such as the ability to make friends) and intellectual skills; Dormant period in terms of psychosexual development	School, play, same-sex friendships	• Ability to get along with others
Genital	Puberty to death	Sexual behavior	Sexual relationship with partner	• Immature love or indiscriminate hate • Uncontrollable working or inability to work

Note: Freud thought that the way a person finds pleasure or is prevented from satisfying urges for pleasure at each stage affects personality. Thus, like Erikson's stage model described in Chapter Ten, Freud's model argues that the way a person deals with particular psychological challenges or potential areas of conflict has long-term effects on personality.

THE NEO-FREUDIANS

11.3 How did Jung, Adler, Horney, and Erikson modify Freud's theory?

◀ **AP*** Identify key contributors to personality theory.

At first Freud's ideas were met with resistance and ridicule by the growing community of doctors and psychologists. Eventually, a number of early psychoanalysts, objecting to Freud's emphasis on biology and particularly on sexuality, broke away from a strict interpretation of psychoanalytic theory, instead altering the focus of **psychoanalysis** (the term Freud applied to both his explanation of the workings of the unconscious mind and the development of personality and the therapy he based on that theory) to the impact of the social environment. At the same time they retained many of Freud's original concepts such as the id, ego, superego, and the defense mechanisms. These early psychoanalysts became the **neo-Freudians**, or "new" Freudian psychoanalysts. This section briefly covers some of the more famous neo-Freudians.

Jung   Carl Gustav Jung ("YOONG") disagreed with Freud about the nature of the unconscious mind. Jung believed that the unconscious held much more than personal fears, urges, and memories. He believed that there was not only a **personal unconscious**, as described by Freud, but a **collective unconscious** as well (Jung, 1933).

psychoanalysis Freud's term for both the theory of personality and the therapy based on it.

neo-Freudians followers of Freud who developed their own competing psychodynamic theories.

personal unconscious Jung's name for the unconscious mind as described by Freud.

collective unconscious Jung's name for the memories shared by all members of the human species.

Watch a classic video on the unconscious with Carl Jung.
www.mypsychlab.com

Carl Jung (1875–1961) was a Swiss psychoanalyst who eventually broke away from Freud's emphasis on the sexual content of the unconscious mind. He formed his own theory of analysis known as analytical psychology.

Dr. Karen Horney (1885–1952) took issue with Freud's emphasis on sexuality, especially the concept of penis envy. She emphasized the importance of feelings of basic anxiety in personality development during early childhood.

archetypes   Jung's collective, universal human memories.

basic anxiety   anxiety created when a child is born into the bigger and more powerful world of older children and adults.

neurotic personalities   personalities typified by maladaptive ways of dealing with relationships in Horney's theory.

According to Jung, the collective unconscious contains a kind of "species" or "racial" memory, memories of ancient fears and themes that seem to occur in many folktales and cultures. These collective, universal human memories were called **archetypes** by Jung. There are many archetypes, but two of the more well known are the *anima/animus* (the feminine side of a man/the masculine side of a woman) and the *shadow* (the dark side of personality, called the Devil in Western cultures). The side of one's personality that is shown to the world is termed the *persona*. **Watch on MyPsychLab**

Adler   Alfred Adler was also in disagreement with Freud over the importance of sexuality in personality development. Adler (1954) developed the theory that as young, helpless children, people all develop feelings of inferiority when comparing themselves to the more powerful, superior adults in their world. The driving force behind all human endeavors, emotions, and thoughts for Adler was not the seeking of pleasure but the seeking of superiority. The defense mechanism of *compensation*, in which people try to overcome feelings of inferiority in one area of life by striving to be superior in another area, figured prominently in Adler's theory. **LINK** *to Chapter Nine: Stress and Health, p. 375.*

Adler (1954) also developed a theory that the birth order of a child affected personality. Firstborn children with younger siblings feel inferior once those younger siblings get all the attention and often overcompensate by becoming overachievers. Middle children have it slightly easier, getting to feel superior over the dethroned older child while dominating younger siblings. They tend to be very competitive. Younger children are supposedly pampered and protected but feel inferior because they are not allowed the freedom and responsibility of the older children. Although some researchers have found evidence to support Adler's birth order theory (Stein, 2001; Sulloway, 1996), and some have even linked birth order to career choices (Leong et al., 2001; Watkins & Savickas, 1990), other researchers point to sloppy methodology and the bias of researchers toward the birth order idea (Beer & Horn, 2001; Freese et al., 1999; Ioannidis, 1998).

Horney   Karen Horney ("HORN-EYE") did not study directly with Freud but studied his work and taught psychoanalysis at the Psychoanalytic Institutes of Berlin and New York (1967, 1973). She left the institute because of disagreements with Freud over the differences between males and females and the concept of penis envy, with which she strongly disagreed. She countered with her own concept of "womb envy," stating that men felt the need to compensate for their lack of childbearing ability by striving for success in other areas (Burger, 1997).

Rather than focusing on sexuality, Horney focused on the child's sense of **basic anxiety**, the anxiety created in a child born into a world that is so much bigger and more powerful than the child. While people whose parents gave them love, affection, and security would overcome this anxiety, others with less secure upbringings would develop **neurotic personalities** and maladaptive ways of dealing with relationships. Some children, according to Horney, try to deal with their anxiety by moving toward people, becoming dependent and clingy. Others move against people, becoming aggressive, demanding, and cruel. A third way of coping would be to move away from people by withdrawing from personal relationships.

Erikson   Erik Erikson (1950, 1959, 1982) was an art teacher who became a psychoanalyst by studying with Anna Freud. He also broke away from Freud's emphasis on sex, preferring instead to emphasize the social relationships that are important at every stage of life. Erikson's eight psychosocial stages are discussed in detail in Chapter Ten. (LINK) *to Chapter Ten: Development Across the Life Span, p. 412.*

It sounds as if all of these theorists became famous by ditching some of Freud's original ideas. Is Freud even worth studying anymore?

CURRENT THOUGHTS ON FREUD AND THE PSYCHODYNAMIC PERSPECTIVE

11.4 How does modern psychoanalytic theory differ from that of Freud?

Although Freud's psychoanalytic theory seems less relevant in today's sexually saturated world, many of his concepts have remained useful and still form a basis for many modern personality theories. As mentioned in Chapter Nine, the idea of the defense mechanisms has research support. The concept of an unconscious mind also has some research support. As strange as the idea of an unconscious mind that guides behavior must have seemed to Freud's contemporaries, modern researchers have had to admit that there are influences on human behavior that exist outside of normal conscious awareness. Although much of this research has taken place in the area of hypnosis and subliminal perception (Borgeat & Goulet, 1983; Bryant & McConkey, 1989; Kihlstrom, 1987, 1999, 2001), other researchers have looked at the concept of implicit memory and implicit learning (Frensch & Runger, 2003). (LINK) *to Chapter Six: Memory, p. 231.*

Criticisms of the Psychodynamic Perspective   This might be a good time to point out a very important fact about Freud's theory: He did no experiments to arrive at his conclusions about personality. His theory is based on his own observations (case studies) of numerous patients. Basing his suppositions on his patients' detailed memories of their childhoods and life experiences, he interpreted their behavior and reminiscences to develop his theory of psychoanalysis. He felt free to interpret what his patients told him of their childhoods as fantasy or fact, depending on how well those memories fit in with his developing theory. For example, many of Freud's patients told him that they were abused by fathers, brothers, and other close family members. Freud was apparently unable to accept these memories as real and decided that they were fantasies, making them the basis of the Oedipal conflict. He actually revised his original perceptions of his patients' memories of abuse as real in the face of both public and professional criticism from his German colleagues (Masson, 1984).

Freud based much of his interpretations of a patient's problems on the interpretations of dreams (LINK) *to Chapter Four: Consciousness: Sleep, Dreams, Hypnosis, and Drugs, p. 148.* and the results of the patient's free association (talking about anything without fear of negative feedback). These "sources" of information are often criticized as being too ambiguous and without scientific support for the validity of his interpretations. The very ambiguity of these sources of information allowed Freud to fit the patient's words and recollections to his own preferred interpretation, as well as increasing the possibility that his own suggestions and interpretations to the patient might alter the actual memories of the patient, who would no doubt be in a very suggestible state of mind during therapy (Grünbaum, 1984).

Although most professionals today view Freud's theory with a great deal of skepticism, his influence on the modern world cannot be ignored. Freudian concepts have had an impact on literature, movies, and even children's cartoons. People who have

It sounds as if all of these theorists became famous by ditching some of Freud's original ideas. Is Freud even worth studying anymore?

never taken a course in psychology are familiar with some of Freud's most basic concepts, such as the defense mechanisms. He was also one of the first theorists to emphasize the importance of childhood experiences on personality development—in spite of the fact that he never studied children.

It has only been in the last several decades that people have had the necessary tools to examine the concepts of the unconscious mind. One can only wonder how Freud might have changed his theory in light of what is known about the workings of the human brain and the changes in society that exist today.

11.2–4

psychosexual stages of personality development
- id exists at birth; ego and superego develop in childhood
- different erogenous zones are sources of conflict as individual ages; unresolved conflicts result in individuals getting stuck or fixated at that stage
  - oral
  - anal
  - phallic ----> see Table 11.1
  - latency
  - genital

a group of Freud's students and followers of the psychoanalytic perspective, called the neo-Freudians, modified his theory and altered the focus of psychoanalysis
- **Jung:** believed in both a personal and collective unconscious that holds universal human memories called archetypes
- **Adler:** focused on having feelings of inferiority and seeking feelings of superiority as opposed to focus on sexuality; birth order also important
- **Horney:** disagreed with concept of penis envy, developed concept of womb envy; rather than sexuality, focused on basic anxiety
- **Erikson:** emphasized social relationships at every stage of life (see Table 10.4)

Psychodynamic Perspective

- modern psychoanalytic theory maintains focus on unconscious mind, concept of defense mechanisms is still useful

- despite several criticisms, Freud's theory still important—first to suggest that personality develops through stages, that we are not always consciously aware of reasons for behavior, and that early life experiences influence who we are later in life

PRACTICE **QUIZ:** PREPARING FOR THE AP* EXAM   ANSWERS ON PAGE AK-3.

Directions: Read each of the questions or incomplete sentences below. Then choose the response that best answers the question or completes the sentence.

1. In which psychosexual stage would fixation most likely result in a person who is excessively neat and fussy?
   a. Oral   d. Latency
   b. Anal   e. Genital
   c. Phallic

2. In which psychosexual stage does the defense mechanism of identification figure prominently?
   a. Oral   d. Latency
   b. Anal   e. Genital
   c. Phallic

3. In which psychosexual stage are sexual feelings repressed?
   a. Oral   d. Latency
   b. Anal   e. Genital
   c. Phallic

4. Which of the following is a way in which Jung's beliefs differed from Freud's?
   a. Jung did not believe in archetypes.
   b. Jung believed in eight psychosocial stages.
   c. Jung did not believe in defense mechanisms.
   d. Jung believed in the collective unconscious.
   e. Jung did not believe in the id, ego, and superego.

5. Which of the following psychologists talked about neurotic personalities as moving toward people, moving against people, or moving away from people?
   a. Freud   d. Erikson
   b. Jung   e. Horney
   c. Adler

The Behaviorist and Social Cognitive View of Personality

At the time that Freud's theory was shocking the Western world, another psychological perspective was also making its influence known. In Chapter Five the theories of classical and operant conditioning were discussed in some detail. *Behaviorists* (researchers who use the principles of conditioning to explain the actions and reactions of both animals and humans) and *social cognitive theorists* (researchers who emphasize the influence of social and cognitive factors on learning) have a very different view of personality.

11.5 How do behaviorists and social cognitive theorists explain personality?

For the behaviorist, personality is nothing more than a set of learned responses or **habits** (DeGrandpre, 2000; Dollard & Miller, 1950). In the strictest traditional view of Watson and Skinner, everything a person or animal does is a response to some environmental stimulus that has been reinforced or strengthened by reward in some way. ❋ Explore on MyPsychLab

So how does a pattern of rewarding certain behavior end up becoming part of some kind of personality pattern? Think about how a traditional behaviorist might explain a shy personality. Beginning in childhood, a person might be exposed to a parent with a rather harsh discipline style (stimulus). Avoiding the attention of that parent would result in fewer punishments and scoldings, so that avoidance response is negatively reinforced—the "bad thing" or punishment is avoided by keeping out of sight and quiet. Later, that child might generalize that avoidance response to other authority figures and adults, such as teachers. In this way, a pattern (habit) of shyness would develop.

Of course, many learning theorists today do not use only classical and operant conditioning to explain the development of the behavior patterns referred to as personality. **Social cognitive learning theorists**, who emphasize the importance of both the influences of other people's behavior and of a person's own expectancies on learning, hold that observational learning, modeling, and other cognitive learning techniques can lead to the formation of patterns of personality. Ⓛ Ⓘ Ⓝ Ⓚ *to Chapter Five: Learning, p. 204.*

One of the more well-researched learning theories that includes the concept of cognitive processes as influences on behavior is the social cognitive theory of Albert Bandura. In the **social cognitive view**, behavior is governed not just by the influence of external stimuli and response patterns but also by cognitive processes such as anticipating, judging, and memory as well as learning through the imitation of models.

BANDURA'S RECIPROCAL DETERMINISM AND SELF-EFFICACY

Bandura (1989) believes that three factors influence one another in determining the patterns of behavior that make up personality: the environment, the behavior itself, and personal or cognitive factors that the person brings into the situation from earlier experiences (see Figure 11.2). These three factors each affect the other two in a reciprocal, or give-and-take, relationship. Bandura calls this relationship **reciprocal determinism**.

As can be seen in Figure 11.2, the environment includes the actual physical surroundings, the other people who may or may not be present, and the potential for reinforcement in those surroundings. The intensity and frequency of the behavior will not only be influenced by the environment but will also have an impact on

So how does a pattern of rewarding certain behavior end up becoming part of some kind of personality pattern?

❋ Explore behaviorists Dollard and Miller's four critical situations. www.mypsychlab.com

habits in behaviorism, sets of well-learned responses that have become automatic.

social cognitive learning theorists theorists who emphasize the importance of both the influences of other people's behavior and of a person's own expectancies of learning.

social cognitive view learning theory that includes cognitive processes such as anticipating, judging, memory, and imitation of models.

◄ AP* Identify key contributors to personality theory.

◄ AP* Identify key contributors in developmental psychology

reciprocal determinism Bandura's explanation of how the factors of environment, personal characteristics, and behavior can interact to determine future behavior.

Figure 11.2 Reciprocal Determinism

In Bandura's model of reciprocal determinism, three factors influence behavior: the environment, which consists of the physical surroundings and the potential for reinforcement; the person (personal/cognitive characteristics that have been rewarded in the past); and the behavior itself, which may or may not be reinforced at this particular time and place.

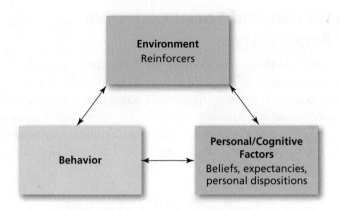

that environment. The person brings into the situation previously reinforced responses (personality, in other words) and mental processes such as thinking and anticipating.

Here's how this might work: Richard walks into a classroom filled with other students, but no teacher is present at this time. (This is the *environment*.) Part of Richard's *personal* characteristics includes the desire to have attention from other people by talking loudly and telling jokes, which has been very rewarding to him in the past (past reinforcements are part of his cognitive processes, or expectancies of future rewards for his behavior). Also in the past, he has found that he gets more attention when an authority figure is not present. His *behavior* will most likely be to start talking and telling jokes, which will continue if he gets the reaction he expects from his fellow students. If the teacher walks in (the *environment* changes), his behavior will change. If the other students don't laugh, his behavior will change. In the future Richard might be less likely to behave in the same way because his expectations for reward (a cognitive element of his *personal* variables) are different.

One of the more important personal variables that Bandura talks about is **self-efficacy**, a person's expectancy of how effective his or her efforts to accomplish a goal will be in any particular circumstance (Bandura, 1998). (Self-efficacy is not the same concept as *self-esteem*, which is the positive values a person places on his or her sense of worth.)

People's sense of self-efficacy can be high or low, depending on what has happened in similar circumstances in the past (success or failure), what other people tell them about their competence, and their own assessment of their abilities. For example, if Fiona has an opportunity to write an extra-credit paper to improve her grade in psychology, she will be more likely to do so if her self-efficacy is high: She has gotten good grades on such papers in the past, her teachers have told her that she writes well, and she knows she can write a good paper. According to Bandura, people high in self-efficacy are more persistent and expect to succeed, whereas people low in self-efficacy expect to fail and tend to avoid challenges (Bandura, 1998).

ROTTER'S SOCIAL LEARNING THEORY: EXPECTANCIES

Julian Rotter (1966, 1978, 1981, 1990) devised a theory based on a basic principle of motivation derived from Thorndike's Law of Effect: People are motivated to seek reinforcement and avoid punishment. He viewed personality as a relatively stable set of *potential* responses to various situations. If in the past, a certain way of responding led to a reinforcing or pleasurable consequence, that way of responding would become a pattern of responding, or part of the "personality" as learning theorists see it.

AP* Identify key contributors to personality theory.

self-efficacy individual's expectancy of how effective his or her efforts to accomplish a goal will be in any particular circumstance.

One very important pattern of responding in Rotter's view became his concept of **locus of control**, the tendency for people to assume that they either have control or do not have control over events and consequences in their lives. (LINK) *to Chapter Eight: Motivation and Emotion, p. 312.* People who assume that their own actions and decisions directly affect the consequences they experience are said to be *internal* in locus of control, whereas people who assume that their lives are more controlled by powerful others, luck, or fate are *external* in locus of control (MacDonald, 1970; Rotter, 1966). Rotter associated people high in internal locus of control with the personality characteristics of high achievement motivation (the will to succeed in any attempted task). Those who give up too quickly or who attribute events in their lives to external causes can fall into patterns of learned helplessness and depression (Abramson et al., 1978, 1989; Gong-Guy & Hammen, 1980).

Like Bandura, Rotter (1978, 1981) also believed that an interaction of factors would determine the behavioral patterns that become personality for an individual. For Rotter, there are two key factors influencing a person's decision to act in a certain way given a particular situation: expectancy and reinforcement value. **Expectancy** is fairly similar to Bandura's concept of self-efficacy in that it refers to the person's subjective feeling that a particular behavior will lead to a reinforcing consequence. A high expectancy for success is similar to a high sense of self-efficacy and is also based on past experiences with successes and failures.

CURRENT THOUGHTS ON THE BEHAVIORIST AND SOCIAL COGNITIVE VIEWS

Behaviorism as an explanation of the formation of personality has its limitations. The classic theory does not take mental processes into account when explaining behavior, nor does it give weight to social influences on learning. The social cognitive view of personality, unlike traditional behaviorism, does include social and mental processes and their influence on behavior. Unlike psychoanalysis, the concepts in this theory can and have been tested under scientific conditions (Backenstrass et al., 2008; Bandura, 1965; Catanzaro et al., 2000; DeGrandpre, 2000; Domjan et al., 2000; Skinner, 1989). Some of this most recent research has been investigating how people's expectancies can influence their control of their own negative moods. Although some critics think that human personality and behavior are too complex to explain as the result of cognitions and external stimuli interacting, others point out that this viewpoint has enabled the development of therapies based on learning theory that have become effective in changing undesirable behavior. (LINK) *to Chapter Thirteen: Psychological Therapies, pp. 524–531.*

The Third Force: Humanism and Personality

11.6 How do humanists such as Carl Rogers explain personality?

As first discussed in Chapter One, in the middle of the twentieth century the pessimism of Freudian psychodynamic theory with its emphasis on conflict and animalistic needs, together with the emphasis of behaviorism on external control of behavior, gave rise to a third force in psychology: the **humanistic perspective**. Humanists such as Carl Rogers and Abraham Maslow wanted psychology to focus on the things that make people uniquely human, such as subjective emotions and the freedom to choose one's own destiny. As Maslow's theory was discussed more fully in Chapter Eight, in this chapter the discussion of the humanistic view of personality will focus on the theory of Carl Rogers.

locus of control the tendency for people to assume that they either have control or do not have control over events and consequences in their lives.

expectancy a person's subjective feeling that a particular behavior will lead to a reinforcing consequence.

humanistic perspective the "third force" in psychology that focuses on those aspects of personality that make people uniquely human, such as subjective feelings and freedom of choice.

"It's always 'Sit,' 'Stay,' 'Heel'—never 'Think,' 'Innovate,' 'Be yourself.'"

©The New Yorker Collection 1990 Peter Steiner from cartoonbank.com. All Rights Reserved.

◄ **AP*** Identify key contributors to personality theory.

◄ **AP*** Identify major figures in psychological treatment

self-actualizing tendency   the striving to fulfill one's innate capacities and capabilities.

self-concept   the image of oneself that develops from interactions with important, significant people in one's life.

self   an individual's awareness of their own personal characteristics and level of functioning.

real self   one's perception of actual characteristics, traits, and abilities.

ideal self   one's perception of whom one should be or would like to be.

positive regard   warmth, affection, love, and respect that come from significant others in one's life.

unconditional positive regard   positive regard that is given without conditions or strings attached.

conditional positive regard   positive regard that is given only when the person is doing what the providers of positive regard wish.

fully functioning person   a person who is in touch with and trusting of the deepest, innermost urges and feelings.

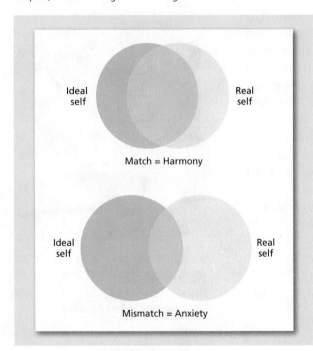

Figure 11.3 Real and Ideal Selves
According to Rogers, the self-concept includes the real self and the ideal self. The real self is a person's actual perception of traits and abilities, whereas the ideal self is the perception of what a person would like to be or thinks he or she should be. When the ideal self and the real self are very similar (matching), the person experiences harmony and contentment. When there is a mismatch between the two selves, the person experiences anxiety and may engage in neurotic behavior.

CARL ROGERS AND SELF-CONCEPT

Like Maslow, Rogers (1961) believed that human beings are always striving to fulfill their innate capacities and capabilities and to become everything that their genetic potential will allow them to become. This striving for fulfillment is called the **self-actualizing tendency**. An important tool in human self-actualization is the development of an image of oneself, or the **self-concept**. The self-concept is based on what people are told by others and how the sense of **self** is reflected in the words and actions of important people in one's life, such as parents, siblings, coworkers, friends, and teachers.

Real and Ideal Self   Two important components of the self-concept are the **real self** (one's actual perception of characteristics, traits, and abilities that form the basis of the striving for self-actualization) and the **ideal self** (the perception of what one should be or would like to be). The ideal self primarily comes from those important, significant others in a person's life, most often the parents. Rogers believed that when the real self and the ideal self are very close or similar to each other, people feel competent and capable, but when there is a mismatch between the real self and ideal self, anxiety and neurotic behavior can be the result. (See Figure 11.3.)

The two halves of the self are more likely to match if they aren't that far apart at the start. When a person has a realistic view of the real self, and the ideal self is something that is actually attainable, there usually isn't a problem of a mismatch. It is when a person's view of self is distorted or the ideal self is impossible to attain that problems arise. Once again, it is primarily how the important people (who can be either good or bad influences) in a person's life react to the person that determines the degree of agreement between real and ideal selves.

Conditional and Unconditional Positive Regard   Rogers defined **positive regard** as warmth, affection, love, and respect that come from the significant others (parents, admired adults, friends, and teachers) in people's experience. Positive regard is vital to people's ability to cope with stress and to strive to achieve self-actualization. Rogers believed that **unconditional positive regard**, or love, affection, and respect with no strings attached, is necessary for people to be able to explore fully all that they can achieve and become. Unfortunately, some parents, spouses, and friends give **conditional positive regard**, which is love, affection, respect, and warmth that depend, or seem to depend, on doing what those people want.

Here is an example: As a freshman, Sasha was thinking about becoming a math teacher, a computer programmer, or an elementary school teacher. Karen, also a freshman, already knew that she was going to be a doctor. Whereas Sasha's parents had told her that what she wanted to become was up to her and that they would love her no matter what, Karen's parents had made it very clear to her as a small child that they expected her to become a doctor. She was under the very strong impression that if she tried to choose any other career, she would lose her parents' love and respect. Sasha's parents were giving her unconditional positive regard, but Karen's parents (whether they intended to do so or not) were giving her conditional positive regard. Karen was obviously not as free as Sasha to explore her potential and abilities.

For Rogers, a person who is in the process of self-actualizing, actively exploring potentials and abilities and experiencing a match between the real self and ideal self, is a **fully functioning person**. Fully functioning people are in touch with their own feelings and abilities and are able to trust their innermost urges and intuitions (Rogers, 1961). To become fully functioning, a person needs unconditional positive regard. In Rogers's view, Karen would not have been a fully functioning person.

What kind of people are considered to be fully functioning? Is it the same thing as being self-actualized? Although the two concepts are highly related, there are some subtle differences. Self-actualization is a goal that people are always striving to reach, according to Maslow (1987). **LINK** to *Chapter Eight: Motivation and Emotion, pp. 316–318.* In Rogers's view, only a person who is fully functioning is capable of reaching the goal of self-actualization. To be fully functioning is a necessary step in the process of self-actualization. Maslow (1987) listed several people that he considered to be self-actualized people: Albert Einstein, Mahatma Gandhi, and Eleanor Roosevelt, for example. These were people that Maslow found to have the self-actualized qualities of being creative, autonomous, and unprejudiced, for example. In Rogers's view, these same people would be seen as having trusted their true feelings and innermost needs rather than just going along with the crowd, a description that certainly seems to apply in these three cases.

◀ What kind of people are considered to be fully functioning? Is it the same thing as being self-actualized?

CURRENT THOUGHTS ON THE HUMANISTIC VIEW OF PERSONALITY

Humanistic views of personality paint a very rosy picture. Some critics believe that the picture is a little too rosy, ignoring the more negative aspects of human nature. For example, would humanistic theory easily explain the development of sociopathic personalities who have no conscience or moral nature? Or could a humanist explain the motivation behind terrorism?

Humanistic theory is also very difficult to test scientifically. Little research support exists for this viewpoint, which is almost more of a philosophical view of human behavior rather than a psychological explanation. Its greatest impact has been in the development of therapies to promote self-growth and help people better understand themselves and others. **LINK** to *Chapter Thirteen: Psychological Therapies, pp. 520–523.*

11.5–6

behavioral and social cognitive
- for behaviorists, personality is set of learned responses and habits, gained through classical and operant conditioning
- in the social cognitive view, both learning (individual and through imitation of models) and cognitive processes (such as anticipation, judgment, and memory) are important

- **Bandura:** concept of self-efficacy; believed three factors were important: the environment, the behavior itself, and personal or cognitive experiences from earlier experiences; each affects the other two in a reciprocal way—reciprocal determinism (see Figure 11.2)
- **Rotter:** theory based on principles of motivation derived from Thorndike's Law of Effect; personality is set of potential responses to various situations, including one's locus of control (internal vs. external) and sense of expectancy

Behavioral, Social Cognitive, and Humanistic Perspectives

humanistic
referred to as the third force in psychology (after psychoanalysis and behaviorism); based largely on work of Rogers and Maslow

- **Rogers:** believed that humans are always striving to fulfill their innate capacities and capabilities (self-actualizing tendency)
- **self-concept** is based on an individual's view of his or her real self and ideal self; when close/similar, people feel capable and competent; when there is mismatch, anxiety and neurotic behavior can occur
- **self-actualization** is facilitated through positive regard, especially unconditional positive regard
- when there is congruence between real and ideal selves, one is considered to be fully functioning and capable of reaching the goal of self-actualization

(continued)

PRACTICE **QUIZ:** PREPARING FOR THE AP* EXAM

Directions: Read each of the questions or incomplete sentences below. Then choose the response that best answers the question or completes the sentence.

1. According to behaviorists, personality is _____.
   a. a set of learned responses or habits
   b. a collection of specific traits
   c. driven by unconscious forces
   d. motivated by a striving for success
   e. determined by biology and heredity

2. What are the three factors in Bandura's model of reciprocal determinism?
   a. Behavior, self-esteem, control
   b. Environment, heredity, self-esteem
   c. Behavior, heredity, personal/cognitive factors
   d. Heredity, self-esteem, personal/cognitive factors
   e. Environment, behavior, personal/cognitive factors

3. Eddie knows that he is pretty good at art, but his parents have never encouraged him to develop art as a career because they don't feel that artists have "real" jobs. As a result, Eddie feels that he should concentrate on a more practical career to please his parents. If Eddie is working to be who his parents think he should be, he is influenced by his _____.
   a. id
   b. superego
   c. ideal self
   d. self-esteem
   e. self-concept

4. Carl Rogers believed that in order for people to become fully functioning, they must receive _____.
   a. a strong sense of self
   b. positive reinforcement
   c. reciprocal determinism
   d. an internal locus of control
   e. unconditional positive regard

5. Which of the following is a weakness of humanistic personality theory?
   a. It is biased against women.
   b. It is unnecessarily pessimistic.
   c. It has no therapeutic application.
   d. It is difficult to test scientifically.
   e. It does not promote healthy relationships.

---

trait theories   theories that endeavor to describe the characteristics that make up human personality in an effort to predict future behavior.

trait   a consistent, enduring way of thinking, feeling, or behaving.

AP* Identify key contributors to personality theory. ▶

"Can't you give him one of those personalities in a bottle I keep reading about?"

⊙ **Watch** classic video footage on personality traits with Allport.
www.mypsychlab.com

Trait Theories: Who Are You?

11.7 What are the history and current views of the trait perspective?

As discussed in the introduction to this chapter, **trait theories** are less concerned with the explanation for personality development and changing personality than they are with describing personality and predicting behavior based on that description. A **trait** is a consistent, enduring way of thinking, feeling, or behaving, and trait theories attempt to describe personality in terms of a person's traits.

ALLPORT

One of the earliest attempts to list and describe the traits that make up personality can be found in the work of Gordon Allport (Allport & Odbert, 1936). Allport and his colleague H. S. Odbert literally scanned the dictionary for words that could be traits, finding about 18,000, then paring that down to 200 traits after eliminating synonyms. Allport believed (with no scientific evidence, however) that these traits were literally wired into the nervous system to guide one's behavior across many different situations and that each person's "constellation" of traits was unique. (In spite of Allport's lack of evidence, behavioral geneticists have found support for the heritability of personality traits, and these findings are discussed in the next section of this chapter.) ⊙ ⎮**Watch** on **MyPsychLab**

CATTELL AND THE 16PF

Two hundred traits is still a very large number of descriptors. How might an employer be able to judge the personality of a potential employee by looking at a list of 200 traits? A more compact way

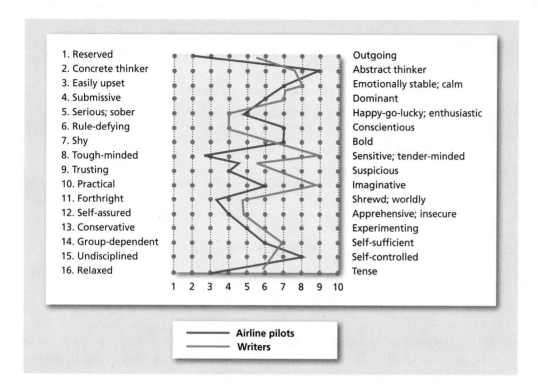

	1	2	3	4	5	6	7	8	9	10	
1. Reserved											Outgoing
2. Concrete thinker											Abstract thinker
3. Easily upset											Emotionally stable; calm
4. Submissive											Dominant
5. Serious; sober											Happy-go-lucky; enthusiastic
6. Rule-defying											Conscientious
7. Shy											Bold
8. Tough-minded											Sensitive; tender-minded
9. Trusting											Suspicious
10. Practical											Imaginative
11. Forthright											Shrewd; worldly
12. Self-assured											Apprehensive; insecure
13. Conservative											Experimenting
14. Group-dependent											Self-sufficient
15. Undisciplined											Self-controlled
16. Relaxed											Tense

—— Airline pilots
—— Writers

Figure 11.4 Cattell's Self-Report Inventory

This is an example of personality profiles based on Cattell's 16PF self-report inventory. The two groups represented are airline pilots and writers. Notice that airline pilots, when compared to writers, tend to be more controlled, relaxed, self-assured, and far less sensitive. Writers, on the other hand, were more imaginative and better able to think abstractly.
Source: Cattell (1973).

of describing personality was needed. Raymond Cattell (1990) defined two types of traits as surface traits and source traits. **Surface traits** are like those found by Allport, representing the personality characteristics easily seen by other people. **Source traits** are those more basic traits that underlie the surface traits. For example, shyness, being quiet, and disliking crowds might all be surface traits related to the more basic source trait of **introversion**, a tendency to withdraw from excessive stimulation.

Using a statistical technique that looks for groupings and commonalities in numerical data called *factor analysis*, Cattell discovered 16 source traits (Cattell, 1950, 1966), and although he later determined that there might be another seven source traits to make a total of 23 (Cattell & Kline, 1977), he developed his assessment questionnaire, *The Sixteen Personality Factor Questionnaire* (16PF) (Cattell, 1995) based on just 16 source traits (see Figure 11.4). These 16 source traits are seen as trait dimensions, or continuums, in which there are two opposite traits at each end with many possible degrees of the traits possible along the dimension. For example, someone scoring near the reserved end of the reserved/outgoing dimension would be more introverted than someone scoring in the middle or at the opposite end.

THE BIG FIVE: OCEAN, OR THE FIVE-FACTOR MODEL OF PERSONALITY

Sixteen factors are still quite a lot to discuss when talking about someone's personality. Later researchers attempted to reduce the number of trait dimensions to a more manageable number, with several groups of researchers arriving at more or less the same five trait dimensions (Botwin & Buss, 1989; Jang et al., 1998; McCrae & Costa, 1996). These five dimensions have become known as the **five-factor model**, or the **Big Five** (see Table 11.2), and represent the core description of human personality—that is, the only dimensions necessary to understand what makes us tick.

surface traits aspects of personality that can easily be seen by other people in the outward actions of a person.

source traits the more basic traits that underlie the surface traits, forming the core of personality.

introversion dimension of personality in which people tend to withdraw from excessive stimulation.

five-factor model (Big Five) model of personality traits that describes five basic trait dimensions.

Table 11.2   The Big Five

HIGH SCORER CHARACTERISTICS	FACTOR (OCEAN)	LOW SCORER CHARACTERISTICS
Creative, artistic, curious, imaginative, nonconforming	Openness (O)	Conventional, down-to-earth, uncreative
Organized, reliable, neat, ambitious	Conscientiousness (C)	Unreliable, lazy, careless, negligent, spontaneous
Talkative, optimistic, sociable, affectionate	Extraversion (E)	Reserved, comfortable being alone, stays in the background
Good-natured, trusting, helpful	Agreeableness (A)	Rude, uncooperative, irritable, aggressive, competitive
Worrying, insecure, anxious, temperamental	Neuroticism (N)	Calm, secure, relaxed, stable

Source: Adapted from McCrae & Costa (1990).

Explore with a simulation on the five-factor model. **www.mypsychlab.com**

openness   one of the five factors; willingness to try new things and be open to new experiences.

conscientiousness   the care a person gives to organization and thoughtfulness of others; dependability.

extraversion   dimension of personality referring to one's need to be with other people.

extraverts   people who are outgoing and sociable.

introverts   people who prefer solitude and dislike being the center of attention.

agreeableness   the emotional style of a person that may range from easygoing, friendly, and likeable to grumpy, crabby, and unpleasant.

neuroticism   degree of emotional instability or stability.

AP* Identify key contributors to personality theory.   ▶

As shown in the table, these five trait dimensions can be remembered by using the acronym OCEAN, in which each of the letters is the first letter of one of the five dimensions of personality. **Explore** on **MyPsychLab**

- **Openness** can best be described as a person's willingness to try new things and be open to new experiences. People who try to maintain the status quo and who don't like to change things would score low on openness.

- **Conscientiousness** refers to a person's organization and motivation, with people who score high in this dimension being those who are careful about being at places on time and careful with belongings as well. Someone scoring low on this dimension, for example, might always be late to important social events or borrow belongings and fail to return them or return them in poor condition.

- **Extraversion** is a term first used by Carl Jung (1933), who believed that all people could be divided into two personality types: **extraverts** and **introverts**. Extraverts are outgoing and sociable, whereas introverts are more solitary and dislike being the center of attention.

- **Agreeableness** refers to the basic emotional style of a person, who may be easygoing, friendly, and pleasant (at the high end of the scale) or grumpy, crabby, and hard to get along with (at the low end).

- **Neuroticism** refers to emotional instability or stability. People who are excessive worriers, overanxious, and moody would score high on this dimension, whereas those who are more even-tempered and calm would score low.

Costa and McCrae believed that these five traits were not interdependent. In other words, knowing someone's score on extraversion would not give any information about scores on the other four dimensions, allowing for a tremendous amount of variety in personality descriptions.

CURRENT THOUGHTS ON THE TRAIT PERSPECTIVE

Some theorists have cautioned that personality traits will not always be expressed in the same way across different situations. Walter Mischel, a social cognitive theorist, has emphasized that there is a **trait–situation interaction** in which the particular circumstances of any given situation are assumed to influence the way in which a trait is expressed (Mischel & Shoda, 1995). An outgoing extravert, for example, might laugh, talk to strangers, and tell jokes at a party. That same person, if at a funeral, would still talk and be open, but the jokes and laughter would be less likely to occur.

As mentioned earlier, the five-factor model has been studied and tested by numerous researchers. Cross-cultural studies have found evidence of these five trait dimensions in 11 different cultures, including Japan, the Philippines, Germany, China, and Peru (Digman, 1990; John et al., 1988; McCrae et al., 2000; 2005; McCrae & Terracciano, 2007; Paunonen et al., 1996; Piedmont et al., 2002). This cultural commonality raises the question of the origins of the Big Five trait dimensions: Are child-rearing practices across all those cultures similar enough to result in these five aspects of personality, or could these five dimensions have a genetic component that transcends cultural differences? The next section will discuss the evidence for a genetic basis of the Big Five.

trait–situation interaction the assumption that the particular circumstances of any given situation will influence the way in which a trait is expressed.

◀ **AP*** Speculate how cultural context can facilitate or constrain personality development.

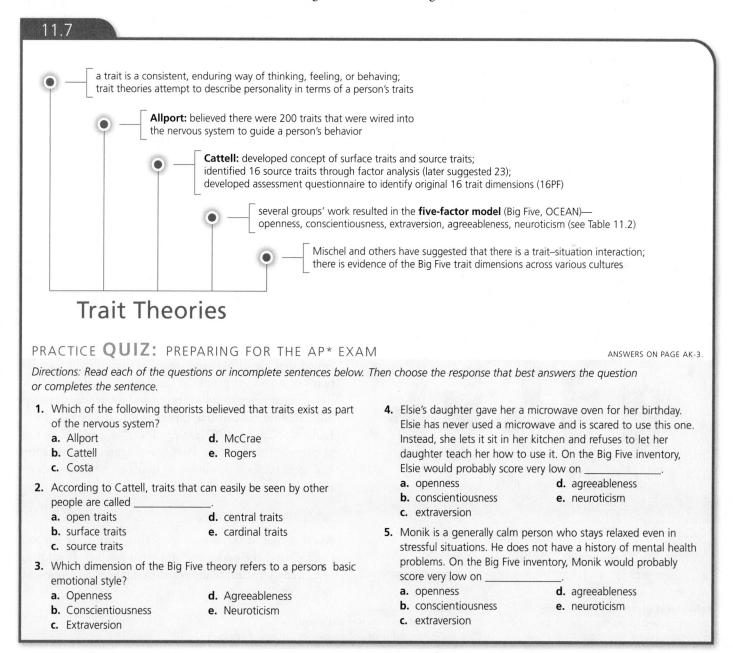

11.7

- a trait is a consistent, enduring way of thinking, feeling, or behaving; trait theories attempt to describe personality in terms of a person's traits

  - **Allport:** believed there were 200 traits that were wired into the nervous system to guide a person's behavior

    - **Cattell:** developed concept of surface traits and source traits; identified 16 source traits through factor analysis (later suggested 23); developed assessment questionnaire to identify original 16 trait dimensions (16PF)

      - several groups' work resulted in the **five-factor model** (Big Five, OCEAN)— openness, conscientiousness, extraversion, agreeableness, neuroticism (see Table 11.2)

        - Mischel and others have suggested that there is a trait–situation interaction; there is evidence of the Big Five trait dimensions across various cultures

Trait Theories

PRACTICE **QUIZ:** PREPARING FOR THE AP* EXAM   ANSWERS ON PAGE AK-3.

Directions: Read each of the questions or incomplete sentences below. Then choose the response that best answers the question or completes the sentence.

1. Which of the following theorists believed that traits exist as part of the nervous system?
   a. Allport
   b. Cattell
   c. Costa
   d. McCrae
   e. Rogers

2. According to Cattell, traits that can easily be seen by other people are called _____.
   a. open traits
   b. surface traits
   c. source traits
   d. central traits
   e. cardinal traits

3. Which dimension of the Big Five theory refers to a person's basic emotional style?
   a. Openness
   b. Conscientiousness
   c. Extraversion
   d. Agreeableness
   e. Neuroticism

4. Elsie's daughter gave her a microwave oven for her birthday. Elsie has never used a microwave and is scared to use this one. Instead, she lets it sit in her kitchen and refuses to let her daughter teach her how to use it. On the Big Five inventory, Elsie would probably score very low on _____.
   a. openness
   b. conscientiousness
   c. extraversion
   d. agreeableness
   e. neuroticism

5. Monik is a generally calm person who stays relaxed even in stressful situations. He does not have a history of mental health problems. On the Big Five inventory, Monik would probably score very low on _____.
   a. openness
   b. conscientiousness
   c. extraversion
   d. agreeableness
   e. neuroticism

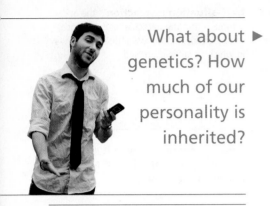

What about ▶ genetics? How much of our personality is inherited?

AP* Describe and compare research methods that psychologists use to investigate personality.

▶

Figure 11.5 Personalities of Identical and Fraternal Twins

Identical and fraternal twins differ in the way they express the Big Five personality factors. The scores of identical twins have a correlation of about 50 percent, whereas those of fraternal twins have a correlation of only about 15 to 20 percent. These findings give support to the idea that some aspects of personality are genetically based. *Source:* Loehlin (1992)

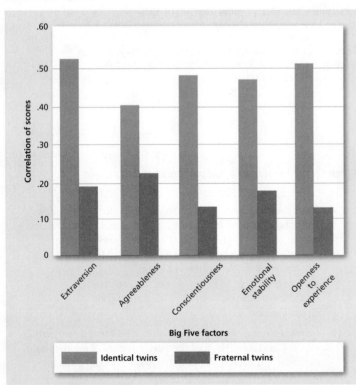

Big Five factors

■ Identical twins　　■ Fraternal twins

behavioral genetics field of study devoted to discovering the genetic bases for personality characteristics.

The Biology of Personality: Behavioral Genetics

What about genetics? How much of our personality is inherited? The field of **behavioral genetics** is devoted to the study of just how much of an individual's personality is due to inherited traits. Animal breeders have known for a long time that selective breeding of certain animals with specific desirable traits can produce changes not only in size, fur color, and other physical characteristics but also in the temperament of the animals (Isabel, 2003; Trut, 1999). As stated earlier in this chapter, temperament consists of the characteristics with which each person is born and is, therefore, determined by biology to a great degree. If the temperaments of animals can be influenced by manipulating patterns of genetic inheritance, then it is only one small step to assume that at least those personality characteristics related to temperament in human beings may also be influenced by heredity.

Animal breeders have an advantage over those who are studying the influence of genes in human behavior. Those who breed animals can control the mating of certain animals and the conditions under which those animals are raised. Human research cannot ethically or practically develop that degree of control and so must fall back on the accidental "experiments" of nature and opportunity, studies of twins and adopted persons.

11.8 What part do biology, heredity, and culture play in personality?

TWIN STUDIES

The difference between monozygotic (identical) and dizygotic (fraternal) twins was discussed in Chapter Ten. ⓛⓘⓝⓚ *to Chapter Ten: Development Across the Life Span, pp. 391–392.* As discussed previously, identical twins share 100 percent of their genetic material, having come from one fertilized egg originally, whereas fraternal twins share only about 50 percent of their genetic material as any other pair of siblings would. By comparing identical twins to fraternal twins, especially when twins can be found who were not raised in the same environment (like Oskar and Jack or the "Jim" twins in the opening story), researchers can begin to find evidence of possible genetic influences on various traits, including personality. (See Figure 11.5.)

The results of the Minnesota twin study have revealed that identical twins are more similar than fraternal twins or unrelated people in intelligence, leadership abilities, the tendency to follow rules, and the tendency to uphold traditional cultural expectations (Bouchard, 1997; Finkel & McGue, 1997); nurturance,* empathy,** and assertiveness (Neale et al., 1986); and aggressiveness (Miles & Carey, 1997). This similarity holds even if the twins are raised in separate environments.

ADOPTION STUDIES

Another tool of behavioral geneticists is to study adopted children and their adoptive and birth families. If studying genetically identical twins raised in different environments

---

*Nurturance: affectionate care and attention.
**Empathy: the ability to understand the feelings of others.

can help investigators understand the genetic influences on personality, then studying *unrelated* people who are raised in the *same* environment should help investigators discover the influence of environment. By comparing adopted children to their adoptive parents and siblings and, if possible, to their biological parents who have not raised them, researchers can uncover some of the shared and nonshared environmental and genetic influences on personality.

Adoption studies have confirmed what twin studies have shown: Genetic influences account for a great deal of personality development, regardless of shared or nonshared environments (Hershberger et al., 1995; Loehlin et al., 1985; Loehlin et al., 1998). Through this kind of study, a genetic basis has been suggested for shyness (Plomin et al., 1988) and aggressiveness (Brennan et al., 1997).

CURRENT FINDINGS

Several studies have found that the five personality factors of the five-factor model have nearly a 50 percent rate of heritability* across several cultures (Bouchard, 1994; Herbst et al., 2000; Jang et al., 1996; Loehlin, 1992; Loehlin et al., 1998). Together with the results of the Minnesota twin study and other research (Lubinski, 2000; Lykken & Tellegen, 1996; Plomin, 1994), the studies of genetics and personality seem to indicate that variations in personality traits are about 25 to 50 percent inherited (Jang et al., 1998). This also means that environmental influences apparently account for about half of the variation in personality traits as well.

Although the five factors have been found across several cultures, this does not mean that different cultures do not have an impact on personality. For more on this topic, see the Classic Studies in Psychology section that follows.

James Arthur Springer and James Edward Lewis, otherwise known as the "Jim" twins. Although separated shortly after birth and reunited at age 39, they exhibited many similarities in personality and personal habits. Although genetics may explain some of these similarities, what other factors might also be at work?

AP* Speculate how cultural context can facilitate or constrain personality development.

---

*Heritability: the degree to which the changes in some trait within a population can be considered to be due to genetic influences.

Classic Studies in Psychology

Geert Hofstede's Four Dimensions of Cultural Personality

In the early 1980s, organizational management specialist Geert Hofstede conducted a massive study into the work-related values of employees of IBM, a multinational corporation (Hofstede, 1980; Hofstede et al., 2002). The study surveyed workers in 64 countries across the world. Hofstede analyzed the data collected from this survey and found four basic dimensions of personality along which cultures differed.

1. **Individualism/collectivism:** *Individualistic cultures* tend to have loose ties between individuals, with people tending to look after themselves and their immediate families only. Members of such cultures have friends based on shared activities and interests and may belong to many different loosely organized social groups. Autonomy,* change, youth, security of the individual, and equality are all highly valued. In a *collectivistic culture,* people are from birth deeply tied into very strong in-groups,

---

*Autonomy: the quality of being self-directed or self-controlled.

typically extended families that include grandparents, aunts and uncles, and cousins. Loyalty to the family is highly stressed, and the care of the family is placed before the care of the individual. Group membership is limited to only a few permanent groups that have tremendous influence over the individual. The values of this kind of culture are duty, order, tradition, respect for the elderly, group security, and respect for the group status and hierarchy.* Whereas the United States and Great Britain are examples of individualistic cultures, Japan, China, Korea, Mexico, and Central America are much more collectivistic.

2. **Power distance:**　This dimension refers to the degree to which the less powerful members of a culture accept and even expect that the power within the culture is held in the hands of a select few rather than being more evenly distributed. Countries such as the Philippines, Mexico, many Arab countries, and India were found to be high in such expectations, whereas countries such as Austria, Sweden, Australia, Great Britain, and the United States were low in power distance.

3. **Masculinity/femininity:**　Referring to how a culture distributes the roles played by men and women within a culture, this dimension varies more for the men within a culture than for the women. "Masculine" cultures are assertive and competitive, although more so for men than for women, and "feminine" cultures are more modest and caring. Both men and women in "feminine" countries have similar, caring values, but in "masculine" countries, the women are not quite as assertive and competitive as the men, leading to a greater difference between the sexes in masculine countries. Japan, Austria, Venezuela, Italy, Switzerland, Mexico, Ireland, Jamaica, the United States, Great Britain, and Germany were found to be masculine countries, whereas Sweden, Norway, the Netherlands, Denmark, Costa Rica, Yugoslavia, Finland, Chile, Portugal, Thailand, and Guatemala were ranked as more feminine.

4. **Uncertainty avoidance:**　Some cultures are more tolerant of uncertainty, ambiguity,** and unstructured situations. Cultures that do not tolerate such uncertainty and lack of structure tend to have strict rules and laws with lots of security and safety measures and tend toward a philosophical/religious belief of One Truth (and "we have it!"). Cultures that are more accepting of uncertainty are more tolerant of different opinions and have fewer rules. They tend to allow many different religious beliefs to exist side by side and are less anxious and emotional than people in uncertainty-avoiding countries. Uncertainty-avoiding countries include Greece, Portugal, Guatemala, Uruguay, Belgium, El Salvador, Japan, Yugoslavia, and Peru, whereas those that are more tolerant of uncertainty include Singapore, Jamaica, Denmark, Sweden, Hong Kong, Ireland, Great Britain, Malaysia, India, Philippines, the United States, Canada, and Indonesia.

Note that the Big Five personality dimensions of Costa and McCrae (2000) are not necessarily in competition with Hofstede's dimensions. Hofstede's dimensions are *cultural* personality traits, whereas those of the Big Five refer to individuals.

Questions for Further Discussion

1. Was your own culture listed for any of these dimensions? If so, do you agree with the personality dimension assigned to your culture?

2. If your culture was not listed for a personality dimension, where do you think your culture would fall on that dimension?

---

*Hierarchy: in this sense, a body of persons in authority over others.

**Ambiguity: the quality of being uncertain and indistinct.

Assessment of Personality

11.9 What are the advantages and disadvantages of the following measures of personality: interviews, projective tests, behavioral assessment, personality inventories, and online personality tests?

With all the different theories of personality, how do people find out what kind of personality they have? The methods for measuring or assessing personality vary according to the theory of personality used to develop those methods, as one might expect. However, most psychological professionals doing a personality assessment on a client do not necessarily tie themselves down to one theoretical viewpoint only, preferring to take a more *eclectic* view of personality. The eclectic view is a way of choosing the parts of different theories that seem to best fit a particular situation, rather than using only one theory to explain a phenomenon. In fact, looking at behavior from all four perspectives can often bring insights into a person's behavior that would not easily come from taking only one perspective. Many professionals will not only use several different perspectives but also several of the assessment techniques that follow. Even so, certain methods are more commonly used by certain kinds of theorists, as can be seen in Table 11.3.

Personality assessments may also differ in the purposes for which they are conducted. For example, sometimes a researcher may administer a personality test of some sort to participants in a research study so that the participants may be classified according to certain personality traits. There are personality tests available to people who simply want to learn more about their own personalities. Finally, clinical and counseling psychologists, psychiatrists, and other psychological professionals use personality assessment in the diagnosis of disorders of personality. Ⓛ Ⓘ Ⓝ Ⓚ *to Chapter Twelve: Psychological Disorders, pp. 504–506.*

With all the different theories of personality, how do people find out what kind of personality they have?

AP* Describe and compare research methods that psychologists use to investigate personality.

AP* Identify frequently used assessment strategies and evaluate relative test quality based on reliability and validity of the instruments.

Table 11.3 Who Uses What Method?

TYPE OF ASSESSMENT	MOST LIKELY USED BY . . .
Interviews	Psychoanalysts, Humanistic Therapists

Projective Tests
  Rorschach
  Thematic Apperception Test
	Psychoanalysts

Behavioral Assessments
  Direct Observation
  Rating Scales
  Frequency Counts
	Behavioral and Social Cognitive Therapists

Personality Inventories
  Sixteen Personality Factor Questionnaire (16PF)
  Neuroticism/Extraversion/Openness Personality Inventory (NEO-PI)
  Myers-Briggs Type Indicator (MBTI)
  Eysenck Personality Questionnaire (EPQ)
  Keirsey Temperament Sorter II
  California Psychological Inventory (CPI)
  Minnesota Multiphasic Personality Inventory, Version II (MMPI-2)
	Trait Theorists

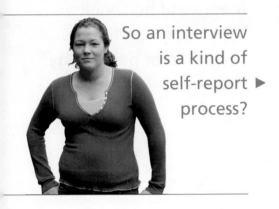

So an interview is a kind of self-report process? ▶

INTERVIEWS

Some therapists ask questions and note down the answers in a survey process called an **interview**. ⓛⓘⓝⓚ *to Chapter One: The Science of Psychology, p. 24.* This type of interview, unlike a job interview, may be *unstructured* and flow naturally from the beginning comments between the client and the psychologist.

Problems with Interviews

So an interview is a kind of self-report process? Yes, when psychologists interview clients, clients must report on their innermost feelings, urges, and concerns—all things that only they can directly know. The same problems that exist with self-report data (such as surveys) exist with interviews. Clients can lie, distort the truth, misremember, or give what they think is a socially acceptable answer instead of true information. Interviewers themselves can be biased, interpreting what the client says in light of their own belief systems or prejudices.

Another problem with interviews is something called the **halo effect**, which is a tendency to form a favorable or unfavorable impression of someone at the first meeting, so that all of a person's comments and behavior after that first impression will be interpreted to agree with the impression—positively or negatively. The halo effect can happen in any social situation, including interviews between a psychological professional and a client. First impressions really do count, and people who make a good first impression because of clothing, personal appearance, or some other irrelevant* characteristic will seem to have a "halo" hanging over their heads—they can do no wrong after that (Lance et al., 1994; Thorndike, 1920). (Sometimes the negative impression is called the "horn effect.")

PROJECTIVE TESTS

Psychoanalysts have a goal in dealing with their clients that other personality theorists do not share: The psychoanalyst wishes to uncover the unconscious conflicts, desires, and urges that affect the client's conscious behavior. No other theorist assigns such importance to the unconscious mind, so psychoanalysts use assessment methods that are meant to "get at" those unconscious, hidden emotions and events.

Think about the definition of the defense mechanism of **projection**: placing, or "projecting," one's own unacceptable thoughts onto others, as if the thoughts actually belonged to those others. What if a person could project unacceptable, unconscious thoughts onto some harmless, ambiguous stimulus, like a picture? For example, have you ever tried to see "shapes" in the clouds? You might see a house where another person might see the same cloud as a horse. The cloud isn't really either of those things but can be *interpreted* as one or the other, depending on the person doing the interpretation. That makes a cloud an ambiguous stimulus—one that is capable of being interpreted in more than one way.

In just this way, psychoanalysts (and a few other psychologists) show their clients ambiguous visual stimuli and ask the clients to tell them what they see. The hope is that the client will project those unconscious concerns and fears onto the visual stimulus, revealing them to the analyst. Tests using this method are called **projective tests**. Although such tests can be used to explore a client's personality, they are more commonly used as a diagnostic tool to uncover problems in personality.

interview method of personality assessment in which the professional asks questions of the client and allows the client to answer, either in a structured or unstructured fashion.

halo effect tendency of an interviewer to allow positive characteristics of a client to influence the assessments of the client's behavior and statements.

projection defense mechanism involving placing, or "projecting," one's own unacceptable thoughts onto others, as if the thoughts actually belonged to those others and not to oneself.

projective tests personality assessments that present ambiguous visual stimuli to the client and ask the client to respond with whatever comes to mind.

---

*Irrelevant: not applying to the case or example at hand.

The Rorschach Inkblots   One of the more well-known projective tests is the **Rorschach inkblot test**, developed in 1921 by Swiss psychiatrist Hermann Rorschach (ROR-shok). There are 10 inkblots, five in black ink on a white background and five in colored inks on a white background. (See Figure 11.6 for an example of a Rorschach-type inkblot.)

People being tested are asked to look at each inkblot and simply say whatever it might look like to them. Using predetermined categories and responses commonly given by people to each picture (Exner, 1980), psychologists score responses on key factors, such as reference to color, shape, figures seen in the blot, and response to the whole or to details.

Rorschach tested thousands of inkblots until he narrowed them down to the 10 in use today. They are still frequently used to describe personality, diagnose mental disorders, and predict behavior (Watkins et al., 1995; Weiner, 1997).

The TAT   First developed in 1935 by psychologist Henry Murray and his colleagues (Morgan & Murray, 1935), the **Thematic Apperception Test (TAT)** consists of 20 pictures, all black and white, that are shown to a client. The client is asked to tell a story about the person or people in the picture, who are all deliberately drawn in ambiguous situations (see Figure 11.7). Again, the story developed by the client is interpreted by the psychoanalyst, who looks for revealing statements and projection of the client's own problems onto the people in the pictures.

These are only two of the more well-known projective tests. Other types of projective tests include the Sentence Completion test, Draw-A-Person, and House-Tree-Person. In the Sentence Completion test, the client is given a series of sentence beginnings, such as "I wish my mother . . ." or "Almost every day I feel . . ." and asked to finish the sentence, whereas in the Draw-A-Person and House-Tree-Person, the client is asked to draw the named items.

But how can anyone know if the interpretation is correct? Isn't there a lot of room for error?

Problems with Projective Tests   Projective tests are by their nature very **subjective** (valid only within the person's own perception), and interpreting the answers of clients is almost an art. It is certainly not a science and is not known for its accuracy. Problems lie in the areas of reliability and validity. In Chapter Seven, *reliability* was defined as the tendency of a test to give the same score every time it is administered to the same person or group of people, and *validity* was defined as the ability of the test to measure what it is intended to measure. Projective tests, with no standard grading

Figure 11.6 Rorschach Inkblot Example

One of the Rorschach inkblots. A person being tested is asked to tell the interviewer what he or she sees in this inkblot. Answers are neither right nor wrong but may reveal unconscious concerns. What do you see in this inkblot? Laura Dwight/Hermann Rorschach, Rorschach®-Test. ©Verlag Hans Huber, Hogrefe AG.

But how can anyone know if the interpretation is correct? Isn't there a lot ◀ of room for error?

Rorschach inkblot test   projective test that uses 10 inkblots as the ambiguous stimuli.

Thematic Apperception Test (TAT) projective test that uses 20 pictures of people in ambiguous situations as the visual stimuli.

subjective   referring to concepts and impressions that are only valid within a particular person's perception and may be influenced by biases, prejudice, and personal experiences.

Figure 11.7 Thematic Apperception Test Example

A sample from the Thematic Apperception Test (TAT). When you look at this picture, what story does it suggest to you? Who are the people? What is their relationship?

scales, have both low reliability and low validity (Gittelman-Klein, 1978; Lilienfield, 1999; Wood et al., 1996). A person's answers to the Rorschach, for example, might be quite different from one day to the next, depending on the person's mood and what scary movie might have been on television the previous night.

Projective tests may sound somewhat outdated in today's world of MRIs and PET scans, but many practicing clinical psychologists and psychiatrists still use this type of testing (Butcher & Rouse, 1996; Camara et al., 2000). Some psychologists believe that the latest versions of these tests and others like them still have practical use and some validity (Ganellen, 1996; Weiner, 1997), especially when a client's answers on these tests are used as a starting point for digging deeper into the client's recollections, concerns, and anxieties. However, more reliable and objective methods for assessing personality are available, as the next section discusses.

Somehow, I can't see a behaviorist using any of these tests, they're too "mental"—do behaviorists even measure personality?

BEHAVIORAL ASSESSMENTS

Behaviorists do not typically want to "look into the mind." Because behaviorists assume that personality is merely habitually learned responses to stimuli in the environment, the preferred method for a behaviorist would be to watch that behavior unfold in the real world.

In **direct observation**, the psychologist observes the client engaging in ordinary, everyday behavior, preferably in the natural setting of home, school, or workplace, for example. A therapist who goes to the classroom and observes that tantrum behavior only happens when a child is asked to do something involving fine motor abilities (like drawing or writing) might be able to conclude that the child has difficulty with those skills and throws a tantrum to avoid the task.

Other methods often used by behavioral therapists and other assessors are rating scales and frequency counts. In a **rating scale**, a numerical rating is assigned, either by the assessor or the client, for specific behaviors (Nadeau et al., 2001). In a **frequency count**, the assessor literally counts the frequency of certain behaviors within a specified time limit. Educators make use of both rating scales and frequency counts to diagnose behavioral problems such as attention deficit/hyperactivity disorder (ADHD) and aspects of personality such as social skill level through the various grade levels.

Problems with Behavioral Assessments   Problems with these assessments can include the observer effect (when a person's behavior is affected by being watched) and observer bias, which can be controlled by having multiple observers and correlating their observations with each other. ⓛⓘⓝⓚ *to Chapter One: The Science of Psychology, pp. 22–23.* As with any kind of observational method, there is no control over the external environment. A person observing a client for a particular behavior may not see that behavior occur within the observation time—much as some car problems never seem to show up when the mechanic is examining the car.

PERSONALITY INVENTORIES

Trait theorists are typically more interested in personality descriptions. They tend to use an assessment known as a **personality inventory**, a questionnaire that has a standard list of questions and only requires certain specific answers, such as "yes," "no," and "can't decide." The standard nature of the questions (everyone gets the same list) and the lack of open-ended answers make these assessments far more

---

> Somehow, I can't see a behaviorist using any of these tests, they're too "mental"—do behaviorists even measure personality?

direct observation   assessment in which the professional observes the client engaged in ordinary, day-to-day behavior in either a clinical or natural setting.

rating scale   assessment in which a numerical value is assigned to specific behavior that is listed in the scale.

frequency count   assessment in which the frequency of a particular behavior is counted.

personality inventory   paper and pencil or computerized test that consists of statements that require a specific, standardized response from the person taking the test.

objective and reliable than projective tests (Garb et al., 1998), although they are still a form of self-report. One such personality inventory is Cattell's 16PF, described earlier in this chapter. Costa and McCrae (2000) have recently revised their original *Neuroticism/Extraversion/Openness Personality Inventory (NEO-PI)*, which is based on the five-factor model of personality traits (discussed on page 454).

Another inventory in common use is the *Myers-Briggs Type Indicator (MBTI)*. This inventory is based on the ideas of Carl Jung and looks at four personality dimensions. The sensing/intuition (S/I) dimension includes people who prefer to rely on what they can see, hear, and so on through their own physical senses (*sensing*) and, on its opposite end, those who look for patterns and trust their hunches (*intuition*). Sensing people are very detail oriented, preferring to work only with the known facts, whereas intuitive people are more willing to use metaphors, analogies, and look for possibilities. The thinking/feeling (T/F) dimension runs from those who prefer to use logic, analysis, and experiences that can be verified as facts (*thinkers*) to those who tend to make decisions based on their personal values and emotional reactions (*feeling*). Introversion/extroversion (I/E) is the same classic dimension that began with Jung and is represented in nearly every personality theory, including the Big Five. Perceiving/judging (P/J) describes those who are willing to adapt and modify decisions, be spontaneous, and who are naturally curious and tend to put off making a final decision so that all possibilities are covered (*perceiving*) as well as those who are the opposite: the action-oriented, decisive, get-the-task-done-and-don't-look-back type (*judging*). These four dimensions can differ for each individual, resulting in 16 (4 × 4) possible personality types: ISTJ, ISTP, ISFP, ISFJ, and so on (Briggs & Myers, 1998).

The Myers-Briggs is often used to assess personality to help people know the kinds of careers for which they may best be suited. For example, a person who scored high on the extravert, sensing, thinking, and judging dimensions would be an ESTJ. A typical description of this personality type would be a person who needs to analyze information and bring order to the outer world. Such people are organizers, energetic in completing tasks, and practical. They also take their responsibilities seriously and expect others to do so as well. School administrators, for example, are often ESTJs.

Other common personality tests include the Eysenck Personality Questionnaire (Eysenck & Eysenck, 1993), the Keirsey Temperament Sorter II (Keirsey, 1998), the California Psychological Inventory (Gough, 1995), and the Sixteen Personality Factor Questionnaire (Cattell, 1994).

The MMPI-2   By far the most common personality inventory is the *Minnesota Multiphasic Personality Inventory, Version II*, or *MMPI-2*, which specifically tests for abnormal behavior patterns in personality (Butcher & Rouse, 1996; Butcher et al., 2000, 2001). This questionnaire consists of 567 statements such as "I am often very tense" or "I believe I am being plotted against." The person taking the test must answer "true," "false," or "cannot say." The MMPI has 10 clinical scales and eight validity scales in addition to numerous subscales. Each scale tests for a particular kind of behavior. The behavior patterns include relatively mild personality problems such as excessive worrying and shyness as well as more serious disorders such as schizophrenia and depression. ⓁⒾⓃⓀ *to Chapter Twelve: Psychological Disorders, pp. 497, 501.* ✸⌐Explore on MyPsychLab

How can you tell if a person is telling the truth on a personality inventory? Validity scales, which are built into any well-designed psychological inventory, are intended to indicate whether or not a person taking the inventory is responding honestly. Responses to certain items on the test will indicate if people are trying to

✸ **Explore** clinical scales of the MMPI-2. **www.mypsychlab.com**

How can you tell if a person is telling the truth on a personality inventory?

make themselves look better or worse than they are, for example, and certain items are repeated throughout the test in a slightly different form, so that anyone trying to "fake" the test will have difficulty responding to those items consistently (Butcher et al., 2001). For example, if one of the statements is "I am always happy" and a person responds "true" to that statement, the suspicion would be that this person is trying to look better than he or she really is. If several of the validity scale questions are answered in this way, the conclusion is that the person is not being honest.

Problems with Personality Inventories   The advantage of personality inventories over projective tests and interviews is that inventories are standardized (i.e., everyone gets exactly the same questions and the answers are scored in exactly the same way). In fact, responses to inventories are often scored on a computer. Observer bias and bias of interpretation are simply not possible because this kind of assessment is objective rather than subjective. The validity and reliability of personality inventories are generally recognized as being greatly superior to those of projective tests (Anastasi & Urbina, 1997).

There are some problems, however. The validity scales, for example, are a good check against cheating, but they are not perfect. Some people are still able to fake their answers and respond in what they feel are the socially appropriate ways (Anastasi & Urbina, 1997; Hicklin & Widiger, 2000). Other problems have to do with human nature itself: Some people may develop a habit of picking a particular answer rather than carefully considering the statement, whereas others may simply grow tired of responding to all those statements and start picking answers at random.

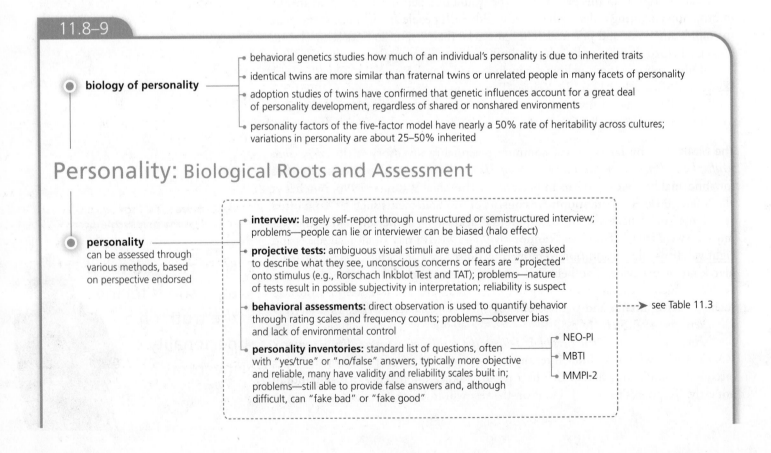

11.8–9

biology of personality

- behavioral genetics studies how much of an individual's personality is due to inherited traits
- identical twins are more similar than fraternal twins or unrelated people in many facets of personality
- adoption studies of twins have confirmed that genetic influences account for a great deal of personality development, regardless of shared or nonshared environments
- personality factors of the five-factor model have nearly a 50% rate of heritability across cultures; variations in personality are about 25–50% inherited

Personality: Biological Roots and Assessment

personality
can be assessed through various methods, based on perspective endorsed

- **interview:** largely self-report through unstructured or semistructured interview; problems—people can lie or interviewer can be biased (halo effect)
- **projective tests:** ambiguous visual stimuli are used and clients are asked to describe what they see, unconscious concerns or fears are "projected" onto stimulus (e.g., Rorschach Inkblot Test and TAT); problems—nature of tests result in possible subjectivity in interpretation; reliability is suspect
- **behavioral assessments:** direct observation is used to quantify behavior through rating scales and frequency counts; problems—observer bias and lack of environmental control
- **personality inventories:** standard list of questions, often with "yes/true" or "no/false" answers, typically more objective and reliable, many have validity and reliability scales built in; problems—still able to provide false answers and, although difficult, can "fake bad" or "fake good"
  - NEO-PI
  - MBTI
  - MMPI-2

----> see Table 11.3

PRACTICE QUIZ: PREPARING FOR THE AP* EXAM

Directions: Read each of the questions or incomplete sentences below. Then choose the response that best answers the question or completes the sentence.

1. Which of the following is not one of the traits found to have a genetic component in studies of identical twins?
   a. Empathy
   b. Antagonism
   c. Intelligence
   d. Aggressiveness
   e. Leadership abilities

2. According to Hofstede, which of the following countries is high in power distance?
   a. India
   b. Austria
   c. Sweden
   d. Great Britain
   e. The United States

3. Which measure of personality assessment offers the most objective measurement?
   a. Interview
   b. Rating scale
   c. Direct observation
   d. Personality inventory
   e. Rorschach inkblot test

4. Which of the following personality assessment methods would most likely be used by a psychoanalyst?
   a. MMPI-2
   b. Rating scales
   c. Myers-Briggs
   d. Frequency counts
   e. Rorschach inkblot test

5. Which of the following is a drawback of behavioral personality assessments?
   a. The assessments can be affected by observer bias.
   b. The assessments are usually neither reliable nor valid.
   c. The assessments do not examine real-world behaviors.
   d. The assessments seem somewhat outdated to most people.
   e. The assessments are scored on a computer rather than by hand.

Applying Psychology to Everyday Life: Personality Testing on the Internet

Most people enjoy finding out something about themselves. In fact, that's part of the attraction of the pseudopsychological methods of astrology and graphology, as discussed in Chapter One. People want to know, "What am I really like?" ((•—Listen on MyPsychLab

((•● **Listen** to the Psychology in the News podcast. **www.mypsychlab.com**

There are a number of online personality tests available, with more appearing on almost a daily basis. Some of these tests are fairly well thought out, based on much larger, validated tests, and can give the casual "surfer" some insight into personality traits. Here are two sample Web sites with fairly serious tests:

- Keirsey Temperament Sorter (based on Jung's theory): **http://www.keirsey.com/sorter/register.aspx**

- Five-Factor Test (based on the five-factor model): **http://users.wmin.ac.uk/~buchant/wwwffi**

One of the more unusual online personality tests is the Color Test, which has the person select certain colored shapes by clicking on them. The Color Test is based on the work of Swiss color psychologist Dr. Max Lüscher, a color consultant for industrial concerns (Lüscher, 1969). Color psychologists study the effects of color on mood, attention, and other human factors, and most often work in the field of consumer or marketing psychology, helping businesses and industries select color schemes for products, Web pages, and physical surroundings that will maximize sales and productivity (Bellizzi & Crowley, 1983; Guerin et al., 1995). There are several Internet sites that allow people to take a free Color Test, such as the one at **www.colorquiz.com**.

The Color Test as devised by Lüscher consists of eight cards, each a different color, which are randomly placed color side up in front of the person to be tested. The person is asked to choose the color card that is most attractive, which is then recorded and removed, and the person is asked to choose the most attractive color from those that remain. This is repeated until only one card is left. Various tables in Lüscher's book are used to interpret the color choices.

Although colors have been shown to have an effect on the body's physical reactions, with red creating higher measurements of blood pressure, respiration, heart rate, and eyeblink frequency and blue the lowest (Dominy & Lucas, 2001; Kaiser, 1984), there is little scientifically derived research to support the association of certain colors with certain personality traits (Brauen & Bonta, 1979; Holmes et al., 1984; McAloon & Lester, 1979). The results of color personality tests sound suspiciously like the general readings given by astrologers and graphologists: "Does not wish to be involved in differences of opinion, contention or argument, preferring to be left in peace. Wants to make a favorable impression and be recognized. Needs to feel appreciated and admired. Sensitive and easily hurt if no notice is taken of him or if he is not given adequate acknowledgment." How many of these statements are true of you or someone you know? This is a good example of the *Barnum Effect* in action—keep the statement general with a little something for everyone, and it will please nearly everyone.

Still, it can be fun to participate in tests like these, so long as people remember that a real personality test should be administered under controlled conditions by an expert. One of the dangers in taking online personality tests (and especially those in magazines) too seriously, for example, is that there is no person-to-person contact to help put the results in perspective, which can lead people to believe that they are in big trouble—even though their results are not that different from other people's results. It can be a little like "medical student disease," in which medical students read up on exotic diseases and become convinced that they have them all until the teacher reassures them. People taking an online personality test may believe they have some serious psychological disorder because they don't know how to interpret the results of the test.

One final word of advice: Online testing can be good entertainment, but real problems should be handled by real professionals.

Questions for Further Discussion

1. What might be some other dangers of taking a personality test online?

2. What should a person look for when trying to judge the quality of an online personality test?

11 — CHAPTER SUMMARY

Theories of Personality

11.1 What is personality, and how do the various perspectives in psychology view personality?

- Personality is the unique way individuals think, feel, and act. It is different from character and temperament but includes those aspects.

- The four perspectives in the study of personality are the psychodynamic, behavioristic (including social cognitive theory), humanistic, and trait perspectives.

The Man and the Couch: Sigmund Freud and the Psychodynamic Perspective

11.2 How did Freud's historical view of the mind and personality form a basis for psychodynamic theory?

- The three divisions of the mind are the conscious, preconscious, and unconscious. The unconscious can be revealed in dreams and Freudian slips of the tongue.

- The three parts of the personality are the id, ego, and superego.

- The id works on the pleasure principle and the ego works on the reality principle.
- The superego is the moral center of personality, containing the conscience, and is the source of moral anxiety.
- The conflicts between the demands of the id and the rules and restrictions of the superego lead to anxiety for the ego, which uses defense mechanisms to deal with that anxiety.
- The personality develops in a series of psychosexual stages: oral (id dominates), anal (ego develops), phallic (superego develops), latency (period of sexual repression), and genital (sexual feelings reawaken with appropriate targets).
- The Oedipus and Electra complexes (sexual "crushes" on the opposite-sex parent) create anxiety in the phallic stage, which is resolved through identification with the same-sex parent.
- Fixation occurs when conflicts are not fully resolved during a stage, resulting in adult personality characteristics reflecting childhood inadequacies.

11.3 How did Jung, Adler, Horney, and Erikson modify Freud's theory?

- The neo-Freudians changed the focus of psychoanalysis to fit their own interpretation of the personality, leading to the more modern version known as the psychodynamic perspective.
- Jung developed a theory of a collective unconscious.
- Adler proposed feelings of inferiority as the driving force behind personality and developed birth order theory.
- Horney developed a theory based on basic anxiety and rejected the concept of penis envy.
- Erikson developed a theory based on social rather than sexual relationships, covering the entire life span.

11.4 How does modern psychoanalytic theory differ from that of Freud?

- Current research has found support for the defense mechanisms and the concept of an unconscious mind that can influence conscious behavior, but other concepts cannot be scientifically researched.

The Behaviorist and Social Cognitive View of Personality

11.5 How do behaviorists and social cognitive theorists explain personality?

- Behaviorists define personality as a set of learned responses or habits.
- The social cognitive view of personality includes the concept of reciprocal determinism, in which the environment, characteristics of the person, and the behavior itself all interact.
- Self-efficacy is a characteristic in which a person perceives a behavior as more or less effective based on previous experiences, the opinions of others, and perceived personal competencies.
- Locus of control is a determinant of personality in which one either assumes that one's actions directly affect events and reinforcement one experiences or that such events and reinforcements are the result of luck, fate, or powerful others.
- Personality, in the form of potential behavior patterns, is also determined by an interaction between one's expectancies for success and the perceived value of the potential reinforcement.
- Behaviorist personality theory has scientific support but is criticized as being too simplistic.

The Third Force: Humanism and Personality

11.6 How do humanists such as Carl Rogers explain personality?

- Humanism developed as a reaction against the negativity of psychoanalysis and the deterministic nature of behaviorism.
- Carl Rogers proposed that self-actualization depends on proper development of the self-concept.
- The self-concept includes the real self and the ideal self. When these two components do not match or agree, anxiety and disordered behavior result.
- Unconditional positive regard from important others in a person's life helps the formation of the self-concept and the congruity of the real and ideal selves, leading to a fully functioning person.
- Humanistic theory is not scientifically researched but has been effective in therapy situations.

Trait Theories: Who Are You?

11.7 What are the history and current views of the trait perspective?

- Trait theorists describe personality traits in order to predict behavior.
- Allport first developed a list of about 200 traits and believed that these traits were part of the nervous system.
- Cattell reduced the number of traits to between 16 and 23 with a computer method called factor analysis.
- Several researchers have arrived at five trait dimensions that have research support across cultures, called the Big Five or five-factor model. The five factors are openness, conscientiousness, extraversion, agreeableness, and neuroticism.
- Cross-cultural research has found support for the five-factor model of personality traits in a number of different cultures.
- Future research will explore the degree to which child-rearing practices and heredity may influence the five personality factors.
- Behavior genetics is a field of study of the relationship between heredity and personality.

The Biology of Personality: Behavioral Genetics

11.8 What part do biology, heredity, and culture play in personality?

- Studies of twins and adopted children have found support for a genetic influence on many personality traits, including intelligence, leadership abilities, traditionalism, nurturance, empathy, assertiveness, neuroticism, and extraversion.

Classic Studies in Psychology: Geert Hofstede's Four Dimensions of Cultural Personality

- Hofstede's cross-cultural management study revealed four basic dimensions of personality along which cultures may vary: individualism/collectivism, power distance, masculinity/femininity, and uncertainty avoidance.

Assessment of Personality

11.9 What are the advantages and disadvantages of the following measures of personality: interviews, projective tests, behavioral assessment, personality inventories, and online personality tests?

- Interviews are used primarily by psychoanalysts and humanists and can include structured or unstructured interviews.

- Disadvantages of interviews can include the halo effect and bias of the interpretation on the part of the interviewer.

- Projective tests are based on the defense mechanism of projection and are used by psychoanalysts. Projective tests include the Rorschach inkblot test and the Thematic Apperception Test.

- Projective tests can be useful in finding starting points to open a dialogue between therapist and client but have been criticized for being low in reliability and validity.

- Behavioral assessments are primarily used by behaviorists and include direct observation of behavior, rating scales of specific behavior, and frequency counts of behavior.

- Behavioral assessments have the disadvantage of the observer effect, which causes an observed person's behavior to change, and observer bias on the part of the person doing the assessment.

- Personality inventories are typically developed by trait theorists and provide a detailed description of certain personality traits. They are objective tests rather than subjective.

- The NEO-PI is based on the five-factor model, whereas the Myers-Briggs Type Indicator is based on Jung's theory of personality types.

- The MMPI-2 is designed to detect abnormal personality.

- Personality inventories include validity scales to prevent cheating, but such measures are not perfect and cheating is sometimes possible.

Applying Psychology to Everyday Life: Personality Testing on the Internet

- There are numerous personality tests available on the Internet, although all of them are not equal in quality, reliability, or validity.

- One danger in taking an online personality test is the lack of professional interpretation of the results of such tests.

TEST YOURSELF: PREPARING FOR THE AP* EXAM

ANSWERS ON PAGE AK-3.

✓• Practice on MyPsychLab   Ready for your test? More quizzes and a customized study plan. www.mypsychlab.com

PART I: MULTIPLE-CHOICE QUESTIONS

Directions for Part I: Read each of the questions or incomplete sentences below. Then choose the response that best answers the question or completes the sentence.

1. According to Freud, which structure of the personality functions on the reality principle?
   a. Id
   b. Ego
   c. Superego
   d. Conscience
   e. Unconscious

2. According to Freud, activities such as overeating and talking too much stem from a fixation in the _____.
   a. oral stage
   b. anal stage
   c. phallic stage
   d. latency stage
   e. genital stage

3. Alfred Adler believed that middle children tend to be _____.
   a. pampered and protected
   b. limited in their freedom
   c. inferior-feeling overachievers
   d. dominating and competitive
   e. unwilling to receive attention

4. To explain an individual's personality, behaviorists would examine _____.
   a. hereditary and genetic clues
   b. early childhood emotional traumas
   c. the amount of parental love and affection
   d. traits that have been evident since birth
   e. early experiences of rewards and punishments

5. For Bandura, one of the most important personal variables in determining personality is _____.
   a. self-control
   b. self-concept
   c. self-efficacy
   d. self-monitoring
   e. self-actualization

6. According to Rogers, anxiety and neurotic behavior result from _____.
   a. learned habits of behavior
   b. chemical imbalances in the brain
   c. unconscious conflicts and desires
   d. receiving too much unconditional positive regard
   e. a mismatch between the real self and the ideal self

7. Which of the following locations is characterized by an individualistic culture?
   a. Japan
   b. Korea
   c. Mexico
   d. Great Britain
   e. Central America

8. Mr. Phillips is constantly late for his classes, leaving students waiting in the hallway outside his door for nearly an hour at times. Which dimension of the five-factor model would show a very low score for Mr. Phillips?
   a. Openness
   b. Conscientiousness
   c. Extraversion
   d. Agreeableness
   e. Neuroticism

9. Which of the following personality assessment methods is most likely to be reliable?
- **a.** Projective test
- **b.** Subjective interview
- **c.** Personality inventory
- **d.** Rorschach inkblot test
- **e.** Thematic Apperception Test

10. Which of the following personality inventories is based on the five-factor model?
- **a.** CPI
- **b.** 16PF
- **c.** MBTI
- **d.** MMPI-2
- **e.** NEO-PI

PART II: FREE-RESPONSE QUESTION

Directions for Part II: Read the essay question that follows. Then, respond to the question in a clear, concise essay. Do not simply list facts. Instead, present a thorough argument based on your critical consideration of the topic. Use proper psychological terminology as necessary.

In a well-organized essay, contrast the psychodynamic approach to personality with the trait approach to personality. Describe each approach, including advantages and disadvantages, and discuss at least one prominent individual associated with each.

11.1 p. 440

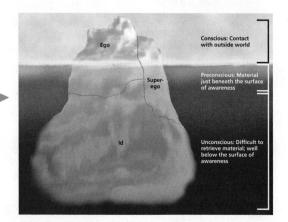

Conscious: Contact with outside world

Ego

Preconscious: Material just beneath the surface of awareness

Super-ego

Id

Unconscious: Difficult to retrieve material; well below the surface of awareness

personality
unique way in which each individual thinks, acts, and feels throughout life

perspectives/theories
different ways of viewing and explaining personality

→ **psychodynamic** →
→ **behavioral and social cognitive views**
→ **humanistic**
→ **trait**

Theories of Personality

psychodynamic perspective
basic aspects

- mind made up of different levels of awareness—conscious, preconscious, and unconscious

- personality stems from interplay and conflict between demands made by the id, restrictions set forth by the superego, and direction by the ego

- disordered behavior is product of constant conflict and anxiety; ego uses unconscious defense mechanisms as ways to manage anxiety/conflict among three parts of personality (see Table 9.3)

Table 11.1 Freud's Psychosexual Stages

STAGE	AGE	FOCUS OF PLEASURE	FOCUS OF CONFLICTS	DIFFICULTIES AT THIS STAGE AFFECT LATER . . .
Oral	Birth to $1\frac{1}{2}$ years old	Oral activities (such as sucking, feeding, and making noises with the mouth)	Weaning	• Ability to form interpersonal attachments • Basic feelings about the world • Tendency to use oral forms of aggression, such as sarcasm • Optimism or pessimism • Tendency to take charge or be passive
Anal	$1\frac{1}{2}$ to 3 years old	Bowel and bladder control	Toilet training	• Sense of competence and control • Stubbornness or willingness to go along with others • Neatness or messiness • Punctuality or tardiness
Phallic	3 to 6 years old	Genitals	Sexual awareness	• Development of conscience through identification with same-sex parent • Pride or humility
Latency	6 years old to puberty	Social skills (such as the ability to make friends) and intellectual skills; Dormant period in terms of psychosexual development	School, play, same-sex friendships	• Ability to get along with others
Genital	Puberty to death	Sexual behavior	Sexual relationship with partner	• Immature love or indiscriminate hate • Uncontrollable working or inability to work

Note: Freud thought that the way a person finds pleasure or is prevented from satisfying urges for pleasure at each stage affects personality. Thus, like Erikson's stage model described in Chapter Ten, Freud's model argues that the way a person deals with particular psychological challenges or potential areas of conflict has long-term effects on personality.

11.2–4 p. 446

psychosexual stages of personality development

- id exists at birth; ego and superego develop in childhood

- different erogenous zones are sources of conflict as individual ages; unresolved conflicts result in individuals getting stuck or fixated at that stage

- a group of Freud's students and followers of the psycho-analytic perspective, called the neo-Freudians, modified his theory and altered the focus of psychoanalysis

→ **Jung**
→ **Adler**
→ **Horney** →
→ **Erikson**

Psychodynamic Perspective

- modern psychoanalytic theory maintains focus on unconscious mind, concept of defense mechanisms is still useful

- despite several criticisms, Freud's theory is still important—first to suggest that personality develops through stages, that is we are not always consciously aware of reasons for behavior, and that early life experiences influence who we are later in life

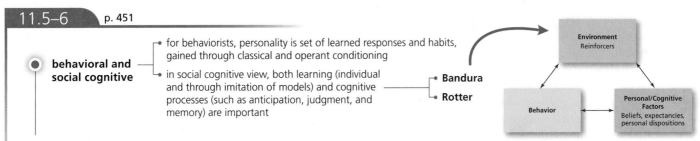

11.5–6   p. 451

behavioral and social cognitive
- for behaviorists, personality is set of learned responses and habits, gained through classical and operant conditioning
- in social cognitive view, both learning (individual and through imitation of models) and cognitive processes (such as anticipation, judgment, and memory) are important
  - **Bandura**
  - **Rotter**

Environment
Reinforcers

Behavior

Personal/Cognitive Factors
Beliefs, expectancies, personal dispositions

Behavioral, Social Cognitive, and Humanistic Perspectives

humanistic
referred to as the third force in psychology (after psychoanalysis and behaviorism); based largely on work of Rogers and Maslow

- **Rogers**
- **self-concept**
- **self-actualization**
- when there is congruence between real and ideal selves, one is considered to be fully functioning and capable of reaching the goal of self-actualization

Ideal self   Real self

Match = Harmony

Ideal self   Real self

Mismatch = Anxiety

11.7   p. 455

- a trait is a consistent, enduring way of thinking, feeling, or behaving; trait theories attempt to describe personality in terms of a person's traits

- **Allport:** believed there were 200 traits that were wired into the nervous system to guide a person's behavior

- **Cattell:** developed concept of surface traits and source traits; identified 16 source traits through factor analysis (later suggested 23); developed assessment questionnaire to identify original 16 trait dimensions (16PF)

- several groups' work resulted in the **five-factor model** (Big Five, OCEAN)—openness, conscientiousness, extraversion, agreeableness, neuroticism (see Table 11.2)

- Mischel and others have suggested that there is a trait–situation interaction; there is evidence of the Big Five trait dimensions across various cultures

Trait Theories

Table 11.2   The Big Five

HIGHER SCORER CHARACTERISTICS	FACTOR (OCEAN)	LOW SCORER CHARACTERISTICS
Creative, artistic, curious, imaginative, nonconforming	Openness (O)	Conventional, down-to-earth, uncreative
Organized, reliable, neat, ambitious	Conscientiousness (C)	Unreliable, lazy, careless, negligent, spontaneous
Talkative, optimistic, sociable, affectionate	Extraversion (E)	Reserved, comfortable being alone, stays in the background
Good-natured, trusting, helpful	Agreeableness (A)	Rude, uncooperative, irritable, aggressive, competitive
Worrying, insecure, anxious, temperamental	Neuroticism (N)	Calm, secure, relaxed, stable

Source: Adapted from McRae & Costa (1990)

11.8–9   p. 464

biology of personality
- behavioral genetics studies how much of an individual's personality is due to inherited traits
- identical twins are more similar than fraternal twins or unrelated people in many facets of personality
- adoption studies of twins have confirmed that genetic influences account for a great deal of personality development, regardless of shared or nonshared environments
- personality factors of the five-factor model have nearly a 50% rate of heritability across cultures; variations in personality are about 25–50% inherited

Personality: Biological Roots and Assessment

personality
can be assessed through various methods, based on perspective endorsed

Table 11.3   Who Uses What Method?

TYPE OF ASSESSMENT	MOST LIKELY USED BY . . .
Interviews	Psychoanalysts, Humanistic Therapists
Projective Tests • Rorschach • Thematic Apperception Test	Psychoanalysts
Behavioral Assessments • Direct Observation • Rating Scales • Frequency Counts	Behavioral and Social Cognitive Therapists
Personality Inventories • Sixteen Personality Factor Questionnaire (16PF) • Neuroticism/Extraversion/Openness Personality Inventory (NEO-PI) • Myers-Briggs Type Indicator (MBTI) • Eysenck Personality Questionnaire (EPQ) • Keirsey Temperament Sorter II • California Psychological Inventory (CPI) • Minnesota Multiphasic Personality Inventory, Version II (MMPI-2)	Trait Theorists

12
Psychological Disorders

The Harsh Reality of Postpartum Psychosis

What could drive a mother to kill her own children? In Toronto, a 37-year-old woman jumped in front of a subway train with her 6-month-old infant in her arms. Another young mother shut herself and her three children in the garage with the car running. Yet another mother in Texas drowned her five children in the bathtub. Experts believe that these women were suffering from a rare form of depression that is caused by sudden hormonal changes just after a woman gives birth. This condition is called postpartum psychosis (Ahokas et al., 2000; Brockington et al., 1982; Hamilton, 1982; Mahe & Dumaine, 2001).

Postpartum psychosis may include actual false beliefs or delusions (such as believing that the baby is possessed by a demon), hallucinations (one woman thought her baby was a rat trying to bite her), frantic energy, and an unwillingness to eat or sleep in addition to **postpartum depression** symptoms (Rohde & Marneros, 1993).

Research into this condition has suggested that postpartum psychosis is most likely caused by internal, biological factors rather than any cultural or societal expectations because this disorder is found in many cultures, both Western and non-Western, as well as in both technological and traditional societies (Kumar, 1994). Other research highlights the possible role of lack of estrogen, the female hormone that is lower than usual right after childbirth (Ahokas et al., 2000; Mahe & Dumaine, 2001).

Whatever the cause, how can the delusions and hallucinations seem real enough to these women to cause them to harm their own children? Why does this condition become so severe in some women, whereas many others have only a mild form of it? What factors cause a person to cross over the line from normal to abnormal behavior?

Why study abnormal behavior? Because it is all around us, which raises many questions: How should one react? What should be done to help? What kind of person develops a mental illness? Could this happen to someone close? The key to answering these questions is to develop an understanding of just what is meant by abnormal behavior and the different ways in which behavior can depart from the "normal" path.

12 Learning Objectives

I've heard people call the different things other people do "crazy" or "weird." How do psychologists decide when people are really mentally ill and not just a little odd?

AP* Describe contemporary and historical conceptions of what constitutes psychological disorders.

postpartum psychosis a rare and severe form of depression that occurs in women just after giving birth and includes delusional thinking and hallucinations.

postpartum depression depression occurring within a year after giving birth in about 10 percent of women and that includes intense worry about the baby, thoughts of suicide, and fears of harming the baby.

psychopathology the study of abnormal behavior.

What Is Abnormality?

I've heard people call the different things other people do "crazy" or "weird." How do psychologists decide when people are really mentally ill and not just a little odd? Exactly what is meant by the term *abnormal behavior*? Abnormal compared to what? Who gets to decide what is normal and what is not? Has the term always meant what it means now? These are just a few questions that come to mind when thinking about the study of abnormal behavior, or **psychopathology** (Wen-Shing & Strelzer, 1997). As can be seen in the following section, definitions of abnormality have depended on cultural ways of explaining behavior down through the ages.

A BRIEF HISTORY OF PSYCHOLOGICAL DISORDERS

12.1 How has mental illness been explained in the past, how is abnormal behavior defined today, and what is the impact of cultural differences in defining abnormality?

Dating from as early as 3000 B.C.E., archaeologists have found human skulls bearing the evidence of an ancient surgical technique. The skulls have holes cut into them, and the holes were made while the person was still living. In fact, many of the holes show evidence of healing, meaning that the person survived the process. The process of cutting holes into the skull of a living person is called *trepanning* (also spelled *trephining*). Although trepanning is still done today to relieve pressure of fluids on the brain, in ancient times the reason may have had more to do with releasing the "demons" possessing the poor victim (Gross, 1999). Ancient peoples might well have assumed that people who were behaving oddly were possessed by evil spirits. As trepanning had to be rather unpleasant, the disordered person may very well have tried hard to be "normal" after treatment, too.

Hippocrates, a Greek physician during the time in which the rest of the world and even many Greeks believed in the demon possession explanation of mental illness, challenged that belief with his assertion that illnesses of both the body and the mind were the result of imbalances in the body's vital fluids, or *humors*. Although Hippocrates was not correct in his assumptions about the humors of the body (phlegm, black bile, blood, and yellow bile), his was the first recorded attempt to explain abnormal behavior as due to some biological process.

These human skulls clearly show the signs of trepanning, a process in which ancient priests or medicine men cut holes into the skulls of a living person, perhaps to release the "demons" making the person's behavior odd or disturbed. Some who were treated in this way must have survived, as the holes show some evidence of healing.

Moving forward in time, people of the Middle Ages believed in spirit possession (through the teachings of the Roman Catholic Church or the remnants of other religious/cultural systems) and the treatment of choice was a religious one: *exorcism*, or the formal casting out of the demon through a religious ritual (Lewis, 1995). During the Renaissance, belief in demon possession (in which the possessed person was at least seen as a victim) gave way to a belief in witchcraft, and mentally ill persons were most likely called witches and put to death. Although there is wide disagreement about exactly how many people were hanged, burned, stoned, or drowned as witches, some estimates place the number at around 100,000 (Barstow, 1995).

WHAT IS ABNORMAL?

Defining abnormal behavior or abnormality is not as simple as it might seem at first. The easy way out is to say that abnormal behavior is behavior that is not normal, but what does that mean?

Statistical Definition   One way to define *normal* and *abnormal* is to use a statistical definition. Frequently occurring behavior would be considered normal, and behavior that is rare would be abnormal. That kind of definition works fine with a behavior such as talking to others, as the two rarer possibilities would be not talking to anyone at all and talking too much to too many people—both of which would be considered abnormal. What about a behavior such as happiness? Is a medium level of happiness really the "norm" most people strive to reach? A total lack of happiness would be abnormal, but should a person who is very happy really be labeled abnormal? Statistical definitions of abnormality wouldn't work for intelligence either, as only mental retardation (the lower end of a distribution of intelligence in a population) would be considered undesirable and abnormal (Troisi & McGuire, 2002). People possessing a higher degree of intelligence than is "normal" are actually highly respected.

Social Norm Deviance   Another way of defining abnormality is to see it as something that goes against the norms or standards of the society in which the individual lives. For example, refusing to wear clothing in a society that does not permit nudity would be seen as abnormal. But deviance (variation) from social norms is not always labeled as negative, abnormal behavior, as in a person who decides to become a monk and live in a monastery in the United States. That would be unusual behavior and not what the society considers a standard behavior, but it wouldn't be a sign of abnormality.

El Hechizo (The Spell), by Spanish artist Francisco Goya. It portrays witches, demons, and other evil spirits tormenting a poor young man and represents what ancient people believed was the cause of mental illness: demon possession.
Francisco Goya, *El Hechizo*, 1787–88, Fundacion Lazaro Gaidiano.

situational context the social or environmental setting of a person's behavior.

subjective discomfort emotional distress or emotional pain.

maladaptive anything that does not allow a person to function within or adapt to the stresses and everyday demands of life.

psychological disorders any pattern of behavior that causes people significant distress, causes them to harm others, or harms their ability to function in daily life.

So how do psychologists decide what is abnormal? ▶

✸ **Explore** psychological disorders. **www.mypsychlab.com**

Using social nonconformity as a criterion for abnormality also creates a problem when dealing with different cultures. Behavior that would be labeled disordered in one culture may be quite acceptable in another. (See the Current Issues in Psychology feature following this section.) Even within one culture, the **situational context** (the social or environmental setting of a person's behavior) can make a difference in how behavior is labeled. For example, if a man comes to a therapist complaining of people listening in on his phone conversations and spying on all his activities, the therapist's first thought might be that the man is suffering from feelings of persecution. But if the man then explains that he is in a witness protection program, the complaints take on an entirely different and quite understandable tone.

Subjective Discomfort   One sign of abnormality is when the person experiences a great deal of **subjective discomfort**, or emotional distress while engaging in a particular behavior. A woman who suffers from a fear of going outside her house, for example, would experience a great deal of anxiety when trying to leave home and distress over being unable to leave. However, all behavior that might be considered abnormal does not necessarily create subjective discomfort in the person committing the act—a serial killer, for example, does not experience emotional distress after taking someone's life, and some forms of disordered behavior involve showing no emotions at all.

Inability to Function Normally   Behavior that does not allow a person to fit into society or function normally can also be labeled abnormal. This kind of behavior is termed **maladaptive**, meaning that the person finds it hard to adapt to the demands of day-to-day living. Maladaptive behavior includes behavior that may initially help a person cope but has harmful or damaging effects. For example, a woman who cuts herself to relieve anxiety does experience initial relief but is harmed by the action. Maladaptive behavior is a key element in the definition of abnormality.

THE FINAL DEFINITION OF ABNORMALITY

So how do psychologists decide what is abnormal? Perhaps the shortest definition of abnormality or **psychological disorders** is any pattern of behavior that causes people significant distress, causes them to harm themselves or others, or harms their ability to function in daily life. To get a clear picture of abnormality, it is often necessary to take all of the factors discussed thus far into account. Psychologists and other psychological professionals must consider several different criteria in determining whether or not a behavior is abnormal (at least two of these criteria must typically be met to form a diagnosis of abnormality): ✸ Explore on **MyPsychLab**

1. Is the behavior unusual, such as experiencing severe panic when faced with a stranger or being severely depressed in the absence of any stressful life situations?

2. Does the behavior go against social norms? (And keep in mind that social norms change over time—e.g., homosexuality was once considered a psychological disorder rather than a variation in sexual orientation.)

3. Does the behavior cause the person significant subjective discomfort?

4. Is the behavior maladaptive?

5. Does the behavior cause the person to be dangerous to self or others, as in the case of someone who tries to commit suicide or attacks other people without reason?

ABNORMALITY VERSUS INSANITY

Psychologists and psychiatrists determine whether or not certain behavior is abnormal, but they do not decide whether a certain person is insane. In the United States, *insanity* is not a psychological term; it is a legal term used to argue that a mentally ill person who has committed a crime should not be held responsible for his or her actions. This argument is called the *insanity defense.*

Like the women we earlier discussed, who suffered from postpartum psychosis and harmed their children as a result, many people are diagnosed with psychological disorders either before or after committing crimes. If a schizophrenic person burns down a house because he believes God has told him to do it, he has certainly committed a crime—but is he truly guilty? Supporters of the insanity defense might argue that he is not.

It is important to keep in mind that not everyone who has been diagnosed with a psychological disorder can use the insanity defense to plead innocent to a criminal charge. The legal definition of insanity is a thorny issue subject to interpretation, but insanity is often defined as the inability to tell right from wrong due to mental illness. Very few people use the insanity defense in court, and of those people, only a small percentage are found innocent by reason of insanity.

While the impact of psychological disorders on society extends to the legal system, lawyers and judges do not have a hand in defining or treating psychological disorders. They are charged with determining how the law should address crimes committed under the influence of mental illness, but only psychological professionals can diagnose disorders and determine the best course of treatment for someone who suffers from mental illness.

AP* Discuss the intersection between psychology and the legal system.

Models of Abnormality

What causes psychological disorders? In Chapter Eleven several different theories of personality were discussed. These theories of personality can be used to describe and explain the formation of not only ordinary behavior and personality but disordered behavior and abnormal personality as well. How one explains disordered behavior, then, depends on which theoretical model is used to explain personality in general.

◄ What causes psychological disorders?

12.2 How can psychological disorders be explained within the biological and psychological models?

AP* Evaluate the strengths and limitations of various approaches to explaining psychological disorders.

THE BIOLOGICAL MODEL: MEDICAL CAUSES FOR PSYCHOLOGICAL DISORDERS

One model that was not discussed in Chapter Eleven is the **biological model**, which proposes that psychological disorders have a biological or medical cause (Gamwell & Tomes, 1995). This model explains disorders such as anxiety, depression, and schizophrenia as caused by chemical imbalances, genetic problems, brain damage and dysfunction, or some combination of those causes. For example, as you may recall from Chapter Eleven's discussion of trait theory and the five-factor theory of personality traits (pp. 453–455), there is a growing body of evidence that basic personality traits are as much influenced by genetic inheritance as they are by experience and upbringing, even across cultures (Bouchard, 1994; Herbst et al., 2000; Jang et al., 1996; Loehlin, 1992; Loehlin et al., 1998). One of the Big Five factors was neuroticism, for example, and it is easy to see how someone who scores high in neuroticism would be at greater risk for anxiety-based disorders.

biological model model of explaining behavior as caused by biological changes in the chemical, structural, or genetic systems of the body.

sociocultural perspective perspective in which abnormal behavior (like normal behavior) is seen as the product of the learning and shaping of behavior within the context of the family, the social group to which one belongs, and the culture within which the family and social group exist.

cultural relativity the need to consider the unique characteristics of the culture in which behavior takes place.

culture-bound syndromes disorders found only in particular cultures.

Current Issues in Psychology

A Look at Abnormality in Various Cultures

As mentioned earlier, what's normal in one culture may be abnormal in another culture. In the **sociocultural perspective** of abnormality, abnormal behavior (like normal behavior) is seen as the product of behavioral shaping within the context of family influences, the social group to which one belongs, and the culture within which the family and social group exist. In particular, cultural differences in abnormal behavior must be addressed when psychological professionals are attempting to treat members of a culture different from that of the professional. **Cultural relativity** is a term that refers to the need to consider the unique characteristics of the culture in which a person with a disorder was nurtured to be able to correctly diagnose and treat the disorder (Castillo, 1997). For example, in most traditional Asian cultures, mental illness is often seen as a shameful thing that brings disgrace to one's family. It may be seen as something inherited and, therefore, something that would hurt the marriage chances of other family members, or it may be seen as stemming from something the family's ancestors did wrong in the past (Ritts, 1999; Ying, 1990). This leads many Asian people suffering from disorders that would be labeled as depression or even schizophrenia to report bodily symptoms rather than emotional or mental ones because bodily ailments are more socially acceptable (Fedoroff & McFarlane, 1998; Lee, 1995; Ritts, 1999).

Some disorders called **culture-bound syndromes** are only found in particular cultures. Here are a few examples, together with the culture in which they are found (Ritts, 1999):

- *Taijin-kyofu-sho (TKS):* TKS is found primarily in Japan and involves the fear that one will do something in public that is socially inappropriate or embarrassing, such as blushing, staring, or having an offensive body odor (Kirmayer, 1991).
- *Susto:* Susto is a kind of magical fright found among the Kechua-speaking Latino Indians of the Andes. It is seen as a "loss of soul" triggered by some frightening experience, after which the person falls to the ground and experiences appetite and weight loss, weakness, problems sleeping, depression, and apathy* (Pfeiffer, 1982).
- *Amok:* The term comes from Southeast Asia but similar concepts are found in Latin America as well as in certain Native American tribes. Amok results from a perceived insult or slight, which is followed by a period of brooding and then a violent or aggressive outburst, during which the person may attack others and may not remember doing so (Pfeiffer, 1982).
- *Anorexia nervosa:* The eating disorder, anorexia, in which individuals starve themselves to become thin, is typically found only in Western cultures such as the United States and Great Britain (Bemporad, 1997; Garner & Garfinkel, 1980). There is some evidence that the incidence rates in other non-Western cultures are changing as exposure to Western culture through the media increases (Ritenbaugh et al., 1992) and that in some cultures starvation is not motivated by a desire to be thin but rather by eccentric nutritional ideas or religious fasting (Castillo, 1997; Rieger et al., 2001).

((●• **Listen** to the Psychology in the News podcast. **www.mypsychlab.com**

Questions for Further Discussion   ((●—**Listen** on **MyPsychLab**

1. Think about your own culture. Is there a disorder or behavior that seems to be unique to your culture?

2. Are there superstitions or magical beliefs in your culture or social group that could become the basis for a disorder?

---

*Apathy: lack of feeling or emotion; indifference to surroundings.

The biological or medical model has had a great deal of influence, especially in the language used to describe disorders: *mental illness*, *symptoms of disorder*, and terms such as *diagnosis, mental patient, mental hospital, therapy*, and *remission* all come from medical terminology. The use of such terms, although still widespread, may tend to bias the assumptions of professionals who are not psychiatrists or medical doctors toward a biological cause for disordered behavior.

THE PSYCHOLOGICAL MODELS

Although biological explanations of psychological disorders are influential, they are not the only ways or even the first ways in which disorders are explained. There are several psychological models that attempt to explain disordered behavior as the result of various forms of emotional, behavioral, or thought-related malfunctioning.

Psychodynamic View: Hiding Problems The psychodynamic model, based on the work of Freud and his followers, L I N K *to Chapter Eleven: Theories of Personality, pp. 437–439*, explains disordered behavior as the result of repressing one's threatening thoughts, memories, and concerns in the unconscious mind (Carducci, 1998). These repressed thoughts and urges try to resurface, and disordered behavior develops as a way of keeping the thoughts repressed. For example, a woman who has unacceptable thoughts of harming her family members might feel "dirty" and be compelled to wash her hands every time those thoughts threaten to become conscious, ridding herself symbolically of the "dirty" thoughts.

Behaviorism: Learning Problems Behaviorists, who define personality as a set of learned responses, have no trouble explaining disordered behavior as being learned just like normal behavior (Skinner, 1971; Watson, 1913). For example, when Joanne was a small child, a spider dropped onto her leg, causing Joanne to scream and react with fear. Her mother came running and made a big fuss over her, soothing her and giving her lots of attention. The next time Joanne saw a spider, she screamed again because of the prior fear-provoking incident. She also was rewarded with the attention of everyone in the room. Eventually, Joanne would experience a fear reaction and scream if someone just said the word *spider*. Behaviorists would say that Joanne's fear of the spider was classically conditioned to occur to the mere sight of a spider or even the word, and her screaming reaction was positively reinforced by all the attention and soothing.

Cognitive Perspective: Thinking Problems **Cognitive psychologists**, who study the way people think, remember, and mentally organize information, see abnormal behavior as resulting from illogical thinking patterns (Mora, 1985). A depressed person, for example, may be taking small problems and blowing them out of proportion: "I flunked my algebra test, my life is ruined!" A cognitive psychologist might explain Joanne's fear of spiders as distorted thinking: "All spiders are vicious and will bite me, and I will die!" Joanne's particular thinking patterns put her at a higher risk of depression and anxiety than those of a person who thinks more logically.

BIOPSYCHOSOCIAL PERSPECTIVE: ALL OF THE ABOVE

In recent years, the biological, psychological, and sociocultural influences on abnormality have no longer been seen as independent causes of abnormal behavior. Instead, these influences interact with one another to cause the various forms of disorders. For

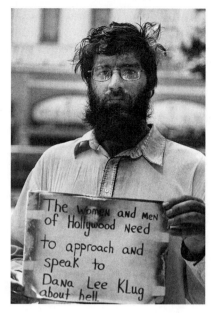

Some homeless people suffer from mental disorders, such as this man, who seems to believe that he has knowledge that others lack—a symptom typical of several serious disorders possibly linked to chemical imbalances or structural defects in the nervous system, according to the biological model.

cognitive psychologists psychologists who study the way people think, remember, and mentally organize information.

biopsychosocial model perspective in which abnormal behavior is seen as the result of the combined and interacting forces of biological, psychological, social, and cultural influences.

example, a person may have a genetically inherited tendency for a type of disorder, such as anxiety, but may not develop full-blown disorder unless the family and social environments produce the right stressors at the right time in development. How accepting of such disorders the particular culture is will also play a part in determining the exact degree and form that anxiety disorder might take. This is known as the **biopsychosocial model** of disorder, which has become a very influential way to view the connection between mind and body.

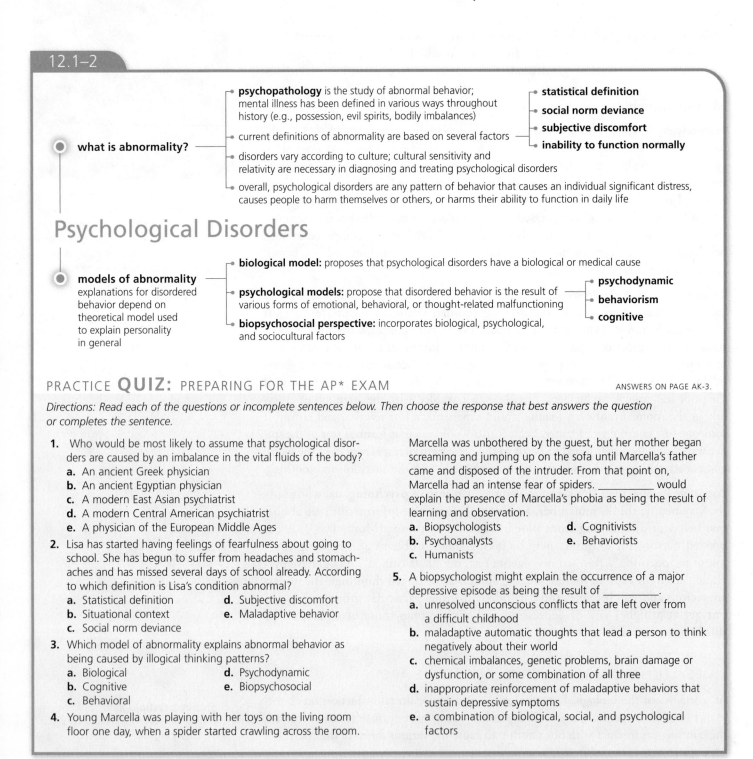

12.1–2

Psychological Disorders

what is abnormality?

- **psychopathology** is the study of abnormal behavior; mental illness has been defined in various ways throughout history (e.g., possession, evil spirits, bodily imbalances)
- current definitions of abnormality are based on several factors
  - **statistical definition**
  - **social norm deviance**
  - **subjective discomfort**
  - **inability to function normally**
- disorders vary according to culture; cultural sensitivity and relativity are necessary in diagnosing and treating psychological disorders
- overall, psychological disorders are any pattern of behavior that causes an individual significant distress, causes people to harm themselves or others, or harms their ability to function in daily life

models of abnormality explanations for disordered behavior depend on theoretical model used to explain personality in general

- **biological model:** proposes that psychological disorders have a biological or medical cause
- **psychological models:** propose that disordered behavior is the result of various forms of emotional, behavioral, or thought-related malfunctioning
  - **psychodynamic**
  - **behaviorism**
  - **cognitive**
- **biopsychosocial perspective:** incorporates biological, psychological, and sociocultural factors

PRACTICE QUIZ: PREPARING FOR THE AP* EXAM

ANSWERS ON PAGE AK-3.

Directions: Read each of the questions or incomplete sentences below. Then choose the response that best answers the question or completes the sentence.

1. Who would be most likely to assume that psychological disorders are caused by an imbalance in the vital fluids of the body?
   a. An ancient Greek physician
   b. An ancient Egyptian physician
   c. A modern East Asian psychiatrist
   d. A modern Central American psychiatrist
   e. A physician of the European Middle Ages

2. Lisa has started having feelings of fearfulness about going to school. She has begun to suffer from headaches and stomachaches and has missed several days of school already. According to which definition is Lisa's condition abnormal?
   a. Statistical definition
   b. Situational context
   c. Social norm deviance
   d. Subjective discomfort
   e. Maladaptive behavior

3. Which model of abnormality explains abnormal behavior as being caused by illogical thinking patterns?
   a. Biological
   b. Cognitive
   c. Behavioral
   d. Psychodynamic
   e. Biopsychosocial

4. Young Marcella was playing with her toys on the living room floor one day, when a spider started crawling across the room.

Marcella was unbothered by the guest, but her mother began screaming and jumping up on the sofa until Marcella's father came and disposed of the intruder. From that point on, Marcella had an intense fear of spiders. _____ would explain the presence of Marcella's phobia as being the result of learning and observation.
   a. Biopsychologists
   b. Psychoanalysts
   c. Humanists
   d. Cognitivists
   e. Behaviorists

5. A biopsychologist might explain the occurrence of a major depressive episode as being the result of _____.
   a. unresolved unconscious conflicts that are left over from a difficult childhood
   b. maladaptive automatic thoughts that lead a person to think negatively about their world
   c. chemical imbalances, genetic problems, brain damage or dysfunction, or some combination of all three
   d. inappropriate reinforcement of maladaptive behaviors that sustain depressive symptoms
   e. a combination of biological, social, and psychological factors

Diagnostic and Statistical Manual of Mental Disorders, Fourth Edition, Text Revision (DSM-IV-TR)

12.3 What are the different types of psychological disorders, and how common are they?

In 1952, the first edition of the *Diagnostic and Statistical Manual of Mental Disorders (DSM)* was published to help psychological professionals diagnose psychological disorders. The current version of the *DSM* is called the *Diagnostic and Statistical Manual of Mental Disorders, Fourth Edition, Text Revision (DSM-IV-TR)* (American Psychiatric Association, 2000). (The Text Revision version did not change any categories from the older *DSM-IV* but added new text material to the existing categories.)

CATEGORIES IN THE *DSM-IV-TR*

The *DSM-IV-TR* describes about 250 different psychological disorders. Each disorder is described in terms of its symptoms, the typical path the disorder takes as it progresses, and a checklist of specific criteria that must be met in order for the diagnosis of that disorder to be made. The manual also divides these disorders and relevant facts about the person being diagnosed along five different categories, or axes (see Table 12.1). A psychologist or psychiatrist assesses the person on each of these five axes.

Axis I, Clinical Disorders, contains the disorders that bring most people to the attention of a psychological professional. With one exception, all of the psychological disorders are listed on this axis. The exception is the personality disorders, which are listed on Axis II along with mental retardation (which is a developmental disorder). The reason for this is that, unlike most psychological disorders that appear at some later point in a person's life, personality disorders are a part of the person's personality and are, therefore, relatively stable and enduring. As an integral part of the personality, affecting relationships, careers, and behavior, personality disorders seem more similar to a condition such as mental retardation, which is a developmental disorder affecting many areas of the individual's life.

Axis III includes physical disorders that affect a person's psychological *adjustment*, such as juvenile diabetes, chromosome disorders such as Klinefelter's syndrome, and high blood pressure. (In psychology, the term *adjustment* refers to a person's ability to function normally in everyday life.) Axis IV contains information about problems in the person's life that might affect adjustment, such as the

AP* Recognize the use of the Diagnostic and Statistical Manual of Mental Disorders (DSM) published by the American Psychiatric Association as the primary reference for making diagnostic judgments.

Table 12.1 The Axes of the *DSM-IV-TR*

AXIS	TYPE OF INFORMATION	DESCRIPTION IN BRIEF
Axis I	Clinical Disorders and Other Conditions That May Be a Focus of Clinical Attention	Psychological disorders that impair functioning and are stressful and factors that are not disorders but may affect functioning, such as academic or social problems
Axis II	Personality Disorders and Mental Retardation	Rigid, enduring, maladaptive personality patterns and mental retardation
Axis III	General Medical Conditions	Chronic and acute illnesses and medical conditions that may have an impact on mental health
Axis IV	Psychosocial and Environmental Problems	Problems in the physical surroundings of the person that may have an impact on diagnosis, treatment, and outcome
Axis V	Global Assessment of Functioning	Overall judgment of current functioning, including mental, social, and occupational

Adapted from the American Psychiatric Association, *DSM-IV-TR* (2000).

Table 12.2 Axis I Disorders of the *DSM-IV-TR*

DISORDER	EXAMPLES
Disorders usually first diagnosed in infancy, childhood, or adolescence	Learning disabilities, ADHD, bed-wetting, speech disorders
Delirium, dementia, amnesia, and other cognitive disorders	Alzheimer's, Parkinson's, amnesia due to physical causes
Psychological disorders due to a general medical condition	Personality change because of a brain tumor
Substance-related disorders	Alcoholism, drug addictions
Schizophrenia and other psychotic disorders	Schizophrenia, delusional disorders, paranoid psychosis
Mood disorders	Depression, mania, bipolar disorders
Anxiety disorders	Panic disorder, phobias, stress disorders
Somatoform disorders	Hypochondria, conversion disorder
Factitious disorders	Pathological lying, Munchausen syndrome
Dissociative disorders	Dissociative identity disorder (formerly multiple personality), amnesia not due to physical causes
Sexual and gender identity disorders	Sexual desire disorders, paraphilias
Eating disorders	Anorexia, bulimia
Sleep disorders	Insomnia, sleep terror disorder, sleepwalking, narcolepsy
Impulse-control disorders not classified elsewhere	Kleptomania, pathological gambling, pyromania
Adjustment disorders	Mixed anxiety, conduct disturbances

Adapted from the American Psychiatric Association, *DSM-IV-TR* (2000).

death of a loved one, the loss of a job, or poverty. Finally, Axis V, Global Assessment of Functioning, is an overall judgment made by the psychological professional of the person's mental health and adjustment, literally a rating on a scale of 0 to 100. For example, scores of 91–100 would be interpreted as superior functioning, 71–80 as temporary problems due to stress, and 41–50 would indicate serious symptoms or impairment in functioning.

For a listing and brief description of the disorders found on Axis I, see Table 12.2.

HOW COMMON ARE PSYCHOLOGICAL DISORDERS?

That table has a pretty long list of disorders, but most people don't get these problems, right?

That table has a pretty long list of disorders, but most people don't get these problems, right? Actually, psychological disorders are more common than most people might think. In any given year, about 22 percent of adults over age 18 suffer from a mental disorder (Narrow et al., 2002; National Institute of Mental Health [NIMH] 2001; Regier et al., 1993). That comes to about 44 million people in the United States. Four of the ten leading causes of disability in the United States and other developed countries are psychological disorders of some kind, with major depression leading the list (Murray & Lopez, 1996; NIMH, 2001). In fact, it is quite common for people to suffer from more than one mental disorder at a time, such as a person with depression who also has a substance abuse disorder, or a person with an anxiety disorder who suffers from sleep disorders as well (NIMH, 2001). Table 12.3 has percentages of selected psychological disorders in the United States. (Note that this table does not include all of the disorders that occur in the 44 million adults in the United States mentioned earlier in this paragraph.)

Table 12.3 Occurrence of Psychological Disorders in the United States

CATEGORY OF DISORDER	SPECIFIC DISORDER	PERCENTAGE/NUMBER*
Depressive disorders	Major depressive disorder	5%/9.9 million
	Dysthymic disorder	5.4%/10.9 million
	Bipolar disorder	1.2%/2.3 million
Schizophrenia	All types	1.1%/2.2 million
Anxiety disorders	Panic disorder	1.7%/2.4 million
	Obsessive-compulsive disorder	2.3%/3.3 million
	Post-traumatic stress disorder	3.6%/5.2 million
	Generalized anxiety disorder	2.8%/4.0 million
	Social phobia	3.7%/5.3 million
	Agoraphobia	2.2%/3.2 million
	Specific phobia	4.4%/6.3 million

*Percentage of adults over age 18 affected annually/actual number within the population where available, in the United States.
Adapted from NIMH (2001).

Before describing the various categories and types of disorders, a word of caution: It's very easy to see oneself in these disorders. As mentioned in Chapter Eleven, medical students often become convinced that they have every one of the symptoms for some rare, exotic disease they have been studying. Psychology students studying abnormal behavior can also become convinced that they have some mental disorder, a problem that can be called *psychology student's syndrome*. The problem is that so many psychological disorders are really ordinary variations in human behavior taken to an extreme. For example, some people are natural-born worriers. They look for things that can go wrong around every corner. That doesn't make them disordered—it makes them pessimistic worriers. It doesn't become a disorder until the worrying gets out of hand or takes place when there's nothing to worry about or go wrong. So if you start "seeing" yourself or even your friends and family in any of the following discussions, don't panic—all of you are *probably* okay.

Statistically speaking, about one out of every five of the people in this crowd probably suffers from some form of psychological disorder.

THE PROS AND CONS OF LABELS

With its lists of disorders and their corresponding symptoms, the *DSM-IV-TR* helps psychological professionals diagnose patients and provide those patients with labels that explain their conditions. In the world of psychological diagnosis and treatment, labels like *depression, anxiety*, and *schizophrenia* can be very helpful: They make up a common language in the mental-health community, allowing psychological professionals to communicate with each other clearly and efficiently. Labels establish distinct diagnostic categories that all professionals recognize and understand, and they help patients receive effective treatment.

However, labels can also be dangerous—or, at the very least, overly influential. In 1972, researcher David Rosenhan asked healthy participants to enter

AP* Identify the positive and negative consequences of diagnostic labels.

psychiatric hospitals and complain that they were hearing voices. All of the participants, whom Rosenhan called "pseudopatients," were admitted into the hospitals and diagnosed with either schizophrenia or manic depression. Once the pseudopatients were admitted, they stopped pretending to be ill and acted as they normally would, but the hospital staff's interpretation of the pseudopatients' normal behavior was skewed by the label of mental illness. For example, hospital workers described one pseudopatient's relatively normal relationships with family and friends as evidence of a psychological disorder, and another pseudopatient's note-taking habits were considered to be a pathological behavior. The pseudopatients had been diagnosed and labeled, and those labels stuck, even when actual symptoms of mental illness disappeared. Rosenhan concluded that psychological labels are long lasting and powerful, affecting not only how other people see mental patients but how patients see themselves (Rosenhan, 1973).

Labels can be time-saving and even life-saving tools, but they can also bias us, affect our judgment, and give us preconceived notions that may very well turn out to be false. Just to be clear, the diagnostic labels listed in the *DSM-IV-TR* are intended to help both psychologists and patients, and they *do* help. As you read about the disorders described in the following pages, though, remember the power that labels have to shape our perceptions of reality.

Anxiety Disorders: What, Me Worry?

AP* Discuss the major diagnostic categories and their corresponding symptoms. ▶

12.4 What are the different types of anxiety disorders, their symptoms, and causes?

The category of **anxiety disorders** includes all disorders in which the most dominant symptom is excessive or unrealistic anxiety. Anxiety can take very specific forms, such as a fear of a specific object, or it can be a very general emotion, such as that experienced by someone who is worried and doesn't know why.

> But doesn't everybody ▶ have anxiety sometimes? What makes it a disorder?

But doesn't everybody have anxiety sometimes? What makes it a disorder? Everyone does have anxiety, and some people have a great deal of anxiety at times. When talking about anxiety disorders, the anxiety is either excessive—greater than it should be given the circumstances—or unrealistic. If final exams are coming up and a student hasn't studied enough, that student's anxiety is understandable and realistic. But a student who has studied, has done well on all the exams, and is very prepared and still worries *excessively* about passing is showing an unrealistic amount of anxiety. People who are in danger of losing their job might experience quite a bit of anxiety, but its source is obvious and understandable. But someone whose life is going well and for whom nothing bad is looming in the future who still feels extremely anxious may be experiencing an anxiety disorder. **Free-floating anxiety** is the term given to anxiety that seems to be unrelated to any realistic, known factor, and it is often a symptom of an anxiety disorder (Freud & Gay, 1977).

Post-traumatic and acute stress disorders are also anxiety disorders but were discussed more thoroughly in Chapter Nine and will not be repeated here.

PHOBIC DISORDERS: WHEN FEARS GET OUT OF HAND

One of the more specific anxiety disorders is a **phobia**, an irrational, persistent fear of something. The "something" might be an object or a situation or may involve social situations. For example, many people would feel fear if they suddenly came upon a live snake as they were walking and would take steps to avoid the snake. Although those same people would not necessarily avoid a *picture* of a snake in a book, a

anxiety disorders disorders in which the main symptom is excessive or unrealistic anxiety and fearfulness.

free-floating anxiety anxiety that is unrelated to any realistic, known source.

phobia an irrational, persistent fear of an object, situation, or social activity.

person with a phobia of snakes would. Avoiding a live snake is rational; avoiding a picture of a snake is not.

Social Phobias (Social Anxiety Disorder)   **Social phobias** (also called *social anxiety disorders*) involve a fear of interacting with others or being in a social situation and are some of the most common phobias people experience (WHO International Consortium in Psychiatric Epidemiology, 2000). People with a social phobia are afraid of being evaluated in some negative way by others, so they tend to avoid situations that could lead to something embarrassing or humiliating. They are very self-conscious as a result. Common types of social phobia are stage fright, fear of public speaking, and fear of urinating in a public restroom. Not surprisingly, people with social phobias often have a history of being shy as children (Sternberger et al., 1995).

Specific Phobias   A **specific phobia** is an irrational fear of some object or specific situation, such as a fear of dogs, or a fear of being in small, enclosed spaces (**claustrophobia**). Other specific phobias include a fear of injections (*trypanophobia*), fear of dental work (*odontophobia*), fear of blood (*hematophobia*), and fear of heights (**acrophobia**). For a listing of common phobias, see Table 12.4.

✻┤**Explore** on **MyPsychLab**

Agoraphobia   A third type of phobia is **agoraphobia**, a Greek name that literally means "fear of the marketplace." Although that makes it sound like a social phobia, agoraphobia is a little more complicated. It is actually the fear of being in a place or situation (social or not) from which escape is difficult or impossible if something should go wrong (American Psychiatric Association, 2000). So agoraphobics are often afraid of not only crowds but also crossing bridges, traveling in a car or plane, eating in restaurants, and sometimes even of leaving the house. To be in any of these situations or to even think about being in such situations can lead to extreme feelings of anxiety and even panic attacks (see the following section about panic attacks).

✻ **Explore** phobias.
www.mypsychlab.com

social phobia   fear of interacting with others or being in social situations that might lead to a negative evaluation.

specific phobia   fear of objects or specific situations or events.

claustrophobia   fear of being in a small, enclosed space.

acrophobia   fear of heights.

agoraphobia   fear of being in a place or situation from which escape is difficult or impossible.

Table 12.4   **Common Phobias and Their Scientific Names**

FEAR OF	SCIENTIFIC NAME
Washing and bathing	Ablutophobia
Spiders	Arachnophobia
Lightning	Ceraunophobia
Dirt, germs	Mysophobia
Snakes	Ophidiophobia
Darkness	Nyctophobia
Fire	Pyrophobia
Foreigners, strangers	Xenophobia
Animals	Zoophobia

Source: Adapted from Culbertson (2003).

Agoraphobia includes a fear of crossing bridges, although this bridge is enough to test anyone's courage.

If a person has ▶ agoraphobia, it might be difficult to even go to work or to the store, right?

www.CartoonStock.com

"RONALD IS EXTREMELY COMPULSIVE."

panic attack sudden onset of intense panic in which multiple physical symptoms of stress occur, often with feelings that one is dying.

panic disorder disorder in which panic attacks occur frequently enough to cause the person difficulty in adjusting to daily life.

panic disorder with agoraphobia fear of leaving one's familiar surroundings because one might have a panic attack in public.

obsessive-compulsive disorder disorder in which intruding, recurring thoughts or obsessions create anxiety that is relieved by performing a repetitive, ritualistic behavior or mental act (compulsion).

If a person has agoraphobia, it might be difficult to even go to work or to the store, right? Exactly. People with specific phobias can usually avoid the object or situation without too much difficulty, and people with social phobias may simply avoid jobs and situations that involve meeting people face-to-face. But people with agoraphobia cannot avoid their phobia's source because it is simply being outside in the real world. A severe case of agoraphobia can make a person's home a prison, leaving the person trapped inside unable to go to work, shop, or engage in any kind of activity that requires going out of the home.

PANIC DISORDER

Fourteen-year-old Anna was sitting in science class watching a film. All of a sudden, she started feeling really strange. Her ears seemed to be stuffed with cotton and her vision was very dim. She was cold, had broken out in a sweat, and felt extremely afraid for no good reason. Her heart was racing and she immediately became convinced that she was dying. A friend sitting behind her saw how pale she had become and tried to ask her what was wrong, but Anna couldn't speak. She was in a state of panic and couldn't move. The friend got the teacher's attention, who motioned to Anna to come over to him. Although she would have sworn she couldn't move, she stood up to go to him and immediately everything returned to normal.

Anna's symptoms are the classic symptoms of a **panic attack**, a sudden onset of extreme panic with various physical symptoms: racing heart, rapid breathing, a sensation of being "out of one's body," dulled hearing and vision, sweating, and dry mouth (Kumar & Oakley-Browne, 2002). Many people who have a panic attack think that they are having a heart attack and can experience pain as well as panic, but the symptoms are caused by the panic, not by any actual physical disorder. Psychologically, the person having a panic attack is in a state of terror, thinking that this is it, death is happening, and many people may feel a need to escape. The attack happens without warning and quite suddenly. Although some panic attacks can last as long as half an hour, some last only a few minutes, with most attacks peaking within 10 to 15 minutes.

Having a panic attack is not that unusual, especially for adolescent girls and young adult women (Eaton et al., 1994; Hayward et al., 1989, 2000). Researchers have also found evidence that cigarette smoking greatly increases the risk of panic attacks in adolescents and young adults (Johnson, 2000; Zvolensky et al., 2003). Regardless of the age of onset, it is only when panic attacks become so frequent that they affect a person's ability to function in day-to-day life that they become a **panic disorder**. When a fear of having panic attacks in a public place prevents the person from going out into unfamiliar or exposed places, it is called **panic disorder with agoraphobia**.

Many people try to figure out what triggers a panic attack and avoid the situation if possible. If driving a car sets off an attack, they don't drive. If being in a crowd sets off an attack, they don't go where crowds are. It is easy to see how having panic disorder can often lead to agoraphobia. Psychologists and psychiatrists will classify a person as having either a panic disorder with agoraphobia or a panic disorder without agoraphobia.

OBSESSIVE-COMPULSIVE DISORDER

Sometimes people get a thought running through their head that just won't go away, like when a song gets stuck in one's mind. If that particular thought causes a lot of anxiety, it can become the basis for an **obsessive-compulsive disorder** or OCD. OCD is a disorder in which intruding* thoughts that occur again and again (obsessions, such as a fear that germs are on one's hands) are followed by some compulsion, a repetitive, rit-

---

*Intruding: forcing one's way in; referring to something undesirable that enters awareness.

ualistic behavior (such as repeated hand washing) or mental act (such as praying or counting). The compulsions are meant to lower the anxiety caused by the thought (Soomro, 2001).

Some other examples of obsessive thoughts and compulsive behaviors include an obsession with having left something undone, resulting in the constant checking and rechecking of one's work, or thinking that one might do something to harm a loved one, leading to counting and recounting the knives in the kitchen.

I knew someone who had just had a baby, and she spent the first few nights home with the baby checking it to see if it was breathing—is that an obsessive-compulsive disorder? No, almost all new parents check their infant's breathing frequently at first. Remember *psychology student's syndrome?* Everyone has a little obsessive thinking from time to time or has some little ritual that just makes them feel better. One woman liked to check on both of her children just before she went to bed, saying a little prayer for their safekeeping each night. She didn't feel *compelled* to do the checking and the prayer, however. If she had been a true obsessive-compulsive, she would *always have to perform the check and the prayer*, even if it meant getting out of bed or going to wherever the children were sleeping. If she had for some reason been unable to complete the ritual, she would also have experienced extreme anxiety or distress. The distress caused by a failure or inability to successfully complete the compulsive behavior or mental act is a defining feature of OCD. In fact, the woman's children might not have been allowed to sleep anywhere else because of her fear that she could not complete the ritual. It's really a matter of degree.

◄ I knew someone who had just had a baby, and she spent the first few nights home with the baby checking it to see if it was breathing—is that an obsessive-compulsive disorder?

GENERALIZED ANXIETY DISORDER

What about people who are just worriers? Can that become a disorder? Remember free-floating anxiety? That's the kind of anxiety that has no real source and may be experienced by people with **generalized anxiety disorder**, in which excessive anxiety and worries (apprehensive expectations) occur more days than not for at least six months. People with this disorder may also experience anxiety about a number of events or activities (such as work or school performance). These feelings of anxiety persist six months or more and have no real source that can be pinpointed, nor can the person control the feelings even if an effort is made to do so.

◄ What about people who are just worriers? Can that become a disorder?

People with this disorder are just plain worriers (Ruscio et al., 2001). They worry about money, their children, their lives, their friends, the dog, and anything else that they think might possibly go wrong. They feel tense and edgy, get tired easily, and may have trouble concentrating. They have muscle aches and tension; they experience sleeping problems and are often irritable—all signs of stress. The problem is that the stress comes from their worrying rather than from any real external source. General anxiety disorder is often found occurring with other anxiety disorders and depression.

Once again, it is a matter of degree and source: People with generalized anxiety disorder worry more excessively than people who are normal worriers, and they worry about things that would cause other people no real concern.

CAUSES OF ANXIETY DISORDERS

Different perspectives on how personality develops offer different explanations for anxiety disorders. For example, the *psychodynamic model* sees anxiety as a kind of danger signal that repressed urges or conflicts are threatening to surface (Freud & Gay, 1977). A phobia is seen as a kind of displacement, in which the phobic object is actually only a symbol of whatever the person has buried deep in his or her unconscious mind—the true source of the fear. A fear of knives might mean a fear of one's own aggressive tendencies, or a fear of heights may hide a suicidal desire to jump.

generalized anxiety disorder
disorder in which a person has feelings of dread and impending doom along with physical symptoms of stress, which lasts six months or more.

magnification the tendency to interpret situations as far more dangerous, harmful, or important than they actually are.

all-or-nothing thinking the tendency to believe that one's performance must be perfect or the result will be a total failure.

overgeneralization the tendency to interpret a single negative event as a never-ending pattern of defeat and failure.

minimization the tendency to give little or no importance to one's successes or positive events and traits.

Anxiety disorders affect children as well as adults.

Behaviorists believe that anxious behavioral reactions are learned. They see phobias, for example, as nothing more than classically conditioned fear responses, as was the case with "Little Albert" (Rachman, 1990; Watson & Rayner, 1920). Ⓛ Ⓘ Ⓝ Ⓚ *to Chapter Five: Learning, p. 183.* Remember Joanne, who was afraid of spiders? She received a lot of attention when she had a phobic reaction. When her friends stopped giving her this attention every time she overreacted to seeing a spider or hearing the word, the reaction was almost completely extinguished.

Cognitive psychologists see anxiety disorders as the result of illogical, irrational thought processes. One way in which people with anxiety disorders show irrational thinking (Beck, 1976, 1984) is through **magnification**, or the tendency to "make mountains out of molehills" by interpreting situations as being far more harmful, dangerous, or embarrassing than they actually are. In panic disorder, for example, a person might interpret a racing heartbeat as a sign of a heart attack instead of just a momentary arousal.

Another distorted thought process is **all-or-nothing thinking**, in which a person believes that his or her performance must be perfect or the result will be a total failure. **Overgeneralization** (a single negative event interpreted as a never-ending pattern of defeat), jumping to conclusions without facts to support that conclusion, and **minimization** (giving little or no emphasis to one's successes or positive events and traits) are other examples of irrational thinking.

Growing evidence exists that *biological* factors contribute to anxiety disorders. Generalized anxiety disorder, for example, has been linked to an imbalance in several neurotransmitters in the nervous system, including lower levels of both serotonin and GABA (Brawman-Mintzer & Lydiard, 1997; Rynn et al., 2000). Lower levels of these neurotransmitters may reduce the ability to calm reactions to stress. Recent research has linked panic disorder to a possible defect in the way serotonin binds to its receptors in the nervous system (Neumeister et al., 2004). Some evidence suggests that these chemical imbalances may have a genetic component, meaning that anxiety disorders such as obsessive-compulsive disorder, phobias, and panic disorder can be passed from parent to child through more than just observational learning (Karayiorgou et al., 1997; Lesch et al., 1996; Logue et al., 2003).

Twin studies have provided more evidence for a genetic basis for anxiety disorders, particularly panic disorder and the phobias, with some studies finding that the heritability of panic disorder is about 44 percent, agoraphobia about 39 percent, and anxiety disorder about 30 percent (Hettema et al., 2001; Tsuang et al., 2004; Villafuerte & Burmeister, 2003). Neuroimaging studies using the scanning techniques of PET and fMRI, Ⓛ Ⓘ Ⓝ Ⓚ *to Chapter Two: The Biological Perspective, pp. 66–68,* have revealed that the amygdala, an area of the limbic system, is more active in phobic people responding to pictures of spiders than in nonphobic people (LeDoux, 2003; Rauch et al., 2003).

Anxiety disorders are found around the world, although the particular form the disorder takes might be different in various cultures. For example, in some Latin American cultures anxiety can take the form of "ataque de nervios," or "attack of nerves," in which the person may have fits of crying, shout uncontrollably, experience sensations of heat, and become very aggressive, either verbally or physically. These attacks usually come after some stressful event such as the death of a loved one (APA, 2000). The Current Issues in Psychology section earlier in this chapter mentioned several syndromes found in certain cultures, such as TKS or Susto, that are essentially types of phobias specific to those cultures. Panic disorder is found almost universally at about the same rate all over the world (Weissman et al., 1997).

12.3–4

Diagnostic and Statistical Manual of Mental Disorders, Fourth Edition, Text Revision (DSM–IV–TR)
- *DSM* first published in 1952, current version (*DSM–IV–TR*) published in 2000
- currently describes approximately 250 different psychological disorders and includes diagnostic criteria along five different categories, or axes (see Tables 12.1 and 12.2)
- in general, approximately 22% of adults over age 18 in the United States suffer from a mental disorder

Psychological Disorders

anxiety disorders
most dominant symptom is excessive or unrealistic anxiety

- anxiety can be free-floating (nonspecific, anxious in general) or more specific, as in the case of phobias
  - social phobias
  - specific phobias (e.g., **claustrophobia, acrophobia**)
  - **agoraphobia**
- **panic disorder** consists of an individual having frequent panic attacks that interfere with normal daily functioning; **panic disorder with agoraphobia** occurs when a fear of having panic attacks in public prevents an individual from going out
- **obsessive compulsive disorder (OCD)** consists of recurring anxiety-provoking thoughts or obsessions that are only relieved through ritualistic or repetitive behaviors or mental events
- **generalized anxiety disorder** involves excessive worry about lots of things and occurs more days than not
- causes
  - **behaviorists:** anxious behavioral reactions are learned
  - **cognitive psychologists:** anxiety is result of illogical, irrational thought processes
    - **magnification**
    - **all-or-none thinking**
    - **overgeneralization**
    - **minimization**
  - **biological:** anxiety is due to imbalance in several neurotransmitters (e.g., serotonin, GABA) and/or difference in brain activation; panic disorder is also hereditary
  - **culture:** anxiety disorders found around the world but particular forms vary across cultures

PRACTICE **QUIZ:** PREPARING FOR THE AP* EXAM

ANSWERS ON PAGE AK-3.

Directions: Read each of the questions or incomplete sentences below. Then choose the response that best answers the question or completes the sentence.

1. In the *DSM-IV-TR*, Axis I contains information about _____.
   a. clinical disorders
   b. general medical conditions
   c. global assessment of functioning
   d. psychosocial and environmental problems
   e. personality disorders and mental retardation

2. On which axis of the *DSM-IV-TR* would you find information about juvenile diabetes?
   a. Axis I
   b. Axis II
   c. Axis III
   d. Axis IV
   e. Axis V

3. Maurice is shopping in the supermarket one afternoon, when he is suddenly gripped with overwhelming dread, tension, and anxiety. He has several physical symptoms—his heart races, his breathing speeds up, he begins to sweat—and he feels an intense desire to escape and run away. Just a few minutes later, when he gets outside and takes several deep breaths, the feelings pass. Maurice has just experienced a(n) _____ attack.
   a. somatoform
   b. panic
   c. phobic
   d. obsessive-compulsive
   e. dissociative

4. Jennifer worries that someone might come into her house at night while she is sleeping. She checks the locks on the doors and windows several times before she can relax enough to go to bed. Her constant checking of the locks is _____.
   a. a phobia
   b. an obsession
   c. a compulsion
   d. a panic attack
   e. a panic disorder

5. Bud's relatives are concerned that Bud worries too much. He worries about little things going wrong, he worries about big things going wrong, and sometimes it seems as though he's worrying because there's nothing to worry about. He worries so much that he has a hard time getting things done. Bud most likely has

   _____.
   a. panic disorder
   b. a social phobia
   c. a specific phobia
   d. generalized anxiety disorder
   e. obsessive-compulsive disorder

AP* Discuss the major diagnostic categories and their corresponding symptoms.

I've heard of something like this— but I thought the name of it was psychosomatic disorder?

Somatoform Disorders: Sickness as a State of Mind

12.5 What are the different kinds of somatoform disorders and their causes?

Another category of abnormal behavior involves the belief that one is physically ill, which is often accompanied by the experience of physical symptoms even though there is no physical illness or problem. Disorders in which people believe they are sick when they are not are called **somatoform disorders**. *Somatoform* means that these disorders take the form of a bodily (somatic) ailment but are not real physical disorders. Although there is no real physical cause, the symptoms are very real to the person experiencing them.

I've heard of something like this—but I thought the name of it was psychosomatic disorder? Somatoform disorders are actually quite different from **psychosomatic disorders**. In a psychosomatic disorder (now called **psychophysiological disorder**), the bodily ailments are real physical ailments caused or worsened by stress. The two disorders are often confused. Unlike psychophysiological disorders, somatoform disorders are *not* real physical ailments, and although the symptoms are real to the person experiencing them, they are quite literally "all in one's head."

HYPOCHONDRIASIS

Hypochondriasis (or the older name *hypochondria*) is one of the better-known somatoform disorders. In this disorder, a person worries excessively and almost constantly about getting ill. Although this may sound like an anxiety disorder, the specific worry about illness is the distinguishing feature of this disorder. People with this disorder become very preoccupied with bodily symptoms, which may be real but unimportant in reality or imagined (Phillips, 2001). They go to doctors and health clinics frequently, looking for some medical professional who will tell them what dreadful disease they have (Magarinos et al., 2002). People with this disorder are often called *hypochondriacs*.

SOMATIZATION DISORDER

A similar somatoform disorder is **somatization disorder**, in which the person complains about a specific physical symptom or symptoms, such as pain, nausea, difficulty swallowing, or trouble catching one's breath (Kellner, 1986). People with this disorder also go to doctors a lot, but they show less worry and more "drama." They tend to get very emotional when describing their symptoms, using phrases like "unbearable" and "beyond description" to describe their pain or other symptom, and they tend to become very dependent on the medical professional, demanding attention and even threatening suicide to get that attention in some cases. The symptoms also seem to multiply and shift frequently, with the main symptom being pain one day and shortness of breath on another, for example (Swartz, 1990). Like the hypochondriac, a person with somatization disorder is not creating symptoms just to fool others. Although it might be obvious to others, people with these disorders do not see the connection between their anxiety and their bodily symptoms.

CONVERSION DISORDER

Conversion disorder is limited to those functions controlled by the somatic nervous system. It is not seen as frequently today as in the past. Symptoms are the loss of motor and/or sensory functions (APA, 2000). A person may experience dramatic, sudden, and specific symptoms such as blindness, paralysis, deafness, or numbness of certain body parts, none of which have real physical causes. Typically, the problems

somatoform disorders disorders that take the form of bodily illnesses and symptoms but for which there are no real physical disorders.

psychosomatic disorder disorder in which psychological stress causes a real physical disorder or illness.

psychophysiological disorder modern term for psychosomatic disorder.

hypochondriasis somatoform disorder in which the person is terrified of being sick and worries constantly, going to doctors repeatedly, and becoming preoccupied with every sensation of the body.

somatization disorder somatoform disorder in which the person dramatically complains of a specific symptom such as nausea, difficulty swallowing, or pain for which there is no real physical cause.

conversion disorder somatoform disorder in which the person experiences a specific symptom in the somatic nervous system's functioning, such as paralysis, numbness, or blindness, for which there is no physical cause.

occur along with some other psychological disorder, such as depression, at a time when there is a stressful situation either already happening or threatening to happen (Hurwitz, 1989).

There are some simple ways to recognize conversion disorders. Organically caused blindness, deafness, and other disorders hardly ever occur with the suddenness that is typical of conversion disorders. People with such disorders tend to exhibit a kind of indifference or lack of concern about the symptom, which is understandable if the person has unconscious knowledge that the symptom is not real (Silver, 1996). Another is that the symptom is anatomically impossible, as is the case with blindness for which there is no corresponding damage to the eyes, optic nerve, or parts of the brain responsible for vision. (See Figure 12.1.) Finally, conversion disorder symptoms disappear when the person is asleep, hypnotized, under anesthesia, or unconscious (Parobek, 1997; Silver, 1996). Like somatization disorder, conversion disorder usually occurs when a stressful situation has also occurred or is threatening to occur, such as a soldier facing the return to combat.

CAUSES OF SOMATOFORM DISORDERS

The psychodynamic view of this type of disorder is that it is a way of making anxiety caused by the repression of traumatic events or unacceptable impulses into a physical symptom. Behaviorists, on the other hand, believe that the behavior of people with somatoform disorders clearly brings them two kinds of reinforcement: positive reinforcement in the form of attention from doctors, family members, and others, and negative reinforcement from being able to avoid whatever stressful situation is associated with the disorder. A hypochondriac, for example, who believes that his heart is about to give out might resist going back to work or doing strenuous chores around the house; a soldier with conversion paralysis need not face combat again; and a child with a somatization stomachache gets to stay home and avoid the big math exam that day. Cognitive psychologists would again point to the tendency of people with these disorders to magnify minor physical symptoms and allow false beliefs about their health to dominate their thinking.

Dissociative Disorders: Altered Consciousness

12.6 How do the various dissociative disorders differ, and how do they develop?

Dissociative disorders involve a break, or dissociation, in consciousness, memory, or a person's sense of identity. This "split" is easier to understand when thinking about how people sometimes drive somewhere and then wonder how they got there—they don't remember the trip itself at all. This sort of "automatic pilot" driving happens when the route is familiar and frequently traveled. One part of the conscious mind was thinking about work, school, or whatever was uppermost in the mind while lower centers of consciousness were driving the car, stopping at signs and lights, and turning when needed. This split in conscious attention is very similar to what happens in dissociative disorders. The difference is that in the disorders the dissociation is much more pronounced and involuntary.

DISSOCIATIVE AMNESIA: WHO AM I?

In **dissociative amnesia**, one cannot remember personal information such as one's own name or specific personal events—the kind of information contained in episodic long-term memory. (L)(I)(N)(K) *to Chapter Six: Memory, p. 232.* This memory loss is

Figure 12.1 Glove Anesthesia
Glove anesthesia is a disorder in which the person experiences numbness from the wrist down (see the drawing on the left). However, real nerve damage would produce numbness down one side of the arm and hand, as shown in the drawing on the right. Thus, because glove anesthesia is anatomically impossible, it is actually a sign of a conversion disorder.

◄ **AP*** Discuss the major diagnostic categories and their corresponding symptoms.

dissociative disorders disorders in which there is a break in conscious awareness, memory, the sense of identity, or some combination.

dissociative amnesia loss of memory for personal information, either partial or complete.

On Christmas Day 1985, James McDonnell came home to his wife in Larchmont, New York, after 14 years of amnesia. After suffering two separate head injuries in auto accidents, he lost his memory. He went to Philadelphia and found a job in a restaurant. On Christmas Eve, Mr. McDonnell bumped his head and recovered all of his memories. This picture shows the happy reunion with his wife. What kinds of emotional and psychological adjustments do you think Mr. McDonnell and his family might have had to make upon his sudden return? Is it possible that his 14-year memory loss may have begun with the head injuries but was maintained for so long because of dissociation from his former life?

dissociative fugue traveling away from familiar surroundings with amnesia for the trip and possible amnesia for personal information.

dissociative identity disorder disorder occurring when a person seems to have two or more distinct personalities within one body.

usually associated with a stressful or emotionally traumatic experience, such as rape or childhood abuse (Chu et al., 1999; Kirby et al., 1993), and cannot be easily explained by simple forgetfulness. It can be a loss of memory for only one small segment of time, or it can involve a total loss of one's past personal memories. For example, a soldier might be able to remember being in combat but cannot remember witnessing a friend get killed, or a person might forget his or her entire life. These memories usually resurface, sometimes quickly, and sometimes after a long delay. In one case, a veteran of the Second World War had amnesia for the time during which he was captured, tortured, and escaped from the Far East. He did not recall these memories, or the fact that he had been an intelligence agent at the time, until 37 years later (Cassiday & Lyons, 1992).

Dissociative amnesia may sound like retrograde amnesia, but it differs in its cause. In retrograde amnesia, the memory loss is typically caused by a physical injury, such as a blow to the head. In dissociative amnesia, the cause is psychological rather than physical. The "blow" is a mental one, not a physical one. People with dissociative amnesia do not forget how to drive or any of the skills they previously had, and they can still talk and use the kind of information found in semantic memory. It is only the personal information that is suppressed.

DISSOCIATIVE FUGUE: WHO AM I AND HOW DID I GET HERE?

The Latin word *fugere* means "flight" and is the word from which the term *fugue* is taken. A **dissociative fugue** occurs when a person suddenly travels away from home (the flight) and afterwards cannot remember the trip or even personal information such as identity. The person may become confused about identity, sometimes even taking on a whole new identity in the new place (Nijenhuis, 2000). Such flights usually take place after an emotional trauma and are more common in times of disasters or war.

As an example, look at the story of John Doe, so named by the physician who first saw him in the emergency room. John had no belongings and didn't know his name. He had no memories about his life before waking up on a park bench that morning, eight hours before. He seemed physically healthy, in his forties, and was dressed neatly and casually. He was clear and coherent* and seemed mentally stable, except for his loss of memory. Following a lead provided by the tag in his jacket, John was identified as a lawyer from a town 500 miles away who had been reported missing by his wife two days earlier. He had been criminally charged with embezzling from his clients and had been under such pressure that he had told his wife, "I don't know if I can take much more of this without losing my mind." Instead of losing his mind, John lost himself (Morrison, 1995).

DISSOCIATIVE IDENTITY DISORDER: HOW MANY AM I?

Perhaps the most controversial dissociative disorder is **dissociative identity disorder**, formerly known as multiple personality disorder. In this disorder, a person seems to experience at least two or more distinct personalities existing in one body. There may be a "core" personality, who usually knows nothing about the other personalities and is the one who experiences "blackouts" or losses of memory and time. Fugues are common in dissociative identity disorder, with the core personality experiencing unsettling moments of "awakening" in an unfamiliar place or with people who call the person by another name (Kluft, 1984).

First reported in the nineteenth century as a clinical disorder, many believe that cases of so-called "spirit" or "demon possession" were possibly people with this dis-

*Coherent: logically and consistently ordered or structured.

order. Freudian psychoanalysts believe that multiple personalities come about as a way of coping with extreme stress, usually in early childhood. Many people who have been diagnosed as "multiples" are women with a history of childhood abuse. It is thought that the dissociation occurs as one aspect of personality emerges to deal with the stress while the rest of the personality remains safely "hidden" in the unconscious mind. Psychoanalysts attempt to "reintegrate" the individual personalities into the core personality, which is a fancy way of saying that the person has to reclaim that part of the personality as part of the whole (Kluft, 1988). (Non-Freudian psychologists, psychiatrists, and therapists use other forms of psychotherapy and/or drugs in the treatment of this disorder.) ◉ Watch on MyPsychLab

With the publication of several famous books such as *The Three Faces of Eve* (Thigpen & Cleckley, 1992) and *Sybil* (Schreiber, 1973) and movies made from those books, dissociative identity disorder became well known to the public. Throughout the 1980s, the publishing world saw numerous books, some fiction, and some a blend of fiction and fact, about this disorder, and psychological professionals began to diagnose this condition at an alarming rate—"multiple personality," as it was then known, had become the "fad" disorder of the late twentieth century, according to some researchers (Aldridge-Morris, 1989; Boor, 1982; Cormier & Thelen, 1998; Showalter, 1997).

In the last decade, the diagnosis of dissociative identity disorder has come under scrutiny* with many (but not all) professionals now beginning to doubt the validity of previous diagnoses. Even the famous case of "Sybil" has been criticized as a case of the therapist actually "creating" the multiple personalities in her client through suggestion and even direct instruction. (For more on this controversial case, see the following Current Issues in Psychology section.) Some psychological professionals believe that dissociative identity disorder is actually a misdiagnosis of borderline personality disorder or some other form of anxiety disorder (Lauer et al., 1993).

Is it a real disorder that some people fake, or is there really no such thing as multiple personality? There are some skeptics who believe that there is no such disorder at all and that clients who demonstrate different "personalities" are simply acting out to get the attention of the therapist or are responding to what the therapist seems to want (Gleaves, 1996). In one study, ordinary people were given instructions in how to play the role of a multiple personality and were able to exhibit the "symptoms" associated with the disorder quite effectively (Spanos et al., 1985). However, just because someone can act out having the flu does not mean that the flu does not really exist, so being able to reproduce the symptoms of dissociative identity disorder by acting does not automatically mean that such a disorder does not exist. The question is not really, "Does dissociative identity disorder exist?" but rather, "What causes a person to exhibit the symptoms of dissociative identity disorder?" If the cause is suggestions from the therapist or deliberate deception, then there is a problem. If the symptoms of dissociative identity disorder are a sign of a person in deep psychological trouble, then the "reality" of those "personalities" becomes somewhat meaningless—the person is in trouble and needs help in either case (Arrigo & Pezdek, 1998; McHugh, 1993).

Christine Costner Sizemore is the real face behind The Three Faces of Eve, the book that first brought dissociative identity disorder into the public eye. Ms. Sizemore is a successful writer and artist and has been free of symptoms for many years.

◉ Watch classic video footage on *The Three Faces of Eve.* www.mypsychlab.com

◀ Is it a real disorder that some people fake, or is there really no such thing as multiple personality?

*Scrutiny: a close examination.

CAUSES OF DISSOCIATIVE DISORDERS

Psychodynamic theory, of course, sees the repression of threatening or unacceptable thoughts and behavior as a defense mechanism at the heart of all disorders, and the dissociative disorders in particular seem to have a large element of repression—motivated forgetting—in them. In the psychodynamic view, loss of memory or disconnecting one's awareness from a stressful or traumatic event is adaptive in that it reduces the emotional pain (Dorahy, 2001).

Cognitive and behavioral explanations for dissociative disorders are connected: The person may feel guilt, shame, or anxiety when thinking about disturbing experiences or thoughts and start avoiding thoughts about them. This "thought avoidance" is negatively reinforced by the reduction of the anxiety and unpleasant feelings and eventually will become a habit of "not thinking about" these things. This is similar to what many people do when faced with something unpleasant, such as an injection or a painful procedure such as having a root canal. They "think about something else." In doing that, they are deliberately not thinking about what is happening to them at the moment and the experience of pain is decreased. People with dissociative disorders may simply be better at doing this sort of "not thinking" than other people are.

Also, consider the positive reinforcement possibilities for a person with a dissociative disorder: attention from others and help from professionals. Shaping may also play a big role in the development of some cases of dissociative identity disorder. The therapist may unintentionally pay more attention to a client who talks about "feeling like someone else," which may encourage the client to report more such feelings and even elaborate on them. In the wake of the books and movies about multiples, many therapists no doubt were looking very hard for signs of multiple personality in their clients.

There are some possible biological sources for dissociations, as well. Researchers have found that people with **depersonalization disorder** (a mild dissociative disorder in which people feel detached and disconnected from themselves, their bodies, and their surroundings) have lower brain activity in the areas responsible for their sense of body awareness than do people without the disorder (Simeon et al., 2000). Others have found evidence that people with dissociative identity disorders (DID) show significant differences in PET scan activity taken when different "personalities" are present (Reinders et al., 2001; Tsai et al., 1999). Another study proposes that the neurological differences might result from the childhood abuse so common to persons diagnosed with DID (Teicher et al., 2002). These studies, if successfully replicated in future research, may one day put an end to the controversy over the validity of dissociative identity disorder.

Dissociative disorders can also be found in other cultures. As mentioned previously, the trancelike state known as *amok* in which a person suddenly becomes highly agitated and violent (found in Southeast Asia and Pacific Island cultures) is usually associated with no memory for the period during which the "trance" lasts (Suryani & Jensen, 1993). But a study that reviewed historical literature throughout the centuries found no mention or tales of what would be labeled as dissociative amnesia in the stories or nonfiction writings of any culture prior to the 1800s (Pope et al., 2007). The authors concluded that dissociative amnesia may be more of a nineteenth-century culture-bound phenomenon than a neuropsychological one.

depersonalization disorder
dissociative disorder in which individuals feel detached and disconnected from themselves, their bodies, and their surroundings.

Current Issues in Psychology

Was "Sybil" a True Multiple Personality?

Shirley Ardell Mason is pictured here as she looked in 1970 while serving as an assistant art professor at Rio Grande College in Ohio. Upon her death in 1998, neighbors in her Lexington, Kentucky, hometown were stunned to discover that Ms. Mason was the famous multiple personality, "Sybil."

Shirley Ardell Mason spent the last 25 years of her life in Lexington, Kentucky, living quietly as the town's resident artist. When she died on February 26, 1998, of breast cancer at age 75, all but a very few people were surprised to learn that the former college art teacher was in fact the most famous psychiatric patient in the world—"Sybil" (Miller & Kantrowitz, 1999). Her diagnosis and treatment for dissociative identity disorder (DID), known then as multiple personality disorder or MPD, became known worldwide with the publication of writer Flora Rita Schreiber's landmark book, *Sybil*, in 1973, followed by a 1976 made-for-television movie starring actress Sally Fields.

But were Shirley's 16 alternate personalities real, or did her psychiatrist, Dr. Wilbur, unintentionally "create" a case of multiple personality? Two sources of evidence suggest strongly that "Sybil" was not a multiple personality until Dr. Wilbur suggested that "Sybil," under hypnosis and the effects of sodium pentothal, a powerful mind-altering drug, talk about her feelings as other people with other names and identities. In an excerpt from audiotapes of the sessions between Wilbur and book author Schreiber, Wilbur says, "And I said, 'Well, there's a personality who calls herself Peggy.' And uh, I said, 'She is pretty assertive. . . . She can do things you can't,' and she (Sybil) was very, uh, obviously perturbed by this . . . And I said . . . 'She wouldn't do anything you wouldn't approve of. She might do something that you wouldn't think of doing.'" This quote seems to have Wilbur actually telling Shirley how she should think of her other "personalities." In another tape, Schreiber is heard dismissing a letter written by Shirley Mason to Dr. Wilbur, in which Shirley denies having multiple personalities (Spiegel & Borch-Jacobsen, 1997).

Evidence was also offered by Dr. Herbert Spiegel, who was Shirley's therapist when Dr. Wilbur was out of town. Spiegel, basing his opinion on both his own sessions with Shirley and the contents of the tapes, concluded that the so-called personalities came out of Wilbur's technique of giving names to various emotional states experienced by her client (Spiegel & Borch-Jacobsen, 1997). More ominous is his recall of telling the book's author, Schreiber, that "Sybil" did not have multiple personalities. He says that Schreiber replied, "If we don't call it multiple personality, the publisher won't want it, it won't sell."

If many cases of dissociative identity disorder are not real, how can the people who are diagnosed with this disorder act so much like different "people" that even professionals are fooled? Spanos (1994, 1996) conducted studies in which he found that ordinary college students, under hypnosis, would show signs of a "second personality." He concludes that many cases of DID may actually be misdiagnosed because of clients' tendencies to "play the role" of a multiple personality, a social role that has become quite well known through books and movies.

Lending further support to the idea that dissociative identity disorder may be a disorder created by therapists in a particular social context, like the hysteria of the Freudian age, is the fact that the disorder is confined to North American culture with very few cases in Britain and none in Asian cultures such as Japan and India (Cohen et al., 1995; Fujii et al., 1998; Merskey, 1992).

One fact is clear: Before the publication of *Sybil*, there were only 76 reported *current* cases of DID (Braun, 1986) and only 200 cases of DID in all recorded medical history up to that time (Ofshe & Watters, 1994). After the book, the number of diagnosed cases of DID began to skyrocket. By 1984, there were 1,000 cases; by 1989, there were 4,000 cases, and in the 1990s psychiatrists and psychologists were estimating that there were 20,000 to 30,000 people suffering from DID (Van Til, 1997).

Questions for Further Discussion

1. If the famous case of "Sybil" turns out to be a mistaken diagnosis, does that mean that all other diagnoses of dissociative identity disorder are also mistaken?

2. What kind of precautions could therapists take to avoid "creating" certain symptoms of disorder in their clients?

12.5–6

● **somatoform disorders**
include disorders in which individuals believe they are sick and may experience physical symptoms but there is no physical illness or problem

- **hypochondriasis:** excessive worry about illness and getting ill
- **somatization disorder:** involves complaints of specific physical symptoms
- **conversion disorder:** not as common, symptoms involve loss of motor and/or sensory functions; may be sudden and dramatic
- causes
  - **psychodynamic:** repressed anxiety is manifest as a physical symptom
  - **cognitive:** magnification of minor physical symptoms coupled with false beliefs

Somatoform and Dissociative Disorders

● **dissociative disorders**
involve a dissociation in consciousness, memory, or sense of identity, often associated with extreme stress or trauma

- **dissociative amnesia:** person cannot remember personal information
- **dissociative fugue:** person takes sudden trip and cannot remember trip or personal information
- **dissociative identity disorder:** person seems to experience at least two or more distinct personalities; validity of actual disorder has been topic of debate
- causes
  - **psychodynamic:** repressed thoughts and behavior are primary defense mechanism and reduce emotional pain
  - **cognitive and behavioral:** trauma-related thought avoidance is negatively reinforced by reduction in anxiety and emotional pain
  - **biological:** support for brain activity differences in body awareness has been found in individuals with **depersonalization disorder**

PRACTICE QUIZ: PREPARING FOR THE AP* EXAM

ANSWERS ON PAGE AK-3.

Directions: Read each of the questions or incomplete sentences below. Then choose the response that best answers the question or completes the sentence.

1. Which of the following is a real physical ailment?
   a. Hypochondriasis
   b. Conversion disorder
   c. Somatoform disorder
   d. Somatization disorder
   e. Psychophysiological disorder

2. Carlos wakes up in an unfamiliar part of town. He doesn't know where he is or how he got there, and he's not sure what day it is. Carlos has most likely experienced an episode of

   _____.
   a. dissociative fugue
   b. dissociative amnesia
   c. somatization disorder
   d. depersonalization disorder
   e. dissociative identity disorder

3. Which of the following explanations would a psychodynamic psychologist most likely give about somatoform disorders?
   a. Somatoform disorders turn repressed anxiety into physical symptoms.
   b. Somatoform disorders give people both positive and negative reinforcement.
   c. Somatoform disorders are caused primarily by biological and genetic factors.

   d. Somatoform disorders occur in people who hold false beliefs about their health.
   e. Somatoform disorders can be evolutionarily advantageous for both men and women.

4. Because the symptoms of dissociative amnesia are not referenced in writing until the 1800s, dissociative amnesia is most likely to be a _____.
   a. nonexistent syndrome
   b. culture-bound syndrome
   c. psychosomatic syndrome
   d. neuropsychological syndrome
   e. genetically inherited syndrome

5. The controversial condition formerly known as multiple personality disorder is now called _____.
   a. agoraphobia
   b. panic disorder
   c. depersonalization disorder
   d. generalized anxiety disorder
   e. dissociative identity disorder

Mood Disorders: The Effect of Affect

12.7 What are the different types of mood disorders and their causes?

◄ **AP*** Discuss the major diagnostic categories and their corresponding symptoms

In psychological terms, the word **affect** is used to mean "emotion" or "mood." **Mood disorders** are a disturbance in emotion and are also referred to as affective disorders. Although the range of human emotions runs from deep, intense sadness and despair to extreme happiness and elation, under normal circumstances people stay in between those extremes—neither too sad nor too happy but content (see Figure 12.2). It is when stress or some other factor pushes a person to one extreme or the other that mood disorders can result. Mood disorders can be relatively mild (straying only a short distance from the "average") or they can be extreme (existing at either extreme of the range).

There are two relatively mild to moderate mood disorders, although their lesser intensity does not mean that people suffering from these disorders do not need help. **Dysthymia** comes from Greek words meaning "bad spirit" and is a form of mild, chronic* depression that lasts for at least two years or more (Klein et al., 2000). **Cyclothymia** means "spirit that moves in circles" and involves a cycle of being sad, then feeling quite happy, and then returning to sad, happy, sad, happy, and so on, with the cycle lasting two years or more. The episodes of elation are called *hypomania*, meaning "low mania." (*Mania* is extremely excessive activity and elation or irritability.) Like dysthymia, it usually begins in childhood or adolescence and includes times of normal feelings that may last less than two months at a time (APA, 2000). Both dysthymia and cyclothymia are usually reactions to external events such as the loss of a job or the death of a loved one.

But doesn't everybody get a little "down" sometimes? When does being sad become a disorder? It is normal to get sad every now and then and even to have a mild "mood swing" on occasion (the "mild" positions on Figure 12.2). But people experiencing normal sadness or moodiness usually return to normal relatively quickly. There's also usually a reason for the sadness—something bad has happened, an opportunity was lost, somebody is sick or has died, and so on. Although both dysthymia and cyclothymia can be triggered by an outside, stressful event, they go on too long to be considered normal reactions that need no treatment or attention.

◄ But doesn't everybody get a little "down" sometimes? When does being sad become a disorder?

MAJOR DEPRESSION

When a deeply depressed mood comes on fairly suddenly and either seems to be too severe for the circumstances or exists without any external cause for sadness, it is called **major depression**. Major depression would fall at the far extreme of sadness on Figure 12.2. People suffering from major depression are depressed for most of every day, take little or no pleasure in any activities, feel tired, have trouble sleeping or sleep

| Extreme sadness | Mild sadness | Normal emotions | Mild elation | Extreme elation |

Figure 12.2 The Range of Emotions

Most people experience a range of emotions over the course of a day or several days, such as mild sadness, calm contentment, or mild elation and happiness. A person with a mood disorder experiences emotions that are extreme and, therefore, abnormal.

*Chronic: long-lasting or occurring frequently over a long period of time.

affect in psychology, a term indicating "emotion" or "mood."

mood disorders disorders in which mood is severely disturbed.

dysthymia a moderate depression that lasts for two years or more and is typically a reaction to some external stressor.

cyclothymia disorder that consists of mood swings from moderate depression to hypomania and lasts two years or more.

major depression severe depression that comes on suddenly and seems to have no external cause.

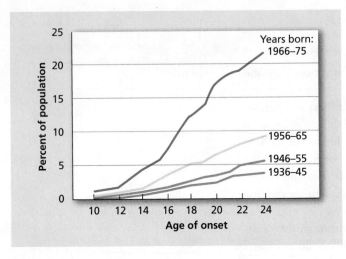

Figure 12.3 Prevalence of Major Depression

As the most common mood disorder, major depression has seen an increase in diagnosis with each decade. From 1936 to 1945, the prevalence of major depression in the population was about 3 percent, with the onset of symptoms occurring at around ages 18 to 20. By 1966 to 1975, the prevalence had jumped to about 23 percent of the population, and the age of onset had dropped to the early teens.

manic having the quality of excessive excitement, energy, and elation or irritability.

bipolar disorder severe mood swings between major depressive episodes and manic episodes.

That sounds almost like a description of an overactive child—can't sit still, can't concentrate—are the two disorders related? ▶

too much, experience changes in appetite and significant weight changes, experience excessive guilt or feelings of worthlessness, have trouble concentrating, and may have thoughts of death or suicide, including suicide attempts. Death by suicide is a real risk faced by people suffering from major depression. Some people with this disorder also suffer from delusional thinking and may experience hallucinations. Most of these symptoms occur on a daily basis, lasting for the better part of the day (APA, 2000).

Major depression is the most common of the diagnosed mood disorders (see Figure 12.3) and is about twice as common in women as it is in men (APA, 2000). This is true even across various cultures (Blazer et al., 1994; Weissman et al., 1993). There are many possible explanations for this gender difference, including the different hormonal structure of the female system (menstruation, hormonal changes during and after pregnancy, menopause, etc.) and different social roles played by women in the culture (Blehar & Oren, 1997). Research has found little support for hormonal influences in general, instead finding that the role of hormones and other biological factors in depression is unclear. Instead, studies have found that the degree of differences between male and female rates of depression is decreasing and is nonexistent in college students and single adults, leading some to conclude that social factors such as marital status, career type, and number of children may have more importance in creating the gender difference than biological differences (McGrath et al., 1992; Nolen-Hoeksema, 1990; Weissman & Klerman, 1977).

BIPOLAR DISORDERS

Major depression is sometimes referred to as a *unipolar disorder* because the emotional problem exists at only one end, or "pole," of the emotional range. When a person suffers from severe mood swings that go all the way from severe depression to **manic** episodes (excessive excitement, energy, and elation), that person is said to suffer from a **bipolar disorder**, meaning that emotions cycle between the two poles of possible emotions (APA, 2000). Unlike cyclothymia (which typically is a reaction to some environmental stressor), there is usually no external cause for the extreme ups and downs of the bipolar person. The depressive phases of a bipolar person are indistinguishable from major depression but give way to manic episodes that may last from a few weeks to a few months. In these manic episodes, the person is extremely happy or euphoric* without any real cause to be so happy. Restlessness, irritability, an inability to sit still or remain inactive, and seemingly unlimited energy are also common. The person may seem silly to others and can become aggressive when not allowed to carry out the grand (and sometimes delusional) plans that are often the hallmark of the manic phase. Speech may be rapid and jump from one topic to another. Oddly, people in the manic state are often very creative until their lack of organization renders their attempts at being creative useless (Blumer, 2002; McDermott, 2001; Rothenberg, 2001).

That sounds almost like a description of an overactive child—can't sit still, can't concentrate—are the two disorders related? The answer to that question is actually part of an ongoing controversy. There does seem to be a connection between attention-

---

*Euphoric: having a feeling of vigor, well-being, or high spirits.

deficit hyperactivity disorder (ADHD) and the onset of bipolar disorder in adolescence (Carlson et al., 1998), but only a small percentage of children with ADHD go on to develop bipolar disorder. The symptoms of bipolar disorder include irrational thinking and other manic symptoms that are not present in ADHD (Geller et al., 1998). Confusion between the two disorders arises because hyperactivity (excessive movement and an inability to concentrate) is a symptom of both disorders. In one recent study, researchers compared children diagnosed with both bipolar disorder and ADHD to children diagnosed with ADHD only on measures of academic performance and a series of neurological tests (Henin et al., 2007). They found that the two groups responded in very similar ways, showing the same deficits in information processing abilities, with only one exception: The children with both disorders performed more poorly on one measure of processing speed when compared to children with only ADHD. The researchers concluded that the neurological deficits often observed in children with bipolar disorder are more likely to be due to the ADHD rather than the bipolar disorder itself. ⊙ Watch on MyPsychLab

⊙ **Watch** a video on bipolar disorder. www.mypsychlab.com

CAUSES OF MOOD DISORDERS

Explanations of depression and other mood disorders come from the perspectives of psychodynamic, behavioral/social cognitive, and biological theories as well as genetics. Psychodynamic theories see depression as anger originally aimed at parents or other authority figures who are too threatening to receive the expressions of anger directly. The anger gets repressed by the child and later is displaced to the self in the form of self-blame and self-hate (O'Conner, 1994; O'Conner et al., 1997).

Behavioral theorists link depression to learned helplessness (Seligman, 1975, 1989), whereas social cognitive theorists point to distortions of thinking such as blowing negative events out of proportion and minimizing positive, good events (Beck, 1976, 1984). In the social cognitive view, depressed people continually have negative, self-defeating thoughts about themselves, which depress them further in a downward spiral of despair. Learned helplessness (discussed in Chapter Five) has been linked to an increase in such self-defeating thinking and depression in studies with people who have experienced uncontrollable, painful events (Abramson et al., 1978, 1980). This link does not necessarily mean that negative thoughts *cause* depression; it may be that depression increases the likelihood of negative thoughts (Gotlib et al., 2001). One study has found that when comparing adolescents who are depressed to those who are not, the depressed group faced risk factors specifically associated with the social cognitive environment: being female or a member of an ethnic minority; poverty; regular drug use (including tobacco and alcohol); and engaging in delinquent behavior (Costello et al., 2008). In contrast, those in the nondepressed group of adolescents were more likely to come from two-parent households, had higher self-esteem, and felt connected to parents, peers, and school. Clearly, learned helplessness in the face of discrimination, prejudice, and poverty may be associated with depression in these adolescents.

Biological explanations of mood disorders focus on the effects of brain chemicals such as serotonin, norepinephrine, and dopamine; drugs used to treat depression and mania typically affect the levels of these three neurotransmitters, either alone or in combination (Cohen, 1997; Cummings & Coffey, 1994; Ruhe et al., 2007).

Genes also play a part in mood disorders. The fact that the more severe mood disorders are not a reaction to some outside source of stress or anxiety but rather seem to come from within the person's own body, together with the tendency of mood

Depression may be caused by conflicts with others, learned reactions, illogical thought patterns, or chemical imbalances—or some combination of all of these factors.

disorders to appear in genetically related individuals at a higher rate, suggests rather strongly that inheritance may play a significant part in these disorders (Barondes, 1998; Farmer, 1996). Evidence exists for specific genes associated with major depression on chromosome 11 and with bipolar disorder on chromosome 18 (McMahon et al., 2001; Stine et al., 1995). More than 65 percent of people with bipolar disorder have at least one close relative with either bipolar disorder or major depression (Craddock et al., 2005; NIMH Genetics Workgroup, 1998; Sullivan et al., 2000). Twin studies have shown that if one identical twin has either major depression or bipolar disorder, the chances that the other twin will also develop a mood disorder are about 40 to 70 percent (Muller-Oerlinghausen et al., 2002).

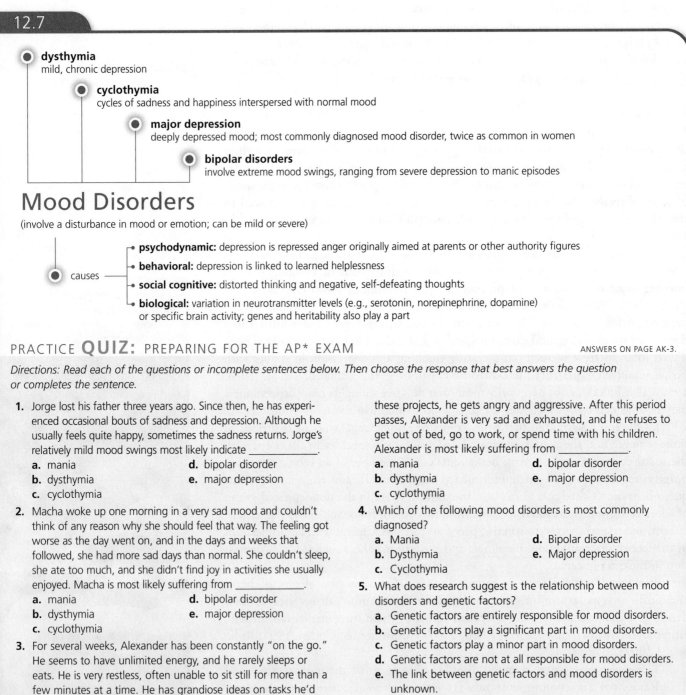

12.7

● **dysthymia**
mild, chronic depression

● **cyclothymia**
cycles of sadness and happiness interspersed with normal mood

● **major depression**
deeply depressed mood; most commonly diagnosed mood disorder, twice as common in women

● **bipolar disorders**
involve extreme mood swings, ranging from severe depression to manic episodes

Mood Disorders
(involve a disturbance in mood or emotion; can be mild or severe)

● causes
- **psychodynamic:** depression is repressed anger originally aimed at parents or other authority figures
- **behavioral:** depression is linked to learned helplessness
- **social cognitive:** distorted thinking and negative, self-defeating thoughts
- **biological:** variation in neurotransmitter levels (e.g., serotonin, norepinephrine, dopamine) or specific brain activity; genes and heritability also play a part

PRACTICE **QUIZ:** PREPARING FOR THE AP* EXAM

ANSWERS ON PAGE AK-3.

Directions: Read each of the questions or incomplete sentences below. Then choose the response that best answers the question or completes the sentence.

1. Jorge lost his father three years ago. Since then, he has experienced occasional bouts of sadness and depression. Although he usually feels quite happy, sometimes the sadness returns. Jorge's relatively mild mood swings most likely indicate _____.
   a. mania
   b. dysthymia
   c. cyclothymia
   d. bipolar disorder
   e. major depression

2. Macha woke up one morning in a very sad mood and couldn't think of any reason why she should feel that way. The feeling got worse as the day went on, and in the days and weeks that followed, she had more sad days than normal. She couldn't sleep, she ate too much, and she didn't find joy in activities she usually enjoyed. Macha is most likely suffering from _____.
   a. mania
   b. dysthymia
   c. cyclothymia
   d. bipolar disorder
   e. major depression

3. For several weeks, Alexander has been constantly "on the go." He seems to have unlimited energy, and he rarely sleeps or eats. He is very restless, often unable to sit still for more than a few minutes at a time. He has grandiose ideas on tasks he'd like to accomplish, and when his wife tells him not to attempt these projects, he gets angry and aggressive. After this period passes, Alexander is very sad and exhausted, and he refuses to get out of bed, go to work, or spend time with his children. Alexander is most likely suffering from _____.
   a. mania
   b. dysthymia
   c. cyclothymia
   d. bipolar disorder
   e. major depression

4. Which of the following mood disorders is most commonly diagnosed?
   a. Mania
   b. Dysthymia
   c. Cyclothymia
   d. Bipolar disorder
   e. Major depression

5. What does research suggest is the relationship between mood disorders and genetic factors?
   a. Genetic factors are entirely responsible for mood disorders.
   b. Genetic factors play a significant part in mood disorders.
   c. Genetic factors play a minor part in mood disorders.
   d. Genetic factors are not at all responsible for mood disorders.
   e. The link between genetic factors and mood disorders is unknown.

Schizophrenia: Altered Reality

Once known as *dementia praecox*, a Latin-based term meaning "out of one's mind before one's time," **schizophrenia** was renamed by Eugen Bleuler, a Swiss psychiatrist, to better illustrate the division (*schizo-*) within the brain (*phren*) among thoughts, feelings, and behavior that seems to take place in people with this disorder (Bleuler, 1911; Möller & Hell, 2002). Because the term literally means "split mind," it has often been confused with dissociative identity disorder, which was at one time called "split personality." A more modern definition of schizophrenia describes it as a long-lasting **psychotic** disorder (involving a severe break with reality), in which there is an inability to distinguish what is real from fantasy as well as disturbances in thinking, emotions, behavior, and perception.

12.8 What are the main symptoms, types, and causes of schizophrenia?

SYMPTOMS

Schizophrenia includes several different kinds of symptoms. Disorders in thinking are a common symptom and are called **delusions**. Although delusions are not prominent in all forms of schizophrenia, they are the symptom that most people associate with this disorder. Delusions are false beliefs about the world that the person holds and that tend to remain fixed and unshakable even in the face of evidence that disproves the delusions. Common schizophrenic delusions include *delusions of persecution*, in which people believe that others are trying to hurt them in some way; *delusions of reference*, in which people believe that other people, television characters, and even books are specifically talking to them; *delusions of influence*, in which people believe that they are being controlled by external forces, such as the devil, aliens, or cosmic forces; and *delusions of grandeur*, in which people are convinced that they are powerful people who can save the world or have a special mission (APA, 2000).

Dr. John Nash is a famous mathematician who won the Nobel Prize for mathematics in 1994. His fame, however, is more due to the fact that Nash once suffered from a form of schizophrenia in which he experienced delusions of persecution. He at one time believed that aliens were trying to contact him through the newspaper (delusions of reference). His life story and remarkable recovery from schizophrenia are portrayed in the 2001 movie *A Beautiful Mind*, which starred Russell Crowe as Nash (Kuhn & Nasar, 2001; Nasar, 1998).

Delusional thinking alone is not enough to merit a diagnosis of schizophrenia, as there is a separate category of psychotic disorders called **delusional disorders**, in which the primary symptom is some form of delusion. In schizophrenia, other symptoms must be present (APA, 2000; Black & Andreason, 1999). Speech disturbances are common: People with schizophrenia will make up words, repeat words or sentences persistently, string words together on the basis of sounds (called *clanging*, such as "come into house, louse, mouse, mouse and cheese, please, sneeze"), and experience sudden interruptions in speech or thought. Thoughts are significantly disturbed as well, with schizophrenic people having a hard time linking their thoughts together in a logical fashion.

People with schizophrenia may also have **hallucinations**, in which they hear voices or see things or people that are not really there. Hearing voices is actually more common and one of the key symptoms in making a diagnosis of schizophrenia. Hallucinations involving touch, smell, and taste are less common but also possible. Although the movie portrayed Nash as having visual hallucinations, he says that he actually heard voices that he eventually learned to ignore (Nasar, 1998).

Emotional disturbances are also a key feature of schizophrenia. **Flat affect** is a condition in which the person shows little or no emotion. Emotions can also be

AP* Discuss the major diagnostic categories and their corresponding symptoms.

How a person with schizophrenia may perceive the world.

Actor Russell Crowe portrayed schizophrenic genius John Forbes Nash in the 2001 film A Beautiful Mind.

schizophrenia severe disorder in which the person suffers from disordered thinking, bizarre behavior, hallucinations, and inability to distinguish between fantasy and reality.

psychotic term applied to a person who is no longer able to perceive what is real and what is fantasy.

delusions false beliefs held by a person who refuses to accept evidence of their falseness.

delusional disorder a psychotic disorder in which the primary symptom is one or more delusions.

hallucinations false sensory perceptions, such as hearing voices that do not really exist.

flat affect a lack of emotional responsiveness.

disorganized type of schizophrenia in which behavior is bizarre and childish and thinking, speech, and motor actions are very disordered.

catatonic type of schizophrenia in which the person experiences periods of statue-like immobility mixed with occasional bursts of energetic, frantic movement, and talking.

paranoid type of schizophrenia in which the person suffers from delusions of persecution, grandeur, and jealousy, together with hallucinations.

positive symptoms symptoms of schizophrenia that are excesses of behavior or occur in addition to normal behavior; hallucinations, delusions, and distorted thinking.

negative symptoms symptoms of schizophrenia that are less than normal behavior or an absence of normal behavior; poor attention, flat affect, and poor speech production.

This photograph shows Keith, Deanna, Joshua, and Luck Laney of New Chapel Hill, Texas, in seemingly happier times. On May 12, 2003, Deanna Laney killed her two young sons because she believed that God had ordered her to kill her children. On the day of the killings, Deanna suffered a number of visual and auditory hallucinations. She was found innocent by reason of insanity in 2004 and has been committed to a maximum security state hospital, where she is undergoing treatment for paranoid schizophrenia.

excessive and/or inappropriate—a person might laugh when it would be more appropriate to cry or show sorrow, for example.

The person's behavior may also become disorganized and extremely odd. For example, some forms of schizophrenia are accompanied by periods of complete immobility, whereas still others may involve weird facial grimaces and odd gesturing. According to the American Psychiatric Association (2000), at least two or more of the following symptoms must be present frequently for at least one month to diagnose schizophrenia: delusions, hallucinations, disturbed speech, disturbed emotions, and disturbed behavior.

Attention is also a problem for many people with schizophrenia. They seem to have trouble "screening out" information and stimulation that they don't really need, causing them to be unable to focus on information that is relevant (Asarnow et al., 1991).

CATEGORIES OF SCHIZOPHRENIA

Although all people with schizophrenia share the symptoms already discussed to a certain degree, the way in which these symptoms show up in behavior can be used to distinguish among several different types of schizophrenia. There are five basic categories and two major types of schizophrenia (APA, 2000). The two types differ in the kind of symptoms that predominate.

Disorganized People suffering from **disorganized** schizophrenia are very confused in speech, have vivid and frequent hallucinations, and tend to have very inappropriate affect (emotion) or flat affect. They are very socially impaired, unable to engage in the normal social rituals of daily life. Giggling, silliness, nonsensical speech, and neglect of cleanliness are common. They may not bathe or change clothing and may have problems with urinating or defecating in public, either because of incontinence or a deliberate wish to shock those watching.

Catatonic Although it is becoming rare, **catatonic** schizophrenia involves very disturbed motor behavior. The person doesn't respond to the outside world and either doesn't move at all, maintaining often odd-looking postures for hours on end (a condition known as *catatonia*) or moves about wildly in great agitation. It's as if there are only two "speeds" for the catatonic, totally off or totally on.

Paranoid People diagnosed with **paranoid** schizophrenia suffer from hallucinations and delusions. Auditory* hallucinations are common, and the delusions are typically persecution, grandeur, or extreme jealousy of another or several other persons. Although their thinking is not as scattered as that of someone with disorganized schizophrenia, their delusions tend to be bizarre** but very systematic.

Another way of categorizing schizophrenia is to look at the kind of symptoms that predominate. **Positive symptoms** appear to reflect an excess or distortion of normal functions, such as hallucinations and delusions. **Negative symptoms** appear to reflect a decrease of normal functions, such as poor attention or lack of affect (APA, 2000).

Positive symptoms are associated with overactivity in the dopamine areas of the brain. Dopamine-reducing drugs used to treat schizophrenia are usually effective on these symptoms, and the outlook for recovery is generally good (Davis et al., 1991; Penn, 1998; Rosenzweig et al., 1996).

Negative symptoms include the inability to filter out stimuli to focus attention, flat affect, problems with producing speech, apathy, and withdrawal from others. Negative symptoms, unlike positive symptoms, are associated with *lower* than normal activity in the dopamine systems of the brain and problems in the functioning of the frontal lobe. Stud-

---

*Auditory: having to do with hearing.
**Bizarre: extremely unusual or weird.

ies have found that those with schizophrenia and primarily negative symptoms have decreased blood flow to the frontal lobe areas (Davis et al., 1991; Perlstein et al., 2001) and enlarged ventricles (the fluid-filled spaces within the brain) when compared to people without schizophrenia (Serban et al., 1990). Unfortunately, this also means that the outlook for recovery from schizophrenia with predominantly negative symptoms is not good, as these symptoms do not respond well to medications that are effective with schizophrenia with predominantly positive symptoms. ✳—📄Explore on MyPsychLab

CAUSES OF SCHIZOPHRENIA

When trying to explain the cause or causes of schizophrenia, the biopsychological model prevails. Biological explanations of schizophrenia have generated a significant amount of research pointing to genetic origins, chemical influences (dopamine), and brain structural defects (frontal lobe defects and deterioration of neurons) as the causes of schizophrenia (Gottesman & Shields, 1982; Harrison, 1999; Kety et al., 1994). Dopamine was first suspected when amphetamine users began to show schizophrenia-like psychotic symptoms. One of the side effects of amphetamine usage is to increase the release of dopamine in the brain. Drugs used to treat schizophrenia decrease the activity of dopamine, and the prefrontal cortex (an area of the brain involved in planning and organization of information) of people with schizophrenia has been shown to produce lower levels of dopamine than normal (Acar et al., 2003; Harrison, 1999).

Further support for a biological explanation of schizophrenia comes from studies of the incidence of the disorder across different cultures. If schizophrenia were caused mainly by environmental factors, the expectation would be that rates of schizophrenia would vary widely from culture to culture. In fact, the rate of schizophrenia is approximately 1 percent of the population, regardless of the culture (Torrey, 1987).

Family, twin, and adoption studies have provided strong evidence that genes are a major means of transmitting schizophrenia. The highest risk for developing schizophrenia if one has a blood relative with the disorder is faced by monozygotic (identical) twins, who share 100 percent of their genetic material, with a risk factor of about 50 percent (Gottesman & Shields, 1976, 1982; Gottesman et al., 1987). Dizygotic twins, who share about 50 percent of their genetic material, have about a 17 percent risk, the same as a child with one schizophrenic parent. As genetic relatedness decreases, so does the risk (see Figure 12.4).

The woman on the right suffers from schizophrenia, as does 1 percent of the population worldwide. Medication, such as that being given by the nurse on the left, can help some people with schizophrenia lead relatively normal lives. Others must remain in institutions.

✳ **Explore** undifferentiated and residual categories of schizophrenia. **www.mypsychlab.com**

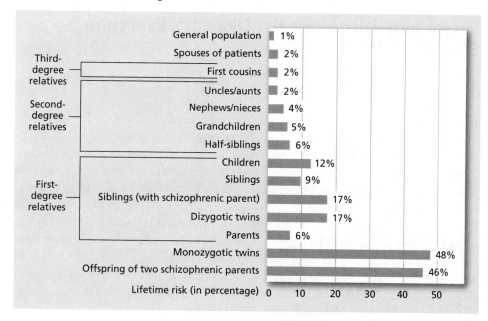

Figure 12.4 Genetics and Schizophrenia

This graph shows a definite pattern: the greater the degree of genetic relatedness, the higher the risk of schizophrenia in individuals related to each other. The only individual to carry a risk even close to that of identical twins (who share 100 percent of their genes) is a person who is the child of two schizophrenic parents.
Source: Gottesman (1991).

There's something I don't understand. If one identical twin has the gene and the disorder, shouldn't the other one always have it, too? Why is the rate ▶ only 50 percent?

Adoption studies also support the genetic basis of schizophrenia. In one study, the biological and adoptive relatives of adoptees with schizophrenia were compared to a control group of adoptees without schizophrenia but from similar backgrounds and conditions (Kety et al., 1994). The adoptees with schizophrenia had relatives with schizophrenia but *only among their biological relatives.* When the prevalence of schizophrenia was compared between the biological relatives of the adoptees with schizophrenia and the biological relatives of the control group, the rate of the disorder in the relatives of the group with schizophrenia was 10 times higher than in the control group (Kety et al., 1994).

There's something I don't understand. If one identical twin has the gene and the disorder, shouldn't the other one always have it, too? Why is the rate only 50 percent? If schizophrenia were entirely controlled by genes, identical twins would indeed both have the disorder at a risk of 100 percent, not merely 50 percent. Obviously, there is some influence of environment on the development of schizophrenia. One model that has been proposed is the **stress-vulnerability model**, which assumes that persons with the genetic "markers" for schizophrenia have a physical vulnerability to the disorder but will not develop schizophrenia unless they are exposed to environmental or emotional stress at critical times in development, such as puberty (Harrison, 1999; Weinberger, 1987). That would explain why only one twin out of a pair might develop the disorder when both carry the genetic markers for schizophrenia—the life stresses for the affected twin were different from those of the one who remained healthy.

The development of brain scanning techniques such as magnetic resonance imaging (MRI) and functional MRI (fMRI), Ⓛ Ⓘ Ⓝ Ⓚ *to Chapter Two: The Biological Perspective, pp. 66–68,* has made studies of the structure as well as the functioning of the brains of those with schizophrenia possible. In one recent study, researchers using a special MRI technique in addition to other neurological testing found that, when compared to healthy control participants, participants with schizophrenia showed structural differences in two particular areas of the brain (Nestor et al., 2008). Specifically, areas known as the cingulum bundle (CB; consisting of fibers linking the thalamus, cortex, and other parts of the limbic system) and the uncinate fasciculus (UF; neural fibers linking the frontal lobe to the temporal lobe) were found to have significantly less myelin coating on the axons of the neurons within the bundle. This makes these areas of the brain less efficient in sending neural messages to other cells, resulting in decreased memory and decision-making ability. ❈ Explore on **MyPsychLab**

❈ **Explore** with a simulation on schizophrenia. **www.mypsychlab.com**

AP❊ Discuss the major diagnostic categories and their corresponding symptoms. ▶

stress-vulnerability model explanation of disorder that assumes a biological sensitivity, or vulnerability, to a certain disorder will result in the development of that disorder under the right conditions of environmental or emotional stress.

personality disorders disorders in which a person adopts a persistent, rigid, and maladaptive pattern of behavior that interferes with normal social interactions.

Personality Disorders: I'm Okay, It's Everyone Else Who's Weird

12.9 How do the various personality disorders differ, and what is thought to be the cause of personality disorders?

Personality disorders are a little different from other psychological disorders in that the disorder does not affect merely one aspect of the person's life, such as a higher than normal level of anxiety or a set of distorted beliefs, but instead affects the entire life adjustment of the person. The disorder is the personality itself, not one aspect of it. In personality disorder, a person has an excessively rigid, maladaptive pattern of behavior and ways of relating to others (APA, 2000). This rigidity and inability to adapt to social demands and life changes make it very difficult for the individual with a personality disorder to fit in with others or have relatively normal social relationships. There are three basic categories of personality disorders listed in the *DSM-IV-TR* (APA, 2000): those in which the people are seen as odd or eccentric by others, those in which the behavior of the person is very dramatic or erratic, and those in which the main emotion is anxiety or fearfulness. There are 10 recognized types of personality disorders (see Table 12.5).

Table 12.5 The Personality Disorders

PERSONALITY DISORDER	DESCRIPTION
Odd or Eccentric Types	
Paranoid	Extreme suspicion of others; mistrustful, often jealous
Schizoid	Loners who are cool, distant, and unwilling and unable to form close relationships with others
Schizotypal	Difficulty in forming social relationships, odd and eccentric behavior, tendency to hold magical beliefs
Dramatic or Erratic Types	
Antisocial	Lacking in conscience or morals; users and con artists who experience no regret or strong emotions
Borderline	Moody, unstable, lacking in a clear sense of identity, clinging to others
Histrionic	Tendency to overreact and use excessive emotions to draw attention from and manipulate others. Love to be the center of attention
Narcissistic	Extremely vain and self-involved
Anxious or Fearful Types	
Avoidant	Fearful of social relationships, tend to avoid social contacts unless absolutely necessary
Dependent	Needy, want others to make decisions for them
Obsessive-Compulsive	Controlling, focused on neatness and order to an extreme degree

Adapted from the American Psychiatric Association, *DSM-IV-TR* (2000).

ANTISOCIAL PERSONALITY DISORDER

One of the most well researched of the personality disorders is **antisocial personality disorder**. People with antisocial personality disorder are literally "against society." The antisocial person, sometimes called a *sociopath*, habitually breaks the law, disobeys rules, tells lies, and uses other people without worrying about their rights or feelings. In Freudian terms, the antisocial personality has no superego or a very weak superego and, therefore, has no real conscience to create guilt feelings when the person does something morally wrong. As a consequence, people with this disorder typically feel no remorse or guilt at lying, cheating, stealing, or even more serious crimes such as murder.

The first thing that usually comes to most people's minds when they hear the term *sociopath* is the *serial killer*, a person who kills others for the excitement and thrill of killing without feeling any guilt. However, most antisocial personalities are not killers. Typically they borrow money or belongings and don't bother to repay the debt or return the items, they are impulsive, they don't keep their commitments either socially or in their jobs, and they tend to be very selfish, self-centered, manipulative, and unable to feel deep emotions.

There is a definite gender difference in antisocial personality disorder with nearly three times to six times as many males diagnosed with this disorder as females (APA, 2000; Paris, 2004).

BORDERLINE PERSONALITY DISORDER

People with **borderline personality disorder** have relationships with other people that are intense and relatively unstable. They are often moody, manipulative, and untrusting of others. Periods of depression are not unusual, and some may engage in excessive spending, drug abuse, or suicidal behavior (suicide attempts may be part of the manipulation the borderline personality uses against others in a relationship).

antisocial personality disorder
disorder in which a person has no morals or conscience and often behaves in an impulsive manner without regard for the consequences of that behavior.

borderline personality disorder
maladaptive personality pattern in which the person is moody, unstable, lacks a clear sense of identity, and often clings to others.

Emotions are often inappropriate and excessive, leading to confusion with *histrionic personality disorder*. What makes the borderline different is the confusion over identity issues, in which the person may be unable to focus on consistent life goals, career choices, friendships, and sexual behavior (APA, 2000).

The frequency of this disorder in women is nearly two to three times greater than in men (APA, 2000; Swartz et al., 1990). Numerous causes such as genetic or hormonal influences, childhood experiences with incest or other abuse, and a poor mother–infant relationship during the years in which the identity is forming have all been suggested as a cause of the disorder (Torgersen, 2000; Widiger & Weissman, 1991; Zanarini, 2000).

CAUSES OF PERSONALITY DISORDERS

Psychodynamic theorists have blamed an inadequate resolution to the Oedipus complex for the formation of personality disorders. In particular, the antisocial personality can be described as lacking a fully developed superego. More recently, these theories focus on problems in the development of the ego in the anal stage as being responsible for disorders such as narcissism and borderline disorders.

Cognitive-behavioral theorists do not talk about innate personality traits—normal, disordered, or otherwise. Instead, these theorists talk about how specific behavior can be learned over time through the processes of reinforcement, shaping, and modeling. More cognitive explanations involve the belief systems formed by the personality disordered persons, such as the paranoia, extreme self-importance, and fear of being unable to cope by oneself of the paranoid, narcissistic, and dependent personalities, for example.

There is some evidence of genetic factors in personality disorders. Close biological relatives of people with disorders such as antisocial, schizotypal, and borderline are more likely to have these disorders than those who are not related, for example (APA, 2000; Battaglia et al., 1995; Faraone et al., 1999; Nigg & Goldsmith, 1994). Adoption studies of children whose biological parents had antisocial personality disorder show an increased risk for that disorder in those children, even though raised in a different environment by different people (APA, 2000). A longitudinal study has linked the temperaments of people at age 3 to antisocial tendencies in adulthood, finding that those children with lower fearfulness and inhibitions were more likely to show antisocial personality characteristics in a follow-up study at age 28 (Glenn et al., 2007). The researchers believe that this study is one of the first to show a possible link between genetically/biologically based temperament and future antisocial personality.

One interesting finding in genetic studies is that some research shows a greater risk of schizophrenia in relatives of people with schizotypal personality disorder (Kendler & Walsh, 1995; Webb & Levinson, 1993). Only a small proportion of people with schizotypal personality disorder go on to develop full-blown schizophrenia, however (APA, 2000).

Other causes of personality disorders have been suggested. Antisocial personalities are emotionally unresponsive to stressful or threatening situations when compared to others, which may be one reason that they are not afraid of getting caught (Arnett et al., 1997; Blair et al., 1995; Lykken, 1995). This unresponsiveness seems to be linked to lower than normal levels of stress hormones in antisocial persons (Lykken, 1995).

Disturbances in family relationships and communication have also been linked to personality disorders and, in particular, to antisocial personality disorder (Benjamin, 1996; Livesley, 1995). Childhood abuse, neglect, overly strict parenting, overprotective parenting, and parental rejection have all been put forth as possible causes, making the picture of the development of personality disorders a complicated one. It is safe to say that many of the same factors (genetics, social relationships, and parenting) that help to create ordinary personalities also create disordered personalities.

12.8–9

schizophrenia
psychotic disorder
involving a break
with reality and
disturbances in thinking,
emotions, behavior,
and perceptions

primary symptoms are often classified
as positive (in excess or in addition
to normal functions) or negative
(absence or decrease in normal functions)

- **delusions:** false beliefs about the world (e.g., delusions of persecution, delusions of grandeur, delusions of reference)
- **disturbed or disorganized thoughts:** often lacking structure or relevance, most often displayed through disorganized speech
- **hallucinations:** can occur in any sensory modality but auditory hallucinations are most common
- **changes in mood:** including flat affect (displaying little or no emotion)
- **disorganized or odd behavior:** ranging from periods of immobility to odd gesturing or facial grimaces

categories
- **disorganized**
- **catatonic**
- **paranoid**

causes
- positive symptoms appear to be associated with overactivity of dopamine areas of brain; negative with lower dopamine activity; related to dopamine hypothesis
- genetics and brain structural defects have been implicated
- biological roots supported by universal prevalence rate of approximately 1% across cultures; genetics supported by twin and adoption studies
- **stress vulnerability model:** suggests people with genetic markers for schizophrenia will not develop the disorder unless they are exposed to environmental or emotional stress at critical times in development

Schizophrenia and Personality Disorders

personality disorders
involve excessively rigid
and maladaptive patterns
of behavior and ways of
relating to others
(see Table 12.5)

- **antisocial personality disorder:** sociopath; minimal to no regard for value of others' rights or feelings; more common in men
- **borderline personality disorder:** relationships with others that are intense and unstable; often moody, manipulative, and untrusting of others; more common in women

causes
- **psychodynamic:** inadequate resolution of Oedipus complex
- **cognitive-behavioral:** specific behaviors learned over time, associated with maladaptive belief systems
- genetic factors play a role, with many showing increased rates of heritability
- variances in stress tolerance and disturbances in family relationships and communication have also been linked to personality disorders

PRACTICE QUIZ: PREPARING FOR THE AP* EXAM

ANSWERS ON PAGE AK-3.

Directions: Read each of the questions or incomplete sentences below. Then choose the response that best answers the question or completes the sentence.

1. Charles believed that a famous song by a popular musical group carried a special, secret message meant only for him. Charles's belief is an example of a delusion of _____.
   a. grandeur
   b. influence
   c. reference
   d. persecution
   e. schizophrenia

2. A person who makes weird faces and sounds, demonstrates inappropriate social behaviors, and giggles constantly is exhibiting behavior typical of _____.
   a. residual schizophrenia
   b. catatonic schizophrenia
   c. paranoid schizophrenia
   d. disorganized schizophrenia
   e. undifferentiated schizophrenia

3. Which type of schizophrenic individual is most likely to have delusions of grandeur?
   a. Catatonic
   b. Paranoid
   c. Residual
   d. Disorganized
   e. Undifferentiated

4. Which of the following is a negative symptom of schizophrenia?
   a. Delusions
   b. Lack of affect
   c. Hallucinations
   d. Distorted thinking
   e. Excessive emotions

5. Jane loves to be the center of attention. She tends to manipulate friends and family members into giving her attention, and she is very emotional. Which type of personality disorder is Jane most likely to have?
   a. Schizoid
   b. Avoidant
   c. Histrionic
   d. Borderline
   e. Dependent

Applying Psychology to Everyday Life: Seasonal Affective Disorder (SAD)

12.10 What is seasonal affective disorder and how can it be treated?

Some people find that they only get depressed at certain times of the year. In particular, depression seems to set in during the winter months and goes away with the coming of spring and summer. If this describes you or someone you know, it could be **seasonal affective disorder (SAD)**. SAD is a mood disorder that is caused by the body's reaction to low levels of light present in the winter months (Partonen & Lonnqvist, 1998).

Think back to Chapter Four and the discussion of the role of the *suprachiasmatic nucleus* (SCN) of the hypothalamus in the brain. **LINK** *to Chapter Four: Consciousness: Sleep, Dreams, Hypnosis, and Drugs, p. 136.* Light entering the eye travels through the optic nerve and through the SCN. The SCN controls the secretion of the hormone *melatonin* from the pineal gland in the brain, and that hormone is released in greater amounts as darkness and the need for sleep cause the SCN to stimulate the pineal gland. When daylight comes, the SCN tells the pineal gland to stop producing melatonin and the body is able to wake up.

What happens in SAD is simple. In some people, especially those who live in northern climates where winter is long and the days are very short, the biological clock that is controlled by the SCN gets out of "step." This can cause feelings of tiredness, lack of energy, and daytime sleepiness that the mind interprets as depression. Other symptoms include excessive eating, a craving for sugary and starchy foods, excessive sleeping, and weight gain. The worst months for SAD are January and February, and true SAD disappears in the spring and summer.

Treatment of SAD can include antidepressant drugs, but one of the most effective treatments is **phototherapy**, or daily exposure to bright light (Terman, 2001). Lamps are used to create an "artificial daylight" for a certain number of hours during each day, and the person with SAD sits under that light. Milder symptoms can be controlled with more time spent outdoors when the sun is shining and increasing the amount of sunlight that comes into the workplace or home (see Figure 12.5).

This woman is experiencing full-spectrum light therapy, one of the main treatments recommended for people suffering from seasonal affective disorder, or SAD.

seasonal affective disorder (SAD) a mood disorder caused by the body's reaction to low levels of sunlight in the winter months.

phototherapy the use of lights to treat seasonal affective disorder or other disorders.

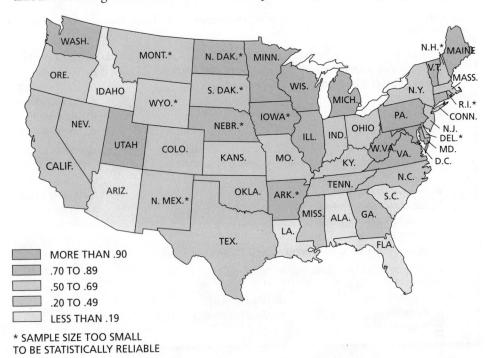

Figure 12.5 **Prevalence of SAD in the United States**

These data, gathered by Steven G. Potkin and his associates (from Wurtman & Wurtman, 1989), indicate considerably higher rates of seasonal affective disorder (SAD) in the northern latitudes. For example, Washington, Minnesota, and Maine have more than three times the levels of SAD as Florida, Louisiana, and Arizona. Shorter winter days in the more northern areas are thought to trigger a change in the brain's biochemistry resulting in SAD.

MORE THAN .90
.70 TO .89
.50 TO .69
.20 TO .49
LESS THAN .19

* SAMPLE SIZE TOO SMALL TO BE STATISTICALLY RELIABLE

12 CHAPTER SUMMARY

What Is Abnormality?

- Psychopathology is the study of abnormal behavior.

12.1 How has mental illness been explained in the past, how is abnormal behavior defined today, and what is the impact of cultural differences in defining abnormality?

- In ancient times holes were cut in an ill person's head to let out evil spirits in a process called trepanning. Hippocrates believed that mental illness came from an imbalance in the body's four humors, whereas in the Middle Ages the mentally ill were labeled as witches.
- Abnormal behavior can be defined as behavior that is statistically rare, is deviant from social norms, causes subjective discomfort, does not allow day-to-day functioning, or causes a person to be dangerous to self or others.

Current Issues in Psychology: A Look at Abnormality in Various Cultures

- Cultural relativity refers to the need to consider the norms and customs of another culture when diagnosing a person from that culture with a disorder.
- Culture-bound syndromes are disorders found only in certain cultures.

Models of Abnormality

12.2 How can psychological disorders be explained within the biological and psychological models?

- In biological models of abnormality, the assumption is that mental illnesses are caused by chemical or structural malfunctions in the nervous system.
- Psychodynamic theorists assume that abnormal behavior stems from repressed conflicts and urges that are fighting to become conscious.
- Behaviorists see abnormal behavior as learned.
- Cognitive theorists see abnormal behavior as coming from irrational beliefs and illogical patterns of thought.

Diagnostic and Statistical Manual of Mental Disorders, Fourth Edition, Text Revision (DSM-IV-TR)

12.3 What are the different types of psychological disorders, and how common are they?

- *Diagnostic and Statistical Manual of Mental Disorders, Fourth Edition, Text Revision (DSM-IV-TR)* is a manual of psychological disorders and their symptoms.
- There are five axes in the *DSM-IV-TR*, which include clinical disorders, personality disorders and mental retardation, general medical conditions, psychosocial and environmental problems, and a global assessment of functioning.
- Over one-fifth of all adults over age 18 suffer from a mental disorder in any given year. Major depression is one of the most common psychological disorders worldwide.

Anxiety Disorders: What, Me Worry?

12.4 What are the different types of anxiety disorders, their symptoms, and causes?

- Anxiety disorders are all disorders in which the most dominant symptom is excessive and unrealistic anxiety.
- Phobias are irrational, persistent fears. The three types of phobias are social phobias, specific phobias, and agoraphobia.
- Obsessive-compulsive disorder consists of an obsessive, recurring thought that creates anxiety and a compulsive, ritualistic, and repetitive behavior that reduces that anxiety.
- Panic disorder is the sudden and recurrent onset of intense panic for no reason, with all the physical symptoms that can occur in sympathetic nervous system arousal, and is sometimes accompanied by agoraphobia.
- Generalized anxiety disorder is a condition of intense and unrealistic anxiety that lasts six months or more.
- Psychodynamic explanations point to repressed urges and desires that are trying to come into consciousness, creating anxiety that is controlled by the abnormal behavior.
- Behaviorists state that disordered behavior is learned through both operant conditioning and classical conditioning techniques.
- Cognitive psychologists believe that excessive anxiety comes from illogical, irrational thought processes.
- Biological explanations of anxiety disorders include chemical imbalances in the nervous system, in particular serotonin and GABA systems.
- Genetic transmission may be responsible for anxiety disorders among related persons.

Somatoform Disorders: Sickness as a State of Mind

12.5 What are the different kinds of somatoform disorders and their causes?

- Somatoform disorders are the belief that one is physically ill, although there is no corresponding physical ailment, and include hypochondriasis, somatization disorder, and conversion disorder.
- Psychodynamic explanations of somatoform disorders assume that anxiety is turned into a physical symptom.
- Behavioral explanations point to the negative reinforcement experienced when the "ill" person escapes unpleasant situations such as combat.
- Cognitive explanations assume that people magnify their physical symptoms and normal bodily changes into ailments out of irrational fear.

Dissociative Disorders: Altered Consciousness

12.6 How do the various dissociative disorders differ, and how do they develop?

- Dissociative disorders involve a break in consciousness, memory, or both. These disorders include dissociative amnesia, dissociative fugue, and dissociative identity disorder.
- Psychodynamic explanations point to repression of memories, seeing dissociation as a defense mechanism against anxiety.

- Cognitive and behavioral explanations see dissociative disorders as a kind of avoidance learning.

- Biological explanations point to lower than normal activity levels in the areas responsible for body awareness in people with dissociative disorders.

Current Issues in Psychology: Was "Sybil" a True Multiple Personality?

- There is taped evidence to suggest that the psychiatrist treating "Sybil," the famous multiple personality case, may have suggested to "Sybil" that she view her emotions as separate personalities.

Mood Disorders: The Effect of Affect

12.7 What are the different types of mood disorders and their causes?

- Mood disorders, also called affective disorders, are severe disturbances in emotion.

- Dysthymia is a moderate depression that is typically a reaction to some external stressor, whereas cyclothymia consists of moderate mood swings usually tied to an external stressor.

- Major depression has a sudden onset and is extreme sadness and despair, typically with no obvious external cause. It is the most common of the mood disorders and is twice as common in women as in men.

- Bipolar disorders are severe mood swings from major depressive episodes to manic episodes of extreme elation and energy with no obvious external cause.

- Psychodynamic theories see depression as anger at authority figures from childhood turned inward on the self.

- Learning theories link depression to learned helplessness.

- Cognitive theories see depression as the result of distorted, illogical thinking.

- Biological explanations of mood disorders look at the function of serotonin, norepinephrine, and dopamine systems in the brain.

- Mood disorders are more likely to appear in genetically related people with higher rates of risk for closer genetic relatives.

Schizophrenia: Altered Reality

- Schizophrenia is a split between thoughts, emotions, and behavior. It is a long-lasting psychotic disorder in which reality and fantasy become confused.

12.8 What are the main symptoms, types, and causes of schizophrenia?

- Symptoms of schizophrenia include delusions (false beliefs about the world), hallucinations, emotional disturbances, attentional difficulties, disturbed speech, and disordered thinking.

- The three types of schizophrenic behavior are disorganized, catatonic, and paranoid.

- Positive symptoms are excesses of behavior associated with increased dopamine activity, whereas negative symptoms are deficits in behavior associated with decreased dopamine activity.

- Psychodynamic theories see schizophrenia as resulting from a severe breakdown of the ego, which has become overwhelmed by the demands of the id and results in childish, infantile behavior.

- Behaviorists focus on how reinforcement, observational learning, and shaping affect the development of the behavioral symptoms of schizophrenia.

- Cognitive theorists see schizophrenia as severely irrational thinking.

- Biological explanations focus on dopamine, structural defects in the brain, and genetic influences in schizophrenia. Rates of risk of developing schizophrenia increase drastically as genetic relatedness increases with the highest risk faced by an identical twin whose twin sibling has schizophrenia.

Personality Disorders: I'm Okay, It's Everyone Else Who's Weird

12.9 How do the various personality disorders differ, and what is thought to be the cause of personality disorders?

- Personality disorders are extremely rigid, maladaptive patterns of behavior that prevent a person from normal social interactions and relationships.

- In antisocial personality disorder a person has no conscience and uses people for personal gain. A rare form is the serial killer.

- In borderline personality disorder a person is clingy, moody, unstable in relationships, and suffers from problems with identity.

- Psychoanalysts blame an inadequate resolution to the Oedipal complex for personality disorders, stating that this results in a poorly developed superego.

- Cognitive-learning theorists see personality disorders as a set of learned behavior that has become maladaptive—bad habits learned early on in life. Belief systems of the personality disordered person are seen as illogical.

- Biological relatives of people with personality disorders are more likely to develop similar disorders, supporting a genetic basis for such disorders.

- Biological explanations look at the lower than normal stress hormones in antisocial personality disordered persons as responsible for their low responsiveness to threatening stimuli.

- Other possible causes of personality disorders may include disturbances in family communications and relationships, childhood abuse, neglect, overly strict parenting, overprotective parenting, and parental rejection.

Applying Psychology to Everyday Life: Seasonal Affective Disorder (SAD)

12.10 What is seasonal affective disorder, and how can it be treated?

- Seasonal affective disorder, or SAD, is a form of depression that is related to low levels of exposure to light during the winter months.

- Treatment consists of light exposure, called phototherapy.

TEST YOURSELF: PREPARING FOR THE AP* EXAM

✔•⎡**Practice** on **MyPsychLab**   **Ready for your test?** More quizzes and a customized study plan. **www.mypsychlab.com**

PART I: MULTIPLE-CHOICE QUESTIONS

Directions for Part I: Read each of the questions or incomplete sentences below. Then choose the response that best answers the question or completes the sentence.

1. Which model of abnormality talks about reinforcement and imitation as ways of developing abnormal behavior?
   a. Biological
   b. Cognitive
   c. Behavioral
   d. Psychodynamic
   e. Biopsychosocial

2. Which axis of the *DSM-IV-TR* would a therapist use to classify the loss of a person's job?
   a. I
   b. II
   c. III
   d. IV
   e. V

3. When anxiety is unrelated to any known, realistic factor, it is called _____.
   a. panic
   b. a phobia
   c. acute anxiety
   d. free-floating anxiety
   e. generalized anxiety disorder

4. When a person experiences sudden attacks of intense fear, racing heart, dizziness, and other physical signs of stress, and refuses to go away from home for fear one of these attacks will happen again, the person's condition is most properly called _____.
   a. dysthymia
   b. hypochondriasis
   c. dissociative fugue
   d. obsessive-compulsive disorder
   e. panic disorder with agoraphobia

5. Henri was a soldier during World War I. He and his best friend were scouting ahead when a mine blew up nearby, killing his friend and wounding Henri in the leg. When Henri woke up after the surgeons repaired his leg, he found that he could not see. The doctors told him that there should be nothing wrong with his eyes, but he was still unable to see anything. Henri most likely suffered from a _____.
   a. conversion disorder
   b. dissociative disorder
   c. somatization disorder
   d. psychosomatic disorder
   e. hypochondriasis disorder

6. Which disorder is characterized by severe mood swings, intense energy, and intense sadness?
   a. Mania
   b. Dysthymia
   c. Cyclothymia
   d. Bipolar disorder
   e. Major depression

7. When compared to unrelated persons, relatives of people who have schizotypal personality disorder have an increased risk of developing _____.
   a. schizophrenia
   b. bipolar disorder
   c. major depression
   d. affective psychosis
   e. antisocial personality disorder

8. Drugs used to treat schizophrenia _____.
   a. decrease blood flow to the brain
   b. restructure the brain's frontal lobe
   c. decrease the activity of dopamine
   d. operate similarly to amphetamines
   e. effectively cure negative symptoms

9. What is the relationship between gender and diagnostic rates of major depression?
   a. Women and men are diagnosed with major depression at the same rate.
   b. Women are diagnosed with major depression twice as often as men are.
   c. Men are diagnosed with major depression twice as often as women are.
   d. Men are diagnosed with major depression three to six times as often as women are.
   e. There seems to be no relationship between gender and diagnostic rates of major depression.

10. Which approach explains major depression as the result of chemical imbalances in the brain?
    a. Genetic
    b. Biological
    c. Behavioral
    d. Psychodynamic
    e. Social cognitive

PART II: FREE-RESPONSE QUESTION

Directions for Part II: Read the essay question that follows. Then, respond to the question in a clear, concise essay. Do not simply list facts. Instead, present a thorough argument based on your critical consideration of the topic. Use proper psychological terminology as necessary.

Two psychologists, Dr. Hashimoto and Dr. Ward, have differing views about the basis of schizophrenia. Dr. Hashimoto believes that schizophrenia has a biological basis, while Dr. Ward believes that schizophrenia is caused primarily by environmental factors. In a well-organized essay, first describe the types and symptoms of schizophrenia. Then, explain which psychologist is more correct and why. Provide detailed evidence to support your argument.

12.1–2   p. 480

psychopathology is the study of abnormal behavior; mental illness has been defined in various ways throughout history (e.g., possession, evil spirits, bodily imbalances)

what is abnormality?

- current definitions of abnormality are based on several factors
- disorders vary according to culture; cultural sensitivity and relativity are necessary in diagnosing and treating psychological disorders
- overall, psychological disorders are any pattern of behavior that causes significant distress, causes them to harm themselves or others, or harms their ability to function in daily life

Psychological Disorders

models of abnormality
explanations for disordered behavior depend on theoretical model used to explain personality in general

- biological model
- psychological models
- biopsychosocial perspective

12.3–4   p. 489

- DSM first published in 1952, current version *(DSM–IV–TR)* published in 2000

Diagnostic and Statistical Manual of Mental Disorders, Fourth Edition, Text Revision (DSM–IV–TR)

- currently describes approximately 250 different psychological disorders and includes diagnostic criteria along five different categories, or axes (see Tables 12.1 and 12.2)
- in general, approximately 22% of adults over age 18 in the United States suffer from a mental disorder

Table 12.1 The Axes of the *DSM-IV-TR*

AXIS	TYPE OF INFORMATION	DESCRIPTION
Axis I	Clinical Disorders and Other Conditions That May Be a Focus of Clinical Attention	Psychological disorders that impair functioning and are stressful and factors that are not disorders but that may affect functioning, such as academic or social problems
Axis II	Personality Disorders and Mental Retardation	Rigid, enduring, maladaptive personality patterns and mental retardation
Axis III	General Medical Conditions	Chronic and acute illnesses and medical conditions that may have an impact on mental health
Axis IV	Psychosocial and Environmental Problems	Problems in the physical surroundings of the person that may have an impact on diagnosis, treatment, and outcome
Axis V	Global Assessment of Functioning	Overall judgment of current functioning, including mental, social, and occupational

Adapted from the American Psychiatric Association, *DSM-IV-TR* (2000).

Psychological Disorders

Table 12.2 Axis I Disorders of the *DSM-IV-TR*

DISORDER	EXAMPLES
Disorders usually first diagnosed in infancy, childhood, or adolescence	Learning disabilities, ADHD, bed-wetting, speech disorders
Delirium, dementia, amnesia, and other cognitive disorders	Alzheimer's, Parkinsonis, amnesia due to physical causes
Psychological disorders due to a general medical condition	Personality change because of a brain tumor
Substance-related disorders	Alcoholism, drug addictions
Schizophrenia and other psychotic disorders	Schizophrenia, delusional disorders, paranoid psychosis
Mood disorders	Depression, mania, bipolar disorders
Anxiety disorders	Panic disorder, phobias, stress disorders
Somatoform disorders	Hypochondria, conversion disorder
Factitious disorders	Pathological lying, Munchausen syndrome
Dissociative disorders	Dissociative identity disorder (formerly multiple personality), amnesia not due to physical causes
Sexual and gender identity disorders	Sexual desire disorders, paraphilias
Eating disorders	Anorexia, bulimia
Sleep disorders	Insomnia, sleep terror disorder, sleepwalking, narcolepsy
Impulse-control disorders not classified elsewhere	Kleptomania, pathological gambling, pyromania
Adjustment disorders	Mixed anxiety, conduct disturbances

Adapted from the American Psychiatric Association, *DSM-IV-TR* (2000).

anxiety disorders
most dominant symptom is excessive or unrealistic anxiety

- anxiety can be free-floating (nonspecific, anxious in general) or more specific, as in the case of phobias
- **panic disorder**
- **obsessive compulsive disorder (OCD)**
- **generalized anxiety disorder**
- causes
  - **behavioral**
  - **cognitive**
  - **biological**
  - **cultural**

12.5–6   p. 496

- **hypochondriasis**
- **somatization disorder**
- **conversion disorder**

somatoform disorders
include disorders in which individuals believe they are sick and may experience physical symptoms but there is no physical illness or problem

- causes
  - **psychodynamic**
  - **cognitive**

Somatoform and Dissociative Disorders

dissociative disorders
involve a dissociation in consciousness, memory, or sense of identity, often associated with extreme stress or trauma

- **dissociative amnesia**
- **dissociative fugue**
- **dissociative identity disorder**
- causes
  - **psychodynamic**
  - **cognitive and behavioral**
  - **biological**

12.7 | p. 500

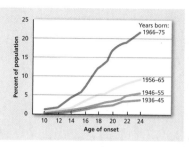

- **dysthymia**
  mild, chronic depression

  - **cyclothymia**
    cycles of sadness and happiness interspersed with normal mood

    - **major depression**
      deeply depressed mood; most commonly diagnosed mood disorder, twice as common in women

      - **bipolar disorders**
        involve extreme mood swings, ranging from severe depression to manic episodes

Mood Disorders

(involve a disturbance in mood or emotion; can be mild or severe)

— **causes**

- **psychodynamic:** depression is repressed anger originally aimed at parents or other authority figures
- **behavioral:** depression is linked to learned helplessness
- **social cognitive:** distorted thinking and negative, self-defeating thoughts
- **biological:** variation in neurotransmitter levels (e.g., serotonin, norepinephrine, dopamine) or specific brain activity; genes and heritability also play a part

12.8–9 | p. 507

- primary symptoms are often classified as positive (in excess or in addition to normal functions) or negative (absence or decrease in normal functions)
  - **delusions**
  - **disturbed or disorganized thoughts**
  - **hallucinations**
  - **changes in mood**
  - **disorganized or odd behavior**

- categories
  - **disorganized**
  - **catatonic**
  - **paranoid**

- **schizophrenia**
  psychotic disorder involving a break with reality and disturbances in thinking, emotions, behavior, and perceptions

- causes
  - positive symptoms appear to be associated with overactivity of dopamine areas of brain; negative with lower dopamine activity; related to dopamine hypothesis
  - genetics and brain structural defects have been implicated
  - biological roots supported by universal prevalence rate of approximately 1% across cultures; genetics supported by twin and adoption studies
  - **stress vulnerability model:** suggests people with genetic markers for schizophrenia will not develop the disorder unless they are exposed to environmental or emotional stress at critical times in development

Schizophrenia and Personality Disorders

- **personality disorders**
  involve excessively rigid and maladaptive patterns of behavior and ways of relating to others (see Table 12.5)

  - **antisocial personality disorder**
  - **borderline personality disorder**
  - causes
    - **psychodynamic**
    - **cognitive-behavioral**
    - genetic factors play a role
    - variances in stress tolerance and disturbances in family relationships and communication have also been linked to personality disorders

Table 12.5 The Personality Disorders

PERSONALITY DISORDER	DESCRIPTION
Odd or Eccentric Types	
Paranoid	Extreme suspicion of others; mistrustful; often jealous
Schizoid	Loners who are cool, distant, and unwilling and unable to form close relationships with others
Schizotypal	Difficulty in forming social relationships, odd and eccentric behavior, tendency to hold magical beliefs
Dramatic or Erratic Types	
Antisocial	Lacking in conscience or morals; user and con artists who experience no regret or strong emotions
Borderline	Moody, unstable, lacking in a clear sense of identity, clinging to others
Histrionic	Tendency to overreact and use excessive emotions to draw attention from and manipulate others. Love to be the center of attention
Narcissistic	Extremely vain and self-involved
Anxious or Fearful Types	
Avoidant	Fearful of social relationships, tend to avoid social contacts unless absolutely necessary
Dependent	Needy, want others to make decisions for them
Obsessive-Compulsive	Controlling, focused on neatness and order to an extreme degree

Adapted from the American Psychiatric Association, *DSM-IV-TR* (2000).

13

Psychological Therapies

Treating Panic Disorder

Marie began having panic attacks at the age of 14. When she started having attacks at school, the school began sending her home. Marie's mother took her to see a child psychiatrist, who diagnosed Marie with mild panic disorder. ⓁⒾⓃⓀ *to Chapter Twelve: Psychological Disorders, p. 486.*

The psychiatrist recommended two types of treatment: cognitive psychotherapy and a carefully monitored drug treatment. (Remember, psychiatrists are medical doctors who can prescribe drugs to treat disorders.) The cognitive psychotherapy included sessions in which the psychiatrist would let Marie talk about her feelings and fears and then he would show her where her thinking was going a little off track. The goal of cognitive therapy is to help clients see how their thinking patterns can be self-defeating and illogical. The psychiatrist explained to Marie that panic disorder did not mean that she was "crazy." A small area in her brain that would normally react to fear-provoking situations was "misfiring," making her body think that there was reason to be afraid and causing the panic symptoms. He explained that it was like having a smoke detector that went off when there was no smoke and no fire.

The drug treatment consisted of daily doses of an antidepressant medication; the dosage was very small at first and was increased gradually until Marie was on an effective dose. During the course of the drug treatment, the cognitive therapy sessions continued. Marie's panic attacks disappeared completely, and she was able to gradually discontinue taking the drug. Within one year, Marie was able to end her therapy, having successfully conquered her panic.

Marie's story is a successful one, but the stories of other people with psychological disorders are not always resolved so simply. Different disorders require different kinds of therapies, and not all disorders can be completely eliminated. Therapies can take many forms, depending on the particular psychological explanation of disorder that is the basis of the therapy and the specific disorder that needs to be treated.

Why is it important to study therapies for psychological disorders?
There are almost as many therapy methods as there are disorders. Correctly matching the type of therapy to the disorder can mean the difference between a cure or a crisis. It is important to know the choices available for treatment and how they relate to the different kinds of disorders so that an informed decision can be made and the best possible outcome can be achieved for mental health and wellness.

13 Learning Objectives

- **13.1** What are the two modern ways in which psychological disorders can be treated, and how have they been treated in the past?

- **13.2** What were the basic elements of Freud's psychoanalysis, and how does psychoanalysis differ today?

- **13.3** What are the basic elements of the humanistic therapies known as person-centered therapy and Gestalt therapy?

- **13.4** How do behavior therapists use classical and operant conditioning to treat disordered behavior?

- **13.5** How successful are behavior therapies?

- **13.6** What are the goals and basic elements of cognitive therapies such as cognitive-behavioral therapy and rational-emotive behavior therapy?

- **13.7** What are the various types of group therapies and the advantages and disadvantages of group therapy?

- **13.8** How effective is psychotherapy, and how is the effectiveness of psychotherapy influenced by cultural, ethnic, and gender differences?

- **13.9** What are the various types of drugs used to treat psychological disorders?

- **13.10** How are electroconvulsive therapy and psychosurgery used to treat psychological disorders today?

- **13.11** What are the dangers of treating children and adolescents with antidepressant drugs?

AP* Describe the central characteristics of psychotherapeutic intervention.

AP* Compare and contrast different treatment formats.

✳ Explore on schools of therapy.
www.mypsychlab.com

therapy treatment methods aimed at making people feel better and function more effectively.

psychotherapy therapy for mental disorders in which a person with a problem talks with a psychological professional.

biomedical therapy therapy for mental disorders in which a person with a problem is treated with biological or medical methods to relieve symptoms.

insight therapies therapies in which the main goal is helping people to gain insight with respect to their behavior, thoughts, and feelings.

action therapy therapy in which the main goal is to change disordered or inappropriate behavior directly.

Two Kinds of Therapy

When talking about treating psychological disorders, there are two main types of **therapy** (treatment methods aimed at making people feel better and function more effectively). In one type of therapy based in psychological techniques, people tell the therapist about their problems, and the therapist listens and tries to help them understand those problems or change the behavior that causes them. The other type of therapy uses medical interventions to bring the symptoms under control.

13.1 What are the two modern ways in which psychological disorders can be treated, and how have they been treated in the past?

The kind of therapy that involves talking things out with a professional is called **psychotherapy**, whereas the kind of therapy that uses medical methods is called **biomedical therapy**. ✳ Explore on MyPsychLab

PSYCHOTHERAPY

Psychotherapy probably began when some tribal shaman (holy man) helped a tribe member whose problems could not be helped by the medicine man of the tribe (Torrey, 1986). Psychotherapy can be performed in many different ways. Sometimes an individual talks with a professional on a one-to-one basis. At other times, a person with certain psychological problems might become part of a group of people with similar problems that is led by a professional. This is known as *group therapy* and is discussed in more detail later in this chapter.

The goal of almost all psychotherapy is to help both mentally healthy and psychologically disordered persons understand themselves better (Goin, 2005; Wolberg, 1977). Because understanding of one's motives and actions is called *insight*, therapies aimed mainly at this goal are called **insight therapies**. A therapy that is directed more at changing behavior than providing insights into the reasons for that behavior (as used by Marie's psychiatrist in the opening story) is called **action therapy**. Most psychological professionals use a combination of insight and action therapeutic methods.

BIOMEDICAL THERAPY

The other main type of therapy uses some biological treatment in the form of a medical procedure to bring about changes in the person's disordered behavior. Biomedical therapies include the use of drugs, as in the case of Marie in the opening story, surgical methods, and electrical shock treatments. It is important to understand that biomedical therapy alone does nothing but alleviate the symptoms of the disorder, such as anxiety, depression, or attentional problems. Although in some cases controlling the symptom may be all that is needed, most professionals would agree that any biomedical therapy of a psychological disorder should be accompanied by some form of psychotherapy as well, as Marie's psychiatrist chose to do (Keller et al., 2000; Rohde et al., 2008). This ensures that any underlying psychological problems that may be the source of the symptoms are also treated, preventing a recurrence of the problem or the development of some other kind of symptom.

The Early Days of Therapy:
Ice-Water Baths and Electric Shocks ⊙ Watch on MyPsychLab

Life for the mentally ill was not pleasant in most parts of the world for many years. As discussed in Chapter Twelve, people with severe mental illnesses were often thought to be possessed by demons or evil spirits, and the "treatments" to rid the person of these spirits were severe and deadly. Even in the supposedly more enlightened times of the last two hundred years or so, the mentally ill did not always receive humane* treatment.

EARLY TREATMENT OF THE MENTALLY ILL

I've seen movies about mental hospitals, and they didn't look like great places to be in even now—how bad was it back then? What did people do with relatives who were ill that way? The first truly organized effort to do something with mentally ill persons began in England in the middle of the sixteenth century. Bethlehem Hospital in London (later known as "Bedlam") was converted into an asylum (a word meaning "place of safety") for the mentally ill. In reality, the first asylums were little more than prisons where the mentally ill were chained to their beds. "Treatments" consisted of bloodletting (which more often than not led to death or the need for lifelong care for the patient), beatings, ice baths in which the person was submerged until passing out or suffering a seizure, and induced vomiting in a kind of spiritual cleansing (Hunt, 1993). This cleansing or purging was meant to rid the body of physical impurities so that the person's mind and soul could function more perfectly.

PINEL'S REFORMS

It was not until 1793 that efforts were made to treat the mentally ill with kindness and guidance—known as "moral treatment"—rather than beating them or subjecting them to the harsh physical purging that had been commonplace. It was at this time that Philippe Pinel personally unchained the inmates at the Bicêtre Asylum in Paris, France, beginning the movement of humane treatment of the mentally ill (Brigham, 1844; Curtis, 1993).

---

*Humane: marked by compassion, sympathy, or consideration for humans (and animals).

◄ **AP*** Compare and contrast different treatment formats.

⊙ **Watch** videos on a history of mental institutions in the United States. **www.mypsychlab.com**

I've seen movies about mental hospitals, and they didn't look like great places to be in even now— how bad was it back then? What did people do with ◄ relatives who were ill that way?

In this famous painting by French artist Robert Fleury, French psychiatrist Dr. Philippe Pinel orders the chains removed from patients at a Paris asylum for insane women. Pinel was one of the first psychiatrists to recommend humane treatment of the mentally ill.

So what exactly happens in psychoanalysis? I've heard lots of stories about it, but what's it really like?

AP* Describe major treatment orientations used in therapy. ▶

AP* Identify major figures in psychological treatment. ▶

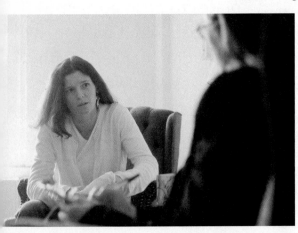

Psychotherapy often takes place one-on-one, with a client and therapist exploring various issues together to achieve deeper insights or to change undesirable behavior.

psychoanalysis an insight therapy based on the theory of Freud, emphasizing the revealing of unconscious conflicts.

manifest content the actual content of one's dream.

latent content the symbolic or hidden meaning of dreams.

free association psychoanalytic technique in which a patient was encouraged to talk about anything that came to mind without fear of negative evaluations.

In the Beginning: Psychoanalysis

▶ *So what exactly happens in psychoanalysis? I've heard lots of stories about it, but what's it really like?* In a sense, Freud took the old method of physical cleansing to a different level. Instead of a physical purge, cleansing for Freud meant removing all the "impurities" of the unconscious mind that he believed were responsible for his patients' psychological and nervous disorders. (Freud was a medical doctor and referred to the people who came to him for help as "patients.") The impurities of the unconscious mind were considered to be disturbing thoughts, socially unacceptable desires, and immoral urges that originated in the id, the part of the personality that is itself unconscious and driven by basic needs for survival and pleasure. ⓛⓘⓝⓚ *to Chapter Eleven: Theories of Personality, p. 437.*

Because these unconscious thoughts were used by the person to prevent anxiety and would not be easily brought into conscious awareness, Freud designed a technique to help his patients feel more relaxed, open, and able to explore their innermost feelings without fear of embarrassment or rejection. This method was called **psychoanalysis**, an insight therapy that emphasizes revealing the unconscious conflicts, urges, and desires that are assumed to cause disordered emotions and behavior (Freud, 1904; Mitchell & Black, 1996). This is the original reason for the couch in Freud's version of psychoanalysis; people lying on the couch were more relaxed and would, Freud thought, feel more dependent and childlike, making it easier for them to get at those early childhood memories. An additional plus was that he could sit behind the patients at the end of the couch and take notes. Without the patients being able to see his reactions to what they said, they remained unaffected by his reactions.

13.2 What were the basic elements of Freud's psychoanalysis, and how does psychoanalysis differ today?

Freud also made use of two techniques to try to get at the repressed information in his patients' unconscious minds. These techniques were the interpretation of dreams and allowing patients to talk freely about anything that came to mind.

DREAM INTERPRETATION

Dream interpretation, or the analysis of the elements within a patient's reported dream, formed a large part of Freud's psychoanalytic method. ⓛⓘⓝⓚ *to Chapter Four: Consciousness: Sleep, Dreams, Hypnosis, and Drugs, pp. 147–148.* Freud believed that repressed material often surfaced in dreams, although in symbolic form. The **manifest content** of the dream was the actual dream and its events, but the **latent content** was the hidden, symbolic meaning of those events that would, if correctly interpreted, reveal the unconscious conflicts that were creating the nervous disorder (Freud, 1900).

FREE ASSOCIATION

The other technique for revealing the unconscious mind was a method originally devised by Freud's coworker, Josef Breuer (Breuer & Freud, 1895). Breuer encouraged his patients to freely say whatever came into their minds without fear of being negatively evaluated or condemned. As the patients talked, they began to reveal things that were loosely associated with their flow of ideas, often revealing what Breuer felt were hidden, unconscious concerns. Freud adopted this method, believing that repressed impulses and other material were trying to "break free" into consciousness and would eventually surface in his patients' **free associations**.

RESISTANCE

A key element in psychoanalysis was the analysis of **resistance**, the point at which the patient becomes unwilling to talk about certain topics. Freud believed that resistance from the patient meant that the conversation was coming uncomfortably close to repressed material.

TRANSFERENCE

In revealing more and more of their innermost feelings to the doctor, patients would begin to trust the therapist who accepted anything they said and did not criticize or punish them for saying it, as they once trusted their parents. Freud believed that the therapist would then become a symbol of a parental authority figure from the past in a process he called **transference**. In transference, the patient would at first transfer positive feelings for some authority figure from the past such as a mother or father. When the therapist remained neutral and seemingly unresponsive, the patient would transfer negative feelings.

"Why do you think you cross the road?"

EVALUATION OF PSYCHOANALYSIS

Freud's original theory, on which he based his interpretations of his patients' revelations, has been criticized for several flaws, as discussed in Chapter Eleven. These included the lack of scientific research to support his claims, his unwillingness to believe some of the things revealed by his patients when those revelations did not fit into his view of the world, and his almost obsessive need to assume that problems with sex and sexuality were at the heart of nearly every nervous disorder.

▶ **AP*** Summarize effectiveness of specific treatments used to address specific problems.

Although some psychoanalysts today still use Freud's original methods, which could take years to produce results, modern psychoanalysts have greatly modified the way a psychoanalytic session is conducted. The couch is gone, and the *client* (a term used to support the active role of the person seeking help and not imply sickness, instead of the doctor–patient concept) may sit across a desk from the therapist or in chairs. The client may stand or walk about. Rather than remaining quiet until the client says something revealing, the modern psychoanalyst is far more **directive**, asking questions, suggesting helpful behavior, and giving opinions and interpretations earlier in the relationship, which helps speed up the therapeutic process. Today's psychoanalysts also focus less on the id as the motivator of behavior, instead looking more at the ego or sense of self as the motivating force behind all actions (Prochaska & Norcross, 2003). Some psychoanalysts also focus on the process of transference more than on other typical aspects of traditional psychoanalysis, leading to the more general method called **psychodynamic therapy**. Psychodynamic therapy is typically shorter in duration than traditional psychoanalysis.

Even so, the psychodynamic technique requires the client to be fairly intelligent and verbally able to express his or her ideas, feeling, and thoughts effectively. People who are extremely withdrawn or who suffer from the more severe psychotic disorders are not good candidates for this form of psychotherapy. People who have nonpsychotic adjustment disorders, such as anxiety, somatoform, or dissociative disorders, are more likely to benefit from psychodynamic therapy.

resistance occurring when a patient becomes reluctant to talk about a certain topic, either changing the subject or becoming silent.

transference In psychoanalysis, the tendency for a patient or client to project positive or negative feelings for important people from the past onto the therapist.

directive therapy in which the therapist actively gives interpretations of a client's statements and may suggest certain behavior or actions.

psychodynamic therapy a newer and more general term for therapies based on psychoanalysis with an emphasis on transference, shorter treatment times, and a more direct therapeutic approach.

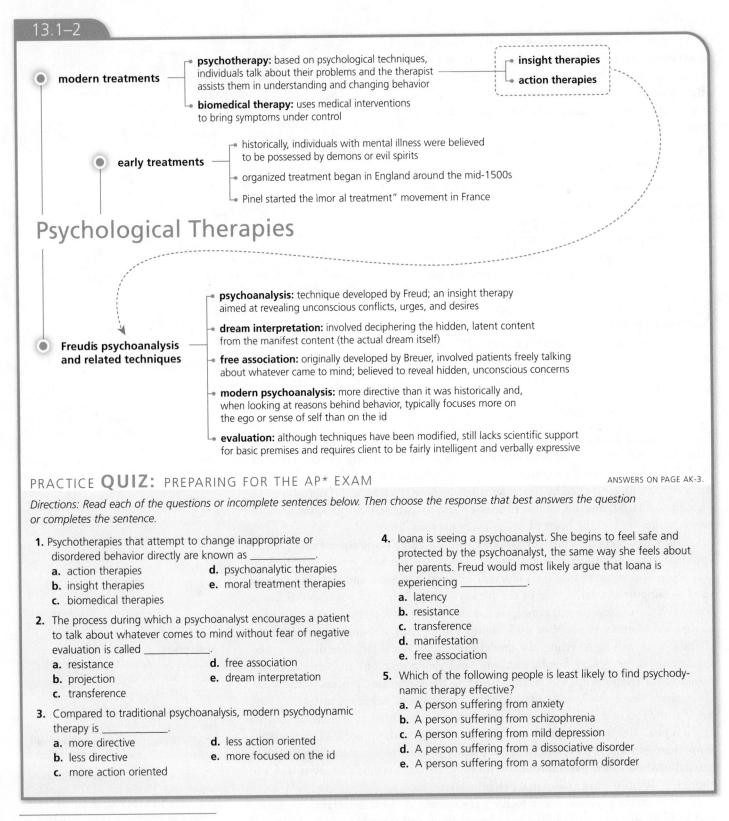

13.1–2

modern treatments
- **psychotherapy:** based on psychological techniques, individuals talk about their problems and the therapist assists them in understanding and changing behavior
  - insight therapies
  - action therapies
- **biomedical therapy:** uses medical interventions to bring symptoms under control

early treatments
- historically, individuals with mental illness were believed to be possessed by demons or evil spirits
- organized treatment began in England around the mid-1500s
- Pinel started the ìmor al treatment" movement in France

Psychological Therapies

Freudís psychoanalysis and related techniques
- **psychoanalysis:** technique developed by Freud; an insight therapy aimed at revealing unconscious conflicts, urges, and desires
- **dream interpretation:** involved deciphering the hidden, latent content from the manifest content (the actual dream itself)
- **free association:** originally developed by Breuer, involved patients freely talking about whatever came to mind; believed to reveal hidden, unconscious concerns
- **modern psychoanalysis:** more directive than it was historically and, when looking at reasons behind behavior, typically focuses more on the ego or sense of self than on the id
- **evaluation:** although techniques have been modified, still lacks scientific support for basic premises and requires client to be fairly intelligent and verbally expressive

PRACTICE **QUIZ:** PREPARING FOR THE AP* EXAM   ANSWERS ON PAGE AK-3.

Directions: Read each of the questions or incomplete sentences below. Then choose the response that best answers the question or completes the sentence.

1. Psychotherapies that attempt to change inappropriate or disordered behavior directly are known as _____.
   a. action therapies
   b. insight therapies
   c. biomedical therapies
   d. psychoanalytic therapies
   e. moral treatment therapies

2. The process during which a psychoanalyst encourages a patient to talk about whatever comes to mind without fear of negative evaluation is called _____.
   a. resistance
   b. projection
   c. transference
   d. free association
   e. dream interpretation

3. Compared to traditional psychoanalysis, modern psychodynamic therapy is _____.
   a. more directive
   b. less directive
   c. more action oriented
   d. less action oriented
   e. more focused on the id

4. Ioana is seeing a psychoanalyst. She begins to feel safe and protected by the psychoanalyst, the same way she feels about her parents. Freud would most likely argue that Ioana is experiencing _____.
   a. latency
   b. resistance
   c. transference
   d. manifestation
   e. free association

5. Which of the following people is least likely to find psychodynamic therapy effective?
   a. A person suffering from anxiety
   b. A person suffering from schizophrenia
   c. A person suffering from mild depression
   d. A person suffering from a dissociative disorder
   e. A person suffering from a somatoform disorder

AP* Describe major treatment orientations used in therapy.

Humanistic Therapy: To Err Is Human

Unlike psychodynamic therapists, humanistic theorists do not focus on unconscious, hidden conflicts. Instead, humanists focus on conscious, subjective experiences of emotion and people's sense of self, as well as the more immediate experiences in their daily lives rather than early childhood experiences of the distant past (Cain & Seeman, 2001; Rowan, 2001; Schneider et al., 2001). **LINK** *to Chapter One: The Science of Psychology, p. 14.* Humanistic therapy emphasizes the importance of the choices made by individuals and the potential to change one's behavior. The two most common therapy styles based on humanistic theory are Carl Rogers's person-centered therapy and Fritz Perls's Gestalt therapy, both primarily insight therapy.

13.3 What are the basic elements of the humanistic therapies known as person-centered therapy and Gestalt therapy?

TELL ME MORE: ROGERS'S PERSON-CENTERED THERAPY

Chapter Eleven discussed the basic elements of Rogers's theory of personality, which emphasizes the sense of self (Rogers, 1961). To sum it up quickly, Rogers proposed that everyone has a *real self* (how people see their actual traits and abilities) and an *ideal self* (how people think they should be). The closer the real and ideal selves match up, the happier and more well adjusted the person. To have these two self-concepts match, people need to receive *unconditional positive regard*, which is love, warmth, respect, and affection without any conditions attached. If people think that there are conditions put on the love and affection they receive, their ideal selves will be determined by those conditions and become more difficult to achieve, resulting in a mismatch of selves and unhappiness.

So the key to getting over unhappiness would be to get the real and ideal selves closer together? How does a therapist do that? Rogers believed that the goal of the therapist should be to provide the unconditional positive regard that has been absent from the troubled person's life and to help the person recognize the discrepancies between the real and ideal selves. He also believed that the person would actually have to do most of the work, talking out problems and concerns in an atmosphere of warmth and acceptance from the therapist, so he originally called the people in this therapy relationship "clients" instead of "patients," to put the therapeutic* relationship on a more equal footing. As a result, Rogers's therapy is very **nondirective** because the person actually does all the real work, with the therapist merely acting as a sounding board. Later, the term *client* was changed to the even more neutral term *person*. His therapy is now called **person-centered therapy** because the person is truly the center of the process.

Four Basic Elements   Rogers saw four key elements as being necessary in any successful person–therapist relationship.

Reflection   **Reflection** refers to the technique the therapist must use to allow clients to continue to talk and have insights without the interference of the therapist's interpretations and possible biases. The only way to ensure that a therapist will not control the stream of ideas coming from clients is for the therapist to simply restate what people have already said in slightly different words but with the same exact meaning. Reflection is literally a kind of mirroring of clients' statements. Here's an example from one of Rogers's own therapy sessions with a client (Meador & Rogers, 1984, p. 143):

> CLIENT: I just ain't no good to nobody, never was, and never will be.
>
> ROGERS: Feeling that now, hm? That you're just no good to yourself, no good to anybody. Never will be any good to anybody. Just that you're completely worthless, huh?—Those really are lousy feelings. Just feel that you're no good at all, hm?
>
> CLIENT: Yeah.

*Therapeutic: providing or assisting in a cure.

---

nondirective therapy style in which the therapist remains relatively neutral and does not interpret or take direct actions with regard to the client, instead remaining a calm, nonjudgmental listener while the client talks.

person-centered therapy a nondirective insight therapy based on the work of Carl Rogers in which the client does all the talking and the therapist listens.

reflection therapy technique in which the therapist restates what the client says rather than interpreting those statements.

◄ **AP*** Identify major figures in psychological treatment.

So the key to getting over unhappiness would be to get the real and ideal selves closer together? How does a therapist do that?

A Rogerian person-centered therapist listens with calm acceptance to anything the client says. A sense of empathy with the client's feelings is also important.

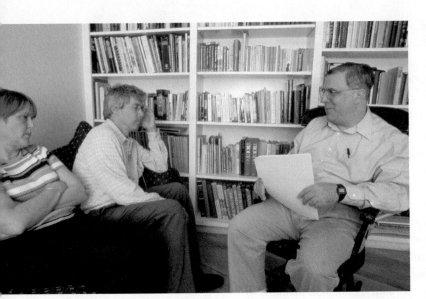

In Gestalt therapy, the therapist looks at the whole person—career, family, relationships, and body language. What do the people sitting on the couch seem to be saying with their body language?

Watch classic video footage on the role of the therapist with Carl Rogers. **www.mypsychlab.com**

That sounds pretty much like the same thing, only with slightly different words. ▶ How is Gestalt therapy different from person-centered therapy?

unconditional positive regard referring to the warmth, respect, and accepting atmosphere created by the therapist for the client in person-centered therapy.

empathy the ability of the therapist to understand the feelings of the client.

authenticity the genuine, open, and honest response of the therapist to the client.

Gestalt therapy form of directive insight therapy in which the therapist helps clients to accept all parts of their feelings and subjective experiences, using leading questions and planned experiences such as role-playing.

Unconditional Positive Regard Another key element of person-centered therapy is the warm, accepting, completely uncritical atmosphere that the therapist must create for clients. Having respect for clients and their feelings, values, and goals, even if they are different from those of the therapist, is called **unconditional positive regard**.

Empathy The therapist also has to be able to acknowledge what clients are feeling and experiencing by using a kind of understanding called **empathy**. This involves listening carefully and closely to what clients are saying and trying to feel what they feel. Therapists must also avoid getting their own feelings mixed up with clients' feelings.

Authenticity Finally, the therapist must show **authenticity** in a genuine, open, and honest response to the client. It is easier for some professionals to "hide" behind the role of the therapist, as was often the case in psychoanalysis. In person-centered therapy, the therapist has to be able to tolerate a client's differences without being judgmental. ⬤ **Watch** on **MyPsychLab**

GESTALT THERAPY

Another humanistic therapy based on Gestalt ideas is called **Gestalt therapy**. The founder of this therapeutic method is Fritz Perls, who believed that people's problems often stemmed from hiding important parts of their feelings from themselves. If some part of a person's personality, for example, is in conflict with what society says is acceptable, the person might hide that aspect behind a false "mask" of socially acceptable behavior. As happens in Rogers's theory when the real and ideal selves do not match, in Gestalt theory the person experiences unhappiness and maladjustment when the inner self does not match the mask (Perls, 1951, 1969).

That sounds pretty much like the same thing, only with slightly different words. How is Gestalt therapy different from person-centered therapy? The two therapy types are similar because they are both based in humanism. But whereas person-centered therapy is nondirective, allowing the client to talk out concerns and eventually come to insights with only minimal guidance from the therapist, Gestalt therapists are very directive. This means that a Gestalt therapist does more than simply reflect back clients' statements; instead, a Gestalt therapist actually leads clients through a number of planned experiences, with the goal of helping clients to become more aware of their own feelings and take responsibility for their own choices in life, both now and in the past. These experiences might include a dialogue* that clients have with their own conflicting feelings in which clients actually argue both sides of those feelings. Clients may talk with an empty chair to reveal their true feelings toward the person represented by the chair or take on the role of a parent or other person with whom they have a conflict so that the clients can see things from the other person's point of view.

The Gestalt therapist actually confronts the client's own statements. For example, if a client complains of tenseness in his hands, the therapist would direct him to talk about how *he* feels, not how his hands feel. Once the client realizes, through active prompting from the therapist, that the tenseness is of his own creation, he can begin to control it and choose not to be tense (Perls, 1969).

*Dialogue: a conversation or exchange of ideas between two or more persons.

But now Gestalt therapy is beginning to sound almost like psychoanalysis with its focus on the past. How are they different? Unlike psychoanalysis, which focuses on the *hidden past*, Gestalt therapy focuses on the *denied past*. Gestalt therapists do not talk about the unconscious mind. They believe everything is conscious but that it is possible for some people to simply refuse to "own up" to having certain feelings or to deal with past issues. The Gestalt therapist is more concerned about the client's "here and now" than some murky early childhood experiences. Part of that "here and now" includes attention to the body language of the client during therapy sessions. Body language, feelings both stated and unstated, and the events going on in the client's life at the time of therapy are the *gestalt* (the "whole picture") that gives this technique its name.

◀ But now Gestalt therapy is beginning to sound almost like psychoanalysis with its focus on the past. How are they different?

EVALUATION OF THE HUMANISTIC THERAPIES

Humanistic therapies have been used not only to treat mental disorders but also to help people make career choices, deal with workplace problems, and serve as a form of marriage counseling. Person-centered therapy in particular can be a very ethical form of therapy because it is so nondirective: There's typically nothing that the therapist says that the client has not already said, so the therapist runs less risk of misinterpretation.

Unfortunately, humanistic therapies have several of the same drawbacks as psychoanalysis. There is little experimental research to support the basic ideas on which this type of therapy is founded, but humanists have always preferred to use case studies to build their theories. People must be intelligent, verbal, and able to express their thoughts, feelings, and experiences in a logical manner, which makes humanistic therapies a somewhat less practical choice for treating the more serious mental disorders such as schizophrenia.

◀ **AP**＊ Summarize effectiveness of specific treatments used to address specific problems.

13.3

person-centered therapy —
- developed by Carl Rogers; focuses on match between real self and ideal self; maladjustment is result of not matching; unconditional positive regard is important for congruence between real and ideal selves
- therapist uses a nondirective approach and four basic elements to develop the person–therapist relationship
  - **reflection**
  - **unconditional positive regard**
  - **empathy**
  - **authenticity**

Humanistic Therapy

(focuses on the conscious, subjective experience of emotion and people's sense of self; promotes insight and emphasizes the importance of individual choice and the potential to change one's behavior)

evaluation: little scientific support for basic premises and requires client to be fairly intelligent and verbally expressive

Gestalt therapy —
- developed by Fritz Perls; focuses on match between actual and ideal self; focuses on the gestalt, or "whole picture"
- therapist uses a very directive approach to lead the client through a number of planned experiences (e.g., self-dialogue, "empty chair" technique), with the goal of increasing self-awareness
- although aspects of the individual's past are examined, the focus is on denied past, not hidden past; everything is conscious but possibly not in the "here and now"

(continued)

PRACTICE **QUIZ:** PREPARING FOR THE AP* EXAM

ANSWERS ON PAGE AK-3.

Directions: Read each of the questions or incomplete sentences below. Then choose the response that best answers the question or completes the sentence.

1. Humanistic therapies are different from psychoanalysis because humanistic therapies are _____.
   a. biomedical
   b. action oriented
   c. insight oriented
   d. focused on childhood events
   e. focused on the conscious experiences

2. Which of the following is not one of the four basic elements of Rogers's person-centered therapy?
   a. Empathy
   b. Reflection
   c. Authenticity
   d. Reinforcement
   e. Unconditional positive regard

3. Which of the following types of therapy makes the greatest use of body language?
   a. Psychoanalysis
   b. Gestalt therapy
   c. Biomedical therapy
   d. Psychodynamic therapy
   e. Person-centered therapy

4. Franklin's therapist has him talk to an empty chair and pretend that he is talking to his father. Franklin's therapist is most likely a _____.
   a. Gestalt therapist
   b. Freudian therapist
   c. behavioral therapist
   d. psychodynamic therapist
   e. person-centered therapist

5. Which of the following would most likely be a person-centered therapist's response to the client's claim, "I feel like a failure"?
   a. "I don't think you're a failure"
   b. "Why do you feel like a failure?"
   c. "Have you always felt like a failure?"
   d. "You feel that you're failing in some way"
   e. "Does this sense of failure cause physical pain?"

AP* Describe major treatment orientations used in therapy.

► The last chapter talked about how behaviorists have a very different way of looking at abnormality—it's all learned. So do behaviorists do any kind of therapy?

► ## Behavior Therapies: Learning One's Way to Better Behavior

The last chapter talked about how behaviorists have a very different way of looking at abnormality—it's all learned. So do behaviorists do any kind of therapy? That's right—the basic concept behind behaviorism is that all behavior, whether "normal" or "abnormal," is learned through the same processes of classical and operant conditioning. Unlike the psychodynamic and humanistic therapies, **behavior therapies** are action based rather than insight based. Their aim is to change behavior through the use of the same kinds of learning techniques that people (and animals) use to learn any new responses. The abnormal or undesirable behavior is not seen as a symptom of anything else but rather is the problem itself. Learning created the problem, and new learning can correct it (Onken et al., 1997; Skinner, 1974; Sloan & Mizes, 1999).

13.4 How do behavior therapists use classical and operant conditioning to treat disordered behavior?

THERAPIES BASED ON CLASSICAL CONDITIONING

Classical conditioning is the learning of involuntary responses by pairing a stimulus that normally causes a particular response with a new, neutral stimulus. After enough pairings, the new stimulus will also cause the response to occur.   *to Chapter Five: Learning, pp. 177–179.* Through classical conditioning, old and undesirable reflex responses can be replaced by desirable ones. There are several techniques that have been developed using this type of learning to treat disorders such as phobias, obsessive-compulsive disorder, and similar anxiety disorders.

Some behavioral therapists now use virtual reality to expose patients to phobic objects and situations—like the cabin of an airplane. As part of systematic desensitization, this patient receives exposure to anxiety-provoking visual displays through a virtual reality headset.
Credit: Charles undermost, Delft University of Technology

Using learning techniques to change undesirable behavior and increase desirable behavior has a long history (Hughes, 1993; Lovaas, 1987; Lovaas et al., 1966). Originally called **behavior modification**, the more recent version of these techniques is **applied behavior analysis**. Both terms refer to the use of conditioning techniques to modify behavior.

Systematic Desensitization **Systematic desensitization**, in which a therapist guides the client through a series of steps meant to reduce fear and anxiety, is normally used to treat phobic disorders and consists of a three-step process. First, the client must learn to relax through deep muscle relaxation training. Next, the client and the therapist construct a list, beginning with the object or situation that causes the least fear to the client and working up to the object or situation that produces the greatest degree of fear. Finally, under the guidance of the therapist the client begins at the first item on the list that causes minimal fear and looks at it, thinks about it, or actually confronts it, all while remaining in a relaxed state. The idea is that the phobic object or situation is a conditioned stimulus that the client has learned to fear because it was originally paired with a real fearful stimulus. By pairing the old conditioned stimulus (the fear object) with a new relaxation response that is incompatible* with the emotions and physical arousal associated with fear, the person's fear is reduced and relieved. The person then proceeds to the next item on the list of fears (called a *hierarchy of fears*) until the phobia is gone. It is even possible to use a computer-generated virtual reality technique for desensitization (Rothbaum et al., 1995).

Aversion Therapy Another way to use classical conditioning is to reduce the frequency of undesirable behaviors, such as overeating, by teaching the client to pair an aversive (unpleasant) stimulus with the stimulus that results in the undesirable response in a process called **aversion therapy**. For example, someone who wants to stop overeating might go to a therapist who allows the client to eat junk foods, but pairs those junk foods with foul-smelling odors. This constant pairing of junk food with bad smells will condition the client to associate junk food with unpleasurable sensations, and the client's new conditioned response to junk food will be nausea rather than hunger.

Another good example of aversion therapy is the use of a drug called *disulfiram*, commonly known by the brand name Antabuse®, to treat alcoholism (Petrakis et al., 2002). This medicine, when properly prescribed and

behavior therapies action therapies based on the principles of classical and operant conditioning and aimed at changing disordered behavior without concern for the original causes of such behavior.

behavior modification or applied behavior analysis the use of learning techniques to modify or change undesirable behavior and increase desirable behavior.

systematic desensitization behavior technique used to treat phobias, in which a client is asked to make a list of ordered fears and taught to relax while concentrating on those fears.

aversion therapy form of behavioral therapy in which an undesirable behavior is paired with an aversive stimulus to reduce the frequency of the behavior.

*Incompatible: referring to two or more things that cannot exist together or at the same time.

Could you use aversion therapy to help someone with a phobia? ▶

monitored by a doctor or psychiatrist, results in several aversive reactions when combined with alcohol. The person may experience nausea, vomiting, anxiety, and even more serious symptoms, making this drug an effective deterrent for drinking for people who are unable to quit by other means.

Could you use aversion therapy to help someone with a phobia? Because phobias are already very unpleasant, aversive conditioning is not the most useful method of therapy. But although desensitization remains one of the more common therapies for phobias, it does not always bring quick results.

Flooding   One method that can help a person deal with a phobia more quickly is **flooding**. Like systematic desensitization, flooding involves exposing the person with a phobia to the phobic object or situation. But this exposure is rapid and intense rather than slow and gradual (Gelder, 1976; Olsen, 1975) and produces extinction of the conditioned fear response rather than replacing the old fear response with a different response. For example, a person who has a phobia of dogs might be exposed to a (very friendly) small dog that is actually in the room with the person. If the person cannot leave the room or avoid the dog (which would actually reinforce the fear through the removal of an unpleasant stimulus, otherwise known as negative reinforcement), the fear will eventually extinguish because *nothing bad happens*. The exposure might have to be repeated several times but usually brings results within a few sessions of only one or two hours each. Notice that there are really two steps in this therapy: exposure to the feared stimulus or situation and prevention of the once typical avoidance response. This technique is also called *exposure and response prevention* for that reason. One danger of flooding may be a strengthening of the phobia if the person is allowed to leave the treatment situation before the fear symptoms have been extinguished. Flooding has also been successfully used to treat post-traumatic stress disorder (Foa et al., 2000; Keane et al., 1989) and obsessive-compulsive disorder through exposure to the anxiety-provoking situations (Foa & Franklin, 2000).

THERAPIES BASED ON OPERANT CONDITIONING

Operant conditioning techniques include reinforcement, extinction, shaping, and modeling to change the frequency of voluntary behavior. (L)(I)(N)(K) *to Chapter Five: Learning, pp. 193–195, 207–208.* In the treatment of psychological disorders, the goal is to reduce the frequency of undesirable behavior and increase the frequency of desirable responses.

One of the advantages of using operant conditioning to treat a problem behavior is that results are usually quickly obtained rather than having to wait through years of more insight-oriented forms of therapy. When bringing the behavior under control (rather than finding out why it occurs in the first place) is the goal, operant and other behavioral techniques are very practical. There's an old joke about a man whose fear of things hiding under his bed is cured by a behavioral therapist in one night. The therapist simply cut the legs off the bed.

Modeling   **Modeling**, or learning through the observation and imitation of a model, is discussed in Chapter Five. The use of modeling as a therapy is based on the work of Albert Bandura, which states that a person with specific fears or someone who needs to develop social skills can learn to do so by watching someone else (the model) confront those fears or demonstrate the needed social skills (Bandura et al., 1969). In **participant modeling**, a model demonstrates the desired behavior in a step-by-step, gradual process. The client is encouraged by the therapist to imitate the

flooding   technique for treating phobias and other stress disorders in which the person is rapidly and intensely exposed to the fear-provoking situation or object and prevented from making the usual avoidance or escape response.

modeling   learning through the observation and imitation of others.

participant modeling   technique in which a model demonstrates the desired behavior in a step-by-step, gradual process while the client is encouraged to imitate the model.

AP * Identify major figures in psychological treatment.   ▶

model in the same gradual, step-by-step manner (Bandura, 1986; Bandura et al., 1974). The model can be a person actually present in the same room with the client or someone seen on videotape. For example, a model might first approach a dog, then touch the dog, then pet the dog, and finally hug the dog. A child (or adult) who fears dogs would watch this process and then be encouraged to repeat the steps that the model demonstrated.

Behavioral therapists can give parents or others advice and demonstrations on how to carry out behavioral techniques. Once a person knows what to do, modeling is a fairly easy technique. Modeling has been effective in helping children with dental fears (Klorman et al., 1980; Ollendick & King, 1998), social withdrawal (O'Connor, 1972), obsessive-compulsive disorder (Roper et al., 1975), and phobias (Hintze, 2002).

Using Reinforcement   **Reinforcement** is the strengthening of a response by following it with some pleasurable consequence (positive reinforcement) or the removal of an unpleasant stimulus (negative reinforcement). Reinforcement of both types can form the basis for treatment of people with behavioral problems.

Token Economies   In a **token economy**, objects that can be traded for food, candy, treats, or special privileges are called *tokens*. Clients earn tokens for behaving correctly or accomplishing behavioral goals and can later exchange those tokens for things that they want. They may also lose tokens for inappropriate behavior. This trading system is a token economy. (L)(I)(N)(K) *to Chapter Five: Learning, p. 201.* Token economies have also been used successfully in modifying the behavior of relatively disturbed persons in mental institutions, such as people with schizophrenia or depressed persons (Dickerson et al., 1994; Glynn, 1990; McMonagle & Sultana, 2002).

Contingency Contracting   Another method based on the use of reinforcement involves making a **contingency contract** with the client (Salend, 1987). This contract is a formal agreement between therapist and client (or teacher and student, or parent and child) in which both parties' responsibilities and goals are clearly stated. Such contracts are useful in treating specific problems such as drug addiction (Talbott & Crosby, 2001), educational problems (Evans & Meyer, 1985; Evans et al., 1989), and eating disorders (Brubaker & Leddy, 2003).

For example, a typical contingency contract between a child and a parent would have one section that states the purpose of the contract (for example, "harmony in the home") and then a specific list of behaviors that the child agrees to complete, such as "completing homework," "making my bed," and "using a respectful tone when speaking to Mom or Dad." There will also be a list of penalties associated with failing to perform each of these tasks. This written statement of the rules and penalties makes it clear to children that if they fail to perform a task, they are choosing the punishment. The parents will also have a section stating the privileges that the child will earn when performing the tasks as agreed, such as free time to watch television, use of the car, or purchase of a special toy. The child and the parents sign the agreement.

Why does it work? The contingency contract puts everything down in "black and white." The stated tasks, stated penalties, and stated rewards are consistent, making discipline easier on both the child and the parents. There is no "wiggle room" for either child or parents to reinterpret the rules or back down on a promised privilege. Consistency is one of the most effective tools in using both rewards and punishments to mold behavior. (L)(I)(N)(K) *to Chapter Five: Learning, p. 193.*

reinforcement   the strengthening of a response by following it with a pleasurable consequence or the removal of an unpleasant stimulus.

token economy   the use of objects called tokens to reinforce behavior in which the tokens can be accumulated and exchanged for desired items or privileges.

contingency contract   a formal, written agreement between the therapist and client (or teacher and student) in which goals for behavioral change, reinforcements, and penalties are clearly stated.

This boy is sitting in the "time-out" corner at his school. By removing the attention that he found rewarding, the teacher is attempting to extinguish the behavior that earned the boy a time-out. Do you see anything in this time-out corner that might make it less effective?

extinction the removal of a reinforcer to reduce the frequency of a behavior.

time-out an extinction process in which a person is removed from the situation that provides reinforcement for undesirable behavior, usually by being placed in a quiet corner or room away from possible attention and reinforcement opportunities.

cognitive therapy therapy in which the focus is on helping clients recognize distortions in their thinking and replace distorted, unrealistic beliefs with more realistic, helpful thoughts.

AP* Summarize effectiveness of specific treatments used to address specific problems.

AP* Describe major treatment orientations used in therapy.

Using Extinction   **Extinction** involves the removal of a reinforcer to reduce the frequency of a particular response. In modifying behavior, operant extinction often involves removing one's attention from the person when that person is engaging in an inappropriate or undesirable behavior. With children, this removal of attention may be a form of **time-out**, in which the child is removed from the situation that provides reinforcement (Kazdin, 1980). In adults, a simple refusal by the other persons in the room to acknowledge the behavior is often successful in reducing the frequency of that behavior. For example, recall Joanne, the spider-phobic woman. ⓁⒾⓃⓀ *to Chapter Twelve: Psychological Disorders, p. 479.* Her friends subjected Joanne to a kind of extinction process by refusing to fuss over her reactions, resulting in a reduction in both the severity and frequency of her phobic reactions.

▶ EVALUATION OF BEHAVIOR THERAPIES

13.5 How successful are behavior therapies?

Behavior therapies may be more effective than other forms of therapy in treating specific behavioral problems, such as bed-wetting, overeating, drug addictions, and phobic reactions (Burgio, 1998; Wetherell, 2002). More serious psychological disorders, such as severe depression or schizophrenia, do not respond as well overall to behavioral treatments, although improvement of specific symptoms can be achieved (Glynn, 1990; McMonagle & Sultana, 2002). Bringing symptoms under control is an important step in allowing a person to function normally in the social world, and behavior therapies are a relatively quick and efficient way to eliminate or greatly reduce such symptoms.

Cognitive Therapies: Thinking Is Believing

13.6 What are the goals and basic elements of cognitive therapies such as cognitive-behavioral therapy and rational-emotive behavior therapy?

Cognitive therapy (Beck, 1979; Freeman et al., 1989) was developed by Aaron T. Beck and is focused on helping people change their ways of thinking. Rather than focusing on the behavior itself, the cognitive therapist focuses on the distorted* thinking and unrealistic beliefs that lead to maladaptive behavior (Hollon & Beck,

---

*Distorted: twisted out of true meaning.

1994), especially those distortions relating to depression (Abela & D'Allesandro, 2002; McGinn, 2000). The goal is to help clients test, in a more objective, scientific way, the truth of their beliefs and assumptions, as well as their attributions concerning both their own behavior and the behavior of others in their lives. (L)(I)(N)(K) *to Chapter Fourteen: Social Psychology, pp. 574–575.* Then they can recognize thoughts that are distorted and negative and replace them with more positive, helpful thoughts. Because the focus is on changing thoughts rather than gaining deep insights into their causes, this kind of therapy is primarily an action therapy.

BECK'S COGNITIVE THERAPY

What are these unrealistic beliefs? Cognitive therapy focuses on the distortions of thinking. (L)(I)(N)(K) *to Chapter Eleven: Theories of Personality, pp. 447–449.* Here are some of the more common distortions in thought that can create negative feelings and unrealistic beliefs in people:

- **Arbitrary inference**: This refers to "jumping to conclusions" without any evidence. *Arbitrary* means to decide something based on nothing more than personal whims. Example: "Suzy canceled our date—I'll bet she's going out with someone else!"

- **Selective thinking**: In selective thinking, the person focuses only on one aspect of a situation, leaving out other relevant* facts that might make things seem less negative. Example: Peter's teacher praised his paper but made one comment about needing to check his punctuation. Peter assumes that his paper is lousy and that the teacher really didn't like it, ignoring the other praise and positive comments.

- **Overgeneralization**: Here a person draws a sweeping conclusion from one incident and then assumes that the conclusion applies to areas of life that have nothing to do with the original event. Example: "I insulted my algebra teacher. I'll flunk and I'll never be able to get a decent job—I'll end up on welfare."

- **Magnification and minimization**: Here a person blows bad things out of proportion while not emphasizing good things. Example: A student who has received good grades on every other exam believes that the C she got on the last quiz means she's not going to succeed in school.

- **Personalization**: In personalization, an individual takes responsibility or blame for events that are not really connected to the individual. Example: When Tara's best friend is in a bad mood because of something that happened at school, Tara immediately assumes that her friend is angry with her.

A cognitive therapist tries to get clients to look at their beliefs and test them to see how accurate they really are. The first step is to identify an illogical or unrealistic belief, which the therapist and client do in their initial talks. Then the client is guided by the therapist through a process of asking questions about that belief, such as "When did this belief of mine begin?" or "What is the evidence for this belief?"

Don't those questions sound like critical thinking, which was discussed in Chapter One? Cognitive therapy really is a kind of critical thinking, but it is thinking specifically about one's own thoughts and beliefs rather than outside events and experiences. Just as cognitive psychology grew out of behaviorism (L)(I)(N)(K) *to Chapter One: The Science of Psychology, pp. 10–11, 14–15,* therapies using cognitive methods have behavioral elements within them as well, leading to the term **cognitive-behavioral therapy (CBT)**.

*Relevant: having importance with regard to the situation.

◄ **What are these unrealistic beliefs?**

arbitrary inference distortion of thinking in which a person draws a conclusion that is not based on any evidence.

selective thinking distortion of thinking in which a person focuses on only one aspect of a situation while ignoring all other relevant aspects.

overgeneralization distortion of thinking in which a person draws sweeping conclusions based on only one incident or event and applies those conclusions to events that are unrelated to the original.

magnification and minimization distortions of thinking in which a person blows a negative event out of proportion to its importance (magnification) while ignoring relevant positive events (minimization).

personalization distortion of thinking in which a person takes responsibility or blame for events that are unconnected to the person.

cognitive-behavioral therapy (CBT) action therapy in which the goal is to help clients overcome problems by learning to think more rationally and logically.

◄ **Don't those questions sound like critical thinking, which was discussed in Chapter One?**

Cognitive-behavioral therapy, or CBT, focuses on the present rather than the past (like behaviorism) but also assumes that people interact with the world with more than simple, automatic reactions to external stimuli. People observe the world and the people in the world around them, make assumptions and inferences* based on those observations or cognitions, and then decide how to respond (Rachman & Hodgson, 1980). As a form of cognitive therapy, CBT also assumes that disorders come from illogical, irrational cognitions and that changing the thinking patterns to more rational, logical ones will relieve the symptoms of the disorder, making it an action therapy. Cognitive-behavioral therapists may also use any of the tools that behavioral therapists use as well to help clients alter their actions. The three basic goals of any cognitive-behavioral therapy follow.

1. Relieve the symptoms and help clients resolve the problems.
2. Help clients develop strategies that can be used to cope with future problems.
3. Help clients change the way they think from irrational, self-defeating thoughts to more rational, self-helping, positive thoughts.

AP* Identify major figures in psychological treatment.

ELLIS AND RATIONAL-EMOTIVE BEHAVIOR THERAPY (REBT)

Albert Ellis proposed a version of CBT called **rational-emotive behavioral therapy (REBT)**, in which clients are taught a way to challenge their own irrational beliefs with more rational, helpful statements (Ellis, 1997, 1998). Here are some examples of irrational beliefs:

- Everyone should love and approve of me (if they don't, I am awful and unlovable).
- When things do not go the way I wanted and planned, it is terrible and I am, of course, going to get very disturbed. I can't stand it!

But I've felt that way at times. ▶ Why are these statements so irrational?

But I've felt that way at times. Why are these statements so irrational? Notice that these statements have one thing in common: It's either all or nothing. Can a person really expect the love and affection of every single person? Is it really realistic to expect things to work as planned every time? REBT is about challenging these types of "my way or nothing" statements, helping people to realize that life can be good without being "perfect." In REBT, therapists take a very directive role, challenging the client when the client makes statements like those listed earlier, assigning homework, using behavioral techniques to modify behavior, and arguing with clients about the rationality of their statements. Take the following example of a hypothetical exchange between a shy client and a REBT therapist:

CLIENT: I'm just so shy, I can't bring myself to talk to anyone.

THERAPIST: Really? You're talking to me, aren't you?
CLIENT: But that's different, I know you.
THERAPIST: You didn't know me when you started coming to see me, yet you were able to talk to me, right? So obviously, you can talk to other people when you want to talk, right?
CLIENT: Well. . . maybe. But it's hard for me to just start up a conversation with someone I've never met.
THERAPIST: But "hard" isn't the same as "impossible," is it? When you go home tonight, I want you to look at some person you don't know on the bus, the train, the sidewalk, and just say, "Hi." That's all, just "hi." Do that at least twice a day until you see me again, and each time you do it, buy yourself a little treat.

rational-emotive behavior therapy (REBT) cognitive-behavioral therapy in which clients are directly challenged in their irrational beliefs and helped to restructure their thinking into more rational belief statements.

---

*Inferences: conclusions drawn from observations and facts.

Table 13.1 Characteristics of Psychotherapies

TYPE OF THERAPY	GOAL	KEY PEOPLE
Psychodynamic therapy	Insight	Freud
Person-centered therapy	Insight	Rogers
Gestalt therapy	Insight	Perls
Behavior therapy	Action	Watson, Jones, Skinner, Bandura
Cognitive therapy	Action	Beck
CBT	Action	Various professionals
REBT	Action	Ellis

EVALUATION OF COGNITIVE AND COGNITIVE-BEHAVIORAL THERAPIES

Cognitive and cognitive-behavioral therapies are less expensive than the typical insight therapy because they are comparatively short-term therapies. As in behavior therapy, clients do not have to dig too deep for the hidden sources of their problems. Instead, cognitive-based therapies get right to the problems themselves, helping clients deal with their symptoms more directly. In fact, one of the criticisms of these therapies as well as behavior therapies is that they treat the symptom, not the cause. However, it should be noted that in the cognitive viewpoint, the maladaptive thoughts are seen as the cause of the problems, not merely the symptoms. There is also an element of potential bias because of the therapist's opinions as to which thoughts are rational and which are not (Westen, 2005).

Nevertheless, cognitive and cognitive-behavioral therapies have considerable success in treating many types of disorders, including depression, stress disorders, eating disorders, anxiety disorders, personality disorders, and even—in addition to other forms of therapy—some types of schizophrenia (Beck, 2007; Clark et al., 1989, in press; DeRubeis et al., 1999; Holcomb, 1986; Jay & Elliot, 1990; Kendall, 1983; Kendall et al., 2008; McGinn, 2000; Meichenbaum, 1996; Mueser et al., 2008). As an offshoot of behaviorism, the learning principles that are the basis of cognitive-behavioral therapies are considered empirically sound (Masters et al., 1987). For a summary of the various types of psychotherapies discussed up to this point, see Table 13.1.

Group Therapies: Not for the Shy

An alternative to individual therapy, in which the client and the therapist have a private, one-on-one session, is to gather a group of clients with similar problems together and have the group discuss problems under the guidance of a single therapist (Yalom, 1995).

13.7 What are the various types of group therapies and the advantages and disadvantages of group therapy?

TYPES OF GROUP THERAPIES

There are also several ways in which group therapy can be accomplished. The therapist may use either an insight or cognitive-behavioral style, although person-centered, Gestalt, and behavior therapies seem to work better in group settings than psychoanalysis and cognitive-behavioral therapies (Andrews, 1989).

AP* Summarize effectiveness of specific treatments used to address specific problems.

AP* Compare and contrast different treatment formats.

In group therapy, several people who share similar problems gather with a therapist to discuss their feelings and concerns. The presence of others who are going through the same kind of emotional difficulties can be comforting as well as provide the opportunity for insights into one's own problems by hearing about the problems of others.

family counseling (family therapy)
a form of group therapy in which family members meet together with a counselor or therapist to resolve problems that affect the entire family.

self-help groups (support groups)
a group composed of people who have similar problems and who meet together without a therapist or counselor for the purpose of discussion, problem solving, and social and emotional support.

Although it appears that the young girl in the middle is the focus of this session, all family members are encouraged to see how their own behavior may contribute to the problem behavior.

In addition to the variations in the style of therapy, the group structure can also vary. There may be small groups formed of related persons or other groups of unrelated persons that meet without the benefit of a therapist. Their goal is to share their problems and provide social and emotional support for each other.

Family Counseling One form of group therapy is **family counseling** or **family therapy**, in which all of the members of a family who are experiencing some type of problem—marital problems, problems in child discipline, or sibling rivalry, for example—are seen by the therapist as a group. The therapist may also meet with one or more family members individually at times, but the real work in opening the lines of communication among family members is accomplished in the group setting (Frankel & Piercy, 1990; Pinsoff & Wynne, 1995). The family members may include grandparents, aunts and uncles, and in-laws as well as the core family. This is because family therapy focuses on the family as a whole unit or system of interacting "parts." No one person is seen as "the problem" because all members of the family system are part of the problem: They are experiencing it, rewarding it, or by their actions or inactions causing it to occur in the first place.

Take the example of the author's cousin, George. George was what most people would label a "brat." He refused to do chores, was rude to his mother and others, and destroyed his toys to gain attention. Why did George need that attention? His father had not wanted children and ignored George—except when George was misbehaving. George's mother would not allow his father to spank him, and she allowed George to be rude. When George destroyed a toy, his mother would buy him a new one. Clearly, the problems within this family system are not all the fault of George alone.

The goal in family therapy, then, is to discover the unhealthy ways in which family members interact and communicate with one another and change those ways to healthier, more productive means of interaction. Family therapists work not only with families but also with couples who are in a committed relationship with the goal of improving communication, helping the couple to learn better ways of solving their problems and disagreements, and increasing feelings of intimacy and emotional closeness (Christensen et al., 1995; Heavey et al., 1993).

Self-Help Groups Therapists are often in short supply, and they also charge money for leading group therapy sessions. Many people may feel that a therapist who has never had an addiction cannot truly understand their problem, for example, and may also feel that someone who has experienced addiction and beaten it is more capable of providing real help. This, rather than just concerns about money, is the main reason some people choose to meet with others who have problems similar to their own on a voluntary basis, with no therapist in charge. Called **self-help groups** or **support groups**, these groups are usually formed around a particular problem. Some examples of self-help groups are Alcoholics Anonymous, Overeaters Anonymous, and

Narcotics Anonymous, all of which have groups meeting all over the country at almost any time of the day or night. There are countless smaller support groups for nearly every condition imaginable, including anxiety, phobias, having a parent with dementia, having difficult children, depression, and dealing with stress—to name just a few. The advantages of self-help groups are that they are free and provide the social and emotional support that any group session can provide (Bussa & Kaufman, 2000). Self-help groups do not have leaders but instead have people who volunteer monthly or weekly to lead individual meetings. So the person who is in charge of organizing the meetings is also a member of the group with the same problem as all the other members.

ADVANTAGES OF GROUP THERAPY

There are several advantages to group therapy:

- Lower cost. Because the therapist can see several clients at one time, this type of therapy is usually less expensive than individual therapy.

- Exposure to the ways in which other people view and handle the same kinds of problems.

- The opportunity for both the therapist and the person to see how that person interacts with others.

- Social and emotional support from people who have problems that are similar or nearly identical to one's own. This advantage is an important one; studies have shown that breast cancer patients who were part of a group therapy process had much higher survival and recovery rates than those who received only individual therapy or no psychotherapy (Fawzy et al., 1993; Spiegel et al., 1989). Another study found that adolescent girls in Africa, suffering from depression due to the stresses of the war in Uganda, experienced significant reductions in depression when treated with group therapy (Bolton et al., 2007).

In this meeting of one of the oldest self-help groups in the country, the person standing at the front of the room is not a specialist or a therapist but just a member of the group. She has the same problem as all of the other people in the room, which is the strength of this type of program—people are more likely to trust and open up to someone who has struggled as they have.

◀ **AP*** Compare and contrast different treatment formats.

DISADVANTAGES OF GROUP THERAPY

Group therapy is not appropriate for all situations, and there can be disadvantages:

- The therapist is no longer the only person to whom secrets and fears are revealed, which may make some people reluctant to speak freely.

- The client must share the therapist's time during the session.

- An extremely shy person may have great difficulty speaking up in a group setting.

- People with severe psychiatric disorders involving paranoia, such as schizophrenia, may not be able to tolerate group therapy settings.

A survey and comparison of the effectiveness of both individual and group therapy found that group therapy is only effective if it is long term and that it is more effective when used to promote skilled social interactions rather than attempting to decrease the more bizarre symptoms of delusions and hallucinations (Evans et al., 2000).

Evaluation of Group Therapy   Group therapy can provide help to people who might be unable to afford individual psychotherapy. It can also provide social and emotional support to people who may improve significantly from simply knowing that they are not the only people to suffer from whatever their particular problem may be. People who are not comfortable in social situations or who have trouble speaking

✱ **Explore** different kinds of self-help groups. www.mypsychlab.com

in front of others may not find group therapy as helpful as those who are more verbal and social by nature. It is also important to note that group therapy can be used in combination with individual and biomedical therapies. ✱⎯Explore on **MyPsychLab**

13.4–6   13.7

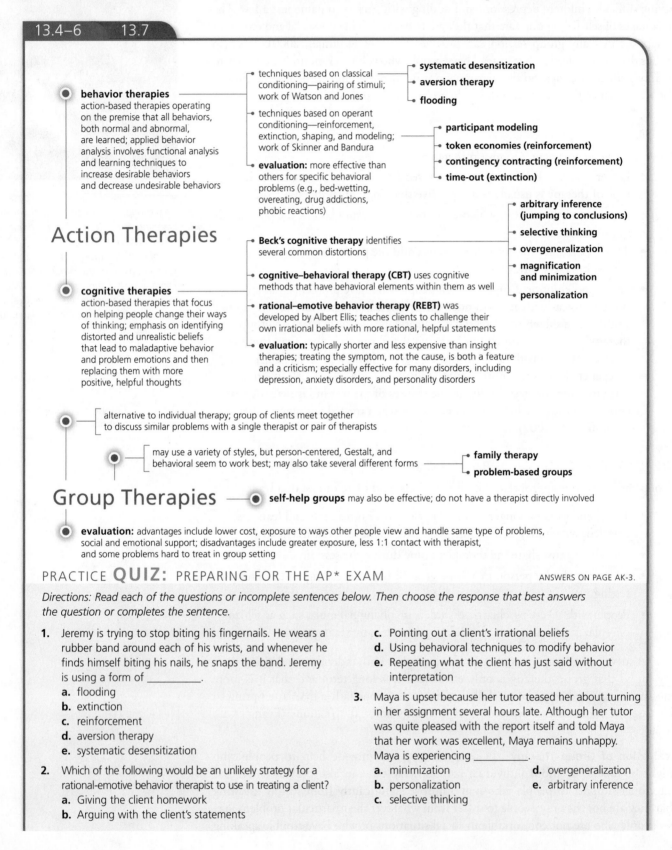

behavior therapies
action-based therapies operating on the premise that all behaviors, both normal and abnormal, are learned; applied behavior analysis involves functional analysis and learning techniques to increase desirable behaviors and decrease undesirable behaviors

techniques based on classical conditioning—pairing of stimuli; work of Watson and Jones
- **systematic desensitization**
- **aversion therapy**
- **flooding**

techniques based on operant conditioning—reinforcement, extinction, shaping, and modeling; work of Skinner and Bandura
- **participant modeling**
- **token economies (reinforcement)**
- **contingency contracting (reinforcement)**
- **time-out (extinction)**

evaluation: more effective than others for specific behavioral problems (e.g., bed-wetting, overeating, drug addictions, phobic reactions)

Action Therapies

cognitive therapies
action-based therapies that focus on helping people change their ways of thinking; emphasis on identifying distorted and unrealistic beliefs that lead to maladaptive behavior and problem emotions and then replacing them with more positive, helpful thoughts

Beck's cognitive therapy identifies several common distortions
- **arbitrary inference (jumping to conclusions)**
- **selective thinking**
- **overgeneralization**
- **magnification and minimization**
- **personalization**

cognitive–behavioral therapy (CBT) uses cognitive methods that have behavioral elements within them as well

rational–emotive behavior therapy (REBT) was developed by Albert Ellis; teaches clients to challenge their own irrational beliefs with more rational, helpful statements

evaluation: typically shorter and less expensive than insight therapies; treating the symptom, not the cause, is both a feature and a criticism; especially effective for many disorders, including depression, anxiety disorders, and personality disorders

alternative to individual therapy; group of clients meet together to discuss similar problems with a single therapist or pair of therapists

may use a variety of styles, but person-centered, Gestalt, and behavioral seem to work best; may also take several different forms
- **family therapy**
- **problem-based groups**

Group Therapies
self-help groups may also be effective; do not have a therapist directly involved

evaluation: advantages include lower cost, exposure to ways other people view and handle same type of problems, social and emotional support; disadvantages include greater exposure, less 1:1 contact with therapist, and some problems hard to treat in group setting

PRACTICE **QUIZ:** PREPARING FOR THE AP* EXAM

ANSWERS ON PAGE AK-3.

Directions: Read each of the questions or incomplete sentences below. Then choose the response that best answers the question or completes the sentence.

1. Jeremy is trying to stop biting his fingernails. He wears a rubber band around each of his wrists, and whenever he finds himself biting his nails, he snaps the band. Jeremy is using a form of _____.
   a. flooding
   b. extinction
   c. reinforcement
   d. aversion therapy
   e. systematic desensitization

2. Which of the following would be an unlikely strategy for a rational-emotive behavior therapist to use in treating a client?
   a. Giving the client homework
   b. Arguing with the client's statements

   c. Pointing out a client's irrational beliefs
   d. Using behavioral techniques to modify behavior
   e. Repeating what the client has just said without interpretation

3. Maya is upset because her tutor teased her about turning in her assignment several hours late. Although her tutor was quite pleased with the report itself and told Maya that her work was excellent, Maya remains unhappy. Maya is experiencing _____.
   a. minimization
   b. personalization
   c. selective thinking
   d. overgeneralization
   e. arbitrary inference

4. Albert Ellis is a key figure in the area of _____.
   a. Gestalt therapy
   b. behavior therapy
   c. psychodynamic therapy
   d. cognitive-behavioral therapy
   e. person-centered therapy

5. Annelina is frightened of water. Her therapist takes her to the beach and forces her to stand by the ocean for an hour at a time over several sessions. This therapeutic technique is called _____.
   a. flooding
   b. extinction
   c. reinforcement
   d. aversion therapy
   e. systematic desensitization

Current Issues in Psychology
What Is EMDR?

Graduate psychology student Francine Shapiro was walking through a local park thinking about some old memories that bothered her. As she moved her eyes rapidly back and forth, she discovered that her disturbing thoughts seemed to disappear. She quickly found 70 volunteers to try this eye-movement technique and they, too, found their disturbing thoughts, fears, and anxieties decreasing as they moved their eyes rapidly back and forth (Butler, 1993). Shapiro eventually earned her doctorate by developing a controlled study in which 22 survivors of rape, war, or childhood abuse were given one hour of what Shapiro called **eye-movement desensitization reprocessing**, or **EMDR**. All participants reported that their memories had lost a great deal of their fearfulness or anxiety and that they felt considerably better after undergoing the process (Shapiro, 1989).

EMDR has since become a popular therapy with many practicing clinicians for treatment of post-traumatic stress disorder or PTSD (LINK to Chapter Nine: Stress and Health, p. 348), phobias, and other anxiety-related disorders, although PTSD remains the disorder for which this new therapy is most commonly used.

Essentially, the client is instructed to think of a negative memory and an image that represents that memory (Shapiro, 1989, 1995). At this point, the client focuses on the memory while visually following the therapist's rapidly moving fingers back and forth, until the anxiety or fear has been eliminated. This is the "eye-movement desensitization" part of the process. The client is also asked to focus on some negative self-statement ("I am unlovable") during the EMDR session, and when the fear and anxiety have been removed, the client focuses on a positive thought ("I am lovable") while looking for signs of stress or tension. If such signs exist, they will be treated with more sessions of EMDR. This is the "reprocessing" part of EMDR, in which the negative cognitions are reprocessed into positive, helpful ones.

But just how new and different is this technique? Shapiro has supporters who have done studies that showed EMDR to be an effective therapy for stress and anxiety disorders of various types (Silver et al. 1995; Wilson et al., 1995). Other researchers have found that EMDR is not always effective (Montgomery & Ayllon, 1994; Muris et al., 1998; Oswalt et al., 1993), nor is it any more effective (as Shapiro and her followers have claimed) than simple muscle relaxation or exposure therapy, which are two more traditional methods (Vaughan et al., 1994). Some researchers and therapists see EMDR as simply another form of exposure therapy (Davidson & Parker, 2001). Still others point to the lack of objectivity in how clients' "recovery" is measured, pointing out that many of the earlier studies were done without actually verifying the presence of a diagnosed disorder in the client and that the therapists themselves personally collected all data (much of it self-report and, therefore, possibly inaccurate) from the clients, leading to the possibility of experimenter bias or the experimenter effect (Hurst & Milkewicz, 2000).

Robert Carroll, in *The Skeptic's Dictionary* article on EMDR (Carroll, 2000), states that each time a new study shows that some part of EMDR does not work the way Shapiro originally theorized that it would, Shapiro changes the theoretical explanation of how EMDR works to

eye-movement desensitization reprocessing (EMDR) controversial form of therapy for post-traumatic stress disorder and similar anxiety problems in which the client is directed to move the eyes rapidly back and forth while thinking of a disturbing memory.

allow the new research to fit. For example, research has shown that the eye movements are not actually necessary; simple finger tapping or alternating tones in each ear also produces the same results (Butler, 1993; Renfry & Spates, 1994). Shapiro then admitted that the eye movements are not essential and shifted the focus of the therapy to the reprocessing of thoughts (Carroll, 2000). This constant revision makes the theory impossible to disprove and sounds suspiciously like what many proponents of pseudopsychologies do when confronted with evidence against their basic ideas (Lohr et al., 1995, 1998). Until enough studies are done that control for experimenter bias and that use objective measurements of recovery, EMDR will no doubt remain a popular but controversial method of therapy (Lilienfeld et al., 2002).

Questions for Further Discussion

1. Could EMDR be a radically different form of systematic desensitization or exposure therapy, or could it be the simple exposure that brings about the relief reported by clients?

2. If a therapy such as EMDR does produce results, what could be the harm in allowing people to take advantage of it? How might that be similar to a placebo effect?

Does Psychotherapy Really Work?

There sure are a lot of psychotherapies, but do any of them really work? One of the earliest studies to look at the effectiveness of psychotherapy was Hans Eysenck's survey of 19 different studies reporting on the improvement or lack of improvement of clients' conditions using psychoanalysis and **eclectic therapies**, in which the therapist used not one but several different techniques of psychotherapy (Eysenck, 1957). (It should be emphasized that nearly all psychological professionals use more than one psychotherapy technique, as methods that work for some people's problems may not work as well with others.) Eysenck compared the results of these studies with studies of people who were institutionalized for mental disorders but given no psychotherapy. Instead, these people received food, shelter, and care for their basic needs and formed the control group. (The studies in question were done in the 1930s, a time period when such custodial care was unfortunately common.) Eysenck concluded that the people receiving psychotherapy did not recover at any higher rate than those who had no psychotherapy and that the passage of time alone could account for all recovery.

> There sure are a lot of psychotherapies, but do any of them really work? ▶

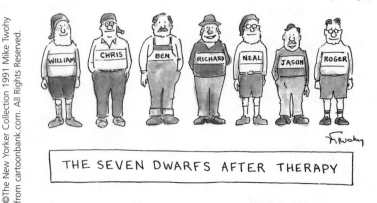

THE SEVEN DWARFS AFTER THERAPY

AP* Identify major figures in psychological treatment.

STUDIES OF EFFECTIVENESS

AP* Summarize effectiveness of specific treatments used to address specific problems.

13.8 How effective is psychotherapy, and how is the effectiveness of psychotherapy influenced by cultural, ethnic, and gender differences?

Eysenck's classic survey created a major controversy within the world of clinical and counseling psychology. Other researchers began their own studies to find evidence that would contradict Eysenck's findings. One such effort reviewed studies that the researchers considered to be well controlled and concluded that the psychotherapies did not differ from one another in effectiveness (Luborsky et al., 1975). Of course, that can mean either that the psychotherapies were all equally effective or that they were all equally ineffective.

There are numerous problems with studying the effectiveness of psychotherapy. Controlled studies can be done using an experimental group of people who receive a particular psychotherapy and a control group of people who are put on a waiting list, but this is less than ideal. The control group is not getting the attention from the ther-

eclectic therapies therapy style that results from combining elements of several different therapy techniques.

apist, for one thing, and so there would be no placebo-effect expectations about getting better because of therapy (Shapiro & Shapiro, 1997). Also, not all therapies take the same amount of time to be effective. For example, psychoanalysis, even in its short form, takes longer than a behavioral therapy. In a short-term study, behavioral therapy would obviously look more effective. Action therapies such as behavior therapy measure the success of the therapy differently than do insight therapies; in a behavioral therapy the reduction of the undesired behavior is easy to objectively measure, but gaining insights and feelings of control, self-worth, self-esteem, and so on are not as easily evaluated (Shadish et al., 2002).

Studies that do not use empirical* procedures but instead try to determine if the clients have been helped by the therapy in general are plagued by problems such as experimenter bias (the therapist expects the therapy to work and is also the one assessing the progress of the client), the inaccuracies of self-report information, and the same placebo effect cited by Shapiro and Shapiro (Seligman, 1995; Wampold, 1997).

"I like to think that each generation will need a little less therapy than the generation before."

Nevertheless, more recent surveys have shown that people who have received psychotherapy believe that they have been helped more often than not (*Consumer Reports*, 1995; Kotkin et al., 1996). The *Consumer Reports* research was a survey of the magazine's readers in which those who had been or were currently clients in psychotherapy rated the effectiveness of the therapy they received. Here are the findings from a summary of this and several other similar surveys (Lambert & Ogles, 2003; Seligman, 1995; Thase, 1999):

- An estimated 75–90 percent of people feel that psychotherapy has helped them.
- The longer a person stays in therapy, the greater the improvement.

Other studies have found that some psychotherapies are more effective for certain types of disorders (Clarkin et al., 2007; Hollon et al., 2002) but that no one psychotherapy is the most effective or works for every type of problem. Remember, all of the survey information is subject to the same flaws as any other survey information: errors in memory, inaccurate self-reporting, deliberate mistruths, and in this case even a placebo effect brought on by cognitive dissonance. **LINK** *to Chapter Fourteen: Social Psychology, p. 570.* Participants who pay for therapy more than likely expect to feel better (whether the therapy works or not).

CHARACTERISTICS OF EFFECTIVE THERAPY

So how does a person with a problem know what kind of therapist to go to? How do you pick a good one? As discussed in Chapter Thirteen, most psychological professionals today take an eclectic view of psychotherapy, using a combination of methods or switching methods to fit the particular client's needs or specific problems. A client with a phobia may benefit from both behavioral therapy and cognitive therapy, for example. Clients who have more long-term goals of understanding themselves better might be more comfortable with psychoanalysis or one of the humanistic therapies. Finding an effective therapy (or therapist) is not so much finding one therapy that works overall but finding a specific therapy that works for a specific problem.

Several factors are important in any successful, effective therapy (Hubble et al., 1999; Seligman, 1998; Stiles et al., 1998). The most important aspect of a successful psychotherapy is the relationship between the client and the therapist, known as the

◄ So how does a person with a problem know what kind of therapist to go to? How do you pick a good one?

*Empirical: capable of being verified or disproved by observation or experiment.

therapeutic alliance   the relationship between therapist and client that develops as a warm, caring, accepting relationship characterized by empathy, mutual respect, and understanding.

AP*   Discuss how cultural and ethnic context influence choice and success of treatment.

therapeutic alliance. This relationship should be caring, warm, and accepting, and be characterized by empathy, mutual respect, and understanding. Therapy should also offer clients a protected setting in which to release emotions and reveal private thoughts and concerns and should help clients understand why they feel the way they do and provide them with ways to feel better. (One of the main problems with radio and television psychologists, of course, is the lack of a private, protected setting for clients. Part of the danger lies in assuming that television or radio therapists actually have any real training in psychology or therapy. Many people call themselves therapists without the proper background, as the term *therapist* is not a licensed term, whereas *psychologist* and *psychiatrist* are.)

▶ CULTURAL, ETHNIC, AND GENDER CONCERNS IN PSYCHOTHERAPY

Consider the following situation (adapted from Wedding, 2004).

> *K. is a 24-year-old Korean American. She lived with her parents, who were both born and reared in Korea before moving to the United States as adults. She came to a therapist because she was depressed and unhappy with her lack of independence. Her father was angry about her plans to marry a non-Korean. Her therapist immediately began assertiveness training and role-playing to prepare K. to deal with her father. The therapist was disappointed when K. failed to keep her second appointment.*

This example of an actual case demonstrates a problem that exists in the therapist–client relationship for many clients when the ethnicity or culture of the client is different from that of the therapist. This cultural difference makes it difficult for therapists to understand the exact nature of their clients' problems and for clients to benefit from therapies that do not match their needs (Matsumoto, 1994; Moffic; 2003; Wedding, 2004). The values of different cultures and ethnic groups are not universally the same. How, for example, could a female therapist who is white, from a upper-middle-class family, and well educated hope to understand the problems of a Hispanic adolescent boy from a poor family living in substandard housing? Gender, ethnicity, and economic background are all vastly different.

In the case of K., for example, the therapist mistakenly assumed that the key to improving K.'s situation was to make her more assertive and independent from her family, particularly her father. This Western idea runs counter to Korean cultural values. Korean culture stresses interdependence, not independence. The family comes first, obedience to one's elders is highly valued, and "doing one's own thing" is not acceptable. K.'s real problem may have been her feelings of guilt about her situation and her father's anger. She may have wanted help in dealing with her family situation and her feelings about that situation, not help in becoming more independent.

For therapy to be effective, the client must continue in treatment until a successful outcome is reached. K. never came back after the first session. One of the problems that can occur when the culture or ethnic backgrounds of the client and therapist are mismatched, as in K.'s case, is that the therapist may project his or her values onto the client, failing to achieve true empathy with the client's feelings or even to realize what the client's true feelings are and causing the client to drop out of therapy. Studies of such situations have found that members of minority racial or ethnic groups drop out of therapy at a significantly higher rate than the majority group clients (Brown et al., 2003; Cooper et al., 2003; Flaherty & Adams, 1998; Sue, 1977, 1992; Sue et al., 1994; Vail, 1976; Vernon & Roberts, 1982).

Traditional forms of psychotherapy, developed mainly in Western, individualistic cultures may need to be modified to fit the more collectivistic, interdependent cultures.

For example, Japanese psychologist Dr. Shigeru Iwakabe has pointed out that the typical "talking cure" practiced by many psychotherapists—including psychodynamic and humanistic therapists—may have to be altered to a nontalking cure and the use of nonverbal tasks (like drawing) due to the reluctance of many traditional Japanese people to talk openly about private concerns (Iwakabe, 2008).

Are differences in gender that important? For example, do women prefer female therapists, but men would rather talk to another man? Research on gender and therapist–client relationships varies. When talking about white middle-class clients, it seems that both men and women prefer a female therapist (Jones et al., 1987). But African American clients were more likely to drop out of therapy if the therapist was the *same* sex as the client (Vail, 1976), male Asian clients seemed to prefer a male therapist, and female Asian clients stayed in therapy equally long with either male or female therapists (Flaherty & Adams, 1998; Flaskerud, 1991). (Although several of the references cited are older ones, they represent the most recent studies for these specific findings.)

Four barriers to effective psychotherapy exist when the culture or ethnic backgrounds of client and therapist are different (Sue & Sue, 2003):

1. **Language.** Speaking different languages becomes a problem in understanding what both client and therapist are saying and in psychological testing (Betancourt & Jacobs, 2000; Lewis, 1996).
2. **Cultural values.** Differing cultural values can cause therapists to fail at forming an empathetic relationship (Sattler, 1977; Wedding, 2004).
3. **Social class.** Clients from impoverished backgrounds may have values and experiences that the therapist cannot understand (Wedding, 2004).
4. **Nonverbal communication.** Body language, or nonverbal communication, can also differ between cultures and ethnicities. The physical distance between the client and therapist, the use of gestures, and eye contact, for example, can cause misunderstandings during the session and in interpretation

of the client's moods and intentions (Galanti, 1997; Like et al., 1996). People in some cultures are content with long periods of silence whereas others are not, direct eye contact is desirable in some cultures and offensive in others, and even facial expressions of emotion vary from very expressive (as with Hispanic people) to nonexpressive (as with many Asian people).

The American Psychiatric Association (2000) has included in the *DSM-IV-TR* a guide for therapists concerning cultural issues and culture-bound syndromes. Ⓛ Ⓘ Ⓝ Ⓚ *to Chapter Twelve: Psychological Disorders, p. 478.* All therapists need to make an effort to become aware of cultural differences, culture-bound syndromes, and possible gender issues.

CYBERTHERAPY: THERAPY IN THE COMPUTER AGE

Although psychotherapy is usually accomplished by the client or clients speaking face-to-face with the therapist, a new type of therapy is now available to people in need who own a computer. **Cybertherapy** refers to psychotherapy that is offered on the Internet, and the people who practice it are called *cybertherapists.* Although this method of delivery may have the advantages of lower or no cost, availability of therapy opportunities for those unable to get to a therapist easily (such as people living in a remote or rural area), access to support groups online, and relative anonymity, there are dangers. There is no guarantee that the cybertherapist has any credentials or training in psychotherapy, and because there may be no face-to-face or even voice-to-voice contact in some forms of

Are differences in gender that important? For example, do women prefer female therapists, but men would rather talk to another man?

◀ **AP*** Compare and contrast different treatment formats.

cybertherapy psychotherapy that is offered on the Internet. Also called online, Internet, or Web therapy or counseling.

cybertherapy, the therapist may not have access to body language or vocal tones in trying to assess a client's emotional and psychological state. For further information on this subject, an excellent list of the various forms that cybertherapy can take and the strengths and weaknesses of each has been developed by Dr. Azy Barak, a psychologist at the University of Haifa in Israel and an expert in Internet psychotherapy (Barak, 1999; Barak & Hen, 2008; Barak & Suler, 2008).

A group of researchers in Germany found that people who were treated as inpatients and then allowed to "meet" with a group therapist in an Internet chat room showed a significantly lower risk of negative changes in their mental status than a control group (Golkaramnay et al., 2007). The dropout rate from the Internet group was very low, and most patients "attended" the chat room sessions, which suggests that the ease of using a computer to connect to a group therapy session may be a viable option for some people needing continued therapy opportunities.

AP* Describe prevention strategies that build resilience and promote competence.

Psychotherapeutic Strategies and Disorder Prevention

So far, we've discussed using psychotherapeutic techniques to counteract the negative effects of existing psychological disorders. But can we use similar techniques to prevent those disorders before they start? Many psychologists argue that we can. When we identify people or communities at risk for psychological disorders and put strategies in place to minimize that risk, we improve people's well-being and avoid the need for expensive drugs and therapy sessions later on.

Many individuals face challenges such as poverty, racism, and sexism every day. These people may not have psychological disorders, but their circumstances encourage them to develop negative thought patterns that could end up triggering a disorder. Further, environmental stressors such as a lack of healthy food, a lack of child care, or a lack of employment can lower people's self-esteem, make them feel helpless, and lead to risky or unhealthy behaviors. To help alleviate these problems, we can use cognitive therapy techniques to help at-risk individuals change their thought patterns and boost their self-esteem. We can use techniques of behavior therapy to provide models of positive behavior and use reinforcement to help families and communities stay together and work together. We can use humanistic techniques to encourage all people to have unconditional positive regard and empathy for each other. Community members can provide job training, parenting help, and other practical skills to increase people's sense of competence, empowerment, and self-worth. On a larger scale, society can move toward eliminating the stresses of everyday life by actively combating poverty, unemployment, and inequality in all its forms.

These actions and many others may help to prevent psychological disorders and also improve the quality of life in our communities. Take a minute to think about it: How can you use some of the psychotherapeutic strategies, which we have discussed in this text, to improve your life and the lives of those around you?

AP* Compare and contrast different treatment formats.

AP* Summarize effectiveness of specific treatments used to address specific problems.

Biomedical Therapies

Just as a therapist trained in psychoanalysis is more likely to use that technique, a therapist whose perspective on personality and behavior is biological will most likely turn to medical techniques to manage disordered behavior. Even psychotherapists who are not primarily biological in orientation may combine psychotherapy with medical treatments that are supervised by a medical doctor working with the psychologist. As medical doctors, psychiatrists are almost inevitably biological in perspective and, thus, use **biomedical therapies** (directly affecting the biological functioning of the body and brain) in addition to any psychotherapy technique they may favor. This was the case with Marie, the young girl from the opening story. The biomedical therapies fall into three categories: drug therapy, shock therapy, and surgical treatments.

PSYCHOPHARMACOLOGY

13.9 What are the various types of drugs used to treat psychological disorders?

The use of drugs to control or relieve the symptoms of a psychological disorder is called **psychopharmacology**. Although these drugs are sometimes used alone, they are more often combined with some form of psychotherapy and are more effective as a result (Kearney & Silverman, 1998; Keller et al., 2000). There are four basic categories of drugs used to treat psychotic disorders, anxiety disorders, the manic phase of mood disorders, and depression. ✴ Explore on MyPsychLab

Antipsychotic Drugs   Drugs used to treat psychotic symptoms, such as hallucinations, delusions, and bizarre behavior, are called **antipsychotic drugs**. The three categories of antipsychotic drugs are *typical neuroleptics, atypical neuroleptics*, and *partial dopamine agonists*. The first of the typical neuroleptics to be developed was *chlorpromazine* (Jones & Pilowsky, 2002). The term *neuroleptic* comes from the French word *neuroleptique*, which means "to have an effect on neurons." Table 13.2 lists several of these antipsychotic drugs and their side effects.

These drugs work by blocking certain dopamine receptors in the brain, thereby reducing the effect of dopamine in synaptic transmission (Csernansky et al., 2002). However, because they block more pathways in the dopamine system than are involved in psychosis, with prolonged use they tend to cause problems such as *tardive dyskinesia*, a syndrome causing the person to make repetitive, involuntary jerks and movements of the face, lips, legs, and body (Jones & Pilowsky, 2002).

biomedical therapies   therapies that directly affect the biological functioning of the body and brain.

psychopharmacology   the use of drugs to control or relieve the symptoms of psychological disorders.

antipsychotic drugs   drugs used to treat psychotic symptoms such as delusions, hallucinations, and other bizarre behavior.

✴ **Explore** with the simulation on drug treatments. **www.mypsychlab.com**

Table 13.2   Types of Drugs Used in Psychopharmacology

CLASSIFICATION	TREATMENT AREAS	SIDE EFFECTS	EXAMPLES
Antipsychotic: Typical Neuroleptic	Positive (excessive) symptoms such as delusions or hallucinations	Motor problems, tardive dyskinesia	Chlorpromazine, Droperidol, Haloperidol
Antipsychotic: Atypical Neuroleptic	Positive and some negative symptoms of psychoses	Fewer than typical neuroleptics; clozapine may cause serious blood disorder	Risperidone, Clozapine, Aripiprazole
Antianxiety: Minor Tranquilizers	Symptoms of anxiety and phobic reactions	Slight sedative effect; potential for physical dependence	Xanax, Ativan, Valium
Antimanic	Manic behavior	Potential for toxic buildup	Lithium, anticonvulsant drugs
Antidepressants: MAOIs	Depression	Weight gain, constipation, dry mouth, dizziness, headache, drowsiness, insomnia, some sexual arousal disorders	Iproniazid, Isocarboxazid, Phenelzine sulfite, Tranylcypromine sulfate
Antidepressants: Tricyclics	Depression	Skin rashes, blurred vision, lowered blood pressure, weight loss	Imipramine, Desipramine, Amitriptyline, Doxepin
Antidepressants: SSRIs	Depression	Nausea, nervousness, insomnia, diarrhea, rash, agitation, some sexual arousal problems	Fluoxetine, Sertraline, Paroxetine

The atypical neuroleptics also suppress dopamine but to a much greater degree in the one dopamine pathway that seems to cause psychotic problems. These drugs also block or partially block certain serotonin receptors, resulting in fewer negative side effects and sometimes even improvement in the more negative symptoms of schizophrenia such as withdrawal, apathy, and reduced communication (Jones & Pilowsky, 2002).

Clozapine, an atypical neuroleptic, can cause a potentially fatal reduction in the white blood cells of the body's immune system in a very small percentage of people. For this reason, the blood of patients on clozapine is closely monitored (Jones & Pilowsky, 2002).

How long do people generally have to take these antipsychotic medications? In some cases, a person might have a psychotic episode that lasts only a few months or a few years and may need drug treatment only for that time. But in most cases, especially in schizophrenia that starts in adolescence or young adulthood, the medication must be taken for the rest of the person's life.

Long-term use of neuroleptics, particularly the older typical drugs, has been associated with a decrease in cognitive functioning (Terry et al., 2002, 2003). A newer class of atypical neuroleptics called partial dopamine agonists affects the release of dopamine rather than blocking its receptors in the brain (Tamminga, 2002). (An *agonist* is any chemical substance that can stimulate a reaction within the synapse.) ⓁⒾⓃⓀ *to Chapter Two: The Biological Perspective, p. 55.* By 2005 the only one of these drugs that had been approved by the Food and Drug Administration for use in the treatment of schizophrenia was aripiprazole (Abilify). The hope is that these newer drugs will not only produce fewer negative side effects but also have less impact on the thought processes of those persons taking these drugs. In one recent study, the atypical neuroleptics were also found to lower the risk of violent behavior in patients with schizophrenia who are receiving their medication through community-based treatment centers (Swanson et al., 2004).

Antianxiety Drugs   There are currently two kinds of drugs used to treat anxiety disorders from mild anxiety to the more serious anxiety of social phobias, simple phobias, and panic disorder. The traditional **antianxiety drugs** are the minor tranquilizers or *benzodiazepines* such as Xanax, Ativan, and Valium. All of these drugs have a sedative effect and in the right dose can relieve symptoms of anxiety within half an hour of taking the drug (Uretsky, 2002). Although many side effects are possible, the main concern in using these drugs is their potential for addiction as well as abuse in the form of taking larger doses to "escape" (National Institute on Drug Abuse [NIDA], 2002).

In the last several years the use of the benzodiazepines to treat anxiety has declined, and physicians and therapists have begun to prescribe **antidepressant drugs** to treat anxiety disorders such as panic disorder, obsessive-compulsive disorder, and post-traumatic stress disorder. Although the antidepressants take from three to five weeks to show any effect, they are not as subject to abuse as the minor tranquilizers and have fewer of the same side effects.

Antimanic Drugs   For many years, the treatment of choice for bipolar disorder and episodes of mania has been *lithium*, a metallic chemical element that in its salt form (lithium carbonate) evens out both the highs and the lows of bipolar disorder. It is generally recommended that treatment with lithium continue at maintenance levels in people with recurring bipolar disorder. Lithium affects the way sodium ions in neuron and muscle cells are transported, although it is not clear exactly how this affects mood. Side effects typically disappear quickly, although the use of lithium has been associated with weight gain. Diet needs to be controlled when taking lithium because lowered levels of sodium in the diet can cause lithium to build up to toxic levels, as can any substance that removes water from the body such as the caffeine in sodas, tea, and coffee.

How long do people generally have to take ▶ these antipsychotic medications?

---

antianxiety drugs drugs used to treat and calm anxiety reactions, typically minor tranquilizers.

antidepressant drugs drugs used to treat depression and anxiety.

Anticonvulsant drugs, normally used to treat seizure disorders, have also been used to treat mania. Examples are carbamazepine, valproic acid (Depakote), and lamotrigine. These drugs can be as effective in controlling mood swings as lithium and can also be used in combination with lithium treatments (Bowden et al., 2000; Thase & Sachs, 2000). When bouts of mania include psychotic symptoms (as in affective psychosis), patients are often treated with antipsychotic drugs in addition to a combination of anticonvulsants or antidepressants (Tohen et al., 2003).

Antidepressant Drugs As is so often the case in scientific discoveries, the first types of drugs used in the treatment of depression were originally developed to treat other disorders. Iproniazid, for example, was used to treat tuberculosis symptoms in the early 1950s and was found to have a positive effect on mood, becoming the first modern *antidepressant* (Trujillo & Chinn, 1996). This drug became the first of the *monamine oxidase inhibitors (MAOIs)*, a class of antidepressants that blocks the activity of an enzyme called monamine oxidase. Monamine oxidase is the brain's "cleanup worker" because its primary function is to break down the neurotransmitters norepinephrine, serotonin, and dopamine—the three neurotransmitters most involved in control of mood. Under normal circumstances, the excess neurotransmitters are broken down *after* they have done their "job" in mood control. In depression, these neurotransmitters need more time to do their job, and the MAOIs allow them that time by inhibiting the enzyme's action.

Some common MAOIs in use today are isocarboxazid (Marplan), phenelzine sufate (Nardil), and tranylcypromine sulfate (Parnate). These drugs can produce some unwanted side effects, although in most cases the side effects decrease or disappear with continued treatment: weight gain, constipation, dry mouth, dizziness, headache, drowsiness or insomnia, and sexual arousal disorders are possible. People taking MAOIs should also be careful about eating certain smoked, fermented, or pickled foods, drinking certain beverages, or taking some other medications due to a risk of severe high blood pressure in combination with these substances (Geddes & Butler, 2002).

The second category of antidepressant drug to be developed is called the *tricyclic antidepressants*. These drugs were discovered in the course of developing treatments for schizophrenia (Trujillo & Chinn, 1996). Tricyclics, so called because of their molecular structure consisting of three rings (cycles), increase the activity of serotonin and norepinephrine in the nervous system by inhibiting their reuptake into the synaptic vesicles of the neurons. **LINK** to *Chapter Two: The Biological Perspective, pp. 56–57.* Some common tricyclics are imipramine (Tofranil), desipramine (Norpramin, Pertofrane), amitriptyline (Elavil), and doxepin (Sinequan, Adapin). Side effects of these drugs, which may also decrease over the course of treatment, are very similar to those of the MAOIs but can also include skin rashes, blurred vision, lowered blood pressure, and weight loss (APA, 2000b; Geddes & Butler, 2002).

The effect of the MAOIs and the tricyclics on the action of the three critical neurotransmitters led researchers to try to develop drugs that would more specifically target the critical neural activity involved in depression with fewer negative side effects. This led to the development of the *selective serotonin reuptake inhibitors (SSRIs)*, drugs that inhibit the reuptake process of only serotonin. This causes fewer side effects while still providing effective antidepressant action, making these drugs relatively safe when compared to the older antidepressants. But like the other two classes of antidepressants, the SSRIs may take from two to six weeks to produce effects. Some of the better-known SSRIs are fluoxetine (Prozac), sertraline (Zoloft), and paroxetine (Paxil).

See Applying Psychology to Everyday Life for a current antidepressant controversy.

13.10 How are electroconvulsive therapy and psychosurgery used to treat psychological disorders today?

ELECTROCONVULSIVE THERAPY

Many people are—well—*shocked* to discover that **electroconvulsive therapy (ECT)** is still in use to treat cases of severe depression. ECT involves the delivery of an electric shock to either one side or both sides of a person's head, resulting in a seizure or convulsion of the body and the release of a flood of neurotransmitters in the brain (APA, 2001). The result is an almost immediate improvement in mood, and ECT is used not only in severe cases of depression that have not responded to drug treatments or psychotherapy but also in the treatment of several other severe disorders that are not responding to those alternate treatments, such as schizophrenia and severe mania (APA, 2001).

In the 1930s, doctors actually were researching the possible uses of inducing seizures in treating schizophrenia, although the seizures were induced through means of a drug (camphor) in those early experiments. It was Italian researchers Cerletti and Bini who first used electricity to induce a seizure in a man with schizophrenia, who fully recovered after only 11 such treatments (Endler, 1988; Fink, 1984; Shorter, 1997). Soon doctors were using ECT on every kind of severe mental disorder. In those early days, no anesthesia was used because the shock was severe enough to result in a loss of consciousness (most of the time). Broken bones, bitten tongues, and fractured teeth were not unusual "side effects."

ECT received more negative attention as it was portrayed in the classic 1975 film *One Flew Over the Cuckoo's Nest*, in which the little understood treatment was applied as a punishment and made to look like one. In reality, today's ECT is far more controlled and humane. It can only be used to treat severe disorders, not to control unruly behavior, and written and informed consent is required in most states. ECT has been found to be most useful for severe depression that has not responded to medications or psychotherapy and in cases where suicide is a real possibility or has already been attempted. ECT works more quickly than antidepressant medications, so it can play an important role in helping to prevent suicide attempts (APA, 2001). However, ECT should not be considered a "cure." It is a way to get a person suffering from severe depression into a state of mind that is more receptive to other forms of therapy or psychotherapy.

What are some of the side effects? Wasn't there something from an earlier chapter about this therapy affecting memory? ECT does have several negative side effects, some of which last longer than others. Memory is definitely affected, as ECT disrupts the consolidation process and prevents the formation of long-term memories. ⓛⓘⓝⓚ *to Chapter Six: Memory, p. 251.* This causes both retrograde amnesia, the loss of memories for events that happen close to the time of the treatment, and anterograde amnesia, the rapid forgetting of new material (APA, 2001; Lisanby et al., 2000; Weiner, 2000). The retrograde effects can extend to several months before and a few weeks after treatment and the older memories may return with time, whereas the anterograde amnesia is more temporary, clearing up in a few weeks after treatment. Only a very few patients suffer more severe and long-lasting cognitive difficulties, and it is not easy to determine whether these difficulties originate with the treatment or the disorder the person exhibits (Smith, 2001).

ECT as it is done today makes an effort to reduce as many side effects as possible. The modern patient is given muscle relaxants to reduce the effects of the convulsion as well as a very short-term anesthetic. In some cases, the electrodes used to induce the shock are placed on both sides of the head (**bilateral ECT**) and in others only on one side and the forehead (**unilateral ECT**). Unilateral ECT causes less severe muscular convulsions and less severe memory and cognitive problems and has been shown to be just as effective as bilateral ECT (Sackeim et al., 2000).

Electroconvulsive therapy consists of applying an electric shock to one or both sides of the head. The result is rapid improvement in mood. It has been shown to be most effective in treating severe depression that has not responded to medication.

What are some of the side effects? Wasn't there something from an earlier ▶ chapter about this therapy affecting memory?

electroconvulsive therapy (ECT) form of biomedical therapy to treat severe depression in which electrodes are placed on either one or both sides of a person's head and an electric current is passed through the electrodes that is strong enough to cause a seizure or convulsion.

bilateral ECT electroconvulsive therapy in which the electrodes are placed on both sides of the head.

unilateral ECT electroconvulsive therapy in which the electrodes are placed on only one side of the head and the forehead.

PSYCHOSURGERY

Just as surgery involves cutting into the body, **psychosurgery** involves cutting into the brain to remove or destroy brain tissue for the purpose of relieving symptoms of mental disorders. One of the earliest and best-known psychosurgical techniques is the **prefrontal lobotomy**, in which the connections of the prefrontal lobes of the brain to the rest of the brain are severed. The lobotomy was developed in 1935 by Portuguese neurologist Dr. Antonio Egas Moniz, who was awarded the Nobel prize in medicine for his contribution to psychosurgery (Cosgrove & Rauch, 1995; Freeman & Watts, 1937). ✱ Explore on MyPsychLab

But I thought lobotomies left most people worse off than before—didn't it take away their emotions or something? Although it is true that some of the early lobotomy patients did seem less agitated, anxious, and delusional, it is also true that some early patients did not survive the surgery (about 6 percent died, in fact) and others were left with negative changes in personality: apathy, lack of emotional response, intellectual dullness, and childishness, to name a few. Fortunately, the development of antipsychotic drugs, beginning with chlorpromazine, together with the results of long-term studies that highlighted serious side effects of lobotomies, led to the discontinuation of lobotomies as a psychosurgical technique (Cosgrove & Rauch, 1995; Swayze, 1995). Some famous recipients of the last decades of lobotomies (and the disorders for which the procedure was performed) were Rosemary Kennedy, sister of John F. Kennedy (mild mental retardation), and Rose Williams, sister of playwright Tennessee Williams (schizophrenia).

Are there any psychosurgical techniques in use today since the lobotomy is no longer used? The lobotomy is gone, but there is a modern replacement called the **bilateral cingulotomy**, in which magnetic resonance imaging, ⒧ⓘⓝⓚ *to Chapter Two: The Biological Perspective, p. 67,* is used to guide an electrode to a specific area of the brain called the cingulate gyrus. This area connects the frontal lobes to the limbic system, which controls emotional reactions. By running a current through the electrode, a very small and specific area of brain cells can be destroyed. This process is called *deep lesioning.* ⒧ⓘⓝⓚ *to Chapter Two: The Biological Perspective, p. 65.* Cingulotomies have been shown to be effective in about one-third to one-half of cases of major depression, bipolar disorder, and certain forms of obsessive-compulsive disorder that have not responded to any other therapy techniques (Dougherty et al., 2002; Spangler et al., 1996). Because this is deliberate brain damage and quite permanent, all other possible treatments must be exhausted before a bilateral cingulotomy will be performed and, unlike the early days of lobotomies, it can be performed only with the patient's full and informed consent (Rodgers, 1992; Spangler et al., 1996). In fact, because of the ethical, social, and legal implications of psychosurgery in general, today only a very small number of such surgeries are carried out in a few medical centers across the world (Cosgrove & Rauch, 1995).

Many psychological professionals today believe that combining psychotherapy with medical therapies—particularly drug therapy—is a more effective approach to treating many disorders. A person dealing with depression may be given an antidepressant drug to alleviate symptoms but may also still need to talk about what it's like to deal with depression and with needing the medication. Cognitive-behavioral therapy in combination with drug therapy has been shown to be particularly effective in treating depression (Dew et al., 2007; Frank et al., 2007; Rohde et al., 2008). Another study has found that women with recurrent depression benefit from a combination of treatment with antidepressants and monthly maintenance psychotherapy (Frank et al., 2007).

◄ **AP*** Identify major figures in psychological treatment

But I thought lobotomies left most people worse off than before—didn't it ◄ take away their emotions or something?

✱ **Explore** the history of lobotomy. www.mypsychlab.com

The woman on the left is Rosemary Kennedy, sister of President John F. Kennedy. The man on the right is her father, U.S. Ambassador to Great Britain Joseph Kennedy. About six years after this photograph was taken, Rosemary, who was mildly mentally retarded and whose behavior had become difficult to control, was subjected to a prefrontal lobotomy. The results were disastrous, and she remained institutionalized until her death on January 7, 2005.

psychosurgery surgery performed on brain tissue to relieve or control severe psychological disorders.

prefrontal lobotomy psychosurgery in which the connections of the prefrontal lobes of the brain to the rear portions are severed.

bilateral cingulotomy psychosurgical technique in which an electrode wire is inserted into the cingulated gyrus area of the brain with the guidance of a magnetic resonance imaging machine for the purpose of destroying that area of brain tissue with an electric current.

13.8 13.9–10

effectiveness is not easy to study due to different theories, techniques, time frames for success, etc.; tendency of some therapists to be eclectic (using variety of techniques) is also a challenge

where effective, greater success is often tied to the relationship between the therapist and client (therapeutic alliance), a sense of safety, and longer time in therapy

psychotherapeutic strategies are useful in fostering resilience and possibly preventing psychological disorders altogether

cultural, ethnic, and gender concerns should also be examined; these factors can affect not only the therapeutic alliance but problem identification and treatment options as well

Does Psychotherapy Work?

psychopharmacology the use of drugs to control or relieve the symptoms of a psychological disorder; may be used alone or in combination with other therapies (see Table 13.2)

antipsychotic drugs: treat psychotic symptoms such as hallucinations, delusions, and bizarre behavior; include the typical neuroleptics, atypical neuroleptics, and partial dopamine agonists; work by blocking certain dopamine receptors in the brain; long-term use has variety of risks, both behavioral and cognitive

antianxiety drugs: address anxiety disorders; include the minor tranquilizers (benzodiazepines) that have a sedative effect; also have potential for addiction and abuse; antidepressant drugs also used to treat anxiety disorders

antimanic drugs: address the manic episodes associated with bipolar disorder; most common is lithium; may also include anticonvulsants and antidepressants used to treat anxiety disorders

antidepressant drugs: are used to treat symptoms of depression and include monoamine oxidase inhibitors (MAOIs), tricyclic antidepressants, and selective serotonin reuptake inhibitors (SSRIs)

Biomedical Therapies

electroconvulsive therapy
- still used to treat severe depression and a few other disorders that have not responded to other forms of treatment
- involves the application of an electric shock and resulting seizure that appears to normalize the balance of neurotransmitters within the brain
- traditional side effects (extreme memory loss, broken bones) have been minimized by lower levels of current and the use of both muscle relaxers and anesthesia

psychosurgery
- used as a last resort, involves cutting into the brain to remove or destroy brain tissues associated with symptoms of a mental disorder
- prefrontal lobotomies were widely used in the mid-1900s up until the development of antipsychotic drugs
- at present, bilateral cingulotomy (involves selective areas of cingulate gyrus) is used, primarily for obsessive-compulsive disorder; has also been used with depression and bipolar disorder

---

PRACTICE QUIZ: PREPARING FOR THE AP* EXAM

ANSWERS ON PAGE AK-3.

Directions: Read each of the questions or incomplete sentences below. Then choose the response that best answers the question or completes the sentence.

1. For psychotherapy to be effective, _____.
  a. the therapist must maintain emotional distance from the client
  b. the therapist must choose one style of therapy for all his or her clients
  c. the therapist must avoid warmth in the relationship with the client
  d. the therapist must provide a protected setting for clients to reveal their feelings
  e. the therapist must prevent the client from engaging in more than one type of therapy

2. According to Sue and Sue (2003), which of the following is not a potential barrier to effective therapy when therapists and clients come from different cultural backgrounds?
  a. Age
  b. Language
  c. Social class
  d. Cultural values
  e. Nonverbal communication

3. The newest drugs being developed to treat psychotic symptoms are called _____.
  a. anticonvulsants
  b. typical neuroleptics
  c. partial dopamine agonists
  d. atypical neuroleptics
  e. selective serotonin reuptake inhibitors

4. Which of the following involves a process in which a current runs through an electrode and destroys a small and specific area of brain cells?
  a. Cybertherapy **d.** Bilateral cingulotomy
  b. Prefrontal lobotomy **e.** Electroconvulsive therapy
  c. Psychopharmacology

5. Tricyclic antidepressants treat depression by _____.
  a. producing a sedative effect
  b. suppressing dopamine receptors in the brain
  c. affecting the transportation of sodium ions in cells
  d. blocking activity of the enzyme monoamine oxidase
  e. inhibiting the reuptake of serotonin and norepinephrine

Applying Psychology to Everyday Life: Should Antidepressants Be Prescribed for Children and Adolescents?

13.11 What are the dangers of treating children and adolescents with antidepressant drugs?

In recent years there has been a growing controversy over the use of antidepressant drugs for treatment of depression and anxiety-related disorders in adolescents (Breggin, 2003, 2004; Breggin & Breggin, 1994). Although such drugs are approved for use by the Food and Drug Administration in adults, in late 2004 the FDA began requiring drug manufacturers to include a "black box" warning (the most serious type of warning in the labeling of prescription drugs) for all antidepressant drugs (FDA MedWatch Safety Alert, 2004). The warning includes a description of an increased risk of suicide in both children and adolescents and suggests that they be closely monitored. Although the new warning does not forbid the use of these drugs in children and teens, it does strongly urge professionals to weigh the possible benefits of the drug against the possible negative effects.
((•─ Listen on **MyPsychLab**

Wait a minute—how can a drug that's meant to help depression increase the risk of suicide? Children and adolescents are often affected differently by drugs used to treat various disorders in adults. The hormonal and neurological systems—including the serotonin systems—of younger people are not yet fully functional, and drugs that would be harmless in an older person may have harmful side effects in young people. The effects of antidepressants on children and adolescents, however, are not clearly understood.

In one major study published in 2001, researchers conducted what was at that time the largest clinical trial of antidepressant use in cases of adolescent depression (Keller et al., 2001). The researchers concluded that using antidepressants in adolescents was both safe and effective. But in April 2004, researchers published the results of a meta-analysis (a comprehensive scientific review) of both the published and unpublished studies conducted by drug companies that produce antidepressants (Whittington et al., 2004). It was found that although

((•● **Listen** to the Psychology in the News podcast. **www.mypsychlab.com**

◄ Wait a minute— how can a drug that's meant to help depression increase the risk of suicide?

the published research supported the safety of these drugs for use with children and adolescents, the unpublished research indicated that four out of the five drugs tested could lead to increased risk of suicide in children from ages 5 to 18. Prozac was the only antidepressant that did not have an increased risk of suicide for this age-group.

Does this mean that children and adolescents should not be given these drugs to treat other conditions? At least one of the drugs in the 2004 study is approved for use in treating obsessive-compulsive disorder in children. When this drug (and possibly others like it) is used to treat anxiety-related disorders rather than depression, there is no apparent increase in risk of suicide.

Obviously, the use of these drugs to treat depression is risky, especially when the research shows that there are safer drugs and alternative treatments. One study found that treating adolescents with a major depression disorder was more successful when the use of the approved antidepressant was combined with psychotherapy (March et al., 2004). Doctors and psychiatrists should exercise caution in prescribing powerful psychoactive drugs meant for adult bodies and nervous systems to younger persons.

Depression is not only an adult disorder; children and adolescents such as this sad young man also suffer from depression. Using antidepressant drugs to treat depression in children and adolescents is controversial. What other methods could be used to treat depression in this age group?

Questions for Further Discussion

1. Why would the combination of psychotherapy and drug therapy be more effective in treating depression in adolescents?

2. How much input should a child be permitted to have in his or her treatment process?

13 CHAPTER SUMMARY

Two Kinds of Therapy

13.1 What are the two modern ways in which psychological disorders can be treated, and how have they been treated in the past?

- Psychotherapy involves a person talking to a psychological professional about the person's problems.

- Psychotherapy for the purpose of gaining understanding into one's motives and actions is called insight therapy, whereas psychotherapy aimed at changing disordered behavior directly is called action therapy.

- Biomedical therapy uses a medical procedure to bring about changes in behavior.

The Early Days of Therapy: Ice-Water Baths and Electric Shocks

- Mentally ill people began to be confined to institutions called asylums in the mid-1500s. Treatments were harsh and often damaging.

- Philippe Pinel became famous for demanding that the mentally ill be treated with kindness, personally unlocking the chains of inmates at Bicêtre Asylum in Paris, France.

In the Beginning: Psychoanalysis

- Sigmund Freud developed a treatment called psychoanalysis that focused on releasing a person's hidden, repressed urges and concerns from the unconscious mind.

13.2 What were the basic elements of Freud's psychoanalysis, and how does psychoanalysis differ today?

- Psychoanalysis uses interpretation of dreams, free association, positive and negative transference, and resistance to help patients reveal their unconscious concerns.

- Freud's original therapy technique is criticized for its lack of scientific research and his own personal biases that caused him to misinterpret much of what his patients revealed.

- Modern psychodynamic therapists have modified the technique so that it takes less time and is much more direct, and they do not focus on the id and sexuality as Freud did.

Humanistic Therapy: To Err Is Human

13.3 What are the basic elements of the humanistic therapies known as person-centered therapy and Gestalt therapy?

- Humanistic therapies focus on the conscious mind and subjective experiences to help clients gain insights.

- Person-centered therapy is very nondirective, allowing the client to talk through problems and concerns while the therapist provides a supportive background.

- The four basic elements of person-centered therapy are reflection of the client's statements by the therapist, unconditional positive regard given to the client by the therapist, the empathy of the therapist for the client, and the authenticity of the therapist in the client's perception.

- Gestalt therapy is more directive, helping clients to become aware of their feelings and to take responsibility for their choices in life.
- Gestalt therapists try to help clients deal with things in their past that they have denied and will use body language and other nonverbal cues to understand what clients are really saying.
- Humanistic therapies are also not based in experimental research and work best with intelligent, highly verbal persons.

Behavior Therapies: Learning One's Way to Better Behavior

- Behavior therapies are action therapies that do not look at thought processes but instead focus on changing the abnormal or disordered behavior itself through classical or operant conditioning.

13.4 How do behavior therapists use classical and operant conditioning to treat disordered behavior?

- Classical conditioning techniques for changing behavior include systematic desensitization, aversion therapy, and flooding.
- Therapies based on operant conditioning include modeling, reinforcement and the use of token economies, and extinction.

13.5 How successful are behavior therapies?

- Behavior therapies can be effective in treating specific problems, such as bed-wetting, drug addictions, and phobias, and can help improve some of the more troubling behavioral symptoms associated with more severe disorders.

Cognitive Therapies: Thinking Is Believing

13.6 What are the goals and basic elements of cognitive therapies such as cognitive-behavioral therapy and rational-emotive behavior therapy?

- Cognitive therapy is oriented toward teaching clients how their thinking may be distorted and helping clients to see how inaccurate some of their beliefs may be.
- Some of the cognitive distortions in thinking include arbitrary inference, selective thinking, overgeneralization, magnification and minimization, and personalization.
- Cognitive-behavioral therapies are action therapies that work at changing a person's illogical or distorted thinking.
- The three goals of cognitive-behavioral therapies are to relieve the symptoms and solve the problems, to develop strategies for solving future problems, and to help change irrational, distorted thinking.
- Rational-emotive behavior therapy is a directive therapy in which the therapist challenges clients' irrational beliefs, often arguing with clients and even assigning them homework.
- Although CBT has seemed successful in treating depression, stress disorders, and anxiety, it is criticized for focusing on the symptoms and not the causes of disordered behavior.

Group Therapies: Not for the Shy

13.7 What are the various types of group therapies and the advantages and disadvantages of group therapy?

- Group therapy has the advantages of low cost, exposure to other people with similar problems, social interaction with others, and social and emotional support from people with similar disorders or problems.
- Disadvantages of group therapy can include the need to share the therapist's time with others in the group, the lack of a private setting in which to reveal concerns, the possibility that shy people will not be able to speak up within a group setting, and the inability of people with severe disorders to tolerate being in a group.
- Group therapy can be accomplished using many styles of psychotherapy and may involve treating people who are all part of the same family, as in family counseling.
- Group therapy can also be accomplished without the aid of a trained therapist in the form of self-help or support groups composed of other people who have the same or similar problems.
- Group therapy is most useful to persons who cannot afford individual therapy and who may obtain a great deal of social and emotional support from other group members.

Current Issues in Psychology:632: What Is EMDR?

- Eye-movement desensitization reprocessing, or EMDR, involves moving the eyes back and forth rapidly while concentrating on disturbing thoughts. The disturbing thoughts are supposed to be controlled or eliminated by this process.
- Although studies seem to show that it is effective in treating stress and anxiety disorders, other research has found that it is not always effective and criticizes the way in which recovery is measured in the supportive studies. More controlled studies are needed.

Does Psychotherapy Really Work?

- Eysenck's early survey of client improvement seemed to suggest that clients would improve as time passed, with or without therapy.

13.8 How effective is psychotherapy, and how is the effectiveness of psychotherapy influenced by cultural, ethnic, and gender differences?

- Surveys of people who have received therapy suggest that psychotherapy is more effective than no treatment at all.
- Surveys reveal that from 75 to 90 percent of people who receive therapy improve, the longer a person stays in therapy the better the improvement, and psychotherapy works as well alone as with drugs.
- Some types of psychotherapy are more effective for certain types of problems, and no one psychotherapy method is effective for all problems.
- Effective therapy should be matched to the particular client and the particular problem, there should exist a therapeutic alliance between therapist and client, and a protected setting in which clients can release emotions and reveal private thoughts is essential.
- When the culture, ethnic group, or gender of the therapist and the client differs, misunderstandings and misinterpretations can occur due to differences in cultural/ethnic values, socioeconomic differences, gender roles, and beliefs.
- The four barriers to effective psychotherapy that exist when the backgrounds of client and therapist differ are language, cultural values, social class, and nonverbal communication.
- Cybertherapy is therapy that is offered on the Internet. Cybertherapists may or may not be trained in psychotherapy, but cybertherapy offers the advantages of anonymity and therapy for people who cannot otherwise get to a therapist.
- Psychotherapeutic strategies in general are useful in promoting resilience and possibly as a preventive measure to avoid psychological disorders altogether.

Biomedical Therapies

- Biomedical therapies include the use of drugs, induced convulsions, and surgery to relieve or control the symptoms of mental disorders.

13.9 What are the various types of drugs used to treat psychological disorders?

- Antipsychotic drugs are used to control delusions, hallucinations, and bizarre behavior and include the typical neuroleptics, atypical neuroleptics, and partial dopamine agonists.
- Antianxiety drugs are used to treat anxiety disorders and include the benzodiazepines and certain antidepressant drugs.
- Antimanic drugs are used to treat bipolar disorder and include lithium and certain anticonvulsant drugs.
- Antidepressant drugs are used in the treatment of depression and include monoamine oxidase inhibitors (MOAIs), tricyclic antidepressants, and selective serotonin reuptake inhibitors (SSRIs).

13.10 How are electroconvulsive therapy and psychosurgery used to treat psychological disorders today?

- Electroconvulsive therapy, or ECT, is used to treat severe depression, bipolar disorder, and schizophrenia and involves the use of a muscle relaxant, a short-term anesthetic, and relatively mild muscular contractions.

- One of the earliest psychosurgeries was the prefrontal lobotomy, in which the front part of the frontal lobe was cut away from the back part of the brain, producing effects ranging from a disappearance of symptoms to a lack of emotional response and mental retardation.
- Modern psychosurgery includes the bilateral cingulotomy, used to treat major depression, bipolar disorders, and certain forms of obsessive-compulsive disorder that have not responded to other forms of treatment.

Applying Psychology to Everyday Life: Should Antidepressants Be Prescribed for Children and Adolescents?

13.11 What are the dangers of treating children and adolescents with antidepressant drugs?

- When both published and unpublished studies are taken into account, research has shown that all but one antidepressant drug has been associated with an increased risk of suicide when used to treat depression in children and adolescents.
- Prozac, the one safe antidepressant for children and adolescents, has been found to be more effective when combined with psychotherapy.

TEST YOURSELF: PREPARING FOR THE AP* EXAM

ANSWERS ON PAGE AK-3.

✔ Practice on MyPsychLab   **Ready for your test?** More quizzes and a customized study plan. **www.mypsychlab.com**

PART I: MULTIPLE-CHOICE QUESTIONS

Directions for Part I: Read each of the questions or incomplete sentences below. Then choose the response that best answers the question or completes the sentence.

1. Larisa is going to a therapist to gain a better understanding of what makes her do the things she does. This type of therapy is known as _____.
   a. action therapy
   b. insight therapy
   c. psychotherapy
   d. behavioral therapy
   e. biomedical therapy

2. Who is most credited with the "moral treatment" movement for using kindness and guidance with the mentally ill?
   a. Fritz Perls
   b. Carl Rogers
   c. Philippe Pinel
   d. Albert Bandura
   e. Sigmund Freud

3. Gestalt therapy differs from person-centered therapy because _____.
   a. it is a form of insight therapy
   b. it is based in humanistic theory
   c. it focuses on the unconscious mind
   d. it is directive rather than nondirective
   e. it is founded on unconditional positive regard

4. Lashonna was afraid of dogs. She wanted to get over this fear, so she began by thinking about seeing a dog but staying calm. Then she walked past her neighbor's dog in its fenced yard until she no longer felt afraid. Next, she visited a pet store and petted a dog while the salesclerk held it. Finally, she bought herself a puppy and was no longer afraid. Lashonna's method of getting over her fear is most similar to _____.
   a. flooding
   b. extinction
   c. reinforcement
   d. aversion therapy
   e. systematic desensitization

5. Carra sat down with her daughter, Morgan, and together they wrote out a list of things that Morgan was expected to do each day and the rewards she would get if she accomplished them, as well as the penalties she would face if she did not do them. This system is most similar to _____.
   a. a time-out
   b. personalization
   c. a token economy
   d. participant modeling
   e. a contingency contract

6. When five-year-old Carson began acting out, her parents took her to a therapist who suggested that her parents may have caused the problem by using the wrong kind of discipline. The kind of therapy that would best help Carson would most likely be _____.

a. family therapy

b. insight therapy

c. cognitive therapy

d. biomedical therapy

e. psychodynamic therapy

7. The use of benzodiazepines to treat anxiety disorders is gradually being phased out in favor of treatment with _____.

a. psychosurgery

b. antimanic drugs

c. antipsychotic drugs

d. antidepressant drugs

e. electroconvulsive therapy

8. Jessica sends a poem she wrote to a magazine for publication, but the magazine rejects her poem. Jessica feels awful about the rejection and tells herself that she'll never be a published writer, she'll never find a good job, and she'll die unhappy and alone. Jessica is engaging in _____.

a. minimization

b. personalization

c. selective thinking

d. overgeneralization

e. arbitrary inference

9. Albert Bandura's research was most influential in the area of _____.

a. Gestalt therapy

b. behavior therapy

c. psychodynamic therapy

d. person-centered therapy

e. cognitive-behavioral therapy

10. According to Carl Rogers, the goal of humanistic therapy is to _____.

a. recognize and adjust distorted ways of thinking and unrealistic beliefs

b. change abnormal behaviors into normal behaviors through conditioning

c. recognize and minimize the differences between the real and ideal selves

d. uncover and eliminate unconscious urges that lead to inappropriate behavior

e. change unhealthy forms of interaction and communication into healthy forms

PART II: FREE-RESPONSE QUESTION

Directions for Part II: Read the essay question that follows. Then, respond to the question in a clear, concise essay. Do not simply list facts. Instead, present a thorough argument based on your critical consideration of the topic. Use proper psychological terminology as necessary.

Matilda becomes anxious whenever she has to speak in public, and she has developed a phobia of public speaking. In a well-organized essay, describe how Matilda's anxiety and phobia would be treated in the context of each of the following therapies:

a. Psychodynamic therapy

b. Behavior therapy

c. Cognitive therapy

d. Biomedical therapy

13.1–2   p. 520

modern treatments →
- **psychotherapy**
- **biomedical therapy**

Psychological Therapies

Freud's psychoanalysis and related techniques →
- **psychoanalysis**
- **dream interpretation**
- **free association**
- **modern psychoanalysis**
- **evaluation**

"Why do you think you cross the road?"

early treatments →
- historically, individuals with mental illness were believed to be possessed by demons or evil spirits
- organized treatment began in England around the mid-1500s
- Pinel started the "moral treatment" movement in France

13.3   p. 523

person-centered therapy →
- developed by Carl Rogers; focuses on match between real self and ideal self; maladjustment is result of not matching; unconditional positive regard is important for congruence between real and ideal selves
- therapist uses a nondirective approach and four basic elements to develop the person–therapist relationship

Humanistic Therapy

(focuses on the conscious, subjective experience of emotion and people's sense of self; promotes insight and emphasizes the importance of individual choice and the potential to change one's behavior)

evaluation: little scientific support for basic premises and requires client to be fairly intelligent and verbally expressive

Gestalt therapy →
- developed by Fritz Perls; focuses on match between actual and ideal self; focuses on the gestalt, or "whole picture"
- therapist uses a very directive approach to lead the client through a number of planned experiences (e.g., self-dialogue, "empty chair" technique), with the goal of increasing self-awareness
- although aspects of the individual's past are examined, the focus is on denied past, not hidden past; everything is conscious but possibly not in the "here and now"

13.7   p. 534

- alternative to individual therapy; group of clients meet together to discuss similar problems with a single therapist or pair of therapists
- may use a variety of styles, but person-centered, Gestalt, and behavioral seem to work best; may also take several different forms

Group Therapies

self-help groups may also be effective; do not have a therapist directly involved

evaluation: advantages include lower cost, exposure to ways other people view and handle same type of problems, social and emotional support; disadvantages include greater exposure, less 1:1 contact with therapist, and some problems hard to treat in group setting

13.4–6 p. 534

behavior therapies
action-based therapies operating on the premise that all behaviors, both normal and abnormal, are learned; applied behavior analysis involves functional analysis and learning techniques to increase desirable behaviors and decrease undesirable behaviors

- techniques based on classical conditioning—pairing of stimuli; work of Watson and Jones
- techniques based on operant conditioning—reinforcement, extinction, shaping, and modeling; work of Skinner and Bandura
- **evaluation:** more effective than others for specific behavioral problems (e.g., bed-wetting, overeating, drug addictions, phobic reactions)

THE SEVEN DWARFS AFTER THERAPY

Action Therapies

cognitive therapies
action-based therapies that focus on helping people change their ways of thinking; emphasis on identifying distorted and unrealistic beliefs that lead to maladaptive behavior and problem emotions and then replacing them with more positive, helpful thoughts

- **Beck's cognitive therapy**
- **cognitive–behavioral therapy (CBT)**
- **rational–emotive behavior therapy (REBT)**
- **evaluation:** typically shorter and less expensive than insight therapies; treating the symptom, not the cause, is both a feature and a criticism; especially effective for many disorders, including depression, anxiety disorders, and personality disorders

Table 13.1 Characteristics of Psychotherapies

TYPE OF THERAPY	GOAL	KEY PEOPLE
Psychodynamic therapy	Insight	Freud
Person-centered therapy	Insight	Rogers
Gestalt therapy	Insight	Perls
Behavior therapy	Action	Watson, Jones, Skinner, Bandura
Cognitive therapy	Action	Beck
CBT	Action	Various professionals
REBT	Action	Ellis

13.8 p. 546

- effectiveness is not easy to study due to different theories, techniques, time frames for success, etc.; tendency of some therapists to be eclectic (using variety of techniques) is also a challenge

Does Psychotherapy Work?

- where effective, greater success is often tied to the relationship between the therapist and client (therapeutic alliance), a sense of safety, and longer time in therapy

- cultural, ethnic, and gender concerns should also be examined; these factors can affect not only the therapeutic alliance but problem identification and treatment options as well

Table 13.2 Types of Drugs Used in Psychopharmacology

CLASSIFICATION	TREATMENT AREAS	SIDE EFFECTS	EXAMPLES
Antipsychotic: Typical Neuroleptic	Positive (excessive) symptoms	Motor problems, tardive dyskinesia	Chlorpromazine, Droperidol, Haloperidol
Antipsychotic: Atypical Neuroleptic	Positive and some negative symptoms of psychoses	Fewer than typical neuroleptics; clozapine may cause serious blood disorder	Risperidone, Clozapine, Aripiprazole
Antianxiety: Minor Tranquilizers	Symptoms of anxiety and phobic reactions	Slight sedative effect; potential for physical dependence	Xanax, Ativan, Valium
Antimanic	Manic behavior	Potential for toxic buildup	Lithium, anticonvulsant drugs
Antidepressants: MAOIs	Depression	Weight gain, constipation, dry mouth, dizziness, headache, drowsiness, insomnia, some sexual arousal disorders	Iproniazid, Isocarboxazid, Phenelzine sulfite, Tranylcypromine sulfate
Antidepressants: Tricyclics	Depression	Skin rashes, blurred vision, lowered blood pressure, weight loss	Imipramine, Desipramine, Amitriptyline, Doxepin
Antidepressants: SSRIs	Depression	Nausea, nervousness, insomnia, diarrhea, rash, agitation, some sexual arousal problems	Fluoxetine, Sertraline, Paroxetine

13.9–10 p. 546

psychopharmacology
the use of drugs to control or relieve the symptoms of a psychological disorder; may be used alone or in combination with other therapies (see Table 13.2)

Biomedical Therapies

electroconvulsive therapy

- still used to treat severe depression and a few other disorders that have not responded to other forms of treatment
- involves the application of an electric shock and resulting seizure that appears to normalize the balance of neurotransmitters within the brain
- traditional side effects (extreme memory loss, broken bones) have been minimized by lower levels of current and the use of both muscle relaxers and anesthesia

psychosurgery

- used as a last resort, involves cutting into the brain to remove or destroy brain tissues associated with symptoms of a mental disorder
- prefrontal lobotomies were widely used in the mid-1900s up until the development of antipsychotic drugs
- at present, bilateral cingulotomy (involves selective areas of cingulate gyrus) is used, primarily for obsessive-compulsive disorder; has also been used with depression and bipolar disorder

14
Social Psychology

The Unresponsive Bystander: Why Did No One Help?

On March 13, 1964, at about 3:15 in the morning, a man who didn't even know Catherine "Kitty" Genovese caught her in the parking lot of her apartment complex, stabbed her, left, and then came back nearly half an hour later to assault and kill her in the entryway of the complex. A police investigation determined that at least 38 people heard or watched some part of the fatal attack from their apartment windows. Not one of these people—Kitty's neighbors—called the police until after the attack was over (Delfiner, 2001; Gado, 2004; Rosenthal, 1964).

Forty-three years later on June 23, 2007, 27-year-old LaShanda Calloway was killed during an argument in a convenience store. It took two minutes for someone to call 9-1-1. Surveillance video captured the attack, including the five shoppers who stepped over her bleeding form and continued shopping. One customer did stop—to take a picture of Ms. Calloway as she lay dying on the floor (Hegeman, 2007).

Why did no one try to help Kitty? How could people coldly and callously step over a bleeding, dying woman and then continue to shop? Were they simply afraid to get involved? Or did all those people simply assume that it was someone else's responsibility? Could LaShanda Calloway have been saved if someone had tried to stop the bleeding or render some kind of first aid?

Why study social psychology? If people lived in total isolation from other people, there would be no reason to study the effect that other people have on the behavior of individuals and groups. But human beings are social creatures—we live with others, work with others, and play with others. The people who surround us all of our lives have an impact on our beliefs and values, decisions and assumptions, and the way we think about other people in general. Why are some people prejudiced toward certain other people? Why do we obey some people but not others? What causes us to like, to love, or to hate others? The answers to all these questions and many more can be found in the study of social psychology.

14 Learning Objectives

- **14.1** What factors influence people to conform to the actions of others?

- **14.2** How is compliance defined, and what are four common ways to gain the compliance of another?

- **14.3** What factors make obedience more likely?

- **14.4** What are the three components of an attitude, how are attitudes formed, and how can attitudes be changed?

- **14.5** How do people react when attitudes and behavior are not the same?

- **14.6** What are social categorization and implicit personality theories?

- **14.7** How do people try to explain the actions of others?

- **14.8** How are prejudice and discrimination different?

- **14.9** Why are people prejudiced, and how can prejudice be stopped?

- **14.10** What factors govern attraction and love, and what are some different kinds of love?

- **14.11** How is aggressive behavior determined by biology and learning?

- **14.12** What is altruism, and how is deciding to help someone related to the presence of others?

- **14.13** Why do people join cults?

---

social psychology the scientific study of how a person's thoughts, feelings, and behavior are influenced by the real, imagined, or implied presence of others.

social influence the process through which the real or implied presence of others can directly or indirectly influence the thoughts, feelings, and behavior of an individual.

conformity changing one's own behavior to match that of other people.

Chapter One defined psychology as the scientific study of behavior and mental processes, including how people think and feel. The field of social psychology also looks at behavior and mental processes but includes as well the social world in which we exist, as we are surrounded by others to whom we are connected and by whom we are influenced in so many ways. It is not the same field as *sociology*, which is the study and classification of human societies. Sociology studies the big picture: how entire groups of people live, work, and play. Although social psychology does look at group behavior, it is more concerned with the individual person within the group and the influence of the group on the person.

Social psychology is the scientific study of how a person's behavior, thoughts, and feelings are influenced by the real, imagined, or implied presence of others. Although there are several sections in this chapter, there are really only three main areas under discussion: *social influence*, the ways in which a person's behavior can be affected by other people; *social cognition*, the ways in which people think about other people; and *social interaction*, the positive and negative aspects of people relating to others.

Social Influence: Conformity, Compliance, and Obedience

People live in a world filled with other people. An infant is born into a world with adults who have an impact on the infant's actions, personality, and growth. Adults must interact with others on a daily basis. Such interactions provide ample opportunity for the presence of other people to directly or indirectly influence the behavior, feelings, and thoughts of each individual in a process called **social influence**. There are many forms of social influence. People can influence others to follow along with their own actions or thoughts, to agree to do things even when the person might prefer to do otherwise, and to be obedient to authorities. The mere presence of others can even influence the way people perform tasks successfully or unsuccessfully.

GREGORY

"Sure, I follow the herd—not out of brainless obedience, mind you, but out of a deep and abiding respect for the concept of community."

CONFORMITY

14.1 What factors influence people to conform to the actions of others?

Have you ever noticed someone looking up at something? Did the urge to look up to see what that person was looking at become so strong that you actually found yourself looking up? This common practical joke always works, even when people suspect that it's a joke. It clearly demonstrates the power of **conformity**: changing one's own behavior to more closely match the actions of others.

In 1936, social psychologist Muzafer Sherif conducted a study in which participants were shown into a darkened room and exposed to a single point of light. Under those conditions, a point of light will seem to move because of tiny, involuntary movements of the eye. ⓁⒾⓃⓀ *to Chapter Three: Sensation and Perception, p. 92.* The participants were not told of this effect and reported the light moved anywhere from a few inches to several feet. When a confederate (a person chosen by the experimenter to deliberately manipulate the situation) also gave estimates, the original participants began to make estimates of motion that were more and more similar to those of the confederate (Sherif, 1936). This early experiment on conformity has been criticized because the judgments being made were ambiguous* (i.e., the light wasn't really moving so any estimate within reason would sound good); would participants be so easily swayed if the judgments were more specifically measurable and certain?

Asch's Classic Study on Conformity   Solomon Asch (1951) conducted the first of his classic studies on conformity by having seven participants gather in a room. They were told that they were participating in an experiment on visual judgment. They were then shown a white card with three black lines of varying lengths followed by another white card with only one line on it. The task was to determine which line on the first card was most similar to the line on the second card (see Figure 14.1). ✱⌐Explore on MyPsychLab

◄ **AP*** Explain how individuals respond to expectations of others.

◄ **AP*** Identify important figures in social psychology.

✱ **Explore** with a simulation on Asch's classic conformity study.
www.mypsychlab.com

Standard line

1   2   3

Comparison lines

Figure 14.1 Stimuli Used in Asch's Study

Participants in Asch's famous study on conformity were first shown the three comparison lines. They were then shown the standard line and asked to determine to which of the three comparison lines the standard line was most similar. Which line would you pick? What if you were one of several people, and everyone who answered ahead of you chose line 3? How would that affect your answer?
Source: Adapted from Asch (1956).

---

*Ambiguous: having no clear interpretation or able to be interpreted in many ways rather than just one way.

In reality, only the next-to-the-last person in the group was a real participant. The others were all confederates (people following special directions from the experimenter) who were instructed to pick the same *incorrect* line from the comparison lines. Would the real participant, having heard the others pick what seemed to be the wrong answer, change to conform to the group's opinion? Surprisingly, the participants conformed to the group answer a little over one-third of the time. Asch also found that the number of confederates mattered: Conformity increased with each new confederate until there were four confederates; more than that did not increase the participants' tendency to conform (Asch, 1951). In a later experiment, Asch (1956) found that conformity decreased if there was just one confederate who gave the correct answer—apparently, if participants knew that there was at least one other person whose answer agreed with their own, the evidence of their own eyes won out over the pressure to conform to the group.

More recent research in the United States has found less conformity among participants, perhaps suggesting that the Asch conformity effect was due to the more conforming nature of people in the era and culture of the United States in the 1950s (Lalancette & Standing, 1990; Nicholson et al., 1985; Perrin & Spencer, 1980). In other cultures, however, studies have found conformity effects similar to those in Asch's study (Neto, 1995). Still others have found even greater effects of conformity in collectivist cultures such as Hong Kong, Japan, and Zimbabwe (Bond & Smith, 1996; Kim & Markus, 1999). This cultural difference may exist only when face-to-face contact is a part of the task, however. A recent study found that when the Asch judgment task is presented in an online format (participants were in communication but not able to see each other), the cultural difference disappears (Cinnirella & Green, 2007).

What about gender—are men or women more conforming? Research shows that gender differences are practically nonexistent unless the situation involves behavior that is not private. If it is possible to give responses in private, conformity is no greater for women than for men, but if a public response is required, women do tend to show more conformity than men (Eagly, 1987; Eagly et al., 2000). This effect may be due to the socialization that women receive in being agreeable and supportive; however, the difference in conformity is quite small.

The Hazards of Groupthink   Shortly after the terrorist attack on the World Trade Center in New York, President George W. Bush and his administration made the decision to invade Iraq, find Saddam Hussein, and stop him before he could use his "weapons of mass destruction" that the administration and its advisors believed were hidden in Iraq. This decision to invade a country that had not committed an open act of war against the United States was made and executed *without* building any broad-based support from allies. Although there were advisors who thought the action to be a mistake, no one person was willing to stand up to the rest of the group and challenge the group's decision and assumptions. Many now see this decision (a costly decision in terms of lost lives and casualties, huge amounts of monetary expenditures, and—according to many—the tarnishing of the diplomatic status of the United States in the eyes of the rest of the world) as a prime example of **groupthink**. Groupthink occurs when people within a group feel it is more important to maintain the group's cohesiveness than to consider the facts realistically (Hogg & Hains, 1998; Janis, 1972, 1982; Schafer & Crichlow, 1996). Other examples include the sinking of the *Titanic* in 1912 (the group responsible for designing and building the ship assumed she was unsinkable and did not even bother to include enough lifeboats on board for all the passengers) and the *Challenger* disaster of 1986 in which a part on the shuttle was known by a few to be unacceptable (but no one spoke up to delay the launch).

What about gender—are men or women more conforming? ▶

groupthink   kind of thinking that occurs when people place more importance on maintaining group cohesiveness than on assessing the facts of the problem with which the group is concerned.

Why does groupthink happen? Social psychologist Irving Janis (1972, 1982), who originally gave this phenomenon its name, lists several "symptoms" of groupthink. For example, group members may come to feel that the group can do no wrong, is morally correct, and will always succeed, creating the illusion of invulnerability.* Group members also tend to hold stereotyped views of those who disagree with the group's opinions, causing members to think that those who oppose the group have no worthwhile opinions. They exert pressure on individual members to conform to group opinion, prevent those who might disagree from speaking up, and even censor themselves so that the group's mind-set will not be disturbed in a "don't rock the boat" mentality. Self-appointed "mind-guards" work to protect the leader of the group from contrary viewpoints. (See Table 14.1.)

Many historical events have been at least partly caused by the phenomenon of groupthink. The invasion of Iraq by the United States, which by some estimates has resulted in over 4,300 deaths of U.S. and allied military personnel and between 83,000 and 90,000 civilian deaths, is now thought to be one of those events. Believing that weapons of mass destruction were hidden in Iraq, President Bush and his advisors chose to invade despite the urgings of Secretary of State Colin Powell and other top military officials for caution—the presidential advisors formed a united front against which dissenting opinions could not prevail.

Several things can be done to minimize the possibility of groupthink (Hart, 1998; McCauley, 1998; Moorhead et al., 1998). For example, leaders should remain impartial and the entire group should seek the opinions of people outside the group. Any voting should be done on secret ballots rather than by a show of hands, and it should be made clear that group members will be held responsible for decisions made by the group.

Other Types of Group Behavior Groupthink is a fairly dramatic example of group effects on human behavior, but it is not the only phenomenon caused by group interaction. Sometimes, the stimulating experience of being in a group combined

Table 14.1 Characteristics of Groupthink

CHARACTERISTIC	DESCRIPTION
Invulnerability	Members feel they cannot fail.
Rationalization	Members explain away warning signs and help each other rationalize their decision.
Lack of introspection	Members do not examine the ethical implications of their decision because they believe that they cannot make immoral choices.
Stereotyping	Members stereotype their enemies as weak, stupid, or unreasonable.
Pressure	Members pressure each other not to question the prevailing opinion.
Lack of disagreement	Members do not express opinions that differ from the group consensus.
Self-deception	Members share in the illusion that they all agree with the decision.
Insularity	Members prevent the group from hearing disruptive but potentially useful information from people who are outside the group.

Source: Janis (1972, 1982).

---

*Invulnerability: quality of being unable to be attacked or harmed.

AP* Describe the structure and function of different kinds of group behavior.

AP* Explain how individuals respond to expectations of others.

I have a friend who watches all those infomercials on the shopping channels and buys stuff that isn't worth the money or that doesn't work like it's supposed to work. Why do people fall for pitches like that?

with the lack of responsibility that comes from being one of the crowd results in *deindividuation*. People who become deindividuated lose, to some extent, their sense of self. Your classmate might be a self-aware, restrained person when she is by herself, but when she gets caught up in the excitement of a group, she might forget her own moral guidelines and restraints: She's no longer an individual—she's just part of the group. Large protests that turn into riots are examples of deindividuation in action: It is unlikely that any single person would act violently against a stranger or an institution, but in large groups of people, self-awareness and self-control are often abandoned in favor of irresponsible, uninhibited group behavior.

If you have ever had a stimulating conversation about your political or religious beliefs with a group of like-minded friends, you may have experienced the effects of *group polarization*, the strengthening of shared beliefs through discussion. For example, if you join a club that promotes racial tolerance and attend weekly meetings at which you discuss the importance of tolerance with other club members, you and the rest of the members are likely to become even more tolerant than you already were. If you spend time chatting online with people who share your political opinions, the whole group will most likely hold those opinions more and more strongly. Like other types of group behavior, group polarization is often harmless and occasionally beneficial, but it can be dangerous when people who promote acts of violence, hatred, or terrorism get together to discuss their radical beliefs.

COMPLIANCE

14.2 How is compliance defined, and what are four common ways to gain the compliance of another?

I have a friend who watches all those infomercials on the shopping channels and buys stuff that isn't worth the money or that doesn't work like it's supposed to work. Why do people fall for pitches like that? Marketing products is really very much a psychological process. In fact, the whole area of **consumer psychology** is devoted to figuring out how to get people to buy things that someone is selling. ⓛⓘⓝⓚ *to Appendix B: Applied Psychology.* But infomercials are not the only means by which people try to get others to do what they want them to do. **Compliance** occurs when people change their behavior as a result of another person or group asking or directing them to change. The person or group asking for the change in behavior typically doesn't have any real authority or power to command a change; when that authority does exist and behavior is changed as a result, it is called *obedience*, which is the topic of the next major section of this chapter.

A number of techniques that people use to get the compliance of others clearly show the relationship of compliance to the world of marketing, as they refer to techniques that door-to-door salespersons would commonly use.

Foot-in-the-Door Technique   Let's say that a neighbor asks you to keep an eye on his house while he is on vacation. You agree, thinking that it's a rather small request. Later that day, or perhaps even in the same conversation, the neighbor asks if you would kindly water his plants while he's gone. This is a little bit more involved and requires more of your time and energy—will you do it? If you are like most people, you probably will comply with this second larger request.

When compliance with a smaller request is followed by a larger request, people are quite likely to comply because they have already agreed to the smaller one and they want to behave consistently with their previous response (Cialdini et al., 1995; Dillard, 1990, 1991; Freedman & Fraser, 1966). This is called the **foot-in-the-door technique** because the first small request acts as an opener. (Salespeople once literally stuck a foot in the door to prevent the occupant from shutting it so they could continue their sales pitch, hence, the name.)

consumer psychology branch of psychology that studies the habits of consumers in the marketplace.

compliance changing one's behavior as a result of other people directing or asking for the change.

foot-in-the-door technique asking for a small commitment and, after gaining compliance, asking for a bigger commitment.

Door-in-the-Face Technique   Closely related to the foot-in-the-door technique is its opposite: the **door-in-the-face technique** (Cialdini et al., 1975). In this method, the larger request comes first, which is usually refused. This is followed by a second smaller and more reasonable request that often gets compliance. An example of this would be if the neighbor first asked you to take care of his dog and cat in your home. After you refused to do so, the neighbor might ask if you would at least water his plants, which you would probably do.

This technique relies on the **norm of reciprocity**, which basically assumes that if someone does something for a person, the person should do something in return (Gouldner, 1960). This is also the principle used by those organizations that give out free, unasked-for samples, such as the free address stickers that come with many requests for charitable donations.

Lowball Technique   Another compliance technique, also common in the world of sales, is called the **lowball technique** (Burger & Petty, 1981). In this technique, once a commitment is made, the cost of that commitment is increased. (In the sense used here, *cost* does not necessarily mean money; *cost* can also mean time, effort, or other kinds of sacrifices.) For example, let's say that a professor agrees to write a textbook for a publishing company. Once committed to that process, the professor discovers that the task involves not only writing but also traveling to meet with editors, working nights and weekends to meet deadlines, and making the commitment to take time off from her teaching job to finish the text on time for publication. (This example is purely hypothetical, of course.)

A more common example will occur to anyone who has ever bought a car. The commitment to buy the car at one low price is quickly followed by the addition of other costs: extended warranties, additional options, taxes and fees, and so on, causing the buyer to spend more money than originally intended.

That's-Not-All Technique   Finally, there is the now familiar technique of the infomercial salesperson: the **that's-not-all technique**. In this compliance tactic, the person doing the persuading makes an offer, but before the target of the offer can make a decision, the persuader throws in something extra to make the deal look even better (Burger, 1986). See if this sounds familiar:

> *"But wait—that's not all! If you act now, we'll send you this 15-piece set of genuine faux carving knives as a bonus!"*

By offering something that the consumer did not ask for in the first place, the persuader has once again activated the norm of reciprocity. Now the consumer feels as though the persuader has "given" something and the consumer should respond by giving in to the persuader's request to buy the product.

Cultural differences exist in people's susceptibility to these techniques. For the foot-in-the door technique in particular, research has shown that people in individualist cultures (such as the United States) are more likely to comply with the second request than are people in collectivist cultures (such as Japan). The research suggests that people in collectivist cultures are not as concerned with being consistent with previous behavior because they are less focused on their inner motivation than are people in individualist cultures, who are more concerned with their inner motives and consistency (Cialdini et al., 1999; Petrova et al., 2003). Ⓛ Ⓘ Ⓝ Ⓚ *to Chapter Eleven: Theories of Personality, pp. 457–458.*

OBEDIENCE

14.3 What factors make obedience more likely?

There is a difference between the concepts of compliance, which is agreeing to change one's behavior because someone else asks for the change, and **obedience**, which is changing one's behavior at the direct order of an authority figure. A salesperson who wants a person to buy a car has no real power to force that person to buy, but an authority

---

door-in-the-face technique   asking for a large commitment and being refused and then asking for a smaller commitment.

norm of reciprocity   assumption that if someone does something for a person, that person should do something for the other in return.

lowball technique   getting a commitment from a person and then raising the cost of that commitment.

that's-not-all technique   a sales technique in which the persuader makes an offer and then adds something extra to make the offer look better before the target person can make a decision.

obedience   changing one's behavior at the command of an authority figure.

◀ **AP*** Explain how individuals respond to expectations of others.

Figure 14.2 Control Panel in Milgram's Experiment

In Stanley Milgram's classic study on obedience, the participants were presented with a control panel like this one. Each participant ("teacher") was instructed to give electric shocks to another person (the "learner," who only pretended to be shocked). Notice the labels under the switches. At what point do you think you would have refused to continue the experiment?

AP* Identify important figures in social psychology. ▶

👁 **Watch** classic video footage on Milgram's obedience study.
www.mypsychlab.com

figure is a person with social power—such as a police officer, a teacher, or a work supervisor—who has the right to demand certain behavior from the people under the authority figure's command or supervision.

How far will people go in obeying the commands of an authority figure? What factors make obedience more or less likely? These are some of the questions that researchers have been investigating for many years. The answers to these questions became very important not only to researchers but also to people everywhere after the atrocities committed by the soldiers in Nazi Germany—soldiers who were "just following orders."

Milgram's Shocking Research   Social psychologist Stanley Milgram set out to find answers to these questions. He was aware of Asch's studies of conformity and wondered how much impact social influence could have on a behavior that was more meaningful than judging the length of lines on cards. He designed what has become one of the most famous (even notorious*) experiments in the history of psychology.

Through ads placed in the local newspaper, Milgram recruited people who were told that they would be participating in an experiment to test the effects of punishment on learning behavior (Milgram, 1964a, 1974). Although there were several different forms of this experiment with different participants, the basic premise was the same: The participants believed that they had randomly been assigned to either the "teacher" role or the "learner" role, when in fact the "learner" was an actor already aware of the situation. The "teacher" was given a sample 45-volt shock from the chair in which the "learner" was strapped during the experiment. The task for the learner was a simple memory test for paired words.

The "teacher" was seated in front of a machine through which the shocks would be administered and the level of the shocks changed. (See Figure 14.2.) For each mistake made by the "learner," the "teacher" was instructed to increase the level of shock by 15 volts. The "learner" (who was not actually shocked) followed a carefully arranged script, showing discomfort, asking for the experiment to end, screaming, and even falling silent as if unconscious—or dead. (See Table 14.2 for samples of the scripted responses of the "learner.") As the "teachers" became reluctant to continue administering the shocks, the experimenter in his authoritative white lab coat said, for example, "The experiment requires you to continue" or "You must continue," and reminded the "teacher" that the experimenter would take full responsibility for the safety of the "learner." 👁 **Watch** on **MyPsychLab**

How many of the participants continued to administer what they believed were real shocks? Milgram surveyed psychiatrists, college students, and other adults prior to the experiments for their opinions on how far the participants

---

*Notorious: widely and unfavorably known.

Table 14.2   Sample Script Items from Milgram's Classic Experiment

VOLTAGE OF "SHOCK"	LEARNER'S SCRIPT
150	"Ugh!! Experimenter! That's all. Get me out of here. I told you I had heart trouble. My heart's starting to bother me now. Get me out of here, please. My heart's starting to bother me. I refuse to go on. Let me out."
210	"Ugh!! Experimenter! Get me out of here. I've had enough. I *won't* be in this experiment any more."
300	(*Agonized scream*) "I absolutely refuse to answer any more. Get me out of here. You can't hold me here. Get me out. Get me out of here."
330	(*Intense and prolonged agonized scream*) "Let me out of here. Let me out of here. My heart's bothering me. Let me out, I tell you. (*Hysterically*) Let me out of here. Let me out of here. You have no right to hold me here. Let me out! Let me out! Let me out of here! Let me out! Let me out!"

Source: Milgram (1964a, 1974).

would go in administering shocks. Everyone predicted that the participants would all refuse to go on at some point, with most believing that the majority of the participants would start refusing as soon as the "learner" protested—150 volts. None of those he surveyed believed that any participant would go all the way to the highest voltage.

So were they right? Far from it—in the first set of experiments, 65 percent of the "teachers" went all the way through the experiment's final 450-volt shock level, although many were obviously uncomfortable and begged to be allowed to stop. Of those "teachers" who did protest and finally stop, not one of them stopped before reaching 300 volts!

So what happened? Were those people sadists? Why would they keep shocking someone like that? No one was more stunned than Milgram himself. He had not believed that his experiments would show such a huge effect of obedience to authority. These results do not appear to be some random "fluke" resulting from a large population of sadistic people residing in the area. These experiments have been repeated at various times, in the United States and in other countries, and the percentage of participants who went all the way consistently remained between 61 and 66 percent (Blass, 1999).

That's incredible—I just don't believe that I could do something like that to someone else.

Evaluation of Milgram's Research   Researchers have looked for particular personality traits that might be associated with high levels of obedience but have not found any one trait or group of traits that consistently predicts who will obey and who will not in experiments similar to Milgram's original studies (Blass, 1991). The people who "went all the way" were not necessarily more dependent or susceptible to being controlled by others; they were simply people like most other people, caught in a situation of "obey or disobey" the authority. Although some have suggested that Milgram's results may have been due to the same kind of foot-in-the-door technique of persuasion as discussed earlier, with participants more likely to go on with each next demanding step of the experiment because they had already agreed to the smaller increments of shock, as yet no research supports this idea (Gilbert, 1981).

Milgram's research also raised a serious ethical question: How far should researchers be willing to go to answer a question of interest? Some have argued that

◄ So what happened? Were those people sadists? Why would they keep shocking someone like that?

◄ That's incredible—I just don't believe that I could do something like that to someone else.

the participants in Milgram's studies may have suffered damaged self-esteem and serious psychological stress from the realization that they were willing to administer shocks great enough to kill another person, just on the say-so of an experimenter (Baumrind, 1964). Milgram (1964b) responded to the criticism by citing his follow-up study of the participants, in which he found that 84 percent of the participants were glad to have been a part of the experiment and only 1.3 percent said that they were sorry they had been in the experiment. A follow-up psychiatric exam one year later also found no signs of harm or trauma in the participants. Even so, most psychologists do agree that under the current ethical rules that exist for such research, this study would never be allowed to happen today. (L)(I)(N)(K) *to Chapter One: The Science of Psychology, pp. 35–36.*

TASK PERFORMANCE: SOCIAL FACILITATION AND SOCIAL LOAFING

In addition to the influence that others can have on a person's actions and attitudes, social influence can affect the success or failure of an individual's task performance. The perceived difficulty of the task seems to determine the particular effect of the presence of others as well: If a task is perceived as easy, the presence of other people seems to improve performance. If the task is perceived as difficult, the presence of others actually has a negative effect on performance. The positive influence of others on performance is called **social facilitation**, whereas the negative influence is sometimes called **social impairment** (Aiello & Douthitt, 2001; Michaels et al., 1982; Zajonc, 1965).

In both social facilitation and social impairment, the presence of other people acts to increase arousal (Zajonc, 1965, 1968; Zajonc et al., 1970). Social facilitation occurs because the presence of others creates just enough increased arousal to improve performance. But the presence of others when the task is difficult produces too high a level of arousal, resulting in impaired performance. (L)(I)(N)(K) *to Chapter Eight: Motivation and Emotion, p. 314.*

All people are not the same, and it would be foolish to expect the rules of social influence to affect different individuals in exactly the same way. For example, people who are lazy tend not to do as well when other people are also working on the same task, but they can do quite well when working on their own. This phenomenon is called **social loafing** (Karau & Williams, 1993, 1997; Latané et al., 1979). The reason for this is that it is easier for a lazy person (a "loafer") to hide laziness when working in a group of people because it is less likely that the individual will be evaluated alone—the group will be the focus of the evaluation, and someone in the group will most likely be concerned enough about the evaluation to make sure that the task is completed successfully. The social loafer doesn't feel the need to make any real effort, preferring to let the other members of the group do the work. But when the social loafer is working alone, the focus of evaluation will be on that person only. In that case, the loafer works harder because there is no one else to whom the work can be shifted.

Social loafing depends heavily on the assumption that personal responsibility for a task is severely lessened when working with a group of other people. One study suggests that although Americans may readily make that assumption, Chinese people, who come from a more interdependent cultural viewpoint, tend to assume that each individual within the group is still nearly as responsible for the group's outcome as the group at large (Menon et al., 1999). Chinese people are, therefore, less likely to exhibit social loafing than are people in the United States.

AP* Predict the impact of the presence of others on individual behavior.

At first the man in the foreground seems to be paying attention to the woman making the presentation. But if you look carefully at his computer screen, you'll see he's actually engaging in some serious social loafing. How do you think his colleagues around the room might feel about his behavior?

social facilitation the tendency for the presence of other people to have a positive impact on the performance of an easy task.

social impairment the tendency for the presence of other people to have a negative impact on the performance of a difficult task.

social loafing the tendency for people to put less effort into a simple task when working with others on that task.

14.1–3

conformity — changing one's own behavior to more closely match the actions of others

- several classic studies (i.e., Sherif, Asch) suggest that individuals will change their behaviors to conform to those of a group
- may be influenced by private vs. face-to-face contact, gender, or culture
- **groupthink:** occurs when people within a group feel it is more important to maintain group cohesiveness rather than critically evaluate facts when making decisions often with dire consequences

compliance — person changing their behavior due to another person or group asking or directing them to change, often in the absence of any real authority or power

- **foot-in-the-door technique**
- **door-in-the-face technique**
- **lowball technique**
- **that's-not-all technique**

Social Influence
(the ways in which a person's behavior can be affected by other people)

obedience — changing one's behavior at the direct order of an authority figure

- a classic study by Milgram (i.e., teacher/learner electrical shock study) indicated that 65% of "teachers" went all the way through shock levels, despite protest from "learners"

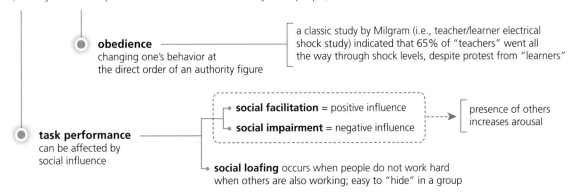

task performance — can be affected by social influence

- **social facilitation** = positive influence
- **social impairment** = negative influence
- → presence of others increases arousal
- **social loafing** occurs when people do not work hard when others are also working; easy to "hide" in a group

PRACTICE **QUIZ:** PREPARING FOR THE AP* EXAM

ANSWERS ON PAGE AK-4.

Directions: Read each of the questions or incomplete sentences below. Then choose the response that best answers the question or completes the sentence.

1. Solomon Asch's 1951 study with a standard line and comparison lines showed the influence of _____.
   a. prejudice
   b. obedience
   c. persuasion
   d. conformity
   e. compliance

2. Which of the following is not a characteristic of groupthink?
   a. Pressure
   b. Insularity
   c. Objectivity
   d. Invulnerability
   e. Rationalization

3. Francisco wants to buy a new computer. He sees a computer being sold for what he thinks is a reasonable price, so he commits to buying it. After he makes this commitment, however, he is forced to spend even more money on a warranty, an anti-theft plan, and required software for the computer. Francisco has been manipulated by the_____.
   a. lowball technique
   b. that's-not-all technique
   c. social loafing technique
   d. foot-in-the-door technique
   e. door-in-the-face technique

4. Which of the following techniques relies on the norm of reciprocity?
   a. Lowball technique
   b. Call-right-now technique
   c. Social loafing technique
   d. Foot-in-the-door technique
   e. Door-in-the-face technique

5. Milgram's classic 1964 experiment found that _____.
   a. the foot-in-the-door technique is rarely effective
   b. stereotyping is a driving force behind groupthink
   c. most people are surprisingly obedient to authority
   d. the presence of others improves the performance of easy tasks
   e. women and men are equally likely to conform in group situations

AP* Discuss attitudes and how they change.

AP* Discuss attitude formation and change.

Social Cognition: Attitudes, Impression Formation, and Attribution

Social cognition focuses on the ways in which people think about other people and how those cognitions influence behavior toward those other people. In this section, we'll concentrate on how we perceive others and form our first impressions of them, as well as how we explain the behavior of others and ourselves.

ATTITUDES

One area of social cognition concerns the formation and influence of attitudes on the behavior and perceptions of others. An **attitude** can be defined as a tendency to respond positively or negatively toward a certain idea, person, object, or situation (Triandis, 1971). This tendency, developed through peoples' experiences as they live and work with others, can affect the way they behave toward those ideas, people, objects, and situations and can include opinions, beliefs, and biases. In fact, attitudes influence the way people view these things *before* they've actually been exposed to them (Petty et al., 2003).

> What do you mean—
> how can an attitude
> have an effect on
> something that hasn't
> happened yet? ▶

What do you mean—how can an attitude have an effect on something that hasn't happened yet? Attitudes are not something people have when they are born. They are learned through experiences and contact with others and even through direct instruction from parents, teachers, and other important people in a person's life. Because attitudes involve a positive or negative evaluation of things, it's possible to go into a new situation, meet a new person, or be exposed to a new idea with one's "mind already made up" to like or dislike, agree or disagree, and so on (Eagly & Chaiken, 1993; Petty et al., 2003). For example, children are known for making up their minds about certain foods before ever tasting them, simply because the foods are "green." Those children may have tried a green food in the past and disliked it and now are predisposed* to dislike any green food whether they've tasted it or not.

THE ABC MODEL OF ATTITUDES

14.4 What are the three components of an attitude, how are attitudes formed, and how can attitudes be changed?

Attitudes are actually made up of three different parts, or components, as shown in Figure 14.3. These components should not come as a surprise to anyone who has been reading the other chapters in this text because, throughout the text, references have been made to personality and traits being composed of the ways people think, feel, and act. By using certain terms to describe these three things, psychologists have come up with a handy way to describe the three components of attitudes (Eagly & Chaiken, 1993, 1998).

Affective Component　The *affective component* of an attitude is the way a person feels toward the object, person, or situation. *Affect* is used in psychology to mean "emotions" or "feelings," so the affective component is the emotional component. For example, some people might feel that country music is fun and uplifting.

Behavior Component　The *behavior component* of an attitude is the action that a person takes in regard to the person, object, or situation. For example, a person who

---

attitude a tendency to respond positively or negatively toward a certain person, object, idea, or situation.

*Predisposed: referring to a tendency to respond in a particular way based on previous experience.

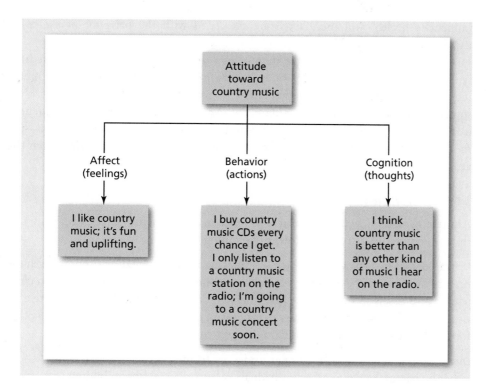

Figure 14.3 Three Components of an Attitude
Attitudes consist of the way a person feels and thinks about something, as well as the way the person chooses to behave. If you like country music, you are also likely to think that country music is good music. You are also more likely to listen to this style of music, buy this type of music, and even go to a performance. Each of the three components influences the other two.

feels that country music is fun is likely to turn to a country music station on the car radio, buy country music CDs, or go to a country music concert.

Cognitive Component   Finally, the *cognitive component* of an attitude is the way a person thinks about the person, object, or situation. These thoughts, or cognitions, include beliefs and ideas about the focus of the attitude. For example, the country music lover might believe that country music is superior to other forms of music.

So if you know what someone thinks or feels about something, you can predict what that person will do, right? Oddly enough, attitudes turn out to be pretty poor predictors of actual behavior in a number of controlled research studies. One survey of such research conducted in the 1960s found that what people say and what people do are often two very different things (Wicker, 1971). Studies conducted in the decades that followed found that attitudes predict behavior only under certain conditions. For example, in one study researchers found that although people indicated on a survey that they believed in protecting the environment and would be willing to pay more for fruits and vegetables raised under such conditions, those same people were seen to buy the ecology-friendly fruit only in grocery stores in areas of higher income levels where consumers actually had the financial means to "put their money where their mouth was" (Clarke et al., 1999). Those who did not live in a higher-income area gave what they probably saw as a socially desirable answer on the survey but then allowed the external influence of a lower income to determine their actual behavior.

Another factor in matching attitudes and behavior concerns how specific the attitude itself is. People may hold a general attitude about something without reflecting that attitude in their actual behavior. For example, doctors generally hold the attitude that people should do everything they can to protect their health and promote wellness, yet many doctors still have unhealthy habits like failing to exercise and getting too little sleep. But a very specific attitude, such as "exercise is important to my

So if you know what someone thinks or feels about something, you can ◀ predict what that person will do, right?

immediate health" will more likely be associated with the behavior of exercising (Ajzen, 2001; Ajzen & Fishbein, 2000).

Some attitudes are stronger than others, and strong attitudes are more likely to predict behavior than weak ones. A person who quit smoking because of failing health might have a stronger attitude toward secondhand smoking than someone who quit smoking on a dare, for example. The importance or salience* of a particular attitude in a given situation also has an impact on behavior—the more important the attitude appears, the more likely the behavior will match the attitude.

ATTITUDE FORMATION

Attitude formation is the result of a number of different influences with only one thing in common: They are all forms of learning.

Direct Contact   One way in which attitudes are formed is by direct contact with the person, idea, situation, or object that is the focus of the attitude. For example, a child who tries Brussels sprouts for the first time and dislikes them will form a negative attitude about Brussels sprouts. Later that negative attitude may be generalized to other foods that are green or have a similar taste.

Direct Instruction   Another way attitudes are formed is through direct instruction, either by parents or some other individual. Parents may tell their children that smoking cigarettes is dangerous and unhealthy, for example. Some children will form a negative attitude about smoking as a result.

Interaction with Others   Sometimes attitudes are formed because the person is around other people with that attitude. Researchers found that a nonsmoking mother, teacher, or brother had a strong influence on both girls and boys (who are less likely to smoke), although the influence of all three on boys seemed to fade over a seven-year follow-up study (Shean et al., 1994).

Vicarious Conditioning (Observational Learning) Many attitudes are learned through the observation of other people's actions and reactions to various objects, people, or situations. Just as a child whose mother shows a fear of dogs may develop a similar fear, a child whose mother or father shows a positive attitude toward classical music may grow into an adult with a similarly positive attitude. The emotional components of an attitude can be learned by observing the emotional reactions of others, and the behavioral components can be observed and imitated.

Attitudes are not only influenced by other people in a person's immediate world but also by the larger world of the educational system (many attitudes may be learned in school or through reading books) and the mass media of magazines, television, and the movies—a fact of which advertisers and marketing experts are well aware (Gresham & Shimp, 1985; MacKenzie et al., 1986).

Don't Get Left in the Rain
Smoking just isn't cool.

AMERICAN CANCER SOCIETY

This public service message is aimed at changing the attitudes of people who smoke. Most nonsmokers will not confront a person who is smoking in an appropriate area, as the young woman outside, looking in the window, is doing. But if the young woman were in a hospital waiting room, others would be more likely to confront her. Smoking in an area that is clearly not appropriate would be more important to those with anti-smoking attitudes.

*Salience: importance or having the quality of being obvious or easily seen.

ATTITUDE CHANGE: THE ART OF PERSUASION

Sometimes people learn attitudes that aren't necessarily good ones, right? So can attitudes change? Because attitudes are learned, they are also subject to change with new learning. The world is full of people, companies, and other organizations that want to change peoples' attitudes. It's all about the art of **persuasion**, the process by which one person tries to change the belief, opinion, position, or course of action of another person through argument, pleading, or explanation.

Persuasion is not a simple matter. There are several factors that become important in predicting how successful any persuasive effort at attitude change might be. These factors include the following:

- **Source:** The *communicator* is the person delivering the message. There is a strong tendency to give more weight to people who are perceived as experts, as well as those who seem trustworthy, attractive, and similar to the person receiving the message (Eagly & Chaiken, 1975; Petty & Cacioppo, 1986, 1996; Priester & Petty, 1995).

- **Message:** The actual message should be clear and well organized (Booth-Butterfield, 1996). It is usually more effective to present both sides of an argument to an audience that has not yet committed to one side or the other (Crowley & Hoyer, 1994; Petty & Cacioppo, 1996; Petty et al., 2003). Messages that are directed at producing fear are more effective if they produce only a moderate amount of fear and also provide information about how to avoid the fear-provoking consequences (Kleinot & Rogers, 1982; Meyrick, 2001; Petty, 1995; Rogers & Mewborn, 1976).

- **Target Audience:** The characteristics of the people who are the intended target of the message of persuasion are also important in determining the effectiveness of the message. The age of the audience members can be a factor, for example. Researchers have found that people who are in the young adult stage of the late teens to the mid-twenties are more susceptible to persuasion than are older people (Visser & Krosnick, 1998).

How easily influenced a person is will also be related to the way people tend to process information. In the **elaboration likelihood model** of persuasion (Petty & Cacioppo, 1986), it is assumed that people either elaborate (add details and information) based on what they hear (the facts of the message) or they do not elaborate at all, preferring to pay attention to the surface characteristics of the message (length, who delivers it, how attractive the message deliverer is, etc.). Two types of processing are hypothesized in this model: **central-route processing**, in which people attend to the content of the message, and **peripheral-route processing**, a style of information processing that relies on peripheral cues (cues outside of the message content itself) such as the expertise of the message source, the length of the message, and other factors that have nothing to do with the message content. This style of processing causes people not to pay attention to the message itself but instead to base their decisions on those peripheral factors (Petty & Cacioppo, 1986; Stiff & Mongeau, 2002). For example, the author once participated on a jury panel in which one woman voted "guilty" because the defendant had "shifty eyes" and not because of any of the evidence presented.

◀ Sometimes people learn attitudes that aren't necessarily good ones, right? So can attitudes change?

persuasion the process by which one person tries to change the belief, opinion, position, or course of action of another person through argument, pleading, or explanation.

elaboration likelihood model model of persuasion stating that people will either elaborate on the persuasive message or fail to elaborate on it and that the future actions of those who do elaborate are more predictable than those who do not.

central-route processing type of information processing that involves attending to the content of the message itself.

peripheral-route processing type of information processing that involves attending to factors not involved in the message, such as the appearance of the source of the message, the length of the message, and other noncontent factors.

How the jurors in this courtroom interpret and process the information they are given will determine the outcome of the trial. Those who listen carefully to what is said by persons involved in the trial are using central-route processing. There may be some jurors, however, who are more affected by the appearance, dress, attractiveness, or tone of voice of the lawyers, defendant, and witnesses. When people are persuaded by factors other than the message itself, it is called peripheral-route processing.

14.5 How do people react when attitudes and behavior are not the same?

As stated earlier, sometimes what people say and what they do are very different. I once pointed this out to a friend of mine who was behaving this way, and he got really upset over it. Why did he get so upset? When people find themselves doing things or saying things that don't match their idea of themselves as smart, nice, or moral, for example, they experience an emotional discomfort (and physiological arousal) known as **cognitive dissonance** (Aronson, 1997; Festinger, 1957; Kelly et al., 1997). When people are confronted with the knowledge that something they have done or said was dumb, immoral, or illogical, they suffer an inconsistency in cognitions. For example, they may have a cognition that says "I'm pretty smart" but also the cognition "That was a dumb thing to do," which causes a dissonance. (*Dissonance* is a term referring to an inconsistency or lack of agreement.)

When people experience cognitive dissonance, the resulting tension and arousal are unpleasant, and their motivation is to change something so that the unpleasant feelings and tension are reduced or eliminated. There are three basic things that people can do to reduce cognitive dissonance:

1. Change their conflicting behavior to make it match their attitude.

2. Change their current conflicting cognition to justify their behavior.

3. Form new cognitions to justify their behavior.

Take the example of Larry, a politically liberal person who takes an internship at a conservative news organization. On one hand, Larry has strong political convictions that he doesn't want to compromise. On the other hand, Larry knows that the internship is a valuable work experience, and he enjoys writing news articles and socializing with his coworkers. His attitude doesn't match his behavior. Larry is experiencing cognitive dissonance and knows he needs to do something to resolve his dilemma.*

If Larry chooses the first way of dealing with cognitive dissonance, he'll quit his internship and try to find a new job that is a better fit with his political beliefs. As long as he is working at changing the conflicting behavior, his dissonance will be reduced. But what if he decides not to quit? He might decide that his original political beliefs were too liberal, which changes his original conflicting attitude (Option Two). He might also form a new attitude by thinking of himself as a "voice of balance" at the news organization (Option Three).

In a classic experiment conducted at Stanford University by psychologist Leon Festinger and colleague James Carlsmith (1959), each male student volunteer was given an hour-long, very boring task of sorting wooden spools and turning wooden pegs. After the hour, the experimenters asked the participant to tell the female volunteer in the waiting room that the task was enjoyable. While half of the participants were paid only $1 to try to convince the waiting woman, the other participants were paid $20. (In the late 1950s, $20 was a considerable sum of money—the average income was $5,000, the average car cost $3,000, and gas was only 25 cents a gallon.)

At the time of this study, many researchers would have predicted that the more the participants were paid to lie, the more they would come to like the task, because they were getting more reinforcement ($20) for doing so. But what actually happened was that those participants who were paid only $1 for lying actually convinced them-

---

As stated earlier, ▶ sometimes what people say and what they do are very different. I once pointed this out to a friend of mine who was behaving this way, and he got really upset over it. Why did he get so upset?

AP* Identify important figures in social psychology. ▶

cognitive dissonance sense of discomfort or distress that occurs when a person's behavior does not correspond to that person's attitudes.

*Dilemma: a problem involving a difficult choice.

selves that the task was interesting and fun. The reason is cognitive dissonance: Participants who were paid only $1 experienced discomfort at thinking that they would lie to someone for only a dollar. Therefore, they must not be lying—the task really was pretty interesting, after all, and fun, too! Those who were paid more experienced no dissonance, because they knew exactly why they were lying—for lots of money—and the money was a sufficient amount to explain their behavior to their satisfaction. Although most people don't want to be thought of as liars, back then, getting paid enough money to fill the gas tank of one's car three or four times over was incentive enough to tell what probably seemed to be a harmless fib. Those who were paid only $1 had to change their attitude toward the task so that they would not really be lying and could maintain their self-image of honesty. (See Figure 14.4.)

Cognitive dissonance theory has been challenged over the last 50 years by other possible explanations. Bem's self-perception theory says that instead of experiencing negative tension, people look at their own actions and then infer their attitudes from those actions (Bem, 1972). New research on dissonance still occurs, much of it focusing on finding the areas of the brain that seem to be involved when people are experiencing dissonance. These studies have found that the left frontal cortex (where language and much of our decision making occurs) is particularly active when people have made a decision that reduces dissonance and then acted upon that decision (Harmon-Jones, 2000, 2004, 2006; Harmon-Jones et al., 2008). Since reducing cognitive dissonance is mainly a function of people "talking" themselves into or out of a particular course of action, this neurological finding is not surprising. But researchers at Yale University have found surprising evidence for cognitive dissonance in both 4-year-old humans and capuchin monkeys—two groups that are not normally thought to have developed the higher-level mental abilities that are thought to be in use during the resolution of dissonance (Egan et al., 2007). Are monkeys and preschool humans more complex thinkers than we had assumed? Or are the cognitive processes used to resolve dissonance a lot simpler than previously indicated? Obviously, there are still questions to be answered with new research in cognitive dissonance.

Inducement	Attitude
$1	+1.35
$20	− 0.5
Control	− .45

*Based on a –5 to +5 scale, where –5 means "extremely boring" and +5 means "extremely interesting"

Figure 14.4 Cognitive Dissonance: Attitude Toward a Task

After completing a boring task, some participants were paid $1 and some $20 to convince others waiting to do the same task that the task was interesting and fun. Surprisingly, the participants who were paid only $1 seemed to change their own attitude toward the task, rating it as interesting, whereas those who were paid $20 rated the task no differently than a control group did. *Source:* Adapted from Festinger and Carlsmith (1959).

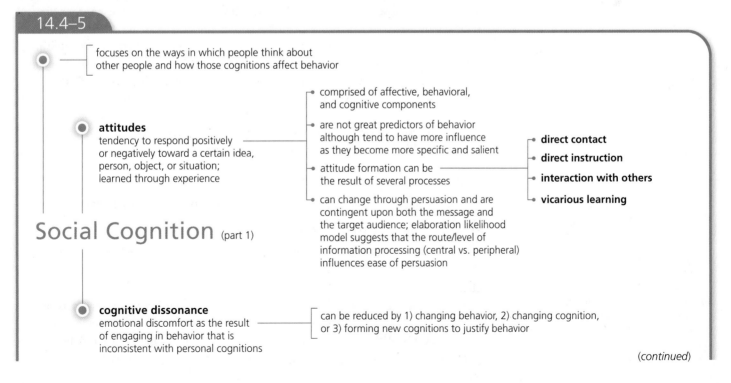

14.4–5

Social Cognition (part 1)

- focuses on the ways in which people think about other people and how those cognitions affect behavior

- **attitudes**
  tendency to respond positively or negatively toward a certain idea, person, object, or situation; learned through experience
  - comprised of affective, behavioral, and cognitive components
  - are not great predictors of behavior although tend to have more influence as they become more specific and salient
  - attitude formation can be the result of several processes
    - direct contact
    - direct instruction
    - interaction with others
    - vicarious learning
  - can change through persuasion and are contingent upon both the message and the target audience; elaboration likelihood model suggests that the route/level of information processing (central vs. peripheral) influences ease of persuasion

- **cognitive dissonance**
  emotional discomfort as the result of engaging in behavior that is inconsistent with personal cognitions
  - can be reduced by 1) changing behavior, 2) changing cognition, or 3) forming new cognitions to justify behavior

(continued)

PRACTICE **QUIZ:** PREPARING FOR THE AP* EXAM

ANSWERS ON PAGE AK-4.

Directions: Read each of the questions or incomplete sentences below. Then choose the response that best answers the question or completes the sentence.

1. Which of the following represents the cognitive component of an attitude?
   a. "I just love Italian food!"
   b. "I'm going to make lasagna tonight."
   c. "Italian food makes me feel warm and happy."
   d. "Italian food is the best of the European cuisines."
   e. "Tonight, we're going to that new Italian restaurant."

2. Lilly's mother always listens to the classic rock station on her car radio, so Lilly has grown up hearing that music and noticing how much her mother enjoys it. Now Lilly says that classic rock is her favorite music, too. Lilly's attitude toward classic rock was most likely acquired through _____.
   a. indirect contact
   b. direct instruction
   c. interaction with others
   d. negative reinforcement
   e. vicarious conditioning

3. Physical attractiveness is most involved in which of the following aspects of persuasion?
   a. The target
   b. The media
   c. The source
   d. The message
   e. The audience

4. Which of the following is an example of central-route processing?
   a. "He has such a negative attitude."
   b. "The logic of his argument doesn't hold up."
   c. "He doesn't seem like a very reliable person."
   d. "I can't believe he's been talking for so long."
   e. "Those other experts don't respect him very much."

5. Pamela hates it when people answer their cell phones during class. One day, however, Pamela gets an urgent call from her mother during class, and she answers the call. Pamela tells herself that answering a phone call during class isn't so bad after all. Pamela is reducing her sense of _____.
   a. attitude formation
   b. social impairment
   c. justified conformity
   d. cognitive dissonance
   e. unwilling compliance

---

impression formation the forming of the first knowledge that a person has concerning another person.

social cognition the mental processes that people use to make sense of the social world around them.

IMPRESSION FORMATION AND ATTRIBUTION

When one person meets another for the first time, it is the first opportunity either person will have to make initial evaluations and judgments about the other. That first opportunity is a very important one in **impression formation**, the forming of the first knowledge a person has about another person. Impression formation includes assigning the other person to a number of categories and drawing conclusions about what that person is likely to do—it's really all about prediction. In a sense, when first meeting another person, the observer goes through a process of concept formation similar to that discussed in Chapter Seven. Impression formation is another kind of social cognition.

There is a *primacy effect* in impression formation: The first time people meet someone, they form an impression of that person that persists even though they may later have other contradictory information about that person (DeCoster & Claypool, 2004; Luchins, 1957). So the old saying is pretty much on target: First impressions do count.

Impression formation is one of a number of phenomena that are all part of **social cognition**, the mental processes that people use to make sense out of the social world around them.

14.6 What are social categorization and implicit personality theories?

AP* Describe processes that contribute to differential treatment of group members.

▶ ## SOCIAL CATEGORIZATION

social categorization the assignment of a person one has just met to a category based on characteristics the new person has in common with other people with whom one has had experience in the past.

One of the processes that occur when people meet someone new is the assignment of that person to some kind of category or group. This assignment is usually based on characteristics the new person has in common with other people or groups with whom the perceiver has had prior experience. This **social categorization** is mostly automatic and occurs without conscious awareness of the process (Macrae & Bodenhausen, 2000). Although this is a natural process (human beings are just born categorizers **LINK** *to Chapter Seven: Cognition: Thinking, Intelligence, and Language,* *pp. 263–266),* sometimes it can cause problems. When the characteristics used to categorize the person are superficial* ones that have become improperly attached to certain ideas, such as "red hair equals a bad temper," social categorization can result in a **stereotype**, a set of characteristics that people believe is shared by all members of a particular social category (Fiske, 1998). Stereotypes (although not always negative) are very limiting, causing people to misjudge what others are like and often to treat them differently as a result. Add the process of stereotyping to the primacy effect and it becomes easy to see how important first impressions really are. That first impression not only has more importance than any other information gathered about a person later on but may include a stereotype that is resistant to change as well (Hilton & von Hipple, 1996; Hugenberg & Bodenhausen, 2003).

It sounds as though we'd be better off if people didn't use social categorization. Social categorization does have an important place in the perception of others. It allows people to access a great deal of information that can be useful about others, as well as helping people to remember and organize information about the characteristics of others (Macrae & Bodenhausen, 2000). The way to avoid falling into the trap of negatively stereotyping someone is to be aware of existing stereotypes and apply a little critical thinking: "Okay, so he's a guy with a tattoo on his arm. That doesn't mean that he's overly aggressive—it just means he has a tattoo."

IMPLICIT PERSONALITY THEORIES

The categories into which people place others are based on something called an **implicit personality theory**. Implicit personality theories are sets of assumptions that people have about how different types of people, personality traits, and actions are all related and form in childhood (Dweck et al., 1995; Erdley & Dweck, 1993). For example, many people have an implicit personality theory that includes the idea that happy people are also friendly people and people who are quiet are shy. Although these assumptions or beliefs are not necessarily true, they do serve the function of helping to organize *schemas*, or mental patterns that represent (in this case) what a person believes about certain "types" of people. (The concept of schema here is similar to the complex patterns proposed by Piaget. (L)(I)(N)(K) *to Chapter Ten: Development Across the Life Span, p. 401.*) Of course, the schemas formed in this way can easily become stereotypes when people have limited experience with others who are different from them, especially in superficial ways such as skin color or other physical characteristics (Levy et al., 1998).

There is some evidence to suggest that implicit personality theories may differ from culture to culture as well as from individual to individual. For example, one study found that Americans and Hong Kong Chinese people have different implicit personality theories about how much the personality of an individual is able to change. Whereas Americans assume that personality is relatively fixed and unchanging, Chinese people native to Hong Kong assume that personalities are far more changeable (Chiu et al., 1997).

stereotype a set of characteristics that people believe is shared by all members of a particular social category.

implicit personality theory sets of assumptions about how different types of people, personality traits, and actions are related to each other.

◄ It sounds as though we'd be better off if people didn't use social categorization.

At this job fair in Shanghai, China, thousands of applicants wait hopefully in line for an opportunity to get a job interview. Making a good first impression is important in any job interview situation, but when the competition numbers in the thousands, the people who will most likely get interviews are those who are neatly dressed and well-groomed.

*Superficial: on the surface.

attribution the process of explaining one's own behavior and the behavior of others.

attribution theory the theory of how people make attributions.

situational cause cause of behavior attributed to external factors, such as delays, the action of others, or some other aspect of the situation.

dispositional cause cause of behavior attributed to internal factors such as personality or character.

fundamental attribution error the tendency to overestimate the influence of internal factors in determining the behavior of others while underestimating situational factors.

But what else determines ▶ which type of cause a person will use? For example, what determines how people explain the behavior of someone they don't already know or like?

ATTRIBUTION

14.7 How do people try to explain the actions of others?

Another aspect of social cognition is the need people seem to have to explain the behavior of other people. Have you ever watched someone who was doing something you didn't understand? Chances are you were going through a number of possible explanations in your head: "Maybe he's sick, or maybe he sees something I can't see," and so on. It seems to be human nature to want to know why people do the things they do so that we know how to behave toward them and whom we might want to use as role models. If no obvious answer is available, people tend to come up with their own reasons. People also need an explanation for their own behavior. This need is so great that if an explanation isn't obvious, it causes the distress known as cognitive dissonance. The process of explaining both one's own behavior and the behavior of other people is called **attribution**.

Causes of Behavior **Attribution theory** was originally developed by social psychologist Fritz Heider (1958) as a way of not only explaining why things happen but also why people choose the particular explanations of behavior that they do. There are basically two kinds of explanations—those that involve an external cause and those that assume that causes are internal.

When the cause of behavior is assumed to be from external sources, such as the weather, traffic, educational opportunities, and so on, it is said to be a **situational cause**. The observed behavior is assumed to be caused by whatever situation exists for the person at that time. For example, if John is late to class, his lateness might be explained by heavy traffic or bad weather.

On the other hand, if the cause of behavior is assumed to come from within the individual, it is called a **dispositional cause**. In this case, it is the person's internal personality characteristics that are seen as the cause of the observed behavior. Someone attributing John's behavior to a dispositional cause, for example, might assume that John was late because he is careless of his and other people's time.

There's an emotional component to these kinds of attributions as well. When people are happy in a marriage, for example, researchers have found that when a spouse's behavior has a positive effect, the tendency is to attribute it to an internal cause ("he did it because he wanted me to feel good"). When the effect is negative, the behavior is attributed to an external cause ("she must have had a difficult day"). But if the marriage is an unhappy one, the opposite attributions occur: "He is only being nice because he wants something from me" or "She's being mean because it's her nature to be crabby" (Fincham et al., 2000; Karney & Bradbury, 2000).

Fundamental Attribution Error

But what else determines which type of cause a person will use? For example, what determines how people explain the behavior of someone they don't already know or like? The most well-known attributional bias is the **fundamental attribution error**, which is the tendency for people to overestimate the influence of another person's internal characteristics on behavior and underestimate the influence of the situation (whereas in explaining our own behavior, the tendency to use situational attributions instead of personal is called the *actor-observer bias*). In other words, people tend to explain the actions of others based on what "kind" of person they are rather than looking for outside causes such as social influences or situations (Blanchard-Fields et al., 2007; Harman, 1999; Jones & Harris, 1967; Leclerc & Hess, 2007; Weiner, 1985). (For example, people hearing about Milgram's "shock" study tend to assume that something is wrong with the "teachers" in the study rather than explaining their behavior within the circumstances of the situation.)

But why do we do that? Why not assume an external cause for everyone? When people observe themselves, they are very aware of the situational influences on their own behavior. For example, Tardy John was actually the one driving to class, and he knows that heavy traffic and an unexpected rainstorm made him late to work—he was *there*, after all. But someone else looking at John's behavior doesn't have the opportunity to see all of the possible situational influences and has only John himself in focus and, thus, assumes that John's tardiness is caused by some internal personality flaw.

Other research has shown that when students are given an opportunity to make attributions about cheating, they demonstrate the fundamental attribution error and actor-observer bias: If others are cheating, it's because they are not honest people, but if the students themselves are cheating it is because of the situation (Bogle, 2000).

Can the tendency to make these errors be reduced? There are several strategies for making errors in attribution less likely. One is to notice how many other people are doing the same thing. As a college professor, the author often has students who come in late. When it is only one student and it happens frequently, the assumption is that the student is not very careful about time (dispositional cause). But when a large number of students come straggling in late, the assumption becomes "there must be a wreck on the bridge," which is a situational attribution. In other words, if a lot of people are doing it, it is probably caused by an outside factor.

Another trick is to think about what you would do in the same situation. If you think that you might behave in the same way, the cause of behavior is probably situational. People should also make the effort of looking for causes that might not be obvious. If John were to look particularly "stressed out," for example, the assumption might be that something stressed him out, and that "something" might have been heavy traffic.

Although the fundamental attribution error has been found in American culture (Jones & Harris, 1967), would the same error occur in a culture that is very different from American culture, such as in Japan? This is the question asked by researchers Masuda and Kitayama (2004), who had both American and Japanese participants ask a target person to read a prewritten attitudinal statement. The participants were then asked to give their opinion on the target's real attitude. American participants made the classic error, assuming that the target's attitude matched the reading. The Japanese participants, however, assumed that the person's attitude might be different from the statement—the person might have been under social obligation to write the piece. Japanese society is a collectivistic culture, and a Japanese person might expect to write a paper to please a teacher or employer even though the paper's contents do not necessarily express the writer's attitudes. A summary of the research in cross-cultural differences in attribution provides further support for the idea that the fundamental attribution error is not a universal one (Peng et al., 2000). The work of Miller (1984) and many other researchers (Blanchard-Fields et al., 2007; Cha & Nam, 1985; Choi & Nisbett, 1998; Choi et al., 1999; Lee et al., 1996; Morris & Peng, 1994; Morris et al., 1995; Norenzayan et al., 1999) strongly suggests that in more interdependent, collectivist cultures found in China, Hong Kong, Japan, and Korea people tend to assume that external situational factors are more responsible for the behavior of other people than are internal dispositional factors—a finding that is exactly the reverse of the fundamental attribution error so common in individualist Western cultures such as the United States.

Even age is a factor in how likely someone is to fall prey to the fundamental attribution error. Several studies (Blanchard-Fields & Horhota, 2005; Follett & Hess, 2002; Leclerc & Hess, 2007) have found that older adults show a stronger bias toward attributing the actions of another to internal causes than do younger people.

◀ But why do we do that? Why not assume an external cause for everyone?

14.6–7

impression formation
forming of first knowledge about another person; influenced by primacy effect

Social Cognition (part 2)
Impression Formation and Attribution

social categorization
automatic and unconscious assignment of a new acquaintance to some category or group

stereotypes: set of characteristics believed to be shared by all members of a particular category; can be useful (by limiting information processing)

categories assigned are based on implicit personality theory, the set of assumptions formed in childhood about different types of people

attribution is process by which we explain both our own behavior and the behavior of others; based on attribution theory (Heider)

situational: cause of behavior is assumed to come from external sources

dispositional: cause of behavior is assumed to come from within the individual

fundamental attribution error is the tendency to overestimate the influence of another person's internal characteristics on behavior and underestimate the external/situational factors; influenced by age and culture

PRACTICE QUIZ: PREPARING FOR THE AP* EXAM

ANSWERS ON PAGE AK-4.

Directions: Read each of the questions or incomplete sentences below. Then choose the response that best answers the question or completes the sentence.

1. Mental patterns that represent what a person believes about certain types of people are called _____.
   a. schemas
   b. attitudes
   c. heuristics
   d. attributions
   e. stereotypes

2. Elizabeth's room is almost always a mess. Her parents attribute this to Elizabeth's laziness, which is an example of a _____.
   a. situational cause
   b. superficial cause
   c. stereotypic cause
   d. fundamental cause
   e. dispositional cause

3. John is late to class, and his friend Raquel assumes that John simply doesn't care about being on time. But when Raquel is late the next day, she blames her lateness on heavy traffic. For John's behavior, Raquel has possibly made the _____.
   a. egocentric error
   b. assumption error
   c. false consensus error
   d. social categorization error
   e. fundamental attribution error

4. In Asian cultures, people tend to explain the behavior of others as a result of _____.
   a. genetics
   b. personality traits
   c. external, situational factors
   d. internal, dispositional factors
   e. unconscious conflicts

5. According to research, which of the following people is most likely to commit the fundamental attribution error?
   a. A younger person from Japan
   b. An older person from Japan
   c. A younger person from the United States
   d. An older person from the United States
   e. Anyone of any age from either Japan or the United States

Social Interaction: Prejudice, Love, and Aggression

Social influence and social cognition are two of three main areas included in the field of social psychology. The third major area has to do with social interactions with others, or the relationships between people, both casual and intimate. Social interactions include prejudice and discrimination, liking and loving, and aggression and prosocial behavior.

AP* Describe processes that contribute to differential treatment of group members.

▶ PREJUDICE AND DISCRIMINATION

14.8 How are prejudice and discrimination different?

In talking about attitudes, the idea that some attitudes—stereotypes—can be formed by using only superficial information about a person or group of people was discussed. When a person holds an unsupported and often negative stereotyped attitude about the members of a particular social group, it is called **prejudice**. When prejudi-

prejudice negative attitude held by a person about the members of a particular social group.

cial attitudes cause members of a particular social group to be treated differently than others in situations that call for equal treatment, it is called **discrimination**. Prejudice is the attitude and discrimination is the behavior that can result from that attitude. Although laws can be made to minimize discriminatory behavior, it is not possible to have laws against holding certain attitudes. In other words, discrimination can be controlled and in some cases eliminated, but the prejudicial attitude that is responsible for the discrimination cannot be so easily controlled or eliminated.

TYPES OF PREJUDICE AND DISCRIMINATION

There are many kinds of prejudice. There are also many kinds of discrimination that occur as a result of prejudice. There's ageism, or prejudicial attitudes toward the elderly or teenagers (among others); sexism; racism, or prejudice toward those from different ethnic groups; prejudice toward those from different religions, those from different economic levels, those who are overweight, those who are too thin, and so on. Prejudice can also vary in terms of what type of people or groups make the most likely targets. In any society, there will always be **in-groups** and **out-groups**, or "us" versus "them." The in-group is all the people with whom a particular person identifies and the out-groups are everyone else (Brewer, 2001; Hewstone et al., 2002; Tajfel & Turner, 1986). The formation of in-groups and out-groups begins in childhood (Ruble et al., 2004) and continues as children become adults.

Once an in-group is established, prejudice toward and discriminatory treatment of the out-group or groups soon follow (Brewer, 2001). Members of the out-groups are usually going to become stereotyped according to some superficial characteristic, such as skin color or hair color, and getting rid of a stereotype once formed is difficult at best (Cameron et al., 2001; Hamilton & Gifford, 1976).

The **realistic conflict theory** of prejudice states that increasing prejudice and discrimination are closely tied to an increasing degree of conflict between the in-group and the out-group when those groups are seeking a common resource, such as land or available jobs (Horowitz, 1985; Taylor & Moghaddam, 1994). Because the examples of this from history and modern times are so numerous, it is possible to list only a few: the conflict between the early Crusaders and the Muslims, between the Jewish people and the Germans, the hatred between the Irish Catholics and the Irish Protestants, and the conflict between the native population of you-name-the-country and the colonists who want that land. The section that follows is a classic study that illustrates how easily in-groups and out-groups can be formed and how quickly prejudice and discrimination follow.

On September 6, 1957, this high school in Little Rock, Arkansas, became integrated, allowing African American students to attend school with white students. The practice of segregating black and white school children was discrimination, and the desegregation laws were aimed at stopping that discrimination. But the attitudes of prejudice persisted even after the legal discrimination was stopped and to some degree still exist today. The courts can make laws against discrimination, but changing prejudicial attitudes is much more difficult.

"First, can we agree that it's a big backyard?"
©The New Yorker Collection 2002 Charles Barsotti from cartoonbank.com. All Rights Reserved.

Classic Studies in Psychology

Brown Eyes, Blue Eyes

In a small town in Iowa in 1968, a few days after the assassination of Dr. Martin Luther King, Jr., a second-grade teacher named Jane Elliot tried to teach her students a lesson in prejudice and discrimination. She divided her students into two groups, those with blue eyes and those with brown eyes.

On the first day of the lesson, the blue-eyed children were given special privileges, such as extra time at recess and getting to leave first for lunch. She also told the blue-eyed children that they were superior to the brown-eyed children, telling the brown-eyed children not to bother taking seconds at lunch because it would be wasted. She kept the blue-eyed children and the brown-eyed children apart (Peters, 1971).

discrimination treating people differently because of prejudice toward the social group to which they belong.

in-groups social groups with whom a person identifies; "us."

out-groups social groups with whom a person does not identify; "them."

realistic conflict theory theory stating that prejudice and discrimination will be increased between groups that are in conflict over a limited resource.

Although Elliot tried to be critical of the brown-eyed out-group, she soon found that the blue-eyed children were also criticizing, belittling, and were quite vicious in their attacks on the brown-eyed children. By the end of the day, the blue-eyed children felt and acted superior, and the brown-eyed children were miserable. Even the lowered test scores of the brown-eyed children reflected their misery. Two days later, the brown-eyed children became the favored group and the effects from the first two days appeared again but in reverse this time: The blue-eyed children began to feel inferior and their test scores dropped.

The fact that test scores reflected the treatment received by the out-group is a stunning one, raising questions about the effects of prejudice and discrimination on the education of children who are members of stereotyped out-groups. That the children were so willing to discriminate against their own classmates, some of whom were their close friends before the experiment, is also telling. In his book about this classroom experiment, *A Class Divided*, Peters (1971) reported that the students who were part of the original experiment, when reunited 15 years later to talk about the experience, said that they believed that this early experience with prejudice and discrimination helped them to become less prejudiced as young adults.

Questions for Further Discussion

1. Is there anything about this experiment that you find disturbing?

2. How do you think adults might react in a similar experiment?

3. Are there any ethical concerns with what Elliot did in her classroom?

4. What kinds of changes might have occurred in the personalities and performances of the children if the experiment had continued for more than two days with each group?

Scapegoating   Conflicts between groups are usually greater when there are other pressures or stresses going on, such as war, economic difficulties, or other misfortunes. When such pressures exist, the need to find a *scapegoat* becomes stronger. A scapegoat is a person or a group, typically a member or members of an out-group, who serves as the target for the frustrations and negative emotions of members of the in-group. (The term comes from the ancient Jewish tradition of sending a goat out into the wilderness with the symbolic sins of all the people on its head.)

Scapegoats are going to be the group of people with the least power, and the newest immigrants to any area are typically those who have the least power at that time. That is why many social psychologists believe that the rioting that took place in Los Angeles, California, in the spring of 1992 occurred in the areas it did. This was the time of the infamous Rodney King beating. Rodney King was an African American man who was dragged out of his car onto the street and severely beaten by four police officers. The beating was caught on tape by a bystander. At the trial, the officers were found not guilty of assault with a deadly weapon. This decision was followed by a series of violent riots (Knight, 1996).

The puzzling thing about these riots is that the greatest amount of rioting and violence did not take place in the neighborhoods of the mostly white police officers or in the African American neighborhoods. The rioting was greatest in the neighborhoods of the Asian Americans and Asians who were the most recent immigrants to the area. When a group has only recently moved into an area, as the Asians had, that group has the least social power and influence in that new area. So the rioters took out their frustrations *not* on the people seen as directly responsible for those frustrations but on the group of people with the least power to resist.

HOW PEOPLE LEARN PREJUDICE

14.9 Why are people prejudiced, and how can prejudice be stopped?

As was clearly demonstrated in the brown eyes–blue eyes experiment discussed in the Classic Studies in Psychology section, even children are, under the right circumstances, prone to developing prejudiced attitudes. Is all prejudice simply a matter of learning, or are there other factors at work? Several theories have been proposed to explain the origins and the persistence of prejudice. In **social cognitive** theory, prejudice is seen as an attitude that is formed as other attitudes are formed, through direct instruction, modeling, and other social influences on learning.

Social Identity Theory   In **social identity theory**, three processes are responsible for the formation of a person's identity within a particular social group and the attitudes, concepts, and behavior that go along with identification with that group (Tajfel & Turner, 1986). The first process is *social categorization*, as discussed earlier in this chapter. Just as people assign categories to others (such as black, white, student, teacher, and so on) to help organize information about those others, people also assign themselves to social categories to help determine how they should behave. The second element of social identity theory is *identification*, or the formation of one's **social identity**. A social identity is the part of one's self-concept that includes the view of oneself as a member of a particular social group within the social category—typically, the in-group. The third aspect of social identity theory is **social comparison**, Festinger's (1954) concept in which people compare themselves favorably to others to improve their own self-esteem: "Well, at least I'm better off than that person." (Members of the out-group make handy comparisons.)

With respect to prejudice, social identity theory helps to explain why people feel the need to categorize or stereotype others, producing the in-group sense of "us versus them" that people adopt toward out-groups. Prejudice may result, at least in part, from the need to increase one's own self-esteem by looking down on others.

Stereotype Vulnerability   As discussed previously, stereotypes are the widespread beliefs a person has about members of another group. Not only do stereotypes affect the way people perceive other people, but also stereotypes can affect the way people see themselves and their performance (Snyder et al., 1977). **Stereotype vulnerability** refers to the effect that a person's knowledge of another's stereotyped opinions can have on that person's behavior (Steele, 1992, 1997). Research has shown that when people are aware of stereotypes that are normally applied to their own group by others, they feel anxious about behaving in ways that might support that stereotype. This fear results in anxiety and self-consciousness that have negative effects on their performance in a kind of **self-fulfilling prophecy**, or the effect that expectations can have on outcomes.

Stereotype vulnerability is highly related to *stereotype threat*, in which members of a stereotyped group are made anxious and wary of any situation in which their behavior might confirm a stereotype (Hyde & Kling, 2001; Steele, 1999). In one study, researchers administered a difficult verbal test to both Caucasian and African American participants (Steele & Aronson, 1995). Half of the African American participants were asked to record their race on a demographic* question before the test, making them very aware of their minority status. Those participants showed a significant decrease in scores on the

---

*Demographic: having to do with the statistical characteristics of a population.

AP* Articulate the impact of social and cultural categories on self-concept and relations with others.

AP* Anticipate the impact of behavior on a self-fulfilling prophecy.

social cognitive   referring to the use of cognitive processes in relation to understanding the social world.

social identity theory   theory in which the formation of a person's identity within a particular social group is explained by social categorization, social identity, and social comparison.

social identity   the part of the self-concept including one's view of self as a member of a particular social category.

social comparison   the comparison of oneself to others in ways that raise one's self-esteem.

stereotype vulnerability   the effect that people's awareness of the stereotypes associated with their social group has on their behavior.

self-fulfilling prophecy   the tendency of one's expectations to affect one's behavior in such a way as to make the expectations more likely to occur.

Intergroup contact is one of the best ways to combat prejudice. When people have an opportunity to work together, as the students in this diverse classroom do, they get to know each other on common ground. Can you think of the first time you had direct contact with someone who was different from you? How did that contact change your viewpoint?

test when compared to the other participants, both African American and Caucasian, who did not answer such a demographic question. They had more incorrect answers, had slower response times, answered fewer questions, and demonstrated more anxiety when compared to the other participants (Steele & Aronson, 1995). Similar effects of stereotype threat on performance also have been found in women (Gonzales et al., 2002; Steele, 1997; Steele et al., 2002), and for athletes in academic settings (Yopyk & Prentice, 2005).

OVERCOMING PREJUDICE

The best weapon against prejudice is education: learning about people who are different from you in many ways. The best way to learn about others is to have direct contact with them and learn to see them as people rather than "as outsiders or strangers." *Intergroup contact* is very common in college settings, for example, where students and faculty from many different backgrounds live, work, and study together. Because they go through many of the same experiences (midterms, finals, and so on), people from these diverse* backgrounds find common ground to start building friendships and knowledge of each other's cultural, ethnic, or religious differences.

Equal Status Contact   Contact between social groups can backfire under certain circumstances, however, as seen in a famous study (Sherif et al., 1961) called the "Robber's Cave." In this experiment conducted at a summer camp called Robber's Cave, 22 white, well-adjusted 11- and 12-year-old boys were divided into two groups. The groups each lived in separate housing and were kept apart from each other for daily activities. During the second week, after in-group relationships had formed, the researchers scheduled highly competitive events pitting one group against the other. Intergroup conflict quickly occurred, with name-calling, fights, and hostility emerging between the two groups.

The third week involved making the two groups come together for pleasant, noncompetitive activities, in the hopes that cooperation would be the result. Instead, the groups used the activities of the third week as opportunities for more hostility. It was only after several weeks of being forced to work together to resolve a series of crises (created deliberately by the experimenters) that the boys lost the hostility and formed friendships between the groups. When dealing with the crises, the boys were forced into a situation of **equal status contact**, in which they were all in the same situation with neither group holding power over the other. Equal status contact has been shown to reduce prejudice and discrimination. It appears that personal involvement with people from another group must be cooperative and occur when all groups are equal in terms of power or status to have a positive effect on reducing prejudice (Pettigrew & Tropp, 2000; Robinson & Preston, 1976).

The "Jigsaw Classroom"   One way to ensure that contact between people from different backgrounds will occur in a cooperative fashion is to make success at a task depend on the cooperation of each person in a group of people of mixed abilities or statuses. If each member of the group has information that is needed to solve the problem at hand, a situation is created in which people must depend on one another to meet their shared goals (Aronson et al., 1978). Ordinarily, school classrooms are not organized along these lines but are instead more competitive and, therefore, more likely to create conflict between people of different abilities and backgrounds.

equal status contact contact between groups in which the groups have equal status, with neither group having power over the other.

————————————

*Diverse: different, varied.

In a "**jigsaw classroom**," students have to work together to reach a specific goal. Each student is given a "piece of the puzzle," or information that is necessary for solving the problem and reaching the goal (Aronson et al., 1978; Clarke, 1994). Students then share their information with other members of the group. Interaction between diverse students is increased, making it more likely that those students will come to see each other as partners and form friendly relationships rather than labeling others as members of an out-group and treating them differently. This technique works at the college level as well as in the lower school grades (Johnson et al., 1991; Lord, 2001).

"jigsaw classroom" educational technique in which each individual is given only part of the information needed to solve a problem, causing the separate individuals to be forced to work together to find the solution.

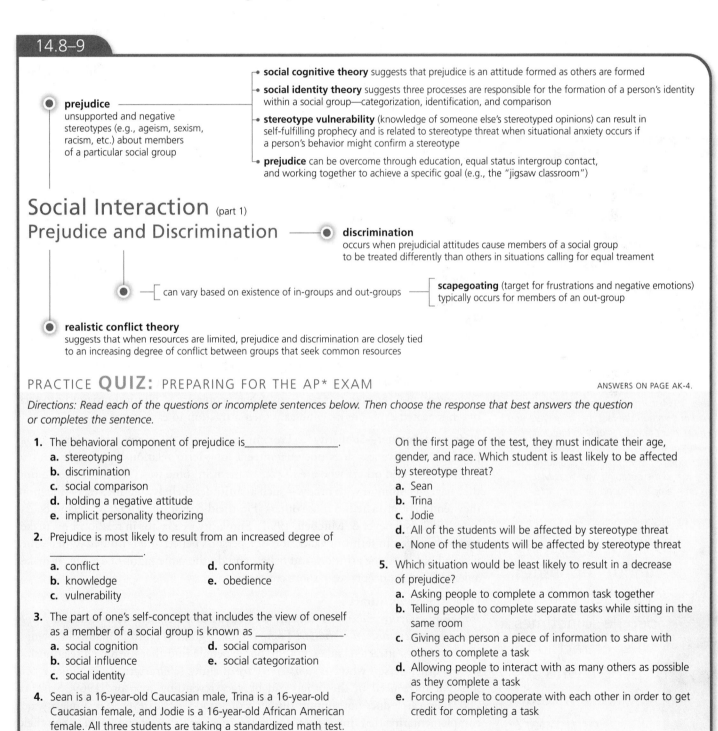

14.8–9

prejudice
unsupported and negative stereotypes (e.g., ageism, sexism, racism, etc.) about members of a particular social group

- **social cognitive theory** suggests that prejudice is an attitude formed as others are formed
- **social identity theory** suggests three processes are responsible for the formation of a person's identity within a social group—categorization, identification, and comparison
- **stereotype vulnerability** (knowledge of someone else's stereotyped opinions) can result in self-fulfilling prophecy and is related to stereotype threat when situational anxiety occurs if a person's behavior might confirm a stereotype
- **prejudice** can be overcome through education, equal status intergroup contact, and working together to achieve a specific goal (e.g., the "jigsaw classroom")

Social Interaction (part 1)
Prejudice and Discrimination

discrimination
occurs when prejudicial attitudes cause members of a social group to be treated differently than others in situations calling for equal treament

can vary based on existence of in-groups and out-groups

scapegoating (target for frustrations and negative emotions) typically occurs for members of an out-group

realistic conflict theory
suggests that when resources are limited, prejudice and discrimination are closely tied to an increasing degree of conflict between groups that seek common resources

PRACTICE QUIZ: PREPARING FOR THE AP* EXAM

ANSWERS ON PAGE AK-4.

Directions: Read each of the questions or incomplete sentences below. Then choose the response that best answers the question or completes the sentence.

1. The behavioral component of prejudice is_____.
   a. stereotyping
   b. discrimination
   c. social comparison
   d. holding a negative attitude
   e. implicit personality theorizing

2. Prejudice is most likely to result from an increased degree of
   _____.
   a. conflict   d. conformity
   b. knowledge   e. obedience
   c. vulnerability

3. The part of one's self-concept that includes the view of oneself as a member of a social group is known as _____.
   a. social cognition   d. social comparison
   b. social influence   e. social categorization
   c. social identity

4. Sean is a 16-year-old Caucasian male, Trina is a 16-year-old Caucasian female, and Jodie is a 16-year-old African American female. All three students are taking a standardized math test.

On the first page of the test, they must indicate their age, gender, and race. Which student is least likely to be affected by stereotype threat?
   a. Sean
   b. Trina
   c. Jodie
   d. All of the students will be affected by stereotype threat
   e. None of the students will be affected by stereotype threat

5. Which situation would be least likely to result in a decrease of prejudice?
   a. Asking people to complete a common task together
   b. Telling people to complete separate tasks while sitting in the same room
   c. Giving each person a piece of information to share with others to complete a task
   d. Allowing people to interact with as many others as possible as they complete a task
   e. Forcing people to cooperate with each other in order to get credit for completing a task

interpersonal attraction liking or having the desire for a relationship with another person.

proximity physical or geographical nearness.

AP * Describe the variables that contribute to altruism, aggression, and attraction.

Liking and Loving: Interpersonal Attraction

Prejudice pretty much explains why people don't like each other. What does psychology say about why people like someone else? There are some "rules" for those whom people like and find attractive. Liking or having the desire for a relationship with someone else is called **interpersonal attraction**, and there's a great deal of research on the subject.

THE RULES OF ATTRACTION

14.10 What factors govern attraction and love, and what are some different kinds of love?

Several factors are involved in the attraction of one person to another, including both superficial physical characteristics, such as physical beauty and proximity, as well as elements of personality.

Physical Attractiveness   When people think about what attracts them to other people, one of the topics that usually arises is the physical attractiveness of the other person. Some research suggests that physical beauty is one of the main factors that influence people's choices for selecting people they want to know better, although other factors may become more important in the later stages of relationships (Eagly et al., 1991; Feingold, 1992; White, 1980).

Proximity—Close to You   The closer together people are physically, such as working in the same office building or living in the same neighborhood, the more likely they are to form a relationship. **Proximity** refers to being physically near someone else. People choose friends and lovers from the pool of people available to them, and availability depends heavily on proximity.

One theory about why proximity is so important involves the idea of repeated exposure to new stimuli. The more people experience something, whether it is a song, a picture, or a person, the more they tend to like it. The phrase "it grew on me" refers to this reaction. When people are in physical proximity to each other, repeated exposure may increase their attraction to each other.

Famed athlete Joe DiMaggio and actress Marilyn Monroe are seen driving away after their 1954 marriage ceremony. While they had in common the fact that they were two of the most famous people in the United States at that time, many people viewed the marriage of the very modest and somewhat shy Joe to the outgoing, vivacious Marilyn as an example of "opposites attract."

Birds of a Feather—Similarity   Proximity does not guarantee attraction, just as physical attractiveness does not guarantee a long-term relationship. People tend to like being around others who are *similar* to them in some way. The more people find they have in common with others—such as attitudes, beliefs, and interests—the more they tend to be attracted to those others (Hartfield & Rapson, 1992; Moreland & Zajonc, 1982; Neimeyer & Mitchell, 1998). Similarity as a factor in relationships makes sense when seen in terms of validation of a person's beliefs and attitudes. When other people hold the same attitudes and beliefs and do the same kinds of actions, it makes a person's own concepts seem more correct or valid.

When Opposites Attract

Isn't there a saying about "opposites attract"? Aren't people sometimes attracted to people who are different instead of similar? There is often a grain of truth in many old sayings, and "opposites attract" is no exception. Some people find that forming a relationship with another person who has *complementary* qualities (characteristics in the one person that fill a need in the other) can be very rewarding (Carson, 1969; Schmitt, 2002). Research does not support this view of attraction, however. It is similarity, not complementarity, that draws people together and helps them stay together (Berscheid & Reis, 1998; McPherson et al., 2001).

Isn't there a saying about "opposites attract"? Aren't people sometimes attracted to people who are different instead of similar?

Reciprocity of Liking   Finally, people have a very strong tendency to like people who like them, a simple but powerful concept referred to as **reciprocity of liking**. In one experiment, researchers paired college students with other students (Curtis & Miller, 1986). Neither student in any of the pairs knew the other member. One member of each pair was randomly chosen to receive some information from the experimenters about how the *other* student in the pair felt about the first member. In some cases, target students were led to believe that the other students liked them and, in other cases, that the targets disliked them.

When the pairs of students were allowed to meet and talk with each other again, they were friendlier, disclosed more information about themselves, agreed with the other person more, and behaved in a warmer manner *if they had been told* that the other student liked them. The other students came to like these students better as well, so liking produced more liking.

The only time that liking someone does not seem to make that person like the other in return is if a person suffers from feelings of low self-worth. In that case, finding out that someone likes you when you don't even like yourself makes you question his or her motives. This mistrust can cause you to act unfriendly to that person, which makes the person more likely to become unfriendly to you in a kind of self-fulfilling prophecy (Murray et al., 1998).

LOVE IS A TRIANGLE—ROBERT STERNBERG'S TRIANGULAR THEORY OF LOVE

Dictionary definitions of love refer to a strong affection for another person due to kinship, personal ties, physical attraction, admiration, or common interests.

But those aren't all the same kind of relationships. I love my family and I love my friends, but in different ways. Psychologists generally agree that there are different kinds of love. One psychologist, Robert Sternberg, outlined a theory of what he determined were the three main components of love and the different types of love that combinations of these three components can produce (Sternberg, 1986, 1988, 1997).

The Three Components of Love   According to Sternberg, love consists of three basic components: intimacy, passion, and commitment.

Intimacy, in Sternberg's view, refers to the feelings of closeness that one has for another person or the sense of having close emotional ties to another. Intimacy in this sense is not physical but psychological. Friends have an intimate relationship because they disclose things to each other that most people might not know, they feel strong emotional ties to each other, and they enjoy the presence of the other person.

Passion is the physical aspect of love. Passion refers to the emotional and physical arousal a person feels toward the other person. Holding hands, loving looks, and hugs can all be forms of passion.

Commitment involves the decisions one makes about a relationship. A short-term decision might be, "I think I'm in love." An example of a more long-term decision is, "I want to be with this person for the rest of my life."

The Love Triangles   A love relationship between two people can involve one, two, or all three of these components in various combinations. The combinations can produce seven different forms of love, as can be seen in Figure 14.5.

Two of the more familiar and more heavily researched forms of love from Sternberg's theory are romantic love and companionate love. When intimacy and passion are combined, the result is the more familiar **romantic love**, which is sometimes called passionate love by other researchers (Bartels & Zeki, 2000; Diamond, 2003; Hartfield, 1987). Romantic love is often the basis for a more lasting relationship.

> But those aren't all the same kind of relationships. I love my family and I love my friends, but in different ways.

◀ **AP*** Identify important figures in social psychology.

reciprocity of liking tendency of people to like other people who like them in return.

romantic love type of love consisting of intimacy and passion.

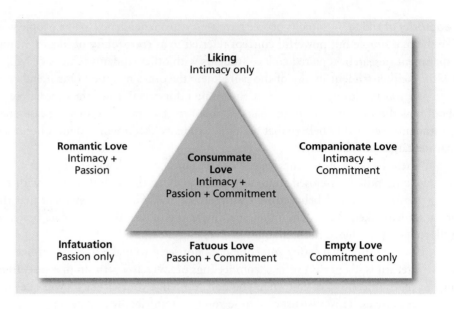

Figure 14.5 Sternberg's Triangular Theory of Love

This diagram represents the seven different kinds of love that can result from combining the three components of love: intimacy, passion, and commitment. Notice that some of these types of love sound less desirable or positive than others. What is the one key element missing from the less positive types of love?
Source: Adapted from Sternberg (1986b).

✳ **Explore** the labeling theory of love— How do we decide we are in love? **www.mypsychlab.com**

companionate love   type of love consisting of intimacy and commitment.

In many Western cultures, the ideal relationship begins with liking, then becomes romantic love as passion is added to the mix, and finally becomes a more enduring form of love as a commitment is made. ✳ Explore on MyPsychLab

When intimacy and commitment are the main components of a relationship, it is called **companionate love**. In companionate love, people who like each other, feel emotionally close to each other, and understand one another's motives have made a commitment to live together, usually in a marriage relationship. Companionate love is often the binding tie that holds a marriage together through the years of parenting, paying bills, and lessening physical passion (Gottman & Krokoff, 1989; Steinberg & Silverberg, 1987). In many non-Western cultures, companionate love is seen as more sensible. Choices for a mate on the basis of compatibility are often made by parents or matchmakers rather than the couple themselves (Duben & Behar, 1991; Hortaçsu, 1999; Jones, 1997; Thornton & Hui-Sheng, 1994).

Finally, when all three components of love are present, the couple has achieved *consummate love*, the ideal form of love that many people see as the ultimate goal. This is also the kind of love that may evolve into companionate love when the passion lessens during the middle years of a relationship's commitment.

14.10

Social Interaction (part 2)
Interpersonal Attraction

- liking or having the desire for a relationship with someone else; can be influenced by a variety of factors
  - **physical attractiveness**
  - **proximity**
  - **similarity**
  - **complementary qualities**
  - **reciprocity of liking**

- **love**
  strong affection for another person due to kinship, personal ties, physical attraction, admiration, or common interests
  - **Sternberg's triangular theory** suggests different components and types of love
    - three components
      - **intimacy**
      - **passion**
      - **commitment**
    - three types
      - **romantic** (intimacy and passion)
      - **companionate** (intimacy and commitment)
      - **consummate** (intimacy, passion, and commitment)

PRACTICE QUIZ: PREPARING FOR THE AP* EXAM

ANSWERS ON PAGE AK-4.

Directions: Read each of the questions or incomplete sentences below. Then choose the response that best answers the question or completes the sentence.

1. Which of the following is not a major cause of interpersonal attraction?

  a. Similarity
  b. Intelligence
  c. Reciprocity of liking
  d. Physical attractiveness
  e. Complementary qualities

2. A person who is very low in self-worth is less likely to be affected by the _____.

  a. halo effect
  b. proximity effect
  c. mere exposure effect
  d. reciprocity of liking effect
  e. need complementarity effect

3. According to Sternberg, which of the following describes the feelings of emotional closeness between two people?

  a. Passion
  b. Intimacy
  c. Friendship
  d. Infatuation
  e. Commitment

4. Greta and Huan have been married for thirty years. They are no longer passionate toward each other, but they feel emotionally close to each other, they nurture their relationship, and they have no intention of leaving each other. Greta and Huan's relationship can best be described as _____.

  a. empty love
  b. fatuous love
  c. romantic love
  d. consummate love
  e. companionate love

5. Romantic love consists of _____.

  a. only passion
  b. intimacy and passion
  c. passion and commitment
  d. intimacy and commitment
  e. passion, intimacy, and commitment

Aggression and Prosocial Behavior

◄ **AP*** Describe the variables that contribute to altruism, aggression, and attraction.

Unfortunately, violence toward others is another form of social interaction. When one person hurts or tries to destroy another person deliberately, either with words or with physical behavior, psychologists call it **aggression**. One common cause of aggressive behavior is frustration, which occurs when a person is prevented from reaching some desired goal. The concept of aggression as a reaction to frustration is known as the frustration–aggression hypothesis (Berkowitz, 1993; Miller et al., 1941). There are many sources of frustration that can lead to aggressive behavior. Pain, for example, produces negative sensations that are often intense and uncontrollable, leading to frustration and often aggressive acts against the nearest available target (Berkowitz, 1993). Loud noises, excessive heat, and even awful smells can lead people to act out in an aggressive manner (Anderson, 1987; Rotton & Frey, 1985; Rotton et al., 1979; Zillmann et al., 1981).

Frustration is not the only source of aggressive behavior. Many early researchers, including Sigmund Freud (1930), believed that aggression was a basic human instinct. In Freud's view, aggression was part of the death instinct that drove human beings to destroy both others and themselves, and he believed that if aggression were not released it would cause illness. But if aggression is an instinct present in all humans, it should occur in far more similar patterns across cultures than it does. Instinctual behavior, as often seen in animals, is not modifiable by environmental influences. Modern approaches try to explain aggression as a biological phenomenon or a learned behavior.

AGGRESSION AND BIOLOGY

14.11 How is aggressive behavior determined by biology and learning?

There is some evidence that human aggression has at least partially a genetic basis. Studies of twins have shown that if one identical twin has a violent temper, the identical sibling will most likely also have a violent temper. This agreement between twins' personalities happens more often with identical twins than with fraternal twins (Miles & Carey, 1997; Rowe et al., 1999). It may be that some gene or complex of genes makes certain people more susceptible to aggressive responses under the right environmental conditions.

aggression behavior intended to hurt or destroy another person.

social role the pattern of behavior that is expected of a person who is in a particular social position.

As discussed in Chapter Two, certain areas of the brain seem to control aggressive responses. The amygdala and other structures of the limbic system have been shown to trigger aggressive responses when stimulated in both animals and humans (Adams, 1968; Albert & Richmond, 1977; LaBar et al., 1995; Scott et al., 1997). Charles Whitman, the Tower of Texas sniper, who in 1966 killed 14 people before finally being killed by law enforcement officers, left a note asking for an examination of his brain. An autopsy did reveal a tumor that was pressing into his amygdala (Lavergne, 1997).

There are also chemical influences on aggression. Testosterone, a male sex hormone, has been linked to higher levels of aggression in humans (Archer, 1991). This may help to explain why violent criminals tend to be young, male, and muscular. They typically have high levels of testosterone and low levels of serotonin, another important chemical found in the brain (Alexander et al., 1986; Brown & Linnoila, 1990; Coccaro & Kavoussi, 1996; Dabbs et al., 2001; Robins, 1996).

Don't some people get pretty violent after drinking too much? Does alcohol do something to those brain chemicals? ▶

Don't some people get pretty violent after drinking too much? Does alcohol do something to those brain chemicals? Alcohol does have an impact on aggressive behavior. Psychologically, alcohol acts to release inhibitions, making people less likely to control their behavior even if they are not yet intoxicated. Biologically, alcohol affects the functioning of many neurotransmitters and in particular is associated with a decrease in serotonin (Virkkunen & Linnoila, 1996). **LINK** *to Chapter Two: The Biological Perspective, p. 56.* In one study, volunteers were asked to administer electric shocks to an unseen "opponent" in a study reminiscent of Milgram's shock experiment. The actual responses to the shock were simulated by a computer, although the volunteers believed that the responses were coming from a real person. The volunteers were told it was a test of reaction time and learning (Bushman, 1997). Volunteers participated both before consuming alcohol and after consuming alcohol. Participants were much more aggressive in administering stronger shocks after drinking.

THE POWER OF SOCIAL ROLES

Although frustration, genetics, body chemicals, and even the effects of drugs can be blamed for aggressive behavior to some degree, much of human aggression is also influenced by learning. The social learning theory explanation for aggression states that aggressive behavior is learned (in a process called observational learning) by watching aggressive models get reinforced for their aggressive behavior (Bandura, 1980; Bandura et al., 1961). **LINK** *to Chapter Five: Learning, pp. 207–209.* Aggressive models can be parents, siblings, friends, or people on television.

There is some evidence to suggest that even taking on a particular *social role*, such as that of a soldier, can lead to an increase in aggressive behavior. A **social role** is the pattern of behavior that is expected of a person who is in a particular social position. For example, "doctor" is a social role that implies wearing a white coat, asking certain types of questions, and writing prescriptions, among other things. A deeply disturbing experiment was conducted by famed social psychologist Philip Zimbardo at Stanford University in 1971.

AP* Identify important figures in social psychology. ▶

The experiment was recorded on film from the beginning to a rather abrupt end: about 70 young men, most of whom were college students, volunteered to participate for two weeks. They were told that they would be randomly assigned the social role of either a guard or a prisoner in the experiment. The "guards" were given uniforms and instructions not to use violence but to maintain control of the "prison." The "prisoners" were booked at a real jail, blindfolded, and transported to the campus "prison," actually the basement of one of the campus buildings. On day 2, the prisoners staged a revolt (not planned as part of the experiment), which was quickly crushed by the guards. The guards then became increasingly more aggressive, using humiliation to control and punish the prisoners. For example, prisoners were forced to clean out toilet bowls with their bare hands. The staff observing the experiment had to release five of the prisoners who became so upset that they were physically ill. The entire experiment was canceled on the fifth day, after one of the prisoners reported to Zimbardo that what the experimenters were doing to the young men was terrible (Zimbardo, 1971).

The conclusions of Zimbardo and his colleagues highlighted the influence that a social role, such as that of "guard," can have on perfectly ordinary people. Although history is full of examples of people behaving horribly to others while filling a particular role, one need not travel very far into the past to find an example.

During the war in Iraq in 2003, an army reserve general was suspended from duty while an investigation into reported prisoner abuses was conducted. Between October and December 2003, investigators found numerous cases of cruel, humiliating, and other startling abuses of the Iraqi prisoners by the army military police stationed at the prison of Abu Ghraib (Hersh, 2004). The "guards" in the Stanford prison study were normal people, but the effect of putting on the uniform and taking on the social role of guard changed their behavior radically. Is it possible that a similar factor was at work at Abu Ghraib? The behavior of the guards at Abu Ghraib was not part of a formal, controlled study, so further research will be needed to determine to what degree the social roles at work in situations like this influence the kind of behavior seen in this real-life example.

Violence in the Media and Aggression

I've heard that violent television programs can cause children to become more aggressive. How true is that? Bandura's early study on the effects of an aggressive model viewed over a movie screen on small children was one of the first attempts to investigate the effect of violence in the media on children's aggressive behavior (Bandura et al., 1963). ⓁⒾⓃⓀ *to Chapter Five: Learning, pp. 207–209.* Since then, researchers have examined the impact of television and other media violence on the aggressive behavior of children of various ages. The conclusions have all been similar: Children who are exposed to high levels of violent media are more aggressive than children who are not (Baron & Reiss, 1985; Bushman & Huesmann, 2000; Centerwall, 1989; Geen & Thomas, 1986; Huesmann & Miller, 1994; Huesmann et al., 1997; Huesmann et al., 2003; Villani, 2001). These studies have found that there are several contributing factors involving the normal aggressive tendencies of the child, with more aggressive children preferring to watch more aggressive media as well as the age at which exposure begins: the younger the child, the greater the impact. Parenting issues also have an impact, as the aggressive impact of television is lessened in homes where aggressive behavior is not tolerated and punishment is not physical. ✲ Explore on MyPsychLab

Violent video games have also come under fire as causing violent acting-out in children, especially young adolescents. The tragic shootings at schools all over the United States have, at least in part, been blamed on violent video games that the

I've heard that violent television programs can cause children ◀ to become more aggressive. How true is that?

✲ **Explore** with a simulation on Bandura's study of the effects of violence and aggression.
www.mypsychlab.com

students seemed to be imitating. In one study, second-grade boys were allowed to play either an aggressive or a nonaggressive video game. After playing the game, the boys who had played the aggressive video game demonstrated more verbal and physical aggression both to objects around them and to their playmates while playing in a free period than boys who had played the nonagressive video game (Irwin & Gross, 1995). **Listen** on **MyPsychLab**

In a massive meta-analysis of research into the connection between violent media and aggressive behavior in children, social psychologist Craig Anderson and colleagues found clear and consistent evidence that even short-term exposure to violent media significantly increases the likelihood that children will engage in both physical and verbal aggression as well as aggressive thoughts and emotions (Anderson et al., 2003). Clearly, violent video games do correlate with increased aggression levels of the children who play them, both young children and adolescents (Anderson, 2003; Anderson & Bushman, 2001). (Remember, correlation does NOT prove causation—the studies mentioned here have not proven that playing violent video games *causes* increased aggression! **LINK** *to Chapter One: The Science of Psychology, pp. 26–28*).

PROSOCIAL BEHAVIOR

Another and far more pleasant form of human social interaction is **prosocial behavior**, or socially desirable behavior that benefits others rather than brings them harm.

14.12 What is altruism, and how is deciding to help someone related to the presence of others?

Altruism   One form of prosocial behavior that almost always makes people feel good about other people is **altruism**, or helping someone in trouble with no expectation of reward and often without fear for one's own safety. Although no one is surprised by the behavior of a mother who enters a burning house to save her child, some people are often surprised when total strangers step in to help, risking their own lives for people they do not know.

Sociobiologists, scientists who study the evolutionary and genetic bases of social organizations in both animals and humans, see altruistic behavior as a way of preserving one's genetic material, even at the cost of one's own life. This is why the males of certain species of spiders, for example, seem to willingly become "dinner" for the female mates they have just fertilized, ensuring the continuation of their genes through the offspring she will produce (Koh, 1996). It also explains the mother or father who risks life and limb to save a child. But why do people risk their own lives to help total strangers? More importantly, why do people sometimes refuse to help when their own lives are not at risk, as in the cases of Kitty Genovese and LaShanda Calloway presented in the opening story?

Why People Won't Help   The opening story about Kitty Genovese's murder shocked most people when reported in the news in March 1964. People were outraged by the apparent indifference and lack of sympathy for the poor woman's plight. Why did those people simply stand by and watch or listen? Social psychologists would explain that the lack of response to Kitty Genovese's screams for help was not due to indifference or a lack of sympathy but instead to the presence of other people. When other people are present at the scene or are assumed to be present, individuals are affected by two basic principles of social psychology: the bystander effect and diffusion of responsibility.

The **bystander effect** refers to the finding that the likelihood of a bystander (someone observing an event and close enough to offer help) to help someone in

---

Listen to the Psychology in the News podcast. www.mypsychlab.com

prosocial behavior socially desirable behavior that benefits others.

altruism prosocial behavior that is done with no expectation of reward and may involve the risk of harm to oneself.

bystander effect referring to the effect that the presence of other people has on the decision to help or not help, with help becoming less likely as the number of bystanders increases.

AP* Describe the variables that contribute to altruism, aggression, and attraction.

AP* Predict the impact of the presence of others on individual behavior.

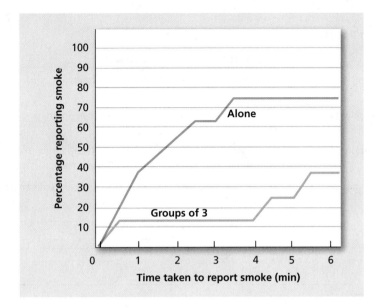

Figure 14.6 **Elements Involved in Bystander Response**
As you can see in the accompanying graph, the time taken to report smoke and the percentage of people reporting smoke both depended on how many people were in the room at the time the smoke was observed. If a person was alone, he or she was far more likely to report the smoke and report it more quickly than when there were three people. *Source:* Latané & Darley (1969).

trouble decreases as the number of bystanders increases. If only one person is standing by, that person is far more likely to help than if there is another person, and the addition of each new bystander decreases the possibility of helping behavior even more (Darley & Latané, 1968; Eagly & Crowley, 1986; Latané & Darley, 1969). In the case of Kitty Genovese, there were 38 "bystanders" at the windows of the apartment buildings, and none of them helped. Five shoppers stepped over the bleeding body of LaShanda Calloway, and none of them helped.

But why does the number of bystanders matter? **Diffusion of responsibility** is the phenomenon in which a person fails to take responsibility for either action or inaction because of the presence of other people who are seen to share the responsibility (Figure 14.6) (Leary & Forsyth, 1987). Diffusion of responsibility is a form of attribution in which people explain why they acted (or failed to act) as they did because of others. "I was just following orders," "Other people were doing it," and "There were a lot of people there, and I thought one of them would do something" are all examples of statements made in such situations. Kitty Genovese received no help because there were too many potential "helpers," and not one of the people listening to her cries for help took the responsibility to intervene—they thought surely someone else was doing something about it.

For more on the bystander effect, the Classic Studies in Psychology section that follows reviews one of the more famous social psychology experiments.

Five Decision Points in Helping Behavior In all of the experiments reported in the preceding section, there were people who did try to help in every condition. What kind of decision-making process might they have gone through before deciding to help? What are the requirements for deciding when help is needed? Darley and Latané (1968) identified several decision points that a bystander must face before helping someone in trouble. These decision points are outlined in Table 14.3.

Aside from the factors listed in the table, there are other influences on the decision to help. For example, the more ambiguity* there is in a situation, the less likely it becomes that the situation will be defined as an emergency. If there are other people nearby, especially if the situation is ambiguous, bystanders may rely on the actions of the others to help determine if the situation is an emergency or not. Since all the

◀ But why does the number of bystanders matter?

diffusion of responsibility occurring when a person fails to take responsibility for actions or for inaction because of the presence of other people who are seen to share the responsibility.

---

*Ambiguity: having the quality of being difficult to identify specific elements of the situation.

Table 14.3 Help or Don't Help: Five Decision Points

DECISION POINT	DESCRIPTION	FACTORS INFLUENCING DECISION
Noticing	Realizing that there is a situation that might be an emergency.	Hearing a loud crash or a cry for help.
Defining an Emergency	Interpreting the cues as signaling an emergency.	Loud crash is associated with a car accident, people are obviously hurt.
Taking Responsibility	Personally assuming the responsibility to act.	A single bystander is much more likely to act than when others are present (Latané & Darley, 1969).
Planning a Course of Action	Deciding how to help and what skills might be needed.	People who feel they have the necessary skills to help are more likely to help.
Taking Action	Actually helping.	Costs of helping (e.g., danger to self) must not outweigh the rewards of helping.

AP* Identify important figures in social psychology. ▶

Classic Studies in Psychology

Latané and Darley

After the Kitty Genovese murder, psychologists became curious about why the bystanders did not call the police right away or try to help in some other way. Two social psychologists, Bibb Latané and John Darley, began a series of research projects to determine the different conditions under which help might or might not be given. In their classic 1969 study, they conducted several experiments, one of which is summarized here.

Participants were filling out questionnaires in a room that began to fill with smoke. Some participants were alone in the room, whereas in another condition there were three participants in the room. In a third condition one participant was in the room with two confederates of the experimenter, who were instructed to notice the smoke but ignore it afterwards. In the "participant alone" condition, three-fourths of the participants left the room to report the smoke. In the "three participants" condition, only a little over one-third of the participants reported the smoke, whereas only one-tenth of the participants who were in the room with confederates did so. Interviews with the participants who failed to report the smoke found that participants did not perceive the smoke as threatening.

In all of the researchers' experiments, participants were less likely to respond to a possible emergency situation when there were others present than when participants were alone. One bystander cannot diffuse responsibility to others, but two or more can.

Questions for Further Discussion

1. What other reasons could participants in this experiment have for not responding?
2. What might be some of the factors that distinguish the participants who did try to help from those who did not?
3. Are there any ethical concerns with research such as this?

◉ **Watch** classic video footage on Latané and Darley.
www.mypsychlab.com

◉⌐**Watch** on **MyPsychLab**

bystanders are doing this, it is very likely that the situation will be seen as a nonemergency because no one is moving to help.

Another factor is the mood of the bystanders. People in a good mood are generally more likely to help than people in a bad mood, but oddly enough, they are not as likely to help if helping would destroy the good mood. Gender of the victim is also a factor, with women more likely to receive help than men if the bystander is male, but not if the bystander is female. Physically attractive people are more likely to be helped. Victims who look like "they deserve what is happening" are also less likely to be helped. For example, a man lying on the side of the street who is dressed in shabby clothing and appears to be drunk will be passed by, but if he is dressed in a business suit, people are more likely to stop and help. Racial and ethnicity differences between victim and bystander also decrease the probability of helping (Richards & Lowe, 2003; Tukuitonga & Bindman, 2002).

14.11–12

aggression may be partly attributed to genetics and can be triggered by variations in brain function (i.e., amygdala activation) and internal or external chemical influences (e.g., testosterone, alcohol)

aggression occurs when one person verbally or physically hurts or tries to destroy another person; often the result of frustration

much of aggression is influenced by learning but not totally deterministic

partially explained by social learning theory—social roles (expected behavior in particular social situation) determine much of behavior (e.g., Zimbardo's Stanford Prison study)

childhood exposure to abuse does not necessarily mean that one will grow up to be an abuser

short-term exposure to violent media (video games, television, movies) has been correlated with increases in both physical and verbal aggression and aggressive thoughts and emotions

Social Interaction (part 3)
Aggression and Prosocial Behavior

prosocial, or socially desirable, behavior benefits others

altruism: helping someone with no expectation of reward and often at personal risk

can be influenced by helper's mood and victim's gender, attractiveness, or "just rewards"; racial and ethnic differences can decrease probability of helping

refusal to help another can be negatively affected by the presence of others (bystander effect/diffusion of responsibility) rather than indifference or a lack of sympathy; also influenced by individual's appraisal of situation (see Table 14.3)

PRACTICE **QUIZ:** PREPARING FOR THE AP* EXAM

ANSWERS ON PAGE AK-4.

Directions: Read each of the questions or incomplete sentences below. Then choose the response that best answers the question or completes the sentence.

1. The area of the brain that is most involved in aggression is the _____.
   a. cortex
   b. medulla
   c. amygdala
   d. cerebellum
   e. pineal gland

2. Research based on the bystander effect suggests that a victim is most likely to get help if _____.
   a. no other people are nearby
   b. only one other person is nearby
   c. three other people are nearby
   d. ten other people are nearby
   e. hundreds of other people are nearby

3. Once a situation has been defined as an emergency, the next step in the decision-making process is _____.
   a. noticing
   b. taking action
   c. taking responsibility
   d. requesting assistance
   e. planning a course of action

4. Which of the following is best classified as an altruistic act?
   a. Conducting a nonviolent protest
   b. Saving a loved one from danger
   c. Making a living by tutoring children
   d. Protecting a stranger from an attack
   e. Using aggression only in self-defense

5. In Zimbardo's classic Stanford prison experiment, participants succumbed to the power of _____.
   a. altruism
   b. social roles
   c. hindsight bias
   d. stereotype threat
   e. self-fulfilling prophecies

Applying Psychology to Everyday Life: Anatomy of a Cult

14.13 Why do people join cults?

cult any group of people with a particular religious or philosophical set of beliefs and identity.

The term **cult** literally refers to any group of people with a particular religious or philosophical set of beliefs and identity. In the strictest sense of the word, the Roman Catholic Church and Protestantism are cults within the larger religion of Christianity. But most people associate the term *cult* with a negative connotation*: a group of people whose religious or philosophical beliefs and behavior are so different from that of mainstream organizations that they are viewed with suspicion and seen as existing on the fringes of socially acceptable behavior. Although many cults exist without much notice from more mainstream groups, at times members of cults have horrified the public with their actions.

One of the most well-remembered and often cited examples of a cult gone horribly wrong was that of the People's Temple in Jonestown, Guyana, headed by Jim Jones. Originally a Christian offshoot, the People's Temple became a cult under Jones's dictatorial leadership. In 1978, when Jones felt threatened by reporters coming to Guyana, he instructed the entire cult of over 900 people to commit suicide. A total of 914 people died, including 274 children (Chidester, 2003).

More recently, the followers of the Heaven's Gate cult, who believed that aliens in a spaceship were coming in the tail of the Hale-Bopp comet in 1997, committed suicide under the leadership of Marshall Applewhite. They believed that their souls would be taken up by the comet aliens.

Why would any person get so caught up in cult beliefs that suicide becomes a desired behavior? What kind of person joins a cult in the first place? Although there is no particular personality profile associated with cult membership, cult members do appear to have been in some psychological distress at the time of recruitment by the cult. People who are under a lot of stress, dissatisfied with their lives, unassertive, gullible, dependent, feel a desire to belong to a group, and who are unrealistically idealistic ("we can solve all the world's problems if everyone will just love each other") are the most likely targets of cult recruitment (Langone, 1996). Young people rebelling against parental authority or trying to become independent of families are prime targets.

Cult leaders also have certain techniques of persuasion that are common to most cult organizations. The first step is usually something called "love-bombing" by current cult members, who shower the recruits with affection and attention and claim to understand just how the potential cult members feel. Then efforts are made to isolate the recruits from family and friends who might talk them out of joining. This is accomplished in part by keeping the recruits so busy with rigid rituals, ways of dress, meditations, and other activities that they do not allow the recruits time to think about what is happening. All of these activities also serve to wear down the resistance of the recruits. Cults also teach their members how to stop questioning thoughts or criticisms, which are typically seen as sins of extremely undesirable behavior. Access to people and information outside the cult is either kept to a well-guarded minimum or totally shut off (Singer & Lalich, 1995; Zimbardo & Hartley, 1985).

---

*Connotation: the meaning of a word or concept that is more suggestive than directly stated.

Commitments to the cult are small at first, such as attending a music concert or some other cult function. Eventually, a major step is requested by the cult, such as quitting one's job, turning over money or property to the cult, or similar commitments. Leaving a cult is quite difficult, as members of the cult in good standing will often track down a "deserter." Parents, friends, and other family members have been known to hire special "deprogrammers" to help their loved one recover from cult membership, willingly or unwillingly. Sometimes people actually have to "kidnap" their loved one out of the cult environment. Nevertheless, as difficult as it is to leave, 90 percent or more of cult members do eventually get out (Barker, 1983; Galanter, 1983).

Marshall Applewhite, leader of the Heaven's Gate cult.

Cults have existed all through recorded history and will probably continue to exist in the future. In 1995, there were between 3,000 and 5,000 cults in the United States alone (Singer & Lalich, 1995). Most cults do not pose a physical threat to their members or others, but the examples of the followers of Jim Jones, David Koresh, and Osama bin Laden clearly demonstrate that cults, like any group of people, can become deadly.

Questions for Further Discussion

1. In what ways are the methods used by cults on new recruits similar to the methods used by the military when training new soldiers?

2. Is it ethical for the family members of an adult to "kidnap" and deprogram a cult member?

3. Which methods of compliance do cults seem to use to recruit new members?

14 CHAPTER SUMMARY

- Social psychology is the scientific study of how a person's thoughts, feelings, and behavior are influenced by the real, imagined, or implied presence of other people.

Social Influence: Conformity, Compliance, and Obedience

14.1 What factors influence people to conform to the actions of others?

- Asch used a set of comparison lines and a standard line to experiment with conformity, finding that subjects conformed to group

opinion about one-third of the time, increased as the number of confederates rose to four, and decreased if just one confederate gave the correct answer.

- Cross-cultural research has found that collectivistic cultures show more conformity than individualistic cultures. Gender differences do not exist in conformity unless the response is not private, in which case women are more conforming than men.

- Groupthink occurs when a decision-making group feels that it is more important to maintain group unanimity and cohesiveness than to consider the facts realistically.

• Minimizing groupthink involves impartial leadership, seeking outside opinions, stating problems in an objective manner, breaking large groups into subgroups, encouraging questions and alternate solutions, using secret ballots, and holding group members responsible for the decisions made by the group.

14.2 How is compliance defined, and what are four common ways to gain the compliance of another?

• Compliance occurs when a person changes behavior as a result of another person asking or directing that person to change.

• Four common ways of getting compliance from others are the foot-in-the-door technique, the door-in-the-face technique, the lowball technique, and the that's-not-all technique.

14.3 What factors make obedience more likely?

• Milgram did experiments in which he found that 65 percent of people obeyed the authority figure of a psychology professor even if it meant hurting, injuring, or possibly killing another person with an electric shock.

• When the performance of an individual on a relatively easy task is improved by the presence of others, it is called social facilitation. When the performance of an individual on a relatively difficult task is negatively affected by the presence of others, it is called social impairment.

• When a person who is lazy is able to work in a group of people, that person often performs less well than if the person were working alone in a phenomenon called social loafing.

Social Cognition: Attitudes, Impression Formation, and Attribution

14.4 What are the three components of an attitude, how are attitudes formed, and how can attitudes be changed?

• Attitudes are tendencies to respond positively or negatively toward ideas, persons, objects, or situations.

• The three components of an attitude are the affective (emotional) component, the behavioral component, and the cognitive component.

• Attitudes are often poor predictors of behavior unless the attitude is very specific or very strong.

• Direct contact with the person, situation, object, or idea can help form attitudes.

• Attitudes can be formed through direct instruction from parents or others.

• Interacting with other people who hold a certain attitude can help an individual form that attitude.

• Attitudes can also be formed through watching the actions and reactions of others to ideas, people, objects, and situations.

• Persuasion is the process by which one person tries to change the belief, opinion, position, or course of action of another person through argument, pleading, or explanation.

• The key elements in persuasion are the source of the message, the message itself, and the target audience.

• In the elaboration likelihood model, central-route processing involves attending to the content of the message itself, whereas peripheral-route processing involves attending to factors not involved in the message, such as the appearance of the source of the message, the length of the message, and other noncontent factors.

14.5 How do people react when attitudes and behavior are not the same?

• Cognitive dissonance is discomfort or distress that occurs when a person's actions do not match the person's attitudes.

• Cognitive dissonance is lessened by changing the conflicting behavior, changing the conflicting attitude, or forming a new attitude to justify the behavior.

• Impression formation is the forming of the first knowledge a person has about another person.

• The primacy effect in impression formation means that the very first impression one has about a person tends to persist even in the face of evidence to the contrary.

• Impression formation is part of social cognition, or the mental processes that people use to make sense out of the world around them.

14.6 What are social categorization and implicit personality theories?

• Social categorization is a process of social cognition in which a person, upon meeting someone new, assigns that person to a category or group on the basis of characteristics the person has in common with other people or groups with whom the perceiver has prior experience.

• One form of a social category is the stereotype, in which the characteristics used to assign a person to a category are superficial and believed to be true of all members of the category.

• An implicit personality theory is a form of social cognition in which a person has sets of assumptions about different types of people, personality traits, and actions that are assumed to be related to each other.

• Schemas are mental patterns that represent what a person believes about certain types of people. Schemas can become stereotypes.

14.7 How do people try to explain the actions of others?

• Attribution is the process of explaining the behavior of others as well as one's own behavior.

• A situational cause is an explanation of behavior based on factors in the surrounding environment or situation.

• A dispositional cause is an explanation of behavior based on the internal personality characteristics of the person being observed.

• The fundamental attribution error is the tendency to overestimate the influence of internal factors on the behavior of other people while underestimating the influence of the situation.

Social Interaction: Prejudice, Love, and Aggression

14.8 How are prejudice and discrimination different?

* Prejudice is a negative attitude that a person holds about the members of a particular social group. Discrimination occurs when members of a social group are treated differently because of prejudice toward that group.

* There are many forms of prejudice, including ageism, sexism, racism, and prejudice toward those who are too fat or too thin.

* In-groups are the people with whom a person identifies, whereas out-groups are everyone else at whom prejudice tends to be directed.

* Conflict between groups increases prejudice and discrimination according to realistic conflict theory.

* Scapegoating refers to the tendency to direct prejudice and discrimination at out-group members who have little social power or influence. New immigrants are often the scapegoats for the frustration and anger of the in-group.

Classic Studies in Psychology: Brown Eyes, Blue Eyes

* A schoolteacher divided her class into brown-eyed children and blue-eyed children to teach them a lesson about prejudice. The children quickly began to discriminate toward whichever group was the out-group during a certain time period.

14.9 Why are people prejudiced, and how can prejudice be stopped?

* Social cognitive theory views prejudice as an attitude acquired through direct instruction, modeling, and other social influences.

* Social identity theory sees a person's formation of a social sense of self within a particular group as being due to three things: social categorization (which may involve the use of reference groups), social identity (the person's sense of belonging to a particular social group), and social comparison (in which people compare themselves to others to improve their own self-esteem).

* Stereotype vulnerability refers to the effect that a person's knowledge of the stereotypes that exist against his or her social group can have on that person's behavior.

* People who are aware of stereotypes may unintentionally come to behave in a way that makes the stereotype real in a self-fulfilling prophecy.

* Intergroup contact is more effective in reducing prejudice if the groups have equal status.

* Prejudice and discrimination can also be reduced when a superordinate goal that is large enough to override all other goals needs to be achieved by all groups.

* Prejudice and discrimination are reduced when people must work together to solve a problem because each person has an important key to solving the problem, creating a mutual interdependence. This technique used in education is called the "jigsaw classroom."

* Interpersonal attraction refers to liking or having the desire for a relationship with another person.

Liking and Loving: Interpersonal Attraction

14.10 What factors govern attraction and love, and what are some different kinds of love?

* People tend to form relationships with people who are in physical proximity to them.

* People are attracted to others who are similar to them in some way.

* People may also be attracted to people who are different from themselves, with the differences acting as a complementary support for areas in which each may be lacking.

* People tend to like other people who like them in return, a phenomenon called the reciprocity of liking.

* Love is a strong affection for another person due to kinship, personal ties, physical attraction, admiration, or common interests.

* Sternberg states that the three components of love are intimacy, passion, and commitment.

* Romantic love is intimacy with passion, companionate love is intimacy with commitment, and consummate love contains all three components.

* Aggression is behavior intended to hurt or destroy another person, which may be physical or verbal. Frustration is a major source of aggression.

Aggression and Prosocial Behavior

14.11 How is aggressive behavior determined by biology and learning?

* Biological influences on aggression may include genetics, the amygdala and limbic system, and testosterone and serotonin levels.

* Social roles are powerful influences on the expression of aggression. Social learning theory states that aggression can be learned through direct reinforcement and through the imitation of successful aggression by a model.

* Studies have concluded that violent television, movies, and video games stimulate aggressive behavior, both by increasing aggressive tendencies and providing models of aggressive behavior.

* Prosocial behavior is behavior that is socially desirable and benefits others.

14.12 What is altruism, and how is deciding to help someone related to the presence of others?

* Altruism is prosocial behavior in which a person helps someone else without expectation of reward or recognition, often without fear for his or her own safety.

* The bystander effect means that people are more likely to get help from others if there are one or only a few people nearby rather than a larger number. The more people nearby, the less likely it is that help will be offered.

* When others are present at a situation in which help could be offered, there is a diffusion of responsibility among all the bystanders, reducing the likelihood that any one person or persons will feel responsibility for helping.

Classic Studies in Psychology: Latané and Darley

- Researchers Latané and Darley found that people who were alone were more likely to help in an emergency than people who were with others.

- The five steps in making a decision to help are noticing, defining an emergency, taking responsibility, planning a course of action, and taking action.

Applying Psychology to Everyday Life: Anatomy of a Cult

14.13 Why do people join cults?

- People who join cults tend to be under stress, unhappy, unassertive, gullible, dependent, idealistic, and want to belong. Young people are also likelier to join cults than are older people.

- Cults use love-bombing, isolation, rituals, and activities to keep the new recruits from questions and critical thinking. Cults also use the foot-in-the-door technique.

TEST YOURSELF: PREPARING FOR THE AP* EXAM

ANSWERS ON PAGE AK-4.

✓•⌐**Practice on MyPsychLab** **Ready for your test?** More quizzes and a customized study plan. **www.mypsychlab.com**

PART I: MULTIPLE-CHOICE QUESTIONS

Directions for Part I: Read each of the questions or incomplete sentences below. Then choose the response that best answers the question or completes the sentence.

1. Which of the following is least likely to prevent groupthink?
   a. Seeking opinions from outside the group
   b. Ensuring that the group leader is impartial
   c. Discouraging questions and alternate solutions
   d. Voting by secret ballot rather than by a show of hands
   e. Encouraging each group member to speak his or her mind

2. Tami asks her mother, Louise, for permission to go to an all-night party at a friend's house while the friend's parents are away. Louise says absolutely not. Tami accepts Louise's decision. Then, she asks instead to go to a smaller party at another friend's house for a few hours that evening. Louise agrees to this request. Which compliance technique has Tami used?
   a. Lowball
   b. That's-not-all
   c. Foot-in-the-door
   d. Door-in-the-face
   e. Attitude adjustment

3. Sandy loves to play pool and has become quite good at the game. Lately, she has noticed that she seems to play better when there are people watching her than when she is playing alone. This difference in Sandy's playing is most likely the result of _____.
   a. social loafing
   b. social identity
   c. social facilitation
   d. social comparison
   e. social impairment

4. Cognitive dissonance arises when _____.
   a. attitudes do not match behaviors
   b. stereotypes do not match reality
   c. spoken words do not match actions
   d. passion does not match commitment
   e. one person's beliefs do not match others' beliefs

5. Alexei does not show up for soccer practice one day. Which of the following explanations for Alexei's absence is dispositional?
   a. He is irresponsible.
   b. He is stuck in traffic.
   c. He has injured himself.
   d. He has a prior commitment.
   e. He has decided to quit the soccer team.

6. Which explanation of prejudice assumes that the same processes that help form other attitudes form prejudiced attitudes?
   a. Scapegoat
   b. Authoritarian
   c. Social cognitive
   d. Psychodynamic
   e. Realistic conflict

7. The self-fulfilling prophecy is a negative outcome of _____.
   a. scapegoating
   b. social identity
   c. equal status contact
   d. reference grouping
   e. stereotype vulnerability

8. According to Sternberg, committed couples who also have intimacy and passion are in the form of love called _____.
   a. empty love
   b. fatuous love
   c. romantic love
   d. consummate love
   e. companionate love

9. The neurotransmitter that seems to be most involved in aggression is _____.

   a. serotonin

   b. dopamine

   c. glutamate

   d. testosterone

   e. norepinephrine

10. According to a large meta-analysis of the existing research into the connections between violent media and aggressive behavior in children, even short-term exposure to violent media was found to significantly increase the likelihood that children would engage in or experience _____.

   a. aggressive thoughts   **d.** physical aggression

   b. verbal aggression   **e.** All of the above

   c. aggressive emotions

PART II: FREE-RESPONSE QUESTION

Directions for Part II: Read the essay question that follows. Then, respond to the question in a clear, concise essay. Do not simply list facts. Instead, present a thorough argument based on your critical consideration of the topic. Use proper psychological terminology as necessary.

In a well-organized essay, describe how each of the following elements could cause or perpetuate prejudiced attitudes and behaviors. Give examples to support your claims:

   a. Groupthink

   b. Cognitive dissonance

   c. Fundamental attribution error

   d. Stereotype threat

14 VISUAL SUMMARY
Social Psychology

14.1–3   p. 565

conformity
changing one's own behavior to more closely match the actions of others

- several classic studies (i.e., Sherif, Asch) suggest that individuals will change their behaviors to conform to those of a group
- may be influenced by private vs. face-to-face contact, gender, or culture
- **groupthink**

compliance
person changing their behavior due to another person or group asking or directing them to change, often in the absence of any real authority or power

- **foot-in-the-door technique**
- **door-in-the-face technique**
- **lowball technique**
- **that's-not-all technique**

Social Influence
(the ways in which a person's behavior can be affected by other people)

task performance
can be affected by social influence

- **social facilitation** = positive influence
- **social impairment** = negative influence
- **social loafing** occurs when people do not work hard when others are also working; easy to "hide" in a group

obedience
changing one's behavior at the direct order of an authority figure

- a classic study by Milgram (i.e., teacher/learner electrical shock study) indicated that 65% of "teachers" went all the way through shock levels, despite protest from "learners"

Table 14.1   Characteristics of Groupthink

CHARACTERISTIC	DESCRIPTION
Invulnerability	Members feel they cannot fail.
Rationalization	Members explain away warning signs and help each other rationalize their decision.
Lack of introspection	Members do not examine the ethical implications of their decision because they believe that they cannot make immoral choices.
Stereotyping	Members stereotype their enemies as weak, stupid, or unreasonable.
Pressure	Members pressure each other not to question the prevailing opinion.
Lack of disagreement	Members do not express opinions that differ from the group consensus.
Self-deception	Members share in the illusion that they all agree with the decision.
Insularity	Members prevent the group from hearing disruptive but potentially useful information from people who are outside the group.

Source: Janis (1972, 1982).

14.4–5   p. 571

- focuses on the ways in which people think about other people and how those cognitions affect behavior

attitudes
tendency to respond positively or negatively toward a certain idea, person, object, or situation; learned through experience

- comprised of affective, behavioral, and cognitive components
- are not great predictors of behavior although tend to have more influence as they become more specific and salient
- attitude formation can be the result of several processes
- can change through persuasion and are contingent upon both the message and the target audience; elaboration likelihood model suggests that the route/level of information processing (central vs. peripheral) influences ease of persuasion

Social Cognition (part 1)

cognitive dissonance
emotional discomfort as the result of engaging in behavior that is inconsistent with personal cognitions

- can be reduced by 1) changing behavior, 2) changing cognition, or 3) forming new cognitions to justify behavior

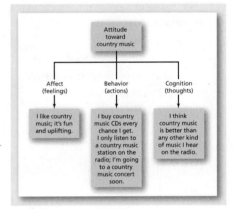

Inducement	Attitude
$1	+1.35
$20	−0.5
Control	−.45

*Based on a −5 to +5 scale, where −5 means "extremely boring" and +5 means "extremely interesting"

14.6–7   p. 576

impression formation
forming of first knowledge about another person; influenced by primacy effect

Social Cognition (part 2)
Impression Formation and Attribution

social categorization
automatic and unconscious assignment of a new acquaintance to some category or group

- **stereotypes**
- categories assigned are based on implicit personality theory, the set of assumptions formed in childhood about different types of people

- attribution is process by which we explain both our own behavior and the behavior of others; based on attribution theory (Heider)
  - **situational**
  - **dispositional**
  - **fundamental attribution error**

14.8–9   p. 581

prejudice — social cognitive theory
unsupported and negative stereotypes (e.g., ageism, sexism, racism, etc.) about members of a particular social group
- social cognitive theory
- social identity theory
- stereotype vulnerability
- prejudice

discrimination
occurs when prejudicial attitudes cause members of a social group to be treated differently than others in situations calling for equal treament

Social Interaction (part 1)
Prejudice and Discrimination
can vary based on existence of in-groups and out-groups — **scapegoating**

realistic conflict theory
suggests that when resources are limited, prejudice and discrimination are closely tied to an increasing degree of conflict between groups that seek common resources

14.10   p. 584

liking or having the desire for a relationship with someone else; can be influenced by a variety of factors
- physical attractiveness
- proximity
- similarity
- complementary qualities
- reciprocity of liking

Social Interaction (part 2)
Interpersonal Attraction

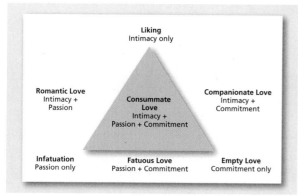

Liking
Intimacy only

Romantic Love
Intimacy + Passion

Consummate Love
Intimacy + Passion + Commitment

Companionate Love
Intimacy + Commitment

Infatuation
Passion only

Fatuous Love
Passion + Commitment

Empty Love
Commitment only

love
strong affection for another person due to kinship, personal ties, physical attraction, admiration, or common interests

Sternberg's triangular theory
suggests different components and types of love

14.11–12   p. 591

aggression may be partly attributed to genetics and can be triggered by variations in brain function (i.e., amygdala activation) and internal or external chemical influences (e.g., testosterone, alcohol)

aggression
occurs when one person verbally or physically hurts or tries to destroy another person; often the result of frustration

much of aggression is influenced by learning but not totally deterministic

Social Interaction (part 3)
Aggression and Prosocial Behavior

prosocial, or socially desirable, behavior benefits others

- **altruism:** helping someone with no expectation of reward and often at personal risk
- can be influenced by helper's mood and victim's gender, attractiveness, or "just rewards"; racial and ethnic differences can decrease probability of helping
- refusal to help another can be negatively affected by the presence of others (bystander effect/diffusion of responsibility) rather than indifference or a lack of sympathy; also influenced by individual's appraisal of situation (see Table 14.3)

Appendix A

STATISTICS IN PSYCHOLOGY

AP* Distinguish the purposes of descriptive statistics and inferential statistics.

A.1 Why do psychologists use statistics?

Why study statistics?

Psychology is a science, and scientists must have ways of describing, summarizing, and analyzing the numerical data gathered through systematic observation and experimentation. Statistics allow researchers to do all of these things in a meaningful, logical fashion.

Many students in psychology wonder why the field uses seemingly such complicated mathematics. The answer is easy. Psychologists base their field on research findings. Data are collected and they have to be analyzed. Statistics is the field that gives us the tools to do that.

Psychologists have to be able to do two things with the data they collect. The first is to summarize the information from a study or experiment. This is the role of **descriptive statistics**. The second is to make judgments and decisions about the data. We are interested if groups differ from each other. We are also interested in how one group of variables is related to another. This second emphasis is known as **inferential statistics**.

Statistical analysis is a way of trying to account for the error that exists in almost any body of data. A **statistic** is typically a number that represents some measure of central tendency or variability. These are described later. Statistics are calculated from a **sample**. The same number calculated from a population is called a **parameter**. If you asked what the average height of teenage males was, and you calculated the average from just your high school, that average would be a statistic. If you tested every teenage male on earth, the average would be a parameter. As you can see parameters are very rarely calculated. Thus, **statistics** is the branch of mathematics that is concerned with the collection and interpretation of data from samples (Agresti & Finlay, 1997; Aron et al., 2005). Psychology is only one of many fields that use the following types of statistics.

Descriptive Statistics

Descriptive statistics are a way of organizing numbers and summarizing them so that they can be understood. There are two main types of descriptive statistics:

- *Measures of Central Tendency.* Measures of central tendency are used to summarize the data and give you one score that seems typical of your sample.

- *Measures of Variability.* Measures of variability are used to indicate how spread out the data are. Are they tightly packed or are they widely dispersed?

The actual descriptive statistics are best understood after we explain the concept of a frequency distribution.

- **A.1** Why do psychologists use statistics?

Descriptive Statistics

- **A.2** What types of tables and graphs represent patterns in data?
- **A.3** What types of statistics examine central tendencies in data?
- **A.4** What types of statistics examine variations in data?

Inferential Statistics

- **A.5** How can statistics be used to determine if differences in sets of data are large enough to be due to something other than chance variation?
- **A.6** How are statistics used to predict one score from another?
- **A.7** Why are skills in statistics important to psychology majors?

---

descriptive statistics a way of organizing numbers and summarizing them so that patterns can be determined.

Inferential statistics statistical analysis of two or more sets of numerical data to reduce the possibility of error in measurement and to determine if the differences between the data sets are greater than chance variation would predict.

statistic a measure of central tendency or variability computed from a sample.

sample group of subjects selected from a larger population of subjects, usually selected randomly.

parameter a number representing some measure of central tendency or variability within a population.

statistics branch of mathematics concerned with the collection and interpretation of numerical data.

AP* Apply basic descriptive statistical concepts, including interpreting and constructing graphs and calculating simple descriptive statistics.

A.2 What types of tables and graphs represent patterns in data?

One way psychologists get started in a research project is to look at their data, but just looking at a list of numbers wouldn't do much good. So we make a graph or chart. Then we can look for patterns.

FREQUENCY DISTRIBUTIONS

A **frequency distribution** is a table or graph that shows how often different numbers, or scores, appear in a particular set of scores. For example, let's say that you have a sample of 30 people, the size of a psychology class. You ask them how many glasses of water they drink each day. You could represent the answers as shown in Table A.1. Just by looking at this table, it is clear that typical people drink between 4 and 8 glasses of water a day.

Tables can be useful, especially when dealing with small sets of data. Sometimes a more visual presentation gives a better "picture" of the patterns in a data set, and that is when researchers use graphs to plot the data from a frequency distribution. One common graph is a **histogram**, or a bar graph. Figure A.1 shows how the same data from Table A.1 would look in a bar graph.

Another type of graph used in frequency distributions is the **polygon**, a line graph. Figure A.2 shows the same data in a polygon graph.

THE NORMAL CURVE

Frequency polygons allow researchers to see the shape of a set of data easily. For example, the number of people drinking glasses of water in Figure A.2 is easily seen to be centered about 6 glasses (central tendency) but drops off below 4 glasses and above 8 glasses a day (variability). Our frequency polygon has a high point and the frequency decreases on both sides.

A common frequency distribution of this type is called the **normal curve**. It has a very specific shape and is sometimes called the **bell curve**. Look at Figure A.3. This curve is almost a perfect normal curve, and many things in life are

Table A.1 A Frequency Distribution

NUMBER OF GLASSES PER DAY	NUMBER OF PEOPLE OUT OF 30 (FREQUENCY)
1	0
2	1
3	2
4	4
5	5
6	6
7	5
8	4
9	2
10	1

frequency distribution a table or graph that shows how often different numbers or scores appear in a particular set of scores.

histogram a bar graph showing a frequency distribution.

polygon line graph showing a frequency distribution.

normal curve a special frequency polygon in which the scores are symmetrically distributed around the mean, and the mean, median, and mode are all located on the same point on the curve with scores decreasing as the curve extends from the mean.

bell curve alternate name for the normal curve, which is said to be shaped like a bell.

Figure A.1 A Histogram

Histograms, or bar graphs, provide a visual way to look at data from frequency distributions. In this graph, for example, the height of the bars indicates that most people drink between 4 and 8 glasses of water (represented by the five highest bars in the middle of the graph).

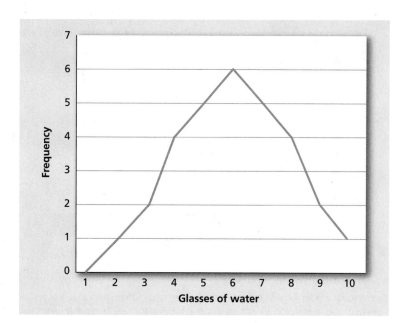

Figure A.2 A Polygon
A polygon is a line graph that can represent the data in a frequency distribution in much the same way as a bar graph but allows the shape of the data set to be easily viewed.

not that perfect. The normal curve is used as a model for many things that are measured, such as intelligence, height, or weight, but even those measures only come close to a perfect distribution (provided large numbers of people are measured). One of the reasons that the normal curve is so useful is that it has very specific relationships to measures of central tendency and a measurement of variability, known as the standard deviation.

Other Distribution Types   Distributions aren't always normal in shape. Some distributions are described as *skewed*. This occurs when the distribution is not even on both sides of a central score with the highest frequency (like in our example). Instead, the scores are concentrated toward one side of the distribution. For example, what if a study of people's water drinking habits in a different class revealed that most people drank around 7 to 8 glasses of water daily, with no one drinking more than 8? The frequency polygon shown in Figure A.4 reflects this very different distribution.

Figure A.3 The Normal Curve
The normal curve, also known as the bell curve because of its unique shape, is often the way in which certain characteristics such as intelligence or weight are represented in the population. The highest point on the curve typically represents the average score in any distribution.

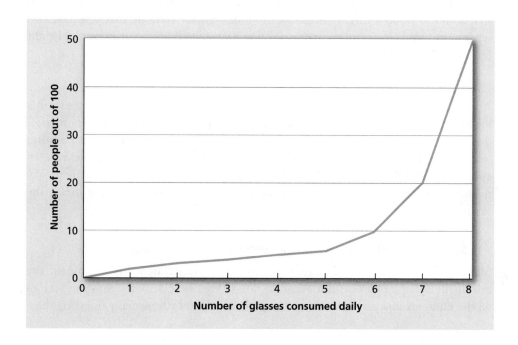

Figure A.4 A Frequency Polygon
Skewed distributions are those in which the most frequent scores occur at one end or the other of the distribution, as represented by this frequency polygon in which most people are seen to drink at least 7 to 8 glasses of water each day.

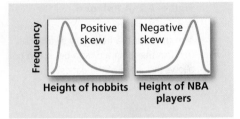

Figure A.5 Skewed Distribution
These frequency polygons show how distributions can be skewed in two different directions. The graph on the left represents the frequency of heights among hobbits (the little people from the fantasy *Lord of the Rings*) and is positively skewed because the long "tail" goes to the right, or positive direction. The graph on the right shows the frequency of heights among NBA basketball players and is negatively skewed—the tail points to the left.

Figure A.6 A Bimodal Distribution
When a distribution is bimodal, it means that there are two high points instead of just one. For example, in the pop-quiz scores represented on this graph there are two "most frequent" scores—6 and 8. This most likely represents two groups of students, with one group being less successful than the other.

In this case, scores are piled up in the high end with most people drinking 7 or 8 glasses of water a day. The graphs in Figure A.5 show a **skewed distribution**. Skewed distributions are called positively or negatively skewed, depending on where the scores are concentrated. A concentration in the high end would be called **negatively skewed**. A concentration in the low end would be called **positively skewed**. The direction of the extended tail determines whether it is positively (tail to right) or negatively (tail to left) skewed. Here's an example. What do you think about the distribution of heights of hobbits (the little guys from the *Lord of the Rings*) and NBA basketball players (who are usually tall)? Might not these frequency distributions of height in Figure A.5 be appropriate?

Some frequency polygons show two high points rather than just one (see Figure A.6) and are called **bimodal distributions**. In this example, we have a distribution of scores from a 10-point pop quiz, and we see that one group of students seemed to do well and one group didn't. Bimodal distributions usually indicate that you have two separate groups being graphed in one polygon. What would the distribution of height for men and women look like?

MEASURES OF CENTRAL TENDENCY

A frequency distribution is a good way to look at a set of numbers, but there's still a lot to look at—isn't there some way to sum it all up? One way to sum up numerical data is to find out what a "typical" score might be, or some central number around which all the others seem to fall. This kind of summation is called a **measure of central tendency**, or the number that best represents the central part of a frequency distribution. There are three different measures of central tendency: the mean, the median, and the mode.

A.3 What types of statistics examine central tendencies in data?

Mean The most commonly used measure of central tendency is the **mean**, the arithmetic average of a distribution of numbers. That simply means that you add up all the numbers in a particular set and then divide them by how many numbers there

skewed distribution frequency distribution in which most of the scores fall to one side or the other of the distribution.

negatively skewed a distribution of scores in which scores are concentrated in the high end of the distribution.

positively skewed a distribution of scores in which scores are concentrated in the low end of the distribution.

bimodal distributions frequency distribution in which there are two high points rather than one.

measure of central tendency numbers that best represent the most typical score of a frequency distribution.

mean the arithmetic average of a distribution of numbers.

are. This is usually the way teachers get the grade point average for a particular student, for example. If Rochelle's grades on the tests she has taken so far are 86, 92, 87, and 90, then the teacher would add 86 + 92 + 87 + 90 = 335, and then divide 355 by four (the number of scores) to get the mean, or grade point average, of 88.75. Here is the formula for the mean:

$$\text{Mean} = \Sigma X/N$$

What does this mean?

- Σ is a symbol called sigma. It is a Greek letter and it is also called the summation sign.

- X represents a score. Rochelle's grades are represented by X.

- ΣX means add up or sum all the X scores or
  $\Sigma X = 86 + 92 + 87 + 90 = 355$.

- N means the number of scores. In this case, there are four grades.

  We then divide the sum of the scores (ΣX) by N to get the mean or

$$\text{Mean} = \Sigma X/N = \frac{355}{4} = 88.75$$

The mean is a good way to find a central tendency if the set of scores clusters around the mean with no extremely different scores that are either far higher or far lower than the mean.

Median *I remember that sometimes my teacher would "curve" the grades for a test, and it was always bad when just one person did really well and everyone else did lousy—is that what you mean about extremely different scores?* Yes, the mean doesn't work as well when there are extreme scores, as you would have if only two students out of an entire class had a perfect score of 100 and everyone else scored in the seventies or lower. If you want a truer measure of central tendency in such a case, you need one that isn't affected by extreme scores. The **median** is just such a measure. A median is the score that falls in the middle of an *ordered* distribution of scores. Half of the scores will fall above the median, and half of the scores will fall below it. If the distribution contains an odd number of scores, it's just the middle number, but if the number of scores is even, it's the average of the two middle scores. The median is also the 50th percentile. Look at Table A.2 for an example of the median.

The mean IQ of this group would be 114.6, but the median would be 101 (the average between Evan with 102 and Fethia with 100, the average of the two middle numbers). This may not look like much of a difference, but it's really a change of about 13.6 IQ points—a big difference. Also, think about measures of income in a particular area. If most people earn around $23,000 per year in a particular area, but there are just a few extremely wealthy people in the same area who earn $1,000,000 a year, a mean of all the annual incomes would no doubt make the area look like it was doing much better than it really is economically. The median would be a more accurate measure of the central tendency of such data.

median the middle score in an ordered distribution of scores, or the mean of the two middle numbers; the 50th percentile.

◄ I remember that sometimes my teacher would "curve" the grades for a test, and it was always bad when just one person did really well and everyone else did lousy—is that what you mean about extremely different scores?

Table A.2	**Intelligence Test Scores For 10 People**								
NAME	ALLISON	BEN	CAROL	DENISE	EVAN	FETHIA	GEORGE	HAL	INGA	JAY
IQ	160	150	139	103	102	100	100	100	98	95

Mode   The **mode** is another measure of central tendency in which the most frequent score is taken as the central measure. In the numbers given in the preceding example, the mode would be 100 because that number appears more times in the distribution than any other. Three people have that score. This is the simplest measure of central tendency and is also more useful than the mean in some cases, especially when there are two sets of frequently appearing scores. For example, suppose a teacher notices that on the last exam the scores fall into two groups, with about 15 students making a 95 and another 14 students making a 67. The mean *and* the median would probably give a number somewhere between those two scores—such as 80. That number tells the teacher a lot less about the distribution of scores than the mode would because, in this case, the distribution is **bimodal**—there are two very different yet very frequent scores (See Figure A.6 for another example.)

Measures of Central Tendency and the Shape of the Distribution   When the distribution is normal or close to it, the mean, median, and mode are the same or very similar. There is no problem. When the distribution is not normal, then the situation requires a little more explanation.

Skewed Distributions   If the distribution is skewed, then the mean is pulled in the direction of the tail of the distribution. The mode is still the highest point and the median is between the two. Let's look at an example. In Figure A.7 we have a distribution of salaries at a company. A few people make a low wage, most make a midlevel wage, and the bosses make a lot of money. This gives us a positively skewed distribution with the measures of central tendency placed as in the figure. As mentioned earlier, with such a distribution, the median would be the best measure of central tendency to report. If the distribution were negatively skewed (tail to the left), the order of the measures of central tendency would be reversed.

Bimodal Distributions   If you have a bimodal distribution, then none of the measures of central tendency will do you much good. You need to discover why you have seemingly two groups in your one distribution.

MEASURES OF VARIABILITY

A.4 What types of statistics examine variations in data?
Descriptive statistics can also determine how much the scores in a distribution differ, or vary, from the central tendency of the data. These **measures of variability** are used to discover how "spread out" the scores are from each other. The more the scores cluster around the central scores, the smaller the measure of variability will be, and the more widely the scores differ from the central scores, the larger this measurement will be.

There are two ways that variability is measured. The simpler method is by calculating the **range** of the set of scores, or the difference between the highest score and the lowest score in the set of scores. The range is somewhat limited as a measure of variability when there are extreme scores in the distribution. For example, if you look at Table A.2, the range of those IQ scores would be 160 − 95, or 65. But if you just look at the numbers, you can see that there really isn't that much variation except for the three highest scores of 138, 150, and 160.

The other measure of variability that is commonly used is the one that is related to the normal curve, the **standard deviation**. This measurement is simply the square root of the average squared difference, or deviation, of the scores from the

---

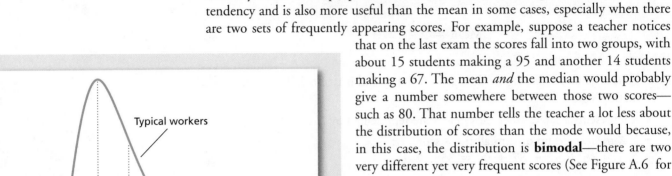

Figure A.7 Positively Skewed Distribution

In a skewed distribution, the high scores on one end will cause the mean to be pulled toward the tail of the distribution, making it a poor measure of central tendency for this kind of distribution. For example, in this graph many workers make very little money (represented by the mode) while only a few workers make a lot of money (the tail). The mean in this case would be much higher than the mode because of those few high scores distorting the average. In this case, the median is a much better measure of central tendency because it tends to be unaffected by extremely high or extremely low scores such as those in this distribution.

mode   the most frequent score in a distribution of scores.

bimodal   condition in which a distribution has two modes.

measures of variability   measurement of the degree of differences within a distribution or how the scores are spread out.

range   the difference between the highest and lowest scores in a distribution.

standard deviation   the square root of the average squared deviations from the mean of scores in a distribution; a measure of variability.

mean of the distribution. The mathematical formula for finding the standard deviation looks complicated, but it is really nothing more than taking each individual score, subtracting the mean from it, squaring that number (because some numbers will be negative and squaring them gets rid of the negative value), and adding up all of those squares. Then this total is divided by the number of scores and the square root of that number is the standard deviation. In the IQ example, it would go like this:

$$\text{Standard Deviation Formula} \quad SD = \sqrt{[\Sigma(X - M)^2/N]}$$

The mean (M) of the 10 IQ scores is 114.6. To calculate the standard deviation we

1. Subtract each score from the mean to get a deviation score $\rightarrow (X - M)$
2. We square each deviation score $\rightarrow (X - M)^2$
3. We add them up. Remember that's what the sigma (Σ) indicates $\rightarrow \Sigma(X - M)^2$
4. We divide the sum of the squared deviation by N (the number of scores) $\rightarrow \Sigma(X - M)^2/N$
5. We take the square root ($\sqrt{}$) of the sum for our final step. $\sqrt{[\Sigma(X - M)^2/N]}$

The process is laid out in Table A.3.

The standard deviation is equal to 41.9. What that tells you is that this particular group of data deviates, or varies, from the central tendencies quite a bit—there are some very different scores in the data set, or in this particular instance, three noticeably different scores.

This procedure may look very complicated. Let us assure you that computers and inexpensive calculators can figure out the standard deviation simply by entering the numbers and pressing a button. No one does a standard deviation by hand anymore.

How does the standard deviation relate to the normal curve? Let's look at the classic distribution of IQ scores. It has a mean of 115 and a standard deviation of 15 as set up by the test designers. It is a bell curve. With a true normal curve, researchers

---

Table A.3 Finding the Standard Deviation

SCORE	DEVIATION FROM THE MEAN ($X \pm M$)	SQUARED DEVIATION ($X \pm M$)^2
160.00	45.40	2,061.16
	(ex. 160 − 114.60 = 45.40)	(45.40^2 = 2,061.16)
150.00	35.40	1,253.16
139.00	24.40	595.36
102.00	−12.60	158.76
102.00	−12.60	158.76
100.00	−14.60	213.16
100.00	−14.60	213.16
100.00	−14.60	213.16
98.00	−16.60	275.56
95.00	−19.60	384.16

Sum of Scores
(ΣX) = 1,146.00   ($\Sigma X - M$) = 0.00   ($\Sigma X - M$)^2 = 5,526.40

Mean = (ΣX)/N Standard Deviation

= 1,146/10 = 114.60   = $\sqrt{[\Sigma(X - M)^2/N]}$

    = $\sqrt{5,526.40/10}$ = 23.5

Standard Deviations	-4	-3	-2	-1	0	1	2	3	4
Wechsler IQ	40	55	70	85	100	115	130	145	160
Stanford-Binet 4 IQ	36	52	68	84	100	116	132	148	164
Cumulative %		0.003	0.135	2.275	15.856	50.00	84.134	97.725	99.865	99.997

Figure A.8 IQ Normal Curve

Scores on intelligence tests are typically represented by the normal curve. The dotted vertical lines each represent one standard deviation from the mean, which is always set at 100. For example, an IQ of 116 on the Stanford-Binet Fourth Edition (Stanford-Binet 4) represents one standard deviation above the mean, and the area under the curve indicates that 34.13 percent of the population falls between 100 and 116 on that test. The Stanford-Binet Fifth Edition was published in 2003 and it now has a mean of 100 and a standard deviation of 15 for composite scores.

know exactly what percent of the population lies under the curve between each standard deviation from the mean. For example, notice that in the percentages in Figure A.8, one standard deviation above the mean has 34.13 percent of the population represented by the graph under that section. These are the scores between the IQs of 100 and 115. One standard deviation below the mean (–1) has exactly the same percent, 34.13, under that section— the scores between 85 and 100. This means that 68.26 percent of the population falls within one standard deviation from the mean, or one average "spread" from the center of the distribution. For example, "giftedness" is normally defined as having an IQ score that is two standard deviations *above* the mean. On the Wechsler Intelligence Scales, this means having an IQ of 130 or greater because the Wechsler's standard deviation is 15. But if the test a person took to determine giftedness was the Stanford-Binet Fourth Edition (the previous version of the test), the IQ score must have been 132 or greater because the standard deviation of that test was 16, not 15. The current version, the Stanford-Binet Fifth Edition, was published in 2003 and it now has a mean of 100 and a standard deviation of 15 for composite scores.

Although the "tails" of this normal curve seem to touch the bottom of the graph, in theory they go on indefinitely, never touching the base of the graph. In reality, though, any statistical measurement that forms a normal curve will have 99.72 percent of the population it measures falling within three standard deviations either above or below the mean. Because this relationship between the standard deviation and the normal curve does not change, it is always possible to compare different test scores or sets of data that come close to a normal curve distribution. This is done by computing a **z score**, which indicates how many standard deviations you are away from the mean. It is calculated by subtracting the mean from your score and dividing by the standard deviation. For example, if you had an IQ of 115, your z score would be 1.0. If you had an IQ of 70, your z score would –2.0. So on any exam if you had a high z score you did well. A low z score means you didn't do that well. The formula for a z score is:

$$Z = (X - M)/SD$$

Inferential Statistics

A.5 How can statistics be used to determine if differences in sets of data are large enough to be due to something other than chance variation?

Descriptive methods of statistics are not useful when it comes to comparing sets of numbers or scores to see if there are differences between them that are great enough to be caused by something other than chance variation. Inferential statistics consist of statistical techniques that allow researchers to determine the difference between results of a study that are meaningful and those that are merely due to chance variations. Inferential statistics also allow researchers to draw conclusions, or make *inferences*, about the results of research and about whether those results are only true for the specific group of animals or people involved in the study or whether the results can be applied to, or *generalized* to, the larger population from which the study participants were selected.

z score a statistical measure that indicates how far away from the mean a particular score is in terms of the number of standard deviations that exist between the mean and that score.

For example, in Dr. Amabile's classic study described in Chapter One, there were a lot of variables that she simply could not control completely, even with random assignment of her participants to the two conditions. (L I N K) *to Chapter One: The Science of Psychology, pp. 32–33.* There was no guarantee that random assignment would take away all of the interfering effects of having children with different artistic abilities at the beginning of the study, or who had breakfast and who didn't, or whether or not some children really didn't want those tacky old prizes anyway. So maybe any difference found between the two groups was due to pure luck or chance and not the independent variable under study.

In any analysis that compares two or more sets of data, there's always the possibility of error in the data that comes from either within the group (all participants in one group, for example, will not be exactly like each other) or differences between groups (the experimental group and the control group are formed with different people, so there are differences between the two groups that have nothing to do with the manipulations of the experimenter). When researchers want to know if the differences they find in the data that come from studies like Dr. Amabile's are large enough to be caused by the experimental manipulation and *not* just by the chance differences that exist within and between groups, they have to use a kind of statistical technique that can take those chance variations into account. These kinds of statistical analysis use inferential statistics.

Inferential statistical analysis also allows researchers to determine how much confidence they should have in the results of a particular experiment. As you might remember, results from other kinds of studies that look for relationships—observations, surveys, and case studies—are often analyzed with descriptive statistics, especially correlations. But experiments look for *causes* of relationships, and researchers want to have some evidence that the results of their experiments really mean what they think they mean.

There are many different kinds of inferential statistical methods. The method that is used depends on the design of the experiment, such as the number of independent and dependent variables or the number of experimental groups. All inferential statistics have one thing in common—they look for differences in group measurements that are **statistically significant**. Statistical significance is a way to test differences to see how likely those differences are to be real and not just caused by the random variations in behavior that exist in everything animals and people do.

For example, in Dr. Amabile's study, her results showed that the collages of the children who were promised the prizes (an extrinsic reward) were judged to be less creative than those of the children who created collages just for fun. But was that difference between the creativity scores of the two groups a real difference, or was it merely due to chance variations in the children's artistic creations? Dr. Amabile used an inferential test on her results that told her that the difference was too big to be just chance variations, which means her results were *significant*—they were most likely to be real differences. How likely? Tests of significance give researchers the probability that the results of their experiment were caused by chance and not by their experimental manipulation. For example, in one test called a ***t*-test**, the scores of the children's artwork would have been placed into a formula that would result in a single number (t) that evaluates the probability that the difference between the two group means is due to pure chance or luck. That number would be compared to a value that exists in a table of possible t values, which tells researchers the probability of the result is due to chance or luck. If the number obtained by the calculation is bigger than the value in the table, there will be a probability associated with that number in the table. The probability, symbolized by the letter p, will tell researchers the probability of the difference was due to chance. In Dr. Amabile's case, the probability was $p < .05$ which means the probability that the results were due to chance alone was less than 5 out of 100. Another way of stating the same result is that Dr. Amabile could be 95 percent

statistically significant referring to differences in data sets that are larger than chance variation would predict.

***t*-test** type of inferential statistical analysis typically used when two means are compared to see if they are significantly different.

significant difference a difference between groups of numerical data that is considered large enough to be due to factors other than chance variation.

correlation coefficient a number that represents the strength and direction of a relationship existing between two variables.

certain that her results were real and not due to chance. Dr. Amabile would, thus, report that the study found a **significant difference**, which means a difference thought not to be due to chance.

There are several statistical techniques to test if groups are different from each other. Here are some common ones you might encounter if you read journal articles.

- *t*-test—determines if two means are different from each other
- *F*-test or analysis of variance—determines if three or more means are different from each other. Can also evaluate more than one independent variable at a time.
- chi-square—compares frequencies of proportions between groups to see if they are different. For example, the proportion of women hired at a company is too low and might indicate discrimination. *Chi* is pronounced like the beginning of the word *kite*. Don't say "chee." It will be ugly.

If you do take a statistics course, you will find out that most analyses are done by computers and you don't have to manually go through the long formulas.

A.6 How are statistics used to predict one score from another?

We've already talked about the correlation coefficient. Let's see how psychologists can predict one variable from another by using it. LINK to *Chapter One: The Science of Psychology*, pp. 26–28.

THE CORRELATION COEFFICIENT

A *correlation* is a measure of the relationship between two or more variables. For example, if you wanted to know if scores on the SAT are related to grade point average, you could get SAT scores and GPAs from a group of people and enter those numbers into a mathematical formula, which will produce a number called the **correlation coefficient**. The correlation coefficient represents the direction of the relationship and its strength. Chapter One (pp. 26–27) discusses correlation in more detail and also emphasizes that correlation does not allow the assumption that one variable causes the other.

> **Is the formula for the correlation coefficient really complicated?**

Is the formula for the correlation coefficient really complicated? Actually, the definitional formula for finding a correlation coefficient is not very complicated. Here it is:

$$r = \frac{\sum Z_x Z_y}{n}$$

The *r* is the *correlation coefficient*, the number representing the strength and direction of the relationship between the two variables. Z_x and Z_y are the *z* scores for each score. If you remember, the *z* score tells you how many standard deviations a score is away from the mean. You would calculate the Z_x and Z_y for each subject, multiply, and add them up. Then divide by the number of subjects. There is a very complicated-looking formula based on the raw scores.

$$r = \frac{\sum XY - \frac{\sum X \sum Y}{N}}{\sqrt{\left(\sum X^2 - \frac{(\sum X)^2}{N}\right)\left(\sum Y^2 - \frac{(\sum Y)^2}{N}\right)}}$$

Don't worry. You can do all this work on inexpensive calculators or on computers using common statistical programs or spreadsheets. Let's take the following example of two sets of scores, one on a test of drawing ability with scores from 1 (poor) to 5 (excellent) and the other on a test of writing ability using the same scale.

	Drawing (X)	**Writing (Y)**
Student 1	3	5
Student 2	1	2
Student 3	2	3
Student 4	4	4
Student 5	1	3
Student 6	4	6
Student 7	2	3
Student 8	3	4
Student 9	5	5
Student 10	1	2

If we plugged our data set into our calculator or spreadsheet, we would find that r (the correlation coefficient) equals 0.86. That would indicate a fairly strong correlation. If you go on in statistics, you will find out how to see if the correlation coefficient we calculated is statistically significant or, if you recall, not due to just dumb luck when we picked our subjects. In our case, the r is very significant and would happen by chance only 1 in 100 times!

Remember that the correlation coefficient has values that range between $+1.0$ and -1.0. The closer the r is to these values, the stronger the relationship. A positive r means a positive relationship, whereas a negative r means a negative relationship.

Our example had us trying to see if two scores were related. It is also possible to see if three or more scores are related with various techniques. The most common one is called multiple regression.

A.7 Why are skills in statistics important to psychology majors?

We have taken a look at describing data, seeing if groups differ from each other and seeing if two variables are related to each other. Those are the basic ideas of psychological statistics. The more advanced techniques are just bigger and better versions of these ideas. Many psych students sometimes panic at the thought of taking statistics. However, it is crucial to the field and not really that hard if you put your mind to it and don't freeze yourself up. Here's a practical hint. Students with good research and statistical skills are much more employable and make more money than those who don't try to master research skills. It's nice to care about people but you need all the skills you can get in today's world. Statistics and research design is one really profitable set of skills.

A CHAPTER SUMMARY

A.1 Why do psychologists use statistics?

• Statistics is a branch of mathematics that involves the collection, description, and interpretation of numerical data.

Descriptive Statistics

• Descriptive statistics are ways of organizing numbers and summarizing them so that they can be understood.

• Inferential statistics are ways of determining if groups are different and if two or more variables are related.

A.2 What types of tables and graphs represent patterns in data?

• Frequency distributions are tables or graphs that show the patterns in a set of scores and can be a table, a bar graph or histogram, or a line graph or polygon.

A.3 What types of statistics examine central tendencies in data?

• Measures of central tendency are ways of finding numbers that best represent the center of a distribution of numbers and include the mean, median, and mode.

- The normal curve is a special frequency polygon that is symmetrical and has the mean, median, and mode as the highest point on the curve.

A.4 What types of statistics examine variations in data?

- Measures of variability provide information about the differences within a set of numbers and include the range and the standard deviation.

Inferential Statistics

A.5 How can statistics be used to determine if differences in sets of data are large enough to be due to something other than chance variation?

- Inferential statistics involves statistical analysis of two or more sets of numerical data to reduce the possibility of error in measurement and determine statistical significance of the results of research.

A.6 How are statistics used to predict one score from another?

- The correlation coefficient is a number that represents the strength and direction of a relationship existing between two variables.

A.7 Why are skills in statistics important to psychology majors?

- Students who understand the process of research and the statistical methods used in research are more desirable to many university and business institutions than those who lack such skills.

TEST YOURSELF: PREPARING FOR THE AP* EXAM

ANSWERS ON PAGE AK-4.

Directions: Read each of the questions or incomplete sentences below. Then choose the response that best answers the question or completes the sentence.

1. Which of following research methods compares sets of numbers or scores to see if the differences between them are greater than chance variations?
   a. Scientific method
   b. Critical thinking
   c. Analytical statistics
   d. Descriptive statistics
   e. Inferential statistics

2. What are researchers able to determine through the use of inferential statistics?
   a. The significant difference
   b. Causes of differences in data
   c. Central tendencies in data
   d. Variability in data
   e. The range of the highest to lowest scores

3. Which of the following cannot be determined through the use of descriptive statistics?
   a. Significant difference
   b. Measures of variability
   c. Frequency distributions
   d. Measures of central tendency
   e. All of the above

4. A table that shows how often different numbers, or scores, appear in a set of scores is called a frequency _____.
   a polygon
   b. histogram
   c. deviation
   d. distribution
   e. normal curve

5. The normal curve is a special kind of _____.
   a. pie chart
   b. scattergram
   c. frequency distribution
   d. inferential statistic
   e. measure of central tendency

6. Which of the following statements describes a normal curve?
   a. The mean, median, and mode are all the same.
   b. The standard deviation is located at the highest point on the curve.
   c. The median is on the highest point while the mean and mode are on either side of the median.
   d. The mean is on the highest point while the median and mode are on either side of the mean.
   e. The standard deviation is located between the mean and the mode.

7. What approximate percent of the population is said to fall between one standard deviation above and one standard deviation below the mean on a normal curve?
   a. 12 percent
   b. 34 percent
   c. 50 percent
   d. 68 percent
   e. 100 percent

8. In a skewed distribution, the scores _____.
   a. are concentrated on both sides of the mean
   b. are concentrated on one side of the distribution
   c. have two low points instead of one
   d. have two high points instead of one
   e. are evenly distributed around the mean

9. In the set of numbers 2, 2, 2, 3, 5, 5, 6, 8, 15, the median would be _____.
   a. 2   d. 5.75
   b. 5   e. 6
   c. 5.33

10. Errors in data _____.
    a. come only from within a group
    b. come only from between different groups
    c. come from both between and within groups
    d. can be completely eliminated by random assignment
    e. all of the above

Appendix B

APPLIED PSYCHOLOGY AND PSYCHOLOGY CAREERS

Why study applied psychology?

Many different kinds of psychologists study or work in many different fields. Whereas early psychologists were still discovering the processes that govern the human mind, today's psychologists are more often applying information and principles gained from research to people in the real world. Why study careers in psychology? With so many different areas of focus, a career in psychology can be varied and exciting. There is much more to psychology than helping people who have mental health problems.

Peggy was a little startled when she received a phone call from her daughter Katy's grade school counselor. The counselor asked Peggy to come to the school the following afternoon for a conference with Katy's teachers. At the conference, Peggy was relieved to learn that Katy, far from being in trouble at school, had been tested and found to be a gifted child. Gifted children are those who score on the upper end of intelligence tests, and Katy had scored very well indeed.

The counselor and teachers explained that Katy, as a gifted child, needed to have a special educational plan drawn up to ensure that she received the education best suited to her abilities. This plan is called an **individualized educational program**, or **IEP** (Sellin & Birch, 1981; U.S. Department of Education, 2000). An IEP is required for children with special needs, such as learning problems or intellectual delay, but many school districts require an IEP for gifted children as well.

Peggy was asked to look at the plan Katy's teachers and counselor had developed, which included a summary of Katy's current performance levels and both short-term and long-term goals for her educational future. For example, the counselor and teachers wanted to work on helping Katy develop better organizational skills and improve her handwriting. Peggy was asked for her input, and then she and the teachers and counselor signed the IEP for Katy. They told Peggy that a new IEP would be developed for Katy each year.

What Is Applied Psychology?

- **B.1** What is the definition of applied psychology?

Psychology as a Career

- **B.2** What are the different types of psychological professionals?
- **B.3** What kinds of careers are available to someone with a bachelor's degree in psychology?
- **B.4** What are the areas of specialization in psychology?

Psychology Beyond the Classroom

- **B.5** How does psychology interact with other career fields?

Psychology and Work

- **B.6** What are industrial/ organizational psychology and human factors psychology?

Applying Psychology to Everyday Life: Techniques Used by Sports Psychologists

- **B.7** What are some techniques used in sports psychology?

individualized educational program (IEP) a special education plan drawn up by teachers for children with special needs such as giftedness or mental retardation.

Peggy's experience with the IEP is one small example of how psychology can be used in the real world, in this case, by those in the field of *educational psychology* who examine the process of learning and look for ways to improve learning in children and adults. Educational psychology is one of many areas in which psychological principles can be applied to issues and concerns of everyday life. This appendix will look at just some of the areas of applied psychology, as well as the types of careers open to someone who studies psychology today.

What Is Applied Psychology?

B.1 What is the definition of applied psychology?

The term **applied psychology** refers to using findings from psychological research to solve real-world problems. The psychological professional, who might be a psychiatrist, psychologist, or even a psychiatric social worker as described here and in Chapter One, may do testing or use some other type of assessment and then describe a plan of action intended to solve whatever problem is of concern. In the opening story, the problem revolved around delivering the best possible education to a gifted child. The counselor tested Katy in several different ways to determine not only her gifted status but also areas in which she needed help, such as her organizational skills. Then the counselor and teachers used that information to devise Katy's IEP. This is a practical application of psychological tools to a real problem—the counselor literally "applies" psychology.

> It seems to me that psychology could be useful in a lot of different areas, not just education. In fact, wasn't that what all those "Applying Psychology" sections at the end of each chapter were about?

It seems to me that psychology could be useful in a lot of different areas, not just education. In fact, wasn't that what all those "Applying Psychology" sections at the end of each chapter were about? Every chapter in this text (and even this appendix) does end with some application of psychology to the real world. The field of applied psychology isn't just one field but rather a lot of different areas that all share the common goal of using psychology in a practical way. A large number of areas can be considered applied psychology, including one of the broadest areas of psychology: clinical and counseling psychology. There are health psychologists who examine the effects of stress on physical as well as mental health, educational and school psychologists, sports psychologists who help athletes prepare themselves mentally for competition, human factors psychologists who deal with the way people and machines interact, forensic psychologists who deal with psychological issues within the legal system, and industrial/organizational (I/O) psychologists who deal with the work environment. There are also environmental psychologists who look at the interaction of people with their surroundings at work, in social settings, and in schools, homes, and other buildings. Those surroundings include not just the physical structures but also the particular population of people who live, work, and play in those surroundings. Other psychologists look at the factors that influence people to buy certain products or the best ways to market a product and examine the buying habits of the typical consumer.

This appendix includes information on the different types of psychological professionals and the type of education required for each profession with a brief overview of many of the specialized areas in psychology. The rest of this appendix briefly explores how psychology can be used in a practical way in several different areas of life: the environment, law, education, sports, and the world of work.

applied psychology the use of psychological concepts in solving real-world problems.

Psychology as a Career

When most people think of psychology as a potential career, they assume certain things about the profession: For example, to help people with their problems one has to be a psychologist, all psychologists are doctors, and all psychologists counsel mentally ill people. None of these assumptions is completely true.

TYPES OF PSYCHOLOGICAL PROFESSIONALS

B.2   What are the different types of psychological professionals?

There are several types of professionals who work in psychology. These professionals have different training with different focuses and may have different goals. Chapter One (pp. 16–17) briefly describes the differences among these types of professionals, and that material is expanded in the following descriptions.

Psychiatrists   A **psychiatrist** has a medical doctorate (M.D.) degree and is a medical doctor who has specialized in the diagnosis and treatment of psychological disorders. Like any other medical doctor who may specialize in emergency medicine, treating the diseases of the elderly, treating infants and children, or any other special area of medicine, psychiatrists are able to write prescriptions and perform medical procedures on their patients. They simply have special training in the diagnosis and treatment of disorders that are considered to be mental disorders, such as schizophrenia, depression, or extreme anxiety. Because they are medical doctors, they tend to have a biopsychological perspective on the causes and treatments for such disorders.

Psychoanalysts   A **psychoanalyst** is either a psychiatrist (M.D.) or a psychologist (doctor of philosophy or Ph.D.) who has special training in the theories of Sigmund Freud and his method of psychoanalysis. (There are nearly three dozen institutes at which this training takes place today.) Today's psychoanalysts may be more direct and take less time to get to the heart of a client's problems, but they still follow many of Freud's original principles and methods.

Psychiatric Social Workers   A **psychiatric social worker** is trained in the area of social work and usually possesses a master of social work (M.S.W.) degree and may be licensed in the state they work as a licensed clinical social worker (L.C.S.W.). These professionals focus more on the environmental conditions that can have an impact on mental disorders, such as poverty, overcrowding, stress, and drug abuse. They may administer psychotherapy (talking with clients about their problems) and often work in a clinical setting where other types of psychological professionals are available.

Psychologists   A **psychologist** has no medical training. Instead, psychologists undergo intense academic training, learning about many different areas of psychology before choosing an area in which to specialize. Psychologists may have either a doctor of philosophy (Ph.D.) or doctor of psychology (Psy.D.) degree. (People who hold a master of science or M.S. degree are not usually called psychologists except in a few states. They can be called therapists or counselors, or they may be teachers or researchers.)

What's the difference between a Ph.D. and a Psy.D.? The Ph.D. is a type of degree that usually indicates the highest degree of learning available in almost any subject area—psychology, the study of languages, education, philosophy, the sciences, and many others. It is typically very research oriented, and earning the degree usually requires a previous master's degree in addition to course work for the doctorate itself,

psychiatrist   a medical doctor who specializes in the diagnosis and treatment of psychological disorders.

psychoanalyst   either a psychiatrist or a psychologist who has special training in the theories of Sigmund Freud and his method of psychoanalysis.

psychiatric social worker   a social worker with some training in therapy methods who focuses on the environmental conditions that can have an impact on mental disorders, such as poverty, overcrowding, stress, and drug abuse.

psychologist   a professional with an academic degree and specialized training in one or more areas of psychology.

Psychologists specialize in many different areas and work in many different settings. This child psychologist is evaluating the young boy by using puppets and dolls to encourage the boy to talk about his feelings.

◄   What's the difference between a Ph.D. and a Psy.D.?

as well as a dissertation—a scholarly work of research in the area of focus that is as long as a book and may even be published as a book.

The Psy.D. is a type of degree developed in the late 1970s that is focused less on research and more on the practical application of psychological principles (Peterson, 1976, 1982). In addition to academic course work such as that required for the Ph.D., this degree may require a major paper instead of a dissertation, with the difference being that the paper is not a report of research designed and conducted by the student but is rather a large-scale term paper. Each year of a Psy.D. program will also require the student to participate in a *practicum,* an actual experience with observing and eventually conducting therapy and treatments under supervision.

Unlike psychiatrists, psychologists typically cannot prescribe medicines or perform medical procedures. Some states allow psychologists to prescribe medication if they have received special education in the use of prescription drugs. The reasoning behind this move, for which the American Psychological Association has been lobbying since 1984, involves both cost and the delay in receiving mental health services. If a person sees a psychologist and then has to go to a psychiatrist for medical prescriptions, the cost can be prohibitive. There are also fewer psychiatrists in some states than in others, causing long waits for mental health services from those doctors— delays that can sometimes lead to an increase in suicide rates for patients who are not getting the help they need.

Although some psychologists take the special training to become psychoanalysts, many do not. Psychologists who are counselors or therapists may use some techniques that have little to do with Freud's original ideas. **LINK** *to Chapter Thirteen: Psychological Therapies, pp. 518–519.* In fact, many psychologists do no counseling at all. There are psychologists who only teach at colleges or universities, those who do only research in those same institutions or for industries, and those who do a combination of teaching and research. Other psychologists are involved in designing equipment and workplaces, developing educational methods, or working as consultants to businesses and the court system.

Although becoming a psychologist requires a doctorate degree of some kind, many career fields can benefit from a four-year college degree in psychology as the basis of that career.

CAREERS WITH A BACHELOR'S DEGREE IN PSYCHOLOGY

B.3 What kinds of careers are available to someone with a bachelor's degree in psychology?

Although people earning only the baccalaureate (bachelor's) degree in psychology cannot be called psychologists or provide therapy in a private practice, there are many career fields open to such a person. A bachelor's degree in psychology can be highly flexible and adaptable to many different kinds of careers (Landrum & Davis, 2007; Schwartz, 2000). In the 1994–1995 *Psychology Baccalaureate Survey* conducted by the American Psychological Association (Grocer & Kohout, 1997), people with bachelor's degrees in psychology found careers in the following areas:
- education and teaching
- consulting and statistical analysis
- administration or clerical services
- professional services
- sales
- health and health-related services
- research and development or research and development management

Constance Newman (left) is a Peace Corps volunteer. Using skills she developed while obtaining a bachelor's degree in psychology, Constance is trying to help this Mbankono woman understand the importance of having her child immunized against diseases such as measles.

Many people with a bachelor's degree in psychology work in mental health related fields, such as this school counselor introducing students to a therapy dog.

Other possible careers include marketing researcher, social worker, and communications specialist (Landrum & Davis, 2007; Schwartz, 2000). With its emphasis on critical thinking and empirical observation, psychology trains people for a variety of potential workplace environments and requirements. Psychology is an excellent undergraduate major even if you intend to do graduate work in some other career: Business, law, child care, teaching, and management are only a few of the areas that relate to psychology.

AREAS OF SPECIALIZATION

You said that some psychologists teach or do research. What kind of research do they do? There are many different areas in which psychologists may focus their energies. They conduct experiments, surveys, observations, and so on to gather more information for their particular field of interest, to find support for current theories, or to develop new ones. Let's look at some of the areas in which psychologists may specialize.

◄ **You said that some psychologists teach or do research. What kind of research do they do?**

B.4 What are the areas of specialization in psychology?

Clinical Psychology Even though not all psychologists do counseling or therapy, many psychologists do. **Clinical psychology** is the most similar of the areas to psychiatry. Clinical psychologists, like psychiatrists, diagnose and treat psychological disorders in people. However, the clinical psychologist cannot prescribe drugs or medical therapies (with the exceptions discussed earlier, of course) but instead relies on listening to the client's problems, administering psychological tests, and then providing explanations for the client's behavior and feelings as well as advising the client on how to make positive changes in his or her life.

◄ **AP*** Distinguish the different domains of psychology.

Counseling Psychology **Counseling psychology** is similar to clinical psychology in that this type of psychologist diagnoses and treats problems. The difference is that a counseling psychologist usually works with people who have less severe problems, such as adjustment to stress, marriage, family life, work problems, and so on. Counseling psychologists and clinical psychologists make up nearly 60 percent of all psychologists currently in the field (NSF/NIH/USED/NEH/USDA/NASA, 2000). (L)(I)(N)(K) *to Chapter One: The Science of Psychology, p. 18.*

clinical psychology area of psychology in which the psychologists diagnose and treat people with psychological disorders that may range from mild to severe.

counseling psychology area of psychology in which the psychologists help people with problems of adjustment.

developmental psychology area of psychology in which the psychologists study the changes in the way people think, relate to others, and feel as they age.

experimental psychology area of psychology in which the psychologists primarily do research and experiments in the areas of learning, memory, thinking, perception, motivation, and language.

social psychology area of psychology in which the psychologists focus on how human behavior is affected by the presence of other people.

personality psychology area of psychology in which the psychologists study the differences in personality among people.

physiological psychology area of psychology in which the psychologists study the biological bases of behavior.

comparative psychology area of psychology in which the psychologists study animals and their behavior for the purpose of comparing and contrasting it to human behavior.

Developmental Psychology **Developmental psychology** is an area that focuses on the study of change, or development. Developmental psychologists are interested in changes in the way people think, in how people relate to others, and in the ways people feel over the entire span of life. These psychologists work in academic settings such as colleges and universities and may do research in various areas of development. They do not provide therapy. ⓁⒾⓃⓀ *to Chapter Ten: Development Across the Life Span, pp. 386–387.*

Experimental Psychology **Experimental psychology** encompasses several different areas such as learning, memory, thinking, perception, motivation, and language. The focus of these psychologists, however, is on doing research and conducting studies and experiments with both people and animals in these various areas. They tend to work in academic settings, especially in large universities. ⓁⒾⓃⓀ *to Chapter One: The Science of Psychology, p. 18.*

Social Psychology **Social psychology** is an area that focuses on how human behavior is affected by the presence of other people. For example, social psychologists explore areas such as prejudice, attitude change, aggressive behavior, and interpersonal attraction. Although most social psychologists work in academic settings, teaching and doing research, some work in federal agencies and big business doing practical (applied) research. In fact, many social psychologists are experimental psychologists who perform their experiments in real-world settings rather than the laboratory to preserve the natural reactions of people. When people are in an artificial setting, they often behave in self-conscious ways, which is not the behavior the researcher wishes to study. ⓁⒾⓃⓀ *to Chapter Fourteen: Social Psychology, p. 556.*

Personality Psychology **Personality psychology** focuses on the differences in personality among people. These psychologists may look at the influence of heredity on personality. They study the ways in which people are both alike and different. They look at the development of personality and do personality assessment. They may be involved in forming new theories of how personality works or develops. Personality psychologists work in academic settings, doing research and teaching. ⓁⒾⓃⓀ *to Chapter Eleven: Theories of Personality, p. 436.*

Developmental psychologists study the changes that occur in children and adults as people age. The researcher in the foreground is videotaping this mother and infant as the infant is tested for various developmental skills. Why do you think the researcher is using a videotape rather than just writing down notes?

Physiological Psychology **Physiological psychology** is an area that focuses on the study of the biological bases of behavior. Many professionals now refer to this area as *behavioral neuroscience* or *biopsychology.* Physiological psychologists study the brain, nervous system, and the influence of the body's chemicals, such as hormones and the chemicals in the brain, on human behavior. They study the effects of drug use and the genetic influences that may exist on some kinds of abnormal and normal human behavior, such as schizophrenia or aspects of intelligence. Most physiological psychologists, like experimental psychologists, work in an academic setting. ⓁⒾⓃⓀ *to Chapter Two: The Biological Perspective, p. 49.*

Comparative Psychology **Comparative psychology** is an area that focuses exclusively on animals and animal behavior. By comparing and contrasting animal behavior with what is already known about human behavior, comparative psychologists can contribute to the understanding of human behavior by studying animals. Studying animal behavior also helps people to learn how to treat animals more humanely and to coexist with the animals in a common environment. Comparative psychologists might work in animal laboratories in a university or may do observation and studies of animals in the animals' natural habitats.

Psychologists in these areas may do research that is directed at discovering basic principles of human behavior (basic research) or they may engage in research designed to find solutions to practical problems of the here and now (applied research). There are many other areas in which psychologists may specialize that focus almost exclusively on applied research. These areas are those most often associated with applied psychology.

Psychology Beyond the Classroom

B.5 How does psychology interact with other career fields?

PSYCHOLOGY AND HEALTH

Health psychology focuses on the relationship of human behavior patterns and stress reactions to physical health with the goal of improving and helping to maintain good health while preventing and treating illness. A health psychologist might design a program to help people lose weight or stop smoking, for example. Stress management techniques are also a major focus of this area. Health psychologists may work in hospitals, clinics, medical schools, health agencies, academic settings, or private practice.

In one study, health psychologists examined the effects of social support and social burden (strain in social activities, negative experiences, and the need for taking care of others) on the number of times women went for breast cancer screening in a special study of breast cancer (Messina et al., 2004). The researchers found that women who had more social support and less of a social burden tended to go for screenings more often than women who had less social support and more social demands. Those with higher social demands and less support tended to rely more on self-examination at home rather than clinical tests. Relying only on self-examination without the support of clinical tests such as mammography puts these women at greater health risk. This is a good example of the kind of research that health psychologists conduct. Other areas studied by health psychologists include the influence of optimistic attitudes on the progress of disease, the link between mental distress and health, and the promotion of wellness and hope in an effort to prevent illness. ⒧ⒾⓃⓀ to *Chapter Nine: Stress and Health, pp. 378–379.*

PSYCHOLOGY AND EDUCATION

Educational psychology is concerned with the study of human learning. As educational psychologists come to understand some of the basic aspects of learning, they develop methods and materials for aiding the process of learning. For example, educational psychologists helped to design the phonics method of teaching children to read. This type of psychologist may have a doctorate of education (Ed.D.) rather than a Ph.D. and typically works in academic settings.

What types of research might an educational psychologist conduct? The November 2009 issue of *Journal of Educational Psychology* included articles on the role that students' oral language and decoding skills play in reading comprehension, a method of teaching anatomy with interactional three-dimensional graphics, and the impact of teacher-student interactions and various prevention strategies in kindergarten and first grade on educational outcomes—just to name a few.

School psychology is related to, but not at all the same as, educational psychology. Whereas educational psychologists may do research and develop new learning techniques, school psychologists may take the results of that research or those methods and apply them in the actual school system. School psychologists work

health psychology area of psychology in which the psychologists focus on the relationship of human behavior patterns and stress reaction to physical health.

educational psychology area of psychology in which the psychologists are concerned with the study of human learning and development of new learning techniques.

school psychology area of psychology in which the psychologists work directly in the schools, doing assessments, educational placement, and diagnosing educational problems.

This woman is a health psychologist. She is helping this girl to control her fear of receiving an injection by letting her act out giving an injection to a special doll.

School psychologists often administer tests to assess a child's intelligence or psychological well-being. Here, a psychologist uses an abstract test for a student with a reading disability.

Sports psychology techniques can help athletes such as Tiger Woods learn to concentrate better and stay focused on the game.

sports psychology area of psychology in which the psychologists help athletes and others to prepare themselves mentally for participation in sports activities.

forensic psychology area of psychology concerned with people in the legal system, including profiling of criminals, jury selection, and expert witnessing.

directly with children in the school setting. They do testing and other forms of assessment to place children in special programs or to diagnose educational problems such as dyslexia or attention deficit disorder. They may act as consultants to teachers, parents, and educational administrators. Counseling students is actually a relatively small part of the job of a school psychologist, although counseling takes a much bigger role when tragedies strike a school. When traumatic events such as the unexpected and tragic death of a classmate or even larger-scale tragedies such as the numerous school shootings of the past decade take place, school psychologists are often called on to offer help and counseling to students.

PSYCHOLOGY AND SPORTS

Sports psychology is a relatively new and fast-growing field in which the main focus is on helping athletes and others involved in sports activities prepare mentally, rather than just physically, for participation in sports. The idea behind this field is that a superior physical performance is not enough to guarantee success; rather, the mind must be prepared for the activity by setting clear, short-term goals, holding positive thoughts, using visualization of the goal, stopping negative thoughts, and other techniques based primarily in the cognitive perspective. For example, a sports psychologist might have a golfer who has been having trouble hitting the ball where he wants it to go do visualization exercises, mentally seeing himself hit the ball down the fairway again and again. The famous golfer, Tiger Woods, must attribute much of his success to his ability to remain focused under the most intense pressure. Sports psychologists work in athletic organizations and may have a private practice or do consulting work. (For more on the techniques used in sports psychology, see the Applying Psychology to Everyday Life section at the end of this appendix.)

PSYCHOLOGY AND THE LAW

Psychologists have often been involved in the world of legal matters in various ways. Social psychologists often do research in the areas of criminal behavior and may consult with attorneys or other agents of the court system on such topics as witness credibility, jury selection, and the kind of influences that exist for decision-making processes. Developmental psychologists may become involved in determining the accuracy of and influences on the testimony of children and adolescents, as well as the needs of children caught up in a custody battle between divorced or divorcing parents. Cognitive psychologists may become expert witnesses on the accuracy of memory and eyewitness testimony or ways to determine the truth or falsehood of statements made by witnesses or defendants. Clinical psychologists may deliver their services directly to prisoners in prisons and jails or may conduct assessments of intelligence and/or mental status to determine whether or not a person charged with a crime should stand trial.

All of the forms of psychological involvement in legal matters mentioned here can be considered as part of the growing field of **forensic psychology**. Forensic psychology is the practice of psychology related to the legal system and involves examining criminal evidence and aiding law enforcement investigations into criminal activities. As discussed earlier, some forensic psychologists provide information and advice to legal officials such as lawyers or judges, some act as expert witnesses, some actually diagnose and treat criminals within the prison system, and others may administer psychological tests to criminal defendants. Forensic psychologists may aid either the prosecution or the defense in a trial by helping determine which potential jurors would be the best or worst choices. This type of professional may do consulting work in addition to a regular private practice in clinical or counseling psychology or may work entirely within the justice system as a police psychologist, a profiler of serial criminals for federal agencies, or a full-time jury expert, for example.

PSYCHOLOGY AND THE ENVIRONMENT

Another broad area in which psychological principles can be applied to solve practical problems is the area of managing the environment. **Environmental psychology** is an area that focuses on the relationship between human behavior and the environment in which the behavior takes place, such as an office, store, school, dormitory, or hospital. Because the concern of researchers in this field deals directly with behavior in a particular setting, research is always conducted in that setting rather than in a laboratory. Environmental psychologists may work with other professionals such as urban or city planners, economists, engineers, and architects, helping those professionals to plan the most efficient buildings, parks, housing developments, or plants, for example.

PRACTICE **QUIZ:** PREPARING FOR THE AP* EXAM

ANSWERS ON PAGE AK-4.

Directions: Read each of the questions or incomplete sentences below. Then choose the response that best answers the question or completes the sentence.

1. Which of the following professionals in psychology focuses most on the environmental conditions that affect mental disorders?
   a. Psychiatrist
   b. Psychologist
   c. Psychoanalyst
   d. Psychology professor
   e. Psychiatric social worker

2. Which of the following specialties in psychology is most similar to the medical field of psychiatry?
   a. Clinical
   b. Counseling
   c. Personality
   d. Experimental
   e. Comparative

3. Max is interested in becoming a psychologist. He is most interested in how people become attracted to other people. He would most likely specialize in _____.
   a. social psychology
   b. counseling psychology
   c. personality psychology
   d. comparative psychology
   e. environmental psychology

4. Which type of psychologist would most likely study the effects of psychological stress on the growth rate of cancer cells?
   a. Sports
   b. Health
   c. Forensic
   d. Educational
   e. Environmental

5. Which type of psychologist would be most likely to administer an IQ test to a child to determine the child's eligibility for a gifted program?
   a. Health
   b. School
   c. Personality
   d. Educational
   e. Developmental

Psychology and Work

B.6 What are industrial/organizational psychology and human factors psychology?

Work is a tremendous part of many people's lives. People often spend more time at work than they do with their families or in social activities. One of the largest branches of applied psychology focuses on how psychology can help people in management, productivity, morale, and many other areas of the world of work.

Industrial/organizational (I/O) psychology is concerned with the relationships between people and their work environments. I/O psychologists may help in personnel selection, administer job performance assessments, design work schedules that help workers adjust to new time periods of work hours with less difficulty, or design new work areas to increase morale and productivity. Psychologists in this field

environmental psychology area of psychology in which the focus is on how people interact with and are affected by their physical environments.

industrial/organizational (I/O) psychology area of psychology concerned with the relationships between people and their work environment.

Human factors psychologists design machines that are more practical and comfortable for people to use. For example, this keyboard is designed to reduce the risk of pain in the wrists and increase accuracy in typing.

human factors psychology area of industrial/organizational psychology concerned with the study of the way humans and machines interact with each other.

These women were participants in one of the early industrial/organizational psychology experiments conducted by Elton Mayo for the Western Electric Company.

may study the behavior of entire organizations. They are often hired by corporations and businesses to deal with the hiring and assessment of employees. They may research and develop ways for workers to be more efficient and productive. They may work in business, government agencies, and academic settings.

A certain kind of I/O specialist, called a *human factors engineer*, focuses on designing machines, furniture, and other devices that people have to use so that those devices are the most practical, comfortable, and logical for human use. **Human factors psychology** consists of these researchers and designers who study the way humans and machines interact with each other. They may work in the design of appliances, airplane controls, and the operation of computers or other mechanical devices. Human factors psychologists tend to work directly in the businesses that design and manufacture the machines they study.

Industrial/organizational psychology got its start near the beginning of the twentieth century with the work of Walter D. Scott, a former student of famed physiologist and founder of the first psychological laboratory, Wilhelm Wundt. Scott applied psychological principles to hiring, management, and advertising techniques (Schultz & Schultz, 2004). He also wrote one of the first books about the application of psychology to industry and advertising, called *The Theory and Practice of Advertising* (Scott, 1908). Another early figure in the newly developing field of industrial/organizational psychology was Hugo Munsterberg, a psychologist also trained by Wundt who conducted research on such varied topics as the power of prayer and eyewitness testimony (Hothersall, 1995). Munsterberg wrote a book about eyewitness testimony called *On the Witness Stand* (1907) and later wrote *Psychology and Industrial Efficiency* (1913).

The field became important during World War I when the army needed a way to test the intelligence of potential recruits. Psychologist Robert Yerkes, who would later become known for his groundbreaking research in comparative psychology while working with the great apes, developed the Army Alpha and Army Beta tests. The Army Alpha test was used with applicants who were able to read, whereas the Army Beta test was administered to applicants who were illiterate (McGuire, 1994; Yerkes, 1921).

In the mid-1920s a series of studies conducted by Elton Mayo for the Western Electric Company (Franke & Kaul, 1978; Parsons, 1992; Roethlisberger & Dickson, 1939) broadened the field. These were the first studies to view the workplace as a social system rather than simply a production line. Rather than treating workers as simply other pieces of equipment, these studies suggested that allowing workers some input into the decision-making process not only improved worker morale* but also reduced workers' resistance to changes in the workplace. These studies led the way for others to examine how management of employees and production could be improved. Management theories and strategies may also be applied to other kinds of settings such as schools, colleges, and universities. The following section takes a closer look at the development of these theories.

---

* Morale: a sense of common purpose, enthusiasm, confidence, and loyalty.

OTHER AREAS IN INDUSTRIAL/ORGANIZATIONAL PSYCHOLOGY

There are many other areas of research and study in the field of industrial/organization psychology. Table B.1 briefly lists some of the areas of specialization.

Table B.1 Areas in I/O Psychology

AREAS IN INDUSTRY	AREAS IN ORGANIZATIONS
Job analysis	Social behavior of work teams
Job evaluation and compensation	Job satisfaction
Characteristics critical to effective management	Personality characteristics critical to job performance
Personnel recruiting, selection, and placement	Relationships between management and workers
Occupational training	Leadership characteristics and training
Examination of working conditions	Consumer psychology
Interviewing and testing	Motivational concerns
Performance appraisal and feedback	Conflict management

PRACTICE **QUIZ**: PREPARING FOR THE AP* EXAM

ANSWERS ON PAGE AK-4.

Directions: Read each of the questions or incomplete sentences below. Then choose the response that best answers the question or completes the sentence.

1. Bernard works in a factory and is responsible for making sure that the office equipment made in the factory is practical and easy to use. He sometimes suggests changes in the design of certain equipment to accomplish this goal. Bernard is most likely what type of psychologist?
   a. Forensic
   b. Human factors
   c. Management/design
   d. Conflict management
   e. Industrial/organizational

2. One of the early figures in I/O psychology who developed the Army Alpha and the Army Beta tests was _____.
   a. Elton Mayo
   b. Hugo Munsterberg
   c. Wilhelm Wundt
   d. Walter D. Scott
   e. Robert Yerkes

Applying Psychology to Everyday Life: Techniques Used by Sports Psychologists

B.7 What are some techniques used in sports psychology?

Many athletes become frustrated when their performance seems to be less than it could be or when they reach some "roadblock" on their way to achieving new goals. The techniques that follow are designed to help athletes get around the roadblocks and get the most out of their performance. The same techniques are also helpful in the careers of acting, musical performance, professional speaking, teaching, or any career in which there is an element of performance in front of others.

1. *Visualization.* In this technique, athletes try to "see" their performance in their minds as if watching from the sidelines before actually doing it.

2. *Imagery/mental rehearsal.* Similar to visualization, imagery can be used to mentally rehearse the desired performance. Instead of visualizing oneself as if from the sidelines, however, imagery/mental rehearsal involves actually "seeing" and "feeling" the performance in one's mind from one's own viewpoint. This helps prepare the muscles that will be used for action.

Current Issues in Psychology

Workplace Violence

Acts of violence in the workplace have increased dramatically in the past few decades—nearly tripling in the eighties alone (Baron, 1993), and psychologists are devoting time and energy to studying the reasons for this violence and ways to recognize and prevent future incidents. Professor John Gambon of Ozarks Technical Community College in Springfield, Missouri, is an industrial/organization psychologist who has been studying this issue and gathering data for presentation to his classes. Here are some highlights from his research into this issue:

- People in some types of jobs face a higher probability of becoming a victim of a crime because of the characteristics of the job. For example, two of the most likely occupations are nighttime convenience store clerk and cab driver. The availability of cash and the solitary nature of these jobs entice many criminals to attempt robbery.
- Other occupations are hazardous because of their very nature. For example, look at the probability of being killed on the job in these areas:
  - Police Officer: 10.3 officers out of every 100,000; police officers were victims of nonfatal crimes while on duty at a rate of 261 per 1,000 officers from 1993 to 1999 (Duhart, 2001).
  - Security Officer: 3.8 officers out of every 100,000.
  - All other workers: 0.7 out of every 100,000.
- Some forms of workplace violence are domestic issues that spill over into the world of work, such as the angry spouse who goes to the employee's place of business and attacks the employee, either on the premises or in the parking lot.
- In some cases, it is not a criminal from the outside who commits the violence but a fellow employee or former employee. Industrial/organizational psychologists have developed a term for the employee who becomes highly violent and commits violent crimes resulting in serious injury or death to other employees: the *berserker*.

On April 20, 2007 at NASA's Johnson Space Center in Houston, Texas, 60-year-old William Phillips, a NASA contract worker, took a handgun into an office building at the center and barricaded himself and at least two hostages for nearly four hours. Phillips apparently had a dispute with one hostage, whom he killed early in the ordeal. The second hostage escaped without harm. The standoff ended when Phillips shot himself. This is a prime example of violence in the workplace.

What are the characteristics of persons who "go berserk" in the workplace? Typically, they have at least a high school diploma or some college. Their self-esteem, or sense of worth as a person, is intimately tied to their job. They tend to like watching violent television or movies. There is a small correlation between berserkers and those with delusional disorders: People who become violent in the workplace are somewhat likely to also suffer from a delusional disorder, such as paranoia. L I N K to Chapter Twelve: *Psychological Disorders, pp. 501–502.*

Prevention of violence in the workplace includes some simple, commonsense items as well as some less simple methods (Arbury, 2005; Harvey & Keashly, 2003; Security Director's Report, 2008; Vandenbos & Bulatao, 1996):

- Entrances and exits that are well lighted
- Presence of video cameras or security guards, especially at night
- Criminal background checks performed on all potential new employees
- Training for managers and supervisors to learn how to identify signs of potential workplace violence, such as
  - Verbal threats by an employee
  - Employee's fascination with/access to firearms
  - Desensitization of an employee to television and movie violence, with a preference for watching such media
  - Employee's low-grade acts of violence, such as pushing or shoving

3. *Distraction desensitization.* Athletes can be trained to ignore distractions, such as the shouts of spectators.

4. *Thought stopping.* People often have negative thoughts about things that might happen: "I'm going to miss it, I just know it!" is a good example of a negative, self-defeating thought. Sports psychologists train athletes to stop such thoughts in the making, replacing them with more positive thoughts: "I can do this. I've done it before and it was easy."

5. *Confidence training.* Another thing that sports psychologists do is try to build confidence and self-esteem in the athletes who come to them for help. Lack of confidence in one's own abilities is a major roadblock.

6. *Focus training.* Athletes can also be trained to focus attention, often through the use of hypnosis, concentrative meditation, or similar psychological techniques.

7. *Relaxation training.* Athletes can be trained to use special breathing methods, tension and relaxation of muscles, and other tricks for relaxation to reduce anxiety and tension before a performance.

8. *Autogenic training.* Autogenic essentially means "from within the self." In the sense used here, autogenic training involves helping athletes learn about their physiological responses to stress. Once learned, athletes can gain control over these responses, such as learning to slow one's heart rate or lower anxiety.

9. *Fostering realistic goals and expectations.* Sports psychologists try to teach athletes that although setting goals is important, setting unrealistic goals can lead to burnout, frustration, and feelings of failure. Sports psychologists try to help athletes modify their expectations and goals to be more realistic.

10. *Fostering team unity.* Sports psychologists may also work with entire teams of athletes, helping them to become a unit that works as one single "organism" while still providing support for each individual athlete.

Relaxation training is becoming a very important part of any athlete's training. Here the Wisconsin Badgers college football team participates in a relaxation exercise before the big game. What other career areas might be improved by relaxation training?

B CHAPTER SUMMARY

What Is Applied Psychology?

B.1 What is the definition of applied psychology?

• Applied psychology refers to using psychological principles and research to solve problems in the real world.

Psychology as a Career

B.2 What are the different types of psychological professionals?

• The different types of psychological professionals are psychiatrists, psychoanalysts, psychiatric social workers, and psychologists.

• Psychologists hold either a Ph.D. or Psy.D. degree.

B.3 What kinds of careers are available to someone with a bachelor's degree in psychology?

• Education, statistical consulting, administration and other business careers, as well as health services are examples of careers that a person with a bachelor's degree in psychology might enter.

B.4 What are the areas of specialization in psychology?

• Areas of specialization include clinical and counseling psychology, developmental, experimental, social, personality, physiological, and comparative psychology.

Psychology Beyond the Classroom

B.5 How does psychology interact with other career fields?

• Health psychology is an area in which the goal is to discover relationships between human behavior, including stress factors, and physical health with the intention of preventing and treating ill health.

• Educational psychologists study the processes of human learning to develop new techniques and methods, whereas school psychologists apply those methods in the school, administer assessments, recommend placement, and provide counseling and diagnosis of educational problems.

• Sports psychologists help athletes prepare themselves mentally for participation in sports.

- Psychologists may act as expert witnesses for legal matters, help in jury selection, provide clinical services to defendants or prisoners, or produce personality profiles of various types of criminals in the field of forensic psychology.
- Environmental psychology looks at the relationship between human behavior and the physical environment in which that behavior takes place.

Psychology and Work

B.6 What are industrial/organizational psychology and human factors psychology?

- Industrial/organizational psychology is concerned with how people function in and are affected by their work environments.

- Human factors is a type of I/O psychology in which the focus is on the way humans and machines interact with each other, designing or helping to design the machines used by people in various science and industrial settings.

Applying Psychology to Everyday Life: Techniques Used by Sports Psychologists

B.7 What are some techniques used in sports psychology?

- Sports psychologists use many techniques to help athletes better their performances, including visualization, imagery, thought stopping, confidence training, relaxation training, and fostering team unity.

TEST YOURSELF: PREPARING FOR THE AP* EXAM

ANSWERS ON PAGE AK-4.

✔ Practice on MyPsychLab   **Ready for your test?** More quizzes and a customized study plan. **www.mypsychlab.com**

Directions: Read each of the questions or incomplete sentences below. Then choose the response that best answers the question or completes the sentence.

1. Carrie would like to work as a psychological professional, but she is not interested in scientific research or in becoming a medical doctor. She would like to be able to call herself a psychologist and provide therapy for her clients. What type of degree should Carrie pursue in order to meet her goals?
   a. A Psy.D.
   b. A Ph.D. in psychology
   c. A master's degree in social work
   d. A master's degree in psychology
   e. A bachelor's degree in psychology

2. The professional most likely to use Freudian concepts in therapy is a _____.
   a. psychiatrist
   b. psychologist
   c. psychoanalyst
   d. psychology professor
   e. psychiatric social worker

3. What type of professional would most likely help people with adjustments to stress, work problems, or marital difficulties?
   a. Social psychologist
   b. Clinical psychologist
   c. Personality psychologist
   d. Counseling psychologist
   e. Developmental psychologist

4. Dr. Trentenelli is studying the changes that occur in people's memories as they age from youth to late adulthood. Dr. Trentenelli's area of specialization is most likely in _____.
   a. social psychology
   b. personality psychology
   c. comparative psychology
   d. environmental psychology
   e. developmental psychology

5. Which psychologists do research and conduct experiments with people and animals in the areas of learning, memory, thought processes, perception, and language?
   a. Experimental psychologists
   b. Comparative psychologists
   c. Developmental psychologists
   d. Social psychologists
   e. Educational psychologists

6. The view that panic attacks occur because of a malfunction in a small area of the brain normally responsible for alerting the person to real danger is most compatible with which area of specialization in psychology?
   a. Health
   b. Counseling
   c. Physiological
   d. Human factors
   e. Developmental

7. What type of psychologist would be most likely to put together a personality profile of a criminal for the FBI?
   a. Clinical
   b. Forensic
   c. Personality
   d. Environmental
   e. Industrial/organizational

8. Workers in which of the following occupations have the highest risk of being killed on the job?
   a. Postal workers
   b. Firefighters
   c. Highway construction workers
   d. Police officers
   e. Security workers

9. Suzanne is about to compete in a gymnastics tournament, and she begins to have second thoughts about her ability. She realizes that such negative thoughts will not help and tells herself that she has done these exercises perfectly in practice, and she can do them perfectly now. Suzanne's ability to replace her negative thinking with more helpful, positive thinking is a form of _____.
   a. visualization
   b. thought stopping
   c. autogenic training
   d. relaxation training
   e. distraction desensitization

10. A sports psychologist tells Michaela, a tennis player, to try to see herself actually hitting the ball over the net. The psychologist is using _____.
    a. focus training
    b. thought stopping
    c. confidence training
    d. autogenic training
    e. imagery/mental rehearsal

Answer Key

CHAPTER 1

Practice Quiz page 13
1. b 2. d 3. a 4. a 5. e

Practice Quiz pages 19–20
1. b 2. d 3. e 4. e 5. c

Practice Quiz page 25
1. d 2. c 3. a 4. d 5. e

Practice Quiz page 34
1. e 2. b 3. a 4. c 5. d

Practice Quiz pages 39–40
1. d 2. b 3. e 4. d 5. c

Test pages 42–43
Part I: 1. b   2. d   3. e   4. c   5. a   6. a   7. c   8. a   9. e   10. c

Part II: Students must answer all parts of the question in a concise, clearly organized essay composed of complete sentences. Students should provide specific details and examples to support their assertions; definitions alone are not sufficient. Psychological perspectives should be discussed in the context of the question rather than abstractly.

Successful essays may include the following arguments:
  a. A psychodynamic theorist might say that Qing's unconscious mind is troubled, causing her conscious behaviors to be negatively affected.
  b. A behavioral theorist might say that Qing has been conditioned to associate painting with positive emotions and sensations.
  c. A sociocultural theorist might say that Qing is struggling to adapt to the norms, values, and expectations of American society because they differ from Chinese norms, values, and expectations.
  d. A cognitive theorist might say that Qing's academic troubles are linked to problems she is having with memory, intelligence, or language learning.
  e. A biopsychological theorist might say that Qing's behavior is caused by hormonal changes or biologically inherited tendencies.

CHAPTER 2

Practice Quiz page 58
1. b 2. e 3. a 4. e 5. b 6. c

Practice Quiz page 65
1. a 2. c 3. d 4. a 5. b

Practice Quiz page 73
1. d 2. e 3. a 4. c 5. a

Practice Quiz page 81
1. c 2. a 3. a 4. e 5. c 6. d

Test pages 86–87
Part I: 1. a   2. d   3. c   4. e   5. d   6. a   7. d   8. b   9. e   10. d

Part II: Students must answer all parts of the question in a concise, clearly organized essay composed of complete sentences. Students should provide specific details and examples to support their assertions; definitions alone are not sufficient.

Successful essays may include the following arguments:
  a. A bicyclist might use the occipital lobe to read road signs and to navigate because this area of the brain processes visual information.
  b. A bicyclist might use the temporal lobe to process street noises and to avoid danger because this area of the brain processes sound and language.
  c. A bicyclist might use the frontal lobe to solve problems like roadblocks or a flat tire because this area of the brain processes higher thinking, like decision making, memory, and planning.
  d. A bicyclist might use the parietal lobe to control the bike because this area of the brain contains the somatosensory cortex, which processes information from the skin for touch and body position.

CHAPTER 3

Practice Quiz page 93
1. b 2. e 3. c 4. e

Practice Quiz page 101
1. c 2. d 3. c 4. a 5. d

Practice Quiz page 106
1. a 2. e 3. a 4. c 5. b

Practice Quiz page 114
1. e 2. b 3. b 4. a 5. c

Practice Quiz pages 124–125
1. b 2. e 3. b 4. c 5. d

Test pages 128–129
Part I: 1. b   2. c   3. d   4. d   5. e   6. c   7. c   8. d   9. a   10. b

Part II: Students must answer all parts of the question in a concise, clearly organized essay composed of complete sentences. Students should provide specific details and examples to support their assertions; definitions alone are not sufficient. Information about sensory processes should be discussed in the context of the question rather than abstractly.

Successful essays may include the following arguments:
  a. Jonah's poor eyesight is most likely due to the age-related hardening of the lenses in his eyes. His lenses are no longer flexible, so he is not able to perform the process of visual accommodation.
  b. Alana most likely has red-green colorblindness: Either the red cones or the green cones in her eyes are not functioning.
  c. Jonah and Alana may be experiencing tinnitus, a ringing in the ears that can result from exposure to loud noises.
  d. Rory's nausea and dizziness may be symptoms of motion sickness, which occurs when the vestibular sense is not coordinated with the other senses.

CHAPTER 4

Practice Quiz page 139
1. d 2. c 3. a 4. b 5. e

Practice Quiz page 147
1. d 2. c 3. e 4. a 5. d 6. b

Practice Quiz page 150
1. b 2. c 3. b 4. a 5. b

Practice Quiz page 154
1. a 2. c 3. a 4. b

Practice Quiz page 166
1. c 2. b 3. a 4. e 5. b 6. a

Test pages 170–171
Part I: 1. c   2. d   3. a   4. b   5. d   6. c   7. a   8. b   9. a   10. b

Part II: Students must answer all parts of the question in a concise, clearly organized essay composed of complete sentences. Students should provide specific details and examples to support their assertions; definitions alone are not sufficient. Information about sensory processes should be discussed in the context of the question rather than abstractly.

Successful essays may include the following arguments:
  a. Alpa was likely drawn to cocaine because it is a stimulant, it made her feel happy, and it made her feel like she had energy.
  b. Alpa likely became addicted to cocaine because she was not able to sustain the feelings of happiness and energy levels after the effects of the cocaine had worn off.
  c. Alpa's friends may have noticed that she is no longer giving as much effort at work or with her relationships because cocaine causes users to disregard the consequences of their actions.
  d. Alpa's friends may have also noticed that Alpa was compulsively using the drug and had lost control of herself.
  e. Cocaine use can cause convulsions and death.

CHAPTER 5

Practice Quiz page 182
1. c 2. b 3. e 4. c 5. b
Practice Quiz page 186
1. a 2. c 3. c 4. a 5. e
Practice Quiz page 195
1. d 2. e 3. c 4. e 5. d
Practice Quiz page 203
1. b 2. c 3. d 4. e 5. a
Practice Quiz page 210
1. d 2. b 3. a 4. b 5. a
Test page 215
Part I: 1. b 2. a 3. e 4. b 5. a 6. c 7. d 8. a 9. b 10. e

Part II: Students must answer all parts of the question in a concise, clearly organized essay composed of complete sentences. Students should provide specific details and examples to support their assertions; definitions alone are not sufficient. Information about each learning concept should be discussed in the context of the question rather than abstractly.

Successful essays may include the following arguments:
  a. The Law of Effect suggests that Owen's parents should create negative consequences for Owen's inappropriate behavior.
  b. Owen's parents could implement punishment by removal by taking away a toy or other desired object when Owen misbehaves.
  c. Owen's parents could implement a fixed interval schedule of reinforcement by providing a treat or reward at the end of every week in which Owen behaves well.
  d. Applied behavior analysis could be used to modify Owen's behavior slowly until he is capable of behaving well independently.
  e. Owen's parents could use a token economy by allowing Owen to earn gold stars for good behavior and exchange those stars for rewards.
  f. If Owen's parents model good behavior in front of Owen, Owen might learn to copy that behavior through observational learning.

CHAPTER 6

Practice Quiz page 223
1. a 2. c
Practice Quiz pages 234–235
1. b 2. e 3. d 4. a 5. c
Practice Quiz page 242
1. c 2. b 3. a 4. d 5. a
Practice Quiz pages 245–246
1. a 2. c 3. e 4. d 5. a
Practice Quiz page 253
1. b 2. a 3. d 4. e 5. d
Test pages 256–257
Part I: 1. d 2. a 3. a 4. c 5. c 6. e 7. a 8. c 9. e 10. c

Part II: Students must answer all parts of the question in a concise, clearly organized essay composed of complete sentences. Students should provide specific details and examples to support their assertions; definitions alone are not sufficient. Information about each topic should be discussed in the context of the question rather than abstractly.

Successful essays may include the following arguments:
  a. Craik and Tulving's research into levels of processing suggests that thinking about meaning encodes a memory more effectively than thinking about its sound or appearance. Lisa should focus on the meanings of the facts she must memorize.
  b. Because elaborative rehearsal makes use of deep processing while maintenance rehearsal makes use of shallow processing, Lisa should use elaborative rehearsal to memorize important dates and historical figures.
  c. Lisa can make use of retrieval cues like encoding specificity by studying in the same room where she will take the test and recreating testing conditions as accurately as possible when she studies.
  d. Lisa will be able to use recognition to answer multiple-choice questions, but she must use recall when she writes an essay.
  e. In order to offset the serial position effect, Lisa can focus her studies on the middle part of her notes. She can take advantage of the recency effect by skimming her notes immediately before the exam.

CHAPTER 7

Practice Quiz page 271
1. c 2. b 3. d 4. a
Practice Quiz page 275
1. c 2. b 3. d 4. a

Practice Quiz page 284
1. a 2. b 3. e 4. e 5. d
Practice Quiz page 293
1. b 2. d 3. e 4. b
Practice Quiz page 298
1. a 2. a 3. e 4. c 5. b
Test pages 302–303
Part I: 1. d 2. c 3. a 4. e 5. c 6. e 7. b 8. e 9. d 10. a

Part II: Students must answer all parts of the question in a concise, clearly organized essay composed of complete sentences. Students should provide specific details and examples to support their assertions; definitions alone are not sufficient. Information about cognitive concepts should be discussed in the context of the question rather than abstractly.

Successful essays may include the following arguments:
  a. If Prashant uses mental sets and tends to solve problems in the same way every time, he will find it difficult to think of creative new solutions to problems, possibly causing his IQ score to suffer.
  b. If Prashant engages often in divergent thinking, he is most likely a creative thinker who can see an object or question in many possible ways, and he will probably score well on the IQ test.
  c. If the IQ test is not valid, it does not accurately measure what it is supposed to measure. Prashant may have a high IQ score, but if the test is invalid, it will not provide useful results.
  d. If the IQ test is written in a manner that is culturally biased rather than culturally fair, and if Prashant was raised in a culture different from the culture in which the test was created, Prashant will be at a disadvantage, no matter what his actual IQ really is.
  e. If Prashant suffers from a developmental delay such as fragile X syndrome, he will most likely not perform well on his IQ test.

CHAPTER 8

Practice Quiz page 313
1. d 2. a 3. c 4. e 5. b
Practice Quiz page 320
1. a 2. b 3. e 4. e 5. c
Practice Quiz page 328
1. e 2. b 3. c 4. d 5. a
Practice Quiz page 337
1. c 2. b 3. a 4. d 5. e
Test page 341
Part I: 1. a 2. c 3. d 4. e 5. a 6. b 7. a 8. b 9. d 10. e

Part II: Students must answer all parts of the question in a concise, clearly organized essay composed of complete sentences. Students should provide specific details and examples to support their assertions; definitions alone are not sufficient. Information about sensory processes should be discussed in the context of the question rather than abstractly.

Successful essays may include the following arguments:
  a. The common sense theory suggests that seeing the snake causes the feeling of fear, which in turn causes physical arousal.
  b. The James-Lange theory suggests that seeing the snake causes physical arousal, which you then label as fear.
  c. The Cannon-Bard theory suggests that seeing the snake leads to subcortical brain activity, and the thalamus sends sensory information to both the cortex and the nervous system, leading to simultaneous physical arousal and cognitive experience of fear.
  d. The Schacter-Singer cognitive arousal theory suggests that seeing the snake leads to simultaneous physical arousal and cognitive appraisal of the arousal based on environmental cues. Both of these events lead to your labeling the emotion as fear.
  e. The cognitive-mediational theory suggests that seeing the snake leads to an appraisal of the threat that the snake poses to you. You see that it is indeed a threat, so you experience fear and your physical arousal increases.

CHAPTER 9

Practice Quiz page 352
1. a 2. e 3. a 4. d 5. b
Practice Quiz page 358
1. a 2. a 3. d 4. c 5. c
Practice Quiz page 369
1. c 2. c 3. d 4. a 5. e
Practice Quiz pages 372–373
1. b 2. d 3. a 4. b 5. c

Practice Quiz page 378
1. e 2. d 3. c 4. e 5. b
Test pages 380–381
Part I: 1. d 2. b 3. e 4. c 5. a 6. e 7. d 8. b 9. d 10. e

Part II: Students must answer all parts of the question in a concise, clearly organized essay composed of complete sentences. Students should provide specific details and examples to support their assertions; definitions alone are not sufficient. Information about the four types of conflict should be discussed in the context of the question rather than abstractly.

Successful essays may include the following arguments:

a. Students must identify the types of conflict as approach-approach, avoidance-avoidance, approach-avoidance, and multiple approach-avoidance.

b. Approach-approach conflicts involve choosing among multiple desirable options, such as two tropical vacation destinations.

c. Avoidance-avoidance conflicts involve choosing among multiple unpleasant options, such as living with a toothache or getting major dental surgery to relieve the toothache.

d. Approach-avoidance conflicts involve one goal or event with both positive and negative aspects, such as moving away from home for the first time.

e. Multiple approach-avoidance conflicts involve choosing among multiple goals or events, each with its own positives and negatives. An example might be choosing one career path from several different options.

f. All conflicts except approach-approach conflicts are likely to result in high amounts of stress. This stress can be minimized through social support, problem- or emotion-focused coping, and the process of secondary appraisal, among other strategies.

CHAPTER 10
Practice Quiz page 393
1. c 2. c 3. d 4. b 5. e
Practice Quiz page 397
1. b 2. d 3. c 4. e 5. d
Practice Quiz page 407
1. d 2. e 3. a 4. e 5. e
Practice Quiz page 413
1. b 2. a 3. e 4. c 5. e
Practice Quiz page 416
1. c 2. d 3. e 4. e 5. b
Practice Quiz page 420
1. a 2. c 3. d 4. d 5. e
Practice Quiz page 425
1. e 2. e 3. c 4. b 5. a 6. e 7. b
Practice Quiz page 427
1. a 2. d 3. c
Test pages 430–431
Part I: 1. d 2. c 3. c 4. e 5. d 6. a 7. c 8. a 9. b 10. b

Part II: Students must answer all parts of the question in a concise, clearly organized essay composed of complete sentences. Students should provide specific details and examples to support their assertions; definitions alone are not sufficient. Information about biological and environmental influences on development should be discussed in the context of the question rather than abstractly.

Successful essays may include the following arguments:

a. Biological factors that may influence the child's development include genetic characteristics passed to the child from both the mother and the father, the rate at which the child develops and grows physically, and the child's temperament (although this can also be affected by environmental factors).

b. Environmental factors that may influence the child's development include the parents' choice of parenting style, cultural expectations regarding gender roles, and the degree to which parents and caregivers provide support for the child's cognitive growth through scaffolding and other strategies.

CHAPTER 11
Practice Quiz page 440
1. d 2. b 3. c 4. e 5. a
Practice Quiz page 446
1. b 2. c 3. d 4. d 5. e
Practice Quiz page 452
1. a 2. e 3. c 4. e 5. d
Practice Quiz page 455
1. a 2. b 3. d 4. a 5. e
Practice Quiz page 465
1. b 2. a 3. d 4. e 5. a

Test pages 468–469
Part I: 1. b 2. a 3. d 4. e 5. c 6. e 7. d 8. b 9. c 10. e

Part II: Students must answer all parts of the question in a concise, clearly organized essay composed of complete sentences. Students should provide specific details, and the elements of personality theory should be discussed in the context of the question rather than abstractly.

Successful essays may include the following arguments:

a. The psychodynamic approach, based on the work of Sigmund Freud, focuses on the role that the unconscious mind plays in the shaping of personality. Personality traits are developed as individuals pass through five psychosexual stages. The idea of the unconscious mind is supported by research, but much of Freud's theory is based on his own observations and interpretations and is not backed up by scientific evidence.

b. Unlike the psychodynamic approach, the trait approach seeks to describe personality rather than explain it. Several theorists have created lists of traits to describe people's personalities; McCrae and Costa's five-factor model is particularly influential. The five-factor model has been tested more rigorously than many aspects of Freud's theories have been, and it's believed that there may be some genetic basis for the five-factor model. However, traits will not always be expressed the same way across different situations.

CHAPTER 12
Practice Quiz page 480
1. a 2. d 3. b 4. e 5. c
Practice Quiz page 489
1. a 2. c 3. b 4. c 5. d
Practice Quiz page 496
1. e 2. a 3. a 4. b 5. e
Practice Quiz page 500
1. c 2. e 3. d 4. e 5. b
Practice Quiz page 507
1. c 2. d 3. b 4. b 5. c
Test page 511
Part I: 1. c 2. d 3. d 4. e 5. a 6. d 7. a 8. c 9. b 10. b

Part II: Students must answer all parts of the question in a concise, clearly organized essay composed of complete sentences. Students should provide specific details, and schizophrenia should be discussed in the context of the question rather than abstractly.

Successful essays may include the following arguments:

a. Types of schizophrenia include disorganized (confused speech, hallucinations, and inappropriate emotions), catatonic (disturbed motor behavior or lack of motion), and paranoid (hallucinations and delusions). Schizophrenia is characterized by both positive and negative symptoms.

b. Dr. Hashimoto is more correct in arguing that schizophrenia has a biological basis. Family, twin, and adoption studies provide strong evidence for a genetic cause of schizophrenia. The rate of schizophrenia is stable across various cultures worldwide, suggesting that it is not a culture-bound syndrome. MRI evidence shows structural abnormalities in schizophrenic brains.

c. Dr. Ward is incorrect; however, the stress-vulnerability model proposes that the environment does have some effect on the onset of schizophrenia.

CHAPTER 13
Practice Quiz page 520
1. a 2. d 3. a 4. c 5. b
Practice Quiz page 524
1. e 2. d 3. b 4. a 5. d
Practice Quiz pages 534–535
1. d 2. e 3. c 4. d 5. a
Practice Quiz pages 546–547
1. d 2. a 3. c 4. d 5. e
Test pages 550–551
Part I: 1. b 2. c 3. d 4. e 5. e 6. a 7. d 8. d 9. b 10. c

Part II: Students must answer all parts of the question in a concise, clearly organized essay composed of complete sentences. Students should provide specific details, and the various therapies should be discussed in the context of the question rather than abstractly.

Successful essays may include the following arguments:

a. Psychodynamic therapists would attempt to uncover the unconscious reasons why Matilda is afraid of public speaking, possibly by analyzing dreams or asking Matilda to engage in free association.

b. Behavior therapists would use conditioning techniques such as systematic desensitization, reinforcement, and flooding to treat Matilda's phobia.

c. Cognitive therapists would explore Matilda's distorted thinking patterns and would encourage her not to magnify the dangers of public speaking or think selectively about the potential problems that public speaking could cause.

d. Biomedical therapists might prescribe an antianxiety drug or an antidepressant drug to treat Matilda's anxiety. This treatment could be prescribed in tandem with a form of psychotherapy.

CHAPTER 14

Practice Quiz page 565
1. d   2. c   3. a   4. e   5. c

Practice Quiz page 572
1. d   2. e   3. c   4. b   5. d

Practice Quiz page 576
1. a   2. e   3. e   4. c   5. d

Practice Quiz page 581
1. b   2. a   3. c   4. a   5. b

Practice Quiz page 585
1. b   2. d   3. b   4. e   5. b

Practice Quiz page 591
1. c   2. b   3. c   4. d   5. b

Test pages 596–597
Part I: 1. c   2. d   3. c   4. a   5. a   6. c   7. e   8. d   9. a   10. e

Part II: Students must answer all parts of the question in a concise, clearly organized essay composed of complete sentences. Students should provide specific details, and the elements of social psychology should be discussed in the context of the question rather than abstractly.

Successful essays may include the following arguments:

a. Groupthink encourages individuals to agree with group members rather than thinking objectively and forming their own opinions. If a person who is not prejudiced joins a group whose members hold prejudiced beliefs, that person will be under pressure to agree with the group's beliefs.

b. If an unprejudiced person is forced to behave in prejudiced ways by members of her group, she will experience cognitive dissonance and may end up adjusting her cognition to make it match her prejudiced behavior.

c. The fundamental attribution error perpetuates prejudiced attitudes when prejudiced people assume that others are weak, lazy, unintelligent, or inferior, when in reality those others are facing external circumstances beyond their control.

d. Stereotype threat can confirm prejudiced people's opinions of an out-group by providing "evidence" that out-group members are less intelligent or talented. In reality, the pressure of the existing stereotype serves to reinforce the stereotype, which may not be founded in fact.

APPENDIX A

Test page A-12
1. e   2. b   3. a   4. d   5. c   6. a   7. d   8. b   9. b   10. c

APPENDIX B

Practice Quiz page B-9
1. e   2. a   3. a   4. b   5. b

Practice Quiz page B-11
1. b   2. e

Test page B-14
1. a   2. c   3. d   4. e   5. a   6. c   7. b   8. d   9. b   10. e

Glossary

absolute threshold: the lowest level of stimulation that a person can consciously detect 50 percent of the time the stimulation is present. 91

accommodation: as a monocular clue, the brain's use of information about the changing thickness of the lens of the eye in response to looking at objects that are close or far away. 120

acculturative stress: stress resulting from the need to change and adapt a person's ways to the majority culture. 370

acquired (secondary) drives: those drives that are learned through experience or conditioning, such as the need for money or social approval. 310

acrophobia: fear of heights. 485

action potential: the release of the neural impulse consisting of a reversal of the electrical charge within the axon. 51

action therapy: therapy in which the main goal is to change disordered or inappropriate behavior directly. 516

activation-information-mode model (AIM): revised version of the activation-synthesis explanation of dreams in which information that is accessed during waking hours can have an influence on the synthesis of dreams. 149

activation-synthesis hypothesis: explanation that states that dreams are created by the higher centers of the cortex to explain the activation by the brain stem of cortical cells during REM sleep periods. 149

activity theory: theory of adjustment to aging that assumes older people are happier if they remain active in some way, such as volunteering or developing a hobby. 426

acute stress disorder (ASD): a disorder resulting from exposure to a major stressor, with symptoms of anxiety, dissociation, recurring nightmares, sleep disturbances, problems in concentration, and moments in which people seem to "relive" the event in dreams and flashbacks for as long as one month following the event. 348

adaptive theory: theory of sleep proposing that animals and humans evolved sleep patterns to avoid predators by sleeping when predators are most active. 138

adolescence: the period of life from about age 13 to the early twenties, during which a young person is no longer physically a child but is not yet an independent, self-supporting adult. 416

adrenal glands: endocrine glands located on top of each kidney that secrete over 30 different hormones to deal with stress, regulate salt intake, and provide a secondary source of sex hormones affecting the sexual changes that occur during adolescence. 80

aerial perspective: the haziness that surrounds objects that are farther away from the viewer, causing the distance to be perceived as greater. 119

affect: in psychology, a term indicating "emotion" or "mood". 497

afferent (sensory) neuron: a neuron that carries information from the senses to the central nervous system. 59

afterimages: images that occur when a visual sensation persists for a brief time even after the original stimulus is removed. 98

aggression: behavior intended to hurt or destroy another person. 354, 585

agonists: chemical substances that mimic or enhance the effects of a neurotransmitter on the receptor sites of the next cell, increasing or decreasing the activity of that cell. 55

agoraphobia: fear of being in a place or situation from which escape is difficult or impossible. 485

agreeableness: the emotional style of a person that may range from easygoing, friendly, and likeable to grumpy, crabby, and unpleasant. 454

alcohol: the chemical resulting from fermentation or distillation of various kinds of vegetable matter. 159

algorithms: very specific, step-by-step procedures for solving certain types of problems. 267

all-or-none: referring to the fact that a neuron either fires completely or does not fire at all. 53

all-or-nothing thinking: the tendency to believe that one's performance must be perfect or the result will be a total failure. 488

alpha waves: brain waves that indicate a state of relaxation or light sleep. 140

altered state of consciousness: state in which there is a shift in the quality or pattern of mental activity as compared to waking consciousness. 135

altruism: prosocial behavior that is done with no expectation of reward and may involve the risk of harm to oneself. 588

amphetamines: stimulants that are synthesized (made) in laboratories rather than being found in nature. 156

amygdala: brain structure located near the hippocampus, responsible for fear responses and memory of fear. 71

anal expulsive personality: a person fixated in the anal stage who is messy, destructive, and hostile. 441

anal retentive personality: a person fixated in the anal stage who is neat, fussy, stingy, and stubborn. 441

anal stage: second stage occurring from about 1 to 3 years of age, in which the anus is the erogenous zone and toilet training is the source of conflict. 441

analytical intelligence: the ability to break problems down into component parts, or analysis, for problem solving. 277

andropause: gradual changes in the sexual hormones and reproductive system of middle-aged males. 421

anorexia nervosa: a condition in which a person reduces eating to the point that a weight loss of 15 percent below the ideal body weight or more occurs. 325

antagonists: chemical substances that block or reduce a cell's response to the action of other chemicals or neurotransmitters. 55

anterograde amnesia: loss of memory from the point of injury or trauma forward, or the inability to form new long-term memories. 230

antianxiety drugs: drugs used to treat and calm anxiety reactions, typically minor tranquilizers. 542

antidepressant drugs: drugs used to treat depression and anxiety. 542

antipsychotic drugs: drugs used to treat psychotic symptoms such as delusions, hallucinations, and other bizarre behavior. 541

antisocial personality disorder: disorder in which a person has no morals or conscience and often behaves in an impulsive manner without regard for the consequences of that behavior. 505

anxiety disorders: disorders in which the main symptom is excessive or unrealistic anxiety and fearfulness. 484

applied behavior analysis (ABA): modern term for a form of behavior modification that uses shaping techniques to mold a desired behavior or response. 201

applied psychology: the use of psychological concepts in solving real-world problems. B-2

approach–approach conflict: conflict occurring when a person must choose between two desirable goals. 356

approach–avoidance conflict: conflict occurring when a person must choose or not choose a goal that has both positive and negative aspects. 356

arbitrary inference: distortion of thinking in which a person draws a conclusion that is not based on any evidence. 529

archetypes: Jung's collective, universal human memories. 444

arousal theory: theory of motivation in which people are said to have an optimal (best or ideal) level of tension that they seek to maintain by increasing or decreasing stimulation. 314

artificial intelligence (AI): the creation of a machine that can think like a human. 269

association areas: areas within each lobe of the cortex responsible for the coordination and interpretation of information, as well as higher mental processing. 75

attachment: the emotional bond between an infant and the primary caregiver. 408

attitude: a tendency to respond positively or negatively toward a certain person, object, idea, or situation. 566

attribution: the process of explaining one's own behavior and the behavior of others. 574

attribution theory: the theory of how people make attributions. 574

auditory canal: short tunnel that runs from the pinna to the eardrum. 102

auditory learners: people who learn best by hearing and saying things out loud. I-2

auditory nerve: bundle of axons from the hair cells in the inner ear. 103

authenticity: the genuine, open, and honest response of the therapist to the client. 522

authoritarian parenting: style of parenting in which parent is rigid and overly strict, showing little warmth to the child. 424

authoritative parenting: style of parenting in which parents combine warmth and affection with firm limits on a child's behavior. 424

autobiographical memory: the memory for events and facts related to one's personal life story. 252

automatic encoding: tendency of certain kinds of information to enter long-term memory with little or no effortful encoding. 239

autonomic nervous system (ANS): division of the PNS consisting of nerves that control all of the involuntary muscles, organs, and glands. 61

autonomy versus shame and doubt: second stage of personality development in which the toddler strives for physical independence. 412

aversion therapy: form of behavioral therapy in which an undesirable behavior is paired with an aversive stimulus to reduce the frequency of the behavior. 525

avoidance–avoidance conflict: conflict occurring when a person must choose between two undesirable goals. 356

axon: tubelike structure that carries the neural message to other cells. 50

axon terminals: branches at the end of the axon. 53

barbiturates: depressant drugs that have a sedative effect. 158

basal metabolic rate (BMR): the rate at which the body burns energy when the organism is resting. 321

basic anxiety: anxiety created when a child is born into the bigger and more powerful world of older children and adults. 444

basic level type: an example of a type of concept around which other similar concepts are organized, such as "dog," "cat," or "pear." 264

behavior modification or applied behavior analysis: the use of learning techniques to modify or change undesirable behavior and increase desirable behavior. 525

behavior modification: the use of operant conditioning techniques to bring about desired changes in behavior. 201

behavior therapies: action therapies based on the principles of classical and operant conditioning and aimed at changing disordered behavior without concern for the original causes of such behavior. 525

behavioral genetics: field of study devoted to discovering the genetic bases for personality characteristics. 456

behaviorism: the science of behavior that focuses on observable behavior only. 10

bell curve: alternate name for the normal curve, which is said to be shaped like a bell. A-2

benzodiazepines: drugs that lower anxiety and reduce stress. 159

bilateral cingulotomy: psychosurgical technique in which an electrode wire is inserted into the cingulated gyrus area of the brain with the guidance of a magnetic resonance imaging machine for the purpose of destroying that area of brain tissue with an electric current. 545

bilateral ECT: electroconvulsive therapy in which the electrodes are placed on both sides of the head. 544

bimodal: condition in which a distribution has two modes. A-6

bimodal distributions: frequency distribution in which there are two highpoints rather than one. A-4

binocular cues: cues for perceiving depth based on both eyes. 119

binocular disparity: the difference in images between the two eyes, which is greater for objects that are close and smaller for distant objects. 121

biofeedback: using feedback about biological conditions to bring involuntary responses, such as blood pressure and relaxation, under voluntary control. 202

biological model: model of explaining behavior as caused by biological changes in the chemical, structural, or genetic systems of the body. 477

biological preparedness: referring to the tendency of animals to learn certain associations, such as taste and nausea, with only one or few pairings due to the survival value of the learning. 184

biological psychology/behavioral neuroscience: branch of neuroscience that focuses on the biological bases of psychological processes, behavior, and learning. 49

biomedical therapies: therapies that directly affect the biological functioning of the body and brain. 541

biomedical therapy: therapy for mental disorders in which a person with a problem is treated with biological or medical methods to relieve symptoms. 516

biopsychological perspective: perspective that attributes human and animal behavior to biological events occurring in the body, such as genetic influences, hormones, and the activity of the nervous system. 16

biopsychosocial model: perspective in which abnormal behavior is seen as the result of the combined and interacting forces of biological, psychological, social, and cultural influences. 480

bipolar disorder: severe mood swings between major depressive episodes and manic episodes. 498

blind spot: area in the retina where the axons of the three layers of retinal cells exit the eye to form the optic nerve, insensitive to light. 95

borderline personality disorder: maladaptive personality pattern in which the person is moody, unstable, lacks a clear sense of identity, and often clings to others. 505

bottom-up processing: the analysis of the smaller features to build up to a complete perception. 124

brightness constancy: the tendency to perceive the apparent brightness of an object as the same even when the light conditions change. 115

Broca's aphasia: condition resulting from damage to Broca's area, causing the affected person to be unable to speak fluently, to mispronounce words, and to speak haltingly. 76

bulimia nervosa: a condition in which a person develops a cycle of "binging," or overeating enormous amounts of food at one sitting, and then using unhealthy methods to avoid weight gain. 326

burnout: negative changes in thoughts, emotions, and behavior as a result of prolonged stress or frustration. 370

bystander effect: referring to the effect that the presence of other people has on the decision to help or not help, with help becoming less likely as the number of bystanders increases. 588

caffeine: a mild stimulant found in coffee, tea, and several other plant-based substances. 158

Cannon-Bard theory of emotion: theory in which the physiological reaction and the emotion are assumed to occur at the same time. 333

case study: study of one individual in great detail. 23

catastrophe: an unpredictable, large-scale event that creates a tremendous need to adapt and adjust as well as overwhelming feelings of threat. 347

catatonic: type of schizophrenia in which the person experiences periods of statue-like immobility mixed with occasional bursts of energetic, frantic movement, and talking. 502

central nervous system (CNS): part of the nervous system consisting of the brain and spinal cord. 59

central-route processing: type of information processing that involves attending to the content of the message itself. 569

centration: in Piaget's theory, the tendency of a young child to focus only on one feature of an object while ignoring other relevant features. 403

cerebellum: part of the lower brain located behind the pons that controls and coordinates involuntary, rapid, fine motor movement. 69

cerebral hemispheres: the two sections of the cortex on the left and right sides of the brain. 73

cerebrum: the upper part of the brain consisting of the two hemispheres and the structures that connect them. 77

character: value judgments of a person's moral and ethical behavior. 436

chromosome: tightly wound strand of genetic material or DNA. 389

circadian rhythm: a cycle of bodily rhythm that occurs over a 24-hour period. 136

classical conditioning: learning to make an involuntary (reflex) response to a stimulus other than the original, natural stimulus that normally produces the reflex. 177

claustrophobia: fear of being in a small, enclosed space. 485

clinical psychology: area of psychology in which the psychologists diagnose and treat people with psychological disorders that may range from mild to severe. B-5

closure: the tendency to complete figures that are incomplete. 116

cocaine: a natural drug derived from the leaves of the coca plant. 156

cochlea: snail-shaped structure of the inner ear that is filled with fluid. 103

cognitive arousal theory: theory of emotion in which both the physical arousal and the labeling of that arousal based on cues from the environment must occur before the emotion is experienced. 333

cognitive development: the development of thinking, problem solving, and memory. 401

cognitive dissonance: sense of discomfort or distress that occurs when a person's behavior does not correspond to that person's attitudes. 570

cognitive neuroscience: study of the physical changes in the brain and nervous system during thinking. 15

cognitive perspective: modern perspective that focuses on memory, intelligence, perception, problem solving, and learning. 15

cognitive perspective: modern theory in which classical conditioning is seen to occur because the conditioned stimulus provides information or an expectancy about the coming of the unconditioned stimulus. 185

cognitive psychologists: psychologists who study the way people think, remember, and mentally organize information. 479

cognitive reserve: The ability of the brain to build and maintain new neurons and the connections between them. 299

cognitive therapy: therapy in which the focus is on helping clients recognize distortions in their thinking and replace distorted, unrealistic beliefs with more realistic, helpful thoughts. 528

cognitive universalism: theory that concepts are universal and influence the development of language. 296

cognitive-behavioral therapy (CBT): action therapy in which the goal is to help clients overcome problems by learning to think more rationally and logically. 529

cognitive-mediational theory: theory of emotion in which a stimulus must be interpreted (appraised) by a person in order to result in a physical response and an emotional reaction. 335

collective unconscious: Jung's name for the memories shared by all members of the human species. 443

College Undergraduate Stress Scale (CUSS): assessment that measures the amount of stress in a college student's life over a one-year period resulting from major life events. 350

companionate love: type of love consisting of intimacy and commitment. 584

comparative psychology: area of psychology in which the psychologists study animals and their behavior for the purpose of comparing and contrasting it to human behavior. B-6

compensation (substitution): defense mechanism in which a person makes up for inferiorities in one area by becoming superior in another area. 375

compliance: changing one's behavior as a result of other people directing or asking for the change. 560

computed tomography (CT): brain-imaging method using computer-controlled X-rays of the brain. 67

concentrative meditation: form of meditation in which a person focuses the mind on some repetitive or unchanging stimulus so that the mind can be cleared of disturbing thoughts and the body can experience relaxation. 375

concept maps: a visual representation of the relationships between key concepts, terms, and ideas. I-8

conception: the moment at which a female becomes pregnant. 391

concepts: ideas that represent a class or category of objects, events, or activities. 263

concrete operations stage: third stage of cognitive development in which the school-age child becomes capable of logical thought processes but is not yet capable of abstract thinking. 404

conditional positive regard: positive regard that is given only when the person is doing what the providers of positive regard wish. 450

conditioned emotional response (CER): emotional response that has become classically conditioned to occur to learned stimuli, such as a fear of dogs or the emotional reaction that occurs when seeing an attractive person. 183

conditioned response (CR): learned reflex response to a conditioned stimulus. 178

conditioned stimulus (CS): stimulus that becomes able to produce a learned reflex response by being paired with the original unconditioned stimulus. 178

conditioned taste aversion: development of a nausea or aversive response to a particular taste because that taste was followed by a nausea reaction, occurring after only one association. 184

cones: visual sensory receptors found at the back of the retina, responsible for color vision and sharpness of vision. 95

confirmation bias: the tendency to search for evidence that fits one's beliefs while ignoring any evidence that does not fit those beliefs. 272

conformity: changing one's own behavior to match that of other people. 556

conscience: part of the superego that produces pride or guilt, depending on how acceptable behavior is. 439

conscientiousness: the care a person gives to organization and thoughtfulness of others; dependability. 454

consciousness: a person's awareness of everything that is going on around him or her at any given moment, which is used to organize behavior. 135

conservation: in Piaget's theory, the ability to understand that simply changing the appearance of an object does not change the object's nature. 403

consolidation: the changes that take place in the structure and functioning of neurons when a memory is formed. 250

constructive processing: referring to the retrieval of memories in which those memories are altered, revised, or influenced by newer information. 243

consumer psychology: branch of psychology that studies the habits of consumers in the marketplace. 560

contiguity: the tendency to perceive two things that happen close together in time as being related. 117

contingency contract: a formal, written agreement between the therapist and client (or teacher and student) in which goals for behavioral change, reinforcements, and penalties are clearly stated. 527

continuity: the tendency to perceive things as simply as possible with a continuous pattern rather than with a complex, broken-up pattern. 117

continuous reinforcement: the reinforcement of each and every correct response. 196

control group: subjects in an experiment who are not subjected to the independent variable and who may receive a placebo treatment. 29

conventional morality: second level of Kohlberg's stages of moral development in which the child's behavior is governed by conforming to the society's norms of behavior. 418

convergence: the rotation of the two eyes in their sockets to focus on a single object, resulting in greater convergence for closer objects and lesser convergence if objects are distant. 121

convergent thinking: type of thinking in which a problem is seen as having only one answer, and all lines of thinking will eventually lead to that single answer, using previous knowledge and logic. 273

conversion disorder: somatoform disorder in which the person experiences a specific symptom in the somatic nervous system's functioning, such as paralysis, numbness, or blindness, for which there is no physical cause. 490

coping strategies: actions that people can take to master, tolerate, reduce, or minimize the effects of stressors. 373

corpus callosum: thick band of neurons that connects the right and left cerebral hemispheres. 73

correlation: a measure of the relationship between two variables. 26

correlation coefficient: a number derived from the formula for measuring a correlation and indicating the strength and direction of a correlation. 26

correlation coefficient: a number that represents the strength and direction of a relationship existing between two variables. A-10

cortex: outermost covering of the brain consisting of densely packed neurons, responsible for higher thought processes and interpretation of sensory input. 72

counseling psychology: area of psychology in which the psychologists help people with problems of adjustment. B-5

creative intelligence: the ability to deal with new and different concepts and to come up with new ways of solving problems. 277

creativity: the process of solving problems by combining ideas or behavior in new ways. 272

critical periods: times during which certain environmental influences can have an impact on the development of the infant. 395

critical thinking: making reasoned judgments about claims. 37

cross-sectional design: research design in which several different age-groups of participants are studied at one particular point in time. 386

cross-sequential design: research design in which participants are first studied by means of a cross-sectional design but are also followed and assessed for a period of time. 386

cult: any group of people with a particular religious or philosophical set of beliefs and identity. 592

cultural relativity: the need to consider the unique characteristics of the culture in which behavior takes place. 478

culture-bound syndromes: disorders found only in particular cultures. 478

curve of forgetting: a graph showing a distinct pattern in which forgetting is very fast within the first hour after learning a list and then tapers off gradually. 246

cybertherapy: psychotherapy that is offered on the Internet. Also called online, Internet, or Web therapy or counseling. 539

cyclothymia: disorder that consists of mood swings from moderate depression to hypomania and lasts two years or more. 497

dark adaptation: the recovery of the eye's sensitivity to visual stimuli in darkness after exposure to bright lights. 96

decay: loss of memory due to the passage of time, during which the memory trace is not used. 248

declarative memory: type of long-term memory containing information that is conscious and known. 231

deep lesioning: insertion of a thin, insulated wire into the brain through which an electrical current is sent that destroys the brain cells at the tip of the wire. 65

delta waves: long, slow waves that indicate the deepest stage of sleep. 141

delusional disorder: a psychotic disorder in which the primary symptom is one or more delusions. 501

delusions: false beliefs held by a person who refuses to accept evidence of their falseness. 501

dendrites: branchlike structures that receive messages from other neurons. 49

denial: psychological defense mechanism in which the person refuses to acknowledge or recognize a threatening situation. 375

dependent variable: variable in an experiment that represents the measurable response or behavior of the subjects in the experiment. 29

depersonalization disorder: dissociative disorder in which individuals feel detached and disconnected from themselves, their bodies, and their surroundings. 494

depressants: drugs that decrease the functioning of the nervous system. 156

depth perception: the ability to perceive the world in three dimensions. 119

descriptive statistics: a way of organizing numbers and summarizing them so that patterns can be determined. A-1

developmental psychology: area of psychology in which the psychologists study the changes in the way people think, relate to others, and feel as they age. B-6

developmentally delayed: condition in which a person's behavioral and cognitive skills exist at an earlier developmental stage than the skills of others who are the same chronological age. A more acceptable term for mental retardation. 284

deviation IQ scores: a type of intelligence measure that assumes that IQ is normally distributed around a mean of 100 with a standard deviation of about 15. 280

diffusion of responsibility: occurring when a person fails to take responsibility for actions or for inaction because of the presence of other people who are seen to share the responsibility. 589

direct observation: assessment in which the professional observes the client engaged in ordinary, day-to-day behavior in either a clinical or natural setting. 462

directive: therapy in which the therapist actively gives interpretations of a client's statements and may suggest certain behavior or actions. 519

discrimination: treating people differently because of prejudice toward the social group to which they belong. 577

discriminative stimulus: any stimulus, such as a stop sign or a doorknob, that provides the organism with a cue for making a certain response in order to obtain reinforcement. 194

disorganized: type of schizophrenia in which behavior is bizarre and childish and thinking, speech, and motor actions are very disordered. 502

displaced aggression: taking out one's frustrations on some less threatening or more available target, a form of displacement. 354

displacement: psychological defense mechanism in which emotional reactions and behavioral responses are shifted to targets that are more available or less threatening than the original target. 354, 375

display rules: learned ways of controlling displays of emotion in social settings. 330

dispositional cause: cause of behavior attributed to internal factors such as personality or character. 574

dissociative amnesia: loss of memory for personal information, either partial or complete. 491

dissociative disorders: disorders in which there is a break in conscious awareness, memory, the sense of identity, or some combination. 491

dissociative fugue: traveling away from familiar surroundings with amnesia for the trip and possible amnesia for personal information. 492

dissociative identity disorder: disorder occurring when a person seems to have two or more distinct personalities within one body. 492

distress: the effect of unpleasant and undesirable stressors. 347

distributed practice: spacing the study of material to be remembered by including breaks between study periods. 247

disuse: another name for decay, assuming that memories that are not used will eventually decay and disappear. 248

divergent thinking: type of thinking in which a person starts from one point and comes up with many different ideas or possibilities based on that point. 273

dizygotic twins: often called fraternal twins, occurring when two eggs each get fertilized by two different sperm, resulting in two zygotes in the uterus at the same time. 391

DNA (deoxyribonucleic acid): special molecule that contains the genetic material of the organism. 389

dominant: referring to a gene that actively controls the expression of a trait. 389

door-in-the-face technique: asking for a large commitment and being refused and then asking for a smaller commitment. 561

double approach–avoidance conflict: conflict in which the person must decide between two goals, with each goal possessing both positive and negative aspects. 357

double-blind study: study in which neither the experimenter nor the subjects know if the subjects are in the experimental or control group. 32

drive: a psychological tension and physical arousal arising when there is a need that motivates the organism to act in order to fulfill the need and reduce the tension. 310

drive-reduction theory: approach to motivation that assumes behavior arises from physiological needs that cause internal drives to push the organism to satisfy the need and reduce tension and arousal. 310

dysthymia: a moderate depression that lasts for two years or more and is typically a reaction to some external stressor. 497

echoic memory: the brief memory of something a person has just heard. 225

eclectic therapies: therapy style that results from combining elements of several different therapy techniques. 536

educational psychology: area of psychology in which the psychologists are concerned with the study of human learning and development of new learning techniques. B-7

efferent (motor) neuron: a neuron that carries messages from the central nervous system to the muscles of the body. 59

ego: part of the personality that develops out of a need to deal with reality, mostly conscious, rational, and logical. 439

egocentrism: the inability to see the world through anyone else's eyes. 403

ego integrity: sense of wholeness that comes from having lived a full life and the ability to let go of regrets; the final completion of the ego. 424

eidetic imagery: the ability to access a visual memory for 30 seconds or more. 225

elaboration likelihood model: model of persuasion stating that people will either elaborate on the persuasive message or fail to elaborate on it and that the future actions of those who do elaborate are more predictable than those who do not. 569

elaborative rehearsal: a method of transferring information from STM into LTM by making that information meaningful in some way. 230

electroconvulsive therapy (ECT): form of biomedical therapy to treat severe depression in which electrodes are placed on either one or both sides of a person's head and an electric current is passed through the electrodes that is strong enough to cause a seizure or convulsion. 544

electroencephalograph (EEG): machine designed to record the brain-wave patterns produced by electrical activity of the surface of the brain. 66

embryo: name for the developing organism from two weeks to eight weeks after fertilization. 395

embryonic period: the period from two to eight weeks after fertilization, during which the major organs and structures of the organism develop. 395

emotion: the "feeling" aspect of consciousness, characterized by a certain physical arousal, a certain behavior that reveals the emotion to the outside world, and an inner awareness of feelings. 328

emotional intelligence: the awareness of and ability to manage one's own emotions as well as the ability to be self-motivated, able to feel what others feel, and socially skilled. 289

emotion-focused coping: coping strategies that change the impact of a stressor by changing the emotional reaction to the stressor. 373

empathy: the ability of the therapist to understand the feelings of the client. 522

encoding: the set of mental operations that people perform on sensory information to convert that information into a form that is usable in the brain's storage systems. 220

encoding failure: failure to process information into memory. 247

encoding specificity: the tendency for memory of information to be improved if related information (such as surroundings or physiological state) available when the memory is first formed is also available when the memory is being retrieved. 236

endocrine glands: glands that secrete chemicals called hormones directly into the bloodstream. 79

environmental psychology: area of psychology in which the focus is on how people interact with and are affected by their physical environments. B-9

episodic memory: type of declarative memory containing personal information not readily available to others, such as daily activities and events. 232

equal status contact: contact between groups in which the groups have equal status, with neither group having power over the other. 580

escape or withdrawal: leaving the presence of a stressor, either literally or by a psychological withdrawal into fantasy, drug abuse, or apathy. 355

eustress: the effect of positive events, or the optimal amount of stress that people need to promote health and well-being. 347

evolutionary perspective: perspective that focuses on the biological bases of universal mental characteristics that all humans share. 16

excitatory synapse: synapse at which a neurotransmitter causes the receiving cell to fire. 54

expectancy: a person's subjective feeling that a particular behavior will lead to a reinforcing consequence. 449

expectancy-value theories: incentive theories that assume the actions of humans cannot be predicted or fully understood without understanding the beliefs, values, and the importance that a person attaches to those beliefs and values at any given moment in time. 315

experiment: a deliberate manipulation of a variable to see if corresponding changes in behavior result, allowing the determination of cause-and-effect relationships. 28

experimental group: subjects in an experiment who are subjected to the independent variable. 29

experimental psychology: area of psychology in which the psychologists primarily do research and experiments in the areas of learning, memory, thinking, perception, motivation, and language. B-6

experimenter effect: tendency of the experimenter's expectations for a study to unintentionally influence the results of the study. 31

explicit memory: memory that is consciously known, such as declarative memory. 232

extinction: the disappearance or weakening of a learned response following the removal or absence of the unconditioned stimulus (in classical conditioning) or the removal of a reinforcer (in operant-conditioning). 180, 528

extraversion: dimension of personality referring to one's need to be with other people. 454

extraverts: people who are outgoing and sociable. 454

extrinsic motivation: type of motivation in which a person performs an action because it leads to an outcome that is separate from or external to the person. 308

eye-movement desensitization reprocessing (EMDR): controversial form of therapy for post-traumatic stress disorder and similar anxiety problems in which the client is directed to move the eyes rapidly back and forth while thinking of a disturbing memory. 535

facial feedback hypothesis: theory of emotion that assumes that facial expressions provide feedback to the brain concerning the emotion being expressed, which in turn causes and intensifies the emotion. 334

false positive: error of recognition in which people think that they recognize some stimulus that is not actually in memory. 239

family counseling (family therapy): a form of group therapy in which family members meet together with a counselor or therapist to resolve problems that affect the entire family. 532

fertilization: the union of the ovum and sperm. 391

fetal period: the time from about eight weeks after conception until the birth of the child. 396

fetus: name for the developing organism from eight weeks after fertilization to the birth of the baby. 396

figure–ground: the tendency to perceive objects, or figures, as existing on a background. 116

five-factor model (Big Five): model of personality traits that describes five basic trait dimensions. 453

fixation: disorder in which the person does not fully resolve the conflict in a particular psychosexual stage, resulting in personality traits and behavior associated with that earlier stage. 441

fixed interval schedule of reinforcement: schedule of reinforcement in which the interval of time that must pass before reinforcement becomes possible is always the same. 196

fixed ratio schedule of reinforcement: schedule of reinforcement in which the number of responses required for reinforcement is always the same. 198

flashbulb memories: type of automatic encoding that occurs because an unexpected event has strong emotional associations for the person remembering it. 240

flat affect: a lack of emotional responsiveness. 501

flooding: technique for treating phobias and other stress disorders in which the person is rapidly and intensely exposed to the fear-provoking situation or object and prevented from making the usual avoidance or escape response. 526

foot-in-the-door technique: asking for a small commitment and, after gaining compliance, asking for a bigger commitment. 560

forensic psychology: area of psychology concerned with people in the legal system, including profiling of criminals, jury selection, and expert witnessing. B-8

formal concepts: concepts that are defined by specific rules or features. 264

formal operations stage: Piaget's last stage of cognitive development in which the adolescent becomes capable of abstract thinking. 404

free association: psychoanalytic technique in which a patient was encouraged to talk about anything that came to mind without fear of negative evaluations. 518

free-floating anxiety: anxiety that is unrelated to any realistic, known source. 484

frequency count: assessment in which the frequency of a particular behavior is counted. 462

frequency distribution: a table or graph that shows how often different numbers or scores appear in a particular set of scores. A-2

frequency theory: theory of pitch that states that pitch is related to the speed of vibrations in the basilar membrane. 104

frontal lobes: areas of the cortex located in the front and top of the brain, responsible for higher mental processes and decision making as well as the production of fluent speech. 74

frustration: the psychological experience produced by the blocking of a desired goal or fulfillment of a perceived need. 353

fully functioning person: a person who is in touch with and trusting of the deepest, innermost urges and feelings. 450

functional fixedness: a block to problem solving that comes from thinking about objects in terms of only their typical functions. 271

functionalism: early perspective in psychology associated with William James, in which the focus of study is how the mind allows people to adapt, live, work, and play. 7

fundamental attribution error: the tendency to overestimate the influence of internal factors in determining the behavior of others while underestimating situational factors. 574

g factor: the ability to reason and solve problems, or general intelligence. 275

gender: the psychological and behavioral aspects of being male or female. 413

gender identity: perception of one's gender and the behavior that is associated with that gender. 414

gender roles: the culture's expectations for masculine or feminine behavior, including attitudes, actions, and personality traits associated with being male or female in that culture. 414

gender typing: the process of acquiring gender role characteristics. 414

gene: section of DNA having the same arrangement of chemical elements. 389

general adaptation syndrome (GAS): the three stages of the body's physiological reaction to stress, including alarm, resistance, and exhaustion. 358

generalized anxiety disorder: disorder in which a person has feelings of dread and impending doom along with physical symptoms of stress, which lasts six months or more. 487

generativity: providing guidance to one's children or the next generation, or contributing to the well-being of the next generation through career or volunteer work. 423

genetics: the science of inherited traits. 389

germinal period: first two weeks after fertilization, during which the zygote moves down to the uterus and begins to implant in the lining. 394

Gestalt psychology: early perspective in psychology focusing on perception and sensation, particularly the perception of patterns and whole figures. 9

Gestalt therapy: form of directive insight therapy in which the therapist helps clients to accept all parts of their feelings and subjective experiences, using leading questions and planned experiences such as role-playing. 522

gifted: the 2 percent of the population falling on the upper end of the normal curve and typically possessing an IQ of 130 or above. 286

glial cells: cells that provide support for the neurons to grow on and around, deliver nutrients to neurons, produce myelin to coat axons, clean up waste products and dead neurons, influence information processing, and, during prenatal development, influence the generation of new neurons. 50

glucagons: hormones that are secreted by the pancreas to control the levels of fats, proteins, and carbohydrates in the body by increasing the level of glucose in the bloodstream. 320

gonads: sex glands; secrete hormones that regulate sexual development and behavior as well as reproduction. 80

grammar: the system of rules governing the structure and use of a language. 294

groupthink: kind of thinking that occurs when people place more importance on maintaining group cohesiveness than on assessing the facts of the problem with which the group is concerned. 558

gustation: the sensation of a taste. 107

habits: in behaviorism, sets of well-learned responses that have become automatic. 447

habituation: tendency of the brain to stop attending to constant, unchanging information. 92

hallucinations: false sensory perceptions, such as hearing voices that do not really exist. 501

hallucinogenics: drugs including hallucinogens and marijuana that produce hallucinations or increased feelings of relaxation and intoxication. 156

hallucinogens: drugs that cause false sensory messages, altering the perception of reality. 163

halo effect: tendency of an interviewer to allow positive characteristics of a client to influence the assessments of the client's behavior and statements. 460

hardy personality: a person who seems to thrive on stress but lacks the anger and hostility of the Type A personality. 366

hassles: the daily annoyances of everyday life. 351

health psychology: area of psychology focusing on how physical activities, psychological traits, and social relationships affect overall health and rate of illnesses. 346, B-7

heroin: narcotic drug derived from opium that is extremely addictive. 162

hertz (Hz): cycles or waves per second, a measurement of frequency. 101

heuristic: an educated guess based on prior experiences that helps narrow down the possible solutions for a problem. Also known as a "rule of thumb." 267

higher-order conditioning: occurs when a strong conditioned stimulus is paired with a neutral stimulus, causing the neutral stimulus to become a second conditioned stimulus. 181

hindsight bias: the tendency to falsely believe, through revision of older memories to include newer information, that one could have correctly predicted the outcome of an event. 243

hippocampus: curved structure located within each temporal lobe, responsible for the formation of long-term memories and the storage of memory for location of objects. 71

histogram: a bar graph showing a frequency distribution. A-2

homeostasis: the tendency of body to maintain a steady state. 310

hormones: chemicals released into the bloodstream by endocrine glands. 79

human development: the scientific study of the changes that occur in people as they age from conception until death. 386

human factors psychology: area of industrial/organizational psychology concerned with the study of the way humans and machines interact with each other. B-10

humanistic perspective: the "third force" in psychology that focuses on those aspects of personality that make people uniquely human, such as subjective feelings and freedom of choice. 449

hypnosis: state of consciousness in which the person is especially susceptible to suggestion. 151

hypochondriasis: somatoform disorder in which the person is terrified of being sick and worries constantly, going to doctors repeatedly, and becoming preoccupied with every sensation of the body. 490

hypothalamus: small structure in the brain located below the thalamus and directly above the pituitary gland, responsible for motivational behavior such as sleep, hunger, thirst, and sex. 71

hypothesis: tentative explanation of a phenomenon based on observations. 20

iconic memory: visual sensory memory, lasting only a fraction of a second. 224

id: part of the personality present at birth and completely unconscious. 438

ideal self: one's perception of whom one should be or would like to be. 450

identification: defense mechanism in which a person tries to become like someone else to deal with anxiety. 375, 442

identity versus role confusion: fifth stage of personality development in which the adolescent must find a consistent sense of self. 419

imaginary audience: type of thought common to adolescents in which young people believe that other people are just as concerned about the adolescent's thoughts and characteristics as they themselves are. 418

immune system: the system of cells, organs, and chemicals of the body that responds to attacks from diseases, infections, and injuries. 360

implicit memory: memory that is not easily brought into conscious awareness, such as procedural memory. 231

implicit personality theory: sets of assumptions about how different types of people, personality traits, and actions are related to each other. 573

impression formation: the forming of the first knowledge that a person has concerning another person. 572

incentive approaches: theories of motivation in which behavior is explained as a response to the external stimulus and its rewarding properties. 315

incentives: things that attract or lure people into action. 315

independent variable: variable in an experiment that is manipulated by the experimenter. 29

individualized educational program (IEP): a special education plan drawn up by teachers for children with special needs such as giftedness or mental retardation. B-1

industrial/organizational (I/O) psychology: area of psychology concerned with the relationships between people and their work environment. B-9

industry versus inferiority: fourth stage of personality development in which the child strives for a sense of competence and self-esteem. 412

infantile amnesia: the inability to retrieve memories from much before age 3. 252

inferential statistics: statistical analysis of two or more sets of numerical data to reduce the possibility of error in measurement and to determine if the differences between the data sets are greater than chance variation would predict. A-1

information-processing model: model of memory that assumes the processing of information for memory storage is similar to the way a computer processes memory in a series of three stages. 221

in-groups: social groups with whom a person identifies; "us." 577

inhibitory synapse: synapse at which a neurotransmitter causes the receiving cell to stop firing. 54

initiative versus guilt: third stage of personality development in which the preschool-aged child strives for emotional and psychological independence and attemps to satisfy curiosity about the world. 412

insight: the sudden perception of relationships among various parts of a problem, allowing the solution to the problem to come quickly. 206

insight therapies: therapies in which the main goal is helping people to gain insight with respect to their behavior, thoughts, and feelings. 516

insomnia: the inability to get to sleep, stay asleep, or get a good quality of sleep. 145

instinct approach: approach to motivation that assumes people are governed by instincts similar to those of animals. 309

instinctive drift: tendency for an animal's behavior to revert to genetically controlled patterns. 200

instincts: the biologically determined and innate patterns of behavior that exist in both people and animals. 309

insulin: a hormone secreted by the pancreas to control the levels of fats, proteins, and carbohydrates in the body by reducing the level of glucose in the bloodstream. 320

intelligence: the ability to learn from one's experiences, acquire knowledge, and use resources effectively in adapting to new situations or solving problems. 275

intelligence quotient (IQ): a number representing a measure of intelligence, resulting from the division of one's mental age by one's chronological age and then multiplying that quotient by 100. 278

interneuron: a neuron found in the center of the spinal cord that receives information from the afferent neurons and sends commands to the muscles through the efferent neurons. Interneurons also make up the bulk of the neurons in the brain. 59

interpersonal attraction: liking or having the desire for a relationship with another person. 582

interview: method of personality assessment in which the professional asks questions of the client and allows the client to answer, either in a structured or unstructured fashion. 460

intimacy: an emotional and psychological closeness that is based on the ability to trust, share, and care, while still maintaining a sense of self. 422

intrinsic motivation: type of motivation in which a person performs an action because the act itself is rewarding or satisfying in some internal manner. 308

introversion: dimension of personality in which people tend to withdraw from excessive stimulation. 453

introverts: people who prefer solitude and dislike being the center of attention. 454

irreversibility: in Piaget's theory, the inability of the young child to mentally reverse an action. 403

James-Lange theory of emotion: theory in which a physiological reaction leads to the labeling of an emotion. 332

"jigsaw classroom": educational technique in which each individual is given only part of the information needed to solve a problem, causing the separate individuals to be forced to work together to find the solution. 58

just noticeable difference (jnd or the difference threshold): the smallest difference between two stimuli that is detectable 50 percent of the time. 91

kinesthetic learners: people who prefer to learn by doing and being active. I-2

kinesthetic sense: sense of the location of body parts in relation to the ground and each other. 110

language: a system for combining symbols (such as words) so that an unlimited number of meaningful statements can be made for the purpose of communicating with others. 294

latency: fourth stage occurring during the school years, in which the sexual feelings of the child are repressed while the child develops in other ways. 442

latent content: the symbolic or hidden meaning of dreams. 518

latent learning: learning that remains hidden until its application becomes useful. 205

Law of Effect: law stating that if an action is followed by a pleasurable consequence, it will tend to be repeated, and if followed by an unpleasant consequence, it will tend not to be repeated. 187

learned helplessness: the tendency to fail to act to escape from a situation because of a history of repeated failures in the past. 207

learning/performance distinction: referring to the observation that learning can take place without actual performance of the learned behavior. 208

learning style: the particular way in which a person takes in information. I-2

leptin: a hormone that, when released into the bloodstream, signals the hypothalamus that the body has had enough food and reduces the appetite while increasing the feeling of being full. 324

levels-of-processing model: model of memory that assumes information that is more "deeply processed," or processed according to its meaning rather than just the sound or physical characteristics of the word or words, will be remembered more efficiently and for a longer period of time. 222

light adaptation: the recovery of the eye's sensitivity to visual stimuli in light after exposure to darkness. 97

limbic system: a group of several brain structures located under the cortex and involved in learning, emotion, memory, and motivation. 70

linear perspective: the tendency for parallel lines to appear to converge on each other. 119

linguistic relativity hypothesis: the theory that thought processes and concepts are controlled by language. 296

locus of control: the tendency for people to assume that they either have control or do not have control over events and consequences in their lives. 449

longitudinal design: research design in which one participant or group of participants is studied over a long period of time. 386

long-term memory (LTM): the system of memory into which all the information is placed to be kept more or less permanently. 229

lowball technique: getting a commitment from a person and then raising the cost of that commitment. 561

LSD (lysergic acid diethylamide): powerful synthetic hallucinogen. 163

magnetic resonance imaging (MRI): brain-imaging method using radio waves and magnetic fields of the body to produce detailed images of the brain. 67

magnification and minimization: distortions of thinking in which a person blows a negative event out of proportion to its importance (magnification) while ignoring relevant positive events (minimization). 529

magnification: the tendency to interpret situations as far more dangerous, harmful, or important than they actually are. 488

maintenance rehearsal: practice of saying some information to be remembered over and over in one's head in order to maintain it in short-term memory. 228

major depression: severe depression that comes on suddenly and seems to have no external cause. 497

maladaptive: anything that does not allow a person to function within or adapt to the stresses and everyday demands of life. 476

manic: having the quality of excessive excitement, energy, and elation or irritability. 498

manifest content: the actual content of one's dream. 518

marijuana: mild hallucinogen (also known as *pot* or *weed*) derived from the leaves and flowers of a particular type of hemp plant. 164

MDMA (Ecstasy or X): designer drug that can have both stimulant and hallucinatory effects. 164

mean: the arithmetic average of a distribution of numbers. A-4

means–end analysis: heuristic in which the difference between the starting situation and the goal is determined and then steps are taken to reduce that difference. 268

measure of central tendency: numbers that best represent the most typical score of a frequency distribution. A-4

measures of variability: measurement of the degree of differences within a distribution or how the scores are spread out. A-6

median: the middle score in an ordered distribution of scores, or the mean of the two middle numbers; the 50th percentile. A-5

meditation: mental series of exercises meant to refocus attention and achieve a trancelike state of consciousness. 374

medulla: the first large swelling at the top of the spinal cord, forming the lowest part of the brain, which is responsible for life-sustaining functions such as breathing, swallowing, and heart rate. 68

memory: an active system that receives information from the senses, puts that information into a usable form, and organizes it as it stores it away, and then retrieves the information from storage. 220

memory trace: physical change in the brain that occurs when a memory is formed. 248

menopause: the cessation of ovulation and menstrual cycles and the end of a woman's reproductive capability. 421

mental images: mental representations that stand for objects or events and have a picture-like quality. 262

mental set: the tendency for people to persist in using problem-solving patterns that have worked for them in the past. 272

mescaline: natural hallucinogen derived from the peyote cactus buttons. 164

microsleeps: brief sidesteps into sleep lasting only a few seconds. 137

minimization: the tendency to give little or no importance to one's successes or positive events and traits. 488

mirror neurons: neurons that fire when an animal or person performs an action and also when an animal or person observes that same action being performed by another. 82

misinformation effect: the tendency of misleading information presented after an event to alter the memories of the event itself. 243

mnemonic: a strategy or trick for aiding memory. I-11

mode: the most frequent score in a distribution of scores. A-6

modeling: learning through the observation and imitation of others. 526

monocular cues (pictorial depth cues): cues for perceiving depth based on one eye only. 119

monozygotic twins: identical twins formed when one zygote splits into two separate masses of cells, each of which develops into a separate embryo. 391

mood disorders: disorders in which mood is severely disturbed. 497

morphemes: the smallest units of meaning within a language. 294

morphine: narcotic drug derived from opium, used to treat severe pain. 162

motion parallax: the perception of motion of objects in which close objects appear to move more quickly than objects that are farther away. 120

motivation: the process by which activities are started, directed, and continued so that physical or psychological needs or wants are met. 308

motor cortex: section of the frontal lobe located at the back, responsible for sending motor commands to the muscles of the somatic nervous system. 75

motor pathway: nerves coming from the CNS to the voluntary muscles, consisting of efferent neurons. 62

Müller-Lyer illusion: illusion of line length that is distorted by inward-turning or outward-turning corners on the ends of the lines, causing lines of equal length to appear to be different. 122

multiple approach–avoidance conflict: conflict in which the person must decide between more than two goals, with each goal possessing both positive and negative aspects. 357

myelin: fatty substances produced by certain glial cells that coat the axons of neurons to insulate, protect, and speed up the neural impulse. 50

narcolepsy: sleep disorder in which a person falls immediately into REM sleep during the day without warning. 146

narcotics: a class of opium-related drugs that suppress the sensation of pain by binding to and stimulating the nervous system's natural receptor sites for endorphins. 156

natural concepts: concepts people form as a result of their experiences in the real world. 264

natural killer cell: immune system cell responsible for suppressing viruses and destroying tumor cells. 361

nature: the influence of our inherited characteristics on our personality, physical growth, intellectual growth, and social interactions. 387

need: a requirement of some material (such as food or water) that is essential for survival of the organism. 310

need for achievement (nAch): a need that involves a strong desire to succeed in attaining goals, not only realistic ones but also challenging ones. 311

need for affiliation (nAff): the need for friendly social interactions and relationships with others. 311

need for power (nPow): the need to have control or influence over others. 311

negative reinforcement: the reinforcement of a response by the removal, escape from, or avoidance of an unpleasant stimulus. 190

negative symptoms: symptoms of schizophrenia that are less than normal behavior or an absence of normal behavior; poor attention, flat affect, and poor speech production. 502

negatively skewed: a distribution of scores in which scores are concentrated in the high end of the distribution. A-4

neo-Freudians: followers of Freud who developed their own competing psychodynamic theories. 443

nerves: bundles of axons coated in myelin that travel together through the body. 50

nervous system: an extensive network of specialized cells that carries information to and from all parts of the body. 48

neurofeedback: form of biofeedback using brain-scanning devices to provide feedback about brain activity in an effort to modify behavior. 202

neuron: the basic cell that makes up the nervous system and that receives and sends messages within that system. 49

neuroplasticity: the ability within the brain to constantly change both the structure and function of many cells in response to experience or trauma. 60

neuroscience: a branch of the life sciences that deals with the structure and function of neurons, nerves, and nervous tissue. 49

neurotic personalities: personalities typified by maladaptive ways of dealing with relationships in Horney's theory. 444

neuroticism: degree of emotional instability or stability. 454

neurotransmitter: chemical found in the synaptic vesicles that, when released, has an effect on the next cell. 53

neutral stimulus (NS): stimulus that has no effect on the desired response. 178

nicotine: the active ingredient in tobacco. 157

night terrors: relatively rare disorder in which the person experiences extreme fear and screams or runs around during deep sleep without waking fully. 143

nightmares: bad dreams occurring during REM sleep. 143

non-REM (NREM) sleep: any of the stages of sleep that do not include REM. 139

nondirective: therapy style in which the therapist remains relatively neutral and does not interpret or take direct actions with regard to the client, instead remaining a calm, nonjudgmental listener while the client talks. 521

norm of reciprocity: assumption that if someone does something for a person, that person should do something for the other in return. 561

normal curve: a special frequency polygon in which the scores are symmetrically distributed around the mean, and the mean, median, and mode are all located on the same point on the curve with scores decreasing as the curve extends from the mean. A-2

nurture: the influence of the environment on personality, physical growth, intellectual growth, and social interactions. 387

obedience: changing one's behavior at the command of an authority figure. 561

object permanence: the knowledge that an object exists even when it is not in sight. 402

objective introspection: the process of examining and measuring one's own thoughts and mental activities. 6

observational learning: learning new behavior by watching a model perform that behavior. 207

observer bias: tendency of observers to see what they expect to see. 23

observer effect: tendency of people or animals to behave differently from normal when they know they are being observed. 22

obsessive-compulsive disorder: disorder in which intruding, recurring thoughts or obsessions create anxiety that is relieved by performing a repetitive, ritualistic behavior or mental act (compulsion). 486

occipital lobe: section of the brain located at the rear and bottom of each cerebral hemisphere containing the visual centers of the brain. 73

Oedipus complex: situation occurring in the phallic stage in which a child develops a sexual attraction to the opposite-sex parent and jealousy of the same-sex parent. 442

olfaction (olfactory sense): the sensation of smell. 108

olfactory bulbs: areas of the brain located just above the sinus cavity and just below the frontal lobes that receive information from the olfactory receptor cells. 71, 109

openness: one of the five factors; willingness to try new things and be open to new experiences. 454

operant: any behavior that is voluntary. 187

operant conditioning: the learning of voluntary behavior through the effects of pleasant and unpleasant consequences to responses. 186

operational definition: definition of a variable of interest that allows it to be directly measured. 28

opium: substance derived from the opium poppy from which all narcotic drugs are derived. 162

opponent-process theory: theory of color vision that proposes four primary colors with cones arranged in pairs: red and green, blue and yellow. 98

optimists: people who expect positive outcomes. 366

oral stage: first stage occurring in the first year of life in which the mouth is the erogenous zone and weaning is the primary conflict. 441

out-groups: social groups with whom a person does not identify; "them." 577

ovaries: the female gonads. 80

overgeneralization: distortion of thinking in which a person draws sweeping conclusions based on only one incident or event and applies those conclusions to events that are unrelated to the original; also the tendency to interpret a single negative event as a never-ending pattern of defeat and failure. 488, 529

overlap (interposition): the assumption that an object that appears to be blocking part of another object is in front of the second object and closer to the viewer. 119

ovum: the female sex cell, or egg. 391

pancreas: endocrine gland; controls the levels of sugar in the blood. 80

panic attack: sudden onset of intense panic in which multiple physical symptoms of stress occur, often with feelings that one is dying. 486

panic disorder: disorder in which panic attacks occur frequently enough to cause the person difficulty in adjusting to daily life. 486

panic disorder with agoraphobia: fear of leaving one's familiar surroundings because one might have a panic attack in public. 486

parallel distributed processing (PDP) model: a model of memory in which memory processes are proposed to take place at the same time over a large network of neural connections. 222

parameter: a number representing some measure of central tendency or variability within a population. A-1

paranoid: type of schizophrenia in which the person suffers from delusions of persecution, grandeur, and jealousy, together with hallucinations. 502

parapsychology: the study of ESP, ghosts, and other subjects that do not normally fall into the realm of ordinary psychology. 125

parasympathetic division: part of the ANS that restores the body to normal functioning after arousal and is responsible for the day-to-day functioning of the organs and glands. 62

parietal lobes: sections of the brain located at the top and back of each cerebral hemisphere containing the centers for touch, taste, and temperature sensations. 73

partial reinforcement effect: the tendency for a response that is reinforced after some, but not all, correct responses to be very resistant to extinction. 196

participant modeling: technique in which a model demonstrates the desired behavior in a step-by-step, gradual process while the client is encouraged to imitate the model. 526

participant observation: a naturalistic observation in which the observer becomes a participant in the group being observed. 23

PCP: synthesized drug now used as an animal tranquilizer that can cause stimulant, depressant, narcotic, or hallucinogenic effects. 163

peak experiences: according to Maslow, times in a person's life during which self-actualization is temporarily achieved. 317

perception: the method by which the sensations experienced at any given moment are interpreted and organized in some meaningful fashion. 114

perceptual set (perceptual expectancy): the tendency to perceive things a certain way because previous experiences or expectations influence those perceptions. 123

peripheral nervous system (PNS): all nerves and neurons that are not contained in the brain and spinal cord but that run through the body itself. 61

peripheral-route processing: type of information processing that involves attending to factors not involved in the message, such as the appearance of the source of the message, the length of the message, and other noncontent factors. 569

permissive indulgent: permissive parenting in which parents are so involved that children are allowed to behave without set limits. 424

permissive neglectful: permissive parenting in which parents are uninvolved with child or child's behavior. 424

permissive parenting: style of parenting in which parent makes few, if any demands on a child's behavior. 424

personal fable: type of thought common to adolescents in which young people believe themselves to be unique and protected from harm. 417

personal unconscious: Jung's name for the unconscious mind as described by Freud. 443

personality: the unique and relatively stable ways in which people think, feel, and behave. 436

personality disorders: disorders in which a person adopts a persistent, rigid, and maladaptive pattern of behavior that interferes with normal social interactions. 504

personality inventory: paper and pencil or computerized test that consists of statements that require a specific, standardized response from the person taking the test. 462

personality psychology: area of psychology in which the psychologists study the differences in personality among people. B-6

personalization: distortion of thinking in which a person takes responsibility or blame for events that are unconnected to the person. 529

person-centered therapy: a nondirective insight therapy based on the work of Carl Rogers in which the client does all the talking and the therapist listens. 521

persuasion: the process by which one person tries to change the belief, opinion, position, or course of action of another person through argument, pleading, or explanation. 569

pessimists: people who expect negative outcomes. 366

phallic stage: third stage occurring from about 3 to 6 years of age, in which the child discovers sexual feelings. 441

phobia: an irrational, persistent fear of an object, situation, or social activity. 484

phonemes: the basic units of sound in language. 294

phototherapy: the use of lights to treat seasonal affective disorder or other disorders. 508

physical dependence: condition occurring when a person's body becomes unable to function normally without a particular drug. 155

physiological psychology: area of psychology in which the psychologists study the biological bases of behavior. B-6

pineal gland: endocrine gland located near the base of the cerebrum; secretes melatonin. 80

pinna: the visible part of the ear. 102

pitch: psychological experience of sound that corresponds to the frequency of the sound waves; higher frequencies are perceived as higher pitches. 104

pituitary gland: gland located in the brain that secretes human growth hormone and influences all other hormone-secreting glands (also known as the master gland). 79

place theory: theory of pitch that states that different pitches are experienced by the stimulation of hair cells in different locations on the organ of Corti. 104

placebo effect: the phenomenon in which the expectations of the participants in a study can influence their behavior. 30

pleasure principle: principle by which the id functions; the immediate satisfaction of needs without regard for the consequences. 438

polygon: line graph showing a frequency distribution. A-2

pons: the larger swelling above the medulla that connects the top of the brain to the bottom and that plays a part in sleep, dreaming, left–right body coordination, and arousal. 69

population: the entire group of people or animals in which the researcher is interested. 24

positive psychology movement: a viewpoint that recommends shifting the focus of psychology away from the negative aspects to a more positive focus on strengths, well-being, and the pursuit of happiness. 338

positive regard: warmth, affection, love, and respect that come from significant others in one's life. 450

positive reinforcement: the reinforcement of a response by the addition or experiencing of a pleasurable stimulus. 189

positive symptoms: symptoms of schizophrenia that are excesses of behavior or occur in addition to normal behavior; hallucinations, delusions, and distorted thinking. 502

positively skewed: a distribution of scores in which scores are concentrated in the low end of the distribution. A-4

positron emission tomography (PET): brain-imaging method in which a radioactive sugar is injected into the subject and a computer compiles a color-coded image of the activity of the brain, with lighter colors indicating more activity. 67.

postconventional morality: third level of Kohlberg's stages of moral development in which the person's behavior is governed by moral principles that have been decided on by the individual and that may be in disagreement with accepted social norms. 418

postpartum depression: depression occurring within a year after giving birth in about 10 percent of women and that includes intense worry about the baby, thoughts of suicide, and fears of harming the baby. 474

postpartum psychosis: a rare and severe form of depression that occurs in women just after giving birth and includes delusional thinking and hallucinations. 474

post-traumatic stress disorder (PTSD): a disorder resulting from exposure to a major stressor, with symptoms of anxiety, nightmares, poor sleep, reliving the event, and concentration problems, lasting for more than one month. 348

practical intelligence: the ability to use information to get along in life and become successful. 277

pragmatics: aspects of language involving the practical ways of communicating with others, or the social "niceties" of language. 295

preconventional morality: first level of Kohlberg's stages of moral development in which the child's behavior is governed by the consequences of the behavior. 418

prefrontal lobotomy: psychosurgery in which the connections of the prefrontal lobes of the brain to the rear portions are severed. 545

prejudice: negative attitude held by a person about the members of a particular social group. 576

preoperational stage: Piaget's second stage of cognitive development in which the preschool child learns to use language as a means of exploring the world. 402

pressure: the psychological experience produced by urgent demands or expectations for a person's behavior that come from an outside source. 353

primacy effect: tendency to remember information at the beginning of a body of information better than the information that follows. 237

primary appraisal: the first step in assessing stress, which involves estimating the severity of a stressor and classifying it as either a threat or a challenge. 362

primary drives: those drives that involve needs of the body such as hunger and thirst. 310

primary reinforcer: any reinforcer that is naturally reinforcing by meeting a basic biological need, such as hunger, thirst, or touch. 188

proactive interference: memory retrieval problem that occurs when older information prevents or interferes with the retrieval of newer information. 248

problem solving: process of cognition that occurs when a goal must be reached by thinking and behaving in certain ways. 266

problem-focused coping: coping strategies that try to eliminate the source of a stress or reduce its impact through direct actions. 373

procedural (nondeclarative) memory: type of long-term memory including memory for skills, procedures, habits, and conditioned responses. These memories are not conscious but are implied to exist because they affect conscious behavior. 230

projection: psychological defense mechanism in which unacceptable or threatening impulses or feelings are seen as originating with someone else, usually the target of the impulses or feelings. 375, 460

projective tests: personality assessments that present ambiguous visual stimuli to the client and ask the client to respond with whatever comes to mind. 460

prosocial behavior: socially desirable behavior that benefits others. 588

prototype: an example of a concept that closely matches the defining characteristics of a concept. 265

proximity: physical or geographical nearness. 582

proximity: the tendency to perceive objects that are close to each other as part of the same grouping 116, or physical or geographical nearness. 582

pseudopsychologies: systems of explaining human behavior that are not based on or consistent with scientific evidence. 38

psilocybin: natural hallucinogen found in certain mushrooms. 164

psychiatric social worker: a social worker with some training in therapy methods who focuses on the environmental conditions that can have an impact on mental disorders, such as poverty, overcrowding, stress, and drug abuse. 17, B-3

psychiatrist: a medical doctor who has specialized in the diagnosis and treatment of psychological disorders. 17, B-3

psychoactive drugs: drugs that alter thinking, perception, and memory. 154

psychoanalysis: Freud's term for both the theory of personality and the therapy based on it. 10, 443, 518

psychoanalyst: either a psychiatrist or a psychologist who has special training in the theories of Sigmund Freud and his method of psychoanalysis. 17, B-3

psychodynamic perspective: modern version of psychoanalysis that is more focused on the development of a sense of self and the discovery of other motivations behind a person's behavior than sexual motivations. 13

psychodynamic therapy: a newer and more general term for therapies based on psychoanalysis with an emphasis on transference, shorter treatment times, and a more direct therapeutic approach. 519

psychological defense mechanisms: unconscious distortions of a person's perception of reality that reduce stress and anxiety. 374

psychological dependence: the feeling that a drug is needed to continue a feeling of emotional or psychological well-being. 155

psychological disorders: any pattern of behavior that causes people significant distress, causes them to harm others, or harms their ability to function in daily life. 476

psychologist: a professional with an academic degree and specialized training in one or more areas of psychology. 18, B-3

psychology: the scientific study of behavior and mental processes. 4

psychopathology: the study of abnormal behavior. 474

psychoneuroimmunology: the study of the effects of psychological factors such as stress, emotions, thoughts, and behavior on the immune system. 360

psychopharmacology: the use of drugs to control or relieve the symptoms of psychological disorders. 541

psychophysiological disorder: modern term for psychosomatic disorder. 490

psychosexual stages: five stages of personality development proposed by Freud and tied to the sexual development of the child. 441

psychosomatic disorder: disorder in which psychological stress causes a real physical disorder or illness. 490

psychosurgery: surgery performed on brain tissue to relieve or control severe psychological disorders. 545

psychotherapy: therapy for mental disorders in which a person with a problem talks with a psychological professional. 516

psychotic: term applied to a person who is no longer able to perceive what is real and what is fantasy. 501

puberty: the physical changes that occur in the body as sexual development reaches its peak. 416

punishment: any event or object that, when following a response, makes that response less likely to happen again. 191

punishment by application: the punishment of a response by the addition or experiencing of an unpleasant stimulus. 191

punishment by removal: the punishment of a response by the removal of a pleasurable stimulus. 191

random assignment: process of assigning subjects to the experimental or control groups randomly, so that each subject has an equal chance of being in either group. 30

range: the difference between the highest and lowest scores in a distribution. A-6

rapid eye movement (REM): stage of sleep in which the eyes move rapidly under the eyelids and the person is typically experiencing a dream. 139

rating scale: assessment in which a numerical value is assigned to specific behavior that is listed in the scale. 462

rational-emotive behavior therapy (REBT): cognitive-behavioral therapy in which clients are directly challenged in their irrational beliefs and helped to restructure their thinking into more rational belief statements. 530

rationalization: psychological defense mechanism in which a person invents acceptable excuses for unacceptable behavior. 375

reaction formation: psychological defense mechanism in which a person forms an opposite emotional or behavioral reaction to the way he or she really feels to keep those true feelings hidden from self and others. 375

real self: one's perception of actual characteristics, traits, and abilities. 450

realistic conflict theory: theory stating that prejudice and discrimination will be increased between groups that are in conflict over a limited resource. 577

reality principle: principle by which the ego functions; the satisfaction of the demands of the id only when negative consequences will not result. 439

recall: type of memory retrieval in which the information to be retrieved must be "pulled" from memory with very few external cues. 237

recency effect: tendency to remember information at the end of a body of information better than the information at the beginning of it. 238

receptive meditation: form of meditation in which a person attempts to become aware of everything in immediate conscious experience, or an expansion of consciousness. 376

receptor sites: holes in the surface of the dendrites or certain cells of the muscles and glands, which are shaped to fit only certain neurotransmitters. 53

recessive: referring to a gene that only influences the expression of a trait when paired with an identical gene. 389

reciprocal determinism: Bandura's explanation of how the factors of environment, personal characteristics, and behavior can interact to determine future behavior. 447

reciprocity of liking: tendency of people to like other people who like them in return. 583

recognition: the ability to match a piece of information or a stimulus to a stored image or fact. 237

reflection: therapy technique in which the therapist restates what the client says rather than interpreting those statements. 521

reflex arc: the connection of the afferent neurons to the interneurons to the efferent neurons, resulting in a reflex action. 60

regression: psychological defense mechanism in which a person falls back on childlike patterns of responding in reaction to stressful situations. 375

reinforcement: any event or stimulus that, when following a response, increases the probability that the response will occur again. 188

reinforcement: the strengthening of a response by following it with a pleasurable consequence or the removal of an unpleasant stimulus. 527

reinforcer: any event or object that, when following a response, increases the likelihood of that response occurring again. 180

relative size: perception that occurs when objects that a person expects to be of a certain size appear to be small and are, therefore, assumed to be much farther away. 119

reliability: the tendency of a test to produce the same scores again and again each time it is given to the same people. 279

REM behavior disorder: a rare disorder in which the mechanism that blocks the movement of the voluntary muscles fails, allowing the person to thrash around and even get up and act out nightmares. 143

REM paralysis: the inability of the voluntary muscles to move during REM sleep. 142

REM rebound: increased amounts of REM sleep after being deprived of REM sleep on earlier nights. 142

replicate: in research, repeating a study or experiment to see if the same results will be obtained in an effort to demonstrate reliability of results. 22

representative sample: randomly selected sample of subjects from a larger population of subjects. 24

repression: psychological defense mechanism in which the person refuses to consciously remember a threatening or unacceptable event, instead pushing those events into the unconscious mind. 375

resistance: occurring when a patient becomes reluctant to talk about a certain topic, either changing the subject or becoming silent. 519

resting potential: the state of the neuron when not firing a neural impulse. 51

restorative theory: theory of sleep proposing that sleep is necessary to the physical health of the body and serves to replenish chemicals and repair cellular damage. 138

reticular formation (RF): an area of neurons running through the middle of the medulla and the pons and slightly beyond that play a role in general arousal, alertness, and sleep. 69

retrieval: getting information that is in storage into a form that can be used. 221

retrieval cue: a stimulus for remembering. 235

retroactive interference: memory retrieval problem that occurs when newer information prevents or interferes with the retrieval of older information. 249

retrograde amnesia: loss of memory from the point of some injury or trauma backwards, or loss of memory for the past. 251

reuptake: process by which neurotransmitters are taken back into the synaptic vesicles. 57

reversible figures: visual illusions in which the figure and ground can be reversed. 116

rods: visual sensory receptors found at the back of the retina, responsible for noncolor sensitivity to low levels of light. 95

romantic love: type of love consisting of intimacy and passion. 583

Rorschach inkblot test: projective test that uses 10 inkblots as the ambiguous stimuli. 461

s factor: the ability to excel in certain areas, or specific intelligence. 275

sample: group of subjects selected from a larger population of subjects, usually selected randomly. A-1

scaffolding: process in which a more skilled learner gives help to a less skilled learner, reducing the amount of help as the less skilled learner becomes more capable. 405

scheme: in this case, a mental concept formed through experiences with objects and events. 401

schizophrenia: severe disorder in which the person suffers from disordered thinking, bizarre behavior, hallucinations, and inability to distinguish between fantasy and reality. 501

school psychology: area of psychology in which the psychologists work directly in the schools, doing assessments, educational placement, and diagnosing educational problems. B-7

scientific method: system of gathering data so that bias and error in measurement are reduced. 20

seasonal affective disorder (SAD): a mood disorder caused by the body's reaction to low levels of sunlight in the winter months. 508

secondary appraisal: the second step in assessing a threat, which involves estimating the resources available to the person for coping with the stressor. 363

secondary reinforcer: any reinforcer that becomes reinforcing after being paired with a primary reinforcer, such as praise, tokens, or gold stars. 188

selective attention: the ability to focus on only one stimulus from among all sensory input. 226

selective thinking: distortion of thinking in which a person focuses on only one aspect of a situation while ignoring all other relevant aspects. 529

self: an individual's awareness of their own personal characteristics and level of functioning. 450

self-actualization: according to Maslow, the point that is seldom reached at which people have sufficiently satisfied the lower needs and achieved their full human potential. 316

self-actualizing tendency: the striving to fulfill one's innate capacities and capabilities. 450

self-concept: the image of oneself that develops from interactions with important, significant people in one's life. 450

self-determination theory (SDT): theory of human motivation in which the social context of an action has an effect on the type of motivation existing for the action. 318

self-efficacy: individual's expectancy of how effective his or her efforts to accomplish a goal will be in any particular circumstance. 448

self-fulfilling prophecy: the tendency of one's expectations to affect one's behavior in such a way as to make the expectations more likely to occur. 579

self-help groups (support groups): a group composed of people who have similar problems and who meet together without a therapist or counselor for the purpose of discussion, problem solving, and social and emotional support. 532

semantic memory: type of declarative memory containing general knowledge, such as knowledge of language and information learned in formal education. 232

semantic network model: model of memory organization that assumes information is stored in the brain in a connected fashion, with concepts that are related stored physically closer to each other than concepts that are not highly related. 233

semantics: the rules for determining the meaning of words and sentences. 294

sensation: the process that occurs when special receptors in the sense organs are activated, allowing various forms of outside stimuli to become neural signals in the brain. 90

sensation seeker: someone who needs more arousal than the average person. 314

sensorimotor stage: Piaget's first stage of cognitive development in which the infant uses its senses and motor abilities to interact with objects in the environment. 402

sensory adaptation: tendency of sensory receptor cells to become less responsive to a stimulus that is unchanging. 92

sensory conflict theory: an explanation of motion sickness in which the information from the eyes conflicts with the information from the vestibular senses, resulting in dizziness, nausea, and other physical discomfort. 113

sensory memory: the very first stage of memory, the point at which information enters the nervous system through the sensory systems. 224

sensory pathway: nerves coming from the sensory organs to the CNS consisting of afferent neurons. 61

serial position effect: tendency of information at the beginning and end of a body of information to be remembered more accurately than information in the middle of the body of information. 237

shape constancy: the tendency to interpret the shape of an object as being constant, even when its shape changes on the retina. 115

shaping: the reinforcement of simple steps in behavior that lead to a desired, more complex behavior. 193

short-term memory (STM): the memory system in which information is held for brief periods of time while being used. 226

significant difference: a difference between groups of numerical data that is considered large enough to be due to factors other than chance variation. A-10

skewed distribution: frequency distribution in which most of the scores fall to one side or the other of the distribution. A-4

similarity: the tendency to perceive things that look similar to each other as being part of the same group. 116

single-blind study: study in which the subjects do not know if they are in the experimental or the control group. 31

situational cause: cause of behavior attributed to external factors, such as delays, the action of others, or some other aspect of the situation. 490

situational context: the social or environmental setting of a person's behavior. 574

size constancy: the tendency to interpret an object as always being the same actual size, regardless of its distance. 115

skin senses: the sensations of touch, pressure, temperature, and pain. 110.

sleep apnea: disorder in which the person stops breathing for nearly half a minute or more. 146

sleep deprivation: any significant loss of sleep, resulting in problems in concentration and irritability. 137

sleepwalking (somnambulism): occurring during deep sleep, an episode of moving around or walking around in one's sleep. 143

social categorization: the assignment of a person one has just met to a category based on characteristics the new person has in common with other people with whom one has had experience in the past. 572

social cognition: the mental processes that people use to make sense of the social world around them. 572

social cognitive learning theorists: theorists who emphasize the importance of both the influences of other people's behavior and of a person's own expectancies of learning. 447

social cognitive theory of hypnosis: theory that assumes that people who are hypnotized are not in an altered state but are merely playing the role expected of them in the situation. 153

social cognitive view: learning theory that includes cognitive processes such as anticipating, judging, memory, and imitation of models. 447

social cognitive: referring to the use of cognitive processes in relation to understanding the social world. 579

social comparison: the comparison of oneself to others in ways that raise one's self-esteem. 579

social facilitation: the tendency for the presence of other people to have a positive impact on the performance of an easy task. 564

social identity: the part of the self-concept including one's view of self as a member of a particular social category. 579

social identity theory: theory in which the formation of a person's identity within a particular social group is explained by social categorization, social identity, and social comparison. 579

social impairment: the tendency for the presence of other people to have a negative impact on the performance of a difficult task. 564

social influence: the process through which the real or implied presence of others can directly or indirectly influence the thoughts, feelings, and behavior of an individual. 556

social learners: people who prefer to learn with other people or in groups. I-2

social loafing: the tendency for people to put less effort into a simple task when working with others on that task. 564

social phobia: fear of interacting with others or being in social situations that might lead to a negative evaluation. 485

social psychology: the scientific study of how a person's thoughts, feelings, and behavior are influenced by the real, imagined, or implied presence of others. 556, B-6

Social Readjustment Rating Scale (SRRS): assessment that measures the amount of stress in a person's life over a one-year period resulting from major life events. 348

social role: the pattern of behavior that is expected of a person who is in a particular social position. 586

social support system: the network of family, friends, neighbors, coworkers, and others who can offer support, comfort, or aid to a person in need. 371

sociocultural perspective: perspective in which abnormal behavior (like normal behavior) is seen as the product of the learning and shaping of behavior within the context of the family, the social group to which one belongs, and the culture within which the family and social group exist. 15, 478

soma: the cell body of the neuron responsible for maintaining the life of the cell. 49

somatic nervous system: division of the PNS consisting of nerves that carry information from the senses to the CNS and from the CNS to the voluntary muscles of the body. 61

somatization disorder: somatoform disorder in which the person dramatically complains of a specific symptom such as nausea, difficulty swallowing, or pain for which there is no real physical cause. 490

somatoform disorders: disorders that take the form of bodily illnesses and symptoms but for which there are no real physical disorders. 490

somatosensory cortex: area of neurons running down the front of the parietal lobes responsible for processing information from the skin and internal body receptors for touch, temperature, body position, and possibly taste. 73

somesthetic senses: the body senses consisting of the skin senses, the kinesthetic sense, and the vestibular senses. 110

source traits: the more basic traits that underlie the surface traits, forming the core of personality. 453

spatial neglect: condition produced by damage to the association areas of the right hemisphere resulting in an inability to recognize objects or body parts in the left visual field. 76

specific phobia: fear of objects or specific situations or events. 485

spinal cord: a long bundle of neurons that carries messages between the body and the brain and is responsible for very fast, lifesaving reflexes. 59

spontaneous recovery: the reappearance of a learned response after extinction has occurred. 180

sports psychology: area of psychology in which the psychologists help athletes and others to prepare themselves mentally for participation in sports activities. B-8

standard deviation: the square root of the average squared deviations from the mean of scores in a distribution; a measure of variability. A-6

statistic: a measure of central tendency or variability computed from a sample. A-1

statistically significant: referring to differences in data sets that are larger than chance variation would predict. A-9

statistics: branch of mathematics concerned with the collection and interpretation of numerical data. A-1

stem cells: special cells found in all the tissues of the body that are capable of manufacturing other cell types when those cells need to be replaced due to damage or wear and tear. 60

stereotype: a set of characteristics that people believe is shared by all members of a particular social category. 573

stereotype vulnerability: the effect that people's awareness of the stereotypes associated with their social group has on their behavior. 579

stimulants: drugs that increase the functioning of the nervous system. 156

stimulatory hallucinogenics: drugs that produce a mixture of psychomotor stimulant and hallucinogenic effects. 164

stimulus discrimination: the tendency to stop making a generalized response to a stimulus that is similar to the original conditioned stimulus because the similar stimulus is never paired with the unconditioned stimulus. 180

stimulus generalization: the tendency to respond to a stimulus that is only similar to the original conditioned stimulus with the conditioned response. 180

stimulus motive: a motive that appears to be unlearned but causes an increase in stimulation, such as curiosity. 313

stimulus substitution: original theory in which Pavlov stated that classical conditioning occurred because the conditioned stimulus became a substitute for the unconditioned stimulus by being paired closely together. 185

storage: holding onto information for some period of time. 220

stress: the term used to describe the physical, emotional, cognitive, and behavioral responses to events that are appraised as threatening or challenging. 346

stressors: events that cause a stress reaction. 346

stress-vulnerability model: explanation of disorder that assumes a biological sensitivity, or vulnerability, to a certain disorder will result in the development of that disorder under the right conditions of environmental or emotional stress. 504

structuralism: early perspective in psychology associated with Wilhelm Wundt and Edward Titchener, in which the focus of study is the structure or basic elements of the mind. 7

subjective: referring to concepts and impressions that are only valid within a particular person's perception and may be influenced by biases, prejudice, and personal experiences. 461

subjective discomfort: emotional distress or emotional pain. 476

sublimation: channeling socially unacceptable impulses and urges into socially acceptable behavior. 375

subordinate concept: the most specific category of a concept, such as one's pet dog or a pear in one's hand. 264

successive approximations: small steps in behavior, one after the other, that lead to a particular goal behavior. 194

superego: part of the personality that acts as a moral center. 439

superordinate concept: the most general form of a type of concept, such as "animal" or "fruit." 264

surface traits: aspects of personality that can easily be seen by other people in the outward actions of a person. 453

sympathetic division (fight-or-flight system): part of the ANS that is responsible for reacting to stressful events and bodily arousal. 62

synapse (synaptic gap): microscopic fluid-filled space between the synaptic knob of one cell and the dendrites or surface of the next cell. 53

synaptic knob: rounded areas on the end of the axon terminals. 53

synaptic vesicles: saclike structures found inside the synaptic knob containing chemicals. 53

synesthesia: disorder in which the signals from the various sensory organs are processed in the wrong cortical areas, resulting in the sense information being interpreted as more than one sensation. 90

syntax: the system of rules for combining words and phrases to form grammatically correct sentences. 294

systematic desensitization: behavior technique used to treat phobias, in which a client is asked to make a list of ordered fears and taught to relax while concentrating on those fears. 525

tactile learners: people who need to touch objects in order to learn about them. I-2

temperament: the enduring characteristics with which each person is born. 408, 436

temporal lobes: areas of the cortex located just behind the temples containing the neurons responsible for the sense of hearing and meaningful speech. 74

teratogen: any factor that can cause a birth defect. 395

testes: the male gonads. 80

texture gradient: the tendency for textured surfaces to appear to become smaller and finer as distance from the viewer increases. 120

thalamus: part of the limbic system located in the center of the brain, this structure relays sensory information from the lower part of the brain to the proper areas of the cortex and processes some sensory information before sending it to its proper area. 71

that's-not-all technique: a sales technique in which the persuader makes an offer and then adds something extra to make the offer look better before the target person can make a decision. 561

Thematic Apperception Test (TAT): projective test that uses 20 pictures of people in ambiguous situations as the visual stimuli. 461

therapeutic alliance: the relationship between therapist and client that develops as a warm, caring, accepting relationship characterized by empathy, mutual respect, and understanding. 538

therapy: treatment methods aimed at making people feel better and function more effectively. 516

theta waves: brain waves indicating the early stages of sleep. 140

thinking (cognition): mental activity that goes on in the brain when a person is organizing and attempting to understand information and communicating information to others. 262

thyroid gland: endocrine gland found in the neck; regulates metabolism. 80

time-out: an extinction process in which a person is removed from the situation that provides reinforcement for undesirable behavior, usually by being placed in a quiet corner or room away from possible attention and reinforcement opportunities. 528

token economy: the use of objects called tokens to reinforce behavior in which the tokens can be accumulated and exchanged for desired items or privileges. 201, 527

top-down processing: the use of preexisting knowledge to organize individual features into a unified whole. 124

trait: a consistent, enduring way of thinking, feeling, or behaving. 452

trait theories: theories that endeavor to describe the characteristics that make up human personality in an effort to predict future behavior. 452

trait–situation interaction: the assumption that the particular circumstances of any given situation will influence the way in which a trait is expressed. 455

transduction: the process of converting outside stimuli, such as light, into neural activity. 90

transference: in psychoanalysis, the tendency for a patient or client to project positive or negative feelings for important people from the past onto the therapist. 519

trial and error (mechanical solution): problem-solving method in which one possible solution after another is tried until a successful one is found. 267

triarchic theory of intelligence: Sternberg's theory that there are three kinds of intelligence: analytical, creative, and practical. 276

trichromatic theory: theory of color vision that proposes three types of cones: red, blue, and green. 97

trust versus mistrust: first stage of personality development in which the infant's basic sense of trust or mistrust develops as a result of consistent or inconsistent care. 412

Type A personality: person who is ambitious, time conscious, extremely hardworking, and tends to have high levels of hostility and anger as well as being easily annoyed. 364

Type B personality: person who is relaxed and laid-back, less driven and competitive than Type A, and slow to anger. 364

Type C personality: pleasant but repressed person, who tends to internalize his or her anger and anxiety and who finds expressing emotions difficult. 365

t-**test:** type of inferential statistical analysis typically used when two means are compared to see if they are significantly different. A-9

unconditional positive regard: positive regard that is given without conditions or strings attached. 512

unconditional positive regard: referring to the warmth, respect, and accepting atmosphere created by the therapist for the client in person-centered therapy. 522

unconditioned response (UCR): an involuntary (reflex) response to a naturally occurring or unconditioned stimulus. 177

unconditioned stimulus (UCS): a naturally occurring stimulus that leads to an involuntary (reflex) response. 177

unconscious mind: level of the mind in which thoughts, feelings, memories, and other information are kept that are not easily or voluntarily brought into consciousness. 437

unilateral ECT: electroconvulsive therapy in which the electrodes are placed on only one side of the head and the forehead. 544

validity: the degree to which a test actually measures what it's supposed to measure. 279

variable interval schedule of reinforcement: schedule of reinforcement in which the interval of time that must pass before reinforcement becomes possible is different for each trial or event. 197

variable ratio schedule of reinforcement: schedule of reinforcement in which the number of responses required for reinforcement is different for each trial or event. 198

vestibular senses: the sensations of movement, balance, and body position. 110

vicarious conditioning: classical conditioning of a reflex response or emotion by watching the reaction of another person. 184

visual accommodation: the change in the thickness of the lens as the eye focuses on objects that are far away or close. 95

visual learners: people who learn best by seeing, reading, and looking at images. I-2

volley principle: theory of pitch that states that frequencies from about 400 Hz to 4000 Hz cause the hair cells (auditory neurons) to fire in a volley pattern, or take turns in firing. 104

waking consciousness: state in which thoughts, feelings, and sensations are clear, organized, and the person feels alert. 135

weight set point: the particular level of weight that the body tries to maintain. 321

Wernicke's aphasia: condition resulting from damage to Wernicke's area, causing the affected person to be unable to understand or produce meaningful language. 76

withdrawal: physical symptoms that can include nausea, pain, tremors, crankiness, and high blood pressure, resulting from a lack of an addictive drug in the body systems. 155

working memory: an active system that processes the information in short-term memory. 227

Yerkes-Dodson law: law stating performance is related to arousal; moderate levels of arousal lead to better performance than do levels of arousal that are too low or too high. This effect varies with the difficulty of the task: Easy tasks require a high-moderate level whereas more difficult tasks require a low-moderate level. 314

zone of proximal development (ZPD): Vygotsky's concept of the difference between what a child can do alone and what that child can do with the help of a teacher. 405

z **score:** a statistical measure that indicates how far away from the mean a particular score is in terms of the number of standard deviations that exist between the mean and that score. A-8

zygote: cell resulting from the uniting of the ovum and sperm. 391

References

AAA Foundation for Traffic Safety. (1997). *Aggressive driving: Three studies.* Washington, DC.

Abadinsky, H. (1989). *Drug abuse: An introduction.* Chicago: Nelson-Hall Series in Law, Crime, and Justice.

Abbott, L., Nadler, J., & Rude, R. K. (1994). Magnesium deficiency in alcoholism: Possible contribution to osteoporosis and cardiovascular disease in alcoholics. *Alcoholism, Clinical & Experimental Research, 18*(5), 1076–1082.

Abe, K., Amatomi, M., & Oda, N. (1984). Sleepwalking and recurrent sleep talking in children of childhood sleepwalkers. *American Journal of Psychiatry, 141,* 800–801.

Abel, G. G., & Osborn, C. A. (1992). The paraphilias: The extent and nature of sexually deviant and criminal behavior. In J. M. W. Bradford (Ed.), *Psychiatric Clinics of North America, 15*(3) (pp. 675–687). Philadelphia: W. B. Saunders Company.

Abela, J. R. Z., & D'Allesandro, D. U. (2002). Beck's cognitive theory of depression: The diathesis-stress and causal mediation components. *British Journal of Clinical Psychology, 41,* 111–128.

Abraham, S., & Llewellyn-Jones, D. (2001). *Eating disorders, the facts.* 5th ed. London: Oxford University Press.

Abraham, W. C., & Williams, J. M. (2003). Properties and mechanisms of LTP maintenance. *The Neuroscientist, 9*(6), 463–474.

Abramson, L. Y., Garber, J., & Seligman, M. E. P. (1980). Learned helplessness in humans: An attributional analysis. In J. Garber & M. E. P. Seligman (Eds.) *Human Helplessness* (pp. 3–34). New York: Academic Press.

Abramson, L. Y., Seligman, M. E. P., & Teasdale, J. D. (1978). Learned helplessness in humans: Critique and reformulation. *Journal of Abnormal Psychology, 87,* 49–74.

Acar, N., Chardigny, J. M., Darbois, M., Pasquis, B., & Sebedio, J. L. (2003). Modification of the dopaminergic neurotransmitters in striatum, frontal cortex and hippocampus of rats fed for 21 months with trans isomers of alpha-linolenic acid. *Neuroscience Research, 45*(4), 375–382.

Adam, K. (1980). Sleep as a restorative process and a theory to explain why. *Progressive Brain Research, 53,* 289–305.

Adams, D. B. (1968). The activity of single cells in the midbrain and hypothalamus of the cat during affective defense behavior. *Archives Italiennes de Biologie, 106,* 243–269.

Adams, R. J. (1987). An evaluation of colour preferences in early infancy. *Infant Behaviour and Development, 10,* 143–150.

Adler, A. (1954). *Understanding human nature.* New York: Greenburg Publisher.

Adler, S. R., Fosket, J. R., Kagawa-Singer, M., McGraw, S. A., Wong-Kim, E., Gold, E., & Sternfeld, B. (2000) Conceptualizing menopause and midlife: Chinese American and Chinese women in the US. *Maturitas 35*(1), 11–23.

Adolphs, R., & Tranel, D. (2003). Amygdala damage impairs emotion recognition from scenes only when they contain facial expressions. *Neuropsychologia, 41,* 1281–1289.

Adolphs, R., Gosselin, F., Buchanan, T. W., Tranel, D., Schyns, P., & Damasio, A. R. (2005). A mechanism for impaired fear recognition after amygdala damage. *Nature, 433,* 68–72.

Aghajanian, G. K., & Marek, G. J. (1999). Serotonin and hallucinogens. *Neuropsychopharmacology, 21,* 16S–23S.

Agnati, L. F., Bjelke, B., & Fuxe, K. (1992). Volume transmission in the brain. *American Scientist, 80,* 362–373.

Aguiar, A., & Baillargeon, R. (2003). Perseverative responding in a violation-of-expectation task in 6.5-month-old infants. *Cognition, 88*(3), 277–316.

Ahern, G. L., & Schwartz, G. E. (1985). Differential lateralization for positive and negative emotion in the human brain: EEG spectral analysis. *Neuropsychologia, 23*(6), 745–755.

Ahlskog, J. E. (2003). Slowing Parkinson's disease progression: Recent dopamine agonist trials. *Neurology, 60*(3), 381–389.

Ahn, W. (1998). Why are different features central for natural kinds and artifacts? The role of causal status in determining feature centrality. *Cognition, 69,* 135–178.

Ahokas, A., Aito, M., & Rimon, R. (2000). Positive treatment effect of estradiol in postpartum psychosis: A pilot study. *Journal of Clinical Psychiatry, 61*(3), 166–169.

Aiello, J. R., & Douthitt, E. A. (2001). Social facilitation from Triplett to electronic performance monitoring. *Group Dynamics: Theory, Research, and Practice, 5*(3), 163–180.

Ainsworth, M. D. S. (1985). Attachments across the life span. *Bulletin of the New York Academy of Medicine, 61,* 792–812.

Ainsworth, M. D. S., Blehar, M. C., Waters, E., & Wall, S. (1978). *Patterns of attachment: A study of the strange situation.* Hillsdale, NJ: Erlbaum.

Aitchison, J. (1992). Good birds, better birds, & amazing birds: The development of prototypes. In P. J. Arnaud & H. Béjoint (Eds.), *Vocabulary and applied linguistics* (pp. 71–84). London: Macmillan.

Ajzen, I. (2001). Nature and operation of attitudes. *Annual Review of Psychology, 52,* 27–58.

Ajzen, I., & Fishbein, M. (2000). Attitudes and the attitude–behavior relation: Reasoned and automatic processes. In W. Stroebe & M. Hewstone (Eds.), *European review of social psychology* (pp. 1–33). New York: John Wiley & Sons.

Akil, M., Kolachana, B. S., et al. (2003). Catechol-o-methyltransferase genotype and dopamine regulation in the human brain. *Journal of Neuroscience, 23*(6), 2008–2013.

Albert, D. J., & Richmond, S. E. (1977). Reactivity and aggression in the rat: Induction by alpha–adrenergic blocking agents injected ventral to anterior septum but not into lateral septum. *Journal of Comparative and Physiological Psychology, 91,* 886–896 [DBA] *Physiology and Behavior, 20,* 755–761.

Alderfer, C. P. (1972). *Existence, relatedness and growth: Human needs in organisational settings.* New York: Free Press.

Aldridge-Morris, R. (1989). *Multiple personality: An exercise in deception.* Hillsdale, NJ: Erlbaum.

Alexander, G., DeLong, M. R., & Strick, P. L. (1986). Parallel organization of functionally segregated circuits linking basal ganglia and cortex. *Annual Review of Neuroscience, 9,* 357–381.

Aligne, C. A., Auinger, P., Byrd, R. S., & Weitzman, M. (2000). Risk factors for pediatric asthma contributions of poverty, race, and urban residence. *American Journal of Respiratory Critical Care Medicine, 162*(3), 873–877.

Alkon, D. (1989). Memory storage and neural systems. *Scientific American, 261*(1), 42–50.

Allen, F. (1994). *Secret formula.* New York: HarperCollins.

Allen, G. E. (2006). *Intelligence tests and immigration to the United States, 1900–1940.* Hoboken, NJ: John Wiley and Sons.

Allen, G., & Parisi, P. (1990). Trends in monozygotic and dizygotic twinning rates by maternal age and parity. Further analysis of Italian data, 1949–1985, and rediscussion of US data, 1964–1985. *Acta Genetic Medicine & Gemellology, 39,* 317–328.

Allen, I. V. (1991). Pathology of multiple sclerosis. In W. B. Matthews (Ed.). *McAlpine's multiple sclerosis.* Edinburgh: Churchill Livingstone, 341–378.

Allen, K., Blascovich, J., & W. Mendes. (2002). Cardiovascular reactivity and the presence of pets, friends, and spouses: The truth about cats and dogs. *Psychosomatic Medicine, 64,* 727–739.

Allen, L. S., & Gorski, R. A. (1991). Sexual dimorphism of the anterior commissure and massa intermedia of the human brain. *Journal of Comparative Neurology, 312,* 97–104.

Allen, L. S., Hines, M., Shryne, J. E., & Gorski, R. A. (1989). Two sexually dimorphic cell groups in the human brain. *Journal of Neuroscience, 9*(9), 496–506.

Alloy, L. B., & Clements, C. M. (1998). Hopelessness theory of depression: Tests of the symptom component. *Cognitive Therapy and Research, 22,* 303–335.

Allport, G. W., & Odbert, H. S. (1936). Trait names: A psycho-lexical study. *Psychological Monographs, 47*(211).

Alm, H., & Nilsson, L. (1995). The effects of a mobile telephone conversation on driver behaviour in a car following situation. *Accident Analysis and Prevention, 27*(5), 707–715.

Alperstein, L. (2001). For two: Some basic perspectives and skills for couples therapy. Paper presented at the XXXIII Annual Conference of the American Association of Sex Educators, Counselors, and Therapists. San Francisco, May 2–6.

Amabile, T. M. (1982). The social psychology of creativity: A consensual assessment technique. *Journal of Personality and Social Psychology, 43*, 997–1013.

Amabile, T. M., DeJong, W., & Lepper, M. R. (1976). Effects of externally imposed deadlines on subsequent intrinsic motivation. *Journal of Personality and Social Psychology, 34*, 92–98.

Amabile, T., Hadley, C. N., & Kramer, S. J. (2002). Creativity under the gun. *Harvard Business Review, 80*(8), 52–60.

American Academy of Pediatrics. (1995). Health supervision for children with Turner syndrome. *Pediatrics, 96*(6), 1166–1173.

American Association for the Advancement of Science. (2007). *AAAS Policy Brief: Stem Cell Research*. Washington, DC. Retrieved from the Internet on November 23, 2007 at **http://www.aaas.org/spp/cstc/briefs/stemcells/**

American Association of University Women. (1992). *How schools shortchange girls*. Washington, DC: American Association of University Women.

American Association of University Women. (1998). *Separated by sex: A critical look at single-sex education for girls*. Washington, DC: American Association of University Women.

American Association on Intellectual and Developmental Disabilities (2009). FAQ on intellectual disability. Retrieved from **http://www.aamr.org/content_104.cfm.**

American Association on Mental Retardation. (2002). Mental retardation: Definition, classification, and systems of supports (10th ed.). Washington, DC: American Association on Mental Retardation.

American Psychiatric Association, DSM-V Neurodevelopmental Disorders Work Group. (2009). *Report of the DSM-V Neurodevelopmental Disorders Work Group*. Retrieved from **http://www.psych.org/MainMenu/Research/DSMIV/DSMV/ DSMRevisionActivities/DSM-V-Work-Group-Reports/Neurodevelopmental-Disorders-Work-Group-Report.aspx.**

American Psychiatric Association. (2000). *DSM-IV-TR: Diagnostic and statistical manual of mental disorders* (4th ed., Text Revision). Washington, DC. [Appendix I: Outline for Cultural Formulation and Glossary of Culture-Bound Syndromes].

American Psychiatric Association. (2000). *DSM-IV-TR: Diagnostic and statistical manual of mental disorders* (4th ed., Text Revision). Washington, DC: APA.

American Psychiatric Association. (2000a). *Diagnostic and statistical manual of mental disorders: DSM-IV-TR*. Washington, DC: American Psychiatric Association.

American Psychiatric Association. (2000b). Practice guidelines for the treatment of patients with major depressive disorder (revision). *American Journal of Psychiatry, 157*(4, Supplement): 1–45.

American Psychiatric Association Committee on Electroconvulsive Therapy. (2001). *The practice of electroconvulsive therapy: Recommendations for treatment, training, and privileging*, 2nd ed. Washington, DC: American Psychiatric Association.

American Psychological Association. (2002). *Ethical Principles of Psychologists and Code of Conduct*. Retrieved from **http://www.apa.org/ethics/code/index.aspx.**

Anand, B. K., & Brobeck, J. R. (1951.) Hypothalamic control of food intake in rats and cats. *Yale Journal of Biological Medicine, 24*, 123–146.

Anastasi, A., & Urbina, S. (1997). *Psychological testing* (7th ed.). Upper Saddle River, NJ: Prentice-Hall.

Anderson, C. A. (1987). Temperature and aggression: Effects on quarterly, yearly, and city rates of violent and nonviolent crime. *Journal of Personality and Social Psychology, 52*(6), 1161–1173.

Anderson, C. A. (2003). Video games and aggressive behavior. In D. Ravitch & J. P. Viteritti (Eds.), *Kid stuff: Marketing sex and violence to America's children* (p. 157). Baltimore and London: The Johns Hopkins University Press.

Anderson, C. A., & Bushman, B. J. (2001). Effects of violent video games on aggressive behavior, aggressive cognition, aggressive affect, physiological arousal, and prosocial behavior: A meta–analytic review of the scientific literature. *Psych Science, 12*(5), 353–359.

Anderson, C. A., & Dill, K. E. (2000). Video games and aggressive thoughts, feelings, and behavior in the laboratory and in life. *Journal of Personality and Social Psychology, 78*(4), 772–790.

Anderson, C. A., Berkowitz, L., Donnerstein, E., Huesmann, R. L., Johnson, J., Linz, D., Malamuth, N., & Wartella, E. (2003). The influence of media violence on youth. *Psychological Science in the Public Interest, 4*, 81–110.

Anderson, M. C., & Neely, J. H. (1995). Interference and inhibition in memory retrieval. In E. L. Bjork & R. A. Bjork (Eds.), *Handbook of perception and cognition, Volume 10, Memory*. San Diego, CA: Academic Press.

Andrews, J. D. W. (1989). Integrating visions of reality: Interpersonal diagnosis and the existential vision. *American Psychologist, 44*, 803–817.

Anschuetz, B. L. (1999). The high cost of caring: Coping with workplace stress. *The Journal, the Newsletter of the Ontario Association of Children's Aid Societies, 43*(3).

Antuono, P. G., Jones, J. L., Wang, Y., & Li, S. (2001). Decreased glutamate [plus] glutamine in Alzheimer's disease detected in vivo with (1)H-MRS at 0.5 T. *Neurology, 56*(6), 737–742.

Archer, J. (1991). The influence of testosterone on human aggression. *British Journal of Psychology, 82*, 1–28.

Argamon, S., Koppel, M., Fine, J., & Shimoni, A. (2003 August). Gender, genre, and writing style in formal written texts. *Text, 23*(3).

Argyle, M. (1986). Rules for social relationships in four cultures. *Australian Journal of Psychology, 38*, 309–318.

Armstrong, R. (1997). When drugs are used for rape. *Journal of Emergency Nursing, 23*(4), 378–381.

Arnett, P. A., Smith, S. S., & Newman, J. P. (1997). Approach and avoidance motivation in psychopathic criminal offenders during passive avoidance. *Journal of Personality and Social Psychology, 72*(6), 1413–1428.

Aronson, E. (1997). Back to the future. Retrospective review of Leon Festinger's—A theory of cognitive dissonance. *American Journal of Psychology, 110*, 127–137.

Aronson, E., Blaney, N., Stephan, C., Sikes, J., & Snapp, M. (1978). *The jigsaw classroom*. Beverly Hills, CA: Sage.

Arrigo, J. M., & Pezdek, K. (1998). Textbook models of multiple personality: Source, bias, and social consequences. In S. Lynn (Ed.), *Truth in memory* (pp. 372–393). New York: Guilford Press.

Asarnow, R. F., Granholm, E., & Sherman, T. (1991). Span of apprehension in schizophrenia. In H. A. Nasrallah (Ed.), *Handbook of Schizophrenia, Vol. 5*, S. R. Steinhauer, J. H. Gruzelie, & J. Zubin, (Eds.), *Neuropsychology, psychophysiology and information processing* (pp. 335–370). Amsterdam: Elsevier.

Asch, S. E. (1951). Effects of group pressure upon the modification and distortion of judgement. In H. Guetzkow (Ed.), *Groups, leadership and men*. Pittsburgh, PA: Carnegie Press.

Asch, S. E. (1956). Studies of independence and conformity: A minority of one against a unanimous majority. *Psychological Monographs, 70* (Whole No. 416).

Aserinsky, E., & Kleitman, N. (1953). Regularly occurring periods of eye motility, and concomitant phenomena, during sleep. *Science, 118*, 273–274.

Ash, M. G. (1998). *Gestalt psychology in German culture, 1890–1967: Holism and the quest for objectivity*. Cambridge: Cambridge University Press.

Asimov, I. (1950, 2008). *I, robot* (reissue). Silverthome, CO: Spectra.

Asimov, I. (1968). *I, robot*. London: Grafton Books.

Associated Press. (2006, September 10). Fergie Recounts Crystal Meth Addiction. *The Washington Post*. Retrieved from **http://www.washingtonpost.com.**

Atkinson, R. C., & Shiffrin, R. M. (1968). Human memory: A proposed system and its control processes. In K. W. Spence & J. T. Spence (Eds.), *The psychology of learning and motivation* (vol. 2, pp. 89–105). New York: Academic Press.

Aylward, E. H., Richards, T. L., Berninger, V. W., Nagy, W. E., Field, K. M., Grimme, A. C., Richards, A. L., Thomson, J. B., & Cramer, S. C. (2003). Instructional treatment associated with changes in brain activation in children with dyslexia. *Neurology, 61*, 212–219.

Backenstraß, M., Pfeiffer, N., Schwarz, T., Catanzaro, S. J., & Mearns, J. (2008). Reliability and validity of the German version of the Generalized Expectancies for Negative Mood Regulation (NMR) Scale. *Diagnostica, 54*, 43–51.

Backer, B., Hannon, R., & Russell, N. (1994). *Death and dying: Understanding and care*, 2nd ed. Albany, NY: Delmar Publishers.

Baddeley, A. (1988). Cognitive psychology and human memory. *Trends in Neurosciences, 11*, 176–181.

Baddeley, A. D. (1986). *Working memory*. London/New York: Oxford University Press.

Baddeley, A. D. (1996). Exploring the central executive. *Quarterly Journal of Experimental Psychology, 49A,* 5–28.

Baddeley, A. D. (2003). Working Memory: Looking back and looking visual forward. *Nature Reviews Neuroscience, 4*(10), 829–839.

Baddeley, A. D., & Hitch, G. (1974). Working memory. In G. A. Bower (Ed.), *The psychology of learning and motivation, 8* (pp. 47–89). New York: Academic Press.

Baehr, E. K., Revelle, W., & Eastman, C. I. (2000). Individual difference in the phase amplitude of the human circadian temperature rhythm: With an emphasis on morningness-eveningness. *Journal of Sleep Research, 9,* 117–127.

Baer, D. M., Wolf, M. M., & Risley, T. R. (1968). Some current dimensions of applied behavior analysis. *Journal of Applied Behavior Analysis, 1,* 91–97.

Bahrick, H. (1984). Fifty years of second language attrition: Implications for programmatic research. *Modern Language Journal, 68,* 105–118.

Bahrick, H. P., Hall, L. K., & Berger, S. A. (1996, September). Accuracy and distortion in memory for high school grades. *Psychological Science, 7,* 265–271.

Bailey, J., Dunne, M. P., & Martin, N. G. (2000). Genetic and environmental influences on sexual orientation and its correlates in an Australian twin sample. *Journal of Personality and Social Psychology Volume, 78*(3), 524–536.

Bailey, J. M., & Pillard, R. C. (1991). A genetic study of male sexual orientation. *Archives of General Psychiatry, 48,* 1089–1096.

Bailey, J. M., & Zucker, K. J. (1995). Childhood sex-typed behavior and sexual orientation: A conceptual analysis and quantitative review. *Developmental Psychology, 31,* 43–55.

Bailey, J. M., Pillard, R. C., Neale, M. C., & Agyei, Y. (1993). Heritable factors influence sexual orientation in women. *Archives of General Psychiatry, 50,* 217–223.

Ball, K., Berch, D. B., Helmers, K. F., Jobe, J. B., Leveck, M. D., Marsiske, M., Morris, J. N., Rebok, G. W., Smith, D. M., Tennstedt, S. L., Unverzagt, F. W., & Willis, S. L. (2002). Advanced Cognitive Training for Independent and Vital Elderly Study Group. Effects of cognitive training interventions with older adults: A randomized controlled trial. *Journal of the American Medical Association, 288,* 2271–2281.

Baltes, P. B., Reese, H. W., & Nesselroade, J. R. (1988). *Introduction to research methods, life-span developmental psychology.* Hillsdale, NJ: Lawrence Erlbaum Associates, Inc.

Bandura, A. (1965). Influence of models' reinforcement contingencies on the acquisition of imitative responses. *Journal of Social Psychology, 1,* 589–595.

Bandura, A. (1980). The social learning theory of aggression. In R. A. Falk & S. S. Kim (Eds.), *The war system: An interdisciplinary approach* (p. 146). Boulder, CO: Westview Press.

Bandura, A. (1986). *Social foundations of thought and action: A social cognitive theory.* Englewood Cliffs, NJ: Prentice Hall.

Bandura, A. (1989). Human agency in social cognitive theory. *American Psychologist, 44,* 1175–1184.

Bandura, A. (1998). Exploration of fortuitous determinants of life paths. *Psychological Inquiry, 9,* 95–99.

Bandura, A., Blanchard, E. B., & Ritter, B. (1969). Relative efficacy of desensitization and modeling approaches for inducing behavioral, affective, and attitudinal changes. *Journal of Personality and Social Psychology, 13,* 173–199.

Bandura, A., Jeffrey, R. W., & Wright, C. L. (1974). Efficacy of participant modeling as a function of response induction aids. *Journal of Abnormal Psychology, 83,* 56–64.

Bandura, A., & Rosenthal, T. L. (1966). Vicarious classical conditioning as a functioning of arousal level. *Journal of Personality and Social Psychology, 3,* 54–62.

Bandura, A., Ross, D., & Ross, S. A. (1961). Transmission of aggression through imitation of aggressive models. *Journal of Abnormal and Social Psychology, 63,* 575–582.

Bandura, A., Ross, D., & Ross, S. A. (1963). Imitation of film-mediated aggressive models. *Journal of Abnormal and Social Psychology, 66,* 3–11.

Barak, A. (1999). Psychological applications on the Internet: A discipline on the threshold of a new millennium. *Applied and Preventive Psychology, 8,* 231–246.

Barak, A., & Hen, L. (2008). Exposure in cyberspace as means of enhancing psychological assessment. In A. Barak (Ed.), *Psychological aspects of cyberspace: Theory, research, applications* (pp. 129–162). Cambridge, UK: Cambridge University Press.

Barak, A., & Suler, J. (2008). Reflections on the psychology and social science of cyberspace. In A. Barak (Ed.), *Psychological aspects of cyberspace: Theory, research, applications* (pp. 1–12). Cambridge, UK: Cambridge University Press.

Bard, P. (1934). On emotional expression after decortication with some remark on certain theoretical views. *Psychological Review, 41,* 309–329, 424–449.

Bargh, J. A., Chen, M., & Burrows, C. (1996). Automaticity of social behavior: Direct effects of trait construct and stereotype activation on action. *Journal of Personality & Social Psychology, 71*(2), 230–244.

Barker, E. (1983). The ones who got away: People who attend Unification Church workshops and do not become Moonies. In E. Barker (Ed.,), *Of gods and men: New religious movements in the West.* Macon, GA: Mercer University Press.

Barkley, R. A. (1998). *Attention deficit hyperactivity disorder: A handbook for diagnosis and treatment.* New York: Guilford Press.

Barkley, R. A., Fischer, M., Fletcher, K., & Smallish, L. (2001). *Young adult outcome of hyperactive children as a function of severity of childhood conduct problems, I: Psychiatric status and mental health treatment.* Submitted for publication.

Barnes, A. M., & Carey, J. C. (2002). Common problems of babies with trisomy 18 or 13. Rochester, NY, *Support Organization for Trisomy 18, 13, and Related Disorders,* January 11.

Barnes, V., Schneider, R., Alexander, C., & Staggers, F. (1997). Stress, stress reduction, and hypertension in African Americans: An updated review. *Journal of the National Medical Association, 89*(7), 464–476.

Barnyard, P., & Grayson, A. (1996). *Introducing psychological research.* London: Macmillan Press.

Baron, J. N., & Reiss, P. C. (1985). Same time, next year: Aggregate analyses of the mass media and violent behavior. *American Sociological Review, 50,* 347–363.

Baron, S. A. (1993). *Violence in the workplace.* Ventura, CA: Pathfinder Publishing of California.

Barondes, S. H. (1998). *Mood genes: Hunting for origins of mania and depression.* New York: W. H. Freeman.

Barone, J. J., & Roberts, H. R. (1996). Caffeine consumption. *Food Chemistry and Toxicology, 34,* 119–129.

Barsalou, L. W. (1992). *Cognitive psychology: An overview for cognitive scientists.* Hillsdale, NJ: Lawrence Erlbaum Associates.

Barsh, G. S., Farooqi, I. S., & O'Rahilly, S. (2000). Genetics of body-weight regulation. *Nature, 404,* 644–651.

Barstow, A. L. (1995). *Witchcraze: A new history of the European witch hunts.* London: Pandora.

Bartels, A., & Zeki, S. (2000). The neural basis of romantic love. *NeuroReport, 11,* 3829–3834.

Barth, J. M., & Boles, D. B. (1999). Positive relations between emotion recognition skills and right hemisphere processing. Paper presented to the *11th Annual Convention of the American Psychological Society,* Denver, CO.

Bartholomew, K. (1990). Avoidance of intimacy: An attachment perspective. *Journal of Social and Personal Relationships, 7,* 147–178.

Bartlett, F. C. (1932). *Remembering: A study in experimental ad social psychology.* Cambridge: Cambridge University Press.

Bartlett, N. R. (1965). Dark and light adaptation. Chapter 8. In C. H. Graham, (Ed.), *Vision and visual perception.* New York: John Wiley and Sons, Inc.

Barton, M. E., & Komatsu, L. K. (1989). Defining features of natural kinds and artifacts. *Journal of Psycholinguistic Research, 18,* 433–447.

Bartoshuk, L. M. (1993). The biological basis for food perception and acceptance. *Food Quality and Preference, 4*(1/2), 21–32.

Basadur, M., Pringle, P., & Kirkland, D. (2002). Crossing cultures: Training effects on the divergent thinking attitudes of Spanish-speaking South American managers. *Creativity Research Journal, 14*(3, 4), 395–408.

Bastien, C. H., Morin, C. M., Ouellet, M., Blais, F. C., Bouchard, S. (2004). Cognitive-behavioral therapy for insomnia: Comparison of individual therapy, group therapy, and telephone consultations. *Journal of Consulting and Clinical Psychology, 72*(4), 653–659.

Bates, J. E. (1989). Applications of temperament concepts. In G. A. Kohnstamm, J. E. Bates, & M. K. Rothbart (Eds.), *Temperament in childhood* (pp. 323–355). New York: Wiley.

Battaglia, M., Bernardeschi, L., Franchini, L., Bellodi, L., & Smeraldi, E. (1995). A family study of schizotypal disorder. *Schizophrenia Bulletin, 21*(1), 33–45.

Baumrind, D. (1964). Some thoughts on ethics of research: After reading Milgram's "Behavioral Study of Obedience." *American Psychologist, 19,* 421–423.

Baumrind, D. (1967). Child care practices anteceding three patterns of preschool behavior. *Genetic Psychology Monograph, 75,* 43–88.

Baumrind, D. (1991). The influence of parenting style on adolescent competence and substance abuse. *Journal of Early Adolescence, 11*(1), 56–95.

Baumrind, D. (1997). Necessary distinctions. *Psychological Inquiry, 8,* 176–182.

Baumrind, D. (2005). Patterns of parental authority and adolescent autonomy. In J. Smetana (Ed.), *New directions for child development: Changes in parental authority during adolescence* (pp. 61–69). San Francisco: Jossey-Bass.

Bayliss, D. M., Baddeley, J. C., & Gunn, D. M. (2005). The relationship between short-term memory and working memory: Complex span made simple? *Memory, 13*(3-4), 414–421.

Beardsley, T. (1995, January). For whom the bell curve really tolls. *Scientific American,* 14–17.

Bechtel, W., & Abrahamsen, A. (2002). *Connectionism and the mind: Parallel processing, dynamics, and evolution in networks* (2nd ed.) Oxford: Basil Blackwell.

Beck, A. T. (1976). *Cognitive therapy and the emotional disorders.* New York: International Universities Press.

Beck, A. T. (1979). *Cognitive therapy and the emotional disorders.* New York: Penguin Books.

Beck, A. T. (1984). Cognitive approaches to stress. In C. Lehrer & R. L. Woolfolk (Eds.), *Clinical guide to stress management.* New York: Guilford Press.

Beck, A. T., Freeman, A., Davis, D. D., & Associates (2007). *Cognitive therapy of personality disorders.* (2nd ed.). New York: Guilford Press.

Beckman, M. & Pierrehumbert, J. (1986). Intonational structure in English and Japanese. *Phonology Year Book III,* 15–70.

Beehr, T. A., Jex, S. M., Stacy, B. A., & Murray, M. A. (2000). Work stressors and coworker support as predictors of individual strain and job performance. *Journal of Organizational Behavior, 21*(4), 391–405.

Beer, J. M., & Horn, J. M. (2000). The influence of rearing order on personality development within two adoption cohorts. *Journal of Personality, 68,* 789–819.

Behne, T., Carpenter, M., & Tomasello, M. (2005). One-year-olds comprehend the communicative intentions behind gestures in a hiding game. *Developmental Science, 8,* 492–499.

Bellizzi, J. A., & Crowley, A. E. (1983). The effects of color in store design. *Journal of Retailing, 59,* 21–45.

Belsky, J. (2005). Differential susceptibility to rearing influence: An evolutionary hypothesis and some evidence. In B. Ellis & D. Bjorklund (Eds.), *Origins of the social mind: Evolutionary psychology and child development* (pp. 139–163). New York: Guilford.

Belsky, J., & Johnson, C. D. (2005). Developmental outcome of children in day care. In J. Murph, S. D. Palmer, & D. Glassy (Eds.), *Health in child care: A manual for health professionals,* 4th ed., (pp. 81–95). Elks Grove Village, IL: American Academy of Pediatrics.

Belsky, J., Vandell, D., Burchinal, M., Clarke-Stewart, K. A., McCartney, K., Owen, M., & NICHD Early Child Care Research Network (2007). Are there long-term effects of early child care? *Child Development, 78,* 681–701.

Bem, D. J. (1972). Self-perception theory. In L. Berkowitz (Ed.), *Advances in Experimental Social Psychology* (vol. 6, pp. 1–62). New York: Academic Press.

Bem, D. J., & Honorton, C. (1994). Does psi exist? *Psychological Bulletin, 115*(1), 4–18.

Bem, S. L. (1975). Sex role adaptability: The consequence of psychological androgyny. *Journal of Personality and Social Psychology, 31,* 634–643.

Bem, S. L. (1981a). Gender schema theory: A cognitive account of sex typing. *Psychological Review, 88,* 354–364.

Bem, S. L. (1981b). The BSRI and gender schema theory: A reply to Spence and Helmreich. *Psychological Review, 88,* 369–371.

Bem, S. L. (1987). Gender schema theory and the romantic tradition. In P. Shaver & C. Hendrick (Eds.), *Review of personality and social psychology* (Volume 7). Newbury Park, CA: Sage.

Bem, S. L. (1993). Is there a place in psychology for a feminist analysis of the social context? *Feminism & Psychology, 3,* 247–251.

Bemporad, J. R. (1997). Cultural and historical aspects of eating disorders. *Theor Med 18*(4), 401–420.

Benjafield, J. J. G. (1996). *A history of psychology.* Boston: Allyn and Bacon.

Benjamin, S. L. (1996). An interpersonal theory of personality disorders. In J. F. Clarkin & M. F. Lenzenweger (Eds.), *Major theories of personality disorder.* New York: Guilford Press.

Benowitz, N. L. (1996). Pharmacology of nicotine: Addiction and therapeutics. *Annual Review of Pharmacology and Toxicology, 36,* 597–613.

Ben-Shakhar, G., Bar-Hillel, M., Bliu, Y., Ben-Abba, E., & Flug, A. (1986). Can graphology predict occupational success? Two empirical studies and some methodological ruminations. *Journal of Applied Psychology, 71,* 645–653.

Benson, H. (1975). *The relaxation response.* New York: Morrow.

Benson, H., Beary, J., & Carol, M. (1974a). The relaxation response. *Psychiatry, 37,* 37–46.

Benson, H., Rosner, B. A., Marzetta, B. R., & Klemchuk, H. M. (1974b). Decreased blood pressure in pharmacologically treated hypertensive patients who regularly elicited the relaxation response. *Lancet, 1*(7852), 289–291.

Berenbaum, S. A., & Snyder, E. (1995). Early hormonal influences on childhood sex-typed activity and playmate preferences: Implications for the development of sexual orientation. *Developmental Psychology, 31,* 31–42.

Berent, S. (1977). Functional asymmetry of the human brain in the recognition of faces. *Neuropsychologia, 15,* 829–831.

Berg, F. (1999). Health risks associated with weight loss and obesity treatment programs. *Journal of Social Issues, 55*(2), 277–297.

Berk, L. E. (1992). Children's private speech: An overview of theory and the status of research. In R. M. Diaz & L. E. Berk (Eds.), *Private speech: From social interaction to self-regulation* (pp. 17–53). Hillsdale, NJ: Erlbaum.

Berk, L. E., & Spuhl, S. T. (1995). Maternal interaction, private speech, and task performance in preschool children. *Early Childhood Research Quarterly, 10,* 145–169.

Berk, L. S., Felten, D. L., Tan, S. A., Bittman, B. B., & Westengard, J. (2001, March). Modulation of neuroimmune parameters during the eustress of humor-associated mirthful laughter. *Alternative Therapy Health Medicines, 7*(2), 62–72, 74–76.

Berkowitz, L. (1993). *Aggression: Its causes, consequences and control.* New York: McGraw-Hill.

Bermond, B., Nieuwenhuyse, B., Fasotti, L., & Schuerman, J. (1991). Spinal cord lesions, peripheral feedback, and intensities of emotional feelings. *Cognition and Emotion, 5,* 201–220.

Bernat, E., Shevrin, H., & Snodgrass, M. (2001). Subliminal visual oddball stimuli evoke a P300 component. *Clinical Neurophysiology, 112,* 159–171.

Berry, J. W., & Kim, U. (1998). Acculturation and mental health. In P. R. Dasen, J. W. Berry, & N. Sartorius (Eds.), *Health and cross-cultural psychology: Toward applications* (pp. 207–236). Newbury Park, CA: Sage Publications.

Berry, J. W., & Sam, D. L. (1997). Acculturation and adaptation. In J. W. Berry, M. H. Segall, & C. Kagitcibasi (Eds.), *Handbook of cross-cultural psychology, Vol. 3: Social behaviour and applications* (2nd ed., pp. 291–326). Boston: Allyn & Bacon.

Berscheid, E., & Reis, H. T. (1998). Attraction and close relationships. In D. T. Gilbert & S. T. Fiske et al. (Eds.), *The handbook of social psychology, Vol. 2* (4th ed., pp. 193–281), New York: McGraw-Hill.

Berteretche, M. V., Dalix, A. M., Cesar d'Ornano, A. M., Bellisle, F., Khayat, D., & Faurion, A. (2004). Decreased taste sensitivity in cancer patients under chemotherapy. *Supportive Care in Cancer, 12*(8), 571–576.

Best, D. L., & Williams, J. E. (2001). Gender and culture. In D. Matsumoto (Ed.), *The handbook of culture and psychology* (pp. 195–212). New York: Oxford University Press.

Betancourt, J. R., & Jacobs, E. A. (2000). Language barriers to informed consent and confidentiality: The impact on women's health. *Journal of American Medical Women's Association, 55,* 294–295.

Beyer, B. K. (1995). *Critical thinking.* Bloomington, IN: Phi Delta Kappa Educational Foundation.

Beyreuther, K., Biesalski, H. K., Fernstrom, J. D., Grimm, P., Hammes, W. P., Heinemann, U., Kempski, O., Stehle, P., Steinhart, H., & Walker, R. (2007). Consensus meeting: Monosodium glutamate, an update. *European Journal of Clinical Nutrition, 61,* 304–313.

Bigler, E. D., Johnson, S. C., Anderson, C. V., Blatter, D. D., Gale, S. D., Russo, A. A., Ryser, D. K., Macnamara, S. E., Bailey, B. R., & Hopkins, R. O. (1996). Traumatic brain injury and memory: The role of hippocampal atrophy. *Neuropsychology, 10,* 333–342.

Binet, A., & Simon, T. (1916). *The development of intelligence in children.* Baltimore: Williams & Wilkins.

Binkofski, F., & Buccino G. (2006). The role of ventral premotor cortex in action execution and action understanding. *Journal of Physiology, 99,* 396–405.

Bivens, J. A., & Berk, L. E. (1990). A longitudinal study of the development of elementary school children's private speech. *Merrill-Palmer Quarterly, 36,* 443–463.

Bjork, R. A., & Bjork, E. L. (1992). A new theory of disuse and an old theory of stimulus fluctuation. In A. Healy, S. Kosslyn, & R. Shiffrin (Eds.), *From learning processes to cognitive processes: Essays in honor of William K. Estes* (vol. 2, pp. 35–67). Hillsdale, NJ: Erlbaum.

Bjork, R. A., & Whitten, W. B. (1974). Recency-sensitive retrieval processes in long-term free recall. *Cognitive Psychology, 6*, 173–189.

Black, D. W., & Andreasen, N. C. (1999). Schizophrenia, schizophreniform disorder, and delusional (paranoid) disorders. In R. E. Hales, et al. (Eds.), *Textbook of psychiatry* (3rd ed., pp. 425–477). Washington, DC: American Psychiatric Press.

Blackmon, L. R., Batton, D. G., Bell, E. F., Engle, W. A., Kanto, W. P., Martin, G. I., Rosenfeld, W. N., Stark, A. R., & Lemons, J. A. (2003). *Apnea, sudden infant death syndrome, and home monitoring.* Committee on Fetus and Newborn. *Pediatrics, 111*(4), 914–917.

Blair, R. J. R., Sellars, C., Strickland, I., Clark, F., Williams, A. O., Smith, M., & Jones, L. (1995). Emotion attributions in the psychopath. *Personality and Individual Differences, 19*(4), 431–437.

Blanchard, M., & Main, M. (1979). Avoidance of the attachment figure and social-emotional adjustment in day-care infants. *Developmental Psychology, 15*, 445–446.

Blanchard-Fields, F., & Horhota, M. (2005). Age differences in the correspondence bias: When a plausible explanation matters. *Journals of Gerontology: Psychological Sciences, 60B*, P259–P267.

Blanchard-Fields, F., Chen, Y., Horhota, M., & Wang, M. (2007). Cultural differences in the relationship between aging and the correspondence bias. *Journals of Gerontology Series B: Psychological Sciences and Social Sciences, 62*(6), 362–365.

Blass, T. (1991). Understanding behavior in the Milgram obedience experiment: The role of personality, situations, and their interactions. *Journal of Personality and Social Psychology, 60*, 398–413.

Blass, T. (1999). The Milgram paradigm after 35 years: Some things we now know about obedience to authority. *Journal of Applied Social Psychology, 25*, 955–978.

Blatt, S. D., Meguid, V., & Church, C. C. (2000). Prenatal cocaine: What's known about outcomes? *Contemporary Ob/Gyn, 9*, 67–83.

Blazer, D. G., Kessler, R. C., McGonagle, K. A., & Swartz, M. S. (1994). The prevalence and distribution of major depression in a national community sample: The National Comorbidity Survey. *American Journal of Psychiatry, 151*, 979–986.

Bledsoe, C. H., & Cohen, B. (1993). *Social dynamics of adolescent fertility in Sub-Saharan Africa.* Washington, DC: National Academy Press.

Blehar, M. C., & Oren, D. A. (1997). Gender differences in depression. *Medscape General Medicine, 1*(2). Retrieved from the Internet on June 27, 2004, at **www.medscape.com/viewarticle/408844**.

Bleuler, E. (1911, reissued 1950). *Dementia praecox or the group of schizophrenias.* New York: International Universities Press.

Blits, B., & Bunge, M. B. (2006). Direct gene therapy for repair of the spinal cord. *Journal of Neurotrauma, 23*(3-4), 508–520.

Block, N. (2005). Two neural correlates of consciousness. *Trends in Cognitive Sciences, 9*, 41–89.

Block, R. I., & Ghoneim, M. M. (1993). Effects of chronic marijuana use on human cognition. *Psychopharmacology, 100*(1–2), 219–228.

Bloom, L. (1974). Talking, understanding and thinking. In R. Schiefelbusch, & L. L. Lloyd (Eds.), *Language perspectives: Acquisition, retardation and intervention.* New York: Macmillan.

Bloom, P. (2000). *How children learn the meaning of words.* Cambridge, MA: MIT Press.

Blumer, D. (2002). The illness of Vincent van Gogh. *American Journal of Psychiatry, 159*(4), 519–526.

Bock, R. (1993). *Understanding Klinefelter Syndrome: A guide for XXY males and their families.* National Institutes of Health, Office of Research Reporting. Publication No. 93-3202 (August).

Bodrova, E., & Leong, D. J. (1996). *Tools of the mind: The Vygotskian approach to early childhood education.* Englewood Cliffs, NJ: Prentice Hall.

Bogle, K. D. (2000). Effect of perspective, type of student, and gender on the attribution of cheating. *Proceedings of the Oklahoma Academy of Science, 80*, 91–97.

Bolton, P., Bass, J., Betancourt, T., Speelman, L., Onyango, G., Clougherty, K. F., et. al. (2007). Interventions for depression symptoms among adolescent survivors of war and displacement in northern Uganda. *Journal of Medical Association, 298*, 519–527.

Bond, R. A., & Smith, P. B. (1996). Culture and conformity: A meta–analysis of studies using Asch's (1952, 1956) line judgment task. *Psychological Bulletin, 119*, 111–137.

Bondarenko, L. A. (2004). Role of methionine in nocturnal melatonin peak in the pineal gland. *Bulletin of Experimental Biological Medicine, 137*(5), 431–432.

Bonnelykke, B. (1990). Maternal age and parity as predictors of human twinning. *Acta Genetic Medicine & Gemellology, 39*, 329–334.

Bonnet, M., & Arand, D. (1995). We are chronically sleep deprived. *Sleep, 18*(10), 908–911.

Boor, M. (1982). The multiple personality epidemic: Additional cases and inferences regarding diagnosis, etiology, dynamics, and treatment. *Journal of Nervous and Mental Disease, 170*, 302–304.

Booth-Butterfield, S. (1996). Message characteristics. *Steve's primer of practical persuasion and influence.* Retrieved from the Internet on August 2, 2004, at **www.as.wvu.edu/~sbb/comm221/chapters/message.htm**.

Borgeat, F., & Goulet, J. (1983, June). Psychophysiological changes following auditory subliminal suggestions for activation and deactivation. *Perceptual & Motor Skills, 56*(3), 759–766.

Borges, M. A., Stepnowsky, M. A., & Holt, L. H. (1977). Recall and recognition of words and pictures by adults and children. *Bulletin of the Psychonomic Society, 9*, 113–114.

Bosworth, H. B., & Schaie, K. W. (1997). The relationship of social environment, social networks, and health outcomes in the Seattle Longitudinal Study: Two analytical approaches. *Journals of Gerontology Series B: Psychological Sciences and Social Sciences, 52*(5), 197–205.

Botwin, M. D., & Buss, D. M. (1989). The structure of act data: Is the five-factor model of personality recaptured? *Journal of Personality and Social Psychology, 56*, 988–1001.

Bouchard, C., Tremblay, A., Nadeau, A., Dussault, J., Despres, J. P., Theriault, G., Lupien, P. J., Serresse, O., Boulay, M. R., & Fournier, G. (1990). Long-term exercise training with constant energy intake. 1: Effect on body composition and selected metabolic variables. *International Journal on Obesity, 14*(1), 57–73.

Bouchard, T. (1994). Genes, environment, and personality. *Science, 264*, 1700–1701.

Bouchard, T. J., Jr. (1997). Whenever the twain shall meet. *The Science, 37*(5), 52–57.

Bouchard, T. J., & Segal, N. L. (1985). Environment and IQ. In B. B. Wolman (Ed.), *Handbook of intelligence: Theories, measurements, and applications* (pp. 391–464). New York: John Wiley.

Bowden, C. L., Calabrese, J. R., McElroy, S. L., Gyulai, L., Wassef, A., Petty, F., Pope, H. G. Jr., Chou, J. C., Keck, P. E. Jr., Rhodes, L. J., Swann, A. C., Hirschfeld, R. M., & Wozniak, P. J. (2000). For the Divalproex Maintenance Study Group. A randomized, placebo-controlled 12-month trial of divalproex and lithium in treatment of outpatients with bipolar I disorder. *Archives of General Psychiatry, 57*(5), 481–489.

Bowers, K. S., & Woody, E. Z. (1996). Hypnotic amnesia and the paradox of intentional forgetting. *Journal of Abnormal Psychology, 105*, 381–390.

Bowman, E. S. (1996). Delayed memories of child abuse: Part II: An overview of research findings relevant to understanding their reliability and suggestibility. *Dissociation: Progress in the Dissociative Disorders, 9*, 232–243.

Boyd, L. A., & Winstein, C. J. (2004). Cerebellar stroke impairs temporal but not spatial accuracy during implicit motor learning. *Neurorehabilitation and Neural Repair, 18*(3), 134–143.

Boyson-Bardies, B., deHalle, P., Sagart, L., & Durand, C. (1989). A cross-linguistic investigation of vowel formats in babbling. *Journal of Child Language, 16*, 1–17.

Bracey, G. (1997). A few facts about poverty. *Phi Delta Kappan, 79*, 163–164.

Brauen, C. M., & Bonta, J. L. (1979). Cross-cultural validity, reliability, and stimulus characteristics of the Luscher Color Test. *Journal of Personality Assessment, 43*, 459–460.

Braun, B. G. (Ed.) (1986). *Treatment of multiple personality disorder.* Washington, DC: American Psychiatric Press.

Braun, S. (1996). *Buzz: The science and lore of alcohol and caffeine.* New York: Oxford University Press, 107–192.

Brawman-Mintzer, O., & Lydiard, R. B. (1997). Biological basis of generalized anxiety disorder. *Journal of Clinical Psychiatry, 58*(3), 16–25.

Brazelton, T. B. (1992). *Touchpoints: Your child's emotional and behavioral development*. Reading, MA: Addison-Wesley Publishing Co.

Brecher, M., Wang, B. W., Wong, H., & Morgan, J. P. (1988). Phencyclidine and violence: Clinical and legal issues. *Journal of Clinical Psychopharmacology, 8*, 397–401.

Breedlove, S. M., Rosenzweig, M. R., & Watson, N. V. (2007). *Biological psychology: An introduction to behavioral and cognitive neurosciences* (5th ed., pp. 23–34). Sunderland, MA: Sinauer Associates, Inc.

Breggin, P. R. (2003/2004). Suicidality, violence and mania caused by selective serotonin reuptake inhibitors (SSRIs): A review and analysis. *International Journal of Risk & Safety in Medicine, 16*, 31–49.

Breggin, P. R., & Breggin, G.R. (1994). *Talking back to Prozac*. New York: St. Martin's Press.

Breier, A., Albus, M., Pickar, D., Zahn, T. P., Wolkowitz, O. M., & Paul, S. M. (1987). Controllable and uncontrollable stress in humans: Alterations in mood, neuroendocrine and psychophysiological function. *American Journal of Psychiatry, 144*, 1419–1425.

Breland, K., & Breland, M. (1961). The misbehavior of organisms. *American Psychologist. 16*, 681–684.

Brennan, J. F. (2002). *History and systems of psychology*, 6th ed. Upper Saddle River, NJ: Prentice Hall.

Brennan, P. A., Raine, A., Schulsinger, F., Kirkegaard-Sorensen, L., Knop, J., Hutchings, B., Rosenberg, R., & Mednick, S. A. (1997). Psychophysiological protective factors for male subjects at high risk for criminal behavior. *American Journal of Psychiatry, 154*, 853–855.

Breslau, N., Chilcoat, H. D., Kessler, R. C., Peterson, E. L., & Lucia, V. C. (1999). Vulnerability to assaultive violence: Further specification of the sex difference in posttraumatic stress disorder. *Psychological Medicine, 29*, 813–821.

Breslau, N., Davis, G. C., Andreski, P., & Peterson, E. L. (1997). Sex differences in posttraumatic stress disorder. *Archives of General Psychiatry, 54*(11), 1044–1048.

Breuer, J., & Freud, S. (1895). *Studies on hysteria (cathartic method). Special Edition, 2*, 1–309.

Brewer, M. B. (2001). Ingroup identification and intergroup conflict: When does ingroup love become outgroup hate? In R. D. Ashmore, L. Jussim, & D. Wilder (Eds.), *Social identity, intergroup conflict, and conflict reduction*. New York: Oxford University Press.

Brick, J. (2003). The characteristics of alcohol: Chemistry, use and abuse. In J. Brick (Ed.), *Handbook of the medical consequences of alcohol and drug abuse* (pp. 1–11). New York: Haworth Medical Press.

Briem, V., & Hedman, L. R. (1995). Behavioural effects of mobile telephone use during simulated driving. *Ergonomics, 38*, 2536–2562.

Briggs, K. C., & Myers, I. B. (1998). *The Myers-Briggs Type Indicator-Form M*. Palo Alto, CA: Consulting Psychologists Press.

Brigham, A. (1844). Asylums exclusively for the incurably insane. Classic article in *The American Journal of Psychiatry, 151*, 50–70.

Broadbent, D. (1958). *Perception and communication*. Elmsford, NY: Pergamon.

Brockington, I. F., Winokur, G., & Dean, C. (1982). Puerperal psychosis. In I. F. Brockington & R. Kumar, (Eds.), *Motherhood and mental illness* (pp. 37–69). London: Academic Press.

Brondolo, E., Rieppi, R., Erickson, S. A., Bagiella, E., Shapiro, P. A., McKinley, P., & Sloan, R. P. (2003). Hostility, interpersonal interactions, and ambulatory blood pressure. *Psychosomatic Medicine, 65*, 1003–1011.

Brooks, J. G., & Brooks, M. G. (1993). *In search of understanding: The case for constructivist classrooms*. Alexandria, VA: The Association for Supervision and Curriculum Development.

Brown, C., Taylor, J., Green, A., Lee, B. E., Thomas, S. B., & Ford, A. (2003). *Managing depression in African Americans: Consumer and provider perspectives*. (Final Report to Funders). Pittsburgh: Mental Health Association of Allegheny County.

Brown, G. L., & Linnoila, M. I. (1990). CSF serotonin metabolite (5–HIAA) studies in depression, impulsivity, and violence. *Journal of Clinical Psychiatry, 51*(4)(suppl), 31–43.

Brown, J. (1958). Some tests of the decay theory of immediate memory. *Quarterly Journal of Experimental Psychology, 10*, 12–21.

Brown, P. K., & Wald, G. (1964). Visual pigments in single rods and cones of the human retina. *Science, 144*, 45.

Brown, R. (1973). *A first language: The early stages*. Cambridge, MA: Harvard University Press.

Brown, R., & McNeill, D. (1966). The "tip of the tongue" phenomenon. *Journal of Verbal Learning & Verbal Behavior, 5*(4), 325–337.

Browne, D. (2004). Do dolphins know their own minds? *Biology & Philosophy, 19*, 633–653.

Brubaker, D. A., & Leddy, J. J. (2003). Behavioral contracting in the treatment of eating disorders. *The Physician and Sportsmedicine, 31*(9).

Brunner, E. J., Hemingway, H., Walker, B., Page, M., Clarke, P., Juneja, M., Shipley, M. J., Kumari, M., Andrew, R., Seckl, J. R., Papadopoulos, A., Checkley, S., Rumley, A., Lowe, G. D., Stansfeld, S. A., & Marmot, M. G. (2002). Adrenocortical, autonomic and inflammatory causes of the metabolic syndrome: Nested case-control study. *Circulation, 106*, 2659–2665.

Brunner, L., Nick, H. P., Cumin, F., Chiesi, M., Baum, H. P., Whitebread, S., Stricker-Krongrad, A., & Levens, N. (1997). Leptin is a physiologically important regulator of food intake. *International Journal of Obesity Related Metabolic Disorders, 21*, 1152–1160.

Bryan, E. B., & Hallett, F. (2001). *Guidelines for professionals. Twins and triplets: The first five years and beyond*. London: Multiple Births Foundation.

Bryan, J., & Freed, F. (1982). Corporal punishment: Normative data and sociological and psychological correlates in a community college population. *Journal of Youth and Adolescence, 11*(2), 77–87.

Bryant, R. A., & McConkey, K. M. (1989). Hypnotic blindness: A behavioral and experimental analysis. *Journal of Abnormal Psychology, 98*, 71–77.

Brzustowicz, L. M., Simone, J., Mohseni, P., Hayter, J. E., Hodgkinson, K. A., Chow, E. W., & Bassett, A. S. (2004). Linkage disequilibrium mapping of schizophrenia susceptibility to the CAPON region of chromosome 1q22. *American Journal of Human Genetics, 74*(5), 1057–1063.

Buccino, G., Binkofski, F., & Riggio, L. (2004). The mirror neuron system and action recognition. *Brain and Language, 89*(2), 370–376.

Buccino, G., Binkofski, F., Fink, G. R., Fadiga, L., Fogassi, L., Gallese, V., et al. (2001). Action observation activates premotor and parietal areas in a somatotopic manner: An fMRI study. *European Journal of Neuroscience, 13*(2), 400–404.

Bucher, B. D., & Lovaas, O. I. (1967). Use of aversive stimulation in behavior modification. In M. R. Jones (Ed.), *Miami Symposium on the Prediction of Behavior 1967: Aversive Stimulation*, 77–145.

Buck, R. (1980). Nonverbal behavior and the theory of emotion: The facial feedback hypothesis. *Journal of Personality and Social Psychology, 38*, 811–824.

Budney, A. J., Hughes, J. R., Moore, B. A., & Novy, P. L. (2001). Marijuana abstinence effects in marijuana smokers maintained in their environment. *Archives of General Psychiatry, 58*, 917–924.

Bullock, T. H., Bennett, M. V. L., Johnston, D., Josephson, R., Marder, E., & Fields, R. D. (2005). The neuron doctrine, redux. *Science, 310*(11), 791–793.

Bunge, M. (1984). What is pseudoscience? *The Skeptical Inquirer, 9*(1), 36–46.

Bunge, M. B., & Pearse, D. D. (2003). Transplantation strategies to promote repair of the injured spinal cord. *Journal of Rehabilitative Research & Development, 40*(4), 55–62.

Bureau of Labor Statistics, U.S. Department of Labor. (2008). *Occupational Outlook Handbook, 2008–09 Edition*. Retrieved from the Internet on May 28, 2008 at http://www.bls.gov/oco/ocos056.htm.

Burger, J. M. (1986). Increasing compliance by improving the deal: The that's not all technique. *Journal of Personality and Social Psychology, 51*, 277–283.

Burger, J. M., & Petty, R. E. (1981). The low-ball compliance technique: Task or person commitment? *Journal of Personality and Social Psychology, 40*, 492–500.

Burger, J. J. M. (1997). The psychoanalytic approach: Neo-Freudian theory, application, and assessment. *Personality* (4th ed.). Pacific Grove, CA: Brooks/Cole.

Burgio, K. L. (1998). Behavioral vs. drug treatment for urge urinary incontinence in older women: A randomized controlled trail. *Journal of the American Medical Association, 280*, 1995–2000.

Burke, D. M., MacKay, D. G., Worthley, J. S., & Wade, E. (1991). On the tip of the tongue: What causes word finding failures in young and older adults. *Journal of Memory and Language, 30*, 542–579.

Burks, N., & Martin, B. (1985). Everyday problems and life change events: Ongoing versus acute sources of stress. *Journal of Human Stress, 11*, 27–35.

Bushman, B. J. (1997). Effects of alcohol on human aggression: Validity of proposed explanations. In M. Galanter (Ed.), *Recent developments in alcoholism. Vol. 13* (pp. 227–243). New York: Plenum Press.

Bushman, B. J., & Huesmann, L. R. (2000). Effects of televised violence on aggression. In D. G. Singer & J. L. Singer (Eds.), *Handbook of children and the media* (pp. 223–254). Thousand Oaks, CA: Sage Publications.

Bushman, B. J., & Huesmann, L. R. (2001). Effects of televised violence on aggression. In D. G. Singer & J. L. Singer (Eds.), *Handbook of children and the media* (Ch. 11, pp. 223–254). Thousand Oaks, CA: Sage.

Buss, D. M., Larsen, R. J., Westen, D., & Semmelroth, J. (1992). Sex differences in jealousy: Evolution, physiology, and psychology. *Psychological Science, 3,* 251–255.

Bussa, B., & Kaufman, C. (2000). What can self-help do? *The Journal of the California Alliance of the Mentally Ill, 2*(2).

Butcher, J. N., & Rouse, S. V. (1996). Personality: Individual differences and clinical assessment. *Annual Review of Psychology, 47,* 87–111.

Butcher, J. N., Graham, J. R., Ben-Poarth, Y. S., Tellegen, A., Dahlstrom, W. G., & Kaemmer, B. (2001). *Minnesota Multiphasic Personality Inventory-2. Manual for administration, scoring, and interpretation* (rev. ed.). Minneapolis, MN: University of Minnesota Press.

Butcher, J. N., Rouse, S. V., & Perry, J. N. (2000). Empirical description of psychopathology in therapy clients: Correlates of MMPI-2 scales. In J. N. Butcher (Ed.), *Basic sources on the MMPI-2* (pp. 487–500). Minneapolis, MN: University of Minnesota Press.

Butler, K. (1993). Too good to be true? *Networker, 6,* 19–31.

Byne, W. (1995). Science and belief: Psychobiological research on sexual orientation. *Journal of Homosexuality, 28,* 303–344.

Cabeza, R., Anderson, N. D., Locantore, J. K. & McIntosh, A. R. (2002). Aging gracefully: Compensatory brain activity in high-performing older adults. *NeuroImage, 17*(3), 1394–1402.

Cain, D., & Seeman, J. (Eds.). (2001). *Humanistic psychotherapies: Handbook of research and practice.* Washington, DC: APA Publications.

Califia, P. (1997). *Sex changes: The politics of transgenderism.* San Francisco: Cleis Press.

Camara, W. J., Nathan, J. S., & Puente, A. E. (2000). Psychological test usage: Implications in professional psychology. *Professional Psychology: Research and Practice, 31*(2), 141–154.

Cameron, J., Banko, K. M., & Pierce, W. D. (2001). Pervasive negative effects of rewards on intrinsic motivation: The myth continues, *The Behavior Analyst, 24,* 1–44.

Cameron, J. A., Alvarez, J. M., Ruble, D. N., & Fuligni, A. J. (2001). Children's lay theories about ingroups and outgroups: Reconceptualizing research on prejudice. *Personality and Social Psychology Review, 5,* 118–128.

Cameron, J. R., Hansen, R., & Rosen, D. (1989). Preventing behavioral problems in infancy through temperament assessment and parental support programs. In W. B. Carey & S. C. McDevitt (Eds.), *Clinical and educational applications of temperament research* (pp. 155–165). Amsterdam: Swets & Zeitlinger.

Cami, J., Farre, M., Mas, M., Roset, P. N., Poudevida, S., Mas, A., San, L., & de la Torre, R. (2000). Human pharmacology of 3,4-methylenedioxymethamphetamine ("ecstasy"): Psychomotor performance and subjective effects. *Journal of Clinical Psychopharmacology, 20,* 455–466.

Campbell, J. C., & Wolf, A. D. (2003). Risk factors for femicide in abusive relationships: Results from a multisite case control study. *American Journal of Public Health, 93*(7).

Campos, J. J., Langer, A., & Krowitz, A. (1970). Cardiac responses on the visual cliff. *Science, 170,* 196–197.

Cannon, W. B. (1927). The James-Lange theory of emotion: A critical examination and an alternative theory. *American Journal of Psychology, 39,* 10–124.

Cannon, W. B., & Washburn, A. L. (1912). An explanation of hunger. *American Journal of Physiology, 29,* 444–454.

Capek, J., & Capek, K. (1923). *"R.U.R." (Rossum's Universal Robots).* London: Oxford University Press.

Carducci, B. (1998). *The psychology of personality.* Pacific Grove, CA: Brooks/Cole Publishing Co.

Carlson, G. A., Jensen, P. S., & Nottelmann, E. D. (Eds.) (1998). Special issue: Current issues in childhood bipolarity. *Journal of Affective Disorders, 51.*

Carnot, M. J., Dunn, B., Cañas, A. J., Gram, P., & Mudloon, J. (2001). Concept maps vs. Web pages for information searching and browsing. Retrieved from the Internet on May 28, 2008, at http://www.ihmc.us/users/acanas/publications/CMapsVSWebPagesExp1/CMapsVSWebPagesExp1.htm

Carpenter, P. A., Just, M. A., & Shell, P. (1990). What one intelligence test measures: A theoretical account of the processing in the Raven Progressive Matrices test. *Psychological Review, 97*(3), 404–431.

Carr, E. G., & Lovaas, O. I. (1983). Contingent electric shock as a treatment for severe behavior problems. In S. Axelrod & J. Apsche (Eds.), *The effects of punishment on human behavior* (pp. 221–245). New York: Academic Press.

Carrion, V. G., Weems, C. F., & Reiss, A. L. (2007). Stress predicts brain changes in children: A pilot longitudinal study on youth stress, posttraumatic stress disorder, and the hippocampus. *Pediatrics, 119*(3), 509–516.

Carroll, R. T. (2000). Eye movement desensitization and reprocessing (EMDR). The Skeptic's Dictionary. Retrieved from the Internet on July 14, 2004, at www.skepdic.com/pseudosc.html.

Carruthers, M. (2001). A multifactorial approach to understanding andropause. *Journal of Sexual and Reproductive Medicine, 1,* 69–74.

Carskadon, M. A., & Dement, W. C. (2005). Normal human sleep overview. In M. H. Kryger, T. Roth, & W. C. Dement (Eds.), *Principles and practice of sleep medicine* (4th ed., pp. 13–23). Philadelphia: Elsevier/Saunders.

Carson, R. C. (1969). *Interaction concepts of personality.* Chicago: Aldine.

Carter, C., Bishop, J., & Kravits, S. L. (2006). Keys to success: Building successful intelligence for college, career, and life (5th ed.). Englewood Cliffs, NJ: Prentice Hall.

Carter, C., Bishop, J., Kravits, S. L., & D'Agostino, J. V. (Ed. consultant). (2002). *Keys to college studying: Becoming a lifelong learner.* Upper Saddle River, NJ: Prentice Hall.

Carver, C. S., & Antoni, M. H. (2004). Finding benefit in breast cancer during the year after diagnosis predicts better adjustment 5 to 8 years after diagnosis. *Health Psychology, 26,* 595–598.

Carver, L. J., & Bauer, P. J. (2001). The dawning of a past: The emergence of long-term explicit memory in infancy. *Journal of Experimental Psychology: General, 130,* 726–745.

Cassiday, K. L., & Lyons, J. A. (1992). Recall of traumatic memories following cerebral vascular accident. *Journal of Traumatic Stress, 5,* 627–631.

Cassidy, A., Bingham, S., & Setchell, K. D. R. (1994). Biological effects of a diet of soy protein rich in isoflavones on the menstrual cycle of premenopausal women. *American Journal of Clinical Nutrition, 60,* 333–340.

Castillo, R. J. (1997). Eating disorders. In R. J. Castillo (Ed.), *Culture and mental illness: A client-centered approach* (p. 152). Pacific Grove, CA: Brooks/Cole Publishing Co.

Catanzaro, S. J., Wasch, H. H., Kirsch, I., & Mearns, J. (2000). Coping-related expectancies and dispositions as prospective predictors of coping responses and symptoms: Distinguishing mood regulation expectancies, dispositional coping, and optimism. *Journal of Personality, 68,* 757–788.

Cattell, R. B. (1950). *Personality: A systematic, theoretical, and factual study.* New York: McGraw-Hill.

Cattell, R. B. (1973). *Personality and mood by questionnaire.* San Francisco: Jossey-Bass.

Cattell, R. B. (1990). Advances in Cattellian personality theory. In L. A. Pervin (Ed.), *Handbook of personality: Theory and research* (pp. 101–110). New York: Guilford.

Cattell, R. B. (1994). *Sixteen Personality Factor Questionnaire* (5th ed.). Champaign, IL: Institute for Personality and Ability Testing, Inc.

Cattell, R. B. (1995). Personality structure and the new fifth edition of the 16PF. *Educational & Psychological Measurement, 55*(6), 926–937.

Cattell, R. B. (Ed.). (1966). *Handbook of multivariate experimental psychology.* Chicago: Rand McNally.

Cattell, R. B., & Kline, P. (1977). *The scientific analysis of personality and motivation.* New York: Academic Press.

Cave, K. R., & Kim, M. (1999). Top-down and bottom-up attentional control: On the nature of interference from a salient distractor. *Perception & Psychophysics, 61,* 1009–1023.

CBS/AP. (March 9, 2009). Obama ends stem cell research ban. Retrieved from the Internet on March 24, 2009 at http://www.cbsnews.com/stories/2009/03/09/politics/100days/domesticissues/main4853385.shtml

Centers for Disease Control and Prevention (CDC). (1992). *Smoking and health in the Americas: The Surgeon General's report.* National Center for Chronic Disease Prevention and Health Promotion.

Centers for Disease Control and Prevention (CDC). (1994). *Addressing emerging infectious disease threats: A prevention strategy for the United States.* Atlanta, GA: U.S. Department of Health and Human Services, Public Health Service.

Centers for Disease Control and Prevention (CDC). (1999). Achievements in public health, 1900–1999: Impact of vaccines universally recommended for children, United States 1990–1998. *Morbidity and Mortality Weekly Report, 48,* 243–248. Atlanta, GA: U.S. Department of Health and Human Services, Public Health Service.

Centers for Disease Control and Prevention (CDC). (2000). *What would happen if we stopped vaccinations?* Atlanta, GA: U.S. Department of Health and Human Services, Public Health Service. Retrieved from the Internet on August 23, 2004, at **www.cdc.gov/nip/publications/fs/gen/WhatIfStop.htm.**

Centers for Disease Control and Prevention (CDC). (2002). Annual smoking-attributable mortality, years of potential life lost, and economic costs—United States, 1995–1999. *Morbidity and Mortality Weekly Report, 51,* 300–303.

Centers for Disease Control and Prevention (CDC). (2004). *Parents' guide to childhood immunization.* Atlanta, GA: U.S. Department of Health and Human Services, Public Health Service.

Centers for Disease Control and Prevention (CDC). (2005). Web-based Injury Statistics Query and Reporting System (WISQARS) [Online]. National Center for Injury Prevention and Control, CDC (producer). Available at **http://www.cdc.gov/ncipc/wisqars/default.htm.**

Centers for Disease Control and Prevention (CDC). (2006). Welcome to WISQARS (Web-based Injury Statistics Query and Reporting System). Retrieved from the Internet on February 27, 2008, from Centers for Disease Control and Prevention, National Center for Injury and Prevention Control Web site: **http://www.cdc.gov/ncipc/wisqars/.**

Centers for Disease Control. (2008). National Health and Nutrition Survey. Retrieved from the Internet on February 8, 2008, at **http://www.cdc.gov/hiv/resources/brochures/livingwithhiv.htm.**

Centers for Disease Control and Prevention. (2009). Health effects of cigarette smoking. Retrieved from **http://www.cdc.gov/tobacco/data_statistics/fact_sheets/health_effects/effects_cig_smoking/index.htm.**

Centerwall, B. S. (1989). Exposure to television as a risk factor for violence. *American Journal of Epidemiology, 129,* 643–652.

Cepeda, N. J., Pashler, H., Vul, E., Wixted, J. T., & Rohrer, D. (2006). Distributed practice in verbal recall tasks: A review and quantitative synthesis. *Psychological Bulletin, 132:* 354–380.

Cermak, L., & Craik, F. (1979). *Levels of processing in human memory.* Hillsdale, NJ: Erlbaum.

Cha, J. H., & Nam, K. D. (1985). A test of Kelley's cube theory of attribution: A cross-cultural replication of McArthur's study. *Korean Social Science Journal, 12,* 151–180.

Chadda, R. K., & Ahuja, N. (1990). Dhat syndrome. A sex neurosis of the Indian subcontinent. *The British Journal of Psychiatry, 156,* 577–579.

Chandola, T., Britton, A., Brunner, E., Hemingway, H., Malik, M., Kumari, M., Badrick, E., Kivimaki, M., & Marmot, M. (2008). Work stress and coronary heart disease: What are the mechanisms? *European Heart Journal,* DOI:10.1093/eurheartj/ehm584.

Chang, P. P., Ford, D. E., Meoni, L. A., Wang, N., & Klag, M. J. (2002). Anger in young men and subsequent premature cardiovascular disease: The precursors study. *Archives of Internal Medicine, 162,* 901–906.

Chapelon-Clavel, F., Paoletti, C., & Benhamou, S. (1997). Smoking cessation rates 4 years after treatment by nicotine gum and acupuncture. *Preventive Medicine, 26,* 25–28.

Charlesworth, W. R., & Kreutzer, M. A. (1973). Facial expression of infants and children. In P. Ekman (Ed.), *Darwin and facial expression: A century of research in review.* New York: Academic.

Chee, M. W. L., & Choo, W. C. (2004). Functional imaging of working memory following 24 hours of total sleep deprivation. Program and abstracts of the 56th Annual Meeting of the American Academy of Neurology; April 24–May 1, 2004, San Francisco, California.

Chen, R., & Ende, N. (2000). The potential for the use of mononuclear cells from human umbilical cord blood in the treatment of amyotrophic lateral sclerosis in SOD1 mice. *Journal of Medicine, 31,* 21–31.

Cheng, H., Cao, Y., & Olson, L. (1996). Spinal cord repair in adult paraplegic rats: Partial restoration of hind limb function. *Science, 273,* 510–513.

Cherry, E. C. (1953). Some experiments on the recognition of speech, with one and with two ears. *Journal of the Acoustical Society of America, 25*(5), 975–979.

Chess, S., & Thomas, A. (1986). *Temperament in clinical practice.* New York: Guilford.

Chesterton, L. S., Barlas, P., Foster, N. E., Baxter, G. D., & Wright, C. C. (2003). Gender differences in pressure pain threshold in healthy humans. *Pain, 101,* 259–266.

Chidester, D. (2003). *Salvation and suicide: Jim Jones, the Peoples Temple, and Jonestown* (rev. ed., pp. 1–51). Bloomington, IN: Indiana University Press.

Chiu, C., Hong, Y., & Dweck, C. S. (1997). Lay dispositionism and implicit theories of personality. *Journal of Personality and Social Psychology, 73,* 19–30.

Choi, I., & Nisbett, R. E. (1998). Situational salience and cultural differences in the correspondence bias and in the actor–observer bias. *Personality and Social Psychology Bulletin, 24,* 949–960.

Choi, I., Nisbett, R. E., & Norenzayan, A. (1999). Causal attribution across cultures: Variation and universality. *Psychological Bulletin, 125,* 47–63.

Chomsky, N. (1957). *Syntactic structures.* The Hague: Mouton.

Chomsky, N. (1964). *Current issues in linguistic theory.* The Hague: Mouton.

Chomsky, N. (1981). Principles and parameters in syntactic theory. In N. Hornstein & D. Lightfoot (Eds.), *Explanation in linguistics: The logical problem of language acquisition.* London: Longman.

Chomsky, N. (1986). *Knowledge of language: Its nature, origin and use.* New York: Praeger.

Chomsky, N. (2006). *Language and mind* (3rd ed.). New York: Cambridge University Press.

Chomsky, N., Belletti, A., & Rizzi, L. (2002). *On nature and language.* New York: Cambridge University Press.

Chou, S. Y., Grossman, M., & Saffer, H. (2004). An economic analysis of adult obesity: Results from the behavioral risk factor surveillance system. *Journal of Health Economics, 23,* 565–587.

Christensen, A., Jacobson, N. S., & Babcock, J. C. (1995). Integrative behavioral couple therapy. In N. S. Jacobson & A. S. Gurman (Eds.), *Clinical handbook of couple therapy* (pp. 31–64). New York: Norton.

Chu, J. A., Frey, L. M., Ganzel, B. L., & Matthews, J. A. (1999). Memories of childhood abuse: Dissociation, amnesia, and corroboration. *American Journal of Psychiatry, 156,* 749–755.

Chwalisz, K., Diener, E., & Gallagher, D. (1988). Autonomic arousal feedback and emotional experience: Evidence from the spinal cord injured. *Journal of Personality and Social Psychology, 54,* 820–828.

Cialdini, R., Vincent, J., Lewis, S., Catalan, J., Wheeler, D., & Darby, B. (1975). Reciprocal concessions procedure for inducing compliance: The door–in–the–face technique. *Journal of Personality and Social Psychology, 31,* 206–215.

Cialdini, R., Wosinska, W., Barrett, D., Butner, J., & Gornik–Durose, M. (1999). Compliance with a request in two cultures: The differential influence of social proof and commitment/consistency on collectivists and individualists. *Personality and Social Psychology Bulletin, 25,* 1242–1253.

Cialdini, R. B., Trost, M. R., & Newsom, J. T. (1995). Preference for consistency: The development of a valid measure and the discovery of surprising behavioral implications. *Journal of Personality and Social Psychology, 69,* 318–328.

Ciardiello, A. (1998). Did you ask a good question today? Alternative cognitive and metacognitive strategies. *Journal of Adolescent & Adult Literacy, 42,* 210–219.

Cincirpini, P. M., Lapitsky, L., Seay, S., Wallfisch, A., & Kitchens, K. V. V. H. (1995). The effects of smoking schedules on cessation outcome: Can we improve on common methods of gradual and abrupt nicotine withdrawal? *Journal of Consulting and Clinical Psychology, 63*(3), 388–399.

Cinnirella, M., & Green, B. (2007). Does "cyber-conformity" vary cross-culturally? Exploring the effect of culture and communication medium on social conformity. *Computers in Human Behavior, 23*(4), 2011–2025.

Clark, A. (1991). *Microcognition: Philosophy, cognitive science, and parallel distributed processing.* Cambridge, MA: MIT Press, reprint edition (1989).

Clark, D. A., Beck, A. T., & Brown, G. (1989). Cognitive mediation in general psychiatric outpatients: A test of the content-specificity hypothesis. *Journal of Personality and Social Psychology, 56,* 958–964.

Clark, D. A., Hollifield, M., Leahy, R. L., & Beck, J. S. (in press). The cognitive theory for psychiatric disorders. In G. Gabbard, J. S. Beck, and J. Wright (Eds.), *Textbook of psychotherapeutic treatments in psychiatry.* Washington, DC: American Psychiatric Press.

Clarke, A., Harvey, M. L., & Kane, D. J. (1999). Attitudes and behavior: Are produce consumers influenced by eco-labels? Paper presented at a National Conference on Eco-labels, "Making Change in the Marketplace," October 22–23, 1998, at the Governor Hotel in Portland, Oregon. Sponsored by the Food Alliance. Retrieved from the Internet on August 1, 2004, at **www.ssi.nrcs.usda.gov/SSIEnvPsy/nrcs/ecopaper.pdf.**

Clarke, J. (1994). Pieces of the puzzle: The jigsaw method. In S. Sharan (Ed.), *Handbook of cooperative learning methods* (pp. 34–50). Westport, CT: Greenwood Press.

Clarkin, J. F., Levy, K. N., Lenzenweger, M. F., & Kernberg, O. F. (2007). Evaluating three treatments for borderline personality disorder: A multiwave study. *American Journal of Psychiatry, 164*(6), 922–928.

Coates, J. (1986). *Women, men, and language.* New York: Longman.

Coccaro, E. F., & Kavoussi, R. J. (1996). Neurotransmitter correlates of impulsive aggression. In D. M. Stoff & R. B. Cairns (Eds.), *Aggression and violence* (pp. 67–86). Mahwah, NJ: Lawrence Erlbaum.

Cohen, L., Berzoff, J., & Elin, M. (1995). *Dissociative identity disorder: Theoretical and treatment controversies.* New York: Human Sciences Library.

Cohen, L. J. (1997). Rational drug use in the treatment of depression. *Pharmacotherapy, 17,* 45–61.

Cohen, N. J., Eichenbaum, R., Decedo, J. C., & Corkin, S. (1985). Preserved learning capacity in amnesia: Evidence for multiple memory systems. In L. S. Squire & N. Butters (Eds.), *Neuropsychology of memory.* New York: Guilford Press.

Cohen, S., & Herbert, T. B. (1996). Health psychology: Psychological factors and physical disease from the perspective of human psychoneuroimmunology. *Annual Review of Psychology, 47,* 113–142.

Cohen, S., Frank, E., Doyle, B. J., Skoner, D. P., Rabin, B. S., & Gwaltney, J. M. (1998). Types of stressors that increase susceptibility to the common cold. *Health Psychology, 17,* 214–223.

Cohen, S., Janicki-Deverts, D., & Miller, G. E. (2007). Psychological stress and disease. *Journal of the American Medical Association, 298*(14), 1685–1687.

Colcombe, S. J., Erickson, K. I., Raz, N., Webb, A. G., Cohen, N. J., McAuley, E., & Kramer, A. F. (2003). Aerobic fitness reduces brain tissue loss in aging humans. *Journal of Gerontology Series A: Biological Sciences and Medical Sciences, 58,* 176–180.

Colligan, J. (1983). Musical creativity and social rules in four cultures. *Creative Child and Adult Quarterly, 8,* 39–44.

Collins, A. M., & Loftus, E. F. (1975). A spreading activation theory of semantic processing. *Psychological Review, 82,* 407–428.

Collins, A. M., & Quillian, M. R. (1969). Retrieval time from semantic memory. *Journal of Verbal Learning and Verbal Behaviour, 8,* 240–247.

Collins, C. J., Hanges, P. J., & Locke, E. A. (2004). The relationship of achievement motivation to entrepreneurial behavior: A meta-analysis. *Human Performance, 17*(1), 95–117.

Colom, R., Shih, P. C., Flores-Mendoza, C., & Quiroga, M. A. (2006). The real relationship between short-term memory and working memory. *Memory, 14*(7), 804–813.

Committee on Animal Research and Ethics. (2004). *Research with animals in psychology.* APAOnline. Retrieved from the Internet on October 12, 2004, at **www.apa.org/science/animal2.html.**

Conrad, R., & Hull, A. J. (1964). Information, acoustic confusion, and memory span. *British Journal of Psychology, 55,* 429–432.

Consumer Reports. (1995, November). Mental health: Does psychotherapy help? 734–739.

Conway, M. A., Cohen, G., & Stanhope, N. (1992). Very long-term memory for knowledge acquired at school and university. *Applied Cognitive Psychology, 6,* 467–482.

Coolidge, F. L. (2006). *Dream interpretation as a psychotherapeutic technique.* London: Radcliffe, Inc.

Cooper, L. A., Gonzales, J. J., Gallo, J. J., Rost, K. M., Meredith, L. S., Rubenstein, L. V., Wang, N. Y., & Ford, D. E. (2003). The acceptability of treatment for depression among African-American, Hispanic, and white primary care patients. *Medical Care, 41*(4), 479–489.

Corbetta, M., Kincade, M. J., Lewis, C., Snyder, A. Z., & Sapir, A. (2005). Neural basis and recovery of spatial attention deficits in spatial neglect. *Nature Neuroscience, 8,* 1603–1610.

Cormier, J. F., & Thelen, M. H. (1998). Professional skepticism of multiple personality disorder. *Professional Psychology: Research and Practice, 29,* 163–167.

Cosgrove, G. R., & Rauch, S. L. (1995). Psychosurgery. *Neurosurgery Clinics of North America, 6,* 167–176.

Costa, P. T., Jr., & McCrae, R. R. (2000). The Revised NEO Personality Inventory (NEO PI-R). In J. Cheek & E. M. Donahue (Eds.), *Handbook of personality inventories.* New York: Plenum.

Costello, D. M., Swendsen, J., Rose, J. S., & Dierker, L. C. (2008). Risk and protective factors associated with trajectories of depressed mood from adolescence to early adulthood. *Journal of Consulting and Clinical Psychology, 76*(2), 173–183.

Courage, M. L., & Howe, M. L. (2002). From infant to child: The dynamics of cognitive change in the second year of life. *Psychological Bulletin, 128,* 250–277.

Cowan, N. (1988). Evolving conceptions of memory storage, selective attention, and their mutual constraints within the human information processing system. *Psychological Bulletin, 104,* 163–191.

Craddock, N., O'Donovan, M. C., & Owen, M. J. (2005). The genetics of schizophrenia and bipolar disorder: Dissecting psychosis. *Journal of Medical Genetics, 42,* 288–299.

Crago, M. B., Shisslak, C. M., & Estes, L. S. (1996). Eating disturbances among American minority groups: A review. *International Journal of Eating Disorders, 19,* 239–248.

Craik, F. I. M. (1970). The fate of primary memory items in free recall. *Journal of Verbal Learning and Verbal Behavior, 9,* 143–148.

Craik, F. I. M. (1994). Memory changes in normal aging. *Current Directions in Psychological Science, 3*(5), 155–158.

Craik, F. I. M., & Lockhart, R. S. (1972). Levels of processing. A framework for memory research. *Journal of Verbal Learning and Verbal Behaviour, 11,* 671–684.

Craik, F. I. M., & Tulving, E. (1975). Depth of processing and the retention of words in episodic memory. *Journal of Experimental Psychology: General, 104,* 268–294.

Cramer, P. (2000). Defense mechanisms in psychology today: Further processes for adaptation. *American Psychologist, 55,* 637–646.

Crawford, M., & Unger, R. (2004). *Women and gender: A feminist psychology* (4th ed.). Boston: McGraw-Hill.

Croft, A. P., & Przyborski, S. A. (2006). Formation of neurons by non-neural adult stem cells: Potential mechanism implicates an artifact of growth in culture. *Stem Cells, 24*(8), 1841–1851.

Crowley, A. E., & Hoyer, W. D. (1994). An integrative framework for understanding two-sided persuasion. *Journal of Consumer Research, 20,* 561–574.

Csernansky, J. G., Mahmoud, R., & Brenner, R. (2002). A comparison of reperidone and haloperidol for the prevention of relapse in patients with schizophrenia. *New England Journal of Medicine, 346,* 16–22.

Csikszentmihalyi, M. (1996). *Creativity: Flow and the psychology of discovery and Invention.* New York: Harper Perennial.

Csikszentmihalyi, M. (1997). *Finding flow: The psychology of engagement with everyday life.* New York: Basic Books.

Cua, A. B., Wilhelm, K. P., & Maibach, H. I. (1990). Elastic properties of human skin: Relation to age, sex and anatomical region. *Archives of Dermatology Research, 282,* 283–288.

Culbertson, F. (2003). *The phobia list.* Retrieved from the Internet on June 22, 2004, at **www.phobialist.com.**

Cummings, J. L., & Coffey C. E. (1994). Neurobiological basis of behavior. In C. E. Coffey & J. L. Cummings (Eds.), *Textbook of geriatric neuropsychiatry* (pp. 72–96). Washington, DC: American Psychiatric Press.

Cummings, S. R., & Melton, L. J., III. (2002). Epidemiology and outcomes of osteoporotic fractures. *Lancet, 359*(9319), 1761–1767.

Curtis, R. C., & Miller, K. (1986). Believing another likes or dislikes you: Behaviors making the beliefs come true. *Journal of Personality and Social Psychology, 51,* 284–290.

Curtis, R. H. (1993). *Great lives: Medicine.* New York: Charles Scribner's Sons Books for Young Readers.

Cytowic, R. E. (1989). Synesthesia and mapping of subjective sensory dimensions. *Neurology, 39,* 849–850.

Czeisler, C. A. (1995). The effect of light on the human circadian pacemaker. In D. J. Chadwick & K. Ackrill (Eds.), *Circadian clocks and their adjustment* (pp. 254–302). West Sussex, England: John Wiley & Sons.

Czeisler, C. A., Moore-Ede, M. C., & Coleman, R. M. (1982). Rotating shift work schedules that disrupt sleep are improved by applying circadian principles. *Science, 217,* 460–463.

Czeisler, C. A., Weitzman, E. D., Moore-Ede, M. C., Zimmerman, J. C., & Knauer, R. S. (1980). Human sleep: Its duration and organization depend on its circadian phase. *Science, 210,* 1264–1267.

Dabbs, J. M., Jr., Bernieri, F. J., Strong, R. K., Campo, R., & Milun, R. (2001). Going on stage: Testosterone in greetings and meetings. *Journal of Research in Personality, 35,* 27–40.

Dalenberg, C. J. (1996). Accuracy, timing and circumstances of disclosure in therapy of recovered and continuous memories of abuse. *The Journal of Psychiatry and Law, 24*(2), 229–275.

Dallman, M., Pecoraro, N., Akana, S., la Fleur, S. E., Gomez, F., Houshyar, H., Bell, M. E., Bhatnagar, S., Laugero, K. D., & Manalo, S. (2003). Chronic stress and obesity: A new view of "comfort food." *Proceedings of the National Academy of Sciences, 100*(20), 11696–11701.

Daly, M., Wilson, M., & Weghorst, S. J. (1982). Male sexual jealousy. *Ethology and Sociobiology, 3,* 11–27.

Damasio, H., Grabowski, T., Frank, R., Galaburda, A. M., & Damasion, A. R. (1994). The return of Phineas Gage: Clues about the brain from the skull of a famous patient. *Science, 264,* 1102–1105.

Dapretto, M., Davies, M. S., Pfeifer, J. H., Scott, A. A., Sigman, M., Bookheimer, S. Y., & Iacoboni, M. (2006). Understanding emotions in others: Mirror neuron dysfunction in children with autism spectrum disorders. *Nature Neuroscience, 9*(1), 28–30.

Darley, J. M., & Latané, B. (1968). Bystander intervention in emergencies: Diffusion of responsibility. *Journal of Personality and Social Psychology, 8,* 377–383.

Darvill, T., Lonky, E., Reihman, J., Stewart, P., & Pagano, J. (2000). Prenatal exposure to PCBs and infant performance on the Fagan test of infant intelligence. *Neurotoxicology, 21*(6), 1029–1038.

Darwin, C. (1859). *The origin of species by means of natural selection.* London: John Murray.

Darwin, C. (1898). *The expression of the emotions in man and animals.* New York: D. Appleton & Co.

Daum, I., & Schugens, M. M. (1996). On the cerebellum and classical conditioning. *Current Directions in Psychological Science, 5,* 58–61.

Davidson, P. R., & Parker, K. C. H. (2001). Eye movement desensitization and reprocessing (EMDR): A meta-analysis. *Journal of Counseling and Clinical Psychology, 69*(2), 305–316.

Davidson, R., Kabat-Zinn, J., Schumacher, J., Rosenkranz, M., Muller, D., Santorelli, S., Urbanowski, F., Harrington, A., Bonus, K. & Sheridan, J. (2003). Alterations in brain and immune function produced by mindfulness meditation. *Psychosomatic Medicine, 65,* 564–570.

Davidson, R. J. (2003). Affective neuroscience and psychophysiology: Toward a synthesis. *Psychophysiology, 40*(5), 655–665.

Davidson, R. J., Ekman, P., Saron, C. D., Senulis, J. A., & Friesen, W. V. (1990). Approach-withdrawal and cerebral asymmetry: Emotional expression and brain physiology I. *Journal of Personality and Social Psychology, 58*(2), 330–341.

Davidson, R. J., Putman, K. M., & Larson, C. L. (2000). Dysfunction in the neural circuitry of emotion regulation—A possible prelude to violence. *Science, 289,* 591–594.

Davies, I. R. L., Laws, G., Corbett, G. G., & Jerrett, D. J. (1998a). Crosscultural differences in colour vision: Acquired "colour blindness" in Africa. *Personality and Individual Differences, 25,* 1153–1162.

Davies, I. R. L., Sowden, P., Jerrett, D. T., Jerrett, T., & Corbett, G. G. (1998b). A cross-cultural study of English and Setswana speakers on a colour triads task: A test of the Sapir-Whorf hypothesis. *British Journal of Psychology, 89,* 1–15.

Davis, K. F., Parker, K. P., & Montgomery, G. (2004). Sleep in infants and young children: Part one: Normal sleep. *Journal of Pediatric Healthcare, 18*(2), 65–71.

Davis, K. L., Kahn, R. S., Ko, G., & Davidson, M. (1991). Dopamine in schizophrenia: A review and reconceptualization. *American Journal of Psychiatry, 148,* 1474–1486.

Davis, M., & Whalen, P. J. (2001). The amygdala: Vigilance and emotion. *Molecular Psychiatry, 6,* 13–34.

Dawood, K., Pillard, R. C., Horvath, C., Revelle, W., & Bailey, J. M. (2000). Familial aspects of male homosexuality. *Archives of Sexual Behavior, 29*(2).

Day, R. H., & McKenzie, B. E. (1981). Infant perception of the invariant size of approaching and receding objects. *Developmental Psychology, 17,* 670–677.

Dean, G., & Kelly, I. W. (2000). Does astrology work? Astrology and skepticism 1975–2000. In P. Kurtz (Ed.), *Skepticism: A 25 Year Retrospective* (pp. 191–207). Amherst, NY: Prometheus Books.

Dean, G., Kelly, I. W., Sakolfske, D. H., & Furnham, A. (1992). Graphology and human judgment. In B. L. Beyerstein & D. F. Beyerstein (Eds.), *The write stuff: Evaluations of graphology—the study of handwriting analysis* (pp. 342–396). Amherst, NY: Prometheus Books.

DeAngelis, T. (2002). Promising treatments for anorexia and bulimia: Research boosts support for tough-to-treat eating disorders. *APA Monitor on Psychology, 33*(3), 38–43.

DeCasper, A. J., & Fifer, W. P. (1980). Of human bonding: Newborns prefer their mothers' voices. *Science, 208,* 1174–1176.

DeCasper, A. J., & Spence, M. J. (1986). Prenatal maternal speech influence on newborns' perception of sounds. *Infant Behaviour and Development, 9,* 133–150.

deCharms, R. (1968). *Personal causation.* New York: Academic Press.

Deci, E. L., & Ryan, R. M. (1985). *Intrinsic motivation and self-determination in human behavior.* New York: Plenum.

Deci, E. L., Eghrari, H., Patrick, B. C., & Leone, D. R. (1994). Facilitating internalization: The self-determination theory perspective. *Journal of Personality, 62,* 119–142.

Deci, E. L., Koestner, R., & Ryan, R. M. (1999). A meta-analytic review of experiments examining the effects of extrinsic rewards on intrinsic motivation. *Psychological Bulletin, 125,* 627–668.

DeCoster, J., & Claypool, H. M. (2004). A meta-analysis of priming effects on impression formation supporting a general model of informational biases. *Personality and Social Psychology Review, 8*(1), 2–27.

DeGrandpre, R. J. (2000). A science of meaning: Can behaviorism bring meaning to psychological science? *American Psychologist, 55,* 721–739.

Dehaene, S., Naccache, L., Cohen, L., Le Bihan, D., Mangin, J. F., Poline, J. B., & Riviere, D. (2001). Cerebral mechanisms of word masking and unconscious repetition priming. *Nature Neuroscience, 4,* 752–758.

Deinzer, R., Kleineidam, C. H., Winkler, R., Idel, H., & Bachg, D. (2000). Prolonged reduction of salivary immunoglobulin A (slgA) after a major academic exam. *International Journal of Psychophysiology, 37,* 219–232.

Delagrange, P., & Guardiola-Lemaitre, B. (1997). Melatonin, its receptors, and relationships with biological rhythm disorders. *Clinincal Neuropharmacology, 20,* 482–510.

Delaney, A. J., Crane, J. W., & Sah, P. (2007). Noradrenaline modulates transmission at a central synapse by a presynaptic mechanism. *Neuron, 56*(6), 880–892.

Delfiner, R. (2001, November 16). "Kitty Left at Death's Door." *The New York Post.*

DeLongis, A., Lazarus, R. S., & Folkman, S. (1988). The impact of daily stress on health and mood: Psychological and social resources as mediators. *Journal of Personality and Social Psychology, 54*(3), 486–495.

Dement, W. (1997). Sleepless at Stanford: What all undergraduates should know about how their sleeping lives affect their waking lives. Article retrieved from the Internet on October 19, 2004, at **www.stanford.edu/~dement/sleepless.html**.

Dement, W. C. (1960). The effect of dream deprivation. *Science, 131,* 1705–1707.

Dement, W. C., Henry, P., Cohen, H., & Ferguson, J. (1969). Studies on the effect of REM deprivation in humans and animals. In K. H. Pribram (Ed.), *Mood, states, and mind.* Baltimore: Penguin.

Demers, R. A. (1988). Linguistics and animal communication. In Newmeyer (Ed.), *Language form and language function* (pp. 314–335). Cambridge, MA: MIT Press.

Dempster, F. N., & Farris, R. (1990). The spacing effect: Research and practice. *Journal of Research and Development in Education 23*(2), 97–101.

Dennett, D. C. (1991). *Consciousness explained.* New York: Little, Brown, & Co.

Denno, D. W. (2002). Crime and consciousness: Science and involuntary acts. *Minnesota Law Review, 87,* 269–399.

Deregowski, J. B. (1969). Perception of the two-pronged trident by two- and three-dimensional perceivers. *Journal of Experimental Psychology, 82,* 9–13.

DeRubeis, R. J., Gelfand, L. A., Tang, T. Z., & Simons, A. D. (1999). Medications versus cognitive behavior therapy for severely depressed outpatients: Megaanalysis of four randomized comparisons. *American Journal of Psychiatry, 156*(7), 1007–1013.

De Valois, R. L., & Jacobs, G. H. (1968). Primate color vision, *Science, 162*, 553–540.

Dew, M. A., Whyte, E. M., Lenze, E. J., Houck, P. R., Mulsant, B. H., Pollock, B. G., Stack, J. A., Bensasi, S., & Reynolds, C. F. (2007). Recovery from major depression in older adults receiving augmentation of antidepressant pharmacotherapy. *American Journal of Psychiatry, 164*(6), 892–899.

Diamond, L. M. (2003). What does sexual orientation orient? A biobehavioral model distinguishing romantic love and sexual desire. *Psychological Review, 110*, 173–192.

Diamond, M. (1995). Biological aspects of sexual orientation and identity. In L. Diamant & R. McAnulty (Eds.), *The psychology of sexual orientation, behavior and identity: A handbook* (pp. 45–80). Westport, CT: Greenwood Press.

Diamond, M., & Sigmundson, H. K. (1997). Sex reassignment at birth. Long-term review and clinical implications. *Archives of Pediatric Adolescent Medicine, 151*(3), 298–304.

Diamond, M. C. (1991). Hormonal effects on the development of cerebral lateralization. *Psychoneuroendocrinology, 16*, 121–129.

Dickens, W. T., & Flynn, J. R. (2001 April). Heritability estimates vs. large environmental effects: The IQ paradox resolved. *Psychological Review, 108*(2), 346–369.

Dickerson, F., Ringel, N., Parente, F., & Boronow, J. (1994). Seclusion and restraint, assaultiveness, and patient performance in a token economy. *Hospital and Community Psychiatry, 45*, 168–170.

Digman, J. M. (1990). Personality structure: Emergence of the five-factor model. *Annual Review of Psychology, 41*, 417–440.

Dillard, J. (1990). Self-inference and the foot-in-the-door technique: Quantity of behavior and attitudinal mediation. *Human Communication Research, 16*, 422–447.

Dillard, J. (1991). The current status of research on sequential–request compliance techniques. *Personality and Social Psychology Bulletin, 17*, 282–288.

Dinges, D. F. (1995). An overview of sleepiness and accidents. *Journal of Sleep Research, 4*(2), 4–14.

Dodge, K. A., Bates, J. E., & Pettit, G. S. (1990). Mechanisms in the cycle of violence. *Science, 250*, 1678–1683.

Doidge, N. (2007). *The brain that changes itself.* New York: Viking.

Dollard, J., & Miller, N. F. (1950). *Personality and psychotherapy.* New York: McGraw-Hill.

Dollard, J., Doob, L. W., Milller, N. E., Mowrer, O. H., & Sears, R. R. (1939). *Frustration and aggression.* New Haven: Yale University Press.

Domagalski, T. A., & Steelman, L. A. (2007). The impact of gender and organizational status on workplace anger expression. *Management Communication Quarterly, 20*(3), 297–315.

Domhoff, G. W. (1996). *Finding meaning in dreams: A quantitative approach.* New York: Plenum Publishing Co.

Domhoff, G. W. (2005). The content of dreams: Methodologic and theoretical implications. In M. Kryger, T. Roth, & W. Dement (Eds.), *Principles and practices of sleep medicine* (4th ed., pp. 522–534). Philadelphia: Saunders.

Dominey, P. F., & Dodane, C. (2004). Indeterminacy in language acquisition: The role of child-directed speech and joint attention. *Journal of Neurolinguistics, 17*(2–3), 121–145.

Dominy, N. J., & Lucas, P. W. (2001). Ecological importance of trichromatic vision to primates. *Nature, 410*, 363–366.

Domjan, M., Cusato, B., & Villarreal, R. (2000). Pavlovian feed-forward mechanisms in the control of social behavior. *Behavioral and Brain Sciences, 23*, 235–282.

Donnerstein, E., Slaby, R., & Eron, L. (1994). The mass media and youth aggression. In L. Eron, J. Gentry, & P. Schlegel (Eds.), *A reason to hope: A psychosocial perspective on violence and youth* (pp. 219–250). Washington, DC: American Psychological Association.

Donovan, J. J., & Radosevich, D. R. (1999). A meta-analytic review of the distribution of practice effect: Now you see it, now you don't. *Journal of Applied Psychology, 84*, 795–805.

Dorahy, M. J. (2001). Dissociative identity disorder and memory dysfunction: The current state of experimental research and its future directions. *Clinical Psychology Review, 21*(5), 771–795.

Dougherty, D. D., Baer, L., Cosgrove, G. R., Cassem, E. H., Price, B. H., Nierenberg, A. A., Jenike, M. A., & Rauch, S. L. (2002). Prospective long-term follow-up of 44 patients who received cingulotomy for treatment-refractory obsessive-compulsive disorder. *The American Journal of Psychiatry, 159*(2), 269–275.

Dove, A. (1971). The "Chitling" Test. In L. R. Aiken, Jr. *Psychological and educational testings.* Boston: Allyn and Bacon.

Dreger, A. D. (1998). "Ambiguous sex"—or ambivalent medicine? Ethical issues in the treatment of intersexuality. *Hastings Center Report, 28*(3), 24–35.

Dreger, A. D. (1999). *Intersex in the age of ethics.* Hagerstown, MD: University Publishing Groups Inc.

Drenth, P. J., Thierry, H., Willems, P. J., & de Wolff, C. J. (1984). *Handbook of work and organizational psychology.* Chichester: John Wiley and Sons, Inc.

Druckman, D., & Bjork, R. A. (Eds.). (1994). *Learning, remembering, believing: Enhancing human performance.* (Study conducted by the National Research Council). Washington, DC: National Academy Press.

Duben, A., & Behar, C. (1991). *Istanbul households: Marriage, family and fertility 1880–1940.* Cambridge: Cambridge University Press.

Dubowitz, H., & Bennett, S. (2007). Physical abuse and neglect of children. *Lancet, 369*(9576): 1891–1899.

Duker, P. C., & Seys, D. M. (1995). *Long-term use of electrical aversion treatment with self-injurious behavior.* Paper presented at BILD Conference.

Duncan, R. M. (1995). Piaget and Vygotsky revisited: Dialogue or assimilation? *Developmental Review, 15*, 458–472.

Dunn, J. C., Whelton, W. J., & Sharpe, D. (2006). Maladaptive perfectionism, hassles, coping, and psychological distress in university professors. *Journal of Counseling Psychology, 53*(4), 511–523.

Durrant, M. (Ed.). (1993). *Aristotle's De anima in focus.* London: Routledge.

Durso, F., Rea, C., & Dayton, T. (1994). Graph-theoretic confirmation of restructuring during insight. *Psychological Science, 5*, 94–98.

Durston, S. (2003). A review of the biological bases of ADHD: What have we learned from imaging studies? *Mental Retardation and Developmental Disabilities Research Reviews, 9*, 184–195.

Dweck, C. (1986). Motivational processes affecting learning. *American Psychologist, 41*(10), 1040–1048.

Dweck, C., & Elliott, E. (1983). Achievement motivation. In P. Mussen (Ed.), *Handbook of child psychology. Vol. 4. Socialization, personality, and social development* (pp. 643–691). New York: Wiley.

Dweck, C. S. (1999). *Self-theories: Their role in motivation, personality and development.* Philadelphia: Psychology Press.

Dweck, C. S., & Leggett, E. L. (1988). A social-cognitive approach to motivation and personality. *Psychological Review, 95*, 256–273.

Dweck, C. S., Chiu, C., & Hong, Y. (1995). Implicit theories and their role in judgments and reactions: A world from two perspectives. *Psychological Inquiry, 6*, 267–285.

Dykens, E. M., Hodapp, R. M., & Leckman, J. F. (1994). *Behavior and development in Fragile X syndrome.* Thousand Oaks, CA: Sage Publications.

Eagly, A., & Chaiken, S. (1975). An attribution analysis of the effect of communicator characteristics on opinion change: The case of communicator attractiveness. *Journal of Personality and Social Psychology, 37*, 136–144.

Eagly, A., & Crowley, M. (1986). Gender and helping behavior: A meta-analytic review of the social psychological literature. *Psychological Bulletin, 100*, 283–308.

Eagly, A. H. (1987). *Sex difference in social behavior: A social-role interpretation.* Hillsdale, NJ: Lawrence Erlbaum.

Eagly, A. H., & Chaiken, S. (1993). *The psychology of attitudes.* Fort Worth, TX: Harcourt Brace.

Eagly, A. H., & Chaiken, S. (1998). Attitude structure and function. In D. T. Gilbert, S. T. Fiske, & G. Lindzey (Eds.), *The handbook of social psychology* (4th ed., pp. 269–322). New York: McGraw–Hill.

Eagly, A. H., Ashmore, R. D., Makhijani, M. G., & Longo, L. C. (1991). What is beautiful is good, but...: A meta-analytic review of the physical attractiveness stereotype. *Psychological Bulletin, 110*, 109–128.

Eagly, A. H., Wood, W., & Diekman, A. B. (2000). Social role theory of sex differences and similarities: A current appraisal. In T. Eckes & H. M. Trautner (Eds.), *The developmental social psychology of gender* (pp. 123–174). Mahwah, NJ: Lawrence Erlbaum.

Eaker, E. D., & Castelli, W. P. (1988). Type A behavior and mortality from coronary disease in the Framingham Study. *New England Journal of Medicine, 319,* 1480–1481.

Eaton, W. W., Kessler, R. C., Wittchen, H. U., & Magee, W. J. (1994). Panic and panic disorder in the United States. *American Journal of Psychiatry 151*(3), 413–420.

Ebbinghaus, H. (1885). *Memory: A contribution to experimental psychology.* New York: Dover Publications.

Ebbinghaus, H. (1913). *Memory: A contribution to experimental psychology.* New York: Teachers College Press. (Translated from the 1885 German original.)

Eddy, J., Fitzhugh, E., & Wang, M. (2000). Smoking acquisition: Peer influence and self-selection. *Psychological Reports, 86,* 1241–1246.

Edelmann, R. J., & Iwawaki, S. (1987). Self-reported expression of embarrassment in five European cultures. *Psychologia: An International Journal of Psychology, 30,* 205–216.

Egan, L. C., Santos, L. R., & Bloom, P. (2007). The origins of cognitive dissonance. Evidence from children and monkeys. *Psychological Science, 18*(11), 978–983.

Egner, T., Strawson, E., & Gruzelier, J. H. (2002). EEG signature and phenomenology of alpha/theta neurofeedback training versus mock feedback. *Applied Psychophysiology Biofeedback, 27*(4), 261–70.

Eich, E., & Metcalfe, J. (1989). Mood dependent memory for internal vs. external events. *Journal of Experimental Psychology: Learning, Memory and Cognition, 15,* 443–455.

Ekman, P. (1973). Darwin and cross-cultural studies of facial expression. In P. Ekman (Ed.), *Darwin and facial expression: A century of research in review.* New York: Academic Press.

Ekman, P. (1980). Asymmetry in facial expression. *Science, 209,* 833–834.

Ekman, P., & Friesen, W. (1969). The repertoire of nonverbal behavior: Categories, origins, usage, and coding. *Semiotica, 1,* 49–98.

Ekman, P., & Friesen, W. (1971). Constants across cultures in the face and emotion. *Journal of Personality and Social Psychology, 17*(2), 124–129.

Ekman, P., & Friesen, W. V. (1978). *The facial action coding system.* Palo Alto, CA: Consulting Psychologists Press.

Ekman, P., Sorensen, E. R., & Friesen, W. V. (1969). Pan-cultural elements in facial displays of emotion. *Science, 164,* 86–88.

Elkind, D. (1985). Egocentrism redux. *Developmental Review, 5,* 218–226.

Ellenbogen, J. M., Payne, J. D., & Stickgold, R. (2006). The role of sleep in declarative memory consolidation: Passive, permissive, active or none? *Current Opinions in Neurobiology, 16,* 716–722.

Elliott, E., & Dweck, C. (1988). Goals: An approach to motivation and achievement. *Journal of Personality and Social Psychology, 54,* 5–12.

Elliott, L., & Brantley, C. (1997). *Sex on campus: The naked truth about the real sex lives of college students.* New York: Random House.

Ellis, A. (1997). *The practice of rational emotive behavior therapy.* New York: Springer Publishing Company.

Ellis, A. (1998). *The Albert Ellis reader: A guide to well-being using rational emotive behavior therapy.* Secaucus, NJ: Carol Publishing Group.

Ellis, B. J., McFayden-Ketchum, S. A., Dodge, K. A., Pettit, G. S., & Bates, J. E. (1999). Quality of early family relationships and individual differences in the timing of pubertal maturation in girls: A longitudinal test on an evolutionary model. *Journal of Personality and Social Psychology, 77,* 387–401.

Ellis, H. D. (1983). The role of the right hemisphere in face perception. In A. W. Young (Ed.), *Functions of the right cerebral hemisphere* (pp. 33–64). London: Academic Press.

Ellis, L., Ames, M. A., Peckham, W., & Burke, D. (1988). Sexual orientation of human offspring may be altered by severe maternal stress during pregnancy. *The Journal of Sex Research, 25,* 152–157.

Ellis, L. K., Gay, P. E., & Paige, E. (2001). Daily pleasures and hassles across the lifespan. Poster presented at the annual meeting of the American Psychological Association, San Francisco, CA.

Endler, N. S. (1988). The origins of electroconvulsive therapy (ECT). *Convulsive Therapy, 4,* 5–23.

Engle, R. W., & Kane, M. J. (2004). Executive attention, working memory capacity, and a two-factor theory of cognitive control. *The Psychology of Learning and Motivation, 44,* 145–199.

Enns, J. T., & Coren, S. (1995). The box alignment illusion: An orientation illusion induced by pictorial depth. *Perception & Psychophysics, 57,* 1163–1174.

Ephraim, P. L., Wegener, S. T., MacKenzie, E. J., Dillingham, T. R., & Pezzin, L. E. (2005). Phantom pain, residual limb pain and back pain in persons with limb loss: Results of a national survey. *Archives of Physical Medicine and Rehabilitation, 86,* 1910–1919.

Epping-Jordan, M., Waltkins, S. S., Koob, G. F., & Markou, A. (1998). Dramatic decreases in brain reward function during nicotine withdrawal. *Nature (Lond), 393,* 76–79.

Erdley, C. A., & Dweck, C. S. (1993). Children's implicit personality theories as predictors of their social judgments. *Child Development, 64,* 863–878.

Erikson, E. (1980). Elements of a psychoanalytic theory of psychosocial development. In S. Greenspan & G. Pollock (Eds.), *The Course of Life, Vol. 1* (pp. 11–61). Washington, DC: U.S. Dept. of Health and Human Services.

Erikson, E. H. (1950). *Childhood and society.* New York: Norton.

Erikson, E. H. (1959). Growth and crises of the healthy personality. *Psychological Issues, 1,* 50–100.

Erikson, E. H. (1982). *The life cycle completed.* New York: Norton.

Erikson, E. H., & Erikson, J. M. (1997). *The life cycle completed.* New York: Norton.

Ertelt, D., Small, S., Solodkin, A., Dettmers, C., McNamara, A., Binkofski, F., & Buccino, G. (2007). Action observation has a positive impact on rehabilitation of motor deficits after stroke. *Neuroimage, 36,* Suppl.(2), T164–T173.

Ertelt, D., Small, S., Solodkin A., McNamara A., Binkofski F., & Buccino, G. (in press). Action observation has a positive impact on rehabilitation of motor deficits after stroke. *Neuroimage.*

Eschenbeck, H., Kohlmann, C-W., & Lohaus, A. (2007). Gender differences in coping strategies in children and adolescents. *Journal of Individual Differences, 28*(1), 18–26.

Eskenazi, B., Bradman, A., & Castorina, R. (1999). Exposures of children to organophosphate pesticides and their potential adverse health effects. *Environmental Health Perspectives, 107*(Suppl. 3), 409–419.

Espiard, M. L., Lecardeur, L., Abadie, P., Halbecq, I., & Dollfus, S. (2005). HPPD after psilocybin consumption: A case study. *European Psychiatry, 20*(5–6), 458–460.

Evans, D., Hodgkinson, B., O'Donnell, A., Nicholson, J., & Walsh, K. (2000). The effectiveness of individual therapy and group therapy in the treatment of schizophrenia. In *Best Practice, 5*(3), 1–54. Published by the Joanna Briggs Institute for Evidence Based Nursing and Midwifery.

Evans, I. M., & Meyer, L. H. (1985). *An educative approach to behavior problems: A practical decision model for interventions with severely handicapped learners.* Baltimore: Paul H. Brookes.

Evans, W. H., Evans, S. S., & Schmid, R. E. (1989). *Behavior and instructional management: An ecological approach.* Boston: Allyn and Bacon.

Everson, S. (1995). Psychology. In J. Barnes (Ed.), *The Cambridge companion to Aristotle* (pp. 168–194). Cambridge, England: Cambridge University Press.

Exner, J. E. (1980). But it's only an inkblot. *Journal of Personality Assessment, 44,* 562–577.

Eysenck, H. (1994). *Test your IQ.* Toronto: Penguin Books.

Eysenck, H. J. (1957). The effects of psychotherapy: An evaluation. *Journal of Consulting Psychology, 16,* 319–324.

Eysenck, H. J. (1994). Synergistic interaction between psychosocial and physical factors in the causation of lung cancer. In C. Lewis, C. O'Sullivan, & J. Barraclough (Eds.), *The psychoimmunology of human cancer* (pp. 163–178). London: Oxford University Press.

Eysenck, H. J., & Eysenck, S. B. G. (1993). *Eysenck Personality Questionnaire [Revised].* London: Hodder & Stoughton Educational.

Fagot, B. I., & Hagan, R. (1991). Observations of parent reactions to sex-stereotyped behaviours: Age and sex effects. *Child Development, 62,* 617–628.

Fahey, V. (1993). How sleep deprived are you? *Health, 7*(5), 3–4.

Fanselow, M. S., & Gale, G. D. (2003). The amygdala, fear, and memory. *Annals of the New York Academy of Sciences, 985,* 125–134.

Fantz, R. L. (1961). The origin of form perception. *Scientific American, 204,* 66–72.

Fantz, R. L. (1964). Visual experience in infants: Decreased attention to familiar patterns relative to novel ones. *Science, 146,* 668–670.

Faraone, S. V., Biederman, J., & Friedman, D. (2000). Validity of DSM-IV subtypes of attention-deficit/hyperactivity disorder: A family study perspective. *Journal of the American Academy of Child and Adolescent Psychiatry, 39*, 300–307.

Faraone, S. V., Biederman, J., Lehman, B. K., Keenan, K., Norman, D., Seidman, L. J., Kolodny, R., Kraus, I., Perrin, J., & Chen, W. J. (1993). Evidence for independent familial transmission of attention deficit hyperactivity disorder and learning disabilities: Result from a family genetic study. *American Journal of Psychiatry, 150*, 891–895.

Faraone, S. V., Tsuang, M. T., & Tsuang, D. W. (1999). *Genetics of mental disorders: A guide for students, clinicians, and researchers.* New York: Guilford Press.

Farmer, A. E. (1996). The genetics of depressive disorders. *International Review of Psychiatry, 8*(4).

Farthing, W. (1992). *The psychology of consciousness.* Upper Saddle River, NJ: Prentice-Hall.

Faucett, J., Gordon, N., & Levine, J. (1994). Differences in postoperative pain severity among four ethnic groups. *Journal of Pain Symptom Management, 9*, 383–389.

Fawzy, F. I., Fawzy, N. W., Hyun, C. S., Elashoff, R., Guthrie, D., Fahey, J. L., & Morton, D. L. (1993). Malignant melanoma effects of an early structured psychiatric intervention, coping, and affective state on recurrence and survival 6 years later. *Archives of General Psychiatry, 50*(9), 681–689.

Fazel-Rezai, R., & Peters, J. F. (2005). P300 wave feature extraction: Preliminary results, in *Proceedings of the 18th Annual Canadian Conference on Electrical and Computer Engineering (CCECE '05, pp. 390–393). Saskatoon, Saskatchewan, Canada.

FDA MedWatch Safety Alert. (October 15, 2004). Public health advisory: Suicidality in children and adolescents being treated with antidepressant medications. Retrieved from the Internet on December 15, 2004, at **www.fda.gov/medwatch/SAFETY/2004/safety04.htm#ssri.**

Fechner, G. T. (1860). *Elemente der Psykophysik.* Leipzig: Breitkopf und Härtel.

Fedoroff, I. C., & McFarlane, T. (1998). Cultural aspects of eating disorders. In S. S. Kazarian & D. R. Evans (Eds.). *Cultural clinical psychology: Theory, research and practice* (pp. 152–176). New York: Oxford University Press.

Feingold, A. (1992). Good-looking people are not what we think. *Psychological Bulletin, 111*, 304–341.

Felder, R. M., & Spurlin, J. E. (2005). Applications, reliability and validity of the index of learning styles. *International Journal of Engineering Education, 21*(1), 103–112.

Feldman, D. H. (2003). Cognitive development in childhood. In R. M. Lerner, M. A. Easterbrooks, et al. (Eds.), *Handbook of psychology: Developmental psychology, Vol. 6* (pp. 195–201). New York: Wiley.

Ferguson, N. B., & Keesey, R. E. (1975). Effect of a quinine-adulterated diet upon body weight maintenance in male rats with ventromedial hypothalamic lesions. *Journal of Comparative Physiological Psychology, 89*(5), 478–488.

Fernald, A. (1984). The perceptual and affective salience of mothers' speech to infants. In L. Feagans, C. Garvey, & R. Golinkoff (Eds.), *The origins and growth of communication.* Norwood, NJ: Ablex.

Fernald, A. (1992). Human maternal vocalizations to infants as biologically relevant signals: An evolutionary perspective. In J. H. Barkow, L. Cosmides, & J. Tooby (Eds.), *The adapted mind: Evolutionary psychology and the generation of culture.* New York: Oxford University Press.

Fernandez, E., & Sheffield, J. (1996). Relative contributions of life events versus daily hassles to the frequency and intensity of headaches. *Headache, 36*(10), 595–602.

Feroah, T. R., Sleeper, T., Brozoski, D., Forder, J., Rice, T. B., & Forster, H. V. (2004). *Circadian slow wave sleep and movement behavior are under genetic control in inbred strains of rat.* Paper presented at the American Physiological Society Annual Conference, April 17–21, 2004, at the Washington, DC, Convention Center.

Ferron, F., Considine, R. V., Peino, R., Lado, I. G., Dieguez, C., & Casanueva, F. F. (1997). Serum leptin concentrations in patients with anorexia nervosa, bulimia nervosa and non-specific eating disorders correlate with the body mass index but are independent of the respective disease. *Clinical Endocrinology (Oxford), 46*, 289–293.

Festinger, L. (1954). A theory of social comparison processes. *Human Relations, 7*, 117–140.

Festinger, L. (1957). *A theory of cognitive dissonance.* Stanford, CA: Stanford University Press.

Festinger, L., & Carlsmith, J. (1959). $1/$20 Experiment: Cognitive consequences of forced compliance. *Journal of Abnormal and Social Psychology, 58*(2), 203–210.

Fiatarone, M. (1996). Physical activity and functional independence in aging. *Research Quarterly for Exercise & Sport, 67*, 70–75.

Fiatarone, M. A., O'Neill, E. F., Doyle, N., Clements, K. M., Roberts, S. B., Kehayias, J. J., Lipsitz, L. A., & Evans, W. J. (1993). The Boston FICSIT study: The effects of resistance training and nutritional supplementation on physical frailty in the oldest old. *Journal of American Geriatrics, 41*, 333–337.

Fieve, R. R. (1997). *Moodswing: Dr. Fieve on depression,* 2nd rev. ed. New York: Bantam Books.

Fincham, F. D., Harold, G. T., & Gano–Phillips, S. (2000). The longitudinal association between attributions and marital satisfaction: Direction of effects and role of efficacy expectations. *Journal of Family Psychology, 14*, 267–285.

Fink, M. (1984). Meduna and the origins of convulsive therapy. *American Journal of Psychiatry, 141*, 1034–1041.

Finke, R. (1995). Creative realism. In S. Smith, T. Ward, & R. Finke (Eds.), *The creative cognition approach* (pp. 301–326). Cambridge: Cambridge University Press.

Finkel, D., & McGue, M. (1997). Sex differences and nonadditivity in heritability of the Multidimensional Personality Questionnaire scales. *Journal of Personality and Social Psychology, 72*, 929–938.

Fischer, A. (1993). Sex differences in emotionality: Fact or Stereotype? *Feminism & Psychology, 3*, 303–318.

Fischl, B., Liu, A., & Dale, A. M. (2001). Automated manifold surgery: Constructing geometrically accurate and topologically correct models of the human cerebral cortex. *IEEE Transactions on Medical Imaging, 20*, 70–80.

Fiske, S. T. (1998). Stereotyping, prejudice, and discrimination. In D. T. Gilbert & S. T. Fiske (Eds.), *The handbook of social psychology* (4th ed., vol. 2, pp. 357–411). New York: McGraw–Hill.

Fivush, R., & Nelson, K. (2004). Culture and language in the emergence of autobiographical memory. *Psychological Science, 15*(9), 573.

Fivush, R., Haden, C., & Reese, E. (1996). Remembering, recounting, and reminiscing: The development of autobiographical memory in social context. In D. C. Rubin (Ed.), *Remembering our past: Studies in autobiographical memory* (pp. 341–359). New York: Cambridge University Press.

Flaherty, J. A., & Adams, S. A. (1998). Therapist–patient race and sex matching: Predictors of treatment duration. *Psychiatric Times, 15*(1).

Flaskerud, J. H. (1991). Effects of an Asian client–therapist language, ethnicity and gender match on utilization and outcome of therapy. *Community Mental Health Journal, 27*, 31–42.

Flavell, J. H. (1999). Cognitive development: Children's knowledge about the mind. *Annual Review of Psychology, 50*, 21–45.

Fleming, M. F., & Barry, K. L. (1992). Clinical overview of alcohol and drug disorders. In M. F. Fleming & K. L. Barry (Eds.), *Addictive disorders.* St. Louis: Mosby Year Book.

Flemons, W. W. (2002). Obstructive sleep apnea. *New England Journal of Medicine, 347*, 498–504.

Foa, E. B., & Franklin, M. E. (2000). Psychotherapies for obsessive-compulsive disorder: A review. In M. Maj, N. Sartorius, A. Okasha, & J. Zohar, (Eds.), *Obsessive-compulsive disorder* (pp. 93–115). New York: John Wiley & Sons.

Foa, E. B., Keane, T. M., & Friedman, M. J. (Eds). (2000). *Effective treatments for PTSD.* New York: Guilford.

Folkard, S., & Tucker, P. (2003). Shift work, safety, and productivity. *Medicine, 53*, 95–101.

Folkard, S., Arendt, J., & Clark, M. (1993). Can melatonin improve shift workers' tolerance of the night shift? Some preliminary findings. *Chronobiology International, The Journal of Biological and Medical Rhythm Research, 10*(5), 315–320.

Folkard, S., Lombardi, D. A., & Spencer, M. B. (2006). Estimating the circadian rhythm in the risk of occupational injuries and accidents. *Chronobiology International, The Journal of Biological and Medical Rhythm Research, 23*(6), 1181–1192.

Folkard, S., Lombardi, D. A., & Tucker, P. (2005). Shiftwork: Safety, sleepiness, and sleep. *Industrial Health, 43*(1), 20–23.

Folkman, S. (1997). Positive psychological states and coping with severe stress. *Social Science & Medicine, 45*, 1207–1221.

Folkman, S., & Chesney, M. A. (1995). Coping with HIV infection. In M. Stein and A. Baum (Eds.), *Perspectives in behavioral medicine* (pp. 115–133). Hillsdale, NJ: Lawrence Erlbaum.

Folkman, S., & Lazarus, R. S. (1980). An analysis of coping in a middle-aged community sample. *Journal of Health and Social Behavior, 21*(3), 219–239.

Follett, K. J., & Hess, T. M. (2002). Aging, cognitive complexity, and the fundamental attribution error. *Journals of Gerontology Series B: Psychological Sciences and Social Sciences, 57*, 312–323.

Förster, J., Grant, H., Idson, L. C., & Higgins, E. T. (2001). Success/failure feedback, expectancies, and approach/avoidance motivation: How regulatory focus moderates classic relations. *Journal of Experimental Social Psychology, 37*(3), 253–260.

Foulkes, D. (1982). *Children's dreams*. New York: Wiley.

Foulkes, D., & Schmidt, M. (1983). Temporal sequence and unit comparison composition in dream reports from different stages of sleep. *Sleep, 6*, 265–280.

Frank, D. A., Augustyn, M., Knight, W. G., Pell, T., & Zuckerman, B. (2001). Growth, development, and behavior in early childhood following prenatal cocaine exposure. *Journal of the American Medical Association, 285*(12), 1613–1625.

Frank, E., Kupfer, D. J., Buysse, D. J., Swartz, H. A., Pilkonis, P. A., Houck, P. R., Rucci, P., Novick, D. M., Grochocinski, V. J., & Stapf, D. M. (2007). Randomized trial of weekly, twice-monthly, and monthly interpersonal psychotherapy as maintenance treatment for women with recurrent depression. *American Journal of Psychiatry, 164*(5), 761–767.

Frankel, B. R., & Piercy, F. P. (1990). The relationship among selected supervisor, therapist, and client behaviors. *Journal of Marital and Family Therapy, 16*, 407–421.

Freedman, J., & Fraser, S. (1966). Compliance without pressure: The foot-in-the-door technique. *Journal of Personality and Social Psychology, 4*, 195–202.

Freeman, A., Simon, K. M., Beutler, L. E., & Arkowitz, H. (Eds.) (1989). *Comprehensive handbook of cognitive therapy*. New York: Plenum Press.

Freeman, J. (2001). *Gifted children grown up*. London: David Fulton Publishers Ltd.

Freeman, W., & Watts, J. W. (1937). Prefrontal lobotomy in the treatment of mental disorders. *Southern Medical Journal, 30*, 23–31.

Freese, J., Powell, B., & Steelman, L. C. (1999). Rebel without a cause or effect: Birth order and social attitudes. *American Sociological Review, 64*, 207–231.

Frensch, P. A., & Runger, D. (2003). Implicit learning. *Current Directions in Psychological Science, 12*, 13–18.

Fresquet, N., Angst, M., & Sandner, G. (2004, August). Insular cortex lesions alter conditioned taste avoidance in rats differentially when using two methods of sucrose delivery. *Behavioral Brain Research, 153*(2), 357–365.

Freud, A. (1946). *The ego and the mechanisms of defense. American Edition*. New York: I.U.P.

Freud, S. (1900). *The interpretation of dreams. S.E., 4–5*. (cf. Joyce Crick, Trans., 1999). London: Oxford University Press.

Freud, S. (1900). *The interpretation of dreams*. Translated by A. A. Brill, 1913. New York: Macmillan.

Freud, S. (1901). *The psychopathology of everyday life, S.E., 6*, 1–290.

Freud, S. (1904). *Freud's psycho-analytic procedure, S.E., 7*, 249–254.

Freud, S. (1904). *Psychopathology of everyday life*. New York: Macmillan; London: Fisher Unwin.

Freud, S. (1915). *Repression, The Standard Edition of the Complete Psychological Works of Sigmund Freud, Vol. 14*. Edited by James Strachey. London: The Hogart Press and the Institute of Psychoanalysis, 1974.

Freud, S. (1923). *The ego and the id, S.E., 19*, 12–66.

Freud, S. (1930). *Civilization and its discontents*. New York: Jonathon Cape and Co.

Freud, S. (1931) Female sexuality. *Pelican Freud Library, 7*, 367.

Freud, S. (1933). *New introductory lectures on psycho-analysis*, London: Hogarth.

Freud, S. (1940). Splitting of the ego in the process of defence. *International Journal of Psychoanalysis, 22*, 65 [1938], S.E., 23:275–278.

Freud, S., & Gay, P. (1977). *Inhibitions, symptoms and anxiety. Standard edition of the complete works of Sigmund Freud*. New York: W. W. Norton.

Freud, S., Strachey, J., & Riviere, J. (1990). *The ego and the id (The Standard Edition of the Complete Psychological Works of Sigmund Freud)*. New York: W. W. Norton and Company.

Friedman, J. M. (2000). Obesity in the new millennium. *Nature, 404*, 632–634.

Friedman, J. M. (2003). A war on obesity, not the obese. *Science, 299*(5608), 856–858.

Friedman, J. M., & Halaas, J. L. (1998). Leptin and the regulation of body weight in mammals. *Nature, 395*, 763.

Friedman, M., & Kasanin, J. D. (1943). Hypertension in only one of identical twins. *Archives of Internal Medicine, 72*, 767–774.

Friedman, M., & Rosenman, R. H. (1959). Association of specific behavior pattern with blood and cardiovascular findings. *Journal of the American Medical Association, 169*, 1286–1296.

Frontera, W. R., Hughes, V. A., Lutz, K. J., & Evans, W. J. (1991). A cross-sectional study of muscle strength and mass in 45- to 78-year-old men and women. *Journal of Applied Physiology, 71*, 644–650.

Fujii, Y., Suzuki, K., Sato, T., Murakami, Y., & Takahashi, T. (1998). Multiple personality disorder in Japan. *Psychiatry and Clinical Neurosciences, 52*(3), 299.

Fulcher, J. S. (1942). "Voluntary" facial expression in blind and seeing children. *Archives of Psychology, 38*, 1–49.

Fumeron, F., Betoulle, D., Aubert, R., Herbeth, B., Siest, G., & Rigaud, D. (2001). Association of a functional 5–HT transporter gene polymorphism with anorexia nervosa and food intake. *Molecular Psychiatry, 6*, 9–10.

Furumoto, L. (1979). Mary Whiton Calkins (1863–1930): Fourteenth president of the American Psychological Association. *Journal of the History of Behavioral Sciences, 15*, 346–356.

Gado, M. (2004). A cry in the night: The Kitty Genovese murder. *Court TV's Crime Library: Criminal Minds and Methods*. Retrieved from the Internet on August 2, 2004, at **www.crimelibrary.com/serial_killers/predators/kitty_genovese/ 1.html?sect=2**.

Galanter, M. (1983). Unification Church ("Moonie") dropouts: Psychological readjustment after leaving a charismatic religious group. *American Journal of Psychaiatry, 140*(8), 984–989.

Galanti, G. A. (1997). *Caring for patients from different cultures* (2nd ed.). Philadelphia: University of Pennsylvania Press.

Galea, S., Resnick, H., Kilpatrick, D., Bucuvalas, M., Gold, J., & Vlahov, D. (2002, March 28). Psychological sequelae of the September 11 terrorist attacks in New York City. *New England Journal of Medicine, 346*(13), 982–987.

Gamwell, L., & Tomes, N. (1995). *Madness in America: Cultural and medical perspectives of mental illness before 1914*. Ithaca, NY: Cornell University Press.

Ganchrow, J. R., Steiner, J. E., & Munif, D. (1983). Neonatal facial expressions in response to different qualities and intensities of gustatory stimuli. *Infant Behavior Development, 6*, 473–478.

Ganellen, R. J. (1996). *Integrating the Rorschach and the MMPI-2 in personality assessment*. Mahwah, NJ: Erlbaum.

Garb, H. N., Florio, C. M., & Grove, W. M. (1998). The validity of the Rorschach and the Minnesota Multiphasic Personality Inventory: Results from meta-analyses. *Psychological Science, 9*, 402–404.

Garcia, J., & Koelling, R. A. (1966). Relation of cue to consequence in avoidance learning. *Psychonomic Science, 4*, 123.

Garcia, J., Brett, L. P., & Rusiniak, K. W. (1989). Limits of Darwinian conditioning. In S. B. Klein & R. R. Mowrer (Eds.), *Contemporary learning theories: Instrumental conditioning theory and the impact of biological constraints on learning* (pp. 237–275). Hillsdale, NJ: Erlbaum.

Gardner, H. (1993a). *Creating minds: An anatomy of creativity seen through the lives of Freud, Einstein, Picasso, Stravinsky, Eliot, Graham, and Ghandi*. New York: Basic Books.

Gardner, H. (1993b). *Multiple intelligences: The theory in practice*. New York: Basic Books.

Gardner, H. (1998). Are there additional intelligences? The case for naturalist, spiritual, and existential intelligences. In J. Kane (Ed.), *Education, information, and transformation* (pp. 111–131). Upper Saddle River, NJ: Merrill-Prentice Hall.

Gardner, H. (1999a). *Intelligence reframed: Multiple intelligences for the 21st century*. New York: Basic Books.

Gardner, H. (1999b, February). Who owns intelligence? *Atlantic Monthly*, 67–76.

Gardner, H., & Moran, S. (2006). The science in multiple intelligences: A response to Lynn Waterhouse. *Educational Psychologist, 41*, 227–232.

Gardner, H., Kornhaber, M. L., & Wake, W. K. (1996). *Intelligence: Multiple perspectives*. Orlando, FL: Harcourt Brace & Co.

Gardner, J., & Oswald, A. J. (2004). How is mortality affected by money, marriage, and stress? *Journal of Health Economics, 23*(6), 1181–1207.

Gardner, R. J. M., & Sutherland, G. R. (1996). Chromosome abnormalities and genetic counseling. *Oxford Monographics on Medical Genetics No. 29.* New York: Oxford University Press.

Garland, E. J., & Smith, D. H. (1991). Simultaneous prepubertal onset of panic disorder, night terrors, and somnambulism. *Journal of American Academic Child and Adolescent Psychiatry, 30*(4), 553–555.

Garner, D. M., & Garfinkel, P. E. (1980). Socio-cultural factors in the development of anorexia nervosa. *Psychological Medicine, 10,* 647–656.

Geary, D. C. (2000). Evolution and proximate expression of human paternal investment. *Psychological Bulletin, 126,* 55–77.

Gebhard, P. H., & Johnson, A. B. (1979/1998). *The Kinsey data: Marginal tabulations of 1938–1963 interviews conducted by the Institute for Sex Research.* Philadelphia: W. B. Saunders.

Geddes, D. P. (Ed.) (1954). *An analysis of the Kinsey reports.* New York: New American Library.

Geddes, J., & Butler, R. (2002). Depressive disorders. *Clinical Evidence, 7,* 867–882.

Geddes, J. R., Carney, S. M., Davies, C., Furukawa, T. A., Kupfer, D. J., Frank, E., & Goodwin, G. M. (2003). Relapse prevention with antidepressant drug treatment in depressive disorders: A systematic review. *Lancet, 361*(9358), 653–661.

Geen, R. G., & Thomas, S. L. (1986). The immediate effects of media violence on behavior. *Journal of Social Issues, 42,* 7–27.

Gelder, M. (1976). Flooding. In T. Thompson & W. Dockens (Eds.), *Applications of behavior modification* (pp. 250–298). New York: Academic Press.

Geliebter, A. (1988). Gastric distension and gastric capacity in relation to food intake in humans. *Physiological Behavior, 44,* 665–668.

Geller, B., Williams, M., Zimerman, B., Frazier, J., Beringer, L., & Warner, K. L. (1998). Prepubertal and early adolescent bipolarity differentiate from ADHD by manic symptoms, grandiose delusions, ultra-rapid or ultradian cycling. *Journal of Affective Disorders, 51*(2), 81–91.

Gelman, S. A. (1988). The development of induction within natural kind and artifact categories. *Cognitive Psychology, 20,* 65–95.

Gelman, S. A., & Markman, E. M. (1986). Categories and induction in young children. *Cognition, 23,* 183–209.

Gershoff, E. (2000). The short- and long-term effects of corporal punishment on children: A meta-analytical review. In D. Elliman & M. A. Lynch. *The physical punishment of children, Archives of Disease in Childhood. 83,* 196–198.

Geschwind, D. H., & Iacoboni, M. (2007). Structural and functional asymmetries of the frontal lobes. In B. L. Miller & J. K. Cummings (Eds.), *The human frontal lobes* (2nd ed., pp. 68–91). New York: The Guilford Press.

Gibbons, J. L., Stiles, D. A., & Shkodriani, G. M. (1991). Adolescents' attitudes toward family and gender roles: An international comparison. *Sex Roles, 25,* 625–643.

Gibson, E. J., & Walk, R. D. (1960). The "visual cliff." *Scientific American, 202,* 67–71.

Giedd, J. N., Blumenthal, J., Jeffries, N. O., Castellanos, F. X., Liui, H., Zijdenbos, A., Paus, T., Evans, A. C., & Rapoport, J. L. (1999). Brain development during childhood and adolescence: A longitudinal MRI study. *Nature Neuroscience, 2*(10), 861–863.

Gilberg, C., & Coleman, M. (2000). *The biology of the autistic syndromes* (3rd ed.). London: Mac Keith Press.

Gilbert, P. B., Peterson, M. L., Follmann, D., Hudgens, M. G., Francis, D. P., Gurwith, M., Heyward, W. L., Jobes, D. V., Popovic, V., Self, S. G., Sinangil, F., Burke, D., & Berman, P. W. (2005). Correlation between immunologic responses to a recombinant glycoprotein 120 vaccine and incidence of HIV-1 infection in a phase 3 HIV-1 preventive vaccine trial. *Journal of Infectious Diseases, 191,* 666–677.

Gilbert, S. J. (1981). Another look at the Milgram obedience studies: The role of the graduated series of shocks. *Personality and Social Psychology Bulletin, 7*(4), 690–695.

Gill, S. T. (1991). Carrying the war into the never-never land of psi. *Skeptical Inquirer, 15*(1), 269–273.

Gillespie, M. A., Kim, B. H., Manheim, L. J., Yoo, T., Oswald, F. L., & Schmitt, N. (2002). The development and validation of biographical data and situational judgment tests in the prediction of college student success. Presented in A. M. Ryan (Chair), *Beyond g: Expanding thinking on predictors of college success.* Symposium conducted at the 14th Annual Convention of the American Psychological Society, New Orleans, LA.

Gillham, B., Tanner, G., Cheyne, B., Freeman, I., Rooney, M., & Lambie, A. (1998). Unemployment rates, single parent density, and indices of child poverty: Their relationship to different categories of child abuse and neglect. *Child Abuse and Neglect, 22*(2), 79–90.

Gilligan, C. (1982). *In a different voice: Psychological theory and women's development.* Cambridge, MA: Harvard University Press.

Gillund, G., & Shiffrin, R. M. (1984). A retrieval model for both recognition and recall. *Psychological Review, 91,* 1–67.

Gilmour, J., & Skuse, D. (1999). A case-comparison study of the characteristics of children with a short stature syndrome induced by stress (hyperphagic short stature) and a consecutive series of unaffected "stressed" children. *Journal of Child Psychology and Psychiatry and Allied Disciplines, 40*(6), 969–978.

Ginzburg, K., Solomon, Z., Koifman, B., Keren, G., Roth, A., Kriwisky, M., Kutz, I., David, D., & Bleich, A. (2003). Trajectories of post-traumatic stress disorder following myocardial infarction: A prospective study. *Journal of Clinical Psychiatry, 64*(10), 1217–1223.

Gittelman-Klein, R. (1978). Validity in projective tests for psychodiagnosis in children. In R. L. Spitzer & D. F. Klein (Eds.), *Critical issues in psychiatric diagnosis* (pp. 141–166). New York: Raven Press.

Gleaves, D. H. (1996). The socio-cognitive model of dissociative identity disorder: A reexamination of the evidence. *Psychological Bulletin, 20,* 42–59.

Glenn, A. L., Raine, A., Mednick, S. A., & Venables, P. (2007). Early temperamental and psychophysiological precursors of adult psychopathic personality. *Journal of Abnormal Psychology, 116*(3), 508–518.

Glick, P., & Fiske, S. (2001). An ambivalent alliance: Hostile and benevolent sexism as complementary justifications for gender inequality. *American Psychologist, 56,* 109–118.

Glynn, S. M. (1990). Token economy approaches for psychiatric patients: Progress and pitfalls over 25 years. *Behavior Modification, 14,* 383–407.

Godden, D. R., & Baddeley, A. D. (1975). Context-dependent memory in two natural environments: On land and underwater. *British Journal of Psychology, 66,* 325–331.

Goel, V., & Grafman, J. (1995). Are the frontal lobes implicated in "planning" functions? Interpreting data from the Tower of Hanoi. *Neuropsychologia, 33*(5), 623–642.

Goin, M. K. (2005). Practical psychotherapy: A current perspective on the psychotherapies. *Psychiatric Services, 56*(3), 255–257.

Goldman-Rakic, P. S. (1998). The prefrontal landscape: Implications of functional architecture for understanding human mentation and the central executive. In A. C. Roberts, T. W. Robbins, & L. Weiskrantz (Eds.), *The prefrontal cortex: Executive and cognitive functions* (pp. 87–102). Oxford: Oxford University Press.

Goldsmith, H. H., & Campos, J. (1982). Toward a theory of infant temperament. In R. Emde & R. Harmon (Eds.), *The development of attachment and affiliative systems: Psychobiological aspects* (pp. 161–193). New York: Plenum Press.

Goldstein, S. (1997). *Managing attention and learning disorders in late adolescence and adulthood: A guide for practitioners.* New York: John Wiley.

Goldston, D. B., Molock, S. D., Whitbeck, L. B., Murakami, J. L., Zayas, L. H., & Hall, G. C. (2008). Cultural considerations in adolescent suicide prevention and psychosocial treatment. *American Psychologist, 63*(1), 14–31.

Goleman, D. (1982). Staying up: The rebellion against sleep's gentle tyranny. *Psychology Today, 3,* 24–35.

Goleman, D. (1995). *Emotional intelligence: Why it can matter more than IQ.* New York: Bantam Books.

Golkaramnay, V., Bauer, S., Haug, S., Wolf, M., & Kordy, H. (2007). The exploration of the effectiveness of group therapy through an Internet chat as aftercare: A controlled naturalistic study. *Pychotherapy and Psychosomatics, 76,* 219–225.

Gong-Guy, E., & Hammen, C. (1980). Causal perceptions of stressful events in depressed and nondepressed outpatients. *Journal of Abnormal Psychology, 89,* 662–669.

Gonsalves, B., Reber, P. J., Gitelman, D. R., Parrish, T. B., Mesulam, M. M., & Paller, K. A. (2004). Neural evidence that vivid imagining can lead to false remembering. *Psychological Science, 15,* 655–660.

Gonzales, P. M., Blanton, H., & Williams, K. J. (2002). The effects of stereotype threat and double–minority status on the test performance of Latino women. *Personality and Social Psychology Bulletin, 28*(5), 659–670.

Gonzalez, J. S., Penedo, F. J., Antoni, M. H., Durán, R. E., Fernandez, M. I., McPherson-Baker, S., Ironson, G., Klimas, N. G., Fletcher, M. A., & Schneiderman, N. (2004). Social support, positive states of mind, and HIV treatment adherence in men and women living with HIV/AIDS. *Health Psychology, 23*(4), 413–418.

Goodglass, H., Kaplan, E., & Barresi, B., (2001). *The assessment of aphasia and related disorders* (3rd ed.). Baltimore: Lippincott, Williams and Wilkins.

Goodman, E. S. (1980). Margaret Floy Washburn (1871–1939) first woman Ph.D. in psychology. *Psychology of Women Quarterly, 5*, 69–80.

Gosselin, R. E., Smith, R. P., Hodge, H. C., & Braddock, J. E. (1984). *Clinical toxicology of commercial products* (5th ed.). Sydney: Williams & Wilkins.

Gotlib, I. H., Sivers, H., Canli, T., Kasch, K. L., & Gabrieli, J. D. E. (2001). Neural activation in depression in response to emotional stimuli. In I. H. Gotlib (Chair), *New directions in the neurobiology of affective disorders.* Symposium presented at the Annual Meeting of the Society for Research in Psychopathology, Madison, WI.

Gottesman, I., & Shields, J. (1982). *Schizophrenia: The epigenetic puzzle.* New York: Cambridge University Press.

Gottesman, I. I. (1991). *Schizophrenia genesis: The origins of madness.* New York: Freeman.

Gottesman, I. I., & Shields, J. (1976). A critical review of recent adoption, twin and family studies of schizophrenia: Behavioural genetics perspectives. *Schizophrenia Bulletin, 2*, 360–401.

Gottman, J. M., & Krokoff, L. J. (1989). Marital interaction and satisfaction: A longitudinal view. *Journal of Consulting and Clinical Psychology, 57*, 47–52.

Gough, H. G. (1995). *California Psychological Inventory* (3rd ed.). Palo Alto, CA: Consulting Psychologist-Press.

Gould, J. L., & Gould, C. G. (1994). *The animal mind.* New York: Scientific American Library.

Gould, S. J. (1981). *The mismeasure of man.* New York: Norton.

Gould, S. J. (1996). *The mismeasure of man.* New York: W. W. Norton.

Gouldner, A. W. (1960). The norm of reciprocity: A preliminary statement. *American Sociological Review, 25*, 161–178.

Graber, J. A., Brooks-Gunn, J., & Warren, M. P. (1995). The antecedents of menarcheal age: Heredity, family environment, and stressful life events. *Child Development, 66*, 346–359.

Grandjean, P., Weihe, P., White, R. F., Debes, F., Araki, S., Yokoyama, K., Murata, K., Sorensen, N., Dahl, R., & Jorgensen, P. J. (1997). Cognitive deficit in 7-year-old children with prenatal exposure to methylmercury. *Neurotoxicology and Teratology, 19*(6), 417–428.

Greenwald, A. G., Draine, S. C., & Abrams, R. L. (1996). Three cognitive markers of unconscious semantic activation. *Science, 273*, 1699–1702.

Gregory, R. L. (1990). *Eye and brain, the psychology of seeing.* Princeton, NJ: Princeton University Press.

Gresham, L. G., & Shimp, T. A. (1985). Attitude toward the advertisement and brand attitudes: A classical conditioning prospective. *Journal of Advertising, 14*(1), 10–17, 49.

Gribbons, B., & Herman, J. (1997). True and quasi-experimental designs. *Practical Assessment, Research & Evaluation, 5*(14).

Gross, C. G. (1999). A hole in the head. *The Neuroscientist, 5*, 263–269.

Grumbach, M. M., & Kaplan, S. L. (1990). The neuroendocrinology of human puberty: An ontogenetic perspective. In M. M. Grumbach, P. C. Sizonenko, & M. L. Aubert (Eds.), *Control of the onset of puberty* (pp. 1–6). Baltimore: Williams & Wilkins.

Grumbach, M. M., & Styne, D. M. (1998). Puberty: Ontogeny, neuroendocrinology, physiology, and disorders. In J. D. Wilson, D. W. Foster, H. M. Kronenberg, & P. R. Larsen (Eds.), *Williams textbook of endocrinology* (9th ed. pp. 1509–1625). Philadelphia: W. B. Saunders Co.

Grünbaum, A. (1984). *The foundations of psychoanalysis: A philosophical critique.* Berkeley, CA: University of California Press.

Guar, A., Dominguez, K., Kalish, M., Rivera-Hernandez, D., Donohoe, M., & Mitchell, C. (2008). Practice of offering a child pre-masticated food: An unrecognized possible risk factor for HIV transmission. Paper presented at the 15th Conference on Retroviruses and Opportunistic Infections, February 3–6, 2008, Boston, MA.

Guerin, D. A., Park, Y., & Yang, S. (1995). Development of an instrument to study the meaning of color in interior environments. *Journal of Interior Design, 20*(2), 31–41.

Guilford, J. P. (1967). *The nature of human intelligence.* New York: McGraw-Hill.

Gupta, M. (1994). Sexuality in the Indian sub-continent. *Sex and Marital Therapy, 9*, 57–69.

Gustavson, C. R., Kelly, D. J., Seeney, M., & Garcia, J. (1976). Prey lithium aversions I: Coyotes and wolves. *Behavioral Biology, 17*, 61–72.

Guthrie, R. V. (2004). *Even the rat was white: A historical view of psychology.* Boston: Allyn and Bacon.

Haber, R. N. (1979). Twenty years of haunting eidetic imagery: Where's the ghost? *The Behavioral and Brain Sciences, 2*, 583–619.

Hajek, P., & Stead, L. F. (2000). *Aversive smoking for smoking cessation.* Oxford, UK: The Cochrane Library.

Halbesleben, J. R. B., & Bowler, W. M. (2007). Emotional exhaustion and job performance: The mediating role of motivation. *Journal of Applied Psychology, 91*, 93–106.

Hall, C. (1966). Studies of dreams collected in the laboratory and at home. *Institute of Dream Research Monograph Series* (No. 1). Santa Cruz, CA: Privately printed.

Hall, W. & Degenhardt, L. (2009). Adverse health effects of non-medical cannabis use. *Lancet, 374*, 1383–1391.

Hamann, S., Herman, R. A., Nolan, C. L., & Wallen, K. (2004). Men and women differ in amygdale response to visual sexual stimuli. *Nature Neuroscience, 7*(4), 411–419.

Hamer, D. H., Hu, S., Magnuson, V. L., Hu, N., & Pattatucci, A. M. L. (1993). A linkage between DNA markers on the X chromosome and male sexual orientation. *Science, 261*, 321–327.

Hamilton, D. L., & Gifford, R. K. (1976). Illusory correlation in interpersonal perception: A cognitive basis of stereotypic judgments. *Journal of Experimental Social Psychology, 12*, 392–407.

Hamilton, J. A. (1982). The identity of postpartum psychosis. In I. F. Brockington, & R. Kumar (Eds.), *Motherhood and mental illness* (pp. 1–17). London: Academic Press.

Hammond, D. C. (2001a). Neurofeedback treatment of depression with the Roshi. *Journal of Neurotherapy, 4*(2), 45–56.

Hammond, D. C. (2001b). Treatment of chronic fatigue with neurofeedback and self-hypnosis. *NeuroRehabilitation, 16*, 295–300.

Hammond, D. C. (2003). QEEG-guided neurofeedback in the treatment of obsessive compulsive disorder. *Journal of Neurotherapy, 7*(2), 25–52.

Hampton, J. A. (1998). Similarity-based categorization and fuzziness of natural categories. *Cognition, 65*, 137–165.

Handel, S. (1989). *Listening: An introduction to the perception of auditory events.* Cambridge, MA: MIT Press.

Hansen, C. P. (1988). Personality characteristics of the accident involved employee. *Journal of Business and Psychology, 2*(4), 346–365.

Harlow, H. F. (1958). The nature of love. *American Psychologist, 13*, 573–685.

Harman, G. (1999). Moral philosophy meets social psychology: Virtue ethics and the fundamental attribution error. *Proceedings of the Aristotelian Society, 1998–99, vol. 99*, 315–331.

Harmon-Jones, E. (2000). Cognitive dissonance and experienced negative affect: Evidence that dissonance increases experienced negative affect even in the absence of aversive consequences. *Personality and Social Psychology Bulletin, 26*, 1490–1501.

Harmon-Jones, E. (2004). Insights on asymmetrical frontal brain activity gleaned from research on anger and cognitive dissonance. *Biological Psychology, 67*, 51–76.

Harmon-Jones, E. (2006). Integrating cognitive dissonance theory with neurocognitive models of control. *Psychophysiology, 43*, S16.

Harmon-Jones, E., Harmon-Jones, C., Fearn, M., Sigelman, J. D., & Johnson, P. (2008). Action orientation, relative left frontal cortical activation, and spreading of alternatives: A test of the action-based model of dissonance. *Journal of Personality and Social Psychology, 94*(1), 1–15.

Harrison, P. J. (1999). The neuropathology of schizophrenia: A critical review of the data and their interpretation. *Brain, 122*, 593–624.

Hart, P. (1998). Preventing groupthink revisited: Evaluating and reforming groups in government. *Organizational Behavior & Human Decision Processes, 73*(2–3), 306–326.

Hartfield, E. (1987). Passionate and companionate love. In R. J. Sternberg & M. L. Barnes (Eds.), *The psychology of love* (pp. 191–217). New Haven, CT: Yale University Press.

Hartfield, E., & Rapson, R. L. (1992). Similarity and attraction in intimate relationships. *Communication Monographs, 59,* 209–212.

Harvey, S. & Keashly, L. (2003). Predicting the risk for aggression in the workplace: Risk factors, self-esteem and time at work. *Social Behaviour & Personality: An International Journal, 31*(8), 807–814.

Hauck, S. J., & Bartke, A. (2001). Free radical defenses in the liver and kidney of human growth hormone transgenic mice. *Journal of Gerontology and Biological Science, 56,* 153–162.

Havighurst R. J., Neugarten B. L., & Tobin S. N. S. (1968). Disengagement and patterns of aging. In B. L. Neugarten (Ed.), *Middle age and aging: A reader in social psychology* (pp. 161–172). Chicago: University of Chicago Press.

Hawks, S. R., Madanat, H. N., Merrill, R. M., Goudy, M. B., & Miyagawa, T. (2003). A cross-cultural analysis of "motivation for eating" as a potential factor in the emergence of global obesity: Japan and the United States. *Health Promotion International, 18*(2), 153–162.

Hay, P., & Bacaltchuk, J. (2002). Bulimia nervosa. *Clinical Evidence,* (8), 914–926.

Hayflick, L. (1977). The cellular basis for biological aging. In C. E. Finch & L. Hayflick (Eds.), *Handbook of biology of aging* (p. 159). New York: Van Nostrand Reinhold Co.

Hayward, C., Killen, J. D., Kraemer, H. C., & Taylor, C. B. (2000). Predictors of panic attacks in adolescents. *Journal of the American Academy of Child and Adolescent Psychiatry, 39*(2), 207–214.

Hayward, C., Killen, J., & Taylor, C. B. (1989). Panic attacks in young adolescents. *American Journal of Psychiatry, 146*(8), 1061–1062.

Hazan, C., & Shaver, P. (1987). Romantic love conceptualized as an attachment process. *Journal of Personality and Social Psychology, 52,* 511–524.

Heavey, C. L., Layne, C., & Christensen, A. (1993). Gender and conflict structure in marital interaction: A replication and extension. *Journal of Consulting and Clinical Psychology, 61,* 16–27.

Hebb, D. O. (1955). Drives and the C.N.S. (Conceptual Nervous System). *Psychological Review, 62,* 243–254.

Hechtman, L., Weiss, G., & Perlman, T. (1984). Hyperactives as young adults: Past and current substance abuse and antisocial behavior. *American Journal of Orthopsychiatry, 54,* 415–425.

Hegeman, R. (2007). Police: Shoppers stepped over victim. *The Associated Press.* Retrieved from the Internet on February 21, 2008, at **http://abcnews.go.com/US/wireStory?id=3342724.**

Heider, F. (1958). *The psychology of interpersonal relations.* New York: John Wiley & Sons.

Heil, G., Maslow, A., & Stephens, D. (1998). *Maslow on management.* New York: John Wiley and Sons, Inc.

Heilman, K., Watson, R., & Valenstein, E. (1993). Neglect and related disorders. In K. Heilman and E. Valenstein (Eds.), *Clinical Neuropsychology.* New York: Oxford University Press.

Heilman, K. M. (2002). *Matter of mind: A neurologist's view of brain-behavior relationships.* New York: Oxford University Press.

Hein, A., & Held, R. (1967). Dissociation of the visual placing response into elicited and guided components. *Science, 158,* 390–392.

Heinicke, C. M., Goorsky, M., Moscov, S., Dudley, K., Gordon, J., Schneider, C., & Guthrie, D. (2000). Relationship-based intervention with at-risk mothers: Factors affecting variations in outcome. *Infant Mental Health Journal, 21,* 133–155.

Heinrich, B. (2000). Testing insight in ravens. In C. Heyes & L. Huber (Eds.), *The evolution of cognition.* Cambridge, MA: MIT Press.

Held, R., & Hein, A. (1963). Movement-produced stimulation in the development of visually guided behavior. *Journal of Comparative and Physiological Psychology, 56,* 872–876.

Helms, J. E. (1992). Why is there no study of cultural equivalence in standardized cognitive ability testing? *American Psychologist, 47*(9), 1083–1101.

Henin, A., Mick, E., Biederman, J., Fried, R., Wozniak, J., Faraone, S. V., Harrington, K., Davis, S., & Doyle, A. E. (2007). Can bipolar disorder-specific neuropsychological impairments in children be identified? *Journal of Consulting and Clinical Psychology, 75*(2), 210–220.

Henning, H. (1916). Die qualitätenreihe des geschmacks. *Zsch. f. Psychol., 74,* 203–219.

Henningfield, J. E. (1995). Nicotine medications for smoking cessation. *New England Journal of Medicine, 333*(18), 1196–1203.

Henningfield, J. E., Clayton, R., & Pollin, W. (1990). Involvement of tobacco in alcoholism and illicit drug use. *British Journal of Addition, 85,* 279–292.

Herberman, R. B., & Ortaldo, J. R. (1981). Natural killer cells: Their role in defenses against disease. *Science, 214,* 24–30.

Herbst, J. H., Zonderman, A. B., McCrae, R. R., & Costa, P. T., Jr. (2000). Do the dimensions of the Temperament and Character Inventory map a simple genetic architecture? Evidence from molecular genetics and factor analysis. *American Journal of Psychiatry, 157,* 1285–1290.

Herman, L. M., Pack, A. A., & Morrell-Samuels, P. (1993). Representational and conceptual skills of dolphins. In H. L. Roitblatt, L. M. Herman, & P. E. Nachtigall (Eds.), *Language and communication: Comparative perspectives.* Hillsdale, NJ: Erlbaum.

Hermann, A., Maisel, M., Wegner, F., Liebau, S., Kim, D-W., Gerlach, M., Schwarz, J., Kim, K-S., & Storch, A. (2006). Multipotent neural stem cells from the adult tegmentum with dopaminergic potential develop essential properties of functional neurons. *Stem Cells, 24*(4), 949–964.

Hernandez, D., & Fisher, E. M. (1996). Down syndrome genetics: Unravelling a multifactorial disorder. *Human Molecular Genetics, 5,* 1411–1416.

Herrnstein, R. J., & Murray, C. (1994). *The bell curve: The reshaping of American life by differences in intelligence.* New York: Free Press.

Hersh, S. M. (2004, May 10). Annals of national security: Torture at Abu Ghraib. *The New Yorker.*

Hershberger, S. L., Plomin, R., & Pedersen, N. L. (1995, October). Traits and metatraits: Their reliability, stability, and shared genetic influence. *Journal of Personality and Social Psychology, 69*(4), 673–685.

Herxheimer, A., & Petrie, K. J. (2001). Melatonin for preventing and treating jet lag. *Cocharane Database of Systematic Reviews,* (1), CD001520.

Heslegrave, R. J., & Rhodes. W. (1997). Impact of varying shift schedules on the performance and sleep in air traffic controllers. *Sleep Research, 26,* 198.

Hetherington, A. W., & Ranson, S. W. (1940). Hypothalamic legions and adiposity in rats. *Anatomical Records, 78,* 149–172.

Hettema, J. M., Neale, M. C., & Kendler, K. S. (2001). A review and meta-analysis of the genetic epidemiology of anxiety disorders. *Amercian Journal of Psychiatry, 158,* 1568–1578.

Hewstone, M., Rubin, M., & Willis, H. (2002). Intergroup bias. *Annual Review of Psychology, 53,* 575–604.

Heyes, C. M. (1998). Theory of mind in nonhuman primates. *Behavior and Brain Science, 21,* 101–148.

Hicklin, J., & Widiger, T. A. (2000). Convergent validity of alternative MMPI-2 personality disorder scales. *Journal of Personality Assessment, 75*(3), 502–518.

Hilgard, E. R. (1991). A neodissociation interpretation of hypnosis. In Lynn & Rhue (Eds.), *Theories of hypnosis* (pp. 83–104). New York: Guilford Press.

Hilgard, E. R., & Hilgard, J. R. (1994). *Hypnosis in the relief of pain* (rev. ed.). New York: Brunner/Mazel.

Hill, D. (1990). Causes of smoking in children. In B. Durston & K. Jamrozik, *Smoking and health 1990—the global war. Proceedings of the Seventh World Conference on Smoking and Health,* 1–5 April. Perth: Health Department of Western Australia, 205–209.

Hill, J. A. (1998). Miscarriage risk factors and causes: What we know now. *OBG Management, 10,* 58–68.

Hill, P. C., & Butter E. M. (1995). The role of religion in promoting physical health. *Journal of Psychology and Christianity, 14*(2), 141–155.

Hilton, J. L., & von Hipple, W. (1996). Stereotypes. *Annual Review of Psychology, 47,* 237–271.

Hinton, G. E., McClelland, J. L., & Rumelhart, D. E. (1986). Distributed representations. In D. E. Rumelhart, J. L. McClelland, & the PDP Research Group (Eds.), *Parallel distributed processing: Explorations in the microstructure of cognition, volume 1: Foundations* (pp. 77–109). Cambridge, MA: MIT Press.

Hintze, J. M. (2002). Interventions for fears and anxiety problems. In M. R. Shinn, H. R. Walker, & G. Stoner (Eds.), *Interventions for academic and behavior problems II: Preventive and remedial approaches* (pp. 939–954). Bethesda, MD: National Association of School Psychologists.

Hobson, J. (1988). *The dreaming brain.* New York: Basic Books.

Hobson, J., Pace-Schott, E., & Stickgold, R. (2000). Dreaming and the brain: Towards a cognitive neuroscience of conscious states. *Behavioral and Brain Sciences, 23*(6), 793–1121.

Hobson, J. A., & McCarley, R. (1977). The brain as a dream state generator: An activation-synthesis hypothesis of the dream process. *American Journal of Psychiatry, 134,* 1335–1348.

Hochman, J. (1994). Buried memories challenge the law. *National Law Journal, 1,* 17–18.

Hodges, J. R. (1994). Retrograde amnesia. In A. Baddeley, B. A. Wilson, & F. Watts (Eds.), *Handbook of memory disorders* (pp. 81–107). New York: Wiley.

Hodgson, B. (2001). *In the arms of Morpheus: The tragic history of laudanum, morphine, and patent medicines.* New York: Firefly Books.

Hodson, D. S., & Skeen, P. (1994). Sexuality and aging: The hammerlock of myths. *The Journal of Applied Gerontology, 13,* 219–235.

Hoebel, B. G., & Teitelbaum, P. (1966). Weight regulation in normal and hypothalamic hyperphagic rats. *Journal of Comparative Physiological Psychology, 61,* 189–193.

Hoffmann, A. (1998). *Paradigms of artificial intelligence: A methodological and computational analysis.* London: Springer-Verlag.

Hoffrage, U., Hertwig, R., & Gigerenzer, G. (2000). Hindsight bias: A by-product of knowledge updating? *Journal of Experimental Psychology: Learning, Memory, and Cognition, 26,* 566–581.

Hofstede, G. H. (1980). *Culture's consequences, international differences in work-related values.* Beverly Hills, CA: Sage Publications.

Hofstede, G. J., Pedersen, P. B., & Hofstede, G. H. (2002). *Exploring culture: Exercises, stories, and synthetic cultures.* Yarmouth, ME: Intercultural Press.

Hogg, M. A., & Hains, S. C. (1998). Friendship and group identification: A new look at the role of cohesiveness in groupthink. *European Journal of Social Psychology, 28*(1), 323–341.

Holahan, C. K., & Sears, R. R. (1996). *The gifted group at later maturity.* Stanford, CA: Stanford University Press.

Holcomb, W. R. (1986). Stress inoculation therapy with anxiety and stress disorders of acute psychiatric patients. *Journal of Clinical Psychology, 42,* 864–872.

Holden, C., & Vogel, G. (2002). Plasticity: Time for a reappraisal? *Science, 296,* 2126–2129.

Hollon, S., These, M., & Markowitz, J. (2002). Treatment and prevention of depression. *Psychological Science in the Public Interest, 3,* 39–77.

Hollon, S. D., & Beck, A. T. (1994). Cognitive and cognitive-behavioral therapies. In A. E. Bergin & and S. L. Garfield (Eds.), *Handbook of psychotherapy and behavior change* (4th ed., p. 428). Chichester, UK: John Wiley & Sons.

Holman, E. A., Silver, R. C., Poulin, M., Andersen, J., Gil-Rivas, V., & McIntosh, D. N. (2008). Terrorism, acute stress, and cardiovascular health: A 3-year national study following the September 11th attacks. *Archives of General Psychiatry, 65,* 73–80.

Holmes, C. B., Wurtz, P. J., Waln, R. F., Dungan, D. S., & Joseph, C. A. (1984). Relationship between the Luscher Color Test and the MMPI. *Journal of Clinical Psychology, 40,* 126–128.

Holmes, T. H., & Masuda, M. (1973). Psychosomatic syndrome: When mothers-in-law or other disasters visit, a person can develop a bad, bad cold. *Psychology Today, 5*(11), 71–72, 106.

Holmes, T. H., & Rahe, R. H. (1967). The Social Readjustment Rating Scale. *Journal of Psychosomatic Research II,* 213–218.

Holroyd, J. (1996). Hypnosis treatment of clinical pain: Understanding why hypnosis is useful. *International Journal of Clinical and Experimental Hypnosis, 44,* 33–51.

Holt-Lunstad, J., Uchino, B. N., Smith, T. W., Cerny, C. B., & Nealey-Moore, J. B. (2003). Social relationships and ambulatory blood pressure: Structural and qualitative predictors of cardiovascular function during everyday social interactions. *Health Psychology, 22,* 388–397.

Hood, D. C. (1998). Lower-level visual processing and models of light adaptation. *Annual Review of Psychology, 49,* 503–535.

Hopfinger, J. B., Buonocore, M. H., & Mangun, G. R. (2000). The neural mechanisms of top-down attentional control. *Nature Neuroscience, 3,* 284–291.

Horne, J. A., & Staff, C. H. (1983). Exercise and sleep: Body heating effects. *Sleep, 6,* 36–46.

Horney, K. (1939). *New ways in psychoanalysis,* New York: W. W. Norton.

Horney, K. (1967/1973). *Feminine psychology.* New York: W. W. Norton.

Horowitz, D. L. (1985). *Ethnic groups in conflict.* Berkeley, CA: University of California Press.

Hortaçsu, N. (1999). The first year of family and couple initiated marriages of a Turkish sample: A longitudinal investigation. *International Journal of Psychology, 34*(1), 29–41.

Hossain, P., Kawar, B., & El Nahas, M. (2007). Obesity and diabetes in the developing world—a growing challenge. *New England Journal of Medicine, 356*(9), 973.

Hu, P., & Meng, Z. (1996). *An examination of infant–mother attachment in China.* Poster presented at the meeting of the International Society for the Study of Behavioral Development, Quebec City, Quebec, Canada.

Hu, S., & Stern, R. M. (1999). Retention of adaptation to motion sickness eliciting stimulation. *Aviation, Space, and Environmental Medicine, 70,* 766–768.

Hu, S., Pattatucci, A. M. L., Patterson, C., Li, L., Fulker, D. W., Cherny, S. S., Kruglyak, L., & Hamer, D. H. (1994). Linkage between sexual orientation and chromosome Xq28 in males but not in females. *Nature Genetics, 11,* 248–256.

Hubble, M. A., Duncan, B. L., & Miller, S. D. (1999). Directing attention to what works. In M. A. Hubble, B. L. Duncan, & S. D. Miller (Eds.), *The heart and soul of change: What works in therapy* (pp. 407–447). Washington, DC: American Psychological Association.

Huesmann, L. R., & Eron, L. (1986). *Television and the aggressive child: A cross-national comparison.* Hillsdale, NJ: Erlbaum.

Huesmann, L. R., & Miller, L. S. (1994). Long-term effects of repeated exposure to media violence in childhood. In L. R. Huesmann (Ed.), *Aggressive behavior: Current perspectives* (pp. 153–183). New York: Plenum Press.

Huesmann, L. R., Moise, J. F., & Podolski, C. L. (1997). The effects of media violence on the development of antisocial behavior. In D. M. Stoff, J. Breiling, & J. D. Maser (Eds.), *Handbook of antisocial behavior* (pp. 181–193). New York: John Wiley.

Huesmann, L. R., Moise-Titus, J., Podolski, C. L., & Eron, L. D. (2003). Longitudinal relations between children's exposure to TV violence and their aggressive and violent behavior in young adulthood: 1977–1992. *Developmental Psychology, 39*(2), 201–221.

Hugenberg, K., & Bodenhausen, G. V. (2003). Facing prejudice: Implicit prejudice and the perception of facial threat. *Psychological Science, 14,* 640–643.

Hughes, J. (1993). Behavior therapy. In T. R. Kratochwill & R. J. Morris (Eds.), *Handbook of psychotherapy with children and adolescents* (pp. 185–220). Boston: Allyn and Bacon.

Hughes, S. M., Harrison, M. A., & Gallup, G. G., Jr. (2007). Sex differences in romantic kissing among college students: An evolutionary perspective. *Evolutionary Psychology 5*(3), 612–631.

Hull, C. L. (1943). *Principles of behavior.* New York: Appleton-Century.

Hummer, R. A., Rogers, R. G., Nam, C. B., & Ellison, C. G. (1999). Religious involvement and U.S. adult mortality. *Demography, 36*(2), 273–285.

Humphries, L. L. (1987). Bulimia: Diagnosis and treatment. *Comprehensive Therapy, 13,* 12–15.

Hunt, E. (2001). Multiple views of multiple intelligence. [Review of Intelligence reframed: Multiple intelligence in the 21st century.] *Contemporary Psychology, 46,* 5–7.

Hunt, M. (1993). *The story of psychology.* New York: Doubleday.

Hurley, D. (1989). The search for cocaine's methadone. *Psychology Today, 23*(7/8), 54.

Hurley, S., & Nudds, M. (Eds.) (2006). *Rational animals?* Oxford: Oxford University Press.

Hurst, S., & Milkewicz, N. (2000). Eye movement desensitization and reprocessing: A controversial treatment technique. Retrieved from the Internet on July 14, 2004, at **www.netpsych.com/health/emd.htm**.

Hurvich, L. M. (1969). Hering and the scientific establishment. *American Psychologist, 24,* 497–514.

Hurwitz, T. A. (1989). Approach to the patient with psychogenic neurological disturbance. In W. N. Kelley (Ed.), *Textbook of internal medicine. Volume 2* (pp. 2518–2521). Philadelphia: J. B. Lippincott.

Hutcheson, J., & Snyder, H. M. (2004). Ambiguous genitalia and intersexuality. *eMedicine Journal, 5*(5). Retrieved from the Internet on November 17, 2004, at **http://author.emedicine.com/PED/topic1492.htm.**

Hvas, L. (2001). Positive aspects of menopause: A qualitative study. *Maturitas 39*(1), 11–17.

Hyde, J. S., & Kling, K. C. (2001). Women, motivation, and achievement. *Psychology of Women Quarterly, 25,* 264–378.

Hyde, J. S., & Plant, E. A. (1995). Magnitude of psychological gender differences. *American Psychologist, 50,* 159–161.

Hyman, I. E., Gilstrap, L. L., Decker, K., & Wilkinson, C. (1998). Manipulating remember and know judgements of autobiographical memories. *Applied Cognitive Psychology, 12,* 371–386

Hyman, I. E., Jr. (1993). Imagery, reconstructive memory, and discovery. In B. Roskos-Ewoldsen, M. J. Intons-Peterson, & R. E. Anderson (Eds.), *Imagery, creativity, and discovery: A cognitive perspective* (pp. 99–121). The Netherlands: Elsevier Science Publishers.

Hyman, I. E., Jr., & Loftus, E. F. (1998). Errors in autobiographical memories. *Clinical Psychology Review, 18,* 933–947.

Hyman, I. E., Jr., & Loftus, E. F. (2002). False childhood memories and eyewitness memory errors. In M. L. Eisen, J. A. Quas, & G. S. Goodman (Eds.), *Memory and suggestibility in the forensic interview* (pp. 63–84). Mahwah, NJ: Erlbaum.

Iacoboni, M., Woods, R. P., Brass, M., Bekkering, H., Mazziotta, J. C., & Rizzolatti, G. (1999). Cortical mechanisms of human imitation. *Science, 286,* 2526–2528.

Imaizumi, Y. (1998). A comparative study of twinning and triplet rates in 17 countries, 1972–1996. *Acta Genetic Medicine & Gemellology, 47,* 101–114.

Ioannidis, J. P. A. (1998, January 28). Effect of the statistical significance of results on the time to completion and publication of randomized efficacy trials. *Journal of the American Medical Association, 279,* 281–286.

Irwin, A. R., & Gross, A. M. (1995). Cognitive tempo, violent video games, and aggressive behavior in young boys. *Journal of Family Violence, 10*(3), 337–350.

Irwin, M., Cole, J., & Nicassio, P. (2006). Comparative meta-analysis of behavioral intervention for insomnia and their efficacy in middle aged adults and in older adults 55+ years of age. *Health Psychology, 25,* 3–14.

Irwin, M., Mascovich A., Gillin, J. C., Willoughby, R., Pike, J., & Smith, T. L. (1994). Partial sleep deprivation reduces natural killer cell activity in humans, *Psychosomatic Medicine, 56,* 493–498.

Irwin, M., McClintick, J., Costlow, C., Fortner, M., White, J., & Gillin, J. C. (1996). Partial night sleep deprivation reduces natural killer and cellular immune responses in humans. *The Federation of American Societies for Experimental Biology Journal, 10,* 643–653.

Isabel, J. (2003). *Genetics: An introduction for dog breeders.* Loveland, CO: Alpine Publications.

Iwakabe, S. (2008). Psychotherapy integration in Japan. *Journal of Psychotherapy Integration, 18*(1), 103–125.

Iwamoto, E. T., & Martin, W. (1988). A critique of drug self-administration as a method for predicting abuse potential of drugs. *National Institute on Drug Abuse Research Monograph, 1046,* 81457–81465.

Izard, C. (1988). Emotion-cognition relationships and human development. In C. Izard, J. Kagan, and R. Zajonc (Eds.), *Emotions, cognition, and behavior* (Chapter 1). New York: Cambridge University Press.

Jackson, R. (2001). *Plato: A beginner's guide.* London: Hodder & Stoughton.

Jackson, T., Iezzi, T., Gunderson, J., Fritch, A., & Nagasaka, T. (2002). Gender differences in pain perception: The mediating role of self-efficacy beliefs. *Sex Roles, 47,* 561–568.

Jacobson, S. G., Cideciyan A. V., Regunath, G., et al. (1995). Night blindness in Sorsby's fundus dystrophy reversed by vitamin A. *Nature Genetics, 11,* 27–32.

Jaeger, J. J., Lockwood, A. H., Van Valin, R. D., Kemmerer, D. L., Murphy, B. W., & Wack, D. S. (1998). Sex differences in brain regions activated by grammatical and reading tasks. *Neuroreport, 9,* 2803–2807.

James, W. (1884). What is an emotion? *Mind, 9,* 188–205.

James, W. (1890). *Principles of psychology.* New York: Henry Holt.

James, W. (1890, 2002). *The principles of psychology (Vols. 1 and 2).* Cambridge, MA: Harvard University Press.

James, W. (1894). The physical basis of emotion. *Psychological Review, 1,* 516–529.

Jameson, M., Diehl, R., & Danso, H. (2007). Stereotype threat impacts college athletes' academic performance. *Current Research in Social Psychology, 12*(5), 68–79.

Jang, K. L., Livesley, W. J., & Vernon, P. A. (1996). Heritability of the Big Five personality dimensions and their facets: A twin study. *Journal of Personality, 64,* 577–591.

Jang, K. L., McCrae, R. R., Angleitner, A., Riemann, R., & Livesley, W. J. (1998). Heritability of facet-level traits in a cross-cultural twin sample: Support for a hierarchical model of personality. *Journal of Personality and Social Psychology, 74,* 1556–1565.

Janis, I. (1972). *Victims of groupthink.* Boston: Houghton-Mifflin.

Janis, I. (1982). *Groupthink* (2nd ed.) Boston: Houghton-Mifflin.

Janos, P. M. (1987). A fifty-year follow-up of Terman's youngest college students and IQ-matched agemates. *Gifted Child Quarterly, 31,* 55–58.

Janowitz, H. D. (1967). Role of gastrointestinal tract in the regulation of food intake. In C. F. Code (Ed.), *Handbook of physiology: Alimentary canal 1.* Washington, DC: American Physiological Society.

Janus, S. S., & Janus, C. L. (1993). *The Janus report on sexual behavior.* New York: John Wiley & Sons, Inc.

Jarusiewicz, B. (2002). Efficacy of neurofeedback for children in the autistic spectrum: A pilot study. *Journal of Neurotherapy, 6*(4), 39–49.

Jay, S. M., & Elliot, C. H. (1990). A stress inoculation program for parents whose children are undergoing medical procedures. *Journal of Consulting and Clinical Psychology, 58,* 799–804.

Jensen, A. R. (1969). How much can we boost IQ and scholastic achievement? *Harvard Educational Review, 39,* 1–123.

Jimerson, D. C., Wolfe, B. E., Metzger, E. D., Finkelstein, D. M., Cooper, T. B., & Levine, J. M. (1997). Decreased serotonin function in bulimia nervosa. *Archives of General Psychiatry, 54,* 529–534.

Joanna Briggs Institute. (2001). Smoking cessation interventions and strategies. In *Best Practice, 5*(3), 1329–1874. Published by the Joanna Briggs Institute for Evidence Based Nursing and Midwifery.

John, O. P., Angleitner, A., & Ostendorf, F. (1988). The lexical approach to personality: A historical review of trait taxonomic research. *European Journal of Personality, 2,* 171–203.

Johnson, D., Johnson, R., & Smith, K. (1991). *Active learning: Cooperation in the college classroom.* Edna, MN: Interaction Book Company.

Johnson, G. (1995, June 6). Chimp talk debate: Is it really language? *The New York Times.*

Johnson, J., Cohen, P., Pine, D. S., Klein, D. F., Kasen, S., & Brook, J. S. (2000). Association between cigarette smoking and anxiety disorders during adolescence and early adulthood. *Journal of the American Medical Association, 284*(18), 2348–2351.

Johnson, W., Bouchard, T. J., Jr., McGue, M., Segal, N. L., Tellegen, A., Keyes, M., & Gottesman, I. I. (2007). Genetic and environmental influences on the Verbal-Perceptual-Image Rotation (VPR) Model of the structure of mental abilities in the Minnesota Study of Twins Reared Apart. *Intelligence, 35*(6), 542–562.

Joiner, W. J., Crocker, A., White, B. H. & Sehgal, A. (2006). Sleep in *Drosophila* is regulated by adult mushroom bodies. *Nature, 441,* 757–760.

Joint United Nations Programme on HIV/AIDS (UNAIDS). (2007). 2007 AIDS epidemic update. Retrieved from the Internet on February 8, 2007, at **http://www.unaids.org/en/KnowledgeCentre/HIVData/EpiUpdate/EpiUpd Archive/2007/.**

Jones, E. E., & Harris, V. A. (1967). The attribution of attitudes. *Journal of Experimental Social Psychology, 3,* 1–24.

Jones, E. J., Krupnick, J. L., & Kerig, P. K. (1987). Some gender effects in a brief psychotherapy. *Psychotherapy, 24,* 336–352.

Jones, G. W. (1997). Modernization and divorce: Contrasting trends in Islamic Southeast Asia and the West. *Population and Development Review, 23*(1), 95–113.

Jones, H. M., & Pilowsky, L. S. (2002). Dopamine and antipsychotic drug action revisited. *British Journal of Psychiatry, 181,* 271–275.

Jones, M. C. (1924). A laboratory study of fear: The case of Peter. *Pedagogical Seminary, 31,* 308–315.

Juffer, F., & Rosenboom, L. G. (1997). Infant–mother attachment of internationally adopted children in the Netherlands. *International Journal of Behavioral Development, 20*(1), 93–107.

Jung, C. (1933). *Modern man in search of a soul.* New York: Harcourt Brace.

Kabat-Zinn, J., Lipworth, L., & Burney, R. (1985). The clinical use of mindfulness meditation for the self-regulation of chronic pain. *Journal of Behavioral Medicine, 8,* 163–190.

Kabat-Zinn, J., Lipworth, L., Burney, R., & Sellers, W. (1986). Four year follow-up of a meditation-based program for the self regulation of chronic pain: Treatment outcomes and compliance. *Clinical Journal of Pain, 2,* 159–173.

Kagan, J. (1998). *Galen's prophecy: Temperament in human nature* (pp. 237–260, 270–274). New York: Basic Books.

Kagan, J., Snidman, N., Kahn, V., & Towsley, S. (2007). The preservation of two infant temperaments into adolescence. *SRCD Monographs, 72*(2).

Kahan, M., & Sutton, N. (1998). Overview: Methadone treatment for the opioid-dependent patient. In B. Brands & J. Brands (Eds.), *Methadone maintenance: A physician's guide to treatment* (pp. 1–15). Toronto, ON: Addiction Research Foundation.

Kahneman, D., & Tversky, A. (1973). On the psychology of prediction. *Psychological Review, 80,* 237–251.

Kahneman, D., Slovic, P., & Tversky, A. (1982). *Judgment under uncertainty: Heuristics and biases.* New York: Cambridge University Press.

Kail, R. & Hall, L. K. (2001). Distinguishing short-term memory from working memory. *Memory & Cognition, 29*(1), 1–9.

Kaiser, P. K. (1984). Physiological response to color: Critical review. *Color Research and Application, 9,* 29–36.

Kakko, J., Svanborg, K. D., Kreek, M. J., & Heilig, M. (2003). 1-year retention and social function after buprenorphine-associated relapse prevention treatment for heroin dependence in Sweden: A randomised, placebo-controlled trial. *Lancet, 361,* 662–668.

Kales, A., Soldatos, C., Bixler, E., Ladda, R. L., Charney, D. S., Weber, G., & Schweitzer, P. K. (1980). Hereditary factors in sleepwalking and night terrors. *British Journal of Psychiatry, 137,* 111–118.

Kamin, L. J. (1995, February). Behind the curve. *Scientific American,* 99–103.

Kamphaus, R. W. (1993). *Clinical assessment of children's intelligence.* Boston: Allyn & Bacon.

Kandel, E. R., & Schwartz, J. H. (1982). Molecular biology of learning: Modulation of transmitter release. *Science, 218,* 433–443.

Kanne, S. M., Balota, D. A., Storandt, M., McKeel, D. W., Jr., & Morris, J. C. (1998). Relating anatomy to function in Alzheimer's disease: Neuropsychological profiles predict regional neuropathology 5 years later. *Neurology, 50*(4), 979–985.

Karau, S. J., & Williams, K. D. (1993). Social loafing: A meta-analytic review and theoretical integration. *Journal of Personality and Social Psychology, 65,* 681–706.

Karau, S. J., & Williams, K. D. (1997). The effects of group cohesiveness on social loafing and social compensation. *Group Dynamics: Theory, Research and Practice, 1,* 156–168.

Karayiorgou, M., Altemus, M., Galke, B., Goldman, D., Murphy, D., Ott, J., & Gogos, J. (1997). Genotype determining low catechol-O-methyltransferase activity as a risk factor for obsessive-compulsive disorder. *Proceeds of the National Academy of Science, 94,* 4572–4575.

Karney, B. R., & Bradbury, T. N. (2000). Attributions in marriage: State or trait? A growth curve analysis. *Journal of Personality and Social Psychology, 78,* 295–309.

Kastenbaum, R., & Costa, P. T., Jr. (1977). Psychological perspective on death. *Annual Review of Psychology, 28,* 225–249.

Katada, E. K., Sato, K., Sawaki, A., Dohi, Y., Ueda, R., & Ojika, K. (2003). Long-term effects of donepezil on P300 auditory event-related potentials in patients with Alzheimer's disease. *Journal of Geriatric Psychiatry and Neurology, 16*(1), 39–43.

Katzman, R., Aronson, M., Fuld, P., Kawas, C. K., Brown, T., Morgenstern, H., Frishman, W., Gidez, L., Eder, H., & Ooi, W. L. (1989). Development of dementing illnesses in an 80-year-old volunteer cohort. *Annals of Neurology, 25*(4), 317–324.

Kaufman, J., & Zigler, E. (1993). The intergenerational transmission of abuse is overstated. In R. J. Gelles & D. R. Loseke (Eds.), *Current controversies on family violence.* Newbury Park, CA: Sage Publications.

Kaufmann, G. R., Bloch, M., Zaunders, J. J., Smith, D., & Cooper, D. A. (2000). Long-term immunological response in HIV-1 infected subjects receiving potent antiretroviral therapy. *AIDS, 14,* 959–969.

Kaveny, M. C. (2001). The case of conjoined twins: Embodiment, individuality, and dependence. *Theological Studies, 62.*

Kazdin, A. E. (1980). Acceptability of time out from reinforcement procedures for disruptive behavior. *Behavior Therapy, 11*(3), 329–344.

Keane, T. M., Fairbank, J. A., Caddell, J. M., & Zimering, R. T. (1989). Implosive (flooding) therapy reduced symptoms of PTSD in Vietnam combat veterans. *Behavior Therapy, 20,* 245–260.

Kearney, C. A., & Silverman, W. K. (1998). A critical review of pharmacotherapy for youth with anxiety disorders: Things are not as they seem. *Journal of Anxiety Disorders, 12,* 83–102.

Keillor, J., Barrett, A., Crucian, G., Kortenkamp, S., & Heilman, K. (2002). Emotional experience and perception in the absence of facial feedback. *Journal of the International Neuropsychological Society, 8*(1), 130–135.

Keller, M. B., McCullough, J. P., Klein, D. N., Arnow, B., Dunner, D., Gelenberg, A., Markowitz, J. C., Nemeroff, C. B., Russell, J. M., Thase, M. E., Trivedi, M. H., & Zajecka, J. (2000). A comparison of nefazodone, the cognitive behavioral-analysis system of psychotherapy, and their combination for the treatment of chronic depression. *New England Journal of Medicine, 342*(20), 1462–1470.

Keller, M. B., Ryan, N. D., Strober, M., Klein, R. G., Kutcher, S. P., Birmaher, B., Hagino, O. R., Koplewicz, H., Carlson, G. A., Clarke, G. N., Emslie, G. J., Feinberg, D., Geller, B., Kusumakar, V., Papatheodorou, G., Sack, W. H., Sweeney, M., Wagner, K. D., Weller, E. B., Winters, N. C., Oakes, R., & Mc-Cafferty, J. P. (2001). Efficacy of paroxetine in the treatment of adolescent major depression: A randomized, controlled trial. *Journal of the Academy of Child and Adolescent Psychiatry, 40*(7), 762–772.

Kellner, R. (1986). *Somatization and hypochondriasis.* New York: Praeger-Greenwood.

Kelly, I. (1980). The scientific case against astrology. *Mercury, 10*(13), 135.

Kelly, J. A., McAuliffe, T. L., Sikkema, K. J., Murphy, D. A., Somlai, A. M., Mulry, G., Miller, J. G., Stevenson, L. Y., & Fernandez, M. I. (1997). Reduction in risk behavior among adults with severe mental illness who learned to advocate for HIV prevention. *Psychiatric Services, 48*(10), 1283–1288.

Kendall, P. (1983). Stressful medical procedures: Cognitive-behavioral strategies for stress management and prevention. In D. Meichenbaum & M. Jaremko (Eds.), *Stress reduction and prevention.* (pp. 159–190). New York: Plenum Press.

Kendall, P. C., Hudson, J. L., Gosch, E., Flannery-Schroeder, E., & Suveg, C. (2008). Cognitive-behavioral therapy for anxiety disordered youth: A randomized clinical trial evaluating child and family modalities. *Journal of Consulting and Clinical Psychology, 76*(2), 282–297.

Kendler, K. S. (1985). Diagnostic approaches to schizotypal personality disorders: A historical perspective. *Schizophrenia Bulletin, 11,* 538–553.

Kendler, K. S., & Prescott, C. A. (1999). A population-based twin study of lifetime major depression in men and women. *Archives of General Psychiatry, 56*(1), 39–44.

Kendler, K. S., & Walsh, D. (1995). Schizotypal personality disorder in parents and the risk for schizophrenia in siblings. *Schizophrenia Bulletin, 21*(2), 47–52.

Kenny, A. (1968). Mind and body. In *Descartes: A study of his philosophy* (p. 279). New York: Random House.

Kenny, A. (1994). Descartes to Kant. In A. Kenny (Ed.), *The Oxford History of Western Philosophy* (pp. 107–192). Oxford, England: Oxford University Press.

Keromoian, R., & Leiderman, P. H. (1986). Infant attachment to mother and child caretaker in an East African community. *International Journal of Behavioral Development, 9,* 455–469.

Kessler, S. (1998). *Lessons from the intersexed.* Piscataway, NJ: Rutgers University Press.

Kety, S. S., Wender, P. H., Jacobsen, B., Ingaham, L. J., Jansson, L., Faber, B., & Kinney, D. K. (1994). Mental illness in the biological and adoptive relatives of schizophrenic adoptees. *Archives of General Psychiatry, 51,* 442–455.

Kiecolt-Glaser, J. K., Fisher, L. D., Ogrocki, P., Stout, J. C., Speicher, C. E., & Glaser, R. (1987). Marital quality, marital disruption, and immune function. *Psychosomatic Medicine, 49,* 13–34.

Kiecolt-Glaser, J. K., Glaser, R., Gravenstein, S., Malarkey, W. B., & Sheridan, J. (1996). Chronic stress alters the immune response to influenza virus vaccine in older adults. *Processes of the National Academy of Science, 93*(7), 3043–3047.

Kiecolt-Glaser, J. K., Marucha, P. T., Malarkey, W. B., & Marcado, A. M. (1995). Slowing of wound healing by psychological stress. *Lancet, 346,* 1194–1196.

Kiecolt-Glaser, J. K., McGuire, L., Robles, T., & Glaser, R. (2002). Psychoneuroimmunology: Psychological influences on immune function and health. *Journal of Consulting and Clinical Psychology, 70,* 537–547.

Kihlstrom, J., Mulvaney, S., Tobias, B., & Tobis, I. (2000). The emotional unconscious. In E. Eich, J. Kihlstrom, G. Bower, J. Forgas, & P. Niedenthal (Eds.), *Cognition and emotion* (pp. 30–86). New York: Oxford University Press.

Kihlstrom, J. F. (1985). Hypnosis. *Annual Review of Psychology, 36*, 385–418.

Kihlstrom, J. F. (1987). The cognitive unconscious. *Science, 237*, 1445–1452.

Kihlstrom, J. F. (1999). Conscious and unconscious cognition. In R. J. Sternberg (Ed.), *The nature of cognition* (pp. 173–203). Cambridge, MA: MIT Press.

Kihlstrom, J. F. (2001). Hypnosis and the psychological unconscious. In Howard S. Friedman (Ed.), *Assessment and therapy: Specialty articles from the Encyclopedia of Mental Health* (pp. 215–226). Adelman (Ed.), San Diego, CA: Academic Press.

Kihlstrom, J. F. (2002). Memory, autobiography, history. *Proteus: A Journal of Ideas, 19*(2), 1–6.

Kim, H., & Markus, H. R. (1999). Deviance or uniqueness, harmony or conformity? A cultural analysis. *Journal of Personality and Social Psychology, 77*, 785–800.

Kimura, D. (1999). *Sex and cognition.* Cambridge, MA: MIT Press.

Kimura, D. (2002, May 13). Sex differences in the brain. *Scientific American.* Special issue "The hidden mind," *12*, 32–37.

Kinsey, A. C., Pomeroy, W. B., & Martin, C. E. (1948). *Sexual behavior in the human male.* Philadelphia: W. B. Saunders.

Kinsey, A. C., Pomeroy, W. B., Martin, C. E., & Gebhard, P. H. (1953). *Sexual behavior in the human female.* New York: W. B. Saunders.

Kirby, J. S., Chu, J. A., & Dill, D. L. (1993). Correlates of dissociative symptomatology in patients with physical and sexual abuse histories. *Comprehensive Psychiatry 34*, 250–263.

Kirmayer, L. J. (1991). The place of culture in psychiatric nosology: Taijinkyofusho and the DSM-III-R. *Journal of Nervous and Mental Disease, 179*, 19–28.

Kirsch, I. (2000). The response set theory of hypnosis. *American Journal of Clinical Hypnosis, 42*, 3/42, 4, 274–292.

Kirsch, I., & Lynn, S. J. (1995). The altered state of hypnosis: Changes in the theoretical landscape. *American Psychologist, 50*, 846–858.

Kitayama, S., & Markus, H. R. (1994). Introduction to cultural psychology and emotion research. In S. Kitayama & H. R. Markus (Eds.), *Emotion and culture: Empirical studies of mutual influence* (pp. 1–22). Washington, DC: American Psychological Association.

Klaver, C. C., Wolfs, R. C., Vingerling, J. R., Hofman, A., & de Jong, P. T. (1998). Age-specific prevalence and causes of blindness and visual impairment in an older population: The Rotterdam Study. *Archives of Ophthalmology, 116*, 653–658.

Klein, D., Schwartz, J., Rose, S., & Leader, J. (2000). Five-year course and outcome of dysthymic disorder: A prospective, naturalistic follow-up study. *American Journal of Psychiatry, 157*(6), 931–939.

Klein, S. B., & Mowrer, R. R. (1989). *Contemporary learning theories: Pavlovian conditioning and the status of traditional learning theory.* Hillsdale, NJ: Lawrence Erlbaum Associates.

Kleinot, M. C., & Rogers, R. W. (1982). Identifying effective components of alcohol misuse prevention programs. *Journal of Studies on Alcohol, 43*, 802–811.

Kligman, A. M., & Balin, A. K. (1989). Aging of human skin. In A. K. Balin & A. M. Kligman (Eds.), *Aging and the skin* (pp. 1–42). New York: Raven Press.

Klorman, R., Hilpert, P. L., Michael, R., LaGana, C., & Sveen, O. B. (1980). Effects of coping and mastery modeling on experienced and inexperienced pedodontic patients' disruptiveness. *Behavior Therapy, 11*, 156–168.

Kluft, R. P. (1984). Introduction to multiple personality disorder. *Psychiatric Annals, 14*, 19–24.

Kluft, R. P. (1988). The phenomenology and treatment of extremely complex multiple personality disorder. *Dissociation, I*, 47–58.

Klüver, H., & Bucy, P. C. (1939). Preliminary analysis of functions of the temporal lobes in monkeys. *Archives of Neurological Psychiatry, 42*, 979–1000.

Knauth, P. (1993). The design of shift systems. *Ergonomics, 36*(1–3), 15–28.

Knight, A. (1996). *The life of the law: The people and cases that have shaped our society, from King Alfred to Rodney King.* New York: Crown Publishing Group.

Knight, J. A. (1998). Free radicals: Their history and current status in aging and disease. *Annals of Clinical and Laboratory Science, 28*, 331–346.

Knight, W. (2003). Man vs. machine chess match ends in stalemate. *NewScientist.com News Service, February.* Retrieved from the Internet on November 4, 2004, at **www.newscientist.com/news/news.jsp?id=ns99993370.**

Kobasa, S. (1979). Stressful life events, personality, and health: An inquiry into hardiness. *Journal of Personality and Social Psychology, 37*(1), 1–11.

Koenig, H. G., Hays, J. C., Larson, D. B., George, L. K., Cohen, H. J., McCullough, M. E., Meador, K. G., & Blazer, D. G. (1999). Does religious attendance prolong survival? A six-year follow-up study of 3,968 older adults. *Journal of Gerontology, 54A*, M370–M377.

Koenig, H. G., McCullough, M. E., & Larson, D. B. (2001). *Handbook of religion and health.* Oxford, UK: Oxford University Press.

Koh, J. K. (1996). A guide to common Singapore spiders. *BP Guide to Nature* series. Singapore: Singapore Science Center.

Kohlberg, L. (1969). Stage and sequence: The cognitive-developmental approach to socialization. In D. A. Goslin (Ed.), *Handbook of socialization: Theory in research* (pp. 347–480). Boston: Houghton-Mifflin.

Kohlberg, L. (1973). Continuities in childhood and adult moral development revisited. In P. Baltes & K. W. Schaie (Eds.), *Life-span development psychology: Personality and socialization.* San Diego, CA: Academic Press.

Kohler, W. (1925, 1992). *Gestalt psychology: An introduction to new concepts in modern psychology (reissue).* New York: Liveright.

Kolodny, R. C. (2001, August). In memory of William H. Masters. *Journal of Sex Research.*

Konowal, N. M., Van Dongen, H. P. A., Powell, J. W., Mallis, M. M., & Dinges, D. F. (1999). Determinants of microsleeps during experimental sleep deprivation. *Sleep, 22* (1 Suppl.), 328.

Korn, S. (1984). Continuities and discontinuities in difficult/easy temperament: Infancy to young adulthood. *Merrill Palmer Quarterly, 30*, 189–199.

Kosslyn, S. M. (1983). Mental imagery. In Z. Rubin (Ed.), *The psychology of being human.* New York: Harper and Row.

Kosslyn, S. M., Alpert, N. M., Thompson, W. L., Maljkovic, V., Weise, S. B., Chabris, C. F., Hamilton, S. E., & Buonano, F. S. (1993). Visual mental imagery activates topographically organized visual cortex: PET investigations. *Journal of Cognitive Neuroscience 5*, 263–287.

Kosslyn, S. M., Ball, T. M., & Reiser, B. J. (1978). Visual images preserve metric spatial information: Evidence from studies of image scanning. *Journal of Experimental Psychology: Human Perception and Performance, 4*, 47–60.

Kosslyn, S. M., Ganis, G., & Thompson, W. L. (2001). Neural foundations of imagery. *Nature Reviews Neuroscience 2*, 635–642.

Kosslyn, S. M., Pascual-Leone, A., Felician, O., Camposano, S., Keenan, J. P., Thompson, W. L., Ganis, G., Sukel, K. E., & Alpert, N. M. (1999). The role of area 17 in visual imagery: Convergent evidence from PET and rTMS. *Science 284*, 167–170.

Kosslyn, S. M., Thompson, W. L., Wraga, M. J., & Alpert, N. M. (2001). Imagining rotation by endogenous and exogenous forces: Distinct neural mechanisms for different strategies. *Neuroreport, 12*, 2519–2525.

Kotkin, M., Daviet, C., & Gurin, J. (1996). The *Consumer Reports* mental health survey. *American Psychologist, 51*(10), 1080–1082.

Kouri, E. M., Pope, H. G., & Lukas, S. E. (1999). Changes in aggressive behavior during withdrawal from long-term marijuana use. *Psychopharmacology, 143*, 302–308.

Kourtis, A. P., Bulterys, M., Nesheim, S. R., & Lee, F. K. (2001). Understanding the timing of HIV transmission from mother to infant. *Journal of the American Medical Association, 285*(6), 709–712.

Krasnowski, M. (2004, June 13). Testimony to begin in "sleepwalking" trial. *The San Diego Union-Tribune.* Retrieved from the Internet on February 14, 2008, at **http://www.signonsandiego.com/uniontrib/20040613/news_1n13sleep.html.**

Kratofil, P. H., Baberg, H. T., & Dimsdale, J. E. (1996). Self-mutilation and severe self-injurious behavior associated with amphetamine psychosis. *General Hospital Psychiatry, 18*, 117–120.

Kreipe, R. E. (1992). Normal somatic adolescent growth and development. In E. McAnarney, R. E. Kreipe, D. Orr, & G. Comerci (Eds.), *Textbook of adolescent medicine* (pp. 44–68). Philadelphia: W. B. Saunders & Co.

Kristensen, P., & Bjerkedal, T. (2007). Explaining the relation between birth order and intelligence. *Science, 316*(5832), 1717.

Kryger, M., Lavie, P., & Rosen, R. (1999). Recognition and diagnosis of insomnia. *Sleep, 22*, S421–S426.

Kübler-Ross, E. (1997). *The wheel of life: A memoir of living and dying.* New York: Touchstone.

Kuhn, H. W., & Nasar, S. (Eds.) (2001). *The essential John Nash.* Princeton, NJ: Princeton University Press.

Kulik, J. A., & Mahler, H. I. M. (1989). Social support and recovery from surgery. *Health Psychology, 8,* 221–238.

Kulik, J. A., & Mahler, H. I. M. (1993). Emotional support as a moderator of adjustment and compliance after coronary bypass surgery: A longitudinal study. *Journal of Behavioral Medicine, 16,* 45–63.

Kumar, R. (1994). Postnatal mental illness: A transcultural perspective. *Social Psychiatry and Psychiatric Epidemiology, 29*(6), 250–264.

Kumar, S., & Oakley-Browne, M. (2002). Panic disorder. *Clinical Evidence, 7,* 906–912.

Küntay, A., & Slobin, D. I. (2002). Putting interaction back into child language: Examples from Turkish. *Psychology of Language and Communication, 6,* 5–14.

Kupfer, D. J., & Reynolds, C. F., III. (1997). Management of insomnia. *New England Journal of Medicine, 336*(5), 341–346.

LaBar, K. S., LeDoux, J. E., Spencer, D. D., & Phelps, E. A. (1995). Impaired fear conditioning following unilateral temporal lobectomy to humans. *Journal of Neuroscience, 15,* 6846–6855.

LaBerge, D. (1980). Unitization and automaticity in perception. In J. H. Flowers (Ed.), *Nebraska symposium on motivation* (pp. 53–71). Lincoln, NB: University of Nebraska Press.

Lacayo, A. (1995). Neurologic and psychiatric complications of cocaine abuse. *Neuropsychiatry, Neuropsychology, and Behavioral Neurology, 8*(1), 53–60.

LaFromboise, T., Coleman, H. L. K., & Gerton J. (1993). Psychological impact of biculturalism: Evidence and theory. *Psychological Bulletin, 114,* 395–412.

Laguna, F., Adrados, M., Alvar, J., Soriano, V., Valencia, M. E., Moreno, V., Polo, R., Verdejo, J., Jimenez, M. I., Martinez, P., Martinez, M. L., & Gonzalez-Lahoz, J. M. (1997). Visceral leishmaniasis in patients infected with the human immunodeficiency virus. *European Journal of Clinical Microbiology and Infectious Diseases, 16,* 898–903.

Lal, S. (2002). Giving children security: Mamie Phipps Clark and the radicalization of child psychology. *American Psychologist, 57*(1), 20–28.

Lalancette, M-F., & Standing, L. G. (1990). Asch fails again. *Social Behavior and Personality, 18*(1), 7–12.

Lambert, M. J., & Ogles, B. M. (2003). The efficacy and effectiveness of psychotherapy. In M. J. Lambert (Ed.), *Handbook of psychotherapy and behavior change* (5th ed.) (pp. 139–193). New York: Wiley.

Lance, C. J., LaPointe, & S. Fisicaro. (1994). Tests of three causal models of halo rater error. *Organizational Behavior and Human Decision Performance, 57,* 83–96.

Landrum, R. E., & Davis, S. F. (2007). *The psychology major: Career options and strategies for success,* 3rd ed. Upper Saddle River, NJ: Prentice Hall.

Lane, R. D., Kivley, L. S., DuBois, M. A. Shamasundara, P., & Schwartz, G. E. (1995). Levels of emotional awareness and the degree of right hemisphere dominance in the perception of facial emotion. *Neuropsychologia, 33,* 525–538.

Lange, C. (1885/1967). The emotions. Reprinted in Lange, C. G. & James, W., (Eds.), *The emotions.* New York: Harner Publishing Co.

Langer, E. J., & Rodin, J. (1976). The effects of enhanced personal responsibility for the aged: A field experiment in an institutional setting. *Journal of Personality and Social Psychology, 34,* 191–198.

Langford, C. (2002). *Sexually transmitted diseases: Frequently asked questions.* National Women's Health Information Center, U.S. Department of Health and Human Services.

Langone, M. C. (1996). Clinical update on cults. *Psychiatric Times, 13*(7).

Lanphear, B. P., Dietrich, K., Auinger, P., & Cox, C. (2000). Cognitive deficits associated with blood lead concentrations <10 micrograms/dL in U.S. children and adolescents. *Public Health Reports, 115*(6), 521–529.

Lapsley, D. K., Milstead, M., Quintana, S. M., Flannery, D., & Buss, R. R. (1986). Adolescent egocentrism and formal operations: Tests of a theoretical assumption. *Developmental Psychology, 22,* 800–807.

Larzelere, R. (1986). Moderate spanking: Model or deterrent of children's aggression in the family? *Journal of Family Violence, 1*(1), 27–36.

Lashley, K. S. (1938). The thalamus and emotion. *The Psychological Review, 45,* 21–61.

Lasnik, H. (1990). Metrics and morphophonemics in early English verse. *University of Connecticut Working Papers in Linguistics, Vol. 3,* 29–40. University of Connecticut, Storrs, CT.

Latané, B., & Darley, J. M. (1969). Bystander "apathy." *American Scientist, 57*(2), 244–268.

Latané, B., Williams, K., & Harkins, S. (1979). Many hands make light the work: The causes and consequences of social loafing. *Journal of Personality & Social Psychology, 37*(6), 822–832.

Lauer, J., Black, D. W., & Keen, P. (1993). Multiple personality disorder and borderline personality disorder: Distinct entities or variations on a common theme? *Annals of Clinical Psychiatry, 5,* 129–134.

Laumann, E. O., Paik, A., & Rosen, R. C. (1999). Sexual dysfunction in the United States: Prevalence and predictors. *Journal of the American Medical Association, 281*(6), 537–544.

Launer, L., Masaki, K., Petrovitch, H., Foley, D., & Havlik, R. (1995). The association between midlife blood pressure levels and late-life cognitive function. *Journal of the American Medical Association, 272*(23), 1846–1851.

Lavergne, G. M. (1997). *A sniper in the tower: The true story of the Texas Tower massacre.* New York: Bantam.

Laws, G., Davies, I., & Andrews, C. (1995). Linguistic structure and nonlinguistic cognition: English and Russian blues compared. *Language and Cognitive Processes, 10,* 59–94.

Lay, C., & Nguyen, T. T. I. (1998). The role of acculturation-related and acculturation non-specific daily hassles: Vietnamese-Canadian students and psychological distress. *Canadian Journal of Behavioural Science, 30*(3), 172–181.

Lazarus, R. S. (1991). *Emotion and adaptation.* New York: Oxford University Press.

Lazarus, R. S. (1993). From psychological stress to the emotions: A history of changing outlooks. *Annual Review of Psychology, 44,* 1–22.

Lazarus, R. S. (1999). *Stress and emotion: A new synthesis.* New York: Springer.

Lazarus, R. S., & Folkman, S. (1984). *Stress, appraisal and coping.* New York: Springer.

Leary, M. R., & Forsyth, D. R. (1987). Attributions of responsibility for collective endeavors. *Review of Personality and Social Psychology, 8,* 167–188.

Leask, J., Haber, R. N., & Haber, R. B. (1969). Eidetic imagery in children: II. Longitudinal and experimental results. *Psychonomic Monograph Supplements, 3,* 25–48.

Le Bars, P. L., Velasco, F. M., Ferguson, J. M., Dessain, E. C., Kieser, M., & Hoerr, R. (2002). Influence of the severity of cognitive impairment on the effect of the Ginkgo biloba extract EGb 761 in Alzheimer's disease. *Neuropsychobiology, 45*(1), 19–26.

Leccese, A. P., Pennings, E. J. M., & De Wolff, F. A. (2000). Combined use of alcohol and psychotropic drugs. A review of the literature. *Academisch Ziekenhuis Leiden (AZL),* Leiden.

Leclerc, C. M., & Hess, T. M. (2007). Age differences in the bases for social judgments: Tests of a social expertise perspective. *Experimental Aging Research, 33*(1), 95–120.

LeDoux, I. (1994). Emotion, memory and the brain. *Scientific American, 270,* 32–39.

LeDoux, J. (2003). The emotional brain, fear, and the amygdala. *Cellular and Molecular Neurobiology, 23*(4–5), 727–738.

Lee, F., Hallahan, M., & Herzog, T. (1996). Explaining real life events: How culture and domain shape attributions. *Personality and Social Psychology Bulletin, 22,* 732–741.

Lee, M., & Shlain, B. (1986). *Acid dreams: The complete social history of LSD: The CIA, the sixties, and beyond.* New York: Grove Press.

Lee, P. A. (1995). Physiology of puberty. In K. L. Becker (Ed.), *Principles and Practice of endocrinology and metabolism* (pp. 822–830). Philadelphia: J.B. Lippincott Company.

Lehnert, B. (2007). Joint wave-particle properties of the individual photon. *Progress in Physics, 4*(10), 104–108.

Lehr, U., & Thomae, H. (Hrsg.) (1987). Patterns of psychological aging. *Results from the Bonne Aging Longitudinal Study (BOLSA).* Stuttgart: Enke.

Leibel, R. L., Rosenbaum, M., & Hirsch, J. (1995). Changes in energy expenditure resulting from altered body weight. *The New England Journal of Medicine, 332,* 621–628.

Leon, P., Chedraui, P., Hidalgo, L., & Ortiz, F. (2007). Perceptions and attitudes toward the menopause among middle-aged women from Guayaquil, Ecuador. *Maturitas, 57*(3), 233–238.

Leonard, L. (1997). *Children with specific language impairment.* Cambridge, MA: MIT Press.

Leong, F. T. L., Hartung, P. J., Goh, D., & Gaylor, M. (2001). Appraising birth order in career assessment: Linkages to Holland's and Super's models. *Journal of Career Assessment, 9,* 25–39.

LePoncin, M. (1990). *Brain fitness.* New York: Ballantine Books.

Leroy, C., & Symes, B. (2001). Teachers' perspectives on the family backgrounds of children at risk. *McGill Journal of Education, 36*(1), 45–60.

Lesch, K. P., Bengel, D., Heils, A., Sabol, S. Z., Greenberg, B. D., Petri, S., Benjamin, J., Muller, C. R., Hamer, D. H., & Murphy, D. L. (1996). Association of anxiety-related traits with a polymorphism in the serotonin transporter gene regulatory region. *Science, 274*(5292), 1527–1531.

Leslie, M. (2000, July/August). The vexing legacy of Louis Terman. *Stanford Magazine.*

LeVay, S. (1991). A difference in hypothalamic structure between heterosexual and homosexual men. *Science, 253,* 1034–1037.

LeVay, S., & Hamer, D. (1994). Evidence for a biological influence in male homosexuality, *Scientific American, 270,* 44–49.

Levenson, R. W. (1992). Autonomic nervous system differences among emotions. *Psychological Sciences, 3,* 23–27.

Levenson, R. W., Ekman, P., Heider, K., & Friesen, W. V. (1992). Emotion and autonomic nervous system activity in the Minangkabau of West Sumatra. *Journal of Personality and Social Psychology, 62,* 972–988.

Levy, B. R., Slade, M. D., Kunkel, S. R., & Kasl, S. V. (2002). Longevity increased by positive self-perceptions of aging. *Journal of Personality and Social Psychology, 83,* 261–269.

Levy, S. R., Stroessner, S. J., & Dweck, C. S. (1998). Stereotype formation and endorsement: The role of implicit theories. *Journal of Personality and Social Psychology, 74,* 1421–1436.

Lewin, K. (1936). *Principles of topological psychology.* New York: McGraw-Hill.

Lewis, D. K. (1996, June). A cross-cultural model for psychotherapy: Working with the African-American client. *Perspectives on Multiculturalism and Cultural Diversity, VI*(2).

Lewis, J. R. (1995) *Encyclopedia of afterlife beliefs and phenomenon.* Detroit, MI: Visible Ink Press.

Like, R., Steiner, P., & Rubel, A. (1996). Recommended core curriculum guidelines on culturally sensitive and competent care. *Family Medicine, 27,* 291–297.

Lilienfeld, S., Lynn, S., & Lohr, J. (2002). *Science and pseudoscience in clinical psychology* (pp. 248–255). New York: Guilford Press.

Lilienfeld, S. O. (1999). Projective measures of personality and psychopathology: How well do they work? *Skeptical Inquirer, 23*(5), 32–39.

Lilienfeld, S. O., Lynn, S. J., & Lohr, J. M. (2004). Science and pseudoscience in clinical psychology: Initial thoughts, reflections, and considerations. In S. O. Lilienfeld, S. J. Lynn, & J. M. Lohr (Eds.), *Science and pseudoscience in clinical psychology.* New York: Guilford Press, p. 2.

Lim, J., Choo, W. C., & Chee, M. W. L. (2007). Reproducibility of changes in behavior and fMRI activation associated with sleep deprivation in a working memory task. *Sleep, 30,* 61–70.

Lin, C. S., Lyons, J. L., & Berkowitz, F. (2007). Somatotopic identification of language-SMA in language processing via fMRI. *Journal of Scientific and Practical Computing 1*(2), 3–8.

Lin, P. J., & Schwanenflugel, P. J. (1995). Cultural familiarity and language factors in the structure of category knowledge. *Journal of Cross-Cultural Psychology, 26,* 153–168.

Lin, P. J., Schwanenflugel, P. J., & Wisenbaker, J. M. (1990). Category typicality, cultural familiarity, and the development of category knowledge. *Developmental Psychology, 26,* 805–813.

Lindau, S. T., Schumm, P., Laumann, E. O., Levinson, W., O'Muircheartaigh, C. A., & Waite, L. J. (2007). A study of sexuality and health among older adults in the United States. *New England Journal of Medicine, 357*(8), 762–764.

Lindemann, B. (1996). Taste reception. *Physiological Review, 76,* 719–766.

Linden, M., Habib, T., & Radojevic, V. (1996). A controlled study of the effects of EEG biofeedback on cognition and behavior of children with attention deficit disorder and learning disabilities. *Biofeedback and Self Regulation, 21*(1), 35–49.

Lisanby, S. H., Maddox, J. H., Prudic, J., Devanand, D. P., & Sackeim, H. A. (2000). The effects of electroconvulsive therapy on memory of autobiographical and public events. *Archives of General Psychiatry, 57,* 581–590.

Livesley, J. W. (Ed.). (1995). *The DSM-IV Personality disorders.* New York: Guilford Press.

Lizskowski, U., Carpenter, M., Striano, T., & Tomasello, M. (2006). 12- and 18-month-olds point to provide information for others. *Journal of Cognition and Development, 7,* 173–187.

Lock, M. (1994). Menopause in cultural context. *Experimental Gerontology, 29*(3–4), 307–317.

Loehlin, J. C. (1992). *Genes and environment in personality development.* Newbury Park, CA: Sage.

Loehlin, J. C., McCrae, R. R., Costa, P. T., Jr., & John, O. P. (1998). Heritabilities of common and measure-specific components of the Big Five personality factors. *Journal of Research in Personality, 32,* 431–453.

Loehlin, J. C., Willerman, L., & Horn, J. M. (1985). Personality resemblances in adoptive families when the children are late-adolescent or adult. *Journal of Personality and Social Psychology, 48,* 376–392.

Loftus, E. (1975). Leading questions and the eyewitness report. *Cognitive Psychology, 7,* 560–572.

Loftus, E. (1987, June 29). Trials of an expert witness. *Newsweek.*

Loftus, E. F., Miller, D. G., & Burns H. J. (1978). Semantic integration of verbal information into a visual memory. *Journal of Experimental Psychology: Human Learning, 4,* 19–31.

Loftus, J. (2001). America's liberalization in attitudes toward homosexuality, 1973 to 1998. *American Sociological Review, 66*(5), 762–782.

Logue, M. W., Vieland, V. J., Goedken, R. J., & Crowe, R. R. (2003). Bayesian analysis of a previously published genome screen for panic disorder reveals new and compelling evidence for linkage to chromosome 7. *American Journal of Medical Genetics, 121B,* 95–99.

Lohr, J. M., Kleinknecht, R. A., Tolin, D. F., & Barrett, R. H. (1995). The empirical status of the clinical application of eye movement desensitization and reprocessing. *Journal of Behavior Therapy and Experimental Psychiatry, 26,* 285–302.

Lohr, J. M., Tolin, D. F., & Lilienfeld, S. O. (1998). Efficacy of eye movement desensitization and reprocessing: Implications for behavior therapy. *Behavior Therapy, 29,* 123–156.

Lord, T. R. (2001). 101 reasons for using cooperative learning in biology teaching. *The American Biology Teacher, 63*(1), 30–38.

Lovaas, O. I. (1964). Cue properties of words: The control of operant responding by rate and content of verbal operants. *Child Development, 35,* 245–256.

Lovaas, O. I. (1987). Behavioral treatment and normal educational and intellectual functioning in young autistic children. *Journal of Consulting and Clinical Psychology, 55,* 3–9.

Lovaas, O. I., Berberich, J. P., Perloff, B. F., & Schaffer, B. (1966). Acquisition of imitative speech by schizophrenic children. *Science, 151,* 705–707.

Lu, S., & Ende, N. (1997). Potential for clinical use of viable pluripotent progenitor cells in blood bank stored human umbilical cord blood. *Life Sciences, 61,* 1113–1123.

Lubinski, D. (2000). Scientific and social significance of assessing individual differences: "Sinking shafts at a few critical points." *Annual Review of Psychology, 51,* 405–444.

Luborsky, L., Singer, B., & Luborsky, L. (1975). Comparative studies of psychotherapies: Is it true that "everyone has won and all must have prizes"? *Archives of General Psychiatry, 32,* 995–1008.

Luchins, A. S. (1957). Primacy-recency in impression formation. In C. Hovland (Ed.), *The order of presentation in persuasion* (pp. 33–40, 55–61). New Haven, CT: Yale University Press.

Lucy, J. A., & Shweder, R. A. (1979). Whorf and his critics: Linguistic and nonlinguistic influences on color memory. *American Anthropologist, 81,* 581–615.

Luria, A. R. (1968). *The mind of a mnemonist* (pp. 24, 25). New York: Basic Books.

Lurito, J. T., Dzemidzic, M., Mathews, V. P., Lowe, M. J., Kareken, D. A., Phillips, M. D., & Wang, Y. (2000). Comparison of hemispheric lateralization using four language tasks. *Neuroimage, 11,* S358.

Lüscher, M. (1969). *The Lüscher Color Test.* New York: Random House.

Lutkenhaus, P., Grossmann, K. E., & Grossman, K. (1985). Infant–mother attachment at twelve months and style of interaction with a stranger at the age of three years. *Child Development, 56,* 1538–1542.

Lykken, D. T. (1995). *The antisocial personalities*. Hillsdale, NJ: Lawrence Erlbaum.

Lykken, D. T., & Tellegen, A. (1996). Happiness is a stochastic phenomenon. *Psychological Science, 7*, 186–189.

Lynch, E. B., Coley, J. D., & Medin, D. L. (2000). Tall is typical: Central tendency, ideal dimensions, and graded category structure among tree experts and novices. *Memory & Cognition, 28*(1), 41–50.

Lytton, H., & Romney, D. M. (1991). Parents' sex-differentiated socialization of boys and girls: A meta-analysis. *Psychological Bulletin, 109*, 267–296.

Lyubomirsky, S. (2001). Why are some people happier than others?: The role of cognitive and motivational processes in well-being. *American Psychologist, 56*, 239–249.

Lyvers, M. (2003). The neurochemistry of psychedelic experiences. *Science & Consciousness Review, 1*, 1–5.

Lyznicki, J. M., Doege, T. C., Davis, R. M., & Williams, M. A. (1998). Sleepiness, driving, and motor-vehicle crashes. Council on Scientific Affairs, American Medical Association. *Journal of the American Medical Association, 279*(23), 1908–1913.

Maccoby, E. E. (1998). *The two sexes: Growing up apart: Coming together*. Cambridge, MA: Belknap Press of Harvard University Press.

MacDonald, A. P. (1970). Internal-external locus of control and the practice of birth control. *Psychological Reports, 27*, 206.

MacDonald, D., Kabani, N., Avis, D., & Evens, A. C. (2000). Automated 3D extraction of inner and outer surfaces of cerebral cortex from MRI. *NeuroImage, 12*, 340–356.

Mack, J. E. (1994). *Abduction*. New York: Scribner.

MacKenzie, S. B., Lutz, R. J., & Belch, G. E. (1986, May). The role of attitude toward the ad as a mediator of advertising effectiveness: A test of competing explanations. *Journal of Marketing Research, 23*, 130–143.

Macquet, P., & Franck, G. (1996). Functional neuroanatomy of human rapid eye movement sleep and dreaming. *Nature, 383*, 163–166.

Macrae, C. N., & Bodenhausen, G. V. (2000). Social cognition: Thinking categorically about others. *Annual Review of Psychology, 51*, 93–120.

Madsen, K. M., Hviid, A., Vestergaard, M., Schendel, D., Wohlfahrt, J., Thorsen, P., Olsen, J., & Melbye, M. (2002). A population-based study of measles, mumps, rubella vaccine and autism. *New England Journal of Medicine, 347*, 1477–1482.

Magarinos, M., Zafar, U., Nissenson, K., & Blanco, C. (2002). Epidemiology and treatment of hypochondriasis. *CNS Drugs, 16*(1), 9–22.

Maguire, E. A., Burgess, N., Donnett, J. G., O'Keefe, J., & Frith, C. D. (1998). Knowing where things are: Parahippocampal involvement in encoding object locations in virtual large-scale space. *Journal of Cognitive Neuroscience, 10*(1), 61–76.

Mahe, V., & Dumaine, A. (2001). Oestrogen withdrawal associated psychoses. *Acta Psychiatrica Scandinavica, 104*(5), 323–331.

Mahowald, M. W., & Schenck, C. H. (1996). NREM sleep parasomnias. *Neurologic Clinics, 14*, 675–696.

Mai, J. K., Triepel, J., & Metz, J. (1987). Neurotensin in the human brain. *Neuroscience, 22*, 499–524.

Maier, S. F., & Watkins, L. R. (1998). Cytokines for psychologists: Implications of bidirectional immune-to-brain communication for understanding behavior, mood, and cognition. *Psychological Review, 105*, 83–107.

Main, M., & Cassidy, J. (1988). Categories of response to reunion with the parent at age 6: Predictable from infant attachment classifications and stable over a 1-month period. *Developmental Psychology, 24*, 415–426.

Main, M., & Hesse, E. (1990). Parents' unresolved traumatic experiences are related to infant disorganized attachment status; Is frightened and/or frightening parental behaviour the linking mechanism? In M. T. Greenberg, D. Cicchetti, & E. M. Cummings (Eds.), *Attachment in the preschool years: Theory, research and intervention* (pp. 161–182). Chicago: University of Chicago Press.

Main, M., & Solomon, J. (1990). Procedures for identifying infants as disorganized/disoriented during the Ainsworth Strange Situation. In M. T. Greenberg, D. Cicchetti, & E. M. Cummings (Eds.), *Attachment in the preschool years: Theory, research and intervention* (pp. 121–160). Chicago: University of Chicago Press.

Maisel, M., Herr, A., Milosevic, J., Hermann, A., Habisch, H-J., Schwarz, S., Kirsch, M., Antoniadis, G., Brenner, R., Hallmeyer-Elgner, S., Lerche, H., Schwarz, J., & Storch, A. (2007). Transcription profiling of adult and fetal human neuroprogenitors identifies divergent paths to maintain the neuroprogenitor. *Cell State Stem Cells, 25*(5), 1231–1240.

Makeig, S., Delorme, A., Westerfield, M., Jung, T., Townsend, J., Courchesne, E., & Sejnowski, T. J. (2004). Electronic brain dynamics following manually responded visual targets. *Public Library of Science: Biology, 2*(6), e176.

Mandler, G. (1967). Organization and memory. In K. W. Spence & J. T. Spence (Eds.), *The psychology of learning and motivation, Vol. 1* (pp. 327–372). New York: Academic Press.

Mandler, J. M. (2000). Perceptual and conceptual processes. *Journal of Cognition and Development, 1*, 3–36.

Mandler, J. M. (2003). Conceptual categorization. In D. H. Rakison & L. M. Oakes (Eds.), *Early category and concept development: Making sense of the blooming, buzzing confusion* (pp. 103–131). Oxford, England: Oxford University Press.

Manson, J., Greenland, P., LaCroix, A. Z., Stefanick, M. L., Mouton, C. P., Oberman, A., Perri, M. G., Sheps, D. S., Pettinger, M. B., & Siscovick, D. S. (2002). Walking compared with vigorous exercise for the prevention of cardiovascular events in women. *The New England Journal of Medicine, 347*(10), 716–725.

Manusov, V., & Patterson, M. L. (Eds.) (2006). *The Sage handbook of nonverbal communication* (p. 289). Thousand Oaks, CA: Sage Publications, Inc.

Manzo, L., Locatelli, C., Candura, S. M., & Costa, L. G. (1994). Nutrition and alcohol neurotoxicity. *Neurotoxicology, 15*(3), 555–565.

Maquet, P., Schwartz, S., Passingham, R., & Frith, C. (2003). Sleep-related consolidation of a visuomotor skill: Brain mechanisms as assessed by functional magnetic resonance imaging. *The Journal of Neuroscience, 23*(4), 1432.

March, J., Silva, S., Petrycki, S., Curry, J., Wells, K., Fairbank, J., Burns, B., Domino, M., McNulty, S., Vitiello, B., & Severe, J. [Treatment for Adolescents with Depression Study (TADS) Team]. (2004). Fluoxetine, cognitive-behavioral therapy, and their combination for adolescents with depression: Treatment for Adolescents with Depression Study (TADS) randomized controlled trial. *Journal of the American Medical Association, 292*(7), 807–820.

Marcus, G. F. (2001). *The algebraic mind: Integrating connectionism and cognitive science (learning, development, and conceptual change)*. Cambridge, MA: MIT Press.

Maren, S., & Fanselow, M. S. (1996). The amygdala and fear conditioning: Has the nut been cracked? *Neuron, 16*, 237–240.

Margolin, S., & Kubic, L. S. (1944). An apparatus for the use of breath sounds as a hypnogogic stimulus. *American Journal of Psychiatry, 100*, 610.

Marik, P. E. (2000). Leptin, obesity, and obstructive sleep apnea. *Chest, 118*, 569–571.

Markovitz, J. H., Lewis, C. E., Sanders, P. W., Tucker, D., & Warnock, D. G. (1997). Relationship of diastolic blood pressure with cyclic GMP excretion among young adults (the CARDIA study): Influence of a family history of hypertension. *Journal of Hypertension, 15*(9), 955–962.

Marks, D. F., Murray, M., Evans, B., Willig, C., Sykes, C. M., & Woodall, C. (2005). *Health Psychology: Theory, research & practice* (pp. 3–25). London: Sage Publications.

Mars, A. E., Mauk, J. E., & Dowrick, P. (1998). Symptoms of pervasive developmental disorders as observed in prediagnostic home videos of infants and toddlers. *Journal of Pediatrics, 132*, 500–504.

Martin, C. L. (2000). Cognitive theories of gender development. In T. Eckes & H. M. Trautner (Eds.), *The developmental social psychology of gender* (pp. 91–121). Mahwah, NJ: Lawrence Erlbaum.

Martin, J. A., & Buckwalter, J. J. (2001). Telomere erosion and senescence in human articular cartilage chondrocytes. *Journal of Gerontology and Biological Science, 56*(4), 172–179.

Martin, L. (2004). Can sleepwalking be a murder defense? Document retrieved from the Internet on October 19, 2004, at: **www.mtsinai.org/pulmonary/Sleep/sleep-murder.htm**.

Maruta, T., Colligan, R. C., Malinchoc, M., & Offord, K. P. (2002, August). Optimism-pessimism assessed in the 1960s and self-reported health status 30 years later. *Mayo Clinic Proceedings. 77*, 748–753.

Maslow, A. (1943). A theory of human motivation. *Psychological Review, 50*, 370–396.

Maslow, A. (1971). *The farther reaches of human nature.* New York: The Viking Press.

Maslow, A. (1987). *Motivation and personality* (3rd ed.). New York: Harper & Row.

Maslow, A., & Lowery, R. (Ed.). (1998). *Toward a psychology of being* (3rd ed.). New York: Wiley & Sons.

Maslow, A. H. (1943). A theory of human motivation. *Psychological Review 50,* 370–396.

Maslow, A. H. (1968). *Toward a psychology of being.* Princeton, NJ: Van Nostrand Reinhold.

Massaro, D. W., & Cowan, N. (1993). Information processing models: Microscopes of the mind. *Annual Review of Psychology, 44,* 383–426.

Masson, J. M. (1984). *The assault on truth: Freud's suppression of the seduction theory.* New York: Farrar, Straus and Giroux.

Masters, J. C., Burish, T. G., Holton, S. D., & Rimm, D. C. (1987). *Behavior therapy: Techniques and empirical finding.* San Diego: Harcourt Brace Jovanovich, Inc.

Masters, W., & Johnson, V. (1966). *Human sexual response.* Boston: Little, Brown.

Masters, W., Johnson, V., & Kolodny, R. (1995). *Human sexuality* (5th ed.). New York: HarperCollins.

Masters, W. H., & Johnson, V. E. (1970). *Human sexual inadequacy.* Boston: Little, Brown.

Masuda, T., & Kitayama, S. (2004). Perceiver-induced constraint and attitude attribution in Japan and the US: A case for the cultural dependence of the correspondence bias. *Journal of Experimental Social Psychology, 40,* 409–416.

Matsumoto, D. (1994). *People: Psychology from a cultural perspective* (pp. 144–147). Pacific Grove, CA: Brooks-Cole.

Matthews, K. A., Gump, B. B., Harris, K. F., Haney, T. L., & Barefoot, J. C. (2004). Hostile behaviors predict cardiovascular mortality among men enrolled in the Multiple Risk Factor Intervention Trial. *Circulation, 109,* 66–70.

Maurer, D., & Young, R. (1983). Newborns' following of natural and distorted arrangements of facial features. *Infant Behaviour and Development, 6,* 127–131.

Mavromatis, A. (1987). *Hypnagogia: The unique state of consciousness between wakefulness and sleep.* London: Routledge & Kegan Paul.

Mavromatis, A., & Richardson, J. T. E. (1984). Hypnagogic imagery. *International Review of Mental Imagery, 1,* 159–189.

Mayer, J. D. (September 1999). Emotional intelligence: Popular or scientific psychology? *APA Monitor Online, 30*(8) [*Shared Perspectives* column]. Washington, DC: American Psychological Association. Retrieved from the Internet on June 12, 2004, at **www.apa.org/monitor/sep99/sp.html**.

Mayer, J. D., & Geher, G. (1996). Emotional intelligence and the identification of emotion. *Intelligence, 22,* 89–113.

Mayer, J. D., Salovey, P., & Caruso, D. R. (2000). Models of emotional intelligence. In R. J. Sternberg (Ed.), *Handbook of human intelligence* (2nd ed., pp. 396–420). New York: Cambridge.

Maziade, M., Bissonnette, L., Rouillard, E., Martinez, M., Turgeon, M., Charron, L., Pouliot, V., Boutin, P., Cliché, D., Dion, C., Fournier, J. P., Garneau, Y., Lavallee, J. C., Montgrain, N., Nicole, L., Pires, A., Ponton, A. M., Potvin, A., Wallot, H., Roy, M. A., & Merette, C. (1997). 6p24–22 region and major psychoses in the Eastern Quebec population. Le Groupe IREP. *American Journal of Medical Genetics, 74,* 311–318.

Mazzoni, G. A. L., Loftus, E. F., & Kirsch, I. (2001). Changing beliefs about implausible autobiographical events: A little plausibility goes a long way. *Journal of Experimental Psychology: Applied, 7*(1), 51–59.

McAloon, M., & Lester, D. (1979). The Luscher Color Test as a measure of anxiety in juvenile delinquents. *Psychological Reports, 45,* 228.

McCann, S. J. H., & Stewin, L. L. (1988). Worry, anxiety, and preferred length of sleep. *Journal of Genetic Psychology, 149,* 413–418.

McCarthy, J. (1959). Programs with common sense. In *Mechanisation of thought processes, proceedings of the Symposium of the National Physics Laboratory* (pp. 77–84). London: Her Majesty's Stationery Office.

McCauley, C. (1998). Group dynamics in Janis's theory of groupthink: Backward and forward. *Organizational Behavior & Human Decision Processes, 73*(2–3), 142–162.

McClelland, D. C. (1961). *The achieving society.* Princeton, NJ: Van Nostrand.

McClelland, D. C. (1987). *Human motivation.* Cambridge, MA: Cambridge University Press.

McClelland, J. L., & Rumelhart, D. E. (1988). Explorations in parallel distributed processing. Cambridge, MA: MIT Press.

McCrae, R. R., & Costa, P. T. (1990). *Personality in adulthood.* New York: Guilford Press.

McCrae, R. R., & Costa, P. T., Jr. (1996). Toward a new generation of personality theories: Theoretical contexts for the five-factor model. In J. S. Wiggins (Ed.), *The five-factor model of personality: Theoretical perspectives* (pp. 51–87). New York: Guilford.

McCrae, R. R., & Terracciano, A. (2007). The Five-Factor Model and its correlates in individuals and cultures. In F. J. R. van de Vijver, D. A. van Hemert, & Y. Poortinga (Eds.), *Individuals and cultures in multi-level analysis* (pp. 247–281). Mahwah, NJ: Erlbaum.

McCrae R. R., Terracciano A., & 78 Members of the Personality Profiles of Cultures Project (2005). Universal features of personality traits from the observer's perspective: Data from 50 cultures. *Journal of Personality and Social Psychology, 88,* 547–561.

McCrae, R. R., Costa, P. T., Jr., Ostendorf, F., Angleitner, A., Hrebickova, M., Avia, M. D., Sanz, J., Sanchez-Bernardos, M. L., Kusdil, M. E., Woodfield, R., Saunders, P. R, & Smith, P. B. et al. (2000). Nature over nurture: Temperament, personality, and life span development. *Journal of Personality and Social Psychology, 78,* 173–186.

McDermott, J. F. (2001). Emily Dickinson revisited: A study of periodicity in her work. *American Journal of Psychiatry, 158*(5), 686–690.

McDonald, J., Becker, D., Sadowsky, C., Jane, J., Conturo, T., & Schultz, L. (2002). Late recovery following spinal cord injury. *Journal of Neurosurgery: Spine, 97,* 252–265.

McDougall, W. (1908). *An introduction to social psychology.* London: Methuen & Co.

McEwen, B. S. (2000). The neurobiology of stress: From serendipity to clinical relevance. *Brain Research, 886,* 172–189.

McGinn, L. K. (2000). Cognitive behavioral therapy of depression: Theory, treatment, and empirical status. *American Journal of Psychotherapy, 54,* 254–260.

McGinnis, J. M., & Foege, W. H. (1993). Actual causes of death in the United States. *Journal of the American Medical Association, 270*(18), 2207–2212.

McGrath, E., Keita, G. P., Strickland, B. R., & Russo, N. F. (1992). *Women and depression: Risk factors and treatment issues.* Washington, DC: American Psychological Association.

McGregor, D. (1960). *The human side of enterprise.* New York: McGraw-Hill.

McHugh, P. R. (1993). Multiple personality disorder. *Harvard Mental Health Newsletter, 10*(3), 4–6.

McKenzie, B. E., Tootell, H. E., & Day, R. H. (1980). Development of visual size constancy during the 1st year of human infancy. *Developmental Psychology, 16,* 163–174.

McLaughlin, S. K. & Margolskee, R. F., (1994). Vertebrate taste transduction. *American Scientist, 82,* 538–545.

McMahon, F. J., Simpson, S. G., McInnis, M. G., Badner, J. A., MacKinnon, D. F., & DePaulo, J. R. (2001). Linkage of bipolar disorder to chromosome 18q and the validity of bipolar II disorder. *Archives of General Psychiatry, 58,* 1025–1031.

McMillan, H. L., Boyle, M. H., Wong, M. Y., Duku, E. K., Fleming, J. E., & Walsh, C. A. (1999). Slapping and spanking in childhood and its association with lifetime prevalence of psychiatric disorders in a general population sample. *Canadian Medical Association Journal, 161,* 805–809.

McMonagle, T., & Sultana, A. (2002). Token economy for schizophrenia (Cochrane Review). In *The Cochrane Library, Issue 2.* Oxford: Update Software.

McPherson, M., Smith-Lovin, L., & Cook, J. M. (2001). Birds of a feather: Homophily in social networks. *Annual Review of Sociology, 27,* 415–444.

Meador, B. D., & Rogers, C. R. (1984). Person-centered therapy. In R. J. Corsini (Ed.), *Current psychotherapies* (3rd ed., pp. 142–195). Itasca, IL: Peacock Publishers.

Meadow, P. W., & Clevans, E. G. (1978). A new approach to psychoanalytic teaching. *Modern Psychoanalysis, 3*(1), 29–43.

Medical Economics Staff. (1994). *PDR family guide to women's health & prescription drugs.* Montvale, NJ: Medical Economics Company.

Medicine, B. (2002). Directions in gender research in American Indian societies: Two spirits and other categories. In W. J. Lonner, D. L. Dinnel, S. A. Hayes, & D. N. Sattler (Eds.), *Online Readings in Psychology and Culture* (Unit 3, Chapter 2), (www.wwu.edu/~culture), Center for Cross-Cultural Research, Western Washington University, Bellingham, WA.

Mehrabian, A. (2000). Beyond IQ: Broad-based measurement of individual success potential or "emotional intelligence." *Genetic, Social, and General Psychology Monographs, 126*, 133–239.

Meichenbaum, D. (1996). Stress inoculation training for coping with stressors. *The Clinical Psychologist, 49*, 4–7.

Meltzoff, A. N. (1990). Foundations for developing a concept of self: The role of imitation in relating self to other and the value of social mirroring, social modeling, and self practice in infancy. In D. Cicchetti & M. Beeghly (Eds.), *The self in transition: Infancy to childhood* (pp. 139–164). Chicago: University of Chicago Press.

Meltzoff, A. N. (2007). "Like me": A foundation for social cognition. *Developmental Science, 10*(1) 126–134.

Meltzoff, A. N., & Moore, M. K. (1989). Imitation in newborn infants: Exploring the range of gestures imitated and the underlying mechanisms. *Developmental Psychology, 25*, 954–962.

Melzack, R., & Wall, P. D. (1965). Pain mechanisms: A new theory. *Science, 150*, 971–979.

Melzack, R., & Wall, P. D. (1996). *The challenge of pain*. London: Penguin Books.

Menon, T., Morris, M., Chiu, C. Y., & Hong, Y. I. (1999). Culture and the construal of agency: Attribution to individual versus group dispositions. *Journal of Personality and Social Psychology, 76*, 701–727.

Merikle, M. P. (2000). Subliminal perception. In A. E. Kazdin (Ed.), *Encyclopedia of Psychology* (vol. 7, pp. 497–499). New York: Oxford University Press.

Merriam-Webster. (2003). *Merriam-Webster's collegiate dictionary*, 11th ed. Merriam-Webster, Publisher. Springfield, MA.

Merskey, H. (1992). The manufacture of personalities: The production of multiple personality disorder. *British Journal of Psychiatry, 160*, 327–340.

Mertens, R., & Allen, J. J. (2007). The role of psychophysiology in forensic assessments: Deception detection, ERPs, and virtual reality mock crime scenarios. *Psychophysiology, 45*(2): 286–298.

Mervis, C. B., & Rosch, E. (1981). Categorization of natural objects. *Annual Review of Psychology, 32*, 89–115.

Meyrick, J. (2001). Forget the blood and gore: An alternative message strategy to help adolescents avoid cigarette smoking. *Health Education, 101*(3), 99–107.

Mezzich, J. E., Kleinman, A., Fabrega, H., & Parron, D. L. (1996). *Culture and psychiatric diagnosis*. Washington, DC: American Psychiatric Association.

Michaels, J. W., Blommel, J. M., Brocato, R. M., Linkous, R. A., & Rowe, J. S. (1982). Social facilitation and inhibition in a natural setting. *Replications in Social Psychology, 2*, 21–24.

Miles, D. R., & Carey, G. (1997). Genetic and environmental architecture of human aggression. *Journal of Personality and Social Psychology, 72*, 207–217.

Milgram, S. (1964a). Behavioral study of obedience. *Journal of Abnormal and Social Psychology, 67*, 371–378.

Milgram, S. (1964b). Issues in the study of obedience: A reply to Baumrind. *American Psychologist, 19*, 848–852.

Milgram, S. (1974). *Obedience to authority: An experimental view*. New York: Harper and Row.

Miller, G. A. (1956). The magical number seven, plus or minus two: Some limits on our capacity for processing information. *Psychological Review, 63*, 81–97.

Miller, J. G. (1984). Culture and the development of everyday social explanation. *Journal of Personality and Social Psychology, 46*, 961–978.

Miller, K., & Doman, J. M. R. (1996, April). Together forever. *Life Magazine*, 46–56.

Miller, K. E., & Graves, J. C. (2000). Update on the prevention and treatment of sexually transmitted diseases. *American Family Physician, 61*, 379–386.

Miller, L. H., & Smith, A. D. (1993). *The stress solution*. New York: Pocket Books.

Miller, M., & Kantrowitz, B. (1999, January 25). Unmasking Sybil: A re-examination of the most famous psychiatric patient in history. *Newsweek*.

Miller, M., & Rahe, R. H. (1997). Life changes scaling for the 1990s. *Journal of Psychosomatic Research, 43*(3), 279–292.

Miller, M. E., & Bowers, K. S. (1993). Hypnotic analgesia: Dissociated experience or dissociated control? *Journal of Abnormal Psychology, 102*, 29–38.

Miller, M. N., & Pumariega, A. (1999). Culture and eating disorders. *Psychiatric Times, 16*(2), 1–4.

Miller, N. E., Sears, R. R., Mowrer, O. H., Doob, L. W., & Dollard, J. (1941). The frustration-aggression hypothesis. *Psychological Review, 48*, 337–342.

Miller, T. Q., Smith, T. W., Turner, C. W., Guijarro, M. L., & Hallet, A.J. (1996). A meta-analytic review of research on hostility and physical health. *Psychological Bulletin, 119*, 322–348.

Miller, T. Q., Turner, C. W., Tindale, R. S., Posavac, E. J., & Dugoni, B. L. (1991). Reasons for the trend toward null findings in research on Type A behavior. *Psychological Bulletin, 110*, 469–485.

Mills, M. A., Edmondson, D., & Park, C. L. (2007). Trauma and stress response among Hurricane Katrina evacuees. *American Journal of Public Health, 97*(1), 116–123.

Milner, B., Corkin, S., & Teuber, H. L. (1968). Further analysis of the hippocampal syndrome: 14-year follow-up study of H. M. *Neuropsychologia, 6*, 215–234.

Milner, J. (1992, January). Risk for physical child abuse: Adult factors. *Violence Update*.

Milton, J., & Wiseman, R. (2001). Does psi exist? Reply to Storm and Ertel (2001). *Psychological Bulletin, 127*, 434–438.

Miner, M. H., & Dwyer, S. M. (1997). The psychosocial development of sex offenders: Differences between exhibitionists, child molesters, and incest offenders. *International Journal of Offender Therapy and Comparative Criminology, 41*, 36–44.

Mintz, L. B., & Betz, N. E. (1988). Prevalence and correlates of eating disordered behaviors among undergraduate women. *Journal of Counseling Psychology, 35*, 463–471.

Mischel, W. (1966). A social learning view of sex differences in behaviour. In E. E. Maccoby (Ed.), *The development of sex differences* (pp. 56–81). Stanford, CA: Stanford University Press.

Mischel, W., & Shoda, Y. (1995). A cognitive-affective system theory of personality: Reconceptualizing situations, dispositions, dynamics, and invariances in personality structure. *Psychological Review, 102*, 246–268.

Mishell, D. R. (2001). Menopause. In M. A. Stenchever, et al. (Eds.), *Comprehensive gynecology* (4th ed., pp. 1217–1258). St. Louis: Mosby.

Mitchell, J. E. (1985). *Anorexia nervosa & bulimia, diagnosis and treatment*. Minneapolis, MN: University of Minnesota Press.

Mitchell, S. A., & Black, M. J. (1996). *Freud and beyond: A history of modern psychoanalytic thought*. New York: HarperCollins Publishers, reprint edition.

Miyatake, A., Morimoto Y., Oishi, T., Hanasaki, N., Sugita, Y., Iijima, S., Teshima. Y., Hishikawa, Y., & Yamamura, Y. (1980). Circadian rhythm of serum testosterone and its relation to sleep: Comparison with the variation in serum luteinizing hormone, prolactin, and cortisol in normal men. *Journal of Clinical Endocrinology and Metabolism, 51*(6), 1365–1371.

Moffic, H. S. (2003). Seven ways to improve "cultural competence." *Current Psychiatry, 2*(5), 78.

Mogil, J. S. (1999). The genetic mediation of individual differences in sensitivity to pain and its inhibition. *Proceedings of the National Academy of Sciences of the United States of America, 96*(14), 7744–7751.

Mokdad, A. H., Bowman, B. A., Ford, E. S., Dietz, W. H., Vinicor, F., Bales, V. S., & Marks, J. S. (2001). Prevalence of obesity, diabetes, and obesity related health risk factors. *Journal of the American Medical Association, 289*, 76–79.

Moldofsky, H. (1995). Sleep and the immune system. *International Journal of Immunopharmacology, 17*(8), 649–654.

Moll, H., & Tomasello, M. (2007). How 14- and 18-month-olds know what others have experienced. *Developmental Psychology, 43*, 309–317.

Möller, A., & Hell, D. (2002). Eugen Bleuler and forensic psychiatry. *International Journal of Law and Psychiatry*, 25, 351–360.

Monastra, V. J., Monastra, D. M., & George, S. (2002). The effects of stimulant therapy, EEG biofeedback, and parenting style on the primary symptoms of attention-deficit/hyperactivity disorder. *Applied Psychophysiology & Biofeedback, 27*(4), 231–249.

Money, J. (1994). *Sex errors of the body and related syndromes*. Baltimore: Paul H. Brookes Publishing Co.

Money, J., & Mathews, D. (1982). Prenatal exposure to virilizing progestins: An adult follow-up study of 12 women. *Archives of Sexual Behavior, 11*(1), 73–83.

Money, J., & Norman, B. F. (1987). Gender identity and gender transposition: Longitudinal outcome study of 24 male hermaphrodites assigned as boys. *Journal of Sex and Marriage Therapy, 13*, 75–79.

Montgomery, R. W., & Ayllon, T. (1994). Eye movement desensitization across subjects: Subjective and physiological measures of treatment efficacy. *Journal of Behavior Therapy and Experimental Psychiatry, 25*, 217–230.

Moody, R., & Perry, P. (1993). *Reunions: Visionary encounters with departed loved ones.* London: Little, Brown and Company.

Moore, T. E. (1988). The case against subliminal manipulation. *Psychology and Marketing, 5*, 297–316.

Moore, T. H., Zammit, S., Lingford-Hughes, A., Barnes, T. R., Jones, P. B., Burke, M., & Lewis, G. (2007). Cannabis use and risk of psychotic or affective mental health outcomes: A systematic review. *Lancet, 370*, 293–294, 319–328.

Moore-Ede, M. C., Sulzman, F. M., & Fuller, C. A. (1982). *The clocks that time us.* Cambridge, MA: Harvard University Press.

Moorhead, G., Neck, C. P., & West, M. S. (1998). The tendency toward defective decision making within self-managing teams: The relevance of groupthink for the 21st century. *Organizational Behavior & Human Decision Processes, 73*(2–3), 327–351.

Mora, G. (1985). History of psychiatry. In H. I. Kaplan & B. J. Sadock (Eds.), *Comprehensive textbook of psychiatry* (pp. 2034–2054). Baltimore: Williams & Wilkins.

Moreland, R. L., & Zajonc, R. B. (1982). Exposure effects in person perceptions: Familiarity, similarity, and attraction. *Journal of Experimental Social Psychology, 18*(5), 395–415.

Morgan, C. D., & Murray, H. A. (1935). A method for investigating fantasies: The Thematic Apperception Test. *Archives of Neurology and Psychiatry, 34*, 298–306.

Morin, C. M., Bootzin, R. R., Buysse, D. J., Edinger, J. D., Espie, C. A., & Lichstein, K. L. (2006). Psychological and behavioral treatment of insomnia: Update of the recent evidence (1998–2004). *Sleep, 29*(11), 1398–1414.

Morris, J. S., Friston, K. J., Buche, L. C., Frith, C. D., Young, A. W., Calder, A. J., & Dolan, R. J. (1998). A neuromodulatory role for the human amygdala in processing emotional facial expressions. *Brain, 121*, 47–57.

Morris, M., Nisbett, R. E., & Peng, K. (1995). Causal understanding across domains and cultures. In D. Sperber, D. Premack, & A. J. Premack (Eds.), *Causal cognition: A multidisciplinary debate* (pp. 577–612). Oxford: Oxford University Press.

Morris, M. W., & Peng, K. (1994). Culture and cause: American and Chinese attributions social and physical events. *Journal of Personality and Social Psychology, 67*, 949–971.

Morrison, J. (1995). *The clinician's guide to diagnosis.* New York: Guilford Press.

Moruzzi, G., & Magoun, H. W. (1949). Brainstem reticular formation and activation of the EEG. *Electroencephalographs in Clinical Neurophysiology, 1*, 455–473.

Mowat, F. (1988). *Woman in the mists: The story of Dian Fossey and the mountain gorillas of Africa.* New York: Warner Baooks.

Mueller, H. H., Donaldson, C. C. S., Nelson, D. V., & Layman, M. (2001). Treatment of fibromyalgia incorporating EEG-driven stimulation: A clinical outcomes study. *Journal of Clinical Psychology, 57*(7), 933–952.

Mueser, K. T., Rosenberg, St. D., Xie, H., Jankowski, M. K., Bolton, E. E., Lu, E., Hamblen, J. L., Rosenberg, H. J., McHugo, G. J., & Wolfe, R. (2008). A randomized controlled trial of cognitive-behavioral treatment for posttraumatic stress disorder in severe mental illness. *Journal of Consulting and Clinical Psychology, 76*(2), 259–271.

Muhlberger, A., Herrmann, M. J., Wiedemann, G. C., Ellgring. H., & Pauli, P. (2001). Repeated exposure of flight phobics to flights in virtual reality. *Behaviour Research and Therapy, 39* (9), 1033–1050.

Muller-Oerlinghausen, B., Berghofer, A., & Bauer, M. (2002). Bipolar disorder. *Lancet, 359*, 241–247.

Munroe, R. (1980). Male transvestism and the couvade: A psychocultural analysis. *Ethos, 8*, 49–59.

Murdock, B. B., Jr. (1962). The serial position effect in free recall. *Journal of Experimental Psychology, 64*, 482–488.

Muris, P., Harald, M., Irit, H., & Sijsenaar, M. (1998). Treating phobic children: Effects of EMDR versus exposure. *Journal of Consulting and Clinical Psychology, 66*, 193–198.

Murphy, C. C., Boyle, C., Schendel, D., Decouflé, P., & Yeargin-Allsopp, M. (1998). Epidemiology of mental retardation in children. *Mental Retardation and Developmental Disabilities Research Reviews, 4*, 6–13.

Murphy, K. R., & LeVert, S. (1995). *Out of the fog: Treatment options and coping strategies for adult attention deficit disorder.* New York: Hyperion.

Murphy, L. R. (1995). Managing job stress: An employee assistance/human resource management partnership. *Personnel Review, 24*(1), 41–50.

Murphy, M., & Donavan, S. (1997). *The physical and psychological effects of meditation: A review of contemporary research with a comprehensive bibliography.* Petaluma, CA: Institute of Noetic Sciences.

Murray, C. J. L., & Lopez, A. D. (Eds.). (1996). *Summary: The global burden of disease: A comprehensive assessment of mortality and disability from diseases, injuries, and risk factors in 1990 and projected to 2020.* Cambridge, MA: Published by the Harvard School of Public Health on behalf of the World Health Organization and the World Bank, Harvard University Press.

Murray, S. L., Holmes, J. G., MacDonald, G., & Ellsworth, P. C. (1998). Through the looking glass darkly? When self-doubts turn into relationship insecurities. *Journal of Personality and Social Psychology, 75*, 1459–1480.

Muter, P. (1978). Recognition failure of recallable words in semantic memory. *Memory & Cognition, 6*(1), 9–12.

Myers, D. (1993). *The pursuit of happiness: Who is happy, and why?* New York: Avon.

Nadeau, K. G. (1995). *A comprehensive guide to attention deficit disorder in adults: Research, diagnosis, and treatment.* New York: Brunner/Mazel.

Nadeau, K. G., Quinn, P., & Littman, E. (2001). *AD/HD Self-Rating Scale for Girls.* Springfield, MD: Advantage Books.

Naitoh, P., Kelly, T. L., & Englund, C. E. (1989). *Health effects of sleep deprivation.* Naval Health Research Centre, Report No. 89–46.

Narrow, W. E., Rae, D. S., Robbins, L. N., & Regier, D. A. (2002). Revised prevalence estimates of mental disorders in the United States. *Archives of General Psychiatry, 59*, 115–123.

Nasar, S. (1998). *A beautiful mind: A biography of John Forbes Nash, Jr., winner of the Nobel Prize in economics 1994.* New York: Simon & Schuster.

National Center for Health Statistics (NCHS) (2007). Alcohol use. Retrieved from the Internet on July 25, 2007, at **http://www.cdc.gov/nchs/fastats/alcohol.htm.**

National College Athletic Association (2002). 2002 NCAA Graduation Rates Report. Retrieved September 21, 2007, from NCAA—The National Collegiate Athletic Association: The Online Resource for the National Collegiate Athletic Association Web site: **http://www.ncaa.org/grad_rates/2002/.**

National Commission on Sleep Disorders. (1997). Lack of sleep America's top health problem, doctors say. CNN Interactive: Health Story Page. Retrieved from the Internet on October 19, 2004, at **www.cnn.com/HEALTH/9703/17/nfm/ sleep.deprivation/index.html.**

National Institute of Mental Health (NIMH). (2001). The numbers count: Mental disorders in America. *NIH Publication No. 01-4584.* Bethesda, MD.

National Institute on Alcoholism and Alcohol Abuse (NIAAA) (2007). Data/ Statistical Tables. Retrieved from the Internet on July 25, 2007, at **http://www.niaaa.nih.gov/Resources/DatabaseResources/QuickFacts/default.htm.**

National Institute on Drug Abuse (NIDA). (2002). Research report series— Prescription drugs: Abuse and addiction. National Institutes of Health (NIH). Retrieved from the Internet on July 19, 2008, at **www.drugabuse.gov/ ResearchReports/Prescription/prescription5.html.**

National Institutes of Health. (1998). *Understanding vaccines.* NIH Publication #98–4219.

National Institutes of Health. (2007). *Stem cell basics.* Retrieved from the Internet on February 6, 2008, at **http://stemcells.nih.gov/info/basics/.**

Neale, M. C., Rushton, J. P., & Fulker, D. W. (1986). The heritability of items from the Eysenck Personality Questionnaire. *Personality and Individual Differences, 7*, 771–779.

Neary, N. M., Goldstone, A. P., & Bloom, S. R. (2004). Appetite regulations: From the gut to the hypothalamus. *Clinical Endocrinology, 60*(2), 153–160.

Neimark, J. (1996). The diva of disclosure, memory researcher Elizabeth Loftus. *Psychology Today, 29*(1), 48–80.

Neimeyer, R. A., & Mitchell, K. A. (1998). Similarity and attraction: A longitudinal study. *Journal of Social and Personality Relationships, 5*, 131–148.

Neisser, U. (1982). Snapshots or benchmarks? In U. Neisser (Ed.), *Memory observed: Remembering in natural contexts* (pp. 43–48). San Francisco: W. H. Freeman.

Neisser, U., & Harsch, N. (1992). Phantom flashbulbs: False recollections of hearing the news about *Challenger.* In E. Winograd & U. Neisser (Eds.), *Affect and accuracy in recall: Studies of "flashbulb memories"* (pp. 9–31). New York: Cambridge University Press.

Neisser, U., Boodoo, G., Bouchard, T. J., Boykin, A. W., Brody, N., Ceci, S. J., Halpern, D. F., Loehlin, J. C., Perloff, R., Sternberg, R. J., & Urbina, S. (1996). Intelligence: Knowns and unknowns. *American Psychologist, 51*, 77–101.

Nelson, D. B., Sammel, M. D., Freeman, E. W., Lin, H., Gracia, C. R., & Schmitz, K. H. (2008). Effect of physical activity on menopausal symptoms among urban women. *Medicine & Science in Sports & Exercise, 40*(1), 50–58.

Nelson, K. (1993). The psychological and social origins of autobiographical memory. *Psychological Science, 4*, 7–14.

Nestor, P. G., Kubicki, M., Niznikiewicz, M., Gurrera, R. J., McCarley, R. W., & Shenton, M. E. (2008). Neuropsychological disturbance in schizophrenia: A diffusion tensor imaging study. *Neuropsychology, 22*(2), 246–254.

Neto, F. (1995). Conformity and independence revisited. *Social Behavior and Personality, 23*(3), 217–222.

Neumarker, K. (1997). Mortality and sudden death in anorexia nervosa. *International Journal of Eating Disorders, 21*, 205–212.

Neumeister, A., Bain, E., Nugent, A. C., Carson, R. E., Bonne, O., Luckenbaugh, D. A., Eckelman, W., Herscovitch, P., Charney, D. S., & Drevets, W. C. (2004). Reduced serotonin Type 1_a receptor binding in panic disorder. *The Journal of Neuroscience, 24*(3), 589–591.

Neville, H. J., & Bavelier, D. (2000). Specificity and plasticity in neurocognitive development in humans. In M. S. Gazzaniga (Ed.), *The New Cognitive Neurosciences* (2nd ed., pp. 83–99). Cambridge, MA: The MIT Press.

Nicholson, N., Cole, S., & Rocklin, T. (1985). Conformity in the Asch situation: A comparison between contemporary British and US students. *British Journal of Social Psychology, 24*, 59–63.

Nickerson, R. S., & Adams, J. J. (1979). Long-term memory for a common object. *Cognitive Psychology, 11*, 287–307.

Nieto, F., Young, T. B., Lind, B. K., Shahar, E., Samet, J. M., Redline, S., D'Agostino, R. B., Newman, A. B., Lebowitz, M. D., & Pickering, T. G. (2000). Association of sleep-disordered breathing, sleep apnea, and hypertension in a large, community-based study. *Journal of the American Medical Association, 283*(14), 1829–1836.

Nigg, J. T., & Goldsmith, H. H. (1994). Genetics of personality disorders: Perspectives from personality and psychopathology research. *Psychological Bulletin, 115*, 346–380.

Nikolajsen, L., & Jensen, T. S. (2001). Phantom limb pain. *British Journal of Anaesthesia, 87*, 107–116.

Nijenhuis, E. R. (2000). Somatoform dissociation: Major symptoms of dissociative disorders. *Journal of Trauma and Dissociation, 1*(4), 7–29.

NIMH Genetics Workgroup. (1998). *Genetics and mental disorders*. NIH Publication No. 98-4268. Rockville, MD: National Institute of Mental Health.

Nisbett, R. E. (1972). Hunger, obesity, and the ventromedial hypothalamus. *Psychological Review, 79*, 433–453.

Nolen-Hoeksema, S. (1990). *Sex differences in depression*. Palo Alto, CA: Stanford University Press.

Norenzayan, A., Choi, I., & Nisbett, R. E. (1999). Eastern and Western perceptions of causality for social behavior: Lay theories about personalities and situations. In D. A. Prentice & D. T. Miller (Eds.), *Cultural divides* (pp. 239–272). New York: Russell Sage Foundation.

Norrbrink Budh, C., Lund, I., Hultling, C., Levi, R., Werhagen, L., Ertzgaard, P., & Lundeberg, T. (2003). Gender-related differences in pain in spinal cord injured individuals. *Spinal Cord, 41*, 122–128.

Norris, S. L., Lee, C. T., Burshteyn, D., & Cea-Aravena, J. (2001). The effects of performance enhancement training on hypertension, human attention, stress, and brain wave patterns: A case study. *Journal of Neurotherapy, 4*(3), 29–44.

Novak, J. D. (1995). Concept mapping: A strategy for organizing knowledge. In S. M. Glynn & R. Duit (Eds.), *Learning science in the schools: Research reforming practice* (pp. 229–245). Mahwah, NJ: Lawrence Erlbaum Associates.

Nyberg, L., & Tulving, E. (1996). Classifying human long-term memory: Evidence from converging dissociations. *European Journal of Cognitive Psychology, 8*(2), 163–183.

Oberman, L. M. & Ramachandran, V. S. (2007). The simulating social mind: The role of simulation in the social and communicative deficits of autism spectrum disorders. *Psychological Bulletin, 133*, 310–327.

Oberman, L. M., Hubbard, E. M., McCleery, J. P., Altschuler, E. L., Ramachandran, V. S., & Pineda, J. A. (2005). EEG evidence for mirror neuron dysfunction in autism. *Cognitive Brain Research, 24*, 190–198.

Ocholla-Ayayo, A. B. C., Wekesa, J. M., & Ottieno, J. A. M. (1993). *Adolescent pregnancy and its implications among ethnic groups in Kenya*. International Population Conference, Montreal, Canada: International Union for the Scientific Study of Population.

Ochsner, K., & Kosslyn, S. M. (1994). Mental imagery. In V. S. Ramaschandran (Ed.), *Encyclopedia of human behavior*. New York: Academic Press.

O'Connor, R. D. (1972). Relative efficacy of modeling, shaping, and the combined procedures for modification of social withdrawal. *Journal of Abnormal Psychology, 79*, 327–334.

Offit, P. A., & Bell, L. M. (1998). *What every parent should know about vaccines*. New York: Macmillan.

Ofshe, R., & Watters, E. (1994). *Making monsters: False memories, psychotherapy and sexual hysteria*. New York: Scribners.

Olin, B. R. (Ed.). (1993). Central nervous system drugs, sedatives and hypnotics, barbiturates. In *Facts and comparisons drug information* (pp. 1398–1413). St. Louis, MO: Facts and Comparisons.

Oliver, J. E. (1993). Intergenerational transmission of child abuse: Rates, research, and clinical interpretations. *American Journal of Psychiatry, 150*, 1315–1324.

Ollendick, T. H., & King, N. J. (1998). Empirically supported treatments for children with phobic and anxiety disorders: Current status. *Journal of Clinical Child Psychology, 27*(2), 156–167.

Olsen, P. (1975). *Emotional flooding*. Baltimore, MD: Penguin Books.

Olson, H. C., & Burgess, D. M. (1997). Early intervention for children prenatally exposed to alcohol and other drugs. In M. J. Guralnick (Ed.), *The effectiveness of early intervention* (pp. 109–146). Baltimore: Brookes.

Oman, C. M. (1990). Motion sickness: A synthesis and evaluation of the sensory conflict theory. *Canadian Journal of Physiological Pharmacology, 68*, 294–303.

Onken, L. S., Blaine, J. D., & Battjes, R. J. (1997). Behavioral therapy research: A conceptualization of a process. In S. W. Henggeler & A.B. Santos (Eds.), *Innovative approaches for difficult-to-treat populations* (pp. 477–485). Washington, DC: American Psychiatric Press.

Oswald, I. (1959). Sudden bodily jerks on falling asleep. *Brain, 82*, 92–103.

Oswalt, R., Anderson, M., Hagstrom, K., & Berkowitz, B. (1993). Evaluation of the one-session eye-movement desensitization reprocessing procedure for eliminating traumatic memories. *Psychological Reports, 73*, 99–104.

Overeem, S., Mignot, E., Gert van Dijk, J., & Lammers, G. J. (2001). Narcolepsy: Clinical features, new pathophysiological insights, and future perspectives. *Journal of Clinical Neurophysiology, 18*(2), 78–105.

Overmier, J. B., & Seligman, M. E. P. (1967). Effects of inescapable shock on subsequent escape and avoidance behavior. *Journal of Comparative Physiology and Psychology, 63*, 23–33.

Owen, M. T., Easterbrooks, M. A., Chase-Lansdale, L., & Goldberg, W. A. (1984). The relation between maternal employment status and the stability of attachments to mother and to father. *Child Development, 55*, 1894–1901.

Padayatty, S. J., & Levine, M. (2001). New insights into the physiology and pharmacology of vitamin C [editorial]. *Canadian Medical Association Journal, 164*(3), 353–355.

Padian, N. S., Shiboski, S. C., & Jewell, N. P. (1991). Female-to-male transmission of human immunodeficiency virus. *Journal of the American Medical Association, 266*(12), 1664–1667.

Paivio, A. (1971). *Imagery and verbal processes*. New York: Holt, Rinehart & Winston.

Paivio, A. (1986). *Mental representations: A dual coding approach*. New York: Oxford University Press.

Palmer, S. E. (1992). Common region: A new principle of perceptual grouping. *Cognitive Psychology, 24*(3), 436–447.

Pan, A. S. (2000). Body image, eating attitudes, and eating behaviors among Chinese, Chinese-American and non-Hispanic White women. *Dissertation Abstracts International, Section B: The Sciences and Engineering, 61*(1-B), 544.

Papousek, I., & Schulter, G. (2002). Covariations of EEG asymmetries and emotional states indicate that activity at frontopolar locations is particularly affected by state factors. *Psychophysiology 39*, 350–360.

Pargament, K. I. (1997). *The psychology of religion and coping: Theory, research, and practice*. New York: Guilford.

Paris, J. (2004). Gender differences in personality traits and disorders. *Current Psychiatry Reports, 6*, 71–74.

Park, J., Turnbull, A. P., & Turnbull, H. R. (2002). Impacts of poverty on quality of life in families of children with disabilities. *Exceptional Children, 68,* 151–170.

Parkinson, W. L., & Weingarten, H. P. (1990). Dissociative analysis of ventromedial hypothalamic obesity syndrome. *American Journal of Physiology: Regulatory, Integrative, and Comparative Physiology, 259,* R829–R835.

Parobek, V. M. (1997). Distinguishing conversion disorder from neurologic impairment. *Journal of Neuroscience Nursing, 29*(2), 128.

Partonen, T., & Lonnqvist, J. (1998). Seasonal affective disorder. *Lancet, 352*(9137), 1369–1374.

Paul, B. M., Elvevåg, B., Bokat, C. E., Weinberger, D. R., & Goldberg, T. E. (2005). Levels of processing effects on recognition memory in patients with schizophrenia. *Schizophrenia Research, 74*(1), 101–110.

Paunonen, S. V., Keinonen, M., Trzbinski, J., Forsterling, F., Grishenko-Roze, N., Kouznetsova, L., & Chan, D. W., et al. (1996). The structure of personality in six cultures. *Journal of Cross Cultural Psychology, 27,* 339–353.

Pavlov, I. (1926). *Conditioned reflexes.* London: Oxford University Press.

Pavlov, I. P. (1906). The scientific investigation of the psychical faculties or processes in the higher animals. *Science, 24,* 613–619.

Peng, K., Ames, D. R., & Knowles, E. D. (2000). Culture and human inference: Perspectives from three traditions. In D. Matsumoto (Ed.), (2001). *The handbook of culture and psychology* (pp. 245–264). New York: Oxford University Press.

Penn, D. L. (1998). Assessment and treatment of social dysfunction in schizophrenia. *Clinicians Research Digest, Supplemental Bulletin, 18,* 1–2.

Peplau, L. A., & Taylor, S. E. (1997). *Sociocultural perspectives in social psychology: Current readings.* Upper Saddle River, NJ: Prentice-Hall.

Pepperberg, I. M. (1998). Talking with Alex: Logic and speech in parrots. *Scientific American Presents: Exploring Intelligence, 9*(4), 60–65.

Pepperberg, I. M. (2005). An avian perspective on language evolution: Implications of simultaneous development of vocal and physical object combinations by a grey parrot (*Psittacus erithacus*). In M. Tallerman (Ed.), *Language origins: Perspectives on evolution* (pp. 239–261). New York: Oxford University Press.

Pepperberg, I. M. (2007). Grey parrots do not always "parrot": The roles of imitation and phonological awareness in the creation of new labels from existing vocalizations. *Language Sciences, 29*(1), 1–13.

Pereira, M. A., Kartashov, A. I., Van Horn, L., Slattery, M., Jacobs, D. R. Jr., & Ludwig, D. S. (2003). Eating breakfast may reduce risk of obesity, diabetes, heart disease. Paper presented March 6 at the American Heart Association's 2003 Annual Conference on Cardiovascular Disease Epidemiology and Prevention in Miami, FL.

Perls, F. (1951). *Gestalt therapy.* New York: Julian Press.

Perls, F. (1969). *Gestalt therapy verbatim.* Moab, UT: Real People Press.

Perlstein, W. M., Carter, C. S., Noll, D. C., & Cohen, J. D. (2001). Relation of prefrontal cortex dysfunction to working memory and symptoms in schizophrenia. *American Journal of Psychiatry, 156,* 1105–1113.

Perrin, S., & Spencer, C. (1980). The Asch effect—a child of its time. *Bulletin of the British Psychological Society, 33,* 405–406.

Persaud, R. (2001). *Staying sane: How to make your mind work for you.* New York: Bantam.

Peters, W. A. (1971). *A class divided.* Garden City, NY: Doubleday.

Peterson, L. R., & Peterson, M. J. (1959). Short-term retention of individual items. *Journal of Experimental Psychology, 58,* 193–198.

Petitto, L. A., & Marentette, P. F. (1991). Babbling in the manual mode: Evidence for the ontogeny of language. *Science, 251,* 1493–1496.

Petitto, L. A., Holowka, S., Sergio, L. E., & Ostry, D. (2001). Language rhythms in baby hand movements. *Nature, 413,* 35.

Petrakis, I. L, Gonzalez, G., Rosenheck, R., & Krystal, J. H. (2002). Comorbidity of alcoholism and psychiatric disorders. *Alcohol Research and Health, 26*(2), 81–89.

Petri, H. (1996). *Motivation: Theory, research and application* (4th ed.). Belmont, CA: Wadsworth.

Petrova, P. K., Cialdini, R. B., & Sills, S. J. (2003). Compliance, consistency, and culture: Personal consistency and compliance across cultures. *Journal of Experimental Social Psychology* [submitted]. Retrieved from the Internet on August 6, 2004, at **www.public.asu.edu/~liulang/Compliance.pdf**.

Pettigrew, T. F., & Tropp, L. R. (2000). Does intergroup contact reduce prejudice? Recent meta-analytic findings. In S. Oskamp (Ed.), *Reducing prejudice and discrimination: Social psychological perspectives* (pp. 93–114). Mahwah, NJ: Erlbaum.

Petty, R., & Cacioppo, J. (1986). *Communication and persuasion: Central and peripheral routes to attitude change.* New York: Springer-Verlag.

Petty, R., & Cacioppo, J. (1996). *Attitudes and persuasion: Classic and contemporary approaches* (reprint). Boulder, CO: Westview Press.

Petty, R. E. (1995). Attitude change. In A. Tesser (Ed.), *Advances in social psychology* (pp. 194–255). New York: McGraw-Hill.

Petty, R. E., Wheeler, S. C., & Tormala, Z. L. (2003). Persuasion and attitude change. In T. Millon & M. J. Lerner (Eds.), *Handbook of psychology: Volume 5: Personality and social psychology* (pp. 353–382). Hoboken, NJ: John Wiley & Sons.

Pezdek, K., & Hodge, D. (1999). Planting false childhood memories in children: The role of event plausibility. *Child Development, 70,* 887–895.

Pezdek, K., Finger, K., & Hodge, D. (1997). Planting false childhood memories: The role of event plausibility. *Psychological Science, 8,* 437–441.

Pfeiffer, W. M. (1982). Culture-bound syndromes. In I. Al-Issa (Ed.), *Culture and psychopathology* (pp. 201–218). Baltimore: University Park Press.

Phan, T., & Silove, D. (1999). An overview of indigenous descriptions of mental phenomena and the range of traditional healing practices amongst the Vietnamese. *Transcultural Psychiatry, 36,* 79–94.

Phillips, K. A. (2001). Somatoform and factitious disorders. *Review of Psychiatry, 20*(3), 27–65.

Piaget, J. (1926). *The language and thought of the child.* New York: Harcourt Brace.

Piaget, J. (1952). *The origins of intelligence in children.* New York: W. W. Norton.

Piaget, J. (1962). *Play, dreams and imitation in childhood.* New York: W. W. Norton.

Piaget, J. (1983). Piaget's theory. In W. Kessen (Ed.), *Handbook of child psychology, Volume 1* (pp. 103–128). New York: Wiley.

Piedmont, R. L., Bain, E., McCrae, R. R., & Costa, P. T., Jr. (2002). The applicability of the Five-Factor Model in a sub-Saharan culture: The NEO-PI-R in Shona. In R. R. McCrae & J. Allik (Eds.), *The Five-Factor Model across cultures* (pp. 105–126). New York: Kluwer Academic/Plenum Publishers.

Pilkington, J. (1998). "Don't try and make out that I'm nice": The different strategies women and men use when gossiping. In J. Coates (Ed.), *Language and gender: A reader* (pp. 254–269). Oxford: Blackwell.

Pinker, S. (1995). Language acquisition. In Gleitman, et al. (Eds.), *An invitation to cognitive science* (2nd ed.) (pp. 135–182). Cambridge, MA: MIT Press.

Pinker, S., & Bloom, P. (1990). Natural language and natural selection. *Behavioral and Brain Sciences, 13*(4), 707–784.

Pinsof, W. M., & Wynne, L. C. (1995). The efficacy of marital and family therapy: An empirical overview, conclusions, and recommendations. *Journal of Marital and Family Therapy, 21,* 585–613.

Pittam, J., Gallois, C., Iwawaki, S., & Kroonenberg, P. (1995). Australian and Japanese concepts of expressive behavior. *Journal of Cross-Cultural Psychology, 26*(5), 451–473.

Pizarro, D. A., & Salovey, P. (2002). On being and becoming a good person: The role of emotional intelligence in moral development and behavior. In J. Aronson (Ed.), *Improving academic achievement: Impact of psychological factors on education* (pp. 247–266). San Diego: Academic Press.

Plomin, R. (1994). The nature of nurture: The environment beyond the family. In R. Plomin (Ed.), *Genetics and experience: The interplay between nature and nurture* (pp. 82–107). Thousand Oaks, CA: Sage.

Plomin, R., & DeFries, J. C. (1998, May). Genetics of cognitive abilities and disabilities. *Scientific American,* 62–69.

Plomin, R. N. L., Pederson, G. E., McClearn, J. R., Nesselroade, C. S., & Bergman, H. F. (1988). EAS temperaments during the last half year of the life span: Twins reared apart and twins raised together. *Psychology of Aging, 4,* 43–50.

Plug, C., & Ross, H. E. (1994). The natural moon illusion: A multi-factor angular account. *Perception, 23,* 321–333.

Plum, F., & Posner, J. B. (1985). *The diagnosis of stupor and coma.* Philadelphia: F. A. Davis.

Polce-Lynch, M., Myers, B. J., Kilmartin, C. T., Forssmann-Falck, R., & Kliewer, W. (1998). Gender and age patterns in emotional expression, body image, and self-esteem. A qualitative analysis. *Sex Roles, 38,* 1025–1050.

Polewan, R. J., Vigorito, C. M., Nason, C. D., Block, R. A., & Moore, J. W. (2006). A cartesian reflex assessment of face processing. *Behavioral and Cognitive Neuroscience Reviews, 3*(5), 3–23.

Pope, H. G., Gruber, A. J., Hudson, J. I., Huestis, M. A., & Yurgelun-Todd, D. (2001). Neuropsychological performance in long-term cannabis users. *Archives of General Psychiatry, 58*(10), 909–915.

Pope, H. G., Poliakoff, M. B., Parker, M. P., Boynes, M., & Hudson, J. I. (2007). Is dissociative amnesia a culture-bound syndrome? Findings from a survey of historical literature. *Psychological Medicine, 37*(2), 225–233.

Pormerleau, C. S., & Pormerleau, O. F. (1994). Euphoriant effects of nicotine. *Tobacco Control, 3*, 374.

Postman, L. (1975). Tests of the generality of the principle of encoding specificity. *Memory & Cognition, 3*, 663–672.

Powers, M. H. (1984). A computer assisted problem solving method for beginning chemistry students. *The Journal of Computers in Mathematics and Science Teaching, 4*(1), 13–19.

PR Newswire Association, Inc. (2000). Con Edison Hosts the U.S. Memory Championship at Corporate Headquarters in New York. Gale Group: Farmington Hills, MI. Retrieved from the Internet on August 15, 2007, at **http://www.highbeam.com/doc1G1-f9201135.html.**

Pratkanis, A. R. (1992). The cargo-cult science of subliminal persuasion. *Skeptical Inquirer, 16*, 260–272.

Pratkanis, A. R., & Greenwald, A. G. (1988). Recent perspectives on unconscious processing: Still no marketing applications. *Psychology and Marketing, 5*, 337–353.

Pratt, J. A. (1991). Psychotropic drug tolerance and dependence: Common underlying mechanisms? In E. Pratt (Ed.), *The biological bases of drug tolerance and dependence* (pp. 2–28). London: Academic Press, Harcourt Brace Jovanovich.

Premack, D. (2004). Is language the key to human intelligence? *Science, 303*(5656), 318–320.

Priester, J. M., & Petty, R. E. (1995). Source attributions and persuasion: Perceived honesty as a determinant of message scrutiny. *Personality and Social Psychology Bulletin, 21*, 637–654.

Prigerson, H. G., Bierhals, A. J., Kasi, S. V., Reynolds, C. F., Shear, M. K., Day, N., Beery, L. C., Newsome, J. T., & Jacobs, S. (1997). Traumatic grief as a risk factor for mental and physical morbidity. *American Journal of Psychiatry, 154I*, 616–623.

Prochaska, J. O., & Norcross, J. C. (2003). *Systems of psychotherapy* (5th ed.). Belmont, CA: Wadsworth.

Puetz, T. W., Flowers, S. S., & O'Connor, P. J. (2008). A randomized controlled trial of the effect of aerobic exercise training on feelings of energy and fatigue in sedentary young adults with persistent fatigue. *Psychotherapy and Psychosomatics, 77*(3), 167–174.

Pullum, G. K. (1991). *The great Eskimo vocabulary hoax: And other irreverent essays on the study of language.* Chicago: The University of Chicago Press.

Pumariega, A. J., & Gustavson, C. R. (1994). Eating attitudes in African-American women: The essence. *Eating Disorders: Journal of Treatment and Prevention, 2*, 5–16.

Purcell, S. (1985). Relation between religious orthodoxy and marital sexual functioning. Paper presented at a meeting of the American Psychological Association, Los Angeles, August 25.

Purdy, D., Eitzen, D., & Hufnagel, R. (1982). Are athletes also students? The educational attainment of college athletes. *Social Problems, 29*, 439–448.

Putnam, J. A. (2001). EEG biofeedback on a female stroke patient with depression: A case study. *Journal of Neurotherapy, 5*(3), 27–38.

Putnam, S. P., & Stifter, C. A. (2002). Development of approach and inhibition in the first year: Parallel findings for motor behavior, temperament ratings and directional cardiac response. *Developmental Science, 5*, 441–451.

Quintero, J. E., Kuhlman, S. J., & McMahon, D. G. (2003). The biological clock nucleus: A multiphasic oscillator network regulated by light. *Journal of Neuroscience, 23*, 8070–8076.

Raaijmakers, J. G. W., & Shiffrin, R. M. (1992). Models for recall and recognition. *Annual Review of Psychology, 43*, 205–234.

Rachman, S. (1990). The determinants and treatments of simple phobias. *Advances in Behavioral Research and Therapy, 12*(1), 1–30.

Rachman, S. J., & Hodgson, R. J. (1980). *Obsessions and compulsions.* Englewood Cliffs, NJ: Prentice Hall.

Radford, B. (2004). New technique used in treating A.D.D. Article retrieved from the Internet on August 28, 2004, at **www.kansascity.com/mld/kansascity.**

Raikkonen, K., Matthews, K. A., & Salomon, K. (2003). Hostility predicts metabolic syndrome risk factors in children and adolescents. *Health Psychology, 22*, 279–286.

Rainforth, M. V., Schneider, R. H., Nidich, S. I., Gaylord-King, C., Salerno, J. W., & Anderson, J. W. (2007). Stress reduction programs in patients with elevated blood pressure: A systematic review and meta-analysis. *Current Hypertension Reports, 9*, 520–528.

Ramachandran, V. S., & Blakeslee, S. (1998). *Phantoms in the brain.* New York: Quill William Morrow.

Ramachandran, V. S., & Hubbard, E. M. (2003). Hearing colors, tasting shapes. *Scientific American, 5*, 52–59.

Ramón y Cajal, S. (1995.) *Histology of the nervous system of man and vertebrates.* New York: Oxford University Press. English translation by N. Swanson and L. M. Swanson.

Randi, J. (1980). *Flim-flam!* New York: Lippincott/Crowell.

Randi, J. (1982). *Flim-flam! Psychics, ESP, unicorns and other delusions.* Buffalo, NY: Prometheus.

Ranke, M. B., & Saenger, P. (2001, July 28). Turner's syndrome. *Lancet, 358*(9278), 309–314.

Rao, S. C., Rainer, G., & Miller, E. K. (1997) Integration of what and where in the primate prefrontal cortex. *Science, 276*, 821–824.

Rauch, S. L., Shin, L. M., & Wright, C. I. (2003). Neuroimaging studies of amygdala function in anxiety disorders. *Annals of the New York Academy of Sciences, 985*, 389–410.

Raynor, H. A., & Epstein, L. H. (2001). Dietary variety, energy regulation and obesity. *Psychological Bulletin, 127*(3), 325–341.

Reason, J. T., & Brand, J. J. (1975). *Motion sickness.* London: Academic Press.

Reder, L. M., Anderson, J. R., & Bjork, R. A. (1974). A semantic interpretation of encoding specificity. *Journal of Experimental Psychology, 102*, 648–656.

Regier, D. A., Narrow, W. E., Rae, D. S., Manderscheid, R. W., Locke, B. Z., & Goodwin, F. K. (1993). The de facto mental and addictive disorders service system. Epidemiologic Catchment Area prospective 1-year prevalence rates of disorders and services. *Archives of General Psychiatry, 50*(2), 85–94.

Reinders, A., Quak, J., Nijenhuis, E. R., Korf, J., Paans, A. M., Willemsen, A. T., & den Boer, J. A. (2001). Identity state-dependent processing of neutral and traumatic scripts in Dissociative Identity Disorder as assessed by PET. Oral Presentation: 7th Annual Meeting of the Organisation for Human Brain Mapping, June 10–14, Brighton, UK. *NeuroImage 13* (supplement), S1093.

Reinders, A. A. T. S., Nijenhuis, E. R. S., Paans, A. M. J., Korf, J., Willemsen, A. T. M., & den Boer, J. A. (2003). One brain, two selves. *Neuroimage, 20*, 2119–2125.

Reiner, W. G. (1999). Assignment of sex in neonates with ambiguous genitalia. *Current Opinions in Pediatrics, 11*(4), 363–365.

Reiner, W. G. (2000). The genesis of gender identity in the male: Prenatal androgen effects on gender identity and gender role. Talk given at New York University Child Study Center, Grand Rounds Summary.

Reiseberg, B., Doody, R., Stoffler, A., Schmitt, F., Ferris, S., & Mobius, H. J. (2003). Memantine in moderate to severe Alzheimer's disease. *New England Journal of Medicine, 348*(14), 1333–1341.

Reisenzein, R. (1983). The Schachter theory of emotion: Two decades later. *Psychological Bulletin, 94*, 239–264.

Reisenzein, R. (1994). Pleasure-arousal theory and the intensity of emotions. *Journal of Personality and Social Psychology, 7*(6), 1313–1329.

Reiter, R., & Milburn, A. (1994). Exploring effective treatment for chronic pelvic pain. *Comtemporary Ob/Gyn, 3*, 84–103.

Renchler, R. (1993). Poverty and learning. *ERIC Digests*, ERIC Clearinghouse on Educational Management, Eugene, OR. Retrieved from the Internet on June 1, 2004, at **www.ed.gov/databases/ERIC_Digests/ed357433.html.**

Renfrey, G., & Spates, R. C. (1994). Eye movement desensitization: A partial dismantling study. *Journal of Behavior Therapy and Experimental Psychiatry, 25*, 231–239.

Renner, M. J., & Mackin, R. S. (1998). A life stress instrument for classroom use. *Teaching of Psychology, 25*, 47.

Rescorla, R. (1988). Pavlovian conditioning—It's not what you think. *American Psychologist, 43*, 151–160.

Rescorla, R. A. (1968). Probability of shock in the presence and absence of CS in fear conditioning. *Journal of Comparative and Physiological Psychology, 66*, 1–5.

Rezvani, A. H., & Levin, E. D. (2001). Cognitive effects of nicotine. *Biological Psychiatry, 49*, 258–267.

Rhine, J. B. (1935). *Extrasensory perception.* Boston: Bruce Humphries.

Richards, C. F., & Lowe, R. A. (2003). Researching racial and ethnic disparities in emergency medicine. *Academic Emergency Medicine, 10*(11), 1169–1175.

Rideout, T. M. (2005). Eating disorders: Anorexia and bulimia. Holistic-online.com: Eating Disorders Infocenter. Retrieved from the Internet on March 30, 2005, at **www.holistic-online.com/Remedies/EatingD/EatD_anorxia-bulemia.htm**.

Ridley, M. (1999). *Genome: The autobiography of a species in 23 chapters.* London: Fourth Estate Ltd.

Rieber, R. W., & Robinson, D. K. (2001). *Wilhelm Wundt in history: The making of a scientific psychology.* New York: Kluwer Academic Publishers.

Rieger, E., Touyz, S. W., Swain, T., & Beumont, P. J. (2001). Cross-cultural research on anorexia nervosa: Assumptions regarding the role of body weight. *International Journal of Eating Disorders, 29*(2), 205–215.

Ritenbaugh, C., Shisslak, C., & Prince, R. (1992). Eating disorders: A cross-cultural review in regard to DSM-IV. In J. E. Mezzich, A. Kleinman, & H. Farega, et al. (Eds.), *Cultural proposals for DSM-IV.* Submitted to the DSM-IV Task Force by the NIMH Group on Culture and Diagnosis. Pittsburgh: University of Pittsburgh.

Ritts, V. (1999). Infusing culture into psychopathology: A supplement for psychology instructors. Retrieved from the Internet on June 19, 2004, at **www.stlcc.cc.mo.us/mc/users/vritts/psypath.htm**.

Rizzolatti, G., Fadiga, L., Gallese, V., & Fogassi, L. (1996). Premotor cortex and the recognition of motor actions. *Cognitive Brain Research, 3,* 131–141.

Robins, L. N. (1996). *Deviant children grown up.* Baltimore: Williams & Wilkins.

Robinson, F. P. (1946). *Effective study.* New York: Harper & Bros.

Robinson, J. W., & Preston, J. D. (1976). Equal status contact and modification of racial prejudice: A reexamination of the contact hypothesis. *Social Forces, 54,* 911–924.

Robinson, P. (1993). *Freud and his critics.* Berkeley, CA: University of California Press.

Rodgers, J. E. (1992). *Psychosurgery: Damaging the brain to save the mind.* New York: HarperCollins.

Rodin, J. (1981). Current status of the internal-external hypothesis for obesity. *American Psychologist, 36,* 361–372.

Rodin, J. (1985). Insulin levels, hunger, and food intake: An example of feedback loops in body weight regulation. *Health Psychology, 4,* 1–24.

Rodin, J., & Langer, E. J. (1977). Long-term effects of a control-relevant intervention among the institutionalized aged. *Journal of Personality and Social Psychology, 35,* 275–282.

Roediger, H. L. (1990). Implicit memory: Retention without remembering. *American Psychologist, 45,* 1043–1056.

Roediger, H. L., III (2000). Why retrieval is the key process to understanding human memory. In E. Tulving (Ed.), *Memory, consciousness and the brain: The Tallinn Conference* (pp. 52–75). Philadelphia: Psychology Press.

Roediger, H. L., III, & Crowder, R. G. (1976). A serial position effect in recall of United States presidents. *Bulletin of the Psychonomic Society, 8,* 275–278.

Roediger, H. L., III, & Guynn, M. J. (1996). Retrieval processes. In E. L. Bjork & R. A. Bjork (Eds.), *Memory* (pp. 197–236). New York: Academic Press.

Roffman, R. A., Stephens, R. S., Simpson, E. E., & Whitaker, D. L. (1988). Treatment of marijuana dependence: Preliminary results. *Journal of Psychoactive Drugs, 20*(1), 129–137.

Roffwarg, H. P., Muzio, J. N., & Dement, W. C. (1966). Ontogenetic development of the human sleep-dream cycle. *Science, 152*(3722), 604–619.

Rogers, C. (1961). *On becoming a person: A therapist's view of psychotherapy.* Boston: Houghton/Mifflin.

Rogers, C. F. (1961). *On becoming a person.* Boston: Houghton/Mifflin.

Rogers, R. W., & Mewborn, C. R. (1976). Fear appeals and attitude change: Effects of a threat's noxiousness, probability of occurrence, and the efficacy of the coping responses. *Journal of Personality and Social Psychology, 34,* 54–61.

Rogoff, B. (1994). Developing understanding of the idea of communities of learners. *Mind, Culture, and Activity, 1*(4), 209–229.

Rohde, A., & Marneros, A. (1993). Postpartum psychoses: Onset and long-term course. *Psychopathology, 26,* 203–209.

Rohde, P., Silva, S. G., Tonev, S. T., Kennard, B. D., Vitiello, B., Kratochvil, C. J., Reinecke, M. A., Curry, J. F., Simons, A. D., & March, J. S. (2008). Achievement and maintenance of sustained improvement during TADS continuation and maintenance therapy. *Archives of General Psychiatry, 65*(4), 447–455.

Roid, G. H. (2003). *Stanford-Binet intelligence scales* (5th ed.). Itasca, IL: Riverside Publishing.

Roos, P. E., & Cohen, L. H. (1987). Sex roles and social support as moderators of life stress adjustment. *Journal of Personality and Social Psychology, 3,* 576–585.

Roper, G., Rachman, S., & Marks, I. (1975). Passive and participant modeling in exposure treatment of obsessive-compulsive neurotics. *Behaviour Research and Therapy, 13,* 271–279.

Rosch, E. (1973). On the internal structure of perceptual and semantic categories. In T. E. Moore (Ed.), *Cognitive development and the acquisition of language* (pp. 111–144). New York: Academic Press.

Rosch, E. (1977). Human categorization. In N. Warren (Ed.), *Advances in cross-cultural psychology, 1* (pp. 1–72). London: Academic Press.

Rosch, E., & Mervis, C. (1975). Family resemblances: Studies in the internal structures of categories. *Cognitive Psychology, 7,* 573–605.

Rosch, E., Mervis, C. B., Gray, W. D., Johnson, D. M., & Boyes-Braem, P. (1976). Basic objects in natural categories. *Cognitive Psychology, 8,* 382–439.

Rosch-Heider, E. (1972). Universals in color naming and memory. *Journal of Experimental Psychology, 93,* 10–20.

Rosch-Heider, E., & Olivier, D. C. (1972). The structure of the color space in naming and memory for two languages. *Cognitive Psychology, 3,* 337–354.

Rose, S., Kamin, L. J., & Lewontin, R. C. (1984). *Not in our genes: Biology, ideology and human nature.* Harmondsworth, UK: Penguin.

Roselli, C. E., Larkin, K., Resko, J. A., Stellflug, J. N., & Stormshak, F. (2004). The volume of a sexually dimorphic nucleus in the ovine medial preoptic area/anterior hypothalamus varies with sexual partner preference. *Endocrinology, 145*(2), 478–483.

Rosenman, R. H., Brand, R. I., Jenkins, C. D., Friedman, M., Straus, R., & Wurm, M. (1975). Coronary heart disease in the Western Collaborative Group Study, final follow-up experience of $\frac{1}{2}$ years. *Journal of the American Medical Association, 233,* 812–817.

Rosenthal, A. M. (1964). *Thirty-eight witnesses: The Kitty Genovese case.* New York: McGraw-Hill.

Rosenthal, R., & Jacobson, L. (1968). *Pygmalion in the classroom.* New York: Holt, Rinehart and Winston.

Rosenzweig, M. R., Leiman, A. L., & Breedlove, A. M. (1996). *Biological psychology.* Sunderland, MA: Sinaur Associates Inc.

Ross, H. E., & Ross, G. M. (1976). Did Ptolemy understand the moon illusion? *Perception, 5,* 377–385.

Rossini, P. M., Altamura, C., Ferreri, F., Melgari, J. M., Tecchio, F., Tombini, M., Pasqualetti, P., & Vernieri, F. (2007). Neuroimaging experimental studies on brain plasticity in recovery from stroke. *Eura Medicophys, 43*(2), 241–254.

Rossiter, T. R., & La Vaque, T. J. (1995). A comparison of EEG biofeedback and psychostimulants in treating attention deficit hyperactivity disorders. *Journal of Neurotherapy,* 48–59.

Rothbaum, B. O., Hodges, L. F., Kooper, R., Opdyke, D., Williford, J. S., & North, M. (1995). Effectiveness of computer-generated (virtual reality) graded exposure in the treatment of acrophobia. *American Journal of Psychiatry, 152,* 626–628.

Rothbaum, R., Weisz, J., Pott, M., Miyake, K., & Morelli, G. (2000). Attachment and culture: Security in Japan and the U.S. *American Psychologist, 55,* 1093–1104.

Rothenberg, A. (2001). Bipolar illness, creativity, and treatment. *Psychiatric Quarterly, 72*(2), 131–147.

Rotter, J. B. (1954). *Social learning and clinical psychology.* New York: Prentice Hall.

Rotter, J. B. (1966). Generalized expectancies for internal versus external control of reinforcements. *Psychological Monographs, 80,* Whole No. 609.

Rotter, J. B. (1978). Generalized expectancies for problem solving and psychotherapy. *Cognitive Therapy and Research, 2,* 1–10.

Rotter, J. B. (1981). The psychological situation in social learning theory. In D. Magnusson (Ed.), *Toward a psychology of situations: An interactional perspective.* Hillsdale, NJ: Lawrence Erlbaum.

Rotter, J. B. (1990). Internal versus external control of reinforcement: A case history of a variable. *American Psychologist, 45,* 489–493.

Rotton, J., & Frey, J. (1985). Air pollution, weather, and violent crime: Concomitant time-series analysis of archival data. *Journal of Personality and Social Psychology, 49,* 1207–1220.

Rotton, J., Frey, J., Barry, T., Milligan, M., & Fitzpatrick, M. (1979). The air pollution experience and physical aggression. *Journal of Applied Social Psychology, 9,* 397–412.

Rouse, B. A. (1998). *Substance and mental health statistics source book.* Rockville, MD: Department of Health and Human Services, Substance Abuse and Mental Health Services Administration (SAMHSA).

Rouw, R., & Scholte, H. S. (2007). Increased structural connectivity in grapheme-color synesthesia. *Nature Neuroscience.* Published online: May 21, 2007.

Rovet, J. (1993). The psychoeducational characteristics of children with Turner's syndrome. *Journal of Learning Disabilities, 26,* 333–341.

Rowan, J. (2001). *Ordinary ecstasy.* Hove, UK: Brunner-Routledge.

Rowe, D. C., Almeida, D. A., & Jacobson, K. C. (1999). School context and genetic influences on aggression in adolescence. *Psychological Science, 10,* 277–280.

Roysircai-Sodowsky, G. R., & Maestas, M. V. (2000). Acculturation, ethnic identity, and acculturative stress: Evidence and measurement. In R. H. Dana (Ed.), *Handbook of cross-cultural and multicultural assessment* (pp. 131–172). Mahwah, NJ: Lawrence Erlbaum.

Ruble, D., Alvarez, J., Bachman, M., Cameron, J., Fuligni, A., Garcia Coll, C., & Rhee, E. (2004). The development of a sense of "we": The emergence and implications of children's collective identity. In M. Bennett & F. Sani (Eds.), *The development of the social self.* New York: Psychology Press.

Rudd, P., & Osterberg, L. G. (2002). Hypertension: Context, pathophysiology, and management. In E. J. Topol (Ed.), *Textbook of cardiovascular medicine* (pp. 91–122). Philadelphia: Lippincott Williams and Wilkins.

Ruhe, H. G., Mason, N. S., & Schene, A. H. (2007). Mood is indirectly related to serotonin, norepinephrine and dopamine levels in humans: A meta-analysis of monoamine depletion studies. *Molecular Psychiatry, 12*(4), 331–359.

Rumelhart, D. E., Hinton, G. E., & McClelland, J. L. (1986). A general framework for parallel distributed processing. In D. E. Rumelhart, J. L. McClelland, & the PDP Research Group (Eds.), *Parallel distributed processing: Explorations in the microstructure of cognition. Vol. 1: Foundations* (pp. 45–76). Cambridge, MA: MIT Press.

Rundus, D. (1971). An analysis of rehearsal processes in free recall. *Journal of Experimental Psychology, 89,* 63–77.

Ruscio, A. M., Borkovec, T. D., & Ruscio, J. (2001). A taxometric investigation of the latent structure of worry. *Journal of Abnormal Psychology, 110,* 413–422.

Russell, D. E. (1986). *The secret trauma: Incest in the lives of girls and women..* New York: Basic Books.

Rutherford, A. (2000). Mary Cover Jones (1896–1987). *The Feminist Psychologist, 27*(3), 25.

Ryan, R. M., & Deci, E. L. (2000). Intrinsic and extrinsic motivations: Classic definitions and new directions. *Contemporary Educational Psychology, 25,* 54–67.

Rynn, M., Scherrer, J., & True, W. R. (2000, November). Generalized anxiety disorder. *Best Practice of Medicine.*

Sackeim, H. A., Prudic, J., Devanand, D. P., Nobler, M. S., Lisanby, S. H., Peyser, S., Fitzsimons, L., Moody, B. J., & Clark, J. (2000). A prospective, randomized, double-blind comparison of bilateral and right unilateral electroconvulsive therapy at different stimulus intensities. *Archives of General Psychiatry, 57,* 425–434.

Sacks, O. (1990). *The man who mistook his wife for a hat and other clinical tales.* New York: HarperPerennial.

Sacks, O. (1995). *An anthropologist on Mars.* London: Picador.

Sadker, M., & Sadker, D. (1994). *Failing at fairness: How America's schools cheat girls.* New York: Scribner.

Sagan, C. (1977). *The dragons of Eden: Speculations on the evolution of human intelligence.* New York: Random House.

Salend, S. J. (1987). Contingency management systems. *Academic Therapy, 22,* 245–253.

Salovey, P., & Mayer, J. D. (1990). Emotional intelligence. *Imagination, Cognition, and Personality, 9,* 185–211.

Salovey, P., Rothman, A. J., Detweiler, J. B., & Steward, W. (2000). Emotional states and physical health. *American Psychologist, 55,* 110–121.

Salthouse, T. A. (1984). The skill of typing. *Scientific American, 250*(2), 128–135.

Sanders, L. D., Weber-Fox, C. M., & Neville, H. J. (2008). Varying degrees of plasticity in different subsystems within language. In J. R. Pomerantz and M. Crair (Eds.), *Topics in integrative neuroscience: From cells to cognition.* New York: Cambridge University Press.

Sands, L. P., & Meredith, W. (1992). Intellectual functioning in late midlife. *Journal of Gerontological and Psychological Science, 47,* 81–84.

Sapir, E. S. (1921). *Language: An introduction to the study of speech.* New York: Harcourt, Brace.

Sapolsky, R. M. (2004). *Why zebras don't get ulcers* (3rd ed., pp. 1, 144–145). New York: Owl Books.

Sarbin, T. R., & Coe, W. C. (1972). *Hypnosis: A social psychological analysis of influence communication.* New York: Holt, Rinehart, & Winston.

Sartori, G., & Umilta, C. (2000). How to avoid the fallacies of cognitive subtraction in brain imaging. *Brain and Language, 74,* 191–212.

Sastry, K. S., Karpova, Y., Prokopovich, S., Smith, A. J., Essau, B., Gersappe, A., Carson, J. P., Weber, M. J., Register, T. C., Chen, Y. Q., Penn, R. B., & Kulik, G. (2007). Epinephrine protects cancer cells from apoptosis via activation of cAMP-dependent protein kinase and BAD phosphorylation. *Journal of Biological Chemistry, 282*(19), 14094–14100.

Satcher, D. (2001). *The surgeon general's national strategy to prevent suicide.* Washington, DC: Office of the Surgeon General of the United States.

Satterly, D. (1987). Piaget and education. In R. L. Gregory (Ed.), *The Oxford companion to the mind* (pp. 110–143). Oxford: Oxford University Press.

Sattler, J. M. (1977). The effects of therapist–client racial similarity. In A. S. Gurman, & A. M. Razin (Eds.), *Effective psychotherapy: A handbook of research* (pp. 252–290). Elmsford, NY: Pergamon.

Saunders, B., & Goddard, C. R. (1998). Why do we condone the "physical punishment" of children? *Children Australia, 23,* 23–28.

Savage-Rumbaugh, S., & Lewin, R. (1994). *Kanzi.* New York: Wiley.

Savage-Rumbaugh, S., Shanker, S., & Taylor, T. J. (1998). *Apes, language and the human mind.* Oxford: Oxford University Press.

Scarmeas, N., Levy, G., Tang, M.-X., Manly, J., & Stern, Y. (2001). Influence of leisure acitivity on the incidence of Alzheimer's disease. *Neurology, 57,* 2236–2242.

Scarmeas, N., Luchsinger, J. A., Mayeux, R., & Stern, Y. (2007). Mediterranean diet and Alzheimer disease mortality. *Neurology, 69,* 1084–1093.

Scarmeas, N., Stern, Y., Mayeux, R., & Luchsinger, J. A. (2006). Mediterranean diet, Alzheimer disease, and vascular mediation. *Archives of Neurology, 63,* 1709–1717

Scarmeas, N., Zarahn, E., Anderson, K. E., Habeck, C. G., Hilton, J., Flynn, J., Marder, K. S., Bell, K. L., Sackeim, H. A., Van Heertum, R. L., Moeller, J. R., & Stern, Y. (2003). Association of life activities with cerebral blood flow in Alzheimer disease: Implications for the cognitive reserve hypothesis. *Archives of Neurology, 60*(3), 317–318.

Scarpa, A., Raine, A., Venables, P. H., & Mednick, S. A. (1995). The stability of inhibited/uninhibited temperament from ages 3 to 11 years in Mauritian children. *Journal of Abnormal Child Psychology, 23,* 607–618.

Schachter, S., & Singer, J. E. (1962). Cognitive, social and physiological determinants of emotional states. *Psychological Review, 69,* 379–399.

Schacter, D. L. (1996). *Searching for memory. The brain, the mind, and the past.* New York: Basic Books.

Schafer, M., & Crichlow S. (1996). Antecedents of groupthink: A quantitative study. *Journal of Conflict Resolution, 40,* 415–435.

Schmitt, D. P. (2002). Personality, attachment and sexuality related to dating relationship outcomes: Contrasting three perspectives on personal attribute interaction. *British Journal of Social Psychology, 41*(4), 589–610.

Schmitz, C., Wagner, J., & Menke, E. (2001). The interconnection of childhood poverty and homelessness: Negative impact/points of access. *Families in Society, 82*(1), 69–77.

Schneider, K. J., Bugental, J. F. T., & Fraser, J. F. (Eds.). (2001). *Handbook of humanistic psychology.* Thousand Oaks, CA: Sage.

Schneider, R. H., Staggers, F., Alexander, C. N., Sheppard, W., Rainforth, M., Kondwani, K., Smith, S., & King, C. G. (1995). A randomized controlled trial of stress reduction for hypertension in older African Americans. *Hypertension, 26*(5), 820–827.

Schneider, W., Dumais, S., & Shriffrin, R. (1984). *Automatic and control processing and attention.* London: Academic Press.

Schneidman, E. (1983). *Death of man.* New York: Jason Aronson, Inc.

Schneidman, E. (1994). *Death: Current perspectives.* New York: McGraw-Hill.

Schols, L., Haan, J., Riess, O., Amoiridis, G., & Przuntek, H. (1998). Sleep disturbance in spinocerebellar ataxias: Is the SCA3 mutation a cause of restless legs syndrome? *Neurology, 51*, 1603–1607

Schreiber, F. R. (1973, reissued 1995). *Sybil.* New York: Warner.

Schroeder, S. R. (2000). Mental retardation and developmental disabilities influenced by environmental neurotoxic insults. *Environmental Health Perspectives 108* (Suppl. 3), 395–399.

Schroth, M. L., & McCormack, W. A. (2000). Sensation seeking and need for achievement among study-abroad students. *The Journal of Social Psychology, 140*, 533–535.

Schwanenflugel, P., & Rey, M. (1986). Interlingual semantic facilitation: Evidence from common representational system in the bilingual lexicon. *Journal of Memory and Language, 25*, 605–618.

Schwartz, B., Ward, A. H., Monterosso, J., Lyubomirsky, S., White, K., & Lehman, D. (2002). Maximizing versus satisficing: Happiness is a matter of choice. *Journal of Personality and Social Psychology, 83*, 1178–1197.

Schweickert, R. (1993). A multinomial processing tree model for degradation and redintegration in immediate recall. *Memory and Cognition, 21*, 168–175.

Schwitzgebel, E. (1999). Representation and desire: A philosophical error with consequences for theory-of-mind research. *Philosophical Psychology, 12*, 157–180.

Scott, S. K., Young, A. W., Calder, A. J., Hellawell, D. J., Aggleton, J. P., & Johnson, M. (1997). Impaired auditory recognition of fear and anger following bilateral amygdala lesions. *Nature, 385*(6613), 254–257.

Searight, H. R., Burke, J. M., & Rottnek, F. (2000). Adult ADHD: Evaluation and treatment in family medicine. *American Family Physician, 62*(9), 2077–2086, 2091–2092.

Security Director's Report (2008). Experts identify four trends in workplace violence. *Institute of Management and Administration, Inc., 8*(6), 1–15.

Segall, M. H., Campbell, D. T., & Herskovits, M. J. (1966). *The influence of culture on perception.* Indianapolis, IN: Bobbs-Merrill Co.

Segerstrom, S. C., Taylor, S. E., Kemeny, M. E., & Fahey, J. L. (1998). Optimism is associated with mood, coping, and immune change in response to stress. *Journal of Personality and Social Psychology, 74*(6), 1646–1655.

Seligman, L. (1998). *Selecting effective treatments: A comprehensive guide to treating mental disorders.* San Francisco, CA: Jossey-Bass.

Seligman, M. (1975). *Helplessness: Depression, development and death.* New York: W. H. Freeman.

Seligman, M. (1989). *Helplessness.* New York: W. H. Freeman.

Seligman, M. E. P. (1970). On the generality of the laws of learning. *Psychological Review, 77*, 406–418.

Seligman, M. E. P. (1975). *Helplessness—On depression, development, and death.* San Francisco, CA: Freeman.

Seligman, M. E. P. (1995). The effectiveness of psychotherapy: The *Consumer Reports* study. *American Psychologist, 50*, 965–975.

Seligman, M. E. P. (1998). *Learned optimism: How to change your mind and your life* (2nd ed.). New York: Pocket Books.

Seligman, M.E.P. (2002). *Authentic happiness.* New York: Free Press.

Seligman, M. E. P., & Maier, S. F. (1967). Failure to escape traumatic shock. *Journal of Experimental Psychology, 74*, 1–9.

Selye, H. (1956). *The stress of life.* New York: McGraw-Hill.

Selye, H. (1976). *The stress of life* (rev. ed.). New York: McGraw-Hill.

Selye, H. A. (1936). Syndrome produced by diverse nocuous agents. *Nature, 138*, 32.

Serban, G., George, A., Siegel, S., DeLeon, M., & Gaffney, M. (1990). Computed tomography scans and negative symptoms in schizophrenia: Chronic schizophrenics with negative symptoms and nonenlarged lateral ventricles. *Acta Psychiatrica Scandinavica, 81*(5), 441–447.

Shackelford, T. K., Buss, D. M., & Bennett, K. (2002). Forgiveness or breakup: Sex differences in responses to a partner's infidelity. *Cognition and Emotion, 16*(2), 299–307.

Shadish, R., Cook, T. D., & Campbell, D. T. (2002). *Experimental and quasi-experimental designs for generalized causal inferences.* New York: Houghton Mifflin Company.

Shafto, P., & Coley, J. D. (2003). Development of categorization and reasoning in the natural world: Novices to experts, naïve similarity to ecological knowledge. *Journal of Experimental Psychology: Learning, Memory & Cognition, 29*, 641–649.

Shafton, A. (1995). *Dream reader: Contemporary approaches to the understanding of dreams (S U N Y series in dream studies)* (pp. 40–46). New York: State University of New York Press.

Shah, P. M. (1991). Prevention of mental handicaps in children in primary health care. *Bulletin of the World Health Organization, 69*, 779–789.

Shapiro, A. K., & Shapiro, E. (1997). *The powerful placebo.* Baltimore, MD: Johns Hopkins University Press.

Shapiro, F. (1989). Eye movement desensitization: A new treatment for post-traumatic stress disorder. *Journal of Behavior Therapy and Experimental Psychiatry, 20*, 211–217.

Shapiro, F. (1995). *Eye movement desensitization and reprocessing: Basic principles, protocols, and procedure.* New York: Guilford.

Shapiro, K. L., Jacobs, W. J., & LoLordo, V. M. (1980). Stimulus relevance in Pavlovian conditioning in pigeons. *Animal Learning and Behavior, 8*, 586–594.

Shaywitz, S. E. (1996). Dyslexia. *Scientific American, 275*(5), 98–104.

Shean, R. E., de Klerk, N. H., Armstrong, B. K., & Walker, N. R. (1994). Seven-year follow-up of a smoking-prevention program for children. *Australian Journal of Public Health, 18*, 205–208.

Sheeber, L. B., & Johnson, J. H. (1992). Child temperament, maternal adjustment, and changes in family life style. *American Journal of Orthopsychiatry, 62*(2), 178–185.

Shekelle, P. G., Hardy, M. L., Morton, S. C., Maglione, M., Mojica, W. A., Suttorp, M. J., Rhodes, S. L., Jungvig, L., & Gagné, J. (2003). Efficacy and safety of ephedra and ephedrine for weight loss and athletic performance: A meta-analysis. *Journal of the American Medical Association, 289*(12), 1537–1545.

Sheldon, S. H. (2002). Sleep in infants and children. In T. L. Lee-Chiong, M. J. Sateia, and M. A. Carskadon (Eds.), *Sleep medicine*, (pp. 99–103). Philadelphia, PA: Hanley & Belfus, Inc.

Shepard, R. N., & Metzler, J. (1971). Mental rotation of three-dimensional objects. *Science, 171*, 701–703.

Shepard, T. H. (2001). *Catalog of teratogenic agents* (10th ed.). Baltimore, MD: Johns Hopkins University Press.

Sherif, M. (1936). *The psychology of social norms.* New York: Harper & Row.

Sherif, M., Harvey, O. J., White, B. J., Hood, W. R., & Sherif, C. W. (1961). *Intergroup conflict and cooperation: The Robber's Cave experiment.* Norman, OK: University of Oklahoma Book Exchange.

Sherry, P. (1991). Person environment fit and accident prediction. *Journal of Business and Psychology, 5*, 411–416.

Sherry, P., Gaa, A., Thurlow-Harrison, S., Graber, K., Clemmons, J., & Bobulinski, M. (2003). Traffic accidents, job stress, and supervisor support in the trucking industry. Paper presented at the International Institute for Intermodal Transportation at the University of Denver, CO.

Shore, L. A. (1990). Skepticism in light of scientific literacy. *Skeptical Inquirer, 15*(1), 3–4.

Shorey, G. (2001). Bystander non-intervention and the Somalia incident. *Canadian Military Journal*, 19–27.

Shorter E. (1997). *A history of psychiatry: From the era of the asylum to the age of Prozac.* New York: John Wiley & Sons.

Showalter, E. (1997). *Hystories: Hysterical epidemics and modern culture.* New York: Columbia University Press.

Shuglin, A. (1986). The background chemistry of MDMA. *Journal of Psychoactive Drugs, 18*(4), 291–304.

Shurkin, J. N. (1992). *Terman's kids; The groundbreaking study of how the gifted grow up.* Boston: Little, Brown & Company Limited.

Siegel, J. M. (2001). The REM sleep-memory consolidation hypothesis. *Science, 294*, 1058–1063.

Siegel, S. (1969). Effects of CS habituation on eyelid conditioning. *Journal of Comparative and Physiological Psychology, 68*(2), 245–248.

Siegler, I. C., Costa, P. T., Brummett, B. H., Helms, M. J., Barefoot, J. C., Williams, R. B., Dahlstrom, G., Kaplan, B. H., Vitaliano, P. P., Nichaman, M. Z., Day, S., & Rimer, B. K. (2003). Patterns of change in hostility from college to midlife in the UNC alumni heart study predict high-risk status. *Psychosomatic Medicine, 65*, 738–745.

Siegler, R. S. (1996). *Emerging minds: The process of change in children's thinking.* New York: Oxford University Press.

Silva, C. E., & Kirsch, I. (1992). Interpretive sets, expectancy, fantasy proneness, and dissociation as predictors of hypnotic response. *Journal of Personality & Social Psychology, 63,* 847–856.

Silver, F. W. (1996). Management of conversion disorder. *American Journal of Physical Medicine and Rehabilitation, 75,* 134–140.

Silver, L. (2000). Attention deficit/hyperactivity in adult lives. *Child & Adolescent Psychiatric Clinics of North America, 9,* 511–523.

Silver, S. M., Brooks, A., & Obenchain, J. (1995). Eye movement desensitization and reprocessing treatment of Vietnam war veterans with PTSD: Comparative effects with biofeedback and relaxation training. *Journal of Traumatic Stress, 8*(2), 337–342.

Simeon, D., Guralnik, O., Hazlett, E. A., Spiegel-Cohen, J., Hollander, E., & Buchsbaum, M. S. (2000). Feeling unreal: A PET study of depersonalization disorder. *American Journal of Psychiatry, 157,* 1782–1788.

Simon, D. A., & Bjork, R. A. (2001). Metacognition in motor learning. *Journal of Experimental Psychology: Learning, Memory, and Cognition, 27*(4), 907–912.

Singer, M. T., & Lalich, J. (1995). *Cults in our midst.* San Francisco: Jossey-Bass.

Singh-Manoux, A., Richards, M., & Marmot, M. (2003). Leisure activities and cognitive function in middle age: Evidence from the Whitehall II study. *Journal of Epidemiology and Community Health, 57,* 907–913.

Skinner, B. F. (1938). *The behavior of organisms: An experimental analysis.* New York: Appleton-Century-Crofts.

Skinner, B. F. (1956). A case history in scientific method. *American Psychologist, 11,* 221–233.

Skinner, B. F. (1961). *Cumulative record: Definitive edition.* New York: Appelton-Century-Crofts.

Skinner, B. F. (1971). *Beyond freedom and dignity.* New York: Alfred A. Knopf, Inc.

Skinner, B. F. (1974). *About behaviorism.* New York: Alfred A. Knopf.

Skolnick, A. (1986). Early attachment and personal relationships across the life course. In P. B. Baltes, D. L. Featherman, & R. M. Lerner (Eds.), *Life-span development and behavior* (vol. 7). Hillsdale, NJ: Erlbaum.

Skrandies, W., Reik, P., & Kunze, C. (1999). Topography of evoked brain activity during mental arithmetic and language tasks: Sex differences. *Neuropsychologia, 37,* 421–430.

Slater, A. (2000). Visual perception in the young infant: Early organisation and rapid learning. In D. Muir and A. Slater (Eds.), *Infant development: The essential readings.* Oxford: Blackwells.

Slater, A. (2001). Visual perception. In G. Bremner & A. Fogel (Eds.), *Blackwell handbook of infant development* (pp. 5–34). Malden, MA: Blackwell.

Slater, A., Mattock, A., & Brown, E. (1990). Size constancy at birth: Newborn infants' responses to retinal and real size. *Journal of Experimental Child Psychology, 49,* 314–322.

Slipp, S. (1993). *The Freudian mystique: Freud, women and feminism.* New York: New York University Press.

Sloan, D. M., & Mizes, J. S. (1999). Foundations of behavior therapy in the contemporary healthcare context. *Clinical Psychology Review, 19,* 255–274.

Smith, D. (2001). Shock and disbelief. *Atlantic Monthly, 2,* 79–90.

Smith, J. D., & Mitchell, A. (2001). "Me? I'm not a drooler. I'm the assistant": Is it time to abandon mental retardation as a classification? *Mental Retardation, 39*(2), 144–146.

Smith, J. W. (1988). Long term outcome of clients treated in a commercial stop smoking program. *Journal of Substance Abuse Treatment, 5*(1), 33–36.

Smith, T. C., Ryan, M. A. K., Wingard, D. L., Sallis, J. F., & Kritz-Silverstein, D. (2008). New onset and persistent symptoms of post-traumatic stress disorder self-reported after deployment and combat exposures: Prospective population based U.S. military cohort study. *British Medical Journal, 336*(7640), 366–371.

Smith-Spark, L. (2005, March 18). How sleepwalking can lead to killing. *BBC News.* Retrieved from the Internet on February 14, 2008, at **http://news.bbc.co.uk/1/hi/uk/4362081.stm.**

Snyder, M., Tanke, E. D., & Berscheid, E. (1977). Social perception and interpersonal behavior: On the self-fulfilling nature of social stereotypes. *Journal of Personality and Social Psychology, 35,* 656–666.

Sodowsky, G. R., Lai, E. W., & Plake, B. S. (1991). Moderating effects of socio-cultural variables on acculturation attitudes of Hispanics and Asian Americans. *Journal and Counseling and Development, 70,* 194–204.

Soomro, G. M. (2001). Obsessive-compulsive disorder. *Clinical Evidence, 6,* 754–762.

Sowell, E. R., Thompson, P. M., Holmes, C. J., Jernigan, T. L., & Toga, A. W. (1999). In vivo evidence for post-adolescent brain maturation in frontal and striatal regions. *Nature Neuroscience, 2*(10), 859–861.

Spangler, W. D. (1992). Validity of questionnaire and TAT measures of need for achievement: Two meta-analyses. *Psychological Bulletin, 112,* 140–154.

Spangler, W. J., Cosgrove, G. R., Ballantine, H. T., Jr., Cassem, E. H., Rauch, S. L., Nierenberg, A., & Price, B. H. (1996). Magnetic resonance image-guided stereotactic cingulotomy for intractable psychiatric disease. *Neurosurgery, 38,* 1071–1076.

Spanos, N. P. (1994). Multiple identity enactments and multiple personality disorder: A socio-cognitive perspective. *Psychological Bulletin, 116,* 143–165.

Spanos, N. P. (1996). *Multiple identities and false memories: A socio-cognitive perspective.* Washington, DC: American Psychological Association.

Spanos, N. P., Weekes, J. R., & Bertrand, L. D. (1985). Multiple personality: A social psychological perspective. *Journal of Abnormal Psychology, 94,* 362–376.

Sparing, R., Mottaghy, F., Ganis, G., Thompson, W. L., Toepper, R., Kosslyn, S. M., & Pascual-Leone, A. (2002).Visual cortex excitability increases during visual mental imagery—A TMS study in healthy human subjects. *Brain Research, 938,* 92–97.

Spearman, C. (1904). "General intelligence" objectively determined and measured. *American Journal of Psychology, 15,* 201–293.

Speca, M., Carlson, L. E, Goodey, E., & Angen, E. (2000). A randomized wait-list controlled clinical trial: The effects of a mindfulness meditation-based stress reduction program on mood and symptoms of stress in cancer outpatients. *Psychosomatic Medicine, 6,* 2613–2622.

Sperling, G. (1960). The information available in brief visual presentations. *Psychological Monographs, 74*(11), 1–29.

Speroff, L., Glass, R. H., & Kase, N. G. (1999). Recurrent early pregnancy loss. In *Clinical gynecologic endocrinology and infertility* (pp. 1042–1055). Philadelphia, PA: Lippincott Williams and Wilkins.

Sperry, R. W. (1968). Mental unity following surgical disconnection of the cerebral hemispheres. *The Harvey Lectures.* Series 62, 293–323. New York: Academic Press.

Spiegel, D., Bloom, J. R., & Gottheil, E. (1989). Effects of psychosocial treatment on survival of patients with metastatic breast cancer. *Lancet, 2,* 888–891.

Spiegel, H., & Borch-Jacobsen, M. (1997). Sybil—The making of a disease. *New York Review of Books, 44*(7).

Springer, S. P., & Deutsch, G. (1998). *Left brain, right brain: Perspectives from cognitive neuroscience* (5th ed.). New York: Freeman.

Squire, L., & Kandel, E. (1999). *Memory: From mind to molecule.* New York: Scientific American Library.

Squire, L. R., & Slater, P. C. (1978). Anterograde and retrograde memory impairment in chronic amnesia. *Neuropsychologia, 16,* 313–322.

Squire, L. R., Knowlton, B., & Musen, G. (1993). The structure and organization of memory. *Annual Review of Psychology, 44,* 453–495.

Squire, L. R., Slater, P. C., & Chace, P. M. (1975). Retrograde amnesia: Temporal gradient in very long-term memory following electroconvulsive therapy. *Science, 187,* 77–79.

Standing, L., Conezio, J., & Haber, R. N. (1970). Perception and memory for pictures: Single-trial learning of 2500 visual stimuli. *Psychonomic Science, 19,* 73–74.

Steele, C. M. (1992). Race and the schooling of black Americans. *The Atlantic Monthly, 269*(4), 68–78.

Steele, C. M. (1997). A threat in the air: How stereotypes shape intellectual identity and performance. *American Psychologist, 52,* 613–629.

Steele, C. M. (1999, August). Thin ice: "Stereotype threat" and Black college students. *The Atlantic Monthly, 284,* 44–54.

Steele, C. M., & Aronson J. (1995). Stereotype threat and the intellectual test performance of African Americans. *Journal of Personality and Social Psychology, 69,* 797–811.

Steele, J., James, J. B., & Barnett, R. C. (2002). Learning in a man's world: Examining the perceptions of undergraduate women in male-dominated academic areas. *Psychology of Women Quarterly, 26,* 46–50.

Steen, C. (1996). Synesthesia. *Health Report with Robin Hughes.* ABC Radio National Transcripts.

Stein, H. T. (2001). Adlerian overview of birth order characteristics. Alfred Adler Institute of San Francisco. Retrieved from the Internet on June 16, 2004, at **http://ourworld.compuserve.com/homepages/hstein/birthord.htm.**

Stein, S. (1984). *Girls and boys: The limits of non-sexist rearing.* London: Chatto and Windus.

Stein-Behrens, B., Mattson, M. P., Chang, I., Yeh, M., & Sapolsky, R. (1994). Stress exacerbates neuron loss and cytoskeletal pathology in the hippocampus. *Journal of Neuroscience, 14*, 5373–5380.

Steinberg, L., & Silverberg, S. B. (1987). Influences on marital satisfaction during the middle stages of the family life cycle. *Journal of Marriage and the Family, 49*, 751–760.

Steriade, M., & McCarley, R. W. (1990). *Brainstem control of wakefulness and sleep.* New York: Plenum.

Sterman, M. B. (2000). Basic concepts and clinical findings in the treatment of seizure disorders with EEG operant conditioning. *Clinical Electroencephalography, 31*(1), 45–55.

Sterman, M. B., & Lantz, D. (2001). Changes in lateralized memory performance in subjects with epilepsy following neurofeedback training. *Journal of Neurotherapy, 5*, 63–72.

Stern, W. (1912). The psychological methods of testing intelligence (translated by G. M. Whipple). *Educational Psychology Monographs*, no. 13.

Sternberg, R. J. (1986). A triangular theory of love. *Psychological Review, 93*, 119–135.

Sternberg, R. J. (1988a). *The triarchic mind: A new theory of human intelligence.* New York: Viking-Penguin.

Sternberg, R. J. (1988b). Triangulating love. In R. Sternberg & M. Barnes (Eds.), *The psychology of love* (pp. 119–138). New Haven: Yale University Press.

Sternberg, R. J. (1996). *Successful intelligence: How practical and creative intelligence determine success in life.* New York: Simon & Schuster.

Sternberg, R. J. (1997a). Construct validation of a triangular love scale. *European Journal of Social Psychology, 27*, 313–335.

Sternberg, R. J. (1997b). The triarchic theory of intelligence. In P. Flannagan, J. L. Genshaft, & P. L. Harrison (Eds.), *Contemporary intellectual assessment: Theories, tests, and issues* (pp. 92–104). New York: Guilford Press.

Sternberg, R. J., & Kaufman, J. C. (1998). Human abilities. *Annual Review of Psychology, 49*, 479–502.

Sternberger, R. R., et al. (1995). Social phobia: An analysis of possible developmental factors. *Journal of Abnormal Psychology, 194*, 526–531.

Stevenson, M. B., Roach, M. A., Leavitt, L. A., Miller, J. F., & Chapman, R. S. (1988). Early receptive and productive language skills in preterm and full-term 8-month-old infants. *Journal of Psycholinguistic Research, 17*(2), 169–183.

Stickgold, R., Hobson, J. A., Fosse, R., & Fosse, M. (2001). Sleep, learning and dreams: Off-line memory reprocessing. *Science, 294*, 1052–1057.

Stiff, J. B., & Mongeau, P. A. (2002). *Persuasive communication* (2nd ed.). New York: Guilford Publications.

Stiles, W. B., Agnew-Davies, R., Hardy, G. E., Barkham, M., & Shapiro, D. A. (1998). Relations of the alliance with psychotherapy outcome: Findings in the second Sheffield Psychotherapy Project. *Journal of Consulting and Clinical Psychology, 66*, 791–802.

Stine, C., Xu, J., Koskela, R., McMahon, F. J., Gschwend, M., Friddle, C., Clark, C. D., McInnis, M. G., Simpson, S. G., Breschel, T. S., Vishio, E., Riskin, K., Feilotter, H., Chen, E., Shen, S., Folstein, S., Meyers, D. A., Botstein, D., Marr, T. G., & DePaulo, J. R. (1995). Evidence for linkage of bipolar disorder to chromosome 18 with a parent-of-origin effect. *American Journal of Human Genetics, 57*(6), 1384–1394.

Stitzer, M. L., & De Wit, H. (1998). Abuse liability of nicotine. In N. L. Benowitz (Ed.), *Nicotine safety and toxicity* (pp. 119–131). New York: Oxford University Press.

Stockhorst, U., Gritzmann, E., Klopp, K., Schottenfeld-Naor, Y., Hübinger, A., Berresheim, H., Steingrüber, H., & Gries, F. A. (1999). Classical conditioning of insulin effects in healthy humans. *Psychosomatic Medicine, 61*, 424–435.

Stowell, J. R., Kiecolt-Glaser, J. K., & Glaser, R. (2001). Perceived stress and cellular immunity: When coping counts. *Journal of Behavioral Medicine, 24*(4), 323–339.

Stratton, K., Gable, A., & McCormick, M. C. (Eds.) (2001a). *Immunization safety review: Thimerosal-containing vaccines and neurodevelopmental disorders.* Washington, DC: The National Academies Press.

Stratton, K., Wilson, C. B., & McCormick, M. C. (Eds.). (2001b). *Immunization safety review: Measles-mumps-rubella vaccine and autism.* Washington, DC: The National Academies Press.

Straus, M. A. (2000). Corporal punishment of children and adult depression and suicidal ideation. *Beating the devil out of them: Corporal punishment in American families and its effects on children.* New York: Lexington Books (pp. 60–77).

Straus, M. A., & Stewart, J. H. (1999). Corporal punishment by American parents: National data on prevalence, chronicity, severity, and duration, in relation to child, and family characteristics. *Clinical Child and Family Psychology Review, 2*, 55–70.

Straus, M. A., & Yodanis, C. L. (1994). Physical abuse. In M. A. Straus (Ed.), *Beating the devil out of them: Corporal punishment in American families* (pp. 81–98). San Francisco: New Lexington Press.

Strawbridge, W. J., Cohen, R. D., Shema, S. J., & Kaplan, G. A. (1997). Frequent attendance at religious services and mortality over 28 years. *American Journal of Public Health, 87*, 957–961.

Strayer, D. L., & Drews, F. A. (2007). Cell-phone-induced driver distraction. *Current Directions in Psychological Science, 16*, 128–131.

Strayer, D. L., & Johnston, W. A. (2001). Driven to distraction: Dual-task studies of simulated driving and conversing on a cellular phone. *Psychological Science, 12*, 462–466.

Strayer, D. L., Drews, F. A., & Crouch, D. J. (2006). A comparison of the cell phone driver and the drunk driver. *Human Factors, 48*, 381–391.

Strober, M., Freeman, R., Lampert, C., Diamond, J., & Kaye, W. (2000). Controlled family study of anorexia nervosa and bulimia nervosa: Evidence of shared liability and transmission of partial syndromes. *American Journal of Psychiatry, 157*, 393–401.

Stromeyer, C. F., III, & Psotka, J. (1971). The detailed texture of eidetic images. *Nature, 237*, 109–112.

Stuss, D. T., Binns, M. A., Murphy, K. J., & Alexander, M. P. (2002). Dissociations within the anterior attentional system: Effects of task complexity and irrelevant information on reaction time speed and accuracy. *Neuropsychology, 16*, 500–513.

Sue, D. W., & Sue, D. (2003). *Counseling the culturally different: Theory and practice* (4th ed.). New York: John Wiley & Sons.

Sue, S. (1977). Community mental health services to minority groups: Some optimism, some pessimism. *American Psychologist, 32*, 616–624.

Sue, S. (1992). Ethnicity and mental health: Research and policy issues. *Journal of Social Issues, 48*(2), 187–205.

Sue, S., Zane, N., & Young, K. (1994). Research on psychotherapy in culturally diverse populations. In A. Bergin & S. Garfield (Eds.), *Handbook of psychotherapy and behavior change* (pp. 783–817). New York: Wiley.

Sullivan, P. F., Neale, M. C., & Kendler, K. S. (2000). Genetic epidemiology of major depression: Review and meta-analysis, *American Journal of Psychiatry, 157*, 1552–1562.

Sulloway, F. J. (1996). *Born to rebel: Birth order, family dynamics, and creative lives.* New York: Pantheon.

Suryani, L., & Jensen, S. (1993). *Trance and possession in Bali: A window on western multiple personality, possession disorder, and suicide.* New York: Oxford University Press.

Sutcliffe, N., Clarke, A. E., Levinton, C., Frost, C., Gordon, C., & Isenberg, D. A. (1999). Associates of health status in patients with systemic lupus erythematosus. *Journal of Rheumatology, 26*, 2352–2356.

Sutherland, P. (1992). *Cognitive development today: Piaget and his critics.* London: Paul Chapman.

Swann, J. (1998). Talk control: An illustration from the classroom of problems in analyzing male dominance of conversation. In J. Coates (Ed.), *Language and gender: A reader* (pp. 185–196). Oxford: Blackwell.

Swanson, H. (1994). Index of suspicion. Case 3. Diagnosis: Failure to thrive due to psychosocial dwarfism. *Pediatric Review, 15*(1), 39, 41.

Swanson, J. W., Swartz, M. S., & Elbogen, E. B. (2004). Effectiveness of atypical antipsychotic medications in reducing violent behavior among persons with schizophrenia in community-based treatment. *Schizophrenia Bulletin, 30*(1), 3–20.

Swartz, M. (1990). Somatization Disorder. In L. N. Robins, (Ed.), *Psychiatric disorder in America* (pp. 220–257). New York: Free Press.

Swartz, M., Blazer, D., George, L., & Winfield, I. (1990). Estimating the prevalence of borderline personality disorder in the community. *Journal of Personality Disorders, 4*(3), 257–272.

Swayze, V. W., II (1995). Frontal leukotomy and related psychosurgical procedures in the era before antipsychotics (1935–1954): A historical overview. *American Journal of Psychiatry, 152*(4), 505–515.

Swenson, D. D., & Marshall, B. (2005, May 14). Flash flood: Hurricane Katrina's inundation of New Orleans, August 29, 2005 (SWF). *Times-Picayune.*

Taglialatela, J. P., Savage-Rumbaugh, E. S., & Baker, L. A. (2003). Vocal production by a language-competent bonobo (Pan Paniscus). *International Journal of Comparative Psychology, 24,* 1–17.

Tajfel, H., & Turner, J. C. (1986). The social identity theory of intergroup behaviour. In S. Worchel & W. G. Austin (Eds.), *The psychology of intergroup relations* (Vol. 2). (pp. 7–24) New York: Nelson Hall.

Takeuchi, T., Ogilvie, R. D., Murphy, T. I., & Ferrelli, A. V. (2003). EEG activities during elicited sleep onset. REM and NREM periods reflect difference mechanisms of dream generation. *Clinical Neurophysiology, 114*(2), 210–220.

Talbott, G. D. & Crosby, L. R. (2001). Recovery contracts: Seven key elements. In R. H. Coombs (Ed.), *Addiction recovery tools* (pp. 127–144). Thousand Oaks, CA: Sage Publications, Inc.

Tamminga, C. A. (2002). Partial dopamine agonists in the treatment of psychosis. *Journal of Neural Transmission, 109,* 411–420.

Tart, C. (1986). *Waking up: Overcoming the obstacles to human potential.* Boston: New Science Library.

Tart, C. T. (1970). Marijuana intoxication: Common experiences. *Nature, 226,* 701.

Taylor, B., Miller, E., Farrington, C. P., Petropoulos, M. C., Favot-Mayaud, I., Li, J., & Waight, P. A. (1999). Autism and measles, mumps, and rubella vaccine: No epidemiological evidence for a causal association. *Lancet, 353,* 2026–2029.

Taylor, D. M., & Moghaddam, F. M. (1994). *Theories of intergroup relations: International social psychological perspectives* (2nd ed.). Westport, CT: Praeger.

Taylor, M. J., Carney, S., Geddes, J., & Goodwin, G. (2004). Folate for depressive disorders (Cochrane Review). In *The Cochrane Library,* Issue 2, 2004. Chichester, UK: John Wiley & Sons, Ltd.

Teicher, M. H., Andersen, S. L., Polcari, A., Anderson, C. M., & Navalta, C. P. (2002). Developmental neurobiology of childhood stress and trauma. *Psychiatric Clinics of North America, 25,* 397–426.

Teigen, K. (1994). Yerkes–Dodson: A law for all seasons. *Theory & Psychology, 4,* 525–547.

Temoshok, L., & Dreher, H. (1992). *The Type C connection: The behavioral links to cancer and your health.* New York: Random House.

Terman, J. S. (2001). Circadian time of morning light administration and therapeutic response in winter depression. *Archives of General Psychiatry, 58,* 69–75.

Terman, L. M. (1916). *The measurement of intelligence.* Boston: Houghton Mifflin.

Terman, L. M. (1925). *Mental and physical traits of a thousand gifted children (I).* Stanford, CA: Stanford University Press.

Terman, L. M., & Oden, M. H. (1947). *The gifted child grows up: 25 years' follow-up of a superior group: Genetic studies of genius (V. 4).* Stanford, CA: Stanford University Press.

Terman, L. M., & Oden, M. H. (1959). *The gifted group at mid-life, thirty-five years follow-up of the superior child: Genetic studies of genius (V. 3).* Stanford, CA: Stanford University Press.

Terry, A. V., Jr., Hill, W. D., Parikh, V., Evans, D. R., Waller, J. L., & Mahadik, S. P. (2002). Differential effects of chronic haloperidol and olanzapine exposure on brain cholinergic markers and spatial learning in rats. *Psychopharmacology, 164*(4), 360–368.

Terry, A. V., Jr., Hill, W. D., Parikh, V., Waller, J. L., Evans, D. R., & Mahadik, S. P. (2003). Differential effects of haloperidol, risperidone, and clozapine exposure on cholinergic markers and spatial learning performance in rats. *Neuropsychopharmacology, 28*(2), 300–309.

Thase, M. E. (1999). When are psychotherapy and pharmacotherapy combinations the treatment of choice for major depressive disorders? *Psychiatric Quarterly, 70*(4), 333–346.

Thase, M. E., & Sachs, G. S. (2000). Bipolar depression: Pharmacotherapy and related therapeutic strategies. *Biological Psychiatry, 48*(6), 558–572.

The Arc (1982). *The prevalence of mental retardation.* Hartford, CT: The Arc.

Thiedke, C. C. (2001). Sleep disorders and sleep problems in childhood. *American Family Physician, 63,* 277–284.

Thigpen, C. H., & Cleckley, H. M. (1992, revised). *The three faces of Eve.* London: Secker & Warburg.

Thomas, A., & Chess, S. (1977). *Temperament and development.* New York: Brunner/Mazel.

Thomas, M., Thorne, D., Sing, H., Redmond, D., Balkin, T., Wesensten, N., Russo, M., Welsh, A., Rowland, L., Johnson, D., Aladdin, R., Cephus, R., Hall, S., & Belenky, G. (1998). The relationship between driving accidents and microsleep during cumulative partial sleep deprivation. *Journal of Sleep Research, 7*(2), 275.

Thomas, N. J. T. (2001). Mental imagery. In E. N. Zalta (Ed.), *The Stanford encyclopedia of philosophy* (Winter 2001 edition) **http://plato.stanford.edu/entries/mental-imagery/Retrieved January 20, 2008.**

Thompson, W. W., Price, C., Goodson, B., Shay, D. K., Benson, P., Hinrichsen, V. L., Lewis, E., Eriksen, E., Ray, P., Marcy, S. M., Dunn, J., Jackson, L. A., Lieu, T. A., Black, S., Stewart, G., Weintraub, E. S., Davis, R. L., & DeStefano, F. (2007). Early thimerosal exposure and neuropsychological outcomes at 7 to 10 years. *The New England Journal of Medicine, 357*(13), 1281–1292.

Thoresen, C. E., & Harris, H. S. (2002). Spirituality and health: What's the evidence and what's needed? *Annals of Behavioral Medicine, 24,* 3–13.

Thorndike, E. L. (1911). *Animal Intelligence: Experimental studies.* New York: Macmillan.

Thorndike, E. L. (1920). A constant error on psychological rating. *Journal of Applied Psychology, vol. IV,* 25–29.

Thornton, A., & Hui-Sheng, L. (1994). Continuity and change. In A. Thornton & L. Hui-Sheng (Eds.), *Social change and the family in Taiwan* (pp. 396–410). Chicago: University of Chicago Press.

Thurstone, L. L. (1938). *Primary mental abilities.* Chicago: University of Chicago Press.

Tobach, E. (2001). Development of sex and gender. In J. Worell (Ed.), *Encyclopedia of women and gender* (pp. 315–332). San Diego, CA: Academic Press.

Toga, A. W., & Thompson, P. M. (2003). Mapping brain asymmetry. *Natural Neuroscience, 4,* 37–48.

Tohen, M., Vieta, E., Calabrese, J., Ketter, T. A., Sachs, G., Bowden, C., Mitchell, P. B., Centorrino, F., Risser, R., Baker, R. W., Evans, A. R., Beymer, K., Dube, S., Tollefson, G. D., & Breier, A. (2003). Efficacy of olanzapine and olanzapine-fluoxetine combination in the treatment of bipolar I depression. *Archives of General Psychiatry, 60*(11), 1079–1088.

Tolman, E. C. (1932). *Purposive behavior in animals and man.* New York: Century.

Tolman, E. C., & Honzik, C. H. (1930). Introduction and removal of reward and maze learning in rats. *University of California Publications in Psychology, 4,* 257–275.

Tomasello, M., Carpenter, M., & Lizskowski, U. (2007). A new look at infant pointing. *Child Development, 78,* 705–722

Torgersen, S. (2000). Genetics of patients with borderline personality disorder. *Psychiatric Clinics of North America, (23),* 1–9.

Torrance, E. P. (1993). The Beyonders in a thirty-year longitudinal study of creative achievement. *Roeper Review, 15*(3), 131–135.

Torrey, E. F. (1986). *Witchdoctors and psychiatrists. The common roots of psychotherapy and its future.* New York: Harper & Raw.

Torrey, E. F. (1987). Prevalence studies in schizophrenia. *British Journal of Psychiatry, 150,* 598–608.

Trappey, C. (1996). A meta-analysis of consumer choice and subliminal advertising. *Psychology and Marketing, 13,* 517–530.

Tremblay, A., Doucet, E., & Imbeault, P. (1999). Physical activity and weight maintenance. *International Journal of Obesity, 23*(3), S50–S54.

Treisman, M. (1977). Motion sickness: An evolutionary hypothesis. *Science, 197,* 493.

Tresniowski, A. (1999, July 12). Troubled sleep. *People Weekly,* 56–59.

Triandis, H. (1971). *Attitude and attitude change.* New York: Wiley.

Trocmé, N., MacLaurin, B., Fallon, B., Daciuk, J., Billingsley, D., Tourigny, M., Mayer, M., Wright, J., Barter, K., Furford, G., Hornick, J., Sullivan, R., & McKenzie, B. (2001). Canadian incidence study of reported child abuse and neglect: Final report, pp. 30–31. Ottawa, ON: Minister of Public Works and Government Services Canada.

Troisi, A., & McGuire, M. (2002). Darwinian psychiatry and the concept of mental disorder. *Human Ethology & Evolutionary Psychology, 23*(4), 31–38.

Trudeau, D. L. (2000). The treatment of addictive disorders by brain wave biofeedback: A review and suggestions for future research. *Clinical Electroencephalography, 31*(1), 13–22.

Trujillo, K. A., & Chinn, A. B. (1996). Antidepressants. *Drugs and the Brain*: California State University. Retrieved from the Internet on July 20, 2004, at **www.csusm.edu/DandB/AD.html#history.**

Trut, L. M. (1999). Early canid domestication: The Farm-Fox Experiment. *Science, 283.*

Tsai, G. E., Condle, D., Wu, M-T., & Chang, I-W. (1999). Functional magnetic resonance imaging of personality switches in a woman with dissociative identity disorder. *Harvard Review of Psychiatry, 7,* 119–122.

Tsai, J. L., Simeonova, D. I., & Watanabe, J. T. (2004). Somatic and social: Chinese Americans talk about emotion. *Personality and Social Psychology Bulletin, 30*(9), 1226–1238.

Tsuang, M., Domschke, K., Jerskey, B. A., & Lyons, M. J. (2004). Agoraphobic behavior and panic attack: A study of male twins. *Journal of Anxiety Disorders, 18*(6), 799–807.

Tucker, E. W., & Potocky-Tripodi, M. (2006). Changing heterosexuals' attitudes toward homosexuals: A systematic review of the empirical literature. *Research on Social Work Practice, 16*(2), 176–190.

Tucker, M. A., Hirota, Y., Wamsley, E. J., Lau, H., Chaklader, A., & Fishbein, W. (2006). A daytime nap containing solely non-REM sleep enhances declarative but not procedural memory. *Neurobiology of Learning and Memory, 86*(2), 241–247.

Tugade, M. M., & Fredrickson, B. L. (2004). Resilient individuals use positive emotions to bounce back from negative emotional experiences. *Journal of Personality and Social Psychology, 86*(2), 320–333.

Tukuitonga, C. F., & Bindman, A. B. (2002). Ethnic and gender differences in the use of coronary artery revascularisation procedures in New Zealand. *New Zealand Medical Journal, 115,* 179–182.

Tulving, E., & Thomson, D. M. (1973). Encoding specificity and retrieval processes in episodic memory. *Psychological Review, 80,* 352–373.

Turner, W. J. (1995). Homosexuality, Type 1: An Xq28 phenomenon. *Archives of Sexual Behavior, 24*(2), 109–134.

Tusel, D. J., Piotrowski, N. A., Sees, K., Reilly, P. M., Banys, P., Meek, P., & Hall, S. M. (1994). Contingency contracting for illicit drug use with opioid addicts in methadone treatment. In L. S., Harris (Ed.), *Problems of drug dependence: Proceedings of the 56th Annual Scientific Meeting. National Institute on Drug Abuse research monograph 153* (pp. 155–160). Washington, DC: U.S. Goverment Printing Office.

Tversky, A., & Kahneman, D. (1974). Judgment under uncertainty: Heuristics and biases. *Science, 185,* 1124–1130.

Tversky, A., & Shafir, E. (1992). The disjunction effect in choice under uncertainty. *Psychological Science, 3*(5), 305–309.

UNAIDS. (2003). AIDS epidemic update. Publication of the Joint United Nations Programme on HIV/AIDS.

Unger, R. (1979). Toward a redefinition of sex and gender. *American Psychologist, 34,* 1085–1094.

Upthegrove, T., Roscigno, V., & Charles, C. (1999). Big money collegiate sports: Racial concentration, contradictory pressures, and academic performance. *Social Science Quarterly, 80,* 718–737.

Uretsky, S. D. (2002). Antianxiety drugs. *Gale Encyclopedia of Medicine.* The Gale Group. Retrieved from the Internet on July 19, at **www.healthatoz.com/healthatoz/Atoz/ency/antianxiety_drugs.html#.**

Vail, A. (1976). Factors influencing lower class, black patients' remaining in treatment. *Clinical Psychology, 29,* 12–14.

Vaillant, G. E. (2002). Adaptive mental mechanisms: Their role in a positive psychology. *American Psychologist, 55,* 89–98.

Valverde, R., Pozdnyakova, I., Kajander, T., Venkatraman, J., & Regan, L. (2007). Fragile X mental retardation syndrome: Structure of the KH1-KH2 domains of fragile X mental retardation protein. *Structure, 9,* 1090–1098.

Van de Castle, R. (1994). *Our dreaming mind.* New York: Ballantine Books.

van der Merwe, A., & Garuccio, A. (Eds.). (1994). *Waves and particles in light and matter.* New York: Plenum Press.

Van Dongen, H. P. A., Maislin, G., Mullington, J. M., & Dinges, D. F. (2003). The cumulative cost of additional wakefulness: Dose-response effects on neurobehavioral functions and sleep physiology from chronic sleep restriction and total sleep deprivation. *Sleep, 26,* 117–126.

Van Til, R. (1997). *Lost daughters: Recovered memory therapy and the people it hurts.* Grand Rapids, MI: Eerdmans.

Vartanian, L. R. (2000). Revisiting the imaginary audience and personal fable constructs of adolescent egocentrism: A conceptual review. *Adolescence, 35*(140), 639–661.

Vaughan, K., Armstrong, M. S., Gold, R., O'Connor N., Jenneke, W., & Tarrier, N. (1994). A trial of eye movement desensitization compared to image habituation training and applied muscle relaxation in post-traumatic stress disorder. *Journal of Behavior Therapy and Experimental Psychology, 25,* 283–291.

Vaughan, S. (2000). *Half empty, half full: The psychological roots of optimism.* New York: Harcourt.

Veasey, S. C. (2003). Serotonin agonists and antagonists in obstructive sleep apnea: Therapeutic potential. *American Journal of Respiratory Medicine, 2*(1), 21–29.

Vernon, S. W., & Roberts, R. E. (1982). Use of RDC in a tri-ethnic community survey. *Archives of General Psychiatry, 39,* 47.

Villafuerte, S., & Burmeister, M. (2003). Untangling genetic networks of panic, phobia, fear and anxiety. *Genome Biology, 4*(8), 224.

Villani, S. (2001). Impact of media on children and adolescents: A 10-year review of the research. *Journal of the American Academy on Child and Adolescent Psychiatry, 40*(4), 392–401.

Vink, T., Hinney, A., Van Elburg, A. A., Van Goozen, S. H., Sandkuijl, L. A., Sinke, R. J., Herpertz-Dahlman, B. M., Henebrand, J., Remschmidt, H., Van Engeland, H., & Adan, R. A. (2001). Association between an agouti-related protein gene polymorphism and anorexia nervosa. *Molecular Psychiatry, 6*(3), 325–328.

Virkkunen, M., & Linnoila, M. (1996). Serotonin and glucose metabolism in impulsively violent alcoholic offenders. In D. M. Stoff, & R. B. Cairns, (Eds.), *Aggression and violence* (pp. 87–100). Mahwah, NJ: Lawrence Erlbaum.

Visser, P. S., & Krosnick, J. A. (1998). Development of attitude strength over the life cycle: Surge and decline. *Journal of Personality and Social Psychology, 75*(6), 1389–1410.

Vogel, G. W. (1975). A review of REM sleep deprivation. *Archives of General Psychiatry, 32,* 749–761.

Vogel, G. W. (1993). Selective deprivation, REM sleep. In M. A. Carskadon (Ed.), *The encyclopedia of sleep and dreaming.* New York: Macmillan Publishing Company.

Vokey, J. R., & Read J. D. (1985). Subliminal messages: Between the devil and the media. *American Psychologist, 40,* 1231–1239.

von Helmholtz, H. (1852). On the theory of compound colours. *Philosophical Magazine, 4,* 519–535.

von Helmholtz, H. L. F. (1863). *Die Lehre von den Tonempfindungen als physiologische Grundlage fur die Theorie der Musik* published in translation (1954). *On the sensations of tone as a physiological basis for the theory of music.* New York: Dover.

Voyer, D., & Rodgers, M. (2002). Reliability of laterality effects in a dichotic listening task with nonverbal material. *Brain & Cognition, 48,* 602–606.

Voyer, D., Voyer, S., & Bryden, M. (1995). Magnitude of sex differences in spatial abilities: A meta-analysis and consideration of critical variables. *Psychological Bulletin, 117*(2), 250–270.

Vygotsky, L. (1998). *Child psychology.* New York: Plenum.

Vygotsky, L. S. (1934/1962). *Thought and language.* Cambridge, MA: MIT Press.

Vygotsky, L. S. (1978). *Mind in society: The development of higher psychological processes.* Cambridge, MA: Harvard University Press.

Vygotsky, L. S. (1987). Thought and word. In R. W. Riebe & A. S. Carton (Eds.), *The collected works of L. S. Vygotsky, Vol. 1: Problems of general psychology* (pp. 243–288). New York: Plenum.

Wahlsten, D. (1997). The malleability of intelligence is not constrained by heritability. In B. Devlin, S. E. Fienberg, & K. Roeder, *Intelligence, genes, and success: Scientists respond to the bell curve* (pp. 71–87). New York: Springer.

Walker, L. J. (1991). Sex differences in moral reasoning. In W. M. Kurtines & J. L. Gewirtz (Eds.), *Handbook of moral behavior and development: Vol. 2. Research* (pp. 333–364). Hillsdale, NJ: Lawrence Erlbaum.

Walker, M. P. (2005). A refined model of sleep and the time course of memory formation. *Behavioral and Brain Sciences, 28,* 51–64.

Wampold, B. E. (1997). Methodological problems in identifying efficacious psychotherapies. *Psychotherapy Research, 7,* 21–43.

Ward, A. S., Li, D. H., Luedtke, R. R., & Emmett-Oglesby, M. W. (1996). Variations in cocaine self-administration by inbred rat strains under a progressive-ratio schedule. *Psychopharmacology, 127*(3), 204–212.

Ward, C., & Rana-Deuba, A. (1999). Acculturation and adaptation revisited. *Journal of Cross-Cultural Psychology, 30,* 422–442.

Ward, I. L. (1992). Sexual behavior: The product of parinatal hormonal and prepubertal social factors. In A. A. Gerall, H. Moltz, & I. L. Ward. (Eds.), *Handbook of behavioral neurobiology, vol. 11, Sexual differentiation* (pp. 157–178). New York: Plenum Press.

Ward, J., Mattic, K. R. P., & Hall, W. (1999). *Methadone maintenance treatment and other opioid replacement therapies.* Sydney: Harwood Academic Publishers.

Ward, M. M., Lotstein, D. S., Bush, T. M., Lambert, R. E., van Vollenhoven, R., & Neuwelt, C. M. (1999). Psychosocial correlates of morbidity in women with systemic lupus erythematosus. *Journal of Rheumatology, 26,* 2153–2158.

Wartner, U. G., Grossmann, K., Fremmer-Bombik, E., & Suess, G. (1994). Attachment patterns at age six in south Germany: Predictability from infancy and implications for preschool behavior. *Child Development, 65,* 1014–1027.

Washburn, M. F., (1908). *The animal mind: A text-book of comparative psychology.* New York: Macmillan.

Wasserman, E. A., & Miller, R. R. (1997). What's elementary about associative learning? *Annual Review of Psychology, 48,* 573–607.

Waterhouse, L. (2006a). Inadequate evidence for multiple intelligences, Mozart effect, and emotional intelligence theories. *Educational Psychologist, 41*(4), 247–255.

Waterhouse, L. (2006b). Multiple intelligences, the Mozart effect, and emotional intelligence: A critical review. *Educational Psychologist, 41,* 207–225.

Watkins, C. E., Campbell, V. L., Nieberding, R., & Hallmark, R. (1995). Contemporary practice of psychological assessment by clinical psychologists. *Professional Psychology: Research and Practice, 26,* 54–60.

Watkins, C. E., Jr., & Savickas, M. L. (1990). Psychodynamic career counseling. In W. B. Walsh & S. H. Osipow (Eds.), *Career counseling: Contemporary topics in vocational psychology* (pp. 79–116). Hillsdale, NJ: Lawrence Erlbaum.

Watson, D. L., Hagihara, D. K., & Tenney, A. L. (1999). Skill-building exercises and generalizing psychological concepts to daily life. *Teaching of Psychology, 26,* 193–195.

Watson, J. B. (1913). Psychology as the behaviorist views it. *Psychological Review, 20,* 158–177.

Watson, J. B. (1924). *Behaviorism.* New York: W. W. Norton and Company.

Watson, J. B., & Rayner, R. (1920). Conditioned emotional responses. *Journal of Experimental Psychology, 3,* 1–14.

Watt, H. M. G. (2000). Measuring attitudinal change in mathematics and English over the 1st year of junior high school: A multi-dimensional analysis. *Journal of Experimental Education, 68,* 331–361.

Webb, C. T., & Levinson, D. F. (1993). Schizotypal and paranoid personality disorder in the relatives of patients with schizophrenia and affective disorders: A review. *Schizophrenic Research, 11*(1), 81–92.

Webb, W. B. (1992). *Sleep: The gentle tyrant* (2nd ed.). Bolton, MA: Ander.

Wechsler, D. (1975). *The collected papers of David Wechsler.* New York: Academic Press.

Wechsler, D. (1981). *Wechsler Adult Intelligence Scale—Revised.* San Antonio, TX: The Psychological Corporation.

Wechsler, D. (1990). *Wechsler Preschool and Primary Scale of Intelligence—Revised.* Sidcup, Kent: The Psychological Corporation.

Wechsler, D. (1991). *Wechsler Intelligence Scale for Children—Third Edition.* New York: Psychological Corporation.

Wedding, D. (2004). Cross-cultural counseling and psychotherapy. In R. J. Corsini & D. Wedding (Eds.), *Current psychotherapies* (7th ed., p. 485). Itasca, IL: Peacock.

Weinberger, D. R. (1987). Implications of normal brain development for the pathogenesis of schizophrenia. *Archives of General Psychiatry, 44,* 660–668.

Weiner, B. (1985). An attributional theory of achievement motivation. *Psychological Review, 92,* 548–573.

Weiner, I. B. (1997). Current status of the Rorschach Inkblot Method. *Journal of Personality Assessment, 68,* 5–19.

Weiner, R. D. (2000). Retrograde amnesia with electroconvulsive therapy: Characteristics and implications. *Archives of General Psychiatry, 57,* 591–592.

Weis, S., Klaver, P., Reul, J., Elger, C. E., & Fernandez, G. (2004). Temporal and cerebellar brain regions that support both declarative memory formation and retrieval. *Cerebral Cortex, 14,* 256–267.

Weisman, A. (1972). *On dying and denying.* New York: Behavioral Publications.

Weiss, J. M. (1972). Psychological factors in stress and disease. *Scientific American, 26,* 104–113.

Weisse, C. S. (1992). Depression and immunocompetence: A review of the literature. *Psychological Bulletin, 111,* 475–489.

Weissman, M. M., & Klerman, G. L. (1977). Sex differences and the epidemiology of depression. *Archives of General Psychiatry, 34,* 98–111.

Weissman, M. M., Bland, R. C., Canino, G. J., Faravelli, C., Greenwald, S., Hwu, H. G., Joyce, P. R., Karam, E. G., Lee, C. K., Lellouch, J., Lepine, J. P., Newman, S. C., Oakley-Browne, M. A., Rubio-Stipec, M., Wells, J. E., Wickramaratne, P. J., Wittchen, H. U., & Yeh, E. K. (1997). The cross-national epidemiology of panic disorder. *Archives of General Psychiatry, 54,* 305–309.

Weissman, M. M., Bland, R., Joyce, P. R., Newman, S., Wells, J. E., & Wittchen, H. U. (1993). Sex differences in rates of depression: Cross-national perspectives. *Journal of Affective Disorders, 29,* 77–84.

Weizenbaum, J. (1976). *Computer power and human reason.* San Francisco, CA: W. H. Freeman and Company.

Wender, P. H., Wolf, L. E., & Wasserstein, J. (2001). Adults with ADHD. An overview. *Annals of the New York Academy of Sciences, 931,* 1–16.

Wenneberg, S. R., Schneider, R. H., Walton, K. G., Maclean, C. R., Levitsky, D. K., Mandarino, J. V., Waziri, R., & Wallace, R. K. (1997). Anger expression correlates with platelet aggregation. *Behavioral Medicine, 22*(4), 174–177.

Wen-Shing, T., & Strelzer, J. (Eds.). (1997). *Culture and psychopathology: A guide to clinical assessment.* Bristol, PA: Brunner/Mazel.

Werker, J. F., & Lalonde, C. E. (1988). Cross-language speech perceptions: Initial capabilities and developmental change. *Developmental Psychology, 24,* 672–683.

Wertheimer, M. (1982). *Productive thinking.* Chicago: University of Chicago Press.

Westen, D. (2005). Cognitive neuroscience and psychotherapy: Implications for psychotherapy's second century. In G. Gabbard, J. Beck, & J. Holmes (Eds.), *Oxford textbook of psychotherapy.* Oxford: Oxford University Press.

Wetherell, J. L. (2002). Behavior therapy for anxious older adults. *Behavior Therapist, 25,* 16–17.

White, G. L. (1980). Physical attractiveness and courtship progress. *Journal of Personality and Social Psychology, 39,* 660–668.

White, S. (2000). *The transgender debate (the crisis surrounding gender identity).* Reading, U. K.: Garnet Publishing Ltd.

Whittington, C. J., Kendall, T., Fonagy, P., Cottrell, D., Cotgrove, A., & Boddington, E. (2004). Selective serotonin reuptake inhibitors in childhood depression: Systematic review of published versus unpublished data. *Lancet, 363*(9418), 1341–1345.

WHO International Consortium in Psychiatric Epidemiology. (2000). Cross-national comparisons of the prevalences and correlates of mental disorders. *Bulletin of the World Health Organization, 78*(4), 413–426.

Whorf, B. L. (1956). *Language, thought and reality.* New York: Wiley.

Wicker, A. W. (1971). An examination of the "other variables" explanation of attitude–behavior inconsistency. *Journal of Personality and Social Psychology, 19,* 18–30.

Widiger, T. A., & Weissman, M. M. (1991). Epidemiology of borderline personality disorder. *Hospital and Community Psychiatry, 42,* 1015–1021.

Williams, M. E. (1995). *The American Geriatrics Society's complete guide to aging and mental health.* New York: Random House, Inc.

Williams, R. B. (1999). A 69-year-old man with anger and angina. *Journal of the American Medical Association, 282,* 763–770.

Williams, R. B., Haney, T. L., Lee, K. L., Kong, Y. H., Blumenthal, J. A., & Whalen, R. E. (1980). Type A behavior, hostility, and coronary atherosclerosis. *Psychosomatic Medicine, 42*(6), 539–549.

Williamson, A. M., & Feyer, A. M. (2000). Moderate sleep deprivation produces impairments in cognitive and motor performance equivalent to legally prescribed levels of alcohol intoxication. *Journal of Occupational and Environmental Medicine, 57*(10), 649–655.

Wilson, R. S., Mendes de Leon, C. F., Barnes, L. L., Schneider, J. A., Bienias, J. L., Evans, D. A., & Bennet, D. A. (2002). Participation in cognitively stimulating activities and risk of incident Alzheimer disease. *Journal of the American Medical Association, 287,* 742–748.

Wilson, S., Becker, L., & Tinker, R. (1995). Eye movement desensitization and reprocessing (EMDR) treatment for psychologically traumatized individuals. *Journal of Consulting and Clinical Psychology, 63,* 928–937.

Winningham, R. G., Hyman, I. E., Jr., & Dinnel, D. L. (2000). Flashbulb memories? The effects of when the initial memory report was obtained. *Memory, 8*, 209–216.

Witelson, S. F. (1991). Neural sexual mosaicism: Sexual differentiation of the human temporo-pariatal region for functional asymmetry. *Psychoneuroendocrinology, 16*, 131–153.

Wolberg, L. R. (1977). *The technique of psychotherapy*. New York: Grune & Stratton.

Wood, J. M., Nezworski, M. T., & Stejskal, W. J. (1996). The comprehensive system for the Rorschach: A critical examination. *Psychological Science, 7*(1), 3–10, 14–17.

Woodhouse, A. (2005). Phantom limb sensation. *Clinical and Experimental Pharmacology and Physiology, 32*(1-2), 132–134.

Wu, C., Tashkin, D., Djahed, B., & Rose, J. E. (1988). Pulmonary hazards of smoking marijuana as compared with tobacco. *New England Journal of Medicine, 318*, 347–351.

Wu, C-C., Lee, G. C., & Lai, H-K. (2004). Using concept maps to aid analysis of concept presentation in high school computer textbooks. *Education and Information Technologies, 9*(20), 185–197.

Wurtman, R., & Wurtman, J. (1989, January). Carbohydrates and depression. *Scientific American*.

Wyman, P. A., Moynihan, J., Eberly, S., Cox, C., Cross, W., Jin, X., & Caserta, M. T. (2007). Association of family stress with natural killer cell activity and the frequency of illnesses in children. *Archives of Pediatric and Adolescent Medicine, 161*, 228–234.

Wynne, C. (1999). Do animals think? The case against the animal mind. *Psychology Today, 32*(6), 50–53.

Yalom, I. (1995). *The theory and practice of group psychotherapy* (4th ed.). New York: Basic Books.

Yamaguchi, S., Isejima, H., Matsuo, T., Okura, R., Yagita, K., Kobayashi, M., & Okamura, H. (2003). Synchronization of cellular clocks in the suprachiasmatic nucleus. *Science, 302*, 1408–1412.

Yerkes, R. M., & Dodson, J. D. (1908). The relation of strength of stimulus to rapidity of habit formation. *Journal of Comparative Neurology and Psychology, 18*, 459–482.

Ying, Y. W. (1990). Explanatory models of major depression and implications for help-seeking among immigrant Chinese-American women. *Culture, Medicine, and Psychiatry, 14*, 393–408.

Yopyk, D., & Prentice, D. A. (2005). Am I an athlete or a student? Identify salience and stereotype threat in student-athletes. *Basic and Applied Social Psychology, 27*(4), 29–336.

Young, S. N. (Ed.) (1996). Melatonin, sleep, aging, and the health protection branch. *Journal of Psychiatry Neuroscience, 21*(3), 161–164.

Young, T. (1802). On the theory of light and colors. *Philosophical Transactions of the Royal Society, 91*, 12–49.

Yuan, Q., Lin, F., Zheng, X. & Sehgal, A. (2005). Serotonin modulates circadian entrainment in *Drosophila. Neuron, 47*, 115–127.

Yule, G. (1996). *Pragmatics*. Oxford: Oxford University Press.

Zajonc, R. B. (1965). Social facilitation. *Science, 149*, 269–274.

Zajonc, R. B. (1968). Attitudinal effects of mere exposure. *Journal of Personality and Social Psychology Monographs, 9*(2), 1–27.

Zajonc, R. B. (1980). Feeling and thinking: Preferences need no inferences. *American Psychologist, 35*, 151–175.

Zajonc, R. B. (1984). On the primacy of affect. *American Psychologist, 39*, 117–123.

Zajonc, R. B. (1998). Emotions. In D. T. Gilbert & S. T. Fiske (Eds.), *Handbook of social psychology* (4th ed., vol. 1, pp. 591–632). New York: McGraw-Hill.

Zajonc, R. B., Heingartner, A., & Herman, E. M. (1970). Social enhancement and impairment of performance in the cockroach. *Journal of Social Psychology, 13*(2), 83–92.

Zamrini, E., McGwin, G., & Roseman, J. M. (2004). Association between statin use and Alzheimer's disease. *Neuroepidemiology, 23*, 94–98.

Zanarini, M. C. (2000). Childhood experiences associated with the development of borderline personality disorder. *Psychiatric Clinics of North America, 23*(1), 89–101.

Zeki, S. (2001). Localization and globalization in conscious vision. *Annual Review of Neuroscience, 24*, 57–86.

Zentall, T. R. (2000). Animal intelligence. In R. J. Sternberg (Ed.), *Handbook of intelligence*. Cambridge: Cambridge University Press.

Zhou, J. N., Hofman, M. A., Gooren, L. J. G., & Swaab, D. F. (1995). A sex difference in the human brain and its relation to transsexuality. *Nature, 378*, 68–70.

Zilles, K. (1990). Cortex. In G. Paxinos (Ed.), *The human nervous system* (pp. 757–802). San Diego, CA: Academic.

Zillmann, D., Baron, R., & Tamborini, R. (1981). Social costs of smoking: Effects of tobacco smoke on hostile behavior. *Psychology Journal of Applied Social, 11*, 548–561.

Zimbardo, P. (1971). The pathology of imprisonment. *Society, 9*(4–8), 4.

Zimbardo, P., Maslach, C., & Haney, C. (2000). Reflections on the Stanford Prison Experiment: Genesis, transformations, consequences. In T. Blass (Ed.), *Obedience to authority: Current perspectives on the Milgram paradigm* (pp. 193–237). London: Lawrence Erlbaum.

Zimbardo, P. G. (1970). The human choice: Individuation, reason, and order versus deindividuation, impulse, and chaos. In N. J. Arnold & D. Levine (Eds.), *Nebraska Symposium on Motivation, 1969*. Lincoln: University of Nebraska Press.

Zimbardo, P. G., & Hartley, C. F. (1985). Cults go to high school: A theoretical and empirical analysis of the initial stage in the recruitment process. *Cultic Studies Journal, 2*, 91–148.

Zisapel, N. (2001). Circadian rhythm sleep disorders: pathophysiology and potential approaches to management. *CNS Drugs, 15*(4), 311–328.

Zorilla, E. P., Luborsky, L., McKay, J. R., Rosenthal, R., Houldin, A., Tax, A., McCorkle, R., Seligman, D. A., & Schmidt, K. (2001). The relationship of depression and stressors to immunological assays: A meta-analytic review. *Brain, Behavior, and Immunity, 15*, 199–226.

Zuckerman, M. (1979). *Sensation seeking: Beyond the optimal level of arousal*. Hillsdale, NJ: Lawrence Erlbaum.

Zuckerman, M. (1994). *Behavioral expression and biosocial bases of sensation seeking*. New York: Cambridge University Press.

Zuckerman, M. (2002). Zuckerman-Kuhlman Personality Questionnaire (ZKPQ): An alternative five-factorial model. In B. De Raad & M. Perugini (Eds.), *Big five assessment* (pp. 377–396). Seattle, WA: Hogrefe & Huber Publishers.

Zuo, L., & Cramond, B. (2001). An examination of Terman's gifted children from the theory of identity. *Gifted Child Quarterly, 45*(4), 251–259.

Zvolensky, M. J., Schmidt, M. B., & Stewart, S. H. (2003). Panic disorder and smoking. *Clinical Psychology: Science and Practice, 10*, 29–51.

Credits

PHOTO CREDITS

Introduction

Page I–1 Courtesy of Myesha Oowtin; Page I–2 Andrew Holrooke/© Andrew Holbrooke/CORBIS All Rights Reserved; Page I–3 David Joel/David Joel/Getty Images, Inc; Page I–4 Joe Sohm/Chromosohm/Stock Connection; Page I–5 Jack Hollingsworth/Corbis RF; Page I–7 (Top Right) Moodboard/Corbis RF; Page I–7 (Bottom Right) Bill Varie/CORBIS- NY; Page I–9 (Top Right) James Marshall/© James Marshall/CORBIS All Rights Reserved; Page I–9 (Bottom Right) Dex Images/© Dex Images/CORBIS; Page I–10 Corbis RF; Page I–11 Pulp Photography/Corbis RF; Page I–12 Andersen Ross/Andersen Ross/Photodisc/Getty Images.

Chapter 1

Page 2 (Top Left) Getty Images; Page 2 (Middle) Thomas Northcut/Thomas Northcut/PhotoDisc/Getty Images; Page 2 (Bottom Left) 3D4Medicalcom/Getty Images, Inc - 3DClinic; Page 2 (Bottom Right) Digital Zoo/Digital Zoo/Getty Images, Inc; Page 3 (Bottom Left) Dave King/Dave King © Dorling Kindersley; Page 3 (Top Left) Photodisc/Getty Images; Page 3 (Middle) Andy Crawford/Andy Crawford © Dorling Kindersley; Page 3 (Top Right) Alperium/Shutterstock; Page 3 (Bottom Right) Dex Image/Jupiter Images Royalty Free; Page 5 Jeff Greenberg/The Image Works; Page 7 (Top) German Information Center; Page 7 (Bottom) Nancy R. Cohen/Getty Images, Inc.- Photodisc./Royalty Free; Page 8 Archives of the History of American Psychology - The University of Akron; Page 9 Getty Images Inc. - Hulton Archive Photos; Page 10 CORBIS- NY; Page 11 (Top) Underwood & Underwood/© Underwood & Underwood/CORBIS All Rights Reserved; Page 11 (Bottom) G. Paul Bishop; Page 14 Nina Leen/Getty Images/Time Life Pictures; Page 16 "Courtesy, Dr. Arthur W. Toga, Laboratory of Neuro Imaging"; Page 17 (Top) Peter Barrett/© Peter Barrett/CORBIS All Rights Reserved; Page 17 (Bottom) Michael Newman/PhotoEdit; Page 20 Bob Daemmrich/The Image Works; Page 22 Michael K. Nichols/Michael K. Nichols/National Geographic Image Collection; Page 23 (Top) Hanna Damasio, M.D./From H. Damasio, T. Grabowski, R. Frank, A.M. Galaburda, A.R. Damasio, The Return of Phineas Gage: Clues about the brain from the skull of a famous patient. Science 264:1102-1105, 1994. Department of Neurology and Image Analysis Facility, University of Iowa; Page 23 (Bottom) The Warren Anatomical Museum, Francis A. Countway Library of Medicine, Harvard Medical School; Page 24 ©The New Yorker Collection 1989 George Price from cartoonbank.com. All Rights Reserved; Page 26 ©The New Yorker Collection 1994 Leo Cullum from cartoonbank.com. All Rights Reserved; Page 29 Bill Aron/PhotoEdit Inc; Page 31 John Henley/© John Henley/CORBIS All Rights Reserved; Page 33 Jeff Greenberg/PhotoEdit; Page 35 ©The New Yorker Collection 1999 Tom Chalkley from cartoonbank.com. All Rights Reserved; Page 37 Roger Ressmeyer/© Roger Ressmeyer/CORBIS All Rights Reserved; Page 38 Stapleton Collection/© Stapleton Collection/CORBIS All Rights Reserved; Page 40 Peter M. Fisher/© Peter M. Fisher/CORBIS All Rights Reserved.

Chapter 2

Page 46 (Top Left) 3D4Medicalcom/Getty Images, Inc - 3DClinic; Page 46 (Bottom Right) 3D4Medicalcom/Getty Images, Inc - 3DClinic; Page 47 Ryan McVay/Ryan McVay/Image Bank/Getty Images; Page 49 Juergen Berger/Max-Planck Institute/Photo Researchers, Inc; Page 54 Science Source/Photo Researchers; Page 55 C.ALLAN MORGAN/Peter Arnold, Inc; Page 56 Image Source/Jupiter Images Royalty Free; Page 60 Secchi-Lecaque/Roussel-

UCLAF/CNRI/Science Photo Library/Photo Researchers, Inc; Page 61 Andrew Paul Leonard/Photo Researchers, Inc; Page 63 Peter Hvizdak/The Image Works; Page 64 Kai Pfaffenbach/CORBIS- NY; Page 66 (Top Left) SPL/Photo Researchers, Inc; Page 66 (Top Right) Alfred Pasieka/Photo Researchers, Inc; Page 66 (Bottom Left) Pete Saloutos/CORBIS- NY; Page 66 (Bottom Middle) Tim Beddow/Photo Researchers, Inc; Page 66 (Bottom Right) Living Art Enterprises/Photo Researchers; Page 69 Moodboard/© Moodboard/CORBIS All Rights Reserved; Page 71 Holger Sceibe/Zefa/© Holger Sceibe/Zefa/CORBIS All Rights Reserved; Page 74 Bettmann/© Bettmann/CORBIS All Rights Reserved; Page 77 Marcello Santos/Getty Images - Photodisc-Royalty Free; Page 82 George Simian/© George Simian/CORBIS All Rights Reserved.

Chapter 3

Page 88 (Top Left) Dave King/Dave King © Dorling Kindersley; Page 89 (Right) Dave King/Dave King © Dorling Kindersley; Page 89 (Middle) PM Images/PM Images/Taxi/Getty Images; Page 91 Steve Taylor/Getty Images Inc. - Stone Allstock; Page 96 (Top) Photo Researchers, Inc; Page 96 (Bottom) Bryan Allen/CORBIS- NY; Page 98 Fritz Goro/Getty Images/Time Life Pictures; Page 99 (Bottom Left) Ishihara, "Test for Color Deficiency". Courtesy Kanehara & Co., Ltd. Offered Exclusively in The USA by Graham-Field Health Products, Atlanta, GA; Page 99 (Bottom Right) Hart-Davis/Science Photo Library/Photo Researchers, Inc; Page 100 (Top Left) ©Copyright Lowell Handler; Page 100 (Top Right) ©Copyright Lowell Handler; Page 101 ©The New Yorker Collection 1998 Charles Barsotti from cartoonbank.com. All Rights Reserved; Page 105 CORBIS- NY; Page 107 Omikron/Photo Researcher, Inc; Page 110 Robin Sachs/PhotoEdit Inc; Page 111 AP Wide World Photos; Page 112 Vince Streano/© Vince Streano/CORBIS All Rights Reserved; Page 118 Mark Richards/Mark Richards/PHOTOEDIT; Page 120 (Top Left) Faint, Grant V./Grant V. Faint/Image Bank/Getty Images, Inc; Page 120 (Bottom left) Shaen Adey/Shaen Adey © Dorling Kindersley; Page 120 (Top Right) ROBIN SMITH/Photolibrary.com; Page 120 (Bottom Right) Tom Mareschal/Creative Eye/MIRA.com; Page 123 Larry Landolfi/Photo Researchers, Inc.

Chapter 4

Page 132 (Top Left) Photodisc/Getty Images; Page 132 (Middle) Photodisc/Getty Images; Page 132 (Bottom Left) Corbis RF; Page 133 Jean Luc Morales/Jean Luc Morales/Image Bank/Getty Images; Page (middle-right) 135 Tim Pannell/© Tim Pannell/CORBIS All Rights Reserved; Page (top) 137 SW Productions/Getty Images, Inc.- Photodisc./Royalty Free; Page (bottom) 137 David Tejada/Tejada Photography, Inc; Page (top) 148 ©The New Yorker Collection 1973 Dana Fradon from cartoonbank.com. All Rights Reserved; Page (top) 138 Kevin Schafer/Corbis/Glow Images; Page 159 ©The New Yorker Collection 1989 George Price from cartoonbank.com. All Rights Reserved; Page (bottom) 138 Stephen Frink/CORBIS- NY; Page 142 Charles Gullung/© Charles Gullung/Zefa/CORBIS All Rights Reserved; Page 143 (Top Right) Mark Seelen/Zefa/© Mark Seelen/Zefa/CORBIS All Rights Reserved; Page 143 (Bottom) ©The New Yorker Collection J. Dator from cartoonbank.com. All Rights Reserved; Page 144 Pool/Pool/Getty Images, Inc; Page 145 Envision/© Envision/CORBIS All Rights Reserved; Page 146 www.CartoonStock.com; Page 148 Sven Hagolani/Zefa/© Sven Hagolani/Zefa/CORBIS All Rights Reserved; Page 153 © Bettmann/CORBIS All Rights Reserved; Page 156 Peter Morgan/AP Wide World Photos; Page 158 Thinkstock/© Thinkstock/CORBIS All Rights Reserved; Page 160 Joefoxphoto/Alamy Images; Page 165 Ed Kashi/© Ed Kashi/CORBIS All Rights Reserved; Page 167 Doug Menuez/Getty Images, Inc. [end] PhotoDisc.

©The New Yorker Collection 1993 George Booth from cartoonbank.com. All Rights Reserved; Page 422 Voisin/Photo Researchers, Inc; Page 426 Mike Greenlar/The Image Works; Page 428 Charles Thatcher/Courtesy of Charles Thatcher.

Chapter 11

Page 434 (Top Left) Thomas Northcut/Thomas Northcut/PhotoDisc/Getty Images; Page 434 (Middle Right) ColoBlind Images/ColorBlind Images/Iconica/Getty Images, Inc; Page 434 (Bottom Right) PureStock/VALUELINE/PUNCHSTOCK/GETTY IMAGES, INC; Page 435 (Top Left) Riko Pictures/Riko Pictures/Digital Vision/Getty Images, Inc; Page 435 (Middle) Emilio Simion/Emilio Simion/PhotoDisc/Getty Images; Page 435 (Bottom Right) Edik Rank/[Photographer]/Image Bank/Getty Images; Page 435 (Bottom Left) Getty Images Inc-Image Source Royalty Free; Page 435 (Bottom Middle) Ron Krisel/Jupiter Images; Page 435 (Bottom Right) Heather Elder Represents/Jupiter Images; Page 437 © Bettmann/CORBIS All Rights Reserved; Page 441 (Top Left) Golden Pixels, LLC/Shutterstock; Page 441 (Bottom Right) Joe Sohm/Chromosohm/Stock Connection; Page 444 (Top Left) © Bettmann/CORBIS All Rights Reserved; Page 444 (Bottom Left) CORBIS- NY; Page 449 ©The New Yorker Collection 1990 Peter Steiner from cartoonbank.com. All Rights Reserved; Page 452 Lee Lorenz/©The New Yorker Collection 1994 Lee Lorenz from cartoonbank.com. All Rights Reserved; Page 457 Bob Sacha Photography; Page 461 (Top Right) Kovalchuk Oleksandr/Shutterstock; Page 461 (Bottom) Don Martinetti; Page 471 Kovalchuk Oleksandr/Shutterstock.

Chapter 12

Page 472 Andy Crawford/Andy Crawford © Dorling Kindersley; Page 473 (Bottom Right) Kevin Mackintosh/Kevin Mackintosh/Stone/Getty Images; Page 475 (Top) American Museum of Natural History; Page 475 (Right) Francisco Goya, "El Hechizo", 1787-88, Fundacion Lazaro Galdiano; Page 479 Jocelyn Bain Hogg/Jocylyn Bain Hogg/VII/Vagrant Dana Lee Klug; Page 483 Alan Schein Photography/© Alan Schein Photography/CORBIS All Rights Reserved; Page 485 (Top Right) Janet Street/Images.com/© Janet Street/Images.com/CORBIS All Rights Reserved; Page 485 (Bottom Right) Owen Franken/© Owen Franken/CORBIS All Rights Reserved; Page 486 www.CartoonStock.com; Page 488 B. Bird/Zefa/© B. Bird/Zefa/CORBIS All Rights Reserved; Page 492 New York Daily News; Page 493 David Longstreath/AP Wide World Photos; Page 495 AP Wide World Photos; Page 499 M. Deutsch/Zefa/© M. Deutsch/Zefa/CORBIS All Rights Reserved; Page 501 (Top Right) Jim Dandy/Images.Com/© Jim Dandy/Images.com/CORBIS All Rights Reserved; Page 501 (Bottom Right) Eli Reed/Everett Collection; Page 502 Getty Images, Inc; Page 503 Spencer Grant/PhotoEdit Inc; Page 508 Michael Newman/PhotoEdit Inc.

Chapter 13

Page 514 Stockbyte/Getty Images - Stockbyte, Royalty Free; Page 515 Stockbyte/Getty Images - Stockbyte, Royalty Free; Page 517 Charles Ciccione/Photo Researchers, Inc; Page 518 Tom Stewart/© Tom Stewart/CORBIS All Rights Reserved; Page 519 ©The New Yorker Collection 1990. Arnie Levin from cartoonbank.com. All Rights Reserved; Page 521 Zigy Kaluzny/Getty Images Inc. - Stone Allstock; Page 522 Michael Newman/PhotoEdit; Page 524 ScienceCartoonsPlus.com; Page 525 (Top Left) Charles Vandermast, Delft University of Technology; Page 525 (Top Right) Charles Vandermast/Charles Vandermast, Delft University of Technology; Page 525 (Bottom Right) Bill Aaron/PhotoEdit Inc; Page 528 Bob Daemmrich/The Image Works; Page 532 (Top Left) George Dodson/Pearson Education/PH College; Page 532 (Bottom Left) Michael Newman/PhotoEdit; Page 533 Mary Kate Denny/PhotoEdit Inc; Page 536 ©The New Yorker Collection 1991 Mike Twohy from cartoonbank.com. All Rights Reserved; Page 537 ©The New Yorker Collection 1999 Barbara Smaller from cartoonbank.com. All Rights Reserved; Page 539 Reprinted with special permission of King Features Syndicate; Page 544 Will & Deni McIntyre/Photo Researchers/Getty Images; Page 545 © Bettmann/CORBIS All Rights Reserved; Page 548 Cleo Freelance/Photolibrary.com; Page 552 (bottom left) Michael Newman/PhotoEdit; Page 553 ((bottom right) Will & Deni McIntyre/Photo Researchers/Getty Images.

Chapter 14

Page 554 Alperium/Shutterstock; Page 555 Ryan McVay/Ryan McVay/Photodisc/Getty Images; Page 555 (Left) Bill Reitzel/Getty Images, Inc. - Photographer's Choice/Bill Reitzel/Photographer's Choice/Getty Images; Page 555

(Middle) Dex Image./Jupiter Images -; Page 555 Bryan Mullennix/Bryan Mullennix/Iconica/Getty Images, Inc; Page 555 (Right) Iconica/Getty Images - Iconica; Page 556 ©The New Yorker Collection 2003 Alex Gregory from cartoonbank.com. All Rights Reserved; Page 559 Rick Bowmer/AP Wide World Photos; Page 564 Javier Pierini/© Bettmann/CORBIS All Rights Reserved; Page 568 Reprinted by the permission of the American Cancer Society, Inc; Page 569 Tim Pannell/Corbis RF; Page 573 Reuters New Media Inc./© Reuters New Media Inc./CORBIS; Page 577 (Top Right) CORBIS- NY; Page 577 (Bottom Right) ©The New Yorker Collection 2002 Charles Barsotti from cartoonbank.com. All Rights Reserved; Page 580 J. Nettis/IPNstock/Nielsen Business Media; Page 582 Jerry Ohlinger/Jerry Ohlinger; Page 586 Philip G. Zimbardo, Inc; Page 593 AP Wide World Photos.

Appendix B

Page B-3 Michal Heron/Michal Heron Photography; Page B-4 Peace Corps; Page B-5 ZUMA Press, Inc./Alamy; Page B-6 Picture Partners/Alamy; Page B-7 Will & Deni McIntyre/Science Source/Photo Researchers, Inc; Page B-8 (Top Left) Photofusion Picture Library/Alamy; Page B-8 (Bottom Left) Chris Trotman/Duomo/© Chris Trotman/Duomo/CORBIS All Rights Reserved; Page B-10 (Top Left) Brian Smith/Brian Smith, Photographer; Page B-10 (Bottom left) Courtesy of AT&T Archives and History Center, Warren, NJ; Page B-12 Aaron M. Sprecher /epa/© Aaron M. Sprecher/epa/CORBIS All Rights Reserved; Page B-13 Dan McCoy/Rainbow Image Library.

TEXT CREDITS

Page 4 Frontis piece Copyright © 2009 by The College Board. Reproduced with permission. http://apcentral.collegeboard.com.

Chapter 1

Page 18 Fig. 1.2a From Hoffer, T.B., M. Hess, V. Welch, Jr., and K. Williams. 2007. *Doctorate Recipients from United States Universities: Summary Report 2006.* Chicago: National Opinion Research Center. http://www.norc.org/NR/rdonlyres/C22A3F40-0BA2-4993-A6D3-5E65939EEDC3/0/06SRFinalVersion.pdf.

Chapter 4

Page 138 Fig. 4.1 Figure 1 from "Ontogenic Development of the Human Sleep-Dream Cycle" by H. P. Roffwarg, J. N. Muzio, W. C. Dement, *Science*, April 29, 1966. Copyright © 1966 by American Association for the Advancement of Science. Reprinted by permission of AAAS; Page 140 Fig. 4.2 Reprinted by permission of Dr. Leslie Sherlin; Page 141 Fig. 4.3 N/A; Page 151 Table 4.2 Courtesy of Henry R. Hilgard; Page 159 Table 4.4 As cited in Barone, J. J. & Roberts, H. R. (1996); Page 161 Table 4.5 Adapted from HOW TO CONTROL YOUR DRINKING by William Miller and Ricardo Munoz.

Chapter 5

Page 210 text Reprinted by permission of Karawynn Long.

Chapter 6

Page 224 Fig. 6.2 Sperling, 1960; Page 226 Fig. 6.7 Graph based on Table 1, p. 328 from "Context-Dependent Memory in Two Natural Environments: On Land and Underwater" by Godden & Baddeley, (1975), *British Journal of Psychology*, 66 (3), pp. 325-331. Copyright © 1975 by The British Psychological Society. Reproduced with permission from the British Journal of Psychology; Page 247 Fig. 6.10 Reprinted from *Cognitive Psychology*, Vol. ll, 1979, pp. 297-307, Nickerson, et al. "Long-Term Memory for a Common Object" with permission from Elsevier.

Chapter 7

Page 278 Table 7.4 Roid, G. H. (2003). *Stanford-Binet Intelligence Scales, Fifth Edition.* Itasca, IL: Riverside Publishing; Page 279 Table 7.5 Wechsler Adult Intelligence Scale®—Third Edition. Copyright © by NCS Pearson, Inc. Reproduced with permission. All rights reserved. "Wechsler", "Wechsler Adult Intelligence Scale," and "WAIS" are trademarks, in the US and/or other countries, of Pearson Education, Inc. or its affiliate(s). Pearson is a trademark, in the US and/or other countries of Pearson Education, Inc. or its affiliates; Page 282 Table 7.6 From PSYCHOLOGICAL TESTING AND ASSESSMENT 10th edition by Lewis R. Aiken. Copyright

Name Index

A

AAA Foundation for Traffic Safety, 369
Abadinsky, H., 155
Abbott, L., 160
Abela, J. R. Z., 529
Abraham, S., 325
Abraham, W. C., 60
Abrahamsen, A., 222
Abramson, L. Y., 449, 499
Abramson, L. Y., 449, 499
Acar, N., 503
Adam, K., 138
Adams, D. B., 586
Adams, R. J., 399
Adams, S. A., 538
Adler, A., 444
Adler, S. R., 421
Adolphs, R., 71, 329
Aghajanian, G. K., 164
Agnati, L. F., 56
Aguiar, A., 404
Ahlskog, J. E., 56
Ahn, W., 264
Ahokas, A., 472
Aiello, J. R., 564
Ainsworth, M. D. S., 409
Aitchison, J., 265
Aito, M., 472
Ajzen, I., 568
Akil, M., 56
Albert, D. J., 586
Alderfer, C. P., 318
Aldridge-Morris, R., 493
Alexander, G., 586
Aligne, C. A., 370
Alkon, D., 250
Allen, F., 157
Allen, G. E., 281, 391
Allen, I. V., 50

Allen, J. J., 67
Allen, K., 372
Alloy, L. B., 207
Allport, G. W., 452
Alm, H., 135
Amabile, T. M., 32, 33, 308, 353
American Academy of Pediatrics, 390, 391
American Association for the Advancement of Science, 61
American Association on Intellectual and Developmental Disabilities, 284
American Association on Mental Retardation, 284
American Psychiatric Association, 284, 285, 286, 325, 326, 348, 481, 482, 485, 502, 505, 539
American Psychological Association, 36
Anand, B. K., 321
Anastasi, A., 464
Anderson, C. A., 585, 588
Anderson, M. C., 248
Andreasen, N. C., 501
Andrews, J. D. W., 531
Anschuetz, B. L., 370
Antoni, M. H., 371
Antuono, P. G., 253
Arand, D., 168
Archer, J., 586
Argyle, M., 415
Arnett, P. A., 506
Aronson, E., 506
Aronson, J., 579, 580
Arrigo, J. M., 493
Asarnow, R. F., 502
Asch, S. E., 557, 558
Aserinsky, E., 139
Ash, M. G., 9
Asimov, I., 269
Associated Press, 156
Atkinson, R. C., 224, 228

Ayllon, T., 535
Aylward, E. H., 6

B

Backenstrass, M., 449
Backer, B., 426
Baddeley, A. D., 220, 226, 227, 236, 238, 242
Baehr, E. K., 135
Baer, D. M., 202
Bahrick, H. P., 229, 243
Baillargeon, R., 404
Balin, A. K., 426
Ball, K., 299
Baltes, P. B., 386
Bandura, A., 184, 207, 208, 447, 448, 449, 526, 527, 586, 587
Barak, A., 540
Bard, P., 332
Bargh, J. A., 92
Barker, E., 593
Barkley, R. A., 427, 428
Barnes, A. M., 390, 391
Barnes, V., 376
Barnyard, P., 229
Baron, J. N., 587
Baron, S. A., B-12
Barondes, S. H., 500
Barone, J. J., 159
Barry, K. L., 155
Barsalou, L. W., 176
Barsh, G. S., 323
Barstow, A. L., 475
Bartels, A., 583
Barth, J. M., 329
Bartholomew, K., 410
Bartke, A., 426
Bartlett, F. C., 242
Bartlett, N. R., 96
Barton, M. E., 264

Subject Index